THE ARABS IN ANTIQUITY

The question of ethnicity continues to be fundamental as we progress into the new millennium. Modern claims of ethnic identities are often supported with historical arguments, and the modern Arab nationalist movements in the Middle East are no exception: they have from the beginning leaned heavily on history to support their cause.

The Arabs in Antiquity describes the history of the people called Arabs from the earliest occurrence of the word around 850 BC until the first century of Islam. It studies all the main instances of the word in Akkadian, Hebrew, Aramaic, Greek, Latin, Ancient and Middle Persian and Epigraphic South Arabian sources during more than 1400 years.

The history of the Arabs in antiquity is described from their first appearance at the battle of Qarqar in Syria in 853 BC via their wars with the Assyrian kings, their appearance in the Bible, their role in the Persian empire and its successor, the Greek empires in the Middle East until the arrival of the Romans. The role of the Arabs in the Nabataean kingdom is thoroughly described as well as their relationship to the Roman emperors. Special attention is paid to their role in ancient South Arabia and the description of them in Jewish literature, both rabbinical and non-rabbinical. An analysis of the context and nature of the sources presents a new interpretation of the identity of the ancient Arabs as they relate to the Arabs of the first Islamic century. Rather than as an ethnic group, they appear as a community worshipping certain gods. They are characterized by being subject to certain taboos, such as prohibition from wine-drinking, and their intimate connection with the camel is another special feature. The Arabs of antiquity thus resemble the early Islamic Arabs more than is usually assumed, being united by common bonds of religious ideology and law.

Jan Retsö gained his PhD from Göteborg University in 1983 and was appointed Professor of Arabic there in 1986. His main field of work is Arabic and Semitic linguistics, especially comparative and diachronic studies, in which he has published two monographs and a series of articles. In addition, he has published several articles on the history of pre-Islamic Arabia and the ancient Near East.

THE ARABS IN ANTIQUITY

Their history from the Assyrians to the Umayyads

Jan Retsö

RoutledgeCurzon
Taylor & Francis Group
LONDON AND NEW YORK

First published 2003
by RoutledgeCurzon
11 New Fetter Lane, London EC4P 4EE

Simultaneously published in the USA and Canada by
RoutledgeCurzon
29 West 35th Street, New York, NY 10001

RoutledgeCurzon is an imprint of the Taylor & Francis Group

Typeset in Times by
M Rules
Printed and bound in Great Britain by
Antony Rowe Ltd, Chippenham, Wiltshire

British Library Cataloguing in Publication Data
A catalogue record for this book is available from the British Library

Library of Congress Cataloging in Publication Data
A catalog record for this book has been requested

ISBN 0–7007–1679–3

CONTENTS

PREFACE

The original aim of this work was to write a textbook for students of Arabic and Middle Eastern studies giving a survey of the history of pre-Islamic Arabia and the Arabs. This turned out to be far more complicated than was expected if the standard views and phrases were not to be followed slavishly. A good textbook for use at a university level should not only state 'facts'. It should also introduce the student to the basics of scholarly thinking and the problems within the field which have been and are subject to discussion among the scholars. The history of Arabs and Arabia in pre-Islamic times soon proved to be a much more problematic matter than it seemed from the general statements found in the scholarly literature. Despite the impressive growth of data and studies on specific regions and periods, overall analyses and syntheses are still very largely lacking. The attempts which exist are almost always caught up in preconceived ways of thinking, which blur rather than clarify important aspects of the history of pre-Islamic Arabia and its inhabitants.

A book with this ambition thus had to be based on primary research and, as a consequence, it could not be retained within the format of an introductory textbook. It has been necessary to re-read all relevant sources in the original languages, re-evaluate and re-analyse them as well as to dig up sources which have been neglected. It has also been necessary to rethink the whole issue about who the pre-islamic Arabs were and of their relationship to other groups in Arabia and adjacent regions. As far as scope and contents are concerned, the book has grown beyond recognition from the original plan. But the intention has remained to write a legible introduction to the subject which can be understood by a reader with some general knowledge about the ancient history of the Mediterranean and the Middle East. There is a fairly generous presentation of the sources and the problems connected with them, which is crucial to any historical investigation and without which no real grasp of history as a science is possible. Specialists in certain fields may find some of the initial remarks concerning their own subjects too elementary, yet it is hoped that they will also find points of interest in the treatment.

The scope of this book is enormous. It deals with essential aspects of the history of a continent during one and a half millennia. Furthermore, the study of the history of Arabia is not organized into a distinct academic discipline. Arabia is treated by specialists in many other, well-established disciplines such as Assyriology, Old Testament studies, Classical studies, Middle Eastern archaeology, Patristic, Judaic and Sabaean studies, and, of course, Arabic and Islamic studies. At the same time Arabia is not a central area in most of these disciplines. Events there are confronted when they intrude into the fields mentioned. The student who wants to acquire a coherent picture of the area's history should, ideally, be a master of all disciplines mentioned. It goes without saying that this is not possible. Anyone who in spite of this ventures the task will expose themselves to the criticism and even scorn of the experts in each topic they dare to penetrate in order to seek the truth. Neverthess, the attempt must be made. As specialization in scholarly fields increases, it becomes more and more necessary to break down disciplinary borders, lift the eyes from minute details and try to comprehend epochs and areas which have played crucial roles in human history. Pre-islamic Arabia is definitely one of them and a deeper understanding of the processes there which gave rise to the world-wide conquests of the tribes and the rise of Islam in the seventh century AD is one of the most urgent tasks of historical science. This book is an attempt to show the way. Nobody realizes the dangers and difficulties of such a task more than its author but the fascination and importance of the subject has been an irresistible impetus and hopefully will inspire both the average student and the specialist.

The book is based upon a scrutiny of all relevant written pre-Islamic sources together with a similar study of a selection of the most important Arabic ones from the Islamic period. These have been read in the original languages from editions as up-to-date as possible and the relevant parts have been rendered in English in order to make them easily available and controllable. In the cases where a translation already exists, it has normally been followed, although often with adjustments of the wording to get as close to the original as possible. This means that on several occasions, technical terms and ethnic and other designations have been left in their original linguistic form in order to give the reader an idea of what the source text looks like and the problems in it.

The transcription of ancient names and terms is made for the expert and the layman alike. The Semitic words are given as close to the original as possible. The transcription of Arabic names basically follows the system in the Encyclopaedia of Islam, 2nd edition. Arabic terms, expressions and sentences are, however, rendered in a Mideastern transcription, following the convention in linguistic literature. This procedure may sometime make a deterrent impression to the reader who is not an expert in Semitic languages. It has, however, been judged necessary to reproduce the terms and words as nearly as possible. An exception are the Hebrew names, where the conventions of the English Bible translations are followed, although not with complete consistency.

A host of persons have, in different ways, contributed to the work and their names deserve to be mentioned. My first thanks go to some of my academic colleagues who have commented upon specific issues, read parts of the work and provided supplementary material. Professors Sven-Tage Teodorsson, Göteborg and Vincent Gabrielsen, Copenhagen, have given substantial assitance in digging up the Greek papyri. Professors Ebbe E. Knudsen, Oslo, and John Huehnergard, Harvard, have given valuable comments on the cuneiform texts used. Professor Walter W. Müller, Marburg, has kindly read the parts on South Arabia and made important corrections and comments. Professor Albert Arazi, Jerusalem, has provided a series of references to ancient Arabic poetry. Professor M. A. Dandamaev, St Petersburg, has put one of his unpublished articles at my disposal and professors Christian Robin, Aix-en-Provence, and François Bron, Paris, have sent me a steady stream of offprints of their works on South Arabia, many of which have been of crucial importance for this work. My thanks also go to professor Avraham Negev, Jerusalem, for generously supplying copies of his works on the Nabataeans. This also holds for Gianfranco Fiaccadori, Bologna, who kindly sent me his work on the history of the Red Sea area, and Robert Hoyland, Oxford who generously provided me with a preliminary version of his book about pre-Islamic Arabia.

Likewise, I have received similar assistance from Professor Thomas Hägg, Bergen and Dr Witold Witakowski, Uppsala. Mohamad Yaacoubi, Damascus, has helped me to enrich my library with many Arabic texts essential for the work. I must also thank my teachers in Greek: Karin Hult and Tryggve Göransson, Göteborg, who have patiently put their ability at my disposal for clarifications of many passages in the Greek sources. Karin has read the whole manuscript with the continuous remarks and commentaries of an intelligent reader. The same applies to Gunnel Hult, Göteborg, who has meticulously scrutinized the text and provided corrections and remarks both on content and form. A tower of strength throughout the whole work has been Ferenc Tafferner, whose computer skill on many occasions has saved the project from ruin. Jon van Leuven has once again brushed up my English. My thanks also go to professor Lars Johanson, Mainz and Uppsala, who provided some important connections with people essential for the publication. I want to thank the University Library and the Classics Department of Göteborg University for putting their inexhaustible resources at my disposal. The Royal Society of Arts and Sciences in Göteborg has supported several research trips to different regions in the Middle East during these years and deserves my gratitude. And finally, my gratitude goes to the Swedish Collegium for Advanced Studies in the Social Sciences, Uppsala, for kindly inviting me as a fellow during spring 2001, which gave me the possibility to finish this work in a quiet and stimulating environment.

Apart from the people and institutions attached to academic life, several others have been of invaluable help during the period of work. The following ones should be singled out: Olav Ljösne, Norwegian Consulate General, Jeddah; Paul Moe, Norwegian Embassy, Riyadh; Claes Spong, Fayed Commercials, Riyadh; Steen Hohwü-Christensen, Swedish Embassy, Riyadh; Sabry and Andrea Saleem, Yemen Language Center, Sanaa; Aud-Lise Norheim and Kjetil Jensehaugen, Norwegian Embassy, Damascus; Göran Berg, Swedish Embassy, Damascus. I especially thank Jonathan Price, Curzon Press, for his helpfulness and enthusiastic support during the publication process.

Perhaps my the greatest inspiration have been the modern Arabs themselves. During 25 years of travel and sojourn in the Arab world I have enjoyed the friendliness, hospitality and helpfulness of ordinary people in restaurants, taxis, hotels, stone palaces in Sanaa, Damascus and Aleppo, clay huts on the countryside of Iraq and Egypt, bedouin tents in the Sinai and in the Arabian peninsula and many other places. If this work has been able to clarify something about their vast history, it should be seen as a modest act of gratitude for having had the privilege to become acquainted with them and their culture.

Jan Retsö
Göteborg, 14 July 2001

Map 1 The Arabian Pensinsula and the adjacent regions

Map 2 Southern Syria and Northwestern Arabia, Sinai and Lower Egypt

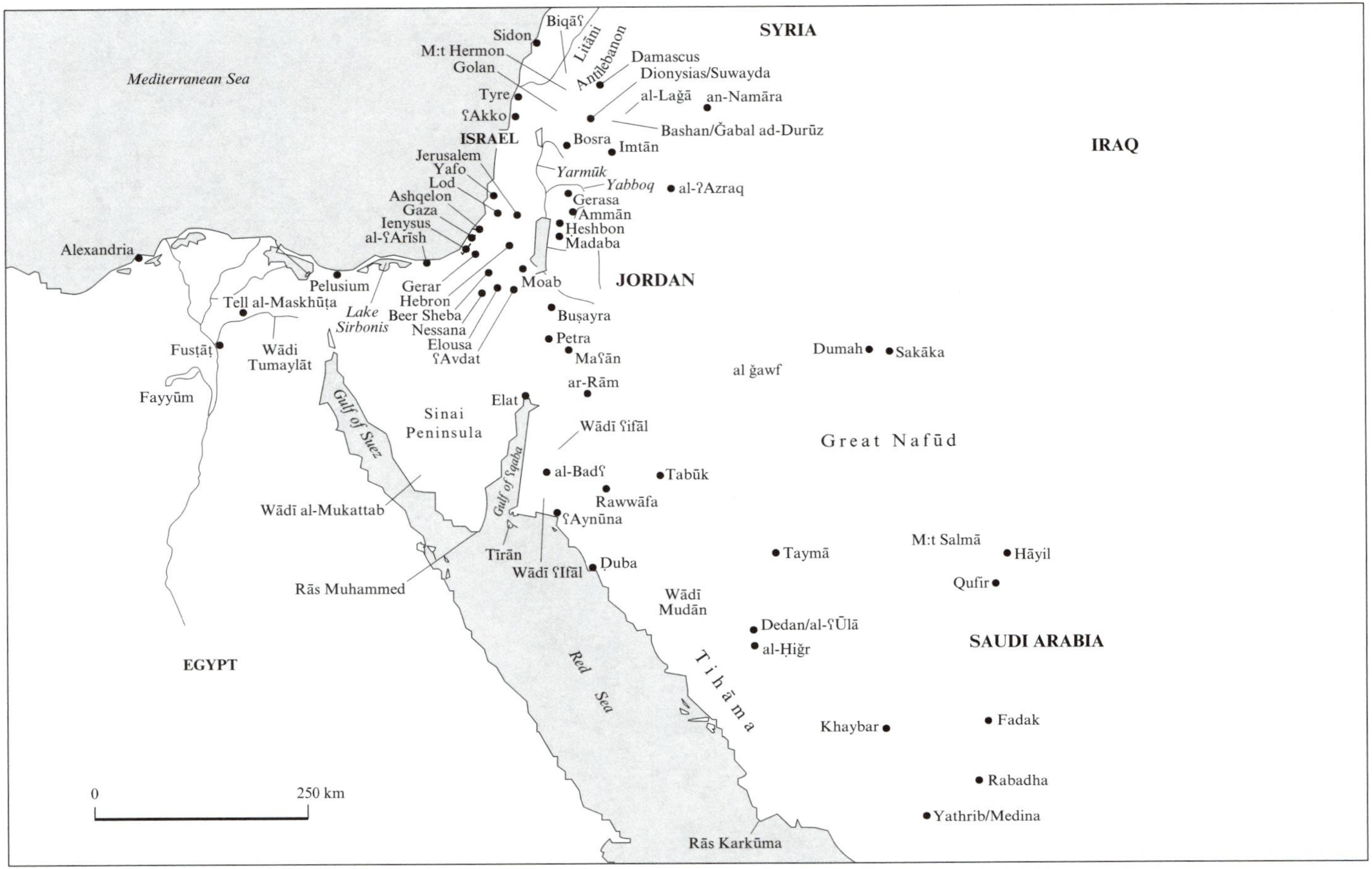

Map 3 Mesopotamia and the Syrian Desert

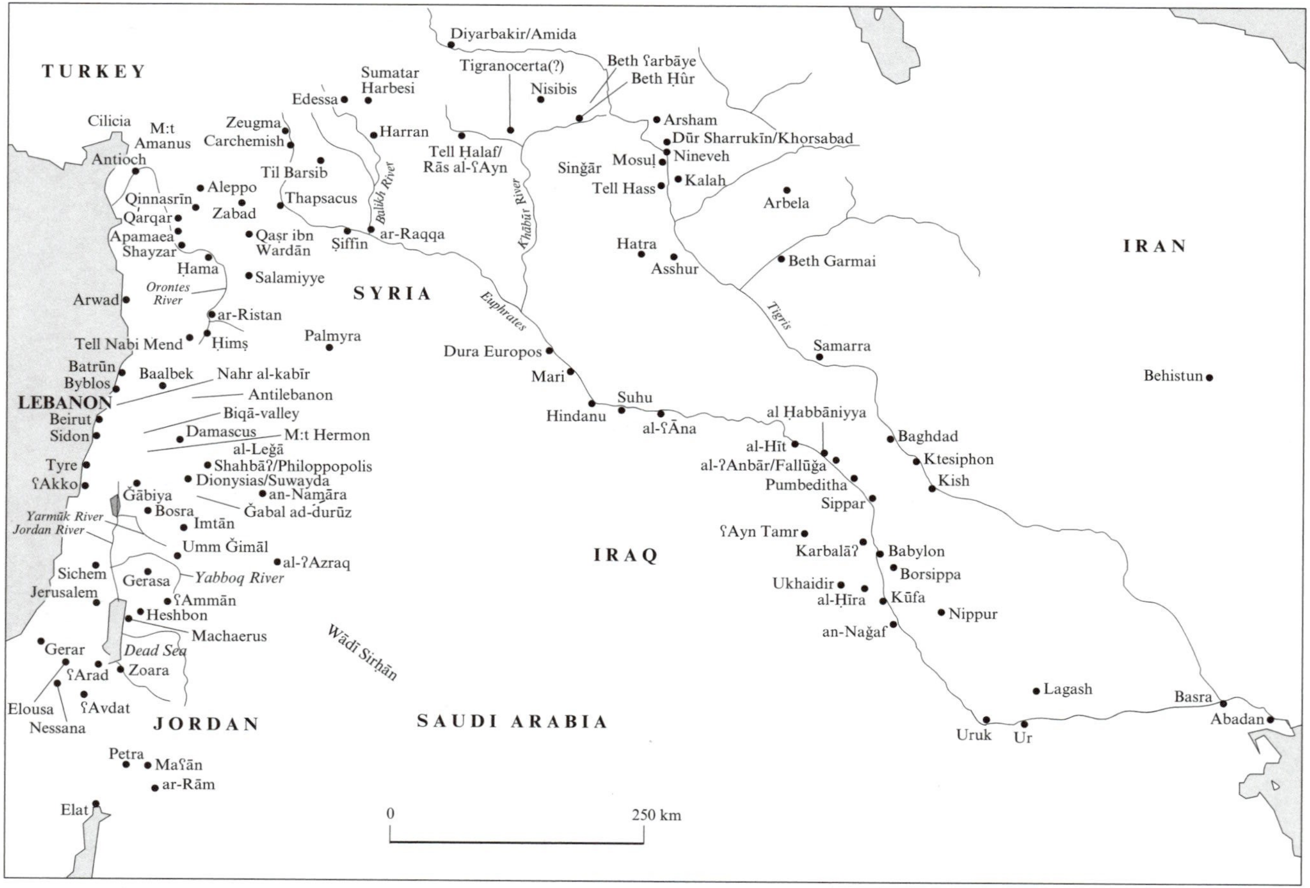

Map 4 Eastern Arabia and the Persian Gulf

Map 5 Southern Arabia

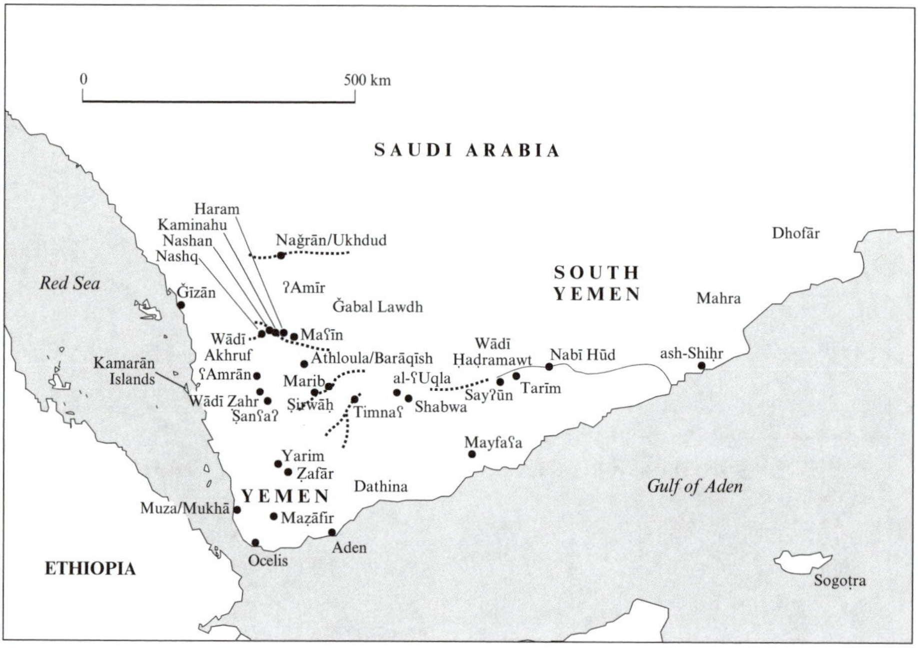

PROLEGOMENA

Man hüte sich vor der Meinung,
dass alle semitische Wüstenvölker
durchaus nur Araber in unsere
jetzige Auffassung des Wortes
gewesen sein könnten.
(Theodor Nöldeke, *Über die Amalekiter* 637)

Which Arabs?

One day in May 1992, when I was travelling north of Salamiyyeh in Syria heading for the impressive sixth-century ruins at Qaṣr ibn Wardān, I saw a group of bedouin tents far away on the plain, still deep green from the winter rains. I asked my driver, an Ismaili from Salamiyyeh, which tribe (*qabīle*) he thought they belonged to. He pondered for a while and then asked: 'You mean: which *ʕarab*?'

This correction of my vocabulary was not completely unexpected, but it was a neat confirmation of an insight which had become clearer during my work for some years with the question of the meaning of the word 'Arab'. It is often alleged that those whom we call the bedouin usually see themselves as *the* Arabs in contrast to the non-bedouin. My driver, who, as a citizen of the Syrian Arab Republic and a user of the Arabiyya language in reading and writing, would probably on other occasions have labelled himself an Arab in accordance with the ruling ideology of modern Arabism, now relapsed into a more traditional linguistic usage when confronted with the tent-dwellers.

It might be a good start to try to find out the actual meaning of the word 'Arab' according to the traditional usage demonstrated by the Syrian taxi-driver. A natural way is to listen to what the inhabitants of those tents in Syria have to say about the matter. We do, in fact, today have a large corpus of texts recorded among the different bedouin tribes in the Syrian desert and the Arabian peninsula, dealing mostly with warfare and with frequent occurrences of the word *ʕarab*. These texts constitute a primary source for how this term is understood among those who often identify themselves as Arabs, in opposition to the modern nationalist meaning of the word.

Arabs and bedouin: present-day evidence

We will begin with a look at the statements made by the great ethnologist Alois Musil, who had first-hand knowledge of the bedouin in the Syrian desert from the beginning of the twentieth century. According to him, the members of the Rwala tribe in the Syrian desert call people living in black, movable tents (including themselves) *ʕarab*. Among them there are different groups. The *ʕarab ad-dīra* are those dwelling on tilled land and its borders. They are identical with the *šwāya* or *šūyān*, who herd sheep and goats and move within a limited area. Another group is the *badw*, who are camel-breeders, moving far into the desert and practising the razzia.[1] Thus, according to Musil, the bedouin are a restricted group within the category *ʕarab*, and they often exercise power over the small-cattle breeders. There is usually a sharp social distinction between the *šwāya* and the bedouin, although both are *ʕarab*. *ʕarab* and bedouin are thus not synonymous.

Musil's picture seems quite coherent. A closer reading of his report will, however, show some cracks. It is said that in the expression *ʕarabna raḥalow*, *ʕarabna nazalow*, 'our Arabs have removed, our Arabs have camped' the word refers to members of the same kin. The plural *ʕurbān* is said to refer to membership of different clans or tribes, and Musil reports a conversation quite similar to the one in the taxi from Salamiyyeh: 'If someone meets a nomad and asks him "Where are you from, lad?" and he answers "From these *ʕarab*", the response may be: "We know that you are from the *ʕarab*, but from which of the various *ʕurbān*?"'.[2]

There are thus in Musil's report signs of at least two definitions of Arabs among the Rwala which are not quite synonymous: one according to way of life, another according to descent. This lack of a unitary concept reappears in the modern documentations of bedouin speech.[3] Most investigators translate the word *ʕarab* with several different expressions according to what they believe the context demands – bedouin, nomad, tribe, camp – or they leave it untranslated.

The Arabic word bedouin (*badw*, *badawī*) occurs now and then in the texts. Its meaning is most clear in the following cases:

> She belongs to the *baduw*, she is not among the *ḥḍiriyyah*.[4]
>
> The *ḥaḍir*, the people of the Mountain [of Shammar] remained but as for the *badyih*, they emigrated to Mesopotamia.[5]
>
> My eyes shed their water;
> Ninety nights' sleep did not delight them;
> I am looking for medicine for them among *ḥaḍar* and *bidwān*.[6]

These three examples contrast the *badw* with the *ḥaḍr*, i.e. the moving peoples with the settled ones. The only reasonable interpretation is that suggested by Musil, namely that *badw* signifies those living as nomads moving between summer and winter pastures, whereas the *ḥaḍr* are people living in villages.

In a story dealing with the conflict between ʕAbdallah ibn Rashīd and Muhammed ibn Rakhīṣ in the Shammar in Central Arabia in the middle of the nineteenth century, the people involved are characterized in the following way:

> [ʕAbdallah] was a *əḥḍəri* man but Ibn Rakhīṣ was a *əbdəwi*.[7]

ʕAbdallah was from the town of Ḥāyel, whereas his adversary was a chief in the nomadic parts of the Shammar tribe. Now, according to the storyteller, these events 'took place among the *ʕarab*'.[8] This statement stands as the conclusion of the whole story, and the meaning must be that both Abdallah and Ibn Rakhīṣ were *ʕarab*. This term would then, for our storyteller, encompass people among both nomads and settlers. This evidence thus goes nicely with the distinction pointed out by Musil: *ʕarab* does not mean nomad or bedouin; both settlers and nomads could be part of the *ʕarab*.[9]

In a story recently recorded among 'bedouin' in Galilee, we find explicit mention of non-bedouin Arabs. It is told about two men from the tribe of Ghrīfāt:

> The origin of al-eġrēfāt is from *ʕarab* called the Muwāli *ʕarab*.[10]

After a quarrel with their cousins, the two seek refuge in a village with a shaykh. One becomes a shepherd, the other ploughs:

> This shaykh had a daughter; an *ʕarabi*, a shaykh, from a village, farmers [*fallāḥīn*].[11]

This shaykh is not a nomad, i.e. a bedouin, but a settler in a village. The two youths, however, are something else:

> We are cut-off folk, we have no one and we are lonely *bedu* in this village.[12]

It is, however, completely clear from the text that all these people are *ʕarab*. Unless one has decided beforehand that bedouin and *ʕarab* are synonymous, there is no difficulty in seeing Arab as a larger category than bedouin in this passage.

Another passage in the same collection of texts should be interpreted in a similar manner.[13] The story begins by presenting a group of villagers sitting one evening in a house – 'the custom of the *ʕarab*!' – when people knock at the door and all come in 'except the *əbduwi*'. This bedouin has a law case and is looking for a judge (*qāḍī*), preferably the shaykh of the village (*šēx al-balad*).[14] If the shaykh is not willing to take the case, the bedouin will transfer it to his brother 'for he is also an *ʕarab qāḍī* like you'.[15] The text thus states clearly that the villagers are *ʕarab* but not necessarily *badw*.[16]

Such passages are clear enough, although not very numerous in the published texts. But the evidence is beyond discussion. It is thus easy to see why *ʕarab* and *badw* can often be found as terms for the same people. Bedouin are Arabs but not all Arabs are bedouin. It must also be kept in mind that the distinction may easily be blurred in daily speech. Among the bedouin it is not difficult to imagine how the two terms may stand for the same people in most cases, the more so since they may tend to look down on settled people in general. One can also imagine that among outsiders the distinction is not always kept up.[17]

Even though the distinctive meaning of the word may not always be upheld, it is the distinction that is of crucial interest for the historical background of the term. It can safely be assumed that in the distinctive meaning we have a clue to the original sense. It is not very likely that two different words are originally synonyms. If *badw* today means migrating shepherds, we can be sure that *ʕarab* originally meant something else. It is also quite possible that *badw* had another meaning earlier. The important point is the difference reflected in the modern semantic distinctions between the two words.

Having thus determined that *ʕarab* does not mean bedouin, although the bedouin may well be included in the term, we may proceed to a definition of what the term *ʕarab* does refer to. We shall turn to the texts from the Aḥaywāt tribe in the Negev, which contain several passages of interest for our problem. In one text, a man tells about his conflict with a man from another tribe. On one occasion, his adversary appears unexpectedly in his camp in an angry mood:

> And my mood wasn't exactly a good one either but I thought to myself: what about my children and my *ʕarab*?[18]

After a heated discussion, the adversary takes his leave. The other one decides to leave his camp-ground and move his children and family elsewhere:

> However, the following morning I said: 'Come on, oh *ʕarab*, come on, women, we're going to move camp.' They said: 'Where to?' I said: 'We're going to move; we'll camp in Wādī Abu Syaylih just below the road. We'll camp [lit. we'll put up (our tent)] by our *ʕarab*.'[19]

Another passage tells about a dispute over a border between two tribes. The man telling the story has gone to Quntilleh in the southern Negev for the spring pasture:

> I reached the *ʕarab* there, my *ʕarab* together with the *ʕarab* of my father-in-law and my cousins.[20]

In these instances it would be absurd to translate *ʕarab* with 'nomad' or 'bedouin'. The meaning is obviously 'kin', 'close relatives', 'people belonging to your family', 'people of the same lineage'.[21]

This use of the term should be compared with passages in an older recording from around 1900, namely the story of Ḥuthrubī, a hero of the ʕAnaza tribe in the Syrian desert. We will adduce two of them.

> When they saw that Ḥuthrubī had taken a horse, they drove their camels until they reached [the] *ʕarab*, their *ahl*.[22]

> They praised God and marched forward until they came close to the *ʕarab*, their *ahl*.[23]

There is no doubt that *ahl* here stands as an explaining gloss to the word *ʕarab*, which then must have a similar, if not identical meaning. If we accept the meaning 'kin' etc. for the term, several expressions in the texts generated by the modern bedouin themselves become more comprehensible. We do, for example, have many instances of the word *ʕarab* with a pronominal suffix: 'our *ʕarab*':

> He said: 'Yes, we are only – our *ʕarab* are not with us . . . our *ʕarab* are not present; now we are only the *ḥamūla* [the family of the shaykh] as one might say.'[24]

If the word *ʕarab* thus means something like 'tribesmen related to each other by blood', it also becomes explicable why editors of the texts have sometimes seen it proper to render *ʕarab* by 'camp', since a camp often (not always) is made up of members of one family or families closely related.[25] That the term *ʕarab* pertains to blood relations is seen from the use of the participle *m(u)ʕarrab* as a designation for both people and animals of pure blood:

> Noble scions of pure-blooded maternal uncles charged against doughty warriors who were close kinsmen.[26]

The best illustration of this meaning of the word is the ample use of *ʕarab* and, more frequently, the plural *ʕurbān* in a genitive construction with a tribal name or the name of a chief as attribute: *ʕarab/ʕurbān Šammar*, *ʕurbān Ibn Rašīd*. It may also be qualified by a place name: *ʕurbān Ḥāyel*, *ʕurbān al-Ǧōf*.[27] In fact, *ʕurbān* is the natural designation for tribesmen belonging to specific lineages.[28]

We may now understand the following text better. Two men, Slēmān and Nağm, belonging to different lineages within the Aḥaywāt, camping together with several other clans, are talking about a girl, ʕIdih, more closely related to Slēmān than to Nağm but whom the latter wants to marry:

> I [Slēmān] said to him: 'Nağm, we have mixed *ʕurbān* with us – and afterwards when they see you – they see you walking with her, the *ʕurbān* will say we are dishonoured'. For we had with us people from outside, distinguished *ʕarab*.[29]

From the context it is clear that by *ʕurbān muxallaṭa* is meant people belonging to different sub-groups among the Aḥaywāt.

It might be legitimate to ask how representative these investigated passages are. Many instances of *ʕarab* in the available texts could also be interpreted in a more traditional way, i.e. a general term for the inhabitants of the desert. The fact that so many authors and scholars have thought that Arab means 'nomad' or that it may mean anything from camp to family may indicate that the word has a very vague meaning or that it indeed means nomad, i.e. it is a term for a way of living. The translation of *ʕarab/ʕurbān* with 'bedouin' is a way of avoiding the problem, since the meaning of this word often seems to remain unspecified. The question might be difficult to settle by direct interrogation of informants. It is likely that our texts are actually very good testimonies for the use of the term since the informants have not been asked to explain this specific word. It is then also likely that the word does indeed have a specific meaning to those producing the texts, even though they never bother to make it explicit. It should also be observed that the meaning arrived at here, namely 'kin' or 'tribesmen', is applicable to all instances of the word *ʕarab*, without any exception, in the modern documentations of 'bedouin' texts, whereas, if one clings to the meaning 'nomad' or 'bedouin', the instances just quoted must be explained as exceptions from the general rule. There is no reason to make things more complicated than they are. It can be stated with a very high degree of probability that *ʕarab* in the texts we have from 'bedouin' in this century means 'kinsfolk', people who are related to each other in a certain way, namely those who can claim membership of a set of tribes and tribe-like groups in the Syrian desert and on the Arabian peninsula. It can then further be assumed that the testimony of these texts is a trustworthy reflex of the actual usage of the word among the real *ʕarab* and others in close contact with them.

This does not necessarily imply that *ʕarab* is a term for some kind of ethnic group.

In the texts studied here so far, it designates a class of people who can show relationship to specific tribes and/or shaykhs, not membership of a nationality. Ethnicity among the *ʕarab* consists of membership in a specific tribe: Shammar, ʕAnaza, Bani Ṣakhr, Rwala etc. One could well call the tribes the nations of the *ʕarab*. One could perhaps compare this categorization of people with that of traditional European nobility. Noblemen all over Europe belonged/belong to specific nations: they are British, Spanish, Belgian, Swedish, Danish etc. But they have one common characteristic, namely that they by birth or sometimes by appointment (knighting) belong to a class of people in which one is entitled to some privileges, nowadays mostly of a symbolic nature, and perform special duties, based on descent and membership in a defined set of families. The criterion of a traditional European aristocrat is membership in certain families. This criterion was acknowledged all over Europe as a definition of a nobleman, regardless of nationality. A closer parallel is the terminology used among the present-day Somali people. The Somali see themselves as a nation of genetically related tribes. Interestingly enough, the Somalis seem not to have had any ethnic designation for themselves. The word 'Somali' is a fairly recent term which seems to have been applied on them by outsiders.[30] The Somalis have always traditionally identified themselves by membership in one of the larger tribal groups: Dir, Hawiya, Ishaak or Darod. Those humans who can trace their genealogy to one of these are Haagi or Hashya, 'of noble lineage'.[31] It is remarkable that the Somali-speaking Sab group in south-western Somalia is not traditionally considered Somalis but Haagi/Hashya. It seems that belonging to the *ʕarab/ʕurbān* is something of this sort. This does not imply that *ʕarab* must mean 'aristocrat' or 'nobleman', only that it is a term of the same kind. An Arab is not one who belongs to an ethnic group called *ʕarab* but one who can claim membership based on blood in this or that ethnic group/well-defined set of ethnic groups. An Arab of this kind may be a settler in a village tilling the soil, or he may be a small cattle-breeder moving to pastures during a part of the year, or he may be a camel-breeder moving across large areas following the seasonal blossoming and withering of the grasslands, or even a city-dweller.[32] The camel-breeders have always been the nobility among the Arab aristocracy whereas the others have constituted the gentry.

The evidence gathered mainly by linguists since Musil's time thus confirms to a large extent his definition of Arabs and bedouin, although we can, from the textual material, get an understanding of the contradictions in Musil's definition. The interpretation presented here explains the obvious difficulties many scholars have had in giving a proper rendering of the terms *ʕarab* and *badw* in their translations of the texts.

The picture emerging from the modern textual sources, adjusting Musil's definitions, thus seems quite coherent and unambiguous. If we lift our eyes and look towards other parts of the Arab world, however, it becomes less clearcut. Unfortunately, there is no authentic documentation available of everyday linguistic usage among 'bedouin' in North Africa, Egypt and South Arabia comparable to that which we have from the central and northern parts of the peninsula, as well as the Syrian desert.[33] We must rely on scattered remarks in dictionaries and studies. It then appears that there is a completely different meaning of the word *ʕarab* around.

At the turn from the nineteenth to the twentieth centuries we find testimonies from South Arabia that *ʕarab* designates settled people and especially city-dwellers.[34] This is said to hold both for Ḥaḍramawt and North Yemen. These *ʕarab* are said to stand outside both the tribal organization with its *mašāyikh* as well as the *sāda*-class, and they are also distinguished from the lower classes in the towns. Today these distinctions may be disappearing, but since this definition of Arabs goes against the one commonly accepted in other parts of the 'Arab' world it is worth noticing.[35] There are some hints of the existence of a similar definition in Tunisia and Morocco, although we also have documentation of the meaning 'tribe'.[36]

Even though the contradictions in the traditional renderings of the word *ʕarab* in texts from the Syrian desert and the central and northern parts of the Arabian peninsula can be straightened out at a closer look, the South Arabian evidence is more difficult to integrate. The traditional South Arabian *ʕarab* are defined as town-dwellers and non-tribalists, which is completely opposite to the traditional northern concept. This contradiction may seem insignificant and also doubtful since its documentation is scanty. It does, however, lead to the formulation of some questions about the term:

1. How far back in time can the meaning 'kin', 'blood-relative' be traced?
2. What is the relationship between the two meanings 'kin' and 'townsman'?

It should be obvious to everybody that these questions must be studied by looking at the evidence from earlier periods of the history of people called Arabs, preferably the earliest evidence available. We will thus now turn to history itself.

Method of investigation

From the preceding survey it has become clear that we should be somewhat cautious before stating what kind of people is meant by Arabs during the course of history. General statements based on more or less realistic ideas about the geographical and ecological conditions in Arabia (since we all know that Arabia is a desert and that all those who live there are nomads, Arab must mean 'desert-dwellers' and 'nomad' or: 'Arabs are all who speak Arabic') are to be avoided until they can be verified by solid and unequivocal documentation from historical sources. Since present-day evidence does not indicate that Arabs are identical either with nomads, bedouin or any other group definable in such general cultural terms, the mere mention of such groups in historical sources constitutes a problem: who are the people designated by this term? Our aim in this study is to find out what the word 'Arab' stands for from its earliest occurrence until the end of the Umayyad period. This will, hopefully, also shed some light on its present-day use. The method chosen is to trace the occurrences of the word itself in the sources. Since the definition of Arab at this stage of the investigation turns out to be rather elusive, we shall consequently read the word as X, i.e. of unknown meaning, wherever it occurs. By studying its context, the character of the source and its historical background, a meaning will, hopefully, emerge. Our working hypothesis will be that if an individual or a group of people are *not* called Arab(s) in the sources, we have no reason to call them so either. Even though they in some sense were *ʕarab* we have no means of proving it, except perhaps in a few special cases.

Designations of people of the kind we are dealing with are problematic as to who uses them. Outsiders may use designations for people which are rejected by those designated. This is quite common with non-ethnic groups like the Quakers or the 'vagrants' of western and northern Europe.[37] Then we have all the cases when outsiders and insiders use completely different terms for the same group like German/Deutsch, Hungarians/Magyar etc. As far as the *ʕarab* are concerned, it will be shown that the tribes in the first Islamic state used this term for themselves, at least to a certain extent, whereas their neighbours called them Saracens, Ishmaelites etc. The relationship between these terms during the preceding centuries will have to be investigated.

It is also crucial to establish the status of the written records. It can be assumed that the terminology found in contemporary official documents like inscriptions, governmental ordinances etc. reflects more faithfully the valid political and juridical conditions than do descriptions by geographers and philosophers and other literary documents based on more theoretical academic or theological views of political and ethnic conditions and often written at a later date. Purely literary documents must thus be judged to have less documentary value than official documents even though, as we shall see, both historians and geographers not seldom have preserved matter-of-fact records by travelling merchants and reports by military men of a more documentary character and, consequently, possessing a high value as a source. Since, as will become evident, almost all contemporary documentation of Arabs before Islam originates from outsiders, i.e. people who were not Arabs in any sense of the word, these distinctions are crucial in order to extract a picture of what was actually meant by Arabs during the period. As we shall see, the historical records are astonishingly rich even with the restrictions we have imposed.

Apart from the distinctions outlined above, the historical records can be divided into two further kinds: the texts in Arabic, codified by Islamic scholars and *litterati* during the Islamic period, and the pre-Islamic sources in which Arabs are mentioned. These latter sources are in many languages: Akkadian, Hebrew, Old and Middle Persian, Greek, Latin, Aramaic and Sabaean. The pre-Islamic sources are thus in non-domestic languages, except a handful of inscriptions from north and central Arabia, which are of less importance since the word ʕRB occurs in only a few of them.[38] The two groups of sources overlap during the period AD 500–700 when we have both Arabic and non-Arabic testimonies.

The following investigation will consequently be divided into two parts: the first analysing the testimony of the sources in Arabic which deal with the history of the tribes of Arabia during the century preceding the rise of Islam until the fall of the Umayyad empire in AD 750; the second studying the non-Arabic evidence from the pre-Islamic period. In medieval Islamic culture, only the stories recorded in the Arabic sources were taken into account. Thus the period before AD 500, from which very few memories were preserved in these sources, was ignored and almost completely forgotten.[39] For an educated Muslim in the Middle Ages, the history of the Arabs began around one century before the Prophet and could be studied in passages scattered in the great works compiled by Islamic historians and antiquarians. For us, the value of this evidence comes largely from the fact that it is the earliest evidence about the meaning of the word among people considering themselves as Arabs or, at least, closely connected with Arabs and the language named after them. It gives a picture of how Arabs and their close associates defined the word during the time of the Prophet and the following century. For the century before Muhammed the value of these sources is more uncertain.

The evidence for the existence of people called Arabs stretches 1,400 years back in time before the rise of Islam. That evidence originates almost completely from people not called Arabs by themselves or others. The picture is thus mainly that of outsiders. This must be kept in mind when studying the context of the evidence. One must be prepared to realize that outsiders may have had different concepts about what Arabs were. The question must always be posed to what extent the understanding of the outsiders may coincide with that of the Arabs themselves, whoever they were. We must also be attentive to the possibility that the concept may have changed over time among both the Arabs themselves and the outsiders.

Equipped with these insights we shall dive into the past, looking for the origins of the Arabs, remembered and forgotten.

Notes

1 Musil, *Customs* 44–45; cf. also Oppenheim, *Beduinen* I:22, for a similar definition.

2 *Fāhmīn annak min hal-ʕarab mār min ayy al-ʕorbān?* (Musil, *Customs* 44).

3 These texts are, apart from those mentioned in the bibliography: A. Socin, *Diwan aus Centralarabien* (1901); R. Montagne, 'Contes poétiques bédouins', *Bulletin d'études orientales de l'Institut Français de Damas* 5 (1935) 33–120; idem, 'Sālfet Šāyeʕ Alemsāḥ, Gyedd errmāl', *Mélanges Gaudefroy-Demombynes*, Le Caire 1935–45 125–130; B. Ingham, *North East Arabian Dialects* (1982); idem, *Najdi Arabic. Central Arabian* (1994); P.M. Kurpershoek, *Oral Poetry and Narratives from Central Arabia 2: The Story of a Desert Knight. The Legend of Šlēwīḥ al-ʕAṭāwi and Other ʕUtaybah Heroes* (1995). The texts from Palva's *Studies* 1976 and onwards are recorded directly from speakers of bedouin dialects. The older ones are either dictations or free compositions in 'bedouin' style. Almost the entire corpus represents the type of story-telling in prose with interfoliated poems dealing with violent conflicts, a literary form well known from the *ʔayyām al-ʕarab* tradition, representing a traditional, stylized language and linguistic usage employed not only by 'pure bedouin' but also by storytellers with settled background. The only texts with a different structure are those of Stewart, which are recordings of judicial cases among the bedouin in the Negev. They contain narrative elements but also dialogues and heated debates.

4 Kurpershoek, *Poetry* 17:11 (p. 154).

5 Sowayan, *Narrative* 64.

6 Palva, *Artistic colloquial* IV:34.

7 Palva, *Studies* § 18 (p. 64).

8 Palva, *Studies* § 100.

9 Cf. Wetzstein, *Zeltlagern* 70: the *ʔahl ad-dīra* are 'die Localstämme', the *ʔahl al-badu* are 'die grosse Wanderstämme der Wüste'.

10 Rosenhouse, *Dialects* 4:1 l.1.

11 Rosenhouse, *Dialects* 180:14. The editor translates freely: He was an Arab, from a village, a farmer's village.

12 Rosenhouse, *Dialects* 4:1 l. 19.

13 Rosenhouse, *Dialects* 4:6 l. 3 (p. 214).

14 Rosenhouse, *Dialects* 4:40.

15 Rosenhouse, *Dialects* 4:10.

16 The editor misses the distinction when translating both *badawī* and *ʕarab* as 'bedouin'.

17 It is no coincidence that the clearest and most explicit instances of the comprehensive use of the word 'Arab' come from Rosenhouse's texts. They originate among Arabs in the proper traditional sense of the word, who live close to the settlers and to whom the distinction between settled and migrant Arabs is more crucial than for those living farther out in the steppes.

18 Stewart, *Texts* 15:70 (§ 4). Stewart's translations are very free and paraphrasing and the version given here is an attempt at coming closer to the original.

19 Stewart, *Texts* 15:102–105 (§ 5).

20 Stewart, *Texts* 36:40 (§ 4).

21 A similar meaning may be intended in Rosenhouse, *Dialects* 4.4 l.1: *ʔamīr ʕarab, famīliya*. These words stand as the introduction of a story, although it is not quite clear what the editor means by putting them within parentheses. Do they belong to the recorded text or not? The word *famīliya* indeed looks like a gloss (by the story-teller himself?) to the word *ʕarab*.

22 Landberg, *ʕAnazeh* 1:13: *elyāma garrabu ʕala ʕarab, ahalhon*. The last word is translated 'leurs familles'.

23 Landberg, *Anazeh* 1:10, 2:30: *alʕarab ahalhon*. The latter is translated 'leurs contribules'.

24 Ingham, *Bedouin* 10:4–5 (p. 77). Cf. also the expression recorded by Musil above. See also Kurpershoek, *Poetry* 3:250, 118 and Landberg, *ʕAnazeh* 1:13, whose rendering of the phrase: *u yōm igbalu ʕala ʕarabhom* with 'lorqu'ils arrivèrent dans leur tribu' is in accordance with this interpretation of the word.

25 Examples are legion, e.g. Sowayan, *Narrative* 395, 404; Stewart, *Texts* 5:23, 69:21; idem, *Narrative* 2:1, 3:2, 8:2, 10:2; Palva, *Studies* X:4; idem, *Narratives* E:29, E:33; Kurpershoek, *Poetry* 1:1:2; Montagne, *Ghazou* 21; Bailey, *Poetry* 31; cf. Stewart, *Texts* 2 Glossary s.v. *ʕrb* (p. 199).

26 Sowayan, *Narrative* 634:

ʕyāl aš-šyūx mʕarribīn al-axwāl
raddaw ʕala rabʕin tidānaw ba-l-ansāb

Cf. the note 56 to this verse (ibid., p. 319). For the term *ʕāribāt* for she-camels of noble race see Kurpershoek, *Poetry*: Vocabulary s.v. *ʕrb*. Cf. also Kurpershoek, *Poetry* 3:488 and Glossary s.v. *ʕirb* with reference to Hess, *Beduinen* 75: *ʔibil ʕirāb*.

27 Palva, *Narratives* A:11, E:1, F:1.

28 Thus also Musil: 'The word *ʕorbân* expresses membership of various clans or tribes' (*Manners* 44).

29 Stewart, *Narrative* 1:2. For the meaning of *ʕarab kibīrih,* see idem, *Texts* 2 Vocabulary s.v. *kbr*.

30 Lewis, *Peoples* 13–14.

31 Lewis, *Peoples* 15–17.

32 Cf. Abu Lughod, *Sentiments* 44–45.

33 In traditional Mauritanian society *ʕarab* is said to denote an aristocracy among the free or the *awlād Ḥassān* (Norris, *Mūrītāniyā* 616, Taine-Cheikh, *Dictionnaire* s.vv. *ʕrab, ʕarbi* : 'guerrier' opposed to 'marabout'; cf. *ʕrab n-ngāb*, 'the Arabs of the turban' = the Touaregs; *ʕrab š-šmāl,* 'the Bambaras'). It is interesting that *ʕarab* may also denote all members of this great tribe. It seems that the limited definition is the older one. Unfortunately it is not clear how these *ʕarab* define themselves.

34 Landberg, *Hadramoût* 653 s.v. ʕRB; Glaser, *Kastengliederung* 202–204; cf. Gerholm, *Market* 141 sqq., Behnstedt, *Dialekte* 814 s.v. ʕRB and Piamenta, *Dictionary* 320–321.

35 Unfortunately, Dresch does not discuss this problem in his book on tribes and government in Yemen. He only adduces the more widespread understanding of Arab as 'tribesmen' in accordance with the northern usage (Dresch, *Tribes* 13–14). It is evident that this usage is also found in Yemen, cf. Caton, *Peaks* 290 verse 3 (cf. ibidem 119) where the guests at a *sahrah*, i.e. the tribesmen, are called *ʕarab*, but it could be suspected that this usage originally is a northern import. The absence of the contrary meaning in Dresch could indicate that the limited sense of the word is an archaic usage which is gradually disappearing.

36 Marçais/Guîga, *Textes* s.v. ʕRB: *ʕrab tūnes* 'les gens de [la ville de] Tunis', *ʕrab al-ḥōma* 'les habitants du faubourg'; cf. Dozy, *Supplément* s.v. ʕRB: *ʔawlād al-ʕarab* 'citadins et villageois'. Sinaceur, *Dictionnaire Colin* 5/1242: *f-la-ʕréb* 'à la campagne'; cf. ibid. *la-ʕrōbīya* 'les campagnards, la campagne'.

37 These call themselves 'Friends' and 'Travellers' respectively.

38 From these texts should be distinguished the inscriptions in South Arabia in which the word ʕRB is frequent. But the South Arabian texts were not written by people belonging to the ʕRB, at least not as far as we can see from the texts themselves. They thus basically belong to the category 'non-domestic'.

39 The only exception was the history of the Iranian kings, where the Sassanid period was fairly well documented by the Muslim historians. The Muslims from Yemen also preserved vague memories of their pre-Islamic kings. Otherwise, the periods before AD 500 were filled out with material ultimately originating from Judaeo-Christian sacral history.

Part I

THE REMEMBERED ORIGINS

1

ARABS IN EARLY ISLAM

Sources

For an investigation of the actual and original meaning of the word *ʕarab* it is natural to start by taking a look at the earliest historical records in the language called Arabic. The relevant parts of these records treat a period beginning *c.* AD 500. As is well known, the general opinion is that Islam arose among 'the Arabs' and that they constituted the main factor in the Islamic conquests resulting in the spread of Islam and the Arabic language outside Arabia. The national and ethnic background is usually seen as unproblematic. In order to determine the role of the Arabs during these fateful events it is necessary to find out what the term meant during the formative period of the Arabo-Islamic civilization, i.e. the period AD 500–750.

The difficulties in mapping out the use of the term during the first centuries covered by the Arabic sources (AD 500–750) are, however, considerable. We have few contemporary sources in Arabic preserved in their original shape from the Umayyad period, i.e. up to AD 750. From the pre-Islamic period we have at best a corpus of poetry which, however, does not give much historical information, but no other certain documents in Arabic. The history of the rise of Islam, the rise and fall of the first Islamic empire and the large conquests has, in modern times, traditionally been written by using records that received their final shape during the subsequent Abbasid period. For a study of the meaning of the term 'Arab' during the formative period before that period, the whole corpus of Arabic texts dealing with the history before 750 should be investigated. This has not been done here. The textual corpus is very large, often deficiently edited, lacking good indices and sometimes linguistically difficult, raising many problems of source criticism and interpretation. The following analysis is based on instances collected from the most important texts. It is clear that in this material we have a corpus of texts and fragments of texts which were actually written or formulated before 750 but which are preserved only in the recensions of later periods. The reliability of these texts, especially for the period before AD 700 is, however, problematic.

The earliest comprehensive Islamic history was that of Ibn Isḥāq (–767), completed around AD 760. It was a kind of world history beginning with the creation and the Biblical prophets, followed by the legends of the kings of Yemen and then the story of Muhammed. It probably also included the history of the Islamic state until the rise of the Abbasids. The work is lost in its original shape but preserved in quotations and an abbreviated recension by Ibn Hishām one generation later. Ibn Isḥāq's book was based on the work of predecessors, one of whom was the Yemeni Wahb b. Munabbih (–728 or –732?), who might himself have written a world history around AD 720. Like Ibn

Isḥāq, Wahb was edited by Ibn Hishām and, apart from a few fragments, his original writings are lost.

The history of pre-Islamic South Arabia is also documented in a work independent of Wahb-Ibn Isḥāq, namely a book ascribed to ʕUbayd b. Shariya which is said to have been composed already in the reign of Muʕāwiya, i.e. before AD 680, but which most likely is a pseudepigraph from the beginning of the Abbasid period. Like Wahb, this book is dominated by legendary and folk-tale-like stories about pre-Islamic Arabia.

Historical writing on the early history of Islam was continued by several authors who were younger contemporaries of Ibn Isḥāq or belonged to the following generations, such as Sayf b. ʕUmar, Abū Mikhnaf and al-Madāʔinī. Only two of these early historians are preserved: al-Wāqidī (–823) and Khalīfa al-Khayyāṭ (–845). Two of Sayf's texts have been discovered lately.

In the more technical Islamic literature there is some *ḥadīth* which is relevant for our problem. It is found in the classical collections ('the six books') and in the *Kitāb al-ʔamwāl*, 'The book on property' by Abū ʕUbayd (–838). The latter contains much interesting material on the structure of the early Islamic state. Important for the earliest Islamic history are also the two large collections from the ninth century of biographies of early Muslims by Ibn Saʕd (–845) and al-Balādhurī (–892).

Ibn Isḥāq's concept of a chronologically ordered world history was followed by other writers, the first of whom was al-Yaʕqūbī (897). The ninth century also saw the history of ad-Dīnawarī (–*c*. 902), written from an Iranian perspective. From the tenth century we have the monumental works by aṭ-Ṭabarī (–923) and al-Masʕūdī (–956), which contain large sections on pre-Islamic and early Islamic periods. In the same century Ḥamza al-ʔIṣfahānī (–961 or –971) wrote a shorter world history with a systematic chronological presentation of pre-Islamic and early Islamic history.

All these comprehensive world histories followed Ibn Isḥāq in moulding Islamic and pre-Islamic history together, basing themselves on the works of their predecessors. As far as the memories of the pre-Islamic period of Arabia outside Yemen are concerned, they were codified by two authors in the early ninth century: Abū ʕUbayda (–824) and Hishām b. al-Kalbī (–819). The material used by later historians for the pre-Islamic period is mostly derived from these two. In the tenth century two large collections of pre-Islamic and early Islamic traditions were made. One of them was collected by the Andalusian Ibn ʕAbd Rabbihi (–940), the other by ʔAbū al-Farağ al-ʔIṣfahānī (–*c*. 972). The latter's *Kitāb al-ʔaghānī* is an immense collection of poetry and accompanying prose texts dealing with both pre-Islamic and Islamic times. Unfortunately, this cornerstone for the information on the whole cultural and political development during the first centuries of Islamic history as well as for the preceding period is still to a large extent uninvestigated as far as sources are concerned. There does not even exist a critical edition of the text.

Information about the beginnings of 'Arab' history is also spread out in other types of literature. Important are the works by some of the earliest representatives of the encyclopaedic *adab* literature in the ninth century: al-Ğāḥiẓ (–868), Ibn Qutayba (–889) and al-Mubarrad (–899). Very valuable material is contained in the big dictionaries compiled from the tenth century onwards. The articles ʕRB in the two classics *Lisān al-ʕarab* by the Tunisian Ibn Manẓūr (–1311) and *Tāğ al-ʕarūs* by the Yemeni az-Zabīdī (–1791) are, like much of the other material in them, more or less compilations from older works like *at-Tahdhīb fī l-luġa*, written by al-Azharī in the tenth century, which, in its turn, is a compilation of lexicographical knowledge from the preceding centuries beginning with al-Khalīl (–791), the father of Arabic lexicography and grammar. These dictionaries thus contain traditions about the Arabic language from the first four centuries of Islam, and the articles ʕRB are a summary of the different meanings of the word known to the Arabic lexicographers during this period. Another important work for the early history of Arabia is the geographical lexicon by al-Bakrī from the tenth century, together with the works of the Yemeni historian al-Hamdānī from the same century, who in his description of Arabia has a wealth of interesting material. These works are completed by Yāqūt's (–1229) *Muʕǧam*, a vast geographical dictionary compiled in the twelfth century with additional material not found in the two earlier geographers.

To the extensive prose texts contained in the mentioned literature can be added the corpus of Arabic poetry attributed to poets starting from the beginning of the sixth century. The authenticity of the oldest parts of this corpus is debated. This discussion is not as relevant for the present study as could be expected, since there are surprisingly few occurrences of the word *ʕarab* and its derivations in it. The poetry turns out not to cast as much light on this question as one would have anticipated.

The Arabic texts telling the history of the period between AD 500 and 700 are all written after that period, most of them after 750.[1] The only preserved texts whose very wording comes from this period itself are the Qurʔān, parts of the poetic corpus and a few documents copied by later historians. It should further be observed that the chronological perspective of the Arabo-Islamic tradition does not go further back than *c*. AD 500. To the Muslim historians and scholars, the history of the tribes that were to constitute the Islamic community in the seventh century starts around this time. For the earlier history of Arabia, they had very vague memories more or less on folk-tale level. The only concrete information from before AD 500 was a series of names of the kings of the Himyarites in Yemen which starts at the end of the third century AD.[2] A similar list existed for the kings of al-Ḥīra in Iraq claiming to reach back to the middle of the third century AD. The series of rulers in al-Ḥīra is connected with tribal rulers in Syria in the third century whose descendants still lived in the beginning of the Islamic period.[3] Apart from the stories and genealogies of the northern tribes claiming to deal with the sixth century, the Arabo-Islamic tradition for earlier periods thus had only two fragile lists with a series of names beginning in the third century AD.

The picture we get in the Arabic literature of the background and origins of Islam and its early history is filtered through the minds of writers who lived long after the events depicted. Even though the Arabo-Islamic historians as a rule refer to eye-witnesses via chains of transmitters, the reliability of the information is questionable and remains uncertain for the period before 700.[4] This holds even more for the picture of the pre-Islamic period given in the Arabo-Islamic sources. The stories about the life of the tribes in Arabia in war and peace are often told in a brilliant literary form, which makes them very suspect as historical documentation. This does not exclude the presence in them of genuine memories of the past, but this material should always be read with an eye on the age when the stories were codified in their present shape.

For an analysis of the pre-Islamic tribal history Caskel's *Aijām* is still fundamental. The historical evaluation remains problematic. The traditions of the pre-Islamic period were revived around AD 700 with the great conflicts between the Qays and Kalb in Syria and the ʕAzd/Rabīʕa and Tamīm in Iraq. We find numerous references to them in the poems from the period and it can be assumed that the *ʔayyām*-stories received their basic shape by then. Dim memories of battles in a distant past were revived and used in the propaganda between the parties in these

> conflicts. In the *khabar*-stories, i.e. the stories dealing with the pre-Islamic history of the tribes, it is possible to discern two strains: one episodic, telling about razzias of plunder of cattle undertaken by a handful of men as a sport, told in a rather strict form, very short; another one heroic, telling about battles for the sake of honour only, involving large groups of warriors and often whole tribes, the stories tending to be spun out into larger epic structures and often connected with the kings in al-Ḥīra or Yemen. A similar division can be found in the poetry, where the short monothematic pieces, the *qiṭaʕ*, often deal with conflicts in everyday life whereas the large ode, the *qaṣīda*, is characterized by a heroic mood reminiscent of the epic *khabar*-stories. The historic evaluation of this dichotomy is difficult. According to Caskel, the epic-heroic strain is the result of the work of tradition during a long period with a corresponding distortion and disappearance of concrete history. The shorter ones would be closer to the events themselves, most of them telling about events having occurred after AD 580. It should, however, not be overlooked that the two strains can have originated and lived in different milieus. The heroic-epic stories represent the ideals of a warrior aristocracy whereas the short razzia stories reflect the realities of people directly involved in cattle breeding.

Due to the compilatory nature of the extant Arabic sources, it is difficult, not to say impossible, to study the transformation of ethnic terms during the first 200 years of Islam by starting with the oldest source and moving on chronologically. Most extant texts are agglomerations of material from different periods, and the dating of specific passages is often not immediately evident from the present version, even though the Islamic system of references by *ʔisnād*, when it occurs, is of great help, although not always reliable. When investigating the use of a term like *ʕarab* in this kind of source material, one has to group the instances according to different kinds of meaning before trying to relate these groups to historical events and persons and thus ultimately grasping the chronological development of the term.

The result arrived at from a study of the Arabic material should then be compared to the texts in Greek and Syriac written in the sixth and seventh centuries AD. Unlike most Arabic material dealing with this period, these texts are written by contemporaries and preserved in more or less original shape. These texts are of two kinds: literary texts, mostly dealing with history or theology, and administrative or private documents. The testimony of these sources is a most important check of the picture of the historical development given by the Muslim historians, even though their objectivity cannot be taken *a priori*.[5]

We have a fairly large corpus of papyri in Greek and Arabic from Aphrodito in Upper Egypt from around 700, and from the town Nessana in the Negev from the end of the sixth century AD onwards, which reflect the economic and administrative conditions in the area before and after the Islamic conquest. These papyri are preserved in their original shape and contain extremely valuable information about conditions in Egypt and southern Palestine during our period, some of which is of immediate relevance to our problem, constituting an important means of checking the Arabic testimony.

Events during the first Islamic period are also reflected in some historical and theological works written during the seventh and the beginning of the eighth centuries AD. There is a conspicuous lack of works in Greek from the period after 630, and the most important sources are in Syriac written by Christians who were direct witnesses to the events. It should be kept in mind that these texts continue a literary tradition reaching back to the second century AD as far as the Syriac is concerned and even further back as far as the Greek is concerned. The ethnic terms used in them may thus well represent traditional literary custom and not contemporary usage. This holds to a much lesser degree for the papyri: everyday economic documents tend to use the official judicial terminology and may thus be a better testimony about actual ethnic conditions than the historians and theologians.

The picture presented on the following pages of the Arabs at the beginning of the Islamic period is not complete since it is based on a study of a selection of the most important sources. It is, however, likely that a fairly good idea of the use of the word can be gleaned from the investigated material. A complete study of the entire source material may well make necessary some adjustments of the results, but it does not seem likely that the basic outlines of the picture would have to be changed.

General historical background

The historical background of the events represented by the Arabo-Islamic tradition comprises the unruly conditions in Arabia in the sixth century, from which the prophet Muhammed and the state founded by him emerged at the beginning of the seventh century. Arabia, which until *c.* 525 had been dominated by the Himyaritic empire, which tried to balance between the two superpowers Rome and Iran, was thrown into a more anarchic state by the overthrow of the Himyarite kingdom by the Ethiopians in 525. The following period was, if we are to believe the picture given by the stories of 'the Wars of the Arabs', characterized by several attempts of local chieftains to control larger areas, and by a growing Iranian influence in the whole peninsula, culminating in the conquest of Yemen in AD 570.[6] This was then followed by the Iranian conquest of Syria and Egypt starting in 610. Arabia and the Middle East were on the verge of being totally taken over by the House of Sasan. The rise of the Islamic state in Medina after AD 622 can be seen as a response to this threat of Iranian hegemony.[7]

Muhammed's activities in Mecca and Medina during some two decades until the year 632 were followed by the first period of conquests under the four caliphs Abū Bakr, ʕUmar b. al-Khaṭṭāb, ʕUthmān b. ʕAffān and ʕAlī b. Abī Ṭālib. After the murder of ʕAlī in AD 661 there follows the period of the first three caliphs from the Sufyanid branch of the Umayyads: Muʕāwiya, Yazīd and Muʕāwiya II. After a civil war between 683 and 695 comes the epoch of the Marwanids, i.e. ʕAbd al-Malik and his descendants, another branch of the same family, whose rule, in spite of continuous convulsions and revolts, lasted until 750 when the Umayyad dynasty was finally overthrown by the Abbasids. Almost the whole period is characterized by severe conflicts, first between different factions among the Muslim tribes themselves and then, from 680, also between the tribes and the growing masses of Muslim converts from the conquered peoples. The division of factions in the Muslim community during these most dramatic decades has turned out never to be forgotten, and in many later conflicts within Islam the parties have identified themselves with the factions during the Umayyad era. Many of these have, as a matter of fact, survived until this day.

In order to understand something of the role of 'Arabs' in this period, it should be kept in mind that the first Islamic caliphate, the state originally founded by the Prophet himself and the subsequent state governed by the four caliphs and the following Umayyads, was a kind of alliance between tribes in Arabia. To be a full citizen in this state it was necessary to be a member of one of these tribes. Outside Arabia, or more properly speaking, outside the territories traditionally belonging to the tribes, the conquered peoples were not full members of the tribal federation unless they in some way or other became members of one of the tribes. The conquered lands were not given over to individual tribes or even individual warriors as property, but remained formally in the hands of the conquered peoples, who thus, being under occupation, had to pay tribute to the tribal federation. This tribute was then distributed to the tribal members, or rather those tribesmen who took part in the conquest. In Iraq warriors from different tribes were garrisoned together in large military camps. In Syria the main tribes were not mixed but remained separate units with control over defined territories. The difference between the tribal rulers and the conquered peoples was at least theoretically upheld in all provinces during the whole Umayyad period. There was, however, a way for non-tribesmen to join the ruling class, namely by becoming a client, a *mawlā*, to a tribesman or a tribe. These clients became an influential part of Muslim society, handling the administration and also at times joining the army. From an ideological point of view, however, the first Muslim state continued to consist of a class of tribesmen whose main task was warfare, who were settled in military camps outside Arabia supported by the labour of subjugated peoples not belonging to the tribal community. The tribesmen were drafted from a well-defined number of tribes, whose habitats mostly remained within traditional tribal areas in Arabia itself, although the drafting of tribesmen to the war front seems, in several cases, to have caused severe depopulation of some of the old homelands. Some tribes, however, moved from Arabia into the conquered land.

This system created growing conflicts between the conquered and the conquerors. But also within the tribal federation development was characterized by growing conflicts and rivalries. This ultimately resulted in the downfall of the tribal federation and abolition of the political system in AD 750. The conflicts were aggravated by the fact that the tribes identified the tribal federation with the Islamic community, so that only members of those tribes belonging to the federation or their clients could be considered real Muslims. Even if the client system made it possible also for non-tribesmen to attain positions of power in the state, its tribal structure remained its basic principle of organization. This system turned out to be unable to handle the conflicts that, for different reasons, increased during the latter part of the history of the Muslim state and which deepened the inter-tribal rivaries. Since the constituting document of Islam, the Qurʔān, did not contain any specific legitimation of such a system, and since its message was interpreted by many in universalistic and egalitarian terms, those opposing the system used arguments based on the Holy Book itself in their opposition to the rule of the tribal federation. This argumentation received increased weight from the fact that many among the subjugated peoples early began to practise Islam as their own religion without becoming clients. The conflicts between the tribal federation and its opponents was thus expressed in ideological and religious terms derived from the source of Islam. Also within the tribal federation the struggle for power between the tribes caused incessant strife, since the Qurʔān itself did not contain any sanction of leadership within the community. The universalistic interpretation turned out to be victorious. The empire established by the Abbasids was not based on a tribal federation but, ideologically, on the consensus of all human beings believing in the message of Muhammed.

The view of a medieval Muslim sociologist: Ibn Khaldūn

When dealing with the sociology of the Middle East in a historical perspective it is difficult to avoid Ibn Khaldūn (–1407) even though he was separated from the earliest

Islamic period by many centuries. In the Introduction, the *Muqaddima*, to his world history, the *Kitāb al-ʕibar*, he presents an elaborate theory about the social developments of the Islamic world, which is one of the most original and independent achievements of medieval thinking in general. Ibn Khaldūn, as an historian, knew the testimony of his predecessors very well and built his analysis of the processes of world history to a large extent on their material. Ibn Khaldūn sees world history as a continuous oscillation of power between nomadic and settled peoples. The political developments, the rise and fall of empires, are explained by the influx into the sown lands of nomadic peoples, who establish political structures kept together by the tribal solidarity which is found among them due to the harsh living conditions. When settled, the nomads gradually lose their virtues, ending with the dissolution of empires and ensuing political crisis. The scene is open for the next invasion.

This view of history has had a great attraction even to modern historians, and there is no doubt that Ibn Khaldūn has grasped some, if not all, basic mechanisms behind the history, if not of the world, then at least of the Middle East. The issue of the nomads is crucial in Ibn Khaldūn's philosophy of history, and he has much to say about bedouin and Arabs. The central passage relevant for the question investigated here is found in Book I Chapter II of the *Muqaddima,* of which a condensed version is given here.[8]

> 1. Different ways of living are the result of different ways of getting food. There are two main ways: *ḥaḍr* and *badw*. The *ḥaḍr* are the inhabitants of cities, some of whom adopt crafts as their living, others commerce. They build large houses and lay out towns and cities with castles and mansions for protection.
>
> 2. The people of *badw* have adopted the natural way of living: agriculture and animal husbandry. Among them are those who live from tilling the soil and are settled people. They live in small communities, villages and mountain regions. Their dwellings are tents of hair and wool or houses of clay, wood or stone. Most of them are Berbers and *ʔaʕāǧim*. Some of them make their living from cattle, travelling around for pasture. These are the *šāwiyya*. They do not go deep into the desert. Among them are Berbers, Turks, Slavs and others. Those who make their living from camels go far into the desert because of the habits of the camel. To these belong the *ʕarab* and the nomadic Berbers as well as Kurds and Turkmens. The *ʕarab* are the most extreme since they live from camel breeding only. The others also have sheep.
>
> 3. The life of the *badw* precedes the life of the *ḥaḍr* and life in towns, and precedes the building of cities and fortresses.
>
> 4. The *badw* lead a more natural life than the *ḥaḍr* because they are closer to nature and have no luxury. Sedentariness is the end of sound living and the beginning of corruption.[9]
>
> 5. The *ḥaḍr* people are corrupted, trusting in the walls that surround them, their ruler and his soldiers who protect them. The people of the *badw* have no walls, no defenders and carry their own weapons.

> 6. The influence of laws is negative since they enslave the subjects. Therefore we find the wild ones among the *ʕarab* from the *badw* people stronger and braver since they obey no laws of any ruler.
>
> . . .
>
> 8. The respect for blood-relations is natural to man. It creates solidarity (*ʕaṣabiyya*). The more extreme the living conditions are, the stronger the blood ties become.
>
> 9. The *ʕarab* are closest to nature and have the strongest respect for blood ties since their living conditions are the toughest. This was the case especially among the Muḍar tribes [i.e. the tribes in central and western Arabia in pre-Islamic times, among them Quraysh] because they had no agriculture, their lineages were not mixed with others and they lived far from the countryside in Iraq and Syria. Other *ʕarab*, like those in Yemen or in Syria, lived among fertile hills or good pastures and mixed their lineages with others.

An immediate insight from this text is that 'bedouin' has a wider meaning to Ibn Khaldūn than we usually think of today. The people of the *badw* are not only the nomadic tent-dwellers but everyone living outside the walled cities. Ibn Khaldūn explicitly states that they are both farmers and cattle-breeders (small cattle or camels). The *bādiya* is the open land of villages and tent camps with no walls. The *ḥāḍira* consists of the walled cities where people make their living from handicrafts or trade. Among the pure nomads of the *badw* we find the *ʕarab*, whose characteristics are said to derive from their primitive way of living. To Ibn Khaldūn the *badw* is the more comprehensive category and the *ʕarab* a sector of it.

Ibn Khaldūn defines *ʕarab* not only as camel nomads but also according to lineage. *ʕarab* are those living outside walled cities who have 'pure' lineage. This is reminiscent of the concept we found among the modern 'bedouin' in the Middle East, and supports the assumption that this is an ancient view. But at the same time, Ibn Khaldūn's *ʕarab* are defined in non-genealogical terms. They are those who live the harshest life farthest from the settled peoples. It is their way of living that, in fact, has created their genealogical system. The consequence is that the genealogical definition of *ʕarab* has been created by the environment.

Ibn Khaldūn does not show acquaintance with the meaning 'townsman', 'city-dweller', of the word *ʕarab.* Or if he knew about it, he discarded it as not fitting for his philosophical system. On the other hand, it can be observed that according to the documentation of modern linguistic usage, the term *ʕarab* or derivations from it seem to have replaced *badw* in large parts of North Africa. The dictionaries of Maghrebine Arabic show that the old meaning still exists but the impression is that the term *ʕarab* has expanded to designate people outside the cities in general, whereas *badw* has received a more limited meaning.[10]

The documented usage from present-day Maghrib can then be seen as closely connected with Ibn Khaldūn's description, which also fits quite well with conditions in the Middle East. The *bādiya* thus constitutes all land outside towns, and its inhabitants are the *badw* encompassing both villagers and shepherds of different kinds. The *ʕarab* would then originally have been people with a special kind of genealogy living mostly as camel-herders. These conditions seem still to be existing in Mauritania. The trend towards amalgamation between *ʕarab* and *badw* in modern linguistic usage in Morocco, and perhaps also in Tunisia, may be due to the paucity of 'real' *ʕarab* there.

The view of a medieval Muslim belletrist: al-Ǧāḥiẓ

Ibn Khaldūn defined *ʕarab* by a combination of criteria: they are characterized by racial purity, i.e. genealogical awareness, but this arises from their way of living in harsh environmental conditions. This awareness of the different factors determining 'Arabness' is, in fact, found in earlier authors as well. A clear statement of this view is found in the great prose-writer al-Ǧāḥiẓ, in the ninth century AD, i.e. in the classical Abbasid age, when describing the relationship between culture and nationality in his essay about the Virtues of the Turks (*Risāla ʕan faḍāʔil at-turk*) which is designed as a letter. The starting-point is the allegation that the army of the Abbasid caliph has united several different groups of people, like the Khurasanians, the Turks, the *ʕarabī* and the *banawī*.[11] The receiver of the letter, Fatḥ b. Khāqān, a high official in the Abbasid caliphate, objects to this classification of nationalities according to genealogy. For him, Khurasanians and Turks are brothers because of the closeness of their territories. He gets the following answer:

> Your opinion is that the difference between the Khurasānī and the Turk is not like the difference between the *ʕağamī* and the *ʕarabī* or that between the Roman and the Slav, or the Zanǧī and the Ethiopian, let alone someone who is more distant in substance and more in difference. Instead it is [more] like the difference between the Meccan and the Medinean or the *badawī* and the settled one, or the inhabitant of the lowland and the mountains and like the difference between the (members of the tribe) Ṭayyiʔ in the mountains and the lowlands. As they say: the (tribe of) Hudhayl are the Kurds of the *ʕarab*; and like the difference between those who have settled in valleys and those who have settled in rugged areas, and those who have settled on hills and those who have settled in caves.
>
> Your opinion is that even though they differ a little in language and they differ between themselves a little in appearances (*ṣuwar*) – for the highlanders of Tamīm and the lowlanders of Qays, the core of Hawāzin and the pure-speakers of Ḥiǧāz differed in a language which in most respects differs from the language of Ḥimyar and the inhabitants of the districts of Yaman, and in the same way (they differed) in physical appearance, characteristics and morals – all of them are still pure *ʕarabī*, unmixed, no low birth, no bastards, and no adoptions. They [the Turks and the Khurasanians] do not [even] differ like Qaḥṭānids and ʕAdnānids in the nature of the peculiar instincts that God has imprinted upon them and in the physical forms and appearances and linguistic differences that God has distributed to the people of every region.
>
> Now if you say: 'How can the children of these two [Qaḥṭān and ʕAdnān] be all *ʕarab* when their fathers are different?'
>
> We say: When the *ʕarab* became one, they became equal as regards living ground, language, characteristics, ambition, pride, violence, and temperament. They were moulded in one mould, and poured out in one instant, and the form was one, the parts were (= became) similar to each other, and the components became related. When this had become a stronger similarity in general and

> particular, in concord and conflict, than between blood-relatives, they reached a decision of agreement about noble descent (*ḥasab*). This became the reason for a second birth until they intermarried according to it, and became in-laws because of it. ʕAdnān prevented everyone from marrying the sons of Isaac, in spite of him being the brother of Ishmael. But they were always generous in that to the sons of Qaḥṭān, who was the son of ʕĀbir, and in uniting the two groups in intermarriage and in-lawing. The fact that they prevented all peoples from that, like Kisrā and those under him [= the Iranians], shows that genealogy among them was agreed and that this concept had arisen among them through birth and close relationship.[12]

The implication of this statement seems to be that nationalities based on kinship in fact arise through intermarriage caused by territorial closeness, common environmental factors etc. The community of *ʕarab* are not originally physical descendants of one forefather. Instead, they are the result of cross-breeding between several groups which has given birth to a new entity claiming common blood-ties. This is, in fact, a very modern view of how larger tribal units originate. al-Ǧāḥiẓ seems to be aware of the fact that the existence of the nation of the *ʕarab* in his days was the result of an historic event and that the incitement to its formation was largely cultural and environmental. al-Ǧāḥiẓ's definition of *ʕarab* is thus largely in agreement with that of Ibn Khaldūn and was obviously a well-known view before al-Ǧāḥiẓ.[13] We have a saying attributed to the second caliph, ʕUmar b. al Khaṭṭāb, who is claimed to have told the Muslim Arabs: 'Learn genealogy (*nasab*) and do not be like the *nabīṭ* of the Sawād who say, when they are asked about their origin: "[We are] from this or that village."'[14] Since the *nabīṭ*, usually identified as the indigenous farming communities in Iraq, are contrasted with the *ʕarab*, genealogical consciousness would thus be a characteristic of the latter. This concept of the *ʕarab* as a community based on kinship goes quite well with the definition among present-day 'bedouin'. It is clear that this definition was known and accepted at least as early as the beginning of the Abbasid age. But it follows from the descriptions by Ibn Khaldūn and al-Ǧāḥiẓ that it was known that *ʕarab* originally could have meant something quite different.

Notes

1 The literature on the early Islamic historiography is extensive. An excellent introduction is now Donner, *Narratives*, with references to the earlier scholarly literature.

2 Caskel (*Ǧamhara* II 69) rejected the idea that any genuine South Arabian traditions were preserved in the tradition about the kings of Yemen, a categorial judgement which was doubted by Henninger (*Genealogie* 70). For the value of the Islamic history of pre-Islamic Yemen in general, see now Piotrovskij, *Predanije*. The king-list is used already by Wahb and is found in different forms in later writers (Pseudo-ʕUbayd, al-ʔAṣmaʕī, al-Yaʕqūbī). Behind the legendary kings Yunʕim/Niʕam Yāsir and his son Shamir Yurʕish in these works stand the Himyaritic rulers YSR YHNʕM and his successor ŠMR YHRʕŠ, now well documented from contemporary inscriptions and dated to *c*. AD 270–310. They are the earliest ones that can be identified with names in the king-list. Many of the successive kings in the lists can be identified with Himyaritic rulers in the fourth and fifth centuries.

3 For the history of al-Ḥīra, see Rothstein, *Dynastie* and the commentaries in Nöldeke, *Tabari*. As will be pointed out later in this study (pp. 476 ff.) the connection between the kings of al-Ḥīra in Iraq and the king mentioned in the Namāra inscription in Syria from AD 328, with whom ancient traditions about other tribal rulers (namely the Fahmids and Ǧadhīma al-

ʔabraṣ of the Tanūkh) are connected in the Arabo-Islamic tradition, is most likely to be secondary.

4 See the basic discussion in Donner, *Narratives* 64–146.

5 This material is now easily accessible in Hoyland, *Islam*.

6 For this date, see Bosworth, *Iran* 606–607 and Shahid, *Byzantium 3* 364–372.

7 For a sketch of this background, see Retsö, *Road*. For a detailed study of events from the Roman perspective, see Shahid's volumes *Byzantium*. The ideological background of the Islamic conquests is still largely unknown and remains one of the puzzles of world history. The Qurʔān, especially in the later suras, has a strong bellicose tone, but it is not very clear which enemy is intended. There are no anti-Roman statements and Iran is not mentioned at all. The hagiographic tradition, on the other hand, gives a very vivid description of the attacks directed against the Romans in Syria during the last years of the Prophet. The numerous discrepancies between the Qurʔānic text and the hagiographic tradition are usually played down by Western as well as Muslim scholarship, but have lately been emphasized (cf. Crone/Cook, *Hagarism*; Crone, *Trade*; Rubin, *Eye*; and Hawting, *Idea*).

8 Ibn Khaldūn, *ʕIbar* 1:101–110. For a full translation, see Rosenthal, *The Muqaddimah* I 249 sqq.

9 Here follows a discussion about the famous ḥadīth prohibiting *taʕarrub* after *hiǧra* (Bukhārī, *Ṣaḥīḥ* IV:373). This will be treated later; see pp. 84 ff..

10 According to Taine-Cheikh, *Dictionnaire*, the word *badawi* has a traditional usage in Mauritania meaning 'campagne, brousse', and *badw* is 'campagnard, nomade, bédouin'. The *ʕarab* in Mauritania are a more limited group of warrior tribes who own slaves etc. Similar usage is documented from Morocco where *bādīya* may be used for all kinds of countryside outside the towns (Sinaceur, *Dictionnaire Colin* s.v. I:59). It should, however, be observed that *bédwi* designates a very special group of travelling merchants and that *ʕrabī* tends to be used like *bādīya* (ibid. and s.v. ʕRB).

11 The *banawī* are here probably an elite group in the Abbasid period composed of people close to the ruling family; cf. Zetterstéen/Lewis, *al-ʔAbnāʔ*.

12 al-Ǧāḥiẓ, *Rasāʔil* I:10–12.

13 Cf. al-Ǧāḥiẓ, *Bayān* III:291.

14 Ibn ʕAbd Rabbihi, *ʕIqd* III:312.

2

THE ARABS AS A PEOPLE

ʕarab and *ʕağam*

In the text quoted above, al-Ǧāḥiẓ opposes *ʕarabī* to *ʕağamī*. The latter is the classical term for Iranians in medieval Arabic texts, and it usually stands for the Iranians who converted to Islam during the two first Islamic centuries.[1] But it also had a wider meaning. The idea of the early Muslim community being composed of two groups, *ʕarab* and *ʕağam*, as well as the conflict between them, is expressed in one of the versions of the final sermon said to have been given by Muhammed during his last pilgrimage:

> 'All of you are from Adam, and Adam is from dust; the most noble among you is he who is most pious. God is knowing, understanding. The *ʕarabī* has no precedence over the *ʕağamī* except in piety.'[2]

This version of the sermon represents a time when the conflict between the leading tribes and the other, non-tribal Muslims had become acute, a conflict which was, at least officially, resolved by the Abbasid revolt. In fact, the Abbasid revolution in 750 was, to a large extent, the final revolt of the non-*ʕarab* Muslims against the *ʕarab* and their taking of power. This revolt was dominated by the Iranian *ʕağam*, and the outcome was the establishment of at least formal equality between the two groups.

In Ibn Manẓūr's large dictionary, the *Lisān al-ʕarab* from the thirteenth century, where the articles on ʕRB and ʕǦM are one of the basic collections of the early Arabo-Muslim traditions about these concepts, we read:

> *al-ʕurb* and *al-ʕarab* is an ethnic group [*ğīl*] known as opposite to *al-ʕağam*.[3]

The word *ğīl* seems to cover what we today would call a nation. Thus, according to the *Lisān*, the Turks, the Chinese and the Romans are *ʔağyāl* like the *ʕarab*. It is equated with *ʔumma* or 'every *qawm* which is characterized by a language'.[4]

The implication of the saying by the Prophet quoted above is, however, that *ʕağam* could be used for others than Iranians since the Islamic community already in the first Islamic century consisted also of people from other countries than Arabia and Iran. When it is said that the first Iranian Muslim, Salmān, belonged to 'the *ʕağam* of the Persians', the meaning must be that there were also other *ʕağam* than the Persians.[5] In Wahb b. Munabbih's book of tales from the pre-Islamic history of Yemen and Syria, it was said that the Jews in Yathrib at the time of the Ghassanid king Ḥāritha b. Thaʕlaba (the beginning of the sixth century AD) are *ʕağam*, and that the Jews are respected only in the land of the *ʕarab*.[6] There is another saying from Wahb b. Munabbih that only four prophets were from the *ʕarab*; the others were from the *ʕağam*.[7] The latter cannot possibly refer to Iranians but must refer to Jews. Thus, *ʕağam* is not quite equal to a *ğīl*, on the same level as the *ʕarab*. It is negatively defined: *ʕağam* are those who are not *ʕarab*, be they Iranians, Romans, Jews etc., i.e. all *ʔağyāl* who are not *ʕarab*.

The *Lisān* further states that *ʕağam* is a collective, the singular of which is *ʕağamī*, the opposite to *ʕarab*.[8] There is, however, another word derived from the same root: *ʔaʕğam* with the plural *ʕuğm* meaning: 'the one whose language is not pure'.[9] In a complementary note in the *Lisān* (from Abū Isḥāq) it is said that 'the *ʔaʕğam* is someone whose language is not pure and clear even though he is *ʕarabī* according to kinship'.[10] The *Lisān* quotes a verse:

> A waterhole for people which cannot be avoided,
> an end-stop for every *ʔaʕğam* and pure-speaker (*faṣīḥ*).

The two words *faṣīḥ* and *ʔaʕğam* here stand antithetically according to the rhetorical figure called *ṭibāq*. Thus, an *ʔaʕğam* is someone who suffers from a fault of speech (*ḥubsa*) even though he is an *ʕarabī*. Consequently, it is independent of the ethnic designation *ʕağam*(*ī*). In pre-Islamic poetry the adjective *ʔaʕğam* is used with this linguistic meaning, and it could obviously be applied to individuals belonging to the tribes but whose speech in some way or other did not conform to the norm.[11]

We thus have two series of derivations of the same root with different meanings: *ʕağamī* (sing.) – *ʕağam* (plur.) meaning 'not belonging to the *ʕarab*-people', and *ʔaʕğam* (sing.) – *ʕuğm* (plur.) meaning 'one whose speech is impure or unclear'.

There is no doubt that the two words *ʕağam* and *ʔaʕğam* are connected since they are derived from the same root. The tenth-century grammarian Ibn Ğinnī claims that the root ʕĞM means 'unclarity', 'opaqueness', which would be a clear indication of which derivation has preserved the original meaning.[12] This goes well with the meaning of the root in other Semitic languages.[13]

In the earliest Arabic dictionary, the *Kitāb al-ʕayn* by al-Khalīl, compiled in the second half of the eighth century, it is said:

> *ʕağam* is the opposite to *ʕarab*. An *ʔaʕğamī* is not an *ʕarabī* . . . the *ʔaʕğam* is someone who does not speak clearly (*yufṣiḥ*).[14]

In this statement the distinction between the two derivations from ʕĞM seems to be blurred. Both *ʔaʕğam* and *ʕağam* are opposed to *ʕarab* and the former is a characterization of speech. In the article ʕĞM in the *Lisān* an anonymous verse is quoted:

> O Sallūm, if you were among the *ʔaʕğam*
> in Rūm or Fāris or in Daylam
> we would visit you even with Sullam![15]

Here both Rūm, i.e. Rome or Byzantium, and Iran are *ʔaʕğam*. In the story of the conflict between Ghassān and Salīḥ, which led to the establishment of Ghassanid power in Syria, the Ghassanid protagonist Ǧidhʕ is reported to have said to the Roman emperor:

> You are a king who is able to speak and then perform. When the *ʔaʕǧamī* is able, he performs. We, the *ʕarab*, are able and we leave benevolence/kindness and mercy.[16]

Here, *ʔaʕǧamī* is applied to the Romans, whom we would rather expect to be called *ʕaǧam*. In a passage in the *Lisān* both Romans and Iranians are, in fact, explicitly described as *ʕaǧam*.[17] But in a verse by al-ʔAʕšā ash-Shaybānī from the beginning of the eighth century, directed to the governor of Kufa, Bishr b. Marwān, we find the following description:

> O chief of people from *ʕuǧm* and *ʕarab*
> and the best of people in religion and honour![18]

By *ʕuǧm*, i.e. the plural of *ʔaʕǧam*, are here meant the non-*ʕarab*, i.e. those not belonging to the tribes in Kufa.[19] The distinction is thus the same as in the farewell speech of the Prophet, but here the non-*ʕarab* are called by the plural of *ʔaʕǧam*, not *ʕaǧam*. The same use is found in a poem said to be composed one century earlier. In a verse dealing with the battle at Dhū Qār around AD 600 it is said:

> They hit the free men the day they encountered them,
> with swords, on the base of the skull;
> *ʕarab*, three thousand, and a troop (*katība*),
> two thousand, *ʔaʕǧam* from those with a mouth-handkerchief.[20]

The *ʔaʕǧam* are here described as wearing the characteristic Iranian outfit. We notice once again that the non-*ʕarab* in the poem are called *ʔaʕǧam,* not *ʕaǧam.*[21]

We have many other examples of how *ʔaʕǧam* is used for people not belonging to the tribes in Arabia, i.e. with the same meaning as *ʕaǧam*. There seems to be no sharp difference between *ʕaǧam* and *ʔaʕǧam*. The *Lisān* in fact says that the adjectives *ʕaǧamī* ('non-*ʕarabī*') and *ʔaʕǧam* ('not speaking pure Arabic') both have *ʕaǧam* as collective. The result is thus that, even to the readers of the *Lisān, ʕaǧam* can have both meanings.[22] The distinction between the two forms and the two meanings of the root ʕǦM tends to be artificial.

All this makes it unlikely that the contrast between tribesmen from Arabia-*ʕaǧam* = Iranians and/or other ethnic groups is original. Judging from the use and the etymology of the word it is likely that the noun *ʕaǧam* does not originally mean Iranians or foreigners. It is quite possible that *ʕaǧam* could be a term not only for Romans, Jews and Iranians but also for tribesmen from Arabia. Originally it must have designated people in Arabia with some kind of linguistic features belonging to dialects deviating from a norm, or caused by physical defects. The original contrast was between *ʔaʕǧam*/*ʕaǧamī* and *faṣīḥ*, 'pure-speaking'. It was then extended as a general designation for people whose speech was incomprehensible. This semantic extension is thus of the same kind as when the Slavs called speakers of German 'the dumb ones' (*nemcy*), i.e. people who cannot speak Slavonic, or when the Greeks classified all non-Greeks as *bárbaroi*, 'people who cannot speak properly'. From this it follows that when *ʕağam* and *ʕarab* are opposed as two different nationalities, this is secondary and the result of the sharp difference between the Muslim tribes and the others in the Umayyad empire. This is probably reflected in the following statement found in the *Lisān* but taken from the tenth-century lexicographer al-ʔAzharī:

> A man is *ʕarabī* when his genealogy among the *ʕarab* is certain even though he is not a speaker of the pure language, and the plural is *ʕarab*. A man is *muʕrib* [speaking the pure language] even though he is an *ʕağamī* according to genealogy.[23]

The meaning must be that if you are born an *ʕağamī* you will always remain one. The same holds for the *ʕarab*. In al-ʔAzharī's dictionary compiled in the tenth century it is said:

> The *ʕağamī* is someone whose kinship (*nisba*) is with the *ʕağam* even though his language is pure (*faṣīḥ*).[24]

Kinship thus overrules cultural affiliation: it is not enough to learn or to be able to speak pure Arabic to become a member of the people called *ʕarab*. You must be a tribesman. These statements look as if they are directed against the older meaning of *ʕağam* as a term for linguistic deficiency, not for tribal affiliation. Even in the Abbasid age there were people who alleged that *ʕarab* is something you can become, namely by learning the 'pure' language of the *ʕarab*. This is for instance the case of the ninth-century poet Bashshār b. Burd who was said to have been *ʕarabī* according to language and outfit but of *ʕağamī*, i.e. Iranian, origin.[25]

ʕağam is originally a collective noun for the group of individuals having the characteristic of being *ʔaʕğam* and could well have been formed as a morphological analogy to *ʕarab*. Since *ʕağam* mostly means 'Iranians' (Muslims or pagans), the reinterpretation of the word as a national designation must have been cemented in Iraq or Khurasān during the early Islamic period. The application of the term *ʔaʕğam*(*ī*) to people not belonging to the tribes of Arabia may however be earlier, although we have no means of documenting it.[26]

It thus turns out that the derivations from ʕǦM have two meanings: non-*ʕarab* nationality, i.e. not belonging to the peninsular tribes, and non-*ʕarabī*-speaking. In this case, we can state with a high degree of certainty that the linguistic meaning is more original than the national one. The definition of *ʕağam* as non-tribal must be secondary. The use of *ʕağam* opposed to *ʕarab* as a term for ethnic identity is thus an example of the reuse of a linguistic category as a national designation. It is a recycling of a linguistic term originating in the cultural and linguistic situation in pre-Islamic Arabia as an expression of politico-ethnic conflicts in a world empire outside Arabia. A consequence of the view expressed by both al-Ǧāḥiẓ and Ibn Khaldūn is that *ʕarab* designates a kinship community which, in a way, is fictitious. Since *ʕağam* does not originally designate a national entity the following question arises: is there any evidence that *ʕarab* as a term for a kinship community is secondary as well? Are there any traces of the use of the term *ʕarab* as, for example, a linguistic concept instead of a designation of a community of genealogically related tribes, a meaning which can be shown to reflect a usage existing before the rise of the kinship community? In order to give an answer we have to take a closer look at the structure and history of the tribal community called *ʕarab* during the first Islamic centuries.

ʕarab as a nation of tribes

The starting point of the preceding paragraph was the use of *ʕarab* as a designation for people defined according to kinship. In a saying attributed to the Abbasid caliph al-Maʔmūn, the son of Hārūn ar-Rashīd, from the year AD 833 (the year of his death) we can get a closer look at the structure of the *ʕarab* kinship community as opposed to the *ʕağam*. al-Maʔmūn is known as a fierce persecutor of the memory of the Umayyads in Syria, which had been their stronghold. During his last visit to Syria it is told that a Syrian approached him:

> 'O commander of the faithful, look after the interests of the *ʕarab* in Syria, just as you look after the interests of the *ʕağam* from the people of Khurasan.' al-Maʔmūn replied: 'O brother from the people of Syria, you have reproached me in strong terms! By God, I have never made the Qays descend from their horses except at times when I saw that there was not a single dirham left in the public treasury. As for Yaman, I have never liked them and they have never liked me. As for Quḍāʕa, their chiefs expect the coming of the Sufyānī and his appearance so they might join his party. As for Rabīʕa, they have been angry with God ever since he sent his prophet from Muḍar, and there have never been two of them going out without one of them being a kharijite. Now get out, may God wreak havoc on you!'[27]

This anecdote, regardless of whether it is genuine or not, gives a good summary of how the relationship between the concept *ʕarab* and the tribes was seen at the beginning of the Abbasid period. According to this dictum, the *ʕarab* consist of five main groups: Qays, Quḍāʕa, Yaman, Rabīʕa and Muḍar to which latter the tribe of the Prophet, Quraysh, and, consequently, the caliph himself belonged. Qays is a term for a group of tribes originally from the areas east and south of Medina. The Quḍāʕa are the tribes that were in Syria already before the Islamic conquest and who were included in the Islamic state as full members. Yaman, of course, stands for the Muslim tribes originating in South Arabia, including those in the mountains south of Mecca. Rabīʕa are the tribes east and north-east of Nağd. Finally, Muḍar, the caliph's own group, represents a chain of tribes starting from Mecca eastwards and encompassing most of the Nağd. These five groups seem to have been constituted as alliances within the Muslim state from the second half of the seventh century AD when they played a crucial role in the conflicts during the Umayyad period.[28] There is no indication that they existed as alliances before that time, even though some of the names may be ancient.[29] The political constellations formed in the Umayyad period seem to have revived names of tribes which had disappeared long ago.

In the anecdote quoted above, *ʕarab* is simply the term for the tribal federation constituting the first Islamic state and is a comprehensive designation for all the tribes belonging to it. We notice the use of *ʕağam* for the citizens of Islam outside the tribal genealogical system in accordance with the statements we have quoted e.g. from the *Lisān*.

The division of the federation into five large components is not the only one documented. Another one is a division into three main groups: ʕAdnān encompassing mainly Rabīʕa and Muḍar, Qaḥṭān as a name for the Yemenis, and Quḍāʕa.

The aggregation of tribes into larger groups is an expression of the concept of genealogical relationships between them. The names Muḍar, Qaḥṭān, Nizār etc. are considered the names of the forefathers of the tribes belonging to these groups. Thus, for example, Muḍar and Rabīʕa were called *ibnā Nizār* 'the two sons of Nizār'.[30] The *ʕarab*, according to this view, constitute several large families which, in their turn, are related. All *ʕarab* are ultimately related genealogically.[31] The basic document where the relationships within the family of the *ʕarab* are given in great detail is Hishām Ibn al-Kalbī's *Ǧamharat an-nasab* from the beginning of the ninth century which, even though it is not explicitly stated, is a complete survey of the tribes and groups that made up the Islamic state before AD 750.[32]

We have already seen how the genealogical definition of *ʕarab* is emphasized in statements preserved in the medieval dictionaries. al-Ǧāḥiẓ spells out the difference between the tribal federation ruling the empire until 750 and their *ʕaǧamī* successors very clearly:

> We have to mention something of what has reached us concerning our caliphs, the sons of ʕAbbās, even though their empire (*dawla*) is *ʕaǧamiyya* and Khurasānian and the empire of the Marwānids was *ʕarabiyya* and 'bedouin' and among Syrian troops.[33]

The meaning is that the Abbasid state is founded mainly on non-tribesmen, mostly Iranians, and the people of Khurasan from where the Abbasid revolt started. The Marwanids, on the other hand, were supported by the *ʕarab* tribesmen and their followers who were based geographically in Syria.

It is obvious that, in a state where full citizenship was based on kinship, it was important to be able to show one's belonging to one of the tribes since it entailed several privileges.[34] The claim of correct *nasab* (genealogy) is a motif often found. We have evidence for a certain rivalry among the tribes of the *ʕarab* as to who had the best genealogy. The competitive striving to show a 'good' genealogy is to be expected in a tribal society where an integral part of someone's honour was descent from renowned ancestors.[35] But it must have received increased weight in the Islamic state where it became tied to one's position in a large political structure of a kind which had not existed in Arabia before. This is apparent in an ancedote about ʕUbayd ʔAbū ʕAliyy Waǧza from the tribe of Sulaym (a tribe later included in the Qays), who was sold as a slave after the battle at Dhū Maǧāz which occurred in the beginning of Muhammed's sojourn in Medina. Much later, when he was maltreated by his master, he went to the caliph ʕUmar b. al-Khaṭṭāb saying:

> 'I am a man from the Sulaym tribe, from the clan of Ẓafar. I was captured during the Time of Ignorance as the *ʕarab* used to capture each other. I am known by my *nasab* . . . I have heard that there is no capturing in Islam and that there is no slavery for an *ʕarabī* in Islam.'[36]

The genealogical system and the ranking between different genealogies reflects the complexity of the tribal structure among the *ʕarab* as well as political rivalry among them.

Even though the opinion was that all *ʕarab* constituted one family, a remarkable feature in this system is that the *ʕarab* are ultimately descended from at least two different patriarchs, Qaḥṭān and ʕAdnān (or Ismāʕīl). This fact is put into relief when we compare with those who, at a certain stage of human history, emerged as the people of Israel. They expressed their concept of a common destiny and heritage by claiming to be the descendants of a man named Israel, calling themselves 'the sons of Israel', *bnē Yisrāʔēl*, which was intended to be understood literally. But there are no traces of a patriarch named ʕArab and the tribes never call themselves 'the sons of ʕArab'. The tribes had their own claimed forefathers and could call themselves 'sons of Tamīm', 'sons of Sulaym' etc., even stretching as far as Qaḥṭān and ʕAdnān. These tribal names could stand for more or less imaginary forefathers, who could be described as acting individuals.

The absence of a commonly accepted forefather led to the introduction of foreigners as the ultimate origin of the tribal family. In the second half of the nineth century Ibn Qutayba remarks:

> All the *ʕarab*, both the Yamanis and the Nizāris come from the children of Sām son of Nūḥ.[37]

The opinion that Sām (= Shem) is the father of the *ʕarab* is ascribed to Sumra b. Ǧundab in the first Islamic century.[38] The *ʕarab* as a whole are here traced back to a common ancestor like the Israelites in the Old Testament. The ancestor himself is, in fact, taken from that book, and the genealogical system of the Israelite/Jewish tradition has obviously been an important example for the early Muslim historians. From the Biblical tradition Ishmael was taken out and made the ancestor of ʕAdnān, whereas Yoqtan was identified with Qaḥṭān, the patriarch of the Yemenis. Both were ultimately the descendants of Sām who consequently could be called 'father of the *ʕarab*'. This was, however, a purely theoretical construction by theologically minded genealogists. There is no evidence that Sām was generally considered the virtual father of the tribes. The introduction of Biblical figures as the ultimate ancestors of the *ʕarab* shows that there was no indigenous tradition among the tribes themselves of a common forefather.[39]

This, together with the obvious origin of the main tribal alliances in the politics of the early Islamic age, leads us to the conclusion that the term *ʕarab* originally did not stand for an ethnic entity of the same kind as ancient Israel, or for most of the individual tribes on the Arabian peninsula.[40] It must have meant something else.[41] *ʕarab* cannot have been a genealogical term since it obviously could designate people of different genealogical descent. Even today the *ʕarab* do not have a patriarch named ʕArab. Among them we saw that *ʕarab* instead are people who have a genealogy of a special kind. The question then is: was the term *ʕarab* used in the same meaning in the early Islamic period? Was not only the concept but also the word coined when the rather special type of kinship community described by al-Ǧāḥiẓ and Ibn Khaldūn came into being?

The 'real' *ʕarab*

If we take a closer look at the classical genealogical system, we find that the Arabs are divided in two groups: the 'real *ʕarab*', *al-ʕarab al-ʕāriba*, and 'the secondary (arabicized) *ʕarab*', *al-ʕarab al-mustaʕriba* or *al-mutaʕarriba*. The meaning of these terms is that the latter are newcomers into the community of *ʕarab*. Thus, the *Lisān* quotes a statement by al-ʔAzharī:

> According to my view (*ʕindī*) the *mustaʕriba* is a tribe from the *ʕağam* who have been assimilated among the *ʕarab* and speak their language and speak in their way but there are no [genealogically] pure ones (*ṣuraḥāʔ*) among them.[42]

The difference between the *ʕāriba* and *mustaʕriba* Arabs is found in most works on history and genealogy in Arabic and is an established fact from a very early period. It should be noticed that the genealogical definition of *ʕarab* is here rejected. Instead the term is tied to the language. It thus stands close to the definition of *ʕarab* as opposed to *ʔağam*/*ʔaʕğam* used in a linguistic sense. Among the 'real' Arabs we find the Qaḥṭān group, i.e. the tribes from Yemen and the Quḍāʕa in northern Ḥiğāz and Syria. The *mustaʕriba* were the descendants of Ismāʕīl, i.e. the ʕAdnān-Maʕadd tribes in central and eastern Arabia.

At least for Muslims in the Abbasid age and onwards, this primary ranking of the Yemenis was an established fact but without any real political or other consequence. Yemenis have played a marginal role in Islamic history from the early Abbasids until this day, and their position in the genealogical system has remained a curiosity and an anomaly. It would have been more in accordance with the Islamic view on history to make Quraysh/Muḍar/Maʕadd, from whom the Prophet emerged, the real *ʕarab*. The explanation for the ranking of the Yemenis as Arabs *par préférence* must be that it has been made very early. The question is: what does the term *ʕarab ʕāriba* stand for and why were the Yemeni tribes and their allies defined by that term?

The high ranking of the Yemen-Quḍāʕa is related to their claimed descent from Qaḥṭān. That is a name of an area in south-western Arabia known from Sabaean inscriptions.[43] It is documented as a designation for Yemenis, Syrian tribes and a few other groups (the *ʔanṣār* in Medina, the ʔAzd and the Ṭayyiʔ tribes) in texts ascribed to poets who were active in the last decades of the seventh and the first decades of the eighth century AD.[44] One of the reasons for the use of the name Qaḥṭān as the patriarch of these tribes was undoubtedly the claim that the Yemenis descended from Yoqtan, the brother of Peleg according to the Table of Nations in Genesis.[45] This idea undoubtedly goes back to early Yemeni converts to Islam with knowledge about the Bible.[46] Among them there were several with a Jewish background, the best known of whom was Kaʕb al-ʔAḥbār.

This effort to connect Yemen and its allies under the early Umayyads with the Biblical world history is paralleled by similar associations with the more obscure Qurʔānic prophets and peoples like Thamūd, ʕĀd and Hūd who were all located in Yemen by the early Yemeni preachers. There is no doubt that this view reflects the leading position of the Muslims from Yemen and the tribes from Syria in the political system created by Muʕāwiya after the middle of the seventh century AD. The ultimate power-base of the early Umayyad caliphate was the Muslim tribes in Syria which consisted of Yemenis and those called Quḍāʕa. The Yemenis could challenge the status of Quraysh and their relatives, who could boast of having produced the Prophet but not much more and whose past was far less glorious than the royal splendour of Yemen.[47]

But even though the Yemenis and their allies emphasized their role by claiming a descent from the earliest Biblical heroes and making Muhammed's predecessors in

Arabia their forebears, the Yemenis cannot have been the first ones to use the term *ʕarab* as a status-designation for themselves. The distinction between real *ʕarab* and secondary *ʕarab* must imply that the term *ʕarab*, in fact, had already been accepted as a general term for all the tribes, both Yemenis and non-Yemenis. The terminology represents a downgrading of one group within an existing *ʕarab* community: nobody could deny that the non-Yemenis were *ʕarab* but they were of a lower kind: all are Arabs but the Yemenis are more Arab than the others.

But the Arabness of the Yemenis was not uncontested. In Wahb's Book of Kings, the Arabness of the Himyarites was stressed many times in a way that makes it suspect. The last Yemeni king, the hero Sayf b. Dhī Yazan, is called the *raʔs al-ʕarab*, 'the head of the Arabs', and all the *ʕarab* and their leading men, the *ʔašrāf*, come to him to pay allegiance just as they did to Muhammed in Medina.[48] The tomb of the great king Shamir Yurʕish has, according to Wahb, an inscription which looks like a direct reply to anyone doubting the Arabness of the Yemenis:

> This is the king of the *ʕarab* – not the *ʕağam*.[49]

The fictional nature of the whole scheme is seen by the ease with which the Quḍāʕa-tribes were incorporated into the genealogy of their Yemeni allies in Syria.[50] According to one testimony, some of the Quḍāʕa tribes were originally *mustaʕriba*.[51] It is further said about ʔAzd, a tribe reckoned among Qaḥṭān by the genealogists:

> They tried to become *ʕarab* but in vain, for they are *ʕağam*.[52]

The rejection of ʔAzd's claim to Arabness is clearly expressed in the following anecdote:

> A man from Quraysh looked at a man from Yemen who said: 'Praise to God who gave me delight in killing Quraysh!' His son said: 'Praise to God who humiliated them through us!' For Quraysh did not consider those from ʔAzd who had settled in Oman to be *ʕarabī*.[53]

The rejection of the claim of the Qaḥṭānids seems to be hinted at in al-ʔAzraqī's history of Mecca, compiled in the ninth century AD, where it is said that the two sons of ʔIsmāʕīl, Qaydar and Nābit, were the fathers of the *ʕarab*, thus ignoring the Yemenis altogether or at least their claims.[54]

Even in the traditions of the Yemenis themselves we find contradictory statements. In Wahb's book on the kings of Yemen, a fictitious inscription from the tomb of a legendary prophet of Rass is quoted:[55]

> I was sent to ʕArīb, Hamdān, and the *ʕarab* of Yemen as a preacher and a warner.[56]

In this text the *ʕarab* are one part of the inhabitants in Yemen, separated from the great Yemeni tribe of Hamdān. We find a similar distinction in South Arabia in the letter said to be sent by Muhammed to the tribe of Hamdān, when they had accepted Islam:

> And he (Muhammed) imposed his treaty on his people Hamdān: their *ʔaḥmūr*, their *ʕarab*, their *xalāʔiṭ* and their *mawālī*, that they should obey him.[57]

According to these two quotations, the *ʕarab* are either part of the larger federation of Hamdān or separate from them.[58] In the genealogical system, on the other hand, the Hamdānids belong to the most prominent among the *ʕarab ʕāriba*.

The picture given in these quotations is that the *ʕarab* originally were only one part of the society in South Arabia and that the large tribes there were not considered *ʕarab*. If we compare this evidence with the pre-Islamic evidence from the Yemenis themselves, the result is unequivocal: most Yemenis were not considered *ʕarab* in any sense of the word. The ʕRB in pre-Islamic Yemen made up a small part of the population restricted to certain border areas.[59] This means that the Yemeni claim to be *ʕarab*, let alone the noblest among them, must be the result of a political development in the early Islamic period. This explains why their claim was not uncontested.

The Qaḥṭān/Yoqtan genealogy of the Yemenis and their allies is documented in poetry quite early, but the distinction between *ʕāriba* and *mustaʕriba* Arabs is not found there. This leads to the assumption that the development of the latter occurred much later than the former. It thus seems clear that the Yemeni Muslims, including the Quḍāʕa, have begun to claim their rank as the foremost of Arabs at a certain period in the history of the Umayyad empire. The *ʕāriba* claim may be connected with the allegation that Ismāʕīl was the ancestor of Quraysh and the other ʕAdnān tribes. It has been shown that the establishment of a genealogy from ʕAdnān back to Ismāʕīl probably goes back to the reign of ʕUmar b. ʕAbd al-ʕAzīz (717–720).[60] This represents the propaganda of Quraysh, as does the allegation that only the descendants of Ismāʕīl were *ʕarab*.[61] It was well known that both Quraysh and Ismāʕīl had not been the original inhabitants of Mecca. When Ismāʕīl was launched as the forefather of Quraysh, he was made a Meccan by the story of his marriage to the daughter of the ruler of Mecca who belonged to the obscure tribe of Ǧurhum, according to one tradition, the earliest inhabitants of the town.[62] But this story could be used by the anti-Qurashi circles, who interpreted it as a confirmation of the secondary status of Quraysh and indeed all the descendants of ʕAdnān. Since nobody knew where Ǧurhum came from, they could easily be made relatives to the Yemenis. The whole distinction between the Yemeni *ʕāriba* and the ʕAdnānī *mustaʕriba* Arabs has the Ismāʕīl story, and consequently also the Qaḥṭān descent, as its prerequisite. It also implies that all the tribes involved in this debate were already called *ʕarab*. If the Ismāʕīli genealogy of Quraysh and ʕAdnān can be dated to the time of ʕUmar b. ʕAbd al-ʕAzīz, the terminological differentiation between real and secondary Arabs must have been made later. In that case the expression of the ranking between ʕAdnanis and Yemenis in the terms *ʕāriba* – *mustaʕriba* was propagated by the latter after the death of the caliph ʕUmar b. ʕAbd al-ʕAzīz, which brings us to the decades after AD 720.

The Yemeni claim to be the foremost among the *ʕarab* thus turns out to be a propagandistic argument launched perhaps after AD 720.[63] The fact that their opponents could be labelled *mustaʕriba*, 'secondary Arabs', and that this designation never seems to have been seriously contested, indicates that their Arabness may not have been very well established. But at the same time this shows that the term *ʕarab* itself must have existed probably as a designation for all the tribes before AD 720. As will be shown later, there is documentation of the term *ʕarab* as being in use as a comprehensive term for all members of the Muslim tribes as well as their dependants around the time of ʕUmar b. ʕAbd al-ʕAziz, which could indicate that it was launched as such during the early Marwanid rulers.[64] The idea of the Biblical Shem as the forefather of all *ʕarab*, both the Yemenis and the others, may well have been formulated at this time.

According to the statement of al-Azharī, *ʔistiʕrāb,* 'Arabization' or 'becoming an Arab' is effected by mastering the language of the *ʕarab*. This is an interesting parallel to the meaning of *ʔaʕǧam* etc. discussed in the previous chapter. It also appears more and more clearly that the debate about the *ʕāriba* and *mustaʕriba* Arabs tacitly operates with a concept of Arabs which is in contradiction to the genealogical one: one can obviously become an *ʕarabī*, according to al-ʔAzharī, by starting to use their language. This language would then have been the original characteristic of the Yemenis and their allies according to this view. Thus, is the term *ʕāriba* originally the designation for those speaking the language of the *ʕarab*? And why did the Yemenis adopt it for themselves?

The original *ʕāriba* peoples

In the work called *ʔAkhbār al-Yaman* attributed to ʕUbayd b. Shariya, who is said to have taught the caliph Muʕāwiya in the AD 660s, we find the following presentation of the components of the community of *ʕarab*.[65]

> Muʕāwiya said: 'Who are the *ʕarab ʕāriba* and who are the *ʕarab mustaʕriba*?' He [ʕUbayd] said: 'O Muʕāwiya! Do you and other learned men not know that they are ʕĀd, Thamūd, Ṭasm, Ǧadīs, ʔIram, al-ʕAmālīq, Ǧurhum, and Qaḥṭan son of Hūd? They were the first peoples and among them was Yaʕrub who spoke the *ʕarabiyya* language. Everyone took it from Yaʕrub son of Qaḥṭān son of Hūd, and the *ʕarabiyya* is traced back to him. It is said [to be] *ʕarabī* because Yaʕrub was the first who spoke it and no one else spoke it before him.'
>
> 'ʔIbrāhīm carried his son ʔIsmāʕīl from his land and made him settle in Makka, and we, Ǧurhum, were the people of the Holy Land. Then ʔIsmāʕīl grew up among us and spoke the *ʕarabiyya* and married among us. All the sons of ʔIsmāʕīl are from the daughter of Muḍāḍ, son of ʕAmr, the Ǧurhumite, and the father of ʔIsmāʕīl is from us, and you, o Quraysh, are from us and the *ʕarab* are [descended] from each other.'[66]

We find here the claims of the Yemenis clearly stated. The *ʕarab* identity is transmitted through their ancestor Yaʕrub to all other *ʕāriba* peoples as well as to the ancestor of the *mustaʕriba*. But it is also clearly stated that the descendants of Qaḥṭān were not the only people belonging to the *ʕāriba* category. The Yemenis shared their rank with seven other peoples. These were by now extinct, and the sons of Qaḥṭān were the only survivors of the ancient inhabitants of Arabia.

The *ʔAhkbār* is a work which probably was written in the beginning of the Abbasid period, even though its contents reflect the Yemeni views developed in the preceding Umayyad age. It belongs to a kind of literature which was frowned upon by many *ḥadīth*-minded historians, who may also have shunned it because of the obvious propagandistic tendency.

The antiquarian and historian Hishām b. al-Kalbī (–AD 819) was a more acceptable authority, who became one of the main transmitters of the prehistory of the *ʕarab* to the later Islamic historians. Ibn al-Kalbī says:

> It is said that ʕImlīq was the the first to speak the *ʕarabiyya* when they travelled

> from Babylon and they and Ǧurhum were called the *ʕarab ʕāriba* . . . God made ʕĀd, ʕAbīl, Thamūd, Ǧadīs, ʕImlīq, Ṭasm, ʔUmaym and the sons of Yaqṭan understand the *ʕarabiyya*.[67]

The Yemenis are here made the descendants of the Biblical figure Yaqṭan, i.e. Yoqṭan. As in the *ʔAkhbār*, it is said that the Yemenis were on line with seven other peoples with whom they shared the understanding of the *ʕarabiyya* language. But here it is not said explicitly that the Qaḥṭānids had the status of *ʕarab ʕāriba*. This is reserved for Ǧurhum and ʕImlīq.

Both the *ʔAkhbār* and Ibn al-Kalbī's writings are testimonies of a similar view on Arab origins, although we notice in the latter a more restricted view on the precedence of the Yemenis. In Ibn Isḥāq's book on the history of prophecy, which was written some decades earlier than the two preceding ones, there was another variant of this tradition:

> Ṭasm, al-ʕAmālīq, ʔUmaym, and Ǧāsim were an *ʕarab* people whose language to which they were created was an *ʕarabī* language . . . ʕĀd . . . Thamūd, and Ǧadīs . . . became close to an *ʕarab* people who spoke this language of ʔLMṢRY. The *ʕarab* used to call these peoples the 'real *ʕarab*' (*al-ʕarab al-ʕāriba*) because [it was] their language to which they were created. The sons of Ismāʕīl, son of Abraham, are called the 'arabicized *ʕarab* (*al-ʕarab al-mutaʕarriba*) because they spoke the language of these peoples when they lived among them. ʕĀd, Thamūd, al-ʕAmālīq, ʔUmaym, Ǧāsim, Ǧadīs, Ṭasm are the *ʕarab*.[68]

Here the Qaḥṭānids or the Yemenis are not mentioned at all. We find the seven peoples only. Ibn ʔIsḥāq seems to have used Yaqṭan, borrowed directly from Genesis 10, as the forefather of Ǧurhum in Mecca. These are not characterized as belonging to the *ʕāriba* peoples and also do not have any primary connection with the *ʕarabiyya* language.

Ibn ʔIsḥāq took most of his material about the prehistory of Arabia from Wahb b. Munabbih. If we compare Ibn ʔIsḥāq's account with the identifiable fragments of Wahb's writings, we find a close similarity. Wahb mentions ʕĀd, Thamūd, Ǧadīs and ʕImlāq as a group clearly separate from the Qaḥṭānids as well as from the sons of Ibrāhīm.[69] Wahb does not call these peoples *ʕarab* but he knows the legend that both Yaʕrub, the son of Hūd, and the seven peoples were speakers of the pure *ʕarabiyya*. He seems to have seen Yaʕrub and Ǧurhum as the first ones in this exclusive society.[70] Wahb thus emphasizes the Arabness of both Ishmaelites and Qaḥṭānids like ʕUbayd but the distinction between *ʕāriba* and *mustaʕriba* is not found in the texts ascribed to him.[71]

The ancient peoples of Arabia are grouped by the historians and genealogists into genealogical schemes which are rather consistent. A characteristic feature is their connection with names, sometimes arabicized, in Genesis 10. A common feature is also the division of 'the seven' into three groups. The first one is constituted by ʕĀd and, according to Wahb and ʕUbayd, completed with ʕAbīl. The second consists of Thamūd. The third is made up by Ṭasm, ʕImlīq/ʕImlāq and ʔUmaym. One people, Ǧadīs, is linked by Ibn al-Kalbī and Ibn ʔIsḥāq with Thamūd in group two, but by Wahb and ʕUbayd with group three.

The difference between the Yemenis (Wahb, ʕUbayd) and the 'Iraqis' (Ibn ʔIsḥāq, Ibn al-Kalbī) is also seen in the overall genealogical scheme. All agree that

Qaḥṭān/Yaqtan, i.e. the Yemenis, are descended from Arfakhshadh son of Sām son of Nūḥ. The Yemeni historians then make all three groups descend from ʔIram b. Sām via ʕAwṣ, ʕĀbir and Lāwudh.[72] The 'Iraqis', on the other hand, elevate Lāwudh to the same rank as ʔIram, giving group three an independent line back to Sām. With the Yemenis, the *ʕāriba* peoples are thus descendants from two patriarchs, ʔIram and Arfakhshadh, whereas with the 'Iraqis' there are three: ʔIram, Lāwudh and Arfakhshadh. Furthermore, Ibn Isḥāq has yet another patriarch, Ashūdh, who is the ancestor of a group of *ʕāriba* peoples headed by Ǧāsim. This difference between the Yemeni and Iraqi school is reflected in all later Arabo-Islamic historians, many of whom give both variants.

Ibn al-Kalbī and Ibn Isḥāq give geographical locations of these peoples which are fairly consistent. ʕĀd is said to have settled in aš-Šiḥr in South Arabia, in the sands up to Ḥaḍramawt. ʕImlīq settled in Ṣanʕāʔ 'before it was called Ṣanʕāʔ', but some went on to Yathrib and drove away ʕAbīl. Thamūd dwelt in al-Ḥiǧr between Ḥiǧāz and Syria to Wādī al-qurā [the Valley of Villages] and what is between. ʕAbīl is placed in the Yathrib area whereas ʔUmaym is connected with the mythical town of Wubar between Ḍufār and Oman. Ǧadīs reached Ṭasm and was with them in the Yamāma and what was around it until Baḥrayn. According to the genealogy also, ʕImlīq belonged to this area but were found elsewhere as well. Ǧāsim belonged to Oman. The Qaḥṭānids of course went to Yemen.[73]

Of these peoples, Thamūd is the only name which appears in pre-Islamic literary texts and inscriptions from the eighth century BC till late antiquity. From these it appears that they had their habitat in the north-western Ḥiǧāz.[74] This fits quite well with the geography of the Arabic sources and shows that the names are not inventions. The Lāwudh group stands for peoples in central Arabia and Ibn Isḥāq's Ashūdh are located south and east of them. ʕĀd are always located in Yemen but the descent from ʕAwṣ and ʔIram makes it likely that the original habitat should be sought in north-western Arabia.

The most important feature in all the variants of this tradition is the definition of *ʕarab* according to language. We do not, in the tradition about the 'real' and 'arabicized' *ʕarab*, find any explanation for the use of the word *ʕarab*, except the connection with the language. According to the classical Yemeni tradition, its first speaker was Yaʕrub, the son of Qaḥṭān:

> The *ʕarabiyya* is this language [which we are reading just now?]. People disagreed about the *ʕarab* why they were called *ʕarab*. Some of them said: The first one whom God made to speak in the language of the *ʕarab* was Yaʕrub b. Qaḥṭān, who was the father of Yemen: they are all the *ʕarab al-ʕāriba*. Ismāʕīl son of Ibrāhīm – peace be upon them – grew up together with them and began to speak their language; he and his children are the *ʕarab al-mustaʕriba*.[75]

This statement represents the strongly pro-Yemeni viewpoint which we have found in, for example, ʕUbayd's *ʔAkhbār*. We should notice the absence in this tradition of any explicit reference to genealogy. According to this definition of *ʕarab*, people become *ʕarab* because they adopt the language called *ʕarabiyya*. This language is seen as inherited from most ancient times. It is a family treasure which makes its possessors *ʕarab*. 'Arabness' is a heritage of non-genealogical nature but within genealogically defined units. The very term *mustaʕriba* must mean that these tribes were not *ʕarab* from the beginning but have become *ʕarab* by adopting the language of the *ʕarab*. This excludes a genealogical definition.[76]

There is, however, something fundamentally wrong with the whole concept of the Arabness of the Yemenis. They were never known as speakers of the pure *ʕarabiyya*. The linguistic situation in Yemen in the tenth century AD was, according to al-Hamdānī, as variegated as it is today, and there is no reason to believe that it was simpler, let alone more 'Arabic', in earlier periods.[77] The impression is that the whole argumentation about the Yemenis being foremost in 'Arabness' is a conscious redefinition of *ʕarab* directed against another already existing concept. The aim seems to have been to make it possible to define *ʕarab* in a way that enabled a ranking of members within the community of *ʕarab* according to some criterion other than tribal descent. We should keep in mind that the Yemenis, including the Quḍāʕa tribes in Syria, were mainly outsiders to the aristocratic circles of the tribes from central Arabia. The history of the Umayyad caliphate is, to a large extent, the story of how the central Arabian tribes gradually took over the leadership in the Muslim state from the Yemenis and the Ḥiğāzis. Their opponents must have felt the need for some other definition of aristocracy which could legitimize their own claims to leadership. The Yemenis launched several different arguments of doubtful value: the claim that the heritage of prophecy before Muhammed had mainly been transmitted by their heroes and glorious kings, or that they were direct descendants from the Biblical patriarchs, or that they were the first ones who had received the language of the *ʕarab*.

The view of the ancestor of the Yemenis, Yaʕrub, as the originator of the *ʕarabiyya* language is found in texts which, like ʕUbayd, represent the extremes of Yemeni propaganda, such as the two works on the kings of Yemen ascribed to Diʕbil and al-ʔAṣmaʕī respectively, both probably written in the beginning of the Abbasid period.[78] Remarkable, however, is the absence of the Yemenis as *ʕarab ʕāriba* in the earliest versions of the traditions of the origins of the *ʕarab*, both in the Yemeni Wahb and the Ḥiğāzi-Iraqi Ibn Isḥāq. This is the more interesting since these sources are strongly influenced by the Yemeni viewpoints.[79] This is one of the decisive arguments leading us to the conclusion that the Yemenis were not originally included among the *ʕāriba* peoples. This is confirmed by their being the eighth people in the list, which looks very much like an addition to a traditional number of seven. Ibn Khaldūn even calls the Yemenis *ʕarab mustaʕriba* since they have learnt the language just like the ʕAdnānis.[80] The absence of the Qaḥṭānids among the *ʕarab ʕāriba* also goes well with what we have already found, namely that there is no evidence that the Yemenis were actually seen as Arabs originally. The conclusion is that, after a closer look at the traditions about the *ʕāriba* and the *mustaʕriba* peoples, it turns out that both Yemenis/Qaḥṭānids and ʕAdnānis should be excluded from the original *ʕarab*. This term originally seems to refer to others who were more or less extinct in the early Islamic period. This is reflected in the distinction between *al-ʕarab al-bāʔida*, 'the perished Arabs', i.e. the seven peoples, and *al-ʕarab al-bāqiya*, 'the remaining Arabs', i.e. Qaḥṭān and ʕAdnān, found in some writers.[81] The next step in our investigation must be to get some idea about the connection between these vanished peoples and the term *ʕarab*.

The ancient *ʕāriba* peoples belong mainly to two geographical regions, Ḥiğāz and Yamāma, which is expressed in the Iraqi tradition by giving them two separate ancestors: ʔIram and Lawdh/Lāwidh. In both groups we find the names ʕĀd and ʕImlīq. These do not stand for ethnic groups at all. The former simply means 'by-gones' and was used for events and peoples in an undifferentiated distant past.[82] ʕĀd is a general term for people living at the dawn of history although it seems to be used mostly for inhabitants of north-western Arabia.[83] This geographical location is expressed by making them sons of ʔIram via ʕAwṣ, who definitely belongs there.[84] It is very likely that ʕImlīq is also a designation for some non-ethnic entity. The name itself is usually seen as an old borrowing from the Old Testament where we find a people called ʕAmāleq.[85] There are, however, reasons to believe that the *ʕamāliqa* in Arabic literature belong to the ancient lore of Arabia and stand for some kind of mythical giants who were the enemies of man. We notice that ʕImlīq are said to have dwelt not only in al-Yamāma but also in the area of Yathrib/Madīna after having expelled ʕAbīl. There are also traces of them elsewhere in Arabia, e.g. in Mecca, where they are even said to have built the Kaʕba.[86] The main allocation is to al-Yamāma and some cities in the Ḥiǧāz. In the same way, Ṭasm and Ǧadīs, both names derived from roots meaning 'disappear, be extinguished', are hardly real ethnic names either. The story told about how they perished is clearly mythical.[87]

Nöldeke argued that the Arabic name *ʕamālīq* is an arabicized form of the Hebrew ʕAmāleq interpreted as an Arabic plural with a back-formation ʕImlīq as singular.[88] His claim that all that is told about ʕImlīq in Arabic tradition is pure fantasy, except that which is borrowed from the Bible, is probably not entirely correct. Even though the claims that peoples all over the world were descendants of ʕImlīq of course belong to the world of folktales, one should look more closely at what is told about them from Arabia. Here they appear as giants and tyrannical rulers. That they are not mentioned in pre-Islamic poetry or the Qurʔān is no argument for their being pure inventions by learned folktale tellers. If the name ʕImlīq stands for mythical actors belonging to the pagan religion of Arabia, their absence from the poetry and the Qurʔān is not sensational since references to that religion are extremely rare in those texts. If we had only the Qurʔān and the poetry, our picture of religious conditions in pre-Islamic Arabia would be very different from what we have, which is based on the reports by the early Islamic philologians (e.g. Ibn al-Kalbī) and archaeological and epigraphical evidence from Arabia.[89]

As far as ʕAmāleq in the Old Testament are concerned, they were probably not an ethnic group either but rather a mythological enemy which appeared in concrete cultic rituals. Nöldeke's characterization of the stories about them as 'fabelhaft' could therefore be more exactly to the point than he realized.[90] ʕAmāleq's first appearance in the Old Testament (the fight by the waters of Refîdîm) bears all resemblances of a ritual, not of history.[91] The same holds for the killing of their king Agag by Samuel at Gilgal.[92] It should be observed that the hero of Ephraim, Joshua bin Nun, plays a central role in the Refîdîm story and that he is the founder of the sanctuary at Gilgal. In the Song of Deborah, Ephraim is somehow connected with ʕAmāleq.[93] ʕAmāleq live in deserts, by wells and on mountains.[94] They are also the oldest people on earth, who will face destruction.[95] Several features point to a ritual fight in order to make water from wells usable. The association with water is also found in Arabic where the noun *ʕamlaqat-* means 'water mixed with mud' and the verb *ʕamlaqa* is 'be scanty' of water.[96] This word can hardly be borrowed from the Old Testament but would be a suitable mythological name for a demon which is defeated in a ritual. The water-demon ruling as a tyrant is a well-known figure in Arabic folklore and may well be a very ancient mythological survival.[97]

The Arabness of ʕImlīq, ʕĀd and the other *ʕāriba* peoples, like that of the descendants of Qaḥṭān, is founded on their mastering of the *ʕarabiyya* language. This is why they are called *ʕarab*. But that the *ʕarab* should have been named after a language called *ʕarabiyya* is untenable linguistically.[98] According to the inflectional system of Arabic, the word *ʕarabiyya* must be a derivation from *ʕarab*, not the other way round. This means that, if we are to believe the tradition, even the non -Yemeni *ʕāriba* peoples, said to be called *ʕarab* because they had learnt the *ʕarabiyya* language, cannot have been the original *ʕarab* either. This is confirmed by external historical records. The only people among them who are documented in pre-Islamic documents are Thamūd, and they are never called Arabs. On the contrary, they are explicitly distinguished from them.[99] There is, in fact, even in Arabic literature some documentation denying the 'Arabness' not only of the South Arabians but also of the ancient peoples in Arabia. In the passage from Ibn Isḥāq about the *ʕāriba* peoples there is a line that must mean that the *ʕāriba* peoples learnt the *ʕarabiyya* from *ʕarab* who were not identical to them. The Prophet himself is reported to have said:

> Some tribes are affiliated to the *ʕarab* but they are not from the *ʕarab*: Ḥimyar is from Tubbaʕ, Ǧurhum is from ʕĀd, and Thaqīf is from Thamūd.[100]

The inconsistency between this dictum and some of the preceding ones is noteworthy. If the meaning is that the tribes mentioned are not *ʕarab* it means that Ḥimyar, ʕĀd and Thamūd are not *ʕarab* either. The saying looks like an argument directed not only against the claims of the Yemenis, but against the whole concept of ancient Arabs.

Behind the entire *ʕāriba* concept lies the idea that the ʕAdnān tribes, i.e. the great tribes in central and eastern Arabia who became the leading power in the later Umayyad period, were not related to the ancient peoples in Arabia. ʕĀd, Thamūd etc. were gone and the ʕAdnānis had replaced them. At the same time, they were united with the Yemenis (including the Syrian tribes) as Arabs. The receding Yemenis then launched the idea about a ranking of the Arabs according to the *ʕarabiyya* language. According to this view, that language was not the property of the ʕAdnānis. It was something they had acquired at a later stage. It was not connected with them originally. Instead it had some obscure connection with the peoples who had disappeared. It is remarkable that ʔIsmāʕīl, in spite of his status as the founder of the Temple in Mecca, is still a *mustaʕrib*, not a 'real' *ʕarabī*.[101] An isolated tradition that alleges him to be the first speaker of the *ʕarabiyya* should be considered an unsuccessful attempt to overcome this fact.[102] In another tradition referred to by Ibn Isḥāq, Ṭasm, ʕAmālīq, ʔUmaym and Ǧāsim seem to have been *ʕarab* before ʕĀd, Thamūd and Ǧadīs.[103] Since they are connected with eastern and central Arabia, this view could reflect an attempt to establish some link between the *ʕāriba* peoples and the great tribes in Naǧd in the Islamic period. But this also failed. None of these suggestions was accepted by those who formed the Islamic picture of history. This is a hint that there is a hard kernel of historical truth hidden in the propagandistic legends about the *ʕāriba* complex: the *ʕarabiyya* language was older than the ʕAdnān tribes and originally belonged to people who were not related to ʕAdnān. Since the language by its name belonged to the *ʕarab*, the ʕAdnāni tribes cannot have been *ʕarab* originally. Like the language, that identity was a late acquisition. This fact made the Yemeni argumentation possible.

The conclusion from all this must be that none of the peoples discussed here, neither the tribes in early Islamic times nor the ancient peoples in Arabia, was considered to have been *ʕarab* from the beginning, not even by those who told the stories about them in the early Islamic period. To the early Islamic story-tellers and historians, the ancient peoples had become *ʕarab* because they had learnt the *ʕarabiyya* language. So too had all other later *ʕarab*. All were, in fact, *mustaʕriba*.

In the 'de-yemenized' version in Ibn ʔIsḥāq quoted above, ʕImlīq is said to have been the first who spoke Arabic and he is even given the epithet ʕArīb.[104] Why were the *ʕamāliqa* seen as the earliest speakers of the *ʕarabiyya*? That language was obviously considered very old, expressed in the statement that the giants at the Dawn of Time, the *ʕamāliqa*, were the first ones to speak it. The *ʕarabiyya* was considered an ancient language, which the earliest inhabitants of Arabia learnt when they arrived there. About Yaʕrub it is said that God gave him the *ʕarabiyya*-language. The *ʔAkhbār* plainly says that Yaʕrub 'pronounced' or 'articulated' (*naṭaqa*) it.[105] But other sources have more obscure phrases.[106] Wahb states that God revealed (*ʔanzala*) the *ʕarabiyya* together with its alphabet with its 29 letters to the prophet Hūd.[107] It is not self-evident that these statements refer to an everyday language. The obscure verbs used by some sources rather seem to indicate a language used for special purposes. In a later source which, however, is founded upon older material, it is said that the sons of Qaḥṭān *ʔaʕrabū* their speech and made good poetry.[108]The meaning of the verb is not altogether clear but it obviously does not refer to everyday vernacular but to formal, elevated speech.[109]

At the same time, the *ʕarabiyya* is a language whose name is derived from *ʕarab*. It can also be assumed that the *ʕāriba* peoples were considered *ʕarab* because they were associated with areas where the *ʕarabiyya* language was originally at home. It cannot be excluded that the story about Yaʕrub son of Qaḥṭān in the same way is based on a tradition about a location in the land of Qaḥṭān where the *ʕarabiyya* was used for oracle-giving and recitation of poetry. We now know from Sabaean inscriptions that Qaḥṭān already around AD 200 was known as an area or an ethnic group, probably north of Kinda, i.e. in ʕAsīr or Wādī Bīsha.[110] The Yemenis might thus after all have had some foundation for their claim that there was an ancient community also in South Arabia where this mystical tongue was in use.

A valuable piece of information gleaned from these stories about the *ʕāriba* peoples is the likely geographical limitation of the mystical *ʕarab* to whom this language somehow is related. The *ʕarabiyya* language is said to have first been spoken by the *ʕamāliqa*. They are said to have dwelt near Medina and in the Yamāma. The Yaʕrub story may point to yet another area closer to Yemen. If the meaning of this is that the *ʕarabiyya* language had its roots in those areas, its original speakers after whom it was named should also be looked for there. We shall now turn to the earliest Arabic testimonies about this remarkable tongue.

The language of the *ʕarab*

In Arabic sources the name of a language named after the *ʕarab* occurs for the first time in the Qurʔān, and the reason why we still call the language of that book and its derivations Arabic is due to this fact.[111] In order to get closer to the original meaning of the term it is necessary to take a more detailed look at this earliest evidence.

> From a purely secular, non-Islamic viewpoint the interpretation of the Qurʔān and the history around it is, of course, a much more open pursuit than among scholars with a Muslim background. The reading of the Holy Book has, however, also in

the West been steered by the Islamic consensus about the course of the history of the Prophet and the rise of Islam. Since this consensus was not the starting point of Islamic scholarship from the beginning but arrived at only after centuries of debate and study, it should not be necessary for western scholars, or even modern Muslim ones, to follow it slavishly. There are, in fact, weighty grounds to liberate oneself from it and look at this historic event with eyes as fresh as possible.

There are three groups of sources for the history of the Prophet and the origins of Islam: (1) the Qurʔān; (2) the contemporary sources, which are basically non-Arabic/non-Muslim, originating with Christian and Jewish contemporaries in the seventh century; (3) the Muslim hagiographic tradition, represented by the biography of Muhammed by Ibn ʔIsḥāq around AD 760, as well as hagiographic material in later texts like the works of al-Wāqidī, al-Balādhurī and the *tafsīr* literature. In practice, western scholarship, following the Muslim tradition, has based its picture of these events on (3). The Qurʔān has been read and interpreted in the light of the hagiographic tradition and has been used as an illustration and a proof text to it. It is easy to see the weakness of this position although few scholars have ventured a serious questioning of it. A turning point was the so-called London school starting in the 1970s with scholars like J. Wansborough and P. Crone. Especially the latter has tried to re-evaluate the whole history of Muhammed by rewriting it based on source-group (2), with results that remain controversial.[112] One lasting result is, however, that the unreliability of the hagiographic tradition for the interpretation of the Qurʔān has been emphasized and demonstrated more clearly than before. [113]At least for the so-called Meccan period, it seems that the hagiographic tradition, including the historical notes in the *tafsīr*, is almost totally founded upon exegesis of the Qurʔānic text, and that these parts of the Book cannot be read in the light of it. In other words, the early Muslim commentators and hagiographers did not know more than we do about the concrete background of the text. Without subscribing to all the views of Crone and her colleagues, we have here tried to read the Qurʔānic text as it stands and tried to see what information can be extracted from it without ogling at the *sīra* literature. Crone's use of contemporary external sources for the rise of Islam is a fascinating exercise. That does not mean that it is the last word. The time has perhaps come to try to construct a history out of the Qurʔānic text itself. This was once made by the Islamic hagiographers. Since we now know more about the contemporary background as well as the vocabulary of the Qurʔān, this achievement should perhaps be attempted once again.

The adjective *ʕarabī* occurs ten times in the Qurʔān and only in suras traditionally dated to the Meccan period, i.e. before AD 622. In all occurrences it refers to a language. The suras in question are considered to belong to the middle and late Meccan periods. This is a group of texts in which we often find references to earlier Prophets as well as to script or a book.

In six passages the adjective *ʕarabī* is a qualification of the word *qurʔān*, a word meaning 'recitation, reading aloud'. We shall start with *sūrat aš-šūrā*, The Consultation (XLII). The sura is introduced by five letters, ḤMʕSQ, followed by the statement: 'Thus (*ka-dālika*) does he reveal (*yūḥī*) to you and to those who have been before you.' They (those before you?) have taken 'protectors' (*ʔawliyyāʔ*) other than Allah. Then it is said:

> Thus we have revealed (*ʔawḥaynā*) to you a *qurʔān ʕarabī* so that you may warn the Mother of Villages (? *ʔumm al-qurā*) and those around her/them and warn of the Day of the Assembly of which there is no doubt, one group in the Garden, one group in the Fire.[114]

The message is directed to people who are divided, not constituting an *ʔumma*, a community. There follows a reference to the *dīn* (religion?) given to Nūḥ and ʔIbrāhīm. To some of their descendants a writing, *kitāb*, has been given as a heritage but they doubt it and quarrel about it. It is Allah who has sent down (*ʔanzala*) the *kitāb* through?/by? the truth (? *bi-l-ḥaqq*) and the balance (? *al-mīzān*). The Prophet is ordered to say that he is a believer (*ʔāmantu*) in this *kitāb*. Allah only speaks through *waḥy*, behind a veil (*ḥiǧāb*), or through a messenger (*rasūl*) who reveals (*yūḥī*) under His protection?/with His permission (? *bi-ʔiḏnihi*). We (Allah?) have revealed a spirit (*ʔawḥaynā rūḥan*) and the Prophet did not know before what the writing or the belief (*ʔīmān*) was.

We are here immediately confronted with the difficulties of the Qurʔānic language and a wealth of terms that during 1,400 years of Islamic exegesis have received a commonly accepted meaning which, however, is not at all self-evident and is often highly uncertain. We must confess that, as soon as we leave the secure waters of traditional Islamic exegesis, which after all was developed by people who were not contemporaries of the Prophet, we are often at a loss. All the italicized terms are, in fact, of very uncertain meaning and an interpretation without the crutches of traditional exegesis is an expedition into the unknown.

In spite of the enigmatic language, some observations relevant to our subject can be made. One is the difference between the *kitāb* and the *qurʔān*. The former refers to writing that has been sent down earlier. The latter is obviously the form of the present message. The former is conveyed by NZL, ‘sending down’, the latter by WḤY. The meaning of the latter root is originally ‘to make a sign, hint’ and then ‘suggest, inspire through speech’.[115] This also suits the meaning of *qurʔān* as recitation. The receivers of the message thus have the *kitāb* already as a heritage from their ancestors, ultimately Noah and Abraham, and it is indicated that there is no discrepancy between it and the Recitation. The Recitation is thus oral, a message spoken in a stylized way, like the liturgical reading in the Syrian church or among the Jews. The audience to this message live in the *ʔumm al-qurā*, usually rendered as ‘the mother of villages’, and the surroundings thereof, and they have Noah and Abraham as their forefathers. According to a reference in the *tafsīr*, *ʔumm al-qurā* refers to the place where the first Temple was built.[116] This place is named Bakka in the Qurʔān.[117]

It must be admitted that this picture does not fit very well with the account of the Meccans in the hagiographic tradition. There the Meccans are said to have been polytheists whereas these people seem to be worshippers of the God of Israel or Allah, although in a corrupt fashion. This is confirmed by other Qurʔānic passages.[118] The name Bakka is always alleged to be identical to Mecca or a place in Mecca. The evidence for this identification is, however, meagre. The term *ʔumm al-qurā* could very well mean ‘a cluster of villages’ and need not refer to one special town.[119] It should also be remarked that the usual translation of *kitāb* as ‘book’ is not self-evident or even likely. In the prologues to classical Arabic odes, *kitāb* mostly means ‘writing’ or, ‘script’, not ‘book’.[120] This seems to have been the the normal meaning and it should be followed in the interpretation of the Qurʔān.

Sūrat zumar, The Crowds (XXXIX), is introduced by a reference to the sending down of the writing *(tanzīl al-kitāb)* 'in truth' (*bi-l-ḥaqq*), thus the same wording as in the preceding quotation. Further along it is said that Allah has sent down the most beautiful speech or story (*ḥadīth*) as writing (*kitāban* v. 23) resembling or similar to (*mutašābihan*) the *mathānī*, a word of uncertain meaning. Then it is said:

> (27) We have put forth for men in this *qurʔān* every kind of example (parable? *matal*) so that they may remember; (28) a *qurʔān ʕarabī* without anything crooked (*ʕiwağ*), so that they will fear.

This is followed by an example of a *mathal*, from which it seems that also here *kitāb* and *qurʔān* refer to different things. The former brings *ḥadīth*, 'story' or 'speech', connected with writing, and is sent down; the latter contains *mathal* which, judging from the adduced example, must be something else (moral admonitions or the like). This interpretation is confirmed by another Qurʔānic passage where a distinction is made between the seven *mathānī* and the *qurʔān*.[121] The *kitāb* may refer to writing that has existed for some time, which is contrasted with the Recitation, which is actually performed 'so that they will fear'. Nothing is said about where the Recitation comes from, although, if *ḥadīth* means 'speech' and not 'story', this word could be more or less identical with the Recitation and thus somehow derived from the Writing. The word *qurʔān* (actually a loan-word) thus means the oral performance of the text. This recitation is in the *ʕarabī* language, which thus is the oral medium of the message. Nothing is said about the form of the Writing so far.

Sūrat az-zukhruf, The Adornments (XLIII), is introduced by the following words:[122]

> (1) ḤM (2) By the clear Writing! (3) Truly, we have made it a *qurʔān ʕarabī* so that you (plur.) may get insight *(taʕqilūn*). (4) Truly, it is [being] in (= contained in?) the Mother of the Writing with us, exalted, wise.[123]

Unfortunately, the exact meaning of 'being in the Mother of the Writing', *ʔumm al-kitāb*, escapes us. The reference of 'it' in verses 3 and 4 is also uncertain. There is, however, no doubt that an intimate connection between Recitation and Writing is described. But they are not identical. The Writing seems also here to be primary and the Recitation some kind of derivation or transformation of it. In two of the most ancient Qurʔānic passages it is said that the Recitation is in (*fī*) a concealed or covered writing or a 'kept tablet'.[124] In this connection it is said that the Recitation is a 'sending down (*tanzīl*) from the Lord of the World'.[125] A similar idea is expressed in *Sūrat Yūsuf* (XII).[126]

> (1) ʔLR (2) These are the *ʔāyāt* of the clear (*mubīn*) Writing. (3) Truly, we have sent it down as a *qurʔān ʕarabī* so that you may get insight.[127]

An unprejudiced reading of these verses gives the conclusion that there is definitely a difference between the 'clear Writing', *al-kitāb al-mubīn*, on the one hand and the *qurʔān* on the other. We now learn that the Writing is characterized as consisting of *ʔāyāt*. This word has several meanings in the Qurʔānic language: natural phenomena (as signs of God's power), events connected with the Prophet's career, words recited by a messenger, and parts of the Book or the Writing itself.[128] The latter two, closely related, meanings have led to the use of the word *ʔāya* for the verses of the text. Now it is striking that in the quoted passages as well as in the other quoted *kitāb* passages we find the mysterious letters (as in verse 1 in sura XII) as an introduction. It lies near at hand to assume that the *ʔāyāt* in fact refer to these very letters.[129] The corresponding word in Hebrew and Aramaic actually means 'letter'.[130] The many meanings of this word in Qurʔānic Arabic may, indeed, partly be the result of semantic influence from outside, from which the meaning 'letter' might have come. There thus seems to be a clear hint that the mysterious letters standing as an introduction to these suras (and several others) are identical with or represent the Writing. The following text is then the oral Recitation. Grammatically, the difference between the Book and the Recitation is expressed by the Arabic accusative here rendered 'as', indicating that the Arabic Recitation is the way the Writing is made manifest to men.

The oral nature of the *qurʔān* clearly stands out in another passage in *sūrat Ṭā Hā* (XX).[131] From its name it can be seen that it too is introduced by letters of unknown meaning. This introduction is followed by mentioning the process of revelation:

> (113) Thus we have sent it down as a *qur ʔān ʕarabī* and we have distributed (? *faṣṣalnā*) in it some warnings so that they will fear or it will cause remembering. (114) High exalted be God, the king, the true one. Do not hasten with the recitation (*qurʔān*) before the revelation (*waḥy*) to you is finished. Say: 'O my Lord, increase my knowledge!'

This leads us to the most difficult of the *ʕarabī* passages in the Qurʔān. *Sūrat Ḥā Mīm* (or *as-sağda* or *fuṣṣilat*, XLI) has the following introduction:

> (1) ḤM (2) A sending down (*tanzīl*) from the merciful, the compassionate (3) a writing whose *ʔāyāt* have been divided (*fuṣṣilat*) to (as?) a *qurʔān ʕarabī* for a people who know (*yaʕlamūn*).

The relationship betwen the Writing and its *ʔāyāt* and the *ʕarabī* Recitation is in these verses described with the verb *fuṣṣilat*. This verb has several meanings, all related to one basic sense: 'to separate, make a division between'. The most common abstract meaning is then: 'to explain, make distinct as to meaning'. The concrete meanings are: 'to put a pearl of a different kind between two of the same kind in a necklace', which therefore can be called *mufaṣṣal*. Or: 'to divide something into portions' like a slaughtered animal or a piece of garment.[132] It is also used as a technical term for dividing the lines in rhymed prose with a rhyme-word, a so-called *fāṣila*, which is the term for such a rhyme-word.[133] In the Qurʔān, the verb is as a rule translated 'to explain, make understandable'. It is, however, evident that in some passages the verb can be read with a more concrete meaning.[134] In general, the verb is frequently used in connection with *ʔāyāt* as in VI:97: 'We [have] *faṣṣalnā* the *ʔāyāt* to a people who knows.'[135] If it means 'explain', one wonders where this explanation is found and what it consists of. And why would a people who already knows need an explanation? It should be tested whether there are other meanings that give a better understanding to these passages. The connection between the verb that can mean 'forming a text as rhymed prose' and the concept 'recitation in the language of the *ʕarab*' should be noted. We would suggest the following interpretation of the verse: writing has been sent down as a divine gift, i.e. it exists physically among men, characterized by or consisting of *ʔāyāt*, which may mean letters ('signs') or sentences/verses. It serves as a basis for an oral performance according to the rules of the language of the *ʕarab*, which may include following the patterns of rhymed prose, *saǧʕ*, used by the soothsayers in Arabia.[136]

Equipped with these insights we move further down in the text until we reach the following verses:

> (41) Those who disbelieve the remembrance (or: the mentioning) when it has come to them – truly, it is a Writing, powerful. (42) Falsehood does not come to it (belong to it?) from before it or from behind it (= from its beginning to its end?); a sending down from a wise, laudable one. (43) To you is said only that which was said to the messengers before you. Truly, the Lord has forgiveness and painful punishment. (44) If we had made it a *qurʔān ʔaʕǧamī* they would have said, if its *ʔāyāt* had not been divided *(fuṣṣilat)* /Or: they would have said: 'Why are its *ʔāyāt* not divided?/: '*ʔaʕǧamī* and *ʕarabī*?' Say: 'It is guidance and healing for those who believe and those who do not believe, in their ears is deafness and it is blindness for them.'[137]

It is clear that verse 44 deals with the relationship between the Writing and the Recitation. The objection treated seems to be that if there were no *tafṣīl* of the *ʔāyāt*, the message would have appeared in a form characterized as *ʔaʕǧamī*, which, as was pointed out above, would not necessarily mean what we today would call non-Arabic language. Rather, it implies that the form of the message would not have conformed to the demands of the rhymed prose of the *ʕarabī* language (taking the verb to have this meaning). The further implication is that, in that case, the authority of the message would be at stake. The two adjectives would then be an answer to this objection: 'Is it (i.e. the Recitation) *ʔaʕǧamī*?', i.e. 'How can you say it is *ʔaʕǧamī*? (Do you not see/hear that) It is *ʕarabī*!'[138] Consequently, it is to be considered as divine guidance.

Both suras XLI and XLIII deal with the relationship between the Writing and the Recitation. In two instances it is said that the Writing 'is made' into a Recitation. In two others, the relationship is expressed by the verb *fuṣṣilat*.[139] This might represent a progressive precision of the message about the Writing and the Recitation. The passages where the latter is said only to 'be in' the Writing or in a Tablet might then be the earliest ones.[140]

Closely related to the verse last quoted are two others where we find the expression 'an *ʕarabī* language' (*lisān ʕarabī*). In the introduction to *sūrat aš-šuʕarāʔ*, The Poets (XXVI), it is assured, after the mention of the three letters ṬSM, that 'these are the *ʔāyāt* of the clear writing' (*kitāb mubīn*, v. 1).[141] Then follow seven stories of earlier prophets: Mūsā, ʔIbrāhīm, Nūḥ, Hūd, Ṣāliḥ, Lūṭ and Šuʕayb. Then it is said:

> (192) Truly it is the sending down *(tanzīl)* of the Lord of the world. (193) The faithful spirit brought it down (194) upon your heart that you may be one of the warners (195) in a clear *ʕarabī* language. (196) Truly it is in the *zubur* of the ancients. (197) Was it not a sign *(ʔāya)* for them that the learned of the Israelites should know it? (198) If we had sent it down to some of the *ʔaʕǧamūn* (199) and he had recited it for them they would not have believed in it.

For the problem discussed here it should first be noted that we have a contrast between *ʕarabī* and *ʔaʕǧam(ī)* which we also found in XLII:44. From what has been shown, it is not very likely that the latter mean what we would call non-Arabic speakers. It could very well be those who speak a language different from what was recognized as a standard, or even those who were not able to use the *ʕarabī* language. The important point is that it is not said that the *ʕarabī* language was incomprehensible to the *ʔaʕǧam*. The meaning of XXVI:198–199 must be that a recitation in their language would not have been authoritative. An unprejudiced reading leads to the conclusion that the recitation of the message in the *ʕarabī* language gives it an authority which it otherwise would have lacked. In fact, this whole sura, like the other verse quoted, is about the authority of the message. It is authentic since (a) it was preached by the seven prophets, (b) it is in the *zubur* of the ancients and (c) it is in the *ʕarabī* language.[142]

The *ʔaʕǧamī* argument is also found in *sūrat an-naḥl*, The Bee (XVI).[143] Also here we find a reference to the sending down of the Writing (v. 89). We hear an admonition to seek protection with God from Satan when reciting the text (v. 98). Then follows one of the passages about the changing and replacement of verses. People are reported to charge the Prophet with forgery since there are passages in the revelation that are contradictory. It is assured that the Holy Spirit brings it down from the Lord. Then it is said (v. 103):

> Indeed we know that they say: 'A human being is teaching him'. The language of him they hint at is *ʔaʕǧamī* and this is a clear *ʕarabī* language (*lisān ʕarabī mubīn*).

Here, too, the point is the authority of the message. The objection from the adversaries has obviously been that the revelation is a fake, i.e. it is made up by a human being and not anyone else, which is shown by the contradictions and even the different versions of the recitation at different times. We have no hint who was actually meant by the human being said to be teaching the Prophet. The only thing that can be said with certainty is that the later commentators did not know for sure.[144] The point of the argument is that the message is of non-human origin because it is recited in the *ʕarabī* language, and the person who was said to teach the Prophet did not use or master that language.

In *sūrat ar-raʕd*, The Thunder (XIII), which is also introduced by mysterious letters and an assertion that 'these are the *ʔāyāt* of the Book which was sent down to you by the Lord' the *kitāb* is characterized in the following way:

> (36) Those whom we have brought the Writing rejoice in what has been sent down to you and among the parties (*ʔaḥzāb*) there are some who reject some of it. Say: 'I have only been commanded to worship God and not to associate with him. Him I call and to him I return.' (37) Thus we have sent it down as a *ḥukm ʕarabī*. If you follow their desires after the knowledge has come to you, you will have no protector against God and no defender. (38) We have sent messengers before you and we have appointed for them wives and offspring, and it was not for any messengers to bring an *ʔāya* except by God's leave. Every term (*ʔaǧal*) has a Writing. (39) God blots out what he will and he makes certain, and with him is the Mother of the Writing.

This text is clearly related to the first one we quoted. The Prophet has brought a message to those who already possess the Writing and who seem to be descendants of earlier messengers. The word *ḥukm* has been translated 'judgement', 'decision', 'illumination'.[145] Even though this is a well-documented meaning of the word it is somewhat awkward. What would 'an Arabic judgement' be? The suggestion 'illumination' shows that some interpreters have been uncomfortable with the common meaning. Even though it cannot be proved, we would suggest that *ḥukm* is a parallel to the Revelation in its linguistic form, written or oral. In the beginning of *sūrat Hūd* (XI) it is said that 'this is a Book whose *ʔāyāt* are put together (*ʔuḥkimat*) and then *fuṣṣilat* by one wise, aware'. The exact meanings of these terms are obscure, if we leave traditional exegesis aside. But the meaning 'composition' or the like would be a more expected meaning of *ḥukm* than 'judgement'.[146]

From what has been shown we can draw some conclusions. (1) It is the Recitation which is characterized as *ʕarabī*, not the Writing; (2) the purpose of its *ʕarabī* character is primarily to make people believe and get wisdom, not to facilitate understanding linguistically; (3) the term *ʔāya* refers to the Writing, not to the Recitation; (4) the Recitation is secondary to the Writing. There is a contrast between the Writing which is 'clear' (*mubīn*) and the Recitation which is *ʕarabī*. The 'tongue' (*lisān*) is characterized by both. The term NZL 'send down' seems originally to belong to the Writing but is also used for the Recitation. The term WḤY is, however, used only for the Recitation.

The division between the mysterious writing and the recitation of it is fundamental to the concept of revelation in the Qurʔān, a contrast which has been toned down by the later theologians.[147] It cannot be excluded that the discrepancy between the actual consonantal text and the reading is somehow connected with this dichotomy. The spelling of the text and the reading of it are not in complete harmony, and they are even partly represented by two different graphic systems. This does not mean that the consonantal text of the Qurʔān as we have it represents the Writing. Also the consonantal text which we possess is in rhymed prose, reflecting for example the case and mood inflection of the *ʕarabī* language, and we do not know anything about what the earliest written Qurʔānic texts looked like. But it is plausible that the idiosyncrasies of Arabic orthography have something to do with the original *tafṣīl* between the Recitation and the Writing.[148]

What do we learn about our problem from the Qurʔānic passages? The first observation is that it has to be pointed out that the recited text is in the *ʕarabī* language. The only purpose of such a statement is the contrast: it is not in another language. The *ʕarabī* statements in the Qurʔān have been interpreted to mean that many previous peoples have received the revelation in their own language and now, finally, the Arabs have received it in their tongue. There is, in fact, one Qurʔānic verse which could be (and has been) used as a confirmation of this idea, namely XIV:4: 'We have sent no messenger except with (*bi-*) the language of his (?) people (*qawm*) in order to make clear to them.' This statement is, however, not as unequivocal as is usually thought. The *ʕarabī* language is, in the Qurʔān, not contrasted with Hebrew, Aramaic and Greek, which were the languages of the earlier revelations, but with *ʔaʕǧamī* which, as we have already seen, is probably a form of the language we today would call Arabic. Further, as we have pointed out, the revelation is *ʕarabī*, not because otherwise it would have been incomprehensible, but to make people believe.[149] The purpose of the use of *ʕarabī* is to authorize the message, not to make it linguistically comprehensible. This is most likely the meaning also of XIV:4: all revelations have been in the language of the *ʕarab*. The implication is that this one is of the same kind.[150]

Another striking feature is that the message is directed to those who already know. If it is recited for the *ʔaʕǧamūn* they will not believe it. The message is for a closed circle, a *qawm*, to whom a message of this kind is authoritative. It is wisdom and warning for them, not necessarily for others.[151] Who were these people?

The land of the *ʕarab* and their villages

The only concrete indication of the identity of the *qawm* who received the divine message is that they belonged to the *ʔumm al-qurā*, usually translated 'the mother of villages', but which can have a quite different meaning: a cluster of villages. The word *qurā* occurs quite frequently in the Qurʔān in the sūras from the Meccan period, which are very negative against 'villages'. God is said in the past to have warned the *qurā* and then destroyed them.[152] Some of them are still left.[153] Now the warning is given to *ʔumm al-qurā*, and those living around it/them.[154] Similar statements are made of individual *qaryas*, one of which is the *qarya* of Lūṭ.[155] No *qarya* except that of Yūnis has believed.[156] The impression from the Qurʔān is that most of God's warners have been sent to *qurā* and that almost none of them has believed in the warning. Let us also remember that the Qurʔān implies that all the prophets have preached in the language of the *ʕarab*, not necessarily to them but to those who were familiar with their language. Where were these villages?

In a tradition preserved in al-Bakrī's geographical dictionary the *Ǧazīrat al-ʕarab* is defined as:

> Makka, al-Madīna, al-Yaman, and their villages *(qurā)*.[157]

In another passage, al-Bakrī enumerates the different regions of the peninsula: Naǧd, Ḥiǧāz, Tihāma/Ghawr, Ǧināb and ʕIrāq. Then it is said:

> Arab villages (*qurā ʕarabiyya*) are every village in the land of the *ʕarab* such as (*naḥw*) Khaybar, Fadak, as-Suwāriqiyya and the like.[158]

According to Yāqūt, *Wādī al-qurā*, 'the valley of the villages', is between Syria and Medina, more exactly between Taymāʔ and Khaybar, where there used to be several settlements which are 'nowadays' ruined and the waters of the wadi flow freely and unused. Wādī al-qurā, al-Ḥiǧr (present-day Madāʔin Ṣāliḥ) and al-Ḥabāb are said to be the land of the Quḍāʕa tribes Ǧuhayna, ʕUdhra and Baliy. Remarkably enough, this is the old homeland of ʕĀd and Thamūd which was later settled by Jewish tribes. These made an agreement with Quḍāʕa, who were to protect them against the *ʕarab*.[159]

Another group of villages is mentioned in a passage dealing with the governors appointed after the expedition to Tabūk in the year AD 629 when ʕAmr b. Saʕīd b. al ʕĀṣ was entrusted with *qurā ʕarabiyya*, which seem not to be those mentioned by al-Bakrī.[160] The geographer Yāqūt says that there were *qurā ʕarabiyya* where the tribe Ṭayyiʔ was settled as well as at the sites Dūma, Sakāka and al-Qāra.[161] They are in the area stretching around the western part of the Great Nafūd desert.

The location in Yāqūt agrees with that of al-Bakrī, and the identity of these villages with those of the *ʕarab* is fairly certain. This expression is encountered in another passage which sheds new light on the identity of the *ʕarab* living in villages. In the year 653, the governor of Iraq, Saʕīd b. al-ʕĀṣ, expelled to Syria a group of men who violently opposed the plans to distribute lands in Iraq to some of the tribal leaders who had fought against Islam in the so-called *ridda* wars after Muhammed's death.[162] These people were a mixture from different parts of Arabia, who had been entrusted with the guardianship of the countryside in Iraq, i.e. the occupied lands outside the garrison towns. There follows a report of a conversation between the Syrian governor, Muʕāwiya, the future caliph, and one of their leaders, Ṣaʕṣaʕa b. Sūḥān from the tribe ʕAbd al-Qays, about the excellence of the expelled ones and Quraysh. Muʕāwiya calls them 'a people from the *ʕarab*' who have achieved rank through the merits of Quraysh.[163] When Ṣaʕṣaʕa points out that Quraysh was insignificant before Islam, Muʕāwiya fiercely denies this and delivers a defence of the precedence of Quraysh over all other groups of Muslims, especially those represented by Ṣaʕṣaʕa:

> As for you, Ṣaʕṣaʕa, your village is surely the worst of the villages of the *ʕarab*, the one whose vegetation is most malodorous, whose wādī is deepest, whose evildoing is most notorious, and whose *ğīrān* are vilest. No one of noble or humble birth has ever dwelt there without being insulted because of it and it became a meanness for him. Further, they had the ugliest nicknames (*ʔalqāb*) among the *ʕarab*, the basest marriage ties, and were the outcasts of nations.[164]

This conversation is reported by Sayf b. ʕUmar, living in the reign of Hārūn ar-Rashīd, and may well, in its present shape, reflect pro-Qurayshite propaganda from later periods. What is interesting is the term 'villages of the *ʕarab*'. That was obviously a term for the settlements of the guardians in the countryside in Iraq. These people belonged to small tribes of Ḥiğāzi and Yemeni origin who had joined the Islamic movement early and remained faithful after Muhammed's death. The first serious conflict in Iraq was in the 650s between them and the tribal aristocracy who had fought against Islam in the *ridda* wars and arrived in Iraq after the conquest. These people are known by the enigmatic term *qurrāʔ* or *ʔahl al-qurrāʔ*. This term was earlier interpreted as 'Qurʔān-reciters' since in some passages they appear to have a special association with the Holy Book.[165] Several scholars have, however, argued that the word, in fact, is a derivation from *qarya*, 'village', thus meaning 'villager'.[166] The description given by Muʕāwiya of Ṣaʕṣaʕa's people does indeed contain all the terms: 'village' (*qarya*), *wādī* – and *ʕarab*. It should also be noticed that a large part of them came from Ḥiğāz.[167] After the above-mentioned conflict, the governor Saʕīd, when effecting his land reform, gave large areas to the tribal aristocrats, and the *qurrāʔ* were given compensation in Ḥiğāz and Yemen, i.e. their original habitats.[168] The definition of *ğazīrat al-ʕarab* in al-Bakrī quoted above might well refer to the villages, *qurā*, settled by these *qurrāʔ*.

We should now recall the *ʔumm al-qurā* in sura XLII:7 to which the Prophet is sent as a warner. If we did not know better from the hagiographic account of Ibn ʔIsḥāq and his successors, we should have good reason to believe that the message in the *ʕarabī* passages in the Qurʔān would have been directed to people in that area. The connecting link, admittedly somewhat fragile, is the use of the word *qurā*, possibly also referring to a group of villages. It is striking that the seven prophets mentioned in sura XXVI as Muhammed's predecessors can all be associated with north-western Ḥiğāz. Disregarding the hagiographic account, which is of a much later date, there is nothing in the Qurʔān that speaks against a location in an area north of Medina. There were the prophets, there were the villages, there were the *ʕarab* and a people, a *qawm*, for whom the *ʕarabī* language was an authority.[169]

The *qurrāʔ*/*ʔahl al-qurā* are associated with Ḥiǧāz. A Qurʕānic passage from the Medinean period prescribes that the booty from the *ʔahl al-qurā* should be given to the Messenger.[170] In the account of early Islamic history, the *qurrāʔ* appear for the first time in the so-called Biʔr Maʕūna incident, when Muhammed in 626 sent 40 of them to the tribe of ʕĀmir b. Ṣaʕṣaʕa, who killed them.[171] Their second appearance is in the story about the main battle during the *ridda* wars, namely that at ʕAqrabāʔ against the 'false' prophet Musaylima and the tribe of Ḥanīfa in AD 633. We hear that the Muslim army before the battle grouped itself according to internal non-military divisions: *muhāǧirūn*, i.e. the Muslims from Mecca, the *ʔanṣār*, i.e. the Muslims from Medina, *ʔahl al-bawādī*, i.e. the people of 'the open land', *ʔahl al-qabāʔil*, i.e. the people from the tribes, and *ʔahl al qurā*.[172] When the *ʔahl al-bawādī* and the *ʔahl al-qurā* quarrelled about their military prowess, the latter said: 'We are better in fighting the *ʔahl al-qurā* than you are.'[173] We thus learn that there were *ʔahl al-qurā* even among the enemy. The enemy at ʕAqrabāʔ was the tribe of Ḥanīfa, whose domicile was al-Yamāma, which, as we have seen, is one of the areas where we find the *ʕāriba* peoples ʕImlīq, Ṭasm and Ǧadīs.

We can thus discern a group in the earliest history of Islam called *qurrāʔ*, probably meaning 'villagers' or 'the people of the villages', *ʔahl al-qurā*. They consisted mainly of people from insignificant tribes in the Ḥiǧāz and most likely in Yamāma together with Yemenis, whose main merit was to have remained faithful to Islam during the *ridda* wars. In Muʕāwiya's speech quoted above they are addressed as *ʕarab*. Since they were villagers from Ḥiǧāz, it lies near at hand to suspect that their villages were none other than the *qurā ʕarabiyya*. Are these villages the home of the original *ʕarab*?

The idea of a limited geographical location of the original *ʕarab* apparent in this tradition does not stand isolated. We have seen that the seven legendary peoples, whose Arabness is secondary, are limited to certain regions in Arabia. A similar limited location of the *ʕarab* is, in fact, found outside the folk-tale tradition. Ibn Qutayba says that the land of the *ʕarab* is between Yemen and Kisrā (i.e. the territory of the Sassanids) close to Rome.[174] The same author gives the measurements of the main countries according to some tradition, and we hear that the whole world has a length of 4,000 parasangs, half of which is possessed by the kings of Sudan. The rest is divided between Rome (8,000), Persia (3,000) and the land of the *ʕarab* encompassing 1,000.[175] Leaving the exact meaning of these measurements aside, it is remarkable that the land of the Arabs is considered so small (*c.* 5,500 km) in comparison to Rome (44,000) and Iran (16,500). It indicates that it was not considered identical with the peninsula, the dimensions of which were well known from Greek geographers at least since the days of Eratosthenes. There are other passages that can be read in the same way. Wahb says that the Ghassanid king al-Ḥāritha leaves Syria for the land of the *ʕarab*, which is Yathrib/Medina.[176] It is told how the first Iranian Muslim, Sālmān al-Fārisī, in his search for truth, asked some people from the Kalb tribe to take him to *ʔarḍ al-ʕarab*, 'the land of the Arabs', and they brought him to Wādī al-qurā.[177] The area around Naǧrān is sometimes referred to as *ʔarḍ al-ʕarab*, 'the land of the *ʕarab*'.[178] The same is said about the region around al-Ḥīra along the Euphrates in stories about pre-Islamic times.[179]

It thus seems possible that the term *bilād*/*ʔarḍ*/*ǧazīrat al-ʕarab*, 'land of the *ʕarab*', may stand for quite small areas and not necessarily always mean the whole peninsula.

The following note in the *Lisān* may contain more interesting information about the language of the *ʕarab* and those who speak it than even Ibn Manẓūr himself was aware of:

> All who live in the land of the *ʕarab* and their *ǧazīra* and speak their language are *ʕarab*.[180]

One could speculate that the word *ǧazīra* did not originally mean 'island', let alone 'peninsula', but 'separate part of land', 'lot' derived from the basic meaning of the root GZR, 'cut off'. The note in the *Lisān* might thus contain an original reference to the limited areas in Arabia where the villages of the *ʕarab* were and where their language was spoken or at least known.

The (Muslim) *qurrāʔ/ʔahl al-qurā* seem to have consisted mainly of two groups: one with roots in Ḥiǧāz and another originating in Yemen. Now we have seen that in the later genealogies, the Yemenis claim to have a close relationship with the *ʕāriba* Arabs, sharing the main characteristic of Arabness, *ʕurūba*, namely the *ʕarabiyya* language. Since the *ʕāriba* peoples can be shown to have been considered the original inhabitants of the land where we find the *qurrāʔ/ʔahl al-qurā*, it seems most likely that the association between the forefathers of the Yemenis and the original dwellers in the villages of the *ʕarab* in fact is a reflection of the alliance between the Yemenis and the *qurrāʔ* documented in the conflicts in Kufa in the 640s and 650s AD.

The most important result of this survey is that we find traces of a far more limited extent of the *ʕarab* than the classical one, which identifies them with all the tribes that had become citizens of the first Islamic empire. We have indications that *ʕarab* could be associated with people who had been settled in villages within limited regions in northern Ḥiǧāz and eastern Arabia and who were, if not extinct, at least unimportant in the first Islamic century. In the same way we have evidence that the *ʕarab* in Yemen constituted only one small sector of society at the time of the Prophet. It is most likely that the limited extension of the term is chronologically prior to the comprehensive one(s) documented from the later Umayyad period. We also begin to discern at least a geographical connection not only between the *ʔahl al-qurā/qurrāʔ* and the *ʕarab* but also between these and the mysterious *ʕarab ʕāriba*.[181]

Excursus: the language of Quraysh

The definition of *ʕarab* according to linguistic proficiency looks very much as if it has developed during the *šuʕūbiyya/ʕaṣabiyya* debate in the early Abbasid period. In Sibawayhi's *Kitāb* from the latter half of the eighth century, the *ʕarab* are constantly referred to as informants for the linguistic description.[182] In Sibawayhi, the striving towards linguistic legislation based on an explicitly defined linguistic canon is not yet prominent. Such a concept presupposes a linguistic norm: one form of a language is considered 'correct', other forms are considered 'incorrect'. Unfortunately, we do not know when such a concept was explicitly formulated for Arabic. Sībawayhi is still a descriptivist, not a prescribist. A linguistic canon is presupposed by the grammarians in Iraq from the ninth century onwards and has remained dominant in Arabic linguistic culture ever since.[183] It is most likely that the definition of *ʕarab* as those mastering the old *ʕarabiyya* received renewed importance during the cultural debate in the early Abbasid period. But, as we have seen, there are clear indications that the language criterion is older and that the term *ʔaʕǧam/ʕaǧam* presupposes a kind of linguistic norm.

For the Muslim hagiographic tradition and the succeding Islamic scholars, as well as most western ones, the identity of the Qurʔānic audience is no problem: it was Quraysh in Mecca from the very beginning. When it is said that the Prophet is sent as 'a warner for the Mother of Villages and those around it (them?)' (XLII:7), this is explained as a reference to Mecca. This would mean that Quraysh had a special acquaintance with the *ʕarabī* language. There is, in fact, a well-known tradition about the linguistic superiority of Quraysh, which is best summarized by the *Lisān*:

> ʔAbū Bakr is said to have said: Quraysh are the middlemost of the *ʕarab* in dwelling [i.e. they dwell in the middle of them], and they are the most prominent in giving protection and they are the most *ʕarab* of them (*ʔaʕrabuhum*) as far as language is concerned.
>
> Qatāda said: Quraysh used to 'harvest', i.e. choose the best of the language of the *ʕarab*, until their language became the best of their languages and the Qurʔān was [then] revealed in it.
>
> al-ʔAzharī said: The Qurʔān was revealed to the Prophet in Arabic (*ʕarabiyyan*) since he was one of the pure *ʕarab (min ṣarīḥ al-ʕarab*).

This view of the origin of the *ʕarab* which, as has become clear, is only one among many others among the learned of early Islam, was later chosen as the true one and hardened into a dogma which is difficult to uproot even among modern scholars.[184] It should be emphasized that the Qurʔān itself does not single out Quraysh, or the mysterious *qawm*, as those with the 'best' Arabic language. The only information we get is that this language was an authority for them. If the audience of the Qurʔān had been the recognized carriers of the genuine linguistic tradition and considered the most 'pure' among the speakers of the *ʕarabī* language, it is difficult to explain why this is not at least alluded to in the Revelation when the *ʕarabī* language is dealt with. As we have seen, the Qurʔānic statements about the *ʕarabī* language go in another direction, namely that that language had an authority as a medium for messages from the non-human world. Instead, this tradition could easily be interpreted as an expression of the ambition to raise the prestige of Quraysh in the struggle for rank with both the Yemenis and the emerging nationalism, the *šuʕūbiyya*, of the Iranian Muslims. Apart from the quoted statements, which are easily explicable by the cultural and political struggle in the Islamic community from the second civil war onwards, there are no indications of the linguistic authority or superiority of Quraysh. On the contrary, it is noticeable that from this tribe we have no poets of any rank, which is indeed strange if they had been the 'most *ʕarab*' of all linguistically.[185]

The linguistic excellence of Quraysh is connected with an attempt at explaining the word *ʕarab* itself, in fact the only attempt in Islamic literature. We turn once more to the *Lisān*:

> It is said that the children of ʔIsmāʕīl lived in *ʕAraba*, which is part of the Tihāma, and that they were named after their land (i.e. *ʕarab*).
>
> al-ʔAzharī said: they are called *ʕarab* after the name of their land: *al-ʕArabāt*.
>
> ʔIsḥāq b. al Farağ said: *ʕAraba* is the plain (*bāḥa*) of the *ʕarab* and it is the

courtyard of the house of The Father of Linguistic Purity (*ʔabū faṣāḥa*), ʔIsmāʕīl [two anonymous verses]:

ʕAraba is a land the sacredness of which is not to be defiled by violence.[186]

The plain of *ʕArabāt* is shaken
so that blood is being mixed in its highlands.

Quraysh lived in *ʕAraba* and multiplied there. The rest of the *ʕarab* were dispersed over their peninsula but they were named after *ʕAraba* because their father ʔIsmāʕīl was born there and his children had thrived (*rabalū*) there and become many. When the land could not bear them they spread, but Quraysh stayed there.

This tradition looks very much as if it belongs to the general trend of exalting the past of Quraysh, which was part of the struggle between Yemen and the northern tribes in the Umayyad period. The question remains whether there is any connection between the name *ʕarab* and the geographical name or designation *ʕAraba*. The latter is, apart from the north and south of the Dead Sea, claimed also to be found in the Tihāma which is alluded to here.[187] The Dead Sea *ʕaraba* is documented already in the Old Testament, whereas the Tihāmī one is found with Arabo-Islamic sources. The derivation of *ʕarab* from *ʕAraba* is linguistically no more likely than the derivation from *ʕarabiyya*. If there indeed is a connection between the two, it should, according to the derivational system in Semitic, be the other way around.

Notes

1 Cf. Goldziher, *Studien* I 102–104.
2 al-Ǧāḥiẓ, *Bayān* II:33; cf. Blachère, *Allocution*. Most versions of the sermon do not contain this passage.
3 *Lisān* s.v. ʕRB beginning; cf. Ibn Durayd, *Ištiqāq* 524 [306].
4 *Lisān* s.v. ǦYL.
5 *Lisān* s.v. ʕRB.
6 Ibn Hishām, *Tīǧān* 301 ll. 2, 4.
7 Wahb, *Papyrus I*; cf. Ibn Qutayba, *Maʕārif* 28; Ibn ʕAbd Rabbihi, *ʕIqd* III:409.
8 *Lisān* s.v. ʕǦM beginning: *xilāfu l-ʕağami*; ibid. s.v. ʕǦM: *wa-l-ʕağamu gayru ʕarabin*.
9 *Lisān*, ibid.: *al-ʔaʕğamu llaḏī lā yufṣiḥu*.
10 *al-ʔaʕğamu llaḏī lā yufṣiḥu wa-lā yubayyinu kalāmahu wa-ʔin kāna ʕarabiyya n-nasabi*.
11 Cf. ʕAnṭara, *Muʕallaqa* 25; idem, nos. 21:2; 27:2 (= Ahlwardt, *Divan* 44, 52); cf. Ibn Qutayba, *ʕUyūn* II:142. According to az-Zawzānī's commentary, *ʔaʕğam ṭimṭim* in verse 25 in ʕAnṭara's *Muʕallaqa* refers to Ethiopian shepherds. This seems unlikely and is probably an attempt to interpret the verse on the view that everybody in Arabia was *faṣīḥ*. An *ʔaʕğam*, consequently, must be a non-*ʕarabī*, i.e. a non-tribesman. This is contradicted by the *Lisān*, which clearly states that even an *ʕarabī* may well be *ʔaʕğam*. The verse instead sheds some light on social conditions in pre-Islamic Arabia: the shepherds, i.e. those who tended the animals for the professional warriors, were *ʔaʕğam*. It was among the warriors that one could find people who were *fuṣaḥāʔ*, masters of the 'pure language'.
12 Ibn Ǧinnī, *Sirr* 36: *ʔinnamā waqaʕat* [namely the root ʕǦM] *fī kalāmi l-ʕarabi li-l-ʔibhāmi wa-li-l-ʔixfāʔi wa-ḍidda l-bayāni wa-l-ʔifṣāḥi*; cf. az-Zabīdī, *Tāğ* s.v. ʕǦM (8:390).
13 The root ʕGM is found in Hebrew, Palestinian Aramaic and, possibly, Akkadian. In Mishnaic Hebrew the participle *ʕagūm* means 'grieving, mourned about', like the Palestinian Aramaic

equivalent *ʕagīm*. A more original meaning seems to be 'bent down, pressed down', from which the meaning 'grieving' is derivable. Thus it is used about the drunken man 'who has a tied tongue' (*lašōn ʕagūm*, *Ba-Midbar Rabbah* 10 = Mirkin IX:298 bottom; cf. Jastrow, *Dictionary*; Sokoloff, *Dictionary* s.vv.). The latter example is interesting and is close to the meaning of Arabic *ʔaʕǧam* as a characterization of speech. The meaning 'bent, crooked' is found with the (Eastern?) Aramaic *ʔagīm*, which is possibly identical with ʕGM. The Akkadian *agāmu(m)*, 'to rage, to be angry' would also belong to this root (= 'to be distorted from anger') as well as to Arabic ʔǦM 'to loathe' (von Soden, *Handwörterbuch* s.v.).

14 al-Khalīl, *Kitāb al-ʕayn* I:237 s.v. ʕGM.

15 *Lisān* s.v. ʕǦM beginning. Sullam is the name of the horse of Zabbān b. Sayyār al-Fazārī, a famous warrior from the Fazāra tribe in Ghaṭafān. There is of course a pun on the name Sallūm.

16 Ibn Hishām, *Tīǧān* 297.

17 *Lisān* s.v. ǦYL.

18 al-Balādhurī, *ʔAnsāb* V:171.

19 ʔAʕshā ash-Shaybānī was active during the period AD 690–720.

20 aṭ-Ṭabarī, *Tārīkh* I:1036; Bevan, *Naqāʔiḍ* 645:3–4, 806:3; Ibn ʕAbd Rabbihi, *ʕIqd* V:265; cf. Nöldeke, *Geschichte* 343 (see the anecdote in aṭ-Ṭabarī, *Tārīkh* I:1040, cf. Goldziher, *Studien* I:113.). The punctuation tries to render the somewhat awkward syntax of the verses. The poet is Bukayr, 'the dumb one from al-Ḥārith'. According to the context, he was a contemporary of the great ʔAʕshā al-Maymūn who died around AD 630. The dating of these poets as well as the poems ascribed to them is, however, highly uncertain, and the great ʔAʕshā is often ascribed poems by other ʔAʕshās of lesser standing.

21 The latter reading is, in fact, found in prose commentaries to the poem and may well be a correction according to the norm of later periods. Cf. Ibn Qutayba, *Maʕārif* 603; Ibn ʕAbd Rabbihi, *ʕIqd* V:262; Ibn Ḥabīb, *al-Muḥabbar* 360 who all have *ʕaǧam*: Dhū Qār was the first battle when the *ʕarab* took vengeance on the *ʕaǧam*. The commentaries go back to Abū ʕUbayda. The reading *ʔaʕǧam* is, however, to be preferred since it is demanded by the metre (*kāmil*).

22 Cf. Lane, *Lexicon* s.v. ʕǦM: *raǧul ʔaʕǧam, qawm ʔaʕǧam.*

23 *Lisān* s.v. ʕRB.

24 al-ʔAzharī, *Tahdhīb* s.v. ʕǦM.

25 Iṣfahānī, *ʔAghānī* 3:138: *ʔammā l-lisānu wa-z-ziyyu fa-ʕarabiyyāni wa-ʔammā l-ʔaṣlu fa-ʕaǧamiyyun.*

26 The story from Wahb about Ǧidhʕ and the Roman emperor is difficult to date. Wahb's book was written around AD 720, and the event is, according to the story, dated to either the beginning of the sixth century or even the middle of the third century AD (the Roman emperor Decius 249–251 is mentioned!). As far as Dhū Qār is concerned, it should be observed that the Iranians according to the account in aṭ-Ṭabarī had several tribes from Arabia in their ranks. The battle was thus not a clearcut confrontation between *ʕarab* tribesmen and the Iranians.

27 aṭ-Ṭabarī, *Tārīkh*, III:1142. The Sufyānī was a Messiah expected in some anti-Abbasid circles, cf. Madelung, *Sufyānī*.

28 See Caskel, *Ǧamhara* I:31–33; Piotrovskij, *Predanije* 10 ff. The only possible exception is Muḍar, which is the name of a cultic league of tribes which existed in the pagan period (Caskel, *Bedeutung* 15; idem, *Ǧamhara* II:417). However, some of the members of the Muḍar group in the Islamic era, like Tamīm, did not belong to the cultic league but were joined to the others during the conflicts in the 680s.

29 The emergence of the Qays in Islamic times is explicitly stated by Ibn Qutayba, *Maʕārif* 64, 79–90; see also Watt, *Qays*. For the others see Kister, *Ḳuḍāʕa*; Kinderman, *Rabīʕa*. For the formation of the Yemeni party, see Piotrovskij, *Predanije* 10–34 and Shaban, *History* I 120–121. For the fictitious nature of the genealogical system, see Bräunlich, *Beiträge*; Henninger, *Genealogie* 54; Caskel, *Stamm*; idem, *Ǧamhara* II 81.

30 Caskel, *Ǧamhara* I:31.

31 A similar concept is found among the Somalis (including the Sab) who define themselves as descendants of patriarchs from Arabia married into the Dir group (Lewis, *Peoples* 18–42).

32 It should be noticed that Ibn al-Kalbī himself does not use the word *ʕarab* as an overall term for the community of tribes listed in the *Ǧamhara*, nor does he adduce the Biblical ancestry. His name-lists start with ʕAdnān as the father of Maʕadd and Qaḥṭān respectively, and there is no trace of differences in rank between the tribes. He was, however, familiar with the term *ʕarab*, as is seen from the titles of many of his other books as well as in the texts preserved in quotations (cf. Ibn an-Nadim, *Fihrist* I 95–98). From the use of the term in those texts it is clear that for him *ʕarab* is a comprehensive term for the tribes.

33 al-Ǧāḥiẓ, *Bayān* III:366. The term 'bedouin' is *ʔaʕrāb*, which will be returned to later; see pp. 82ff.

34 The basis for the detailed register of tribes by Ibn al-Kalbī is probably the *dīwān*, i.e. the register of tribes and tribesmen entitled to shares in the booty taken by the Muslim army, set up under the reign of ʕUmar b. al-Khaṭṭāb. That document (or rather, those documents) is lost but it is likely to have had an important political role during most of the Umayyad period, being the actual confirmation of someone's citizenship in the Muslim community. For a study of the extant evidence, see Puin, *Diwan*.

35 Cf. Goldziher, *Studien* I 40 ff.

36 Iṣfahānī, *ʔAghānī* 12:240 line 6 ff.

37 Ibn Qutayba, *Maʕārif* 28.

38 aṭ-Ṭabarī, *Tārīkh* I:222. Sumra died in AD 679, which makes the ascription somewhat doubtful. Also Wahb b. Munabbih has subscribed to this view, cf. aṭ-Ṭabarī, *Tārīkh* I:211.

39 Once again, the Somalis provide a close parallel, also claiming descent from several forefathers some of whom may well be fictitious (Lewis, *Peoples* 18 ff.).

40 In the Old Testament, the nisba-adjective *yisrʔelī* is quite rare. The everyday designations were obviously formed from local tribes and districts like Yehūdī, Binyamīnī, Gilʕadī, Reʔūvenī etc. In Arabia nisba-forms from tribal names are also very frequent, such as Sulamī, Tamīmī, ʕAbsī, Qaysī etc. Unlike in Israel, the overall term for the tribes is also very often used in a nisba form: *ʕarabī*.

41 It might be objected that, for example, Quraysh does not have an eponymous patriarch with that name. In their genealogy a certain Fihr appears as a forefather. Neither do we find the expression banū Qurayš, 'the sons of Quraysh'. But the question is whether Quraysh was indeed a tribe like those named after a forefather. According to a note by Ibn ʔIsḥāq (Ibn Hishām, *Sīra* 61, cf. Ibn ʕAbd Rabbihi *ʕIqd* III:312), the name Quraysh is derived from a verb *taqarraša*, a synonym to *taǧammaʕa*, 'to get together'. Ibn ʕAbd Rabbihi even adduces a verse: /Quṣayy, your father, was called *muǧammiʕ* //through him God gathered the tribes of Fihr/. There are reasons to suspect that Quraysh, in fact, was some kind of association that originally was not based on claims of common kinship and genealogy. This might also hold for certain other 'tribes' in Arabia like the Shalamians; see p. 439, cf. p. 527.

42 *Lisān* s.v. ʕRB.

43 E.g. Ja 635:27. von Wissmann (*Zur Geschichte* 181–182) locates them between present-day Bīsha and the ʕArid/Ṭuwayq mountains.

44 Cf. Ṭirimmāḥ, *Dīwān* nos. 8:6, 13, 26; 47:54, 48:10; ʔAʕshā Hamdān no. 4 (= Geyer, *Díwán* 312); ʕAdī b. Ruqāʕ al-Ǧudhamī in Iṣfahānī, *ʔAghānī* 9:305, 314–315: 'Qaḥṭān is our father and by him we are named'; Caskel, *Ǧamhara* I 34; Piotrovskij, *Predanije* 13–17; Crone, *Qays* 45 ff.

45 Genesis 10:25.

46 The equivalence between the two names is evident from aṭ-Ṭabarī, *Tārīkh* I:219–220, a quotation from Ibn al-Kalbī; see p. 35.

47 For this propaganda see Goldziher, *Studien* I 78–100; Piotrovskij, *Predanije* 10 ff.

48 Ibn Hishām, *Tīǧān* 319.

49 Ibn Hishām, *Tīǧān* 246. Cf. ibid. 107, 232, 242, 239. This king is without doubt identical to ŠMR YHRʕŠ known from Sabaean inscriptions, reigning *c*. AD 270–310.

50 al-Yaʕqūbī, *Tārīkh* I:230 f.

51 aṭ-Ṭabarī, *Tārīkh* I:2347; al-Balādhurī, *Futūḥ* 135; al-Masʕūdī, *Tanbīh* 265. See Crone, *Qays* 48 n. 259 for further examples. For the tribes counted among the *Quḍāʕa* see Kister, *Ḳuḍāʕa*. For the phrase *al-ʕarab min Quḍāʕa* in the Ṭabarī passage see pp. 76, 615.

52 Iṣfahānī, *ʔAghānī* 14:288.
53 Iṣfahānī, *ʔAghānī* 23:230.
54 al-ʔAzraqī, *ʔAkhbār* 44.
55 One of the locations of ar-Rass is the area between Yemen, al-Yamāma and Ḥaḍramawt; see Bakrī, *Muʕǧam* s.vv. Rass and Ṣayhad; al-Hamdānī, *ʔIklīl* I:52.
56 Ibn Hishām, *Tīǧān* 174.
57 Ibn Saʕd, *Ṭabaqāt* I:73, cf. Wellhausen, *Skizzen* IV 65, 179; Hamidullah, *Waṯāʔiq* no. 112 (pp. 232–233). Cf. p. 563.
58 The reading of this passage is somewhat problematical. The printed text to Ibn Saʕd has GRB, which is meaningless. The emendation to ʕRB is then most likely and is followed by Robin (*L'Arabie* 87). Also *xalāʔiṭ* is problematical. It must be (an undocumented) plural of *xalīṭ* (or rather *xalīṭa* which is undocumented), which means 'people with whom one has common but temporary affairs' like sharing of water or pasture (Lane, *Lexicon* s.v.).
59 For the documentation, see Chapter 19.
60 Dagorn, *Geste* 217; cf. ibid. 7 ff.
61 Dagorn, *Geste* 208–209.
62 The basis for the claim that Quraysh were descendants of Ismāʕīl was the verses in the Qurʔān II:124 ff., which, however, do not say so.
63 For the political situation, especially the relations between Yemenis and non-Yemenis at this time, see Crone, *Qays* 28 ff. The antagonism between the two factions seems to have increased, cf. ibid. 42–43, 50–54.
64 See p. 69.
65 For the origins of ʕUbayd, see Crosby, *ʔAkhbār* 5–18, 93–106. Crosby seems to advocate a dating to the time of Muʕāwiya with possible later additions (cf. also Donner, *Narrative* 196, 224). This is highly doubtful. The violent pro-Yemeni propaganda in it as well as the reference to Wahb b. Munabbih (392) points to a time at least after AD 720. The references to Ibn ʕAbbās and Ibn ʔIsḥāq point to the Abbasid age. The prophecy about a Fāṭimid *mahdī* coming from the land of the Berbers (336) might even reflect the rise of the Fatimids. In spite of this, the work undoubtedly contains some of the main arguments of Yemeni propaganda during the second civil war and perhaps even before that.
66 ʕUbayd, *ʔAkhbār* 327–328: *al-ʕarab baʕḍuhā min baʕḍ*. This emphasis on the unity of the *ʕarab* reflects conditions in the later Umayyad period. On the other hand it is worth remarking that ʕUbayd does not speak about other North Arabian tribes than Quraysh. This feature is also found in Wahb and might well be an archaic feature preserved from the time before all the northern tribes were seen as a unity.
67 aṭ-Ṭabarī, *Tārīkh* I:219–220. In Ibn Ḥabīb (*al-Muḥabbar* 384) Ibn al-Kalbī is quoted as saying that God first taught ʕĀd and ʕAbīl to understand the *ʕarabiyya*.
68 aṭ-Ṭabarī, *Tārīkh* I:214–215, cf. ibid 231. This passage belongs to those which were excluded by Ibn Hishām when he edited Ibn ʔIsḥāq's text; see Newby, *Making* 44 ff. The word ʔLMṢRY has been emended to ʔLMḌRY which would make the language belong to the northern groups of tribes, the Muḍar. Parallels in al-Balādhurī, *ʔAnsāb* I:3–4.
69 Ibn Hishām, *Tīǧān* 32–33; 36–37; 107; cf. Ibn Qutayba, *Maʕārif* 26–28, which is based on Wahb.
70 Ibn Hishām, *Tīǧān* 37, 107; Ibn Qutayba, *Maʕārif* 26–27 (quoting Wahb).
71 Thus, in the fragment of his *maghāzī*-book (PH 3:10, 13 = Khoury, *Wahb* I 126–127) we find the contrast between *ʕarab* and *ʕaǧam*, which obviously reflects the terminology of the beginning of the eighth century. There is only one passage in the *Tīǧān* (107) where the sons of Hūd are said to be *al-ʕarab banū Qaḥṭān*. It is, however, not entirely clear if there is identity between the two terms (*banū Qaḥṭān* being an apposition to *al-ʕarab*) or if the latter is a part of the former.
72 Wahb has Lāwī.
73 aṭ-Ṭabarī, *Tārīkh* I:221. This author (I:216–217) has one anonymous version of the genealogy of the ancient peoples of Arabia which, however, does not mention the word *ʕarab* at all. It more or less follows the mentioned ones. ʕĀd is the son of ʕAwṣ, and Lawdh has four sons: Ṭasm, Ǧadīs, ʕImlīq and ʔUmaym. Thamūd is not mentioned.

74 van den Branden, *Histoire* 13–14.
75 *Lisān* s.v. ʕRB.
76 A conclusion from all this is that it is doubtful that the adjective *ʕāriba* would mean 'genuine'. It cannot be excluded that it has the same meaning as *mustaʕriba/mutaʕarriba*, i.e. 'behave *ʕarab*-like' (cf. *layl – lāʔil*). One could associate it with the modern meaning established earlier in this investigation. But since the Arabness of the *ʕāriba* peoples was obviously not constituted by descent, one should beware of attributing this meaning to the word at this stage.
77 al-Hamdānī, *Ṣifa* 134–136; cf. Corriente, *Marginalia* 55–56 note 2; Robin, *Langues* 104–106.
78 al-ʔAṣmaʕī, *Tārīkh* 7-8; Diʕbil, *Waṣāyā* 26-27. That this view represents a Yemeni opinion is explicitly stated by al-Masʕūdī, *Tanbīh* 80.
79 Ibn Isḥāq actually came from Medina, the town of the *ʔanṣār* who were close to the Yemenis. This makes the absence of the *ʕāriba* argument even more interesting.
80 Ibn Khaldūn, *Tārīkh* II:86.
81 al-Masʕūdī, *Tanbīh* 184–185, idem, *Murūǧ* III:103–104.
82 Cf. Wellhausen, *Diwan* 596–597. Thus, for example, the well at Qaryat al-Fāw was called ʕĀdiyya (al-Hamdānī, *Ṣifa* 265), which must simply mean 'the very old one'. According to al-Hamdānī, the *ʕarab* call everything old *ʕādī* (*ʔIklīl* I 38).
83 According to Wahb quoted by Ibn Qutayba, the dwelling of ʕĀd was identical with that of Sām: ad-Dahnāʕ, ʕĀliğ, Yabrīn, Wubār, Oman, Ḥaḍramawt and Yemen (*Maʕārif* 28 cf. 26), i.e. central, eastern and southern Arabia.
84 ʔIram has been identified with present-day ar-Ramm in southern Jordan and is probably mentioned already in the Old Testament (see p. 000). ʕAwṣ is the same as Biblical ʕUṣ, south of Edom. The traditional location of ʕĀd in Yemen is a reflex of the Yemeni propaganda.
85 Lāwudh is associated with the *lûdîm* in Genesis 10, thus giving a Biblical ancestry. It cannot be excluded, however, that the Arabic root LWḎ, 'taking refuge', has some old connection with these peoples. For Amaleq etc. see Nöldeke, *Amalekiter* 651; Meyer, *Israeliten* 389 ff.; Mattingly, *Amalek*.
86 According to Ibn ʔIsḥāq, they were scattered over the land, aṭ-Ṭabarī, *Tārīkh* I:213; cf. al-ʔAzraqī, *ʔAkhbār* 28, 22. Cf. also Ibn Qutayba, *Maʕārif* 27. al-Masʕūdī (*Murūǧ* III:92) says that Ismāʕīl married an *ʕamlaqī* woman and the dwelling place of the *ʕamālīq* in Mecca is pointed out.
87 The story is found, for example, in aṭ-Ṭabarī, *Tārīkh* I:219–222.
88 Nöldeke, *Amalekiter* 644.
89 See Hawting, *Idea*, for a convincing analysis of the Qurʔānic evidence.
90 Nöldeke, *Amalekiter* 641.
91 Exodus 17:8–16.
92 1 Samuel 15.
93 Judges 5:14.
94 Numbers 13:29; 1 Samuel 15:17, cf. Genesis 14:7; Judges 12:15, cf. Numbers 14:45, 1 Samuel 15:12 and Josephus, *Antiquities* 2.1.2.
95 Numbers 24:7.
96 *Lisān*, s.v. ʕMLQ, cf. Numbers 24:7.
97 We have a remarkable story referring to the tyrannical rule of ʕAmlūq, a chief from Ṭasm, over Ğadīs. When the latter revolt and kill the tyrant, Ṭasm calls in the king of Himyar, Ḥassān b. Tubbaʕ, who attacks Ğadīs and kills them. The story, which reappears in the legend of Macbeth, is attributed to Ibn Isḥāq via Ibn al-Kalbī (aṭ-Ṭabarī, *Tārīkh* I:771 ff.; cf. Ibn Qutayba, *Maʕārif* 632–633).
98 The derivation is explicitly stated in al-ʔAṣmaʕī, *Tārīkh* 8.
99 See pp. 199, 437 f., 511 f.
100 Iṣfahānī, *ʔAghānī* 4:307. The question about the genuineness of this *ḥadīth* is not important; the main point is that it has been formulated, by the Prophet or someone else.
101 It should be noticed that the Arabo-Islamic scholars did not claim the *ʕarabiyya* to have

been the oldest language of mankind. Most of them considered Syriac as the language of Adam and Eve, cf. e.g. al-Yaʕqūbī, *Tārīkh* I 17.

102 This tradition is reported by al-Yaʕqūbī (*Tārīkh* I:252). Nöldeke's scepticism about the relevance of the distinction between the different kinds of *ʕarab* (*Amalekiter* 641 n. 1) is not altogether justified. He is right that the different ranking was probably not generally accepted by all the affected groups of tribes. On the other hand it is clear that the ranking was not 'blosse Träume von Gelehrten'. There is no doubt that the ranking represents political struggles and propagandistic arguments. One weakness in Nöldeke's (and indeed most of his successors') analysis of the ethnic conditions in Arabia and adjacent lands is the tacit assumption that all gentilic names stand for the same kind of ethnic units, i.e. 'peoples'. From such a viewpoint, his scepticism about the stories from pre-Islamic Arabia is to a large extent justified. If, however, it can be shown that many of these stories are not pseudo-history but survivals and reflections of the myths of pre-Islamic Arabia, their importance is greatly increased.

103 All are, however, *ʕarab* according to Ibn ʔIsḥāq; see Ibn Hishām, *Sīra* 5.

104 This epithet is also found in the genealogies of the Qaḥṭānids; see below.

105 ʕUbayd, *ʔAkhbār* 328.

106 Diʕbil, *Waṣāyā* 27: *tabaḥbaḥa*; al-ʔAṣmaʕī, *Tārīkh* 7: *sḥyʕ* = *sağaʕa*?; al-Hamdānī, *ʔIklīl* I:116: *ʔalhamahu llāh*.

107 Ibn Hishām, *Tīğān* 43.

108 Ibn Saʕīd, *Nashwa* 81.

109 *ʔaʕraba* most often means to follow the rules of the *ʕarabiyya*, especially its inflectional system, which presupposes the existence of language forms without that system. This is one of the many passages which hint at the existence of several different related languages in Arabia, of which the *ʕarabiyya* was one but with a special status, probably used for poetry and oracle-giving but not as a spoken idiom.

110 The inscription Ja 635:27 mentions a campaign against ṮWRM MLK KDT WQḤṬN, 'Thawr, king of Kinda and Qaḥṭān', and against 'the lords of the town of QRYTN'. The latter is probably Qaryat al-Fāw. Since that site was the main residence of Kinda, QḤṬN could be west of it on the eastern slopes of ʕAsīr, where we today know a site by that name. It deserves to be mentioned that the same inscription mentions ʔʕRB near Nağrān, which should be in the same area; cf. p. 564.

111 The term Arabic for a language does, in fact, occur in non-Arabic pre-Islamic sources (Greek, Latin, Syriac); see further p. 591.

112 See Crone/Cook, *Hagarism*.

113 See especially Crone, *Trade*.

114 XLII:17.

115 Nöldeke, *Geschichte* I 21 n. 2; Horowitz, *Untersuchungen* 67–68; Watt, *Introduction* 20–25.

116 al-Bayḍāwī, *Tafsīr* ad loc.

117 III:96.

118 E.g. XXIX:61, 63; XXXI:25; XXXIX:38.

119 Thus, for example, *ʔumm an-nuğūm* means 'The Milky Way', i.e. an agglomeration of stars (Lane, *Lexicon* s.v. ʔMM). Cf. Bell, *Commentary* I 198.

120 Cf. Horowitz, *Untersuchungen* 67, for some references to the old poetry. Cf. also the Qurʔān itself in XXVII:28–29 and Bell, *Commentary* II 211, 237. See *Wörterbuch* s.v. KTB for the different meanings of *kitāb*. Welch (*Qurʔān* 401–402, 403–404) denies that *kitāb* in the Qurʔān refers to a heavenly book. Instead it is a term for the revelation as such. It is, however, difficult not to take the use of *qurʔān*, 'recitation', and *kitāb*, 'scripture', as indications of two different forms of the revelation, even though Welch is right that the idea of a heavenly prototype is absent.

121 XV:87. *maṯānī* obviously refers to some kind of narrative; cf. Lane, *Lexcicon* s.v. ṮNY.

122 Middle Meccan period; cf. Nöldeke, *Geschichte des Korans* 131–132.

123 The verse is difficult but should be read in the light of *sūrat al-wāqiʕa* (LVI) v. 78: 'Truly, it is a noble *qurʔān* / in a hidden book', and *sūrat al-burūğ* (LXXXV) v. 22: 'Nay, it is a glorious *qurʔān* / in a preserved tablet.' Cf. also above XXVI:196: 'it is in the *zubur* of the

ancients'. The locative *fī ʔummi l-kitābi* can be taken as a kind of *ḥāl*-complement to the nominal sentence: 'it is wise and exalted because/since it is with us'. The Recitation has these two divine attributes because of its intimate connection with the Divine Book. Blachère's rendering distorts the structure of the the verse : 'En vérité, cette écriture, dans l'Archétype auprès nous, est certes sublime et sage!' Paret is more aware of the difficulty: 'Sie (or 'Er', i.e. the Qurʔān) gilt in der Urschrift bei uns als erhaben und weise.'

124 Cf. LVI:77–80; LXXXV:21–22.

125 LVI:80.

126 Third Meccan period; cf. Nöldeke, *Geschichte des Korans* 152–153.

127 It should be observed that the word *laʕalla* often means 'so that, in order that' in the Qurʔān and not 'perhaps' as in later Arabic.

128 See Bell/Watt, *Introduction* 121–127; Welch, *Qurʔān* 401.

129 For the various interpretations of these letters, see Nöldeke, *Geschichte des Korans* II 68–78; Welch, *Qurʔān* 412–414 points out that the occurrence of the letters is closely connected with the concept of the *kitāb*, namely the written revelation.

130 Hebrew *ʔot*, Aramaic *ʔāṯā*.

131 From the second Meccan period; see Nöldeke, *Geschichte des Korans* 124–125.

132 From this comes the designation *al-mufaṣṣal* for the latter part of the Qurʔān due to the frequent divisions between the suras because of their increasing shortness.

133 See Lane, *Lexicon* s.v. FṢL and *Tāǧ al-ʕarūs* s.v. SǦʕ.

134 E.g. VI:119: 'You should only eat from that over which God's name has been mentioned, for God has *faṣṣala* (separated?) for you that which he has forbidden for you.' Or in VII:133: 'We have sent over them the Flood, locusts, lice, frogs and blood as signs *mufaṣṣalāt*' (= separated from each other, Paret, *Koran*: 'eines nach dem anderen'). Or VI:114: 'He is the one who has sent down to you the Book (or the writing) *mufaṣṣalan*' (i.e. in separate parts?). Cf. Bell, *Commentary* I 349 (to XI:1) who renders it 'distinctly separated'.

135 Cf. VI:126; VII:32, 133, 174; IX:11, X:5, 24; XXX:28.

136 This interpretation means that the relationship between the Book and the Recitation is much freer and more distant than supposed by the later orthodoxy.

137 The translations: Arberry: If we had made it a barbarous Koran, they would have said: 'Why are its signs not distinguished? What, barbarous and Arabic?' Say: . . . Paret: Wenn wir sie (die Mahnung) zu einem nichtarabischen Koran gemacht hätten, würden sie sagen: 'Warum sind seine Verse nicht (im einzelnen) auseinandergesetzt (so dass jedermann sie verstehen kann)? (Was soll das:) ein nichtarabischer Koran und ein arabischer (Verkünder)?' Sag: . . . Blachère (= 72): Si Nous avions fait de [cette Révélation] une prédication en [langue] barbare, ils auraient dit: 'Pourquoi ces aya n'ont-elles pas été rendues intelligibles? Pourquoi [sont-elles en langue] barbare alors que [notre idiome] est arabe?' – Réponds: . . . Cf. Horowitz, *Untersuchungen* (75): Wenn wir ihn zu einen fremdsprachigen Quran gemacht hätten, . . . 'Warum sind seine Verse nicht wohl gebaut? Ist er fremdsprachisch und arabisch [zugleich]?'. The first crux is the phrase *lawlā fuṣṣilat* etc. *lawlā* has two meanings (1) 'unless, if not', (2) 'why . . . not' (warum nicht). As is seen, the modern translators follow the second one. With this is connected the question whether that clause is a quotation of what 'they' say or whether it is a commentary. Then the function of the two adjectives is unclear. The textual tradition is uncertain, one version having the interrogative particle *ʔa* before the first one, another lacking it. As far as their reference is concerned, Horowitz takes both adjectives as referring to the Qurʔān, not *ʕarabī* as referring to the Prophet as is usually done by the traditional exegesis. All other instances of this adjective in the Qurʔān refer to the Revelation, not to the Prophet. Horowitz's reading is thus defensible and likely.

138 In Arabic one could fill out the missing links: *ʔa-*[*taqūlūna ʔinnahu*] *ʔaʕǧamiyyun wa-*[*huwa*] *ʕarabiyyun*! 'Do you say (claim) that it is *ʔaʕǧamī*? Do you not see that it is *ʕarabī*?' The underlying construction would be like *kayfa . . . wa* – 'how . . . while?'.

139 Cf. also X:37: 'this *qurʔān* . . . is a *tafṣīl* of the Writing (*kitāb*)'.

140 For the difference between the Book and the Revelation, see Buhl, *Forkyndelse* 56–62, a passage unfortunately not included in the German translation (*Das Leben Muhammeds*).

141 For the dating, see Nöldeke, *Geschichte des Korans* 126.

142 The *zubur* is some kind of scripture. The word is of South Arabian origin and, as we now know, the Sabaean term for the cursive South Arabian script (see W.W. Müller, *L'Écriture.*).

143 Nöldeke, *Geschichte des Korans* 145–146.

144 The traditional *tafsīr* has many suggestions: a Roman (Byzantine) slave, a Christian blacksmith in Mecca named Balʕām (Bileam?), a slave from Ḥaḍramawt belonging to the family of Mughīra in Quraysh named Yaʕīsh, a Christian Ḥaḍramī (!) named Ǧabr, two Yemeni slaves named Yasār and Ǧabr, Salmān the Persian (see aṭ-Ṭabarī, *Tafsīr* ad loc. 7:647–652). The most substantial information from these suggestions is the definition of which people were considered *ʔaʕǧam*: Iranians, Romans and Yemenis!

145 Arberry, *Koran* 244; Blachère, *Coran* 2 717; Paret, *Koran* 205.

146 Cf. Horowitz, *Untersuchungen* 75 Anm. 2. The traditional exegesis equates it with *ḥikma*, 'wisdom'; cf. aṭ-Ṭabarī, *Tafsīr* ad.loc. and Lane, *Lexicon* s.v. ḤKM.

147 Cf. Buhl, *Forkyndelse* 56–62.

148 The concept *kitāb* in the Qurʔān is in fact more complex than usually realized. From several passages it seems that by this term some kind of cosmic alphabet is intended by which God governs the entire universe (cf. Buhl, *Forkyndelse* 60–64 cf. 42 ff.; Pedersen, *Meyer* 114). This explains why both *kitāb* and *ʔāya* seem to be used both in the sense of 'writing' and 'letters' respectively, and in the sense of 'cosmic principles', 'signs of divine will' etc. Behind it lies a concept of writing similar to the one found, for example, in Jewish Qabbalah. That concrete writing could be seen as miraculous is clear from the famous verses in *sūrat al-ʕalaq*, The Blood-clot (XCVII), and in *sūrat al-baqara*, The Cow (II) verse 282. The meaning of these passages must be that writing itself is of divine origin. We should also notice the connection between QRʔ and writing (*qalam*) in sura XCVII. Against orthodox Islamic dogma it has, on good grounds, been assumed that written Qurʔānic texts existed already in the time before the Hiǧra; cf. Watt, *Introduction* 30–39.

149 Cf. XXVI:198–199.

150 The idea that God has sent a prophet to every people with the message in their own language is quite un-Qurʔānic. There is no indication in the Holy Book that the people of Firʕawn, ʕĀd, Thamūd, Saba etc. were considered to have their own languages (cf. e.g. *sūrat an-naml*, The Ant XXVII, especially 28–31). The earlier prophets are implicitly seen as preaching in the *ʕarabiyya* just like Muhammed. This is in accordance with the geographical scope of the Holy Book which is limited to the western parts of Arabia. The expression *lisān qawmihi* in XIV:4 most likely refers to the *lisān ʕarabī*: all prophets have used this language.

151 This is quite remarkable and explains many strange features in the early Qurʔānic passages. The purpose is not to convert the 'Arabs', i.e. the tribes of the peninsula, to monotheism, but to warn a closed group, a *qawm*. The violently polemic tone of the Qurʔān arises from the fact that many of the *qawm* in question rejected the message. The bitterness of the polemic shows that it seems to have been reasonable to expect that they would accept it. In spite of its aggressive tone, the criticism of the unbelievers in the Meccan suras is strangely vague. Above all there is surprisingly little criticism, if any at all, of polytheism. It is very unlikely that the term *širk* actually means polytheism. The cardinal sin of the opponents is their *hybris*, their complete trust in their own ability, which is hardly a characteristic of polytheists. The *qawm* has divided itself in not accepting the message (XLII:6, 13). As a *qawm*, it would have been their duty to accept. In fact, the *qawm* in the Meccan suras appear as worshippers of God, *ʔAllāh*, not of the pagan deities of Arabia, against whom we find very little criticism. The only polytheistic feature of the opponents is their worship of the three goddesses who are considered the daughters of ʔAllāh (LIII:19–23). It is highly doubtful if such worship was a characteristic feature of pagan religion in Arabia. At least it is not a characteristic of 'paganism' in general. It rather seems to be a special form of monotheism (cf. Krone, *Gottheit* 538–539 and Hawting, *Idea*). On the whole, the conditions reflected in the Qurʔān do not fit very well with what is found in the hagiographic account.

152 XVIII:59, VI:131, VII:94–98, XII:109, XXVIII:59, XLVI:27, XXXIV:18.

153 XI:100–102, 117.

154 XLII:7, VI:92. The suffix *-hā* in *ḥawla-hā* may mean 'it' or 'they'.

155 XXVII:34, 56, XXIX:31, 34.
156 X:98.
157 al-Bakrī, *Muʕǧam* 5, l. 20. The tradition is ascribed to al-Mughīra b. ʕAbd ar-Raḥmān. Cf. ll. 17–18.
158 al-Bakrī, *Muʕǧam* 11 ll. 16 ff. as-Suwāriqiyya is a village between Medina and Mecca belonging to the Sulaym tribe. Abū Bakr is said to have been born there; cf. Yāqūt, *Muʕǧam* III:180–181.
159 Yāqūt, *Muʕǧam* IV:81.
160 al-Yaʕqūbī, *Tārīkh*, II:81. The MS. has ʕZNYH, which is meaningless. The emendation is most likely from the context.
161 Yāqūt, *Muʕǧam* IV:76.
162 aṭ-Ṭabarī, *Tārīkh* I:2907 ff.; al-Balādhurī, *ʔAnsāb* V:39–47.
163 aṭ-Ṭabarī, *Tārīkh* I:2909 bottom.
164 aṭ-Ṭabarī, *Tārīkh* I:2911.
165 Cf. Wellhausen, *Oppositionsparteien* 8–11.
166 Shaban, *History* I 23, 51; Juynboll, *Qurrāʔ*; idem, *Qurʔān reciters*. Cf. Hinds, *Alignments* 358 ff., 363 ff.; Nagel, *Qurrāʔ*. Shaban's derivation of the word *qurrāʔ* from QRY and not QRʔ has a parallel in Hebrew, where there is constant contamination between QRʔ 'call, read aloud' and QRY 'encounter'. The word *qarya* (Hebrew *qiryā*) probably means 'meeting place', i.e. 'market'. There could then be an original connection between the two roots: '[the place of] calling [together]'.
167 Ṣaʕṣaʕa himself belonged to the tribe of ʕAbd al-Qays, whose habitat was in al-Ḥasā, present day al-Hufūf, in eastern Arabia. As will be shown later (pp. 290–294, 307), this is one of the areas especially associated with Arabs in pre-Islamic times.
168 See note 55.
169 There is a tradition that parts of Quraysh originated in the *Wādī l-qurā,* cf., pp. 614–615.
170 LIX:7. This is the only occurrence of the word *qurā* in the Medinan suras. This sura is, according to traditional exegesis, about the conflict with the Jewish tribe of B. Naḍīr in AD 626.
171 Juynboll, *Qurrāʔ* 124 ff.
172 It is said that *ʔahl al-qurā* separated themselves from *ʔahl al-ḥāḍir*, i.e. the settled ones. It is not clear if they were a sixth group or if the term is a summary of some of the others.
173 aṭ-Ṭabarī, *Tārīkh* I:1946. Donner's translation (*History* X, 122) misses the terminological distinctions since he does not distinguish between *ʔahl al-qurā* and *ʔahl al-ḥāḍir*.
174 Ibn Qutayba, *ʕUyūn* I:179, 198.
175 Ibn Qutayba, *ʕUyūn* I:215.
176 Ibn Hishām, *Tīǧān* 297.
177 Ibn Hishām, *Sīra* 140.
178 Ibn Hishām, *Sīra* I:19; 'the middle of the land of the *ʕarab*' (from Wahb?).
179 Iṣfahānī, *ʔAghānī* 2:144.
180 *Lisān* s.v. ʕRB.
181 Basing himself on other kind of evidence Henninger (*Genealogie* 58) stated that there existed no Arab people before the eighth century AD.
182 Cf. Levin, *Attitude*. The impression from Sibawayhi is that these masters of the language of the *ʕarab* were found among the tribes around Basra in his time. His informants would thus have been tribesmen who had learnt this idiom in a traditional way, perhaps through oral training in public speaking and poetry making and not through the study of grammar. It is not possible from the evidence in Sibawayhi to decide whether the *ʕarabiyya* actually was the everyday vernacular of these tribesmen or not. The important point for Sibawayhi was that they were first-class informants about the inherited idiom.
183 It should be kept in mind that, from a purely linguistic point of view, it is difficult to uphold the sharp distinction between correct and incorrect languages. Language is a form of human behaviour manifesting itself in certain linguistic patterns (phonological, morphological, syntactical and lexical), some of which are frequent, some infrequent or very rare, and some of which are possible in the language but still never found at all. How the speakers

evaluate these patterns is a different thing altogether. All speech-communities make such evaluations considering some patterns acceptable, some unacceptable and some (quite many) somewhere in between. The bases for these evaluations are not necessarily always linguistic. From the meanings of the term *ʕağam*/*ʔaʕğam* it is clear that at some time, the Arabic-speaking community introduced a system of linguistic evaluation where certain linguistic patterns were considered on the same level as faults of speech or incomprehensible foreign tongues. From this background comes the meaning of the word *ʕarab* lurking behind some passages in the *Lisān*, namely 'clear', 'unmixed'. There is no indication that the word originally had such a meaning. As we shall see, the oldest known meaning of the root is almost the opposite. The definition of *ʕarab* as meaning 'those with pure descent' or 'speakers of the pure language' is thus most likely to be secondary and the result of documentable political and ideological events. As is evident from what has been shown, the Arabs are *not* of 'pure' descent even according to the genealogists. Most of them were of 'impure' descent, i.e. not Yemenis.

184 Cf. the saying about ʔIsmāʕīl as the first speaker of the *ʕarabiyya* quoted p. 39.

185 The interpretation of *ʕarabī* in XLI:44 as referring to the nationality of Muhammed ('an Arabic prophet') is due to this pro-Qurashi tendency. In all the other instances where the word occurs the reference is clearly to the language. We should thus prefer a reading of this verse that allows the same reference.

186 Cf. Yāqūt, *Muʕğam* III:634.

187 Yāqūt, *Muʕğam* III:633 f.

3

THE ARABS AS A SECTION OF SOCIETY

ʕarab and Muslim

We have already seen that the tribes in the latter part of the Umayyad period were seen as *ʕarab*, a concept which was the basis for the Yemeni claims of being the foremost of *ʕarab*. We have also indicated that this pan-tribal meaning was not invented by the Yemenis but existed before the time of Wahb b. Munabbih, i.e. before AD 720. The identification of the tribes as *ʕarab* should be compared to another, namely that between *ʕarab* and Muslims. The identity of Muslims and *ʕarab* was drastically expressed in a poem which Naṣr b. Sayyār, the last Umayyad governor in Khurasān, is said to have sent to the caliph Marwān II, informing him about the rapidly growing Abbasid revolt:

> I see among ashes the gleaming of coal;
> It is on the verge of flaring up;
> For fire is kindled by two pieces of wood,
> and the beginning of war is speech,
> and if you do not quench it it will cause a war.
> It is ready for a work from which young men will get white-haired.
> I say from astonishment: I wish I knew
> whether the Umayyads are awake or asleep.
> If they are our people may they wake up.
> Then say: 'Stand up! for the time of arising has come!
> Flee [o woman] from your men and say
> to Islam and the *ʕarab* "farewell!"'[1]

According to these verses, the impending fall of the Umayyad dynasty would also include the fall of both Islam and the *ʕarab*. Even though we may have here a poetic hyperbole, the terminology reflects official political realities. It is, however, problematic. By this time, more than one century after the death of the Prophet, many non-tribesmen in the conquered territories had joined Islam. Does it mean that non-tribesmen were not considered Muslims by certain circles? Or does it mean that *ʕarab* in fact is employed as an ideological term without any genealogical implication? The non-tribal Muslims would thus be terminologically integrated into the community and, at least by some, called *ʕarab* like the full tribal members. This is supported by the fact that it was possible to become an *ʕarabī* in the later period of the kingdom of the *ʕarab* by converting to Islam. The Muslims/*ʕarab* were, in principle, exempted from taxes on person and land. When al-ʔAshras, the governor in Khurasān, appointed by the caliph Hishām, in the year 110 H (= AD 728–729) sent a missionary, ʔAbū aṣ-Ṣaydāʔ, to Samarkand, he went there on the condition that people who converted to Islam should not pay tax (*ǧizya* or *kharāǧ*). Not surprisingly, his mission was a success. Local dignitaries then complained to al-ʔAshras:

> From whom will you collect *kharāǧ*-tax? All people have become *ʕarab*![2]

The historian al-Madāʔinī is reported to have told the following from the time of the second civil war around AD 690:

> When ʕAbd al-Malik was busy with the crisis with Muṣʕab b. az-Zubayr, the Roman nobles assembled to their king and said: 'Chance has given you power over the *ʕarab* when they are engaged in conflict with each other.'[3]

Another example of the use of the term *ʕarab* in a similar vein in the same period is the story of the killing of ʕAmra, the wife of Mukhtār, the revolt leader in Kūfa, by Ibn az-Zubayr's men, thus for a while securing the latter's hold on the caliphate. The killing was commented upon in the following verses:

> Did not the troops wonder about the killing of a free woman,
> one of those who had insight, faith and honour?
> one of the insightful ones, one of the believers, one pious,
> with doubt, slander, guilt and uncertainty,
> as if, when they brought her out and she was cut to pieces
> with their swords, they won the kingdom of the *ʕarab*?[4]

Undoubtedly, the meaning of *ʕarab* is here simply the Muslim state. Ibn al-Kalbī is reported to have called the Muslims *ʕarab* when telling about the conquest of Iran in the 650s AD.[5] Whether this is an historically correct terminology for such an early period remains to be seen. But according to many reports by the later Islamic historians one could be *ʕarab* even without belonging to the Islamic state. There were whole tribes in the early days of Islam who, in our sources, are called *ʕarab* without being Muslims. The following is just one example:

> Yūsuf b. Yazīd al-ʔAylī said: I asked Ibn Shihāb: 'Did the Messenger – GSGP – accept tribute (*ǧizya*) from anyone from the idolators of the *ʕarab*?' He said: 'The sunna is that *ǧizya* is accepted from those of the People of the Book who were Jews and Christians belonging to the *ʕarab*, this because they are from them [the People of the Book] and belong to them [the *ʕarab*].'[6]

In the same work there are more specific notes about the identity of some of these *ʕarab*:

> The Messenger – GSGP – accepted *ǧizya* from the people of Yemen – they are namely *ʕarab* – when they were People of the Book. He also accepted it from the people of Naǧrān who belonged to the tribe of al-Ḥārith b. Kaʕb.
>
> Ibn Shihāb said: The first ones who gave *ǧizya* were the people of Naǧrān who were Christians.[7]

> From Zurʕa b. Nuʕmān or Nuʕmān b. Zurʕa – He asked ʕUmar b. al Khaṭṭāb when he had talked to him about the Christians of the Taghlib tribe. For ʕUmar had had in mind to take *ǧizya* from them and they had dispersed in the land. Nuʕmān or Zurʕa b. Nuʕmān said to ʕUmar: 'O Prince of the Believers! The Taghlib tribe are an *ʕarab* tribe/a tribe from the *ʕarab* who rejects *ǧizya*. They have no property for they are owners of land and cattle, and they are a damage to the enemy. Do not give your enemy help over you with them.' So ʕUmar b. al-Khaṭṭāb made a deal with them that he should diminish the tribute (*ṣadaqa*) for them on the condition that they should not make their children Christians.[8]

We have here a quite generous definition of *ʕarab*. In this group could obviously be included all the tribes who had paid allegiance to the Prophet himself, regardless of whether they had confessed Islam or not. The identity between *ʕarab* and Muslim was thus not complete. This becomes even more apparent when we turn to what the Islamic historians told about the pre-Islamic period in Arabia. In the prose texts dealing with that heroic age we are often told about the poets and the poetry of the *ʕarab*, the pagan religion of the *ʕarab*, the proverbs among the *ʕarab*, the most famous heroes of the *ʕarab*, the battle-days of the pre-Islamic *ʕarab* and, not least, the language of the *ʕarab* named after them: the *ʕarabiyya*.[9] It has been said that the impression from the records is that *ʕarab* in this period designates a kind of general public consisting of all the members of the tribes.[10]

We should, however, be somewhat cautious in drawing too far-reaching conclusions from this material. The texts describing the life and history of the tribes in Arabia before the rise of Islam were, with very few exceptions, written down in their present form around AD 800 or later. We know very little about how the contents of these texts reached the earliest known historians, Hishām b. al-Kalbī and ʔAbū ʕUbayda, and consequently even less about the history of their content. What is certain is that what was told about the pre-Islamic period served to illustrate the background of the Prophet and the past glory of the tribes that had carried the Umayyad empire. We cannot exclude a quite high degree of projection backwards of conditions in the late Umayyad era. Such projections are not infrequent in history. Thus, the Yemeni Muslims, who were the main supporters of the Umayyad power in Syria, projected the whole empire back into the times of their own pre-Islamic kings, who are said to have made conquests suspiciously similar to those of the Umayyads.[11]

In ninth-century Baghdad, we know that there was a fierce dispute between those who considered the Iranians superior due to their cultural and historical heritage, and those who claimed that the Arabs had at least similar merits.[12] This led to an interest in the poetry and history of the inhabitants of the Arabian peninsula, especially before the rise of Islam. This interest is the main reason why we have a large documentation of the pre-Islamic poetry as well as a wealth of information about pre-Islamic period preserved. The 'pro-Arabists' emphasized both the language and the genealogy of the *ʕarab* when their opponents, the 'pro-Iranians', defined the Iranian supremacy in cultural terms: literary excellence and a glorious past of imperial splendour.

If the 'arabization' of the pre-Islamic history of Arabia reflects the cultural debate in ninth-century Baghdad, it cannot be excluded that the identification of the earliest Islamic state as composed of *ʕarab* is also a projection backwards of conditions in the later Umayyad period. It seems fairly certain that the equation of *ʕarab* and Muslim was accepted, at least in certain circles, after the 720s AD. It should also be emphasized that this identification is not completely parallel to the definition of the tribes composing the Umayyad state as *ʕarab*. In the Yemeni propaganda we have referred to, there is no trace of identification of the two branches of the *ʕarab*, *al-ʕāriba* and *al-mustaʕriba*, as Muslims, nor is there any interest in the position of the non-tribesmen. The *ʕāriba/mustaʕriba* quarrel is an affair betwen tribal aristocrats and politicians; the *ʕarab*/Muslim debate has a more theological flavour and can be seen as partly directed against the propaganda of the traditional tribal aristocrats. The use of the term *ʕarab* for the tribesmen in the stories about the pre-Islamic period is connected with the view of the aristocrats rather than with that of the theologians. It can be suggested that the identification of all Muslims with the *ʕarab* could have its origin in the conflicts in the reigns of Sulaymān b. ʕAbd al-Malik and ʕUmar b. ʕAbd al-ʕAzīz during the first two decades of the eighth century AD when an attempt was made to bridge the difference between the traditional tribesmen and their clients, the *mawālī*, mostly Muslim converts of non-tribal origin, who were looked down upon by the real tribesmen.[13] It would then be another instance of a non-genealogical use of the term *ʕarab*. We must thus investigate the use of the two terms *ʕarab* and *mawlā*.

ʕarab and *mawlā*

In the texts dealing with the history of the first centuries of Islam we often find a distinction between *ʕarab*, obviously meaning 'tribesmen', and *mawlā*, plural *mawālī*, people attached to them in some way. During the early phase of that history, *mawlā* status was a means of assimilating individuals converted to Islam who did not have any affiliation to any tribe of the Islamic tribal federation.[14] Thus emerged a situation where the Islamic community consisted of two different parts: the original tribal members, the *ʕarab*, and the converts from non-tribal societies, mostly outside Arabia, the *mawālī*. This appears clearly in the poem said to have been sent by Naṣr b. Sayyār to the troops in Marw in Khurasān, fighting a civil war between themselves when the Abbasid revolt had started:

> Tell [the tribes of] Rabīʕa in Marw and their brothers
> that they should show wrath before wrath is of no use;
> may they prepare war, for people have prepared
> war which burns the edges of the wood.
> Where are your wits? You make war pregnant among you
> as if people of wisdom were absent from your doings.
> You leave an enemy who has overshadowed you,
> who is a hotchpotch, without religion or honour.
> If they are asked about descent, they are not traced to *ʕarab* from us so that we may know them, and not to the honourable of *mawālī*.
> Woe to a people practising a religion of which I have never heard,
> far from the Prophet, to whom no books have come!
> If someone asks me about their religion [I answer]:
> 'Lo, their religion is that the *ʕarab* are killed!'[15]

A few years earlier, in AD 736, we hear about the general Khudayʕā al-Kirmānī conquering a fortress in Balkh held by the Barzā clan from the tribe of Taghlib:

> He killed their warriors (*muqātila*), killed the tribe of Barzā and captured all their people: *ʕarab*, *mawālī* and children.[16]

In the historical texts this terminology, distinguishing between *ʕarab* and *mawālī*, appears frequently in the reports about the revolt of Mukhtār in Kūfa in 685–687, and this event was the first major appearance of the non-tribal elements in the Islamic community.[17] Mukhtār himself belonged to the tribal aristocracy, which he is said to have stated himself, as quoted by ʔAbū Mikhnaf:

> 'I belong to the *ʕarab*; I have seen Ibn az-Zubayr fall upon the Ḥiğāz, and I have seen Nağda [one of the leaders of the *khāriğiyya* movement] fall upon the Yamāma and Marwān [falling upon] Syria. I am not inferior to any of these *ʕarab* men, so I have seized this town [Kūfa].'[18]

The relationship between the *ʕarab* and the *mawālī* is nicely illustrated by a story from the revolt. A man named ʔAbū Saʕīd aṣ-Ṣayqal fought with Mukhtār against Shabath b. Ribʕī but lost and was captured together with two others, Siʕr b. Abū Siʕr al-Ḥanafī and Khulayd, the *mawlā* of a man from the Dhuhl, a tribe in the Bakr. Now Shabath killed Khulayd but pardoned Siʕr:

> Then I [ʔAbū Saʕīd] said to myself: He killed the *mawlā* and left the *ʕarabī*! By God! if he knew that I am a *mawlā* he would kill me! When I was brought before him he said: 'Who are you?' I said: 'I am from the tribe of Taym Allāh'. He said: 'Are you an *ʕarabī* or a *mawlā*?' I said: 'Indeed no! I am an *ʕarabī* from the family of Ziyād b. Khaṣafa.' He said: 'Well, well! You mentioned the noble, well-known man! Join your people!'[19]

The picture of Mukhtār's movement emerging from these passages is that it consisted of two classes of people: those called *ʕarab* and those called *mawālī*. They were obviously the two juridically acknowledged classes in Muslim society, at least in Iraq and Iran during the second civil war and thereafter. Interestingly, the term *mawlā* appears in some passages as a synonym to *ʕağam*. Thus, the historian al-Wāqidī tells the following about Muṣʕab b. az-Zubayr's final struggle against Mukhtār in the year (67):

> When they [Mukhtār's men?] went out, Muṣʕab wanted to kill the *ʕağam* and leave the *ʕarab* but those who were with him said: 'What kind of religion is this? How can you expect victory when you kill the *ʕağam* and leave the *ʕarab*, in spite of their religion being the same?'[20]

The historian of the Mukhtār revolt, ʔAbū Mikhnaf, told an anecdote quoted by aṭ-Ṭabarī which catches the mood. The tribal chiefs, the *ʔašrāf*, fled from Kufa when the insurrection broke out and came to al-ʔAzdī in Basra, asking him to fight Mukhtār. His answer is:

> 'With this man [Mukhtār] are your brave ones and your horsemen from among yourselves . . . and also your slaves and your *mawālī* . . . Your slaves and your *mawālī* are stronger in hatred against you than your enemies. He will thus

> fight you with the bravery of the *ʕarab* and the enmity of the *ʕağam*!'[21]

Slaves and *mawālī* are here summed up as *ʕağam*. A comparison with the preceding quotations shows that *ʕağam* could be used more or less as a synonym for *mawlā*.

We have already indicated that the opposition between *ʕarab* and *ʕağam* may not be ancient since the latter originally is a term characterizing language considered in some way deficient, the original oppositional term being *faṣīḥ*. We may now ask if the opposition between *mawlā* and *ʕarab*, documented from the time of the second civil war and possibly even before that, goes further back in time. We hear about the same division inside individual tribes, for example, in the report of the following conversation between Saʕīd b. Ğubayr (–714) and Ibn ʕAbbās:

> Ibn ʕAbbās said to me [Saʕīd]: 'From which [tribe] do you come?' I said: 'From the tribe of (*banū*) ʔAsad.' He said: 'From their *ʕarab* or their *mawālī*?' I said: 'Indeed, from their *mawālī*!' He said: 'Say then: I belong to those of the tribe of ʔAsad to whom God has shown his grace!'[22]

We have a notice about the demographic conditions in al-Kūfa in Iraq just after the battle of Ṣiffīn in 657, even though we cannot be completely certain that the terminology reflects the actual usage:

> The *ʕarab* were 50,000 of the inhabitants of Kufa, and of their *mawālī* and their slaves (*mamālīk*) there were 8,000.[23]

Here, *ʕarab* is still the term for the traditional tribal members opposed to the *mawlā* class.[24] But the latter are not necessarily people coming from outside Arabia. They belong to the traditional society in Arabia, living with the tribes but of a lower status. We hear about a certain ʔAbū Ḍamīra in the time of the Prophet:

> [He was] the *mawlā* of the Messenger. He was one of those whom God gave to the Messenger as booty. He was from the *ʕarab*; then the Prophet emancipated him.[25]

The meaning must be that he became a *mawlā* to Muhammed after his emancipation from slavery. Here *mawlā* designates a special social status on a lower level than the full members of tribal society, a status which, however, could also be possessed by an *ʕarabī*.[26] This contradicts the conditions during the second civil war in Iraq and later periods and must represent an earlier stage of the *mawlā* concept.

Originally, *mawlā* was a term for a relative in general, entitled to the protection of other relatives within a clan or a tribe. It could also designate a person who gave such protection.[27] If *ʕarab* was used at that time as a designation for a tribesman it could thus not have been opposed to *mawlā*. This was obviously a tribal institution which had nothing to do with foreign nationality. Tribesmen could be *mawālī* to each other. As we have seen, tribesmen could also be *ʕağam*/*ʕuğm*.

The division between *mawālī* and *ʕarab* would thus have arisen during a period when becoming a *mawlā* was the only means for a non-tribesman to become a recognized Muslim. After the severe conflicts between the *ʕarab* and the *mawālī* in the time of Mukhtār, the *mawālī* were accepted as *ʕarab*. Instead, the conflict between those

Muslims who were absorbed into the traditional tribes and the others who remained outside the tribal system was now expressed by the use of the terms *ʕarab* and *ʕağam*. *ʕağam*, originally a characteristic that could be given to both *ʕarab* and non-*ʕarab* like *mawlā*, now suffered a similar fate in being reserved for people outside the tribal organization. Unlike the *mawālī*, however, the *ʕağam* were never reabsorbed into the community of the *ʕarab* but remained a term for non-*ʕarab* within the Muslim community even after the fall of the state of the *ʕarab* in AD 750.

For both Mukhtār and his rivals, Arabness and tribal descent coincided, at least according to the accounts of the historians. The insurrection of the *mawālī* was subdued but was followed by an ambition to try to upgrade the status of the *mawālī* in order to avoid further disturbances, a policy which culminated under the caliph ʕUmar b. ʕAbd al-ʕAzīz (717–720). This could explain why the term *mawālī*, on the whole, was not used as frequently by the later Umayyads as during the second civil war. Instead, the contrast *ʕarab/ʕağam* appears. The extension of the *ʕarab* in the later Umayyad period thus included the *mawālī* but excluded the *ʕağam*.

The question that still remains is: was *ʕarab* the original general designation for all members of those tribes that later became Muslims, thus originally including both *mawālī* and *ʕağam* in the original meaning of these two terms? Was the use of *ʕarab* as a term for the whole community of Muslim tribes only taken over from a similar pre-Islamic usage of it as a designation for a community of tribes encompassing most of the tribes in Arabia? In other words: did there, in the pre-Islamic period, exist a concept of a nation of *ʕarab* consisting of the tribes, similar to the nation of Israel?[28] As we have seen, such a concept definitely existed at least during the latter part of the Umayyad period but, from what we have seen so far, probably not earlier.[29] Among the Muslims in Abbasid times and onwards, however, there was a general agreement that *ʕarab* had been the common designation for the tribes even before the appearance of Muhammed; this is evident from what is told about their history and culture in 'the Time of Ignorance', the *Ǧāhiliyya*. If this indeed were the case, the identification between Muslims, both tribesmen and *mawālī*, and *ʕarab* making its appearance in the later Umayyad period would have been a formal reversion to the original terminology.

But, as we have tried to point out, the linking of 'Arabness' with Islam, which we find in one set of passages, is clearly the result of dramatic developments in the Umayyad period. The same holds for the definition of *ʕarab* in genealogical terms. We have also seen that the concept of *ʕarab* as tribesmen was not the only one even in later times, which also explains how it could be used as a political weapon: integrating the *mawālī* and countering the cultural claims of the Iranians. In certain periods at least you could become an *ʕarabī*: by learning the *ʕarabiyya* language or by becoming a Muslim. We must keep our scepticism about the use of *ʕarab* as a general term for all the tribes in pre-Islamic times as well as before the revolt of Mukhtār.

ʕarab and *muhāğirūn*

In a non-Muslim Arabic text from *c*. AD 700 the Muslims are called *ʔummatu l-hiğra l-ʕarabiyya*, 'the Arabian *hiğra* community'.[30] Also in Abū Nuʕaym's *Kitāb al-fitan*, a remarkable collection of apocalyptic prophecies, most of which go back to the decades around AD 700, we find a similar expression referring to the Yemeni *ʕarab* in Syria.[31] In sources from the early Marwanid period we thus find the term *ʕarab* associated with *muhāǧirūn*. The same association appears in the report from the earliest phase of the conquest of Iraq. It is told that the caliph ʕUmar b. al-Khaṭṭāb ordered his general Saʕd b. al-Waqqāṣ to establish a camp for the army, which afterwards was to become the town of al-Kūfa. This report is preserved in several versions which are interesting for our purposes:

> ʕUmar b. al Khaṭṭāb wrote to Saʕd b. al Waqqāṣ ordering him to take a house for *hiǧra* and a camp (*qayrawān*) for the muslims.[32]

> Saʕd b. al Waqqāṣ . . . stayed with the army at al-Qādisiyya until ʕUmar's letter came to him ordering him to put up for the *ʕarab* who were with him a house for *hiǧra*.[33]

> ʕUmar wrote to him [Saʕd]: 'Stop where you are and do not pursue them. Take for the Muslims a house for *hiǧra* and a dwelling for *ǧihād*. Do not put an ocean between me and the Muslims!' Saʕd went with the people to al-ʔAnbār . . . and it did not suit them. Saʕd wrote to ʕUmar and told him about it. ʕUmar wrote to Saʕd telling him that the *ʕarab* only thrive where the cattle and small cattle thrive in grasslands.[34]

ʕarab is thus associated not only with *hiǧra* and *muhāǧirūn* but also with *ǧihād*. *Hiǧra* is the established term for Muhammed's transition from Mecca to Medina in AD 622 and the *muhāǧirūn* are those Meccans from the tribe of Quraysh who followed him. It is, however, well known that the terms were used not only for this unique event but also as a general term for joining the Islamic movement as a full member in the time after 622 and even long after the death of the Prophet. It seems to have been especially current among the Muslims in Syria, as is reflected in the *Kitāb al-fitan*.[35]

In the Qurʔān we find exhortations to the believers to perform *muhāǧara*, i.e. to make *hiǧra* and become *muhāǧirūn*, in order to take part in war.[36] Medina is not mentioned explicitly as a goal for this *muhāǧara*/*hiǧra*. The traditionally accepted interpretation of the Qurʔānic statements has been that the exhortation for *muhāǧara* is a commandment to come and settle in Medina during the Prophet's lifetime. There is even a statement ascribed to the Prophet that the duty to perform *hiǧra* was abolished after the conquest of Mecca in AD 630.[37] It has been convincingly argued that the *hiǧra* spoken about in the Qurʔān does not refer to Muhammed's emigration in AD 622, at least not as it is usually understood. Instead, the Qurʔānic *hiǧra* should be understood as an instruction for preparation for war and the *muhāǧara* as a kind of mobilization for *gihād*. The *hiǧra* of the Prophet as well as the *hiǧra*/*muhāǧara* demanded from the believers was of the same kind.[38] There are several ḥadīths stating that the commandment was still valid during the rulers following after Muhammed's death.[39] This idea seems to have been cultivated especially among the Muslims in Syria during the first Islamic century.[40]

In the Qurʔān the *muhāǧara* commandment is not connected with *ʕarab*. As a matter of fact, the word *ʕarab* does not occur in the Qurʔān at all. The apparent connection is between *hiǧra* and warfare, *ǧihād*, in the name of Islam. In the passages dealing with the settlement in Iraq as well as the *Kitāb al-fitan*, we see the Muslims and the *ʕarab* being practically identical with the *muhāǧirūn*. From the Arabic sources it looks very much as if the application of the term *ʕarab* for the Muslim warriors is secondary, and that the earliest Islamic army was known as *muhāǧirūn*, not *ʕarab*. This is exactly the picture found in the non-Arabic sources contemporary with the first Islamic century, which will receive a special treatment later in this study.[41] It is not certain when the latter term was introduced, but it seems to have been in use at the time of the second civil war. It still took some decades before it penetrated to the Greek and Syriac-writing historians.

ʕarab, Quraysh and the early Muslims

If the conclusion arrived at in the preceding section is correct, namely that the original designation of the earliest Muslim army was *muhāǧirūn*, not *ʕarab*, it is worthwhile looking into the relationship between Quraysh, the tribe to which the earliest *muhāǧirūn* belonged, and the *ʕarab*. The following anecdote deals with Nāfiʕ b. Ǧubayr, a famous Islamic scholar belonging to Quraysh, living in Medina until his death in AD 717:

> There were people in Quraysh who were rough and offensive. Nāfiʕ b. Ǧubayr, one of the B. Nawfal b. ʕAbd Manāf, when he was passed by a funeral procession, used to ask about it. If it was said: 'A Qurayshite!' he said: 'Woe to his family!' If it was said: 'An *ʕarabī*!' he said: 'Woe to his property!' If it was said: 'A *mawlā*!' or: 'An *ʕaǧamī*!' he said: 'O God! Since they are your servants you take from them what you want and give to whom you want!'[42]

The anecdote mentions four different terms. One interpretation is to take the first two terms as referring to members of individual tribes and *ʕarabī* as the more inclusive term. Another way is to take Quraysh as the term inclusive of the three others. This is somewhat less attractive if the reference is to conditions in cosmopolitan Medina. For the traditionalist historian the first alternative is self-evident. But the preceding discussion ought to have made us slightly suspicious about the unreflected identification of all inhabitants in Arabia as *ʕarab*. Is it possible that the terms actually stand for four separate groups?

In a verse ascribed to the pre-Islamic poet Qays b. Ḥidādiyya from the Khuzāʕa tribe, the non-Qurashi *ʕarab* seem to reappear. Qays says to his adversary, a warrior from the Kināna tribe:

> You have put a too heavy burden upon yourself, oh son of aẓ-Ẓarib
> and you have imposed on them [your tribe] an enterprise which turned out to be difficult.
> You put a pressing burden on them
> of load when you led them to battle
> in war against the Khuzāʕa, an elevated people,
> a people of fame, a people of honourable descent.
> They are the defenders of the Temple, driving away
> from the sanctuary all *ʕarab*.
> They ousted Ǧurhum and ousted after them
> Kināna violently, with white [bows] of quṣub-wood.[43]

The Khuzāʕa were associated with the cult of the goddess al-ʕUzzā in Nakhla. But they are also said to have conquered Mecca from its first inhabitants, the Ǧurhum.[44] Even though the verses may be apocryphal, they give the impression that *ʕarab* could be used for groups of people with whom, in this case the Khuzāʕa, associated with the Qurashi sanctuaries, did not identify themselves.

The differentiation between Quraysh and the *ʕarab* in the anecdote about Nāfiʕ is also found in some stories dealing with pre-Islamic times. Ibn Qutayba tells us that the first who paid 100 camels as blood money was the Prophet's uncle ʕAbd al-Muṯṯalib, and that this custom was taken up 'by Quraysh and the *ʕarab*'.[45] This could very well mean 'Quraysh as well as the *ʕarab*'. When the Kaʕba was being restored by the same ʕAbd al-Muṯṯalib its treasure disappeared. The suspect was taken by Quraysh 'to a *kāhina* (i.e. a female oracle-giver) of the *ʕarab*'.[46] Ibn Ḥabīb has the following to tell about the market in ʕUkāẓ:

> ʕUkāẓ was one of the largest markets of the *ʕarab*. Quraysh used to stay at it as well as Hawāzin and groups of the undifferentiated *ʕarab*: Ghaṭafān, ʔAslam and the *ʔaḥābīš*.[47]

In ʕUbayd's *ʔAkhbār* it is said that in the pre-Islamic period the *ʕarab* and other polytheists used to pray for rain at the Kaʕba.[48] Nothing prevents us from interpreting this as an indication that the *ʕarab* were only one group among the pilgrims from different parts of Arabia to the sanctuary.[49]

We also notice the antithesis between the *ʕarab* and the Temple in Mecca in ʕUbayd's *ʔAkhbār* and in the poem by Qays. This corresponds to the characterization of the non-Muslims as *ʕarab* in several stories dealing with the events in the later Medinan period of Muhammed. In Abū ʕUbayd al-Qāsim's (–838) *Kitāb al-ʔamwāl*, which preserves much valuable information on conditions in the earliest Islamic period, it is said:

> al-Ḥasan [the son of ʕAlī] said: The Messenger – GSGP – ordered that the *ʕarab* should be fought because of Islam and that only that should be accepted from them and he ordered that the People of the Book should be fought until they gave tribute . . . We think that al-Ḥasan here by *ʕarab* meant the idolators among them [the *ʕarab*] who were not the People of the Book.[50]

The contrast here seems to be of the Muslims in Medina and, possibly, Quraysh against the *ʕarab*. We should note the explanatory gloss which seems to adjust the meaning to a more common one. In a report from the battle at Ḥunayn in 630, fought against the Hawāzin tribes south of Mecca, the difference is spelled out clearly:

> God's messenger gave away those gifts [the booty from the battle] among Quraysh and the tribes of the *ʕarab*, but the *ʔanṣār* received nothing of it.[51]

In the aftermath of the battle, the Prophet sent warriors to pursue the enemy. He sent a certain ʔAbū ʕĀmir against Durayd b. aṣ-Ṣimma, who was killed. ʔAbū ʕĀmir was then wounded by an arrow. ʔAbū Mūsā, one of those who was with him, says:

> I went for him and sought him and got hold of him. When he saw me, he turned away from me and went away. I pursued him and I started to shout at him: 'Do you not defend yourself? Are you not an *ʕarabī*?'[52]

ʔAbū ʕĀmir was from the tribe of ʔAšʕar, thus one of the allied tribes of the Muslims. He is properly designated as an *ʕarabī*.

When the delegations of the tribes to Muhammed in Medina in the year 630 are described, Ḥassān b. Thābit is reported to have seen 'a large amount of those of the *ʕarab* who came to the Prophet and became Muslims'.[53] These passages give the impression that the *ʕarab* were people outside the Islamic community proper which consisted of the *muhāǧirūn*, originally Qurashis from Mecca, and the *ʔanṣār*, the people from Medina who had joined the *muhāǧirūn* after Muhammed's *hiǧra* in AD 622. One could compare the following passage concerning a campaign against the Tamīm tribe who had refused to pay the *ṣadaqa*:

> ʕAyniyya b. Badr volunteered, and the Prophet sent him with fifty riders from the *ʕarab* among whom there was no *muhāǧirī* and no *ʔanṣārī*.[54]

Saʕd b. ʕUbāda, who was the candidate of the *ʔanṣār* as the Prophet's successor, delivered a speech during the days immediately after Muhammed's death in which he is reported to have said:

> 'O *ʔanṣār*! You have rank in religion and merits in Islam which no tribe of the *ʕarab* has . . . You were the strongest of men against his [the Prophet's] enemies among you and the most difficult to his enemies not from you until the *ʕarab* became upright for God, willingly or unwillingly, and the distant one gave submission in abjection and humility until God made slaughter in the earth and made the *ʕarab* close to him by your swords.'[55]

A plain reading of this passage suggests that there was a dividing line between the *ʕarab* and the two leading groups in the Islamic movement. When the *ʔanṣār* claimed the leadership, ʕUmar responded to them saying:

> The *ʕarab* will not be content to give you the leadership when their prophet is not from you; but they would not prevent their affairs from being led by one of those among whom prophethood appeared and the entrusting of their matters from them. In this there is for us a clear argument against those of the *ʕarab* who deny it.[56]

After the Prophet's death, the so-called *ridda* wars broke out, when the tribes apostacized from the alliance with Islam. It is described in the following way:

> and the *ʕarab* apostacized except a small number of them.[57]

> The *ʕarab* had apostacized, either generally or as particular individuals in every tribe . . .; the Muslims were like sheep on a cold and rainy night because of the loss of their Prophet and because of their fewness and the multitude of the enemy. So the people said to ʔAbū Bakr: 'These are the majority of the Muslims. The *ʕarab*, as you see, have mutinied against you.'[58]

ʕAmr b. al ʕĀṣ, the conqueror of Egypt, had been an adversary of ʕUthmān. When the news of the murder of ʕUthmān in AD 656 reached him he is reported to have said:

> O you host of Quraysh! There was between you and the *ʕarab* a solid gate but now you have broken it down.[59]

Some thirty years later ʕUthmān is criticized by Ibn az-Zubayr in the following terms:

> He divided [God's booty] between the godless of Quraysh and the shameless of the *ʕarab*![60]

There are thus plenty of instances where we find quite a sharp division between Quraysh and the *ʕarab*. This division looks similar to that within the Muslim community: the *muhāğirūn* and the *ʔanṣār* on the one hand, and the *ʕarab* on the other. In the latter case, the *ʕarab* are the tribes, mostly from southern and central Arabia, that made alliances of different kinds with the Medinan community during the latter part of Muhammed's life. Most of these tribes considered the treaties with the Muslims annulled by the death of the Prophet. These reports occur in contexts dealing with the earliest Islamic period, from the time when tribes started to seek the company of the Prophet until the definitive establishment of the Islamic state after the *ridda* wars. Most of the quoted instances also come from one historian, namely Abū Mikhnaf (AD 774).[61] The question to be posed is: do these instances reflect the time of Muhammed or are they a back-projection of conditions in later times? In that case, which time? The opposition between *muhāğirūn*/Quraysh and *ʕarab* seems to reflect conditions earlier than the second civil war when, as we have seen, *ʕarab* was used as a designation for the Muslim warriors in general, including the *muhāğirūn*. This leads us to the suggestion that the *ʕarab* concept somehow was connected with the aristocracy of the great tribes who joined the Islamic movement at the time of Muhammed, then left the alliance after his death but were forced to rejoin it during the *ridda* wars. During the following decades the internal development was characterized by the leadership of Quraysh and its Yemeni, Ḥiğāzi and Syrian allies, which, however, was steadily undermined by the rising power and influence of the old aristocracy of Arabia: the great central Arabian tribes. But in the notes on *ʕarab* as opposed to Quraysh and the *muhāğirūn* one might discern another layer where the *ʕarab* are the closer neighbours of Quraysh in the surroundings of Mecca and Ṭāʔif.

ʕarab, *ʔanṣār* and their successors

In the passages quoted so far, the *ʔanṣār*, i.e. the Muslims from Medina, are grouped together with Quraysh or the *muhāğirūn* against the *ʕarab*. There are, however, other statements. The poet Thābit b. Qays in debating with the delegation from Tamīm says:

> The Prophet called to faith and from his people and from those with brotherly love the *muhāğirūn* answered him, men of the noblest descent, with the most brilliant chiefs and the noblest deeds. Then the first of the *ʕarab* who followed the messenger of God and responded to him were we, the host of *ʔanṣār*.[62]

The poet ʕAdī b. ar-Ruqāʕ was asked by a man to mention him in his poetry. The poet asked:

> 'From which *ʕarab* are you?' He answered: 'I am a man from the *ʔanṣār*.'[63]

After the battle at Ḥunayn, an *ʔanṣārī* was seen plundering the body of a young man from Thaqīf, who turned out to be uncircumcised. When al-Mughīra passed by and saw it, he called on the *ʔanṣār* not to tell it among the *ʕarab*. In al-Wāqidī's version he says: 'O you throng of *ʔanṣār*!'[64] In Ibn ʔIsḥāq's version he says: 'O you throng of *ʕarab*.'[65] One tradition could obviously replace *ʔanṣār* with *ʕarab*. From the time of the first civil war we have some statements where the *ʔanṣār* are counted as *ʕarab*. Thus, Ṣaʕṣaʕa b. Ṣūḥān, one of the leaders of the pro-ʕAlī party during the first civil war, says to his followers slandering the *khawāriǧ*, i.e. those who had left ʕAlī after the battle of Ṣiffīn in AD 657:

> 'No people are more hostile to God, to you and to the Holy Family, your Prophet and all Muslims than these sinful apostates who have separated themselves from our Imām (ʕAlī), profaned our blood and testified falsely against us. Beware of giving them shelter in your houses, rather hide away from them. No tribe of the *ʕarab* should be more hostile to these apostates than you.'[66]

Among the most ardent supporters of ʕAlī were the *ʔanṣār* from Medina, who are definitely included among the tribes of the *ʕarab* in this speech. An explicit equation between *ʔanṣār* and *ʕarab* appears in a speech that ʕAlī b. ʔAbī Ṭālib is said to have delivered before the battle of Ṣiffīn when he had heard that some of his men had had contacts with his adversary, Muʕāwiya:

> 'Furthermore, oh host of Rabīʕa, you are my *ʔanṣār*, giving response to my call and among the most faithful of the tribes of the *ʕarab*.'[67]

We can thus see that not only were the *ʔanṣār* included among the *ʕarab*, but the concept itself could be expanded to encompass the 'helpers' of ʕAlī, among whom were many of the Prophet's *ʔanṣār*. The meaning of this stands out clearly in a story from the battle at Ṣiffīn, told by ʔAbū Mikhnaf. When the right wing of ʕAlī's troops gave in, Mālik al-ʔAshtar rallied the tribe of Madḥḥiǧ around him and put some Yemenis from Hamdān around the standard of ʕAlī. Several standard-bearers were then killed. Then one anonymous warrior says to the surviving standard-bearer, Wahb b. Kurayb:

> 'Retire with this standard. God have mercy upon you! The chiefs of your tribe have been killed around it. Do not kill yourself and those who remain of your people!' They retired saying: 'Would that we had a number of *ʕarab* swearing alliance with us [to fight] till death. Then we and they would put ourselves in the vanguard, and we would not retire until we were killed or had victory!'[68]

Then they retire passing al-ʔAshtar, telling him this. He says: 'Come here! I do indeed swear alliance to you and make a pledge with you that we shall never retire until we shall have victory or perish!' Al-ʔAshtar is then joined by 'people of steadfastness, decency, and loyalty' with whom he attacks the enemy and drives them back.

The composition of ʕAlī's army at Ṣiffīn stands out in some of the hortatory speeches by some of the leaders. Thus Qays b. Fahdān:

> 'When you attack, do it together; and if you retire go together; put down your eyes and be few in words; stop the adversary and may not the *ʕarab* be overcome through you.'[69]

Or Khālid b. al-Muʕammar:

> And if you shrink away from your enemy, oh Rabīʕa . . . God will be pleased with your action. Then you will not come to anyone, young or old, who does not say: 'Rabīʕa disgraced honour and ran away from battle, and the *ʕarab* were overcome through them. Beware that the *ʕarab* and the Muslims should see you as an evil omen!'[70]

There is in these passages an equation of *ʔanṣār* and *ʕarab*, which seems to have originated during the first decade of the caliphate. The reason for this stands out quite clearly: the *ʕarab* that came to the Prophet during the last years of his life were indeed a kind of 'helpers', although of a different standing than the *ʔanṣār*. When the *ʔanṣār* were put aside during the political development after the death of Muhammed, their rank became similar to that of the *ʕarab* who had defected in the *ridda* wars. The latter, however, were on their way up in the ranking list, and it may be suggested that the adoption of the *ʕarab* designation by the *ʔanṣār* was partly due to the fact that the designation was gaining prestige. A stimulus for this upgrading of the *ʕarab* status was the fact that the *ʕarab* appear as a kind of helpers to the divinely guided Prophet.[71] It is interesting to notice that in the pro-Yemeni traditions in the *Kitāb al-fitan*, the Prophet is reported to have called Ḥimyar, i.e. the *ʕarab* in Syria, his 'helpers' (*ʔaʕwān*).[72] Was it, in fact, the status as such helpers that originally constituted the *ʕurūba*?

The *ʕarab* among the tribesmen

Ibn al-Kalbī believed the legendary pre-Islamic king of al-Ḥaḍr (Hatra) aḍ-Ḍayẓan to be 'from the *ʕarab* from Quḍāʕa'.[73] This could be understood in at least two ways.[74] But a similar thing is said about Nuṣayb b. Rabāh, a *mawlā* of ʕAbd al-ʕAzīz b. Marwān (a brother of the caliph ʕAbd al-Malik):

> He belonged to some of the *ʕarab* from the tribe of Kināna, the inhabitants of Waddān.[75]

Once again we find an *ʕarabī* as a *mawlā*. But the meaning of the rest must be that the Kināna tribe contained some *ʕarab*, not that all of them were such. This brings us to the cases when there is talk about an individual of the *ʕarab*. The poet Zuhayr and his son Kaʕb, two of the most famous poets in the ancient Arabic literature, were travelling together:

> and they passed by a woman of the *ʕarab*.[76]

Or when it is said about the Prophet and a companion:

> The prophet . . . stopped by a shaykh of the *ʕarab*.[77]

It is told in a story about the father of the poet Marwān b. ʔAbī Ḥafṣa, who had been a *mawlā* to the caliph Marwān b. Ḥakam, the founder of the Marwanid dynasty after the second civil war, that he came to the caliph together with a Tamīmī and a Sulamī, i.e. men from the tribes of Tamīm and Sulaym, in order to give themselves as slaves to the caliph because of the famine raging at the beginning of the 690s. It is said that only the Sulamī was accepted and/for he was from the *ʕarab*.[78] The genealogy of ʔAbū Ḥafṣa was debated. Some said he was an Iranian or a Jew; others said he was from Kināna, by the later genealogists and historians considered a genuine 'Arab' tribe like Sulaym and Tamīm. One could ask here what was special about the Sulamī. Why is his *ʕurūba* emphasized? Was not the Tamīmī also from the *ʕarab*? When it is said about Marwān b. ʔAbī Ḥafṣa that he went to Minā at Mecca in order to visit a woman 'who was from the *ʕarab*' this could allude to his foreign roots or the fact that his father had been a *mawlā* or that the woman, in fact, belonged to a class of people in Arabia to which neither Marwān nor his father or his companions did.[79]

If everybody on the peninsula or at least all tribesmen were *ʕarab*, these are strange expressions. It is as if in a description of travel in China you are informed that the story-teller suddenly encounters a Chinese. It would be more sensible to note if he had met someone not belonging to the Han people. The characterization of a person as belonging to the *ʕarab*, especially when moving among the tribes on the peninsula, would not be necessary or even likely unless *ʕarab* were a sector of the population and not a general designation.[80]

If it is correct that the *ʕarab* were a part or a section of some tribes and not identified in genealogical terms as other clans or families, one can begin to suspect that the use of the term by the *muhāǧirūn*, the *ʔanṣār* and the Yemenis tells us something of what the word meant. It is a designation of a status that an individual could achieve which was not necessarily received through birth. It also seems clear that its adoption by the *muhāǧirūn* and the *ʔanṣār* indicates that it is somehow connected with war. At the same time, the Qurʔān as well as the Yemeni propaganda about the *ʕāriba* Arabs show that there was a language associated with the *ʕarab* which had the status of divine speech. The oldest *ʕarab* are thus connected with military and mantic activities.

A preliminary sketch of the development of the *ʕarab* term during the first century of Islam looks as follows: originally, the *muhāǧirūn*, basically from the tribe of Quraysh, formed an alliance with the *ʔanṣār* in Medina. This alliance was soon joined by people from the neighbouring tribes in Ḥiǧāz who were designated as *ʕarab*. This term was also used for the tribes from central Arabia who joined the growing Islamic polity but who defected after Muhammed's death. *ʕarab* thus seems to have designated a kind of helpers or supporters to the Muslim warrior-community. When the *ʔanṣār* began to lose their position, they also started to call themselves *ʕarab* and the term obviously had some status. Both the *ʕanṣār* and the great tribes in central and eastern Arabia were groups of secondary rank during the first decades of Islamic history but, unlike the former, the influence of the latter was growing during the seventh century, which must be the reason for the application of the term *ʕarab* to the Muslim tribal warriors as a whole. This process seems to have been completed during the second civil war, i.e. around AD 690. It created a new opposition, namely between *ʕarab*/Muslim/ and *mawālī*. The struggle between the former and the latter resulted in the extension of the term *ʕarab* to all citizens of the Muslim state, possibly as a conscious political act in the reign of ʕUmar b. ʕAbd al-ʕAzīz (AD 717–720).

During the reign of the Marwanids, the power and influence of the Yemeni faction, i.e the tribes from Yemen and Syria (among which were also counted the main tribes of Medina, in other words the *ʔanṣār*) started to decline. They countered this process in the same way as the *ʔanṣār* had done, by launching themselves as the foremost among the *ʕarab*, claiming descent from ancient peoples in Arabia who were dimly remembered as having had some relationship to the *ʕarab*.

According to these passages, *ʕarab* are those who live in villages, cities and garrison towns. We recognize the village-dwelling *ʕarab*. The cities are, unfortunately, not specified. We should, however, notice that being an *ʕarabī* is connected with the performance of the *hiǧra* to Medina (i.e. 'the city') or to the fortified towns outside Arabia, i.e. outside the tribal territories.[81]

The statement in the *Lisān* just quoted also presupposes that *muhāǧirūn* are found not only in one city, Medina, but also in 'cities' together with the garrison towns outside Arabia. We have evidence from Arabic sources that especially the Yemenis in Syria called themselves *muhāǧirūn* at least during the first century after the Prophet.[82]

Thus, it seems that *ʕarab*, at a certain time during the seventh century, after 632 and before the 680s, was introduced as a synonym to *muhāǧirūn*. It also seems that this took place outside Arabia, i.e. in Iraq and/or Syria.

We can thus see that there were at least three different terms for the warriors in the garrison towns: *muqātila, muhāǧirūn*, and *ʕarab*. To these is added the term Muslim/Islam. The first two clearly presuppose membership in an association or participation in an activity which has been deliberately chosen. But if *ʕarab* were a synonym for *muqātila* and *muhāǧirūn*, it would imply the same. This makes it unlikely that *ʕarab* was a term indicating tribal descent. In analogy with the two other terms it would be possible to become an *ʕarabī* just like you became a *muqātil* or a *muhāǧir* when joining the Muslim warriors in the *ʔamṣār*.

Since those who performed this kind of *hiǧra* were members of the tribes constituting the Islamic community, they would, at least in principle, be able to show a tribal genealogy. But the definition given by the *Lisān* does not give any indication that Arabness *per se* has to do with genealogy or tribal status. A consequence of this tradition is that you could very well be a full member of a tribe, Islamic or pagan, without belonging to the *ʕarab*, even though this is not explicitly stated anywhere. Arabness is constituted by becoming a *muhāǧir* by an act of swearing a special kind of allegiance (*bayʕat al-hiǧra*) followed by settling in a well-defined group of towns, the most important of which were the *ʔamṣār*, the garrison towns in Iraq and possibly also in Syria and Egypt. In this way, you became a member of the class of professional warriors, the *muqātila*.[83] If you did not perform this act, you remained a non-*ʕarabī*.[84]

One detail is worth singling out. It is said that the *muhāǧirūn* and the *ʔanṣār* are *ʕarab* because they live in *qurā ʕarabiyya*, 'Arab villages'. This term we have already met: it is the villages north of Medina as indicated by Bakrī in his geographical lexicon. This is also the homeland of the mysterious *ʕarab ʕāriba*, 'the genuine Arabs', with whom the Yemeni Muslims felt so close that they applied this designation to themselves. We should, perhaps, look for a connection between that area and the Yemenis on the one hand, and the Islamic warriors outside Arabia on the other.

It thus seems certain that the members of the Islamic movement in the beginning were not called *ʕarab*. There is no trace of any proclamation of Arabness or indeed any use of the term either at the conquest of Mecca in 630, with the ensuing alliances between the most important tribes in Arabia, or in connection with the restoration of the tribal alliance after the *ridda* wars under the first caliph Abū Bakr. As we shall see, the *ʕarab* mentioned in the sources dealing with these events are of a very special kind.

Notes

1 al-Masʕūdī, *Murūǧ* VI:62; Ibn ʕAbd Rabbihi, *ʕIqd* II:359; ad-Dīnawarī, *ʔAkhbār* 356; cf. Nöldeke, *Delectus* 87–88.
2 aṭ-Ṭabarī, *Tārīkh* II:1508. In the passage the two terms *ǧizya* and *xarāǧ* are used as it seems with the same meaning. The question whether there were differences need not concern us here.
3 Ibn Qutayba, *ʕUyūn* I:116.
4 al-Balādhurī, *ʔAnsāb* V:264. Cf. also the passage from al-Ǧāḥiẓ quoted on p. 29.
5 aṭ-Ṭabarī, *Tārīkh* I:2281, cf. 2284; I:2897.
6 Abū ʕUbayd, *ʔAmwāl* no. 62, 63 (p. 99).
7 Ibid. nos. 66, 67 (p. 100).
8 Ibid. no. 71 (p. 102).
9 For an early survey of these cultural phenomena among the *ʕarab*, see al-Yaʕqūbī, *Tārīkh* I:294–315. See also the essays on 'the merits of the Arabs' (*faḍāʔil al-ʕarab*) by Ibn Qutayba (*Kitāb al-ʕarab*) and in Ibn ʕAbd Rabbihi's *ʕIqd al-farīd* III:312–417. Wahb b. Munabbih listed five prophets from the pre-Islamic *ʕarab*: Hūd, Ṣāliḥ, ʔIsmāʕīl, Šuʕayb and Muḥammed (Wahb, *Papyrus* I v.l.4).
10 Cf. Von Grunebaum, *Nature* [17–19].
11 In Middle Eastern history the great example of such a back-projection of contemporary conditions into a distant past is that of ancient Israel. The story of the Exodus, the wanderings in the desert and the conquest of Canaan is, in the Biblical account, performed by the twelve tribes, who act as a movable nation-state. Historical research has long since established that this picture is largely fictional, based on the ideals and views of the final days of the kingdom, the Exile and the Achaemenid period, when the idea of Israel as composed of twelve tribes descending from Jacob was commonly accepted.
12 Cf. Goldziher, *Studien* I 147–216.
13 Even if the *mawālī* had attained a considerable position and influence in the Umayyad state, they were often despised by the tribal aristocracy, cf. Crone, *Mawlā* 876–878; eadem, *Qays* 14–15.
14 Cf. Goldziher, *Studien* I 104 ff.; Crone, *Mawlā*.
15 Nöldeke, *Delectus* 88.
16 aṭ-Ṭabarī, *Tārīkh* II:1589.
17 Cf., for example, aṭ-Ṭabarī, *Tārīkh* II:623, 653, 660, 689.
18 aṭ-Ṭabarī, *Tārīkh* II:732, cf. II:524.
19 aṭ-Ṭabarī, *Tārīkh* II:623.
20 aṭ-Ṭabarī, *Tārīkh* II:749.
21 aṭ-Ṭabarī, *Tārīkh* II:651.
22 Ibn Saʕd, *Ṭabaqāt* VI:178.
23 aṭ-Ṭabarī, *Tārīkh* I:3372. This note probably goes back to the history of Abū Mikhnaf. For the different figures given in the sources, see Donner, *Conquest* 229.
24 One should notice the terminology in a piece of information in Yāqūt, *Muʕǧam* IV:324 on al-Kūfa, saying that in it there were 50,000 houses (*dār*) for the *ʕarab* of Rabīʕa and Muḍar, 24,000 houses for the rest of the Arabs (*sāʔir al-ʕarab*) and 60,000 for al-Yaman. The information is dated to the year 262 AH but the terminology seems to be older (the Yemenis still not Arabs?). In aṭ-Ṭabarī's text (preceding note) *ʕarab* stands as a synonym to *muqātil* as opposed to *mawālī*.
25 Ibn Qutayba, *Maʕārif* 148 l.9.
26 Cf. Golziher, *Studien* I 106. We should compare the note by Ibn Qutayba preceding this one, about Abū Kabsha who was also a *mawlā* to Muhammed. He had been bought by him and later been emancipated. This man was a *muwallad*, i.e. 'not of mere Arabian extraction'

(Lane, *Lexicon* s.v. WLD) or born among the ʕ*arab* without belonging to them.

27 Goldziher, *Studien* I 105. Crone, *Mawlā*; eadem, *Slaves* 197–200. Cf. Qurʔān XXXIII:5 where God himself is said to be the *mawlā* of the believers.

28 The only relevant question for a historical study like this one is whether the concept as such existed, not whether the nation existed as such.

29 Cf. Henninger, *Genealogie* 58.

30 Samuel, *Apocalypse*, Texte ll. 377:11, cf. 382:3, cf. Crone, *Concept* 358 nr. 20. In Samuel's text ʕ*arab* is confused with ʔ*aʕrāb*, 376, 377:18, 382:2, cf. especially 379:12 and 13; see further pp. 92–93.

31 *Kitāb al-fitan* 275 (fol. 124a).

32 al-Balādhurī, *Futūḥ* 275.

33 ad-Dīnawarī, ʔ*Akhbār* 131.

34 aṭ-Ṭabarī, *Tārīkh* I:2360.

35 Crone, *Concept* 352 ff.

36 See Crone, *Concept* 353–355.

37 Cf. Crone, *Concept* 371 for the references.

38 See basically Crone, *Concept*, especially 364 ff.

39 See the references by Crone, *Concept* 356–363. Cf., for example, Abū Dawūd, *Sunan* no. 2479 (= III:5 ff., *Kitāb al-Ǧihād*, beginning).

40 Cf. Madelung, *Prophecies* 153.

41 Cf. pp. 96–99.

42 Mubarrad, *Kāmil* I:712.

43 Iṣfahānī, ʔ*Aghānī* 14:149–150.

44 Kister, *Khuzāʕa*.

45 Ibn Qutayba, *Maʕārif* 551. There are no weighty arguments against this reading except those based on a different concept of what ʕ*arab* were. It is not even necessary to assume that Ibn Qutayba knew exactly what it meant. The original distinction between ʕ*arab* and others may very well have been ignored in the ninth century. The linguistic usage could, however, have survived.

46 aṭ-Ṭabarī, *Tārīkh* I:1135. The note comes from Ibn Isḥāq.

47 Ibn Ḥabīb, *al-Muḥabbar* 267. The word 'undifferentiated', ʔ*afnāʔ*, means people whose tribal origin is unkown (Lane, Lexicon s.v. FNW). It is also used for the ʕ*arab* in al-Ḥīra according to ʔAbū ʕUbayd, ʔ*Amwāl* § 67 (p. 101).

48 ʕUbayd, ʔ*Akhbār* 344.

49 The question of the historical value of the ʔ*Akhbār* does not interfere with the point at stake here. Other similar passages referring to the *Ǧāhiliyya* are Ibn Hishām, *Sīra* 122; Iṣfahānī, ʔ*Aghānī* 4:123; Ibn al-Kalbī, ʔ*Aṣnām* 16, 22 (Arabic text; observe the erroneous translation by Klinke-Rosenberger, German text 47, where no ʕ*arab* are mentioned in the Arabic text).

50 ʔAbū ʕUbayd, ʔ*Amwāl* no. 63 (p. 99).

51 aṭ-Ṭabarī, *Tārīkh* I:1683.

52 aṭ-Ṭabarī, *Tārīkh* I:1667.

53 Iṣfahānī, ʔ*Aghānī* 4:155. Cf. ibid., 6:1.

54 Wellhausen, *Sendschreiben* no. 78 p. 31 (Arabic text).

55 aṭ-Ṭabarī, *Tārīkh* I:1838.

56 aṭ-Ṭabarī, *Tārīkh* I:1841. These arguments reappear later during the insurrection of Shabīb b. Yazīd and Muṭarrif in the 690s; see ibid. II:984.

57 Ibn Qutayba, *Maʕārif* 170.

58 aṭ-Ṭabarī, *Tārīkh* I:1848; cf. Ibn Qutayba, ʕ*Uyūn* II:313.

59 aṭ-Ṭabarī, *Tārīkh* I:2968; cf. ibid. I:3250 f.

60 aṭ-Ṭabarī, *Tārīkh* II:516.

61 It should, of course, be pointed out that there are plenty of passages where both Quraysh and the first Muslim community are reckoned as ʕ*arab* in accordance with the classical usage in the latter half of the Umayyad period. For example, in Iṣfahānī, ʔ*Aghānī* IV:124 (3:188) Muhammed is called 'the prophet of the ʕ*arab*'; in Ibn Ḥabīb, *Muḥabbar* 178 the tribes of the *ḥums* to which Quraysh belonged are 'from the ʕ*arab*' etc.

62 Iṣfahānī, *ʔAghānī* 4:147; cf. the saying of the *ʔanṣārī* Kaʕb b. Mālik quoted by Farrukh, *Bild* 128.
63 Iṣfahānī, *ʔAghānī* 8:272.
64 al-Wāqidī, *Maghāzī* III:911.
65 Ibn Hishām, *Sīra* 850.
66 aṭ-Ṭabarī, *Tārīkh* II:34.
67 aṭ-Ṭabarī, *Tārīkh* I:3311.
68 aṭ-Ṭabarī, *Tārīkh* I:3296 ('our number'); al-Minqarī, *Ṣiffīn* 253 ('a number').
69 aṭ-Ṭabarī, *Tārīkh* I:3308.
70 aṭ-Ṭabarī, *Tārīkh* I:3313.
71 The adoption of the term *ʕarab* by the *ʔanṣār* is reflected in the verses of the *ʔanṣārī* poets quoted by Farrukh, *Bild* 128 ff. Even though several of them are ascribed to Ḥassān b. Thābit, they could very well be apocryphal, reflecting terminology current some decades after the death of the Prophet.
72 *Kitāb al-fitan* 302 (fol. 139a, cf. Madelung, *Prophecies* 152).
73 aṭ-Ṭabarī, *Tārīkh* I:827.
74 Either the Quḍāʕa is seen as part of a larger unit of *ʕarab*, or the *ʕarab* are a part of the Quḍāʕa. In the light of the next quotation we hold the latter interpretation to be more likely.
75 Iṣfahānī, *ʔAghānī* 1:324 line 2.
76 Iṣfahānī, *ʔAghānī* 10:313.
77 Ibn Qutayba, *ʕUyūn* I 194; cf. ibid. II:323 and Iṣfahānī, *ʔAghānī* 4:179 (from Ibn ʔIsḥāq).
78 Iṣfahānī, *ʔAghānī* 10:73.
79 Iṣfahānī, *ʔAghānī* 10:78.
80 It is another question whether the writers who have written down these sayings understood them according to this analysis. It is more likely that they reproduced a common way of expression, the exact meaning of which was no longer noticed.
81 It should be observed that not all *muhāǧirūn* and *ʔanṣār* are *ʕarab*, namely those who come from the *badw* and some who have gone back to the *badw*.
82 Cf. the references to the *Kitāb al-fitan* in Madelung, *Prophecies* 162–163.
83 Cf. Crone, *Hiǧra*.
84 I.e. an *ʔaʕrābī*. For this term see pp. 89–93.

4

THE NEGLECTED COUSINS

The *ʔaʕrāb*

There remains one peculiar designation of inhabitants in Arabia to analyse. We start with a note in the *Lisān*:

> The *ʔaʕrābī* is the *badawī* and they are the *ʔaʕrāb*.
> Those who have settled in the *bādiya* or have sought refuge by the people of the *bādiya* (*bādūn*), journeyed like them, moving around with them, they are *ʔaʕrāb*.[1]

We have here a word derived from the root ʕRB which is equated with the word borrowed into European languages as 'bedouin'. These *ʔaʕrāb* thus, at a first glance, seem to be identical to those we call bedouin, i.e. nomads, and the word is also usually translated as such in modern scholarly literature.[2] It might be worth while to see how *bādiya/badw/badawī* is explained by medieval writers before proceeding with the *ʔaʕrāb*. Once again we shall start with the *Lisān*:

> 1. al-Layth said: *bādiya* is the name of a land (*ʔarḍ*) where there are no settlers (*ḥaḍar*) and when people go out from the *ḥaḍar* to pasture grounds in the desert (*ṣaḥārā*), you say that they *qad badaw*. The noun is *badw*.
>
> 2. Abū Manṣūr said: *bādiya* is the opposite to *ḥāḍira*. The *ḥāḍira* are people who live by waters and put their camps at them in the summer heat. When the season becomes cold, they leave these waters and *badaw*, i.e. look for pasture. The people are then *bādiya* after having been *ḥāḍira* . . . The places to which the *bādūn* go out are also called *bādiya*.
>
> 3. He (Ibn Manẓūr) said: the *ʔaʕrāb*, living in the *bādiya*, belong to the *ʕarab* who do not dwell in fortified towns (*ʔamṣār*) and only enter them for business.
>
> He (Ibn Manẓūr) said: the *ʕarab* are the people of the fortified cities (*ʔamṣār*), and the *ʔaʕrāb* among them are especially the dwellers of the *bādiya*.

The *bādiya* is contrasted to *ḥāḍira* but it is evidently defined in three different ways. According to no. 1, *bādiya* is identical with the desert where no one dwells and where there are only pasture-grounds; no. 2 must include the winter camps in *bādiya*, whereas no. 3 extends *bādiya* to all regions outside the fortified cities. Of these three definitions we have already encountered no. 3 in Ibn Khaldūn, to whom the *badw* are those living outside fortified cities, living on agriculture and/or cattle husbandry.[3]

A notable feature is the identification of the *ʔaʕrāb*/*bādiya* people as part of the *ʕarab* in no. 3. This is elaborated further in the *Lisān*:

> A man is *ʔaʕrābī* . . . if he is a *badawī*, searching for food . . . and pasture, following the rainfall, regardless whether he belongs to the *ʕarab* or their *mawālī* . . . If it is said to him 'o, *ʕarabī*!' he rejoices and is cheered. But the *ʕarabī*, if it is said to him: 'o, *ʔaʕrābī*!', gets angry at it.

In spite of the identification, there is a clear hint that it was not accepted by everyone. The last sentence shows that another more limited definition of *ʕarab*, excluding the *ʔaʕrāb,* was current. This is reminiscent of Ibn Khaldūn, to whom *ʕarab* and the people living in the *bādiya* were not identical. To him, the *ʕarab* were those living in the most distant parts of the *bādiya*. It is noteworthy that in the oldest Arabic dictionary extant, namely that of al-Khalīl, compiled in the eighth century AD, the identification is absent:

> The *bādiya* is the land in which there is no permanent settlement (*ḥaḍar*), i.e. there is no permanent dwelling there. When you leave the settled area (*ḥaḍar*) for the pasture grounds (*marāʕī*) and the deserts (*ṣaḥārā*), you say *badaw badwan*. You speak about the people of the *badw* and the people of the *ḥaḍar*.
>
> *ḥaḍar* is the opposite to *badw*, as *ḥāḍira* is the opposite to *bādiya*. For the people of the *ḥāḍira* have settled in fortified towns (*ʔamṣār*) and settlements (*diyār*).[4]

Here we find at least definitions 1 and 3, but the latter without the identification with *ʕarab*, which thus can be traced back to the eighth century. In fact, the explanation of the *ḥāḍira* as those living in fortified cities equates them with the *ʕarab*/*muhāǧirūn*, whom we have investigated earlier.

The association between *ʔaʕrāb* and *ʕarab* which we find in the passages in the *Lisān* is quite rare in the older sources. The attempt to see *ʔaʕrāb* as part of a larger unit, the *ʕarab*, is explicitly attributed to the author of the *Lisān* himself, Ibn Manẓūr, and can be seen as governed by the victorious concept of *ʕarab* as a designation for all tribal members on the peninsula, inherited from the late Umayyad period.

In most of the existing evidence dealing with the first two Islamic centuries, *ʕarab* and *ʔaʕrāb* are sharply separated and are not associated except in a few cases.[5] Thus, in Ibn ʕAbd Rabbihi's *ʕIqd al-farīd*, we find several chapters on the *ʕarab*, their merits, their wars, their proverbs, and one on the *ʔaʕrāb* who are clearly distinguished from the former.[6] The *Lisān* also gives a linguistic commentary indicating that the identity is not self-evident:

> It is said that *al-ʔaʕrāb* is not the plural of *ʕarab* as *al-ʔanbāṭ* is the plural of *an-nabaṭ* because al-*ʕarab* is a nomen generis and the derivation from *al-ʔaʕrāb* is *al-ʔaʕrābī*.

Instead, *ʔaʕrāb* is connected with the *hiǧra* concept. This distinction is, in fact, emphasized in a quotation from al-ʔAzharī in the *Lisān* commenting upon a verse in the Qurʔān (sūra IX) mentioning the *ʔaʕrāb*:

> al-ʔAzharī said: 'He who does not distinguish between the *ʕarab* and the *ʔaʕrāb* and the *ʕarabī* and the *ʔaʕrābī,* he may be prejudiced against the *ʕarab* in his commentary to this verse in that he does not distinguish between the *ʕarab* and the *ʔaʕrāb*. It is not possible to call the *muhāǧirūn* and the *ʔanṣār ʔaʕrāb* for they are *ʕarab* because they settled in the Arab villages (*qurā ʕarabiyya*) and lived in cities, no matter whether some of them originated from *al-badw* and then settled in the villages or some of them originated from Mecca. Then they emigrated to Medina. If parts of them adhered to the people of the *badw* after their *hiǧra* and acquired cattle, shepherding where the rain falls, after having become settlers (*ḥāḍira*) or emigrants (*muhāǧira*) it is said that they "arabicized themselves" (*taʕarrabū*), namely they became *ʔaʕrāb* after having been *ʕarab*.' In the ḥadīth he quoted in his speech, a *muhāǧir* is not *ʔaʕrābī*. He put the *muhāǧir* against the *ʔaʕrābī*.

Thus, on the one hand, we have the *muhāǧirūn*, who, as we have seen, in the course of time received the designation *ʕarab*, and who were the warriors of Islam settled in fortified cities; on the other, we have the *ʔaʕrāb*, who are opposed to them. They are opposed because the *ʔaʕrāb* are seen as having defected from the status of the *muhāǧir*, i.e. the *ʕarab*. This defection is called *taʕarrub baʕda al-hiǧra* and is condemned in a ḥadīth ascribed to the Prophet.[7] The *Lisān* has the following commentary:

> In the ḥadīth there are three great sins, one of which is 'arabicizing after emigration' (*at-taʕarrub baʕda l-hiǧra*). This is if someone returns to the *bādiya* and lives with the *ʔaʕrāb* after having become an emigrant (*muhāǧir*). He who returns after the *hiǧra* to his place is without forgiveness and he is considered an apostate.

The sin is even called *ʔaʕrābiyya baʕda l-hiǧra*.[8] The basis for this condemnation was the existence of two pleas of allegiance, *bayʕāt*, in the the early Islamic period.[9] It is clearly stated in a saying ascribed to Muhammed:

> When you meet an enemy from the idolators, call them to three things: . . . Call them to enter Islam. If they do it, accept them (?) and keep away from them. Then call them to change their habitat to the House of the *muhāǧirūn*. And if they do so tell them that they will have the advantages and obligations of the *muhāǧirūn*. But if they enter Islam and choose [to stay in] their houses, tell them that they will become like the *ʔaʕrāb* of the Muslims and it will be proceeded with them according to the ruling of God and they will have no share in the booty if they do not wage war (*yuǧāhidū*) with the Muslims. And if they refuse call them to pay tribute (*ǧizya*).[10]

We see here two classes of Muslims ranked according to their participation in the war. The classes within the community are described in several passages like this one ascribed to Ibn ʕAbbās:

> The Messenger – GSGP – left the people, on the day he died, in four ranks (*manāzil*): believer-emigrant (*muʔmin muhāǧir*), the Helpers (*ʔanṣār*) and the *ʔaʕrābī* who had not emigrated . . . and the fourth was the Followers (*at-tābiʕūn*).[11]

A similar one is ascribed to ʕUmar b. al-Khaṭṭāb:

> ʕUmar used to say: Four things in Islam I have never neglected nor ignored: The control over the property of God and the gathering of it until it was gathered and we put it where God had ordered, and we, the family of ʕUmar, remained without anything of it in our own hands; the *muhāǧirūn* who are under the shade of the swords that they should not be imprisoned and not remain more than half a year in the army, and that the booty of God should be distributed among them and their families, and that I shall support the families until they arrive; the Helpers (*al-ʔanṣār*) who have given God a share and fought against everybody that they will be before those that honour them and pass over those who do evil to them, and that they are asked for counsel; the *ʔaʕrāb* who are the root of the *ʕarab* and the core of Islam that their tribute (*ṣadaqa*) is taken from them according to their rank and not one dinar or dirham is taken from them, and that they may be given to their poor ones.[12]

This latter is, in its present shape, definitely not from ʕUmar but rather from the time of ʕUmar II (717–20), when the equality of all members of Islam was emphasized in a drive to moderate the growing conflicts within it. Thus we have in the biography of ʕUmar II a decree aiming at abolishing the differences between the classes of Muslims, the statement that 'the Book . . . calls all mankind to Islam and the gate of the *hiǧra* is open to the people of Islam' and the people of the Book who have converted should not be discriminated against. It is even said:

> We have opened the *hiǧra* to the *ʔaʕrābī* who has performed it, who has sold his cattle and moved from the House of his *ʔaʕrābiyya* to the House of the *hiǧra* and to the fighting of our enemy. Everyone who has made this has the status (*ʔuswa*) of the *muhāǧirūn* to that which God gives as booty.[13]

The positive ranking of the *ʔaʕrāb* is quite unique;[14] usually they are given very low credentials and appear, even in other sayings from the time of Umar II, as a despised group within Islam.[15]

The important point is the realization that the *ʔaʕrāb* were a group belonging to the early Islamic community. Their status was regulated by the special allegiance called *bayʕat al-ʔaʕrāb* or *bayʕa ʔaʕrābiyya* or *bayʕat al-ḥāḍira*. This *bayʕa* is opposed to the *bayʕat al-hiǧra*, and the main contrast is thus between the *muhāǧirūn* and the *ʔaʕrāb*.[16] The contrast is spelled out in one of the most famous speeches in Arabic, which is said to have been delivered by al-Ḥaǧǧāǧ in the mosque in al-Kūfa when he was appointed governor of Iraq in AD 694/5:

> I am well known,
> striving for fame.
> When I put on the turban you know me.

> I do indeed carry evil,
> and I put its sandal on it
> and cut it according to its size.[17]
> I do indeed see heads which are ripe,
> whose harvest has come.
> I do indeed see blood between turbans and beards.
> She [my riding animal] has bared her thighs.[18]
> This is the noon of harshness so be strong, o Ziyam![19]
> The night has put on her a cruel driver,
> who is not a shepherd of camels or cattle,
> nor a butcher at a slaughter's bench.
> The night has put on her a strong one,
> the most fearsome of the cunning ones from the desert,
> a *muhāğir* who is not an *ʔaʕrābī*.[20]

One should observe that the *muhāğir* is said to be from the desert (*ad-dawiyy*). The difference between the *muhāğir* and the *ʔaʕrābī* is thus not that between desert-dwellers and others. Instead there is a difference of rank: al-Ḥağğāğ is an equal of his listeners, he belongs to the warriors as they do, not to those who do not take part in the struggle. In the *Kitāb al-fitan* it is said that, before the eschatological battle between the Muslims and Rome, 'everyone who owns a *faddān* [i.e. who is a landowner] or a tent pole (*ʕamūd*) shall defect from the battle'. These defectors are called *ʔaʕrāb*.[21] The contrast is thus between the professional warriors, the *muhāğirūn*/*ʕarab*, and those who are farmers and shepherds, the *ʔaʕrāb*.[22]

This makes it unlikely that *ʔaʕrāb* was ever a term for what we call bedouin. Linguistic usage points definitely to some kind of judicial status, not a way of living. The following statement is also said to come from the time of al-Ḥağğāğ:

> Salama b. al-ʔAkwaʕ one day went to al-Ḥağğāğ. The latter said to him: 'O, Ibn al-ʔAkwaʕ! You have turned back (= become an apostate) and made yourself an *ʔaʕrābī* (*taʕarrabta*)!' He said: 'No! The Prophet – GSGP – allowed me to go to the *bādiya*' . . . When ʕUthmān b. ʕAffān had been killed, Salama b. al-ʔAkwaʕ went out to ar-Rabadha/az-Zabadha, married a woman there, who bore him children. He stayed there until one night before his death, when he went to Medina.[23]

The second half of the story gives the background to al-Ḥağğāğ's remark. There is no question here of Ibn al-Akwaʕ becoming a nomad or a bedouin. ar-Rabadha was a luxuriant oasis with a flourishing settlement.[24] We have a similar notice from a somewhat later time (AD 738). It is said to a Tamīmī who had emigrated:

> The house of your *ʔaʕrābiyya* [status] is al-Ḥīra and the house of your *hiğra* is al-Baṣra.[25]

Even though al-Ḥīra at this time was no longer what it once had been, it was still a city with palaces and gardens like ar-Rabadha. The point of this story is that the Tamīmī had not come from a place sufficiently far away. The value of his *muhāğara* could thus be considered low. *ʔaʕrābī* does not signify nomad (even though many may actually have practised a nomadic lifestyle) but one who achieves a certain judicial status.

The association with desertion from the army leads to a negative attitude towards the *ʔaʕrāb*, which is a prominent feature in the Islamic sources. The *Lisān* quotes a ḥadīth:

> He who *badā*, has escaped, run wild, i.e. settled in the *bādiya* and has acquired the uncivilized manners of the *ʔaʕrāb*.[26]

The negative attitude towards the *ʔaʕrāb* is explicable from the connection with desertion from a vow of military duties. There is, however, no indication that the original meaning of *ʔaʕrābī* is 'deserter'. There is nothing in the etymology of the word indicating such a meaning. The fact that they, in the earliest Arabo-Islamic testimonies, are characterized as deserters is no clue to the actual meaning of the word. The main fact is that they are connected with the concept of *hiǧra* and represent the opposite to those who make *muhāǧara*.

If we read the quoted passages of the *Lisān* closely, we can see that the identification of the *ʔaʕrāb* with the moving nomads of the *bādiya* is not unproblematic. It is said that those who have joined the people of the *bādiya* are *ʔaʕrāb*. This could very well imply that the people of the *bādiya* was a larger group than the *ʔaʕrāb*. In one passage, *ʔaʕrāb* are included in the *ʕarab*/*mawālī* complex. *ʔaʕrāb* are members of these groups, i.e. the Muslim community, who have 'defected', i.e. joined the people of the *bādiya*. In other words, they have left the community of warriors and escaped. This is the definition we find in the *Kitāb al-fitan*, where those Syrian tribes who defect and leave the camp of the Yemeni *muhāǧirūn*, i.e. the *ʕarab*, before the last eschatological battle with Rome, are called *ʔaʕrāb*.[27]

The negative evaluation as well as the obligation of military duties upon the *ʔaʕrāb* is found already in the earliest Arabic source where they are mentioned, namely the Qurʔān, which must be investigated for a full picture of the *ʔaʕrāb* in the Islamic tradition.

The *ʔaʕrāb* in the Qurʔān

Unlike *ʕarab*, *ʔaʕrāb* are mentioned in the Qurʔān. The passages in question constitute the earliest certain documentation of the word in Arabic. It appears in four sūras, all from the late Medinean period. The earliest passage is the one in *sūrat al-ʔaḥzāb*, The Confederates (XXXIII), which according to traditional exegesis deals with the aftermath of the siege of Medina in April AD 627 /5 H. by Quraysh and their allies, the so-called Battle of the Trench.[28] Some who had kept themselves back from the fighting (*al-muʕawwiqūn*) are chided for cowardice:

> (20) They think that the confederates (*al-ʔaḥzāb* = the anti-Muslim alliance) have not withdrawn; and if the confederates would come [again] they would wish they were in the deserts (*bādūn*) among the *ʔaʕrāb* seeking news about you, and if they were in your midst, they would fight only a little.

According to this verse, the *ʔaʕrāb* are people living in *al-bādiya*.[29] They do not participate in the war, and they seem to be without any connection with the Muslim community. Those who do not want to participate in the war against the confederates can escape it by seeking refuge among the *ʔaʕrāb*. These *ʔaʕrāb* are thus not supposed to have any obligation to side with the Muslims and their allies at the Battle of the Trench. It is worth noting that the *ʔaʕrāb* do not appear in the traditions about the battle at Badr three years earlier, and they are not mentioned in the so-called Constitution of Medina. This document speaks about those who 'follow and attach themselves to and strive together with them' (the *ʔumma* of Muhammed).[30] These are not *muʔminūn*, 'believers', which is the designation for the *muhāǧirūn* and *ʔanṣār* in that document, but they are allied with them. They are, however, not *ʔaʕrāb*.

A similar view of the state of the *ʔaʕrāb* at the time of the Prophet is found in an anecdote preserved by Ibn Saʕd attributed to ʕĀʔisha:

> al-Mālikiyya were brothers from ʔAslam from the Khuzāʕa who had converted (*ʔaslamat*) and paid allegiance to the Messenger of God – GSGP. ʕĀʔiša . . . said: 'When we had come to Medina, the Messenger forbade us to receive gifts from an *ʔaʕrābī*. Then ʔUmm Sunbula from ʔAslam brought *laban* and came to us with it. But we refused to accept it and continued to do so until the Messenger of God came together with ʔAbū Bakr.' He said: 'What is this?' I said: 'O Messenger of God, this ʔUmm Sunbula brought us *laban*, and you have forbidden us to accept anything from the *ʔaʕrāb*.' The Messenger of God said: 'Accept her. For the ʔAslam are not *ʔaʕrāb*; they are the people of our *bādiya*, and we are the people of their *qāriya*. If we call for them they answer, and if we ask them for assistance they assist us. Pour, o ʔUmm Sunbula!'[31]

The point here is that the ʔAslam, by coming to the assistance of the believers when summoned, behave differently from the *ʔaʕrāb,* with whom the *ʔumma*, the Islamic community, does not have any connection at all and who do not have any obligations to it. By accepting Muhammed and entering into an alliance with him, the ʔAslam thus have left the status of being *ʔaʕrāb* and have entered into that of *hiǧra*.[32] A point in the anecdote is that ʕĀʔisha and the others have not realized that this change has taken place. It should be noted that the *ʔaʕrāb* are supposed to live quite close to Medina: *laban* cannot be transported long distances.[33] But it would obviously be absurd to translate *ʔaʕrāb* with 'nomad' in this anecdote: the ʔAslam did not change their way of living, only their status from *ʔaʕrāb* to *muhāǧirūn*.[34]

The next Qurʔānic passage is, according to the traditional exegesis, a comment on the expedition to Ḥudaybiyya in March 628 when Muhammed made a deal with the Meccans about peace and free passage for pilgrims to the Temple.[35] In *sūrat al-fatḥ*, The Victory (XLVIII), it is stated that an oath to the Prophet is in fact an oath to God, which cannot be broken. This can be seen as an argument against some who opposed the Ḥudaybiyya treaty. Then it is said:

> (11) Those left behind (*al-mukhallafūn*) of the *ʔaʕrāb* will say to you: 'Our property and our families made us busy; ask forgiveness for us!' They say with their tongues what is not in their hearts. Say: 'Who can protect you against God if He desires hurt for you or if He desires profit for you? Nay, God is acquainted with what you do.'
>
> (12) Nay, you thought that the Messenger and the Believers would not return to their families; this was pleasing to your hearts. You thought an evil thought, and you were a people ruined (literally 'fallow').

> (15) Those who were left behind will say when you have set out for the booty to take it: 'Let us follow you!', wishing to change the word of God. Say: 'Do not follow us like that!' God has spoken before. Then they will say: 'Nay, you are jealous of us!' Nay, they only understand a little.
>
> (16) Say to those left behind of the *ʔaʕrāb*: 'You will be called against a people with strong might, whom you will fight or who will surrender. If you obey God will give you a good reward, and if you turn back as you turned back before, he will punish you painfully.'

Here, the *ʔaʕrāb* have a different position than in the preceding verses. It is clear that they are accused of some kind of deceit or not fulfilling a duty, probably contained in the oath mentioned in verse 10. This duty must have been to take part in a military expedition since later there is a reference to the taking of booty.[36] The Ḥudaybiyya expedition is described in Ibn ʔIsḥāq's biography of the Prophet:

> He [Muhammed] summoned the *ʕarab* and those around him from the people of the *bādiya* of the *ʔaʕrāb* to go out together with him because he feared Quraysh, who had designed to hinder him by war or to bar him from the Temple. Then many of the *ʔaʕrāb* delayed against him. God's Messenger – GSGP – went out with those he had of the *muhāǧirūn* and the *ʔanṣār* and of the *ʕarab* who had attached themselves to him.[37]

If we accept the identification of the incident mentioned in the sūra with what is described by Ibn ʔIsḥāq, the latter casts light on the former. The clear difference between *ʕarab* and *ʔaʕrāb* should be noted. The *ʔaʕrāb* are now in some way or other connected with the groups around the Prophet and having some obligations to him. Something seems to have happened between our two passages. If this is true, it also shows that *ʔaʕrāb*, if they were an institution, were not established by Islam but existed before it.[38]

Also the next passage is connected with the events at Ḥudaybiyya but is said to have been revealed a couple of years later, i.e. in AD 630/9 H.[39] *Sūrat al-ḥuǧurāt*, The Chambers (XLIX), deals with the authority of the Prophet, his role as a moderator among the members of the community. The unity of the *ʔumma* and the equality of all its members and, actually, all mankind, is stressed in words that recur in the Sermon of Farewell.[40] Then it is said:

> (14) The *ʔaʕrāb* have said: 'We believe!' Say: You do not believe but say: we have surrendered (*ʔaslamnā*); belief has not entered your hearts. If you obey God and his Messenger he will not diminish anything from your work. God is indeed forgiving, merciful.
>
> (15) For the believers are those who have believed in God and his Messenger; then they have not doubted but strived (*ǧāhadū*) with their property and themselves on the way of God; they are the truthful.

According to this text, the *ʔaʕrāb* do not belong to the *muʔminūn*, the believers, even though they claim to do so. The believers appear as a kernel troop of the community, whose main characteristic is that they have taken part in the wars. This is clearly indicated by the terminology in verse 15. The *ʔaʕrāb* have surrendered, which does not imply participation in the war. There is thus a difference between *ʔīmān* and *ʔislām*, where the latter is wider than the former. *ʔIslām* is an external, formal adherence to the authority of the Prophet, *ʔīmān* is the vanguard of warriors.[41] This means that the *ʔaʕrāb* definitely now belong to the movement around Muhammed, although with a marginal status.[42]

The last, and most extensive, reference to *ʔaʕrāb* in the Qurʔān is in *sūrat at-tawba*, The Repentance (IX), traditionally connected with the great campaign against Tabūk and Dūma in the year AD 630/9 H.[43] The text is said to have been revealed before, during and after this campaign. There are some cracks in the text as we have it, showing a complicated history. Verses 42–48 and 82–97 are alleged to have been revealed during the campaign. In the latter part we have the same criticism of 'those left behind' (*al-mukhallafūn*) as we have seen earlier. They are accused of having refused 'to strive with their property and themselves on the way of God', i.e. take part in the war. Then it is said:

> (90) and those from the *ʔaʕrāb* who made excuses came in order that it should be allowed for them [to stay behind]; and those of them who were unbelieving sat still; a painful punishment will hit those of them who were unbelieving.
>
> . . .
>
> (97) The *ʔaʕrāb* are the strongest in disbelief and hypocrisy and most deserving not to know the bounds of what God has sent down to His Messenger; God is all-knowing, all-wise.

The following verses are thought to have been revealed after the return from the campaign:

> (98) There are some of the *ʔaʕrāb* who take that which they spend for a fine and wait for calamities for you. On them [may come] the calamity of Evil! God is hearing, knowing.
>
> (99) There are some of the *ʔaʕrāb* who believe in God and the Last Day and take what they spend for offerings to God and the service (?) (*ṣalawāt*) of the Messenger. Indeed! They are a merit for them and God will bring them into his mercy; God is forgiving, merciful.
>
> (100) The vanguard, the first of the *muhāǧirūn* and the *ʔanṣār* and those who followed them (*ttabaʕūhum*) in good doing – God is pleased with them and they are pleased with him. He has prepared for them gardens under which the rivers flow, forever dwelling there. This is the great gain.
>
> (101) Of those of the *ʔaʕrāb* who are around you there are hypocrites, and from the people of Medina who have rebelled against hypocrisy (?). You do not know them; we know them; we shall punish them twice, then they will be returned to a mighty punishment.

> . . .
>
> (120) It was not for the people of Medina and those of the *ʔaʕrāb* around them to stay behind (*yataxallafū*) God's Messenger and to prefer their lives to his. This is because thirst and fatigue or hunger do not hit them in the way of God.

We now learn that the *ʔaʕrāb* were obliged to contribute economically to the campaign, apart from the obligation to take part in the operations. They are here equated with the hypocrites, who were the people in Medina who did not practise Islam even though they belonged to tribes that had officially paid allegiance to Muhammed. We also hear explicitly that they live around Medina. This information is, in fact, supported by some other later passages. Thus Ibn ʔIsḥāq reports in the biography of the Prophet that when Jesus sent out his disciples he sent Ibn Thalmā (Bartholomew) 'to the *ʔaʕrābiyya* [land], which is in Ḥiğāz'.[44]

Abū Mikhnaf reported that when Ibn az-Zubayr tried to seize power during the second civil war and established himself in Mecca and was attacked by the troops of Mukhtār from al-Kūfa, he turned to the *ʔaʕrāb* for support:

> And he sent ʕAbbās b. Sahl b. Saʕd from Mecca to Medina with two thousand men and ordered him to summon the *ʔaʕrāb*.[45]

There was obviously a tradition that the *ʔaʕrāb* belonged to an area around Medina. It is not likely that this tradition was the result of exegesis. The reference to the *ʔaʕrāb* around Medina in sūra IX:120 is made very *en passant* and has not influenced the commentators of the Qurʔān.

The *ʔaʕrāb* are thus one of the groups around Muhammed from a period shortly after AD 627. In the Qurʔān they are condemned for not having fulfilled their obligations. In spite of this the community does not fight them. They belong to the Muslim movement in some way, which is also indicated by the term *ʔaʕrāb al-muslimīn*, 'the *ʔaʕrāb* of the Muslims'.[46] In sūra IX they are said to live around Medina. We also find terms like the *ʔaʕrāb* of Ghifār, Muzayna, Ğuhayna, ʔAšğaʕ, ʔAslam and ad-Dayl.[47] These are all tribes in western Arabia, and it thus goes well with the notice that the *ʔaʕrāb* belong to Ḥiğāz. As far as the most famous tribe in Ḥiğāz is concerned, we have an interesting note in the *Lisān*, commenting on a verse by Ğarīr praising the caliph ʕAbd al-Malik:

> The trees of your forest, among Quraysh
> do not have poor branches and are not bare (= without leaves).[48]

The last word is *ḍawāḥin*, plural of *ḍāḥiya*, the lexical meaning of which is 'open land without vegetation of bushes or trees'. The *Lisān* has the following comment on the use of this word in the verse:

> Ğarīr intends with *ḍawāḥin* in his verse Quraysh of the *ẓawāhir*. They are those who do not live in the valley (*šiʕb*) of Mecca and its river-bed. Ğarīr wants to say that ʕAbd al-Malik is from Quraysh of the river-beds (*Qurayš al-ʔabāṭiḥ*), not from Quraysh of the exterior parts (*Qurayš aẓ-ẓawāhir*). The Quraysh of the river-bed have greater honour and are nobler than Quraysh of the exterior parts,

> because the river-bed Qurayshites are settled (*ḥāḍira*), being the residents of the Sanctuary, and the exterior [Qurayshites] are *ʔaʕrāb* of the open land (*bādiya*).[49]

This sounds like a piece of solid historical information, showing clearly the relationship between the noblemen of a tribe and their *ʔaʕrāb*, having a low status and living outside the regulated land. The parallel with the situation in Medina is evident.

We do find traces of such *ʔaʕrāb* even outside western Arabia. When the Sassanian king Sābūr ḏū l-ʔaktāf (= Shāpur II) undertook a campaign in eastern Arabia around AD 330, he is said to have beaten the *ʔaʕrāb* around the town of Hağar in present-day al-Hufūf.[50] When the Iranian general Wahriz marched against the Ethiopian kings in Yemen *c.* AD 570, the enemy is characterized as Ḥabaša, Ḥimyar and *ʔaʕrāb*.[51] These two stories were originally told by Ibn al-Kalbī. At least as far as the latter one is concerned, it fits nicely into the picture put together from the inscriptions from the Himyaritic period, where the ʔʕRB are frequently mentioned.[52] If the *ʔaʕrāb* were an institution, they existed even outside western Arabia. As we shall see later in this investigation, there is ample evidence that they did.[53]

There emerges a picture of the *ʔaʕrāb* in the Qurʔān as people who originally stood in some kind of dependence on some of the tribes in Medina and around it, and who automatically were attached to the Islamic *ʔumma* when those tribes entered into the alliance with Muhammed. Such dependent people would have been attached to other tribes in Ḥiğāz and also to the tribes in the highlands of Yemen. Judging from the regulations about the two different types of allegiance, *bayʕa*, it could be suspected that the status of *ʔaʕrāb* was tied to individuals. At least in later times the choice between allegiance for *hiğra* and *ʔaʕrāb* was individual. The latter were supposed to be some kind of assistants to the *muhāğirūn*, who could be summoned for military duties on special occasions. There is nothing that indicates that *ʔaʕrāb* is a designation for nomadic life. It means to live outside the place of *hiğra* or the *ʔamṣār*, i.e. the military camps, but to have certain obligations and to be available for military activities.

The *ʔaʕrāb* are one of the groups belonging to the early Islamic movement. In the lifetime of Muhammed this movement was far from being a community of equals. Instead, it was an agglomeration of groups with different degrees of loyalty to the Prophet and his message. Around the kernel, which in its turn was divided into two sharply different groups, the *muhāğirūn* and the *ʔanṣār* with different ranking, there were alliances with tribes some of which recognized the authority of Muhammed by performing the *ṣalāt* and paying the *zakāt*. Others were only his military allies and some, like the large Jewish tribes of Medina, only recognized him as their arbiter in conflicts and common defence against enemies. To these obviously were added the *ʔaʕrāb*, a group who very early were criticized and despised, without any action being taken against them. Their low position and reputation has contributed to the neglect of their role, as well as of an understanding of what they were, by Islamic and western scholars. As we shall see later, there are strong reasons to suppose that they were an institution whose history goes far back into pre-Islamic Arabia.

There are, in the Arabic sources, cases where *ʔaʕrāb* and *ʕarab* appear to be identical. In the passage from al Ğāḥiẓ quoted earlier, the empire of the *ʕarab* is said to be a *dawla ʔaʕrābiyya*, in contrast to that of the Abbasids which is Khurasāniyya. In the same way, the *ʔaʕrāb* are said to be the root of the *ʕarab*. In the Apocalypse ascribed to Samuel of Qalamūn, written at the beginning of the eighth century AD, there is a consistent confusion between the two terms.[54] Against these passages stands a massive testimony that the words designate two different groups. It looks as if the distinction between them was forgotten, and that later authors and, perhaps even more, copyists did not have any feeling for the *ʔaʕrāb* as being different from the *ʕarab*.[55] The attempts to reconcile the two meanings by the lexicographers may be due to this fact. The *ʔaʕrāb* in Hağar in the time of Shāpur II may be due to such a confusion, since the point seems to be that the *ʔaʕrāb* did not belong to the *hiğra/hağar* institution. It is explicable that it is the *ʔaʕrāb* whose characteristics disappeared since they were a peripheral group from the beginning with a low status. Even the word itself died out and has not survived among the modern *ʕarab* tribesmen. But the testimonies of their existence cannot be denied or ignored.

Notes

1 *Lisān* s.v. ʕRB.

2 E.g. Watt, *Muhammed* 143; Thamina, *ʔaʕrāb*; Madelung, *Prophecies* 163 ff.; Crone, *Concept*.

3 The etymology of the word *badw* etc. seems to support Ibn Khaldūn rather than Ibn Manẓūr. The meaning is 'being open, unprotected' and does not necessarily imply desert, i.e. desiccated land. It is equivalent to Greek *érēmos* and Hebrew *midbar,* meaning 'pasture ground and desert', i.e. land with no permanent settlements or regular villages. In Geez *bädw* (occurring already in the Bible translation and probably not borrowed from Arabic, cf., for example, Exodus 13.20, Matthew:12.43 etc.) means 'uninhabited land'; cf. Dillmann, *Lexicon* s.v. BDW; Leslau, *Dictionary* s.v. BDW. A word BDT is documented in Sabaean (CIH 191:2: BDTHMW WʔRḌHMW) probably with a similar meaning, see Beeston *et al.*, *Dictionary* s.v. BDW.

4 al-Khalīl, *Kitāb al-ʕayn* s.vv. BDW and ḤḌR.

5 Cf. aṭ-Ṭabarī's *tafsīr* to *sūrat al-ʔaḥzāb* (XXXIII:20):
ʔaʕrābī is said to the people of the *badw* when we distinguish between the people of the *bawādī* and the *ʔamṣār*. The *ʔaʕrāb* is given to the people of the *bādiya* and *ʕarab* to the people of the garrison (*miṣr*).
For this Qurʔānic passage, see further below.

6 E.g. Vol. III.

7 ʔAbū Dāwūd, *Sunan*: Ğihād 2780 (= III:3–4); Crone, *Concept* 371.

8 Cf. Kister, *Land property* 279 n. 40; Meyer, *Pflicht* 73–74.

9 Crone, *Concept* 369–370.

10 al-Wāqidī, *Maghāzī* II:256; cf. ʔAbū Dāwūd, *Sunan* Bāb 936 (2606).

11 Abū ʕUbayd, *al-ʔAmwāl* no. 563 p. 318.

12 aṭ-Ṭabarī, *Tārīkh* I:2775–76. Cf. Ibn Saʕd, *Ṭabaqāt* III/1 239.

13 ʕAbd al-Ḥakam, *Sīrat ʕUmar* 94–95.

14 Cf. ʔAbū ʕUbayd, *ʔAmwāl* no. 570 p. 322.

15 Cf. Madelung, *Prophecies* 163–165.

16 Cf. Madelung, *Hijra* 229 ff. Ibn Saʕd (*Ṭabaqāt* IV/1:66) has the story of ʕUqba b. ʕĀmir from the Ğuhayna tribe, who came to the Prophet in order to join him. The Prophet then asked: '[Do you want] the allegiance of the *ʕarab* (*bayʕa ʕarabiyya*) or that of the *hiğra*?' He chose the latter and stayed with him. In light of the evidence the expression *bayʕa ʕarabiyya* is strange; we would have expected *ʔaʕrābiyya*. This is the form found in the variant of the story in *ʔUsd al-ghāba* (III:417; see Sachau's remark ad loc. IV/1:xcix). Ibn Saʕd's text is here most probably wrong, and the *ʔUsd* is right.

17 = I distribute it according to measure.

18 = She is ready to run.

19 = his riding animal = the subjects in al-Kūfa.

20 aṭ-Ṭabarī, *Tārīkh* II:864. The introduction to this speech is, in fact, a collection of quotations

from earlier poets. The latter part (from the invocation of Ziyam) is from Ruwayshid b. Rumaydh al-ʕAnbarī (cf. al-Mubarrad, *Kāmil* 215; al-Masʕūdī, *Murūğ* V:294; Ibn ʕAbd Rabbihi, *ʕIqd* II:187, III:8). His identity is, unfortunately, not ascertained. Judging from the terminology, he must have lived in the (early?) seventh century, perhaps at the time of the Prophet.

21 *Kitāb al-fitan* 282 (fol. 127b).

22 Madelung's analysis of these passages is contradictory. The *ʔaʕrāb* are said to be bedouin Arabs, but at the same time they are villagers, i.e. farmers (*Prophesies* 164).

23 al-Bukhārī, *Ṣaḥīḥ*: Fitan 14 (p. 2597) = Kremer/Juynboll 373); *Lisān* s.v. ʕRB.

24 Cf. Bosworth, *Note* 358–59. For ar-Rabadha, see al-Rashīd, *Al-Rabadha,* especially pp. 2–4/161–162.

25 al-Balādhurī *ʔAnsāb* Ms. Istanbul nos. 597–598 part 2 fol. 732b, quoted by Thamina, *ʔaʕrāb* 10 n. 33.

26 *Lisān* s.v. BDW.

27 *Kitāb al-fitan* 216, 261 (fol. 96a, 117a). Madelung's translation does not keep the distinction between *ʕarab* and *ʔaʕrāb* in this text, although it is quite clear that they are two different groups.

28 See Nöldeke, *Geschichte des Korans* 206 f.

29 The modern western translations (Arberry, Paret, Blachère) render *ʔaʕrāb* as 'bedouin'. The differing reading preserved by Ibn Masʕūd ('they think that the confederates have withdrawn and when they see that the confederates have not withdrawn, they wish . . .' (cf. Blachère, *Coran* 2 987) does not have any implication for the interpretation discussed here.

30 Ibn Hishām, *Sīra* I:1 341, cf. Wellhausen, *Gemeindeordnung* 1 (§ 1).

31 Ibn Saʕd, *Ṭabaqāt* VIII:215. The rare word *qāriya* is said to mean *ḥāḍira*, i.e. the settled ones. The *qārī* is the one who lives in a *qarya* (village) opposite to the *bādiya* (*Lisān* s.v. QRʔ). One should observe the connection with *qurā/qurrāʔ* (above, p. 49).

32 Cf. Watt, *Medina* 82–84.

33 Cf. the story of Ḥārith b. ʕAmr (Iṣfahānī, *ʔAghānī* 11:85). He has been informed about the whereabouts of Zuhayr b. Ğadhīma, who has insulted both him and the B. ʕĀmir tribe. He has been obliged by his informers not to refer to them. By letting the B. ʕĀmir taste his *laban* they find that it is sweet. He has, consequently, not travelled a long distance. The enemy is close by.

34 Cf. Ibn Saʕd, *Ṭabaqāt* I/1 24 ll.14 ff.: The Messenger of God – GSGP – wrote to ʔAslam from the Khudāʕa to those who believed and performed the prayer and brought the alms and were sincere in the religion of God, that they should have assistance against those who suddenly invaded them unjustly and that they were obliged to assist the Prophet – GSGP – when he summoned them and that the people of their *bādiya* would have the same [rights] as the people of their *ḥāḍira* and that they were *muhāğirūn* where they were.

35 Nöldeke, *Geschichte des Korans* 215–216; Watt, *Medina* 46 ff.

36 This verse is applied to the defectors before the eschatological battle in the *Kitāb al-fitan* 270 (fol. 121a).

37 Ibn Hishām, *Sīra* 740.

38 We should observe the identification of 'those who have attached themselves to him' (*man laḥiqa bihi*), a phrase also occurring in the Medina constitution (*man tabiʕahum fa-laḥiqa bihim*), with the *ʕarab* (see note 37). This use of *ʕarab* deviates from the passages where *ʕarab* are the *muhāğirūn*. As has been pointed out already, there are instances where *ʕarab* are the allies of the *muhāğirūn/ʔanṣār*, especially in connection with the tradition about the 'year of Delegations', i.e. AD 630, when it is said that the *ʕarab* came to pay allegiance to the Prophet and his community (see p. 73). These *ʕarab* must thus be the tribes who pay allegiance to the Prophet without becoming members of the *ʔumma* like the *muhāğirūn* and the *ʔanṣār*.

39 Nöldeke, *Geschichte des Korans* 221 f.

40 Verse 13: 'O mankind! We have created you male and female, and appointed you races and tribes, that you may know one another. Surely the noblest among you in the sight of God is the most God-fearing of you. God is all-knowing, all-aware'. Cf. Blachère, *Allocution*.

41 Cf. Ringgren, *aslama* 31.
42 There are two traditional interpretations of the verse. One is that it refers to the B. ʔAsad, who came to Muhammed during the famine in the year 9 demanding food, referring to their voluntary conversion earlier (aṭ-Ṭabarī, *Tārīkh* I:1637, 1687; cf. Wellhausen, *Skizzen* IV 77). The other is that it is a general reference to those who did not take part in the Ḥudaybiyya expedition. The former interpretation is difficult to verify. There is no support in the Qurʔānic text for it, and it may well be the result of the ambition among certain *mufassirūn* to find (or even invent) concrete historical backgrounds of doubful historicity for vague statements in the Holy Book.
43 Nöldeke, *Geschichte des Korans* 222 ff.
44 Ibn Hishām, *Sīra* II:1027.
45 aṭ-Ṭabarī, *Tārīkh* II:689.
46 Cf. the passage in al-Wāqidī above, p. 84.
47 See az-Zamakhsharī, *Kashshāf* to 9:90 (II:2:300, II:4:236).
48 Ğarīr, *Dīwān* 99.
49 *Lisān* s.v. ḌḤY (14:471).
50 aṭ-Ṭabarī, *Tārīkh* I: 839, cf. Nöldeke, *Geschichte* 56.
51 aṭ-Ṭabarī, *Tārīkh* I:955.
52 See pp. 562 ff.
53 Cf. Chapter 19.
54 See p. 80.
55 An interesting case is the variants in the passage in Ibn Saʕd quoted on p. 85.

5

ARABS IN THE EYES OF OUTSIDERS

Arabs and Muslims in non-Arabic sources from the first century AH

In the evidence discussed in the preceding section we have seen that the monolithic concept of *ʕarab* as a term for all Muslims or all full members of the Muslim tribes or even all the pre-Islamic tribes in Arabia begins to crumble. The 'Arabness' of many tribes was contested, and there are enough hints that the designation may originally have encompassed people in much smaller areas than usually imagined. Such a limitation of the *ʕarab* should be studied more closely, since one can suspect that it may be older than the commonly accepted, wider definition. The term *ʕarab* as used for the Muslim community is definitely a politically and religiously charged term, and it is not difficult to imagine that it is the result of a development of an older, more restricted usage.

One major problem with the Arabic sources is that very few of them, if any, can be dated to the formative period of the earliest Islamic history. It is then worthwhile to compare the terminology in Greek and Syriac documents contemporary with the rise of Islam.[1] In these we get glimpses of the use of the term 'Arab' in sources which are not distorted by later political and ideological transformations. In the Greek papyri from Nessana in the Negev, written between the end of the sixth century and the beginning of the eighth, the 'Arabs' are called Saracens.[2] This is a designation for tribes in northern Arabia which at this time had been in use during more than three centuries by Greek and Latin authors, and the writers of the papyri follow established terminological practice. There are, however, a few contemporary texts where Arabs appear. A Greek inscription from Ḥammat Gader in the Golan is dated 'according to the era of the *árabes*' to a year corresponding to AD 662/663.[3] One limited group of bilingual papyri at Nessana, from the chancellery of the Muslim governor of Gaza, al-Ḥārith b. ʕAbd, from the years AD 674 to 677, written in both Arabic and Greek, have the same dating in the Greek version whereas the Arabic is according to *Hiğra*.[4] To the Greek-speaking reader of these documents, the Muslims, at this time ruled by Muʕāwiya, thus appear as *árabes*.

The dates in the papyri from Aphrodito in Upper Egypt are from AD 685 to 712, and also the undated texts in that collection can be supposed to originate in this period. The Aphrodito documents are in Greek and Coptic, dealing with the taxation in the province. The Muslims have three different designations. In the Coptic and some Greek papyri, all dated between AD 706 and 709, they are called Saracens, i.e. the traditional, literary term well known to Greek readers.[5] In another group, we find personal names, all Arabic, with the epithet *maulos*, i.e. *mawlā*.[6] Finally, there are several passages where the Muslims are called *mōagarîtai*, i.e. a grecized form of *muhāğirūn*.[7] In quite a few we hear about *mōagarîtai toû Phossátou*.[8] This corresponds to Arabic *muhāğirū Fusṭāṭ*, i.e. the Muslim troops garrisoned in the camp in present-day Old Cairo. We thus have the connection between the *muhāğirūn* and the garrison towns, which goes well with the Arabo-Islamic documentation. Only a couple of times do we find mentioned an *arabikòs notários*, who was a secretary to the governor in Fusṭāṭ.[9] There is also once a mention of 'Arabian fodder' (*khórtos arabikós*).[10]

The testimony from these documents clearly indicates that the Muslims were not spoken of as Arabs by the non-Muslim subjects. Instead we find, together with the traditional term 'Saracens', the new Arabic words *muhāğirūn* and *mawlā*. The latter appear in the Egyptian documents from AD 700. The Arabs in the Nessana papyri are connected with the town of Gaza. As will become evident later on in this study, the area around Gaza was, in fact, the first to be called Arabia by the Greeks, a usage which survived into the seventh century.[11]

The limited extent of Arabia and Arabs is also apparent in three contemporary literary sources where a country called Arabia is mentioned. In the history of the reign of the emperor Heraclius, written by a bishop named Sebeos around AD 670, we find one of the earliest testimonies of the beginning of the Islamic conquests.[12] It appears from these passages that Arabia to this author is Transjordan, which corresponds to the province of Arabia established by the emperor Diocletian.[13] This province was what was left of the larger *Provincia Arabia* established by the Romans in AD 106, which also encompassed the areas south of Palestine. The tribes in the north-western parts of the peninsula before and after the rise of Islam are called the Children of Ismael by Sebeos, according to an old identification ultimately going back to pre-Christian Jewish Bible interpretation.[14] In passages dealing with pre-Islamic times, the tribes in the Syrian desert are also called *Tačik* and their land *Tačkastan* in the Armenian translation.[15] The Greek original may have had *taēnoí* or *taiēnoí*, a term related to the Syriac *ṭayyāyē* for the tribes in northern Arabia, which, in its turn, is supposed to be identical with the Arabic tribal name *Ṭayyiʔ*.[16]

The concepts 'Arabs' and 'Arabia' were thus known to Sebeos, but designated a very limited area corresponding to the Roman province in Transjordan. In another chronicle from the end of the seventh century, written by Johannes of Nikiou, originally in Greek or Coptic but preserved only via a lost Arabic version in an Ethiopic translation, Arabia (*ʕārăbyā*) is mentioned in connection with Decius' persecution of the Christians in the middle of the third century.[17] We also hear about barbarians from Arabia (*ʔārăbyā*) in the reign of the emperor Anastasius (491–518).[18] In contrast, the Muslim conquerors of Egypt are called *ʔəslām*.[19] From the context it is clear that the first two passages refer to the traditional Arabia, i.e. the ancient Roman province between Egypt, Palestine up to Transjordan and north-western Ḥiğāz.

The last author from the first Islamic century mentioning Arabia is the Syrian Jacob of Edessa, who wrote a chronicle ending in AD 692 and preserved in fragments.[20] In the passage about the seventh century, Arabia or Arabs are mentioned three times:

> . . . and MḤMṬ (Muhammed) went for trading to the land of Palestine, Arabia and Phoenicia in Syria.
>
> [Headline:] The first kingdom of Arabia: MḤMṬ arose . . .

> The kingdom of Arabia, those whom we call ṬYYʕ [*ṭayyāyē*], began . . .[21]

The first passage sees Arabia as the province in Transjordan. It alludes to the well-known legend of Muhammed's visit to Bosra in Syria before he became a prophet. This Arabia is the same as in Sebeos' chronicle. It is also evident that the Muslim conquerors are called *ṭayyāyē* in accordance with established Syriac practice for inhabitants of the Syrian desert since centuries before. The term 'Arabia' in the two other passages is more puzzling. The name is obviously not a Syriac word and is borrowed from Greek.[22] Its alienness to the Syrian reader is indicated by the gloss. This Arabia could thus be an adaptation to a Greek usage of the term not only for the Roman province but for the whole Arabian peninsula. The *ṭayyāyē*, the new rulers of the Middle East, would thus be the inhabitants of the Arabia of the Greek geographers. In that case, we have here a testimony of the Greek terminology, not the Middle Eastern one and definitely not that of the Muslims at this time.

In all the other sources written by contemporaries to the rise of the Islamic state in the seventh century, the Muslims are called by the names traditionally used for the inhabitants of the Syrian desert and the northern parts of the Arabian peninsula. The Greek texts use *sarakēnoí*, the Syriac ones use *ṭayyāyē*. A few times one encounters Ishmaelites.[23] There are two interesting exceptions. We have a Syriac letter written around AD 640 reporting a discussion between the patriarch Johannes and ʕAmr b. al-ʕĀṣ, the conqueror of Egypt. This is a first-hand document about what the Christians knew about the Muslims after the first decade of conquests. In this document, the Muslims are consistently called *mahgrāyē*.[24] Islam is said to be 'the law of the *mahgrāyē*'.[25] A strict distinction is made between these and the Christian groups Tānūkāyē, Ṭawʕāyē and ʕAqūlāyē. The first is the name of a well-known tribe with a long history before the seventh century, included in the genealogy of the later Arabs. The second represents nomadic tribes in the Ǧazīra and the last stands for Christian groups in al-Ḥīra near the Euphrates. The other instance is found in the so-called 'Book of Caliphs' ending with the year 724, which uses the term *ṭayyāyē* for the Muslims except in one passage, where it is said that the empire founded by Muhammed is of the *mahgrāyē*.[26] That passage may be taken from an older source closer to the beginning of the conquests.

During the last decades of the Umayyad dynasty, the term 'Arabs' used for the Muslims began to appear in Graeco-Latin texts. The earliest occurrence seems to be from the late seventh century in works originating from Anastasius of Sinai, where the Muslims are twice called *árabes*.[27] John of Damascus (dead *c.* 750) still calls them Ishmaelites and Saracens and does not use *árabes*.[28] But his contemporary, Iohannes Monachus, writing in the reign of Hishām (724–743), calls them 'godless Arabs'.[29] In the historical work *Continuatio Byzantina Arabica*, originally written in Syria, ending with the year 741, the Muslims are still *sarraceni*.[30] But in the continuation of this work, the *Continuatio Hispanica*, written under the Umayyads in Spain, ending with the year AD 754, the Muslims have become *arabes*.[31] The *Continuatio Byzantina* mentions Arabs only once, when telling about the accession of the caliph Sulaymān in AD 715.[32] Interestingly enough, Iohannes Monachus also calls Sulaymān 'the tyrant of the godless *arabes*'.[33]

If we had only possessed the contemporary non-Muslim testimony for the first Islamic century, no one would have called the Muslim conquerors Arabs. It is obvious that those who were conquered by them did not call them so. As we have seen, there are plenty of indications even in the Arabo-Muslim sources written down later that 'Arab' was not originally an unproblematic ethnic term for the tribes from the Arabian peninsula but may have evolved in the latter half of the Umayyad period. Even in the sources in Arabic we have seen that there are many indications that the Muslims were not called *ʕarab* originally. The non-Muslim evidence and the Arabo-Islamic testimony thus point in the same direction.

Arabs in the early Arabo-Islamic tradition: attempt at a summary

The picture emerging from this survey is contradictory. The word *ʕarab* stands for different and partly opposed meanings. It may mean those who are able to speak the *ʕarabī* language, regardless of whether they have a background as tribesmen or not; it may designate all members of the tribes constituting the Islamic state; it may designate only the full tribal members and not those associated with them as clients (*mawālī*); or it may stand for the Muslim warriors encamped in the garrison cities in the occupied territories. All these meanings bear the characteristic of being developed during the reign of the caliphs from the House of ʔUmayya, i.e. after *c.* AD 660.

Then there are other meanings that look older. Thus, *ʕarab* seems to be associated with some specific villages in Ḥiǧāz and possibly also in Yamāma but it is also used as a designation of the tribes that came to Muhammed as supporters in the years around AD 630. A few years later, the *ʔanṣār* are included among these 'helpers' to the Prophet.

Apart from the *ʕarab* we have the *ʔaʕrāb*, who appear in a very different light. They seem to consist of smaller groups that live outside cities and villages but are dependent upon them, having certain obligations which are not altogether clear. They often (not always) lead a nomadic or semi-nomadic life, thus following the lifestyle of the larger groups of nomads in Arabia. Even though their designation is clearly derived from the same root as *ʕarab,* they are not identified with the latter group. On the contrary, whereas *ʕarab* gives the impression of having been a term with a certain status, which also explains why it was extended, the *ʔaʕrāb* were evidently a despised group of people, subject to criticism and scorn already in the Qurʔān.

An important insight gathered in the investigation so far is that the term *ʕarab* during the first two Islamic centuries was highly charged with values, positive to some and negative to others, and that it was used in the political and cultural conflicts. It is also evident that its scope could vary according to the ideological trends. It could have purely political as well as more cultural meanings. al-Ǧāḥiẓ has already taught us not to have any preconceived ideas about the origins of nations, however they are defined.

Another remarkable fact that can be gathered from the discussion is the association between *ʕarab* and towns. This meaning is, as we have seen, preserved up to our own time. In the early Islamic period, we found that *ʕarab* was indeed associated with a special kind of town in the 'House of War' of Islam in Iraq and elsewhere, and that this might well be one of the oldest meanings if not the oldest documentable in Arabic sources. At the same time we find that from a study of the use of the term in genealogy we are led to the assumption that the original *ʕarab*, with whom the Yemenis claimed a special close relationship, in fact seem to have belonged to certain areas mostly in western Arabia which were characterized by settlements called 'the villages (or: towns?) of the *ʕarab*'.

This would mean that *ʕarab* originally was a term for people who lived in or in some way were associated with certain towns or villages in Arabia. We do not yet know what set these people apart from the others and what the term itself meant. During a very early phase of the Islamic conquests, the term was transferred to designate tribes from other parts of Arabia that paid allegiance to the Prophet and his community in Medina. Then it was extended to those Muslims who moved to the garrison cities outside Arabia in order to take part in the gigantic military process that resulted in the Islamic conquests of large parts of the urbanized regions of the ancient world. The original term for these warriors was *muhāǧirūn* in accordance with Qurʔānic terminology. This term was replaced during the second part of the seventh century by *ʕarab*. The synonymity between the two terms is clearly visible in, for example, the Nessana papyri, as well as in literary sources. In the military camps, these *ʕarab* in practice came to be identified with people belonging to the tribes, united in a kind of federation around the Muslim leadership with their roots in Mecca and Medina. From the Second Civil War 683–692 onwards, the term *ʕarab* was increasingly used as a term for all members of the tribes constituting the Islamic state. Since membership in a tribe as full member or *mawlā* was the only legal way of joining the Muslim community, *ʕarab*, tribesmen, and Muslims became more or less synonymous during the later part of the Umayyad caliphate. The connection between Muslim and *ʕarab* was finally broken by the fall of the Umayyad state in AD 750. However, it seems that the synonymity established between *ʕarab* and tribesmen survived. This heritage from the empire of the Umayyads is still with us today and has obviously survived even among the heirs of the tribes that carried the empire. How this preservation has been accomplished we do not know. The present-day bedouin are much more different from their forefathers 1,400 years ago than is usually realized. It seems that the term *ʕarab* had achieved such a status that it was kept as the designation of a tribesman.[34]

Those who look for evidence for the existence of an *ʕarab* nation, as we would define it today, will not find what they are looking for except perhaps among the Arabophone cultural élite in Iraq in the ninth century and onwards. And there is no indication that the concept of the *ʕarab* 'nation' found in their writings ever had any relevance outside the literary salons.

Those who look for an *ʕarab* nation analogous with ancient Israel will find it during the later Umayyad period, but all evidence indicates that it was a recent formation due to the special political circumstances in that era (just as had previously been the case with Israel). The absence of an 'Arab' patriarch speaks very clearly against this being an ancient concept.

Those who believe that *ʕarab* means bedouin, i.e. nomads living in tents and roaming around for pasture, will look in vain for this definition in our material. On the contrary, it is explicitly stated in many sources that *ʕarab* are not bedouin or nomads. Even if it were to turn out that the tribes in Arabia indeed called themselves *ʕarab* and had done so since time immemorial and saw themselves as a nation of *ʕarab*, this 'nation' could definitely not be characterized as consisting of nomads.

The *ʔaʕrāb* are close to the nomadic lifestyle but a careful reading of the sources shows clearly that the term itself cannot mean 'nomad' or bedouin. It indicates some kind of subordinated judicial status of people living outside walled cities. They were a peripheral group with a low status already during the first decades of the Islamic movement and seem to have disappeared before the end of the Umayyad period.

Our survey of the evidence in Arabic sources has thus clarified certain issues but it will be obvious to everybody that it raises a number of new questions:

> If the designations derived from the root ʕRB can mean (1) speaker of pure *ʕarabī*-language, (2) people descending from certain tribes, (3) people living in fortified cities, (4) people living in certain villages in the Ḥiǧāz, (5) people who are 'helpers' to a divinely inspired prophet, (6) people living outside villages and towns in the Ḥiǧāz, and perhaps even (7) people originating in a place called ʕAraba, which one is the original meaning? Indeed, was there ever an original meaning?
>
> If there was an original meaning, how do we explain the multifarious meanings documented by the Arabo-Islamic sources?
>
> What is the meaning of the morphological and semantic difference between *ʕarab* and *ʔaʕrāb*? Where does it come from?
>
> How do we explain the peculiar status of the *ʕarabī* language apparent in the Qurʔān? What is the relation between that language and the original *ʕarab*?

These questions cannot be answered immediately from the Arabic sources, although, even though we did not possess any other evidence, it would be possible to put up some hypotheses. Now 'Arabs' are mentioned in sources far older than the Arabo-Islamic ones. The terms derived from the root ʕRB have a long history behind them when they appear in the sources compiled by the early Islamic historians and philologists. The evidence in the oldest sources must be studied and related to the ones we have surveyed so far, before a synthesis can be attempted. This will be the task of the next part of this book.

Notes

1 For a survey of the whole material from the first two centuries of Islam, see now Hoyland, *Islam*.
2 Kraemer, *Excavations* 3:89 l. 22, 35 (possibly from *c*. AD 600): *sarakain-/saraken-/sarakēn-*, idem 3:51, 3:58.
3 Ḥammat Gader no. 3 = Green/Tsafrir, *Inscriptions* 94–96.
4 Kraemer, *Excavations* 60:14; 61:14; 62:15; 63:10; 64:15; 66:9.
5 Bell, *Aphrodito* 1464 vs. 7; 1508:15; 1509; 1510; 1518; 1521:11 (Coptic); 1433 (*passim*); 1441:53; 1457:24 (Greek).
6 Bell, *Aphrodito* 1368:7; 1441 *passim* (AD 706); 1447 *passim*; 1449:53, 57; 1486.
7 Bell, *Aphrodito* 1404:7; 1433 *passim*; 1434:165; 1435:122; 1441:84; 1449: *passim*; 1581.
8 Bell, *Aphrodito* 1335:5; 1349:15; 1357:1; 1373 frgm. 9.1394:8; 1407:3; 1447:32.
9 Bell, *Aphrodito* 1434:229; 1447:140, 190.
10 Bell, *Aphrodito* 1435:84. According to Bell, this could be hay sent from Arabia.
11 See pp. 249 ff..
12 The History of Sebeos was originally written in Greek. The original is lost and we know it through an Armenian translation. The story goes from the end of the fifth century AD until Muʕāwiya's accession (AD 661); cf. Hoyland, *Islam* 124–133.
13 Sebeos, *Histoire* 95–97, 102; Hoyland, *Islam* 586.
14 Sebeos, *Histoire* 95–96. The French translator often adds an explicit subject for clarification. On p. 98 he suddenly starts to write [les Arabes] instead of [les Ismaélites]; cf. also Hoyland, *Islam* 586. For the identification with Ishmael see pp. 335 ff.
15 Sebeos, *Histoire* 13–14, 20.
16 Ṭayyiʔ is said to be derived from ṬWʕ meaning 'go away', especially 'walk far out on the

pasture ground' (*Lisān* s.v. ṬWʕ). The Iranian *tāčīk* is usually associated with a root meaning 'to attack, assault'. For this problem, see Sundermann, *Attestation*; cf. p. 525, n. 126.

17 Johannes, *Chronique* 188:24/416; Hoyland, *Islam* 152–156.

18 Johannes, *Chronique* 259–260/492.

19 Johannes, *Chronique* 145/357; Hoyland, *Islam* 156.

20 The actual text continues until 710 by an unknown hand.

21 Yaʕqub, *Cronicon* fol. 23v. pp. 326–327; Hoyland, *Islam* 399, 584.

22 The first letter is an *ʔālaf*: ʔRBYʔ whereas the word 'Arab' in Syriac is always written (correctly) with an *ʕēn*: ʕRB-. The latter is, as in all Semitic languages, always a designation for people, not a country; cf. pp. 447–448.

23 Greek: Sophronius, *Oratio* (from AD 634) III:3206:C, 3207B; idem, *Epistula ad Sergium*; 3197D *(sarakēnoí, agarēnoí, Ismaēlîtai)*; Anastasius Sinaites, *Sermo* 1156C (Amalek); *Vita Gregorii Chozebitae* 134 (*sarakēnoí*); see further Hoyland, *Islam* 57, 59, 63, 75 105, 217–219, 221, 348, 354, 370. Syriac: Nöldeke, *Kämpfe* I:12; idem, *Bruchstücke* I:4, 24, 31–32; II:2, 4, 20, 22, 24, 33 (ṬYYʔ); II:11, 16 (SRQYʔ); *Pseudo-Methodius* 23:12/X:6 (BNY HGR), 8:2-3/V:1 etc. (BNY ʔYŠMʕYL); *Liber Calipharum* 147, 148. See further Hoyland, op. cit. 116–215, 273, 275 etc.

24 Johannes, *Colloque* 248:16; 251:7.

25 Ibid. 251:20.

26 *Liber Calipharum* 155.

27 Anastasius, *Viae Dux* 41A; idem, *Dialogus* 1224 C–D. For these texts, see Hoyland, op. cit. 79 note 78; 84, 94.

28 Sahas, *John* 132, 142 ff.

29 Iohannes, *Narratio* 517:2: *átheoi árabes.*

30 *Continuatio Byzantina* 12, 13 (*sarraceni*), 21 (ʕUmar is *Hismaelitarum dux*), 24 Muʕāwiya governs *Hismaelitarum plebes*), 29 (Marwān divides *Hismaelitarum provinciae* between his sons).

31 See, for example, *Continuatio Hispanica* 12, 43, 65, 74, 79, 80, 81, 84, 89.

32 *Continuatio Byzantina* 36 (p. 355).

33 Iohannes, *Narratio* 517:2.

34 The use of the term *ʔarab* in the Arabo-Islamic sources lends much credibility to those scholars who claim that the historiography of early Islam started to develop in the age of the Marwanids, i.e. after the second civil war. For this process, see Donner, *Narrative* 203–230, 255–290. The common meaning of the term in most texts is 'member of a tribe belonging to the Islamic state'. This tradition has thus been formulated at a time when *ʕarab* had become the designation for the members of all the tribes making up the Islamic empire. It is worth observing that this employment of the term is also even more dominant in the literature on the pre-Islamic *ʔayyām al-ʕarab*, which would be an indication of when these stories were formulated and codified. In contrast, the sparse use of the word *ʕarab* in the alleged pre-Islamic poetry would be one argument in favour of its genuineness, which, of course, also holds for the Qurʔān. The occurrences of the word with meanings deviating from the comprehensive one in the texts of the historians is further an indication that the historical tradition is not as monolithic as could be expected: there are obvious instances where the historians have preserved material whose terminology reflects conditions prior to the second *fitna*. Donner (*Narrative* 99 note 1, 284) has underlined that, for example, the terms *muʔmin* and *muslim* originally were not synonyms, which can be seen from their use in the historiography (cf. also Ringgren, *Islam* 31, referring to Qurʔān XIL:14–17). The same would hold for *ʕarab*, *muhāğir* etc.; cf. further Donner, *Narrative* 276–285.

Part II

THE FORGOTTEN ORIGINS

6

THE PROBLEM OF THE EARLIEST ARABS

Introduction

The word 'Arab' is documented in written sources as a term for groups of people in the Middle East continuously from the ninth century BC until this day. The enormous outburst of political, military and ideological energy from the Arabian peninsula, which resulted in the birth of Islam and the rise and fall of the Umayyad empire, events that transformed the Middle East and whose reverberations are still with us today, chronologically lies almost exactly in the middle of this period. For the Islamic Middle Ages, the history of the tribes stretched only one century back from the time of the Prophet.[1] This century was called the *Ǧāhiliyya*, 'the Ignorance'. For modern Arabs and Muslims in general, it deserves to be pointed out that the history of groups designated as Arabs goes much further back than was known to the Muslim medieval scholars. Before the activities of the Islamic Prophet there lie almost 1,400 years of history in which 'Arabs' appear in historical sources. A mapping of the use of the word 'Arab' in the period from the time of the Neo-Assyrian empire until the sixth century AD is a prerequisite to understanding its meaning when it appears in the Arabo-Islamic sources and then later through the Middle Ages into our own time.

Pre-Islamic Arabs in modern scholarship: a short survey

Before diving into the vast material relevant for the history of the pre-Islamic Arabs, it is worthwhile to have some idea of the position of modern scholarship on the question. In general it can be said that there are astonishingly few attempts at writing a comprehensive history of the pre-Islamic Arabs. The most substantial work remains, in fact, the first modern one: Caussin de Perceval's *Histoire des Arabes avant l'Islamisme* published around the time of the February Revolution in 1848. This book has a lasting value in that it gives the western reader a detailed presentation of the view of classical Islam on the history of the forebears of the Muslim tribes in Arabia. It is based upon the Islamic historians known in Europe in the first half of the nineteenth century, which means the late medieval historians such as Ibn al-ʔAthīr, Ibn Khaldūn and Abū al-Fidāʔ, who are often closely paraphrased or even quoted directly. Luckily, Caussin also drew heavily upon the *Kitāb al-ʔAghānī*, which gave him access to the ancient poetry. Since these historians as a rule copied their predecessors quite meticulously, Caussin is a fairly reliable guide to what the medieval Muslim *hommes lettrés* knew about pre-Islamic Arabs. This should not, of course, conceal the deficiencies of the work, which, as far as historical criticism is concerned, did not even reach the level of its day. Caussin very rarely shows any deeper understanding of what kinds of source the Arab historians were based upon, and his attempts at critical analyses cannot be taken seriously. He occasionally refers to classical Greek and Latin sources, but on the whole, the work remains within the closed walls of medieval Islamic historiography.

No work of this kind has been written in the West since Caussin. Of the more comprehensive works following him should be mentioned the monographs on geography by A. Sprenger (1875) and E. Glaser (1890). The former is a thorough commentary on Claudius Ptolemy's description of Arabia, whereas Glaser covers all the main geographical texts in antiquity from Theophrastus to Ptolemy. Even though many details in these two works are now outdated, they are still useful when studying the classical texts on Arabia. An early complete survey of Arabia in antiquity was made by D. H. Müller for the *Realencyklopädie der Altertumswissenschaften* (1896). An attempt at a complete survey of Arabs before Islam was made by D. O'Leary (1927). That work treats Arabia as a whole, thus including the city cultures in Yemen. Another work is that of J. A. Montgomery (1934), who tried to write the history of Arabia from an Old Testament viewpoint. Both these works, written as they are by enthusiasts, are characterized by rather opaque ideas about ethnography and social conditions in Arabia. Characteristic is the tendency to identify the pre-Islamic Arabs with modern bedouin, with the ensuing romantization of life in pre-Islamic Arabia. They also share a feature which seems to be common to most authors on the subject in general, namely negligence or uninterest in giving a thorough chronological exposition. One can jump from an Old Testament text to a Syriac chronicle and then to an Islamic text, all being seen as testimonies of the unchanging conditions in Arabia. Source criticism is also completely absent, which is remarkable since at this time both classical and Old Testament studies had developed this tool to a high degree of sophistication. This is a feature which has followed the study in this field, having begun to change only during recent decades.

The works of O'Leary and Montgomery belong to a genre which seems to be shunned by most authors. The tradition of a comprehensive view on Arabia has been continued in short articles named 'Arabia' in Biblical, Assyriological, Egyptological, Islamic and Classical encyclopaedias dealing with different regions of the Middle East. These articles often contain valuable observations but as a whole they shed little light on what Arabs originally were. This also holds for the latest substantial attempt at a comprehensive view on ancient Arabia by A. Grohmann (1963). The copious modern scholarly work on pre-Islamic Arabia and its inhabitants is scattered in a bewildering mass of periodicals, *Festschriften*, encyclopaedias and monographs often dealing with other themes. These works, most of which are enumerated in the bibliography of this book, signify a gigantic leap forward as far as new data are concerned, but the picture of the history of Arabia in general, and the Arabs in particular, still remains very fragmented since few, if any, scholars have a full survey of the field. The study of pre-Islamic Arabia has suffered from the fact that much of the scholarly work has been done within the framework of Old Testament studies, Assyriology, Egyptology, Classical studies, Sabaean studies, Islamology etc. The few attempts at a comprehensive perspective are, as a rule, characterized by sweeping generalizations (Arabs are nomads, Arabia is the cradle of the Semitic race etc.) and lack of understanding of the specific historical, sociological and geographical conditions in Arabia. A common fault has been the careless projection backwards in time of conditions prevalent in modern bedouin society, which have been assumed to be typical of life in Arabia from time immemorial.

While the broad perspective on the history of Arabia has as a rule been absent, there are studies of limited periods and areas which have greatly increased our knowledge. To these belong the studies on the Ghassanid kings in Syria by Nöldeke (1887) and Smeaton (1940) and G. Rothstein's monograph on the kings of al-Ḥīra (1899). In recent times the penetrating works of H. von Wissmann on pre-Islamic South Arabia and I. Shahid's monumental study on the interaction between the tribes in Arabia and the late Roman empire stand out. There is also a steady stream of studies on the history of the two main cities in Ḥiğāz as the birthplace of Islam.

The subject of this book is the history of people called Arabs, not the history of Arabia. This distinction has, however, seldom been made and no one seems to have seen it as a problem worth attention. From the preceding part of this book it has hopefully been made clear that this distinction should be maintained and might tell something important about the history of this part of the world. It will appear that, rather than contradicting Shahid's study on the Romans and Arabs in late antiquity, this work supplements it since Shahid does not deal with Arabs but with Saracens.

The scholarly work on Arabia during the last century has increased the amount of data to an astonishing degree. Penetrating studies of limited geographical areas as well as specific periods based on textual, archaeological and anthropological evidence have created a solid basis for a more comprehensive study of the identity of the people called Arabs in the written sources. In spite of such progress, this question has never really been problematized, although it turns out that several scholars have uttered their opinions on the meaning of the word, both etymologically and historically.[2]

It is possible to discern four main schools among the scholars who have commented on the pre-Islamic history of the 'Arabs'. The distinction between etymology and actual meaning of the term itself is not always made, as is evident from the following.[3]

1 Arab means 'desert-dweller', 'nomad', 'bedouin'

This is the dominating view, which is found in different variants with most scholars.[4] A variant of this concept is a more strictly etymological approach deriving the word 'Arab' from the name *ʕarabat-/ʕarabā*, which is said to mean 'desert'. This definition is already found with Theodor Nöldeke at the end of the twentieth century.[5] He is followed by some modern scholars.[6] From *ʕarabat-* we would then have the derivation *ʕarabī*, 'Arab' = 'one who belongs to *ʕarabat-*'.

We recognize this latter argument without any difficulty as found already among Muslim scholars in the tenth century AD. Strangely enough, none of the modern scholars refers to the medieval Arabo-Islamic discussion of this interpretation. Both schools seem to have conceived it independently of each other.

There are several problems with this interpretation, which should be completely obvious from the preceeding investigation. To start with the latter part of it, there is no indication that *ʕaraba(t)* means 'desert'. It is a name for some very specific areas in Palestine and, possibly, in western Arabia. In no documented Semitic language is this word used as a general term for desert. As a matter of fact, the etymology of the word is opaque, but nothing leads us to assume that it has anything to do with 'desert'. As we have pointed out earlier, the derivation of *ʕarabī* from *ʕarabat-* is possible but does not explain *ʕarab*.[7]

One should also ask what is meant by 'desert'. Geographers have usually defined deserts as areas with less than 250 mm precipitation per year. The Arabs would thus have been those living in the areas bordered by a line indicating this limit. As we have seen, there is no indication in the Arabo-Islamic sources that this was the case. If there was ever a common Semitic word for 'desert', there is no proof that it came from the root ʕRB and there is no proof that Arabs lived only there or that only Arabs lived there. If we are willing to look at the evidence with fresh eyes, it should be agreed that, whatever the original meaning of the word 'Arab' is, it can never have meant 'desert-dweller', in spite of the views of many scholars in East and West. And as we have already seen, there is no clearcut evidence in the documented occurrence of the word *ʕarab* in the Arabo-Islamic sources that it was ever used exclusively for people living as nomads or as camel bedouin etc. Even people in oases and fortified cities can be called *ʕarab*.[8]

This points to a more general weakness in this concept. A common opinion seems to be that 'desert-dweller', 'nomad', semi-nomad' and 'bedouin' are more or less synonymous. This is a view which dominates in older literature on the history of Arabia.[9] Modern research has, however, drastically changed the picture of the relationship between nomads and settlers in the Middle East.[10] Nomads and desert-dwellers need not at all be synonymous. Nomads may well live in areas not classifiable as deserts. People living in deserts do not necessarily have to be nomads. There have in historical times been large sections of the population in Arabia (also outside Yemen) who have not been nomads but farmers. Unfortunately for the adherents of this interpretation, there is no indication that the difference between agriculturalists and nomads was ever expressed in reserving the term *ʕarab* for the latter. Large sections of the population in Arabia and adjacent regions have led lives alternating between pastoralism and agriculture.[11] Only a portion of the shepherding groups have been nomads in the proper meaning of the word. Social organizations like tribes etc. often encompass people leading all these types of life.[12] Further, we can now discern a historical development of nomadism in the Middle East passing through different stages from the time of the shepherding groups appearing in the texts from Mari *c.* 1,700 BC until the camel bedouin of Arabia. There is some evidence that the latter did not emerge until late antiquity.[13] The horse- and camel-riding warriors, documented by the Arabic sources studied in Part I of this investigation, most probably represent a very special type of society, a warrior caste controlling both shepherds and settlers as a base for their own position. These warriors should probably be seen as neither settlers nor nomads. The complex relationship between shepherding, nomadism, agriculture and professional warfare in Arabia makes it impossible to assume that *ʕarab* means 'nomadic bedouin' since these concepts are not identical. Furthermore, if the razzia-loving camel warriors, as we know them from the classical bedouin society in Arabia, originated in the Roman period, *ʕarab* cannot refer to this group since the word is documented already in the ninth century BC. If it was a special term for camel-herders it cannot be a general term for nomads let alone desert-dwellers, since nomadism of different kinds in different kinds of 'desert' existed in the Middle East long before. In sum: there is no evidence that *ʕarab* means desert-dwellers, shepherds, nomads, bedouin or camel- and horse-riding warriors. As we have already seen, it does not mean that even today.

2 Arab is a nationality

This concept was developed by Von Grunebaum, who has been followed by a few but important modern scholars.[14] In the words of one of them, Arabs are 'one people who remain recognizably Arab in spite of the various forms of political, social, and cultural life which they adopt'.[15] Von Grunebaum uses the term *Kulturnation* for this community which 'is kept together by common expectations, associations and tooling' (sic).[16] Such a *Kulturnation* remains unaffected by political shifts but may make itself manifest by establishing a *Staatsnation*, i.e. a political structure expressing the collective will and the identity of the community.[17] According to Von Grunebaum, the Arabs were considered as such 'by common consent'.[18] It can thus be said, for example, about the Nabataeans, that, in spite of the strong influence from neighbouring Hellenistic and Semitic cultures, 'they remained Arab in ethos and mores and above all in their use of the Arabic language'.[19]

This definition seemingly solves the problem posed by the fact that *ʕarab* in both Islamic and pre-Islamic sources can stand for both nomads and farmers and all varieties in between.[20] It also implicitly rejects the idea of some kind of genetic relationship between the 'Arabs', although this is an idea which many scholars are somewhat reluctant to give up completely.[21] In fact, these scholars try to see the Arabs in antiquity as a nation in the modern sense of the word. Von Grunebaum explicitly refers to the concepts developed by European nationalist thinking in the nineteenth century.

A disadvantage is, of course, that the modern idea of nationhood is extremely vague. There are, in short, no objective criteria for defining such a concept. Some of its supporters seem to think of nations as something like biological species, which continue to exist under changing circumstances through centuries and millennia, but it is self-evident that this is only a metaphor – and not a particularly good one. If we pose the question about the modern Europeans – what is an Englishman, a German etc? – no clearcut, objectively valid answer can be given, if we do not accept the formal criterion of citizenship in a modern state, which in fact goes against the concept of *Kulturnation*, since one can be a British or German citizen, while remaining alien to most aspects of what is considered British or German national culture. After all, membership in a *Kulturnation* is constituted by a kind of personal consent which does not even have to be demonstrated in a public act.

The main objection against the definition of the ancient Arabs in terms of a *Kulturnation* is that there is no evidence that they or anyone else in antiquity had such a concept.[22] In antiquity, ethnicity is defined in concrete juridical, political and religious institutions. We do find here and there vague ideas of cultural fellowship similar to the modern European idea of nations, like the concept of 'Hellene' in Greek antiquity or, as we have seen, the *ʕarab* in the early Abbasid period. But unlike the European concept, these ideas in antiquity did not have any real political impact, and it is highly doubtful if they had any relevance outside a small élite populating the literary salons. It is extremely unlikely that the 'Arabs' would have been identified by themselves or by others in terms of a modern nation. Since the idea of nationhood as defined by the quoted scholars in practice did not exist in antiquity, it becomes most unlikely that the term 'Arab' had such a meaning. If a concept does not exist, it is unlikely that there is a word for it. If we identify the Arabs of antiquity as a nation in the modern sense of the word, we run the great risk of imposing a modern concept on a past world where it did not have any relevance, with the consequent distortion of historical facts.

Sometimes the attempts at explaining what the *ʕarab* were give very confused results. Thus, for example, Trimingham rejects the claim that 'Arab' would mean camel-nomads, farmers or speakers of a specific language.[23] Instead they are to be defined as a cultural community based on kinship and customs. But a few lines further down it is said that the Arabs were nomads on the steppes from the beginning, and that the term 'Arab' distinguishes the nomad from the settler. Then it is said that *ʕarab* means speaker of Arabic, whereas *ʔaʕrāb* are the nomads proper.[24] It is even claimed that the pre-Islamic Yemenis were Arabs according to 'culture and social order'. It is symptomatic that the whole passage completely lacks references to sources or secondary literature.

Eph'al's definitions are also highly contradictory. 'Arabs' in the Assyrian period is said to be the designation for 'desert nomads', even used by themselves, or desert-dweller, bedouin, which terms are obviously considered synonyms. The term has later expanded and designates all inhabitants of the peninsula, including the settled ones. The definition according to language is explicitly rejected.[25] But when the peoples in Babylonia in the time of Sennacherib are treated, they are suddenly defined as Arabs according to 'onomastic and linguistic criteria as well as on way of life'.[26] Since these groups obviously lived in fortified settlements called *dūr* and, consequently, were not nomads, this whole concept of Arabs breaks down.

A similar confusion reigns in Robin.[27] It is said that *ʔaʕrāb* in the Sabaean inscriptions means nomads [who are?] 'en principe *arabes*'. The Sabaean texts are said to use the term 'land of the *ʕarab*' to designate the desert in general, thus implying the identification of *ʕarab* as desert-dwellers. But later it is said that *ʔaʕrāb* may signify 'soit les populations (allogènes) de langue arabe, soit les nomades des diverses régions'.

Shahid seems to adhere to the definition of 'Arabs' in terms of modern nationhood: he speaks about 'the ethnic affiliation of these groups', 'their own identity' developed during a long historical period; they belong to 'the same ethnic stock'; they have an 'ethnic and cultural identity'; they 'remain Arab in ethos and mores and above all in their use of the Arabic language'; in short, concepts commonly used for defining a nation in the romantic European sense.[28] These not too clear statements are then countered with others like 'the Arabs . . . of this period [the Roman empire] . . . were not a nation . . . but consisted of various groups, disunited'.[29] Unlike the Germans, the Arab identity was concealed or 'obscured by terminology, both gentilic and geographic'.[30] The meaning of all this is not very transparent, and the consequence seems to be that the ancient Arabs were indeed a nation in the modern sense of the word – without knowing it! But if they did not know they were a nation, they cannot have had a word for such a concept, at least not as applied to themselves. It also becomes very unlikely, to say the least, that outsiders would have known that they were a nation but not the Arabs themselves! Consequently 'Arab' cannot have been a designation for such a nation.

It is only too obvious that these scholars try to reconcile widely different concepts about nationality and ethnicity without realizing that they are different and, in fact, irreconcilable. The only certain conclusion from the discussion is that the scholars in question do not have any clear idea at all about the meaning of *ʕarab* and its derivations, which is not surprising since nobody has ever investigated it extensively.[31]

3 Arabs are those speaking the Arabic language

A way of circumventing the uselessness of the modern concept of nationhood is the argument that those who speak Arabic must be Arabs, and as soon as we have signs of the Arabic language we also have evidence for Arabs.[32] This argument encounters insurmountable difficulties. The definition of Arabic is far from unproblematic. The modern definition of the Arabic language as the inherited *ʕarabiyya* with its modernized variants plus the colloquials between the Atlantic and the Persian Gulf has no relevance for premodern times. In the Islamic Middle Ages, Arabic was the language of the Qurʔān and the written litteraure. The spoken language was something else, and even sometimes considered to be no language at all. Even today not every speaker of Arabic in its modern linguistic sense, i.e. a colloquial, is an 'Arab', as is shown, for example, by the Jews and the Maltese. We have no reason to assume that those in antiquity who spoke a language which *we* classify as Arabic according to modern linguistic criteria considered it to be so, or saw themselves as Arabs, or were considered Arabs by their neighbours, unless we can clearly document it. As we have seen already, the evidence from the Qurʔānic terminology clearly favours such caution. We should also be aware of the difficulties in defining an Arabic language in antiquity. There is no agreement among modern scholars on how to delimit a language which they call Arabic. All experts nowadays make a clear separation between the languages in South Arabia, like Sabaean etc., and those in other parts of the peninsula, reserving the term 'Arabic' for the latter, but no agreement has been reached concerning the languages documented outside South Arabia in the pre-Islamic inscriptions. Are Thamudic, Lihyanitic, Safaitic and Hasaitic Arabic or not? It all depends on the linguistic criteria one uses for the definition of a language, and such criteria are rarely unproblematic and definitely not in this case. Furthermore, documentation of the presence of speakers of English is no proof of the existence of the English. Therefore, historical evidence for the presence of people speaking a language classified by modern linguists as Arabic cannot be taken as a sign of the presence of 'Arabs' in the ancient sense of the word before the sense is found out.

4 Arab means 'mixed people'

This idea is found in Lane's *Lexicon*, where it is connected with the Hebrew *ʕereb* meaning 'mixed people', which is used in the Old Testament about the people who followed the Israelites out of Egypt.[33] This suggestion, which is a purely etymological one, stands quite isolated, and almost no scholar has taken it up. It does have some attractions. Even the Muslim genealogists saw the *ʕarab* as composed of several different genealogical lines, which would suit this meaning. It is clear that already the Old Testament transmitters made the association between *ʕarab* and *ʕereb*.[34] The medieval Arabic dictionaries give the meaning 'pure, unmixed' to some derivations of the root.[35] We would thus have to do with a so-called *ḍidd*-word, a root with derivations of contrasting meanings.

This is an interesting suggestion but it remains to be verified. If *ʕarab* originally meant 'mixed people', it must have been coined by outsiders, i.e. people who did not consider themselves as *ʕarab*. Even though such an interpretation can be defended etymologically, it remains to be proved whether this meaning was valid during documentable history. At least this definition has the advantage of not being bound up with modern politically inspired concepts of nationhood or pseudo-sociology.

It is quite obvious that a main reason for the confusion in defining the word 'Arab' is that no one has bothered to distinguish between modern and traditional concepts of group identities. One factor which has obscured the view is the rise of the modern Arabic nationalist ideology. Its basis is the idea of an Arab nation which encompasses the inhabitants of the modern Arab states from the Atlantic to the Sea of Oman.

Membership in this nation is, according to its founding fathers, constituted by common language and common cultural heritage. The modern Arab identity is thus of the same kind as that claimed for most European nations. It is, in the same manner, rather vague and ultimately based on private consent. It is also well known that large groups within the Arab world reject the idea of an Arab nation altogether and rather see themselves as members of the Egyptian nation or the Lebanese nation or other nations. These nations are then defined as vaguely as the Arab one.

This is not the context to give a thorough analysis of the ideology of modern Arab nationalism. This has been done by others.[36] The achievements of this movement are indeed remarkable and impressive: the revivification of the *ʕArabiyya* language and the abolition of European political control of the area from Mauritania to Oman. It is a fact that vague and unclear thoughts, based on conscious or unconscious distortions of history, can have an enormous effect as popular movements with political goals. This is a truism as far as modern nationalism is concerned, be it the ideology behind the unification of Italy and Germany, Zionism, Arabism or any other nationalistic ideology.

Our aim will instead be to seek the roots of the traditional usage of the term 'Arab' as demonstrated by the driver from Salamiyyeh and amply documented among the present-day bedouin. We have seen that the early Islamic testimony clearly points to definitions and meanings of Arabs current during the first two Islamic centuries that differ not only from the modern nationalist concept but also from the more traditional ones still current today. It is a good starting point to assume that these traditional meanings of the term are primary, compared to that of modern Arab nationalistic ideology. The latter is thus a recycling of a traditional term in a new political and cultural context. The study of the meaning of the traditional term and its history may be of considerable historical interest if one considers national and ethnic terms not as designations for entities similar to unchanging biological species, but rather as terms capable of being transferred and reinterpreted according to political, ideological, ethnic and social changes throughout the centuries.

Such a view of national terms is not uncontroversial in a world where nationalism is growing as a political factor. As we have seen, there is also an almost unified common opinion among scholars that the term is unproblematic. At least there has never been a thorough scholarly discussion of its meaning or its use. When we encounter ethnic designations in antiquity we should, however, always, instead of mechanically applying modern ideas of national identity or other concepts, look for some concrete institution which makes it definable, not by romantic ideas of common culture but by jurisdiction and cult in accordance with what is known about societies in antiquity. If we take the example of the Jews, we can see that during most of their history they have indeed had such institutions: Jews are those who stand under Jewish law. Such definitions hold for most ethnic entities in antiquity of whom we have any deeper knowledge. As far as our Arabs are concerned, we have, in fact, in the Umayyad period found such an institution: the Islamic state and its register of citizens, the *dīwān*. We can say that in those days there existed an Arab people definable in terms similar to the Romans, the Athenians, the Jews and others. Before that time we do not immediately catch sight of anything similar. There is no religious, political or social institution immediately visible defining who is an Arab during the 1,400 years from the first appearance of the term in a text until the rise of the Muslim state. This does not necessarily mean that such institutions cannot have existed. There must have been a reason for using the word 'Arab' as a designation for a group or groups of people during this long period. The question is who these people were and what it was that constituted the identity and its continuity. This question can only be answered after a perusal and an analysis of the testimony of history. It is somewhat remarkable to notice that none of the scholars whose views of this question have been presented here seems to have bothered to look into the concrete evidence, either the Arabo-Islamic or the pre-Islamic. The time has now come to do so.

Excursus: nomadism in the Middle East

There has been a widespread notion in the literature on the history of the Middle East that one of its main themes, if not *the* main theme, is the continuous conflict between the settled peoples in villages and towns on the one hand, and on the other unruly, war-loving nomads who have continuously broken into the settled lands, causing devastation and plundering. Traditionally, the border between nomad and settler has been seen as very sharp, economically and politically. The nomad is completely dependent upon animals, incessantly roaming around looking for pasture. His society is characterized by tribal organization. Nomadic culture is conflict-ridden because of competition for the scarce resources, and becomes anarchic, filled by tribal warfare and blood revenge. Nothing of this belongs to agricultural society, which has to be protected by empires and their armies against the aggressive hunger for land and booty of the nomad. This notion has been connected with the great linguistic changes in the Middle East and a picture has been created of a history where the nomads of Arabia at regular intervals, because of lack of subsistence due to the very limited ecological framework, have set out on large invasions into the agricultural regions, conquering them and effecting changes in language, culture and political structures. Thus a picture was established of the invasions of the Canaanites, the Amorites, the Aramaeans (among which many wanted to find also the Israelites) and the Muslim Arabs, all originating in Arabia, the cradle of 'the Semitic race'.[37]

This picture, which was primarily derived from the knowledge of two major historical events, the Israelite conquest of Palestine and the Muslim conquests, was satisfactory as long as the concept of massive migrations was a main tool for explaining cultural changes in ancient times. One might also observe that a similar concept was basic to Ibn Khaldūn's view on history as early as the Middle Ages. As far as Israel is concerned, the picture was cast into serious doubt in the 1920s by the studies of A. Alt and later of his pupil M. Noth on the traditions about the Israelite conquest. The picture resulting from the work of Alt and his successors was that of a continuous peaceful infiltration of nomads into Palestine rather than a dramatic conquest. A similar picture emerged from the study of J. Kupper in the 1950s on the evidence from the archives of Mari on the middle Euphrates, which, unlike that of Alt and his colleagues, had the advantage of being based on a large corpus of contemporary written documents.[38] Kupper retained the concept of the land-hunger of the nomads but emphasized the peaceful character of their infiltration into farmlands. According to him, the urge to settle down was the main striving of nomads, which led to a continuous pressure on the farmlands and an ever on-going process of settling. This conclusion seemed to be a nice confirmation of the results arrived at by Alt and his colleagues. The peacefulness of the Mari nomads was emphasized even more strongly in the studies that followed Kupper.[39]

In the 1960s, this new picture of the nomads was integrated into a comprehensive model of the role of nomadism and agriculture in the Middle East in a succession of articles by M. Rowton. The picture is as follows:[40] agriculture demands a precipitation of at least 400 mm per year. If it is less than 100–200 mm per year, only pasturage is possible; agriculture in such an area needs irrigation. In the area having between 200 and 400 mm precipitation, there is uncertain agriculture and relatively certain nomadism. Rowton calls this latter zone the dimorphic zone. In it originates what he calls enclosed nomadism, a process which starts in Syria in the Early Bronze age, i.e. the third millennium BC. Because of progressive desiccation, this nomadism increased and reached a climax in the transition from Early to Middle Bronze age around 2000 BC and played an important role during the second millennium BC. In the first millennium BC a new kind of nomadism arose: that of the camel-breeders which was different from the enclosed nomadism. The characteristic feature of enclosed nomadism is that it is a symbiosis with farming culture. The two ways of living complement each other, and the nomads and the farmers are dependent on each other's products. This results in a common socio-political structure, namely the dimorphic tribe, which works as an organization for regulating distribution of resources, marital rules, distribution of property etc. The tribe may encompass cities but mainly it interacts outwards with cities which are organized in a completely different way with tribal structures absent.

Rowton's model cancels the opposition between farmer and nomads, at least in the dimorphic regions. Instead they live in a symbiosis, and individuals within a tribe may well change between farming and shepherding or pursue both activities. A dimorphic tribe may contain all kinds of shepherds: full nomads and semi-nomads or settled shepherds.[41] The relationship between the elements within such a tribal structure is not always frictionless and may be disrupted, but on the whole the system itself turns out to be stable and has continued to function until this day. The main opposition in Middle Eastern history, according to this scenario, is thus not between nomad and farmer but between town-dwellers and tribesmen.

Rowton's abolition of the conflict between the desert and the sown as a main factor in Middle Eastern social and political history was a major step forward. In a later study P. Briant has pointed out that the concept of the hostile nomadic hordes threatening the peaceful farmer has its roots in antiquity, where it was clearly stated by none other than Aristotle.[42] It probably reflects the imperial ideology at the time, inherited by the Achaemenids from the Assyrians, who waged long wars against the desert-dwellers, most likely not out of need for defence but out of purely imperialistic ambitions. It was neither the first nor the last time in history that imperialistic aggression was covered by the claim of an exterior threat to peace, law and order. The quite peaceful life within a dimorphic society is probably in a unique way reflected in the patriarchal stories in the Old Testament. It should be remembered that this is no proof that those stories must be very old. This way of living is not limited in time, only in space, and has been pursued by large sections of Middle Eastern society until this day.

It is nevertheless doubtful whether the conflict between the desert and the sown can be replaced by one between cities and countryside as is done by Rowton. The latter's relationship oscillates between associating in the market-place at the city gate, which is the normal practice, and attempts by the city and its political elite to extend its control over the countryside ruled by the dimorphic tribes. But there are also cases where a larger city may be integrated into the dimorphic tribe or have a kind of treaty or alliance with it. Nor does the relationship exclude military clashes. In other words, all kinds of relationships are possible and indeed also documented.

On the other hand, the dichotomy between city and countryside will remind the reader of this study of the opposition in the Arabo-Islamic sources between the people of the *bādiya* defined as the shepherds and the village farmers, and those of the *ḥāḍira*, the inhabitants of the fortified cities. In Arabo-Islamic sources we find the *ʕarab* among the former and the *ʔaʕrāb* among the latter. But this does not mean that those groups are identical.

In Arabia in the early Islamic period, we find several well-documented cases fitting very nicely into the model of dimorphic structure: the tribes of Ǧuhayna and Sulaym in the Ḥiǧāz, Ḥanīfa in the Yamāma and the tribes in ʕAsīr all show this dichotomy between farmers and shepherds, and it is well documented even among tribes existing today.[43] Things may, however, have been more complicated than Rowton assumes. There were in early Islamic Arabia cities which do not seem to belong to dimorphic tribes: Quraysh in Mecca and Thaqīf in aṭ-Ṭāʔif do not seem to be integrated with their surroundings. Nevertheless they are characterized as tribes. Interesting are the tribes in Medina who appear as oasis-dwellers, i.e. were non-dimorphic, but who must have had some kind of relationship to peoples outside the oasis, namely the *ʔaʕrāb*.

The picture is thus complex even though Rowton has caught one important aspect of the relations between nomads and settlers in the Middle East. Later scholars have emphasized the multifariousness of ways of living on the edge between the desert and the sown, and one should rather look for a continuum of different ways of living, often overlapping, instead of a dichotomy between nomadism and agriculture.[44]

Rowton also distinguished his dimorphic tribes from those living by camel breeding (1974). According to him, the latter are comparable to independent states, not dependent on the settled lands or agriculture, and represent a break with the traditional dimorphic system, similar to that between cities and countryside. It is true that people who have the camel as their main domestic animal must become much more mobile than tenders of sheep and goat. The camel needs a very wide pasturing ground, and the camel-breeder has to follow it. The camel also moves far into the arid lands outside the area suitable for enclosed nomadism, into areas where no sheep or goat can survive. This does not, however, mean that the camel-breeders are independent of the settlers.[45] They may well remain dependent upon them, even more than the sheep and goat tenders since they become tied to their animals in a way that makes it difficult for them to do anything else. Their freedom and mobility is that of the camel. Unlike the small-cattle breeders, they have difficulties in taking up other activities than tending the animal. They will need the services of the farmers and the small-cattle tenders.

It is thus doubtful whether the separation between camel-breeders and others was so definite as Rowton assumes. Also the tribes based on agriculture and small-cattle breeding may well have seen themselves as independent states and only reluctantly succumbed to the empires. The earliest camel-breeders documented in the Assyrian texts also have large numbers of small cattle. Instead it can be assumed that camel breeding may well be developed within Rowton's dimorphic society but that those in charge of it very early constitute a specialized group within the community because of the peculiar demands that the tending of the camel puts on its tender. This does not necessarily mean that they cut all the ties with their shepherding and farming colleagues. It deserves to be pointed out that even today there are differences between the camel-holding tribes in Arabia and adjacent lands as far as the role of the camel is concerned. There are large tribes like the Āl Murrah, the Shammar and the Rwala who are almost exclusively concerned with camel breeding. Others use the camel for transport and labour but also tend small cattle and often have sown fields and pursue commerce, like the tribes in the Negev.[46] The earliest documented *ʕarab* are definitely of this latter type, and the purely camel-holding groups appear quite late in history.

The consequence is that it becomes unlikely that one can analyse historical processes in the Middle East according to a pattern of innate conflict between different patterns of production. All groups are intertwined and dependent on each other in different ways. Middle Eastern societies have always been a continuum of life-patterns, where not seldom different means of subsistence are united in one individual.[47] Members of larger social units like city-dwellers, farmers and shepherds of different kinds often belong to the same political or ethnic unit (states and tribes). The main political conflicts are between these, not between cities and farmers, farmers and nomads, or cities and nomads. And as has been pointed out, the most dramatic political upheaval in Middle Eastern history, namely the Muslim conquest, was not performed by shepherds, nomads, farmers or city-dwellers. The *muhāǧirūn/ʕarab/muslimūn* were a caste of professional warriors, who were recruited among farmers in Medina and Yemen, traders in Mecca and Ḥiǧāz, shepherds and camel-breeders from central Arabia and the Syrian desert. The conquest did not originate from the traditional ambitions of some of those groups but from the fact that these people had left their traditional occupation and become professional warriors led by a militant ideology.

The *ʕarab*, from their first appearance in the sources, are connected with the camel and this animal follows them through their history. This does not necessarily mean that the word itself means just camel-breeders, only that the people called *ʕarab* were closely connected with the camel. They do, in fact, appear in the sources not only as camel-breeders but also as shepherds of small cattle and even farmers. This makes it somewhat unlikely that *ʕarab* was a special designation for camel-breeders or, more exactly, that camel breeding was the origin of the designation *ʕarab*. Second, if *ʕarab* from the beginning designated a group of peoples characterized among other things by being camel-breeders, it cannot have been a general term for nomads. Large-scale camel breeding combined with riding was an innovation, probably developed around 1000 BC, with which the *ʕarab* somehow were connected, but it was never until this day a general characteristic of nomads in Arabia. Consequently, *ʕarab* cannot mean nomads.[48]

Notes

1 See p. 15.

2 A very recent attempt at a comprehensive view on pre-Islamic Arabia is R. Hoyland's *Arabia* (2001). It contains much of the new material and has some up-dated views on some problems. It remains, however, conventional as far as the problem discussed in this study is concerned. There is a considerable number of books on pre-Islamic Arabia and the pre-Islamic Arabs in Arabic. The most important of these is still Ǧ. ʕAlī, *al-Mufaṣṣal fī tārīkh al-ʕarab qabla l-ʔislām* 1–10 (1950–1959). Of other works one should mention U. Farrūkh, *Tārīkh al-Ǧāhiliyya* (1964); A. Sālim, *Tārīkh al-ʕarab fī l-ʕaṣr al-ǧāhilī* (1971); idem, *Tārīkh al-ʕarab qabla l-ʔislām* (1973); S. Z. ʕAbd al-Ḥamīd, *Fī tārīkh al-ʕarab qabla l-ʔislām* (1975); L. ʕAbd al-Wahhāb Yaḥyā, *al-ʕArab fī ʕuṣūr al-qadīm. Madkhal ḥaḍārī fī tārīkh al-ʕarab qabla l-ʔislām* (1979); M. al-ʕAbādī, *Muḥaḍarāt fī tārīkh al-ʕarab qabla l-ʔislām* (1981); F. Barrū, *Tārīkh al-ʕarab al-qadīm* (1984); B. Dallū, *Ǧazīrat al-ʕarab qabla l-ʔislām. at-tārīkh al-iqtiṣādī, al-iǧtimāʕī, aṯ-ṯaqāfī wa-s-siyāsī* (1989); B. Mihrān, *Dirāsāt fī tārīkh al ʕarab al-qadim* (1993); idem, *Tārīkh al-ʕarab al-qadīm* 1–2 (1994). Many of these works are rich in content, reflecting the deep knowledge of their authors of classical Arabic literature, which makes them useful also for the western scholar. On the

other hand, they mostly lack critical analyses of the sources and they do not discuss the problem dealt with in this study. All of them take the modern, nationalistic definition of Arabs for granted. A useful survey of the thinking of modern Arab writers on the history and the origins of the Arabs is Choueiri, *Nationalism* 23–55.

3 For a discussion of this question, see Retsö, *Early Arabs*, and idem, *Xenophon*.

4 Weiss-Rosmarin, *Aribi* 1; Montgomery, *Arabia* 28; Nallino, *Arabi* 179; Dussaud, *Pénetration* 14–15; Grohmann, *Kulturgeschichte* 3; Altheim/Stiehl, *Araber* passim, e.g. II 269, III 257 etc.; Irvine, *Arabs* 287 ff. Donner, *Conquests* 11; cf. idem, *Xenophon* 1–14; Eph'al, *Arabs* 5–7 (cf. Frame, *Review*); idem, *Ishmael* 124; Zadok, *Arabians* 44; Lipinski, *Arabie* 124; W. W. Müller, *Araber* 143; Knauf, *Midian* 109; Zwettler, *Imra'alqays* 10–11; Conrad, *Arabs* 680; more cautious is Nallino, *L'Arabia* 5. Dostal (*Development* 134–135) states that Arab in the Akkadian texts means camelherdsmen, later transformed into an ethnic term. A similar process was suggested by Nallino (*Arabi* 179). Hoyland (*Arabia* 8) seems to take an opposite view.

5 Nöldeke, *Arabia*.

6 Montgomery, *Arabia* 28–29; Nallino, *L'Arabia* 5; Irvine, *Arabs* 287; H. P. Müller, *Arabien* 571; W. W. Müller, *Araber*.

7 See pp. 52 f. This derivation is also, correctly, rejected by Eph'al, *Arabs* 7.

8 Cf. Dostal, *Araber* 3–5.

9 Cf. the classic description of the life of the desert-dweller in Arabia in Hitti, *History* 23–29; O'Leary, *Arabia* 19 ff.

10 Cf. the criticism of the traditional romantic view by Briant, *Etat* 12–56, summing up the ground-breaking works of Kupper, Luke and Rowton. See also Knauf, *Bedouin*.

11 Cf. Dostal, loc. cit.; Morony, *Iraq* 222; Knauf, *Bedouin*.

12 Cf. Dostal, *Araber* 4–5 and the following excursus.

13 Cf. Dostal, *Development* 125; Caskel, *Beduinisierung*; idem, *Bedeutung*; Knauf, *Midian* 9–15.

14 Von Grunebaum, *Nature. passim*; Shahid, *Pre-Islamic Arabs* 18; idem, *Rome* 3–16; Kennedy, *Prophet* 16; Morony, *Iraq* 222. Also Dostal, *Araber* 1–5, seems to adhere to this view. An earlier supporter of this thesis was Guidi, who saw all inhabitants of the peninsula as 'la race arabe' (*L'Arabie* 64, cf. 3).

15 Shahid, *Arabia* 18.

16 Von Grunebaum, *Nature* 7, 10.

17 Ibid. 6.

18 Ibid. 1.

19 Shahid, *Rome* 9.

20 Cf. Shahid, *Arabia* 18 ff.

21 Kennedy still adheres to it: 'united by . . . the idea of common kinship'; Shahid speaks of 'the same ethnic stock' (*Rome* 6).

22 Cf. the discussion in Lemche, *Israelites* 8–21 which, however, is still very much influenced by modern sociological theories of ethnicity as a rather fluid concept. It might well be that to a modern scholar the ethnic identities in antiquity may be difficult to grasp. But for the ancients themselves the borders were, in general, quite sharp and distinct. The famous statement in Herodotus 8:144 is hardly representative, formulated as it is in a nationalistically intoxicated Athens between the Persian and Peloponnesian wars.

23 Trimingham, *Christianity* 1–5.

24 Cf. Mārbākh, *ʕarab*, who from another starting point arrives at a similar distinction.

25 Eph'al, *Arabs* 5–9.

26 Ibid. 115 n. 386.

27 Robin, *L'Arabie* 73.

28 Shahid, *Rome* 6.

29 Shahid, *Rome* xx n. 4.

30 Shahid, *Rome* 6 and n. 15.

31 Good examples of the confusion reigning among scholars on this issue are the articles *al-ʕArab* in *EI*[2] I 524–57 and *al-Badw*, ibidem I 872–892. These articles are written by several

competent scholars (W. Caskel, H. von Wissmann, W. M. Watt, G. Rentz, B. Spuler, G. Wiet, G. Marçais, C. S. Coon). But in spite of this posse of experts it is impossible to extract a definition of what an Arab is or was from their texts, which is somewhat disappointing since they are published in an authoritative framework.

32 This is the main criterion used by Hommel, *Ethnographie* 129 ff. He is followed by Shahid (*Rome* 9) and Zadok (*Semites* 192, 314) who, like Hommel, identifies 'Arabians' as speakers of South-west Semitic. This is somewhat unfortunate since South Arabian and Arabic are quite different language-groups and also the Ethiopian languages belong to the South-west Semitic branch. See also Hoyland, *Arabia* 230 f.

33 Lane, *Lexicon* s.v. ʕRB 1993, cf. Exodus 12:38.

34 See Jeremiah 25 and p. 173.

35 Cf. the summary by Lane, loc. cit.

36 A good introduction to the thinking of modern Arab nationalism is Cleveland, *Nationalist* 92–127, especially 99–105.

37 Classic statements in Hitti, *History* 8–13; cf. Shahid, *Rome* 11. For the debate, see Lemche, *Israel* 148–152.

38 J. R. Kupper: *Les nomades en Mésopotamie au temps des rois de Mari*, Paris 1957. Alt and Noth basically had the Amarna letters as the contemporary evidence, the Biblical texts being written centuries later. By meticulous scrutiny of these and comparison with the picture emerging from the letters, they claimed that it was possible to discern the oldest traditions about Israelite settlement in Palestine, describing it as a peaceful process of nomads settling down. The idea of the violent conquest by Joshua was a much later, largely fictional view, created by the Deuteronomistic theologians in the Neo-Babylonian and early Achaemenid period. See the survey of the debate in Lemche, *Israel* 35–48 and Thompson, *History* 25–76.

39 J. T. Luke, *Pastoralism and Politics in the Mari Period*, Diss., Chicago 1965; V. H. Matthews, *Pastoral Nomadism in the Mari Kingdom (c. 1830–1730 BC)*, Diss., Cambridge, Mass. 1978. See Lemche, *Israel* 159–161, for an evaluation of the debate on nomads in Mari.

40 The following is a condensed summary of the main ideas set forth in Rowton's articles mentioned in the bibliography.

41 Cf. Lemche, *Israel* 152 ff.

42 Briant, *État* 9–56.

43 Rowton, *Enclosed*. For Sulaym, see Lecker, *Banū Sulaym*, especially 221–228.

44 Cf. Lemche, *Israel* 129 f.

45 Lemche, *Israel* 124.

46 Cf. Sweet, *Pastoralism*, especially 130 f.; idem, *Camel raiding* 1133–1134; Marx, *Tribe*; idem, *Organization.*

47 Cf. Lemche's summary in *Israel* 198–201.

48 For the early use of the camel, see Retsö, *Domestication* 199–205. Se also Knauf, *Bedouin* 636 f.

7

ARABS IN CUNEIFORM SOURCES

Syria at the beginning of the first millennium BC: sources

People designated as Arabs first appear in sources connected with events in Syria in the first centuries of the first millennium BC. The main ones are the texts in Akkadian from Assyria: the records of the kings telling about their campaigns to Syria and the Syrian desert from the middle of the ninth century down to the fall of the empire. They are supplemented by some letters from officials. The Assyrian sources are on the whole of good quality. They are often written shortly after the events, and the contents are derived from eye-witnesses and people belonging to the leading class of the Assyrian kingdom with first-hand information. There are propagandistic distortions in them, but the ethnic and political terminology can be assumed to be in accordance with the factual conditions. These distortions have occurred only once, i.e. when the text was conceived, whereas most other, literary sources have often undergone repeated extensive revision by later redactors, apart from corruptions by copyists. Some of the royal Assyrian records do, however, present intricate problems of source criticism which will be commented upon during our presentation. But as we shall see, the Assyrian texts belong to the best and most informative sources we have dealing with our problem, and there are, in fact, few others in antiquity that equal them.[1]

The other group of sources for the period down to the time of the Achaemenids is the literature of ancient Israel collected in what is known as the Old Testament.[2] These texts are far more problematic than the Assyrian ones. Their dating is mostly uncertain, but what is certain is that most of them are written long after the events depicted. The Old Testament as we have it is basically a product of Palestinian Jews during the Achaemenid period, although much of the material used by the redactors is older, reflecting conditions during the time of the Israelite monarchy, called by many Jewish scholars the First Temple period. The sifting of old and recent material is a difficult task yielding uncertain results, and the disagreement among scholars not only about dating but also about historical validity seems to be greater than ever. It can, however, be assumed that short notes on genealogy and political conditions in the Old Testament texts which are not central to the theological and ideological framework or the tendency of the narratives have a larger value as historical documents than the material which has continously been reworked and reinterpreted by the Sages of Israel for centuries. As will be shown, there are reasons to believe that in the notes scattered through the Books of Kings and Chronicles, texts which are basically theological tractates on history, ancient material has been preserved, whereas the theologically highly charged narratives about the origins of Israel, the patriarchs, the Exodus and even the hero kings David and Solomon wholly or mostly consist of mists of legend and theology.[3]

From the mid-1970s the so-called deconstructivist school has put the whole Biblical account about the history of Israel from the patriarchs to the end of divided kingdom in question. This school sees the entire Old Testament as a collection of popular tales used in a framework of theology. Since popular tales are the most unreliable of all historical sources, and the theological framework can be shown to reflect conditions after 700 BC at the earliest, and probably mostly the Achaemenid period, it becomes impossible to use the entire collection of Biblical texts as a source for the history of Israel before that date, and applying traditional methods of historical source-criticism on them is meaningless. To the deconstructivists, traditional scholarly accounts of the history of Israel up to the mid-1970s appear on the same level as Caussin's *Histoire des Arabes* from the 1840s: analysing folktales as if they were historical documents. To this is added the wide discrepancy, especially for the periods before 850 BC, between what the Biblical texts say and the testimony of archaeology. According to this school, the history of southern Syria-Palestine can only be written from archaeological evidence and contemporary textual witnesses, i.e. mainly Assyrian and Babylonian records.[4]

These views have not yet won common acceptance and are met with strong opposition from several scholars. In this investigation a cautious attitude towards the Biblical sources is taken, basically in agreement with the deconstructivist principle that, in the present situation of research, statements about historical events in the period before 700 BC should not be built upon Biblical evidence *only*. But one can assume that, if the Biblical texts dealing with a specific period or event give a picture which is quite coherent with what is found in contemporary sources and/or is in tune with archaeological evidence for the same period and no other, then it is legitimate to adduce the Biblical text as supplementary evidence, assuming that it indeed has preserved memories of the event or period in question.[5] One can also assume that certain genealogical lists, as well as the order of the kings of Israel and Judah, in fact reflect actual historical conditions.[6] Several kings of Israel and Judah are mentioned in contemporary Assyrian and Babylonian sources from 853 to 586 BC.[7] If we analyse the numbers indicating the reigns of all kings mentioned in the Books of Kings and Chronicles, we can pin down the ten kings to dates that roughly correspond to their dating according to the Akkadian sources.[8] This makes it likely that the succession of kings in the Books of Kings and Chronicles is based on an authentic list of kings of Israel and Judah with very short notices about major events during their reigns. The Biblical texts themselves, in fact, refer to earlier sources for the history of the divided monarchy, the existence of which thus gains likelihood.[9]

One could compare similar evidence for the history of pre-Islamic Arabia. In Wahb b. Munabbih's book about the kings of Yemen we have a series of names of kings said to have reigned there until the time of Sayf b. Dhī Yazan at the end of the sixth century AD. The stories told by Wahb about these kings are mostly very legendary and folktale-like, much more so than the narratives in the Book of Kings in the Old Testament. This king-list also appears in later Islamic historians. Deconstructivists would have had an easy task in rejecting Wahb's Yemeni history as 100 per cent fictitious and the whole idea of pre-Islamic kingdoms in Yemen as invented by the pro-Yemeni propagandists in the Umayyad period, were it not for the evidence from both contemporary inscriptions and some literary sources. Of the seventeen names mentioned by Wahb as the kings of Ḥimyar, seven appear in the contemporary inscriptions, and the earliest is dated to *c*. AD 270. The order in which they are mentioned in Wahb's book and the following historians mostly corresponds to the order established from the inscriptions. This shows that the Yemeni story-tellers in the first two Islamic centuries worked with material containing some historical facts and even preserving a chronological framework (without, however, regnal years or chronological notes).[10]

A similar list of the kings of al-Ḥīra was used by Hishām b. al-Kalbī when he wrote a history of the town at the beginning of the ninth century AD which, to a large extent, is preserved by aṭ-Ṭabarī. We here find a list of kings from the third century AD until the end of the sixth century with (sometimes probably correct) regnal years and short notes about events during the reigns of the kings, which in fact makes this text reminiscent of the basic framework in the Books of Kings and Chronicles in the Old Testament. Many of the kings in al-Ḥīra, at least from the sixth century AD, are further documented in contemporary sources, which gives the story of Ibn al-Kalbī status as a supplementary source to the history of the *manāḏira*-kings.[11]

This does not mean that all such lists of rulers preserved in much later versions are useful for reconstructing history. A good example of the opposite are the lists of the kings of Axum in the pre-Solomonic period (i.e. before AD 1270), preserved in several versions in late medieval manuscripts. These lists are a hopeless mess and almost completely unusable for historical purposes.[12] This is shown by the fact that only a couple of the names are identifiable with names of Axumite rulers known from contemporary sources (inscriptions, coins, non-Ethiopian narrative sources).[13]

This kind of historiography thus shows a wide spectrum of historical reliability: from the almost useless Ethiopian king-lists with imaginary names and only faint traces of verifiable chronology, via Wahb's collection of popular legends about pre-Islamic Yemen spun around a series of rulers in an, on the whole, correct chronological order, to the stories of the kings of al-Ḥīra containing a not negligible amount of concrete historical memory. Reading the Books of Kings in this context shows them rather to belong to the last type, whereas Chronicles look more like a combination of Wahb and Ibn al-Kalbī.

Political outline

The twelfth century BC had witnessed major changes in the Syro-Palestinian area.[14] The sway of the Hittites and the Egyptians over Syria had ceased, and a wave of unrest swept the eastern shores of the Mediterranean. In spite of this, the political dividing line between the Hittite sphere of influence in the north and the Egyptian one in the south, established already in the Amarna period (fourteenth century BC) and cemented under Ramses II and Muwatallish in 1259, continued to exist.[15] Local, Neo-Hittite dynasts continued to rule in the north, while indigenous groups, mostly Semitic-speaking, took over in the south and along the coast. That this border, stretching from the Mediterranean north of Byblos, passing the northern entrance to the Biqāʕ valley and running eastwards into the Syrian desert, was a political dividing line of major importance is clearly seen from the fact that it was also later considered the northern border of the Promised Land by the Israelites.[16] Two ethnic migrations started in this period which had a decisive influence: the invasion of the so-called Sea-Peoples in the twelfth century and the appearance of the Aramaeans in the eleventh.

The emergence of independent political structures in Syria after the fall of Egypt and the Anatolian Hittites was closely connected with economic developments. It seems that one decisive factor was the spread of the use of iron for weaponry. Since iron was found in south-eastern Anatolia, the local rulers there could profit from the know-how of mining and preparation, as well as from the trade of iron to neighbouring areas. That iron was an important economic factor in the states in northern Syria/south-eastern Anatolia is clearly seen from the fact that in the ninth century the Assyrian king, Ashurnasirpal II, brought with him 250 talents of iron (i.e. 7.5 tons) from his campaign to Carchemish on the upper Euphrates.[17]

Another development with far-reaching consequences in the future was the beginning of trade with the Arabian peninsula. This is connected with a general economic renaissance during the early Iron Age, when the rise of a new Mediterranean economy involved the inhabitants of the steppes south and east of Syria-Palestine, who became large-scale providers of animal products to the settled societies.[18] The increased importance of the regions south of Syria, visible in the growing concern of the rulers for the two main routes – the coastal route, the Via Maris, and the desert route from southern Transjordan, the King's Highway, through Damascus across the desert via Tadmor to the Euphrates – is probably an indication of the increased weight of north-western Arabia. The Assyrian king Tiglath Pileser I (1115–1076 BC) reports in his annals that he fought with the Aramaeans on the road leading from Suhu on the Middle Euphrates westwards.[19] It may be no coincidence that this text also happens to contain the first mention of Aramaeans ever.[20]

It has often been claimed that the main purpose of this trade was frankincense, which only grows in Ḥaḍramawt and Somaliland. There is, however, no certain indication that such products from South Arabia were used in Syria in the beginning of the first millennium BC. All evidence points to the fact that the frankincense trade from Yemen was established much later.[21] This early stage of Syrian overland trade with Arabia did not yet reach that far south and must have encompassed goods of other kinds.[22] Tukulti Ninurta II's (891–884 BC) list of tribute from the tribes at the end of the route by the Euphrates may give an idea of what was at stake: '10 minas of gold, 10 minas of silver, 2 talents of lead, 1 talent of myrrh, 60 . . . of bronze, 10 minas of the *zadidu*-herb, 8 minas of the *shimzida*-stone, 30 camels, 50 oxen, 30 donkeys . . . 200 sheep'.[23] An indication of the importance of southern Syria is the fact that around 930, the Egyptians revived their dormant military capacity and made a futile attempt at establishing control not only of the Via Maris, a standing point on the agenda of Egyptian foreign policy since time immemorial, but also of the King's Highway.[24]

Goods of great value were carried along this road, a traffic in which the camel was probably beginning to be used as a pack-animal. This made it possible to cross the desert from Damascus directly to the Euphrates via Tadmor, a route which had not been viable before the access to domesticated camels. Those who knew the noble art of camel breeding and handling would thus have a place in the sun guaranteed, both literally and symbolically speaking. The thirty camels received by Tukulti Ninurta are, however, no certain indication of the use of camels from Arabia, since the word used rather indicates two-humped camels.[25] It is after 900 BC that the one-humped camel began to be used much more extensively, for both transport and riding.[26] Especially the latter innovation is likely to have occurred in Syria around this time. At least, the earliest documentation comes from there, although different preliminary stages of domestication and the technical devices for loading and riding the animal seem to have been developed in south-eastern Arabia.[27]

According to the earliest documentation, the kings in northern Syria and the Assyrians used the camel for military transport. Its main use was probably as a pack-animal, which could be used for long journeys in the desert. In the Old Testament it appears as a beast of burden in a notice about events in Damascus in 841, which might be the earliest certain mention in Israelite literature.[28]

The Old Testament has a lot to tell about the tenth century, when the Israelite kingdom arose and, according to this evidence, for a short time dominated Syria. According to the general picture found until recently in almost all textbooks on the history of Israel, iron weaponry was introduced by the Philistines, one of the Sea Peoples, who also triggered off the formation of the Israelite kingdom, which soon grew into the main political power in Syria. It had a predecessor, namely the state of Aram Ṣobah based in the Biqāʕ around the year 1000. From the name of this realm we can see that it was considered dominated by Aramaeans. The kings of Aram Ṣobah are said to have controlled the Syrian desert up to the middle and upper Euphrates, including Tadmor (Palmyra) and Damascus. At the same time they tried to expand southwards in Transjordan, perhaps in order to reach the Gulf of ʕAqabah. This expansion in Transjordan made them clash with the Israelites under David. The result was the conquest of Aram Ṣobah by David, the establishment of an alliance with the Neo-Hittite king in Hama, north of the old border, and Israelite control of Transjordan and probably also parts of the Syrian desert. This Israelite empire was upheld by Solomon, at least during the first part of his reign. It is said that he built (fortified) Tadmor, controlled Hama and was in charge of the horse-trade from Egypt 'to the kings of the Hittites and Aram', and he is said to have controlled the Euphrates up to Thapsacus. The Davidic–Solomonic empire appears as an heir to Aram Ṣobah. To this picture also belongs Solomon's alliance with the king of Tyre, the main sea power on the Syrian coast. Together, these two gentlemen were able to launch a major commercial thrust into the Red Sea, namely the expedition to Ophir.

Unfortunately, we have no contemporary sources verifying the existence of either Aram Ṣobah or David and Solomon, let alone their empire.[29] The Biblical texts that tell the story are written centuries later than the events they purport to depict. While one cannot exclude the possibility of historical memories or even fragments of older documents in them, we have, at present, no means of verifying it.[30]

The Aramaeans' dominance in southern Syria, together with their ties with other Aramaeans on the left bank of the Euphrates, is not documented for this period either. The Aramaean expansion in Transjordan cannot be verified until a much later date. In the genealogy of the sons of Nahor in the book of Genesis, however, we have a list of Aramaean tribes and sites part of which is probably quite old. In the names of the sons of Reʕumah, which are place-names in the Biqāʕ valley, we may well have the kingdom of Aram Ṣobah. Interestingly enough, the Aramaic identity of these seems to be secondary and they are secondarily united with the Transeuphratean Aramaeans represented by Nahor. They might thus constitute a pre-Aramaic layer.[31]

Another problem is the lack of archaeological evidence for the Davidic and Solomonic empires. The absence of epigraphical testimonies from the two kings is remarkable. There seem to be no traces of the cities claimed to be built by Solomon. Judaea, the province said to have been the basis of the Davidic conquest, seems to have been practically uninhabited in the tenth century BC.[32] The scanty archaeological remains show Jerusalem as a small hamlet of peasants rather than the centre of an empire.

Against this negative evidence stands the Biblical account of David and Solomon, which is a conglomeration of texts of very differing kinds. Even though the picture given by them is not very exact, the existence of political structures in Palestine at this period is not impossible. The absence of archaeological evidence is perhaps not as crucial as alleged by the deconstructivists. The Islamic conquest and the early caliphate are not documented archaeologically either. It could very well be alleged that archaeology indicates that the Islamic conquests never happened, and that the whole picture of the conquests and the Umayyads is a propagandistic creation legitimizing the Abbasid empire.

The description of David's empire has several quite realistic traits. It is described as a patchwork of provinces, vassal-states and allies, which is not very likely to be the product of later times in need of a founder and a conqueror. It is, in fact, not unlike the picture of Muhammed's state in Medina, which in the sources appears as a multifarious aggregation of tribes and groups with varying degrees of dependency on the Prophet himself. Like that of David, this state is undocumented, and probably undocumentable archaeologically. As in Jerusalem, the spot in Medina where one can expect archaeological evidence is buried under buildings of high ideological importance, which may never be excavated. Even ʕUmar b. al-Khaṭṭāb, who nominally ruled an empire far bigger than that of David, did not have any governmental offices or bureaucracies: when camels came in as tribute from Mesopotamia he is said to have gone out to count them personally. It is not difficult to imagine David as a ruler of this kind.[33]

It should further be noted that neither David nor Solomon carries a Yahwistic name; they thus differ from practically all the kings said to have succeeded them in Judaea. If the Davidic kingdom was only a projection backwards for legitimizing a later Judaean state in the seventh century which by then worshipped Yahweh as its national god, one would expect at least a Yahwist straw-man as the founder of it, and even more so a pure Yahwist as the builder of the temple. If, on the other hand, we see both David and Solomon as well as their temple as pagan from the viewpoint of the later Israelite religion, their existence becomes more probable even though it cannot be verified by contemporary sources. The presentation of David's religious tenets is, as a matter of fact, quite remarkable and he is consistently described as doing things not expected from a real Israelite. This was once pointed out by J. Pedersen who, however, tended to see him as an early quietist, regarding the later stories about him as real documents of the man himself.[34] David's erratic behaviour in the classical stories about him might, however, be a memory of a figure who was an outsider of a more unruly kind, considerably toned down by the artful hagiographic account.

The road to Qarqar

In the first half of the ninth century we have contemporary evidence of the existence of independent powers in southern Syria. The most important events during the period were the consolidation of an Aramaean power in Damascus and the establishment of the dynasty of Omri in Samaria, perhaps around 880 BC. Omri or his successor formed alliances with the kings of Tyre which now during the ninth century had its political and economic heyday, with the rulers in Damascus and, according to the Old Testament, also with the kings in Jerusalem. An alliance was extended even to the rulers of central and northern Syria as in Hamat.

In 876 BC Syria witnessed the campaign of the Assyrian king Ashurnasirpal II to northern Syria.[35] This was the first Assyrian appearance in this part of the Middle East since the days of Tiglath Pileser I 200 earlier and it was a portent of what was to come.[36] The rising Assyrian power was from now on to dominate Syrian politics during the next 200 years in a terrifying and brutal way that had not been experienced by anybody earlier.

These two events, the formation of the southern Syrian alliance and the entry of Assyria on the Syrian scene, are probably related. It has been suggested that the alliance took its final shape around 858 BC when Ashurnasirpal's successor, Shalmaneser III, arrived in Syria.[37] Both are results of the new mercantile role of the region which is discernible during the preceding centuries of the Iron Age. The most striking element of this was the unparalleled flowering of the Phoenician cities along the coast and their colonial expansion in the Mediterranean basin. But the economic boom also benefited both northern and southern Syria. It is also characteristic that the campaigns of the Assyrian kings in the ninth century were all directed towards the north-west. No campaigns to Babylonia or Media were undertaken in this period. The establishment of the southern Syrian alliance was not only a military enterprise but also a means of reciprocal protection of common trade interests. The membership of Tyre, the economic superpower of the age, in the alliance is a clear indication of its aim.

The reason for the Assyrian expansion towards the west seems to have been pure greed. That is, the new Assyrian kingdom was built on the foundation of a continuous supply of goods robbed from surrounding countries. The Assyrian campaigns in the ninth century were accordingly gigantic razzias, expeditions of plundering, effected with, at least according to the Assyrian sources, appalling cruelty. After a while, the plunderings were replaced by tribute-paying, since it obviously became clear even to the Assyrians that it was more profitable to have a regular income than just to grab what was at hand. The tribute system started under Ashurnasirpal II, who claims to have taken tribute from the Aramaic kings of Bît Adînî and some coastal cities.[38] The third step was the incorporation of foreign territory as provinces, a process which started under Shalmaneser III.[39]

Ashurnasirpal's successor, Shalmaneser III (858–824 BC), initiated regular attacks on Syria during twenty years in order to reduce it to subservience.[40] In his first campaign in 858–57 BC he managed to crush an alliance of states in northern Syria headed by Carchemish, reducing Bît Adînî to the status of province and imposing heavy tribute on the other north Syrian states. Having thus established Assyrian control over the northern iron-trading states, his next step was to gain control of the coastal cities. The foresight of the Tyrian rulers now appears in full light. Their alliance with the land-based powers forced the Assyrian king to attack them before he could deal with the Phoenician cities.

Shalmaneser III is perhaps the best documented of all Assyrian kings. We have at least six recensions of the story of his achievements, each of which is found in several copies.[41] The most detailed account of the campaign to central Syria in 853 BC is found in Recension A with its best-preserved copy consisting of the so-called Monolith Inscription.[42]

In the year 853 BC Shalmaneser III crossed the Euphrates by Carchemish as his predecessors had also done. He made sacrifices to the god Hadad in Aleppo. This city was part of the kingdom of Bît Agûsî, which since 857 had been one of Assyria's tribute-payers. From Aleppo he then continued his march through the Orontes valley, thus entering the territory of the kingdom of Hamat. He took three royal cities belonging to the king of Hamat, Irhuleni. He then claims to have conquered and burnt a fourth royal city, Qarqar.[43] The A version then continues:

> 1200 chariots, 1200 cavalrymen, 20,000 footsoldiers of Adad-'id-ri (91) of Damascus, 700 chariots, 700 cavalrymen, 10,000 footsoldiers of Ir-hu-le-e-ni the a-ma-ta-a-a (the one from Hamat), 2000 chariots, 10,000 footsoldiers of a-ha-ab-bu, (92) the sir-'a-la-a-a (the Israelite), 500 soldiers from the gu-a-a (the Byblian?), 1000 soldiers from the mu-uṣ-ra-a (the Musrian), 10 chariots, 10,000 soldiers from the ir-qa-na-ta-a-a, (93) 200 soldiers of Ma-ti-nu Ba-'-li, the ar-ma-da-a-a (the Arwadian), 200 soldiers from the u-sa-na-ta-a-a, 30 chariots, 1[0?]000 soldiers (94) of A-du-nu Ba-'-li, the si-[a]-na-a-a, 1000 camels of Gi-in-di-bu-'u the ar-ba-a-a, . . . 000 soldiers (95) of Ba-'-sa son of Ru-hu-bi, the a-ma-na-a-a (the Ammonite), these twelve kings he [Irhuleni] brought along to help him. They rose against me for (96) a decisive battle. I fought against them with the mighty forces of Ashur, which Ashur, my lord, has given to me, and the strong weapons which Nergal, my leader, (97) has presented to me; I did inflict a defeat upon them between the towns Qarqara and Gilzau . . .[44]

This famous passage not only contains the earliest reference to an Israelite king in non-Biblical sources but also the first mention of people called Arabs. Both names occur in the Monolith Inscription only, i.e. Recension A of the annals, which is the earliest version of Shalmaneser's annals, compiled already one year after the events. The term *ar-ba-a-a* should probably be pronounced [*ʕarbāy*(*a*)] and is a so-called nisba-adjective to a noun *ʕarab*, thus: [the man] Gindibu belonging to the *ʕarab*.[45]

While there is no doubt that the word is the same as the *ʕarab* we have already investigated, the identity of the people designated by it is not self-evident. The name of the leader of the *ʕarab* is a good Arabic name, which is found many centuries later in the classical Arabic onomasticon. *ǧundub*, *ǧundab* or *ǧindab* means 'grasshopper' and the use of designations of animals as personal names is a characteristic of Arabic names, being rare in other Semitic languages.[46] There is thus an indication that these *ʕarab* spoke a form of the language we would call Arabic or at least closely related to it.

It may be noted that there are prominent rulers lacking in the list. Thus neither Tyre nor Sidon is mentioned, although the Old Testament tells us that Tyre was allied to Israel and probably to Damascus as well. It is noteworthy that Shalmaneser mentions twelve kings but only eleven units are found in the actual list.[47] The list itself is obviously a document which was originally independent of its present context. One may note the discrepancy between line 95 where Irhuleni is said to have called the listed rulers for help, and line 91 where Irhuleni himself is included among these helpers. The list must thus go back to an independent document listing the army units of the enemy taking part in the battle.[48] The units are not listed haphazardly. The two strongest military forces, Damascus and Israel, stand first together with the ruler of Hamat on whose territory the battle was fought. The strength of the Syrians was largely due to their numerous chariotry headed by Ahab of Israel.[49] Then follows a list of cities along the coast. The discussion about the identity of Muṣri and Gu-a-a does not affect this basic classification: regardless of whether they are Egypt and Byblos or two kingdoms in Cilicia they still belong to the same geographic area, namely west of central Syria.[50] The last two names are Gindibu and Ba'sa. The latter is in all likelihood a ruler in Transjordan.[51] It follows from this that Gindibu and his Arabs are likely to have come from the same area. This is confirmed by what we know from later Assyrian sources stating that the Assyrian province of Haurina (= Ḥawrān) established by Tiglath Pileser III in 732 had the *ʕarab* on its eastern border.[52]

We may thus conclude that these *ʕarab* people had their habitat in the north-eastern parts of the present-day Hashemite kingdom of Jordan. The great oasis of al-ʔAzraq and the Wādī Sirḥān, stretching south-eastwards to Dumah, which appears later as the stronghold of the *ʕarab*, immediately comes to mind as a proper place for the keeping of camel-herds.[53]

The link between Arabs and camels is found here already when the former make their first appearance in history. What did Gindibu and his camels do at Qarqar? On the bronze gates of Shalmaneser's palace in Balawāt we see pictures of camels during the campaign to northern Syria in 858 BC.[54] These camels are thus geographically close to those from Carchemish and Tell Ḥalaf. The Assyrian artist had problems in drawing this strange animal, which he perhaps saw for the first time, but it is clearly visible that these camels have the so-called south Arabian saddle, the *ḥawlānī*-saddle consisting of a pad behind the hump.[55] This equipment excludes the use of the animal in the front line. A rider on a cushion on top of the hump is depicted on the reliefs from Tell Ḥalaf and Carchemish from *c.* 900 BC and reappears on the reliefs depicting Sennacherib's conquest of Lachish in 701 BC.[56] The cushion-saddle was a device enabling the rider to use his bow or spear from a very elevated position. The military function is clearly visible in the Carchemish relief. The use of the South Arabian saddle on the Balawāt reliefs indicates that the camels used at Qarqar must have been for transport and also kept in the rear as a means of swift retreat.[57]

The battle at Qarqar was a success for the Syrian alliance. Behind the boasting rhetoric of the Assyrian inscription it emerges clearly that the Assyrians did not achieve anything.[58] These fights in Syria were probably the last great battles in which victory depended on supremacy in chariotry. From the later Assyrian pictures we can see that the army of the king is more and more dominated by infantry. This change was a major factor in the later Assyrian military strength: Assyria had larger resources of manpower than Syria.

In the days of Shalmaneser III this was still in the future. During the decade after Qarqar, the Assyrians repeated their efforts in Syria, but as long as the alliance lasted they had only modest success.

In the report from this campaign we thus catch a glimpse of the role and position of the *ʕarab* in the Syrian desert. The camel was by now becoming more and more important as a means of transport in the desert areas. That the routes through the deserts had also become important we have already seen in the inscription of Tukulti Ninurta II.[59] It may be supposed that the group of states in southern Syria took a keen interest in the growing trade overland from the Arabian peninsula. Gold and myrrh are mentioned by Tukulti Ninurta and may also be the historical kernel in the Queen of Sheba story.[60] In order to get access to the goods from Arabia, camels were necessary. The *ʕarab* people appear in this crucial battle as the experts on the new means of transport, which must have been a technical innovation equivalent to the introduction of cars in the twentieth century. Unlike the handling of cars, the secrets of camel breeding could easily be monopolized, and the *ʕarab* were thus potentially a major force in trade and, as the cushion saddle was developed, also in warfare.[61]

Excursus: the sons of Qeṭurah

Genesis 25:1–7 contains a list of the sons that Abraham is said to have begotten with an otherwise unmentioned woman named Qeṭurah. The name is obviously a derivation from the root meaning 'smoke', and it has been assumed on good grounds that the name has something to do with the transport of incense from Arabia to Syria.[62]

The list gives six names for the sons of Qeṭurah and Abraham: Shuaḥ, Yishboq, Midyān, Medān, Yoqshān and Zimrān. Shuaḥ is likely to be the town Suhu at the middle Euphrates, well known in Assyrian texts from the Old Babylonian period onwards.[63] Yishboq is mentioned in the Monolith Inscription of Shalmaneser III in the description of his first campaign in 858–857 BC as *ia-as-bu-qa-a-a*, i.e. 'the man from Yashbuq', in connection with his conquests of Carchemish and Sam'al, thus in northern Syria.[64] Midyān is well known from the Old Testament. Its kernel area was the Wādī ʕIfāl east of the Gulf of ʕAqabah and the Ḥisma plateau behind.[65] Medān is often seen as a faulty variant of Midyān but may, in fact, be an area south-east of Midyān, still known as Wādī Mudān by medieval Muslim geographers.[66] The last name, Zimrān, cannot be identified with certainty but one should point out that the Septuagint, according to a variant reading of 2 Chronicles 22:1, obviously knew about someone named Zambri close to the *alimazoneîs*. The latter lived around present-day Ḍubā on the coast south-east of the inlet to the Gulf of ʕAqabah, and we should perhaps look for Zimrān there.[67]

These names seem to be distributed along a route from north-western Arabia to the Euphrates. The name of the route, Qeṭurah, indicates that perfumes of different kinds may have been one of the principal goods transported. From the times of Tukulti Ninurta II we have details about the goods available in Suhu: gold, silver, ivory and meshkannu wood, many of which must have come via the Qeṭurah road.[68] There is no indication that the route stretched further south to Yemen.[69]

Of the four sons, who are to be considered groups living in the land of Midian, Yoqshān is given two sons by the Massoretic text: Sheba' (LXX: Saba) and Dedān (LXX: Daidan), to which the Septuagint adds Taima. Midyān's son ʕEphah probably appears in a text by Tiglath Pileser III from 732 BC.[70] Also the Yoqshanid Saba appears in the same list, which is the earliest certainly dated occurrence of that name. From around the same period or shortly before, we find Saba mentioned together with Taymāʔ in a text from Suhu on the Euphrates.[71] Since these are added to the list as sons, it is reasonable to assume that they historically represent a replacement of older groups by new ones. This implies that the six names of the first generation in the list reflect conditions before the time of Tiglath Pileser, i.e. before 750 BC. The list has then been updated, reflecting new conditions in the eighth century and onwards.[72]

A striking feature in the Qeṭurah list is the gap between Midyān and Yishboq in northern Syria. This can be explained in several ways. In the Old Testament the gap is filled with several names of peoples and states: Edom, Moab, Ammon and the Aramaean kingdom of Damascus. If the list is from a time when these entities did not exist as independent states, we are led to a period before the middle of the ninth century BC, since at least the existence of Moab is documented from that time.[73] The Old Testament describes the kingdom of the house of Omri as ruling the entire area from the gulf of ʕAqabah unto Ḥawrān. This is also, by the way, the area said to have been under the rule of David and Solomon. The extension of their empire is, however, very uncertain. The list could thus be a memory of the political conditions east of the empire ruled by Omri. The attachment of the six names to Abraham is made much later, when Abraham had emerged as the patriarch of Judaea, from which David's dynasty is said to have come.[74]

Another possibility is that the list reflects a dominance from Midian northwards into Transjordan, reaching groups in southern Syria. Such a dominance is, in fact, supposed in the Old Testament for the pre-monarchic period and preserves historical memories.[75] The Qeṭurah list could thus, together with the list of the sons of Reʕumah, belong to the oldest ethnographic documents in the Old Testament, describing political conditions before the rise of the empires in southern Syria.[76] It would be a documentation of a trade route from northern Ḥiğāz to the Euphrates, the oldest trade route in western Arabia.[77] The gold and silver coming to Suhu could well originate in western Arabia: Midian was later known as a land of gold. The ivory (if this is really the meaning of the word) indicates African origins.[78] In that case, one can imagine a shipping route from the Egyptian side of the Red Sea to a harbour near Ḍubā. Shipping of gold along the Arabian coast is also conceivable from the story about Solomon's expedition to Ophir. Interesting also is the association of camels with Midian. Even though this association is not so substantial as has been assumed, it can be used as an argument that the camel traffic between Syria and South Arabia was originally initiated from the north. Documented evidence points to Syria as the region where the camel was first used for transport and riding on a larger scale. The point of origin could well have been Wādī Ṣirḥān/Dumah, from where the use of the animal spread to northern Syria and to Midian, thus the habitat of the sons of Qeṭurah. Even though all this is somewhat hypothetical in the absence of solid archaeological documentation, the picture given by the texts is quite coherent and likely.

Tiglath Pileser III

Like the first appearance of the Arabs in historical records, the next primary evidence comes from Assyrian sources. And the reason is once again Assyrian imperialistic ambitions in Syria. The Old Testament evidence for the history of at least southern Syria may, however, be judged more trustworthy for this period than for the preceding one.

The alliance that had successfully withstood the Assyrian attacks in the ninth century BC was definitely dissolved in the year 841 BC, replaced by bitter enmity between Damascus and Israel. The *coups d'état* in both Israel and Damascus, probably in the year before 841 BC, are connected with this event.[79] In Israel Jehu eradicated the house of Omri, including the killing of the unfortunate Ahaziah of Jerusalem who, after all, was an Omrid, while in Damascus the usurper is said to have killed the ailing king with his own hands.[80] It is in this connection that D (the Book of Kings) mentions the camel as a pack-animal in Damascus, a fact which fits nicely with the evidence presented here.[81] It may be assumed that the close relations between the camel-herders and the kings in Damascus and Samaria continued under the new regimes, whose demand for their services had not decreased.

The new king in Damascus, Ḥazaʔel, soon established himself as the leading politician in Syria in spite of the fact that the alliance definitely seems to have fallen apart after 841. This can be judged from the fact that he had to face two Assyrian attacks more or less alone (841 and 838), without the former allies. The Assyrians forced the coastal cities as well as the new ruler in Israel to pay heavy tribute, whereas Ḥazaʔel obviously repelled the attack. Ḥazaʔel's time was the heyday of the power of Damascus, which lasted to the beginning of the following century.[82] Then its power was drastically reduced by renewed Assyrian attacks.

In the year 746, after a period of interior strife and external passivity in Assyria, Tiglath Pileser III ascended the Assyrian throne. His main task was to restore the Assyrian dominion over surrounding countries and reduce them to final submission. This king started the transformation of the conquered areas from tribute-paying vassals to Assyrian provinces.

The sources for Tiglath Pileser's reign are mainly texts put up in at least five halls in his palace in Kalah.[83] He also set up stelae in various parts of the empire, one of which has been preserved, which is of great importance to our subject.[84] The palace was dismantled by Esarhaddon, and the slabs with the texts partly destroyed and reused for building Esarhaddon's own palace. When they were discovered in the 1840s and 1850s they were in great disorder and suffered further destruction.[85] One of the great achievements of modern Assyriology is the reconstruction of Tiglath Pileser's texts by H. Tadmor.[86]

The texts are of two kinds: the Annals recording the activities of the king for each year in chronological order, and the Summary inscriptions listing his achievements according to geographical regions. The latter are all written in the late years of the king, i.e. at the beginning of the 720s BC.[87] The Annals in the palace listed his activities until the seventeenth year of his reign, i.e. 730–729.[88] In the stela found in Iran we have an annalistic text ending with his ninth year, i.e. 737 BC, thus an early version of what we find in the final redaction of the Annals in the Kalah palace.[89]

In 743 Tiglath Pileser started his campaigns to Syria, which in ten years' time would result in the abolition of political independence in the area and its total submission to a foreign power, a situation which was to last until AD 1946. The immediate cause of the renewed Assyrian interest in Syria was the emergence of a mighty rival in eastern Anatolia, namely the kingdom of Urartu with similar interests in the rich northern Syrian kingdoms. The clash occurred here when Tiglath Pileser shattered an alliance between Urartu and kingdoms of northern Syria and south-eastern Anatolia: Melid (= Malatya), Gurgum, Kummuh (= Kommagene), Agusi (= Aleppo) and Umqi (= Zincirli). The city of Arpad, capital of Agusi, Urartu's main ally, was besieged for two years. Its final surrender in 740 was a major political event that echoes to this day in the Bible.[90]

Tiglath Pileser then turned his attention to Armenia and spent the year 739 campaigning there. During his absence the Syrians formed a new alliance, this time headed by the king of Sam'al, Azriya.[91] The exact course of the campaign that Tiglath Pileser undertook in Syria in 738 is not known, but the participants in the anti-Assyrian alliance are mentioned in his Annals.[92] It turns out that, apart from the Phoenician cities from Arqa north of Byblos to Simir south of Arwad, a group of cities from Sam'al in the north to nineteen districts of Hama in the south took part in the struggle. The cities were crushed and their territory was transformed into four Assyrian provinces.[93] In connection with these events Tiglath Pileser received tribute from a host of rulers in the West now eager to wag their tails before the man of the day.[94]

The list of the tribute-payers exists in several versions, the earliest one found on the Iran stela, erected in the year 737, and the final versions in the Annals, edited in

727 BC.[95] The stele is thus the oldest document and fortunately also well preserved. The passage relevant for our purposes runs:[96]

1. On the kings of Hatti, [on] the Aramaeans (ar-ri-me), [on those living] on the seashore,
2. on the Sunset coast, [on] *qid-ri*, [on] *a-ri-bi*[97]
3. Kushtashpi the Kommagenian (ku-mu-ha-a)
4. Raqianu from Damascus
5. Menahem the Samarian (sa-me-ri-i-na-a-a)
6. Tubail the Ṣur-a-a (the Tyrian)
7. Shipit-ba'al the Byblian (gub-la-a-a)
8. Urik the Qu-ú-a-a
9. Shulumal the Malatyan (mi-lid-a-a)
10. Washshurme the Tabalian (ta-bal-a-a)
11. Ushit the A-tú-na-a-a
12. Urpalla the Tú-ha-na-a-a
13. Tuhame the Iš-tu-un-di-a-a
14. Wirimi the Hu-bi-iš-na-a-a
15. Dadilu the Kás-ka-a-a
16. Pishirish the Carkemishian (gar-ga-miš-a-a)
17. Panammu the Sam'alian (sa-ma-al-la-a-a)
18. Tarhularu the Gúr-gu-ma-a
19. Zabibe (Za-bi-bi-e), queen of the *a-ri-bi*
20. tribute and gifts, [namely] silver, gold, tin, iron,
21. (elephant) skin, ivory, blue and red purple,
22. clothes of various colours, linen, camels (*ibilē*)
23. and she-camels (*naqāti*) I imposed . . .[98]

In the Annals, the list belongs to the passage dealing with the king's 9th *palû,* i.e. 738–737 BC. In the three versions there are some minor differences in the order of the names, which need not concern us here.[99] We may, however, notice that the Annals do not have the headline mentioning *qid-ru* and the *a-ri-bi*. All names in the list, including the *aribi*, are preceded by the determinative KUR, 'land', except Kommagene, Tyre and Carchemish, which are characterized as URU, 'city'.

This list has become famous because it is the fourth time an Israelite king is mentioned outside the Old Testament.[100] It deserves additional fame because it contains the second mention of Arabs in world history in a dated contemporary source. Also the first appearance of Qid-ru, identical with the tribe called Qedar in the Old Testament, marks the entrance on the stage of a most important factor in the history of the Arabs.

We can notice some interesting features of these Arabs. No lively imagination is required to conclude that the camels mentioned in the following list of tribute must have been their contribution to Tiglath Pileser's treasures. The very terms for camels used in the list are most likely to be Arabic loan-words in Akkadian. We should also notice the absence of frankincense or perfumes. The Arabs had not yet become involved in this business, otherwise its absence here is difficult to account for. Most important, however, is the fact that they are said to be ruled by a queen. Her name is also a good Arabic word: *zabībat* in later Arabic means 'raisin' and is a name of the same type as Gindibu a century earlier.[101] This first, but not last, Arab queen is designated by the Akkadian word for queen: *šarrat*. We shall see later that there is evidence that this was not the term used by the Arabs themselves.

Certain aspects of the political position of these Arabs can also be gleaned from the list. It is well worth noticing that the list of tributaries does not contain any name of the insurgents of the Azriya alliance. Typical is that the king of Hama gives tribute, and at the same time it is explicitly stated in the Annals that he did not take part in the war. We can see that Commagene, Gurgum and Milid, who fought against Tiglath Pileser in 743–740 BC, this time have remained loyal to Assyria. The tribute-list thus contains Assyria's allies or vassals from at least after 740. As we shall see later, in 733 the Arabs are accused of having broken their oath to Shamash. From the list we can see that our old friends Damascus and Israel are on the same side as the Arabs, which is no coincidence. As a hundred years earlier, the Arabs have followed their closest allies in Syria, then by taking part in the war against the invader, now by paying tribute together to the same power.[102] Does the absence of Judah from the tribute-list together with the breaking up of the alliance with the Arabs in the 840s indicate a consistent anti-Syrian policy on the part of the Jerusalemite kings? It seems that in 738 Judah had just regained her independence from her vassalage under Jeroboam II. Surely a pro-Samarian party in Jerusalem, which in those days would be the same as a pro-Assyrian party, was certain to have to spend most of its time in the political desert.

The order established by Tiglath Pileser in 738 not unexpectedly turned out to be unstable. During his three-year absence webs of intrigue were probably spun between the Syrian rulers with the ultimate goal of throwing off the Assyrian yoke. In 734 BC he had to interfere again, this time to settle the Syrian question once and for all. The immediate cause then was the revolt of the coastal cities, which refused to pay the tribute. The mind behind it was Rezin of Damascus, supported by Hiram of Tyre and the king of Israel.[103]

Tiglath Pileser's campaign in 734 concerned the southern Levantine coast. There is evidence that the immediate goal was to control the trade between the Phoenician cities and Egypt and Philistia. The result of the operations was full Assyrian control of the coast down to Wādī al-ʕArīsh ('The Brook of Egypt'). This result thus severely disturbed the interests of Tyre, Damascus, Israel and, presumably, the Arabs in the east. On the other hand, the tribute list from 734 shows that some of the coastal cities and many south Palestinian states supported the Assyrian dominion: Arwad, Ashqalon and Gaza joined by Judah, Ammon, Moab and Edom, now emerging as partners in the political game in Syria, probably aiming at balancing the 'axis' Tyre–Damascus–Samaria–Arabia.[104]

The agitation of the anti-Assyrian axis, however, made the Assyrian alliance dissolve. Ashqalon defected and, according to the Old Testament, also Edom.[105] When Judah stuck to the Assyrian alliance, the leaders of the anti-Assyrian front, Rezin in Damascus and Menaḥem's successor in Samaria, Peqaḥ, started the famous Syro-Ephraimitic war in order to force Judah to join them. According to 2 Kings 16:5–9, this was the immediate cause of Tiglath Pileser's intervention. The Assyrian eponym-list attributes both 733 and 732 to the operations against Damascus. In connection with Tiglath Pileser's Syrian campaigns in these years, we also possess a report about dealings with Arabs. The text about the Syrian campaigns of 734–732 BC in general is badly damaged in the Annals.[106] The summary inscriptions, however, mention them several times and from the different versions a coherent text of the *arab* episode can be restored. We follow the analysis of these passages made by I. Eph'al, complemented by H. Tadmor:

> As for Shamsi (sa-am-si), the queen of the KUR *a-ri-bi*, at Mount Shaqurri 9400 of [her] warriors I killed. 1000+x hundred people, 30,000 camels, 20,000 cattle, . . . 5000 [bags] of all kinds of spices, . . . pedestals, the resting places of her gods, . . . weapons (?), sceptres of her goddess [and] her property I seized. And she for the rescue of her life . . . to the desert, an arid place, like a wild-ass set her face. The rest of her tents, the might of her people, within her camp I set on fire. And Sa-am-si, who became terrified of my powerful weapons, brought camels, she-camels together with their young, to Assyria before me. I appointed a *qēpu* over her and 10,000 warriors . . . I made bow to my feet.[107]

The number of warriors and animals at the queen's command are considerable, if we are to believe the scribes in the Assyrian Ministry of Information and Propaganda. Even though the figures are exaggerated, it is obvious that the Arabs must have been an important partner in the alliance. We may also notice the first explicit occurrence of spices (*riqqē*) in connection with the Arabs. Unfortunately no information is given on which kinds of spice the bags contained. Noteworthy also is the emphasis laid on the capture of certain cultic utensils, as well as the capture of the queen's property. Shamsi was, however, obviously left intact as ruler, and she was thus luckier than her allies, the kings in Damascus and Samaria. Her status as a vassal was indicated by the appointment of a *qēpu*, an Assyrian politruk usually installed with the vassals to keep them alert in paying the tributes. Unfortunately, the exact position of Mount Shaqurri is not known, but it seems reasonable to place it somewhere in present-day Ǧabal ad-Durūz.[108]

We have another source for this episode, namely the reliefs from Tiglath Pileser's palace in Kalah, the so-called Central Palace. Although in a fragmentary state, they contain important supplementary information.[109] The Arab campaign was shown in a series of slabs which also described three other campaigns. The pictures were arranged in four parallel horizontal rows of which those depicting the Arab campaign were the second from the top. It shows the king himself seated on his throne in the centre. To his left we have pictures of the battle; to the right is shown the tribute paid by the Arabs after the defeat. In the battle scene should be noted two camels with riders.[110] At least one of them is riding on a cushion saddle, thus sitting on top of the hump, as on the relief from Tell Ḥalaf 150 years earlier.[111] The cushion saddle rider seems to be a woman, and it is tempting to identify her as Shamsi herself. One is reminded of the scene with ʕĀʔisha on the camel's back in the 'Battle of the Camel' at Baṣra in AD 657 Shamsi probably also appears among the tribute-payers, dressed in a long gown with her head covered.[112] She keeps a kind of bag in her right hand, which may well be one of the bags with spices mentioned in the text. In front of her, captive warriors are led, and behind her the animals are shown: camels, bovines, sheep and goats.[113]

The very fragmentary Annals insert the Shamsi episode in a chronological framework. In the thirteenth *palû* (= 733 BC) a siege of Damascus was followed by the campaign against Shamsi.[114] The Arab operation would thus have occurred late in the year 733 BC. After this followed the campaign through Galilee against Peqaḥ in Israel and the defeat of Mitinti in Ashqelon.[115]

The anti-Assyrian forces were thus crushed in Syria and the Arabs now appear as vassals of the Assyrian king. The impression gained from the Shamsi affair is that the wealth and power of the Arabs had increased and that Tiglath Pileser treated them rather mildly, being interested in the products they could provide: camels, cattle and spices. That the arrangement was to mutual satisfaction can be seen from the fact that Shamsi remained loyal to Assyria as late as the year 716.[116]

The relationship between Assyria and Shamsi during the reign of Tiglath Pileser is documented in a somewhat fragmentary letter:

> (1´) [. . . Ia]-ra-pa-a (2´) . . . the *rab kiṣir* (5´) will bring the (3´) . . . of the KUR *ar-ba-a-a* (4´) [up] to (the lady) Sam-si; (8´) he will bring (6´) those of (the lady) Sam-si (7´) [up] to the KUR *ar-ba-a-a*. (9´) Ia-ra-pa-a, the *rab kiṣir*, (10´) Ha-šil-a-nu, the *rab kiṣir*, (11´) Ga-na-bu, (12´) Ta-am-ra-a-nu, (13´) in all 4 people for the fugitives. (2) 62 Ha-šil-a-nu, (3) 63 Ia-ra-pa-a, (4) in all 124 stray camels.[117]

The *rab kiṣir* was an officer in command of smaller units.[118] The names may very well be Arabic.[119] In spite of the the fragmentary state of the text, some interesting conclusions can be drawn. If the names are Arabic, it looks as if the Assyrians have employed local people for handling camel traffic between Shamsi's Arabs and others, thus indicating peaceful relations. Most important is also the clear distinction between Shamsi and the *arbāya*. The text clearly speaks about some kind of exchange between Shamsi, queen of the *aribi,* and the *arbāya*, who are thus not identical.

In Tiglath Pileser's Summary Inscriptions there follows, immediately after the Shamsi episode, an account of the bringing of tribute from seven peoples in the same region. The names are the following:

1. Ma-as-'a-a-a
2. Te-ma-a-a
3. Sa-ba-'a-a
4. Ha-a-a-ap-pa-a-a
5. Ba-da-na-a-a
6. Ha-at-te-e-a
7. I-di-ba-'a-il-a-a[120]

Name no. 3 has the determinative LÚ, 'people', in one version and KUR, 'land', in the others. All other names have the 'land' sign, except no. 7 which has 'people' only. These groups are said to dwell 'on the border of the land of sunset' and '[their] dwelling is distant'. They are further said to bring gold, silver, camels, she-camels and all kinds of spices (*riqqē*) to the king.

The 'land of sunset' is Syria in general, and its border should be the line between the desert and the sown. One of the names we have already met, Hayapa, which is most likely to be the same as Ephah (ʕēpā), is one of the sons of Midyān, son of Qeṭurah (and Abraham).[121] As pointed out earlier, the sons of Midyān in the list of Qeṭurah's sons are likely to be later additions to the list of names of groups emerging later. The addition to that list represents changed ethnic conditions in the area from the latter half of the eighth century BC and a couple of centuries onwards, visible for the first time in this passage from Tiglath Pileser.

The name Sheba, written sa-ba-'a-a and probably pronounced Shabaʔ, which now appears for the first time in a dated source, is also found in the Qeṭurah complex as one of the two sons of Yoqshan, thus of the same 'generation' as the sons of Midian. We may conclude that this reflects their appearance in the same period as the 'sons of Midyan'. Since they are grouped together with Dedan, which is the present-day oasis al-ʕŪlā north of Medina, it is reasonable to assume that Shabaʔ in Tiglath Pileser's text are to be found not far from there. There is no indication that these are the South Arabian Sabaeans. This excludes neither a S(h)abaʔ in South Arabia at this period nor a connection between them and the Shabaʔ mentioned by Tiglath Pileser, but his Sabaeans are definitely in the Ḥiğāz.[122]

The presence of Sabaeans in north-western Ḥiğāz is sometimes seen as a proof of the frankincense traffic through western Arabia already in the eighth century BC and even before that date. The Sabaeans would thus have established a trading post in Dedan for control of the traffic.[123] It should, however, be observed that there is no mention of frankincense in the texts from this period, and that frankincense from South Arabia is explicitly mentioned for the first time in Syro-Palestinian and Greek sources from the end of the seventh century BC.[124]

The only clue to the identity of Badana so far is the mention of a tribe BDN in a Thamudic inscription in Sakāka close to Dumah, and in Ṣafaitic inscriptions closer to Syria, probably referring to the same tribe.[125] Of the others in the list, Masʔa, Tema and Idība'ila, are found in the Old Testament as three of Ishmael's twelve sons: Massā', Têmā' and ʔAdbʔel.[126] Têmā' is no doubt to be identified with present-day Taymāʔ, the famous oasis north-east of al-ʕŪlā. Massā' is mentioned in a somewhat later inscription from Taymāʔ.[127] In the list of Ishmael's sons, Massā' stands between Dumah on the northern shore of the Nafūd sand-desert and Taymāʔ.[128] The most likely location for them is thus around the western end of that desert.

The most interesting of these names for our purposes is Idibaʔil. In other passages in the Summary Inscriptions, Idibiʔilu is said to have been installed as *atûtu*, literally 'gatekeeper', 'in front of Muṣri'.[129] In the Annals we find a LÚ Idibiʔilu KUR *a-ru-bu* mentioned after the account of the campaign in Galilee and the defeat of the king of Ashqelon in Tiglath Pileser's thirteenth *palû,* thus: 'the tribe/the man Idibiʔil of the land of the Arabs'.[130] The identical form of the name of the gatekeeper in the Summary Inscriptions and the *arubu* in the Annals makes it most likely that both refer to the same man or group.

In the list of Ishmael's sons in the Old Testament, ʔAdbʔel stands as number three after Nebayot and Qedar and before Mibsam and Mishmaʕ, two groups located in the Negev by the Chronicler.[131] If we assume that Qedar at this time is found west of Dumah, and that Mibsam and Mishmaʕ before the time of the Chronicler were also east of the ʕArabah, ʔAdbʔel should also be looked for in that region.[132] In the Septuagint, ʔAdbʔel in the list of Ishmael's sons appears as Nabdeēl. This name reappears as an addition to the sons of Dedan together with Ragouēl in the list of the sons of Qeṭurah in the Septuagint. The latter is identical with Reʕuʔel, a name alternating with that of Jethro, the Midianite father-in-law of Moses. The updated list in the Septuagint seems to reflect a period when people in or at Dedan had some kind of control over ancient Midian. The Septuagint texts would thus reflect the Achaemenid period, when the Mineans in al-ʕŪlā controlled the frankincense traffic in north-western Arabia. ʔAdbʔel would thus, in that period, be located somewhere around ancient Midian.

Since Idibaʔil, the tribute-bearer in Tiglath Pileser's list, occurs together with other names known as the 'sons of Ishmael', the identification with ʔAdbʔel is quite certain. The identity of Idibi'il, the *arubu* and the gatekeeper against Egypt, with Idibaʔil/ʔAdbʔel the tribute-bringer is assumed by the most recent scholars, but is somewhat more uncertain.[133] According to the Annals, the appointment of Idibiʔil the *arubu* took place at the end of the campaign in 733 BC after the siege of Damascus, the Shamsi episode, the campaign in Galilee and the fall of Ashqelon.[134] This would indicate that the domain of this/these *arubu* was the western Negev just south-west of Ashqelon. Since the seven tributaries including Idibaʔil, who is most likely to be identical with ʔAdbʔel, probably lived east of the Arabah, the conclusion is that Idiba'il in the tribute list is not identical with Idibi'il the *arubu*.

The similarity of names, however, makes it reasonable to assume that they still have some kind of identity. A tentative interpretation is that Idibiʔil the gatekeeper in fact was a group or perhaps a chief from Idibaʔil who were/was transferred from the original habitat east of the ʕArabah and installed between Philistaea and the Egyptian border as guard. This would mean that the tribute of the seven peoples had occurred before the operations in Philistaea. In that case their pledge of subjugation would most probably have occurred as a direct consequence of the Shamsi episode. It would indicate a quite friendly relationship between Assyria and the shepherding peoples of north-western Arabia at this time.

None of the seven peoples in Tiglath Pileser's list are said to be Arabs. If Idibi'il on the Muṣri border is indeed to be understood as a group of Arabs, we have here, for the first time, documentation of Arabs as guardians of frontiers, a function which, as we shall see, they often performed in antiquity. In that case, one could speculate whether the designation *arubu* has something to do with this function.

Excursus: the earliest Arabs in the Old Testament

There is more than one century between the appearance of Arabs on the Syrian side in the battle of Qarqar and their mention in Tiglath Pileser's inscriptions. In the account of the Chronicler covering the century between these two dates, we find four passages mentioning Arabs. We do not find any reference to Arabs in the corresponding passages in the Deuteronomistic history (the Books of Kings). The identification and geographical location of the Arabs are dependent upon the mentioning of other identifiable groups in the same context. There is also the question about the historical reliability of the reports of the Chronicler which, generally, has been estimated as very low, although there is agreement that he had access to sources not used by the Deuteronomists.[135]

Three passages deal with conditions in the middle of the ninth century BC and the fourth with the time of Tiglath Pileser. The first passage claims to refer to an event roughly contemporary with the battle at Qarqar during the reign of Jehoshaphaṭ of Judah (*c*. 870–845 BC):[136]

> Also some of the Philistines brought Jehoshaphaṭ presents and tribute in silver; and the *ʕarbîʔîm* [*ʕarbîm* MSS] brought him flocks, seven thousand and seven hundred rams, and seven thousand and seven hundred goats.[137]

The Chronicler adduces another notice dealing with the reign of Jehoshaphaṭ's successor, J(eh)oram (–843/42 BC), which is more precise:

> Moreover, the Lord stirred against Jehoram the spirit of the Philistines, and of the *ʕarbîm* that were near the *kûšîm*: and they came up into Judah, and broke into it, and carried away all the substance that was found in the king's house,

> and his sons also, and his wives, so that there was never a son left him, save Jehoʔaḥaz, the youngest of his sons.[138]

We are told some more details about this event in a notice about the succession of J(eh)oram in 843 BC:

> MT: And the inhabitants of Jerusalem made *ʔAḥazyā*, his [i.e. Jehoram's] youngest son, king after him; for all the others the throng (*ha-gdûd*) who had brought the *ʕarbîm* to the camp had killed.
>
> LXX: And the inhabitants of Jerusalem made Okhozias, his young son, king after him; for all the older ones the band of robbers had killed which had come over them: the *arábioi* [var.: *zambri*] and the *alimazoneîs*.[139]

ʔAḥazyā and Yehoʔaḥaz are two forms of a name with identical meaning and refer to the same person. The Masoretic text talks about two entities, the *gdûd* and the *ʕarbîm*, where the latter seem to be in some kind of dependence upon the former: the *gdûd* 'has brought the *ʕarbîm*'. The Septuagint, however, talks about two equal groups.[140] The variant reading *zambri* reflects a name pronounced Zimri in Masoretic Hebrew, a name found in the Arabic onomasticon.[141] The ruler toppled by Omri was called Zimri. Was he an *ʕarbî* too? We are also reminded of Zimrān, who is the southernmost entity in the Qeṭurah list, i.e. south of Midian, where also the *alimazoneîs* are located.[142]

The fourth passage deals with the Judaean king Uzziah/Azariah (788–736 BC). Due to inner weakness in Assyria at the beginning of the eighth century BC, the Israelite kingdom was allowed to exercise a short-lived domination over the whole of southern Syria under Jeroboam II until his death in 748.[143] One hundred years after the fall of the house of Omri, the house of Jehu had a short time of supremacy in southern Syria.[144] Also the kings of the house of David were able to strengthen their positions. The Chronicler tells the following about king Uzziah in Judah:

> (6) And he went forth and warred against the Philistines, and broke down the wall of Gath, and the wall of Jabneh, and the wall of Ashdod, and built cities about Ashdod, and among the Philistines. (7) And God helped him against the Philistines, and against the *ʕarbiyîm* (K)/*ʕarbîm* (Q) that dwell in Gur-Baʕal [LXX: the *árabes* living on 'the rock'] and the *meʕûnîm* [LXX: the *minaîoi*; Vulgate: *Ammonitae*]. (8) And the Ammonites [LXX: the *minaîoi*] gave gifts to Uzziah; and his name spread about even to the entering in of Egypt; for he strengthened himself exceedingly.[145]

The textual tradition is shaky in this passage. The Septuagint renders verse 7: 'the '*árabes* on (*epì*) the rock (*pétra*) and against the *minaîoi*'. The Vulgate gives Turbaal for Gur Baʕal, thus indicating a reading *ṭûr*, the Aramaic word for 'mountain'. We may notice that the Septuagint has not read *baʕal* but *w-ʕal* 'and against'. The Targum says that the 'Arabs' live 'in Gerar' (*bi-grar*), i.e. a city in the north-western Negev close to Philistaea.[146]

Scholars commenting on these passages have more or less explicitly agreed upon the location of the *meʕûnîm*, the *kûshîm* and, consequently, the *ʕarbîm* in the western

Negev, close to Philistaea.[147] In the notes about Jehoshaphaṭ and Uzziah, the *ʕarbîm* are mentioned after the Philistines, which is taken as an indication that they must have lived close to their land. Since, in the first note about Jehoram, the *ʕarbîm* are explicitly said to dwell near the *kûshîm*, a location of these could be a clue to the whereabouts of the *ʕarbîm*. Similarly, the exact location of the *meʕûnîm* in the Uzziah story might also be of help in determining where the Arabs dwelt.

These two groups are mentioned by the Chronicler in other contexts as well. He reports that Jehoshaphaṭ's predecessor, Asa, was attacked by the *kûshîm* under their leader Zeraḥ. After having beaten them 'in the valley of Ṣfātā, at Mārešā', he pursued them until the town in the Masoretic text called Gerar, in the Septuagint and the Syriac Peshitta called Gedōr/Gdārā. Asa is said to have taken booty consisting of small cattle and camels.[148] The last verse of the story reads:

> MT: And even tents of cattle they slew and took small cattle as booty, exceedingly, and camels. Then they returned to Jerusalem.
>
> LXX: And having taken the tents, they cut down the *amazoneîs* and took much small cattle (sheep) and camels and turned back to Jerusalem.
>
> Peshitta: And even the tents of the *ʕarbāyē* they brought and took small cattle as booty, a great number for good and camels and they brought [them?] to Jerusalem.[149]

The *meʕûnîm* are mentioned twice in the Masoretic texts to the Old Testament: the one about king Uzziah just quoted, and in 1 Chronicles 4:41. In the latter, we have a notice connected with the traditions of the tribe of Simeon. The Chronicler gives a list of thirteen names intended to be understood as Simeonites (vv. 34–37). Then it is said:

> (38) These bringing names (?), chiefs in their clans and their lineages spread out and became numerous. (39) And they went to the entrance of Gedor (*limbo' gdor*; LXX: Gerar; Peshitta: Gādār), unto the east side of the valley (*ʕad lmizraḥ haggayʔ*), to seek pasture for their flocks. (40) And they found fat and good pasture, and the land was wide and quiet and peaceable; for some Hamites dwelt there before. (41) And these written by name came in the days of Hezekiah, king of Judah, and smote their tents and the Meunites (K: *hammeʕînîm*; Q: *hammeʕûnîm*; LXX: *minaíous*; Targum: *mʕntʔ*, 'dwellings') that were found there and destroyed them utterly unto this day. (42) And some of them, some of the sons of Simeon, went to mount Seʕir (Peshitta: the mountain of Gbal), five hundred men . . . and smote the rest of the refugees of the ʕAmāleq and dwelt there to this day.

In the story of Uzziah's conquests the *meʕûnîm* are mentioned together with the Ammonites, i.e. a Transjordanian people. That constellation may also originally have appeared in another passage dealing with a war during the reign of Jehoshaphaṭ:

> After that came the Moabites, the Ammonites and with them some **meʕûnîm* (MT *mehāʕammônîm*, LXX: *ek tōn meinaíōn*) to wage war against Jehoshaphaṭ.[150]

This story is almost pure theology and probably goes back to descriptions of a religious rite rather than an historical event. The appearance of the peoples reflects, however, historical realities. The MT has 'Ammonites' as the third people among the attackers, which is usually emended to *meʕûnîm* in accordance with the Septuagint, a most likely emendation.[151]

The commentators have accepted the mention of the town Gerar in the Masoretic text to the Asa story and in the Septuagint text to the story about the Simeonites and located the *kûshîm* and *meʕûnîm* in the south-west, south of Philistaea, near Gerar.[152] As we have seen, the Targum can also be adduced as a proof for the location of the *meʕûnîm* near Gerar, since it locates the *meʕûnîm* and the *ʕarbîm* in the Uzziah story there. In that story, the *ʕarbîm* are followed by the *meʕûnîm* and the Ammonites, of which the first are likewise claimed to have dwelt near Philistaea, i.e. in the western Negev.[153]

A further argument for this south-western location of the *meʕûnîm* and, consequently, also of the *ʕarbîm* and the *kûshîm* is a passage in the Summary Inscriptions of Tiglath Pileser, thus a contemporary source. Having described his actions against Gaza, the king tells about Si-ru-at-ti, king or chief of the the KUR *mu-'-na-a-a*. They are said to dwell *šapal* (= below) *KUR Muṣri*.[154] Since Muṣri is said to be Egypt, the *mu-'-na-a-a*, identified with the *meʕûnîm*, must have dwelt between Gaza and the Egyptian border.[155]

We shall here argue for another location, suggesting that all the passages in question deal with areas south-east of Palestine, south-east of the ʕArabah, which is south of the Dead Sea. The *ʕarbîm, kûshîm* and *meʕûnîm* all belong to the area between Ammon-Moab and Midian, i.e. partly the land of Edom.[156] The location close to Philistaea is due to an early interpretation of the Asa story, locating the events told in it in south-western Judaea. This interpretation has influenced the versions of some of the other passages to replace the town name Gedor by Gerar. The arguments are the following:

There is no doubt that the Masoretic text as it now stands locates Asa's battle with the *kûshîm* in south-western Judaea/Philistaea/western Negev. This is shown by the mention of the town Maresha. These *kûshîm* have often been identified with Ethiopians, or rather Nubians, and the story of Asa's war has therefore been rejected either as unhistorical or as perhaps referring to the Egyptian pharaoh Osorkon of the 22nd Libyan Dynasty. The identification with Osorkon seems, however, to have lost its supporters nowadays.[157] Further, the term Kush in the Old Testament does not only designate Nubia. In certain passages it is used for a region in Midian, i.e. northern Ḥiǧāz.[158] The name of their leader in the battle against Asa, Zeraḥ, occurs as the name of a clan variously attributed to Edom/Esau, Judah, Simeon and Levi, all tribal groups living south or south-east of Palestine.[159] The name is in fact likely to refer to the same entity. In that case one could suspect that they were originally settled close to the ʕArabah but in later times moved into the eastern Negev. Not only Zeraḥ but also the *kûshîm* should be found there. The *arbîm* would then also belong to the same area.

As far as the location of the *ʕarbîm*, the *kûshîm* and the *meʕûnîm* in the western Negev is concerned, the main argument is the location of the latter close to Gerar in the story about the wanderings of Simeon and the operations of Asa around the same town. In all passages the name Gerar alternates with Gedor in the textual tradition. The Asa story originally dealt with a 'royal razzia' against shepherding groups south of Judah, later reworked into one about a battle against a gigantic army beaten by Asa with divine help. The latter version is the expansion of the Chronicler, the former probably the story found in his source.[160] The battle takes place in 'the valley towards Ṣephat'.

Ṣephat is mentioned once more, namely in Judges 1:17, i.e. in a collection of short texts about the wars of the Judaean tribes. It was conquered by Judah and Simeon and renamed Ḥormah. The latter is situated in the Negev. In Judges 1 it is mentioned together with ʕArad, which is actually in the eastern Negev, and it is most likely that Ḥormah was in the same region. It has been identified with either Tell el-Milḥ or Tell Mashāsh/Masos between Beer Shevaʕ and ʕArad.[161] The name of the town Gedor preserved in the versions is probably the original and represents a *lectio difficilior*: Gerar is well known from the stories about Abraham and Isaac but nobody has ever heard of Gedor.[162]

If Gedor etc. are the original names in the story, we are so close to the ʕArabah that the origin of the *kûshîm* etc., Gedor included, east of the ʕArabah becomes most likely. But if Gedor was the original reading in all passages, whence comes Gerar? A plausible explanation is that a later targumic-minded scribe or commentator associated the *kûshîm* in the Asa story with the better-known Nubians. Perhaps the existence of the North Arabian *kûshîm* was forgotten. If he interpreted Kûsh as belonging to the Nile valley, a location of the battle at Mareshah in south-western Judaea was very natural: that was the entrance from Egypt to Syria from times immemorial. He also knew of the well-known town of Gerar there and he might well have seen the name Gedor as a misspelling of the more famous town.[163] The association of the *kûshîm* with Philistaea was easy since it was mentioned in the context.[164]

The story about Asa's battle with the *kûshîm* would thus be the source of the confusion between Gedor and Gerar and, consequently, the transfer of the *kûshîm*, the *ʕarbîm* and the *meʕûnîm* from the areas around ʕArabah to the border between Philistaea, Judaea and the western Negev.[165]

In the Jehoshaphaṭ story in 2 Chronicles 20 the 'Ammonites', i.e. the *meʕûnîm*, are called 'the sons of the inhabitants of Mount Seʕir' or 'the sons of Mount Seʕir' in vv. 10, 22 and 23. They are said to come 'from ʔAram beyond the sea' which indicates an area east or south-east of the Dead Sea.[166] Seʕir probably referred originally to the mountains on the western side of the ʕArabah but is also identified with Edom, thus encompassing the areas on both sides.[167] Musil identified 'the valley' with present-day al-Ǧī by Petra, but the *gayʔ* could also be the ʕArabah itself.[168] In both cases the *meʕûnîm* would have been living on its eastern side. Not far from Petra on the eastern side there is an area named Kdhūr, which is an expected Arabic form of Gedor.[169] One should also compare the name Maʕān in southern Jordan not far from Wādī Ram. The Gur where the *ʕarbîm* lived has been identified with Yagûr in Joshua 15:21, which was situated somewhere south of Judaea, but this is highly uncertain.[170] Another suggestion locates it east of Beer Sheba, which is more attractive.[171] As we have seen, both the LXX and the Vulgate have read 'mountain' like the Peshitta, which might be an identification from the early Hellenistic period.[172]

The location of the *mu-'-na-a-a* in Tiglath Pileser's inscription in the western Negev only holds if Muṣri is defined as the part of Egypt that stretches along the Mediterranean. If Muṣri, in fact, covers not only the Nile valley but the entire area counted as the Egyptian sphere of interest in the Negev and the Sinai peninsula, we are not obliged to locate the *meʕûnîm* at the border to Philistaea. The expression 'below Egypt' is quite vague. If the expression means 'close to the border of' (which is not certain) we could as well be in the ʕArabah. There is a clear break in the text indicated by a straight line after the mention of the king of Gaza. In the new paragraph, the *mu-'-na-a-a* are followed by the story of the campaign against the queen of the *aribi*, Shamsi, who are definitely to be located in Transjordan.[173] Since the Summary Inscriptions do not treat the military activities in chronological order but according to geography, the *mu-'-na-a-a* episode could as well be connected with the Shamsi episode as with that about Gaza. It is difficult to see that Tiglath Pileser's inscription definitely settles the *mu-'-na-a-a* close to Philistaea.

In the story about Jehoshaphaṭ's war, as well as in the Uzziah story and in Tiglath Pileser's inscription, the *meʕûnîm* are mentioned together with Transjordanian peoples. The fact that in the textual tradition they even alternate with Ammonites is another indication that they are to be located close to them.[174]

The only definite argument for locating the *meʕûnîm* in the western Negev is the mention of the town Gerar in the Septuagint version of the story about the Simeonites in 1 Chronicles 4. But that text cannot be taken as an unequivocal testimony about the settlement of the *meʕûnîm* at Gerar. Gerar is not mentioned in the MT in this passage, only in the LXX. Considering the documented tendency of that text to update geographical data, one should not accept its testimony unless with very good reason. The reading Gedor in MT is *lectio difficilior*, supported by the Peshitta, and is to be preferred. There is an authentic ring in the realistic figure of 500 men, a realism which is not according to the practice of the Chronicler. One could also point to the names in the introduction to the texts (vv. 34–37). Many of them end in *-ʔel*, which is a type of name that reappears in Numbers 3 and 7, i.e. the Priestly writings. To this source also points the term for the chiefs, *nasî*. It is obvious that the story represents a special source, different from the others in Chronicles.[175] A closer reading of the whole story reveals several interesting cracks. The names in vv. 34–37 do not occur in other lists of the Simeonites and they are abruptly introduced after the enumeration of the (other) Simeonites. There are unclear references in the text: whose are the tents which are destroyed together with the *meʕûnîm* in v. 41? A solution to these problems is to assume that the text does not deal with the Simeonites at all but is a fragment of a story that has been secondarily attached to the traditions about Simeon. The expression 'even the sons of Simeon' in v. 42 is a gloss gluing the story to that of Simeon. According to this analysis, the story should be read as follows: an unnamed group (the introduction to the story is lost) became numerous and settled around Gedor, inhabited by Hamites, because of the rich pasture (vv. 38b–41). Then the people represented by the thirteen names in vv. 34–37 came and destroyed the unnamed people together with the *meʕînîm*/*meʕûnîm* living there. Some of them, either the people of the thirteen or perhaps a remnant of the unnamed one, went on to Mount Seʕir, which means that they crossed the ʕArabah, killed ʕAmāleq and settled there.

> According to P. Welten, the passage about Uzziah in 2 Chron. 26:7–8 reflects conditions in the Chronicler's own time, and the mention of the *meʕûnîm* refers to the settlement of Edom in southern Judaea, which took place in the period of the Exile and later.[176] This is, however, a circular argument. Since the Arabs in the passage are located in the south-west, the *meʕûnîm* have to be there too since they occur in the same context. Conversely, since the *meʕûnîm* are the Edomites settled in Judaea after the exile, the Arabs must also be living in the same area. But it cannot be categorically stated that the passage only deals with the south-west since the Ammonites are mentioned too. The identification of Gur with Yagur is not certain. And if the *meʕûnîm* are the Edomites, why does the Chronicler not call them so, as he was very familiar with them? In fact, the *meʕûnîm* are not explicitly called Edomites anywhere in the Chronicles. That they seem to come from the same area is another matter.

> One scholar, E. A. Knauf, has seen the difficulties and has dissolved the *meʕûnîm* into three different groups: those in Tiglath Pileser's inscriptions in southern Palestine or northern Sinai (which are not quite the same), those in 2 Chronicles 20:1 in Moab in Transjordan, and those in 1 Chronicles 4: 41 and 20:7 around Gaza, identical with the South Arabian Mineans.[177] But this solution is unnecessary if one can show that all point to southern Transjordan. *Entia non sunt multiplicanda praeter necessitatem.*

In the reports about events in the middle of the ninth century, the Septuagint clearly associates the *ʕarbîm* of the MT with areas in ancient Midian. The *alimazoneîs* in the ʔAḥazyah story are most probably to be connected with the *amazoneîs* in the Asa story and should be compared to the *Banizomeneîs* or *Batmizomaneîs* mentioned by Agatharcides from Cnidus in the second century BC as living east of the inlet to the Gulf of ʕAqabah.[178] The variant reading *zambri* in the LXX text to the story about the attack against J(eh)oram might likewise reflect an identification with people from Midian. In the same way, the LXX locates the *árabes* as well as the *minaîoi* in the passage about Uzziah east of the ʕArabah. In the latter passage, there is no direct contradiction to the Masoretic text, even though we have no immediate information where Gur Baʕal is. The Septuagint shows a tendency to update the text in accordance with conditions of the day, a tendency often found both there and in the targums. The identification of the *meʕûnîm* with the Mineans, who from the fourth century BC dwelt in Dedan, also has a targumic flavour, reflecting the time of the LXX. The Masoretic text is, on the whole, preferable in the Uzziah passage, offering *lectiones difficiliores* which are comprehensible, and supports a location of the *meʕûnîm* east of the ʕArabah.[179]

It is also worthwhile to quote the version of Uzziah's campaign found in Josephus' *Antiquities*. He describes Uzziah's operations against the Philistines. Then it is said:

> After this campaign he went against the *árabes* who were neighbours to Egypt and having founded a city by the Red Sea he stationed a garrison there. Then he subdued the *Ammanîtai*.[180]

Even though the passage can be interpreted in different ways, the most natural interpretation is that the campaign against the Philistines and the *árabes* are separated, and that the founding of a city by the Red Sea is connected with the operation against the *árabes*. The location of both would thus be the ʕArabah and Elath. The association between the Arabs and the Red Sea is found neither in the Masoretic text nor in the versions and may well preserve a concrete historical memory. A fortification of Elath by Uzziah is, in fact, mentioned in both Kings and Chronicles without mentioning the Arabs.[181] The closeness to Egypt, the Muṣur of Tiglath Pileser, explicitly mentioned by Josephus, should be observed.

The testimony of the Chronicler shows the *meʕûnîm* as dwellers in the southern ʕArabah or on its eastern slopes, i.e. in the land of Edom, perhaps in the region around modern Maʕān.[182] This does not mean that the *meʕûnîm* were Edomites. The Chronicler makes a clear distinction between Edom and *meʕûnîm*. The latter may well represent a pre-Edomite population in the region, memories of which are preserved in Chronicles. All evidence taken together makes it likely that the *ʕarbîm* mentioned in the story about Uzziah are to be located close to the *meʕûnîm* and the Ammonites, i.e. east of the ʕArabah. Since the presence of peoples called Arabs in that area is well documented in the contemporary inscriptions of Tiglath Pileser III, it becomes likely that the Chronicler has indeed preserved historical memories going back to that period.[183]

It seems that the Chronicler had access to an old source, which he transformed for his own theological puposes.[184] An indication of an old source for the report about the attack of the *ʕarbîm* in the days of Joram is the fact that in the D-version in the Book of Kings, Joram's marriage to Athaliah is the only notice about his family life.[185] The name of their son and Joram's successor is Ahaziah = *ʔaḥaz-yah*, 'YHWH has taken'. This information is repeated by the Chronicler. But in our passage we notice that Joram's and Athaliah's son is called Yeho-ʔaḥaz, thus another form of the name (with the same meaning). The Chronicler also mentions the *wives* of Joram. In a preceding passage (vv. 2–4) six brothers of Jehoram are mentioned as being killed by him. It is clear that we have here a tradition different from the one found in 2 Kings, which is unlikely to be an invention by the Chronicler.

The stories about the *ʕarbîm* in Chronicles belong to a larger group of stories about the wars of the Judaean tribes and the Judaean kings against the surrounding peoples. In Chronicles we find at least two accounts of the wars of the tribes: the story about Simeon and the war of Reuben against peoples in Transjordan.[186] These stories are very similar to those in Judges, Chapter 1, which deal with the same matter. All these very short stories have a Judaean perspective. The Judaean tribes are the actors and the operations are often seen as divinely ordained.[187] The latter also holds for the stories where the Judaean kings are the leaders. The 'stories of royal razzias' belong to the same type as those of David and his wars with the Philistines, where divine oracles also play a main role.[188] The royal, tribal and Judaean perspectives in this material lead to the assumption that it was collected in the late Judaean period, i.e. between the time of Ezekiah and the destruction of the Temple.

This insight increases the value of these stories as a historical source. Several scholars have expressed the opinion that the Chronicler in the story of the tribute to Jehoshaphaṭ had access to old sources not used by the Deuteronomistic authors of the Book of Kings.[189] One scholar, N. Na'aman, has convincingly argued for the existence of ancient source material at least for the war of Asa, the wanderings of the Simeonites and the conquests of Uzziah.[190] The transfer of the Arabs to the western Negev probably also reflects conditions in the Achaemenid age. The source material used by the Chronicler must thus be older, describing conditions before the rise of the Edomite kingdom.

Even though the report about the tribute to Jehoshaphaṭ and the attack of the *ʕarbîm* on Jehoram are influenced by other passages, there is nothing unlikely in the stories themselves. The fact that the Arabs appear as shepherds of small cattle in the middle of the ninth century BC is reminiscent of the reports by the Assyrian kings from Tukulti Ninurta from the same age onwards and especially Tiglath Pileser in 738 BC, where, as we have seen, Arabs pay tribute in animals: camels and small cattle. Such tribute is also reported to have been paid by other surrounding peoples to the Judaean kings in the ninth century BC, such as the Moabite king Meshaʕ.[191] The *ʕarbîm* paying tribute to Jehoshaphaṭ fit nicely with the documented presence of shepherding Arabs in the ninth century BC and later. There are thus good indications that the participation of Arabs at Qarqar reflects the importance of the small cattle herdsmen and camel-keepers for the main powers of southern Syria. We catch a glimpse of these Arabs providing mainly the kings and their housholds with food and clothing, together with access to the new means of transportation: the camel. We should notice the absence of any reference to frankincense or gold in connection with them, another fact which supports the historicity of the accounts.

The friendly relations between the Israelite kings and the Arabs in the days of Jehoshaphaṭ calls to mind a rather remarkable fact, namely that Omri, who founded a strong Israelite dynasty lasting from *c.* 885 to 841 BC, has a name which reappears centuries later as Arabic. Names formed from the root ʕMR like ʕUmar and ʕAmr are well-known Arabic names to this day. The use of the -ī suffix is found in the Arabic names in Tiglath Pileser's texts, like Shams-i and probably Zabib-ie. The name Ahab (ʔAḥ-ʔab = the 'Father' (= the protecting god) is the brother) is also found in the later Arabic onomasticon.[192] That Omri was a usurper to the throne is evident and it is indeed a fascinating hypothesis that the presence of Arabs at Qarqar may have been due not only to common political and economic interests but also to personal ties between them and the Israelite king.[193]

From the reports in the Book of Kings it is evident that Jehoshaphaṭ was a partner in the south Syrian alliance, since he was united with king Ahab through the marriage of his son Joram to Ahab's daughter Athaliah, who was probably the granddaughter of the king of Tyre.[194] In reality he may have been Ahab's vassal. A reflection of their common interests and influence in Transjordan is found in the difficult story of the war against king Meshaʕ of Moab in 2 Kings 3, in which one may notice the role played by domestic animals.[195] It has been suggested that there was an attempt to revive the Solomonic routes to Arabia in the days of Jehoshaphaṭ and to re-establish a route Arabia–Judah–Tyre in collaboration with the large Syrian alliance.[196] We remember the attempts of the same king to build ships at Eṣyon Geber by the Red Sea for sailing to Ophir.[197]

The attack by the *ʕarbîm* under Joram could be a repercussion of the political changes in the middle of the 840s BC when the south Syrian alliance broke up after having successfully withstood several Assyrian attacks. There are reports in the Book of Kings, repeated by Chronicles, that Edom revolted and established a kingdom during Joram's reign.[198] This must have been a serious reduction in the power of Judah, which now lost the remaining control it may have had over the trade route to Arabia as well as its port by the Red Sea. The break-up of the alliance with the Arabs is thus in tune with what we know about the development in Syrian politics in this period.[199]

The presence of Arabs in the neighbourhood of Judah in the middle of the eighth century BC is thus probably not an anachronism. The expansion of Judah to the south-west and south-east in the reign of Uzziah (783–742) is fully likely and may even be supported by archaeological evidence.[200] These activities may be dated to the late period of Uzziah's reign when the control by Israel under Jeroboam II of Judaean affairs began to weaken. The names in the quoted passage obviously list the enemies of Judah from the west (Philistaea) eastwards. The *ʕarbîm* and the *meʕûnîm* thus appear to dwell somewhere between the Philistines and the Ammonites. Evidence shows that they were closer to the latter than to the former.

We may thus conclude that the *ʕarbîm* mentioned in four passages in Chronicles originate in an old source containing short notices about the conflicts between settled Judaea and the surrounding peoples down to the time of Ezekiah. These *ʕarbîm* dwelt somewhere east of the ʕArabah in, or close to, the lands of Edom and Midian. They may well be identical with those governed by queen Shamsi. Close to them lived the *kûshîm* and the *meʕûnîm*. Since the former are associated with Midian and the latter could be located just south of Ammon-Moab, the *ʕarbîm* could be located in between.

In the Greek version of Isaiah, Chapter 10, there is an interesting paragraph not found in the Masoretic text. In a speech describing the haughtiness and self-confidence of Assyria, the MT says: 'For he will say: "Are not all my generals together kings?/Is not Kalneh like Carchemish?/Is not Hamath like Arpad?/Indeed! Samaria is like Damascus!"' The meaning is, of course, that all these cities have been taken by Assyria and Samaria will go the same way. This refers mainly to Tiglath Pileser's activities in Syria in the 730s BC. The LXX version reads:

> And if they say to him: 'You are sole ruler', he will say: 'Did I not take the land above Babylon and Kalannē whose tower was built? And I took Arabia, Damascus and Samaria'.[201]

The LXX is obviously based on a *Vorlage* different from the Masoretic text. It is not easy to say whether one is better than the other. The MT refers to several known victories of Tiglath Pileser and possibly his successor Sargon II in northern Syria, whereas LXX only mentions Kalneh, taken by Tiglath Pileser in 740 BC. But in adding Arabia to the conquests in the south, it looks very much as if it has preserved a concrete piece of information confirmed by Tiglath Pileser's own records. Nowhere in the Hebrew tradition do we hear about the conquest of Arabia by this Assyrian king. Nor is it known from Greek sources. It is only known from his own annals and summary inscriptions, which do not seem to have been available for reading after the reign of Esarhaddon until 1850 AD.[202]

There are, however, traces of a source which may have told about Tiglath Pileser's conquest, which was transmitted among the Jews and thus may have influenced the Biblical text reflected in the LXX. The book of Judith is assumed to have been written in the Hasmonean period *c.* 100 BC.[203] The many anachronisms and inconsistencies in the historical references of the book have given grey hairs to many scholars who have tried to see it as an historical document.[204] The setting of the story is a war waged by Nebuchadnezzar, 'king of the Assyrians in Nineveh', against 'Arpachsad, king of Media'. When Nebuchadnezzar calls upon all other kings to assist him, those in Syria, Palestine and Egypt refuse to take part. After having defeated Media, he sends out his general Holophernes to inflict punishment on the recalcitrant Westerners. The description of the route of the army runs as follows:

> (21) They marched from Nineveh three days to the plain of Bektileth and put their camp at Bektileth by the mountain that is north of Upper Cilicia. (22) And he (Holophernes) took his whole army, the foot soldiers, the cavalry and his chariots and marched from there to the hill country. (23) He broke through Phud and Lud and took booty from all the sons of Rassis and the sons of Ismael [living] towards the desert, southwards of [the land] of Kheleōn. (24) And he crossed the Euphrates, marched through Mesopotamia, destroying all the fortified cities along the river Abronas until the sea. (25) He conquered the borders of Cilicia and struck down all who withstood him and then went to the lands of Iapheth southwards against *Arabía*. (26) And he surrounded all the sons of Madiam and burnt their tents and plundered their encampments [*mándra*]. And he descended unto the plain of Damascus at the time of the harvest and burnt all their fields.[205]

The Mesopotamian ruler in this story is the Babylonian king Nebuchadnezzar. He is known to have made a campaign against the Arabs in the western Syrian desert in 599 BC, and it would have been reasonable to see the text in Judith as a reflection of that event. But it is worth observing that the campaign against the Arabs in this story is not performed by him but by another ruler. A closer look at the geography also gives some interesting hints. The plain of Bektileth near Cilicia has been identified with a people south of Antioch called *bakataïlloi* by Ptolemy.[206] Phud and Lud are more uncertain but are probably an echo from verses in Jeremiah and Hezechiel.[207] It will be shown below that the Lûdîm in Genesis 10:13 are to be sought in Palestine.[208] The sons of Rassis should be linked with the name ar-Rass found in aṭ-Ṭabarī's story of Nebuchadnezzar's campaign, located in the western Syrian desert, as well as with the Septuagint reading Rhōs instead of Buz in Jeremiah's wine-cup vision in Jeremiah 25:18–26.[209] They are close to the Ismaelites who live 'towards the desert'. The following expression is ambiguous. Literally the text says 'southwards of that (fem.) of Kheleōn'.[210] It is unclear whether this pertains to the desert or to the Ishmaelites. The expression probably means 'the southern part of Kheleōn' (or of the *Kheleoi). The name is uncertain but it should be compared with the name Khelous in Judith 1:9. This is, according to the context, located between Batane, i.e. Bashan, and Qadesh on the way to 'the Brook of Egypt'. We seem to be somewhere south or south-east of Palestine.[211] Since Ishmael in the Old Testament is said to live 'from Ḥawilah to Shur which is towards Egypt', it may be suggested that Kheleōn in Judith is a form of the name Ḥawilah. This name appears in much later Greek sources as Khaulotaîoi and is located in the Syrian desert.[212] This suits quite well the picture given in Judith.

The Mesopotamian campaign (verse 24) can be left out for the moment. It has been suggested that Iapheth is in fact Midianite Ephah (ʕEphā).[213] On the other hand, Japheth is an old designation for the Philistines and may well stand for their land. As is well known, Holophernes' campaign ends at a place called Bethoulia, which according to the book should be located somewhere in Samaria. There the end of the career of the brutal general is told in terms definitely belonging to the world of mythology.

The description of Holophernes' route fits remarkably well with what we know about Tiglath Pileser's activities in the years 734–732 BC, even though the identification of some of the place-names remains somewhat uncertain. It is much further from what we know about Nebuchadnezzar's campaign in 599 BC. The mustering of all the kings in the west reported in the first chapter of Judith fits well with the picture of Tiglath Pileser's activities in northern Syria in 743–738 BC although the war with Arpachsad of Media seems to reflect the Assyrian campaigns against Urartu.[214] If we leave out verse 24, we have an account of a campaign from Cilicia down the Levantine coast to Philistaea and the western Negev, followed by the operations against Arabs in Midian and the capture of Damascus. And since the story is a Jewish version of the event, it is natural that the main part revolves around operations in Samaria, which is miraculously saved. There are good reasons to assume that behind the story in the book of Judith lies a popular account of the dramatic events during the final Assyrian conquest of Syria in the 730s BC. The author of the book of Judith has used a novel or collection of stories about Nebuchadnezzar and combined it with a story of the chaste woman who kills an enemy by cutting off his head and saving her people from thirst.[215] This is a well-known folk-tale motif in Near Eastern literature, ultimately going back to a myth.[216] But it is not impossible that this story is in fact a mythological expression of the memories of the very events in Samaria in 733–732 BC.

As the story stands, Nebuchadnezzar is the king, but this is the result of the story's incorporation in a Nebuchadnezzar romance which ascribes episodes from several Mesopotamian rulers like Sargon II and Nabonidus to him.[217] If the original protagonist of the story is Tiglath Pileser III, this would explain why Nebuchadnezzar is king of Assyria, not Babylonia. It then becomes very likely that the quoted passage in the Septuagint alludes to the contents of this source. The memory of the dramatic events in the 730s BC was transmitted outside the walls of the palace in Kalah, which were torn down by Esarhaddon, and the blocks of which, containing Tiglath Pileser's inscriptions, were reused for a new building and remained unread for 2,500 years.

Sargon II

Nothing is known about Arabs from the reign of Tiglath Pileser's successor, Shalmaneser V. The next appearance of Arabs in datable sources is during the reign of Sargon II (722–705 BC). In order to be able to judge the data from Sargon, we have to give an orientation about the problems of the sources for his reign.

From Sargon II we have a large corpus of annalistic texts. These include the Annals proper, which were put up in the palace in his new capital Dūr Sharrukīn, present-day Khorsabad. Annals are also found on several prisms from different parts of the empire. Together, these form the basis for the chronology of Sargon's reign. The contents are then supplied with non-chronological summary inscriptions, as a rule also written on prisms.

A problem with Sargon's annalistic texts is, however, that the dating differs between the Khorsabad annals and the annalistic prisms. For example, one of Sargon's campaigns against Urartu is said to have occurred in his seventh *palû* (i.e. 715 BC) in the Annals but in his sixth *palû* (716 BC) on an annalistic prism.[218] This discrepancy is regular, the annalistic prisms always dating events one year earlier than the Annals.

The background for this is the circumstances around Sargon's accession to the throne. All evidence indicates that it was the result of a *coup d'état*. According to other, non-annalistic sources, Sargon did not undertake any military campaigns during his first year (721 BC) due to domestic troubles. It obviously took some time before he had established his power.[219] When the annalistic prisms give a dating one year earlier than the Khorsabad annals do, this indicates that the scribes of the prisms simply changed the dating by one year in order to fill in the vacant first year. That the Khorsabad annals have a correct dating is shown by the fact that the campaign against Hama in Syria is said to have occurred in the second *palû*, i.e. 720 BC, both in the Khorsabad annals and in the so-called Assur-charter.[220] Annalistic prism texts with notices about this campaign are not preserved, as it happens, but would have dated the Hama campaign to Sargon's first *palû* (721 BC).

Equipped with these insights we can approach the Arab passages in Sargon's official reports. The first one is from the so-called Nimrud D prism, a text of the summary type, i.e. a non-chronological record:

> (37) The city of Samaria I restored and greater than before (38) I caused it to become. People of lands conquered by my two hands (39) I brought within it; my officer (40) as prefect over them I placed and (41) together with the people of Assyria I counted them. (42) The peoples of KUR Muṣur and the LÚ *a-ra-bi* (43) I caused the blaze *(sa-lum-mat)* of Ashur my lord to overwhelm them

> (*ušaššip-ma*). (44) At the mention of my name their hearts (45) palpitated, their arms collapsed. (46) . . .? of KUR Muṣur I opened the sealed (treasury?). (47) The people of KUR Assyria and of KUR Muṣur (48) I mingled together (49) and let them bid (for the contents).[221]

Since this is a summary text, no dating is found in it. A comparison between the Annals and a Summary Inscription shows, however, that lines 37–41 and 46–49 are part of the record of Sargon's first year as recorded in the Khorsabad annals.[222] Even though the quoted passage does not occur in these Annals, there seems to be no doubt that this event, according to the Annals, should be dated to Sargon's first year, i.e. 721 BC.

This is, however, problematic. As we have seen, there are good reasons to assume that Sargon did not undertake any military activities at all, and especially not in the west, in the year 721. This implies that the activities reported for this year in the Annals are faked or taken from other years in order to fill out the empty first year. The authors of the annalistic prism chose another solution as we have seen, lowering the chronology by one year. The compilers of the Annals preserved the correct chronology but had to fill in the empty space left by the year 721. The Annals for this year are thus not to be trusted.

The solution is given by a fragment of an annalistic prism text first published by E. Weidner and now reconstructed by H. Tadmor.[223] According to this text, the so-called Weidner prism, Sargon has settled peoples 'in the cities on the borders of the City of the Brook of Muṣur, a province which is on the shore of the Western sea'. The king of Muṣur, Shilkanni, was overwhelmed (*išpušu-ma*) by the fear of the splendour of Assur and brought presents to the Assyrian king, '12 big horses of Muṣur, their like not to be found in Assyria'. Tadmor supposes, as it seems with good reason, that this episode is a more detailed account of what is told in the annalistic passage quoted above.[224] In the Weidner prism we also have a dating: this passage is preceded by the story of a campaign in the north (the Mannai and the Pattira-land) and is followed by the account of a campaign against Ursa in Urartu said to have happened in Sargon's sixth *palû*. Since this is an annalistic prism text, the sixth *palû* must be equivalent to the seventh in the Khorsabad annals. This is also correct.[225] This implies that the Mannai campaign should have taken place in the fifth *palû* according to the Weidner prism and the sixth according to the Annals.[226] The Annals do not mention the *arabi*-Muṣur episode for this year, with good reason: it had been moved to the first year to fill out an otherwise empty space. The conclusion must be that the event with the Arabs and the Muṣur occurred in Sargon's sixth *palû*, i.e. 716 BC.

The interpretation of these texts depends on the exact locations of both the land of Muṣur and the Arabs. As we have suggested already, the former is Egypt or, more exactly, the delta and the lands east of it stretching to Palestine and the ʕArabah.[227] If the Arabs are to be located close to Muṣur as defined here, they could be identical with Idibiʔil, settled by Tiglath Pileser between Gaza and Eypt. The latter part of the texts speaks about dealings between Assyria and Egypt without mentioning the Arabs, which should perhaps be expected if they were posted at the frontier. Since Idibiʔil was an Assyrian vassal of some kind, it would perhaps be unnecessary to say that also they (he?) were overwhelmed by the Assyrian power. We would rather look for a more substantial enemy. They could be members of Queen Shamsi's people who had been paying tribute to Tiglath Pileser. They appear in the next passage of Sargon to be discussed.

This occurrence is far less problematic than the former, at least as far as chronology is concerned. In the Khorsabad annals we find the following in the account of the seventh *palû*, i.e. 715 BC:

> (94) LÚ Tamudi, LÚ Ibadidi, (95) LÚ Marsimanu, LÚ Hayapa, the distant KUR *ar-ba-a-a*, dwellers of the desert, who did not know learned men or scribes, (96) who had not brought tribute to any king I slew with the help of my lord Ashur; their remnant I dragged away, (97) I settled them in Samaria. From Pir'u, king of Muṣuri, Shamsi, queen of the KUR *a-rib-bi*, Itamra, king of Saba (KUR Sa-ba-'a-a-a), (98) the kings of the coast and the desert I received gold, products (?) from the mountain, precious stones, ivory, *ushu*-seed, all kinds of perfumes, horses, (99) and camels as their tribute.[228]

Of the rulers involved in these events we already know Shamsi, who had been Assyria's ally since 733. Muṣur may well include the territories under Egyptian sovereignty and is thus not limited to the Nile valley at this period. The brook of Muṣur is the Brook of Egypt in the Old Testament, i.e. Wādī l-ʕArīsh. There are, however, some uncertainties concerning the identity of the king of Muṣur. It seems likely that Pir'u is the same as the Hebrew *parʕō*, namely the title pharaoh.[229] In that case we would have the name of the Egyptian king in the Weidner prism: Shilkanni.[230] This name is difficult to find in Egyptian sources, but it should be kept in mind that conditions in Egypt during these years were rather chaotic. The country had for many decades been divided between the Nubian kings of the 25th dynasty in the south and small local kings in the north. The Nubian king Shabako was busy conquering the north and it is not impossible that the tribute to Assyria was a means for the local ruler in the north-west to ensure Assyrian support against the impending danger from the south. It is clear that the giving of *mandattu* from the Muṣur-king, as well as from the Queen of the Arabs, was more a part of the obligations of an alliance than submission to Assyrian rule.

Among the enumerated kings we also find a named king of Saba. YṮʕʔMR is the name of several early rulers in the Sabaean kingdom in Yemen, and it has been supposed by many that this passage refers to one of them.[231] The name is, however, also occasionally found in Dedan (Liḥyān) and in Thamudic inscriptions.[232] The name ʔItāmār occurs in the Old Testament as one of the sons of Aaron the priest, and could be the same as found in Sargon's inscription, which, in that case, is not necessarily identical with the Sabaean name.[233] This would point to Midian or an adjacent territory as the origin. As has been pointed out earlier, there were Sabaeans at Dedan (al-ʕŪlā), whose relationship to their namesakes in Yemen remains unclear. If the name is Sabaean, it would perhaps mean that Assyrians and Sabeans were on trading terms via the agents of the Sabaean king in northern Arabia. It remains, however, somewhat hypothetical. The three rulers mentioned in the Annals ll. 97–99 were thus not under Assyrian rule but rather partners in an alliance. This makes it more likely that the *arabi* mentioned in the text from 716 BC, in fact, are queen Shamsi's Arabs. We thus have three rulers mentioned in an order from north-west to south-east: one over Egypt or/and the Sinai, Queen Shamsi and the Sabaean king, most likely the same as mentioned by Tiglath Pileser. This would put Shamsi's Arabs between Dedan and ʕArabah, perhaps between the Ḥisma and the Great Nafūd.

> Eph'al is sceptical about the information on the transfer of nomads to the hill country of Samaria, which, according to him, does not fit into the deportation

> system of the Assyrians.[234] This objection loses its force if it is acknowledged that there is no evidence that Arab means 'nomad'. Shamsi's Arabs may well have had other virtues that were interesting to the Assyrians. On the contrary, the presence of Arabs from the interior of the Syrian desert becomes very likely when we hear from the Biblical account that one of the gods introduced into Samaria after its fall was ʔAšîma'.[235] This name, which has survived in the Samaritan tradition, is now documented as a divine name from Taymāʔ, i.e. the area where we have located Shamsi.[236] There is thus a definite connection.

As we can see, the *arbāya* are distinguished from the *arab*. The former are grouped together with four other tribes or peoples, two of which are known. *Hayapa* we have encountered already in the reports by Tiglath Pileser from 732 BC *Tamudi* is a tribe which we from now on will be able to follow until the fourth century AD, and whose memory lives on to this day through its inclusion in the Qurʔānic sacral history. We know that Hayapa belongs to Midian, and Thamūd is known in later times to reside in the Wādī l-Qurā area north of Medina.[237] The remaining names are not known from other sources; *Marsimani* could be analysed as an Arab name: *marʔ simān*. A divine name SMN is later known from northern Ḥiğāz.[238] It is tempting to associate this name with the *maisameneîs/alimazoneîs/banizomeîs/batmizománeis* known from Hellenistic geographers and the Septuagint, just south of Midian east of ʕAynūna.[239] Even though this identification remains hypothetical, the location of these peoples in north-western Arabia seems certain.

It is not immediately clear from the text whether *arbāya* is a common designation of the four peoples or constitutes a fifth one. The text can be read both ways. From the picture that will emerge from this study, there will be good arguments in favour of seeing the *arbāya* as a separate group.[240] Important to notice is that the form of the word differs from that found with the queens Zabibe and Shamsi: *arab-*. Instead, it looks like the epithet of Gindibu: *arbāya*. There seems to be no doubt that we have to do with two different groups.

In Sargon's Annals there is one further mention of Arabs which is most remarkable. In the report from the eighth *palû*, i.e. 714 BC, we have an account of a campaign in Kurdistan. In lines 161–162 we find the following:

> (160) . . . U-ia-da-ú-i, Bu-us-ti-is, A-ga-zi, Am-ba-an-da, Da-na-nu, (162) distant regions by the border of the KUR *a-ri-bi* of the rising sun.[241]

Some of these names are identifiable. Bustis is a city in Parsu, i.e. present-day Fars, the homeland of the Persians. According to Ptolemy, there was a city Agaza in Atropatene (present-day Azerbaijan) which could be identical with Agasi.[242] Ambanda is a place today called Chammabādān, south-west of Hamādān.[243]

The existence of Arabs in the interior of Kurdistan is rather surprising and this passage has been adduced as a proof that the word 'Arab' must be a general designation for a nomad or bedouin.[244] Akkadian does, however, have a term for 'tent-dweller', *āšib kuš/ltari*, which is found also in Hebrew, *šôken ʔohalîm*, and which was translated into Greek, *skēnítēs*, and one would have expected this term if these people had been nomads in a general sense. There is no reason to assume that Arab, tent-dweller and shepherd are synonyms in Akkadian texts.[245]

That the '*aribi* of the rising sun' may indeed have been connected with those we know from the Syrian desert is indicated by some evidence. There are at least two seals found in Iran with short inscriptions with letters in South Semitic script.[246] Unfortunately, the exact provenance of these seals is not known. These two inscriptions are of the same type as several others found in Mesopotamia.[247] These seals are dated to the seventh to sixth centuries BC on palaeographical grounds. We thus find inscriptions with similar letters on a small group of seals from lower Mesopotamia and Iran from the last centuries of the Assyrian empire. As we shall see, the area in question in southern Mesopotamia was in fact inhabited by peoples related to our Arabs in the Syrian desert. Although they are never called Arabs, we find names of an Arabic type among them. It is also evident that the South Semitic script was widely spread in Arabia already at the beginning of the first millennium BC.

The evidence of these inscriptions together with the note in Sargon's Annals thus makes the presence of Arabs in western Iran probable at this period. The question is whether there is any explanation for the presence of people from northern Arabia in Iran.

A suggestion near at hand is that the presence of Arabs is connected with the introduction of the domesticated camel. We have evidence that the one-humped camel was known and used in the regions north and north-east of Assyria already during the first part of the first millennium BC.[248] Since as far as we know the Assyrians themselves did not breed camels, it is reasonable to assume that when the new animal was introduced in the north it was accompanied by those who knew how to handle it.[249] The evidence is admittedly scanty but sufficient to support the indication in Sargon's text that Arabs from the Syrian desert were indeed present in Iran at this time. As we have seen, a similar policy might have been behind the installation of Idibiʔil, the Arab, in south-western Palestine under Tiglath Pileser.[250]

From the reign of Sargon we have several letters preserved in which Arabs are mentioned. The first one is to the king from a certain Ṭāb-ṣil-Ešarra who was eponym for the year 716 BC, referring to a report from Nâbu-bêl-Shumâte, the governor of the town Birat just south of Asshur in the Ǧazīra. The governor says:

> I got a royal message: 'Why is it that all city rulers come and stood in my presence but you have not come? Also, why is it that the KUR *ár-pa-a-a* plundered Sippar but you did not go out with your servants but kept [them] away?'[251]

Another is sent by the same Ṭāb-ṣil-Ešarra but is more fragmentary. It is clear, however, that he reports on raids and plundering in the areas around Suhu and Hindanu in the middle of the Ǧazīra because of failed rains. He has been sent to the land of (KUR) *ar-[pa-a-a]*. There is mention of camels *(gamallê)*, which are allowed to graze there. Then Ṭāb-ṣil-Ešarra describes conditions around Hindanu, where plundering and raids have taken place. The governor of Kalah has lost control. He exhorts someone (them) to establish a eunuch in charge of the land of *ar-pa-a-a*. Important is the information that the *arbāya* are under the control of the governor of Calah and that they dwell in his territory (*taḫūmu*).[252] The status of the *arbāya* is illuminated by a list of precious items given by the king to visiting delegations, in which we, among people like Ekronites, Byblians, people from Tabal in Anatolia etc., also find Ilâ-nasaka, LÚ *na-si-ku ar-ba-a-a*.[253] *Nasīkunasikku* is obviously a title of the ruler of the *arbāya*. Like the others in the list, they had a spokesman before the king, although they were subjects to him. The *arbāya* in this list can be assumed to be those dwelling in the territory of the governor of Calah.

They also appear in letters to the king from a certain Bēl liqbi, demanding permission to transform a place called Hi-e-sa from a camp for archers to a caravanserai, which it has been before the stationing of the archers there. Bēl liqbi, who is in the town of Ṣupite, suggests transferring the archers to a place called Argite. He then remarks:

> the LÚ *ar-ba-a-a* as before (yesterday) go in and out; [this is] very good.[254]

Ṣupite is Ṣoba just north-east of the Antilebanon, known from the story about the empire of David. Not far from that is a modern village named Ḥasye.[255] We are thus north of Damascus on the Ḥimṣ plain, which stretches eastwards into the Syrian desert towards Palmyra. Here the *arbāya* played a role in the caravan traffic with the permission of the Assyrian authorities.

The Arabs and their camels appear in a third letter from the same period in which it seems that they are given permission to graze their camels 'in the midst of the land'.[256] A similar statement occurs in a letter from Bēl liqbi saying:

> LÚ ar-b[a-a-a] have entered into the interior (of the province) but the rains have arrived and they are coming and going.[257]

This confirms the picture of close co-operation between Assyrian authorities in Syria and the people called *arbāya* who were obviously active in the Ḥimṣ area. One is reminded of Gindibu the *arbāya*, who seems to have had a similar relationship to the local Syrian rulers a century earlier.

A most interesting piece of information on the position of the Arabs in Syria at this time is found in one more letter from Bēl liqbi to the king. He reports that 'the LÚ *ar-ba-a-a* are settled on the other side of the Hadina river where they come and go'. But then we hear that the king has received information that people in the town of Huzaza sell iron to the LÚ *ar-ba-a-a*. Bēl liqbi, however, claims to be innocent of this business, selling only copper to the LÚ *ar-ba-a-a*. In order to stop the business he has placed a toll collector at the city gate of Huzaza who has scared away the LÚ *ar-ba-a-a*.[258] One might suspect that the prohibition of selling iron to the Arabs in Syria was a way of controlling the development of their weaponry. The access to iron was a major concern for the Assyrians, to whom it may have been crucial for the armament of their troops.[259]

Two facts can be discerned from these texts. One is that the *arbāya* belong to the central parts of the Ǧazīra and that the raid against Sippar is an extraordinary expedition towards the south-east. It is not so certain that these *arbāya* should be identified with the people with Arabic names documented from southern Babylonia in the Neo-Assyrian period.[260] The second observation is that they seem to have been the subjects of the Assyrians. The plundering is seen as something extraordinary, and it is, in fact, not clear if the plundering in the second letter is performed by the *arbāya*. The plundering in the first letter seems to have been done in co-operation with Assyrian officials. Usually the *arbāya* stand under Assyrian officers or officials and it is likely that they were allowed to use the grasslands of the Ǧazīra for raising their camels. It goes nicely with the evidence from Tiglath Pileser about the peaceful employment of the *arbāya* in the area of present-day Ḥimṣ, probably for the same purpose. The second letter seems to indicate that camel-herders have been allowed to graze their animals in the region between Assur and Hindanu, just as they were on the Ḥimṣ plain.

One should now connect these *arbāya* with the groups mentioned in the Khorsabad annals from 715 BC. There Sargon tells about the 'distant *arbāya*, dwellers of the desert' together with the Sabaeans. They were among those settled in Samaria most likely as colonists and subjects to the king. Their appearance together with the Sabaeans recalls the presence of the Sabaeans at Suhu, documented in an earlier quoted text from the eighth century BC.[261] If compared with the evidence for *arbāya* in Tiglath Pileser's time, the impression is that the *arbāya* under both rulers were very much subject to the Assyrians and appear as some kind of specialised colonists and employees. We would thus suggest that the difference between the *arab* and the *arbāya* was that the former was a group formally allied to Assyria like other foreign peoples, whereas the latter were people, perhaps individuals, who were employed more or less as officials. As we shall see, there is further evidence that such a distinction has also existed in other parts of Arabia.[262]

Sennacherib

The presence of people from Arabia in Mesopotamia proper is connected with a development of far-reaching consequences that started at the end of the eighth century BC, namely the resurgence of Babylonia. When Tiglath Pileser III was proclaimed king of Babylonia in 729 BC, this was a sign of the increased importance of southern Mesopotamia that was to reach its peak in the Chaldaean empire in the sixth century. This found its political expression in the successive revolts in the south by the Aramaean Merodach-Baladan and supported by Elam. It is evident that this resurgence was connected with the establishment of new commercial ties with the Persian Gulf and adjacent areas.[263] With the economic revitalization go the complex ethnic conditions in the area. Aramaean tribes had been around for quite a while, and their language was rapidly becoming dominant. But there are also traces of Semitic-speaking groups who did not have Aramaean names but used a language which we would classify as a form of Arabic. There is documentation of a great number of settlements in Babylonia, named after tribes with Arabic names.[264] The presence of these groups in southern Mesopotamia is further corroborated by the so-called Proto-Arabic inscriptions already mentioned. These inscriptions also show that connections were established with South Arabia.

This is some of the background for the events in the year 703 BC. In that year a rebellion broke out in Babylonia led by Merodach-Baladan, who returned from Elam and recaptured the city of Babylon. The course of events is related in an annalistic report of Sennacherib's first campaign.[265] Sennacherib, according to his own words in this text, 'raged like a lion, stormed like a tempest' when attacking the insurgents and devastating the land. In a great battle at Kish in southern Mesopotamia the enemy was scattered and in connection with this we are told:

> Adinu, son of the wife of Merodach-Baladan, together with Bashqanu (ba-as-qa-a-nu), brother of Yathīʕe (Ia-ti-'-e), queen of LÚ *a-ri-bi* along with their armies I seized as living captives.[266]

It is tempting to assume that these Arabs are the same who were made vassals to Assyria by Tiglath Pileser III after the conquest of Syria. Later in the text (ll. 36–49) we find several of the 'Arabian' settlements in Babylonia listed as victims of the Assyrian's wrath.

We also find mentioned two other groups, the LÚ *ha-ga-ra-a-nu* and the LÚ *na-ba-tu*.[267] These names somehow seem to be related to the *hagrîm*, known from the Old Testament, and the *nabaṭ*, the Nabataeans. We will later hear more about both.[268] There is, however, no indication that these settlements were ruled by the queen of the Arabs. The queen could be a successor to Zabibe and Shamsi. In that case she and her Arabs would be located in the same area, i.e. somewhere around the western or north-western shores of the Great Nafūd. In connection with the operations it is related that the Assyrian king took booty consisting of camels, and it is a good guess that these animals were provided by the Arabs from North Arabia, not the Arabic-speakers settled in Mesopotamia.

It is not impossible that there were people called Arabs settled in southern Mesopotamia already at the end of the eighth century BC, since we hear some 150 years later about a 'town of the Arabs' near Nippur.[269] These Arabs would have had some connection with those farther out in the Syrian desert. This possible involvement of the Arabs in Babylonian affairs, siding with Assyria's enemies in the now emerging struggle for the Persian Gulf, seems to represent a definite change of policy on their side. We have seen that the Arabs for 150 years had striven to have good relations with the powers who governed Syria. Now, when Syria is definitely under Assyrian rule, they face Assyria as an enemy. In the following century we shall see that the Arabs were to be involved in the revolts in Babylonia. This would have been a means of easing the Assyrian pressure on North Arabia in general.

The outcome of the events in 703 was renewed Assyrian control of Babylonia. This did not, however, last long. A new insurrection supported by Elam started in 694. The military operations in Babylonia were comprehensive and resulted in the destruction of Babylon in 689. These campaigns are described in detail in several versions of Sennacherib's Annals. In one fragment, describing his activities in 691 during his eighth campaign, we find a somewhat mutilated record of an operation against the Arabs, placed after the completion of the campaign, which is not found elsewhere:

> (53') . . . Telhunu, queen of LÚ *a-ra-bi* in the midst of the desert,
> (54') . . . x thousand camels I took from her hand. She, with Hazaʔil,
> (55') . . . the terror of my battle overcame them, they left their tents,
> (56') . . . to the . . . of A-du-um-ma-te they fled for their lives
> (57') . . . A-d]u-um-ma-tu, whose dwellings are situated in the desert
> (58') . . . of thirst, wherein there are no feeding nor drinking places.
> . . .
> (3") . . . the town Ka-pa-a-nu, the town . . .
> (4") . . . the place of her hiding in . . .
> (5") . . . Telhunu, que]en of LÚ *a-ra-bi* together with [her/their] gods . . .[270]

This is the only reference to the involvement of the Arabs in the war with Assyria at the end of the 690s which comes from Sennacherib's own reign. Since the other versions of his Annals all end with the eighth campaign in 691, without mentioning the Arab operation, this must have taken place after 691 and before the destruction of Babylon in 689. We do, however, find two more references to this adventure in the inscriptions of later Assyrian kings, because the trouble with the Arabs in question turned out to be endemic. When Sennacherib's successor, Esarhaddon, reports his dealings with these people, the story begins with a reference to his father's clash with them:

> [As to] Adumutu, the fortress of the LÚ *a-ri-bi* which Sennacherib, king of Assyria, my father, my creator, had conquered, and whose goods, possessions and gods together with the *apkallatu,* queen of the LÚ *a-ri-bi*, he had taken to Assyria.[271]

A further reference to the same episode is given by Esarhaddon's successor Assurbanipal in the so-called Letter to Ishtar:

> To Dilbat [i.e. Ishtar] . . . who raged against Hazaʔil (ha-za-ilu), king of the KUR *a-ri-bi* . . . who gave him into the hands of Sennacherib, my father's father, my creator and effected his defeat, who said that she would not dwell with the people of the KUR *a-ri-bi* and took the road to Assyria.[272]

We thus learn that Sennacherib undertook a major military expedition into the desert in order to bring down the Arabs, who had sided with the insurgents in Babylonia. The fortress of Adummatu has long since been identified with Dumah in Biblical and classical sources and Dūmat al-ǧandal in Islamic sources, i.e. the oasis today called al-Ǧawf, situated in the southern Syrian desert on the northern edge of the Great Nafūd desert.[273] We have every reason to believe that this was the residence of the Arab queens whom we encountered earlier. The town Kapānu has been identified with a site in the northern Wādī Sirḥān.[274] In connection with Sennacherib's campaign we also learn more about who these queens actually were. Esarhaddon calls the Arab queen *apkallatu*. This is a priestly title well known from Babylonia as well as from North and South Arabia.[275] The queen in Dumah thus appears to have had priestly functions, perhaps predominantly such functions.

We may notice that the Arabs seem to have a new queen after the capture of Yathīʕe and her brother in 703. Telhunu now appears together with somebody called by the Syrian name Hazaʔil. In Assurbanipal's time he is designated 'king of the Arabs'. Due to the dubious character of many of the texts produced by Assurbanipal's scribes, we cannot be certain if this title is correct. We will return to the question.

Sennacherib is best known from his campaigns against Judah when he failed to capture Jerusalem, an event which obviously had a crucial importance for the world-view of the Judaeans. In his Annals, where he reports the campaign against King Ezekiah in Jerusalem, we find the following passage:

> This Ezekiah (Ha-za-qi-a-ú) was overwhelmed by the terrifying splendour of my lordship, and LÚ *úr-bi* and his strong army, which he had brought into Jerusalem to strengthen it, deserted him.[276]

The word *urbi* also occurs in the passage of Sennacherib dealing with operations in Chaldea, i.e. southern Babylonia, where Bashqanu and Yathīʕe had appeared:

> LÚ *ur-bi*, Aramaeans (*ar-a-mu*), Chaldaeans (*ka-al-du*) who were in Uruk, Nippur, Kish, Harsagkalamma together with the citizens, the rebels, I brought forth and counted as spoil.[277]

Some fifty years later, Assurbanipal mentions these groups in the account of his fifth campaign in southern Babylonia:

> The other sons of Bêl iqīsha . . . the sons of Nabû-shum-eresh . . . the bones of their father, their procreator together with LÚ *ur-bi*, the insurgents of the inhabitants of URU Gambuli . . . I carried away to Assur as booty.[278]

Gambuli was an Aramaean tribe in southern Babylonia and the *urbi* were obviously still where they had been under Sennacherib fifty years earlier.[279]

The word *urbi* has been understood in two ways: (1) Arabs, i.e. an ethnic entity, (2) mercenary soldiers.[280] These two meanings are seen as mutually exclusive. The latest scholar who has dealt with the question, I. Eph'al, states categorically that an ethnic meaning is excluded. From the context of the three passages he concludes that the meaning must be some kind of military unit. His argumentation is supported by the assumption that Arab in fact means 'nomad' etc., a meaning which is impossible to ascribe to *urbi* in the context. Eph'al's interpretation of the *urbi* passages may well be correct. But if Arab does not mean 'nomad' and is no ethnic designation, the question comes into a different light. We have indicated earlier that there is evidence that the word, in fact, does mean some kind of warrior.[281] In that case, both suggestions are correct and the debate has arisen from a misunderstanding of the word itself; *urbi* would then be identical with *ʕarab*/*ʕurb*, but the meaning 'mercenary' should be seriously considered, since it is obvious that it means neither 'nomad' nor a specific tribe or groups of tribes.

If we accept the identity of the *urbi* and our Arabs, the question arises about their role in Ezekiah's Judah. From the two other passages in the Assyrian texts it is clear that the *urbi* were more or less subject to the Assyrians (like the *arbāya*). Sennacherib says that the *urbi* deserted the Judaeans, which means that they may have had a similar position there. On the famous reliefs in Sennacherib's palace in Nineveh depicting his siege of Lachish in Judaea, we can see camels being used by the Assyrians for transport.[282] There is also archaeological evidence of extensive camel breeding at Tell Jemmeh in south-western Palestine from *c.* 700 BC.[283] This is the area where Idibiʔil was stationed by Tiglath Pileser. Even though it is somewhat speculative, it cannot be excluded that the documented presence of Arabs and camels in south-western Judaea is reflected in the note on the *urbi* mercenaries of Ezekiah.[284]

The presence of Arabs in Judah in the days of Ezekiah may be reflected in the Old Testament. In 1 Chronicles 27:30 there is a notice about ʔObil *ha-yišmeʕelî*, the Ishmaelite, who was 'over the camels' in King David's administration. In the following verse is mentioned Yaziz *ha-hagrî*, 'the Hagarite', as being 'over the small cattle'. It is very unlikely that the description of David's government in Chronicles goes back to documents from the tenth century BC. It has been argued that the descriptions instead reflect conditions in the later Judaean kingdom.[285] It is very likely that the notices about Obil and Yaziz should be seen as a transfer to the time of David of officials belonging to later times. The appearance of the enigmatic *urbi* in documents contemporary with Ezekiah together with the archaeological documentation of extensive camel breeding in Judaea at this time make it likely that we have here a memory preserved by the Chronicler of the presence of experts on camel breeding and small-cattle holding which could very well be identical with Ezekiah's *urbi*, i.e. the Arabs.[286] Obil's name looks very much like a derivation from the Arabic word *ʔibil* meaning 'camels'.

The political relations between Assyria and different Arab groups seem to have undergone a drastic change in the time of Sennacherib. The Assyrians launched a great expedition to crush the Arabs in Dumah who were involved in the growing unrest in southern Babylonia. The attack against Dumah must have been a daring enterprise which would not have been reasonable if no serious matter had been at stake. The Arabs were obviously seen as an enemy significant enough to be worth a strenuous military campaign further into the Syrian desert than any Assyrian army had gone before.

The presence of Arabs in lower Mesopotamia as early as 700 BC may be remembered even by much later historians. In aṭ-Ṭabarī's account of the earliest history of the *ʕarab* he says that 'Bukht Nuṣṣur' settled some tradesmen of the *ʕarab* in a *ḥayr,* a fenced-in camp near an-Nağaf in Iraq. Other *ʕarab* from the Iraqi countryside submitted to him and were settled in a place close to the Euphrates called al-ʔAnbār, situated just north of present-day al-Falūğa. After the death of the king, all *ʕarab* settled in al-ʔAnbār, where they remained until the founding of the Lakhmid kingdom in al-Ḥīra in the third century AD.[287] This story is transmitted by Hishām b. al-Kalbī, who had access to sources from al-Ḥīra, and it belongs to a corpus of traditions about Nebuchadnezzar in early Arabic literature. Also in another variant, aṭ-Ṭabarī tells that Nebuchadnezzar settled some of the *ʕarab* he had defeated in al-ʔAnbār, which was called *ʔanbār al-ʕarab*.[288] It might be suggested that there was a very old settlement of *ʕarab* by the middle Euphrates about which it was said that they had been settled there by Nebuchadnezzar. This is obviously part of the Nebuchadnezzar traditions, reflected also in the book of Judith, transmitted in the form of a novel or collection of stories about the king.

As we have seen, the presence of people called *arab* or *arbāya* in Akkadian is well documented around the middle Euphrates, at least from the days of Sargon II.[289] We have no documentation about Sargon actually settling *arbāya* in Mesopotamia. But we hear about him settling them in Palestine. His successor, Sennacherib, made a grand campaign against the Arabs in Dumah and took their gods to Assyria. He also led operations in southern Mesopotamia against the *urbi*. We remember the verse in Judith telling about Holophernes' campaign in Mesopotamia, which rather abruptly breaks the context of the operations in Syria and may well originally refer to Sennacherib.[290] In a strange note in Herodotus this king is called 'the king of Assyrians and *arábioi*' and his dealings with the latter may have prompted the notice about his Mesopotamian campaign to be included in the story about Holophernes'/Tiglath Pileser's Syrian campaign.[291] In an even later Greek source 'the phylarchs of the *árabes*' along the Euphrates enter into history.[292] Sennacherib is, by Herodotus, even credited with a conquest of Egypt with an army of Assyrians and *arábioi*. It is told that Sanakharibos, by whom is clearly meant Sennacherib of Assyria, advanced towards Egypt with a great host of *arábioi* and Assyrians. At Pelusium this army was beaten by a swarm of mice which devoured their bows after an invocation of Hephaestus by the priest Sethos.[293] The story is evidently related to the one about the same king's siege of Jerusalem in the days of Isaiah, which also failed due to a miracle.[294] This expedition was actually performed by Sennacherib's successor Esarhaddon, and later by the Achaemenid Cambyses, but it shows that Sennacherib was seen as having close ties with the Arabs and is presented in later legends as being aided by them.

Sennacherib's involvement with the Arabs may also be reflected in the legend about Ninus transmitted by the Greek historian Ctesias, writing the history of the Orient in the fourth century BC. Ninus, who married the famous

Semiramis and who is said to have been the founder of Nineveh and the conqueror of Babylonia, started his career by making a covenant with a certain Ariaios, king of Arabia or the ruler of the *árabes*.[295] These *árabes* aided him in his conquests and were honoured by gifts after the fighting. Also Berossus told about a series of nine Arab kings before the reign of Semiramis.[296] The figure of Ninus has absorbed traits from several of the neo-Assyrian kings, among them Sennacherib, the conqueror of Babylon. One of these traits is definitely his dealings with the Arabs. Noteworthy is that they are transformed from enemies to assistants.

It thus seems quite possible that the *ʕarab* who lived along the middle Euphrates during the centuries before the Islamic conquest had been settled there by several of the great Mesopotamian kings, Assyrians and Babylonians, during the two centuries preceding the Achaemenid conquest. In popular legend all these settlements were ascribed to Nebuchadnezzar, who may well have been responsible for one of them. But it is likely that Sargon II and Sennacherib had initiated this policy long before. The memories have survived in the popular legend spun around the great Nebuchadnezzar.

Esarhaddon

The situation for the Arabs at Esarhaddon's ascension to the Assyrian throne in 681 BC was that the gods of Dumah were kept in Asshur, probably in some temple. The queen and priestess of the Arabs, Telhunu, had been taken to Assyria as well. Before following the course of events we have to make a short survey of the sources from Esarhaddon's reign which are relevant for the Arabs.[297]

The oldest source is an annalistic text probably written in 676 BC. This text is known from two prisms, the so-called Heidel prism and prism B from Nineveh. Another text, written some three years later, is found on several prisms from Nineveh, the most important being the so-called Thompson prism. This text is called Nineveh A. Nineveh A is more detailed than the earlier one and also covers a longer period. Parallels to Nineveh A are the so-called Monument B, a prism from Tell Barsip, and Fragment A from Nineveh.[298] To these should be added two other fragments, F and G, which must have been written around the year 670 BC. We thus have five different annalistic texts dealing with events in the 670s and partly overlapping each other according to the following scheme:

		Heidel prism	Nin. B	Nin. A	Mon. B	Frg. A	Frg. F/G
I	681–676	X	X	X	X	X	–
II	677	X	X	X	X	–	–
III	676–673	–	–	X	X	X	–
IV	673	–	–	–	–	–	–
V	671	–	–	–	–	–	X

The earliest passage runs as follows in the Heidel-prism:

> Hazaʔil, the king of the KUR *a-ri-bi*, with costly gifts came to Nineveh, my lordly city, kissed my feet, (55) begging me to give his gods. I had mercy upon him, the damages on these gods I repaired; the might of Asshur, my god and my name I wrote on them and returned and gave them to him. (60) Tabua (Tabu-u-a), the growth of my palace, I put in power over them and returned her to

> her country with her gods [A-tar-sa-ma-a-a-in, Da-a, Nu-ha-a-a, Ru-ul-da-a-a-u, A-bi-ri-il-lu, A-tar-qu-ru-ma-a (Nin. A, Mon. B)]. (1) Another sixty-five camels on the tribute of my father I imposed on him . . . Afterwards, Hazaʔil passed away and I placed his son Yaʕlu (Ia-'-lu-ú) /Yathaʕ (Nin. A: Ia-ta-', Frg. A: Ia-ta-a)/Yawthiʕ (Ia-u-ti-' Mon. B) (5) on his throne, imposing upon him ten minas of gold, one thousand birutu-stones, fifty camels, one thousand leather bags with spices, in addition to the tribute of my father.[299]

Is this Hazaʔil identical with the companion of the queen of the Arabs in 691, who is said to have fled with her to Dumah? It seems that Assurbanipal's scribes thought so and it is not impossible. In that case he now emerges more than ten years later as king of the Arabs. How he had reached this position we do not know; perhaps he had filled the vacuum in the aftermath of Sennacherib's plundering of Dumah in 691. In Esarhaddon's record he clearly emerges as a vassal of the Assyrians.

There is a notice about Arabs in connection with Esarhaddon's Egyptian campaign in 671 BC which resulted in the Assyrian conquest of the Nile valley. In Frg. F (and other sources) we read how the king sets out from Ra-pi-hi in Philistaea:

> I gathered camels from all the kings of KUR *a-ri-bi* and made them carry watersacks; I marched X 15 days through great dunes of sand.[300]

Eph'al has pointed out the interesting parallel between this piece of information and what we know of later military operations in the area between Palestine and Egypt.[301] We shall see that a similar arrangement was made by the Achaemenid king Cambyses when he conquered Egypt in 525 BC.[302] We should note that this is the first time we hear about several kings of the Arabs, which might indicate some kind of alliance between several groups. It is not certain that all the Arabs were dwelling in the northern Sinai.[303] But Idbiʔil settled there by Tiglath Pileser might well have been included.

In a letter from Esarhaddon's time, containing a report of an eclipse with a concomitant oracle, these kings appear again:

> If someone brings this sign to the kings of Hatti or of Chaldea or of KUR *a-ri-bi*, the king my lord will be well.[304]

The kings of the Arabs are mentioned on the same level as those of Syria (Hatti) and Chaldea. The latter are vassals of the Assyrians, and the Arabs would have had the same status. This means that the Arabs mentioned here must be those living in the Syrian desert, governed by queens known from the time of Tiglath Pileser, Sargon and Sennacherib, and by Hazaʔil and Yathaʕ/Yawthiʕ/Yaʕlu in the time of Esarhaddon. They should be distinguished from the *arbāya* in Syria and Babylonia, who were Assyrian officials and did not have any rulers of their own. This report presupposes harmonious relations between Assyria and the vassals, the Arabs included, and goes well with the notice about the assistance by the Arabs in the Egyptian campaign.

The good relations between Esarhaddon and the Arabs were, however, disrupted by events later in his reign. One could speculate that Hazaʔil's position as king was rather shaky and that he needed support from others to remain in power. The impression given by the passage quoted is that from now on he definitely becomes an Assyrian ally or, more properly speaking, a puppet. Perhaps his shaky position as 'king of the Arabs' was due to his being a usurper. The insecure position of Hazaʔil becomes evident in the immediately following passage in the Esarhaddon texts:

> (23) After this, Wabu (U-a-bu), in order to become king, (24) made all LÚ *a-ru-bu* revolt against Yathaʕ (Ia-ta-'). (25) I, Esarhaddon, king of Assyria, king of the four corners, (26) who loves righteousness and to whom lie is repugnant (?), (27) sent my army to help Yathaʕ (28). They conquered the whole of LÚ *a-ru-bu*, (29) put Wabu and those who were with him in chains (30) and brought them to me. I put a neck-chain on them (31) and tied them at my gate.[305]

One can imagine how Hazaʔil and his son were regarded as quislings by the Arabs and it was not difficult for an enterprising leader to find support for a revolt against Assyria and her puppets. It is perhaps of interest that the leader of this revolt seems to have a genuine Arabic name, Wahbu, whereas Hazaʔil, as has been pointed out, is a Syrian, probably Aramaic name.

The failed revolt of Wabu is the last notice about the Arabs in Dumah and their allies from the reign of Esarhaddon. We hear about more troubles in texts from his successor, Assurbanipal. In the letter to Asshur, as an introduction to the story about the dealings with the Arabs in his own reign, Assurbanipal reports an insurrection against Esarhaddon which must have occurred during the later part of his reign:[306]

> When [Yawthiʕ (Ia-ú-te-')] son of Hazaʔil king of the KUR *a-ri-bi* in the days of Esarhaddon king of Assyria, the firstling of the work of your hands, revolted, broke the yoke of his power, Esarhaddon, king of Assyria, the father, my creator, gathered his troops with your great power, your great force and sent them against him. In the battlefield he effected his defeat and took his gods as booty. [Yawthiʕ] left his camp in order to escape and fled alone and escaped.[307]

One might ask if Yawthiʕ's revolt was due to the fact that the Assyrian army was busy conquering Egypt.[308] This is the only reference we have about the further relations between Esarhaddon and his vassal in Dumah. From the events under Assurbanipal (see below) we must conclude that the Arabs in Dumah remained without a king during the latter part of Esarhaddon's reign and the beginning of that of Assurbanipal, and that the gods were once more taken away. These events should be dated somewhere between the years 673 and 669 BC. The arrangement set up by Esarhaddon at the beginning of his reign thus seems to have broken down.

One important point is the name of Hazaʔil's successor. The Heidel prism is the only source calling him Yaʕlu. In all the others we have a name derived from the root YṮʕ: Yawthiʕ or Yathaʕ.[309] Now we see that Hazaʔil's successor had to face an insurrection from the Arabs and later on, after having failed with his own enterprise in that business, had to disappear. As we shall see below, a Yawthiʕ reappears in the beginning of Assurbanipal's reign as Hazaʔil's successor as king of the Arabs. It may be that Hazaʔil in fact had two sons, Yaʕlu, who had a short career, and Yawthiʕ/Yawthaʕ, who was to try his luck under Assurbanipal, also without lasting success. As we shall see from the texts from Assurbanipal's reign, the scribes were not too scrupulous with names when writing the records, which, after all, even the kings probably could not read. The king who fled under Esarhaddon could, in fact, have been Yaʕlu, and Yawthiʕ appearing under Assurbanipal could have been an Arab 'false Dmitry' claiming the heritage of

Haza?il. Even though this is very speculative, it is not at all impossible and would explain the two names of Haza?il's successors.

We have at least two letters from the reign of Esarhaddon where *arbāya* is mentioned. One is a list of people associated with the palace, among whom we find an (M) *ar-ba-a-a* 'son of the palace', together with a DIŠ *mu-ṣur-a-a*, 'a man from Muṣur', likewise 'son of the palace'.[310] In the second one, a certain Marduk-shum-uṣur tells the king about a 'seer' (*barû*) who was appointed 'before DIŠ *ár-ba-a-a*'.[311] The close association between the *arbāya* and the Assyrian state is further confirmed.

Assurbanipal: the sources

Assurbanipal was the last Assyrian king of importance. He was not the expected successor and this fact after some years led to the severest internal crisis during his reign, a crisis which in the long run contributed to the downfall of the Assyrian empire once and for all. His older brother, Shamash-shum-ukīn, had been appointed governor of Babylon and lurked waiting for his chance to capture the throne. After many years he started the insurrection in 652 BC, which developed into a violent war which also involved Elam and lasted till after 648. Assurbanipal was victorious but the days of Assyria were numbered. As we have seen, Babylon was by this time becoming more and more prosperous and we have also observed that the Arabs now tended to support the local insurgents in the south-east against Assyria.

In the sources from Assurbanipal's reign, the events involving Arabs appear entwined in the Babylonian revolt. In his attempts at restoring and keeping the empire together, Assurbanipal also had to face the Arab problem. His dealings with the Arabs and other peoples of North Arabia are reported in several texts which, however, are contradictory and difficult to interpret. In order to follow the dramatic story of the Arabs under Assurbanipal we have to take a close and critical look at the sources as a whole.[312]

The following texts from Assurbanipal's time contain information on the Arabs:

1. *Prism B*. This is an account consisting of several parallel texts on prisms written in the year 649 BC. The text has been reconstructed by A. C. Piepkorn.[313] The passage about Arabs occurs in VII:93–VIII:63.[314]
2. *Prism C*. In this fragmentary text written *c*. 646 BC, Arabs are mentioned in X:27–66.[315]
3. *The Ishtar letter*. The text belongs to the type where the Assyrian king reports his deeds to a god.[316]
4. *The Assur letter*. The text in this report to Assyria's national god stands rather close to the prism inscriptions, especially *Prism C*. The whole text is reconstructed from three different documents.[317]
5. *Prism A = The Rassam cylinder*. This is the longest and latest edition of Assurbanipal's annals, filling ten columns on the cylinder. The earliest date possible is 643/2 BC.[318] The epic story of the Arab campaign is found in columns VII:82–X:5, 17–19.[319]
6. *The Ishtar slab*. This text was found in Ishtar's temple in Nineveh and is the latest

of the inscriptions in question, written *c*. 640 BC. Arabs are not mentioned in it but, as will become evident, its content is important in order to interpret some details in the others.[320]

To these texts can be added fragments of two more unnamed texts.[321] Both are probably earlier than the Rassam cylinder. All texts except one, namely Prism B, are written after Shamash-shum-ukīn's revolt, i.e. after 648 BC. Another source of importance are the pictures of Assurbanipal's campaigns with accompanying texts from Room L in the palace in Kuyuncık (= Nineveh).[322] There are also a group of letters where a person named *arbāya* is mentioned.

Before attempting to disentangle the historical events from these sources, we should recapitulate the situation of the Arabs at the beginning of Assurbanipal's reign. Their gods had once more been taken to Assyria by Esarhaddon; the king of the Arabs, Yawthiʔ Yawthaʕ (or Yaʕlu) had fled and it seems that there was no king at all. It should be noticed that this information about events in Esarhaddon's later years comes from the Assur letter (source 4) only, i.e. from Assurbanipal's own time.

It is reasonable to start with the earliest source, Prism B. We will give a resumé of the passages, providing a literal translation only of the parts directly mentioning the Arabs:

1. Yawthaʕ (Ia-u-ta-') son of Hazaʔil, king of KUR qa-da-ri/qi-id-ri, is serving the king, asking for the return of his gods. He is given Attar-shamāyīn (VII:93–98).

2. (VII:99) 'Later, he violated his oath to me and (VIII:1) showed no regard of my favours and threw off the yoke of my dominion. (2) He restrained his feet from asking my health and (3) kept back from me (his gifts). (4) The people of KUR *a-ri-bi* he incited to revolt with him, and (5) they repeatedly plundered Amurru. (6) My troops which dwelt in the territory of his land (7) I dispatched against him. (8) Their defeat they accomplished; the people of KUR *a-ri-bi*, (9) as many as had advanced, they struck down with weapons. (10) Their tents, their dwellings, (11) they set on fire, allotted them to flames. (12) Cattle, sheep, asses, camels (*gamallē*), slaves without number they took . . . (Here follows a passage about the distribution of the booty) . . . (23) Yawthaʕ together with the rest of the LÚ *a-ri-bi* who had fled before my weapons, (24) mighty Ira struck down. (25) Famine broke out among them and (26) to still their hunger they ate the flesh of their children. (27) The curses, as many as were written in their oath (28) Asshur, Sîn, Shamash, Bêl, Nabû, (29) Ishtar of Nineveh, Ishtar of Arbela, the great gods, (30) my lords, brought upon them suddenly. As for Yawthaʕ, evil (31) befell him, and he fled by himself.'

3. Someone called Abyathiʕ (A-bi-a-te-') son of Te-'-ri comes to Nineveh, pays homage to Assurbanipal and is installed as king instead of Yawthaʕ (VIII:32–38).

4. Ammuladin king of KUR qa-ad-ri, who had plundered Amurru together with Yawthaʕ, is defeated by Kamash-halta, king of Moab (KUR Ma-'a-ab), who is a follower of the Assyrians. Ammuladin is captured and taken to Nineveh (VIII:39–50).

5. Natnu (Na-at-nu) king of Nabayāti (KUR Na-ba-a-a-ti) who live far away, who has

not earlier been subject to Assyria, sends ambassadors and pays tribute to Assurbanipal (VIII:51–63).

Qi-id-ri and Qa-ad-ri must be Qidri in Tiglath Pileser's tribute list from 738, where they occur together with the Arabs, and must also be the same name as Qedar in the Old Testament, the second eldest son of Ishmael. Ishmael's eldest son appears in episode 5: Nabayāti must be identical with the Nebayot in the list of Ishmael's sons.[323] Of the other names we identify a king Kamāsh Ḫaltu of Moab, acting as Assyria's ally in Transjordan.

According to this account, Qedar and its king Yawthaʕ have been subject to Assyria from the beginning of Assurbanipal's reign but revolted. They plunder Amurru, i.e. central Syria, but are defeated by the Assyrian troops stationed in the area. Another chieftain of Qedar, Ammuladin, is defeated by Moab. Abiyate is installed as a loyal puppet of Assyria. The formal treaty between Abiyate and Assurbanipal, which is implied in item 3, is documented in a text which probably is that of the treaty itself:

> . . . ia-ú-[ta-aʔ]
> . . . the gods of Asshur and of KUR Qi-id-[ri . . .]
> [(Swear by) Asshur], Mulissu, and Sh[erua]:
> [Considering th]at Ia-ú-ta-aʔ (your) malef[actor] handed all [*arub*]*u* over to destruction [through] the iron sword, and put you to the sword,
> [and that Assur]banipal, king of Assyria, your lord, put oil on you and turned his friendly face towards you,
> you shall not strive for peace with Ia-ú-ta-aʔ
> you shall not . . . your brothers, [your] unc[les . . .]
> . . .
> you shall . . .
> [you] sh[all keep] his feet [off . . .], and shall not send . . . after him by the hand of anyone,
> but considering the terrible things which he did, you shall make every effort to kill him.
> [May Asshur, Mu]llissu, Sin, Shamash, [Bel, Na]bu, Ishtar [of Nineveh. Ish]tar [of Arbela], Nergal . . .[324]

Even if the text is damaged it is very reasonable to identify Ia-ú-ta-aʔ with the king of Qidru in Prism B.[325] It can be supposed that Abiyate (Abyathiʕ) was mentioned in the damaged introduction.[326]

If we keep in mind the mention of Arabs and Qedar in the time of Tiglath Pileser, we remember that they appear as separate entities.[327] An unprejudiced reading of the passage in Prism B allows a similar interpretation. Yawthaʕ incites the Arabs to join him and appears as their leader, but it is not necessary to assume identity between Qedar and the Arabs. On the contrary, when another chief, Ammuladin, appears as the ally of Yawthaʕ, he is king of Qedar, and no Arabs are mentioned together with him. The treaty text can be read likewise. It says that Yawthaʕ handed over someone (ending in *-u*!) to destruction, *as well as* the Qedarites. The others must have been the Arabs (*arubu*). The picture is thus of a revolt led by chiefs from Qedar, one of whom mobilized the Arabs and the other led Qedar. We discern a close connection between the Arabs and Qedar but not necessarily identity.

The account in Prism B, which unfortunately is very fragmentary, is closely paralleled by that in Prism C. More informative is the Assur letter, which is also close to the prisms but has a continuation of the story involving the further careers of Natnu and Abyathiʕ. It is most likely that the letter was written at a later date and thus has updated the story with the later events.

The first part of it, which gives the same story as in Prisms B and C, has some interesting deviations and additions. The introduction to Assurbanipal's reign runs:

> (13) From the moment when Asshur, king of the whole heaven and earth, (14) by lifting his pure eyes chose me (15) and wanted me for kingship (16) and gave me sovereignty over Assyria . . . (17) Yuhaythiʕ (Ú-a-ate-'), son of Hazaʔil, king of KUR *a-ri-bi*, (18) heard that I had become king (19) and returned and . . .[328]

We notice that Yawthaʕ, king of Qedar, here appears as Yuhaythiʕ, king of the Arabs. Further, in Prism B, Yawthaʕ together with the Arabs is hit by Ira, the god of death and pestilence, but in the Assur letter it is only the Arabs who suffer from the god's ire. The misery among the Arabs caused by the war is expressively described:

> (II:13–18) A young camel, a young donkey, a calf, a lamb could suck seven milk animals but could not satisfy their stomachs (16) The people among/in the KUR *a-ri-bi* asked each other: 'Why has such a mischief happened? (19) [Which evil has struck KUR *a-ru-bu*?] (20) Because we have not kept the oaths to Assur (21) we have sinned against the goodness of Assurbanipal, the king according to Enlil's heart.'[329]

The Assur letter further has an episode not mentioned in Prism B. After the account about the defeat of Ammuladin, king of Qedar, by Moab, it is said:

> (II:45–49) A-ṭi-ia, queen of KUR *a-ri-bi*, her I defeated greatly. Her tents I set afire. Her I caught alive with my hands. With the booty from her country I took her to Assyria.[330]

Since Ammuladin, king of Qedar, has been mentioned in the immediately preceding passage, it is most likely that the Arabs governed by Aṭiya were distinct from Ammuladin's people although they were allies in the struggle against Assyria. Perhaps the other Qedarite chief is called king of the Arabs, because he did not lead the Qedar to war but the Arabs. How was he related to Aṭiya? We remember that his father, Haza'il, also appears closely related to a queen of the Arabs and is even called king of the Arabs.

This action against the Arabs may also be referred to in a letter from a certain Nabū-shum-lishir, who was some kind of officer of Assurbanipal.[331] He reports:

> Concerning the order which the king my lord has given me saying: 'send whatever report which you hear about LÚ *ar-a-bi*!' When this caravan/expedition went out from LÚ ni-ba-'-a-ti, a-a-ka-ma-ru, son of am-me-'-ta-', the LÚ bar-'-a-a, attacked them, killed people and took captives. When one of them (from the caravan) escaped, he entered into the city of the king. Now I have sent him to the king. May the king hear from his mouth.[332]

The letters from Nabū-shum-lishir seem to be written in a dialect different from the official records. The Niba'āti are probably those called Nabayāti in the other texts.[333] Is Amme'ta' identical with Abyathiʕ? We cannot be sure, but it is not impossible.[334] In that case, we would have a nice confirmation of the difference between the Nabayāti/Nebayot and the Arabs. As we shall see below, both joined in a revolt against Assyria after a short period of peace and treaty.

There are two more differences in the Assur letter which are important. One is the form of the name of the king of Qedar/the Arabs, namely Yuhaythiʕ (instead of Yawthaʕ), and the other the information that he joined the insurrection of Shamash-shum-ukīn. This event is not mentioned at all in Prisms B and C, which is remarkable if Yawthaʕ had indeed joined the revolt. The solution is probably found in the Ishtar slab (source 6) where we have a resumé of the events down to 640 BC. Lines 110–126 deal with our period. The passage starts with a recapitulation of the Shamash-shum-ukīn revolt and in connection with this it is said:

> 1. Yuhaythiʕ king of Shumuʔil who had intrigued with him (i.e. Shamash-shum-ukīn) alive I captured.
>
> 2. Yawthiʕ the king of Shumuʔil who by the command of Asshur, Ninlil and Ishtar of Arbela my hands conquered.
>
> 3. Yawthiʕ who unto Nabayāti had trusted and withheld his gifts . . . by the command of Ashur and Ninlil, the great gods my lords who protected me, I accomplished his defeat: his cities I turned to ruins and heaps, his sons and daughters . . . robes . . . the rich spoil of his land I carried off to Assyria.[335]

Yawthiʕ in passage 2 must be Yawthaʕ, king of Qedar/the Arabs, in Prism C, whereas Yuhaythiʕ, king of Shumuʔil in passage 1, is the one who sided with Shamash-shum-ukīn. In passage 2 these two have been confused by the Assyrian scribes. The confusion may well come from the Assur letter and the Rassam cylinder (Prism A), where both Yawthaʕ, king of Qedar/the Arabs and Yuhaythiʕ, king of Shumuʔil, are called Yuhaythiʕ, and thus not distinguished. The scribes who wrote the Ishtar slab may have been influenced by the Assur letter and Prism A together with Prisms B and C. We would thus originally have to do with two figures and two different series of events: Yawthaʕ, king of Qedar/the Arabs, who fought against Assyria before 652 BC, and Yuhaythiʕ, king of Shumuʔil, who joined the revolt by Shamash-shum-ukīn. Shumuʔil seems to have been a tribe in or around Taymāʔ, documented in a text from Sennacherib's time as well as in inscriptions from Taymāʔ itself.[336]

The Assur letter describes the events following Natnu's alliance with Assurbanipal in the following way:

1. (II:50–III:14) In spite of Yuhaythiʕ's (i.e. Yawthaʕ king of Qedar/the Arabs!) attempt to incite him to war against Assyria, Natnu concludes the treaty.

2. (III:15–56) Assurbanipal sets out on a second campaign, crosses the Euphrates, marches through the deserts in the month of Siwan, attains the mount Hu-ra-ri-na and defeats I-sa-am-me-', the people of A-tar-sa-ma-a-a-in and the LÚ Na-ba-a-a-ta-a-a.

3. (III:57–IV:10) 'From URU A-za-al-li to URU Qu-ra-ṣi-ti, sixty miles of land of thirst and hunger they marched. The people of A-tar-sa-ma-a-a-in, and the LÚ qid-ra-a-a of U-a-a-te-' son of Bir-da-ad-da, king of KUR *a-ri-bi*, and LÚ qid-ra-a-a I surrounded.' They are then taken to Damascus.

4. (IV:11–33) In the month of Ab, Assurbanipal takes off from Damascus, marches to Hul-hu-li-ti. On the mountain of Hu-uk-ku-ru-na he defeats the people of Abiyate, son of Te'ri, the Qedarite (LÚ qid-ra-a-a), captures Abiyate and his brother Ayammu (A-a-mu) and takes them to Assyria with a large booty.[337]

The reason for Assurbanipal's actions in passage 2 is not clearly stated. We could, however, adduce the parallel in the Rassam cylinder (Prism A), which has probably preserved complementary information. It states that Abyathiʕ, Yawthaʕ's successor as king of the Arabs, and Natnu start a war against Assyria.[338] They would thus have joined the insurrection in Babylonia. The geographical names indicate that their operations took place in southern Syria: Hukurina has been identified with Ḥawrān, and Damascus appears as Assurbanipal's base. Hulhuliti can probably also be identified as Khulkhula, north of the Ǧabal ad-Durūz.[339]

The most important passage in the latter part of the Assur letter is no. 3. The king of the Arabs, who is also somehow connected with Qedar, would be Yawthaʕ, who at this time had fled to Natnu. It is likely that we here get the patronymic of Yuhaythiʕ, king of Shumuʔil, who does not really belong to this context: he is son of Birdadda. We note that Qedar is mentioned twice in the passage: belonging to [Yawthaʕ son of Hazaʔil, king of Qedar/the Arabs] and [other] Qedarites, probably those of Ammuladin.

A final piece of information comes from the Rassam cylinder. That text, like the Assur letter, tells about Aṭiya, the queen of the Arabs, who is defeated together with Ammuladin. But we get the additional information that she was the wife of Yuhaythiʕ [i.e. Yawthaʕ], king of the Arabs.[340] Here we have a confirmation of the close relationship between the chiefs of Qedar and the Arabs. This is not the first time we hear about it: Yawthaʕ's father, Hazaʔil, is also mentioned together with a queen of the Arabs and he also appears sometimes as king of the Arabs and sometimes as king of Qedar.[341] Yawthaʕ's relationship with the Arabs was thus inherited.

The course of events

We may now give the main outlines of the relations between Assyria and the Arabs during the reign of Assurbanipal. After his accession to the throne in 669 BC, the chief of Qedar, Yawthaʕ, son of Hazaʔil, is reinstalled as king of the Arabs, and his relation to Assyria is confirmed by a formal treaty. At least one of the gods of the Arabs, Attarshamain, is returned, probably to Dumah. The connection between Yawthaʕ and the Arabs is that Aṭiya, queen of the Arabs, was Yawthaʕ's wife. After some years (we do not know how many) Yawthaʕ tries to shake off the Assyrian yoke by starting an insurrection supported by the Arabs. The main activities seem to have taken place in Syria. Another chief of Qedar, Ammuladin, joins the attack but is beaten by the king of Moab, Assyria's ally in Transjordan. Yawthaʕ and Aṭiya are defeated as well, and Yawthaʕ has to seek refuge with the Nebayoth and their king Natnu, whereas Aṭiya is taken captive to Assyria. Assurbanipal now appoints another chief, Abiyate, as king of Qedar instead of Yawthaʕ. Natnu, king of Nebayot, enters into an alliance with Assyria, in spite of his protection of Yawthaʕ, son of Hazaʔil. The latter seems to have been extradited to Assyria.

These events must have been concluded before 652 BC. It is obvious that the Assyrian influence was decisive among the tribes in northern Arabia and that they tried to control them by appointment of puppets. It is also evident how difficult it was to make these puppets remain loyal. Hazaʔil and his son Yawthaʕ were both Assyria's agents and both revolted twice during their careers. What can we learn about the relations between Arabs and other tribes from their history?

We may observe that Hazaʔil and his son in the sources are called kings of Qedar and kings of the Arabs alternatively. We should also observe that the other figures in this drama are not called kings of the Arabs, with one exception which will be analysed later. It is thus not possible to say that Arab is a general designation for nomads or inhabitants in general in northern Arabia by this time.[342] A close reading of the sources shows that there seems to be a special relation between the Arabs and Qedar. Hazaʔil and Yawthaʕ are designated as kings of the Arabs and/or Qedar. The queens we have encountered during these hundred years are only queens of the Arabs. None of them is called anything else. This must be interpreted in the following way: Arab and Qedar, although connected, are not identical. The exact nature of their relationship is not clear from the Assyrian evidence, but we shall see later in this study that it is possible to get a more exact view from later sources.[343]

One must ask if any 'real' Arabs took part in the Shamash-shum-ukīn revolt which broke out in 651 BC. No Arabs are mentioned in the official sources dealing with this incident. One of the three leaders, however, Abyathiʕ, is connected with the Arabs since he is said to be the successor of Yawthaʕ. The operations against the Arabs are also mentioned in two letters written by Nabū-shum-līshir. In the first one he says:

> The men of Asshur, the king's servants, who were stationed to/prevent/the casting away of the king at the town of the *bi-bar-bar* language, LÚ *a-ra-bu* attacked them, the men of Asshur, lords of the town Ha-lu-li-e and 20 men from Bir-ta-a-a, the king's servants together with them he (?) wounded. A man from their midst escaped . . . with the fate of the king my lord . . . a slaughter among them I wrought. In order to make a treading down they attacked. In their midst for the sake of the people, I established as overseers servants of the king. There is no breakdown there. I have set things right. 7 among them with the language I captured and sent to the king . . .[344]

From another letter of Nabū-shum-līshir we know that the scene is Babylonia: the town Birta is situated near 'the swamps of Bâbili'.[345] It is reasonable to assume that the letters refer to the operations in Babylonia during the insurrection of Shamash-shum-ukīn. In that case these Arabs may have been the people of Abyathiʕ. Of considerable interest is the reference to the different language of the Arabs, 'the *bi-bar-bar* language', perhaps the first mention of an Arabic language in any historical source.[346]

Finally, in five documents from Assurbanipal's time a certain *arbāya* is mentioned who is a *rab kiṣir* and who seems to have been in charge of horses belonging to the king. He appears together with a high official named Bêl eṭir in southern Babylonia[347]. It is uncertain if *arbaya* is a personal name or a designation for someone belonging to the Arabs. The word is also used in somewhat later sources in the same way and could be a designation for an official of some kind. There emerges the picture of individuals called *arbāya* in the service of the Assyrians and in charge of animals in the same way as Gindibu, the camel-tender of the Syrians at Qarqar.

In the Shamash-shum-ukīn revolt, we see that many tribes in North Arabia took part and were drawn into the events in Babylonia. This shows that they must have had interests there. A further indication of this are many forts and settlements in lower Babylonia named after persons well known from the events we have surveyed. Already from the time of Sennacherib we hear about Dūr Yuhaythiʕ (U-a-a-te-'), Dūr Birdadda and Dūr Abyathiʕ.[348] These names, together with the documented presence of people with names of a clearly Arabic type, show that during the seventh century the tribes of North Arabia had established a presence in Mesopotamia. Among them were also the real Arabs.

Excursus: the people of Attar-shamayin

In the texts from Assurbanipal we twice hear about the *aʔlu (ša) a-tar-sa-ma-a-a-in*, 'the people of Attar of Heaven', being defeated together with the Nebayot, the Qedar led by Yuhaythiʕ son of Birdadda, king of the Arabs, and [the rest of?] Qedar.[349]

The two passages where the expression 'people of Attarshamāyīn' occurs, namely the Assur letter III:52 = the Rassam cylinder VIII:111 and IV:1 = IX:1, are problematic. Since references to this episode do not occur in the sources written before Shamash-shum-ukīn's insurrection, they certainly refer to events after that time.

Assurbanipal tells of his wrath when hearing about Uwayte's words to Natnu, king of Nebayot, with whom he had sought refuge. The Assyrian king crosses the Two Rivers into a wilderness of forests and deserts, hunting Yuhaythiʕ, king of the Arabs. In the month of Siwan he sets out from Hadatta, passing Laribda. Having reached Hurarīna between Iarqi and Azalla he continues: 'I made a killing among I-sa-am-me-', LÚ the *aʔlu* of Attarshamāyīn and LÚ Nabayāte'. Having returned to Azalla, he marches against Quraṣat and then recounts: 'the *aʔlu* of Attarshamāyīn and LÚ Qidray of Yuhaythiʕ son of Birdadda, king of KUR *aribi,* and Qidray I surrounded'. Then he heads towards Damascus.

This passage is directly followed by another one which tells about a campaign against Abyathiʕ, son of Te'eri, and his brother Ayammu. Abyathiʕ had been installed as king of the Arabs when Yuhaythiʕ was defeated and had fled to Natnu, king of Nebayot, and had later together with Yuhaythiʕ, son of Birdadda, king of Shumuʔil, participated in the revolt of Shamash-shum-ukīn. Assurbanipal starts from Damascus, marching against Hulhulat in the mountainous country of Hukkurina. Here he defeats Abyathiʕ and Ayammu and takes them to Assyria.[350]

The geographical setting is obviously somewhere in southern Syria. Unfortunately, the only certainly identifiable name is Damascus. The mention of Qedar and Nebayot indicates that the first battle should be located somewhere not too far from Wādī Sirḥān, perhaps east of al-Laǧā in the south-western Syrian desert.[351] The second is more certain to be located south of Damascus, close to the northern slopes of the Ǧabal ad-durūz.

The confusion between Yawthaʕ, son of Hazaʔil, king of the Arabs, and Yuhaythiʕ, son of Birdadda, king of Shumuʔil, is obvious in this passage. The first refers to two battles: one against Ishamme, *aʔlu ša Attarshāmāyīn* and Nebayot, the other against *a'lu ša Attarshamāyīn*, the Qedar of Yuhaythiʕ, son of Birdadda, king of the Arabs and Qedar(enes). The king should be Yawthaʕ, son of Hazaʔil. In the parallel passage in the Rassam cylinder, the second mention of Qedar is missing. It cannot be excluded that there are overlaps between the two battles. Since two of the protagonists, Nebayot and Qedar, together with the Arabs, were the main actors in Assurbanipal's first Arab war, one would expect the Arabs to emerge here too. One would thus suspect that they are hidden under the designation *aʔlu ša Attarshamāyīn*. Another argument for this is the fact that Yawthaʕ is given the (image of the) divinity Attarshamāyīn by Esarhaddon. His father, Hazaʔil, was king of the Arabs and had received the six gods from Esarhaddon. Yawthaʕ excites the Arabs when starting his revolt against Assyria.[352] There is no reasonable doubt that the Arabs belonged to the *aʔlu ša Attarshamāyīn*. Since the other two protagonists, Qedar and Nebayot, are mentioned as separate from the *a'lu ša Attarshamāyīn*, the Arabs seem to be the ones intended by that term.[353]

Excursus: a short historical and redactional survey of the text of the Rassam cylinder

The Rassam cylinder (= Prism A), which may have been the final official version of the account of Assurbanipal's reign, contains a long, coherent story of the operations in North Arabia. This passage is, in fact, one of the longest texts about conditions in North Arabia written before the rise of Islam, and it can be read as an 'Arabiad', an epic story about the wars against the Arabs. From a comparison with the other records it is clear that the text is an amalgamation of two separate series of events, with confusion of the names of two of the main protagonists. The reason for this may have been the fact that two others, Natnu, king of Nebayot, and Abiyate, king of the Arabs, were involved in both. We present the main outline of the story as given in the Rassam cylinder, with adjustments according to the evidence from the other sources.[354]

1. (VII:82–106) Assurbanipal's ninth campaign is against Ú-a-a-te-', king of KUR *a-ri-bi*, who has broken his treaty with Assyria. He has joined the Shamash-shum-ukīn revolt together with Akkad and Elam and incited the people of KUR *a-ri-bi*.

Only the title of Uayte and the last words do, in fact, belong to the first series of events, before the revolt of Shamash-shum-ukīn. The rest refers to that latter event.

2. (VII:107–124) Assurbanipal marches via U-da-me (Edom?), bīt am-ma-ni (ʕAmmān), through the regions of ha-u-ri-na (Ḥawrān), mu-'-a-ba (Moab) and ṣu-pi-te (Soba) where Ú-a-a-te-' is beaten. He escapes to KUR/URU na-ba-a-a-te.

This is an account of the final operations against the allies of Shamash-shum-ukīn and follows the Assur letter closely, except the final words which deal with Yawthaʕ's flight after the first revolt.

3. (VIII:1–14) Ú-a-a-te-', son of Ha-za-ilu, cousin of Ú-a-a-te-', son of Bir-Dadda, who has installed himself as king of the KUR *a-ri-bi*, changes his mind and renders himself to Assurbanipal, who puts him in a cage and exposes him at one of the gates of Nineveh.

This seems to refer to an event after the defeat of Shamash-shum-ukīn, when Yawthaʕ gives himself up to the Assyrian king. This is not reported in any other source. Another important piece of information is that of the family relationship between Yawthaʕ, son of Hazaʔil, and Uayte, son of Birdadda.

4. (VIII:15–29) Am-mu-la-di, king of KUR qí-id-ri, starts a war against Assyria. He is also defeated, captured together with A-di-ia-a, wife of U-a-a-te-', king of KUR *a-ri-bi*.

This passage refers to events in the first revolt only, succeeding the revolt and flight of Yawthaʕ son of Hazaʔil. Also here we get a precious piece of information about personal relationships between the main protagonists, which is not found in any of the other sources. Uayte should, of course, be replaced by Yawthaʕ.

5. (VIII:30–41) A-bi-ia-te and his brother A-a-mu, sons of Te-'-e-ri, have come to support the besieged troops of the insurgents in Babylon. Abiyate is defeated and flees alone. A-a-mu is taken captive.

This passage corresponds to the final account of the Shamash-shum-ukīn revolt in the other sources.

6. (VIII:42–47) Abiyate comes to Assurbanipal and is made king of KUR *a-ri-bi* instead of Ú-a-a-te-', son of Ha-za-ilu.

We are back in the first series of events when Yawthaʕ, son of Hazaʔil, was replaced by Abiyathiʕ.

7. (VIII:48–64) Abiyate allies himself with Nebayot. Their king, Na-at-nu, makes a treaty with Assurbanipal but breaks it after a while. Abiyate son of Teeri and Natnu, king of Nebayot, begin a new war against Assyria.

8. (VIII:65–IX:8) Assurbanipal crosses the Euphrates and chases the troops of Abiyate and Ú-a-ate-', king of KUR *a-ri-bi*. In the month of Siwan, Assurbanipal marches into the desert and defeats I-sa-am-me-', 'the people of Attarshamain', and the Nebayot. Returning he also defeats 'the people of Attarshamain', the LÚ qid-ra-a-a (Qedar) together with Ú-a-ate-' son of Bir-Dadda, king of KUR *a-ri-bi*. The latter is captured and taken to Damascus.

9. (IX:9–52) In the month of Ab, Assurbanipal leaves Damascus. On the mountain Hu-ka-ri-na he overtakes Abiyate, son of Teeri, the Qedarite, who is defeated and taken captive. The rest of his men are besieged on the mountain and perish from hunger and thirst. An immense booty is taken to Assur.

10. (IX:55–128) Ú-a-ate-' (son of Hazaʔil) and his troops are beaten by the god Erra. The punishments mentioned in the treaty oaths hit them. Ú-a-ate-''s troops revolt against him and he seeks refuge in Asshur. He is taken captive and put in a cage at a gate in Nineveh.

11. X:1–5: A-a-mu son of Teeri, who has followed his brother Abiyate, is taken in battle, taken to Nineveh and his skin is peeled off.

These passages follow the story in the Assur letter fairly closely. Only in 10 do we have an intrusion from the first revolt and the defeat of Yawthaʕ son of Hazaʔil. We also notice that the fact that Uayte was king of Sumu'il and not of the Arabs has left no trace in this text.

The Rassam cylinder is a merger of the accounts of two different events. Two different leaders have been made one. The result is after all a fairly coherent story, not without literary qualities. It is a most interesting example of the manipulation of facts into a narrative structure which has taken place very shortly after the events themselves. There are many good parallels from Arabia, both ancient and modern. Suffice it to point out the stories about the famous heroes of the *Ǧāhiliyya* period, as well as the Shammar chief ʕAbdallāh ibn Rashīd, whose career in the middle of the nineteenth century AD became the stuff legends are made of.

The late Judaean kingdom and Arabia

The Deuteronomistic Book of Kings as well as Chronicles contain the following report about the reign of Solomon:

The gold that came to Solomon every year weighed six hundred and sixty six talents, apart from [that coming from] travelling commerciants (*tûrîm*) and [from] the trade of peddlars (*misḥar roklîm*) and [from] the kings of *ʕereb* and [from] the *paḥôt* of the land.	The gold that came to Solomon every year weighed six hundred and sixty six talents, apart from [that coming from] travelling commerciants (*tûrîm*) and [from] merchants (*soḥarîm*) and [from] the kings of *ʕarab* and [from] the *paḥôt* of the land who brought gold and silver to Solomon.
(1 Kings 10:14–15)	(2 Chronicles 9:13–14)

It is obvious that the passage goes back to a common *Vorlage* dealing with the reign of Solomon in the tenth century BC. As it now stands, it is part of a series of notices, the main theme of which is the wealth of Solomon and how he gained it. Eight of the twelve verses in question deal with activities in the Red Sea and adjacent regions: the expedition to Ophir (1 Kings 9:26–28, 10:11–12) and another expedition, probably to the African shore, made with the so-called *ʕoniyê taršîš*, the 'Tarshish-ships' (1 Kings 10:22). Our passage stands between these two (1 Kings 10:14–15). To complicate things even further, the story of the Queen of Sheba is intermingled with these notices, ending just before our passage.

The text of the Book of Kings is the result of the Deuteronomistic redaction, probably accomplished in the sixth century BC. Chronicles is even later, probably the fourth century BC. The historicity of the information given must therefore be problematic, unless it can be shown that the redactors had access to older sources and used them. It is obvious that the Deuteronomists had various such sources. The Chronicler in his turn used the Deuteronomistic version of Kings but supplied it with material of his own, some of which is old.

In the story of the precious metals brought to Solomon we may notice the differences: C has an addition to the note saying that the kings of the *ʕarab* and the *paḥôt* brought gold and silver to Solomon. C also has the form *ʕarab* while D has *ʕereb*. D has the term *roklîm* for merchants while C has *soḥarîm*.

The central part of this whole passage is 1 Kings 10:23–25: 'So king Solomon exceeded all the kings of the earth for riches and for wisdom. And all the earth sought to Solomon to hear his wisdom, which God had put in his heart. And they brought every man his present, vessels of silver, and vessels of gold, and garments, and armour, and spices (*besamîm*), horses, and mules, a rate year by year.'

The theme of Solomon's wealth and wisdom is clearly the reason why the notices about his commercial enterprises are adduced. It also explains the rather unorganized way they are given in the present text. The emphasis on Solomon's status as a superman is also the purpose of the Queen of Sheba story. It is most likely that this theme comes from a popular legend about Solomon. The wisdom-theme may have had a basis in the original sources about Solomon, but its present shape is clearly a development.[355] One cannot escape the impression that the panegyric tone in parts of the Solomon narrative is somewhat alien to the flavour of the Deuteronomistic history, which is on the whole very critical towards Solomon. We know that the Solomonic legend later grew into a wonderful tree, notwithstanding the severe judgement of the official Deuteronomistic history. The sapling of this tree is clearly discernible in our text and shows that the tree started to grow within the covers of the canonical parts of the Old Testament.

This implies that the Arab passage in the Solomonic history is part of a panegyric legend which may be older than the Deuteronomistic redaction. The legend has fed on material some of which may go back to the time of the famous king. The Arab passage, however, is open to doubt. The weight of 666 talents of gold (= *c*. twenty tons) is quite unrealistic, and it is worth noticing that this is the only passage in the Old Testament where *ʕarab* are said to be involved in the gold business. The number may well be the sum of all the gold given to Solomon, mentioned in the text.[356]

The word *roklîm* seems to belong to a later strain in the language. Interestingly enough, out of twenty-two occurrences in the Old Testament of the root with the meaning 'trade', sixteen are found in Chapter 27 of Ezechiel, which deals with international business. In this connection, the *ʕarab* are explicitly said to be dealers in cattle (sheep and goats) and not in gold, which is the business of the Sabaeans. We may further notice that the expression 'all the kings of *ʕarab/ʕereb*' reappears in a passage in the Book of Jeremiah, where we also find the hesitation between the two forms.[357] The Septuagint version of Kings, instead of 'the kings of *ʕereb*', has 'the kings of the other side' (namely of the river Euphrates), going back to a reading *ʕeber*. Finally, the word *paḥôt*, which is an Akkadian loan-word in Hebrew, occurs in eighteen out of twenty occurrences in texts from the sixth century or later. The Assyrian *pi/pahūtu* was hardly used in Palestine before the time of Tiglath Pileser III.[358] It was especially used in the Assyrian empire as a designation for governors of provinces. We may note that Solomon's own governors are designated as *niṣabîm* in other passages.[359]

It is thus clear that the passage reflects Neo-Assyrian times at the earliest. The early version of the legend of king Solomon which we have documented in the Old Testament was probably formed during the last century of the Judaean kingdom, starting in the reign of Ezekiah.[360] The text about the riches of Solomon, as well as the one about the visit of the Queen of Sheba, were incorporated by the Deuteronomistic historians writing the history of Israel during the Exile. That history book was later used by the Chronicler. The alternation between *ʕarab* and *ʕereb* found in the narrative about Solomon and in Jeremiah Chapter 25 seems to reflect an early interpretation of the word *ʕarab*: the root ʕRB in Hebrew means 'mix', and the Septuagint renders *ʕereb* by words derived from the verb 'mix' in other instances.[361] There are thus arguments in favour of seeing *ʕarab* in 2 Chronicles as a better reading than the *ʕereb* in 1 Kings.[362] If the story as we have it has been conceived in the time of Ezekiah or the last century of the Judaean kingdom, and if the reading found in Chronicles is the better one, the mention of Arabs could be inspired by knowledge about those in the Syrian desert otherwise known from the contemporary Assyrian texts.[363]

In short: this Arab passage should be interpreted as a creation by later legend in order to extend the realm of Solomon's reputation to areas that had become better known around 700 BC. The use of vocabulary from the seventh century BC or later indicates that this is the case. The presence of an Assyrian term for governor, as well as the designation 'the other side of the Euphrates', point to the late Assyrian period when the latter was the regular term for Syria. Interestingly enough, 'the other side' as a designation for Syria occurs once more in the texts dealing with Solomon, namely 1 Kings 5:4. The absence of the word *roklîm* in 2 Chronicles may in fact indicate that the text was still growing as late as the fourth century BC, and that the present version in 1 Kings represents a later accretion. C could also be older than D in its use of the term *ʕarab*. On the other hand, C underlines the bringing of gold twice in his version. This may indicate that the original notice just registered the gold received by Solomon without giving any origin, a notice which may in the present text be represented by the introduction. The power of Solomon was obviously seen in the seventh century in terms of that period, and the political entities existing then were projected backwards into the tenth century BC. The employment of the Assyrian terms for Syria and its governors points to *c.* 730 as a *terminus a quo* and might well represent the original Deuteronomistic terminology. And it is of course more glorious for a great king to receive twenty tons of gold per year than herds of sheep and goats, however numerous they may be.

Excursus: the Queen of Sheba

We cannot leave the Old Testament without commenting on the story of the Queen of Sheba from our viewpoint. That the story is part of the panegyric legend about Solomon is completely evident from its whole flavour, its purpose being eloquently expressed in 1 Kings 10:6–9. The question is whether there are any historical facts behind the present version.

We may first notice the absence of any reference to *ʕarab* in the story. As in the rest of the Old Testament, as well as in the Assyrian texts, there is no evidence whatsoever that the Sabaeans or Sheba were designated as *ʕarab*. Further, we have seen that the Old Testament indicates the existence of a Sheba in North Arabia around the oasis of Dedan, present-day al-ʕUlā. The northern Sheba occurs in the list of the descendants of Qeturah as a brother to Dedan. In the Table of Nations in Genesis 10 we find Sheba and Dedan as sons of Raʕmah.[364] This part of the genealogy belongs to the so-called Priestly Code.[365] In Chapter 27 in Ezechiel, originating from a prophet, who in his outlook is close to the Priestly Code, the topos 'tribute from the ends of the earth' is applied to the city of Tyre: 'The merchants of Sheba and Raʕmā, they were thy merchants: they occupied in thy fairs with chief of all spices, and with all precious stones and gold.' Here we find the same association between Sheba and Raʕmah. In the following verse we have a list of merchants in Syria and adjacent regions: 'Haran, and Canneh, and Eden, the merchant of Sheba, Asshur, and Chilmad, were thy merchants'. Most names in that list can be located in northern Syria. Especially noteworthy is the juxtaposition of Asshur and Sheba, which we also find in the Qeṭurah list. The Sheba in Ezechiel 27 must be the northern one.[366] From this Sheba came the Sabaeans appearing as Job's enemies.[367]

On the other hand, in a eulogy to a king in Jerusalem, probably from the later period of the Judaean monarchy, it is said: 'The kings of Tarshish and the isles shall bring presents; the kings of Sheba and Seba shall offer gifts.'[368] These names symbolize the farthest ends of the earth, probably the Straits of Gibraltar and the Straits of the Bāb al-Mandab. If Seba is a kingdom on the African side, which is the common opinion, possibly in present-day Eritrea, Sheba in the psalm should be on the South Arabian side and is likely to be the kingdom of Saba in Yemen.[369] Seba appears among the sons of Kush in the great genealogy in Genesis 10 as the brother of Raʕmah and the uncle of Sheba.[370] This note, which belongs to the Priestly Code, is probably from the same period as the psalm, i.e. not earlier than 700 BC, but it is not certain whether this Sheba is in northern or southern Arabia.[371] A similar juxtaposition of Sheba and Kûsh is made by Deutero-Isaiah in the middle of the sixth century: 'Thus saith the Lord: The labour of Egypt, and merchandise of Kush (*sḥar kûš*) and of Sheba, men of stature, shall come over unto thee'.[372] If Kush here is Nubia, it is likely that Sheba is the South Arabian Saba.

A definite knowledge of the South Arabian Saba is found in the Book of Jeremiah, where we read: 'To what purpose cometh there to me (= the Lord) frankincense (*lebônā*) from Sheba, and the sweet cane from a far country?'.[373] Further in Trito-Isaiah from the end of the sixth century BC: 'The multitude of camels shall cover thee, the dromedaries of Midian and Ephah; all they from Sheba shall come: they shall bring gold and frankincense (*lebônā*); and they shall show forth the praises of the Lord'.[374] The mention of the South Arabian frankincense, even using the South Arabian loanword *lebônā*, proves that from *c.* 600 BC the people of Judah knew about the South Arabian Saba. This knowledge is also documented by the list of the sons of Yoqṭan in the genealogy in Genesis 10, which comes from another source than the Priestly Code.[375]

The Old Testament thus clearly indicates the existence of two Shebas, one in the north around Dedan, which is documented already from the ninth century BC, and one in the south, most probably identical with the Sabaean empire in Yemen, known to have existed at least from the eighth century BC but certainly documented in the Old Testament in the seventh century BC at the earliest. Taking into account the supposed date of the Qeṭurah list above, the Israelites first must have had contacts with the northern Sabaeans and later, perhaps through them, established contacts with the Sabaeans in Yemen. This gradual acquaintance with political conditions in western Arabia may explain the different genealogies of Sheba in the Old Testament. The Qeṭurah version is likely to be the oldest one, supposing Sheba to be a group in North Arabia, later incorporated into the genealogy of the Priestly writers and still remembered by Hezechiel and the author of the Book of Job.

Outside the Old Testament, the northern Sabaeans are documented earliest in the time of Tiglath Pileser III in the year 738 BC.[376] The southern Sabaeans may be documented in Sabaean inscriptions from the eighth century BC.[377] The relationship between these two Sabaean groups is not altogether clear.[378] Since the Assyrian kings mention names of Sabaean kings that we also find in the inscriptions of the southern Sabaeans, it must be supposed that they were somehow related. That the Assyrian kings should have made military campaigns to Yemen and had direct military encounters with the Sabaean kings residing there is completely out of the question. It has been suggested that the northern Sabaeans were some kind of commercial agents for the southern kings or constituted a colony of merchants for them in Dedan like the later Minaeans.[379]

If we now return to the issue of the visit of the Queen of Sheba to Solomon in the tenth century BC, we can say that the presence of Sabaeans in Dedan at that time is undocumented if we disregard the account in 1 Kings 10/2 Chron. 9, the authenticity of which has still to be proved. The Qeṭurah list indicates a close relationship between Israelites/Judaeans and northern Sabaeans around *c.* 850 and perhaps even earlier. But it is most unlikely that Solomon or any other ruler in Syria in the tenth century BC would have had trade connections with Sabaeans in Yemen, since at present there is hardly any evidence for a Sabaean kingdom there before the ninth or even eighth century BC.[380] On the other hand, the story itself belongs to the literary topos documented in several other texts. Of these, psalm 72 may be considered the earliest, since it presupposes the existence of a Jerusalemite king as well as knowledge about South Arabian Saba but without mentioning any frankincense. Since the psalm praises a king in Jerusalem and seems to presuppose acquaintance with Saba in South Arabia, it must have been composed after the establishment of contacts between the South Arabian Sabaeans and Syria and before the fall of the Judaean kingdom in 587 BC.[381] In the light of this, the absence of frankincense in psalm 72 as well as among the queen's gifts to Solomon is remarkable. It is very unlikely indeed that the authors would not have mentioned this expensive and exclusive perfume if they had known that it came from the South Arabian Saba. It can be argued that the psalm is somehow connected with the Messianic hopes surrounding the kings Ezekiah or Josiah, i.e. a period when contacts with South Arabia are much more likely than in the time of Solomon. The story of the Queen of Sheba would consequently have been conceived in the same period. Both texts would be older than the establishment of frankincense trade with South Arabia in the late seventh century and belong to the time of Ezekiah.

Another nail in the queen's coffin is the absence of documented Sabaean queens. We now have an almost complete series of South Arabian Sabaean rulers, from the eighth century until the Ethiopian conquest in the sixth century AD in contemporary documents.[382] No queens are found in this list or indeed mentioned at all in any of the thousands of inscriptions from South Arabia. On the other hand, as we have seen, we do have names preserved of queens belonging to the Arabs in the Syrian desert in the north from the year 738 down to *c.* 650 BC. But as has been pointed out, the Arabs and the Sabaeans are two different groups in this period. The fact remains: no Sabaean queens are documented. That such a queen could have existed in the tenth century (in Dedan?) is of course always possible in the absence of evidence but it cannot be verified.

Since the story about the queen can be analysed in terms of literary topoi and royal ideology, one has to demand very solid contemporary evidence to verify it as history and not fiction. Since such evidence to date has not appeared, the Queen of Sheba story must be seen as literary fiction, like the whole passage on the wealth and wisdom of Solomon. The poet has used evidence at hand: knowledge of the queens in Arabia in the eighth century BC, the legendary riches of the distant land of Yemen and the role of the Sabaeans, southern and northern, in the Pan-Arabian trade as well as the role of the tribute-paying peoples from the ends of the world in the ideology of the late Israelite kings. A concrete historical fact may have been knowledge of connections between Israelites and the northern Sabaeans in the early period of the kings, as reflected in the Qeṭurah-list. The story is thus a projection backwards to the time of Solomon of the royal ideology of the Jerusalemite kingship towards the end of the Monarchy. An indication of the time of its composition may be found in the absence of frankincense. It is most unlikely that the poet would have failed to mention this perfume if he had known that it came from the land of Sheba. Since frankincense appears in Israel first in the late seventh century BC, our story may be older than that but also younger than the middle of the eighth century, when the Arab queens became prominent in the political events in North Arabia.[383]

Nebuchadnezzar II

The campaigns of Assurbanipal against the Arabs is their last appearance in Assyrian sources. We have no information on whether the Arabs took part in the great events around 612 BC when the Assyrian empire was crushed by an alliance between Babylon, the Medes and Egypt. But the disappearance of the hated Assyrians did not lead to peaceful conditions. The allied forces were soon entangled in a fierce struggle among themselves for the now vacant supremacy over the Middle East. After a few years Babylon gained the upper hand, taking control of upper Mesopotamia and wrestling Syria out of the hands of Egypt in a series of campaigns that look strangely similar to the Assyrian ones in the ninth and eighth centuries. The new rulers of Mesopotamia, Nabopolassar and his son Nebuchadnezzar, found themselves confronted with the same geopolitical situation as their Assyrian predecessors.

The Egyptian attempt at taking control of Syria after the fall of Nineveh suffered a major setback in 605 BC, when they were defeated by the Babylonians at Carchemish. The latter took control of the coastland down to Gaza. The Judaean king Jehoiakim, who had been an Egyptian ally until then, had to change his sympathies to the new power in the north and became a vassal of Nebuchadnezzar. When the Babylonian king, in a renewed attempt to conquer Egypt, was defeated by pharaoh Necho in 601, the Babylonian grip on southern Syria loosened for a while, and Jehoiakim once again changed sides. For a short while, Judah and her immediate neighbours, supported by Egypt, could act independently of the Babylonian king. This alliance, encompassing Egypt, Judah, Edom, Ammon, Moab and 'those with cropped hair living in the desert', is probably reflected in what seems to be a condemnation of the whole project by the prophet Jeremiah.[384]

After two years of rearmament, Nebuchadnezzar returned to Syria in 599 BC in order to settle things according to his will. The operations are described in a chronicle from his own time:

> (9) In the sixth year in the month of Kislev the king of Akkad mustered his army and marched to the Hatti-land. From the Hatti-land he sent out his companies (10) and scouring the desert (*madbaru*) they took much plunder from LÚ *a-ra-bi*, their possessions, animals and gods. In the month of Adar the king returned to his own land.[385]

This expedition took place during the winter months Kislev (December)–Adar

(March) 599–598 BC. Judging from the text, Nebuchadnezzar established a base in Syria, perhaps in Damascus, and then started operations against the Arabs. It is remarkable that this is the only activity recorded for the campaign. The text indicates that its main purpose was the pacification of the desert, the Arabs included. It must have been in connection with this operation that Moab and Ammon defected and started to attack Judah, together with the Babylonian vassals in Damascus.[386] Edom is not mentioned.[387]

In his next campaign in 597 BC, Nebuchadnezzar attacked Judah and reduced her to vassalage and took the king prisoner. When unrest broke out in Babylonia in 594, the new Judaean king, Sedeqiah, gathered the local leaders to a summit meeting in Jerusalem. Tyre and Sidon also took part, together with the three neighbours in Transjordan.[388] No result emerged from this meeting, since Nebuchadnezzar soon mastered the domestic situation. Sedeqiah's plots, supported by Egypt, against the Babylonian superpower ended in disaster for Judah in 587 BC.[389]

It seems that the background for these operations was a desire to break up and control a constellation of powers in southern Syria, consisting of Judah, Ammon, Moab and Edom, later joined by Sidon and Tyre, to which the Arabs also belonged. The reason for this policy was not only the ambition to keep Egypt away. When the siege of Tyre had started in 587 BC, the prophet Ezechiel composed a song about the greatness of Tyre, which now was to disappear.[390] A later hand interpolated into the song a list of the trade partners of Tyre, which gives a good picture of its trading connections towards the south:

> (16) Aram (= Edom?) was thy merchant by reason of the multitude of the wares of thy making: they dealt in thy fairs with emeralds, purple, and embroidered work, and fine linen, and coral, and agate.
>
> (17) Judah, and the land of Israel, they were thy merchants: they traded in thy market wheat of Minnith, and Pannag, and honey, and oil, and balm.
>
> . . .
>
> (20) Dedan was thy merchant in precious clothes for chariots.
>
> (21) *ʕarab* and all the princes of Qedar, they dealt in thee lambs, and rams, and goats: in these were they thy merchants.
>
> (22) The merchants of Sheba and Raʕmah, they were thy merchants: they dealt in thy fairs with chief of all spices, and with all precious stones, and gold.[391]

Even though the list has been interpolated after the song was composed, the list itself has been put together some time between 722 and 587.[392] The list is closely related to those in Genesis 10, which will be discussed later. The text is thus a resumé of the position of Tyre during the years before the Babylonian conquest. There is no doubt that we have here one of the reasons for the Babylonian interest in the area and also in the *ʕarab*. The trade through the northern Ḥiǧāz and the Negev and along the coast was obviously important. Both strategic and economic reasons lay behind Nebuchadnezzar's attack against the Arabs.

There is a text in the book of Jeremiah where *ʕarab* occur which must be discussed in connection with the events around the year 600 BC since it may shed more light on the Babylonian campaigns to southern Syria. In Chapter 25 in the Masoretic text, which is Chapter 32 in the Septuagint, we find the report of a vision by the prophet Jeremiah, in which he was ordered to give his own people and their neighbours a cup of wine to drink. This wine would make them deadly drunk as a sign of the divine wrath against them, since they had tried to withstand the Babylonian power which, according to Jeremiah, was the divine tool for punishment of the unfaithful Israelites.[393] The peoples to receive this unpleasant drink are the following:

> (18) Jerusalem with the cities of Judah and its kings and chiefs . . .
>
> (19) Pharaoh, the king of Egypt, and his servants and chiefs and his entire people (20) and the whole mixed throng [*ʕereb*] ([MT: and all the kings of the land of ʕUṣ]), and all the kings of the land of the Philistines, [MT: and] Ashqelon, and Gaza, and Eqron, and the remnant of Ashdod;
>
> (21) [LXX: and] Edom, and Moab, and the Ammonites,
>
> (22) and all the kings of Tyre, and all the kings of Sidon, and the kings of the island that is [LXX: of those who are] beyond the ocean;
>
> (23) [LXX: and] Dedān, and Têmā', and Buz [LXX: Rōs],
>
> and all with cropped hair [*qṣûṣê peʔā*], (24) [MT: and all the kings of *ʕarab*], and all the kings of the *ʕereb* who dwell in the desert [*midbar*],
>
> (25) [MT: and all the kings of Zimri [Peshitta: Zemrān]],
>
> and all the kings of Elam, and all the kings of Media [LXX: the Persians],
>
> (26) and all the kings of the north, close and distant between each other, and all the kingdoms of the world (which are upon the earth),
>
> [MT: and the king of Sheshak shall drink after them].[394]

The differences in the textual tradition show that the text has been tampered with, probably several times. It is clear that the description of the vision itself (= the passages preceding and following the quoted one) has also been revised on at least two occasions.[395] The whole vision is thus likely to have been updated in accordance with the dramatic political developments during the final years of the Judaean kingdom and, possibly, even long after the fall of Jerusalem. Thus the appearance of Elam and Media reflects events many years after AD 587 and is most probably not due to Jeremiah.[396]

The insight that this text has been growing for a long time allows us to analyse it and judge its historical value. The earliest layer would be the doom over Egypt, Judah and Philistaea, reflecting the anti-Babylonian alliance before 604 BC. Edom, Moab and the Ammonites in v. 21 would then represent the first updating, reflecting the constellation of anti-Babylonian powers in southern Syria between 601 and Nebuchadnezzar's campaign in 599–98.[397] The Phoenicians in v. 22 would represent their presence at the anti-Babylonian summit meeting in Jerusalem in 594 BC. The two towns in northern Ḥiǧāz, Dedān and Têmā', are not mentioned otherwise in the book of Jeremiah and may well be a later addition.[398] This also holds for Buz, which belongs together with ʕUṣ in v. 19, which is obviously misplaced.[399] All these names designate places in the northern Ḥiǧāz, probably south of Edom, which makes it very likely that Zimri also belongs to the same group and should be identified with Zimrān in the Qeṭurah list, an identification which is explicitly made by the Peshitta.

What is of primary interest for us is the mention of the *ʕarab* in v. 24. Do they belong to the original Jeremianic sayings and, in that case, to which layer? The answer to these two questions will give the clue to their identity.

The expression 'the kings of *ʕarab*' occurs in one other passage in the Old Testament, namely the passage in Chronicles dealing with the tribute to Solomon, which should be dated to the late Judaean monarchy.[400] This means that the term 'the kings of the *ʕarab*' was known in Israel during the late Judaean monarchy and could very well have been used by Jeremiah. We may notice that the wine-cup vision above all condemns the kings of the peoples. The original wording of the passage about the 'Arabs' may thus have sounded:

> all with cropped hair, all the kings of the *ʕarab* who live in the wilderness.[401]

The expression 'those with cropped hair living in the desert' is also found in the passage in Jeremiah referring to the anti-Babylonian alliance in 601 BC.[402] Although not absolutely certain, this makes it likely that in Jeremiah 25/32 they should be connected with Ammon, Moab and Edom in verse 21, thus the second layer of names.

The expression 'those with cropped hair living in the desert' turns up in yet another text in Jeremiah. In MT chapter 49/LXX 30, an oracle against them is preserved:

> MT (28)/LXX (23) To Qedar and to the kingdoms of *ḥaṣôr*/LXX: To Kedar,
> queen of the courtyard (*aulē*)/ whom Nebuchadnezzar defeated.
> /MT: Thus YHWH has said:/
> Rise up, advance against Qedar!
> Destroy the people of the east (*bnê qedem*)!
> (29)/(24) Their tents and their flocks they shall take,
> their tent-curtains and all their goods,
> their camels they shall carry for them/LXX: themselves/.
> They shall shout against them:
> 'terror on every side!'
> (30)/(25) Flee, wander far away,
> dwell in the depths,
> O inhabitants of *ḥaṣôr*! (/MT: the oracle of YHWH/)
> For he has made a plan against you (/MT: Nebuchadnezzar,/the king of
> Babylon),
> he has formed a purpose against you.
> (31)/(26) Rise up, advance
> against a nation at ease (/MT: the oracle of YHWH/),
> that dwells securely,
> that has no gates,

that has no bars,
that dwells alone.
(32)/(27) Their camels shall become a booty,
their herds of cattle spoil.
I will scatter to every wind those with cropped hair,
and I will bring their doom from every side of them (MT: the oracle of YHWH/LXX: says the Lord).
33/28) *ḥaṣôr* will become a haunt of jackals,
an everlasting waste;
no man shall dwell there,
no man shall sojourn there.[403]

There is agreement that the passages within brackets are secondary additions not belonging to the original poem.[404] It seems that the Septuagint on the whole has a better text than the MT. It has also long since been assumed that *ḥaṣôr* does not refer to the famous city in upper Galilee (or to another city with this name) but is a word related to Arabic *ḥaẓīra* or even *ḥilaẓār*, meaning 'enclosure', 'fold for animals', which is well reflected in the Greek translation into *aulē*, 'enclosed courtyard'.[405]

The mention of those with cropped hair, together with several typical Jeremianic phrases, makes it most likely that the poem deals with the same shaved sons of the desert as those mentioned in the condemnation of the alliance in 601 and in the wine-cup vision.[406] In that case it becomes very likely that the oracle, in fact, does refer to Nebuchadnezzar's operations in southern Syria in 599–598 BC.[407]

A *crux* is that the victim of the Babylonians are called Qedar in the Jeremianic poem but *arab* by Nebuchadnezzar. It has been suggested that the oracle did not originally refer to the campaign in 599 BC but to an earlier event, but the argument for this is weak.[408] Certain is that the early redactors of the book of Jeremiah have associated it with operations by Nebuchadnezzar, as expressed in the headline to the poem. We have also seen that in Assyrian sources from the first half of the seventh century BC, Hazaʔil and his son Yawthaʕ are called kings of Qedar as well as kings of the Arabs. But we have also pointed out that this does not mean that Qedar and the Arabs were identical. Instead we have assumed some kind of close association between them, also documented by the marital links between Hazaʔil and one of the queens of the Arabs. There might in fact be indications in our poem that it deals with two entities. In the MT this is explicitly stated in the headline. It is remarkable that the Septuagint has read 'queen of' (MLKT) instead of 'kingdoms' (MMLKWT) in the headline. A close reading of the poem also shows that it is divided in two parts: one against Qedar and one against 'those with cropped hair', both introduced by the words 'rise up, advance!' A suggested reconstruction of the headline is: 'For Qedar and for the queen(s) of the enclosures'.[409] We would then have a reference to the Arabs, who were ruled by at least six named queens in Assyrian times and who were closely allied with Qedar.

The peoples mentioned in the wine-cup vision have their own separate oracles in the Book of Jeremiah. These oracles are arranged by the redactors in an order roughly corresponding to that in the vision. The order is (with probable later additions in parentheses): MT: Egypt, Philistaea, Moab, Ammon, Edom, Damascus, Qedar, (Elam, Babylon)/LXX: Egypt, (Babylon), Philistaea, Edom, Ammon, Qedar, Damascus, Moab.[410] Qedar is clearly intended by the early redactors of the book of Jeremiah to correspond to the group of names in which the kings of the *ʕarab* are included.

These facts indicate that the *ʕarab* mentioned in the wine-cup vision in the book of Jeremiah are in fact those closely associated with Qedar in the Assyrian inscriptions, and against whom Nebuchadnezzar sent out his troops in 599 BC. From the Qedar oracle in Jeremiah 49 we learn that the Babylonian campaign was not only against the Arabs but also against their close allies, Qedar, who are included under this label by the Babylonian scribe.

We should, however, admit that the identification between the *arab* in Nebuchadnezzar's chronicle and the *ʕarab* in Jeremiah's wine-cup vision on the one hand, and those with cropped hair mentioned three times in the book of Jeremiah on the other, is not completely certain. It cannot be wholly excluded that the *ʕarab* in the vision, in fact, belong to the fourth group of names: Dedan, Temā, Buz, ʕUṣ and Zimrān. Those names probably belong to a later age, namely that of Nabonidus, when we also hear about Arabs in the Ḥiǧāz in the Babylonian sources.

According to a much later tradition, Nebuchadnezzar had one more dealing with Arabs. The Christian historian Eusebius, writing at the beginning of the fourth century AD, quotes an earlier writer, Abydenus, who, in the second century AD, wrote a book on Assyrian and Chaldaean history. According to Eusebius, Abydenus had written the following about Nebuchadnezzar:

> He also put a bulwark against the flooding of the Red Sea and founded the town of Teredon against the attacks of the *árabes*.[411]

The town Teredon existed at the time of Nearchus, the admiral of Alexander the Great, who mentions it by the name Diridotis and describes its close connections with Gerrha further down in the Gulf.[412] In a source from the third century BC, Nicander of Colophon, we hear about 'the *nomádes* of Gerrha' and a commentary to this text talks about the Gerrhaeans as a marauding tribe on the Euphrates.[413] As we shall see, there is evidence in later periods for the presence of Arabs in the oasis of Hufūf, which is situated not far from Gerrha.[414] Abydenus could thus have modernized the nomads in his source to the Arabs of his own time and Nebuchadnezzar's involvement in Arab affairs in the Gulf may be apocryphal. On the other hand, the term 'Red Sea' for the Persian Gulf sounds archaic and may well have stood in Abydenus' source, which may have been old. We should also observe the notice in Judith about the king's campaign to the Gulf and the statement in aṭ-Ṭabarī that he fought the *ʕarab* from ʔUbulla to ʔAyla, of which the first is on the shore of the Persian Gulf.

Nabonidus

The attempts by the Assyrian empire to control southern Syria and northern Ḥiǧāz were continued by the Neo-Babylonians. Nebuchadnezzar clashed with the Arabs just as Sennacherib and Assurbanipal had done. Even though the record of this enterprise gives the impression of having been of the same kind as those of the Assyrian predecessors, we know that at the beginning of the fifth pre-Christian century things were rapidly changing. Dramatic events took place in southern Arabia and an explosive development in the trade between Yemen and the Middle East was soon to change the political and economic patterns in a way which was to be of crucial importance for many centuries ahead.

The heirs to the Assyrian empire were, however, to have one more encounter with the Arabs before the scene changed and with that also the imperial policy towards them. But even this last attempt shows features indicating the dawn of a new age. The final revolt in Judah had ended in disaster and the destruction of the Temple in 587 BC. The result was that the kingdom of Edom now became the leading power and the prolonged arm of Babylonia in southern Syria and northern Ḥiǧāz. Edom had, in fact, been a most obedient servant to Mesopotamian powers from the days of Tiglath Pileser III. Now she seems to have become the bastion of Babylonia in Arabia. From the Old Testament we know that Edom controlled the area down to Dedan.[415] The expansion of Edom southwards is reflected in the incorporation of Nebayot in her pedigree: part of Edom is descended from Basemat, sister of Nebayot.[416] Nebayot was, as we shall see, a tribe in the eastern Ḥisma area, whose territory stretched down to Taymāʔ.[417] There is also evidence of Edom's close connections with Ammon, Moab and the Phoenician towns Sidon and Tyre.[418] Unfortunately we do not know anything about the relations between Edom and Qedar.

It is uncertain how long this arrangement lasted. In the Old Testament there is a series of oracles indicating destruction and disaster in Edom.[419] We know from archaeological excavations that the main cities in Edom, present-day Buṣayra, Ṭawīlān and Tell Khleifeh, were destroyed during the sixth century BC.[420] In contemporary historical sources there are some reports that might tell us what actually happened.

In 556 BC, the ageing Nabonidus ascended the throne in Babylon. From the records it appears that he pursued a traditional Mesopotamian imperialist policy, although with some idiosyncrasies. This is not the place to analyse his religious outlook and the reasons for his ten years' stay in Taymāʔ, which constitute one of the most difficult and fascinating problems in the history of the Ancient Near East. We will concentrate on his encounter with the Arabs and on what we can learn about them from it.

The sources from his reign that concern us are three: the Nabonidus Chronicle, the Royal Chronicle and the second of the Harran inscriptions, H2. Of these, H2 was written during the last years of Nabonidus' reign (*c*. 543–540 BC), whereas the other two are known from copies written in the Seleucid period.[421] To these sources in Akkadian should perhaps be added two texts from the Old Testament, which are more or less contemporary, and a text in Greek, Xenophon's *Cyropaedia*, written almost 200 years after Nabonidus but using old sources.

In the spring of his third year, i.e. 553 BC, Nabonidus set out for Syria.[422] After having stayed there during the summer and autumn, he marched against U-du-mu, which is probably Edom, in December.[423] He then conquered the city of Rug-di-ni.[424] After that, he reached Da-da-nu (= Dedan), whose king was defeated.[425] In the two chronicles we do not hear anything about Taymāʔ but in the text from Harran, H2, we are told that the king left Babylon and went to the cities of Te-ma-a', Da-da-nu, Pa-dak-ku, Hi-ib-ra-a, Iá-di-hu and Ia-at-ri-bu, between which he is said to have moved during ten years.[426] These towns are easily identifiable as Taymāʔ, Dedan, Fadak, Khaybar, Yadīʕ and Yathrib, all in the Ḥiǧāz.[427] Then it is said:

(I:38) At the word
(39) of Sin, also Ishtar, lady of battle, without whom hostility and peace
(40) do not exist in the land and a weapon
(41) is not forged, crossed (?) her hands over them [the people of Babylonia and Syria],
(42) and the king of (KUR?) Miṣir, URU Ma-da-a-a,

(43) KUR *a-ra-bi,* and all the kings hostile
(44) sent messengers for peace and good relations
(45) before me. People of KUR *a-ra-bi* who . . .
(46) of KUR Akkad
(47) .
(48) plunder and capture of property . . .
(II:1) at the word of Sin, Nergal shattered
(2) their weapons, and all of them bowed down [at my feet].[428]

As we can see, the text is damaged in a crucial passage but it is still clear that the Arabs figure in two events: asking for peace together with the two others, and a military encounter with the Babylonians. Another observation is that the six cities in Ḥiǧāz were not in the land of the KUR *aribi*. The Babylonian king first establishes himself in the cities of which at least one (Dedan) was conquered militarily.[429] After that come the delegations. Miṣir and Madāy are identified with Egypt and Media, which were not subject to Babylonia.[430] If this is correct, the Arabs also must represent an entity not conquered by Nabonidus.

The events in north-western Arabia under Nabonidus may be reflected in another contemporary text, namely two enigmatic oracles, preserved in the book of Isaiah.

The oracle 'Dumah'
[To me cry the refugees from Seʕir][431]
'Watcher, how much of the night?'
The watcher has said: 'The morning has come, and so the night;
if you wish to ask, return/do it again'.[432]

The oracle 'among/against *ʕrab*'
In the wilderness, among the *ʕrab* spend the night, o caravans of Dedanites!
To the thirsting ones they have come with (LXX bring!) water;
the inhabitants of the land of Têmā' have given bread to the refugee.
For before the sword they have fled;
before the drawn sword, before the drawn bow;
yea, for the violence of war.
For thus has the Lord said to me:
In one wage-laborer's year the glory of Qedar will have ended;
and the number of bows of heroes in Qedar will have become small.
Thus has YHWH, Israel's god spoken.[433]

The combination of these two oracles may be due to the key-word principle: two different pieces of poetry or prose are transmitted together since they have one or more word in common. In these two poems, the word 'night' (*laylā*) is common. Forms of the rare verb ʔTY occur in both. Judging from the LXX also, the word *noded*, 'refugee', might have been common. This does not prove that the two texts originally belong together. Since the first oracle is called 'Dumah', it is likely that at least one more verse where the name of the oasis was mentioned has fallen out.[434] In that case both texts thus deal with events in the area between Edom, Dumah and Dedan.[435] The oracles, which in fact may be extracts from non-Israelite poems, deal with the effects of military actions against Seʕir = Edom, and Dedan.[436]

It seems that those fleeing from Dedan have been assisted by the *ʕrab* 'in the land of Têmā''. Those giving assistance to the refugees must then have had the same enemy. The latter part of the second text refers to Qedar and is an announcement of doom of a type common in Israelite prophetic literature.[437] If these lines belong to the text, it lies near at hand to assume that the *ʕrab* are identical or closely related to Qedar.[438] The message is then that the *ʕrab*/Qedar have given assistance to those fleeing from the warfare in Dedan, but that they will face a similar fate after one year. The *ʕrab*/Qedar must then have been enemies of the Babylonians.

A war against Dedan is documented in some of the inscriptions from Ǧabal Ghunaym near Taymāʔ, which are dated to the sixth century BC.[439] The identification of the events reflected in these texts with Nabonidus' activities in north-western Arabia has been suggested before and is attractive, although, of course, somewhat speculative, as is the connection between these events and the two oracles in Isaiah.[440] In Nabonidus' own texts it is stated that the Babylonians put an end to Edom which included Dedan, which at the beginning of the sixth century BC was Edom's southernmost outpost.[441] If the *ʕrab* oracle is to be read in this context, it would mean that Qedar and, possibly, the Arabs associated with them were reduced to obedience under the Babylonians partly because of their assistance to the Dedanites. Judging from the H2 inscription, the Arabs(/Qedar?) sought a peaceful solution, although perhaps some did not agree with this policy. There are even indications that Dedan and Edom were conquered the year before Nabonidus settled in Taymāʔ.[442]

It is clear that one of the aims of the operations was the control of the road southwards from Taymāʔ to Yathrib: the six cities mentioned in Nabonidus' inscription form a line from the north to the south which is part of the famous frankincense road. The road, in Akkadian *urhu*, is mentioned in the three Babylonian texts and may also be hinted at in the word 'caravans', Hebrew *ʔorḥôt*, in the *ʕrab* oracle in Isaiah.

In order to grasp the implications of these events, the general political situation in the Middle East in the 550s BC should be understood. Since the days of the downfall of the Assyrian empire there had existed an alliance between Media and Babylonia. It seems that Edom also belonged to this alliance. With the accession of Nabonidus the scene changed. This king seems to have pursued an anti-Median policy from the beginning. Connected with this is probably his explicit identification with the Assyrian kings, as well as his ambitions to restore the temple in Harran which was in Median hands.[443] When the king of the Persian tribes in Pasargadae, Cyrus, in 553 BC revolted against his Median overlord, king Astyages, Nabonidus set out on his campaign to Syria. The events actually caused the liberation of Harran.[444] Even though there was not a formal alliance between Cyrus and Nabonidus, they surely had common interests and acted along common lines.[445] The Babylonian campaigns against Syria, including Edom, in the first years of Nabonidus' reign might be the result of the Syrians holding on to the traditional alliance with Media, perhaps as a means of regaining political freedom. The downfall of Edom was thus most certainly effected by the Babylonians and is, as we have seen, indicated in the contemporary texts themselves. The Syro-Arabian campaign was thus a means of securing the continued control of the new régime in Babylon in its traditional sphere of interest in front of the dramatic developments in Iran.

Nabonidus, Cyrus the Great and the Arabs

The Babylonian campaign to Syria and the subjugation of the Arabs are also reflected in a much later source. In the first half of the fourth century, the Athenian Xenophon wrote a biography of the Achaemenid king Cyrus the Great. The book, the *Cyropaedia*, is actually an historical novel, depicting Cyrus as the ideal king, the incarnation of all the virtues of the good ruler. The course of events deviates in a rather drastic way from what we know from the contemporary sources, as well as from Herodotus and Xenophon's contemporary Ctesias of Cnidus.[446] Xenophon used a source which seems to have been a traditional Iranian epic, mixing together facts from the story of Cyrus' forefather, Cyrus I, with the story of the conqueror of Babylon.[447] Xenophon, who does not mention Nabonidus by name, links the Babylonian activities in Syria at the beginning of Nabonidus' reign, i.e. the years 556–553, with Cyrus' later war against Lydia in 547–546 BC. According to Xenophon's story, Cyrus was a loyal son-in-law to the Median king Astyages. When Astyages passes away, he is succeeded by his son Cyaxares, who is unknown from contemporary sources. The 'king of Assyria', who is unnamed, now plans a war against Media. In order to strengthen his position, he advances into Syria:

> The king of the Assyrians subjugated all the Syrians, a very large nation, and made the king of the *arábioi* obedient.[448]

His main ally is Croesus of Lydia, who forms an alliance against the Medians and advances with an enormous army, which, as Cyaxares tells, consists of Assyrians, Babylonians, Phrygians, Cappadocians and Greeks from Asia:

> and the *arábios* Aragdos has about ten thousand horsemen, about a hundred chariots of war and a great host of slingers.[449]

The battle results in a great victory for the Medo-Persian army led by Cyrus, and the enemy is massacred:

> But the king of Cappadocia and the king of the *arábioi*, as they were still near by and stood their ground though unarmed, were cut down by the Hyrcanians. But the majority of the slain were Assyrians and *arábioi*. For as these were in their own country, they were leisurely about getting away.[450]

After this crushing defeat, Croesus gathers a new army and advances against Cyrus once more with contingents from, for example, the *arábioi*, Phoenicians, Greeks and Assyrians under the king of Babylon. This ends with a new defeat for the anti-Median alliance.[451] Then Cyrus sets out on his campaign to conquer Babylon:

> On the way to Babylon, he [Cyrus] subdued the Greater Phrygia and Cappadocia and reduced the *arábioi* to submission.[452]

The *arábioi* now join Cyrus, who divides his army in twelve parts during his preparations for the conquest of the city:

> But the Babylonians, when they heard about that, laughed much more scornfully still at the thought of Phrygians, Lydians, *arábioi*, and Cappadocians keeping guard against them, for they considered all these to be more friendly towards them than the Persians.[453]

When the Babylonian empire is conquered, Cyrus appoints satraps over his own empire. Among them we find Megabyzus as satrap of *Arabía*.[454]

Undoubtedly, the 'king of the Assyrians' in the *Cyropaedia* is none other than Nabonidus. Its pro-Cyrus tendency results in a cover-up of Cyrus' anti-Median activities. According to the *Cyropaedia*, Cyrus conquered Babylon as a Median vassal and then received the full kingship as a gift. In reality, he defeated Astyages, probably in co-operation with Nabonidus, and made him prisoner.[455] His war against Media is transformed into a war against Babylonia and her allies in Anatolia. Also in the book of Daniel, it is the Medians who receive the kingship over Babylon after her conquest and the killing of Belshazzar.[456] In the notice in Xenophon of how the Assyrian king subjugated the Syrians and the *arábioi*, we most probably have a memory of Nabonidus' actions against Syria and the northern Ḥiğāz during his first years. It is probably also correct that these were operations partly directed against Media. That Cyrus also acted against his overlord during these years is, however, passed over in silence. When the great alliance is formed with, for example, Croesus of Lydia, we have reached the years 547–546 BC. Participants in this alliance are the *arábioi* under their king Aragdos. The name has a similarity to that of the town Rug-di-ni, mentioned in the Nabonidus Chronicle as conquered by the Babylonians in the campaign in 553–552 BC.[457] This might well be a solid historical fact and should be combined with the information about the defeat of the Arabs in the Harran inscription. It look as if the Arabs later joined forces with the Babylonians in the war against Cyrus.[458] Cyrus says himself in the official record that 'the kings of Amurru who dwell in tents (*āšib kuštarī*) brought their tribute to Babylon and kissed my feet'.[459] It is likely that the Arabs are included among these kings and that the *Cyropaedia* is right when it claims that the Arabs took part in the siege and conquest of Babylon.[460] On the other hand, Herodotus says that Cyrus had camels in his army at the siege of Sardis in 546 BC.[461] It is difficult to imagine that these animals could have been enrolled without their tenders. This makes it likely that Arabs were on Cyrus' side already before the conflict with Croesus. As we shall see, the relationship between the Arabs and the new rulers of the Orient was to be much more hearty than it had been with the preceding ones. Nabonidus seems in fact to have pursued a traditional Mesopotamian policy of conquest and subjugation against the Arabs. That they joined the new victorious king in his final settlement with the last empire based in the Mesopotamian plain is very likely, even though it is documented only in a somewhat spurious source.

Who were the *arábioi* following Cyrus? Xenophon says that the *arábioi* and the Cappadocians were in their own country when defeated in the first battle. Later, when Cyrus proceeds towards Babylon, he is said to have subjugated the Cappadocians and the *arábioi* on his way, which explains their appearance before the walls of Babylon. The impression is that these Arabs were somewhere in north-western Mesopotamia. Were the Rugdini/Arágdos Arabs transferred from northern Ḥiğāz to northern Mesopotamia by Nabonidus? We know that in the time of Xenophon, i.e. at the end of the fifth century BC, there were *arábioi* in the Ğazīra east of the Khābūr river.[462] Perhaps they had been transferred there by Nabonidus as a preparation for the great struggle with the new Iranian superpower.

Nebuchadnezzar's campaign against the Arabs in 599 BC, reflected in Jeremiah's wine-cup vision and the poem against Qedar, as well as Nabonidus' activities in the northern Ḥiğāz some fifty years later, have had a quite remarkable literary *Nachleben* which also has importance for the understanding of the very events. In aṭ-Ṭabarī's world history, written one and a half millennia after these events, we find a story telling how the *ʕarab* were settled in al-Ḥīra. aṭ-Ṭabarī refers to two sources which both attribute this event to Nebuchadnezzar. According to the first source, Hishām ibn al-Kalbī, a certain Barakhyā ibn Ḥananyā is told by God:

> 'Go to Bukht Nuṣṣur (Nebuchadnezzar) and command him to raid the *ʕarab*, whose houses have no locks, nor gates. Let him conquer their land with soldiers, slay their fighting men, and despoil their wealth. Tell him that they do not believe in me, that they have taken other deities, and that they deny my prophets and messengers.'[463]

According to the other source, which is anonymous, the reason for the expedition was that the Israelites had slain their prophets:

> This does not include those slain by the men of ar-Rass and the people of Ḥaḍūr. When they had the audacity to attack God's prophets, He decreed the destruction of that generation, to whose prophets Maʕadd ibn ʕAdnān . . . The king was urged in a dream – or some prophet was instructed to command him to do it – to enter the land of the *ʕarab,* wipe out man and beast, and obliterate it completely, leaving no sign of life there. Bukht Nuṣṣur concentrated cavalry and infantry between ʔAyla on the gulf of ʕAqabah and al-ʔUbullah on the Shaṭṭ al-ʕarab. They invaded the *ʕarab* and massacred every living being they had come upon and seized. God had revealed to ʔIrimyā (Jeremiah) and Barakhyā: 'God has warned your people but they did not desist, so after having had a kingdom they became slaves, and after an affluent life they became beggars. Similarly I warned the people of ʕArabah but they were obstinate. I imposed Bukht Nuṣṣur's rule over them to take revenge upon them. Now rush to Maʕadd ibn ʕAdnān of whose progeny will be Muhammed, whom I shall bring forth at the end of time to seal the prophethood and lift humility.' Setting out, the two rushed through the lands as the earth folded under them miraculously. They preceded Bukht Nuṣṣur and met ʕAdnān, who received them, whereupon they rushed him to Maʕadd who was then twelve years old. Barakhyā carried him on al-Burāq and sat behind him. At once they reached Harran. The earth miraculously folded up and rushed ʔIrimyā to Harran. Thus ʕAdnān and Bukht Nuṣṣur met in battle. Bukht Nuṣṣur put ʕAdnān to flight, and he proceeded through the land of the *ʕarab* down to Ḥaḍūr in pursuit of ʕAdnān. Most of the *ʕarab* of the ʕArabah area gathered at Ḥaḍūr, and the two forces established defensive trenches. Bukht Nuṣṣur set an ambush, some assert the very first ambush ever. A heavenly voice called out: 'Woe to the slayers of the prophets'. Swords struck them from behind and in front. They repented their sins and called out in distress. ʕAdnān was prevented from reaching Bukht Nuṣṣur, and the latter from reaching ʕAdnān. Those who were not at Ḥaḍūr, and had escaped before the defeat, split into two groups; one force betook itself to Rasyūt/Rasyūb under ʕAkk, the other set out for Wabār and a group of settled (*ḥaḍr*) *ʕarab*.[464]

There are several elements in both stories which are connected with the events in 599 BC. We observe the participation of Jeremiah and his secretary, Baruch, here called Barakhyā, which indicates contemporaneity with the historical Nebuchadnezzar. The geographical designation of the campaign is between ʔUbulla near Basra and ʔAyla by the Red Sea. The mention of ʕArabah as the main target points to areas south-east of Palestine. More important are the place-names ar-Rass and Ḥaḍūr. ar-Rass is a rather common name in Arabia. One instance is a dwelling place for a clan of Thamūd.[465] This ar-Rass should be connected with one of the earliest known tribes in north-western Ḥiğāz, mentioned in the Qurʔān together with ʕĀd and Thamūd and later counted among the *ʕarab al-ʕāriba*.[466] It should be noticed that the Septuagint reads Rhōs instead of Buz in Jeremiah 25:23, which might reflect a name appearing as ar-Rass in Arabic. As far as Ḥaḏūr is concerned, the medieval Islamic writers locate it in Yemen, where we also find an ar-Rass.[467] We should, as usual, be somewhat sceptical about the location in Yemen of all places important for the protohistory of the *ʕarab*. Ḥaḏūr has a striking similarity with the word *ḥaṣôr* found in Jeremiah 49. That this story should be associated with Jeremiah 49 and Nebuchadnezzar's campaign in 599 BC is also indicated by literal parallels between the two texts. In Jeremiah 49:31 it is said that Qedar is a people 'who has neither gates nor bars'. In aṭ-Ṭabarī the *ʕarab* are a people 'whose houses have no locks nor gates'.[468] The name Nabūxaḏ naṣr occurs in at-Ṭabarī's text and must be explained, which also shows that a foreign source has been present.[469] What kind of source preserved this memory for Islamic historiography during 1,200 years?

The anonymous source used by aṭ-Ṭabarī was obviously known also to his predecessor Ibn Ḥabīb in the middle of the ninth century AD.[470] It definitely has a Judaeo-Christian origin, shown by the appearance of two well-known Biblical personalities from the time of Nebuchadnezzar: Jeremiah and Baruch, as well as direct quotations from the Qedar oracle in the book of Jeremiah[471]. The source is not, however, totally based on the Old Testament. Qedar is mentioned neither by aṭ-Ṭabarī nor by Ibn Ḥabīb. Instead we hear only about the *ʕarab*, in accordance with the terminology in Nebuchadnezzar's own chronicle. The account of the the two Arabo-Islamic writers is based on a source coming from al-Ḥīra, which is seen from its insertion in a context telling about the origins of the *ʕarab* in al-Ḥīra and the establishment of the dynasty of the Lakhmids there.[472] It seems that there once existed a chronicle about the history of the kings in al-Ḥīra, most probably written by Christians, who incorporated a source dealing with Nebuchadnezzar's campaign against the *ʕarab* and completed with legendary stories about Jeremiah and Baruch. The name Ḥaḏūr looks like an Aramaic rendering of the Hebrew *ḥaṣôr*. This could also hold for the form ʔIrimyā as well as the forms of the name of the Babylonian king, which reflects a Hebrew-Aramaic pronunciation.[473] The al-Ḥīra chronicle may thus have been in Aramaic or, at least, been based on an older Aramaic source, probably of Jewish origin.

We would suggest that this source is identical with the one discussed earlier, which was shown to have preserved memories of the campaign of Tiglath Pileser III and the activities of Sennacherib, and documented in the book of Judith. From Judith it is clear that we have to do with popular stories with Nebuchadnezzar as the protagonist, to whom many achievements of other Mesopotamian rulers are attributed. We know, for example, from the book of Daniel, that Nebuchadnezzar and Nabonidus were fused together quite early.[474] There may have existed a written novel about Nebuchadnezzar, originally in Aramaic but drawing details from chronicles in Akkadian and attributing deeds of rulers from Tiglath Pileser III to Nabonidus to Nebukadnezzar. The existence of this kind of literature is well-documented and specimens of it have, interestingly enough, been preserved in Jewish circles.[475] It was intermingled early with legends about Jeremiah and Baruch by these Jewish transmitters.

There are perhaps a couple of traces also in Judith of the events in 599 BC.

There is a parallel between the word *ḥaṣor* in the Qedar oracle and *mándra* in Judith, which both mean 'encampment'. Unlike the transmitters of the Masoretic text, the author of Judith, like the Septuagint, has understood it correctly and rendered it by the corresponding Greek *mándra*.
The existence of a Nebuchadnezzar novel may also be reflected in the Hellenistic Babylonian writer Berossus in his *Babyloniaca*, written at the beginning of the third century BC. The original work is lost, but parts of it are known from quotations in later Greek texts.[476] Berossus had access to original documents from Babylonian archives. In Josephus' *Against Apion* we find a note taken from Berossus about Nebuchadnezzar's activities in Syria. According to this, the Babylonian monarch conquered Egypt, Syria, Phoenicia and Arabia.[477] Nebuchadnezzar, however, never conquered Egypt, and this conquest was probably transferred from the records of Esarhaddon. This would thus be the earliest testimony of how the name Nebuchadnezzar has attracted the deeds of other Mesopotamian kings, not only those of Nabonidus.[478]

It can thus be assumed that there existed an Aramaic Nebuchadnezzar novel preserved by Jewish circles, which was known to those who wrote the history of al-Ḥīra and which was ultimately based on popular legends and reports from Akkadian chronicles, fusing together deeds of many famous Mesopotamian kings under Nebuchadnezzar's name. The author of Judith has used the Nebuchadnezzar story in order to create the prerequisites for his own. For this purpose he has, for example, taken the name Holophernes from the Achaemenid history.[479] In aṭ-Ṭabarī the purpose is to give an account of the origins of the *ʕarab* in al-Ḥīra in Iraq. It is worth noting that al-Ḥīra has the same meaning as *ḥiẓār*/*ḥaṣôr*.[480] This fact may have been one strong reason for using the Nebuchadnezzar story as a background for the origins of al-Ḥīra. Connected with this is probably also the name of the town further upstream on the Euphrates. The river name Abronas in Judith, which was probably found in the Aramaic source, may also have prompted the early Islamic traditionalists to associate the two stories.[481]

Nebuchadnezzar's campaign in 599 BC is the earliest dated event that has been recorded by the Arabo-Islamic historians and incorporated in the Islamic picture of the history of the *ʕarab*. It is not surprising that the exegetes of the Qurʔān think that they have found references to this story even in the Holy Book, or that the Yemenis have transplanted it to South Arabia. It can perhaps be seen as a symbol that the last attempt to control the Arabs in the Syrian desert, undertaken in a traditional way by a traditional Middle Eastern empire, is also the oldest datable historical memory in the later Arabo-Islamic world history.[482]

Individual Arabs in the Chaldaean and early Achaemenid periods

Jeremiah mentions *ʕarab* once more. In one of the earliest texts of the prophet, probably from before 604 BC, we hear the following when the behaviour of the Judaeans is likened to that of a prostitute who has had many customers[483]:

Lift up your eyes to the barren hills
and see: where have you not been raped?

On the roads you have sat down for them
like an *ʕarabī* in the wilderness (*midbar*)[484]

The individual *ʕarabī* in the open, uninhabited pasture-land was obviously a well-known figure to the prophet and his listeners. The last line sounds like a formulaic saying. It is well worth adducing a similar saying which is definitely a proverb, documented in a text from perhaps the same century. In the proverbs ascribed to the wise Aḥīqar, preserved in an Aramaic story about his career, we read:

Do not show an ʕRBY the ocean and a Sidonian the [dry land]
for their work is different.[485]

Although occurring in a text from perhaps the middle of the sixth century, the following also belongs to this characterization of the *ʕarab*:

19) Babel, the flower of kingdoms, the wonder of the glory of the Chaldeans, shall become
like God's overturning of Sodom and Gomorrah;
20) she shall never dwell [securely]/LXX: be inhabited/,
and not lay down/LXX: none shall enter her/as long as men live.
no *ʕarābī*/LXX *árabes*/Pesh. *ʕarbāyē* shall pitch [his] tent there;
shepherds shall not lay down there.[486]

This text belongs to the great oracle about the fall of Babylon preserved in the book of Isaiah, which was composed sometime shortly before 539 BC.[487] The *ʕarabī* here, as in the two other quoted texts, is characterized as a lonely stranger, living in the wilderness, *midbar*, i.e. in the areas used for pasture.[488] One is reminded of 'the *arbāya* who live far away' in the text from Sargon II. It is also striking that both Sargon and the three texts quoted here use the nisbah form of the word, i.e. it is the individual *ʕarabī* who is characterized as a dweller in the distant wilderness making his living from herds. One is reminded of the *ʔaʕrāb* in the Arabo-Islamic sources almost one millennium and a half later.

The Arab presence in southern Mesopotamia discernible during the reigns of Sennacherib and Assurbanipal comes into more light in the Neo-Babylonian and early Achaemenid periods. From the three towns Nippur, Sippar and Uruk we have at least twenty letters in which LÚ *arbāya* are mentioned. Most letters are dated to a period between 563 and 420 BC, and the few undated ones can be assumed to belong to this time as well.[489] These unique documents show Arabs in many different activities: they own land and slaves, they can be slaves themselves, they are involved in business. In one text, an Arab is a shepherd, working for the temple in Sippar. In a text from Nippur they are referred to as warriors standing under a special official. This official is mentioned also from Sippar. In Nippur we hear about a special Arab settlement, *ālu ša arbāya*.[490] Among the names we find good Arabic names such as Abdu and Zabdiya as well as Akkadian ones. On two occasions, a person is called simply *arbāya*, 'the Arab'. An interesting case is an instance when a person is called *te-mu-da-a ar-ba-a-a*, which has been interpreted as a reference to Thamūd. There are also references in the letters to Taymāʔ, which makes the presence of people from Thamūd in Assyria as well not unlikely. In that case, this person is called by two ethnic terms: 'the Thamudean', 'the

Arab'. It recalls the association between Thamūd and the Arabs in the Annals of Sargon, and could be another hint that there was a close connection between Thamūd and Arabs, although they were not identical. The Arabs in southern Mesopotamia are probably mentioned already in texts from the time of Sennacherib.[491] Their presence there was thus well established in the Chaldaean period, which gives support to the equation between Sennacherib's *urbi* and the *arbāya* of the letters.

The evidence in these documents from the sixth and fifth centuries BC is quite unique in giving a glimpse of Arabs in everyday life in lower Mesopotamia. We shall find a similar documentation from Ptolemaic Egypt, where a corpus of contemporary papyri gives a similar insight. The evaluation of this documentation is, however, difficult since one would need a more thorough picture of life and society in general in these regions in order to be able to determine the exact role of Arabs. The impression from the Akkadian letters is that the Arabs were well integrated into society, although they remained a distinct group.[492] Their presence there obviously goes back to Assyrian times and might be connected with the great military upheavals in southern Mesopotamia under Sennacherib and Assurbanipal. As will become apparent later, the existence of a supervisor of the Arabs as well as their settlement in a special area, together with their occasional function as warriors, does not go against evidence from other regions and epochs. It is also worthwhile once again to remember the *hagaranu* and the *nabaṭu*, who appear in the same region in Sennacharib's accounts. The substantial and well-documented presence of Arabs in southern Mesopotamia, together with these two other names, should be kept in mind: we shall encounter all three together in later ages in many different regions. That the *hagaranu* and *nabaṭu* are not mentioned in the letters may be a pure coincidence.

Arabs down to the rise of the Achaemenids: attempt at a summary

People called Arabs appear on the stage of world history in connection with the rise of Syria as an economic and political region of weight, a process which started during the first centuries of the Iron Age. This led to the growing interference in Syrian affairs by the empires in the east, first Assyria, then her successor the Babylonian kingdom. The local Syrian kings seem to have drawn Arabs into their service quite early. The camel riders pictured on the two stelae from Carchemish and Tell Ḥalaf respectively from around 900 BC may well be the first testimony of the presence of Arabs who knew how to handle the new mobile animal, the camel. In texts, they appear for the first time some fifty years later together with their camels siding with the Syrians against the Assyrian aggressor.

At the beginning of the first millennium BC we dimly perceive efforts by local Syrian powers to control Edom, as it seems, in order to reach the Red Sea and thus get a foot into Arabia. The traditions about the Qeṭurah road and the stories about the attempts to reach Ophir by the Israelite kings may reflect a competition between seaborne and overland traffic in western Arabia. In the end of the century, the Assyrians under Adad Nirari III made the first attempt to control Edom. During the interlude of Assyrian absence from southern Syria in the first half of the eighth century, local powers tried to expand southwards: King Uzziah rebuilt Elath *c.* 750 BC which was probably supported, if not ordered, by the king of Israel. These ambitions were finally thwarted by the intervention of Tiglath Pileser III in 734–732. Edom, probably allied with Assyria, recaptured Elath.[493] A new stage now commenced with Assyria as dominating power and Edom acting as her agent. The 'King's Highway' was built through Transjordan and Assyrian forts were established in Rās an-Naqb, i.e. the southern border of Edom.[494] Edom thus became an Assyrian outpost towards Arabia and started to expand southwards and westwards.[495]

The increased Assyrian pressure against the Syrian desert and northern Ḥiğāz led to a continuous conflict between the Arabs and the Assyrian empire, culminating in the occupation of Dumah by Sennacherib and, possibly, his settlement of Arabs in the Ğazīra. That policy dragged other groups into the conflict: the Nebayot, Massa and Shumuʔil tribes south of Wādī Sirḥān and the ʔAzraq oasis, i.e. groups at the western shore of the Great Nafūd. The Arabs sought refuge and support with these tribes, which in turn made them a target for vindictive strikes from the superpower. The ambitions of the Mesopotamians to control the area in north-western Arabia where the Arabs lived continued under their Babylonian successors. The result was the destruction of all local small powers in Palestine, incuding Babylon's main agent and bastion towards the northern Ḥiğāz: Edom. Then followed the sojourn of Nabonidus in Taymāʔ between 553 and 543 BC, an event still not completely understood. It is, however, in many ways a consequence of Assyro-Babylonian policy towards southern Syria/northern Ḥiğāz. Through its presence by its agent Edom and the continued conflict with the Arabs, Babylon had been drawn into the affairs of northern Ḥiğāz. But in the activities of Nabonidus we see the beginnings of change. One dramatic factor is the destruction of Edom at the beginning of the sixth century BC. Although we do not know the exact reason, it meant the end of a long-term policy and signalled new concepts. By this event, a vacuum was created in northern Ḥiğāz which had to be filled and it seems that the Arabs and their close allies Qedar now took the opportunity and poured in. We now hear about peaceful treaties between the Arabs and the Babylonians. It is consistent that we find Arabs fighting with the Mesopotamian empire, not against it, in the war with Cyrus. The whole new political scene in southern Syria/northern Ḥiğāz may be one explanation for the strange Taymāʔ episode.

The ambitions of the Assyrians in the northern Ḥiğāz and the southern Syrian desert, which became evident from the 730s BC, were not directed against the Arabs only but against several other groups as well. The increased pressure by the Mesopotamian powers was obviously due to the growing economic importance of the region. In the earliest period, down to the middle of the eighth century, northern Ḥiğāz was a transit area for transports of goods from the African side of the Red Sea and perhaps, if we are to trust the tradition about the expedition to Ophir, also ʕAsīr. An old document, the Qeṭurah-list in Genesis, describes the overland routes from the northern Red Sea ports to Syria and to the Euphrates.

Just before 700 BC, the seaborne traffic began to face competition from a new means of transport, the camel, probably handled mainly by the Arabs. The camel made it possible to extend the overland expeditions farther south and, sometime in the seventh century, a regular transport of frankincense from the newly established kingdom of Saba to Syria through western Arabia was established. The northern Ḥiğāz as well as the regions around Palestine and the Syrian desert became important as the final stretch of the traffic, and control of it received increased urgency. In the following period, that of the Achaemenids, this would lead to the establishment of new political structures in north-western Arabia which were to have a decisive importance for the history of the Arabs during the following centuries.

Notes

1 The first survey of the Mesopotamian evidence was by Weiss-Rosmarin, *Aribi* (1932). A much updated study is Eph'al, *'Arabs'* (1985). A wealth of new evidence was presented by Zadok, *Arabians* (1981); cf. also idem, *West Semites* 192–239. A thorough up-to-date analysis of the Akkadian sources as a basis for historical conclusions is found in Eph'al, *Arabs* 21–59.

2 See the survey of relevant passages in Eph'al, *Arabs* 60–72.

3 For this view of the historical traditions of Israel, see Thompson, *History* 365–366.

4 For an introduction to deconstructivist arguments, see Thompson, *History* 105 ff. and Lemche, *Israelites* 22 ff.

5 Thompson, *History* 81, 152. Even though the criticism against traditional writing of Israelite history by Thompson and Lemche is relevant, it is difficult to accept the latter's more or less outspoken allegation that the Old Testament writings are without any value at all for writing the history of Palestine before the Babylonian exile, cf. Lemche, *Israelites* 35–85. This at least before he or someone else can show by detailed and convincing analysis that the whole Old Testament is a fiction based on the theology of the post-exilic community, a difficult and perhaps impossible task since we have no datable contemporary documentation at all from that community. But these scholars are right in that one should be much more cautious in using the Biblical texts as a basis for reconstruction of history than has been the case until now.

6 For the historical value of the genealogical material both in general and in the ancient Middle East in particular, see Wilson, *Genealogy*, especially the very instructive example on pp. 46–55.

7 Omri, Ahab, Jehu, Joash, Jehoahaz/Ahaz, Menahem, Peqah, Hosea, Ezeqiah, Menasseh, Jehojaqin.

8 For the latest attempt, see Galil, *Chronology*. For a survey of the Assyrian texts see Kuan, *Inscriptions.*

9 It is worth recalling the existence of similar king-lists with short notices in Tyre, reaching back to the tenth century BC, preserved in quotations by Josephus; see Katzenstein, *History* [77] ff.

10 For the relationship between history and legend in the Yemeni story-telling tradition, Piotrovskij's study (*Predanije*) of the legends around the king ʔAsʕad Kāmil, known to have reigned in the year AD 451, is fundamental.

11 The basic study is still Rothstein, *Dynastie*. See also Shahid, *Byzantium* 3. For the secondary attachment of the Ḥīra kings to rulers in Syria in the third century AD see pp. 483–735. Some of the traditions about these rulers are analysed in Piotrovskij, *Versija*.

12 Cf. Dillmann, *Geschichte* 339–355; Conti Rossini, *Listes*.

13 Cf. Munro-Hay, *Axum* 61–103.

14 See Klengel, *Syria* 181–218, for a general survey of sources and events for the period 1200–745 BC.

15 Klengel, *Syria* 110–112, 119.

16 Numbers 34:1–12; cf. Ezekiel 40:13–17; cf. Aharoni, *Land* 61–70.

17 Baciyeva, *Bor'ba*, 20; Klengel, *Syria* 187.

18 See Thompson, *History* 233.

19 Weidner, *Tiglatpileser* Text I:29–35; Text II:34–43.

20 The story of Solomon's expedition to Ophir (1 Kings 9:26–28, 10:11–12 = 2 Chron. 8:17–18, 9:10–11) could also be connected with the increased importance of Arabia. For the location of Ophir in ʕAsīr see Groom, *Frankincense* 51; von Wissmann, *Geschichte I* 54–65; Gray, *Kings* 256–257. The historicity of the story is accepted by many commentators (see Gray, *Kings* 254–257), but cannot, of course, be verified by non-Biblical, contemporary evidence.

21 Groom, *Frankincense* 32–37, 53–54; Bawden/Eden, *History* 88–91; Retsö, *Domestication.* This goes against Knauf, *Midian* 28–29, Eph'al, *Arabs* 14–15, and Liverani, *Caravan Trade.*

22 It is well worth pointing out that settled occupation seems to disappear in the main sites in north-western Arabia between 1100 and 500 BC, cf. Parr, *Aspects,* especially 43–46, 55, 59 ff., 65 ff. If large-scale overland trade with South Arabia started at the same time, one won-

ders why there are no archaeological remains hinting at this activity. A change to nomadic lifestyle is not the same as long-distance overland trade.

23 Scheil, *Annales* 76–78; cf. Luckenbill, *Annals* 130. According to Liverani (*Caravan Trade* note 16) dromedaries were also included. These may well have come from North Arabia. Gold from Arabia is mentioned in connection with the account of Solomon. In a source commonly considered late, the Old Testament also tells about tribute consisting of animals: sheep and goats paid to the kings of Judah in the middle of the ninth century BC by tribes south-east of Palestine, i.e. in north-western Arabia (2 Chronicles 14:14–15 (Asa), 17:11; 2 Kings 3:4). As will be seen, there are some reasons to see this information as genuine. For a certain economic upswing in northern Ḥiǧāz in the early first millennium BC, see Knauf, *Midian* 25–26 (mining), 10 (camels), 6–8 (irrigation). But cf. also Parr, *Pottery, Peoples*, for the general archaeological picture of north-western Arabia in this period.

24 Gardiner, *Egypt* 330. This is the campaign of Shishaq mentioned to have occurred after the death of Solomon and resulting in the plundering of Jerusalem (2 Kings 14:25–26/2 Chronicles 12:2–10). Shishaq, i.e. Sheshonq, does not mention either Jerusalem or its king in his own account of the campaign (cf. Aharoni, *Land* 283–290). Supporters of the traditional view of the history of Israel make a harmonizing explanation (Aharoni, *Land* 285, 290). The deconstructivists see this as a proof that neither Jerusalem nor its king existed at this time.

25 *ud-ra-te* (Scheil, *Annales* 78).

26 Retsö, *Domestication* 201.

27 Bulliet, *Camel* 28 ff.

28 2 Kings 8:9. In Judges 6:5;12; 8:26 we have a notice about the use of camels in the eleventh century BC which has been interpreted as a sign of the extensive use of the animal among the Midyanites at this time (Bulliet, *Wheel*; Knauf, *Midian* 9–15; cf. idem, *Supplementa 12*). The story is, however, definitely much later and the camels reflect usage in the eighth century at the earliest. This also holds for its appearance in the Patriarchal stories (Genesis 12:16, 24 ff.: dowry; Genesis 31:34: riding by women) as well as in the Joseph story (Genesis 37:25). For an analysis of the Old Testament evidence, see Retsö, *Domestication* 201–205.

29 The only possible exception might be the mention of Solomon in connection with Josephus' account of Hiram of Tyre (Josephus, *Apion* 1.113; idem, *Antiquities* 7.145–149) which is derived from two authors, Menander and Dius, who are said to have used Tyrian archives. It is remarkable that the notice about Solomon only refers to an exchange of riddles between the two kings, an event which is not found in the Biblical account, whereas Solomon's building activities are not mentioned at all. Solomon also appears as a ruler of the city of Jerusalem, not an Israelite empire.

30 E.g. Malamat, *Königreich* states the problem clearly (6) but he builds his account on the Biblical sources, thus avoiding an *Auseinandersetzung* with the source problem. For a critical investigation of the factual archaeological foundations, see Jamieson-Drake, *Scribes* 72, 104, with conclusions supporting the deconstructivists.

31 Genesis 22:20–24; cf. Aharoni, *Land* 190, and Noth, *Beiträge* 22–25; Westermann, *Genesis* 2 450–451.

32 Jamieson-Drake, *Scribes* 138 ff.

33 aṭ-Ṭabarī, *Tārīkh* I:736–737; cf. ibidem I:2742–2745. Solomon's temple remains a difficulty. As described in the Old Testament, it demanded a large administrative apparatus, being the largest building in Syria before the Hellenistic age, which is difficult to harmonize with the scanty archaeological remains of the 'Solomonic' period. A realistic feature is the information that it was built by foreigners. The Old Testament also has a tradition about a predecessor (the Tabernacle) of much more modest dimensions.

34 Pedersen, *Israel* vol. 1: 143 f.; vol. 2: 344 ff.

35 Klengel, *Syria* 194.

36 Klengel, *Syria* 194 f.

37 Cf. Tadmor, *Assyria* 39.

38 Tadmor, *Assyria* 37.

39 For this interpretation, see Grayson, *Studies* 134 ff.

40 Klengel, *Syria* 196 ff. ; Yamada, *Construction*.
41 See Schramm, *Einleitung* 70–105; Kuan, *Inscriptions* 27 n. 70; Yamada, *Construction* 9–58.
42 Schramm, *Einleitung* 70–73.
43 For the route cf. Noth, *Lehrkursus* 39. For the date of the battle, see Brinkman, *Note*.
44 Salmanassar, *Monolith* II:90–97 = Grayson, *Rulers* 23; Kuan, *Inscriptions* 29–31; Yamada, *Construction* 156–157, 368.
45 For the linguistic aspects, see pp. 595 f.
46 Lane, *Lexicon* s.v. ǦDB. See Eph'al, *Arabs* 75 note 225 (*jindub* is not documented in early Arabic). Petráček (*Gindibu'*) suggested a form *ka-nadību-hu* in analogy with Safaitic names. This is most unlikely for several reasons.
47 Pitard (*Damascus* 130 n. 87), Kuan (*Inscriptions* 32–33) and Yamada (*Construction* 159–161) suggest that Ba'sa son of Ruhubi is separate from the following *amānāya*, 'the Ammonite', which would represent the missing ruler. In that case, one must suppose that the scribe has forgotten to write the name, which remains unprovable.
48 For different views on the nature of the list see Michel, *Assur-Texte* 70 n. 13, and Kuan, *Inscriptions* 38–40. The usual explanation has been either carelessness of the copyist or adaptation to the number twelve; cf. Tadmor, *Assyria* n. 29. Tadmor has pointed out the bad quality of the text in general with many names misspelt (id., *Que* 144).
49 Elat, *Campaign*, claims that the strength of the Syrians was largely due to the numerous chariotry under Ahab of Israel. The figure 2,000 has, however, been put into doubt by Na'aman who sees it as totally unrealistic and not fitting into the context. Since the inscription is full of mistakes, the number 2,000 could well be a much lower one, such as 200 (Na'aman, *Notes* 97–102). The text is defended by Pitard, *Damascus* 128 n. 81, and Kuan, *Inscriptions* 34–35.
50 For this debate, see Tadmor, *Que*, cf. idem, *Assyria* 31, Yamada, *Construction* 157 ff. According to Tadmor, Gu-a-a is a scribal error for Gu-bal-a-a, i.e. Byblos. The most controversial element has been the name Muṣri, which has been seen as (1) a region in Cilicia, (2) a region in north-western Arabia, (3) Egypt. Tadmor claims that there is no doubt that Muṣri, whenever mentioned, is Egypt and nothing else. There seem, however, still to be scholars who are uncomfortable with this definition. Winckler's thesis about an Arabian Muṣri (see Winckler, *Land*), although thoroughly rejected by von Bissing (*Bedeutung*), refuses to die completely; cf. Hommel, *Ethnologie* 600–608; Rosmarin, *Aribi* 3–4; Klengel, *Syria* 198 n. 72. What seems clear is that Muṣri is not identical with the Nile valley but rather is a term for areas under Egypt's political control or reckoned as her sphere of interest (cf. Garelli, *Muṣur*), especially the delta and adjacent regions towards the east, which may stretch eastwards to the copper mines in the ʕArabah. When Moses escapes from Pharao he has to go to Midian, i.e. east of the ʕArabah (cf. von Wissmann, *Geschichte* 1 52 f.). It can also be asked whether certain passages in the Old Testament mentioning Pharao and Miṣrayim in fact refer to an area east of the delta, e.g. Genesis 12:10–20 (Abraham in 'Egypt'), 1 Kings 7:8 (Pharao's daughter married to Solomon) etc. The word itself means 'fortress', and we have already encountered its Arabic plural *ʔamṣār* with this meaning. It may thus have been the name of the border region towards Egypt in the Sinai peninsula and the Negev. In that region we still have the name *ʕAqabat Miṣr* (Schmidt/Kahle, *Volkserzählungen* 136). Cf. also the Old Testament term Shûr for the Egyptian border in the Negev, which seems to mean 'wall' (Meyer, *Israeliten* 101 n. 1, 325, perhaps identical with the Asshurim in Genesis 25:6 ibidem 322) and could refer to a line of fortresses protecting the delta in the east.
51 The name occurs as the name of the third king of northern Israel (Baʕsha, 1 Kings 15–16; Gray, *Kings* 358–362).
52 Noth, *Hamath* 40; cf. Asshurbanipal, *Prism A* VII:108–123; Forrer, *Provinzeinteilung*, 62–63.
53 Eph'al, *Arabs* 76.
54 The Syrian campaign in 853 is depicted on plates XLVIII–LIII (King, *Reliefs*). No camels are found in the pictures. They appear on plate XXIV from the campaign in 858 BC. Cf. Bulliet, *Camel* 75.
55 For this saddle, see Bulliet, *Camel* 68–80; Dostal, *Evolution* 15–21.
56 See Bulliet, *Camel* 81.

57 Cf. Knauf, *Midian* 11, 15.
58 See Elat, *Campaign*.
59 See p. 122.
60 See pp. 173–176. We do not know exactly where these goods came from. Gold had been found in Ophir, and if the identification of Solomon's and Hiram's Ophir with ʕAsīr is correct, the gold mentioned from the time of Tiglath Pileser III (the middle of the eighth century BC) may have come from there. One should, however, not exclude the possibility that gold and myrrh may have been shipped from Egypt across the Red Sea to Arabia, then carried to Dedan for further transport northwards. But the archaeological evidence for this is scanty in the extreme; cf. Parr, *Pottery, Peoples*.
61 Retsö, *Domestication* 205 ff.
62 Cf., for example, Groom, *Frankincense* 44.
63 A survey of the evidence is found in Brinkman, *History* 183–184 n. 1127. Cf. Háklár, *Stellung*, and the recent evidence for the importance of Suhu in Cavigneaux/Ismail, *Statthalter*, and Liverani, *Caravan Trade*.
64 Salmaneser, *Monolith* I:54; II:4; cf. Knauf, *Midian* 168.
65 Knauf, *Midian* 1–6.
66 al-Bakrī, *Muʕǧam* 517; Yāqūt, *Muʕǧam* IV 445. Von Wissmann (*Madiama* passim) wanted to see two Midyans, one in Wādī ʕIfāl and one inland from Ḍubā, because Ptolemy puts Madiama there on his map. The latter is probably Medan/Mudān, as pointed out by Knauf, *Madiama*. The oasis Mudān is identified with al-ʔAyka mentioned in the Qurʔān 15:78; 26:175; 38:13; 50:14 (al-Bakrī, *Muʕǧam* 135; *Lisān* s.v. ʔYK).
67 von Wissmann, *Madiama* 538. Cf. Jeremiah 25:25; Numbers 25:14. See p. 142.
68 Tukulti Ninurta, *Annals* I:69–73, cf. 76–79 (= Scheil 18–19); The *meshkannu* wood is identified with *Dalbergia Sisoo* (Liverani, *Caravan Trade* 112 note 19).
69 As assumed by, for example, Eph'al, *Arabs* 231–233, and Liverani, *Caravan Trade*. Macdonald (*Trade Routes* 339) points out that the goods mentioned as coming from western Arabia in Assyrian texts do not contain any typical South Arabian items.
70 Ha-a-a-pa-a-a; see pp. 134 f.
71 Lavigneax/Ismail, *Statthalter* 2:iv:27; Galter, *Grenze* 30–31; cf. Macdonald, *Trade Routes* 338–339.
72 For an early dating see Albright, *Dedan* 9–10; Dumbrell, *Midian* 330; Knauf, *Midian* 168; Westermann, *Genesis* II 484–485. Observe that, contrary to Knauf's allegation, frankincense is not mentioned in connection with these names.
73 Namely the Mesha stone.
74 For this tradition, see Wallis, *Tradition,* esp. 28–33, 39.
75 Eissfeldt's hypothesis about a Midianite 'protectorate' over large parts of north-western Arabia and Palestine (*Protektorat*) was met with some scepticism. The idea, however, lives on in a more moderate form; see Knauf, *Midianites*; idem, *Midian* 31–42; Payne, *Arc*.
76 Commentators agree that they do not belong to the so-called P-layer (e.g. Westermann, *Genesis* II 448–451; 483, 488). In the genealogical system of P, the areas east and south of Palestine are dominated by the sons of Ishmael, which reflects conditions after 700 BC; see pp. 220 f. The earliest empire in southern Syria documented in contemporary sources is that of the house of Omri, which was followed by that of Ḥazaʔel in Damascus after *c*. 840 BC. If the Davidic empire did not exist, as is assumed by the deconstructivists, the Qeturah list could reflect a Midianite domination in Transjordan before the rise of the House of Omri. For a survey of conditions in the area in the early Iron Age see Thompson, *History* 295–300.
77 This route is described by Macdonald, *Trade Routes*, who identifies Saba in the Qeṭurah-list with the Sabaeans in Yemen (ibid. 337–338). For arguments against, see pp. 217 f.
78 Cf. Macdonald, *Trade Routes* 344–345; Parr, *Pottery* 82 ff.
79 Cf. Klengel, *Syria* 199; Elat, *Campaign* 31; Kuan, *Inscriptions* 69–106.
80 2 Kings 8:7–15.
81 2 Kings 8:9.
82 For this period in general see Pitard, *Damascus* 132–160; Kuan, *Inscriptions* 68–106.
83 Tadmor, *Inscriptions* 23–25; Schramm, *Einleitung* 125ff.

84 Tadmor, *Inscriptions* 91–93.
85 Tadmor, *Inscriptions* 9–16.
86 Tadmor's work has reduced the value of Rost's edition (L. Rost: *Die Keilschrifttexte Tiglat-Pilesers* III I, Leipzig 1893); cf. Schramm, *Einleitung* 126–127.
87 Tadmor, *Inscriptions* 117–118.
88 Tadmor, *Inscriptions* 27–38.
89 Tadmor, *Inscriptions* 91–92.
90 Isaiah 10:9; Tiglath Pileser III, *Annals* 17:1'–16'.
91 For the debate around this king, see Kuan, *Inscriptions* 149 n. 57.
92 Tiglath Pileser III, *Annals* 19*:1–20; 13*:1–9.
93 Cf. Forrer, *Provinzeinteilung* 56–59 and preceding note.
94 For a survey of the events, see Kuan, *Inscriptions* 142, 186–189.
95 For a survey of the texts, see Kuan, *Inscriptions* 138–157.
96 For the circumstances around the stela, see Kuan, *Inscriptions* 150–152.
97 Weippert's translation of the first lines runs: 'Den Königen von Hatti, der Aramäer vom Ufer des Meeres des Westens, der Kedrener (von) Arabien . . . [legte ich Abgabe und Tribut]' (Weippert, *Menahem* 30). All evidence points to the fact that the Aramaeans were considered to live in interior Syria and not along the coast. If these lines are taken as an introduction and a summary of the following kings, we have to distinguish between the inhabitants of the coast (= the Phoenicians) and those of the interior (= the Aramaeans) since the ensuing list contains both Phoenician towns and Aramaean kingdoms. The inscription would thus, according to this, make a distinction between the Hatti in south-eastern Anatolia, the Aramaeans in Syria proper (including Damascus and Israel in the south) and the Phoenicians along the coast. Another interpretation is that Hatti is in fact the including term and that the following four represent subcategories of it, i.e. the inhabitants of the entire Hatti-land, namely the lands west of Assyria. It is, however, difficult to see how the Anatolians could ever have been designated as Aramaeans. Weippert further takes *aribi* as apposition to Qidri (cf. his somewhat hesitant commentary to l. 2 '*wohl* Apposition zu' (op. cit. 31, my italics)). This is based on the definition of Arabs as a general designation for nomads. Weippert is followed by Knauf, I*smael* 96 sqq., whereas Eph'al sees the difficulty but follows Weippert as well (*Arabs* 83). Even Tadmor seems hesitant: 'the Aramaeans of the western seashore, the Qedarites (and) the Arabs' in his translation (his brackets) but gives an alternative in his note to the passage: 'Or the Arab Qedarites'. It is a pseudo-problem arising from the preconceived idea that Arab must mean 'nomad'. Since there is no evidence for this, it is proper to take this text as it stands and see the *aribi* as a group alongside the four main ones: Hatti, Aramaeans, Phoenicians and Qidri. This is also correctly realized by Kuan (*Inscriptions* 147 n. 50). For the relationship between Arab and *qidri* in the time of Assurbanipal, see pp. 163 f.
98 For the stela see Tadmor, *Inscriptions* Stele III A:1–30; cf. Weippert, *Menahem*. *Annals* 13*:9–12; 14*:1–5. In Rost's earlier edition of the Annals the list occurs twice: ll. 83–91 and 150–157. It was thought that the two versions represent two different tributes, one in 740 and the other in 738. Tadmor (*Remarks*) showed that the two lists refer to the same occasion.
99 Tiglath Pileser, *Annals* Version A: 3:6 (Tadmor, *Inscriptions* 87); Version C: 27:8 (ibid. 89); Version B: 14*:2 (ibid. 68); cf. Kuan, *Inscriptions* 139–157 for a comparison between the texts.
100 Menahem's tribute to Tiglath Pileser III is mentioned in 2 Kings 15:19–20.
101 Eph'al, *Arabs* 82 n. 247.
102 Eph'al, *Arabs* 86–87.
103 The Assyrian eponym-list for the years 734–732 BC has the notes: 'to Philistaea, to Damascus' (Kuan, *Inscriptions* 137). For the course of events, see Tadmor, *Philistia* 87–90.
104 *Summary inscription* 7:10'–12' (= Tadmor, *Inscriptions* 170–171); Kuan, *Inscriptions* 189–192. Eph'al claims that the Arab queen Shamsi took her oath of allegiance to Assyria, which we know she broke in 733 or 732, in the course of the 734 campaign (*Arabs* 84).

The argument is that she could not have done so before that, since Tiglath Pileser was busy in Armenia in 737–735 BC. There is, however, nothing that speaks against the possibility that such a token of alliance could have been made to Assyrian representatives without the personal presence of the king. Judging by the events in 738, Shamsi's oath must have been a renewal of the allegiance already existing between the Arabs under Zabibe, most likely in connection with Shamsi's succession as queen of the Arabs (on the assumption that *arab* refers to the same group). If this allegiance was established only after the 734 campaign, it is difficult to explain the absence of any reference to it in the tribute-list from that year.

105 2 Chronicles 28:17. The Philistine attacks described in verse 18 are in accordance with the defection of Mitinti of Ashqelon as described in the Annals.

106 Tadmor, *Inscriptions* 78–83.

107 Eph'al, *Arabs* 33–36; Tadmor, *Inscriptions* 225–230.

108 So Eph'al, *Arabs* 85.

109 See Barnett/Falkner, *Sculptures* Plates XIII–XXX (pp. 60–79).

110 Ibid., Plates XIII–XVII (pp. 60–64).

111 Ibid., Plate XVII.

112 Ibid., Plates XXV–XXVI (pp. 74–75).

113 Ibid., Plates XXVII–XXX (pp. 76–79).

114 See the discussion in Eph'al, *Arabs* 24–27. Cf. also Galil, *Chronology* 69–70.

115 Kuan (*Inscriptions* 190–191) has another sequence of events. From the siege of Tyre, Tiglath Pileser moved into Galilee and Samaria and installed Hosea as king there. Then came the campaign against Shamsi followed by the capture of Damascus.

116 See pp. 149 f.

117 Harper letter 631 = Waterman, *Correspondence* I 440, 441 = Fales/Postgate, *Records* II no. 162 (pp. 101–102).

118 Fales/Postgate translate 'cohort commander'.

119 Cf. Eph'al, *Arabs* 99 n. 332.

120 Summary 4:27'–28'; 7:3'; 13:9'–10'; cf. the reconstructed text in Eph'al, *Arabs* 33–36, and Tadmor, *Inscriptions* 228, 229 (§§ 7–8).

121 Genesis 25:1–4; cf. Musil, *Ḥeǧâz* 288–289; Knauf, *Midian* 79–80.

122 The original pronunciation of the name is undoubtedly šăbăʔ. The first sound is in Sabaean written with S[1] which in South Arabia may have been pronounced s already in this period. In Arabic the form is săbăʔ. We follow general custom and use the forms Saba and Sabaeans. For the identity of the Sabaeans, see the discussion in Garbini, *Sabei,* especially [7]. Thus also Irvine, *Arabs* 299; Groom, *Frankincense* 45–46; Eph'al, *Arabs* 88–89, 229; Galter, *Grenze* 30–31, 36. There is no doubt that there was an entity in South Arabia in the eighth century BC named Sabaʔ; see, for example, Robin, *Sheba* 1048. Liverani's arguments against are not convincing (*Caravan Trade*). For Sabaeans in al-ʕŪlā see Knauf, *Heimat*, 26–27; von Wissmann, *Geschichte* I 81–85; idem, *Grossreich* 44–45.

123 Cf., for example, Musil, *Ḥeǧâz* 288–289; Rosmarin, *Aribi* 2; Knauf, *Midian* 28–29; Groom, *Frankincense* 44–45; Macdonald, *Trade Routes*.

124 There is no immediate reason to assume that South Arabian frankincense (LBN) is alluded to in the name Qeṭurah or that it is included in the *riqqē* mentioned in the Assyrian texts (against Liverani, *Caravan Trade* 111). Cf. Retsö, *Domestication* 194 ff. for the references and arguments.

125 Winnett, *Records* 79: Inscriptions from Jawf nr. 18; cf. Eph'al, *Arabs* 89. In Pliny 6:157 most manuscripts read Badanatha as the name of a town between the Tamudaei and Cariata. The former is well known from the time of Sargon II, and the latter could be identical with Wādī l-qurā. The reading is, however, uncertain; cf. Glaser, *Geographie* § 329 (pp. 202–203); Musil, *Ḥeǧâz* 290. There is a modern Wādī Badana documented north-east of Dumah, which could be the same name; see Macdonald, *Trade Routes* 335.

126 Genesis 25:12–15.

127 Ǧabal Ghunaym 16 (Winnett, *Records* 101–102).

128 Eph'al, *Arabs* 219, alternatively suggests an area south-west of Babylonia. Since he argues from evidence from the time of Assurbanipal, i.e. in the middle of the seventh century BC,

it is possible that conditions had changed and that Massā had moved north-eastwards. Albright's suggestion (*Tribe* 2) of the identity between Massā and Mash in the list of the Aramaeans in Genesis 10:23 is most unlikely.

129 *ina muhhi Muṣri*, *Summary* 4:34', 7:6', 13:16'.

130 *Annals* 18:13' = Tadmor, *Inscriptions* 82–83. The syntactic relation between the name and *arubu* is not clear due to the fragmentary state of the text.

131 1 Chronicles 4:25.

132 A Ǧabal Mismaʕ is found *c*. 100 km east of Taymāʔ; see Winnett, *Genealogies* 194. If this name is related to Mishmaʕ, it is unlikely that the tribe in the Ishmael list lived there in the eighth and seventh centuries BC. The position in the Ishmael list indicates a more western location. It is possible that Mishmaʕ has wandered westwards, ending up in the Negev, although this is highly speculative; cf. Knauf, *Ismael* 68. For the location of Idibiʔil in southern Syria see ibid. 66–68. The identification with Nodab in 1 Chronicles 5:19 is less likely.

133 Eph'al, *Arabs* 215–216; Knauf, *Ismael* 66–68.

134 *Annals* 23, 18 = Tadmor, *Inscriptions* 78–83.

135 Japhet, *Chronicles* 18–23.

136 The dates of the kings of Israel and Judah are, according to Galil, *Chronology*, and remain very tentative. For Jehoshaphaṭ, see Miller/Hayes, *History* 275–280.

137 2 Chronicles 17:11.

138 2 Chronicles 21:16–17; Miller/Hayes, *History* 280–284.

139 2 Chronicles 22:1.

140 The Syriac Peshitta has only the 'Arabs' as actors: 'because the ʕRBYʔ [ʕarbāyē] came and destroyed Israel's camp'. So also the Vulgate: *Arabes latrones*, taking *gdûd* as a characterization of the 'Arabs'.

141 The name ZMR is quite frequent in Safaitic; see Harding, *Index* 301.

142 Cf. p. 128.

143 Pitard, *Damascus* 160–179.

144 Klengel, *Syria* 211–212.

145 2 Chronicles 26:6–8.

146 Targum to Chronicles ad loc. = Sperber, *Bible* IVa 56.

147 Cf. the survey in Williamson, *Chronicles* 263–265; Dillard, *2 Chronicles* 135; Japhet, *Chronicles* 709–710, 751, 814.

148 2 Chronicles 14:9–15.

149 2 Chronicles 14:15.

150 2 Chronicles 20:1.

151 Josephus mentions *Moabítes*, *Ammanítes* and *árabes* as the attacking force (*Antiquities* 9.2).

152 Cf. Welten, *Geschichte* 143–145; Japhet, *Chronicles* 712.

153 Eph'al, *Arabs* 77–78.

154 Tiglath Pileser, *Summary* 8:22'.

155 See Borger/Tadmor, *Meuniter*; Tadmor, *Meʕûnîm*; Eph'al, *Arabs* 79–80, 91, cf. however ibid. p. 30 n. 80.

156 Such an interpretation was suggested by Musil, *Ḥeǧâz* 243–247.

157 Cf. Williamson, *Chronicles* 263–264, and the references in Japhet, *Chronicles* 709.

158 For the Cushites as Ethiopians, see Myers, *Chronicles* II 85, 122. It is likely that the land of Cush, like the land of Ḥawilah in Genesis 2:11–14, originally designated areas in the northern Ḥiǧāz (cf. von Wissmann, *Ophir*; Hidal, *Land* 100–102; Knauf, *Midian* 52). In the same manner this Arabian Cush may be reflected in the P genealogy in Genesis 10:6–7. Nimrod is a hunter, which makes him a parallel to Esau, the mythical hero of Edom. Since Nimrod is son of Cush, there seems little doubt that he originally belongs to the same area as Esau. One of his cities is Reḥobot ʕIr, which might be identical with Reḥobot Nahar, from which one of the ancient kings of Edom is said to have come (Genesis 36:37). The story of the oppression of Israel by Kushan Rishʕatayim in the age of the Judges (Judges 3:7–11) also reflects events in the south-east and in the land of Edom (in spite of the

mention of Aram-Naharayim). Musil (*Ḥeğâz* 212) points out that there is a wādī called al-Kūs which encompasses the wide sandy plain between Wādī ʕIyāl and Khreybeh/ʕAynūna.

159 Genesis 36:13, 17; 1 Chronicles 1:37 (son of Reʕûʔel son of Esau), 33; 38:30, 46:12; Numbers 26:20; Joshua 7:1; 1 Chronicles 2:6 (son of Judah); Numbers 26:13; 1 Chronicles 4:24 (son of Simeon); 1 Chronicles 6:21 (son of Levi); cf. Astour, *Sabtah* 422 and n. 4.

160 For the analysis, see further Na'aman, *Nawwadîm*; cf. Rudolph, *Aufbau*; Williamson, *Chronicles* 264; Japhet, *Chronicles* 703, 710; Eph'al, *Arabs* 78.

161 Aharoni, *Land* 28; Hamilton, *Hormah.*

162 Genesis 20; 26:1–22. In Joshua 12:13–14 we find a town Geder mentioned together with Arad and Ḥormah which most likely is identical with Gedor (against Aharoni, *Land of Gerar* 27). Aharoni's remark about Gerar in the Table of Nations (Genesis 19:19, ibid. note 1) is probably not relevant.

163 The difference between GRR and GDR in the Hebrew script is minimal.

164 Also Judges 1:17 is followed by an account of the conquest of the Philistine cities.

165 The confusion between Gerar and a site far east in the ʕArabah is probably reflected in the story of the bishop Marcianus from Iotabe, an island in the Gulf of ʕAqabah, participating in the council of Chalcedon in AD 451 but appearing in the documents as the bishop from Gerar (Alt, *Meinungen* 444–449).

166 This is one of the instances where ʔAram should be read either as Edom or as referring to ʔIram/Wādī Ramm.

167 Bartlett, *Edom* 44; Edelman, *Geography* 8–10.

168 Musil, *Ḥeğâz* 243–247. The word *gayʔ* seems to be particularly used for valleys around the Dead Sea.

169 Musil, *Ḥeğâz* 246.

170 Welten, *Geschichte* 159, n. 226.

171 Japhet, *Chronicles* 880.

172 For the mountain in the Negev and the Arabs, see pp. 285–289. Musil (*Ḥeğâz* 245) suggested that *gûr* in Gur Baʕal is to be connected with the Arabic *qāra*, plural *qūr*, meaning 'mountain', and that it refers to the mountains around Wādī Ramm, i.e. ʔAram in the Old Testament. The Aramaic rendering would thus be correct. The solution is attractive although difficult to verify.

173 Cf. Eph'al, *Arabs* 30 n. 80. See p. 133.

174 In 2 Chronicles 26:8 the Vulgate renders *meʕûnîm* with *Ammonitae*, whereas the Septuagint renders *ʕammônîm* with *minaîoi* in the same passage. The two peoples seem to have been mixed up early in the textual tradition.

175 The alienness of 1 Chronicles 4: 34–43 to the rest of C has been pointed out by Mittmann, *Ri. 1:16*. According to him, the piece is a later addition to C; cf. Braun, *1 Chronicles* 66. Japhet's idea (*Chronicles* 710) that 'black Arabs' are intended by the term 'Hamites' is wayward. It is likely that we have here a memory of the original meaning of the name Ham, designating some groups south of Palestine after which the whole southern third of the world was named by the Priestly writers. They used the term 'Yephet', originally a designation of the Philistines, in the same way.

176 Welten, *Geschichte* 145.

177 Knauf, *Meunäer.*

178 Agatharchides § 90, see pp. 150 f., 297 f.; Musil, *Ḥeğâz* 292–293, 304, 355; von Wissmann, *Madiama*. This name, which tends to appear in many different forms, may also be reflected in the *Marsimani* in Sargon's inscription from 715 BC; cf. p. 149.

179 It should be observed that this passage is absent in the Syriac Peshitta.

180 Josephus, *Antiquities* 9.217.

181 2 Kings 14:22; 2 Chronicles 26:2.

182 Pointed out by Musil, *Ḥeğâz* 243 ff.; cf. Dillard, *2 Chronicles* 155–156. Cf. 2 Chronicles 20:1 with 20:22–23 and 2 Chronicles 25:11, 14 with 1 Chronicles 1:30. See further Welten, *Geschichte* 143–145. The two names could be related.

183 As is usual with information found in Chronicles only, scholars have been sceptical about

the Uzziah story as well; cf. Curtis, *Chronicles* 449–452, 394; Welten, *Geschichte* 159.

184 For a thorough analysis of C's handling of his material, see Na'aman, *Nawwadîm*; cf. Japhet, *Chronicles* 14–19.

185 2 Kings 8:26.

186 1 Chronicles 5:18–22.

187 Reuben belongs to the Judaean tribes as the brother of Simeon and Judah.

188 2 Samuel 5:17–25.

189 Cf. Curtis, *Chronicles* 391–395. The historicity of this passage is defended by Rudolph, *Chronikbücher* 251; Myers, *Chronicles II* 100; Williamson, *Chronicles* 283; Japhet, *Chronicles* 703. Welten, *Geschichte* 186, underlines the *topos* character of the tribute passages in C but does not exclude the possibility of historical facts being preserved in some of them (although not 17:11). Na'aman (*Nawwadîm* 269–270) doubts its historicity, claiming it to be a calque on the account of king Uzziah. Miller/Hayes (*History* 278) assume ancient sources specific for the Chronicler.

190 Na'aman, *Nawwadîm*.

191 2 Kings 3:4.

192 Noth, *Personennamen* 63, 222 n. 7; Nöldeke, *Beiträge* 92–96.

193 One might observe that Omri's immediate predecessor was Zimri, i.e. another person of what looks like an Arabic name. This man, like Omri, was an officer in the chariotry. Two Arabic-looking names are thus found in the Israelite army. Gindibu may have felt quite at home among his Israelite colleagues at Qarqar.

194 2 Kings 8:16–18.

195 2 Kings 3:4. The historicity of the account is defended by Williamson, *Chronicles* 283.

196 Yeivin, *Yehôšafaṭ* 11.

197 1 Kings 22:49; 2 Chronicles 20:35–37 (more detailed).

198 2 Kings 8:20–22; 2 Chronicles 21:8–10.

199 Cf. Kuan, *Inscriptions* 53 ff.

200 Myers, *Chronicles II* 152–153; Aharoni, *Land* 311–314.

201 Isaiah 10:8–9.

202 According to W. W. Müller (*Araber*) the reference is to an area south of Damascus (al-Lağā) to which Paul fled and which was inhabited by the people who have left the Safaitic inscriptions. The impression from Tiglath Pileser's own texts is that Shamsi and her Arabs were further to the south than al-Lağā. For an Arabia in al-Lağā see pp. 417, 437, 612 f.

203 Moore, *Judith* 67. Grünfeld, *Masaʕ* [204] assumes a much earlier date: the end of the fourth century BC.

204 Cf. in general Stummer, *Geographie*; Grünfeldt, *Masaʕ*; Moore, *Judith* 38–56. Brunner, *Nabuchodonosor* esp. 56–137 sees Holophernes' campaign as a historical event after the year 529 BC; cf. ibid. 131 ff. For a positive view, see Eph'al, *Arabs* 173–174. There is, however, no reason to identify Arabia in Judith 2:25 with that of Xenophon in *Anabasis* 1.2; cf. pp. 252, 303.

205 Judith 2:21–27.

206 Ptolemy 5.14; cf. Moore, *Judith* 137.

207 Jeremiah 46:9; Hezechiel 27:10, 30:5. Grünfeld (*Masaʕ* [204]) identifies Phud with Pisidia.

208 It is the same name as the town of Lod, which was used by the Egyptians as a name for Palestine; see p. 214.

209 See p. 178.

210 Moore translates 'Ishmaelites living on the edge of the desert south of Cheleon'.

211 Brunner, *Nabochodonosor* 112, and Stummer, *Geographie* 23, suggest the Syrian desert. Stummer's location of Rassis in the Iskenderun area (25), followed by Moore (*Judith* 138), is less convincing. Stummer also suggested Ḥalḥūl north of Hebron or Elousa in the Negev as a location for Khelous (*Geographie* 12–13), which again is unlikely.

212 Strabo 16.4.2; see pp. 302 f.

213 Stummer, *Geographie* 23–24.

214 According to Schedl, *Nabochodonosor* 248–249, Arpaxad is a Median military title: *arpa-kšad*', leader of the knights'.
215 For a similar view, see Grünfeld, *Masaʕ* [206]–[207].
216 An example in the Old Testament is the story of David and Goliath. The motif is frequent in the Yemeni folk-tales collected by W. Daum in his *Märchen aus dem Jemen*, 2 Aufl. München 1992. The killer is a young man/child or a woman, since these are categories not affected by blood-guilt, which always follows a free adult man.
217 For this romance, see pp. 184–189. It is not impossible that some elements come from the events in 521 BC, as alleged by Schedl, *Nabochodonosor*. It is, however, unlikely that the whole story of Judith is founded on them. A similar romance obviously existed about Sennacherib; see Frahm, *Einleitung* 21–28.
218 Annals 101 (= Lie, *Inscriptions* 16–17); Prism VA 8424 B:12 (= Weidner, *Šilkan(he)ni* 46); cf. Eph'al, *Arabs* 37.
219 See Tadmor, *Campaigns* I.
220 Assur-charter l. 16 (Winckler, *Forschungen* I 403); Sargon, *Annals* l. 23, see Tadmor, *Campaigns* I 25.
221 Nimrud prism DE IV:37–49 (= Gadd, *Prisms* 179–180).
222 For the reconstruction of this passage in the Annals, see Tadmor, *Campaigns* 34.
223 Tadmor, *Campaigns* 77–78; cf. Weidner, *Šilkan(he)ni*, esp. 42.
224 One could observe the occurrence of the verb *šapāšum* in both.
225 Annals l.101 (= Lie, *Inscriptions* 16).
226 Annals l.78, 84 ff. (= Lie, *Inscriptions* 12 ff.).
227 See note 50.
228 Annals 120–125 (= Lie, *Inscriptions* 20–23). Parallel text in the Summary inscription: Winckler, § 27 (Winckler, *Keilschrifttexte* 100, 101) where, however, the perfumes are missing.
229 According to Weiss-Rosmarin, *Aribi* 3–4, *pir'u* is a proper name, cf. 1 Kings 11:18 where it is also used as a proper name: Parʕo, king of Miṣrayim. This seems to be the case in several pasages in the Old Testament, most remarkably in the Exodus story.
230 Cf. Eph'al, *Arabs* 109 n. 371; Hommel, *Ethnologie* 607.
231 E.g. von Wissmann, *Geschichte I* 108; idem, *Geschichte II* 147–150; idem, *Geschichte* 329–330/(22)–(23); Galter, *Grenze* 32–33.
232 Harding, *Index* 658; W. W. Müller, *Abiyaṯaʕ*.
233 Exodus 6:23.
234 Eph'al, *Arabs* 105–106.
235 2 Kings 17:30; cf. Amos 8:14.
236 Knauf, *Administration* 212 n. 49. This makes the identification with *sēmeion* etc., known from the Hellenistic period, less likely, whereas the ʔŠMBYTʔL in the Elephantine papyri is most probably identical with the god(dess) in Amos 8:14 and the god(dess) in Taymāʔ.
237 van den Branden, *Histoire*.4, 13–14 (confusing epigraphy with ethnology).
238 van den Branden, *Histoire* 106.
239 Agatharchides § 89; cf. p. 149 and Eph'al, *Arabs* 89, 218. It seems that in the varying forms of the name there is a confusion between **may*(*r*?)*samen* and the Bathymi/Bythēmanos mentioned in Agatharchides/Photius and Pliny (6.150; cf. Musil, *Ḥeǧâz* 292, 304, 535).
240 Eph'al (*Arabs* 7) inserts an 'and' between 'Marsimani' and Ephah' and takes the following *arbāya rūqūti* as an apposition summing up the preceding names. All are thus, according to his view, to be defined as 'Arabs'. Unless one has decided that this is the case, the text may well be read differently, enumerating five separate entities.
241 Annals ll. 187–188 (= Lie, *Inscriptions* 30–31).
242 Ptolemy 6.2.8.
243 Cf. Behistun II 27.
244 So Streck, *Gebiet* 353–354.
245 See Retsö, *Arabs.*
246 For these inscriptions, see Garbini, *Iscrizioni* 169–171.

247 For the Mesopotamian inscriptions, see Garbini, *Iscrizioni*; Sass, *Studia* 38–58; Bron, *Vestiges*.
248 Cf. Retsö, *Domestication* 200, with further references.
249 Retsö, *Domestication* 205 ff.
250 See p. 135.
251 Harper letter 88 = Waterman, *Correspondence* I:58 (cf. idem III:44) = Parpola, *Correspondence* no. 84 (p 75); cf. also Eph'al, *Arabs* 116 note 392.
252 Harper letter 547 = Waterman, *Correspondence* I:388, 389. Cf. Eph'al, *Arabs* 116 n. 393, and Parpola, *Correspondence* no. 82 (p. 74), with improved readings.
253 Fales/Postgate, *Records* I no. 58 (p. 75).
254 Harper letter 414 = Waterman, *Correspondence* I 288, 289 = Parpola, *Correspondence* no. 177 (p. 139). LÚ (= Sumerian 'man') is the determinative indicating persons. Eph'al, *Arabs* 96–97, argues for a dating of Bēl liqbi and the letter to the time of Tiglath Pileser which has not been accepted by later scholars; see Radner, *Prosopography* s.v. Bēl liqbi 2 (I:2 K. Fabritius).
255 Alt, *Nachrichten* 154, 158–159. Cf. Eph'al, *Arabs* 97.
256 Nimrud letter XXXIII = Saggs, *Letters* II 142–143; cf. Eph'al, *Arabs* 94.
257 Harper letter 953 = Parpola, *Correspondence* no. 178 (pp. 139–140).
258 Parpola, *Correspondence* no. 179 (pp. 140–141).
259 The latest editor of the letters from Sargon's time assumes that a couple of letters signed by Adda-hati, the governor of Hama in Sargon's days (Radner, *Prosopography* I:1 s.v. Adda ḫāti) also mention or deal with Arabs (Parpola, *Correspondence* nos. 174, 175). The word itself is, however, not mentioned in these letters.
260 Thus Eph'al, *Arabs* 116.
261 See p. 128.
262 The *arbāya* may also have been mentioned in Harper letter 642 (= Waterman, *Correspondence* I:446–449), but the passage is so damaged that the reading is uncertain.
263 For this development, see especially Brinkman, *Prelude* 31 ff.
264 See Eph'al, *Arabs* 113–116; Zadok, *West Semites*, 210–39; idem, *Arabians*.
265 BM 113203 published by Luckenbill, *Annals* 48–55, 94–98.
266 BM 113203:28 (= Luckenbill, *Annals* 51); cf. Eph'al, *Arabs* 113. For the interpretation of the name, see W. Müller, *Abyaṯaʕ* 29. In this study Müller's suggestions of the original forms of the ancient Arabian names from the root YṮʕ are followed.
267 Luckenbill, *Annals* 25, 57.
268 See pp. 253 f., 378–383. The *nabaṭu* are already mentioned by Tiglath Pileser: Summary Inscriptions 2:5, 7:6, 11:16.
269 See in general, Cole, *Nippur* 34 ff. and below pp. 190–191.
270 VA 3310 rev. 22–27 (= Luckenbill, *Annals* 92–93) + K 8544 rev. 3–6. The text is here given according to Frahm, *Einleitung* 131; cf. Eph'al, *Arabs* 118 ff., who does not include K 8544.
271 The text is found in two inscriptions: Nineveh A, IV1–5 (Borger, *Inschriften* 53), and the Heidel prism 45–50 (Heidel, *Prism* 18–19). For the reading *ap-kal-la-tu* based on the Heidel prism, see Borger, *Miszellen*.
272 Ishtar Letter = K 3404:1–4 (Streck, *Assurbanipal* 222).
273 For the identification, see Musil, *Arabia Deserta* 531 ff.; Eph'al, *Arabs* 120–121; Frahm, *Einleitung* 135.
274 Frahm, *Einleitung* 135.
275 Cf. Hoftijzer, *Lexicon* s.v. ʔPKL; Höfner, *Religion* 372; Teixidor, *Notes 3*; Borger, *Miszellen*; Beeston *et al.*, *Dictionary* s.v. ʔFKL; Scagliarini, *Chronologie* 129.
276 Luckenbill, *Annals* 33 f.; cf. Neiman, *Urbi* 137–138.
277 Luckenbill, *Annals* 27, 54 (= First campaign 52).
278 Rassam cylinder III:63–67 (= Streck, *Assurbanipal* II:28, 29).
279 Streck, *Assurbanipal* III:783–784.
280 For a survey, see Neiman, *Urbi*, and Eph'al, '*Arabs*' 110 note 16.
281 See pp. 74, 76.

282 Room XXXVI:8 = Paterson, *Sculpture* Plate 71.
283 The remains of camels begin to occur already in the Late Bronze Age but reach a culmination in Iron Age II; see Wapnish, *Caravans* esp. 102; Retsö, *Domestication* 199.
284 It is worth noticing that among the booty taken by Sennacherib from Ezekiah we also find camels (Sennacherib, Prism III:25).
285 See the survey of the discussion in Japheth, *Chronicles* 468–474. Both she (ibid. 472), Myers (*I Chronicles* 185) and Williamson (*Chronicles* 177) favour a dating of 1 Chronicles 27:25–31 to David's time. Japhet is right in that there are no characteristics of C's style in the list of these officials. This supports the assumption that the list is based on an original document and that it is not a composition by C. But the presence of Ishmaelites and Hagarites shows that it must originate in the eighth century BC at the earliest. Cf. also Welten, *Geschichte* 98 ff., with weighty arguments against an early dating of the description of the Judaean army, by C attributed to David's time.
286 Ishmaelites and Hagarites are mentioned as Israel's enemies in Psalm 83:6.
287 aṭ-Ṭabarī, *Tārīkh* I:671 l.5–672 l.8; 744 l. 19–745 l. 3.
288 *ʔanbār* is plural of *nibr*, meaning 'granary', 'store-house'.
289 See p. 149.
290 Judith 2:24. The Abronas river mentioned has been identified differently. Stummer (*Geographie* 26) identifies it with Khabūr whereas Grünfeld suggests ʕAfrīn in the Antioch valley (*Masaʕ* [207]). It may be connected with the river Aborras, present-day Balīkh, mentioned by Strabo (16.1.27).
291 Herodotus 2.141.
292 Strabo 16.1.27–28, a passage which comes from Posidonius in the middle of the first century BC. Cf. further pp. 353 ff.
293 Herodotus 2.141.
294 2 Kings 18–13–19:37/2 Chronicles 32/Isaiah 36–37.
295 Diodorus 2.1.5, 7; 3.2.
296 Schnabel, *Berossos* 267 text 39. The passage is badly preserved only in the Armenian translation of Eusebius' Chronicle; see Schnabel, *Berossos* 141.
297 For the following see Eph'al, *Arabs* 43–46.
298 For these texts except the Heidel prism, see Borger, *Inschriften.* For the relevant passage in the Heidel prism, see Heidel, *Prism* II:46–66, III:1–8.
299 Heidel, *Prism* II:51–III:8, Nineveh A IV ep. 14 10–11 (Borger, *Inschriften* 53); Mon. B:16 (Borger, *Inschriften* 100); Frg. B:8 (Borger, *Inschriften* 111). For the different forms of the name formed from the root YṮʕ, see W. Müller, *Abyaṯaʕ* 28. The name Yaʕlu is from another root and originally belongs to another person, see p. 160.
300 Frg. F Rev. 2 ff. (Borger, *Inschriften* 112). For the Egyptian campaign, cf. also the Babylonian Chronicle IV 23–26 (Grayson, *Chronicle* 1) and the Esarhaddon Chronicle 25–26 (Grayson, *Chronicle* 14).
301 Eph'al, *Arabs* 137–141. For the role of the camels, see the archaeological evidence of extensive presence of camels documented by Wapnish, *Camels*.
302 Eph'al's scepticism towards Herodotus 2.141 about 'Sennacherib, king of Assyrians and Arabs' is fully justified. We shall return to Herodotus in connection with the Achaemenids and their dealings with the Arabs.
303 Assumed by Eph'al, *Arabs* 140–141.
304 Harper letter 629 = Waterman, *Correspondence* I:438, 439. The syntactic structure is not clear.
305 Nin. A:14:23–31 (= Borger, *Inschriften* 54).
306 For details about this source, see p. 161.
307 For this passage in the Ashshur letter, see Streck, *Assurbanipal* 376–378 (= VAT 5600); Weippert, *Bericht* 75–76. For the reading Ia-ú-te-' (=Yawthiʕ and not U-a-a-te-' (= Yuhaythiʕ) see p. 165.
308 So Eph'al, *Arabs* 129.
309 For names with this root, see W.W. Müller, *Abyaṯaʕ*.
310 Harper letter 512 = Waterman, *Correspondence* I:358, 359. The determinative DIŠ is the sign for the numeral 'one' often used with male individuals.

311 Harper letter 773 = Waterman, *Correspondence* II: 40, 41.
312 The following presentation is mainly based upon Eph'al, *Arabs* 46–52, 142–169, and Weippert, *Kämpfe*, especially 48–61.
313 Piepkorn, *Prism Inscriptions* 80–87.
314 Borger, *Beiträge* 113–117.
315 Bauer, *Inschriftenwerk* 13–18. For the dating, see Eph'al, *Arabs* 47 n. 139.
316 The reverse side of tablet K 3405 deals with Assurbanipal. The obverse side deals with Sennacherib and Esarhaddon; see p. 155. For the reverse text of K 3405 see Bauer, *Inschriftenwerk* 45, and Cogan, *Imperialism* 16–19.
317 K 2802, VAT 5600, BM 98591, cf. Streck, *Assurbanipal* 196–207 (Tontafelinschrift 8 = K 2802), ibid. 376–379 (Tontafelinschrift 22 = VAT 5600); Bauer, *Inschriftenwerk* 20 (Th. 1905–4–9.97 = BM 98591). For the reconstruction see Borger, *Miszellen* 1–2; Weippert, *Kämpfe* 74–85 and Borger, *Beiträge* 76–82.
318 Streck, *Assurbanipal* 2–91.
319 Streck, *Assurbanipal* 65–83; Weippert, *Kämpfe* 39–73; Borger, *Beiträge* 60–69. For an incomplete English translation, see Luckenbill, *Records* II 869–870 (= pp. 337–339).
320 Thompson/Mallowan, *Excavations* 80–98; reconstructed in Borger, *Beiträge* 258–296.
321 (a) Bauer, *Inschriftenwerk* 34–35 (= K 2664), 20 (= K 3090); (b) ibid. 64 (= K 4687); Streck, *Assurbanipal* 224–225; Borger, *Beiträge* 168–169 (= K 2664 + 3090), 113-116 (= K 4687).
322 Weidner, *Beschreibungen*; Borger, *Beiträge* 297–319.
323 Genesis 25:13.
324 The translation is according to Parpola/Watanabe, *State Archives II* 68 (no. 10). For earlier treatments of the text, see Grayson, *Treaties* 147–150, Borger, *Staatsvertäge* 177, and Buis, *Traité*.
325 Deller/Parpola, *Vertrag*; Campbell, *Prologue*.
326 Parpola/Watanabe's reconstruction runs: 'The treaty of Assurbanipal, king of the world, king of Assyria, son of Esarhaddon, likewise king of the world, king of Assyria, with Abiyate son of Te'ri, his sons, grandsons, brothers and nephews, with all Qedarites, young and old and with . . .'
327 See p. 131.
328 Paragraphs according to the text in Weippert, *Kämpfe* 75.
329 Cf. Weippert, *Kämpfe* 76–77, 82.
330 Cf. Weippert, *Kämpfe* 77–78, 83.
331 Eph'al, *Arabs* 56–58. In Harper letter 350 (= Waterman, *Correspondence* 242, 243) he figures in a fight against qí-dar-a-a, which probably refers to the war with Ammuladin.
332 Harper letter 260 = Waterman, *Correspondence* I 174, 175.
333 For a discussion see Eph'al, *Arabs* 56–59; cf. also Albright, *Massa'* 4–5.
334 Eph'al (*'Arabs'* 115 note 48) and W. Müller (*Abyaṯaʕ* 29) assume that it is ʕMYṮʕ, well documented in Epigraphic South Arabian. The reading of bar-'-a-a is doubted by Eph'al, who renders it Massa' (*Arabs* 56), whereas Waterman, in his translation, gives Mash. Cf. Albright, *Massa'* 4–5.
335 Ishtar slab 113, 119, 123–126 (Thompson/Mallowan, *Excavations* 86–87, 95–96); Borger, *Beiträge* IIT §§ 113 (p. 279, 293–294), §§ 123–129 (= pp. 281–282).
336 Luckenbill, *Annals* 113; Winnet/Reed, *Records* 93–95. The relation between Shumu'il/ŠMʕL and Yišmāʕel in the Old Testament remains problematic; cf. Eph'al, *Arabs* 166–177, who rejects the identification, and Knauf, *Ismael* (24 n. 101, 40, 60), who accepts it and sees it as a confederation of tribes in North Arabia. Linguistically, the identification is doubtful, and the geographical location is rather Taymāʔ than Wādī Sirḥān. Shumuʔil/ ŠMʔL should instead be associated with the name of the mythical Arab poet of Taymāʔ, as-Samawʔal, who is said to have lived in the first half of the sixth century AD. The name is also found in a Nabataean inscription from al-ʕUlā, dated to the middle of the fourth century AD (JS I 149) as the name of a chief in Taymāʔ. The names are obviously identical.
337 References according to Weippert, *Kämpfe*.

338 VIII:48–64 (= Streck, *Assurbanipal* 68–71; Borger, *Beiträge* 63).
339 Eph'al, *'Arabs'* 163. For the location of Khulkhula see the map in MacAdam, *Studies* 63.
340 Rassam cylinder VIII:24 (Streck, *Assurbanipal* 68–69).
341 King of Qedar: Piepkorn B VII:93–94 (Piepkorn, *Prism Inscriptions* 80). King of the Arabs: Heidel prism, Nineveh A, Mon. B., Frg. B, all from Esarhaddon's time (see note 316); Ishtar letter, Assur letter, all from Assurbanipal.
342 Eph'al (*Arabs* 168) claims that *šar aribi* is a general term for the leaders of the 'nomads', including Qedar and ShumuSil. See Retsö, *Xenophon,* and idem, *Arabs*, for arguments against.
343 See Chapter 13.
344 Harper letter 262 obv. 7–rev. 9 = Waterman, *Correspondence* I 176, 178.
345 Harper letter 259 = Waterman, *Correspondence* I 174, 175.
346 Eph'al (*Arabs* 56) reads *bi-maš-maš.*
347 The documents are Harper letters nos. 273, 543, 1108 and 1244 (= Waterman, *Correspondence* I 184–185, 384–386, II 270–271, 366–367), together with an ostrakon written in Aramaic (Dupont-Sommer, *Ostrakon* 31–34). The interpretation of *rab kiṣir* differs among the commentators. Some (Zimmern, Dupont-Sommer) take it as the designation of a third person, whereas Waterman sees it as the title of the *arbaya*. An argument in favour of Waterman's reading is the mentioning of Ia-ra-pa in the time of Tiglath Pileser III who was *rab kiṣir* of the KUR *ar-ba-a-a* (see p. 134).
348 Sennacherib, 1st Campaign 37, 43, 44 (Luckenbill, *Annals* 52–53).
349 Assur letter III:52; IV:1 (Weippert, *Kämpfe*); Rassam cylinder VIII:111, 124 (= Streck, *Assurbanipal* 72, 73).
350 Assur-letter III:12–IV:10 (= Weippert, *Kämpfe* 79–80, 84–85).
351 The location somewhere in the environs of Palmyra (Weippert, *Kämpfe* 63–65; cf. Eph'al, *Arabs* 161–163) is uncertain and that oasis is not mentioned at all by name.
352 See p. 162.
353 See further pp. 586 f., 610 ff., on the implications of this notice for the religion of the Arabs.
354 The text is found in Streck, *Assurbanipal* 64-83. A new complete edition is Borger, *Beiträge* 61–69. A modern translation with commentary is given by Weippert, *Kämpfe* 39–48.
355 See Scott, *Wisdom, passim*; Gray, *Kings* 120–124 and note 29 above.
356 120 from Hiram of Tyre (1 Kings 9:14), 420 from Ophir (ibid. 9:28), 120 from the Queen of Sheba (ibid. 10:10).
357 Jeremiah 25:24. See further below for an analysis of this passage.
358 Cf. Gray, *Kings* 265.
359 1 Kings 4:5; 5:7, 30; 9:23.
360 An argument for this is, for example, the absence of frankincense (*lebonah*) in the stories about Solomon, which shows that they were formed before 600 BC; cf. Retsö, *Domestication* 203–204. In Psalm 72, which is ascribed to Solomon, depicting him in similar terms as in 1 Kings 10/2 Chronicles 9, the geography reflects conditions in the seventh century at the earliest.
361 In Exodus 12:38; Numbers 11:4; 2 Esdras 23:3 (= MT Nehemiah 13:3): *epímiktos*; Jeremiah 32:18 (= MT 25:20); 27:37 (= MT 50:37): *hoi symmiktoi, ho symmiktos.*
362 So Montgomery, *Commentary* 220; Rudolph, *Chronikbücher* 222; Gray, *Kings* 265. The Septuagint reads 'the kings from the other side' in 1 Kings 10:15.
363 Musil (*Ḥeğâz* 273–274) assumed that the Arabs bringing gold to Solomon came from Midian.
364 Genesis 10:7.
365 See p. 216.
366 RaSmah is identified with Nağrān by W. Müller (*Arabien* 181). The identification is based on an equation of the Hebrew RSMH [RaSmā] with RGMT mentioned in Sabaean texts, which refers to the Nağrān oasis. This identification is highly doubtful; see p. 231, n. 46.
367 Job 1:14–15, 6:19. In Job 6:19 Sheba is mentioned in parallelism with Tema' which supports the northern location.

368 Psalm 72:10.
369 von Wissmann, *Geschichte* I 87–88. In the South Arabian inscriptions the name of the kingdom is written S_1Bʔ. Judging from the writing in the Assyrian texts, its northern namesake was, in the eighth and seventh centuries BC, pronounced *šabaʔ*. The Tiberian Hebrew *š(ə)vå* (in English Sheba) is clearly derived from that form, but looks more Aramaic than Hebrew. The Samaritan reading is *šābā*, which is the expected Hebrew form. Cf. also the Samaritan *dādan* for Tiberian *d(ə)dån* (LXX *Dadan*/*Daidan*). For this linguistic issue, see p. 595.
370 Genesis 10:7.
371 For the dating of this notice, see p. 215.
372 Isaiah 45:14.
373 Jeremiah 6:20.
374 Isaiah 60:6.
375 Genesis 10:26–30; see pp. 219–220.
376 See p. 134.
377 The oldest inscription mentioning the name SBʔ is dated by von Wissmann (*Geschichte* II 63 ff.) to *c*. 780 BC.
378 According to Eph'al (*Arabs* 88) they are independent of each other. Cf. also von Wissmann, *Geschichte* I 81 ff.
379 von Wissmann, *Geschichte* I 85–86. Galter (*Grenze*) also admits the existence of Sabaeans in the north but seems to see them as agents from the southern kingdom. The assumption of a Sabaean merchant colony in Dedan is based on the idea that the name Saba must designate a 'nation' or a 'people' in the modern sense. Consequently, when the name is found in a text, it must indicate the presence of (in this case) 'ethnic Sabaeans'. The very foundation of this argumentation is, of course, highly questionable. The Sabaean problem has to be investigated in a separate study.
380 As we have pointed out, there are also scholars who doubt the existence of a Solomonic kingdom.
381 For this dating of the psalm, see von Wissmann, *Geschichte* I 102–103, and pp. 218, 220.
382 See now the survey in Kitchen, *Documentation* 190–222. The 'husband of the queen of Sheba' (190) is of course a ghost.
383 For the use of vocabulary from the sixth century in this story, see Scott, *Wisdom*.
384 Jeremiah 9:25–26: *qṣûṣê peʔā ha-šoknîm ba-midbar*.
385 Wiseman, *Chronicles* 70–71 = BM 21946 rev. 9–10.
386 2 Kings 24:2.
387 It has been suggested that the Aramaeans in 2 Kings 24:2 in fact were Edom, which is the reading of the Peshitta. The MT, however, makes good sense in this passage and should be followed; cf. Bartlett, *Edom* 148–149.
388 Jeremiah 27:2 ff.
389 For the events, see Miller/Hayes, *History* 406–415.
390 For the events leading up to the siege of Tyre, see Katzenstein, *History* [295]–[319].
391 Ezechiel 27:16–22. For a thorough analysis and reconstruction of the Song of Tyre see Zimmerli, *Ezechiel* 624–661.
392 For the dating, see Zimmerli, *Hezechiel* 661.
393 For the 'cup of wrath' passage as a vision, see Holladay, *Jeremiah* 673.
394 Jeremiah MT 25:18–26/LXX 32:18–25.
395 Holladay, *Jeremiah* 672–673.
396 The parallel to the Qurʔān is striking, e.g. the story behind sūra 53:19–25 and the testimonies of the reinterpretation of 30:1: *ġulibati r-rūm*, 'Rome has been defeated'; *ġalabati r-rūm*, 'Rome has been victorious'; cf. Paret, *Koran: Kommentar* ad. loc.
397 Cf. Jeremiah 9:25 and 2 Kings 24:2.
398 See pp. 220 ff., for their possible historic context.
399 They are mentioned together once more in Genesis 22:21 as two sons of Nahor, probably to be located in southern Edom or in northern Ḥiǧāz; see Westermann, *Genesis* 2 450.
400 Cf. p. 17.

401 Even the passage about Solomon has a variant reading, 'kings of the *ʕereb*' (1 Kings 10:15).
402 Jeremiah 9:25.
403 Jeremiah MT 49:28–33/LXX 30:23–28.
404 Jeremiah 49:28–33. For textual studies on this poem, see Dumbrell, *Jeremiah*, and Holladay, *Jeremiah* 2 382–386.
405 Cf. Dumbrell, *Jeremiah* 102–103; Lane, *Lexicon* s.v. ḤẒR. The Arabic *ḥaẓār* corresponds directly to the Hebrew *ḥāṣôr*. Holladay's suggestion (following Rudolph, *Jeremia* 253) that it instead represents Arabic *ḥāḍir* etc. 'settled people' (*Jeremiah* 2 282-283) should not be accepted since it is founded on an erroneous interpretation of the text. Eph'al (*Arabs* 175) hesitatingly takes it as a proper name 'until a satisfactory explanation . . . is found'.
406 Jeremiah 9:25 and 25:23/32:23.
407 For the identification of the events in Jeremiah 49 with Nebuchadnezzar's campaign in 599–598 and a reconstruction of the oracle, see Dumbrell, *Jeremiah*. Cf. also Eph'al, *Arabs* 172–173; Holladay, *Jeremiah* 2 385.
408 Bright, *Jeremiah* 336. Rudolph (*Jeremia* 253–254) suggested that Qedar is secondary and that the text originally did not even refer to them.
409 The differences in the original writing may have been only one letter: MLKT vs. MMLKT. The reading could be [malkat] 'queen of' or [mlaxōt] (from *malakōt) 'queens (of)'. The Septuagint has read the singular.
410 In the MT they are found in Chapters 46–50 and in LXX in Chapters 28–31 followed directly by the 'wine-cup vision', which is probably the original arrangement.
411 Eusebius, *Praeparatio* IX:41; Müller, *Fragmenta* IV 284–285.
412 Arrian, *Indica* 41:6–7.
413 Cf. Potts, *Gulf* II 85–86.
414 For the location of Gerrha, see pp. 273–274.
415 Ezechiel 25:12 ff.; Jeremiah 49:7 ff.; Lamentations 4:20–21; cf. Knauf, *Supplementa* 4 27; Bartlett, *Edom* 157–161.
416 Genesis 36:3.
417 A war against NBYT is mentioned in inscriptions from Ğabal Ghunaym in the Taymāʔ area; see Winnett/Reed, *Records* 99–101 (Taymāʔ inscriptions 11, 13, 15). The clan Nabīt in the Medinean tribe of ʔAws may have been related to them; cf. Wellhausen, *Medina* 6.
418 Cf. Bartlett, *Edom* 150–151; Knauf, *Supplementa* 13 72–75.
419 Ezechiel 25:13 ff., Jeremiah 34, 49:7 ff.; Obadiah; Maleachi 1:2 ff.
420 Bartlett, *Edom* 157–161.
421 For a survey of the sources for Nabonidus' reign, see Tadmor, *Inscriptions of Nabunaid*; Beaulieu, *Reign* 1–65. For the H2 inscription, see ibid. 32, 209 ff., and Röllig, *Erwägungen*.
422 Nabonidus Chronicle I:11 ff.; Royal Chronicle rev. IV: 57 ff. For the campaign, see Eph'al, *Arabs* 180–188; Beaulieu, *Reign* 165–169.
423 Cf. Lambert, *Nabonidus* 55; Eph'al, *Arabs* 185 ff.
424 Nabonidus Chronicle I:11 ff. Smith rendered the name as Shin-di-ni.
425 Royal Chronicle rev.V:13–22. The passage is fragmentary.
426 Harran stele 2 I:22–25.
427 See Gadd, *Harran* 80–84; Beaulieu, *Reign* 173.
428 Harran stele 2 I:38–II:2; cf. Beaulieu, *Reign* 172–173.
429 So the two chronicles. According to the so-called Verse-account (II:22–26 = Smith, *Texts* 84, 88), an anti-Nabonidus propaganda text from the Persian period, Taymāʔ too was conquered by force.
430 So Gadd, *Harran* 76 ff.; Röllig, *Erwägungen* 228–229.
431 This verse is found in the later Jewish Greek translations (Aquila, Symmachus, Theodotion) and probably belongs to the original version; cf. Galling, *Jesaia* 60.
432 Isaiah 21:11–12. The distribution of lines between speakers is tentative.
433 Isaiah 21: 13–17. The form of the word *ʕrāb* is unusual. The Septuagint reads 'night' *ʕereb*. Galling (*Jesaia* 60 n. 35) suggests the meaning 'steppe', which however is based on

the assumption that the word *ʕarab* has this meaning. As has been shown already, this is most unlikely.

434 The naming of a poem after a key-word in the text is common in Semitic literature; cf., for example, the name 'The Bow' for David's lament over Jonathan and Saul (2 Sam. 1:18) or the naming of the sūras of the Qurʔān.

435 Seʕir was originally an area in the eastern Negev but was early identified with Edom, i.e. the area east of the ʕArabah; cf. pp. 138 ff.

436 Especially the second text uses words which are not common in Biblical Hebrew.

437 Cf. Isaiah 16:13 ff.

438 Galling, *Jesaia* 62, assumes that the two did not originally belong together, and that the announcement refers to a much later date. This might be correct in that a prophet has used an existing poem and added the announcement. It is, however, not necessary to assume a long time-span between the two texts.

439 Winnett, *Records*, inscriptions no. 20–24, 30.

440 Galling, *Jesaja* 61 ff. A war against Dedan (ḌRR DDN) is documented in some of the inscriptions from Ǧabal Ghunaym near Taymāʔ (Winnett, *Records*, inscriptions nr. 20–24, 30). Winnett originally supposed this was connected with Nabonidus' activities in Arabia. Later, he has backed down on the question (Winnett, *Reconsideration* 72). The recent discovery of texts in the area mentioning NBND MLK BBL may, however, increase the likeliness of the connection between the event recorded in the Ghunaym text and Nabonidus.

441 Cf. Bartlett, *Edom* 160–161.

442 Cf. Beaulieu, *Reign* 169 and his preceding discussion.

443 Beaulieu, *Reign* 139–140, 143, 214.

444 Dandamaev, *History* 18.

445 Dandamaev, *History* 17 ff.

446 Herodotus' story is based upon information from the descendants of the Median general, Harpagus, who sided with Cyrus in the revolt against Astyages of Media (see Dandamaev, *History* 15). A similar version was told by Ctesias, transmitted through Nicolaus of Damascus (Dandamaev, *History* 16; König, *Persika* 176–185).

447 See Christensen, *Gestes* 123–135. Xenophon himself refers explicitly to such epics extolling the virtues of Cyrus in the *Cyropaedia* 1.2.1. It is likely that this source goes back to the propaganda of Cyrus the Great himself, who seems to have maintained the fiction that Media still existed. This idea is widely reflected in later popular literature (Herodotus, the Book of Daniel), where Cyrus is seen as the king of the Medes; cf. Dandamaev, *History* 19. The picture of Cyrus given by Herodotus is far more negative, which derives from the fact that Herodotus drew his information from Median sources, critical towards the Persian conqueror (Herodotus 1.95–96).

448 Xenophon, *Cyropaedia* 1.5.2.

449 Xenophon, *Cyropaedia* 2.1.5.

450 Xenophon, *Cyropaedia* 4.2.31.

451 Xenophon, *Cyropaedia* 6.2.10.

452 Xenophon, *Cyropaedia* 7.4.16.

453 Xenophon, *Cyropaedia* 7.5.14.

454 Xenophon, *Cyropaedia* 8.6.7.

455 Xenophon, *Cyropaedia* 1.5–6; cf. Dandamaev, *History* 14–19.

456 Daniel 5:30–31; cf. 6:28.

457 See note 424.

458 The location of Rugdini/Aragdos is not certain. Pliny (6.32.157) much later mentions a tribe named Ar(r)aceni somewhere in the northern Ḥiǧāz, which could be the same name.

459 Cyrus Cylinder 29–30.

460 For a positive evaluation of historical facts in the *Cyropaedia*, i.e. its Iranian *Vorlage*, see Christensen, *Gestes* 123–124.

461 Herodotus 1.80.

462 For the Arabs in Mesopotamia in Xenophon's time, see p. 252.

463 aṭ-Ṭabarī, *Tārīkh* I:671.

464 aṭ-Ṭabarī, *Tārīkh* I:672–674.
465 Yāqūt, *Muʕǧam* II:778.
466 Qurʔān 25:38; 50:12.
467 Yāqūt, *Muʕǧam* II:289.
468 *al-ʕarabu lladīna lā ʔaġlāqa li-buyūtihim wa-lā ʔabwāba* (I:671 l. 10).
469 aṭ-Ṭabarī, *Tārīkh* I:671 l. 13.
470 Cf. Ibn Ḥabīb, *Muḥabbar* 5: 'The reason for the dispersion [of the *ʕarab*] was that Bukht Nuṣṣur was ordered to make a campaign against the people of Ḥaḍūr and the people of *Bāʕarabāyā* (sic) to whose gates there are no locks. So he went against them and massacred the *ʕarab* by sword until he reached Ḥaḍūr.' Cf. also ibid. 7.
471 It is worth pointing out that there exists a seal dated to *c.* 600 BC with the name BRKYHW BN NRYHW HSPR (Avigad, *Bullae* 28–29). It has been suggested that the seal belonged to Baruch, son of Neriah, Jeremiah's secretary (SPR), and we would thus have the original form of his name documented. In that case it is remarkable that the original form, which at this time probably was pronounced [bărăkyăh], is preserved in the source used by aṭ-Ṭabarī whereas the Biblical text has another form (BRWK, Baruch). It would indicate that the legend preserved in Arabic represents a tradition independent from the Biblical one.
472 See pp. 474 ff.
473 In the prophet's own time the name would have been pronounced something like *yĕrĕmĭyāh[ū], reflected in the Septuagint form Ieremias, which in Tiberian Hebrew regularly gives yirm[ə]yáhu and in Aramaic ʔīrəmyā. Both Bukht Nuṣṣur and Nabūxaḏ naṣr must come from a language where k > x, i.e. the *begadkefat* shift, characteristic of Hebrew and Aramaic (but no other Semitic language), has occurred. This shift is quite late in Aramaic (and Hebrew), probably starting in the first century BC; see Beyer, *Texte* 126–128.
474 For example, Nebuchadnezzar's seven years' living as an animal, as well as the setting up of the statue in the plain of Dura, probably refer to activities by Nabonidus; cf. Beaulieu, *Nabonidus* 133–136, 141. The Assyrian identity of the king might belong to this identification. Nabonidus saw himself as a successor to the Assyrian kings; cf. Beaulieu, op. cit. 139–140, 143, 214.
475 A good example is the Aḥīqar-novel, originally in Akkadian but preserved in an Aramaic translation in a papyrus from the fifth century BC, found in the Jewish colony at Elephantine in Egypt. From there we also have an Aramaic translation of Darius' inscription at Behistun. One could also refer to the tale of Tobith. For the sources to the book of Judith, see Priebatsch, *Buch*. Cf. Grünfeld, *Masaʕ* [205]–[206], [208].
476 For the dating of Berossus and his *Babyloniaca* see Schnabel, *Berossos* 8–12.
477 Josephus, *Apion* 1:19; cf. Schnabel, *Berossos* frg. 49 (p. 272).
478 Grünfeld, *Masaʕ* [205]–[206]. Scholars have tended to identify the story in Judith with events after the fall of Assyria. The war against Arpachsad of Media could then be connected with the last king of Assyria who lost Nineveh to the Medes in 612 BC, but also with Nabonidus, fighting against them, supporting Cyrus' revolt in 556 BC and recapturing Harran, which is in the land of Arpachsad according to the Table of Nations in Genesis 10. There is no doubt that the terminology in Judith 1 may be influenced by these events. The different campaigns put under the command of Holophernes may also be distributed to different rulers. The campaign to Cilicia may refer to that of Nabonidus in his first regnal year 556–555 (Beaulieu, *Nabonidus* 116, 127). The one down Mesopotamia may be mentioned in the Nebuchadnezzar chronicle. If we read Iaphet as a reflection of Ephah, the fourth campaign may, in fact, refer to Nabonidus' activities in North Arabia between 553 and 543 BC (Brunner, *Nabuchodonosor* 116–117; Stummer, *Geographie* 23). Finally, the operation against the sons of Rassis and the Ismaelites would be Nebuchadnezzar's campaign in 599 BC. Also here the wording may be influenced by this event. Finally, it should be observed that Nebuchadnezzar's conquest of Egypt is hinted at also in the book of Judith (cf. 1:10–12).
479 For other possible elements from the time of Darius the Great, see Schedl, *Nabochodonosor*.

480 Rothstein, *Dynastie* 12–13.

481 Shahid (*Byzantium* 3:1 358) suggests that Ambaron and Abaron mentioned by early Byzantine writers in connection with the invasion of the Lakhmid kings in Syria in AD 569–570 are identical with ʔAnbār. This identification seems likely. The form of the name looks similar to Abronas in Judith 2:24 and the connection between Nebuchadnezzar and the place-name is made both in Judith and in aṭ-Ṭabarī. This could be another indication that the settlement of Arabs in ʔAnbār in fact goes back to the Neo-Babylonian period.

482 Qurʔān 21:11–15. See, for example, aṭ-Ṭabarī, *Tafsīr* ad loc.

483 For an analysis of the whole passage 2:1–4:4 see Holladay, *Jeremiah* 1 47–131. For the dating, see especially ibid. 63–68.

484 Jeremiah 3:2. For the meaning of *šfayim*, 'barren hill', see Köhler/Baumgartner, *Lexikon* s.v. ŠPY.

485 Sachau col. XIV:208 = Porten, *Textbook* 52–53. The word 'dry land' (BRʔ) is not visible in the papyrus manuscript but is reconstructed by most editors except Porten/Yardeni; cf. Cowley, *Papyri* 219, and Lindenberger, *Proverbs* 209. Cf. Jeremiah 2:10 where the world's end is marked by Kittim and Qedar. This phrase lies behind the passage in Acts 2:11; see p. 418.

486 Isaiah 13:20.

487 Chapters 13:1–14:23. Most commentators and translators read the verbs in v. 20a in the passive: 'It will not be inhabited' etc. The MT as it stands means that Babylon will never dwell but become a wandering nomad. The Targum's rendering of the first verb is ambiguous, but the second favours the active: *lā tiṯyattab l-ʕālam w-lā tišrē l-dār w-dār*. The Peshitta has the active: *lā teṯeb l-ʕālam w-lā tešrē l-dārdārīn*.

488 Eph'al (*Arabs* 196 n. 668) sees the Aḥîqar saying as an illustration of the difference between sailors and caravaneers.

489 For a complete survey see Dandamaev, *Aravit'ane*. Eight of them are mentioned by Eph'al, *Arabs* 188–91. Cf. also Zadok, *West Semites* 224–237; Livingstone, *Arabians;* and Cole, *Nippur* 34–44. It should be remembered that the large onomastic material gathered by Zadok is a testimony of names-giving, reflecting languages among which we might find one we would call Arabic. The terminology among the scholars also varies (Arabs, Arabians, West Semites, Aravit'ane) which reflects the problem. The names themselves are not evidence of the presence of people called Arabs by their contemporaries, although there may be many who actually were Arabs, according to our definition without this being stated explicitly. There is, however, no way of tracing these Arabs who disappear among other 'West Semites'.

490 Cf. Zadok, *West Semites* 224–226; 227.

491 See pp. 153 ff.

492 Correctly emphasized by Livingstone, *Arabians* 100–101.

493 2 Kings 16:6.

494 Bartlett, *Edom* 136–137.

495 Numbers 20:14, 23; 21:4; 33:37.

8

THE OLD TESTAMENT AND ARABIA

Introduction

Of the peoples in Arabia mentioned in the Assyrian texts from Tiglath Pileser onwards, several appear in the Old Testament: Saba/Sheba, Ephah, *meʕûnîm*, Nebayot, Qedar, Adbeʔel and Massa'. As we have emphasized, the contemporary Assyrian sources do not indicate identity between Arabs and any of these tribes, except perhaps Qedar. We find the same picture in the Old Testament. Even though *ʕarab* are mentioned, they are never explicitly identified with any of the other entities mentioned as living in Arabia. In much later Jewish tradition, reflected in the works of Josephus, we find the identification between the sons of Ishmael and *árabes*. Among the former we find Qedar and Dumah which, as is plainly documented from Assyrian sources, are either Arabs or closely connected with them. But the extension of the concept to all other Ishmaelites, and even to everybody living on the peninsula, is not documented until Hellenistic times. We should thus not *ohne weiteres* apply the ideas of later centuries to ethnic conditions in Assyrian, Chaldaean and Achaemenid times.[1]

Nevertheless, it is well worth studying the picture of ethnic conditions in Arabia given by the Old Testament, since it is in fact the earliest attempt at a systematic description of peoples living on the peninsula. The central documents are the genealogies in the Pentateuch, which represent an Israelite view of the ethnic and political situation in the Middle East in the centuries around 500 BC. To these are added a few notices in the Pentateuch and in other Old Testament texts. The exact dating of these texts is still far from settled, but the general view among scholars is that the whole material of the Pentateuch was codified in its present shape towards the end of the fifth century BC at the latest, and that the preceding written tradition may reach back a few centuries. The Pentateuch itself, as is well known, purports to give an account of the prehistory of Israel, i.e. the periods before 1100 BC. Even though the Pentateuch does contain older layers and sometimes very archaic ones, it is very difficult at present to use the Pentateuch as a real historical source for the pre-monarchic period of Israelite history. The texts basically reflect the time in which they were conceived, retold and committed to writing. Bearing this in mind, it is important to single out the elements in the Pentateuchal tradition which are older than the final redaction.

As far as the ethnographic and genealogical material in the Pentateuch relevant for this study is concerned, it is usually ascribed by modern scholars to three different sources or rather layers of tradition: the Priestly code, P, the Yahwist, J, and the Elohist, E.[2] Which one of these is the oldest is in fact not so important for our purpose, since they all accumulate material from several different periods. Even if those scholars are right who see J and E as older, written down already before the destruction of Jerusalem in 587 BC, and P as later, codified together with the rest of the Pentateuch in the fifth century BC, this has no decisive bearing on the ethnographic outlook of the sources. There are, in fact, signs that in the genealogies of P there is a layer which may go back much earlier than anything found in the two others. The basic difference between them is their organization of the material and their general outlook.

The hypothesis of three continuous layers of tradition in the first four books of the Pentateuch, each giving its own coherent view of Israel's origins, originally independent of each other but later worked together by different redactors, came under growing criticism during the twentieth century, without, however, there being a total revision of traditional views. In particular, the existence of continuous J and E sources has been called into doubt. On the other hand, it is difficult to deny the existence of a basic scheme in the Pentateuch ascribed to the traditional P source. Whether J and E have existed as continuous stories, or whether the passages attributed to them are instead separate anecdotes and genealogical and aetiological notices without any connections, is not crucial to our investigation. As far as the ethnographic and geographical outlook is concerned, the structure identified as the P source is the core around which the other material is grouped.[3]

P, and also the J source according to the traditional analysis, are world histories, beginning with the creation of the world and ending with the establishment of Israel. Common to both is also that they see world history in genealogical terms: peoples are descended from related patriarchs, whose families have branched out in different directions. This implies that the peoples of the world can be grouped together according to family relationships, just like normal families. Some peoples are more closely related than others. To us it is obvious that the resulting different clusters of peoples are constituted not from common descent but from political alliances, trade relations, wars etc. For example, the two peoples in Transjordan, Moab and Ammon, were closely connected because of geographical proximity, common enemies (Israel) and possibly common culture (language, cults etc.). To the Biblical authors this was the result of their having a common ancestor, the patriarch Lot. The closeness of these two peoples that had arisen from neighbourhood during a long time is explained by a common heritage. Yet we have no indications from these two peoples themselves that they in fact had ideas of a common father, and the whole idea of their common ancestry is certainly an invention by the Biblical writers. The Biblical genealogies should thus be seen not as based on actual historical knowledge about the history of the peoples involved, but as a means of describing international relations between political entities. The genealogical relationships are thus dependent on and derived from actual political and ethnic conditions and not vice versa. This is clear from the fact that a people can have different ancestors in different texts, as we have already seen in the case of Sheba. Such ancestral variation often reflects political conditions at different periods and is a valuable clue to historical developments.

The method of describing political alliances etc. in terms of family relationships is not specific to Israel. We have already studied how it worked during the first centuries of Islam, and it is found in many societies. But the system found in the Pentateuch is unique in its scope: all the peoples of the earth ultimately belong to one family. There are no barbarians. Together with this goes the fact that Israel is seen as not belonging to the family from the beginning, since it did not exist from the beginning. Both P and J depict a world which, in different ways, is complete and finished without the existence of their own people. Israel is the last people in the world to emerge, the little brother of all the others. This folk-tale motif was turned by the thinkers behind the Pentateuch into a deep and far-reaching symbol and explanation of the faith and destiny of their own people.

The P tables

We will start with the genealogical system of P, since this is the most complete one. P's world history begins with two successive lines of descent.[4] The first enumerates ten names, starting with Adam and ending with the story of Noah and the Flood and the succeeding emergence of the peoples of the earth.[5] This is followed by the second line, with another ten names from Shem, ending with the emergence of the sacred family, i.e. Abraham and his descendants.[6] The connection between the two successive lines of descent is the Table of Nations in Genesis Chapter 10 which, in its present shape, is intermingled with notices usually ascribed to J. The latter seems to function as a kind of complementary commentary to that of P.[7] According to P's system, all peoples, except Israel and her closest neighbours, already existed when Abraham left Harran.

The P Table of Nations comprises Genesis 10:1a, 2–7, 20, 22–23, 31–32.[8] It is divided into three parts according to the three sons of Noah: Japheth, Ham and Shem. The description of each is introduced by the formula: 'The sons of X'.[9] The latter two are concluded by the formula: 'These are the sons of X after their families, after their tongues, in their countries, in their nations.'[10] There are good reasons to suppose that even the passage of Japheth originally had the same conclusion.[11] The insertions by J stand just before these concluding formulas.[12] Also in the P lists, additions to the original names are clearly visible.[13]

A basic observation is that the peoples belonging to the sons of Shem and Ham respectively are listed with the most distant ones first and the ones closest to Israel last. Thus the Hamites consist of Kush, Miṣrayim, Put and Kanaan. All are easily identifiable: Nubia, Egypt proper (the lower Nile valley), Libya and Palestine.[14] The Hamites seem to represent the Egyptian empire with its borders during the Ramessides at the latest, when Egypt controlled an area from Nubia to Palestine, i.e. down to the middle of the twelfth century BC.

The list of the Semites follows the same principle. The 'sons' of Shem are Elam, Asshur, Arpachsad, Lud and Aram. Elam and Asshur are well-known powers in Mesopotamia. Arpachsad must be situated between Asshur and Lud/Aram. Since the descendants of Arpachsad in the following P list of patriarchs down to Abraham definitely belong to northern Syria and northern Mesopotamia, Arpachsad is most likely a designation for that area. The name might be identical with the city Arrapha mentioned in connection with the fall of Nineveh in 612 BC and Arrapakhitis, mentioned much later by Ptolemy as a region south of Armenia.[15] Among the descendants of Arpachsad we find Serug and Haran, which are place-names in the northern Ǧazīra.[16] In that case, Lud and Aram should be looked for in the neighbourhood of Palestine. Lud would not be the Lydians in Asia Minor but some entity in Syria. In J's list, *lûdîm* are clearly part of the so-called Sea Peoples, which supports their location somewhere on the Syrian coast. It might be noted that the name R(W)ČN, which in Egyptian is the term for Palestine and Syria, also stands for the town of Lod (Lydda), for example, in the lists of Thutmosis III.[17] It is thus most likely that the Egyptian word is equivalent to Lud and *lûdîm* and originally was a term for the lowlands of Palestine and the Levantine coast.

In that case, Aram should also be sought near Palestine/Kanaan. Yet this is in conflict with the evidence that Aram is northern Syria and Mesopotamia between the Euphrates and the Khābūr. It has, however, long since been observed that certain passages in the Old Testament where Aram is mentioned do not seem to refer to northern Syria but to a region south-east of Palestine.[18] It has also been suggested that Aram in these passages should instead be read Edom; the difference in spelling between the two is very slight in the Hebrew text. But it should be noted that there is documentation of an old name ʔRM in the same area from inscriptions found at Rām in present-day southern Jordan, which should be the same name.[19] This is probably also the area where ʔIram ḏātu l-ʕimād, 'Iram with the pillars', mentioned on several occasions in the Qurʔān, should be sought.[20] This indicates that the 'false Aram' passages are not false at all, but instead preserve an ancient name of the areas south-east of Palestine including Edom, which has been confused with the Mesopotamian Aram.[21] That an Aram, different from the one in upper Mesopotamia, should be looked for in these regions, is supported by the addition to the P list of the 'sons of Aram', among whom we find ʕUṣ and Ḥul.[22] The former definitely belongs to the Midianite area, whereas the latter must somehow be related to Ḥawilah, the eastern border of the Ishmaelites, identifiable with present-day Nafūd.[23]

The list of the Semites thus establishes five entities from the east to the west. Geographically it could represent the Assyrian empire after 640 BC when Elam was conquered. In that case, Lud cannot be identified with the Lydians, who were never subject to Assyrian dominance. But the absence of Babylon remains an enigma, since it existed as a recognized entity during the Assyrian period. As we have seen, Arpachsad cannot be Babylon. There is also no reflection of the Assyrian conquests in Anatolia and Iran.

In the twelfth century BC, however, Babylon was under Elamite rule.[24] At the same time Assyria was independent, as were the Neo-Hittite city-states in northern Syria. The three entities from the south-east to the north-west, as they are described in Genesis, existed in that period. As we have seen, the constellation of the Hamites also seems to fit into the same period.

The Japhethites may also be brought into the picture. They are Gomer, Magog, Maday, Yawan, Tubal, Meshek and Tiras. The absence of any reference to the Hittite empire shows that it was gone already when the scheme was conceived, which thus must have taken place after 1200 BC. The first name in the list is Gomer, equivalent to Akkadian Gimirrai, documented from the time of Sargon II and known as the Cimmerians in Greek sources.[25] The name is usually connected with Crimea.[26] The last name is to be connected with Tw-rw-šʔ mentioned as one of the Sea Peoples in Merenphtah's time, i.e. at the end of the thirteenth century BC.[27] Of the others, Tubal and Meshek are found in Assyrian sources from the time of Tiglath Pileser I (1117–1077) and have been located in Cilicia and Phrygia respectively.[28] Yawan is, of course, the Ionian Greeks and Maday must be the Medes, whereas Magog is unknown.[29] These latter names are not documented in extrabiblical sources before the 9th century BC. According to the overall scheme, we thus find the Cimmerians far in the north and Tiras somewhere in the Levant. Between them there is a panorama of peoples in Anatolia from the western coast eastwards into Iran. We observe the total absence of reference to the Philistines, which is one of several indications which also set this scenario in the period around 1200 BC or shortly after.

To the original list of peoples there are later additions. Thus, the Semitic Aram is given four sons who, as we have seen, are located east and south-east of Palestine.[30] In the same manner, among the Hamites, Kush is given five sons: Sebā, Ḥawilah, Sabtah, Raʕmah and Sabtekah. Among these, Raʕmah has two sons, Shebā and Dedan, who may be a still later addition.[31] We have an indication about the time of the additions to Kush. It has been shown that the names Sabtah and Sabtekah are probably identical with the two pharaohs of the twenty-fifth 'Ethiopian', i.e. Nubian, dynasty, namely Shabaka (*c.* 712–700) and Shebitku (*c.* 700–695).[32] It may also be noticed that the additions to the sons of Japheth include Ashkenaz, son of Gomer, probably the Scythians, who appear in texts from *c.* 700 BC, Elishah which is probably Alasia in Cyprus, and Kittim, sons of Yawan, all of which betrays increased familiarity with the Greeks. We may assume that the additions are from around 700 BC. or shortly after that.[33] We can thus conclude that the Table of Nations of the Priestly Code seems to contain two basic layers, reflecting political conditions around 1200 and 700 BC. respectively.

The world history of the Priestly Code has a complicated story behind it. It has been claimed that the formula 'these are the generations (*tôledôt*) of . . .' followed by genealogical enumerations, which runs as a refrain through Genesis and sporadically also occurs in Exodus and Numbers, comes from one source, the so-called 'Toledot book', which divided world history into different generations, starting with the descendants of Adam (Genesis 4:1) and ending with the family of Aaron (Numbers 3:1–3). This source thus saw world history as culminating in the establishment of the Israelite cult led by a priesthood claiming Aaronite descent.[34] In the Pentateuch as we have it, this cult, as well as most sacral and civil institutions in Israel, is initiated by Moses, and Aaron appears as a secondary figure. Together with this goes the almost complete absence of references to Aaron in the Deuteronomistic history, as well as the negative judgement of him in Deuteronomy itself.[35] Even more surprising is the complete lack of references to Aaron in the priestly prophet Hezechiel. Also in the Priestly Code, which sees Aaron in quite positive terms, he is chastised for attempts to challenge the authority of Moses.[36] The Aaronite priesthood may originally have been one of several priestly clans in pre-exilic Israel and Judah. During the restoration of the community at the end of the sixth century BC, several different priestly groups seem to have claimed Aaronite descent.[37] This movement of priests was, however, opposed by more lay-minded groups, represented by the Deuteronomistic tradition, where Moses was the unchallenged authority. The Priestly Code as we have it is the result of a compromise between these movements where Moses has been made the protagonist and initiator of all institutions of Israel. The priestly clans claiming Aaronite descent kept their position as the only legitimate priesthood in the new temple, but their forefather was reduced to an obedient servant of Moses and performer of his divine commandments.[38] This would mean that the Toledot book was conceived and composed as a legitimation of these priestly groups during their heyday, which must have been at the beginning of the Second Temple period, i.e. the end of the sixth century BC.[39] The final redaction of P with the Mosaic revision would then belong to the following period, i.e. the fifth century BC.

The material in the Toledot book was not taken out of the air. The concept of the ten antediluvian fathers, the Flood story and the threefold division of the world after the Flood, as well as the ten postdiluvian patriarchs, are much older than the end of the sixth century BC. A close parallell is found in the *Babyloniaca* by the Hellenistic writer Berossus, who also knows about ten antediluvian patriarchs followed by the Flood, and who is certainly independent of the Pentateuchal tradition.[40] As has been shown, the basis of the Table of Nations may go back to the twelfth century BC, reflecting the new political order in the Middle East after the fall of the Hittite and Kassite empires. Among the names in the double series of patriarchs before and after the Flood, we find south Syrian/Palestinian heroes like Shet, Ḥanok, Qenan and Lemek, but there are also names belonging to northern Syria. Noah is probably a north Syrian name as are Metushelaḥ, Shelaḥ, Serug and Haran, and it is likely that the story of Noah and the ark, as well as the idea of the ten antediluvian rulers, originally came from northern Syria.[41]

There is also a layer in the Table of Nations reflecting political conditions not earlier than 700 BC. This pertains not only to the addition of new names but also to the obvious Palestinian world-view of the Table: the peoples of the world are arranged, starting with those farthest away and ending with those closest to the Promised Land. The insertion of local patriarchs in the lists also indicates an Israelite–Judaean revision and adaptation of the older north Syrian scheme. It can be assumed that this revised version originally ended with the three sons of Teraḥ, analogous to those of Noah, one of whom is the Judaean patriarch Abra(ha)m. This revision could then represent ideologies in Judah around 700 BC, i.e. the time of king Ezekiah. We have, in fact, documentation in the Old Testament of substantial cultural and religious imports from Syria under Ezekiah's predecessor Ahaz.[42] The elaboration of the idea that Israel originally came from the northern Ǧazīra may have started in this period.

This Judaean reworking of north Syrian myths, which might have been the first attempt to write a comprehensive Israelite world history and geography, thus an Israelite counterpart to Wahb b. Munabbih 1,400 years later, was used by the priestly writers of the Toledot book two centuries after Ezekiah. The *tôledôt* formula was probably introduced by them, and they also added new peoples to the scheme finishing with their forebear, Aaron. Remarkable is the absence of a *tôledôt* formula with Abraham. Perhaps this is an intentional down-play of the Judaean patriarch who, after all, was originally the hero of the Judaeans headed by the zadokite priests in Jerusalem, the rivals of the Aaronids. Instead we hear about the *tôledôt* of Isaac, Ishmael, Esau and Jaacob. Abraham was installed as the great patriarch of Israel in one of the final revisions of this work, which is the text we have.

Starting from these insights, we can now proceed to P's picture of Arabia, which originates around 700 BC. We first notice, of course, that P does not mention Arabs or Arabians as a people either in the Table of Nations or anywhere else. This may be due to the conservative outlook of the lists, resulting in an unwillingness to incorporate new peoples who had entered the stage. Against this speak the just-mentioned additions, which reveal an ambition to update the list. The *ʕarab* cannot have been unknown to those who added the names around 700 BC. The more likely explanation is instead that the *ʕarab* were indeed not a people on the same level as the others.

According to the later addition to the Table of Nations, which we dated to *c.* 700 BC, Sheba and Dedan belong to the Cushite branch of the Hamitic family. Both are found in western Arabia in the seventh century BC.[43] Raʕmah has been identified with the Rhammanîtai, mentioned much later by Strabo as a tribe around Marsiaba in Yemen, which, however, is doubtful.[44] There is no doubt that Sheba, Dedan and Raʕmah belong together, since they are also mentioned outside the P work in Hezechiel.[45] Since Dedan is present-day al-ʕŪlā in the northern Ḥiǧāz and Sheba is likely to be located immediately south of it, it looks as if by the sons of Raʕmah is meant western Arabia in general.[46] This is supported by the identification of another of the sons of Kush's sons, namely Ḥawilah, Raʕmah's brother, by which is meant the Great Nafūd.[47] As we have already seen, two of the Cushites are pharaohs from the upper Nile valley. Sebā is mentioned in Psalm 72, probably composed around 700 BC, representing the end of the world together with Sheba.[48] According to a note in Strabo, Sabaí is a colony in Eritrea and in Josephus Saba is identified with Meroe, the capital of Nubia.[49] The conclusion is that, according to P, Kush encompasses the land on both sides of the Red Sea and that western Arabia consequently belongs to it.

In P's geography both Palestine and the known parts of the Arabian peninsula belong to the land of Ham, i.e. the southern third of the world. The land of Kush encompasses the land on both sides of the Red Sea. On the western side are explicitly mentioned Sabtah, Sabtecha and Sebā, which stand for traditional Nubia and the Red Sea coast. On the eastern side we have two main parts, Ḥawilah and Raʕmah. If Ḥawilah is the Great Nafūd desert, the eastern, 'Arabian' part of Kush is thus divided in an eastern and a western part: Ḥawilah and Raʕmah respectively. The latter is, in its turn, divided in two parts: one northern, Dedan, and one southern Sheba. How far south this Sheba stretched is not known from the P text. As we shall see, there are further additions to the names from another source, which was far better informed about South Arabia than the P-authors. It looks as if the horizon of the P scheme did not extend very far southwards.[50]

The allocation of both sides of the Red Sea to Ham, i.e. Egypt, is probably older than the seventh century BC. There are no indications of Egyptian dominance in the region during that period. In earlier times, however, we know that Egypt was heavily involved in the business of north-western Ḥiğāz.[51] As we have seen, there was also a Kush in northern Ḥiğāz which made it easy to subsume all under Ham.[52] Once again we find ourselves in the thirteenth to twelfth centuries BC.

According to the Table of Nations, the Levantine coast with its hinterland is divided between the Hamitic Kanaan and the Semitic Lud, with the likewise Semitic Aram between Lud and the Ğazīra. The southern part of Syria along Kanaan and the adjacent Syrian desert down to the border of the Hamitic Cushites does not have any inhabitants. The P writers fill out this area by introducing two more *tôledôt*, namely that of Ishmael and that of Esau. This is, however, done after the Table of Nations has been drawn up. Both are attached to Teraḥ's family. Ishmael is a direct offspring from Abraham and is the first of his descendants who gives birth to twelve tribes. The Edomites have to wait until Abraham's son Isaac begets two sons, one of which becomes the father of the twelve tribes of Edom. Last of all, Isaac's son Jacob brings forth the twelve tribes of Israel. The Ishmaelites and the Edomites are both descendants of the eldest son whereas Israel is from the youngest, in accordance with the folk-tale motif used as a framework for this story. According to this very symmetrical scheme, Noah, the last name in the list of the ten antediluvian patriarchs, has three sons, from whom all the peoples of the world are descended. Teraḥ, the ninth name in the list of the postdiluvial patriarchs, also has three sons, from whom three peoples are descended. From one of the sons likewise three peoples emerge, each consisting of twelve subdivisions: Ishmael, Edom and Israel.

A closer analysis of how the P writers imagined the border between Hamites and Semites may take its base in the description of the borders of the Promised Land in Numbers 34, a text which indicates borders that correspond to the Egyptian domination of Palestine before 1200 BC, which also seem to be the borders assumed in the Table of Nations.[53] Present-day Lebanon and southern Syria are included in the Promised Land, but not Transjordan. From the southern end of the Dead Sea the border goes southwestwards past 'the desert Ṣin' to Qadesh Barneaʕ, and from there towards the north-west, out to the Mediterranean along 'the Brook of Miṣrayim', i.e. present-day Wādī al-ʕArīsh.[54] The eastern border of Egypt (Miṣrayim) is said in the Old Testament to be close to the desert Shur, which is close to Qadesh.[55] Shur is also east of Miṣrayim.[56] ʕAmāleq is said to have dwelt 'from Ḥawilah to Shur' together with Qayin.[57] The latter had their habitat in the eastern Negev around ʕArad.[58] When Saul defeated ʕAmāleq, he put up a stela at Karmel somewhere in the north-eastern Negev, which indicates that the Amalekites were thought to have lived not far from there.[59] The desert Shur is thus probably an area between the ʕArabah and Qadesh Barneaʕ and perhaps stretching southwards towards Qunṭillat ʔAğrud. Since the border of Egypt (Miṣrayim) reached the gulf of ʕAqabah, we get a large triangular area with the ʕArabah south of the Dead Sea as its base and Qadesh Barneaʕ as its apex, which, according to P's system, belonged to the Semites.[60] Since the Hamitic part of Arabia is named Kush by P, it is most likely that the land of Midian was considered Hamitic territory, since, as we have seen, Kush is associated with Midian. In that case, the border between Hamites and Semites would run south-westwards from the Dead Sea to Qadesh, then turn towards the south-east to Elath, then continue south-eastwards into Arabia, passing just south of Taymāʔ to reach the mystical land of Ḥawilah.[61]

The lists of J

The traditional J source is the great story-teller in the Pentateuchal tradition and is not very much concerned about systematic genealogy or geography. J has no continuous or consistent scheme for the political structure of the surrounding world. His main interest in other peoples is as an illustration of his main thesis: the world has been filled with violence (*ḥamas*), in spite of the undeserved grace that God has shown from the beginning. From scattered notices about tribes and names in J one can, however, glean a picture of the main outlines of J's ethnographic world. Unlike the system we find in P, J is much more difficult to fit into actual geographical conditions, which shows that J takes his facts from the popular views, not from the learned circles. J's basic geography is perhaps found in the fragment in Genesis 2:11–12. From the Garden of Eden four mythical rivers spread and give water to the earth. The two central ones are the Euphrates and the Tigris, which are obviously thought to flow 'in the middle of the earth'. The two others are Pishon and Giḥon, which together constitute the waters that surround the *oikoumēnē*. Pishon surrounds or goes around the whole land of Ḥawilah 'where the gold is', while Giḥon surrounds the whole of Kush. By Ḥawilah and Kush are probably meant the farthest ends of the *oikoumēnē*, and it is futile to try to adjust this landscape to the factual geography of the Middle East.[62] It is a mythical landscape, which may very well once have had a concrete physical representation in some sanctuary, perhaps Jerusalem, showing the world as the believers knew it to be, not as what it actually looked like. Kush and Ḥawilah are obviously markers of the borders of the inhabited world. We may then observe that the two names for the extreme corners of the world are geographical names that can be localized. If Ḥawilah is the Great Nafūd, Kush must be the tribes in northern Ḥiğāz rather than Nubia. This North Arabian Kush is, as we have seen, quite well documented. Ḥawilah is then in the south-east and Kush in the south-west. The geographical horizon of J is then similar to that of P, as far as the south is concerned, and may well be older than 700 BC.[63]

The other passages with geographical information are the J insertions in the Table of Nations in Genesis 10. The insertion in the Hamitic list need not concern us here.[64] The insertion in the Semitic list concerns Arpachsad, where J offers a genealogical tree similar to that of P down to Eber.[65] According to P, Eber had one son, Peleg, whereas J adds a second son: Yoqṭān. This is a midrashic element: the name Peleg is interpreted as 'division' (from the root PLG), and a second son is introduced in order to illustrate how the line of inheritance of the earth, hitherto strictly limited to one patriarch, is now divided in two, giving rise to conflict and strife among the descendants of Noah. The name of the second son, Yoqṭān, is derived from the root meaning 'small', probably meaning that he is Peleg's younger brother. It is, however, strikingly similar to the second son of Qeṭurah: Yoqshān. Since Sheba appears as son of both Yoqshān and Yoqṭān, one may suppose that the names are variants of the same. In that case everything speaks for the originality of Yoqshān, since its etymology is far less transparent than the other's.[66] Yoqṭān is then a calque on Yoqshān, intentionally derived from a root designating him as the little brother. This derivation of Yoqṭān from Yoqshān may also explain the vocalism in the former, which is not the one expected for a verb meaning 'he is small'.[67]

This implies that Yoqshān is the older and that the Qeṭurah list is older than the list of the Yoqtanids. The list contains thirteen names: Almodad, Sheleph, Ḥaṣarmawet, Yeraḥ, Hadoram, Uzal, Diqlah, ʕObal, Abimaʔel, Sheba, Ophir, Ḥawilah and Yobab. Only four or perhaps five are identifiable. Sheleph may be identical with SLFN found in a late South Arabian inscription, designating an entity between Ḥaḍramawt and Qatabān.[68] There is no doubt that Haṣarmawet is Ḥaḍramawt. Uzal has since early Islamic times been identified with Ṣanʕāʔ, which, however, is probably secondary.[69] A name ʕObal is found in Sabaean inscriptions, 'the sons of ʕBLM', and ʕAbālim is mentioned by al-Hamdānī between Sanʕāʔ and ʕAsīr.[70] The order of the last four names, Sheba, Ophir, Ḥawilah and Yobab, together with the earlier mention of Haḍramawt suggests that this list also represents a geographical order, beginning with the farthest lands and ending with the land closest to Palestine. This is supported by the fact that Yobab is mentioned as one of the semi-mythical kings of Edom.[71]

The most important information found in the Yoqtanid list is the South Arabian connection. This passage, together with the Ophir story in the first book of Kings/second book of Chronicles, is the only certain documentation of Yemen in the Old Testament.[72] Unfortunately, the details in the list escape our understanding. Many names are unidentifiable.[73] There is, however, no doubt that this list reflects overland connections with South Arabia. Since the overland trading between Yemen and Syria starts quite suddenly in the seventh century, the list can hardly be older than that. It may be noticed that Sheba appears as one region among several others, which may point to a period later than the fifth century BC. when the first Sabaean empire was dissolved.[74] This is also supported by the absence of Dedan. We know that at the beginning of the sixth century Dedan was conquered by Edom and ceased to exist.[75] In the list we find Yobab, the king of Edom, where we would have expected Dedan (and the northern Sheba).[76]

Ishmael and his descendants

Of the three peoples emerging from Abraham's family according to the P scheme, the descendants of Ishmael and Esau are given the south-western corner of the Semitic lot, whereas Israel does not have any land. Instead he is given a lot outside the area of Shem, namely the Hamitic Kanaan. P attributes the area 'from Ḥawilah to Shur to Asshur' to the twelve sons of Ishmael.[77] This would constitute the south-westernmost part of the lot of the Semites, bordering on the lot of the Hamites. In other Biblical texts this area belongs to the mythical ʕAmāleq.[78] The location of several tribes known from *c.* 700 BC onwards in the area of ʕAmāleq may reflect increased knowledge in Judaea about conditions in the Syrian desert and northern Arabia towards the end of the monarchy. Myth has given way to history. The names of the sons of Ishmael fit well into the area. Yeṭur and Naphis can be located in northern Transjordan, Tema' and possibly Ḥadad close to the Great Nafūd in the far south, Dumah in the east, and Mibsam and Mishmaʕ in the Negev.[79] Qedar is definitely located in the Negev in the Achaemenid period. The descendants of Esau are then, according to the P scheme, squeezed in between the area of the Ishmaelites and the Hamitic Promised Land with the Ishmaelites in the south, east and north. According to both the P and the J sources, Ishmael lived *ʕal pnê ʔeḥaw*, 'close to his brothers'.[80]

It has been claimed that there actually existed a tribal federation consisting of twelve 'Arab' Ishmaelite tribes in the Syrian desert, which is reflected in P's list of Ishmael's twelve sons.[81] We have, however, no extra-Biblical indication of such a federation and, in fact, no intra-Biblical evidence either. Among the names of Ishmael's sons we find Dumah and Tema, which are not tribes but cities. *Qédmā* is no name at all but a noun with an adverbial suffix meaning 'eastwards'.[82] It is evident that to P the scheme of twelve tribes is crucial, and that he applies it without bothering too much about realities. Thus even Esau is given twelve male descendants.[83] We know, however, that the tribal structure of Israel itself was much more complicated than P's scheme of twelve tribes. There were many more than twelve tribes in Israel. The description of Israel as a tribal federation is also doubtful. In the same way, the enumeration of Ishmaelite tribes should not *prima facie* be taken as an indication of the existence of a tribal federation. The Ishmaelite family is most probably a construction by the P writers, to whom scheme was more important than reality. They used names of tribes and places in the Syrian desert to create a twelve-tribe system, similar to the Israelite one.

Among these tribes we find Nebayot, Qedar and Massa', as well as the towns Tema and Dumah, which are mentioned in the Assyrian texts from Tiglath Pileser III onwards. Naphis is documented together with Massa' in the time of Assurbanipal.[84] Yeṭur appears in such a late text as Chronicles.[85] The list of Ishmael's sons reflects conditions after the fall of Assyria and down into the Chaldaean and early Achaemenid periods. A closer look reveals that it may have had a complicated history. The names, in fact, fall into separate groups, according to the use of the connective particle *w-* 'and':

1. Nebayot + Qedar + ʔAdbeʔel + Mibsam + Mišmaʕ + Dumah + Massa'
2. Ḥadad + Temā'
3. Yeṭur + Naphis + Qédmā.[86]

The first group contains seven names, which of course is no coincidence. In it we find the names known from the Assyrian texts in the eighth and seventh centuries BC, and they might well originate from a list of tribes involved in the Assyrian wars against groups in the Syrian desert in the seventh century. Temā's geographical location may have separated it from being included in group 1. Finally, group 3 is definitely located in Transjordan, according to a note in the Chronicler.[87] One might wonder why the term 'eastwards' is used instead of a tribal name. An explanation may be that it is the number three which has hindered the original compilators from enumerating more tribal names. Qedmā may be a transformation of the expression *bnê qédem*, 'the easterners', the traditional designation for those living east of Bashan and Gilead.

Ouside the P source, the Old Testament gives some hints about a more exact localization of Ishmael. In a psalm, *yišmeʕelîm* and *hagrîm* are mentioned together with Transjordanian peoples.[88] In the Joseph story, *yišmeʕelîm* carry perfumes to Egypt from Gilead, i.e. Transjordan.[89] The Chronicler provides us with a detailed description of the settlement of the *hagrîm*. They live in huts all along the eastern Gilead. The tribe of Gad lives opposite them in Bashan, i.e. present-day Ǧabal ad-Durūz. The tribe of Reuben waged war against the *hagrîm*, Yeṭur, Naphis and Nodab in the time of Saul.[90] These verses could well come from the same source as the *ʕarab* passages in Chronicles discussed above. One could also refer to the verse in the book of Judith, where Holophernes plunders the Rass and the Ishmaelites 'living on the edge of the desert in the southern Kheleōn', which seems to indicate the Syrian border against the desert.[91] This evidence shows that Hagar, Ishmael, Yeṭur and Naphis, from the last century of the Judaean monarchy onwards, were groups on the fringe between the desert and the sown from Ǧabal ad-Durūz southwards, perhaps down to the upper Yabboq, present-day Wādī Zarqāʔ.

This localization of Ishmael leads us to the assumption that the list of Ishmael's descendants originally consisted of only the names of the tribes in northern Transjordan, namely Yeṭur, Naphis and Qédmā. These may thus have been the original Ishmaelites. The number three also occurs in P's enumeration of the family of Esau/Edom. Of Esau's three wives, Oholibamah had three sons: Yeʕush, Yaʕlam and Qoraḥ.[92] It is therefore possible to discern an older layer in the traditions about Ishmael as well as Esau/Edom/Seʕir, where they were given only three sons. They would then have fitted well into the scheme represented by the three sons of Noah and Teraḥ respectively. As far as the three Ishmaelite sons are concerned, they lived, together with their 'father' and 'mother', in Transjordan.[93]

The result of this analysis is that Ishmael and Esau originally referred to rather small groups in northern Transjordan and eastern Negev respectively, which for certain reasons were considered close relatives to Israel. Later, the Ishmaelites were enlarged and came to be a cover term for all tribes outside the sown, east and south of Palestine, a typical feature of P's ethnology. A reflection of this enlargement is found in a late note in the story of Gideon that even the Midianites were Ishmaelites.[94] In a similar fashion, Esau became the father of the Edomites, as well as of several groups in the Negev.[95]

The story about Ishmael

In spite of the Ishmaelites being a group living on the periphery of the sown in northern Transjordan, they are, by the Old Testament writers, given a unique position in relation to the people of Israel, a relationship they share to a certain extent with the Edomites, the descendants of Esau. We shall start by looking at the P writers, who have incorporated a story of the origins of the Ishmaelites as a prelude to the Table of Ishmael's sons:

> Saray, the wife of Abram, has given Hagar, her Egyptian maid, *šipḥā*, as wife to Abram and she has given birth to Yishmaʕʔel, Ishmael. Later, God reveals himself to Abram as El Shadday, changes his name to Abraham and that of his wife to Sarah, promises another son and the possession of the land of Kanaan

> and gives the commandment of circumcision. The new son, Yiṣḥaq, Isaac, will carry the covenant with God, but also Ishmael will have a divine blessing and twelve sons, who will be great chiefs. Then Ishmael and Abraham are circumcised.[96]

Of the three pentateuchal sources, P shows the most positive attitude towards Israel's two south-eastern neighbours. In particular, Ishmael has a very prominent position, being the only one who, together with the people of Israel, is explicitly said to share the outward sign of the covenant with God. At the same time, the point of the story is to tell how Ishmael, in spite of being entitled to the inheritance of Abraham, had to cede from the first place, although with preserved privileges and a rank above everybody else, except the descendants of Isaac.

The story of the early career of Abraham's and Hagar's son and the reduction of his rank is also a basic theme in the two other narratives in Genesis, that in Chapter 21 attributed to E, and that in Chapter 16 traditionally attributed to the J source. According to the E version, Sarah admonishes Abraham to expel (GRŠ), the child of Hagar, the Egyptian (*miṣrît*) *ʔamā*, slave-girl. He is not to have any inheritance together with Isaac. God speaks to Abraham and orders him to do as Sarah wants, since Isaac is the one who will carry Abraham's name. But the boy of the *ʔamā* will also become a great people (*goy*). Hagar and the child come to the desert of Beer Sheba. They are short of water, but the divine messenger, the *malʔak* of God, hears (ŠMʕ) them and promises to make a great people of the boy. Then Hagar sees the well filled with water, and they drink. God is with the boy when he grows up and becomes a bowman (*robē qaššāt*) living in the Paran desert. His mother takes a wife for him from the land of Miṣrayim.[97]

This story is quite close to that of P, although the vocabulary is different. The descendants of Hagar's son are also in this story very close to those of Isaac: they too carry a promise. The story runs smoothly without any breaks or cracks. The Israelite flavour is shown in that the whole drama is staged by the divinity. Even in the most difficult situation, God leads the course of events. The psychological subtlety characteristic of many of the stories ascribed to E is also found here: Abraham can expel Hagar into the desert because God has told him that she somehow will be saved. The reader is prepared for the drama in the following chapter in Genesis: after the sacrifice of Ishmael follows the sacrifice of Isaac. The dramatic effect is increased by Hagar being kept ignorant of the divine plan. The story also has an aetiological point: it wants to give the background for some bowmen associated with the Paran desert – a desert which in several texts is connected with Qadesh in the southern Negev.[98]

According to the J version, Hagar flees out into the desert because Saray has chastised her for showing *hybris* over the fact that she has become pregnant by Abram while Saray remains infertile. On the road to Shur, at a well in the desert, Hagar meets the *malʔak* of YHWH. This figure gives her three sayings: (1) that she shall return to her mistress and humble herself under her; (2) YHWH shall make her seed numerous; (3) she is pregnant and shall bear a son and call him Ishmael, 'for YHWH has heard (*šamaʕ*) her suffering'. This son shall become like a wild ass (*pere' ʔadam*), his hand shall be against everyone, and the hand of everyone shall be against him. Then Hagar gives a name to YHWH: *ʔEl roʔî*. That is why the well is called Beʔer Laḥay roʔî. It is between Qadesh and Bered.[99]

This text is problematic and contains many obvious cracks, and seems to be an amalgamation of different points.[100] The negative tone is striking and much stronger than in the other two: Hagar has done wrong, she must return as a slave, her son will become a savage in the desert. There is a contradiction between saying (1) and (2): the second is an unequivocally positive announcement, echoing the prophecies in P and E, the first a purely negative one. The point seems to be that the future savagery of Hagar's son is a punishment for her disobedience. The introduction to (3) is also illogical: does not Hagar herself know that she is pregnant? The style is that of the traditional birth oracle where the divinity announces that a woman is pregnant, a device meaningful only if uttered before she has noticed it herself.[101] All three announcements are introduced by the words: 'and the *malʔak* of YHWH said'. This may be a sign that at least (2) and (3) do not originally belong to the story but are later additions. This impression is supported by the remarkable fact that, apart from (3), Ishmael's name is not mentioned. This also holds for the E story, where the absence of the name is striking since the child is already born. In both texts there seems to be an allusion to the name by the use of the verb 'hear', ŠMʕ, from which the name Ishmael is derived.

All three stories thus presuppose that (a) Abra(ha)m's first-born son belonged to the most prominent of his family, and (b) his status has been reduced for different reasons. A further complication is that in E and J and probably also in P, he is connected with the Negev, not with northern Transjordan. In P and E, Hagar, his mother, is said to have been *miṣrît*, which underlines the Negev connection.[102] The three accounts seem to contradict the other traditions about the Transjordanian Ishmael, in locating him in the Negev and making him a descendant of an 'Egyptian' mother.

The first step in the analysis of these contradictions is the observation that J and E do not mention Ishmael by name except in J's birth oracle, which may not belong to the original text. It can further be shown that both of them have used an existing story, or rather a motif, which is clearly discernible when we bring together the features which are common to both stories. Both tell about a woman who ends up in a desert with her son and encounters a divinity. Water is produced. In the E version a wedding is hinted at, which does not appear in J. Following the J story, however, P introduces the story about the circumcision of Ishmael, a ceremony which, in fact, is connected with nuptial rituals. Undoubtedly, the redactors have arranged the narratives in a sequence which was logical to them.

The E story is based on an old salvation story, telling how an ancient hero was threatened by dangers but saved by a divinity, a motif which lies behind many of the episodes told about the desert wanderings of the Israelites. The hero is connected with some kind of bowmen in the Paran desert, probably south-east of the Negev. This latter element, together with the foreign wife of Hagar's son, has a clear parallel in the story of Esau, another hero from the south, who has a status similar to that of Ishmael in the Biblical scheme. There is yet another parallel to an element in the story, namely the encounter with the unknown divinity. This is told about Moses' son Gershom and his mother Ṣipporah.[103] In that passage, as in the story about Hagar and Ishmael at the well, the father of the boy is strangely absent. In the Gershom story, the boy is saved by being circumcised and a wedding rite is hinted at. There is a clear allusion to an archaic myth connected with circumcision and wedding. After the wedding most naturally follows the foundation of a dynasty or the generation of a people, a motif that we have in the E version, which, on the whole, is the one closest to the Gershom story. The story about the circumcision of Ishmael, as told by P, is clearly an echo of this motif. Since circumcision originally is connected with wedding rituals, the connection between all these motifs becomes clear. One might well ask if the bowman in E originally is not a bow-hunting tribe but instead a mythical figure, like the Arabian god Quzaḥ with his bow, or the Edomite god Qos, meaning 'bow', a figure which also lurks behind the hunting Esau.[104]

We may thus venture the following conclusions: in southern Palestine, stories were told about the origin of the people living in the desert outside the sown lands. They are related to the settled peoples, but have a lower status. It is described how their forefather goes out into the wilderness, encounters an unknown divinity, marries a foreign woman and establishes a community of desert-dwellers living by hunting. One such story, which is preserved in quite an original shape in the E version, has been associated with Ishmael by the Biblical writers.

The question still remains why the Transjordanian Ishmael was associated with this story, which must have belonged to the lore of southern Judaea. The main point is probably the brotherhood between Ishmael and Isaac. There are some hints in the Old Testament that the shadowy figure of Isaac was once more prominent than he appears in the Biblical text as we have it. Isaac in the Biblical tradition is intimately connected with Beer Sheba.[105] When the prophet Amos stood forth in the sanctuary at Bethel about a decade before 722 BC, he referred to a vision of Israel's God who told him: 'Isaac's high places shall be deserted // Israel's sanctuaries shall be destroyed' and he is said to have preached 'against Israel // and against the house of Isaac'.[106] In the sacral history of the Pentateuch, Israel, i.e. the northern kingdom, is the son of Isaac and thus subordinated to him. The mention of Isaac in the sanctuary of Bethel is perhaps not a poetic phrase but refers to some real association between this temple and the patriarch of Beer Sheba.

If Isaac was venerated in Bethel, he must somehow have had a prominent position also in the sanctuary at Dan in the north, because the connection between them is well documented. In several instances in the Old Testament we encounter the formula 'from Dan to Beer Sheba', which also occurs in Amos.[107] The connection between the two sanctuaries is also evident from the story of King Jerobeam's establishment of the cults at both places.[108]

The linking between Israel, Ishmael and Esau, together with the attribution of three sons to each of the latter two, is found in the Pentateuchal text in connection with the *tôledôt* formula. This makes it most likely that this view of the relationship between Israel, Esau/Edom and Ishmael belonged to the original Toledot book. In that case the scheme could represent the views of the circles around the Aaronite priesthood. These priests claimed their origins in the south: one tradition locates Aaron's tomb somewhere west or east of the ʕArabah, i.e. in the land inhabited by the descendants of Esau.[109] Of Esau's three sons, the name of the last one, Qoraḥ, looks suspiciously like that of one of the sons of Aaron, i.e. one of the ancient priest-clans among the Levites.[110] That name is associated with Qadesh and the Negev, which shows that this Esau belonged to the Seʕir, i.e. the eastern Negev. The Chronicler mentions a group Nodab in connection with Hagar, Yeṭur and Naphis in Transjordan.[111] One of Aaron's sons was named Nadab, who also was a son of king Jerobeam who, like Aaron, established a cult of golden calves.[112] We would venture the claim that in all these cases we have to do with the same entity, namely a priestly clan claiming Aaronite genealogy connected with the cult at Dan.[113] Just as Qoraḥ was marginalized in the south, Nodab/Nadab declined in the north and was later found together with other future members of the Ishmaelite family in Transjordan.

The connection between the two sanctuaries is also described in the story of the migration of the tribe of Dan from the border between Israel and Judah to Dan.[114] Dan is unique among the Israelite tribes in that it consists of only one clan, the Ḥushîm.[115] These Ḥushîm are in the lists of the Chronicler located in Benjamin, i.e. in the area where Bethel is situated.[116] In an old verse, Dan is said to be 'like a lion rushing down from Bashan'.[117] It is also worth noticing that Dan is the brother of Naphtali, thus originally located in the north, at the foot of Mount Hermon and perhaps in the direction of Ḥawrān. Both are, in their turn, sons of Bilha, the *šipḥā* of Rachel. Rachel belongs to the area of Ramah, i.e. at the southern border of northern Israel near Bethel. The Danites may thus have been a very special breed involved in the cult at Dan and perhaps also Bethel, where Isaac was venerated. In the genealogy the tribe is subordinated to the sanctuary in the south, since it is the son of the maid-servant of Rachel, the wife of one of the patriarchs, who established the cult there. In a late notice, however, the maid-servant Bilha is a clan within Naftali and thus a native in upper Galilee.[118] Striking in the traditions about Dan is the negative tone: the Danites are often condemned, a motive which is reminiscent of J's condemnation of Ishmael. On the other hand, there is a hint at a connection between Dan and the Aaronites: Oholiab, a Danite, took part in the construction of the Tabernacle, the Aaronite sanctuary.[119]

It is worth noticing that the original priesthood at Dan was in the hands of the sons of Gershom, the son of Moses. The Gershomites, in fact, lived in the border lands in the north: Golan, Bashan and Ashtarot. They also possessed the town Qedesh in Naphtali in upper Galilee.[120] At a certain point of time the same story was told about Gershom and Ishmael. Judging from the names, Gershom is probably more original in the story than Ishmael.[121]

Ishmael may thus have been a local patriarch in northern Transjordan, connected with the sanctuary at Dan and the priesthood there. This priesthood had close links to another sanctuary, namely that in Bethel which, in turn, was connected with Beer Sheba and its patriarch Isaac. This is the background for the brotherhood between Isaac and Ishmael. This brotherhood, in turn, is the prerequisite for the introduction of the Transjordanian Ishmael into the stories about the forebears of the wilderness people in the south.

The fact that Ishmael's name is absent from both the E and J versions shows that these stories were not about Ishmael from the beginning. Both deal with peoples and places in the deserts south of Judaea. The E narrative deals with the origins of certain groups in the southern deserts connected with Beer Sheba, the home of the patriarch Isaac, following the old mythical story rather closely. The point of the original narrative of J might have been an aetiological explanation of the name of the well Beʔer Laḥay Roʔî: that was the place where a disobedient and runaway slave-girl encountered and saw a divinity, who ordered her to return to her mistress. The narrative would thus originally have been quite different from that of E. Common to both is the name of the mother of the child, Hagar, although it might be secondary in the J story. This word is definitely connected with the Arabic root HǦR, which means not only 'to escape', 'to flee' but also 'protection'. In South Arabia HGR designates many of the large settlements, although a translation 'town' may not be altogether correct since it might also involve some kind of juridical status. It is most likely that the name Hagar is a personification of some kind of asylum institution which is traceable in many parts of Arabia.[122] Since the basic story is definitely connected with mythology, the name Hagar in the E variant could originally have indicated some kind of taboo, under which the bowman stood. The location of a Hagar in the areas between Egypt and Palestine is well documented, and Hagar in the E and J stories must be separated from the *hagrîm* in northern Transjordan.

This is then the starting point for the position of Ishmael in the P work: the ancient relation between Isaac and Ishmael, based on the connection between the sanctuaries in south and north, and the stories told about peripheral groups in the Negev. It seems that P has had the E version or a text close to it before him. A decisive factor for his development of it may have been the occurrence of the verb in verse 17: *wayyišmaʕ*, 'then he (= God) heard'. This, together with the fact that the story dealt with groups seen as close to Isaac, even as his half-brother, made it easy to identify P's Ishmael with the boy in the E story. Through this process Hagar became Ishmael's mother, which was facilitated by the fact that there was obviously also a Hagar in the north.[123] Hagar's Egyptian nationality, as well as the servant-maid motif, P also got from the E story. By this device, the P author(s) could integrate their Ishmael into the family of Abraham. They found a model for Ishmael's degradation, as well as a way of preserving his status by applying the prophecy of a future great people issuing from the son of Hagar. The tribes in the Syrian deserts were adapted to the twelve-tribe scheme, and in P's system they were declared the descendants of Ishmael; hence the fulfilment of the prophecy. The present enumeration of the descendants of Ishmael clearly has cracks showing that it has been tampered with.[124] One could speculate whether the attribution of the habitat of the mythical ʕAmāleq to these descendants of Ishmael may have been due to a dim memory that the bowman in the E story was originally the mythical slayer of ʕAmāleq. That a bow was indeed associated with a divinity in these regions is shown by the name of the god of Edom: Qos means 'bow'.

Later hands have inserted oracles about Ishmael into J's story about Hagar, which originally seems to have dealt with a different motif altogether. One of them adapts the story to the E–P concept by introducing the prophecy of the numerous descendants. It cannot be excluded that even the name Hagar was introduced at this stage into a story which originally dealt only with a nameless maid-servant. Another oracle, probably later, describes Ishmael in quite negative terms as a consequence of his mother's *hybris* and disobedience, causing the savagery and uncivilized way of life of the Ishmaelites.

The elevated status of Ishmael with his three sons probably existed prior to the conception of the Toledot book and was obviously included in it. The elaboration of the covenant/circumcision motif, as well as the 'Ishmaelization' of the E story, is definitely later and belongs to the final redaction of the P work, when Ishmael has been degraded. The final 'Ishmaelization' of the J story probably belongs to the last stage of the redaction of the Pentateuch.

The location of Ishmael in the Negev had the consequence that he became the patriarch of the tribes that appeared there in the Achaemenid period. The list of Ishmael's twelve sons belongs to the *tôledôt* tradition, which was formulated at the beginning of Achaemenid rule of Palestine. It unites the original Ishmaelite tribes in northern Transjordan with those now established south of Palestine, the most prominent of which was Qedar. But we can also see an extension of the scheme to tribes farther out in the Syrian desert, such as Nebayot and Massa', and oases such as Dumah and Taymāʔ. It is most likely that the whole concept, which makes the Holy Land surrounded in the south and the east by Israel's closest relatives, the descendants of Esau and Ishmael, was created before the conflicts with Qedar in the time of Nehemiah, i.e. the latter half of the fifth century BC.[125] The tolerant attitude towards Israel's neighbours apparent in P's geographical outlook is sharply contrasted with the more particularistic views of the Deuteronomists and the circles around Ezra the scribe, but is in tune with the general political climate in the early Achaemenid period. One could perhaps speculate whether the very negative judgement of Ishmael in the J story might reflect the conflict with Qedar, documented in the book of Nehemiah in the fifth century during the reconstruction of the walls of Jerusalem. By this time, the Ishmaelite descent of Qedar would have been commonly accepted by the Judaeans.

Arabs in the Old Testament: a summary

We can now sketch the history of the western Syrian desert and north-western Arabia as it is presented in the two main Old Testament sources, J and P. The ancient popular view was that the farthest southern corners of the *oikoumēnē* were the Kushites in the north-western Ḥiǧāz and the land of Ḥawilah in the south-east. A learned geographical tradition ascribed the Arabian land south of Edom to the same realm as Egypt. This might in fact reflect ancient Egyptian involvement in the Midianite area before 1000 BC. In the middle of the First Temple period we find a series of tribes east and south-east of the settled areas of Palestine/Transjordan which are included under the title 'Sons of Qeṭurah'. Since the name Qeṭurah means 'incense' (not frankincense), these tribes may somehow have been involved in a traffic with perfumes of different kinds originating in the area. This traffic is reflected in the presence of the Midianite traders in the Joseph story.[126] It may also be noted *en passant* that the friends of Job seem to belong to the Qeṭurah group.[127] The Qeṭurah tribes are also included among 'the Sons of the East', an old designation for the non-agricultural tribes east of the ʕArabah. We may observe that the Israelites thus made a sharp division between two main groups in the east: the settled ones (Ammon, Moab, Edom and, of course, the Transjordanian tribes) and those east of them, the Sons of the East.

Another picture is presented in sources from 700 BC and later. Outside the ancient settlers, Ammonites, Moabites and now also Edomites, we encounter new names of tribes in a vast area, stretching from the Negev in the west to Dedan in the south, Nafūd in the south-east and Dumah in the east. All these tribes, exept the ones around Dedan, are arranged by the priestly writers into one family with Ishmael as father. There is no indication that these tribes actually were a confederation or that they were related in some other way. Among them we find the oasis of Dumah and the Qedarites, both of which are designated as Arabs in contemporary Assyrian sources. From those sources many other tribes are known. Even though all these tribes did not constitute any political entity, they probably differed from those of the earlier period: they had camels which they could ride, they were armed with bows and arrows, which made them militarily more efficient than their predecessors, and they were involved in the traffic with perfumes and spices, but also with gold, which now began to appear overland, probably from ʕAsīr. We can observe that the Joseph story was brought up to date by the introduction of the Ishmaelites in the role of traders. The Ishmaelite family constructed by P did thus have a certain correspondence with realities: they represented a new stage of development among the inhabitants of the Syrian desert.

Finally, it should be underlined once more that Arabs do not appear as a people on the same level as the others in these lists. Most remarkable is their absence from the list of Ishmael's sons. This absence cannot be explained by ignorance of the writers about the Arabs. We know from texts, at least from the end of the seventh century, that they were well known among the Israelites. Their absence cannot be due to their belonging to the new peoples in contrast to the old ones. Even though the Pentateuchal writers to a certain extent worked with the fiction of *Urgeshichte*, we have seen that there were no restrictions in bringing the ethnographical registers up to date by adding peoples who had become known to them during the seventh century. The only explanation is that the term 'Arab' did not denote membership of a tribe like Midianite or Israelite. The question remains what it did denote.

Notes

1 This is usually done without any further considerations, for example by Montgomery, *Arabia*, 37–53; Winnett, *Genealogies* 171. Both state as a fact not to be discussed that there are several genealogies in Genesis dealing with Arabia and the Arabs.
2 The so-called D source does not contain any references to Arabia except the story of the Queen of Sheba; see pp. 173 ff.
3 For a recent survey of the debate about the J source, see de Pury, *Yahwist*.
4 Genesis 5:1–32; 11:1–26.
5 Genesis 6:1–10:32.
6 Genesis 11:27–32.
7 Westermann, *Genesis* I 533–534.
8 For the following analysis, see Westermann, *Genesis* I 622 ff.
9 vv. 2 (Japheth), 6 (Ham), 22 (Shem).
10 vv. 20 (Ham), 31 (Shem).
11 Cf. Westermann, *Genesis* I ad loc. As it stands now, verse 5b has only the latter part of the formula.
12 vv. 8–19, 24–30.
13 To Japheth: vv. 3–5. To Ham: v. 7. To Shem: vv. 23.
14 Säve-Söderberg, *Kusch*.
15 Luckenbill, *Records* 2 418 (§1171), Ptolemy, 6.1.2. Cf. Thompson, *Historicity* 306–307. It is not impossible that the Biblical name also reflects the Median title *arpa-kšad* as claimed by Schedl, *Nabochodonosor* 248 f. But the location is clearly Mesopotamia, not Media.
16 This fact makes the identification of Arpachsad with Babylon impossible. Of the descendants of Arpachsad in Genesis 11:10–26, ʕEber probably belongs to northern Syria and may be identified with the king of Ebla mentioned in the tablets from Tell Mardīkh; cf. Westermann, *Genesis* I 747 ff.
17 Aharoni, *Land* 60, 149 item 64.
18 Numbers 23:7, Judges 3:10, 2 Kings 16:6, 2 Chronicles 20:2.
19 Savignac, *Note*: Inscr. no. 3 (p. 593); idem, *Sanctuaire*: Inscr. nabat. no. 3 (pp. 408–411).
20 Qurʔān LXXXIX:6, cf. Musil, *Ḥeǧâz* 273; Astour, *Sabtah* note 4. Ptolemy (6.7.27) mentions an Aramaua together with Makna and Madiama. This name should thus be located close to Midian, which here is probably present-day al-Badʕ, not very far from ʔRM/Rām/Ramm.
21 2 Samuel 10:6–19/1 Chronicles 19:6–19.
22 v. 23. In 1 Chronicles 1:17 they are brothers of Aram instead of his sons. The prophet Bilʕam (Bileam) came 'from ʔArām // from the mountains of the east' (Numbers 23:7). The 'east' (*qedem*) in the Old Testament stands for the areas just outside the settled lands of Transjordan. In Genesis 36:32 we hear about a chief in Edom named Belaʕ, son of Beʕor. Bilʕam is called son of Beʕor in the old poems ascribed to him in Numbers 24:3 and 24:15 and is likely to be the same person. Aram must thus have been somewhere south-east of Palestine. It is tempting to connect this ʔArām with another name, namely Elihu, who appears among the north-west Arabian friends of Job, who in his turn dwells in ʕUṣ in north-western Ḥiǧāz, belongs to the clan of Rām and is, in addition, called 'he from Buz' (*ha-bûzî*, Job 32:2, 6). One manuscript of the LXX (Ephraemi rescriptus) has read *ʔaram* as the clan of Elihu. The Peshitta reads Rmûn. In 1 Chronicles 2:9–10 we hear about a clan Rām, belonging to the tribe of Judah, in which we find many names of clans and tribes who have originally come from the south-east (cf. Meyer, *Israeliten* 328 ff., 348 ff.). The MT has

Yeraḥmeʔel, Rām and Kelûbay; the LXX has Irameēl, Ram, Khaleb and Aram. One is reminded of the inscriptions in Wādī Rām; cf. p. 57, n. 84 and also 2 Kings 16:6 and 2 Chronicles 28:17.

23 Genesis 25:18. For the location of ʕUṣ, see Musil, *Ḥeǧâz* 248–249. The Samaritan text reads ḤWYL [ḥabbəl] instead of MT ḤWL in Genesis 10:23. Some later Muslim genealogists located Ghāthir, son of Thamūd, in north-western Ḥiǧāz; cf. al-Hamdānī, *ʔIklīl* I:34. For an identification of Ḥawilah with an area north-east of Dedan, see von Wissmann, *Geschichte* I 83; Astour, *Sabtah* 423; Knauf, *Ismael* 64.

24 Brinkman, *History* 86 ff.

25 Sargon, Annals l. 116 (= Lie, *Inscriptions* 20).

26 So already by Herodotus 4.12. Cf. Dhorme, *Peuples* 168–170; *Westermann*, Genesis I 674.

27 Dhorme, *Peuples* 180–181; Westermann, *Genesis* I 675.

28 Dhorme, *Peuples* 176–180; Zimmerli, *Hezechiel* 652; Westermann, *Genesis* I 675; cf. the king of Tabal among the tribute-bearers to Tiglath Pileser III in 738 BC (p. 131). In a text from Sargon II we hear about a king Mi-ta-a in the land of Mu-uš-ki, which is identical to the name of the kings of Phrygia, Midas (Dhorme, *Peuples* 177). According to Aro, *Tabal* 80, Tabal appears in Assyrian texts between 836 and 639 BC. Tibarēnoí are mentioned together with Móskhoi in Herodotus 3.94 and as late as Cicero (*Ad Familiares.* 15.4.10, ibid. 298–301).

29 Dhorme, *Peuples* 171–176; Westermann, *Genesis* I 675. In Hezechiel 38:2 and 39:6 it is connected with the name Gog, where it occurs together with Tubal and Meshek. Gog has been associated with Gyges, king of Lydia (Herodotus 1.8 ff.); see Zimmerli, *Hezechiel* 940–942; Westermann, *Genesis* I 674.

30 Genesis 10:23. The names are ʕUṣ, Ḥul, Geter and Mash.

31 Genesis 10:7.

32 Astour, *Sabtah*; Gardiner, *Egypt* 340–345, 350.

33 This might be confirmed by the fact that Shebā and Dedān have been transferred from the Qeṭurah group to P's Kushites (see pp. 128 ff.). If the Qeṭurah list reflects local views in the ninth century BC, P's more cosmopolitan outlook may be later.

34 See Johnson, *Purpose* 14–28.

35 Deuteronomy 9:15–16. The only remarkable exception is Joshua 21:4, 13, 19, but this passage, like most of those dealing with the distribution of land between the tribes, is probably of P origin. Aaron also appears in a quite unfavourable light in the story of the Golden Calf (Exodus 32), a story which is related to material used by the Deuteronomists (1 Kings 12:25–32).

36 Numbers 12.

37 Cf. Hayes/Miller, *History* 456–460.

38 Spencer, *Aaron*, especially §§ B and C.

39 It should be observed that the *tôledôt* formula does not occur with Abraham but with his descendants Isaac, Ishmael, Esau and Jacob/Israel. A parallel is found in the book of Amos where the two patriarchs mentioned are Isaac and Israel. This could reflect a period when Abraham had not yet been made the forefather of all peoples round Palestine, i.e. around 700 BC.

40 Berossus Fragm. II:29 (= Schnabel, *Berossos* 261–262); ibid. III:34 (= Schnabel, *Berossos* 264–267). The ten antediluvian kings reigning before the Flood appear already in the Sumerian king-list from *c.* 2000 BC.

41 Nāh/Nāhā and Shalaḥ are probably names of gods; cf. Lewy, *Nāh*. Also Teraḥ is most likely a divine name related to the moon (*warḫ*, *yeraḥ*) and would represent the Moon-god in Haran. It deserves to be pointed out that the tripartition of the world in the P scheme has a parallel in Hecataeus and Herodotus from the beginning of the fifth century BC, who represent a tradition originating in Asia Minor not too far from northern Syria. Hecataeus/Herodotus' Europe, Asia and Libya match Japheth, Shem and Ham in P rather well.

42 2 Kings 16:10–11; 2 Chronicles 28:23.

43 See pp. 134, 177 ff.

44 See Astour, *Sabtah* 423. Rhammanîtai are mentioned by Strabo (16.4.24) in connection with the report about the campaign of Aelius Gallus to Yemen.
45 Namely in the additions to the Tyrus song, Hezechiel 27:15–22; cf. p. 177 for the background of this text.
46 Both von Wissmann (*Geschichte* 465) and W. Müller (*Altsüdarabien* 366 n. 13) claim that Raʕmā is identical with Nağrān, based upon the name RGMT documented in ancient South Arabian texts. This is claimed to be supported by the Ethiopic text of Aretas' martyrdom, which says that *Nägran hägär* means 'the city of thunder' (*hägärä näg^{w}ädg^{w}ad*) in Hebrew (Esteves Pereira, *Historia* § 3 81 l. 22). The Hebrew and Aramaic words for thunder are derived from the root RʕM, which is then connected with RGMT. Linguistically this is untenable, and it is much more likely that we have an ancient popular etymology of the South Arabian name RGMT, probably made by people with knowledge of Aramaic and/or Hebrew, who identified the South Arabian town with a Biblical name. The same process lies behind the identification of ʔUzal in Genesis 10:27 with Ṣanʕāʔ, which definitely is secondary, going back to Jews and/or Christians in Yemen.
47 Cf. Genesis 25:18 and note 21 above. For the area of the Ishmaelites, see p. 220.
48 Psalm 72:10.
49 Strabo 16.4.10. This notice comes from Agatharcides of Cnidus, i.e. the third century BC; Josephus, *Antiquities* 2.249, cf. Isaiah 43:3, 45:14. For the identification of Sebā with a port in Eritrea and the possible dating of Psalm 72 in the early seventh century BC see von Wissmann, *Geschichte* I 102–103.
50 The P authors do not exhibit any knowledge about conditions in South Arabia. The gold-land Ophir is not mentioned, nor is Ḥaḍramawt. On the other hand, Sebā on the African coast was known to them. This supports the assumption that the information about the Red Sea and adjacent lands available to these authors came from shipping and not from trans-Arabian caravan traffic. P's picture of Arabia is derived from reports by caravans down to Dedan only, the meeting place between Syria-Mesopotamia and western and southern Arabia. Before the use of the camel for large-scale overland traffic in Arabia, trade with the coastal lands around the Red Sea was made by sea. We have suggested elsewhere that the camel-based trade between Syria and South Arabia did not begin before the year 700 BC (Retsö, *Domestication*). The dating of the P version of the Table of Nations to this period, together with the absence of any concrete reference to South Arabia in it, lends support to this hypothesis.
51 Knauf, *Midian* 110–114; Rothenberg/Glass, *Pottery*, especially 68–69 and 114–115; Parr, *Pottery* 74 ff., 81 ff.
52 The medieval Arab author of the description of South Arabia called *Tārīkh al-mustabṣir* knew about a tradition that at least the southern Tihāma (from Mecca southwards) was called Kūš (Ibn Muğāwir, *Tārīkh* 83) by some (the inhabitants of ʕAmrān = Jews?). It is likely that Kush, Ham, Lud and other names were originally names of rather small areas, used by the P writers as labels for their own divisions of the earth.
53 Aharoni, *Land* 61–70.
54 Numbers 34: 11–12.
55 Genesis 20:1.
56 1 Samuel 15:7, 27:8.
57 1 Samuel 15:6–7.
58 Halpern, *Kenites*, especially § B.
59 1 Samuel 15:12. ʕAmāleq appear as inhabitants of a border land.
60 The exact position of Qadesh is not relevant for this discussion. For a new suggestion, see pp. 287–289.
61 It seems that the latter part of this borderline also appears in Eratosthenes' division of Arabia into *éremos* and *eudaímōn* (see pp. 302 ff.). In Akkadian texts we also hear about a country called *māt tāmtim*, 'the Sea-land' or rather 'the desert land', which stretches south of the Fertile Crescent and may be identical with *Arabía éremos* (cf. Dougherty, *Sealand* 7–8, 24). This division may thus be very ancient and may also explain the geography of the J source (see the following).

62 von Wissmann (*Zur Geschichte* 191 note 401) connected Ḥawilah with ḪWLN in northern Yemen and Pishon with Wādī Baysh or Bayḍ north of it. It is, however, difficult to see how these South Arabian names have ended up in the Jerusalemite mythology.
63 One might observe that according to this location, the borders of the earth seem to coincide with the southern border of the Semites in the P scheme and also, as it seems, with the division between *Arabía érēmos* and *Arabía eudaímōn* in Eratosthenes.
64 Genesis 10:8–19.
65 Genesis 10:24–30.
66 The most likely etymology is a derivation from YQŠ, 'catch' with the gentilic suffix *-ān*, an old plural or collective suffix which is common in north-west Arabia; cf. the names Zimrān, Yoqshān's brother, Midyān, and later Liḥyān.
67 This would be *yiqṭon* or *yaqṭon*. LXX has Iektan.
68 CIH 621; cf. the discussion by von Wissmann in *Geschichte* 1 78 note 1. Ibn Qutayba (*Maʕārif* 103 l. 11) mentions as-Salaf as a son of Saʕd b. Ḥimyar.
69 Cf. the discussion by von Wissmann loc. cit. note 3.
70 W. Müller, *Obal*; al-Hamdānī, *ʔIklīl* 116:12, 21; 189:12. An ʕAbal is mentioned in the same area (ibid. 118:10; 121:18).
71 Genesis 36:33. Glaser (*Skizze* II 303 f.) followed by von Wissmann (*Zur Geschichte* 278–279; idem, *Geschichte* 1 78 n. (2)) identified it with a South Arabian entity YHBB mentioned in the inscription CIH 37. The location is SMʕY in the Yemeni highland around Ṣanʕāʔ. If Ophir is ʕAsīr, as assumed by von Wissmann, the identification of Ḥawilah with ḪWLN and Yobab with YHBB becomes less likely, since it seems that the names stand in a special order with Haṣarmawet as the farthest and Yobab as the closest to Palestine. The identification with the mythical king of Edom in Genesis 36:33–34 is much more likely.
72 1 Kings 9:26–28, 10:11; 2 Chronicles 8:17–18, 9:10. The Sheba mentioned in Psalm 72:10, 15 and Isaiah 60:6 could also refer to Yemeni Saba.
73 The Yoqtanids are said to have lived 'from Meša' to Sfar, the mountain of the east' (Genesis 10:30). Sfar probably means 'border country' (cf. Geez *səfra* 'region'). Unfortunately, the exact location of these sites remains unknown.
74 The final downfall of the first Sabaean empire is dated by von Wissmann (*Geschichte* 2 351 ff., 365 ff.) to *c.* 375 BC. Kitchen puts it back to *c.* 450 BC (*Documentation* 43–57).
75 Jeremiah 49:8; Hezechiel 25:13; Lamentations 4:21.
76 Cf. Knauf, *Supplementa* 4.
77 Genesis 25:18.
78 Cf. 1 Samuel 15:7.
79 For a survey of the evidence, see Knauf, *Ismael* 68–81.
80 For this meaning of the expression, see Drinkard, *ʕal pĕnē*.
81 E.g. Winnett, *Genealogies*, 193–195; Noth, *Ismael*; Knauf, *Ismael* 2; idem, *Ishmaelites* A1. Knauf sees Ishmael as identical with Su-mu-il in the Assyrian texts of Assurbanipal (see p. 205). Linguistically this is untenable. Šumuʔil is rather equivalent to Hebrew Šmûʕʔel = Samuel (cf. Eph'al, *Ishmaelites*). The name of this tribe has survived in the name of the famous Jewish-Arab pre-Islamic poet of Taymāʔ: as-Samawʔal. Eph'al sees Ishmael as a tribal federation in southern Palestine prior to the tenth century BC (*Ishmael* 226) but rejects the existence of any such confederation in Neo-Assyrian times (*Arabs* 237). Needless to say, the existence of a confederation of Ishmaelites in the tenth century or earlier is even more uncertain, due to the absence of any text from this period mentioning them.
82 Cf. Genesis 25:6, where Abraham is said to have sent the sons of Qeṭurah 'eastwards, to the land of the east' (*qédmā ʔel ʔéreṣ qédem*).
83 Genesis 36:1–19.
84 See Knauf, *Supplementa* 1.
85 1 Chronicles 1:31; 5:19.
86 It should be observed that this use of *w-* is not upheld in the Chronicler's version of the list (1 Chronicles 1:29–31): Nebayot + Qedar + Adbeel + Mibsam; Mishmaʕ + Dumah; Massa'; Ḥadad + Tema'; Yeṭur; Naphis + Qedmah. C seems to use two different ways of enumeration: connecting all units in a group with *w-* or connecting only the two last ones. In that

case, the three last units in the list would constitute a group also in C's list.

87 1 Chronicles 5:10.

88 Psalm 83:7. For a juxtaposition of Ishmaelites and Hagarites, see also 1 Chronicles 27:30–31: Obil the *yišmeʕelî* is in charge of David's camels and Yaziz the *hagrî* tends his small cattle.

89 Genesis 37:25.

90 1 Chronicles 5:10–11, 19–22. This may be anachronistic and reflect events which occurred much later.

91 The difference between the Ishmaelites of P and the other instances in the Old Testament is also stressed by Eph'al, who considers the extra-P passages not later than the ninth century BC. The dating of the sources to such an early period is, however, most dubious. E.g. Ps. 83 presupposes the story about the Midianites in Judges 7–9 in its present shape, which puts it quite late, probably around 500 BC at the earliest. The Ishmaelites in Chronicles are camel-breeders, which is not documented before the end of the eighth century. The Joseph story, at least in its present shape, cannot be dated before 700 BC and could be much later.

92 Genesis 36:5.

93 An argument in favour of this suggestion is the fact that the identification of Ishmael as the father of the Arabs, which was made by Jewish midrashists in the Hellenistic age, originally seems to have pertained to the Arabs in Transjordan only (see pp. 335 ff.). This may be a memory that the original home of Ishmael was there.

94 Judges 8:25.

95 Esau is a complex figure, uniting at least two different regions: Seʕîr in the eastern Negev, and Edom on the eastern side of the ʕArabah. He is provided with three wives. Of these, ʕAdā seems to represent the south-eastern Negev down towards Elath (she is the origin of Timnaʕ and ʕAmāleq, and in Genesis 4:19–24 she is connected with the tribe of Qayin). Basemat is the sister of Nebayot and mother of Reʕuʔel. Both definitely belong to the land east of the ʕArabah. The third wife, Oholibamah, is explicitly located in Seʕîr, i.e. the eastern Negev. Her three sons thus represent groups living there, i.e. east of Beer Sheba, the home of Isaac.

96 Genesis 16:3, 15–17:27.

97 Genesis 21:8–21.

98 Knauf (*Ismael* 23 and n. 98) identifies it with present-day Wādī Fīrān in the south-western Sinai peninsula. This ignores both linguistic and geographical difficulties. The impression from other Old Testament texts mentioning this name is that it was an area in the Negev around Qadesh-Barneaʕ (Numbers 13:3; 26, Deuteronomy 1:22, Genesis 14:6–7; 21:15, 21; 1 Kings. 11:8); cf. Musil, *Ḥeǧâz* 275–278, who locates Paran in the southern ʕArabah. Whether it encompassed the entire Sinai peninsula we do not know. The wilderness of Sinai in Numbers 12:16 is probably east of the Gulf of ʕAqaba.

99 Genesis 16:1–2, 4–14. Verses 3 and 15–16 are attributed to P.

100 Knauf's analysis and evaluation of these two latter stories are difficult to understand (*Ismael* 16–45). He uses a strange mixture of aesthetic (which are, of course, most difficult to counter) and linguistic arguments (the introduction of new unexpected lexemes in a passage shows that it is of less value!) to claim that the J story is a masterpiece, whereas the E version is rejected with the characteristic invective 'midrashic'.

101 Cf. Judges 13:3 (the birth of Samson), Isaiah 7:14 (Immanuel), Luke 1:31 (Jesus).

102 For the meaning of MṢR in the Old Testament, see p. 195.

103 Exodus 4:24–26.

104 This probably also explains the Kushite descent of Nimrod in Genesis 10:8–9. Nimrod is originally a variant of the hunting bowman south of Palestine, where the Kushites also lived. His transfer to Babylonia is due to theology, where he, however, found figures like Sargon I and the god Ninurta with whom he could be associated.

105 Both J and E locate him in Beer Sheba: Genesis 26 (J); 21 (E).

106 Amos 7:9, 16.

107 Amos 8:14.

108 1 Kings 12:26–32.

109 Numbers 20:23–29; 33:36–39; Deuteronomy 32:50; cf. another tradition in Deuteronomy 10:6–7.
110 Numbers 16.
111 1 Chronicles 5:20.
112 1 Kings 14:1; 15:25; Leviticus 10:1–3.
113 Nodab is rendered in LXX as *Nadabaîoi*. For the connection, see Albright, *Tribe*, and Knauf, *Nôdab* (where Nabadaioi should be corrected to Nadabaîoi).
114 Judges 17–18.
115 Genesis 46:23. The Shuḥam mentioned in Numbers 26:42 is a variant of the name.
116 1 Chronicles 7:12: the Ḥûshîm are 'the sons of another' (*bnê ʔaḥer*), who perhaps is ʔAḥîrām, one of Benjamin's sons in Numbers 26:38. In 1 Chronicles 8:8, Ḥûshîm are said to have been the wife of someone in Benjamin called Shaharayim, who left them/her? and emigrated to Moab with a new wife.
117 Deuteronomy 33:22.
118 1 Chronicles 7:13.
119 Exodus 31:6; 35:34; 38:23.
120 Joshua 21: 27, 32; 1 Chronicles 6:71–72, 76.
121 It is obviously a derivation from GRŠ, 'drive out', and looks like a cultic name originally connected with the rites of circumcision and wedding.
122 See Beeston, *Significance*. The South Arabian word was pronounced [hagar] like its counterpart in Geez. It is worth observing that al-Hamdānī, when enumerating examples of *haǧar* (*Ṣifa* 86), mentions only the *haǧar* in al-Baḥrayn (= Hufūf), Naǧrān, Ǧāzān and Ḥaṣiba.
123 If Hagar is some kind of institution, the *hagrîm* in Transjordan may be a testimony of the existence of such an institution also there. For the name HKR and Akhoris in Egypt, see pp. 238, 253.
124 Cf. the double introduction vv. 12 and 13.
125 See pp. 250 ff. The position of Esau as subordinated to Isaac and brother of Jacob/Israel may reflect an original Transjordanian constellation where Jacob was a patriarch in central Transjordan (Gilead?) and Esau represents groups further south, thus a parallel to Isaac and Ishmael in the Negev, which would explain the similar stories told about them.
126 Genesis 37:28, 36. The Midianites in the Joseph story are present for theological reasons. Just as they offered a haven for Moses and received the Israelites when they had left Egypt, they also saved Joseph and brought him down to Egypt. With the help of the Midianites Israel descended to Egypt; with the help of the Midianites they left it.
127 They are from Shuaḥ, Têman and Naʕamah respectively, which seem to indicate the extremes of the Qeṭurah tribes.

9

THE AGE OF THE ACHAEMENIDS

Introduction

The rise of the empire of the Achaemenids initiated a new era in the history of the Middle East. For the first time in history, the whole area from the Aegean to India was unified under one government. The Persian state was supra-national, i.e. it tolerated the existence of a large number of local states and tribes. There was no quest for total subjugation or extermination of other peoples. Rather, the Achaemenid empire resembled a federation more than a totalitarian empire like the Assyrian one. There was a ruling class of warriors and aristocrats belonging to the Persian and, to a certain extent, the Median peoples. They occupied a special and privileged position within the empire and were appointed as rulers over large provinces. Below this level, local governments and religious practices of the different peoples were tolerated and even supported, and the administration did not interfere in local affairs more than necessary. On the whole, the Achaemenid rule seems to have been popular among the subjugated peoples, and the Persians receive almost incredibly good credentials from, for example, the notoriously querulous Israelite prophets. It is likely that the almost 250 years of Achaemenid rule for the common people was one of the longest and most prosperous periods of peace in the history of the Middle East, comparable only to the 400 years of internal peace established by the Ottoman Turks many centuries later.

The order created by the Persians continued after the fall of their rule. Alexander's spectacular conquest of the empire was exactly what the word means: a military conquest, an event for journalists if such had existed. But Alexander did not create an empire; he took over one. The structure of the Persian state remained to a large extent untouched, and the Seleucids obviously founded their power on already existing structures.[1] The great change occurred when the Seleucid government in Iran and Mesopotamia broke down in the middle of the second century BC and the Parthian empire arose in the east. This process resulted in the Roman occupation of Syria and inaugurated a new period when the Middle East was divided again between rival political entities. There are thus good reasons to treat the period from 539 to *c*. 130 BC as one coherent time span spectacularly broken in the middle by the meteoric career of Alexander. As will become evident, the relation between the empire and the Arabs seems to have remained the same the whole time, and the change of governments that took place at the end of the fourth century BC was somewhat cosmetic.

The sources for the period 540–335 BC

The sources dealing with Arabs during the period from Cyrus to Alexander are more sparse than during the preceding one, a fact which reflects the fairly peaceful conditions.

From the Arabian peninsula, especially Ḥiǧāz, there is a large corpus of inscriptions from the Achaemenid period. As a matter of fact, the Babylonian expedition to Taymāʔ seems to have given an impetus to the use of writing, both Aramaic and domestic scripts. The word 'Arab' is, as far as is known, not mentioned in any of these inscriptions, and we do not even know if any of them were written by 'Arabs' (with possibly one exception). These texts are valuable for the history of literacy among the inhabitants of the peninsula as well as the languages spoken but they contain disappointingly little historical information.

The contemporary Persian documents are limited to the mention of 'Arabs' in the lists of subjugated peoples under the earliest rulers, Darius I and Xerxes I. To this is added some pictorial material from the tombs and palaces of these rulers as well as their successors. There is also a note in the autobiography of Nehemiah written around 430 BC. Most of the data are found in Greek sources. Of these, the most important is Herodotus, writing his *Historíē* after the middle of the 440s BC. Herodotus had visited at least Egypt and the Levant, probably also Babylonia, and had first-hand information about conditions there. He also had access to the work of Hecataeus, an Ionian geographer who compiled a map and a description of the world known to the Ionians around 500 BC. This work used information from a description of the route around the Arabian peninsula made by Scylax of Caryanda who sailed around it *c.* 517 BC. Also Herodotus used Scylax's work. Another important source is the Athenian Xenophon. He had in his youth taken part in a great adventure, namely the attempt by Cyrus, son of Darius II, to wrest power from his brother Artaxerxes II in the year 401 BC. As we have already seen, Xenophon knew a lot about Persia both from reading and from personal experience. His most important literary source was the *Persica* by Ctesias, a rather dubious historical source as we have noted. From the fourth century BC we have a description of the coastline of the whole Mediterranean including Palestine–Egypt, ascribed to the above-mentioned Scylax of Caryanda but in fact compiled *c.* 350 BC. Finally, Arabs are mentioned sporadically in some other fourth-century Greek texts.

Cambyses and the Arabs

According to Xenophon, Cyrus the Great had dealings with Arabs during his conquest of Babylonia. As has been pointed out, these Arabs are likely to have been living in Mesopotamia around the Khābūr river. From the time of Cyrus' son and successor, Cambyses, we have information about Arabs. They appear in Herodotus' report about Cambyses' conquest of Egypt in 525 BC:

> Phanes . . . counselled Cambyses to send and ask the king of the *arábioi* for a safe passage [along the coast from Palestine to Egypt].[2]
>
> Wherefore Cambyses . . . sent messengers to the *arábios* and asked and obtained safe conduct, giving and receiving *pístis* from him.[3]
>
> Afterwards, when the *arábios* had made a covenant (*pístis*) with the messengers who had come from Cambyses, he [the *arábios*] planned the following: he filled camel-skins with water and loaded all his camels with these; having done this he drove them into the waterless land and there awaited Cambyses' army.

> This is the most credible of the stories told. But a less credible tale is also told. There is a great river in Arabia called Kórys, issuing into the sea called Red. From this river, it is said, the king of the *arábioi* carried water by a duct of sewn oxhides and other hides of length sufficient to reach to the dry country, and he had great tanks dug in that country to receive and keep the water. It is a twelve days' journey from the river to that desert. By three ducts, it is said, he led the water to three different places.[4]

This story has a familiar ring. A similar tale was told about Esarhaddon's campaign to Egypt when he too was assisted by Arabs.[5]

Herodotus tells this story in connection with his account of his stay in Egypt, and it is likely that it is based on an Egyptian source. There is nothing unlikely in the *arábioi* aiding the Persian conqueror even though the details in Herodotus' story cannot be trusted. He himself says that many versions of this event were circulating. The *arábioi* and their king are said to have assisted only with water supply. One wonders where the river Korys was. A possible location is somewhere in Transjordan. If this is true, we have an important piece of information about the extent of the area where the *arábioi* exercised some kind of control. Another possibility is, however, Wādī l-ʕArīsh. The digging of water reservoirs brings later usage documented from the Negev into mind.[6] We thus have evidence for the key role of the Arabs between Syria and Palestine which actually went back to the days of Tiglath Pileser III.[7]

The testimony from the Persians

In several Old Persian texts originating from the Achaemenid kings of the late sixth and fifth centuries BC, the names of different ethnic and other entities are mentioned. Among them we find the word *arabāya* in five monumental inscriptions from the reign of Cambyses' successor Darius I (522–486 BC): Behistun (DB), Persepolis E (DPe), Susa E (DSe), Susa M (DSm) and Naqsh-e-Rustam A (DNa), the tomb of the king.[8] There is also an instance in one of the so-called foundation tablets from Susa, as well as a fortification text in Elamitic from Persepolis.[9] The tomb of Darius I at Naqsh-e-Rustam has, apart from the main text, a picture showing representatives of the peoples of the empire carrying the throne of the King of Kings with a text identifying each carrier, among them the *arabāya*.[10] The oldest text is the one at Behistun, finished around 519/518 BC. This text contains twenty-three names. DPe is from shortly after the conquest of the Indus valley in 517 BC and contains twenty-four names. DNa and the Susa texts mention the Scythians and Thracians in Europe, and are probably from at least after 512 BC or even reflect the conquests in the 490s BC. They contain twenty-nine and twenty-seven names respectively.

The foundation tablet from Susa is in Akkadian. The Behistun inscription as well as the text from Naqsh-e-Rustam are also found in an Akkadian version.[11] In these texts, the word *arabāya* is rendered *arab*. There is thus little doubt that the *arabāya* of the Old Persian texts basically refers to the same kind of people as *arab-*, not only in the Persian texts in Akkadian but also in the earlier Assyrian ones.

In most texts the *arabāya* are mentioned together with other peoples from the Middle East. In DB, DSe, DSm and DNa the peoples in the Middle East proper are listed in the following order:

Babirush (Babylonia) – Athurā (Assyria/Syria) – Arabāya (Arabs) – Mudrāya (Egypt).[12]

This is also the order in which the Arabs occur in the reliefs of the throne carriers at Naqsh-e-Rustam. Only in DPe is the order different:

Babirush – Arabāya – Athurā – Mudrāya.[13]

Yet another text is on one of the statues of Darius set up to celebrate the completion of the canal between the Nile and the Gulf of Suez, which was effected in 516 BC. The statues contain a list of the subjugated peoples in hieroglyphic script. In one of these, on a statue that was later carried to Susa, we find the following series (no. 17–20):

ʔŠR (= Assyria/Syria) – ḤGR – KM(T?) (= Egypt)[14]

Since ḤGR stands in the same position as *arabāya* in the Old Persian texts, it must be its equivalent.[15]

From Darius' successor, Xerxes I (486–465 BC), there is one inscription in Persepolis, the so-called Daiva inscription, a list of subjugated peoples containing thirty-two names, among which the *arabāya* are mentioned.[16] Further, on the great staircase leading up to the Apadana hall in the palace built by Xerxes at Persepolis, we can still see a large relief showing different peoples bringing tribute to the king, among them Arabs.[17] In these two documents the Arabs are not associated with the peoples from the Middle East. In the reliefs of Xerxes' tomb at Naqsh-e-Rustam, on the other hand, they stand in the same position as in that of Darius.

There are four more royal tombs with the same scene as in those of Darius and Xerxes I: Artaxerxes I (465–424 BC) and Darius II (424–404 BC), both at Naqsh-e-Rustam, Artaxerxes II (404–358 BC) and Artaxerxes III (358–337 BC), both in Persepolis.[18] Only the picture on the tomb of Artaxerxes II has a text similar to the one of Darius I.[19]

The Old Persian term for the twenty-three entities mentioned in the inscriptions is *dahyāuš*, pl. *dahyāva*, meaning 'land', 'province', 'district' (modern Persian *dih*, 'village'). A comparison with the pictorial evidence shows that the *dahyāva* were represented with ethnic characteristics, i.e. as peoples. The term could be used for different levels of entities. Thus Bactria is a *dahyāuš*, but when the *dahyāuš* Margiana revolts, the governor of Bactria is sent to crush it and it becomes clear that the *dahyāuš* Margiana, not mentioned among the twenty-three entities, is part of the *dahyāuš* Bactria.[20] In the same way, within the *dahyāuš* Armenia there was another one called Autiyāra, not appearing among the twenty-three.[21] We hear about two *dahyāva* in eastern Iran, Bactria and Arachosia, which were ruled by a *xšačapāvan*, a term rendered *satrápēs* by the Greeks.[22] The term *dahyāuš* could obviously be used for the provinces ruled by a *xšačapāvan*/satrap as well as for smaller units within the province.

The first impression given by these lists and pictures is that they represent an official ideology that was not changed during the Achaemenid era. The fact that Egypt was independent for long periods or that India was lost quite soon is not reflected in the texts. The ideological flavour is a heritage from the first of them, namely the Behistun inscription. That text is a piece of political propaganda which was translated to other languages in the realm and distributed. Its aim was to legitimize the rule of Darius. We should thus not expect these texts and pictures to be a sensitive reflection of political and administrative changes. Instead it is a testimony of the system created by Darius I, upheld by his successors.[23] It has lately been argued that the texts and reliefs represent a state ceremony, a parade of peoples acknowledging the king by bringing him tribute, *bāǧiš*.[24] This word would not necessarily be a designation for regular taxes but rather a ceremonial gift delivered on special occasions. The lists would thus not be an exact geographical or administrative description of the empire.

The different position of the *arabāya* in the lists of Darius need not have any special meaning. A comparison of the lists shows that such irregularities occur also with other names, such as Elam and Media, without this having any significance.[25] There is nothing in these texts and pictures to indicate that the *arabāya* did occupy any special or privileged position. They appear on the same level as all the others, which could then reflect their function in the ceremony.

We do not obtain any detailed information about the *arabāya* from these lists and pictures. In most texts, the *arabāya* belong to the complex Babylon – Assyria – Egypt, which shows that they were geographically part of or close to that area.[26] It is, however, doubtful if the *dahyauš* of the *arabāya* was extended over the whole of North Arabia from the Nile to the Persian Gulf.[27] There is no textual evidence for this, and from what we know about later periods there are strong contrary arguments. It is more likely that it was more or less identical with the Arabia described by Herodotus stretching from the eastern Nile Delta to Palestine, perhaps including the Sinai peninsula and eventually parts of northern Ḥiǧāz. We know from somewhat later evidence that there was a Persian governor, a *pihātu*, in Taymāʔ, but the relations between him and the *arabāya* is far from clear. The *arabāya dahyāuš* would then have corresponded roughly to the later Arabo-Nabataean kingdom. It is worth noticing that the *arabāya* did not take part in the revolts against Darius in the first years of his reign. On the contrary, when he crossed the Tigris to attack Babylon he says that he used, among other things, camel-riders.[28] Such camel-riders are very likely to have included *arabāya*, who by now were specialists in handling this animal. They could thus have performed the same service as they gave to Cambyses in his crossing of the isthmus of Suez a few years earlier.[29]

In one of the so-called fortification tablets from Persepolis written in the reign of Darius, we hear about *harba* = *ʕarbay* receiving grain as provision.[30] They would thus have been employees of the government or the court. From the time of Xerxes, we have another picture of these Arabs. Herodotus describes the army of Xerxes when he went against Greece in 480 BC. This information he must have gathered from people who had participated, since he himself was only a child at the time. It is told that Xerxes mustered his troops at Doriscus in Thrace and Herodotus gives a list of all the peoples that composed the Persian army. This review could, in fact, have been a ceremony similar to the one reflected in the inscriptions and reliefs from the capitals, but this time a military one, not civilian.[31] The *arábioi* are said to have been posted beside the Ethiopians and both under the command of Arsames.[32]

> The *arábioi* were clad in girded-up mantles and carried bows curving backwards, big ones.[33]

This passage pertains to the infantry. There were also mounted troops in the army:

> The *arábioi* had the same equipment as the[ir] infantry, all riding on camels no less swift than horses.[34]

> The *arábioi* were posted hindmost; for the horses not enduring the sight of the camels, their place was in the rear, so that the horses might not be affrighted.[35]

This information gives a realistic impression and is obviously drawn from the testimony of someone who had seen the Persian army. The picture of the *arábioi* is reminiscent of what we have learnt about the *arab* in Assyrian times. It is unfortunate that we do not hear anything about their performance or function in the battles.[36] The presence of the *arábioi* in the line together with all the other peoples goes very well with their appearance in the *dahyāva* lists of the Achaemenid kings.

Scylax of Caryanda

The picture derived from the Persian sources is completed but also made more complex by the Greek sources from the fifth century BC. Scylax's voyage was made after the completion of the Behistun inscription and before the conquest of India, i.e. 517 BC. He sailed down the Indus, then followed the coast of the Arabian peninsula until he landed in Egypt.[37] He wrote a report, a *períplous*, of his journey, which is lost but from which there are preserved quite a few fragments, among them some interesting notes about Arabian matters.[38] One is the mention of the Kamarēnoí islands 'of the *arábioi*'.[39] These are still known as the Kamarān islands off the Red Sea coast of Yemen. Another is the information that it takes forty days to sail through the Red Sea.[40] This is substantial geographical knowledge, obviously based on experience from sailing around the Arabian peninsula. It is most likely that Scylax also mentioned the Persian Gulf, although this knowledge disappeared with the authors who used his Periplus, Hecataeus and Herodotus, who do not mention it.[41] We know from an inscription by Darius found in Suez that at this time ships also went from the canal between the Nile and the Red Sea to Persia, which definitely presupposes knowledge of the Gulf.[42]

Hecataeus of Mytilene

The knowledge that Scylax had presented about Arabia was partly blurred and distorted by the first Greek geographer, Hecataeus, who shortly before 500 BC drew a map of the world with an accompanying description.[43] This work, the *Periēgēsis*, is lost, like Scylax's *Periplus*, but is known from quotations by several later authors, such as Strabo writing in the time of Augustus, and Stephanus of Byzantium writing in the sixth century AD.[44] Also Herodotus used it extensively, although he often polemicizes against his older compatriot. Hecataeus saw the world as a circular agglomeration of land surrounded by a river, the Okeanos. The land was divided in a northern half, Europe, and a southern half. The latter was then divided into two parts, Asia and Libya. This assymmetry has led some scholars to doubt if Hecataeus really operated with three continents. There seem, however, to be good arguments in favour of the tripartition.[45] One of them is that the tripartition, as we have seen, was an ancient world-view in the Middle East. The geographical foundation of the Table of Nations in Genesis 10 is very similar to that of Hecataeus: Japheth covers the entire northern hemisphere like Europe in Hecataeus, whereas the southern is divided between Shem (= Asia) and Ham (= Libya).

Hecataeus' three continents were divided by rivers: the river Phasis, flowing from the east into the Black Sea, separated Asia from Europe, and the Nile was the border between Asia and Libya.[46] Four peoples inhabited the utmost parts of the earth: Celts in the west, Scythians in the north, *arábioi* in the south and, probably, Indians in the east.[47] We thus seem to find both the numbers three and four as basic to this system, which clearly points to an eastern origin of the whole concept.

Herodotus quotes a passage which looks like a description of a map. It is thus very likely that it is, in fact, taken from Hecataeus. According to the description, the Asian continent had two *aktaí*, 'coasts' or rather 'promontories', pointing westwards from Persia. The northern one was Asia Minor. The southern one is described like this in Herodotus' text:

> But the second [*aktē*], beginning with Persia, stretches to the Red Sea [the Indian Ocean], being Persian land, and next the neighbouring country of Assyria [Mesopotamia + Syria?], and after Assyria Arabia . . . In this peninsula there are but three nations (*éthnea*).[48]

Noteworthy is that the Levantine coast seems to run from east to west and not from north to south. This is another indication that the description does not originate with Herodotus, who had sailed along that coast himself.[49] There is no explicit mention of the Arabian peninsula.[50] Instead Arabia is the westernmost part of the southern *áktē*, a peninsula stretching westwards from the Asian mainland, inhabited by three nations: Persia, Assyria and Arabia.[51]

Herodotus polemicizes against the concept of the Ionians about world geography in a way that enables us to get a more detailed picture of the Hecataean view on this question:

> All the rest of Egypt [apart from the Delta] is, as they [namely the Ionians, i.e. Hecataeus] say, partly Libya and partly Arabia.
>
> If we follow the belief of the Greeks, we shall consider all Egypt, down from the cataracts and the city Elephantine, to be divided into two parts, one part belonging to Libya and the other to Asia.[52]

In other passages Herodotus simply reports the geographical conditions of Arabia in Hecataean terms without comments and it is likely that he has, at least partly, copied his older colleague:

> Beyond and above Heliopolis is a narrow land. For it is bounded on one side by the mountains of Arabia, which bear from the north to the south, ever stretching towards the sea called Red Sea. In these mountains are the quarries that were hewn out for the making of the pyramids at Memphis. This way then the mountains turn and end in the places of which I have spoken; their greatest breadth from east to west, as I learnt, is a two months' journey, and their easternmost boundaries yield frankincense. Such are these mountains.[53]

> Now in the *arabíē khōrē* (Arabian land), not far from Egypt, there is a gulf of the sea entering it from the sea called Red, of which the length and narrowness are such as I shall show: for length, it is a forty days' voyage for a ship rowed by oars from its inner end out to the wide sea; and for the breadth, it is half a day's voyage at the widest.[54]

> When the Nile is in flood, it overflows not only the Delta but also the lands

called *libykós* and *arábios*, in places as far as two days' journey from either bank.[55]

In the reign of Psammetichus there were garrisons posted at Elephantine on the side of Ethiopia, at Daphnae of Pelusium on the side of Arabia and Assyria and at Marea on the side of Libya.[56]

[The Canal between the Nile and the Red Sea] is fed by the Nile and is carried from a little above Bubastis by the Arabian town of Patoumos (Pithom); it issues into the Red Sea (sic!). The beginning of the digging was in the part of the Egyptian plain which is nearest to Arabia; the mountains that extend to Memphis, in which mountains are the stone quarries, come close to this plain.[57]

According to this view, Arabia stretched to the eastern shore of the Nile, and Libya began on the opposite shore. Egypt was only the delta, 'the place to which the Greeks sail'.[58] Also this points to an Oriental origin: as we have seen, there is evidence that during the centuries preceding the Persian conquest, the term Miṣir/Muṣur/Miṣrayim was limited to the delta.[59]

Hecataeus' successors

Hecataeus' idea that Arabia belonged to the countries at the extremes of the inhabited world was, most probably, due to Scylax, who had circumnavigated the peninsula. It was accepted in the Greek world. It is referred to by at least two of the dramatic poets from the fifth century BC. Thus in *Prometheus Bound*, all the lands of the world are said to bemoan the hero's fate:

And the flower of Arabia in arms that holdeth
high-cragged citadel near by Caucasus
a hostile host that roareth in the medley of
sharp pointed spears.[60]

In the first scene of Euripides' *Bacchae*, Dionysus tells about his wanderings around the world:

By Bactrian stronghold, Media's storm-swept land,
still pressing on, by Arabia the Blest,
and through all Asia.[61]

The geography in *Prometheus Bound* is admittedly awkward and the poetic function of Arabia there is to indicate the farthest possible end of the world, thus in a way agreeing with the Hecataeus/Scylax view. The very term 'Arabia the Blest', *Arabía eudáimōn, Arabia felix*, a term which we now meet for the first time, clearly points to Scylax as the ultimate source. It is, however, worth remarking that Euripides also seems to locate Arabia in the east: it stands in an enumeration of countries from Bactria to Asia Minor.

The extension of Arabia to the eastern Nilotic shore was a concept that was also widely accepted. From the fifth century BC is preserved a fragment of a commentary by Hellanicus, a compatriot of Hecataeus, to a verse in the *Odyssey* where Menelaos tells Telemachus about his journeys.[62]

> Then to Aethiopia, to the Sidonians, *eremboí*, and then to Libya's coast.[63]

There were several suggestions for the identification of *eremboí,* one of which is ascribed to Hellanicus:

> He [Hellanicus] says that the *eremboí* live along the stream of the Nile; they come from *Araps*, the king of Babylon. It is said that the *eremboí* are the *árabes*.[64]

This identification is most doubtful but it shows the common concept of *árabes* as living east of the Nile.[65] The question is: what is the reality behind this extension of Arabia to the Nile in Hecataeus' time? Is it just a construction by the Ionian geographer, or does it represent political or ethnic realities? We have to take the other testimonies from the fifth century BC into account before attempting an explanation.

Herodotus of Halicarnassus

In the middle of the fifth century, Herodotus, the father of history, visited Egypt and travelled, probably by ship, from Pelusium to Tyre. From there he proceeded to Babylonia.[66] Herodotus' reports of Arabia have a variegated background. Some are, as we have seen, dependent upon Hecataeus, other details are probably taken directly from Scylax's Periplus. Some may even come from Persian sources. We further find several notes and one long passage dealing with Arabia and its inhabitants with contents obviously gathered by Herodotus himself during his travels. This information is derived from his own observations and stories told by locals.

Herodotus explicitly states his disagreement with the Hecataean world-view:

> We put the Ionians' opinion aside and our own judgement is this: Egypt is all that country which is inhabited by Egyptians, even as Cilicia and Assyria are the countries inhabited by Cilicians and Assyrians severally, and we know of no frontier (rightly so called) below Asia and Libya save only the borders of the Egyptians.[67]

The disagreement is built on personal experience. It is supported with notes on Arabia stemming from Herodotus' own journey from Pelusium to Tyre. The journey was probably undertaken by ship, since it is clear that Herodotus has not seen Ashqelon.[68] First, one note correcting Hecataeus' description of the southern *aktē*:

> For the seaboard of Arabia is inhabited by Syrians.[69]

Thus, there are more than three nations inhabiting the southern Asian peninsula.[70] This is also said as a commentary inserted into Hecataeus' description of the southern *aktē*.

> this *aktē* ends, yet not truly but only by common consent, at the Arabian Gulf

> [the Red Sea and the Gulf of Suez] whereunto Darius brought a canal from the Nile. Now from the Persian country to Phoenice there is a wide and great tract of land; and from Phoenice this *aktē* runs beside our sea by the way of the Syrian Palestine and Egypt, which is at the end of it . . .[71]

The mention of Phoenicia, Syrian Palestine and the Syrians seems to be Herodotus' own commentary, thus indicating more than three peoples on the *aktē*. The passage about the land between Persia and Phoenicia and the extent of the Palestinian coast must come from Herodotus himself, who knew the Levantine coast from autopsy, and not from Hecataeus.[72] He has tried to adapt his own knowledge of the area to the abstract scheme of Hecataeus, a strategy found in other parts of his work as well. It is also likely that by 'common consent' is meant Herodotus' own concept: from his comments about the geography of Egypt we know that he thought Arabia to end at the Red Sea.

In connection with the story of Cambyses' invasion, Herodotus gives some more details about the coast:

> The road [to Egypt] runs from Phoenice as far as the borders of the city Cadytis, which belongs to the Syrians of Palestine. From Cadytis, which, as I judge, is a city not much smaller than Sardis, to the city of Ienysus, the seaports belong to the *arábioi*; then they are Syrian again from Ienysus as far as the Sirbonian marsh, beside which the Casian promontory stretches towards the sea. From this Sirbonian marsh, where Typho is said to be hidden, from there is already Egypt. Between the city of Ienysus and Mount Casius and the Sirbonian marshes, there is quite a large territory, for as much as three days' journey, terribly waterless.[73]

Cadytis is present-day Gaza. Ienysus has been identified with present-day Khān Yūnis, south-west of Gaza.[74] Thus a short stretch of the coast was by the consent of the Persians in the hands of the *arábioi*.

From these pieces of information about the extent and borders of Arabia it is evident that the *arábioi* must have had a strategic key position, since Egypt was ruled by the Persians. This must reflect a very cordial relationship between the *arábioi* and the Achaemenids.

To this strategic privilege was added another one. Herodotus presents a document which, at first glance, looks very similar to the *dahyāva* lists of the Achaemenid kings, namely a list of tribute-paying entities in the Persian empire.

This list, which is one of the most discussed historical texts dealing with the ancient Middle East, raises many problems which cannot be solved here. The list contains sixty-four names of peoples plus two purely geographical designations.[75] Three peoples also have their capitals mentioned: Susa (the Cissians), Babylon (the Assyrians) and Ecbatana (the Medes). Among these names most of those mentioned in the Achaemenid inscriptions can be found, although there are some remarkable gaps. Thus Arachosia is not found in Herodotus' list and, most important for this study, the *arabāya* are absent. On the other hand, the Indians are mentioned as well as the central Asian *Sákai* (= *sakā hōmavargā*) and the Balkan Scythians (*orthokorybántioi* = *sakā tigraxoḍā*). Further, the South Russian Scythians (*sakā paradaryā*) are absent as are the Thracians (*Skudra*). Herodotus' list thus stands closer to DB and DPe than to DNa and the Susa inscriptions.[76]

Herodotus arranges these names into twenyy groups. This, he declares, was the work of Darius himself:

> He established twenty *arkhaí* which they call *satrapēíai*. Having thus established the *arkhaí* and appointed governors (*árkhontes*) he imposed taxes (*phóroi*) to be brought to him from the peoples (*éthnea*) uniting to these peoples those who were close neighbours.[77]

As can immediately be seen, the terminology is problematic. Later, when Herodotus starts to enumerate the twenty units, he calls them *nomoí*. The word 'satrapy' does not have any equivalent in Persian and is obviously a Greek derivation.[78] In the Old Persian lists, satraps (*xšačapāvā*) are mentioned only as rulers of Bactria and Arachosia. The latter is absent from Herodotus' list, and Bactria is coupled with the *aigloí*, forming *nomós*/*arkhē* no. XII. Herodotus' list has a clear Ionian perspective: the enumeration starts with the inhabitants of western Asia Minor going down to Egypt via the Levant (*nomoí*/*arkhaí* nos. I–VI). The lists of the Achaemenids all start with the homeland Parsā, which is absent altogether in Herodotus. It has been shown that Herodotus' nos. I–VI and VIII–IX in fact fairly well correspond to the western provinces of the empire, whereas nos. X–XV are ethnic groups some of which belonged to the same province.[79]

The list is obviously derived from a local, Ionian enumeration of units of the Persian empire, perhaps originating in the archives at Sardis.[80] As we have it in Herodotus, it is a confusion of entities, mostly in the western parts of the empire, ruled by satraps, and an enumeration of the host of peoples under the authority of the King of Kings. It cannot be taken as a survey of the administration of the Persian empire at any period. There are, however, features in it that might indicate that it was derived from a list similar to those in DB and DPe.[81]

It is most likely that Herodotus himself has tampered with a document he had at his disposal. The number twenty could have had some symbolic significance already in the original source. Methodologically, the starting point must be the primary sources, i.e. the Achaemenid lists. From these we learn that the basic units in the empire were the *dahyāva*, at least some of which had a satrap over them. From evidence from the latter half of the fifth century it is clear that the satrap could have authority over several of the *dahyāva* mentioned in the lists. Thus, Tissaphernes was satrap over Lydia, Ionia and Caria, of which at least the former two are mentioned as separate *dahyāva* in the lists (Sparda, Yōnā). The son of Darius II, Cyrus, was made satrap over Lydia, Phrygia and Cappadocia when Tissaphernes was deposed in 408 BC.[82] Also Cappadocia is a separate *dahyāuš* in the lists (Katpatuka). The satrap was a kind of viceroy and his office need not have been limited by the ethnic structure of the empire. He could be in charge of one or more *dahyāva* according to the needs of the central administration. This also means that there might even have been *dahyāva* which did not always stand under the authority of a satrap. The picture given by Herodotus is basically correct in that the division into *éthnea*/*dahyāva* was independent of the satrapy system, even though it is uncertain whether he can be trusted in all details. The former were the peoples acknowledging the supremacy of the Achaemenid king; the latter was a device for tax gathering and military administration.[83]

In the list of the tribute-paying *nomoí*/*arkhaí* of Darius, the description of nomós no. V runs as follows:

> Beginning from the town Posideion, which Amphilokhos son of Amphiaros founded on the border between the Cilicians and the Syrians, from this town to Egypt except the part of the *arábioi*, for that was taxfree (*ateléa*), the *phóros* was three hundred and fifty [talents]. In this *nomós* were all Phoenice, entire Syria called the Palestinian, and Cyprus.[84]

Thus the *arábioi* not only occupied a unique strategic position in the empire; they also enjoyed freedom from taxes. This sensational privilege was otherwise given only to the Persians themselves according to our Ionian author. In a commentary at the end of this list, we get a somewhat different picture of the position of the *arábioi*:

> The Persian country is the only one which I have not recorded as tributary; for the Persians dwell free from all taxes (*ateléa*). As for those on whom no tribute (*phóros*) was laid, but who rendered gifts (*dōra*) instead, they were firstly the Ethiopians . . . Gifts were also required from the Colchians . . . [the] *arábioi* rendered a thousand talents' weight of frankincense yearly. Such were the gifts of these peoples to the king, in addition to the tribute.[85]

If the 'gift', i.e. the tribute paid by the *arábioi*, really amounted to 1,000 talents of frankincense (*c*. 30 tons) per year, as Herodotus claims, the dimensions of the trade can be imagined. It might indeed be doubted whether the *arábioi* had a more lenient regime than the *phóros*-payers. The impression is rather that they were under strict orders to bring voluntary gifts. On the other hand, they must have had a dominant position in the frankincense trade if a gift of such dimensions could be imposed on them.[86]

The reason for the special position of the *arábioi* stems from the time of Darius:

> So Darius son of Hystaspes was made king, and the whole of Asia, which Cyrus first and Cambyses after him had subdued, was made subject to him. But the *arábioi* did not yield the obedience of slaves to the Persians, but became allies (*xeînoi*), having given Cambyses passage into Egypt, which the Persians could not enter without the consent of the *arábioi*.[87]

This picture of Arabs as equals of the Persians also appears in Herodotus' legendary account of Sennacherib's conquest of Egypt. This ruler is said to have been king of Assyrians and Arabs. Both reports obviously come from an Egyptian source. In later Egyptian tradition, Cambyses is seen as a ruthless and cruel ruler, a judgement transmitted already by Herodotus himself in the story of the king.[88] It cannot be excluded that the position of the Arabs here on the same level as the Persians themselves is exaggerated, a concept which is transferred to the legends about Sennacherib as well. It definitely represents Egyptians' perspective, expressing a certain negative attitude towards their guardians to the north-east. One should also keep in mind that Egypt herself had revolted against Darius during the first years of his reign.[89] We have seen that the Arabs probably supported Darius during his struggle for the throne, which may be reflected in their appearance as a *dahyāuš* in the lists. It is further worth noticing that the Egyptians are absent from the units of Xerxes' army at Doriscus, in which we find both Arabs and Ethiopians, two of the peripheral peoples outside the taxation system described by Herodotus. It is not impossible that we have an explanation for the special position of the Arabs: they were guardians of the Egyptians. It is tempting to assume that the Ethiopians also had a similar role. Herodotus, in fact, says explicitly that Cambyses offered the status of *xeînoi* to the Ethiopians, i.e. the Nubians.[90] Unfortunately not much is known about the relations between Persians and Nubians. We know, however, that Cambyses failed to conquer Nubia and that Nubia remained independent during the Achaemenid period.[91] In spite of this, the Nubians appear together with the *arabāya* among the *dahyāva* hailing Darius as world ruler in the Naqsh-e-Rustam inscription. Had they assisted Darius in crushing the Egyptian insurrection, just as the Arabs had supported his operations in Babylonia? We do not know for sure, but the special position in the Achaemenid empire of the two *dahyāva* controlling the two entrances to Egypt looks quite sensible from a Persian viewpoint. This may also explain the Arab presence in the eastern Nile Delta. This is where Darius' canal between the Nile and the Red Sea was built, and one of the tasks of the Arabs may have been to act as guardians of this important waterway. We would thus suggest that the Arabs, together with the Nubians, were employed by the Achaemenids as border guards against Egypt. This would have been an extension of a function they performed already under the Assyrians.

The story about the *pístis* of the *arábioi* with Cambyses gave Herodotus the opportunity for the following digression:

> There are no men who respect a covenant (*pístis*) more than the *arábioi*. They make them in the following way: another man stands between the two parties that want to make a covenant, and he cuts with a sharp stone the palms of the hands of those who make the covenant, by the thumb; then he takes a wisp from the cloak of each and smears with blood seven stones that lie between them, calling the while on Dionysus and the Heavenly [goddess]; and when he has fully done this, he who has made the covenant entrusts to the friends (*phíloi*) the stranger (*xeînos*) or the countryman/townsman (*astós*) if it is done with such a one. The friends hold themselves bound to honour the covenant. They consider only Dionysus and the Heavenly [goddess] as gods, and they say that the cropping of their hair is like the cropping of the hair of Dionysus, cutting it round the head and shaving their temples. They call Dionysus *Orotalt*; and the Heavenly [goddess] *Alilat*.[92]

Herodotus repeats his remark about the gods of the *arábioi* in connection with his report about Cyrus the Great:

> They [the Persians] have learnt later to sacrifice to the Heavenly [goddess], from the Assyrians and *arábioi*. The Assyrians call Aphrodite *Mylitta*, the *arábioi* [call her] *Alilat*, and the Persians *Mitra*.[93]

The ceremony described is not so easy to interpret, since the exact meanings of Herodotus' terms *pístis*, *xeînos*, *astós* and *phíloi* are not clear. The impression is that we have to do with exact legal terminology and not the general meaning of these words. It seems clear that *pístis* in Herodotus means 'treaty', 'covenant made by exchange of assurances and oaths'. *xeînos* is a designation for persons or states not belonging to a community but bound to it by a treaty or an obligation. *Phíloi* would be 'clansmen', 'members of a juridically defined community'. *astós* is a member of an *ásty*, a town, and is often opposed to *xeînos*. It seems reasonable to interpret the ceremony described as the admission of an individual *xeînos* or an *astós* into the fellowship with the *phíloi* who are identical with the *arábioi*.[94] We have evidence that a blood-rite as described by Herodotus with no sacrificial animal involved was sporadically performed in Arabia even much later.[95] It is also most likely that the mention of the two gods in connection with the description of the ritual is not fortuitious. One of them is identified with the Persian Mitra, who is the guardian of covenants. The cropping of the hair was perhaps performed when someone entered this kind of covenant. Remarkable also is the denial of other gods than the two mentioned. It sounds similar to the much later monotheistic formulas.

The description of the *pístis* ceremony among the *arábioi* is a most valuable document and originates from trustworthy informants. We shall return to it later on when discussing the question of what the *ʕarab* actually were.[96]

On the whole, the picture of the *arábioi* given in the Cambyses episode fits well into the picture of them in Xerxes' army as well as with the earlier evidence from Assyrian times. The report about their involvement in the frankincense trade is a new feature not encountered earlier. Herodotus mentions frankincense in connection with *arábioi* also in another context:

> Whenever a Babylonian has had intercourse with his wife, they both sit before a burnt offering of incense (*thymímēma*), and at dawn they wash themselves; they will touch no vessel before this is done. This is the custom also in Arabia.[97]

The note on the frankincense gift of the *arábioi* to the Persian king leads to a larger digression about Arabia, which is one of the more entertaining passages in the *Historíē* and in which the connection between *arábioi* and perfumes is treated:

> Again, Arabia is the most distant to the south of all inhabited countries: and it is the only country that yields frankincense and myrrh and cassia and cinnamon and gum-mastic. All these but myrrh are difficult for the *arábioi* to get. They gather frankincense by burning that storax which Phoenicians carry to Hellas; this they burn and so get the frankincense; for the spice-bearing trees are guarded by small winged snakes of varied colour, many around each tree; these are the snakes that attack Egypt.[98]

Then follow descriptions of how frankincense (*libanōtós*), cassia, cinnamon and gum-mastic are gathered by the *arábioi*, sometimes with quite remarkable methods. Finally the fat-tailed sheep of the *arábioi* are described in terms worthy of Odysseus.[99]

The full story about the winged serpents hinted at in the Arabian *lógos* is found in the description of Egypt:

> Not far from the town of Buto, there is a place of Arabia to which I went to learn about the winged serpents. When I came thither, I saw innumerable bones and backbones of serpents; many heaps of backbones there were, great and small and smaller still. This place, where lay the backbones scattered, is where a narrow mountain pass opens into a great plain, which is joined to the plain of Egypt. Winged serpents are said to fly at the beginning of spring from Arabia, making for Egypt; but the ibis birds encounter the invaders in this pass and kill

> them. The *arábioi* say that this ibis is greatly honoured by the Egyptians for this service.[100]

One of Herodotus' most famous stories belongs to this layer in his work:

> Another bird is also sacred; it is called *phoínix*. I myself have never seen it, but only pictures of it; for the bird comes but seldom to Egypt, once in five hundred years, as the people of Heliopolis say . . . He comes, they [the Egyptians] say, from Arabia bringing his father to the Sun's temple enclosed in myrrh, and there buries him.[101]

These stories are of variegated origin and full of unrealistic and folktale-like features, and thus quite different from those dealing with geographical and political matters. This Arabia is a distant legendary country where everything is possible. The first passage seems to have a vague reference to South Arabia, which may indicate an origin in Scylax. The two others deal with Arabia east of Egypt and are explicitly from Herodotus himself. A concrete feature is the association between Arabia and myrrh and frankincense. This does not mean that we have to go to the peninsula itself, since myrrh is found also on the western shores of the Red Sea. It does show that there were vague ideas about a distant myrrh- and frankincense-producing Arabia, which, in fact, could include Eritrea and Somaliland. Arabia is thus a designation for the areas on both sides of the Red Sea, thus reminiscent of Hecataeus. At the same time they have the flavour of popular tales, stemming from sailors, Egyptian caravaneers or dragomans.[102]

As is apparent, Herodotus is operating with two different Arabias. The first one is situated between the eastern Nile Delta and Palestine. He does not give any concrete limits to the south or south-east. This Arabia was obviously a political entity governed by a king who was an ally of the Achaemenid empire and who ruled an area around the town of Cadytis (= Gaza) as a trade station for frankincense. This Arabia Herodotus knew from personal experience. The other Arabia is a vaguely defined vast area stretching far south on both sides of the Red Sea probably down to the Indian Ocean. This Arabia included the myrrh- and frankincense-producing areas, i.e. South Arabia, Eritrea and Somaliland. The information about this Arabia comes from the voyage undertaken by Scylax of Caryanda and, probably, also from Egyptians. In connection with these passages we see that Herodotus disagrees with Hecataeus and considers Ethiopia, i.e. the lands beyond the first cataract, as the farthest. This reveals an Egyptian perspective, which is that of Herodotus.[103]

The information given by Herodotus on Arabia is of great importance for the following history. We note that from now on Arabia is a geographical designation, a name of a territory. Earlier, *ʕarab* is basically a designation for groups of people. The creation of the geographical name Arabia is the work of the Greeks. It is also the work of outsiders. Until this day, Arabia has never existed as a term among the peoples of the Middle East and in their languages. It is also clear that the application of it to the large areas around the Red Sea, and later to the peninsula, is made by scientists, in this case the Greek geographers starting with Hecataeus. Hence it is an academic term which originally had no meaning for those living in the Arabia of the schoolmasters and was probably even unknown to them. There is no indication whatsoever that all the inhabitants of the peninsula considered themselves Arabs.[104] The 'academic' Arabia was, however, used amply by Greeks and others down the ages as a designation for the peninsula, and the inhabitants were consequently called Arabs; but it is important to bear in mind that this was a theoretical construction by outsiders, especially when studying the Greek sources for the history of the area. It remains to be seen which of the groups actually living there were called Arabs by themselves and by others close to them and what it meant.

Geshem the Arab

Hecataeus mentioned a place called Pathoumos as a town in Arabia. It may be identical to present-day Tell al-Maskhūṭa in the eastern Nile Delta, from which are preserved some spectacular silver bowls.[105] On one of them we find an inscription in Aramaic which leads us closer to the identity of the *arabāya/arábioi*:

> That which QYNW son of GŠM king of QDR offered to HN-ʔLT.[106]

The bowls have been dated to the latter half of the fifth century BC.[107] The inscription shows that there was a kingdom in Qedar in that period whose ruler offered gifts to the goddess worshipped in Pithom, i.e. in the land attributed to Arabia by Hecataeus. That Qedar mentioned in the Tell al-Maskhūṭa bowl were actually called Arabs as well is clear from the passages in the book of Nehemiah describing the unrest among Israel's neighbours when Nehemiah rebuilt the walls of Jerusalem:

> But when Sanballat the Horonite, and Tobiah the servant the Ammonite, and Geshem the *ʕarbî*, heard it, they laughed us to scorn and despised us.[108]

> And it came to pass that when Sanballat, and Tobiah, and the *ʕarbîm*, and the Ammonites, and the Ashdodites heard that the walls of Jerusalem were made up, and that the breaches began to be stopped, then they were very wroth.[109]

> Now it came to pass, when Sanballat, and Tobiah, and Geshem the *ʕarbî*, and the rest of our enemies, heard that I had built the wall, and that there was no breach left therein . . . that Sanballat and Geshem sent unto me saying, come let us meet together . . . Then sent Sanballat his servant unto me in the like manner the fifth time with an open letter in his hand wherein it was written: It is reported among the heathen and Gashmû saith it that thou and the Jews think to rebel.[110]

Most scholars agree that these events took place in 445 BC.[111] The story comes from Nehemiah's own report, which was written a decade or two afterwards and must be considered a good historical source. The opposition to the restoration of the walls of Jerusalem came from Judah's northern neighbours in Samaria where Sanballat was governor, from Transjordan, and from the south where Geshem the *ʕarbî* obviously dwelt.[112] The reason was probably not the building activities as such but rather the establishment of a separate entity in Judaea which could be a threat to those already existing.

It has long been assumed that the Geshem mentioned in Nehemiah is identical with the father of Qaynu who donated the bowl in Tell al-Maskhūṭa.[113] This seems very plausible and in fact gives us a means of determining the extent of the area of the *arábioi*. It is striking that the Edomites are not mentioned by Nehemiah. Since they were the immediate neighbours of Judaea in the south, it can be assumed that they were subjects of the Arabian king. In that case, the kingdom stretched from the eastern Nile Delta to southern Judaea. Since eastern Egypt and some cities in the eastern delta are said already by Hecataeus to be in Arabia, this extent of the Arabian kingdom was probably already established in the sixth century BC, probably in connection with the Persian conquest. Further, we learn from this that the Arabia of Hecataeus and his successor, Herodotus, was in fact the land of Qedar or at least was governed by rulers from Qedar, whose influence obviously stretched unto the shores of the Nile.[114] This was remembered long after the disappearance of Geshem. When Genesis was translated into Greek in the third century BC, the passage about how the sons of Jacob settled in the land of Goshen was rendered:

> and they settled in the land of Gesem of Arabia.[115]

The land of Goshen was in fact the area around the town of Patoumos, and the passage in the Septuagint is a strong indication that the GŠM in the bowl inscription is identical with the one mentioned by Nehemiah.

Greeks and Arabs from the end of the fifth century BC until Alexander

In the period after Herodotus and Nehemiah until the time of Alexander we have three instances where this Arabian kingdom is explicitly documented. One of them originates from the history book of Ephorus, which is lost but which was used by Diodorus Siculus for the history of Greece down to 355 BC.[116] The passage should be read together with the list of arkhonts in the Persian empire attached to Xenophon's *Anabasis*. For the interpretation of them, a short survey of the political conditions is necessary.

Since *c*. 530 BC Cyprus had been under Persian rule. During the Persian wars one of the ambitions of Athens was the liberation of the island. The attacks were as a rule thwarted by the Persians by the use of the Phoenician fleet. The Phoenician towns seem generally to have been loyal to the King of Kings and their influence in Cyprus increased until the establishment of a Tyrian king in Kition in 448 BC. After the Athenian *débâcle* in Syracuse in 413 BC, Persia joined Sparta in the struggle against Athens, supported by the exiled Athenian rake and politician Alcibiades, who was a bosom friend of the satrap of Phrygia, Pharnabazus. Alcibiades was, however, not interested in Sparta and the Persians becoming too strong against Athens, since he never gave up the ambition of returning to his home town and resuming his career there. When the Athenian fleet pursued the Spartan one in the Dardanelles in 410, Alcibiades according to Diodorus/Ephorus ensured that Pharnabazus withheld 300 Phoenician ships from the battle:

> He [Pharnabazus] explained to them [the Spartans] that he had done so on receiving information that the king of the *árabes* and the king of the Egyptians had designs upon Phoenicia.[117]

Even though this is described as being the result of a trick by Alcibiades, it fits into a larger pattern and it can, in fact, be doubted if Alcibiades really had the influence ascribed to him by Ephorus. It is very likely that there was a real threat against Phoenicia from Egypt which, probably at this time, had revolted against the Achaemenid rule and established the twenty-eighth dynasty.[118] Since Phoenicia had been the instrument used by the satraps in Asia Minor against Athens, it stands to reason that Athens was also interested in pacifying its dangerous fleet. With this go other events. In the same year, 410 BC, the Phoenician rule on Cyprus was overthrown by Euagoras, who established himself at Salamis and who was definitely the man of Athens. Since a king of the *árabes* is mentioned, it is most likely that one of the dynasty of Geshem the Arab is intended.

The notice thus gives us a glimpse of an axis of common interests between Athens, Cyprus, Arabia and Egypt against the Persian empire and its ally at this time, namely Sparta.[119] During the reign of Darius II (424–404 BC) it is obvious that the rule of the Achaemenids in the eastern Mediterranean was shaken, which is also reflected in the very independent activities of the two satraps in Asia Minor, Tiribazes and Pharnabazus. These troubles culminated in the attempt by Cyrus the younger to overthrow his brother Artaxerxes II in 401 BC, immortalized by Xenophon in his account of the expedition of the Ten Thousand. Many years later Xenophon wrote the account of the great adventure of his youth when he travelled through central Mesopotamia in the long, hot summer of 401 BC together with the army of Cyrus, son of Darius II, during the latter's attempt to seize power in the Persian realm:

> Thence [from Thapsacus where the Euphrates was crossed] he [Cyrus] marched through Syria nine stages, fifty parasangs, and they arrived at the Araxes river (i.e. the Khābūr) . . . Thence they marched through Arabia, keeping the Euphrates on the right, five stages through desert country, thirty-five parasangs . . . Marching on through this region they arrived at the Mascas river, which is a plethrum in width. There in the desert was a large city named Corsote, completely surrounded by the Mascas . . . Thence Cyrus marched thirteen stages through the desert country, ninety parasangs, keeping the Euphrates river on the right and arrived at Pylae.[120]

The vividness and concretion of the description reveals the personal experience behind it. There is no reason to doubt the correctness of the description. This Arabia is in Mesopotamia, i.e. between the two rivers.[121] It also seems clear that Arabia did not belong to Syria and that the border ran along the Khābūr river. The south-eastern border of Arabia was at the city of Pylae, which was close to present-day al-Hīt. We have observed that already in Assyrian times there is ample evidence for the presence of Arabs in central Mesopotamia, who later played a role in the campaigns of Cyrus the Great. These Mesopotamian Arabs do not have any documented connections with those between Palestine and Egypt, and there is no evidence that they stood under the same administration.

From this period date the silver bowls from the sanctuary in Tell al-Maskhūṭa, which are an eloquent testimony of the wealth of the king of the *arábioi*. The fact that the main goddess of the Arabs was worshipped in a temple on the main road between the Gulf of Suez and the delta shows that they must have had a substantial influence also in Egypt itself. This is supported by the rise of the successors to Amyrtaeus as rulers of Egypt, the so-called twenty-ninth dynasty, probably in 399 BC. The third ruler is in

Greek called Akhoris, in Egyptian HKR/HGR, reigning 393–380 BC. This king pursued a policy of alliance with Cyprus and Athens against Persia, Phoenicia and Sparta. Important is that the same name is used as the designation for the area called Arabia by Herodotus.[122] In an indigenous Egyptian source, the myth about the Eye of the Sun, it is said about the sun-goddess:

> Her living is among the HGR birds
> her food is in the land of ʕR[B . . .][123]

The text is preserved in a demotic version from the Roman period but its contents and terminology are much earlier and it shows clearly an identification between Arabia and Hagar which we also find in the Achaemenid period.[124] Akhoris came from the town of Mendes in the centre of the delta. Was he in fact an Arab? His name seems to be an ethnic rather than a personal name.[125]

We are, of course, also immediately reminded of Hagar, the name of Ishmael's mother in the three stories in Genesis about his birth. The existence of a group called *hagrîm* in northern Transjordan cannot be doubted. It also seems that Ishmael is a patriarch who originally belonged to the same area. We have already pointed out that the name Ishmael is very loosely connected with the J and E stories, and that the patriarch does not originally have anything to do with the Negev. Hagar occurs in both stories as well as her epithet 'Egyptian' (*miṣrît*). The bowman in the Paran desert, Hagar's son, has a wife from Miṣrayim. If Hagar is the designation for some kind of institution, an asylum or some kind of protection, it seems evident that there were 'Hagarites', even 'Egyptian Hagarites', also in the wilderness south of Palestine. The story told about Ishmael in the north, calqued on the old myth about the encounter with the divinity and the protective circumcision undertaken by his mother/bride, was also known in the south. Deliverance stories belonged to the figure of the patriarch. The story about the bowman in the south may not have been about a patriarch from the beginning but has, in the Biblical tradition, been integrated into this genre.

It is thus likely that the Hagar concept was somehow connected with the 'Arabs' between Egypt and Palestine. This does not necessarily mean that the Hagarites there were connected or identical with those in northern Transjordan. As we shall see, there were several 'Hagars' in later periods and it might well have been the same case in this one. What is clear is that the Biblical writers thought them to be related and made all the tribes from Ḥawrān to the eastern delta sons of Ishmael. This picture is undoubtedly conceived in the period treated here, i.e. the fifth to the fourth centuries BC, and documented in the list of Ishmael's sons.

The narratives about Ishmael and his mother Hagar are thus Israelite literary creations. The question remains whether the concept of all the sons of Ishmael, i.e. tribes in north-western Arabia, as one unit reflects any political reality in our period. The identification of the river Korys in Herodotus' report about Cambyses as one of those in Transjordan would be an argument in favour. Unfortunately, the identification is most uncertain. More concrete are the definite testimonies of Achaemenid influence and even administration in Transjordan and as far south as Taymāʔ and Dedan.[126] It is, however, difficult to grasp the exact nature of Persian presence in north-western Arabia.[127] We have some kind of governor mentioned for Dedan in an inscription together with a name GŠM BN ŠHR 'in whose days' (B-ʔYM) the inscription was made.[128] If GŠM is identical with Geshem in the time of Nehemiah, we would have evidence for a governor in Dedan in that time. It is, however, not certain that the governor is an Achaemenid one. The identification of the two GŠM is not certain either, and the dating of the inscription remains somewhat unsettled.[129] The Aramaic inscriptions found in Taymāʔ probably also belong to this period and reveal close contacts with the settled countries in the north.[130]

Given this evidence, it is not impossible that the Israelite historians, by the 'land from Ḥawilah to Shur, even to Asshur', had the *dahyāuš* of the *arabāya* in mind. Into this framework they put a selection of names and places known to be located there in order to reach the magic number twelve and made all sons of Ishmael. As we have noted, there are signs in the list that names have been added successively to an original number of three.

During the fifth century BC, the Arabs between Egypt and Palestine emerged as supervisors of the frankincense trade, a role which is clearly documented already in the middle of the century by Herodotus. This role was due to their presence on the Suez isthmus and in eastern Egypt, which perhaps stretched into Transjordan. They would thus have had complete control over the end-stations of both the overland route and the sea route from South Arabia. A most interesting testimony of the role of the Arabs in western Arabia is the mention of a ʕRBYT BN QDR, 'an Arabian [woman] from Qedar', in a South Arabian inscription originating in the South Arabian kingdom of Maʕīn in present-day al-Ğawf in Yemen, probably to be dated to the fourth century BC.[131] The name is of considerable interest for our theme. It shows the relationship between Qedar and the Arabs but also seems to show that the Arabs were perhaps not identical with all Qedar.

Did Qedar/*arabāya*/*arábioi* have their own satrap? There is a notice in Xenophon's *Cyropaedia* where it is said that Cyrus, after his conquest of Babylon, dispatched his men to different parts of the empire. One of them is Megabyzus, who is sent as satrap to Arabia.[132] The satrapies mentioned cannot, however, have existed in Cyrus' time. The note reflects later conditions. We know that one Megabyzus, who took part in Xerxes' campaign in 480, was later appointed satrap of Syria/Athura. It is not impossible that he also had some command over the *arabāya*, although the evidence from the *Cyropaedia* is most untrustworthy. What is certain is that the *arabāya*/*arábioi* had their own king, just like the three Phoenician towns Sidon, Tyre and Arwad. These latter had a satrap over them, as had Egypt at the same time. The privileged position of the *arábioi* in Herodotus may be revealed by the fact that they were not under a satrap.

Sparta, which together with the Persians had defeated Athens in the Peloponnesian war, had supported Cyrus in 401 BC hoping to gain control of the cities in Ionia. When Cyrus failed, Sparta had to face the Persians as enemies now supported by Athens and Euagoras. The alliance had the Phoenician fleet on its side, and Egypt sided with Euagoras in 395. When Sparta was defeated in 394, the anti-Spartan alliance started to break up and Euagoras, Athens and the new Egyptian ruler Achoris continued on their own for a while, until Athens and all the Greek cities made peace with the Persians in the Antalcidas treaty in the year 386 BC. Euagoras, who now controlled Tyre and other cities in Phoenicia, continued the struggle against Persia together with Egypt.

In connection with the preparations for further operations in 386 it is said:

> In addition to these [the allies of Euagoras] not a few soldiers were sent to him by the king of the barbarians and by certain others of whom the Persian king was suspicious.[133]

The text of Diodorus has the word barbarians (*barbárōn*), which by modern editors has been emended to Arabians (*arábōn*). Even though the emendation is good and gives a good meaning to the text, we should be aware that we cannot say for sure if the *árabes* were involved in Euagoras' activities. We do not have more information about the role of these suggested *árabes*, in the subsequent operations that ended in 380 BC with a peace treaty between Egypt, Cyprus and Persia. If Arabia is intended, it is reasonable to assume that these soldiers came from the Arab kingdom between Palestine and Egypt, although, admittedly, we have no definite proof. It is, however, clear that to Ephorus Arabia was this area.

Shortly after Achoris' death in 380, his dynasty fell and a new one came to power. An attempt by the Persians to conquer Egypt failed in 373 BC and was followed by the great insurrection of the satraps, which lasted for more than ten years. The Egyptians under Tachos, now allied with Sparta, attempted an invasion of Persia in 362/361 BC, which ended in failure. Tachos was overthrown by Nectanebo II and fled to Artaxerxes II 'through Arabia'.[134] This must be the Arabia of Geshem.[135]

This Arabia is mentioned in another text from the fourth century as well, namely the description of the entire Mediterranean coast erroneously ascribed to Scylax of Caryanda, compiled after 350 BC, perhaps as late as in the 330s.[136] Unfortunately, the text is badly preserved. After having described the Phoenician and Palestinian coast it says:

> A[rabia. After Syria is the people *árabes*]
> nomads, horsemen [with herds of all kinds of cat-]
> tle, sheep, goa[ts] . . .
> camels. This [region] is [unfertile and deserted]
> and mostly [it lacks water. The western part is towards]
> the Egyptian [region washed by a narrow sea].
> There are [two bays in it: the Aelanite and the Heroonpolitan. Further]
> there is from the sea [called the Red or from the ex-]
> terior sea [Arabia protruding to our ocean] . . .
> . . . of Arabia from the borders of Syria to the mouth of the [Nile which is] at Pelusium (this is the border of Arabia) it is 1200 stadia
> . . . [It is said that] the Egyptian part of Arabia is to the Nile from the [Arabian sea]
> . . . [There are] Egyptian [*árabes*] who give tribute to the Egy[ptians] . . . [who are] always [attacked] by the *árabes*.[137]

The text as found in Müller's edition is, as is evident, heavily restored by conjecture and should be used with caution. It is certain that the name Heroonpolis was not mentioned since this city was founded by Alexander the Great. It is, however, evident that we have to do with a description of the area between the Mediterranean and the Red Sea between Egypt and Palestine. According to the preceding passage about Syria, the last town on the coast belonging to Syria was Ascalon. This implies that Gaza was in the hands of the *árabes*. Compared to Herodotus' description, Arabia now extends beyond Ienysus further westwards to the Egyptian border at Pelusium. The latter part of the text seems to indicate some kind of close connection between the Egyptian king and the *árabes*. As we have seen, this goes nicely with the picture of close common interests between Egypt and the *árabes* during the fourth century BC, which is probably the explanation of the extended Arab control of the coast. In Müller's text we find an identification of Arabs with nomads. But this is the result of Müller's conjecture.[138] Since horsemen (*hippeúontes*) are mentioned, it is far from certain that all the people in Arabia were nomads. Instead, it points towards a rather advanced stage of settled society.

The contacts between Arabia and Greece, which had grown steadily during the Persian period, are also reflected in literary works from the fourth century. The frequent mention of frankincense in Greek literature is one clear indication of this.[139] When the First Delphic Hymn to Apollo describes how 'the Arab smoke (*áraps atmós*) is spread towards Olympus', it is a testimony to the use of incense, probably frankincense imported from Arabia, in the cult at Delphi in the fourth century BC.[140] In Aristotle's *History of Animals*, we find the earliest description of the camel in Greek. The one-humped camel is distinguished from the two-humped Bactrian one, and the mating season is defined as the months October–November.[141] This seems to reflect conditions in South Arabia rather than in the north.[142] In his treatise about meteorology, Aristotle says that the rainy season in Arabia and Ethiopia is in the summer, which also indicates a southern location for Arabia.[143] One could suspect that this piece of information had already been given by Scylax. But it could also originate from people who had met with caravaneers from Yemen in Gaza much later. This information is much more precise than the fantastic stories in Herodotus a century earlier.

Excursus: Arabia in the list of arkhonts in Xenophon's *Anabasis* VII:8

At the end of Xenophon's *Anabasis* we find a list of arkhonts in the Persian empire. It is likely that this list is not from Xenophon, at least not in its present shape, but is added to the text or completed by another hand.[144] It is a problematic text in many respects. First, it is said to list arkhonts who are not identical with satraps, and the question is what is actually the status of these arkhonts. Second, the names are not always identical with known areas and their governors, and not all of them appear in Xenophon's own text. One of these names is Dernes, who is said to have been the arkhont of Phoiníkē and Arabía.[145] This constitutes the third problem. Which Arabia is meant? Among the known names we find Belesys as arkhont of Syria and Assyria and he is also mentioned in Xenophon's account.[146] According to everything we know, Syria, Assyria and Phoinike belonged to the same satrapy, namely the A̱tūra in the royal inscriptions.[147] Its satrap during the Cyrus expedition was Abracomas.[148] Arabia and Phoenicia were thus united under a subordinated governor, whereas the rest was under another. Arabia in this list has been identified with Xenophon's Arabia between the Khābūr and Pylae.[149]

Arabia in the list of arkhonts may, in fact, be two areas: the kingdom between Egypt and Palestine or the area by the Antilebanon, later conquered by Alexander the Great. If the former were intended, it would mean that the Persians had somehow conquered at least parts of the kingdom of Geshem around 400 BC and united them with Phoenicia. There is no evidence for such an assumption. Another possibility is that the Arabo-Phoenician *arkhē* of Dernes did not exist in Xenophon's time but represents later conditions. We also know that a Belesys was ruling Syria around 350 BC.[150] At this time the great rebellion of the satraps had been crushed by Artaxerxes III Ochus. This new ruler also waged a war against rebellious Phoenicia, which ended with the destruction of Sidon. In 350 he then made the first attempt to reconquer Egypt, which failed. Seven years later the Persians were successful and Artaxerxes Ochus emerged as the restorer of the empire of the Achaemenids. A unification of Phoenicia and Arabia in connection with these events seems likely. When Alexander besieged Gaza in 332 BC the town was defended by Persians and *árabes* together, which may show that the town now, unlike in the preceding century, was under Persian military control.[151]

The Arabs in the Antilebanon are mentioned for the first time in sources dealing with Alexander but it is most likely that they had been there for some time.[152] It is told that this encounter took place in connection with the siege of Tyre, and thus after the occupation of Aradus and Sidon. The impression is that the actions of the Persians against the Phoenician towns led to conflicts with these *árabes*, which implies some connection between the latter and the coastal cities.

It is not possible to settle the question of which *árabes* are hiding under the Arabia of the arkhont list, but it seems likely that it reflects a situation in the latter half of the fourth century BC. It is tempting once again to compare with testimonies from the Old Testament. We remember the report about the war of the tribe of Reuben against the *hagrîm*, Yeṭur, Naphis and Nodab.[153] The scene of that war is in the northern Transjordan and areas close to Mount Hermon. Yeṭur and Naphis are counted among the sons of Ishmael, i.e. they are the brothers of Qedar. Hagar is of course the grandmother of them all. We have here another hint of a real link between the tribes around Mount Hermon and the Qedar Arabs in Gaza. Is the link connected with the stratagems of the king of the Arabs against Phoenicia in 410 BC? It would in that case have been natural, when Persian supremacy was restored, to put the Arabs in the hinterland under the control of the governor, who at the same time should keep his thumb in the eye of the Phoenicians. At this time Egypt had liberated itself from Persian rule, and Amyrtaeus had established himself as the twenty-eighth dynasty. Xenophon reports that Artaxerxes was preparing an attack on Egypt when Cyrus' insurrection took place. Arabia in the arkhont list could thus be the Antilebanese Arabs connected with those between Palestine and Egypt.

Notes

1 Cf. Briant, *Histoire* I 895–896; Wolski, *Seleucids* 10, 15–18, 22.
2 Herodotus 3:4.
3 Herodotus 3:7.
4 Herodotus 3:9.
5 Cf. p. 159. Eph' al, *Arabs* 137–142.
6 See p. 284.
7 Briant, *État* 163–164.
8 Kent, *Old Persian* 116–134 (DB), 136–138 (DPe, DNa), 141–142 (DSe), 145 (DSm).
9 Vallat, *Table*.
10 Walzer, *Völkerschaften* 33–36, and Falttafel 1. For the (fragmentary) text, see Kent, *Old Persian* 140–141.
11 Weissbach, *Keilinschriften* 9 ff., 87 ff.; Malbran-Labat, *Version*.
12 DB I:14–15; DSe 25–26; DSm 7; DNa 26–27.
13 DPe 10–11.
14 Yoyotte, *Inscriptions* 256–259.
15 For this word in Egyptian, see Posener, *Achoris*.
16 XPh 25 (= Kent, *Old Persian* 150–152).

17 Walzer, *Völkerschaften* 68 ff.
18 Walzer, *Völkerschaften* 51 ff.
19 For the text, see Kent, *Old Persian* 155–156. For the identification of the owner, see Walzer, *Völkerschaften* 52 with references.
20 Cf. DB I:16 with III:10–21 (Kent, *Old Persian* 56).
21 DB II:58–59.
22 The Greeks got the word not from Old Persian but from another dialect, probably Median or one close to it, seen from the preservation of *tr* which in OP had become *č*, cf. Sanskrit *kṣatriyā*, 'prince' (Kent, *Old Persian* 31). The basis for the Greek form must have sounded **xšatrapā*.
23 Cf. a similar view in Cook, *Rise* 245.
24 Briant, *Histoire* 196–213.
25 This is a correction of the view expressed in Retsö, *Xenophon*, where it was supposed that the *arabāya* in DPe refers to the Arabs in Mesopotamia, whereas the others refer to those between Palestine and Egypt. For this view, see Briant, *État* 168; Eph'al, *Arabs* 202.
26 Cf. Briant, *Histoire* 192, where they belong to his second 'axis', together with Persia and Elam constituting the centre of the empire.
27 Assumed by Högemann, *Alexander* 12–13.
28 DB I:86–87: *uša-barim. uša* (from *uštra*) is the Iranian word for camel, originally designating the two-humped variant and borrowed into Akkadian as a term for that (*udr*[*at*]-). The Akkadian version (§ 17 = Malbran-Labat, *Version* 96, cf. 129) writes the Sumerian ideograms ANŠE.A.AB.BA, 'sea-donkey', which in Akkadian should be read *ibilu* or *gammalu*, not *udru* (cf. von Soden, *Handwörterbuch* s.vv.). The Akkadian version thus supports the assumption that *arabāya* were involved.
29 Herodotus 3.5–9.
30 PFa 17 = Hallock, *Texts* 122. The text is in Elamitic. For the tablets, see Hallock, *Evidence.*
31 Briant, *Histoire* 207–212.
32 Herodotus 7.69, 70.
33 Herodotus 7.69.
34 Herodotus 7.86.
35 Herodotus 7.87.
36 Four hundred years later, Dio Chrysostom (*4th Discourse on Kingship* 45) mentions the *árabes* among the host of Persians, Medes, Scythians and Egyptians who invaded Greece under Xerxes. The *árabes* were thus quite prominent in the army according to Dio. This might, however, reflect the position of the 'Arabs', namely the Arabo-Nabataean kingdom in his day. We notice the mentioning of Egyptians in Dio. They are absent in Herodotus' list. It is, however, possible that Dio by Egyptians intends the Libyans and the Ethiopians = Nubians.
37 Herodotus 4.44.
38 For the fragments, see Jacoby, *Fragmente* 3C:2 587—592 (no. 709). Cf. von Arnim, *Skylax* 625.
39 Hecataeus frgm. 271 (Jacoby, *Fragmente* I 36 = Stephanus of Byzantium, *Ethnika* 351) quoted by Pliny 6.151; cf. von Arnim, *Skylax* 630.
40 Herodotus 2.11; cf. Jacoby, *Fragmente* I 362.
41 Jacoby, *Fragmente* I 281 cf. ibid. 363.
42 DSzc § 3 = Weissbach, *Keilinschriften* 104, 105.
43 Cf. von Radinger, *Hekataios* 2702–2707, 2718–2734.
44 The direct quotations are found in Jacoby, *Fragmente* I 16–47.
45 Hekataeus, Fragment 36 = Herodotus 4.36 (Jacoby, *Fragmente* I 16). Cf. von Radinger, *Hekataios* 2703 ff.; Pearson, *Historians* 31, 86. The main source for the tripartition is Herodotus 2:16; cf. 4: 42, 45 where he ascribes it to the Ionians.
46 von Radinger, *Hekataios* 2704, 2718 f.; cf. Herodotus 2.16, 21, 23; 4:45.
47 For *arábioi*, see Herodotus 3.107, beginning.
48 Herodotus 4.39. For the excluded passage, which is probably Herodotus' own comment, see pp. 243 ff.
49 Cf. Jacoby, *Fragmente* I 362. Potts (*Gulf* II 2) assumes that the Greeks knew about the

Persian Gulf already in the time of Hecataeus. A proof is said to be a passage in Stephanus where Hecataeus is quoted speaking about an island in the *persikòs póntos* (*Ethnika* 396:15). The Peutinger map indeed shows a small bay on the southern shore of the Arabian coast which may be the water referred to by Hecataeus (cf. the description in Pomponius Mela discussed pp. 400 ff). At the same time, it is obvious that this bay does not create an Arabian peninsula.

50 Cf. Jacoby, *Fragmente* I 362.

51 According to Jacoby (*Fragmente* I 362) the map is totally lost. The design of the Middle East, especially Arabia, Palestine and Egypt, on the Peutinger map, however, looks almost as if it is drawn from Herodotus' description and is a good illustration to his text. This map is based on maps from late antiquity but it is tempting to assume that these, in their turn, were late versions of Hecataeus' work. The map drawn by Högemann, *Alexander* 18, is somewhat misleading.

52 Herodotus 2.15, 17.

53 Herodotus 2.8.

54 Herodotus 2.11. The note about the length of the voyage is probably from Scylax.

55 Herodotus 2.19.

56 Herodotus 2.30.

57 Herodotus 2.158.

58 Herodotus 2.5. For this as a quotation from Hecataeus, see Jacoby, *Fragmente* I 367. The view is found also in *Prometheus* 813; cf. Strabo 17.1.22, 30.

59 See p. 195, n. 50.

60 *Prometheus* 420.

61 Euripides, *Bacchae* 15–17.

62 See Jacoby, *Hellanikos*.

63 Odyssey 4.84.

64 Hellanicus frgm. 154a = Jacoby, *Fragmente* I 143; cf. ibid. 469.

65 See Tkač, *Eremboi*. According to him, *eremboí* are to be sought somewhere on the Mediterranean coast (414).

66 Jacoby, *Herodotos* 266–267.

67 Herodotus 2.18.

68 Herodotus 1.105.

69 Herodotus 2.12.

70 One should compare with the gloss in 4:39; see p. 000.

71 Herodotus 4.39.

72 Cf. Jacoby, *Fragmente* I 363. It should be observed that *Palaistínē* in Herodotus, as in all Greek texts down to the time of Hadrian, designates only the coast of later Palestine. It is thus equivalent to Philistaea; cf. pp. 296 f., n. 91.

73 Herodotus 3.5.

74 Mittmann, *Küste* 133–135, instead suggests Khirbet Maʕīn further inland. The toponymic arguments are worth noticing but Herodotus' text (*tà empória tà epí thalássēs*, 'the ports by the sea') seems to indicate a stretch of the coast Gaza-Ienysus as belonging to the *arábioi*. Khirbet Maʕīn is far from the coast.

75 'The inhabitants of the islands in the Red Sea; the Armenians and their neighbours' (3.93).

76 Herodotus has Libya, Cyrenia and Barka. Libya (Pūtiyā) is not mentioned in the two oldest lists but occurs in DNa.

77 Herodotus 3.89.

78 Cf. Herodotus 1:192. Schmitt, *Sprachgut* 2.2.5.

79 Junge, *Satrapie* 36 note 6. Especially noteworthy is *nomós* no. XVI, containing Parthians, Khorasmians, Sogdians and Arians, all of which appear as separate *dahyāva* in the Achaemenid lists. In a similar manner, no. VI contains the equivalents of Mudrāya and Pūtiyāya, no. X Mādā and Sakā tigraxodhā (= the *orthokorybántioi*), no. XIV Asagarta, Zranka and Ūta dahyāva.

80 Briant, *Histoire* I 403.

81 The scholarly debate has been moving to and fro between two differing views: (1)

Herodotus' *nomoí/arkhaí* are equivalent to satrapies and the *dahyāva* in the Old Persian lists which are thus identical (Leuze, *Satrapieeinteilung*; Herzfeldt, *Empire*; Toynbee, *Study* 583f.; (2) the Herodotean entities are satrapies which were a supra-ethnic division of the empire. Consequently, they are not identical with the *dahyāva* (Cameron, *Satrapies*; Junge, *Satrapie* 48–49; Young, *Consolidation* 87; Briant, *Histoire* II 956). Common to everybody is the assumption that both Herodotus and the lists are 'correct', i.e. reflect administrative and ethnic structures in the empire.

82 Xenophon, *Anabasis* 1.1.2.

83 Briant, *Histoire* I 403–404.

84 Herodotus 3.91.

85 Herodotus 3.97.

86 Briant (*Histoire* I 406) suggests that the Arabs paid their gifts directly to the king independently of the satrap over *nomós* V.

87 Herodotus 3.88.

88 Briant, *Histoire* I 70–72.

89 DB II:5–7.

90 Herodotus 3.21.1.

91 Morkot, *Nubia* 326–327; *Fontes* I 329; Briant, *Histoire* I 65–66.

92 Herodotus 3.8.

93 Herodotus 1.131. The Assyrian Mylitta is most likely Ishtar, who is known by the epithet *ummu ālittu*, 'the birth-giving mother' (Tallqvist, *Götterepiteta* 334). This term might be the origin of both Mylitta and Alitta in Herodotus.

94 This was suggested by Robertson Smith, *Religion* 315.

95 See Wellhausen, *Reste* 125–126; Robertson Smith, *Kinship* 56-62.

96 Cf. p. 6080.

97 Herodotus 1.198.

98 Herodotus 3.107.

99 Herodotus 3.108–113.

100 Herodotus 2.75.

101 Herodotus 2.73.

102 For the story of the Phoenix, see van den Broek, *Myth*. The home of the bird varies a lot in the ancient sources and India is often given as its homeland (van den Broek, *Myth* 146–150). But in many sources, especially those dependent on reports from before Alexander's campaigns in the east, India is a vague designation for all countries east and south-east of Babylonia. In one version of the story (Pliny 10.4 quoting from Manilius), the Phoenix comes from Arabia and lands at Panchaea which, as will be shown below (pp. 290–294), is to be identified with Baḥrayn. In the reports by Euhemerus and Iambulus, Panchaea is said to be close to India. This would also mean that the Indian version of the story of the Phoenix is originally associated with Arabia, which means that the origin of the story in some way or another is linked to that region and probably also to the frankincense traffic between Arabia in Egypt and Arabia in the Persian Gulf and South Arabia. One is reminded of the story of Luqmān in Arabic literature where a bird (a *nasr*) is the symbol of regenerating eternal life.

103 Cf. Högemann, *Alexander* 105.

104 As claimed by, for example, Högemann, *Alexander* 20–21.

105 According to Redmount, *Frontier* 294 ff., textual and new archaeological evidence indicates that Pithom was originally a name of a fortress at present-day Tell er-Raṭāba from the time of pharaoh Merneptah (end of the thirteenth century BC). In Saitic times, i.e. shortly before the Persian conquest, the name was transferred to Tell al-Maskhūṭa.

106 Rabinowitz, *Inscriptions*; cf. Dumbrell, *Tell el-Maskhuṭa* 36.

107 Cross, *Geshem*.

108 Nehemiah 2:19.

109 Nehemiah 4:7 (4:1 in MT).

110 Nehemiah 6:1–2, 6.

111 Miller/Hayes, *History* 468–469.

112 Alt, *Nachbarn* [73]–[74].
113 Eph'al, *Arabs*, 210–214; Knauf, *Ismael* 104 f., note 569. It is more uncertain whether he is identical with the Persian governor GŠM, son of SHR, in Dedan in the inscription JS 349. Knauf, *Ismael* 105, accepts the identification; Eph'al, *Arabs*, rejects it. Since GŠM is a rather common Arabic name and since we have no other indications that the Arabian kingdom really extended to Dedan or that Geshem was a Persian governor, caution is recommended.
114 For Qedar in the Persian period, see Knauf, *Ismael* 103–108.
115 Genesis 45:10, cf. 46:34: 'in the land of Gesem, *Arabia*'.
116 Cf. Schwarz, *Ephoros* 1–16; idem, *Diodorus*. In Diodorus, books 11–16 are mainly from Ephorus.
117 Diodorus 13.46. 6.
118 Gardiner, *Egypt* 371–373.
119 For the economic aspects of this axis, see Retsö, *Connection*.
120 Xenophon, *Anabasis* 1.4.19–5.1.
121 For a discussion of this question, see Retsö, *Xenophon*. Cf. also Lendle, *Kommentar* 43–46.
122 Yoyotte, *Inscriptions* (item no. 19) 256–258; Roaf, *Peoples* 135–136. Cf. Posener, *Achoris* 148 (bottom). Knauf, *Administration* 203, identifies it with Hagar in eastern Arabia, present-day al-Hufūf. This is difficult to follow since no arguments are given except, perhaps, the identity of names, and it seems most unlikely.
123 Spiegelberg, *Mythus* III:32 (pp. 16–17).
124 For the dating of the text, see Spiegelberg, *Mythus* 10.
125 Cf. Posener, *Achoris* 149.
126 Graf, *Arabia* 137: the qanāt system in al-ʕŪlā; Knauf, *Administration* 205–207. Knauf's arguments for a Persian administration as far down as Yathrib (*Administration* 210–211), based on an identification of LḤYN HʕLY in the inscription TA 20 with a Liḥyān in Hudhayl, documented much later in Arabo-iskamic sources, remains somewhat unlikely.
127 Cf. Edens/Bawden, *History* 67 note 64.
128 JS Lih 349: PḤT DDN.
129 For arguments for a dating of the text to *c.* 450 BC, see Knauf, *Administration* 205–206.
130 From Tayma itself there are twenty-one texts, and eight from other places in northern Ḥiǧāz. TA 1 mentions the twenty-second year of a king which may be 443/442 BC (Artaxerxes I) or 383/382 BC (Artaxerxes II). TA 22 is dated to year 16, which may be 449/448 BC (Artaxerxes I), 408/407 BC (Darius II) or 389/388 BC (Artaxerxes II); cf. Knauf, *Administration* 206; Edens/Bawden, *History* 62.
131 RÉS 2771; Mlaker, *Hierodulenlisten* 34. This text is a list of people dedicated to a sanctuary in Maʕīn and contains names from, among others, QDR, MṢR and also HGR.
132 Xenophon, *Cyropaedia* 8.6.7.
133 Diodorus 15.2.
134 Diodorus 15.92.5.
135 It cannot reasonably have been the Arabia close to Phoenicia (see below), since Nectanebo was operating in that area (Diodorus 15.92.4).
136 Giesinger, *Skylax* 640-643.
137 Müller, *Geographie* 79–80.
138 The conjecture is based on Strabo 16.3. That passage most probably comes from Eratosthenes but it deals with *árabes* in Mesopotamia, not on the Suez isthmus. It also refers to conditions after Alexander. All this adds a question mark to the reconstruction of the text, which is obviously based on preconceived ideas about Arabia and Arabs.
139 Cf. Retsö, *Connection*, for a survey of all passages in early Greek literature referring to frankincense.
140 *Delphic hymn* I v. 11.
141 Aristotle, *Historia animalium* I:387–389; II:24.
142 Gauthiers-Pilters/Dagg, *Camel* 92–93. The rutting season of the dromedary tends to coincide with the latter half of the wet season, which suits conditions in Yemen.
143 Aristotle, *Meteorologia* 34–35 (349a).

144 Cf. Leuze, *Satrapieeinteilung* 321 ff. Lendle, *Kommentar* 486–487, defends the Xenophontian origin of the list but admits that some names are of unknown origin.
145 The others are Artimas of Lydia, Aratakamas of Phrygia, Mithradates of Lyaconia and Cappadocia, Roparas of Babylonia, and Korylas of Paphlagonia.
146 Xenophon, *Anabasis* 1.1.10.
147 Cf. Leuze, *Satrapieeinteilung* 319 ff.
148 Xenophon *Anabasis* 1.4.4, 5, 12; 1.3.20.
149 Xenophon, *Anabasis* 1.5; see p. 252. So Eph'al, *Arabs* 202.
150 Diodorus 16.42.1.
151 Arrian, *Anabasis* I2.25.4; 27.1; Curtius 4.6.30.
152 Arrian, *Anabasis* 2.2; Plutarch, *Alexander* 24.6; Curtius 4.2.24–3.1.
153 1 Chronicles 5:10, 19.

10

ALEXANDER THE GREAT AND THE ARABS

Sources

The political line *vis à vis* Arabia that we tried to discern in Greek politics during the fifth and fourth centuries BC culminated in the time of Alexander. It turns out that other parts of Arabia also played an important role in his plans and that he envisioned a comprehensive military action against it when he died.

When we turn to Alexander's career we are confronted by a problem with sources which we have already been acquainted with, but which now becomes acute and will remain so during our reconstruction of the history of the Arabs from classical sources. For the events that concern us, contemporary documents are often lost. Instead, they are quoted with varying fidelity to the originals by authors who often lived centuries after the events themselves. Quite often, information about a certain event has reached us through several stages of digestion by different authors. A large part of the discussion of historical sources in Greek and Latin consists of speculation about what once could be read in books no longer extant. This problem, apparent already with Scylax and Hecataeus, will from now on return frequently. As far as Alexander the Great is concerned, his career was documented by at least six contemporaries who had known him personally and taken part in the great Oriental campaign. Of these, Chares, Alexander's chamberlain, Nearchus, his admiral during the voyage from Indus to Susa, Aristobulus, employed by Alexander as a technical expert during the later part of his career, and Ptolemy, son of Lagus, one of Alexander's generals, who ended as king of Egypt and founder of the dynasty in Alexandria, all told about Alexander's relation to Arabs.[1] The reports by both Aristobulus and Ptolemy were sober stories containing much matter-of-fact. The last of the contemporaries, Cleitarchus, wrote a work on Alexander's life, which, unlike those of the predecessors, presented the story in melodramatic epic and dramatic style, according to the taste of emergent Hellenism.[2]

All these books are lost. The texts telling the story about Alexander to us were all written more than 300 years after Alexander's death and are based upon the contemporary sources which by then were still extant and accessible. Quotations from or digests of the original sources where Arabs and Arabia are mentioned are found in Strabo (*Geography*), Plutarch (*Life of Alexander*), Quintus Curtius (*Life of Alexander*) and Arrian (*Anabasis*, *Indica*), all of them written during the first two centuries of the Roman Caesars.[3] These authors used the sources now lost, and it is often possible to say, with some degree of certainty, which passages are built on which source.[4] Traditionally, the works of Arrian and Plutarch have been considered more trustworthy than the others because they mainly follow Ptolemy and Aristobulus.[5] This holds especially for the reports about Alexander's campaign along the Phoenician coast to Egypt, where the information traceable to Ptolemy, which dominates in Arrian and Plutarch, should have the upper hand. The same holds for what is told about activities concerning Arabia during Alexander's last years, which were summarized by Aristobulus who in his turn had access to documents from Alexander's admirals. Some of these activities resulted in a mass of new information on the peninsula and especially South Arabia, which from now on became better known to the Greeks. This information was used in the books on botany and geography written by Theophrastus and Eratosthenes respectively during the third century BC. Unfortunately, Eratosthenes' work is not preserved, but its contents can to a large extent be reconstructed from the *Geography* of Strabo, written during the reign of Augustus.

The Mediterranean campaign

The first act in Alexander's *Blitzkrieg* against the Persians culminated in the battle at Issus in Cilicia in November, 333 BC. From Issus he started to march southwards along the Phoenician coast. Of the cities, Tyre did not succumb to him and he began the famous siege that lasted seven months. It was during the siege that he had his first encounter with Arabs, which is rendered in a similar way by Plutarch and Arrian:

> When the siege of the city was in progress, he made an expedition against the *árabes* who dwelt in the neighbourhood of Mount Antilibanus.[6]

> When his engines were fitted together and his ships were being equipped for attack and for trying the issue of a naval battle, Alexander marched with some of the cavalry squadrons, the hypaspists, the Agranians and the archers in the direction of Arabia to the mountain called Antilibanus. Here he stormed and destroyed some places and brought others to terms; in ten days he was back in Sidon.[7]

This note in Plutarch and Arrian would be enigmatic if we did not have a fuller version of it in Quintus Curtius. He says that Alexander needed wood for building the siege tower on the mole out to Tyre and that he sent expeditions to Mount Libanus to fetch it:

> On Mount Libanus also the peasants (*agrestes*) of the *árabes* attacked the Macedonians when they were in disorder, killed about thirty and took a smaller number of prisoners. This state of affairs compelled Alexander to divide his forces, and lest he should seem slow in besieging one city, he left Perdiccas and Craterus in charge of that work and himself went to Arabia.[8]

Plutarch adds an anecdote of how Alexander, separated from the main force in the night, rushed into a camp of barbarians and was nearly killed. This romantic episode is explicitly said to have been told by Chares, Alexander's chamberlain. The whole tenor of this story is, however, in the pathetic style attributed to Cleitarchus, and it is likely that it originates from him, which makes it of doubtful historical value. It is not impossible that an anecdote by Chares has been the starting point.[9] The description of the other operations reveals a professional soldier and it is likely that this information comes from Ptolemy.[10] The picture emerging is quite clear. The conflict with the *árabes* became acute due to the intrusion of Macedonian troops in the cedar forests of Lebanon. The skirmishes were so serious that Alexander himself left the troops on the shore and directed a punitive expedition against the enemies.[11]

We learn from all variants of this story that the *árabes* dwelt in the Antilebanon, i.e. quite far from the cedar forests exploited by the Macedonians. This is a new entity of *árabes* that now emerges into the light of history and is added to those known previously in the Ǧazīra, in Dumah and between Palestine and the Nile Delta. The attack from these *árabes* on the Macedonians must have been a strategic device, not an improvised act of defence. It should be remembered that Alexander's friend Parmenion had already taken Damascus, having been sent there immediately after Issus.[12] The presence of the Macedonians in the west and in Damascus thus encircled the areas of the *árabes* in the Antilebanon. We have suggested that these *árabes* may be identical to those mentioned in the list of arkhonts added to Xenophon's *Anabasis*. As we shall see, the Arabs in the Antilebanon are mentioned quite often later in antiquity.[13]

Alexander had to conduct two complicated sieges during his campaign along the Levantine coast, and Arabs were involved in both. After having conquered Tyre in the summer of 332 BC he advanced to Gaza, which also refused to surrender. Gaza was under the command of a certain Batis or Betis, and the siege lasted for two months, September and October of 332 BC.[14] Arrian and Plutarch mention only Arab mercenaries (*árabas misthōtoús*).[15] According to Diodorus the city was also defended by Persian troops, and according to Curtius also by both Persians and *arabes*.[16] From Arrian we understand that Gaza now did not belong to any Arabia, the western border of which is 'towards (*epì*) the sea along (*katà*) Phoenicia and Palestine'.[17] Since Gaza belonged to Palestine, the information that a Persian garrison was there is trustworthy, in spite of the fact that Arrian and Plutarch do not mention it. There are indications that the Persian governor in Egypt would have admitted the Macedonian army into the country, which gives sense to Batis' resistance if he was defending the Persian interests.[18]

Curtius tells us that it was an Arab who wounded Alexander himself in the battle and thus almost changed the course of world history.[19] This information, however, almost certainly originates from Cleitarchus, thus being of doubtful historical value.[20] Arrian and Plutarch tell us that Alexander was wounded by a bolt from a catapult, an incident which Cleitarchus has dramatized and personalized like a modern tabloid journalist.[21]

According to Plutarch, Alexander sent 500 talents of frankincense and 100 talents of myrrh to his old teacher Leonidas after the capture of Gaza.[22] This reveals one of the reasons why the capture was judged to be worth the effort.[23]

Arrian says that from now on Phoenicia, Syria and the greater part of Arabia were in Alexander's hands.[24] The meaning is probably that Alexander had control over the Arabia stretching along the coast to the Egyptian border.[25] There is no report that the Macedonian army penetrated further into the Sinai peninsula or northern Ḥiǧāz. This limitation of the Greek sphere is indirectly confirmed when we hear that Alexander's successor Antigonus made a campaign into the regions south-east of the Dead Sea in the year 312.[26] That area was consequently not under Greek control.

After the conquest of Egypt, Arrian reports about governors appointed by the new regime:

> He appointed for Arabia around Heroonpolis Cleomenes from Naucratis.[27]

Heroonpolis is the name given by the Greeks to a town whose location is not altogether clear. It has been identified with Patoumos/Pithom, the main town in Wādī Tumīlāt. At the time of Alexander the name was probably designating present-day Tell al-Maskhūṭa.[28] The town was to play an important role in the Greek communications with Arabia.

In the period between the conquest of Gaza in 332 and Nearchus' return from India in 325, we only hear about Arabia once, namely in Curtius when he describes the route taken by Alexander after the surrender of Arbela in Assyria:

> As they went on, Arabia was on their left hand, a region famous for its abundance of perfumes; the route is through plains in the land lying between the Tigris and the Euphrates, which is so fertile and rich that the flocks are said to be kept from feeding there, for fear that they might die of satiety.[29]

At a first glance the passage seems to be dependent upon Xenophon's description of Arabia in the *Anabasis*.[30] As we have tried to show, Xenophon was basically right when he called the area between the two rivers 'Arabia'. The passage in Curtius may be simply a literary loan from Xenophon, if not by Curtius himself, then by his source. We may notice, however, that in that case the location of Arabia is wrong since Alexander marched on the eastern side of the Tigris where there was no Arabia according to Xenophon. Further, the description of the fertility of Arabia is not consistent with the picture given by Xenophon. Now Arbela is the capital of the country later known as Adiabene. In the first century AD we have good evidence for the presence of Arabs there.[31] Curtius' description may have two explanations: (1) he simply refers to conditions of his own time, i.e. probably around AD 100, which are projected backwards and mixed up with literary reminiscences from Xenophon; (2) the Arab presence in Adiabene goes back to Achaemenid times, and Curtius' note is based on a good source contemporary with Alexander. This latter alternative is not impossible: we have already heard about how Cyrus the Great passed Arabs and Assyrians in their land when advancing towards Babylon.[32] If these Arabs are those mentioned by Curtius, they are probably related to those mentioned by Xenophon. Perhaps the Achaemenids settled Arabs from the Ǧazīra on the eastern shore of the Tigris.[33]

Alexander and the Arabian peninsula

Alexander's taking control of the Arabian coastline along the Mediterranean was a major event in the history, if not of the Arabs, then of the peninsula. Alexander had to settle other questions before he could turn to Arabian affairs. But when the empire of the Achaemenids was finally conquered and the Indian campaign was finished, Arabia became the main target for his ambitions.

One of the impetuses for this was the discovery included in the report by Nearchus about his voyage from the Indus estuary up to the Persian Gulf. The report, which was written before 310 BC, was incorporated in the story of Aristobulus, which in its turn was used by Eratosthenes, Strabo and Arrian. The contents must have been known to Alexander.[34] There is still a scent of exploration and unexpected adventure in the passage in Arrian's book about India, which is built on that report of the moment one day in the autumn of 325 BC, when an unknown land was sighted before the beam to port:

> Thence they set out [from Carmania] and voyaged eight hundred stadia and moored off a desert shore; and they sighted a long cape jutting out far into the ocean; it seemed as if the headland itself was a day's sail away. Those who had knowledge of the district said that this promontory belonged to Arabia and was called Máketa; and that thence the Assyrians imported cinnamon and other spices. From this beach, off which the fleet anchored in the open roadstead, and the promontory which they sighted opposite them running out into the sea, the bay . . . runs back into the interior and would seem to be the Red Sea.[35]

The promontory sighted by Nearchus was no doubt Rās Musandam, the northern part of Oman that projects towards the Persian coast and forms the Hormuz straits. The discovery of the Persian Gulf (called the Red Sea by Nearchus) was also new.[36] At last, in the early spring of 324 BC, Nearchus' expedition reached the town of Diridotis at the innermost shore of the Persian Gulf. This town is identical with Teredon, which, according to a late source, had been founded by Nebuchadnezzar as protection against Arabs.[37] According to Arrian, who must have had his information from Nearchus' report, the town was a centre for the frankincense trade from Arabia and the land of Gerrha.[38] For the first time we hear the name of this legendary city, and once again Alexander's expedition is confronted with frankincense from Arabia.

Arrian has quite an explicit statement of the reasons behind Alexander's plans for Arabia, originally told by Aristobulus. The first two are the following[39]:

> [Alexander] was planning to colonize the coast along the Persian Gulf and the islands close to it: for he thought that it would be just as prosperous a country as Phoenicia.[40]
>
> Then the prosperity of the country incited him, since he heard that in their oases (*ek tōn límnōn*) cassia grew, and from the trees came myrrh and frankincense (*libanōtós*); and from the bushes, cinnamon was cut; and that from their meadows spikenard grew self-sown. Then there was also the size of their [the Arabs'] territory, since the sea-coast of Arabia was reported to him [through Nearchus] to be not less long than that of India, and that there were several islands adjacent and harbours all over the coast, large enough to give anchorage for his fleet, and to permit cities to be built on them, and those cities likely to be rich.[41]

The *árabes* along the coast were obviously people who lived along the newly discovered southern shore of the Persian Gulf, a land which from now on was known to the Greeks as part of Arabia. The description, which most probably Aristobulus had from Nearchus, is basically of the Arabian side of the Gulf, although the mention of frankincense and myrrh hints at regions more distant.[42] There are indications that the plans for colonization took shape during the year 324 BC.[43]

The sources also mention another motive for Alexander's plans against the southern shore of the Gulf. This motive is explicitly connected with the political events during Alexander's last year. Our oldest preserved source, Diodorus Siculus, reports about delegations (*présbeis*) of peoples from the entire *oikoumēnē* coming to Alexander in Babylon in the year 323 BC.[44] Apart from 'the peoples, cities and rulers of Asia' we hear about representatives from the southern shore of the Mediterranean from Libya to Gibraltar as well as from most peoples on the northern shore. In our second earliest source, Strabo, there is a description of Alexander's preparations for operations in Arabia, which is explicitly taken from Aristobulus. The reason is given as follows:

> He [Aristobulus] says that he [Alexander] alleged as the cause for the war that of all [peoples] only the *árabes* did not send any ambassador (*presbeúsainto*) to him.[45]

If read together, these passages in Diodorus and Strabo clearly indicate that the reason for Alexander's Arabian plans was the absence of ambassadors from Arabia in Babylon in the spring of 323 BC.

Strabo then goes on to adduce yet another motive. He says that the real cause was Alexander's ambition 'to be lord of all'. When he heard that the Arabs worshipped two gods, Zeus and Dionysus, he assumed that they would worship him as a third one if he submitted them to his rule. In Arrian we find the same point in a more elaborate version:

> There is a story current that Alexander heard that the tribes of *árabes* reverenced only two gods, Uranus and Dionysus; Uranus, because they behold him and he contains within him all the stars and especially the sun, from which the greatest and most obvious benefits, in all directions come to mankind; Dionysus, in view of his journey to India. Alexander therefore thought himself worthy to be regarded as a third god by the *árabes*, since he had achieved even more famous deeds than Dionysus, at any rate if he should conquer Arabia and permit them, as he had the Indians, to be governed according to their own customs.[46]

Both Strabo and Arrian have the story about Alexander's ambition to become a god among the Arabs from the same source. That source was not Aristobulus.[47] Its emphasis on the personal vainglory of the king, bordering on *hybris*, makes it likely that we have to do with Cleitarchus, who reflects the fast-growing Alexander legend at the beginning of the Hellenistic era.[48]

Arrian also reports the arrival of delegations, but his version gives a more variegated and complex picture. According to him, delegations from the countries in the western Mediterranean were already starting to come to Alexander when he was proceeding from Susa to Babylon in the spring of 323 BC.[49] Other embassies (*presbeîai*), this time from the Greeks, came when he had reached Babylon.[50] Immediately after the reception of the delegations, Arrian tells about grand-scale preparations for naval operations in the Gulf:

> His naval preparations were chiefly directed at the majority of the *árabes*, on the ground that they alone of the barbarians in it [the coastal region of the Persian Gulf] had sent no envoys, nor had anything complimentary, or any honour to him been made by the *árabes*.[51]

Arrian's report about the motive for a campaign against the Arabs is based on the same source as that of Strabo, namely Aristobulus. The motive for the conquest as reported by Aristobulus was obviously a direct consequence of the rally of delegations.

But we observe that Arrian's version gives a somewhat different picture: the action was aimed against the Arabs living along the southern shore of the Persian Gulf. It is thus closely connected with the colonization project, and there is no hint about any conquest of the peninsula as a whole. Arrian's version, which gives a concrete and limited aim for the project, is likely to be more correct than that of Strabo, which is influenced by the idea of Alexander's divine aspirations, which were not mentioned by Aristobulus. That motive most likely reflects the development of the Alexander legend after his death.

The conclusion is thus that we can discard the religious motive. Aristobulus adduced two motives for operations against Arabia: colonization and conquest, which probably go back to Alexander himself. There remains, however, a certain contradiction between the two. A plausible interpretation is that the original idea of colonizing and exploiting the Gulf, conceived by Alexander when he learned about the existence of the southern shore, received an ideological justification through the absence of representatives of its inhabitants among the delegations that later turned up in Babylon.[52] But it should be observed that it is still the southern shore of the Persian Gulf which is in focus, not the entire peninsula. There is no explicit mention of South Arabia.[53]

It has been shown that the reports about the delegations to Alexander in Babylon were tampered with in the Hellenistic period by adding names which were not mentioned from the beginning.[54] There is, however, no doubt that they reflect a real political event.[55] Parts of the list go back to Aristobulus, who had been an eye-witness. In Diodorus' report 'the peoples, cities, and rulers of Asia' are mentioned first, before he goes on to list the peoples in the west.[56] It is reasonable to assume that the Asiatics must be those originally under the authority of the Achaemenid kings. It has been argued that this pageant could, in fact, be the same ceremony as that behind the name-lists and reliefs of the Achaemenid king, now taken over by Alexander.[57] Undoubtedly, Alexander saw himself as an heir to the royal ideology of the Achaemenids.[58] The absence of the 'Arabs' along the southern shore of the Gulf triggering off a military action could have had two reasons: they had been under Achaemenid rule but now tried to liberate themselves, or they had never been under the rule of the Persians and had no reasons to pay homage to their successor. The impression given by the text is that they were expected to turn up. This would then be an argument in favour of the first alternative.[59]

The presence of specific groups called Arabs in the Gulf area in the time of the Greek conquest cannot be confirmed with certainty. It is therefore most likely that when the texts about Alexander speak about the *árabes* living along the coast, this refers to the inhabitants of the newly discovered Arabian peninsula, which means that there is no good reason to assume that this term refers to people who were Arabs in the sense we are looking for.[60] When Nearchus heard that the land sighted was Arabia, the fate of its inhabitants was sealed. They were from now on to be labelled *árabes* by the Greeks and their successors. Arrian's use of the word reflects the usage he found in his sources, which in its turn goes back to the jargon among Alexander's closest friends and counsellors.

The Arabian expeditions

Alexander and his generals, with their experience of the expedition from India to Mesopotamia, realized that a similar expedition along the Arabian side of the Gulf needed meticulous preparation. Reconnoitring was necessary before the army could be sent away. We know of four successive expeditions exploring the coasts of the Arabian peninsula. These expeditions vastly increased the knowledge among Alexander's staff about Arabia and, most likely, also changed their plans. Three of them were sent out from Mesopotamia.[61] Arrian says, referring to Aristobulus:

> . . . Archias, who was sent with a thirty-oared ship to reconnoitre the coastal voyage towards Arabia and arrived at the island of Tylus, but did not venture further.[62]

There is consensus that Tylus is present-day Baḥrayn.[63] The expedition was launched in the early half of the year 324 BC.[64] It would thus have had as its main aim to explore the possibilities for colonization. Arrian gives a long description of the southern shores of the Persian Gulf derived from Aristobulus' account of the Archias expedition.[65] Apart from Baḥrayn, there is a description of the sacred island of Icarus, which is present-day Faylaka off the Kuwaiti coast.[66] The sanctuary of Artemis, described by Archias in terms much like that of a pre-Islamic *ḥimā*, with sacred, unmolested animals, is probably to be sought at the two temples found during the excavations on the site.[67]

According to Arrian/Aristobulus, Archias was followed by Androsthenes from Thasos:

> Androsthenes was despatched with another thirty-oar, and sailed round part of the Arabian peninsula.[68]

This short note is complemented by the log from the expedition, which was used by Eratosthenes half a century later for his description of eastern Arabia.[69] From there we can learn that Androsthenes reached 'the mouth at Makai', i.e. the straits of Hormuz.[70] It is likely that this expedition was undertaken during the winter of 324–323 BC.[71] The colonization project was still the main purpose.[72]

The third expedition was that of Hieron of Soli:

> Farthest of all those who were sent out, Hieron of Soli, the steersman, advanced, who also received a thirty-oar from Alexander. For his sailing orders were to coast the whole Arabian Peninsula till he reached the Arabian Gulf on the Egyptian side, near Heroonpolis; yet he did not dare to advance further, though he had sailed round the greater part of Arabia; but he turned back and reported to Alexander the size of the peninsula as vast and not far short of that of India; and that a projection ran far into the ocean.[73]

Arrian mentions the expeditions in this order when summarizing them in his book on Alexander. Arguments have been put forward that the order of Androsthenes and Hieron should be reversed.[74] It has been claimed that it is unlikely that Hieron would have started in the spring of 323 because that would have made his *períplous* of the peninsula impossible due to the summer monsoon. Now the fact is that he did not succeed in circumnavigating Arabia, probably because of the south-west monsoon as well as the lack of fresh water along the coast.[75] It seems that he was not able to proceed far beyond Rās Musandam. According to Arrian, nobody had ever rounded this cape.[76] As a matter of fact, the Greeks did not get a clear idea of the winds in the Indian Ocean until centuries later. It is thus very likely that Arrian presents the expeditions in correct order.[77]

The Hieron expedition was obviously based on the new knowledge of the size of Arabia derived from the preceding one. Perhaps information of the circumnavigation of Arabia under Darius had also become better known to Alexander and his staff. The plans may have been changed: the finding of another way to India receded into the background. Instead, the circumnavigation of the new continent became the central issue.

Both Plutarch and Curtius mention a plan for circumnavigation of Africa, which is said to have been conceived already when Alexander met Nearchus in Carmania on the return from India.[78] It is difficult to judge the value of this information. What is certain is that Nearchus received orders to continue exploring the coast from Carmania to the Tigris.[79] By then, Arabia had already been sighted, which was reported to Alexander. The exploration of the new land could thus have been conceived already by then. The information in Plutarch and Curtius could be a back-projection of ideas that evolved later during the Arabian expeditions.

Of the expeditions from Mesopotamia, that of Androsthenes was the most important as far as documentation of the geography is concerned. The knowledge of the Greeks concerning Arabia was increased by the report from this expedition, together with the one from the expediton sent out from Egypt in 324 BC. From there, the Achaemenids had already circumnavigated Arabia.[80] The information was used by Theophrastus and Eratosthenes. It is evident that most information about Arabia in both these authors was based mainly on reports from expeditions in the Red Sea. As far as can be seen from the sources, there were at least two expeditions. Theophrastus says, when describing the myrrh tree:

> These [those who have seen the tree with their own eyes] said that on the coasting voyage which they made from the bay of the Heroes they landed to look for water on the mountains and so saw these trees and the manner of collecting their gums.[81]

It is not quite clear from this account how far the expedition reached. In another passage, Theophrastus, referring to the same expedition, tells about the extreme dryness of a place on the Red Sea coast 'a little above Coptos in Arabia'.[82] Unfortunately, the name is textually corrupt, and the reading Coptos is an emendation based on the name Capto in Pliny, who quotes the same passage.[83] Coptos is present-day Qift on the eastern shore of the Nile just north of Luxor. Finally in Arrian, we probably have a reference to the same expedition:

> Yet from the Arabian Gulf [the Gulf of Suez], which runs along Egypt, people have started and have circumnavigated the greater part of Arabia (*tēn pollēn Arabíēn*) hoping to reach the sea nearest to Susa and Persia, and thus have sailed so far round the Arabian coast as the amount of fresh water taken aboard their vessels has permitted, and then have returned home again.[84]

There is no doubt that the Heroonpolis expedition reached the Bāb al-Mandab, left the Red Sea and continued along the South Arabian coast before it had to return.

In Strabo we find a reference to yet another expedition. The passage comes from Eratosthenes' description of Arabia:

> The part of the Arabian Gulf along the side of Arabia, beginning at the Aelanites recess (the Bay of ʕAqaba) is, as recorded by Alexander's associates (*hoi perì Alexándrou*) and by Anaxicrates, fourteen thousand stadia, though this figure is excessive; and the part opposite the Troglodytic country [i.e. the African shore] which is on the right as one sails from Heroonpolis, as far as Ptolemais and the country where elephants are captured, extends nine thousand stadia towards the south and slightly in the direction of the east; and thence as far as the straits [i.e. Bāb al-Mandab], four thousand five hundred stadia, in a direction more towards the east. The straits are formed towards Aethiopia by a promontory called Deire, and by a town bearing the same name which is inhabited by the fish-eaters (*ikhtyóphagoi*).
>
> The straits at Deire contract to a width of sixty stadia. However, it is not these that are called straits now, but a place farther along the voyage, where the voyage across the gulf between the two continents is about two hundred stadia, where are six islands, which follow one another in close succession, fill up the channel, and leave between them extremely narrow passages; through these merchandise is transported from one continent to the other; and for these the name 'straits' is used. After the islands, the next voyage, following the sinuosities of the bays, along the myrrh-bearing country in the direction of south and east as far as the cinnamon-bearing country, is about five thousand stadia; and to the present time, it is said, no one has arrived beyond that country; and though there are not many cities on the coast, there are many in the interior that are beautifully settled. Such, then, is Eratosthenes' account of Arabia.[85]

It is possible that Eratosthenes has fused information from two different expeditions in this passage. One of them, headed by Anaxicrates, started from the Bay of Aelanites. Perhaps Anaxicrates reached the Bāb al-Mandab, whereas the Hieroonpolis expedition is the 'next voyage' mentioned as reaching beyond this point.[86]

The most dramatic result of these expeditions must have been the realization of the existence of South Arabia. Archias and Androsthenes had explored the coast opposite the one along which Nearchus had sailed. During their voyages they must have begun to realize the true dimensions of the Arabian peninsula and, perhaps, the existence of a hitherto unknown culture there with cities, temples, kings and armies guarding the frankincense and myrrh. This must have become definite knowledge through Hieron's voyage. It is likely, then, that in the spring of 323 BC South Arabia became the main target for Alexander. Orders went out to launch expeditions from Heroonpolis and the bay of Aelanites. These expeditions actually reached the coasts of Yemen and sailed out through the Bāb al-Mandab. Now Alexander knew where the land of frankincense was, which from the days of Herodotus had been one of the ends of the world to the Greeks.

The question remains, however, whether Alexander intended a military conquest of South Arabia.[87] Even though the launching of the expeditions from Egypt clearly shows that, at the latest from early in the year 323 BC, Yemen was known to him, it should be noticed that there is no hint at a military conquest in any of the reliable sources. The texts explicitly say that the planning in Babylon was for the Gulf region.

The question about Alexander's Arabian plans has been connected with a larger issue, namely the plans for a conquest of the Mediterranean. Diodorus reports that after Alexander's death his successor Perdiccas found notes, the so-called *hypomnēmata*, with elaborate plans for a conquest of the lands around the Mediterranean.[88] There has been a long debate about the authenticity of the *hypomnēmata*, German scholars as a rule tending to accept them as an expression of Alexander's plans, others doubting them.[89] Relevant for our theme is that Arabia is not mentioned in the *hypomnēmata* as reported by Diodorus. In spite of this, Wilcken in 1937 included the Arabian project as an 'upbeat' for the 'Western Plans', conceived already in Ecbatana in 324 BC.[90] Weighty objections have, however, been launched against the Arabian project being part of a western conquest.[91] As we have seen, there seem to have been two main motives for it: colonisation of the Gulf, later to be completed by a military occupation, and exploration of the Gulf coast, later extended to an exploration of the coasts of the entire Peninsula.

The preparations for the Arabian campaign were in full swing when Alexander suddenly died in Babylon in June 323 BC. The preparations included gathering troops, transporting ships from the Mediterranean to Babylon and building a fort at the Pallacopas canal in southern Mesopotamia on the border to Arabia.[92] With the death of the protagonist, the plans remained unrealized.

Excursus: the location and role of Gerrha

In Strabo we find a notice from Eratosthenes, originating from Aristobulus, about the town of Gerrha:

> After sailing along the coast of Arabia for a distance of two thousand four hundred stadia, one comes to Gerrha, a city situated on a deep gulf; it is inhabited by Chaldaeans, exiles from Babylon; the soil contains salt, and the people live in houses made of salt . . .
>
> The city is two hundred stadia distant from the sea, and the Gerrheans traffic . . . in the Arabian merchandise and aromatics . . .; Aristobulus says . . . that the Gerrheans import most of their cargoes on rafts to Babylonia and thence sail up the Euphrates with them and then convey them by land to all parts of the country.[93]
>
> The Gerrhaeans arrive at Chatramotitis in forty days.[94]

It is very likely that this description comes from one of the two expeditions sent out from Mesopotamia by Alexander. The exact location of Gerrha is still debated.[95] Recent authors seem to favour an identification with Thāǧ, 90 kilometres inland from Ǧubayl.[96] It has also been argued that Gerrha is the same name as Hagar.[97] Further, it has been alleged that the HGR mentioned on some of the coins found in eastern Arabia refers to Thāǧ, 'the only site in north-eastern Arabia which merits the South Arabian designation HGR'.[98] Nothing of this is tenable. Linguistically the equation Hagar = Gerrha is difficult to accept.[99] That HGR must have the same meaning as the corresponding word in South Arabia or that it must be a word imported from there remains to be proved. From Islamic sources we are well informed about Hağar in north-eastern Arabia, which is identical with present-day Hufūf. It is most likely that the epigraphic HGR is identical with this site. In that case it cannot be identical with Gerrha since Hufūf is *c*. 80 kilometres from the sea, i.e. twice the distance given for Gerrha.[100]

According to the notices in Strabo, ultimately going back via Aristobulus to Archias and/or Androsthenes, Gerrha was 2,400 stadia, i.e. *c*. 390 kilometres, from Teredon and 200 stadia, i.e. *c*. 32 kilometres, from the sea.[101] If Teredon is situated at Basra we would, after 390 kilometres, end up at Ğubayl, which is not situated at a deep gulf. On the other hand, the location of Teredon is not settled and it could very well have been further down along the coast.[102] Certain is that Gerrha was near Tylus, i.e. Baḥrayn.[103] When Antiochus III returned from India in 205 BC, he sailed to Antiochia in Persis, then to Gerrha and then to Tylus and Seleucia.[104] Pliny says that Tylus was opposite Gerrha, 75 kilometres from the mainland.[105] From northern Baḥrayn (Manāma) to the mainland sites Qaṭīf or ʕUqayr is *c*. 70 kilometres. From the southern tip of the island to the mainland (ʕUqayr) is *c*. 40 kilometres. We should probably look for the City of Salt some 30 kilometres inland from ʕUqayr or Qaṭīf, preferably the latter, which fits better with the bay. This is the only location that takes the distances given by the sources into full account.[106] This also means that Teredon should be located south-east of Basra.

A description of the route between Gerrha and Ḥaḍramawt is found in a much later source, namely Pliny, who had copied it from Iuba's book on Arabia, written in the time of Augustus.[107] Since Iuba used older sources extensively, the description is probably valid also for the end of the fourth century BC and gives a concrete background to the plans for Alexander's Arabian campaign. It is likely that this route had existed for a considerable time. In favour of this speaks the use of South Semitic script in southern Babylonia already at the end of the seventh century BC.[108] The discovery of another route to South Arabia than the one through Ḥiğāz, known from the emporium at Gaza, probably gave Alexander and his staff the first idea to achieve the same control over its end point as they had already established on the Mediterranean.

Arabs from Cambyses to Alexander: a preliminary synthesis

In the period 525–323 BC people called Arabs appear in several regions. Apart from the Arab/Qedar kingdom between Egypt and Palestine we find Arabs in the Antilebanon, in the Ğazīra, in the region of Nağrān and, perhaps, on the southern shore of the Persian Gulf. It is not at all certain that it is the same 'people' that appears in different parts of the peninsula. The most important of these groups is the first one. From the Persian texts, Hecataeus' description discernible in Herodotus' text together with the inscriptions from Tell al-Maskhūṭa and the reports by Nehemiah, we can sketch a picture of a political entity, called *Arabía* by the Greeks and *arabāya* by the Persians, that encompassed an area from the eastern delta of the Nile to southern Judaea. In the middle of the fifth century one ruler is called the *ʕarbí*, the 'Arab'. His successor is called king of Qedar. At least in the time of Darius I and Xerxes I, this Arabia belonged to the peoples ruled by the Achaemenid king. In the 440s, we hear for the first time about Arab involvement in the frankincense trade from South Arabia to Gaza. At the same time, the king of these Arabs dared to oppose the envoyé of the King of Kings to Judea. In 410 BC we catch a glimpse of this entity threatening the Persians in the eastern Mediterranean and allied with Athens and an emerging independent Egypt. At the beginning of the following century Egypt is ruled by a king who is named after this Arabia and firmly allied with Cyprus and Athens.

The emergence of a tight alliance between Arabia and Egypt at the beginning of the fourth century BC should not be seen isolated from events further south on the peninsula. It is now generally assumed that a change in the political set-up of Ḥiǧāz took place at this time. The Aramaic-speaking dominance in Taymāʔ seems to have ceased and the importance of the town began to wane. Dedan was taken over by a new tribe or dynasty, Liḥyān. We also find the presence of another new entity there, namely the Minaeans who came from South Arabia and set up a colony in Dedan, obviously in co-operation with Liḥyān.

The frankincense trade through western Arabia had since the seventh century BC been controlled by the Sabaean empire. It seems though that there was a competing route through central Arabia to the Persian Gulf. Shortly after 400 BC the Sabaean dominance disappeared and the western route was taken over by two new entities, Qataban and the Minaeans.

The emergence of Arabia on the shore of the Mediteranean thus goes together with these events. Later the kings of Liḥyān have close contacts with the Ptolemies in Egypt, which might be the continuation of a policy already initiated in the fourth century BC. This would mean that Achaemenid presence in North Arabia ended shortly after 400 BC together with the break-up of the Sabaean empire in the south. One should also observe that the rise of an Arabian kingdom in control of the Suez isthmus seems to be intimately connected with the independence of Egypt. This political scenario will become very visible in the centuries after Alexander.

This Arabia is explicitly connected with the tribe Qedar. We have seen that Qedar was already exerting pressure on the Transjordanian areas in Assurbanipal's day and that Nebuchadnezzar tried to pacify them in 599 BC. It is tempting to assume that Nabonidus' Arabian sojourn also had to do with their power in northern Ḥiǧāz, even though they are not mentioned in documents from his time. The disappearance of Edom and the attempt of Babylon to dominate northern Ḥiǧāz were followed by a vacuum in the area, into which Qedar seems to have poured. If the interpretation of the oracles in Isaiah 21 is correct, we have documentation that Qedar was operating militarily south of Edom in the middle of the sixth century BC.[109] This Arabia was a considerable political force, exerting influence not only in Egypt but in the whole eastern Mediterranean. It seems that the Achaemenids allowed them to grow, using them as a kind of police force in Egypt as well as guardians of the road between Syria and Egypt. They are also explicitly associated with frankincense trade. The trade was in full swing at the time and it can be assumed that Gaza became the emporium for this perfume at the beginning of the Achaemenid period. Control of the traffic would have greatly increased the political and economic weight of the Arabian rulers. A sign of this importance may be the coins that were minted, probably at Gaza, in the fourth century BC.[110] Arabia was practically independent during the first two-thirds of the fourth century and probably allied with Egypt, thus posing a severe threat to the Achaemenids in the Levant. The reconquest of Egypt by Artaxerxes III in 343 BC must have included Arabia and possibly abolition of its political independence.

This event would have affected Greek interests if our assumption of the close contacts between Arabia, Cyprus and Greece is correct. A re-emerging Achaemenid control of the Suez isthmus and Egypt would not have been appreciated in Athens. On the whole, it is striking that Alexander after defeating the Persian army at Issus did not attack the heartlands of the empire. Instead he directed his army along the Phoenician coast and used a great deal of energy to pacify the cities, besieging Gaza and conquering Egypt. Alexander in fact fulfilled the programme already discernible in Athenian politics at the beginning of the fifth century by establishing control of the whole coast from Asia Minor to the Nile.

There is no doubt that the frankincense trade was a main impetus. When Alexander took Gaza in 332 BC he had 500 talents of frankincense and 100 talents of myrrh sent to his old tutor Leonidas, as already mentioned.[111] Unfortunately, we do not know much about the role of, for example, Cyprus in this traffic. In 530 Euelthon of Salamis gave an incense burner to the sanctuary in Delphi.[112] It would be interesting to have more archaeological evidence for the role of Phoenicia and Cyprus as trading stations between the Arab kingdom and Greece.[113] The economic considerations and motivations are not very visible in the person-centred Greek historical writings which are our main sources for the period. But it is clear from the activities of Alexander concerning Arabia that they were a central issue on the political agenda in his day and must have been so for a long time.

The term 'Arabia' as a designation for a territory was first coined by the Greeks, referring to the kingdom between Egypt and Palestine. Later, when the existence of the peninsula had become confirmed, the term was extended to encompass all the areas behind the kingdom of Qedar. A most important consequence of this was that Greek and Latin authors from now on often see all inhabitants of Arabia, including South Arabia, as 'Arabs'. This must be kept in mind when investigating the Greek and Latin sources for documentation of Arabs. We have seen already, and shall see further on, that there are good reasons to assume that the term in fact refers to one group among others in Arabia. The passages in the sources which deal with smaller entities called Arabs must thus be considered of higher value for our purpose than those using it as a general designation for everybody living on the Arabian peninsula.

The designation 'Arabia' for the area between Egypt and Palestine, documented for the first time in Herodotus, must be connected with the fact that Qedar were called Arabs and had been so for a long time. As we have seen, Qedar were already called Arabs in the seventh century BC as well as in Nebuchadnezzar's time. Hazaʔil is king of Qedar and of the Arabs. The people attacked by Nebuchadnezzar in 599 BC are called Arabs by him and Qedar by Jeremiah. Geshem is king of Qedar in the inscription from Tell al-Maskhūṭa and the *ʕarbî* in Nehemiah. In the latter case, we notice that *ʕarab* is used by the foreigners whereas the domestic term is a gentilic, Qedar. This dichotomy will reappear in the following history of the area.

Arabs are also mentioned in South Arabia for the first time in this period, and perhaps also in eastern Arabia. More detailed information is, however, accessible only for those between Egypt and Palestine. As we have seen, they are governed by kings. They worship two gods, identified as ʔAllāt and Ruḍāw, with traces of a certain exclusiveness; they are involved in international trade although their exact role is difficult to determine; coins are minted within the realm. According to Pseudo-Scylax they had cattle, camels and also horses. This last detail is of considerable interest and raises the question about the military capacity of the Arabs. It was originally assumed that the camel was ridden on the hump with a cushion saddle at least from the tenth century BC until the third century AD, when the classic *shadād* saddle appears in pictorial documents.[114] Mention of Arabs fighting from a camel's back with long spears or swords are, however, documented as early as around 200 BC, which would indicate that the more steady *shadād* saddle was in use by then.[115] Diodorus Siculus has preserved a passage from Ctesias writing in the fourth century BC, describing men fighting with long swords from camels together with the mythical Semiramis. Such fighters are depicted on one of the coins from Gaza.[116] Since Semiramis was said to have conquered Arabia, this seems to show that Arabs already in the fourth century BC could ride on the camel's hump on a steady saddle. It has been assumed that this saddle was introduced from horse riding and it is interesting that the Arabs are said to have had horses at this time. It should also be observed that the Arabs in Xerxes' army in 480 had only bows, not swords and spears.

The picture of the Arabian kingdom between Egypt and Palestine does not fit very well into the idea of a 'desert kingdom' ruled by bedouin shaykhs wandering around looking for pastures and attacking every one who comes in their way. Instead we find an entity armed with horses and swords, issuing its own coinage, involved in international politics, having a key position in an international economic network.

Notes

1 Chares: Jacoby, *Fragmente* 2 B 657–665 (no. 125); Nearchus: ibid. 677–722 (no. 133); Aristobulus: ibid. 769–799 (no. 139); Ptolemy: ibid. 752–769 (no. 138). Jacoby's excerpts consist mainly of the explicit quotations.

2 Jacoby, *Fragmente* 2B 741–752 (no. 137). The two other authors were Callisthenes and Onesicritus. For the latter see Jacoby, *Fragmente* 2B 723–736 (no. 134). For a survey of these authors, see in general Pearson, *Histories.*

3 The story of Alexander was also told by Diodorus Siculus and Trogus Pompeius, again writing in the beginning of the Roman imperial period. Trogus is lost but known through a digest by Iustinus from the third century AD. Neither of these authors reproduces the passages about Arabs and Arabia.

4 The basic modern studies of this subject are the two books by Hammond (*Historians*, *Sources*). The result of these studies is that we know that we have more from the original sources than what is evident from Jacoby's excerpts.

5 See Hammond, *Historians* 1 ff.

6 Plutarch, *Alexander* 24.6.

7 Arrian, *Anabasis* 2.20.4.

8 *Curtius*, 4.2.24–3.1.

9 Pearson, *Histories* 56. See Hammond, *Historians* 71, 149, 165; idem, *Sources* 56.

10 Hammond (*Historians*, *Sources*) does not comment on the Arab episode during the siege of Tyre. According to Högemann (*Alexander* 27), the Arabs were on one of their usual razzias, so that Alexander had to interfere. This is against plain evidence: Curtius says they were settled farmers.

11 For the episode, see Bosworth, *Conquest* 65.

12 Curtius 3.12.27–13.17.

13 See Schürer, *History* I 561–573, and pp. 407–408, cf. 612–613.

14 See in general Romane, *Siege*.

15 Arrian, *Anabasis* 2.25.4, cf. 27.1. According to Altheim/Stiehl, these Arabs were Nabataeans (*Araber* I 35–36) and also Ba/etis was an Arab/Nabataean. For a refutation of this view, see pp. 375 ff.

16 Diodorus, 17.48.9; Curtius, 4.6.7, cf. 15, 30.

17 Arrian, *Anabasis* 2.25.4; idem, *Indica* 8.43.1. Cf. Bosworth, *Government* 48. The context in the *Anabasis* shows that Gaza was reckoned as a part of 'Palestinian Syria' which had submitted to Alexander, 'but a eunuch named Batis, ruling the town of the Gazaeans, had not submitted to Alexander'. The meaning is that Batis could thus have been expected to do so, together with the rest of Palestine. This indicates that Gaza was part of it. Cf. Bosworth, *Commentary* I 257–258.

18 Bosworth, *Conquest* 67. Batis is a name said to be Persian or Babylonian (ibid. note 134). Much later we hear about the arabarch Manesos in Dura on the Euphrates who also carries the title *bátēsa*. According to Chaumont (*Chute* 230) it is the Persian word *bitaxš*, meaning 'border-guard', which fits very well with the role of the commander in Gaza who might have been a direct descendant of the *atūtu* installed there by the Assyrian kings. Hammond (*Historians* 126) thinks that Batis was acting on his own and that the notice of Persians in Gaza is wrong, which in the light of the etymology of Batis becomes unlikely. The characterization of the *árabes* as mercenaries is an indication that they at least did not rule the city.
19 Curtius 4.6.15.
20 See Hammond, *Historians* 126–128; idem, *Source* 57.
21 Arrian, *Anabasis* 2.27.2.
22 Plutarch, *Alexander* 25:4.
23 For the literary antecedents of this incident, see Pearson, *Histories* 11. Potts (*Gulf* II 9) claims that Alexander made a raid into north-western Arabia and got the frankincense there. This raid is said to be the same as that referred to in connection with the siege of Tyre. There is no support in the texts for this assumption.
24 Arrian, *Anabasis* 3.1.2: *tēs Arabías tà pollá.*
25 This is the conquest of Arabia referred to by Pliny (12.32.62).
26 Cf. pp. 283 ff.
27 Arrian, *Anabasis* 3.5.4.
28 On the other hand, Heroonpolis also seems to be located on the Red Sea, which, however, may be a confusion with Clyzma. Heroonpolis may have been somewhere along the canal from the Nile to the Red Sea. That would explain its location in Arabia and its connections with the ocean. For this discussion, see Redmount, *Frontier* 299–301.
29 Curtius, 5.1.11.
30 Xenophon, *Anabasis* 1.4.19–5–1.
31 See pp. 413 f.
32 Cf. pp. 185.
33 The name of Gaugamela east of the upper Tigris where Alexander finally defeated Darius III seems to mean 'the region of the camel'. At least it is interpreted in this way by Greek writers; see Strabo 16.1.3; Plutarch, *Alexander* 31.7.
34 For the dating of Nearchus see Hammond, *Histories* 83–84.
35 Arrian, *Indica* 8.32.6–8. A shorter parallel version is found in Arrian, *Anabasis* 7.20.9-10: And this [i.e. the promontory] Nearchus' crews, when sailing from India, sighted, before they altered course for the Persian Gulf, stretching out not far away.
36 According to Arrian, Alexander had an idea about a land mass in the Indian Ocean already when he arrived at the estuary of the Indus (*Anabasis* 6.19.5; cf. Strabo 15.1.25). This sounds like an apocryphal story emphasizing the superhuman foresight of the king, and its historicity is doubtful. According to Bosworth (*Commentary* II 361 note 1) the information comes from Nearchus. The actual geographical information may well be from him, but the story as it stands belongs to a more fanciful writer, perhaps Cleitarchus.
37 Cf. p. 181; Potts, *Gulf* I 349, II 89.
38 Arrian, *Indica* 41:6–7.
39 Fragment 55 in Jacoby, *Fragmente* II B 792–793; cf. Hammond, *Sources* 301.
40 Arrian, *Anabasis* 7.19.5.
41 Arrian, *Anabasis* 7.20.2; cf. Strabo 16.1.11.
42 Cf. Högemann, *Alexander* 120–125. Högemann (ibid. 86) assumes that the islands and harbours are identical with Aden, which is against the wording of the text.
43 Bosworth, *Conquest* 159.
44 Diodorus 17.113.
45 Strabo 16.1.11.
46 Arrian, *Anabasis* 7.20.1. The story is repeated by Origenes, *Contra Celsum* 5.37.38.
47 Hammond, *Sources* 302. In Strabo it is clear from the context that the absence of ambassadors was told by Aristobulus. Arrian introduces the motive about divinization with the phrase *lógos dè katékhei*, 'there is a story', which is his way of referring to sources different

from Aristobulus and Ptolemy.

48 Högemann (*Alexander* 130–132, 135–143) assumes that this motive goes back to Alexander himself. It tastes more of Cleitharchus, who tended to paint Alexander in terms of a megalomaniac. According to Högemann the role of the two gods in the Alexander story is not compatible with the ethnological insight of the early Hellenistic period and must go back to Alexander himself (141–143). Alexander's identification with Dionysus and its role for his self-concept is debated (cf. Högemann, *Alexander* 124-126 and the debate referred to in his notes 23–31) and its role for the Arabian conquest remains doubtful. The argument that the passage in Euripides' *Bacchae* quoted above (p. 242) was decisive is unlikely.

49 Arrian, *Anabasis* 7.15.4: *presbeîai entygkhanon.*

50 Arrian, *Anabasis* 7.19.1.

51 Arrian, *Anabasis* 7.19.5–6.

52 Cf. Högemann, *Alexander* 128. According to Högemann (ibid. 52) Alexander was awaiting an Arab delegation in Babylon before the beginning of the Indian campaign. The support is Strabo 16.4.27 (end), where it is said that the *árabes* had not sent ambassadors to him *mēte próteron mēth' hysteron*, 'either before or after'. The 'Arabs' would, according to Högemann, have been those in the Ǧazīra. This is, however, highly doubtful, and it is not unproblematic what Strabo's words refer to. As we have seen, the Arabs mentioned in connection with Alexander's last year were people on the shores of the Gulf, who did not have any relation to those in the Ǧazīra. Just before, Strabo has mentioned that Alexander intended to see whether they would receive him voluntarily or if he would have to go to war with them. This could reflect some kind of attempt to negotiate with the 'Arabs' on the Gulf or calling upon them to submit. Obviously there was no reaction from them 'either before or after'. Högemann's interpretation is based upon erroneous ideas about what Arabs were.

53 The absent Arabs cannot have been those between Egypt and Palestine or those in the Ǧazīra. Bowersock (review of Högemann) seems to have this opinion, which is to be rejected: Alexander had already received the frankincense tribute from the Arabs at Gaza. Those Arabs, i.e. the *arabāya* of the Achaemenids, were already subjected to him. Arrian says that Alexander's first plans were against 'the many Arabs' (*árabas toùs polloús*) who belonged to the tribes 'on it' (*taútēi*), i.e. the southern shore (*paralía*) of the Gulf. There is no doubt that these terms refer to parts of the new continent. It is symptomatic that *taútēi* in Arrian has been changed to *hapántōn*, 'all', in Strabo. Undoubtedly Arrian has the original reading.

54 Tarn, *Alexander* II 374–378.

55 Arrian mentions four western countries plus the Greeks, which comes from Ptolemy and Aristobulus. He then adds several others which he explicitly says do not come from these sources (*légetai*). Diodorus has another variant, where all delegations have been fused together into one occasion.

56 Diodorus 17.113; cf. Iustinus 12.13.1. They are not mentioned in Arrian. According to Tarn (*Alexander* II 375) the expression belongs to the Seleucid period. Even though this is true, it is no argument against the event having taken place; cf. Brunt, *Arrian* II 499, and Bosworth, *Conquest* 165–167. Aristobulus said that Cyrus, Alexander's idol, was 'king of Asia', quoting his tomb inscription (Jacoby, *Fragmente* 139 frg. 51 = Strabo 15.3.7). Alexander is given the same title in Arrian, *Anabasis* 7.15.4 f.

57 For this interpretation, see Briant, *Histoire* 206–207. According to Arrian, *Anabasis* 4.15.5, Alexander's explicit ambition was to restore Darius' kingdom; cf. Tarn, *Alexander* II 398–399.

58 Tarn, *Alexander* II 376; Högemann, *Alexander* 121–126.

59 According to Potts, *Gulf* I 350–353 referring to Herodotus 3.93, there might have been some Achaemenid presence in Baḥrayn.

60 Högemann's equation of Arabs and nomads (*Alexander* 129) is misleading and erroneous: the sources never identify Arabs and nomads; on the contrary, the *árabes* said to live on the shores of the Gulf live in cities and oases.

61 They are summarized in Arrian, *Indica* 43.8:
Those, whom Alexander sent from Babylon, in order that, sailing as far as they could on the

right side of the Red Sea, they might reconnoitre the country on this side – these explorers sighted certain islands lying on their course and very possibly put in at the mainland of Arabia.

62 Arrian, *Anabasis* 7.20.7 = Fragment 55 in Jacoby, *Fragmente* II B 795.
63 Högemann, *Alexander* 88–89; Potts, *Gulf* II 125–153. Tylos is probably the same name as Dilmun.
64 For the dating, see Högemann, *Alexander* 88–89, 92.
65 Arrian, *Anabasis* 7.20.1–6.
66 Potts, *Gulf* II 179–183.
67 Potts, *Gulf* II 157–161; 164–165.
68 Arrian, *Anabasis* 7.20.7.
69 Strabo 16. 3.2–4.
70 Strabo 16.3.4.
71 Wilcken, *Pläne* 191–197; Högemann, *Alexander* 92.
72 Högemann (*Alexander* 135) makes the likely suggestion that the finding of a sailing route between Mesopotamia and India might have been an important issue behind Nearchus' journey. This might, in fact, also hold for the two first expeditions along the southern shore of the Gulf.
73 Arrian, *Indica* 7.7–8. Potts' allegation (*Gulf* II 6) that Hieron reached Heroonpolis is incorrect.
74 Högemann, *Alexander*, 92–93.
75 Arrian, *Anabasis* 7.20.10.
76 Arrian, *Indica* 43.9. This remark must refer to the time of the composition of Arrian's source, not to the second century AD.
77 Cf. Potts, *Gulf* II 5–6.
78 Curtius 10.1.17–18; Plutarch, *Alexander* 68.
79 Arrian, *Anabasis* 6.28.6; idem, *Indica* 36.4–5.
80 Cf. p. 240.
81 Theophrastus, *Plants* 9.4.4.
82 Theophrastus, *Plants* 4.7.1.
83 Pliny 13.139.
84 Arrian, *Indica* 43:7.
85 Strabo 16.4.4.
86 Potts, *Gulf* II 6, assumes that Anaxicrates sailed from Heroonpolis and that there was just one expedition from the Red Sea. It is, however, obvious from the sources that there were two. So also Högemann, *Alexander* 81–82.
87 Against: Tarn, *Alexander* II 386–387; in favour: Högemann, *Alexander* 157–162.
88 Diodorus,18.4.4; cf. Curtius,10.
89 The most prominent doubter is Tarn, e.g. *Alexander* II 378–398. In favour are, for example, Schachermeyr, *Alexander* 547–556; idem, *Pläne*; Högemann, *Alexander* 121–126 (without reference to the *hypomnēmata*); Bosworth, *Conquest* 151–152.
90 Wilcken, *Pläne* 195–197.
91 Basic is Hampl, *Hypomnemata* 826, who, however, accepts the genuineness of the *hypomnēmata*; Schachermeyr takes the same position (*Pläne* 136–138) as does, it seems, Högemann (*Alexander* 121 ff.). Bosworth (*Conquests* 169) follows Wilcken.
92 Högemann claims that Alexander prepared a military operation against the 'Arab nomads' in Babylonia proper (*Alexander* 128–29, 148, 151, 154–155). This interpretation is built on the idea that Arabs = nomads = all the inhabitants of 'Arabia' = the Arabian peninsula (cf. ibid. 43), although he is aware that the natives may not have called their land Arabia (ibid. 74). His idea about the Arabs distorts his picture of the Arabian campaign. It is evident that the sources do not speak about any operations against Arabs in Babylonia. The fort in southern Mesopotamia is built by the lakes *epì tēn Arábōn gēn*, 'in the direction of the land of the *árabes*' (Arrian, *Anabasis* 7.21.7); the lakes in southern Mesopotamia continue *epì tēn synekhēn tēi tōn Arábōn gēi*, 'up to the territory nearest to the land of the *árabes*' (ibid. 7.21.3). The concept of Arabia is that its borders run along southern Mesopotamia. This is the

concept we find in Eratosthenes and all subsequent ancient geographers. That strong military action would have been prepared towards nomads in southern Mesopotamia is most unlikely. The fort with its garrison might, among other purposes, have been intended to keep an eye on the few, probably peaceful, shepherds who in any case did not know that they were classified as 'dangerous Arab bedouin' by learned geographers and historians, ancient or modern.

93 Strabo 16.3.3. The text in Strabo is interfoliated with notices, probably from Eratosthenes, reflecting a somewhat later period, when the Gherraeans had cancelled the sea traffic to Babylonia; see pp. 307 f.

94 Strabo 16.4.4.

95 For the references in ancient literature, see Tkač, *Gerrha*; for the discussion, see Potts, *Thaj* 87 and idem, *Gulf* II 85–97.

96 W. W. Müller in von Wissmann, *Geschichte* II 29 note 21a; Potts, *Thaj*; idem, *Gulf* II 90; Bowersock, Review of Högemann.

97 W. W. Müller, loc. cit. Cf. Potts, *Thaj* 89.

98 Potts, *Thaj* 88–89.

99 Beeston (*Observations* 7 note 5) derives it from *qarya* 'village', which at least linguistically is a better solution. According to al-Hamdānī (*Ṣifa* 137) there was a site in the area of Tamīm named al-Ǧarʕā, which looks like the same name although the location is uncertain; cf. Sprenger, *Geographie* 135; James, *Location*. von Wissmann (*Grundlagen* 100 note 55, idem, *Geschichte* I 12) identifies HGR with TMLḤ in the list of hierodules from Maʕīn.

100 The identification is also rejected by von Wissmann, *Geschichte* I 12.

101 This is based on the common equation of a *stadion* with between 180 and 190 metres. For the problem with different *stadia*, see Potts, *Thaj* 87.

102 Cf. the survey of suggestions in Potts, *Thaj* 87.

103 Strabo 16.3.3,4: one reaches Tylus and Aradus = Baḥrayn and Muḥarraq when sailing 'farther on' (*epì pléon*) from Gerrha.

104 Polybius 13.9.4–5.

105 Pliny 6.28.147.

106 According to von Wissmann (*Geschichte* I 12), Gerrha was the harbour whereas the town (*hē pólis* in Strabo's text) is identical with Haǧar in al-Hufūf. The distance, however, does not fit, since Hufūf is 80 km from the sea, not 32 km as said by Strabo. It is likely that the whole complex of Gerrha and the Gerrhean bay has nothing to do with either Thāǧ or Hufūf-Haǧar.

107 Pliny 6.159, analysed by von Wissmann in *Zamareni* I and II.

108 Cf. pp. 150 f.

109 Cf. Knauf, *Supplementa* 13 75 ff.

110 Knauf, *Supplementa* 8, especially 27–28.

111 Plutarch, *Alexander* 25.

112 Herodotus 4.162.

113 Cf. Retsö, *Connection*.

114 Dostal, *Evolution* 20; idem, *Development* 129; idem, *Frage* 7, 9–12.

115 Bulliet, *Camel* 95.

116 Diodorus 2.17.2 cf. Högemann, *Alexander* 37–38; Knauf, *Supplementa* 8 23.

11

THE HEIRS OF ALEXANDER

Antigonus

After Alexander's death, there followed a struggle between those who wanted to preserve a unified empire, led by Perdiccas, Antipater and Polyperchon, and some of the generals like Ptolemy in Egypt, and Lysimachus and Cassander in Europe, whose ambitions were mainly to carve out kingdoms of their own. The last upholder of the imperial idea was Antigonus 'the One-eyed' (Monophthalmos), who emerged around 316 BC as Alexander's successor. He installed Seleucus as governor in Babylonia, a measure which was to have lasting consequences. In 307 BC Antigonus, together with his son Demetrius Poliorcetes, started his project of restoring the unity of the empire of Alexander and the Achaemenids, which, however, ended in failure and defeat at Ipsus in 301 BC. The Middle Eastern part of the empire was divided into two: Egypt ruled by Ptolemy and his successors in Alexandria, and the rest, i.e. Syria, Mesopotamia and Iran, together ruled by Seleucus and his successors residing in northern Syria. Palestine and adjacent regions were under Egypt, but became from now on a borderland and a strategic key region for the kings in both Alexandria and Antioch. This division of the Middle East had a certain similarity to the situation during late Neo-Assyrian and Neo-Babylonian times. Palestine and the Suez isthmus, together with the people who lived there, were once again drawn into the strategic and political hot air. The area became a bone of contention between the Seleucids in Syria and the Ptolemies in Egypt. It is likely that the frankincense traffic from South Arabia was one of the key factors that placed control of this area on the agenda of the governments in both kingdoms. The struggle was to have consequences for world history, not only because it involved Arabs and gave them a crucial role in international politics, but also for the effect it had on conditions in Jewish Palestine where a new religion arose which was not to remain a local, although eccentric, Syrian cult but evolved into a world religion.

On the Arabian peninsula proper the situation seems to have remained more stable, with an Egyptian presence in Dedan and attempts to revive the trade routes in the Red Sea and the Seleucids showing their ambitions in the Gulf but otherwise on the whole leaving Arabia in peace. In South Arabia, the four kingdoms continued their existence, the situation, as it seems, remaining quite stable for almost two centuries.

The contemporary sources for this period, the Hellenistic era, relevant for our purpose are somewhat scarce. The only original documents from the third century BC where Arabs are mentioned are papyri from Egypt. An important document from the same century is the Greek translation of the holy book of the Jews, according to the legend initiated in Alexandria under Ptolemy's successor Ptolemy Philadelphus

(285–247). From the middle of the second century BC there are preserved samples of Jewish literature: the Book of Jubilees, which has one passage about Arabs, and the First and Second Books of Maccabees, two Jewish historical works in Greek. First Maccabees, originally written in Hebrew around the year 100 BC in Palestine, tells the story of the Maccabaean wars in the middle of the century, where Arabs were involved. Second Maccabees, written in Greek somewhat later, also contains some relevant passages derived from a Jewish historian, Jason of Cyrene, writing in Greek. From the second century we have the Greek historian Polybius who wrote the history of the now rising Roman superpower, in which he dealt at length with the conflict between Rome and the Seleucids, involving Arabs.

Apart from these contemporary sources, preserved more or less in their original shape and wording, we have a number of authors writing in the early Roman imperial period who have preserved information and quotations from works written in the Hellenistic period which are otherwise lost. We have already used Diodorus Siculus and Strabo, who are gold mines in this respect. A most important author is Flavius Josephus who, at the end of the first century AD, wrote the history of the Jews where he quoted earlier writers at length. In the following century Plutarch wrote biographies of some of the protagonists of the Hellenistic age in which he often mentions Arabs. His contemporary Appian wrote a history about the wars of the Romans, dealing with their conquest of the Orient. From all these works we can dig out information originating with writers whose works are otherwise lost: Agatharchides from Cnidus, who incorporated a description of the Red Sea in his account of the early Ptolemaic kings, written in the middle of the second century BC, and the Jewish writers Eupolemus and Artapanus, who told the history of the Jews in Greek probably at the same time. These two writers are quoted not only by Josephus but also by the Christian historian Eusebius at the beginning of the fourth century AD. Agatharchides is quoted by three different writers: Diodorus, Strabo and Photius.

The events of 312 BC: Antigonus in Arabia

When he had expelled the troops of his rival Ptolemy in Egypt from Palestine in 312 BC, Antigonus Monophthalmus was faced by a coalition headed by Ptolemy and including also Seleucus, the former governor of Babylonia whom Antigonus had sacked. The battle fought at Gaza was lost by Antigonus, and Seleucus proceeded towards Babylonia and established himself there in his former province. Antigonus now had to consolidate his position in Syria before launching a new attack on Ptolemy. It is in connection with this we hear about his activities south-east of the Dead Sea. The data come from one of Antigonus' close associates, Hieronymus of Cardia. Hieronymus wrote a book on the history of Alexander's successors *c.* 280 BC. Since he himself had been a minister under Antigonus, he had first-hand information of the events.[1] Hieronymus' book belongs to those lost, but large parts of it were rather slavishly copied by Diodorus Siculus 300 years later.[2] We thus possess a good contemporary source for the important events in 312.

Hieronymus' general view of the geography of his day is found in a survey of the satrapies of the empire as it looked after Alexander's death.[3] He sees Asia divided by a mighty mountain range from east to west, on whose northern and southern slopes the satrapies are situated. The southern chain of satrapies are, from the east westwards, India, Arachosia, Cedrosia, Carmania and Persia:

> Next comes Babylonia [extending] unto the uninhabited [area] towards/at/close to *Arabía*.[4]

On the other side of Babylonia, i.e. northwards, is Mesopotamia to which Syria is adjacent.[5] This would imply that there is a stretch of uninhabited lands between Babylonia and Arabia proper. The latter could be Arabia around Palestine with the Syrian desert in between, but also the later *Arabía Eudaímōn*, which, in fact, encompassed most of what we call Arabia. In that case, the uninhabited land would be more or less the Syrian desert, including the areas south-west of Mesopotamia.

According to Diodorus' digest of Hieronymus, Antigonus in the year 312 BC initiated two military expeditions against 'the land of the *árabes* called *nabataîoi*' followed by an attempt to exploit the resources of asphalt in the Dead Sea.[6] As an introduction to the account of the campaigns stands an ethnographic description of the *árabes/nabataîoi*. Such ethnological excursus in an historical work we have already found in Herodotus, and it became a standard theme in this genre with both Greeks and Romans. There is thus no reason to doubt its authenticity.[7]

> It is useful for the sake of those ignorant to present the customs of those *árabes* following which they think they preserve their freedom. They lead a life in the open air claiming as homeland the uninhabited land without rivers and abundant springs from which an army of enemies could get water. It is a custom for them not to sow grains and not to cultivate any fruit-bearing plant, not to use wine and not to construct houses. He who is found doing against this, to him death is the punishment. They follow this custom, believing that those who have got possession of these things are easily forced by the powerful, because of the use of them, to do that which is ordered. Some of them raise camels, some sheep, pasturing in the desert.
>
> While there are quite many Arabic peoples (*arabiká ethnē*) who use the desert as pasture, these (*hoûtoi*) far surpass the others in wealth, being not more than ten thousand in number. For not a few of them usually bring frankincense, myrrh and most valuable perfumes to the sea having acquired them from those bringing them from the Arabia called *eudaímōn*.
>
> They are extremely freedom-loving, and whenever a strong force of enemies come near they flee to the desert, using it as a fortress. For being waterless it is inaccessible to others, offering safety only to them since they have prepared plastered reservoirs dug under ground. Since the earth is sometimes clayey and sometimes of soft rock they make large excavations in it, the mouths of which they make very small but towards the deep constantly making more digging, in the end finishing with the size so large that each side is one *pléthron*. Filling these reservoirs with rain water they close the openings and make it even with the rest of the ground and leave signs recognizable to themselves but incomprehensible to others. They water their cattle every other day so that when fleeing through waterless places they may not be in need of continuous supply of water. They themselves use as food meat and milk and those of the suitable plants that grow from the ground. For among them grow pepper and plenty of what is called wild honey from the trees, which they use as drink with water.
>
> There are also other tribes of *árabes* (*génē tōn arábōn*), some of whom even

> till the soil, mingling with the tribute-paying peoples, and have the same customs as the Syrians, except that they do not dwell in houses. Such are the customs of the *árabes*.
>
> When their gathering is near, to which those who dwell around usually come, some to sell goods and some to buy things needful to them, they travel to this meeting, leaving on a certain rock their possessions and their old men and also their women and children. This place is extremely strong but unwalled and two days' journey distant from the inhabited land.[8]

Then follows the account of the campaigns. The first one was led by Antigonus' general Athenaeus, who earlier had conquered Damascus for him. Athenaeus waited for the season of the gathering and then went out from Idumaea in three days, covering a distance of 2,200 *stadia*, i.e. *c.* 400 kilometres, and seized the rock mentioned in the ethnographic description. He left with a booty of frankincense, myrrh and 500 talents of silver, but was caught up by 8,000 *árabes/nabataîoi*, who killed most of the army with their javelins and took back the booty.[9]

The *árabes/nabataîoi* wrote to Antigonus 'in Syrian letters', complaining about the attacks. After a period of peace, Antigonus, probably eager to take revenge for the defeat, sent a new army under his son Demetrius into Arabia. Demetrius reached the rock after three days. The inhabitants defended themselves successfully, and the outcome was an agreement. Demetrius received hostages, retired and reached the Dead Sea 300 *stadia*, *c.* 55 kilometres, from the rock.[10]

When Demetrius returned, Antigonus found out that it would be profitable to exploit the asphalt in the Dead Sea. Hieronymus was entrusted with the task. The *árabes*, however, 6,000 men sailing on rafts, managed to kill most of Hieronymus' men with arrows and the enterprise was abandoned.[11] Thus ended Antigonus' business with people in Arabia.

The expedition in 312 BC: analysis

This account has usually been seen as a very trustworthy testimony and documentation of Nabataean, i.e. Arab, presence south-east of the Dead Sea already at the end of the fourth century BC.[12] It has never really been questioned and scholars usually forget that we do not have the words of the presumed eye-witness to the events but rather a version from an author writing two and a half centuries later and, as it seems, not even having the original text before him. It turns out, though, that in the cases when we can check Diodorus, i.e. when we have access to the texts he used for compiling his digest of ancient history, he often seems to have followed his source quite closely.[13] Another matter is, however, that his text is often founded upon several sources, between which he moves rather freely, picking out what he thinks will amuse the reader most.

A first critical reflection when reading the text is the striking difference between the people depicted here and what we hear about the Nabataeans in later periods.[14] In the 60s BC, a certain Athenodorus visited the Nabataean kingdom and its capital, Petra. Strabo has preserved details from his report, and the contradictions with that of Hieronymus are indeed striking.[15] According to Athenodorus, the Nabataeans held magnificent drinking-bouts, whereas Hieronymus states that they did not drink wine at all. In Athenodorus' time they lived in houses of stone, but Hieronymus' *árabes* do not construct houses, not even those who till the soil. The Nabataean kingdom was well supplied with fruit-trees and watered gardens according to Athenodorus, but in Hieronymus' days they did not cultivate any fruit-bearing tree or sow any cereals.

These contradictions may be explained by the time gap between the two accounts: the Nabataean Arabs were originally nomads, who later became permanently settled and adopted the ways of sedentary life.[16] This is not an impossible historical scenario. On the other hand, Hieronymus' description gives the impression that these *árabes* deliberately avoided certain civilizational features, practising a kind of taboo against some important features of settled life. The idea of an ideological anti-civilizational attitude of barbarian peoples is a standing theme in Greek and Roman ethnographic literature, where it is often presented as an example of the moral strength of the barbarians and an example for the degenerate city-dwellers of the Hellenistic world, without necessarily having any real foundation among the peoples described.[17] Hieronymus may very well have followed this moralistic practice. The fact is, however, that such anti-civilizational attitudes are indeed documented in the ancient Middle East. In Israel, there was a group, the 'sons of Yonadab ben Rekab', who followed a life-style strikingly similar to that of Hieronymus' *árabes/nabataîoi*.[18] It is not at all certain that the life-style of the Rechabites was a survival of nomadism. They seem rather to have constituted some kind of guild.[19] Hieronymus' description of the enemies of Athenaeus and Demetrius need not have been taken out of thin air. Instead they look quite similar to the Rechabites, and it is probably a fairly correct description of their life-style.[20]

If we take a closer look at some details in Hieronymus' description we find that the *árabes/nabataîoi* are indeed depicted as camel-holders and shepherds living in a waterless desert. On the other hand, we are told about their fabulous wealth in silver and their activities as tradesmen in the international frankincense trade, as well as their mastery of an advanced kind of water-storing technique. They also know how to write 'in Syrian letters', which obviously means that they use Aramaic. Most remarkable is their military skill. They were able to throw units of the Macedonian army, the world's foremost military machine in that age, out of their land. Even though Athenaeus' failure could be explained as due to bad luck and bad planning from the Greek side, this becomes very unlikely in the second attack. It is difficult to imagine Demetrius Poliorcetes not being able to ward off a second attack from unsophisticated shepherds. There are clear hints that these people were not so unsophisticated and that they possessed considerable military skill. We thus have one more indication that these *árabes*, even though showing nomadic features in their way of living, were not common nomads.

This leads us to the most eye-catching complication of the text: the use of two terms, *árabes* and *nabataîoi*. Both are used as designations for the people involved in the events. The term *nabataîoi* is used alternately with *árabes* in the account of the military operations, but it is absent from the ethnographic excursus as well as from the story of the asphalt project, where we only hear about *árabes*.[21] Since the two attacks are made against a stronghold on a rock, there has never been any doubt about the identity of the enemy: the common identification of the rock with Petra, the later capital of the Nabataean kingdom, confirms the presence of Nabataeans in the text.[22] It should be observed, however, that Diodorus/Hieronymus speaks about 'a (certain) rock' (*pétra tis*), which of course could mean any rock. The location of this rock according to the text as it stands (55 kilometres from the Dead Sea, 400 kilometres from Idumaea) does not support an identification with the later Nabataean capital Petra or with as-Silʕ between Bosra and aṭ-Ṭafīla. In fact, the text as it stands is difficult to harmonize, and even more so if one starts from the idea that the rock must be Nabataean Petra.[23] One valuable piece of information is that the rock was outside the eparchy of Idumaea. In the description of the Dead Sea, Diodorus (i.e. Hieronymus) says: 'it [the Dead Sea] lies towards the middle of (*katà mésēn*) the satrapy of Idumaea'.[24] The only plausible explanation for this piece of information is that the sub-province Idumaea, which must have been a creation of the late Achaemenid rulers, encompassed the areas on both sides of the southern tip of the Dead Sea, i.e. both the territory of the ancient Edomite kingdom destroyed by Nabonidus in 552 BC, and the areas west of the ʕArabah/the eastern Negev.[25] This location excludes the identification of the rock with Petra or as-Silʕ, which are both within the former kingdom of Edom.[26]

A suggestion for a location of the rock may begin with the assumption that Athenaeus' campaign started from present-day southern Syria, perhaps Damascus.[27] If we combine the two distances and take the 400 kilometres as an indication of the whole distance, placing the target outside Edom, we end up in the southern Negev, which was outside the province of Idumaea.[28] An exact identification of the rock is perhaps not possible at the moment, but the following is a tentative suggestion. Around 50 kilometres from the Dead Sea we find the spectacular site ʕAvdat or, in Greek sources, Oboda. This site, which is located on a quite prominent elevation, did have a special status in the later Arabo-Nabataean kingdom. The very site of Avdat fits quite well into the description 'the rock'.[29] Even though it cannot be proved, the candidacy of Avdat as the rock mentioned by Hieronymus is quite strong.

In the book on Arabia by Uranius, written in the third or fourth century AD, which is lost and known only through quotations in later works, it was said that this place 'of the Nabataeans' was the burial place of a deified king named Obodas. It is explicitly said that there was a cult around the dead king. His identity unfortunately remains somewhat obscure, since there are several known kings with that name.[30] It has been assumed that another note from Uranius about the death of Antigonus the Macedonian, who is said to have been killed by Rabilus, the king of the *árabes*, at a place called Mothó, 'Death', should be connected with the events in 312 BC.[31] Both these notes are legendary. An historical fact which has been connected with them is that in the year 88/87 BC the Seleucid king Antiochus XII Dionysius was defeated in the Negev by a king Obodas.[32] The Seleucid king is said to have died at a place located south-west of the Dead Sea, which makes it likely that the battle took place not far from there. It seems that the defeat of a Seleucid by a Nabataean king made such an impression on the inhabitants of the Nabataean kingdom that it was transferred back in time, combining Antigonus (who did not fall in battle in Nabataea) with an early ruler named Rabbel.[33] Behind the transfer of the event to the time of Antigonus may have been the memory of the military operations south of Palestine by this king.

Nabataean presence in the Negev already in the fourth century BC has indeed been suggested but has not found acceptance among scholars.[34] On the other hand, everybody has accepted the Diodorus/Hieronymus testimony of Nabataeans in Petra in 312 BC. But if *pétra tis* in Hieronymus is not the later Nabataean capital, and the presence of Nabataeans in the Negev this early is rejected, we are faced with a problem since the text does talk about the Nabataeans. If, however, we look at the textual tradition of Diodorus, an interesting detail appears. The text to Book XIX, in which we find the account about Antigonus and Demetrius in Arabia, exists in two versions, one represented by manuscript R (Parisinus Graecus 1665) and one by manuscript F (Laurentianus 70.12). The latter, in the text to Book XIX, is based on a lost prototype different from R. R was written in the tenth century AD, whereas F is from the late fifteenth. Both manuscripts have several daughter-manucripts. There are thus, in practice, two textual traditions to take into account for the text of Book XIX. In the six instances where MS R has *nabataîoi*, it turns out that MS F instead has *nomádes*, 'shepherds, nomads'. In other words, in the F manuscript, the Nabataeans are not mentioned, either in the military account or in the ethnographic excursus or the story of the asphalt project.[35]

So what did Diodorus write? Considering the fact that in Diodorus' time and the following centuries the Nabataeans were known as settled empire-builders and partners in international big business, not as nomads, it is less likely that scribes would have changed Nabataeans into nomads. In late antiquity and early Byzantine times the former Nabataea (*Palaestina Tertia* and *Provincia Arabia*) was scattered with well-built, prosperous cities, the ruins of which impress us even today. A strong support for arguing that *nabataîoi* have replaced *nomádes* in the text is the fact that both R and F have the phrase 'the *árabes* called *nabataîoi*' in the introductory passage to Hieronymus' account. This expression is found in another part of Diodorus' book, which is a quotation from Diodorus' somewhat older contemporary Posidonius.[36] The identification of Nabataeans with Arabs was current in the first century BC and Diodorus follows the terminology of his time. But it seems that having finished his introduction to Hieronymus' account, slavishly following the terminology of his own time, he proceeded mechanically to copy Hieronymus' text without bothering about the resulting inconsistencies. The inconsistency between the introduction and the following paragraph led a later copyist to replace *nomádes* with *nabataîoi*, since the paragraph, according to the introduction, dealt with them. F's *nomádes* is *lectio difficilior*, since it goes against common opinion about ethnic conditions in antiquity as well as in Byzantine times but fits quite well into the picture emerging from an unprejudiced reading of the source material.

There is a text from Egypt dated to 259 BC which almost certainly mentions the Nabataeans in the Ḥawrān, i.e. far from the Negev.[37] The story about the king Obodas and its connection with the legend about the Macedonian campaigns in 312 BC shows that the later Nabataeans had absorbed these operations into their own history. There are thus weighty arguments in favour of the conclusion that the Nabataeans did not originally belong to Hieronymus' account. Instead the terminology of the R manuscript in the stories of the two campaigns reflects much later ages, when it was known that the Negev had been firmly in the hands of the Nabataean kings, one of whom had even defeated a successor to Antigonus. The adjustment of terminology by introducing the Nabataeans in the story of the campaigns against the *árabes* reflects conditions and views in the first century BC and onwards, not earlier.

The *árabes* in the Negev were not numerous, but they obviously played a central role in the trade with perfumes from South Arabia. It lies near at hand to assume that they, in fact, are closely related to or identical with those who had been in charge of this business in Gaza for a long time. Their use of Syrian letters is a reminder of the Aramaic letters on the bowls presented to the goddess at Tell al-Maskhūṭa by the king of Qedar.

Antigonus launched two campaigns through Transjordan across the ʕArabah into the Negev. Perfumes like frankincense and myrrh are main parts of the booty taken, which is a clear hint of what the conflict was about. A very plausible interpretation is that Antigonus tried to take control of the frankincense road, which had earlier gone through Transjordan but which now ran through the Negev to Gaza. The conflict was not only about trade. We should keep in mind that Antigonus was involved in a severe conflict with Ptolemy in Egypt, who had just devastated the Syrian coast, and the operations in

Transjordan and the Negev might well have been a preparation for an attack on Egypt from an unexpected direction. Antigonus thus appears as a successor to Nebuchadnezzar who had operated in the same area, as it seems with the same meagre results.

> In the Old Testament we find several passages which testify to the existence of a 'rock' in the Negev. There are two variants of the story of a battle of the Judaean king Amasiah, reigning around 800 BC, against the Edomites 'in the Valley of Salt', taking 'the rock' and hurling the survivors down from it.[38] This valley has usually been identified with the ʕArabah south of the Dead Sea, but this is by no means certain.[39] There is, in fact, today a 'Valley of Salt', Wādī al-Milḥ, east of Beer Sheba, which could well be a better candidate. The rock would then be not far from there.
>
> In a note about the southern borders of Judaea it is said that 'the border of the Amorite,/LXX: the Edomite/, is from/LXX above/ the Ascent of Scorpions, from /LXX: on/ the 'rock' (*selaʕ*) and upward'.[40] The Ascent of Scorpions is the steep road from the ʕArabah westwards into the Negev. The impression is that the two geographical locations are the southernmost outposts of the region of the Amorites who live 'upward', i.e. in the highlands of Judaea rising northwards from the Negev.[41]
>
> The rock in this passage is clearly a border marker, which makes sense if we compare with the description of the southern border of the Promised Land preserved in the book of Numbers. The south-eastern border is said to run from the southern end of the Dead Sea, past the Ascent of Scorpions and the desert Ṣin unto Qadesh Barnea. It is also said to run along Edom.[42] The rock is thus somewhere along this borderline.
>
> The Biblical tradition does, in fact, contain an explicit identification of 'the rock' with the stronghold of *árabes*. In the report of the conquests of the Judaean king Uzziah discussed earlier in this study, it is said that he attacked the *ʕarbîm* in Gur Baʕal.[43] We have argued that these Arabs probably dwelt east of the ʕArabah. The Septuagint, however, renders the passage: 'the *árabes* that [were] on the rock' (*epì tēs pétras*). The same expression has, in fact, intruded into the LXX text to Judges 1:36 as well, where the rock in the Negev is undoubtedly referred to. The Septuagint has obviously updated the passage and together with Diodorus' rendering of Hieronymus there is a clear testimony that Arabs at some time before 312 BC had taken hold of the obviously famous rock in the Negev, well known to the Israelite tradition.

The same *árabes* appear once more in Hieronymus' account of Antigonus. When the latter made a renewed attempt at conquering Egypt in 306 BC he encountered the same problems as his predecessors:

> He [Antigonus] himself, since he was encamped at Gaza and was eager to forestall the preparations by Ptolemy, ordered his soldiers to provide themselves with ten days' rations, and loaded the camels, which had been gathered by the *árabes*, one hundred and thirty thousand measures of grain and a good stock of fodder for the beasts, and carrying his ordinance in waggons he advanced through the wilderness with great hardship because many places in the region were swampy, particularly near the spot called Barathra.[44]

The assistance given to the Macedonian king makes sense when we remember that Demetrius had made a treaty with the *árabes* in the Negev. Arabs obviously still inhabited the areas between Palestine and the Nile Delta. Despite their assistance, Antigonus failed to defeat Ptolemy and had to return to Syria, while Ptolemy secured his hold on Egypt.

Two early Hellenistic authors on Arabia: Euhemerus and Iambulus

The reports from Alexander's expeditions to Arabia not only provided facts for Hellenistic scientists but also stimulated the imagination of other writers. We have preserved digests of two, Euhemerus and Iambulus, probably writing at the beginning and the end of the third century BC respectively. Digests of both of them are preserved by Diodorus Siculus in his *Bibliotheca*. Euhemerus is also quoted by Eusebius at the beginning of the fourth century AD.

Euhemerus wrote a book called *The Holy History*, which seems to have been a philosophical treatise on the origin of the gods.[45] The book, which was perhaps originally a poem, was written shortly before 280 BC.[46] Euhemerus' thesis was that the gods were originally kings and remarkable personalities who later were transformed to gods by priests. As proof of this, he depicts a utopian society that is said to have real existence on islands that lie off Arabia. After his treatment of the islands in the west, the north and the ocean in general, Diodorus introduces the new item:

> We shall, in turn, discuss the islands towards the south, [those] in the ocean belonging to the Arabia which inclines towards the east and borders upon the so-called Kedrōsía. This region contains many villages and notable towns, of which some are situated upon mounds, others on small hills or in plains. The largest of them are constructed in a costly way with a multitude of inhabitants and ample estates. Their entire country abounds with domestic animals of all kinds, bearing fruits and offering no lack of pasturages for the fatted animals. Many rivers flow through the land and irrigate a great part of it, contributing to the full maturing of the fruits. Therefore, the most prominent part of Arabia has, because of its excellency, received an appropriate name being called *eudaímōn*.[47]
>
> Off this Arabia lie three islands, one called *Hierá* 'the holy' and also Pankhaítis or Pankhaía, another where the dead from Hiera are buried, and a third one far in the east, from which one can discern India.[48] It is further said that the inhabitants of the island Hiera trade with frankincense and myrrh, which is sold to *árabes* on the mainland.[49] In the island there is a well with abundant water, which is called 'Sun water'.[50] The two main gods are Uranus and Zeus, of which Uranus was the first to reign on the island. He is said to have resided on top of a mountain, close to a temple and the main spring.[51]

Eusebius quoted Euhemerus in two of his works: the *Praeparatio Euangelica*, a kind of world history where he told the prehistory of Christianity, and in his commentary to the book of Isaiah. In the latter he agrees with the location attributed to Euhemerus by Diodorus and it is very likely that the notice is taken from Euhemerus:

> There is also another [Arabia] called *eudaímōn Arabía* lying near the land of the Persians.[52]

In the *Praeparatio*, Eusebius gives an explicit reference to Euhemerus which shows that he was familiar with his work (or a version of it). He says that Euhemerus was a friend of king Cassandrus, one of Alexander's successors, and was entrusted with several tasks by him, among them travels:

> He [Euhemerus] says that he went far away towards the south into the Ocean setting out from *eudaímōn Arabía* and sailing through the Ocean for several days and landing on some islands in the sea. One of these is the one called Pankhaía on which the Panchaean inhabitants are distinguished by pious living, honouring the gods with magnificent sacrifices.[53]

Then follows the description of the island and the temple to Zeus with an altar to his father Uranus.

One is immediately struck by the resemblance between these accounts and the description of the Arabia which Alexander the Great, according to Arrian, i.e. Aristobulus, intended to colonize and conquer. Even the association between Uranus and the sun is found in both accounts. As has been shown already, Alexander's Arabia was the region along the southern shore of the Persian Gulf. If we are to believe the indications given in Diodorus, Euhemerus' *Arabía eudaímōn* must be the same area. According to Eusebius, *Arabía eudaímōn* was situated near Persia and the statement that this Arabia 'inclined towards the east and Kedrōsía', i.e. the Iranian province Gedrosia north-east of the Hormuz straits, leaves no doubt.[54] With this goes the fact that India is said to be visible from the easternmost of the islands, which could thus reflect the view from Rās Musandam eastwards.[55] Euhemerus seems to have been the first to give an exact location of *Arabía Eudaímōn*, an expression first used by Euripides.[56] According to Eusebius' quotation, Euhemerus had visited the area himself. It was situated in eastern Arabia along the Persian Gulf, not in Yemen.[57]

Euhemerus locates his ideal state in a region well documented by the expeditions of Alexander the Great. It has been pointed out that Euhemerus wanted to give his depiction a documentary colouring.[58] The Happy Arabia was not a myth. It existed like Greece. In the same way, the gods were not mythical beings; they had existed too, like the Greeks.

A similar story was composed somewhat later by a certain Iambulus. His name looks Semitic and even Arabic, but we do not know exactly from where he came.[59] We do not even know exactly when he lived, but he is clearly dependent upon Euhemerus and is tentatively dated to the end of the third century BC. His book is a Utopia: he depicts a society with communist social conditions. According to the text as preserved in Diodorus, Iambulus had travelled in 'spice-bearing Arabia' and from there after many adventures ended up on 'The Happy Island' (*nēsos eudaímōn*).[60] On it there are many springs, hot and cold.[61] The water of the surrounding sea is said to be sweet in taste.[62] The inhabitants worship 'that which encompasses all things, both the sun and, in general, all heavenly bodies'.[63] Like the island of Euhemerus, it is situated 'in the ocean in the south'.[64] When Iambulus leaves the island he ends up in India.[65] All these details make it very likely that Euhemerus and Iambulus have the same island in mind, which consequently should be looked for in the Persian Gulf.[66]

It might now be asked why these authors chose Arabia and, more specifically, the Persian Gulf, as the location for their utopias. A more traditional Greek concept was that the Isles of the Blessed were in the west. The concept of the 'Happy City' on the Red Sea was, however, already known to the Greeks. The idea of a utopian metropolis in this area is in fact already documented in the fifth century BC. In Aristophanes' comedy *The Birds*, two Athenians are looking for a better place than their conflict-ridden hometown to live in. They visit a bird who earlier has been a king, Tereus. When asked about his preferences, one of the Athenians, Peithetairos, says he wants a place with more sexual liberty than Athens. The bird answers that 'there is such a happy city (*eudaímōn pólis*) by the Red Sea (*erythrà thálassa*)'.[67] This is actually the background for the term 'the ocean to the south', in which both Euhemerus and Iambulus say the happy island of the sun is situated. We must remember that in Aristophanes' days the Persian Gulf was more or less unknown to the Greeks. According to Hecataeus' map, the coast ran in a straight line from India to the bay of Suez. The ocean washing this coast was called the Red Sea, which thus lay south of the land mass inhabited by men. It should also be kept in mind that the knowledge about the Gulf in Euhemerus' and Iambulus' days was still very recent, and the geography of eastern Arabia was not known in all details by everybody. On the other hand, it should be remembered that Aristophanes' contemporary, Euripides, mentions *Arabía eudaímōn* and seems to locate it in the east.[68]

But where did the idea of a happy island in this region come from? The unequivocal location in the Persian Gulf makes it incumbent to associate it with one of the oldest myths of the ancient Orient, namely that of Dilmun. This name is mentioned in cuneiform texts from the late Uruk period until Seleucid times.[69] There is no doubt that Dilmun was the name of a specific area. It has been assumed that it originally included the present-day eastern province of Saudi Arabia.[70] But in most cases, it refers to present-day Baḥrayn, whose Greek name Tylos is identical with Dilmun. The island of Dilmun figures in several mythical texts going back to the Sumerian period. It is said to be the place where Ziusudra, the Sumerian Noah, landed after the Deluge. In that story it is the sun god, Utu, who saves Ziusudra and who is worshipped by him in Dilmun after the Flood.[71] This is a striking parallel to what is told about Zeus worshipping his father Uranus in Euhemerus' account. The most interesting myth in this context is the introduction to the story about Enki and Ninhursag, the Sumerian paradise myth. Dilmun is here the pure land where there is no death or sickness. In the beginning there is no water, but this is amended by divine action:

> Utu, standing in heaven . . .
> from the mouth that pours out the earth's water
> he brought sweet water from the earth.
> He pumps the water into her large cisterns.
> From them the city drinks the wealth of water;
> Dilmun drinks from them the waters overflowing.
> Her well of bitter water is now a well of sweet water.
> Her crop-yielding fields and farms turn out heaps of grain.
> Her city is now the floodgate of the land.
> Dilmun is the floodgate of the land.
> Now by Utu, on this day, it has become just that.[72]

This scene bears a strong resemblance to what Euhemerus says about Uranus on the mountain above the temple and the holy spring of the island of Pankhaía. In short, there is no doubt that the picture of the Happy Island described by Euhemerus and Iambulus is dependent upon the age-old Sumerian concept of Dilmun which is located on

Baḥrayn. The description of the site given by them has many features which are surprisingly realistic: the sweet-water springs, which even today flow in the ocean around the island; the abundant greenery and forests of palm trees, until recently a prominent feature of Baḥrayn. The report about the burials on a special island brings the vast ancient graveyards on Baḥrayn into mind. It seems that Baḥrayn in antiquity was a holy place where people were brought to be buried from the surrounding regions.

All this explains how references to the Happy City could appear in both Aristophanes and Euripides before the Persian Gulf was known to the Greeks: they knew about the Dilmun myth locating a paradisiacal city in the 'Red Sea', i.e. somewhere in the large southern ocean as described in Euripides' *Bacchae*. The Dilmun mythology also affected Alexander's concept about the Gulf, as is already documented in Aristobulus. His ambitions there suddenly appear in a new light, and the motive in the later Alexander romance about his quest for the end of the world where the two oceans of sweet and salt waters meet and the source of life is to be found, may, in fact, go back to the great Macedonian king himself.

It thus turns out that the earliest mentions of *Arabía eudaímōn* locate it in the Persian Gulf as lying opposite the island of Baḥrayn. It seems that the epithet *eudaímōn* is originally connected with the island and originates from the role it plays in the ancient Mesopotamian myths about Dilmun. The myth was obviously known to the Greeks as early as the fifth century BC, as well as its location in a land called Arabia. The application of the epithet *eudaímōn* to the shore opposite Dilmun/Baḥrayn may, in fact, reflect an ancient inclusion of that area in the region called Dilmun, although there is little doubt that the epithet originally pertains to the island, as is explicitly stated by Iambulus.

In the Alexander story, the report of the sun-worship among the 'Arabs' is connected with his plans for conquest of Arabia, which, in its turn, was due to their absence among the embassies to Alexander in Babylon. The sun-god Utu/Shamash was in Mesopotamia, since time immemorial, the guardian and guarantor of law, order and justice. It can be suggested that this absence was seen in certain radical and anti-despotic circles as a sign of rejection of the despotic state ideology as a whole. The fact that Arabs were said to have been the only ones not to submit to Alexander made their land the home of freedom and a justice administered not by a capricious human ruler but by the god manifest in the sun, the age-old guarantor of a just world-order.

This means that the absence of the 'Arabs' in Babylon in 323 BC, which is probably an historical fact, gave political utopists a peg upon which they could hang an entire alternative political ideology. When the Arab affair was integrated into the *hypomnēmata* complex, namely Alexander's ambition to conquer the whole world, the behaviour of the Arabs received increased significance. They appear in the legend and the utopian propaganda as the only ones who never submitted to the despotic world ruler, who in fact died when preparing his campaign against them. Arabia became the antithesis of the despotic state. For the radicals the world became divided in two: the land of freedom and justice in Arabia, and the realm of despotism and repression in the rest of the world. Needless to say, this world-view was relevant only to a few thinkers and political utopists, but they seem to have played a not insignificant role in the Hellenistic era. We know that the most dramatic social revolution in antiquity, namely that of Aristonicus in Pergamon in the 140s BC, explicitly had the aim of creating 'the republic of the Sun', and the members of the movement called themselves Heliopolitans, citizens of the City of the Sun.[73] Diodorus' digests of Euhemerus and Iambulus are literary monuments from this movement.

The symbol of the City of the Sun where justice reigns had an impact on later ages and has never been completely forgotten. In Europe, its most remarkable manifestation is, of course, Tommaso Campanella's *La città del sole* from the beginning of the seventeenth century, one of the great utopias of the Renaissance. In the east it also had a remarkable literary *Nachleben*. In *sūrat an-naml,* 'The ant', in the Qurʔān, we read the story of the Queen of Sheba (Sabaʔ) and Solomon (Sulaymān). The latter is the world ruler to whom everybody, even animals and spirits, submit. There is, however, one exception: the kingdom of Sabaʔ whose people 'worship the sun excluding God'.[74] This makes Sulaymān threaten the only remaining independent kingdom with war if it does not surrender, just as Alexander the Great did. Instead of trying to see this verse as a reference to sun-worship in historical Saba, we should realize the traces of ancient revolutionary ideology behind it: this is a survival of the idea of the city ruled by the sun documented by Iambulus, developed from the historical fact that the people on the Gulf coast did not turn up with Alexander the Great in Babylon 323 BC, and ultimately going back to the myth about Dilmun. The location of these sun-worshippers in South Arabia is due to the later reinterpretations of the term *Arabía eudaímōn*.[75]

There is a detail that perhaps takes us even further. In the Muslim tradition about Sulaymān and the Queen, his throne is described more or less like a kind of aeroplane, with which he can travel all over the earth.[76] On the reliefs at Persepolis and Naqsh-e-Rustam we can still see the Achaemenid kings, to whom Alexander explicitly saw himself as an heir, enthroned on daises carried by representatives of the peoples of the *oecumene*. In representations of the story about Sulaymān and Bilqīs in modern popular art in Muslim countries, the animals and demons can be seen as carriers of the throne, much like the subject peoples on the Achaemenid reliefs.[77] Over it hovers the bird that, according to the Qurʔān, informed Sulaymān about the existence of sun-worshipping Sabaʔ. This bird is the *hudhud*, the hoopoe. The bird that tells Peithetairos about the *eudaímōn pólis*, 'the happy city', in Aristophanes' comedy is the *épops*, the hoopoe.

The Ptolemies and the Arabs

The career of Antigonus ended at Ipsus in 301 BC when he was defeated and killed by a coalition of his rivals. This was the end of the attempt to keep Alexander's empire under one ruler. In Syria, Seleucus had emerged as sovereign, whereas Ptolemy secured control of Egypt and southern Syria. One can see this as the final failure of the policy initiated by Esarhaddon aiming at the political integration of both the ancient river-cultures in the East. Already in the fourth century BC Egypt had liberated herself of political control from Asia and Alexander's conquest of her was only a last attempt that did not prevail. Esarhaddon's aims were not to be fulfilled until the Muslim conquest of Egypt in the 640s AD.

Both the Ptolemies and the Seleucids ended up with Arabs within their borders. The former kept control over the coastal region and the road to Palestine. We hear about an overseer of the frankincense trade in Gaza in the reign of the second king in Alexandria, Ptolemy II Philadelphus (283–246).[78] Arabs, perhaps those in the Negev, had supported Antigonus in 306 BC, but it is reasonable to assume that they now joined the new power in Egypt. The Ptolemies also controlled Transjordan, which is probably reflected by the Greek names of the regions all ending in *-itis*, which is characteristic of the Ptolemaic administration: Gobolitis, Ammonitis, Galaaditis, Golanitis and Auranitis.[79] From the papyrus dated to 259 BC referred to above, we hear about the Nabataeans in the last-mentioned region, which would then indicate that they were under Ptolemaic rule or, at least, closely allied with it. North of Auranitis was the region of Damaskēnē, which reveals the Seleucid administrative practice with provincial names in *-ēnē*. The border thus ran just south of Damascus. These names remained in use into the Roman period and were a memory of the political conditions in the area at the beginning of the Hellenistic era.

The Arabs were well known among *hommes littérés*, as we can see from Hecataeus of Abdera, a writer in the third century BC who wrote a fanciful description of Egypt, the *Aegyptiaca*, large parts of which are preserved by the diligent Diodorus in the first book of his *Bibliotheca*.[80] Most of what this Egyptomaniac told is of highly doubtful historicity and the notices about Arabia have only some value as testimony of a not too sophisticated intellectual's understanding of Arabia from an Egyptian perspective. His Arabia is identical with that of his greater namesake from Ionia 200 years earlier, i.e. Egypt between the Nile and the Red Sea, including the land between the delta and Palestine.[81]

The Red Sea expedition of Ptolemy II

The Seleucids in Antioch seem to have given up ambitions in southern Syria. Instead they started to increase their influence in the Persian Gulf. It was these activities that induced the second Ptolemy with the name Philadelphus to start an expansionist policy in the Red Sea and north-western Arabia.[82] As a preparation for a military action in Arabia, Philadelphus sent out an expedition, headed by a certain Ariston, to explore the western coast of Arabia in 280 BC. It is mentioned by later writers like Eratosthenes.[83] Its importance comes from the fact that substantial parts of the report from the expedition are preserved. The report was used by a second-century writer, Agatharchides from Cnidus, who wrote a book, *On the Red Sea*, dealing with the history of the Ptolemies, incorporating the description of the Arabian coast in his fifth book. Agatharchides' original text is lost, but extracts and digests of it are found in three later authors: Diodorus Siculus, Strabo and the collection of extracts from ancient literature made by the Byzantine theologian Photius in the ninth century AD.[84] Of these three witnesses to Agatharchides' work, the Photius text is considered closest to the original. Unfortunately, its author has skipped over many passages; these have to be supplied by Diodorus' fuller version, which, however, is more distant from the original wording. The least important is Strabo, who used an abridgement of Agatharchides made by Artemidorus of Ephesus around 100 BC.[85]

This complicated textual tradition should be kept in mind when we try to find out what was reported about Arabs in western Arabia around 280 BC. From the three versions we may be able to form an opinion of what Agatharchides wrote, but we should then remember that he was at least one century remote from the text of Ariston. It is wise to adduce the three variants together in the passages relevant for our study:

I

> Diodorus: We shall take up the other part of the opposite shore which leans towards Arabia and start with the innermost recess. This is called Poseídeion since Ariston, who was sent out by Ptolemaios to investigate the Arabia stretching as far as the Ocean, founded an altar to Poseidon of the sea.

Strabo: He [Artemidorus] returns to the *árabes* and first he describes those who border on the Arabian Gulf.

Photius: –

Photius' *Bibliotheca* has not preserved the introduction to the description of Arabia. In Diodorus and Strabo we find the *árabes* on the eastern side of the Gulf of Suez.[86] We might tentatively recognize the Arabs encountered by Herodotus 200 years earlier.

II

Diodorus: The promontory (*akrōtērion*) of the island stretching out in front/the promontory stretching out in front of the island lies towards (*katà*) the so-called 'Rock' (*pétra*) and Palestine. To this, according to report, the Gerrhaeans and the Minaeans bring from what is called Upper Arabia frankincense and the other goods having to do with aromatics.

Strabo: Near the island is a promontory, which stretches towards (*pròs*) the Rock (*pétra*) of the *árabes* called *nabataîoi* and Palestinian country, to which Minaeans and Gerrhaeans and all the neighbouring peoples bring the aromatic goods.

Photius: This 'duck' lies close to a promontory richly forested, and it (the 'duck') stretches/points, observed in a straight line, towards (*pròs*) both the so-called 'Rock' *(pétra*) and Palestine, to which Gerrhaeans and Minaeans and all the *árabes* living nearby bring frankincense, according to report, and the goods having to do with aromatics from the upper country.

This passage has always been taken as evidence of the presence of the Nabataeans at Petra at this time.[87] Since, as we have shown, the Nabataeans were not mentioned by Hieronymus of Cardia, and we have evidence from the middle of the third century BC that they were in Ḥawrān, this passage should be examined closely.

The island mentioned in Diodorus and Strabo has been identified with Tīrān at the inlet to the Gulf of ʕAqabah.[88] The promontory has been sought either at Rās al-Qaṣba on the Arabian side or Rās Muhammed on the Sinai peninsula.[89] Both these promontories point towards the south, not to the north, which does not help our understanding of the text. The text is, however, not immediately comprehensible in itself and is probably not in good order. Diodorus' version is the most comprehensible. According to him, the promontory is part of the island, not the opposite mainland, and it is that promontory which points towards Petra and Palestine. Photius says that the island itself points in that direction. Since the Gulf of ʕAqabah is mentioned immediately afterwards, it is difficult to avoid the conclusion that the passage is a description of Rās Muhammed, the southernmost tip of the Sinai peninsula.[90]

If we draw a straight line from there towards *Palaistínē*, which seems to be a reasonable interpretation of the wording, we do not pass the later Nabataean capital. No one seems to have remembered that Palestine at this time is primarily Philistaea, i.e. the coastal region between Gaza and Jaffa not including Judaea and definitely not Transjordan.[91] The 'rock', *hē pétra*, should then be somewhere on a line from the inlet to the Gulf of ʕAqabah to Philistaea. Now Hieronymus mentions a rock which, as we have shown above, must be somewhere in the Negev, perhaps identical with Avdat, and which is a habitat of *árabes*. This fits, in fact, quite well with what Agatharchides seems to have written. The *árabes* living nearby must thus be those mentioned by Hieronymus. We notice that only Strabo, who is the most unreliable of the three, has the phrase 'the *árabes* called *nabataîoi*'. This phrase occurs in other parts of Diodorus' book which clearly come from Posidonius.[92] Diodorus does not have the identification with the Nabataeans. Both he and Photius must be considered better witnesses to Agatharchides than Strabo in this passage.

A very important detail in this passage is the expression 'according to report' (*hōs lógos*). The 'report' is obviously about the frankincense traffic of the Minaeans and the Gerrhaeans. Since it is found in both Diodorus and Photius, it is quite certain that it comes from Agatharchides. But it is also fairly certain that it does not come from Ariston. This expression shows that Agatharchides, in the note about the frankincense traffic, refers to a source different from Ariston, a source which is closer to his own time. The context also makes it very likely that Agatharchides here has not received his information from Ariston, who, sailing in the Red Sea and not entering the Gulf of ʕAqabah, is unlikely to have said anything about frankincense traffic through Transjordan and the Negev. We shall return to the dating of this note below.

III

> Diodorus: The Laianítēs Gulf then follows, inhabited by many villages of the *árabes* called *nabataîoi*.
>
> Strabo: Then [comes] the Ailanítēs Gulf and Nabataía, being a country well populated and with good pastures.
>
> Photius: After the gulf called Laianítēs, around which *árabes* live.

The Laeanites/Aelanites Gulf is no doubt the Gulf of ʕAqabah.[93] Photius mentions only *árabes* living around it. Diodorus has the common phrase identifying Nabataeans as Arabs which, as has been pointed out, probably reflects later times. The *árabes* east of the Gulf remind us of the Arabs mentioned in Chronicles against whom king Uzziah fought.[94]

IV

> Diodorus: Those who shepherd the country beyond (*katà*) the gulf who are called Banizomeneîs get their food by hunting and eating the meat of the land animals. A very holy sanctuary has been built there, exceedingly revered by all the *árabes*.
>
> Strabo: Thereafter [comes] a gulf about five hundred *stadia* in extent, enclosed by mountains and a mouth difficult to enter. Around it live men hunting land animals. Then [come] three uninhabited islands.
>
> Photius: . . . is the land of Bythemanéoi, a large plain . . . There is a gulf directed to the interior of the land, not more than five hundred stadia deep. Those who

> live inside the gulf are called Batmizomaneîs. They are hunters of land animals. After the mentioned land come three islands which form several harbours. Of these they call the first the sanctuary of Isis.

The gulf mentioned by Photius and Strabo is probably the bay at ʕAynūna, beyond which is a large plain and outside of which are several islands.[95] Only Diodorus mentions *árabes* and that in a very general way: the sanctuary is revered by all inhabitants of Arabia as he sees it.[96] The other two versions do not mention Arabs, which probably reflects Agatharchides' own text. The Banizomaneîs in Diodorus, and the Bythemanéoi and the Batmizomaneîs in Photius can be suspected to refer to the same entity.[97] We have suggested earlier that they are identical with the Amazoneîs attacked by king Asa according to the Septuagint, as well as the Alimazoneîs mentioned in the Septuagint in the account of the attack against Jerusalem in the days of king J(eh)oram.[98] In the latter story, the LXX also has a variant reading of *árabes*: *zámbroi* which should be compared to Zimrān, one of the sons of Qeṭurah and brother of Midian. One should also refer to the Mar-si-ma-nu mentioned by Sargon II in 715 BC together with Ha-a-a-pa and Ta-mu-di [and?] 'the distant ar-ba-a-a'.[99] Of the latter three, Hayappa belongs to the Midian of the Old Testament (ʕEphah) and, as is seen from the next paragraph, Thamūd appears in Agatharchides to be located not far from the Banizomeneîs etc. We would suggest that we have to do with the same entity in the north-western Ḥiğāz. The ethnography of that area between the end of the eighth and the beginning of the third century BC can thus to some extent be reconstructed from Sargon's annals, the list of Qeṭurah's sons in Genesis, the Book of Chronicles and Agatharchides.

V

> Diodorus: This coast is inhabited by the *árabes* called Thamoudēnoí.
>
> Strabo: –
>
> Photius: After the separated islands one can see a stony and large shore: this is the land of the Thamoudēnoí *árabes*.

The description fits the stony coast between al-Muwayliḥ and Rās Karkūma just south of al-Wağh.[100] Strabo mentions the stony shore but no ethnic names. We see that both Diodorus and Photius identify Thamūd as *árabes*. Before analysing this passage, we should also adduce another coming shortly afterwards:

VI

> Diodorus: Those of the *árabes* called Débai inhabit the mountainous area . . . The land which comes next is inhabited by *árabes* Alilaîoi and Gasandoí.
>
> Strabo: After that one comes . . . to a country of nomads . . . They are called Débai; some are nomads and some are farmers.
>
> Photius: The Debaí inhabit the area neighbouring the mountainous region;

> some are nomads and some are farmers . . . Their neighbours are Alilaîoi and Kasandreîs.

The coast described here is identified with the coast of the southern Saudi Arabian Tihāma between al-Qunfudha and al-Baysh.[101] One can observe that the Débai according to Photius inhabit the Tihāma itself, whereas Diodorus locates them in the mountains of ʕAsīr. The wording in Strabo supports Photius, and it is much more likely that Ariston had contacts with inhabitants of the coastal region than with the mountain country. Of the others, the Gasandoí/Kasandreîs might be connected with the present-day town of Ǧīzān just north of the Yemeni border.

Photius does not identify the three following peoples as *árabes*, which Diodorus does. The epithet *árabes* given by Photius to the Thamūd would indicate that they had a status similar to Qedar, which, as we have seen, are definitely identified as Arabs. On the other hand, the identification of Thamūd as Arabs also stands isolated in Photius' text, and given the carelessness with which this term is handled by many ancient writers, let alone copyists, we would like to have some more substantial evidence before acknowledging Thamūd as Arabs. One should not, however, forget the first appearance of Thamūd in a historical document. Sargon's writers put the expression 'the distant *arbāya*' just after their name. Does it refer to Thamūd, to all the three peoples mentioned, or to none of them? Meanwhile, there should be no doubt that the Arab identity of the Débai, the Alillaîoi and the Gasandoí is the work of Diodorus and not of Agatharchides.

Then there follow sections on South Arabia of which the following are of importance for this study:

VII

> Diodorus: After these are the Sabaeans, being the most numerous of the Arabic peoples (*arabikà éthnē*) and inhabiting the Arabia called *eudaímōn* . . . This tribe [the Sabaeans] surpasses not only the neighbouring *árabes* but also all other men in wealth.

> Strabo: Bordering [upon this region] is the very fertile (*eudaimonestátē*) [country] of the Sabaeans, a very large tribe (*éthnos*) . . . From their trafficking both the Sabaeans and the Gerrhaeans have become richest of all.

> Photius: Just after this comes the people (*génos*) of the Sabaeans, the largest of those in (*katà*) Arabia, possessing all kinds of wealth (*eudaimonía*) . . . No people seems to be better provided than the Sabaeans and the Gerrhaeans, who profit from all the exceptional things from Europe and Asia.

This passage is quite revealing as far as Diodorus' method is concerned. Both Strabo and Photius have a wording which is much more original than that of Diodorus. The latter has taken the derivations of *eudaímōn*, 'fertile', 'wealthy' etc., and transformed it to a more well-known phrase often used about Arabia in his time. There is no doubt that Strabo and Photius are closer to Agatharchides' original text than Diodorus' more watered-down version.

A comparison of the different versions of Agatharchides shows that he originally spoke of Arabs only in the regions around the two northern tips of the Red Sea: just immediately east of present-day Suez, in the Negev by 'a rock' somewhere between the inlet to the Gulf of ʕAqabah and Philistaea, and on the eastern shore of the same Gulf. Thamūd remains an uncertain card. The presence of people called Arabs in these three regions is confirmed by other reports, independent of Agatharchides and his source. There is an observable tendency to 'arabicize' the other inhabitants of the peninsula in the transmission of Agatharchides' text, which is evident in the earliest witness, Diodorus. There is, however, no doubt that Photius had a text very close to Agatharchides' original before him, whereas Diodorus, and, to a lesser degree Strabo, updated the information according to the current ethnic concepts in their own time. Photius gives the impression of being based on a most unprejudiced and matter-of-fact account of conditions in the Red Sea, which, as we know, goes back to or is identical with Ariston's report of his expedition in 280 BC.

In Photius there is a final important note. In a description of different aromatic plants in South Arabia, one is mentioned which 'in Arabic' (*arabistí*) is called *larimna*. If this note is original from Agatharchides, it is the earliest reference in history to a language named after Arabs. Unfortunately, it is impossible to identify which language is meant since also the identity of the plant is also uncertain.[102] It is tempting to see the initial /l/ as the definite article. This element, which was also documented in Herodotus' report of the goddess Alilat, would make this *arabistí* refer to an Arabic l-dialect, distinct from the h-dialects documented in the epigraphy.[103] To the group of l-dialects also belonged the language visible in the later Nabataean inscriptions and the ʕArabiyya of the Qurʔān and the old poetry. As we shall soon see, there is another testimony from the third pre-Christian century of an l-dialect in North Arabia.

According to a stele put up by Ptolemy II Philadelphus, a military expedition in the Red Sea was made shortly after Ariston's expedition.[104] The Egyptian interests in north-western Arabia reached Dedan, where at this time a dynasty of rulers called Liḥyān was established. It has been suggested that the name of the Gulf of ʕAqabah in Diodorus' and Photius' versions of Agatharchides, Laeanites, is in fact the name Liḥyān, which would testify to the role of the Liḥyanites in the sea traffic in the northern Red Sea.[105] Among their rulers we find the name TLMY, which has been interpreted as a form of Ptolemaíos, another testimony to the Egyptian connection.

Arabs in Ptolemaic Egypt

From the reign of Ptolemy II Philadelphus onwards down into the Roman period we have several contemporary documents testifying to the role of Arabs in Egypt. For the first time since the early Achaemenids we have texts which are not transmitted through copyists over many centuries but preserved in their original shape. Most of them are papyri. From these we know that in 259 BC there was already a province, a *nomós*, named Arabía, established around Wādī Tumaylāt with Pithom/Pathumos as capital under Ptolemy Philadelphus.[106]

This might be the explanation for a remark made by Egypt's great Hellenistic historian, Manetho, writing his history of Egypt in the third century BC, thus a contemporary of the Septuagint translators. Josephus quotes a line from his lost work where he told of the Hyksos rulers that some say they were *árabes*.[107] The identification should be explained by the fact that the Hyksos rulers resided in Avaris in the eastern Nile Delta, not very far from Wādī Tumaylāt. If the Arabs dominated this part of Egypt in the third century BC, it is very likely that Manetho's remark reflects these contemporary conditions.

The province is also mentioned in the Greek translation of the Pentateuch, where it is told how the sons of Jacob settled in the land of Goshen. The translators, working in the time of Philadelphus, rendered it 'the land of Gesem of Arabia' or 'in the land of Gesem, in Arabia'.[108] It is thus obvious that they identified the land of Goshen with Wādī Tumaylāt and the *nomós* Arabía. It also confirms the connection between GŠM, king of Qedar, mentioned on the bowl from Tell al-Maskhūṭa, and the Arabs. The fact that the *nomós* in the wādī was named Arabia shows that there must have been some kind of Arab presence there.

There is no reasonable doubt that Gesem in the Septuagint is connected with GŠM, and there is further no reasonable doubt that he is identical with the Geshem in the book of Nehemiah. The king of Qedar was thus called 'Arab' and had been able to interfere in both Judaean and Egyptian affairs in the fifth century BC to such a degree that the Egyptian authorities named a province after the groups he belonged to. What was the role played by the Arabs in Egypt?

The papyri from the time of Ptolemy Philadelphus where Arabs are mentioned come from the archive of Zenon, who was the manager of the domains of Apollonius, Ptolemy's minister of finance. Zenon was in charge of Apollonius' estate in the town of Philadelphia in Fayyum. In the large collection of documents and letters from Zenon's archive there are nineteen mentioning Arabs written in the 250s and 240s BC. One of the earliest, dated to the year 258/257 BC, is from Demetrios and Petekhon, the *dekatárkhai* of the *árabes* in Philadelphia, to Apollonius.[109] The title shows these two as some kind of officers in charge of ten persons. In another papyrus from 253 BC, Zenon sends a servant to instruct some workers together with an *áraps*.[110] Another one, dated three years later, is a receipt for payment of guards (*phylakîtai*) and ten *árabes* in Philadelphia.[111] It lies near at hand to see these people as some kind of guards or police force organized in units of ten. As we shall see, Arabs in this function are documented for later periods in Egypt, and it is quite possible that *árabes* were used for this purpose in the time of Philadelphus and perhaps even earlier. The rest of the papyri deal with *árabes* employed by Zenon/Apollonius as shepherds.[112] We hear about goats and sheep rented by *árabes* on contract.[113] Some *árabes* paid a sum in copper as rent and/or probably also gave a part of the wool from the sheep but were then entitled to use the animals for their own profit.[114] Others were paid a salary for attending the animals.[115]

The names of these *árabes* are worth studying. We find the following Greek names: Dēmētrios, Hermias, Apollōnios, Phthēreus, Hērō, Herieus, Drakōn and Hermōn. Three others, namely Petekhōn, Peteminios and Nekhthembēs, are clearly Egyptian. No Arabic name appears in the Zenon documents. It was obviously possible to be an 'Arab' and carry a non-Arabic name. Were these individuals speaking an Arabic language and did they have genuine Arabic names for private use? We do not know, but since the use of double names is documented for later periods among both 'Arabs' and Jews, it is quite possible also in Egypt at this time. A few decades later, in the year 220 BC in the reign of Ptolemy III Euergetes, we have a claim from a barber named Parates demanding payment for his performance on a certain Malikhos.[116] In spite of calling himself an *áraps*, Parates seems to have an Egyptian name whereas his niggardly customer has a name that looks highly Arabic, in that case the first of its kind documented from Egypt.

Eratosthenes from Cyrene

In the latter half of the third century BC, one of the greatest Greek scientists,

Eratosthenes, based in Alexandria, wrote a world geography, which summed up the knowledge of the age about the world and its peoples. Unfortunately, his text belongs to the many lost ones, and we have to try to reconstruct relevant parts of it from quotations and digests in preserved works, the most important of which is Strabo's *Geography*, written in the reign of Augustus.

Eratosthenes built his description of the Arabian peninsula on the evidence from the expeditions of Alexander and in it he gathered most of what was known about Arabia in his days.[117] This description was to have a decisive influence on the views of the Graeco-Roman culture on this part of the world, and it is to a certain extent with us even today. The concrete material which Eratosthenes used came from Hecataeus, Herodotus and the admirals of Alexander as well as from Hieronymus of Cardia, but also some other information from the third-century writers, among them probably also Ariston. The data originating with them have been treated earlier in this work. As far as we know, Eratosthenes did not have any personal experience of Arabia. He was not a traveller but a scientist, mostly working at his desk.

The most important passages from Eratosthenes dealing with Arabia are found in Book XVI of Strabo. This book contains four sections describing Babylonia, Syria, the Arabian shore of the Persian Gulf and the Arabian Peninsula respectively. For the general geographical outlook as well as the measures of distances, the size of countries, borderlines etc., Strabo in general used Eratosthenes. In his descriptions of different regions, he uses Eratosthenes too, but mixes his text with quotations from other writers, both earlier and later than Eratosthenes. We have already seen that Alexander's admirals are quoted by Strabo in the passage on the Persian Gulf. Strabo usually (not always) adduces the names of his sources, which makes it possible to disentangle facts originating in different periods of time. In fact, Book XVI, as well as many others in Strabo, is a patchwork of sources from Alexander's generals down to Strabo's contemporaries.

In the relevant passages in Book XVI, Eratosthenes is mentioned only in connection with one, but there are good arguments in favour of attributing some other passages to him.[118] According to Strabo, Eratosthenes introduced his description of Arabia in the following way:

> He [Eratosthenes] says concerning the northern and deserted (*érēmos*) part which is between *eudaímōn Arabía* and the [land of] Coelesyrians and the [land of] Judaeans to the innermost part of the Arabian Gulf, that from Heroonpolis, which is [at?] an innermost part of the Arabian Gulf near the Nile, towards Petra/the Rock of the *nabataîoi* to Babylon, is five thousand six hundred *stadia,* the whole towards the summer sunrise and through the adjacent Arabian peoples (*arábia éthnē*) as well as *nabataîoi* and *khaulotaîoi* and *agraîoi*. Above these is the *eudaímōn* [*Arabía*] which extends for a distance of twelve thousand stadia southwards to the Atlantic (= Indian) ocean. The first ones after the Syrians and Judaeans who occupy this [= *Arabía eudaímōn*] are farming people. After them there is a sandy and barren land having a few palm-trees, thorns, tamarisks, and dug wells as in Gedrosia. Tent-dwelling (*skēnîtai*) *árabes* and camel herds occupy it. The extreme parts towards the south, lying opposite to Ethiopia, are watered by summer rains and are sown twice, like India.[119]

In the description of South Arabia immediately following, we encounter four South

Arabian kingdoms. These had, in fact, already been mentioned by Theophrastus at the beginning of the third century BC.[120] Eratosthenes has new information: for example, the names of their capitals as well as the correct name of the fourth kingdom, the Minaeans, which comes from the Ariston expedition.[121]

In the introduction to the third chapter of Book XVI, the description of the Persian Gulf, Strabo has a passage which is a somewhat abbreviated variant of the one just quoted and thus most probably also comes from Eratosthenes:

> Above Judaea and Coele Syria to Babylonia and the river country of the Euphrates towards the south, lies the whole of Arabia except the tent-dwellers (*skēnîtai*) in Mesopotamia . . . [Of] those parts that follow after Mesopotamia as far as Coele Syria, the tent-dwelling (*skēnîtai*) *árabes* occupy the one closest to the river and Mesopotamia, who are divided in small sovereignties living in regions barren because of lack of water. They farm a little or not at all but they keep herds of all kinds, especially camels. Above these people there is a vast desert (*érēmos*). The parts further south of these are occupied by those who inhabit that which is called *Arabía eudaímōn*. The northern side of this above-mentioned [*Arabía*] is a desert (*érēmos*); the eastern is the Persian Gulf; the western, the Arabian Gulf; the southern is the great sea which is outside the two gulfs, which as a whole is called *erythrá* (the red).[122]

In Strabo's description of the borders of Babylonia and Syria in the first chapter of Book XVI, we find passages which fit very well into the picture given by the two just quoted, and it is most probable that they, too, go back to Eratosthenes:

> Syria . . . is bounded on the east by the Euphrates and by the tent-dwelling (*skēnîtai*) *árabes* inside/on this side of the Euphrates and on the south by *eudaímōn Arabía* and Egypt and on the west by the Egyptian and Syrian seas as far as Issus.[123]

> The land of the Babylonians is surrounded on the east by the Susians, the Elymaeans and the Paraetacenians, and on the south by the Persian Gulf, the Chaldaeans as far as the *árabes elesēnoí/alesēnoí*, and on the west by the *árabes skēnîtai* as far as Adiabene and Gordyaea, and on the north by the Armenians and the Medes as fas as the Zagrus and the tribes around it.[124]

This should be supplemented with a paragraph from Strabo's Book II, where he uses Eratosthenes extensively:

> Mesēnē is the beginning of the promontory (*ísthmos*) that separates *Arabía eudaímōn* from the rest of the continent.[125]

The meaning must be that Mesene is on the borderline betwen Arabia and the (Asian) continent.

Eratosthenes' general view of Arabia emerges quite clearly from these passages. Basic is the division in two parts: the Arabia of desert, *Arabia Deserta* (*érēmos*), and the Arabia of prosperity, *Arabia Felix* (*eudaímōn*), a division which has survived until our time. It is worth noticing that *Arabia Felix* begins far north, close to Syria and Judaea.

Most of the peninsula is thus *Arabia Felix*.[126] We obviously have here an extension of the traditional term which we have met with in connection with Euhemerus, where it designated only the southern shore of the Persian Gulf. It is perhaps a characteristic feature of Eratosthenes' method to name large areas after well-known places.

Details about inhabitants called Arabs are found only in *Arabia Deserta*, perhaps with one exception. *Arabia Deserta* consists of two entities: the parts inhabited by the tent-dwellers, the *skēnîtai*, and the parts of the peoples between Heroonpolis and Babylon: the Arabian peoples, the Nabataeans, the Khaulotaeans and the Agraeans. The names of these latter obviously come from a description of a route connecting Egypt with eastern Arabia, avoiding Palestine and Syria. This is supported by the fact that the distance (*c*. 1,000 kilometres) is not too far from the correct one from Suez to Kuwayt. This means, however, that Babylon cannot stand for the city, but must refer to the whole of lower Mesopotamia.[127]

In Strabo's text we have another notice, probably from Eratosthenes, which we have treated already, and which should be read together with the enumeration of the peoples in the Syrian desert. In his description of Gerrha, Strabo has mixed two accounts, one from Aristobulus telling about the traffic of the Gerrhaeans up the Euphrates, and one from Eratosthenes saying that the Gerrhaeans travelled overland for the most part, with the merchandise and aromatics of the *árabes*.[128] This seems to indicate a route across the desert, i.e. south of the Euphrates. We remember that Agatharchides mentioned the Minaeans and the Gerrhaeans bringing frankincense to the rock in the Negev.[129] As we pointed out, this piece of information probably did not belong to Agatharchides' main source, Ariston. Instead it is a supplementary note added by Agatharchides and taken from another source. It is not unlikely that both Eratosthenes and Agatharchides have this information from the same source. Interestingly, the traffic on the road between the ancient territory of Edom and Gaza through the Negev is documented from *c*. 240 BC onwards.[130] On the whole, the later Nabataean sites in the Negev, like Elusa and Nessana, are traceable from the late third century onwards, not earlier.[131] Thus there is much that speaks in favour of the assumption that a route through northern Arabia from the Gulf to Suez was established in the latter half of the third century BC.

This route also appears in a document copied by Pliny in the first century AD, but which explicitly contains information about conditions before the rise of the Parthians in the second century BC. It is said that the caravaneers started at Carra and proceeded to Gabba twenty days' journey from Carra and then travelled towards Syrian Palestine.[132] Carra is undoubtedly Gerrha.[133] Gabba could be a good Arabic word, in the *ʕArabiyya* pronounced *ǧubb* meaning 'well', 'pit'. It has been connected with *Agubēnoí* in Claudius Ptolemy, in whose land Dumah was situated, but might well be south of the Nafūd beyond present-day Ḥāyil.[134] There is still a place named al-Ǧubb in Mount Salmā a few kilometres south-east of Ḥāyil, which would be a candidate for the home of Ptolemy's *Agubēnoí*.[135]

The names in Eratosthenes thus constitute the earliest documentation of this route and the ethnographic conditions along it. According to the text it goes 'towards the summer sunrise', i.e. more or less straight eastwards. In that case one would expect it to end at the inner corner of the Persian Gulf, which is also supported by the distance given. The 5,600 *stadia,* equivalent to *c*. 1,000 kilometres, eastwards from Heroonpolis bring us to the shore of the Persian Gulf.[136]

The *agraîoi* could be the inhabitants of the al-Ḥasā oasis, where we know of a town named Hağar from early Islamic times.[137] On several coins from that oasis dated to the beginning of the third century BC, we find the inscription MLK HGR, 'the king of HGR', which probably refers to the same town.[138] On the other hand, the *agraîoi* seem not to be located in *Arabía eudaímōn*. Pliny mentions a town Haegra near Domata which seems to be close to the Thamudaei and their town Baclanaza/Badanatha.[139] This location may be supported by a passage in Dionysius Periegetes' geographical poem composed at the beginning of the second century AD. This poem is to a large extent a versification of Eratosthenes.[140] In it we find the following passage:

> The first who live beyond the slopes of Libanos
> are the rich ones called *nabataîoi*
> and thereupon *khaulásioi* and *agrées*. After them is
> the land of Khatramis, a part of the land of Persis.
> Thereafter, on the shores of the Red Sea dwell
> Minaîoi, Sabai, the close Khitabenoí;
> Thus many strong peoples inhabit Arabia.[141]

The dependence of these verses on Eratosthenes is beyond doubt. We notice the direct transition from *agrées* to the South Arabian Khatramis (= Ḥaḍramawt). In Strabo's version on the other hand, the mention of the *agraîoi* is directly followed by a description of the western parts of *Arabia eudaímōn*, ending with the four South Arabian kingdoms. This supports the assumption that the *agraîoi* are not those in al-Ḥasā but people further westwards, perhaps not far from Dumah. It seems that there is a confusion between two groups of *agraîoi* here: one belonging to HGR in al-Ḥasā, at the end of the route from Ḥaḍramawt belonging to *Arabía eudaímōn*, and another one with a similar designation near Dumah and Thamud in Ḥiğāz.

The Khaulotaeans have been associated with Ḥawilah in the Old Testament, i.e. the present-day Nafūd, and could refer to tribes west and south-west of Dumah. The name could also be reflected in present-day Ḥāyil on the southern shore of the Nafūd and could designate the people around the great sand-desert.

The Nabataeans occur in Strabo's quotations from Eratosthenes between the *khaulotaîoi* and the *árabes*.[142] This would mean that the Nabataeans had expanded considerably during the third century and were now able to interfere on the route through northern Arabia from Egypt to the Gulf. A dramatic extension of their rule is indicated when Strabo mentions the rock of the Nabataeans, thus giving the picture that the Nabataeans were now in charge of the later so famous pink city. From what has been said about the rock earlier, we should be a little sceptical about this notice and wonder if Strabo had got it right. We remember that the Nabataeans only a couple of decades before Eratosthenes were a small group in Ḥawrān. We should observe that in Dionysius' poem the *nabataîoi* are said to dwell beyond the slopes of Libanos, which fits very well with a location in Ḥawrān or immediately south of it. The mention of Petra immediately after Heroonpolis could be a hint that it is the rock in the Negev that is intended. The suggested reading of the phrase *te kaì* in Strabo 16.4.2, together with the earlier evidence from Hieronymus of Cardia and Agatharchides of Cnidus, would speak very strongly against the Nabataeans as possessors of the rock. In that case, the Nabataeans are an addition by Strabo reflecting his time. As a matter of fact, Strabo has preserved the earliest certain testimony of the name Petra for the Nabataean capital, coming from Athenodorus, who visited Petra in the first century BC, and it would be natural if he identified the *pétra* found in Eratosthenes, probably without any further attributes, with the now famous Nabataean capital.[143] As we have seen, he was not the last to do so.

Eratosthenes' enumeration starts with the *árabes*. The most natural and unprejudiced reading of Strabo's text indicates that they controlled the westernmost part of the route between the Nabataeans and Heroonpolis. These *árabes* must thus be identical with those described by Hieronymus and Agatharchides as having their centre in the Negev, and the rock mentioned in Strabo's text may, in Eratosthenes' original version, have referred to their stronghold and not the Nabataean capital.

A document which gives a description of conditions in Arabia similar to what we find in Strabo is a passage in Pliny's *Natural History* which, unfortunately, like so much in that work, is a mess of distorted names and unclear references. This document may, in fact, be a digested and distorted passage from Eratosthenes himself. The description of Arabia goes as follows:

> Beyond the Pelusiac [mouth of the Nile] is Arabia extending to the Red Sea, and [also?] that perfume-producing, wealthy [land], famous by the name 'Happy' (*beata*). This [the latter] is called [the Arabia] of the Cattabani, of the Esbonitae and of the *scenitae arabes*, barren except where it adjoins the Syrian frontier, remarkable only by Mount Casius. To these [borders] *arabes* are joined, from the east the Canchlei, from the south the Cedrei, these both then by the Nabataei.[144]

The terminology is clearly Erastothenian ('Happy Arabia', *scenitae*). Pliny obviously merges Eratosthenes' two Arabias together. At least the Cattabani seem to belong to South Arabia (*Arabia Beata*). This is a parallel to Dionysius' poem, where we find the same juxtaposition of North and South Arabia. The latter part of the passage describes peoples around the southern Syrian border, i.e. east and south of Palestine. It is likely that we have here a passage in Eratosthenes corresponding to Strabo's description of *Arabía eudaímōn*. It is reasonable to assume that the Cedrei are the Qedar south of Palestine, and thus identical with or closely connected with the Arabs of Hieronymus of Cardia. The name Esbonitae is probably derived from Ḥeshbon/Ḥisbān east of the Dead Sea.[146] The Canchlei could be a distortion of the Khaulotaîoi in Eratosthenes. Important is that we also in this passage find the Arabs in the Negev, separated from the Nabataeans. The mention of Ḥeshbon and Qatabān is a reminder of the list of the sons of Yoqṭān in Genesis 10, which could be interpreted as the remains of a description of the route from South Arabia to southern Syria. The two names in Pliny could indicate the extremes of *Arabia Beata*.

The impression from Dionysius' verses is that the Nabataeans live directly beyond Antilebanon, i.e. in northern Transjordan, and that the route described goes from the *khaulásioi* through present-day Wādī Sirḥān down to the *agrées* around Dumah. As a matter of fact, Dionysius' versification gives a much clearer picture than Strabo, let alone Pliny, and may in fact be the closest rendering of Eratosthenes' original description, albeit a very condensed one. In particular, the location of the Nabataeans goes well with what is known about them from original sources from the third century BC. The route would thus have run from Heroonpolis through the Negev and its Arabs on the Rock, through Transjordan south of Ḥawrān, where Nabataeans dwelt, into the southern Syrian desert, through the land of Ḥawilah to the Agraeans in the region of

Dumah.[147] From there it might have run north-eastwards to the Euphrates, which it followed down to Teredon on the Persian Gulf, where it met the route from Gerrha and Ḥaḍramawt.

Eratosthenes has obviously operated with a much wider concept of Arabs than the one used in the enumeration of peoples along the route just described: *árabes skēnîtai*, 'tent-dwelling Arabs'. These inhabit most of *Arabia Deserta* between Syria and Mesopotamia. They are also found in parts of *Arabia Felix* and, interestingly enough, in Mesopotamia proper. It can be doubted if Eratosthenes had any detailed information about ethnicity and society among these desert-dwellers. In his time, the whole peninsula was called Arabia, and a logical consequence was that all the inhabitants became Arabs for the foreigners. The Greeks knew about *árabes* in Mesopotamia and between Egypt and Palestine, among whom cattle-herding and tent-dwelling were eye-catching activities. It was natural that the designation was extended to all others in the adjacent land who practised the same way of living. We should thus be cautious in assuming that Eratosthenes always tells us anything about the Arabs we are looking for. Indeed, the idea of the identity between Arabs, camel-herders and desert-dwellers, which is still with us today, comes from the great geographer in Alexandria.

If we read the Eratosthenian fragments in Strabo in this way, it becomes obvious that the notice about *árabes* in the description of the route between Egypt and the Persian Gulf is a most precious document, preserving a more authentic report about ethnic conditions in the Syrian desert in the third century BC than the sweeping generalizations in the geographical systems of the scholars. Moreover, the admission of the existence of *árabes* in Mesopotamia does not quite fit into the geographical scheme. In both these cases we can check Eratosthenes against other sources independent of him, which confirm the existence of minor groups called *árabes* in these areas.

These considerations make it likely that we have yet another genuine documentation of Arabs from Eratosthenes. In the passage about the borders of Babylonia, we hear about *árabes elesēnoí/alesēnoí*. They are explicitly distinguished from the *scenitae*. The meaning of the text seems to be that Babylonia is bordered on the south by the Persian Gulf and the Chaldaeans to/as far as (*mékhri*) these *árabes*; i.e. the region of the Chaldaeans stretches as far as the *árabes*, not that of the Babylonians. The latter element in the phrase is usually emended to *mesēnoí*, a derivation from the name Mesēnē, a region stretching from the estuary of the Two Rivers down to Qaṭīf.[149] But the emendation is not only unnecessary but also wrong: *alesēnoí* is derived from Alesēnē, i.e. al-Ḥasā.[150] We thus learn that there were Arabs in the oasis around the Town, the HGR. Since they were in the oasis, they were not quite like the tent-dwellers, and they are also explicitly separated from them by Eratosthenes.

In Eratosthenes we thus find three groups called *árabes*: the tent-dwellers in the desert parts of *Arabia Deserta* and *Arabia Felix*, called *skēnîtai*; the *árabes* between the Nile Delta and the Nabataeans; and the *árabes* in al-Ḥasā. Of these, the latter two were originally mentioned in route descriptions used by Eratosthenes as a means of measuring distances. This is genuine information on groups within limited areas called *árabes* in the third century BC. The tent-dwellers are labelled *árabes* by Eratosthenes as a general term for people in his great Arabia, which does not reflect any ethnic or social entity conscious of a distinct identity of its own. We shall see from the testimony of a native Syrian two centuries later, namely Posidonius, that this analysis is correct.

The rise of the desert route route from Gerrha to Heroonpolis obviously took place in the latter half of the third century BC. The fact that it is said to run from Egypt to the

Persian Gulf through northern Arabia shows that Egyptian interests must have been involved. It can be assumed that this new route was connected with the new political constellations after Alexander's death. Egypt was now independent and unthreatened. She had all kinds of interests in circumventing her rival in Asia, the Seleucids, and reaching Arabia and India on roads inaccessible to them. The expedition to the Red Sea, the Egyptian connections with Dedan and the new route through northern Arabia are all the results of these ambitions. Egyptian rulers had had close ties with the Arabs east of the delta long before Alexander's time. By their control of Palestine they had secured the northern flank and could expand their contacts with the Arabs and the Nabataeans. The ruler in Syria had failed to take control of Palestine and north-western Arabia in 312 and 306 BC. For more than a century, the Ptolemies had a free hand eastwards.

The Seleucids and the Arabs

Unlike the case of Ptolemaic Egypt, we have scarce evidence for Arabs in the Seleucid empire during the first century of its existence. This is of course partly due to the general scarcity of sources for the Seleucid empire, especially in this period, but it also reflects the general policy of the rulers of Antioch: they seem to have had no ambitions in Arabia. Instead, Seleucus and his successors embarked on the same policy of peaceful co-operation as their Achaemenid predecessors.

We have a description of the extent of Seleucus' empire preserved by Appian in his Roman history written in the second century AD. After having taken Syria and Phrygia,

> he acquired Mesopotamia, Armenia, the so-called Seleucid Cappadocia, the Persians, Parthians, Bactrians, *arábioi*, Tapyri, Sogdians, Arachotes, Hyrcanians, and all the other adjacent peoples that had been subdued by Alexander.[151]

The information in this notice is, however, of doubtful authenticity. It is difficult to determine which Arabs are intended. Arabs are mentioned by Appian in other passages and always appear as *árabes*. It has been suggested that it is a corruption of *araîoi* which would be the *hairawa* in the lists of the Achaemenid kings, an Iranian people around present-day Herat, a town in fact named after them.[152]

Arabs appear in Seleucid politics for the first time under Antiochus III, called 'the Great' (226–188 BC). Our main source for the activities of this king is Polybius, writing his world history probably around 150 BC. Polybius is usually considered a good source since he had access to documents in Roman archives, but a detailed analysis of different passages is difficult because he does not indicate his sources.[153]

When Antiochus ascended the throne, the empire was in dire straits. The Iranian provinces had more or less liberated themselves, and the Ptolemies had got a firm foothold on the southern and western coast of Asia Minor. Antiochus decided first to deal with Egypt. After an initial failure, Antiochus in the year 218 BC marched along the Phoenician coast, conquering the cities. Then he traversed Galilee and crossed the river Jordan. The cities in northern Transjordan were occupied. Polybius continues:

> When this had happened, those who inhabited the adjacent Arabia incited each other and adhered to him [Antiochus] unanimously.[154]

The cities of Galatis, Abila and Gadara were taken. The latter two were situated east of Lake Kinneret, and Galatis must be the Ptolemaic province known as Galaaditis in other sources, i.e. Biblical Gilead, present-day ʕAğlūn.

> After this he heard that a large force of the enemy had gathered in Rabbatámana and was pillaging the country of the *árabes* who had joined him.[155]

Antiochus immediately advanced towards Rabbatámana, present-day ʕAmmān, and conquered the town. Polybius uses the old name of the city, even with the local pronunciation.[156] The Ptolemies had founded cities with Greek names in Transjordan and Rabbat ʕAmmon had been renamed Philadelphia after Ptolemy Philadelphus.[157]

Having thus established his control of the Syrian provinces, we find Antiochus in the next year at Raphia, close to Gaza, on the threshold of Egypt, facing the Egyptian army. In Polybius' description of the participants in Antiochus' army at Raphia we have these notices:

> The *árabes* and some of the tribes neighbouring them were about ten thousand, commanded by Zabdibelos.

> On his left wing he posed . . . the Cissians, the Medes, and the Carmanians, and close to them the *árabes* and their neighbours, in contact with the phalanx.[158]

The performance of the Arabs at Raphia was not their greatest:

> Phoxidas [one of the Egyptian commanders] and his men met with the same success: for charging the *árabes* and the Medes they forced them to headlong flight.[159]

Antiochus' defeat at Raphia resulted in the loss of Phoenicia and Palestine. He now directed his attention eastwards, where during the following years he restored the Greek rule in Iran. According to Polybius, Antiochus, in connection with his eastern campaign, made an expedition to eastern Arabia and reached the town of Gerrha.[160]

The *árabes* mentioned in the campaign in 218 BC appear in connection with operations in northern Transjordan. The cities Abila and Gadara are both situated in the valley of Yarmūk, and the conquest is made after a march through Galilee.[161] Polybius' words can be interpreted in the terms that these *árabes* had originally paid some allegiance to the Ptolemies but now changed sides. It is not impossible that the Ptolemies had employed *árabes* in this region as border troops against the Seleucids in adjacent Damascene. These *árabes* seem to have been stationed somewhere between ʕAmmān and Yarmūk, since their land could be harassed by enemy troops in Rabbatámana. It should be remembered that Rabbatámana had been renamed Philadelphia after Ptolemy Philadelphus, and it is reasonable to assume that the Arabs had been located there by him.[162] As we have seen, there is documentation from his time that Arabs were employed as troops by the Egyptian government.

There is some other evidence for a substantial and enduring Arab presence in Biblical Gilead during this period. In some of the inscriptions found in Gerash we read invocations of 'the /holy/ Arabian God': *theōi* [*hagiōi*] *arabikōi*.[163] The inscriptions were not found *in situ* but are found on blocks reused in the Nymphaeum.[164] This shows that they must be older than that building from the second century AD. There was obviously a special cult in Gerash devoted to a deity explicitly associated with Arabs. We know from Herodotus that there were such gods not very far from Gerasa. It is thus quite likely that the god mentioned should be connected with the Arabs in Transjordan documented by the Hellenistic historians.

The *árabes* lined up together with the troops from Iran and Asia Minor at Raphia must have belonged to a more established part of the imperial army. The only clue to their identity is perhaps the name of the commanding officer at Raphia. Names composed with the element Zab(a)d- in fact also occur later. From much later times there are several places in central and northern Syria called Zabad.[165] Another indication is the second element in the name: Bel. Later the gods of Palmyra are known by names composed with the same element. These Arabs might thus have dwelt in the Syrian desert somewhere between present-day Salamiyyeh and Palmyra. Arabs from this region were to play an important role in the history of the next two centuries, and it is likely that these are the ones now appearing for the first time in the reign of Antiochus.

The participation of the Arabs in the Seleucid army shows that the kings in Antioch pursued the same policy as their predecessors, the Achaemenids. They established some kind of alliance with the Arabs and did not try to crush them as Alexander had done. The whole composition of the Seleucid army makes it clear that there is a remarkable continuity in politics from the Achaemenids to the Seleucids.

This evidence thus points to two groups of Arabs in Syria at the end of the third century BC: one in central Syria, taking part in the operations of the royal army, and one in Transjordan. The Arabs in Transjordan are probably documented in another source dealing with the same period. Josephus has preserved a novel, probably written in Alexandria at the end of the second century BC, about the Jewish family of the Tobiads who rose to prominence as tax-farmers under the Ptolemies in the middle of the third century BC.[166] Due to a struggle for power within the Tobiad family, the young Hyrcanus fled from his elder brothers and settled in the Transjordanian region in a palace in present-day ʕArāk al-ʔAmīr, west of ʕAmmān, where the family had large land-possessions:

> Hyrcanus therefore gave up his intention of returning to Jerusalem, and settled in the country across Jordan, where he continually warred on the *árabes*, until he killed many of them and took many captive.[167]

> This place [i.e. Hyrcanus' palace] is between Arabia and Judaea across the Jordan, not far from Essebonitis.[168]

Hyrcanus' settling in Transjordan occurred at some time between 210 and 205 BC, and thus in a period when the *árabes* in the area had shown their sympathies for the Seleucids, whereas Hyrcanus was a man of the Ptolemies.[169]

Antiochus III finally conquered Syria in 198 BC, having returned from his activities in the east. The Seleucids were soon to realize that their new province was indeed a cuckoo's nest. Then followed campaigning in Asia Minor, resulting in the intervention of Rome. When the Seleucid armies finally, in the year 190 BC, rallied against the legions at Magnesia in Asia Minor, Antiochus again, according to the late sources Livy and Appian, had Arabs in his front line:

> In front of this cavalry [of Syrians, Phrygians and Lydians] were scythe-bearing chariots and camels of the breed called dromedaries. These were ridden by Arab archers (*arabes sagittarii*) carrying slender swords four cubits long so that they might be able to reach the enemy from so great a height.[170]

> There were also other mounted archers (*hippotoxótai*) among them: Daaeans, Mysians, Elymaeans, *árabes* who riding on swift camels, shoot arrows with dexterity from their high position, and use very long, thin knives when they come close to combat.[171]

This information obviously comes from the same source (Polybius?). We should note the military role of the *árabes*. They are archers, as they had always been, but we also now hear about another weapon: the slender swords (*gladii tenues*) in Livy and the long, slender knives (*makhaírai epimēkē kaì stenaí*) in Appian, which allowed them to hit the enemy soldiers from the camel's back.

The battle of Magnesia was the first encounter in history between a people called Arabs and the Romans. From now on, these two were to have a great deal to do with each other until the decisive victory of the late relatives of the Arabs of Magnesia in the battle of Yarmūk 800 years later.[172]

Hyrcanus had been very close to the court in Alexandria and definitely represented Ptolemaic interests. This provides a good explanation of his conflict with the *árabes* in Transjordan, who may have acted as a kind of fifth column for the Seleucids. His life consequently became unbearably complicated after the Seleucid conquest of Syria:

> As for Hyrcanus, seeing how great was the power which Antiochus had, and fearing that he might be captured by him and punished for what he had done to the *árabes*, he ended his life by his own hand.[173]

This happened in 175 BC when a new king ascended the throne of the Seleucids, Antiochus IV Epiphanes, who was to put an end to the last stronghold of Ptolemaic sympathizers in southern Syria.

The *árabes* with whom Hyrcanus had fought were probably those in Transjordan who had already joined Antiochus III in 218 BC. It can then be assumed that those siding with Antiochus at Magnesia were those who had fought with him at Raphia. We thus find two new groups of Arabs emerging around 200 BC, together with those already known from the time of Alexander in the Antilebanon, who also must have come under Seleucid rule in 198 BC: those in Transjordan around ʕAmmān, and those of Zabdibelos in central Syria. Both are allies of the Seleucid king, and there is no reason to assume that those in Antilebanon were not so as well. To these were added the Arabs between the Euphrates and the Tigris, about whom we do not hear much in Seleucid times except in Eratosthenes' *Geography*. The Seleucids thus allowed Arabs to settle in the central lands of their realm and co-operated with them.

Arabs around Palestine in the age of the Maccabees

The pro-Seleucid stand taken by the *árabes* in Transjordan is also documented later. In the 160s BC, the conflicts in Palestine exploded in the Maccabaean insurrection. The origin of the conflict was a struggle within the Jewish community between Hellenizers and conservatives. The main Hellenizer, Iason, seized power in Jerusalem around 171 but was ousted by a rival, Menelaos. Iason tried to seize power once again but had to flee when the king, Antiochus IV, took the city and reinstalled Menelaos in 169 BC.[174] He had once earlier fled to Transjordan, and now he returned there:

> At last, he met with a disastrous end. He was informed against to Aretas, the *tyrannos* of the *árabes*, and had to flee from town to town, persecuted and hated by all as an apostate from the laws and detested as the hangman of his land and its inhabitants and was thrown out into Egypt.[175]

This ruler is usually identified as an early Nabataean king, although the text does not mention the Nabataeans.[176] That the pro-Seleucid Transjordanian *árabes* would persecute an enemy of the Seleucid king is to be expected from what we have learnt about their earlier behaviour. As we shall see soon, there are good reasons to believe that the Nabataeans were pro-Egyptian, and there are thus no reasons to believe that Aretas was a Nabataean ruler. The name turns up among the later Nabataean rulers, but it is a very common name in all parts of Arabia in pre-Islamic times and need not be a sign of this *tyrannos* being a Nabataean.

The *árabes* in Transjordan thus acted as supporters of the Seleucid king once again when they chased Iason out of the country. Obviously, it could be unhealthy to be a supporter of the Ptolemies among the *árabes* in Transjordan.

The conflict in Judaea between Hellenizers and conservatives developed into one between the conservatives and the Seleucid king himself. The story is well known. The attempt by Antiochus IV and the Hellenizers to modernize the Jewish temple to a more up-to-date Hellenistic sanctuary failed. The anti-Hellenists, led by Judas Maccabaeus and his brothers, established themselves in Judaea, purified the temple and started to wage war in all directions in order to protect the Jews living outside Judaea.

We have two accounts of a campaign led by Judas Maccabaeus against a local Transjordanian chief named Timotheus in 163 BC. One version is given in 1 Maccabees which is paraphrased by Josephus, and the other one is found in 2 Maccabees. 1 Maccabees was written in Palestine between 104 and 63 BC, probably at the beginning of the first century BC.[177] 2 Maccabees is a digest of a larger work about the history of the Hasmonaeans written by Jason of Cyrene not long after 160 BC. The epitome was made several decades later, probably by a non-Palestinian Jew.[178]

The two versions are quite different from each other. The most detailed is version 1, found in 1 Maccabees and Josephus' *Antiquities*:

> It is told that Judas made a raid into Transjordan against the Ammonites under a certain Timotheus. Judas conquered the town of Iazor and retired to Judaea.[179]
>
> The Jews in Galaad had taken refuge in the fortress of Dathema (M)/Diathema (J) because of persecution from neighbouring peoples after Judas' victory. The enemies were led by Timotheus.[180]
>
> Judas and his brother Jonathan crossed the Jordan and marched three days into the wilderness. They met the Nabataeans, who welcomed the Jews as friends and informed them about how the Jews in Galaatis were locked up in many

> places (M:) like Bosora, Bosor, Alema, Khaspho, Maked, and Karnain. Judas marched against Bosora and reached the Fortress (= Dathema?). Timotheus' troops were beaten, and Judas then took (M:) Alema/(J:) Mella, (M:) Khaspho/(J:) Khaspomakē, (M:) Maked, Bosor and other towns.[181]
>
> Then Timotheus gathered his army by a river close to (M:) Raphon/(J:) Romphon. Among his troops there were many *árabes* who are hired (M: *memisthōtai*) to help him/persuaded by payment (J: *misthōi peísas*). Judas' troops were victorious and Timotheus' army took refuge in the sanctuary in Karnain, which was also taken by the Jews.[182]

In the second book of Maccabees we find version 2, an account which differs from the one just quoted, especially in the first part. It tells about operations in the region of Jaffa and Yabneh, and is immediately followed by this account:

> From there [Yabneh], when they had marched nine stadia in the direction of Timotheus, *árabes* attacked him [Judas], not less than 5,000 foot soldiers and 500 riders. After a fierce battle which, with the help of God, was successful for Judas' men, the nomads were defeated and asked Judas for peace. They promised to bring cattle to the Jews and to help the Jews in other ways. Judas, who reckoned that they could be of considerable profit in the future, agreed to keep peace with them, and after having received his confirmation of this, they retired to their tents.[183]

After this follows an account of a fight around places called Kaspin and Kharax (= the Fortress, Dathema?), ending up at Karnion (Karnain).[184]

The difference between these two versions, which is important for our study, is the absence of *árabes* in the fighting around Karnion in 2 Maccabees and their presence at the same battle in 1 Maccabees/Josephus. At the same time we hear about a hostile encounter between *árabes* and Jews at the beginning of the campaign in 2 Maccabees, and a peaceful co-operation between Nabataeans and Jews in 1 Maccabees/Josephus.

The *árabes* at Karnion/Karnain may, however, be referred to in 2 Maccabees. In a fragment about the operations against Timotheus, preserved in that source in another context, we note the mention of a *phylarkhos* of the men of Timotheus that was taken and killed 'because he had done much evil to the Jews'.[185] It cannot be proved, but this could well be a reference to a leader of the *árabes* fighting with Timotheus at Rapho.

It has, on good grounds, been assumed that Timotheus acted on behalf of the Seleucids.[186] In that case, the appearance of *árabes* from Transjordan in his ranks is not surprising. The hostility between Jews and *árabes* fits into a pattern. This also holds for the Judaeo-Nabataean alliance. We saw earlier that the Nabataeans are mentioned by Eratosthenes on the route from Egypt to the Persian Gulf. Since this route ended in Ptolemaic Egypt, it is most likely that the Nabataeans were on good terms with the Egyptians. This is also the picture we get from the earliest mention of them, namely in the Zenon papyrus from 259 BC. The political situation in Palestine and adjacent countries at this time thus shows a division between a Judaean–Nabataean–Egyptian bloc and an Arabo-Seleucid one. There was also the Arab entity in the Negev and the northern Sinai to the eastern Nile Delta, which would still be within the Egyptian sphere of interest.

This scenario makes the picture of the Judaeo-Nabataean friendship in

1 Maccabees/Josephus most likely. Why then do hostile *árabes* appear instead of Nabataeans in 2 Maccabees? Even for those who assume an unproblematic identity between Nabataeans and Arabs, this constitutes a problem since the two stories are also contradictory in other details.[187] A solution may be found in another account in 1 Maccabees/Josephus, illustrating the continuing distrust between the Transjordanian Arabs and the Maccabees. In 160 BC, after the death of both Judas Maccabaeus and Antiochus IV, the new Syrian king, Demetrius I Soter, through his general Bacchides, had taken Jerusalem, and the remaining brothers John, Jonathan and Simeon had to start all over again as guerrilla warriors with a base in Transjordan, supported, not surprisingly, by the Nabataeans.[188] When John was sent to his brothers with their luggage, he was attacked near Madeba by the 'Sons of (I)ambri/Amaraios' and killed.[189] Jonathan and Simeon took revenge, killing several of them.[190] It is likely that these people belonged to the *árabes* allied to Timotheus, who considered themselves as having a bone to pick with the Maccabaeans.[191] It is not impossible that this story has in fact influenced the 2 Maccabees version of Judas' encounter with the Nabataeans. The author, Jason, could have replaced the unheroic account of Judas' relations with the Nabataeans with a more dramatic and pathetic one, better suiting the picture of Judas as Israel's greatest warrior since the days of David.[192]

Arabs in Syria in the age of the Maccabees

The conflict between the Jews and the Arabs in Transjordan was after all a minor one, compared to what was happening in the Seleucid realm as a whole. In the period 170–140 BC dramatic events took place in the east, namely the rise of Parthia, which signalled the definite end of Greek control of the eastern parts of the ancient Achaemenid empire. The exact process is not clear from the scanty sources, but in the 140s the Parthian king Mithradates I had a firm hold on the whole Iranian plateau, Media included: Greek coins in Ecbatana cease in 148 BC.[193]

The Seleucid kings could not keep Iran, due to the strong tendencies of dissolution in the central lands, namely in Syria proper. The violent struggle for the throne that commenced in 164 with the death of Antiochus IV, himself a usurper, was the sign of deeper ailments and signalled that the Seleucid state could no longer cope with the political realities of the day. In the process of dissolution, Arabs sometimes played a prominent role. We have seen that in the days of Antiochus III Arabs are already found in central Syria integrated into the army. In 153 BC Alexander Balas, who claimed descent from Antiochus IV, rose against Demetrius I, who was killed in battle three years later. Alexander was supported by the Maccabaean guerrillas led by Jonathan, behind whom stood the Ptolemies and Rome.[194] Alexander became king and reinstalled Maccabaean rule in Jerusalem. In 145 BC, the son of Demetrius, Demetrius II, overthrew Alexander with help from Ptolemy Philometor in Egypt. The story of Alexander's end is told by three different writers: 1 Maccabees, Diodorus Siculus and Josephus. The latter largely follows 1 Maccabees as his main source:

1 Maccabees:

> And Alexander fled to Arabia to seek protection there, and King Ptolemy triumphed. And Zabdielos the Arab (*ho áraps*) chopped off Alexander's head and sent it to the king. And two days later King Ptolemy died and the garrisons in

> the fortified cities were killed by the inhabitants. Thus Demetrius became king in the year 167 [= 145 BC].[195]

Josephus:

> They [Ptolemy and Demetrius] defeated Alexander and put him to flight. And so he fled to Arabia . . . The *dynástēs* of the *árabes*, Zábeilos, cut off Alexander's head and sent it to Ptolemy.[196]

Diodorus:

> Alexander, worsted in battle, fled with five hundred of his men to Abai in Arabia, to take refuge with Diocles, the *dynástēs* in whose care he had earlier placed his infant son Antiochus. Thereupon Heliadus and Casius, two officers who were with Alexander, entered into secret negotiations for their own safety and voluntarily offered to assassinate Alexander. When Demetrius consented to their terms, they became, not merely traitors to their king, but his murderers. Thus was Alexander put to death by his friends.[197]

The sending of one's heir to be raised among Arabs is here documented for the first time. But it was done many times afterwards, the most famous example perhaps being the Sassanian king Vahram V, who was raised among the aristocrats in al-Ḥīra at the beginning of the fifth century AD.

The different names of the Arab *dynástēs* are interesting. It should be observed that the Arab who is blamed for the murder of Alexander in 1 Maccabees, and consequently in Josephus, is called Zabdielos or Zabeilos, whereas the one charged with the upbringing of Antiochus in Diodorus has the Greek name Diocles. In Diodorus' version it is explicitly said that Diocles was *not* guilty of the murder. Further, Diocles is said to dwell at a place called Abai, whereas the other names may point to a place called Zabad. This is reminiscent of the Zabad documented from the time of Antiochus III.[198]

Before trying to explain these differences, we should consider the political development that followed, as told in the three sources. After the death of Alexander Balas, one of his generals, named Tryphon, upheld the claims of Alexander's son, the young Antiochus VI, against the new king, Demetrius II.

1 Maccabees:

> Among those who had served Alexander there was a man called Tryphon. He noticed that the soldiers complained about Demetrius. Then he went to Imalkoue, the Arab [*ho áraps*], who was educating Alexander's little son, Antiochus, visited him in order to take care of the boy and make him king after his father. He told Imalkoue about all the ordinances of Demetrius and about the extant enmity against him among his soldiers.[199]

Josephus:

> It was natural, therefore, that when this disaffection of the soldiers toward Demetrius was perceived by one of Alexander's generals, Diodotos, surnamed

> Tryphon, who was a native of Apamea, he went to Malkhos, the Arab [*ho áraps*], who was bringing up Alexander's son Antiokhos, and, after revealing to him the army's dissatisfaction with Demetrius, persuaded him to give Antiochus over to him and he would restore him to his father's throne. Now Malkhos at first opposed this because of distrust, but finally, after Tryphon had pleaded with him a long while, he was won over to the plan which Tryphon was urging him to accept.[200]

Diodorus:

> A certain Diodotos, also called Tryphon, who stood in high esteem among the king's friends, perceiving the excitement of the masses and their hatred for the prince, revolted from Demetrius, and soon finding large numbers ready to join him, [enlisted first] the men of Larissa . . . He also made an ally of the *dynástēs* of Arabia, Iamblikhos, who happened to have in his keeping Antiochus called Epiphanes, a mere child, the son of Alexander. Setting a diadem on his head and providing him with the retinue appropriate to a king, he restored the child to his father's throne . . . Having collected a modest host he first encamped around Chalcis, a city situated on the Arabian border.[201]

The three variants of the Arab's name, Imalkoue, Iamblikhos and Malkhos, all point to the same name: Malik or Yamlik. It must be this man who is called Diocles in Diodorus. It reflects the degree of integration of these Arabs into the Seleucid state; apart from his Arab name, the Arab chieftain obviously also had a Greek one.[202]

Jonathan Maccabaeus, who had successively supported Alexander Balas and Demetrius II, now changed sides once again and supported Tryphon and the young Antiochus VI. After several combats, Jonathan defeated Demetrius not far from Ḥamā in Syria.[203] Jonathan had thus emerged as one of the leading *condottieri* in the now rapidly crumbling Seleucid kingdom. Immediately after this battle it is said in 1 Maccabees:

> Jonathan turned against the *árabes* called Zabadaîoi, defeated them and took their belongings. And he marched from there and reached Damascus and marched through the entire land.[204]

Jonathan was, at this moment, supposed to be in alliance with Antiochus VI and Tryphon, who were supported by the Arab Malik/Yamlik/Diocles. It is thus most unlikely that the Zabadaîoi were those governed by Malik.[205] The conclusion must be that there were two groups of Arabs in Syria, that at Abai supporting Antiochus VI and Tryphon together with Jonathan Maccabaeus, and that of the Zabadaîoi supporting Demetrius II.[206] Now Tryphon and Antiochus were the heirs of Alexander Balas, with whose help Maccabaean rule had been reinstalled in Jerusalem with Jonathan as leader. It is then striking that the information that Alexander was killed by the Zabadaîoi comes from Jewish sources, namely, 1 Maccabees and Josephus. Since it was known that Alexander Balas had been killed while dwelling with Arabs, and since the Zabadaîoi Arabs were fighting against his heirs, it is not surprising that they are blamed for the murder. If these Zabadaîoi are identical with those fighting at Raphia and Magnesia, thus having a tradition of supporting the Seleucids, their low credentials among the Jews become even more explicable. Once again, the often underrated Diodorus Siculus stands out as the most trustworthy of the sources. In fact, it is clear that Diodorus built his account on a good source, probably Posidonius of Apamaea.[207]

That Abai should be located in northern Syria is confirmed by the notice that Tryphon, having enlisted men from Larissa, camped at Chalcis. These towns were founded by Seleucus Nicator in the northern part of Syria.[208] Chalcis is present-day Qinnasrīn, south-east of Aleppo, whereas Larissa is present-day Shayzar on the Orontes south of Apamea.[209] Abai of the *árabes* would then be not far from there, since Chalkis is said to be on the border to Arabia.[210] The Zabadaîoi, on the other hand, seem, from the text in 1 Maccabees, to have been further south, in the Ḥimṣ region. After his victory over Demetrius, Jonathan attacked them by the river Eleutherus, present-day Nahr al-Kabīr on the northern Lebanese border, and before he reached Damascus.[211] Although there is a well-known Zabad today south-east of Aleppo (not far from Qinnasrīn) there are also other places further south with that name. In the Antilebanon we find Zabdāni and Kafr Zabad even today.[212] In an early rabbinic text which contains much ancient material, we hear about enemies of Israel in the land of Chalcis and Bêt Zabdaʔî, which is most likely to be located in the Antilebanon.[213] This supports the location of the Zabadaîoi in central Syria since this Chalcis undoubtedly is in the Biqāʕ valley and was probably conquered by Jonathan.[214] The Zabadaîoi might have had their dwellings around the Antilebanon, perhaps even to the plain around Ḥims.[215]

In the movement around Alexander Balas and Tryphon for taking power in the Seleucid kingdom, we find both Arabs and Jews playing central roles. It shows that the political power in Antioch from now on was a plaything in the hands of the *condottieri*, many of whom represented the non-Greek elements of the kingdom. The great days of the Seleucid empire were over and with them the whole political structure created by Cyrus the Great 400 years earlier. Demetrius II managed to defeat Tryphon and kill Jonathan Maccabaeus but suffered the final blow himself at the hands of the Parthians in 140 BC. Shortly before that, Simeon Maccabaeus had proclaimed himself king in Jerusalem. The central power of the great empire unifying most of the Middle East for 400 years was gone. The scene lay open for new actors.

Arabs from Alexander to Demetrius: attempt at a summary

During the period from Alexander to the dissolution of the Seleucid empire around 140 BC Arabs are found in several areas where we have not heard about them earlier. We find them already in the Antilebanon in Alexander's days. Around one century later they appear in Transjordan, and in the middle of the second century BC we find one group in central Syria and one in the north. All of these Arab groups are heavily involved with the two empires governed from Alexandria and Antioch respectively. Intimately connected with the former is the Arab kingdom between Palestine and the Nile Delta.

We do not hear much about the Arabs reported by Xenophon in this period. From the events during the next century it will become clear, however, that the *árabes* in northern Syria probably had connections with the Ǧazīra and had perhaps been imported from there by some Seleucid king. For the first time we now also hear about Arabs in other parts of the peninsula: in al-Ḥasā in eastern Arabia, in the area of Naǧrān in Yemen and, somewhat more uncertain, in the northern Ḥiǧāz in the land of Thamūd.

In spite of the Greek designation of the whole peninsula as Arabia, we find many groups there who are not called Arabs. This makes it likely that the name of the country is a geographical term launched by Greek geographers. For the Greeks it originally designated the region between Palestine and Egypt. It can be observed that the Greeks still continued to call the smaller areas where the 'real' Arabs lived Arabia.

The Arabs in the Syro-Palestinian region appear closely allied with the empires. This is especially well documented from Egypt, where we already find them employed as police forces and cattle-tenders in the first half of the third century BC. The great bastion of Arabism, the kingdom between Palestine and the Nile, probably founded by the tribe of Qedar perhaps as early as the late Neo-Babylonian period, seems to have had a fruitful co-operation with the Ptolemies in Egypt both in military and in civil affairs. They were obviously involved in caravan traffic between Egypt and the Persian Gulf and many were also the providers of cattlemen and police sergeants in Egypt proper. It can be assumed that the Arab presence in Transjordan was in fact the result of the founding of military colonies there by Ptolemy Philadelphus, employing his Arab allies as defenders of the border against the Seleucids in Syria. The Syrian ruler Antiochus III seems to have paid him back in the same coin: Arabs from central Syria were used by him in his army not only against the Egyptian arch-enemy but also against the Romans, and it is likely that the Arabs were settled in central Syria in his reign. It can be assumed that the Arabs in Antilebanon were also involved in the fight between the two eastern Mediterranean powers, since they dwelt on the very border between them. In the end of our period we thus find Arabs concentrated in three regions in Syria: Antilebanon with the Transjordanian Arabs not far from there, central Syria around Ḥimṣ, and northern Syria around Chalcis/Qinnasrīn.

A most important result of this investigation so far is the absence of documented identity between Arabs and Nabataeans. On the contrary, they appear explicitly as separate entities in the sources dealing with the period. The Nabataeans are found in Ḥawrān in the second century BC and in (southern) Transjordan around 160 BC, and in the latter as the enemies of the then pro-Seleucid Arabs there. This indicates that they, like the Arabs between Palestine and Egypt, belonged to the Egyptian sphere of interest, and we also have documentation of their involvement in the trade route to Gerrha. It is possible that they were already in Reqem, the later Petra, at this time. The fragment preserved by Pliny quoted above, which could originate with Eratosthenes, seems to show the Nabataeans south-east of Palestine, which would locate them in ancient Edom, i.e. around the later Petra, at the end of the third century BC.[216]

This raises a problem not hitherto faced by any historian dealing with this period: since Nabataeans and Arabs seem to be identified in later sources, and if they were separate entities from the beginning, when were they identified and what does the identification mean? We shall try to answer this question in the course of this investigation.

We do not get much information about other aspects of the life of these Arabs during the period. The most important document is the ethnographic excursus by Hieronymus. Their involvement in cattle breeding is well documented, as is their service as mercenaries to different rulers (Antigonus, Antiochus III, Timotheus). According to Hieronymus, there are also Arabs who are farmers, a piece of information that is also found in the sources dealing with Alexander the Great. They do, however, tend to appear in military contexts. Apart from the traditional armament with bows, we hear, for the first time, about the use of another weapon, namely a long, narrow sword, which was used at Magnesia. Such a weapon is hardly documented in other sources as a characteristic of the *árabes*. It could perhaps be a kind of spear that is intended, a weapon well known among Arabs in later periods. In order to use a long sword or a spear from the camel's back, one would need to be more steadily seated than was possible on the old cushion saddle. The classical North Arabian saddle is probably documented on a coin from Gaza from the early third century BC, as well as in literary texts (Ctesias) from the same period.[217] It then appears in a picture on Roman coins from the middle of the first century BC, where the surrender of the Arabo-Nabataean king Aretas to the Romans is shown.[218] The weaponry described by Polybius indicates that the use of this saddle when riding a camel was well established in the Seleucid period.[219]

Notes

1 Hornblower, *Hieronymus* 11–15. For the extant fragments, see Jacoby, *Fragmente* II B 828–835.

2 For the parts of Diodorus taken from Hieronymus, see the discussion by Schwarz, *Diodorus* 684–685 (very sceptical), Jacoby, *Hieronymus* 1556, Hammond, *Historians* 80–81,and Hornblower, *Hieronymus* 27–32, 144–153 (much more positive).

3 Diodorus 18.5–6. For Hieronymus as author of this text, see Tarn, *Alexander* II 309 ff., 381; Hornblower, *Hieronymus* 80–87. It is assumed that Diodorus did not copy Hieronymus directly but used an expanded version of his text; cf. Schachermeyr, *Pläne* 119–120.

4 Diodorus 8.6.3. According to Leuze, *Satrapieeinteilung* [310–311] *Arabia deserta* is immediately west of Babylonia. This hardly follows from Diodorus' text. It says that beyond Babylonia is the uninhabited area towards (*katà*) Arabia which is not identical with it.

5 This according to a conjecture suggested by Leuze, loc. cit. The text actually has: adjacent to Babylonia.

6 Diodorus 19.94.1. Cf. Plutarch, *Demetrius* 7.1.

7 Cf. Hornblower, *Hieronymus* 144. This passage has often been commented on; see, for example, Abel, *L'expédition* 374–380; Bowersock, *Arabia* 12 ff.; Negev, *Nabateans* 523–529.

8 Diodorus 19.94.2–95.2.

9 Diodorus 19.95.2–7.

10 Diodorus 19.96.1–98.1.

11 Diodorus 19.100.1–3.

12 Cf. Dussaud, *Pénétration* 23; Kammerer, *Pétra* I 2, 116–117; Starcky, *Pétra* 903; Grohmann, *Nabataioi* 1454, Altheim/Stiehl, *Araber I* 31–34; Merkel, *Festsetzungen* 282 ff.; Negev, *Beginnings* 125–127; idem, *Nabateans* 522–529; Hammond, *Nabateans* 12–13; Parr, *Pottery* 204; Lindner, *Geschichte* 39; Roschinski, *Geschichte* 134–135; Bowersock, *Arabia* 12–17; Knauf, *Ismael* 93 note 505, 109; idem, *Herkunft* 75.

13 Hornblower, *Hieronymus* 40–62.

14 Merkel, *Festsetzungen* 284–286.

15 Strabo 16.4.21, 26.

16 For example, Merkel, *Festsetzungen* 282–285. The problems with these texts were clearly seen by Dijkstra, *Life* 297–307.

17 Cf. Graf, *Origin* 51–53.

18 Jeremiah 35:6–7; cf. 2 Kings 10:15–17; 1 Chronicles 2:55 (LXX), 4:11–12.

19 Frick, *Rechab*.

20 The parallel with the Rechabites is pointed out by Hornblower, *Hieronymus* 145–146. Worth remarking is that the life-style of the Rechabites is in fact used by the prophet Jeremiah as a moral example to the Judaeans of his day, whose faithlessness is contrasted with the tenacity with which the Rechabites stick to their traditional way of life. There are indications that the Rechabites were closely related to the Qenites, who are known to have been attached to the Negev. Cf. also Knauf, *Dushara* 177–178.

21 The difference must go back to Hieronymus' text. He had encountered the *árabes* personally in connection with the asphalt project, and the ethnographic description is his own work. The

two campaigns he knew through reports from the generals involved, which obviously used a more variegated terminology.

22 Thus Abel, *L'expédition* 380–385. The rock is identified with ʔUmm al-Biyāra in present-day Petra, cf. idem, *Géographie* 2 407–408; *Histoire* 1 34; Altheim/Stiehl, *Christentum* 233; Wenning, *Nabatäer* 197 cf. ibid. 200.

23 For the different identifications of the rock, see Starcky, *Pétra* 886–900. Buhl *(Geschichte* 34–35) rejected the identification and suggested Shawbak.

24 Diodorus 19.98 beginning.

25 Briant, *Histoire* 737. That the province is pre-Ptolemaic can be assumed from its name Idoumaía, which probably goes back to an Aramaic form. The expected Ptolemaic designation would be *Idoumitis; cf. Jones, *Cities* 239–240.

26 Diodorus 19.95.2. The text says that Athenaeus finished 2,200 *stadia* in three days and three nights from the *eparkhía* of Idoumaía before reaching the rock. The number has been supposed to be wrong since the rock in the account of Demetrius' campaign is said to be 300 *stadia* from the Dead Sea. An argument in favour of the Achaemenid province of Edom encompassing the entire eastern side of the ʕArabah is the documented presence of a Persian governor in Taymāʔ (Knauf, *Ismael* 75–76 note 395). The picture is of an entity extending from the northern Ḥiǧāz to Wādī Ḥasā and including an area south of Judaea to Beer Sheba forming a large L. *Arabāya* would then be another, separate entity encompassing most of the Negev and the northern Sinai. Both Petra and as-Silʕ would be included in Edom.

27 In Diodorus' account preceding the campaign against the *árabes*, we are told that Demetrius after the defeat at Gaza was encamped in 'upper Syria' (*tēn ánō Syrían*) which is contrasted to 'hollow Syria' (*koílēn Syrían*), having returned there from Cilicia. After a surprise attack he defeated Ptolemy who was in Coele Syria. Antigonus himself then crossed the Taurus and joined Demetrius 'after a few days'. Ptolemy retired from Syria, destroying a series of towns starting with Akko, ending with Gaza. Then Athenaeus' campaign was launched (Diodorus 29.93; cf. 19.86 and 18.6). It is reasonable to assume that the defeat of Ptolemy took place somewhere in central Syria in or close to present-day Lebanon, perhaps near Damascus. Antigonus, Demetrius and Atheneaeus are thus likely to have camped not far from there; cf. Abel, *L'expédition* 387 note.

28 For the southern border of Idumaea as we know it from the first century BC, see Gihon, *Idumea*, and Abel, *Géographie* II 135; idem, *Histoire* I 33–37. The border documented in the time of Herod probably goes back several centuries, perhaps even to Achaemenid times. The text of Diodorus says that Athenaeus marched 2,200 *stadia* from the eparchy of Idumaea in three days and three nights before reaching the *árabes*. Usually the number 2,200 is considered wrong. The phrase '2,200 *stadia*' would need some complement indicating that it refers to the entire distance from Syria to the Negev. If it gives a meaning, it is better to keep the text as it stands than try to emendate drastically. A suggested rendering: 'After having marched during *(en)* three days and the same number of nights from the eparchy of Idoumaía, 2200 *stadia* [altogether from his base], he came upon the *árabes* unawares.' This rendering demands a slight change of word order in the text. It is possible that the intermediary between Hieronymus and Diodorus had confused the text.

29 Negev has underlined the fact that Hieronymus' description of Arabia as a waterless desert does not fit conditions in Edom/Nabataea on the eastern side of the ʕArabah but far better the areas west of that region (*Nabateans* 527–528, idem, *Beginnings* 127–128). This was seen already by Buhl (*Geschichte* 34–35). Cf. also Dijkstra, *Life* 297–307. The rock is said to be located at a distance of two days from settled lands, which fits very well with Avdat. The earliest strata of Avdat lie under the later Nabataean and Roman acropolis but the site was already in use around 300 BC; cf. Wenning, *Nabatäer* 159–161. Cf. Athenodorus' description of Petra with that of Hieronymus.

30 Stephanus 482:15–16; cf. Negev, *Nabateans* 537. The information comes from Uranius; cf. pp. 491–493. As will be pointed out below (p. 377), Obodas is probably a deity after whom some Nabataean kings were named; cf. Dijkstra, *Life* 319–321.

31 Stephanus 466:5–7; cf. Starcky, *Pétra* 903–904; Roschinski, *Geschichte* 16; Negev,

Nabateans 529–530, and Wenning, *Nabatäer* 47, who identify it with al-Mawta in Moab or Imtān in southern Syria.

32 Josephus, *War* 13.101–102; cf. Negev, *Nabateans* 536–537.

33 Starcky, *Pétra* 905–906.

34 A. Negev went as far as to suggest that their origins were in the Negev (*Beginnings* 127 ff.)

35 Cf. Chamoux/Bertrac, *Introduction générale* to Diodorus' Book I: CIX–CXXIII; Bizière, *Notice* to Book XIX: XX–XXII. In a daughter-manuscript to F, we find *nybataîoi* in one instance instead of *nomádes*. This is without doubt an influence from the R text. The fact that F was written much later than R cannot be decisive: *recentiores non deteriores*. The two variant traditions are obviously based on two different prototypes.

36 Diodorus 2.48; cf. also Plutarch, *Demetrius* 7.1, which probably also comes from Posidonius. Cf. Strabo 16.4.18, which stands in a passage built on Agatharcides (second century BC) but transmitted by Artemidorus writing around 100 BC. For the origin of this phrase see pp. 369, 377 f.

37 Vitelli, *Papiri* IV no. 406 l. 22–23.

38 2 Kings 14:7; 2 Chronicles 25:11–12.

39 Gray, *Kings* 605.

40 Judges 1:36.

41 'The Edomite' in LXX A is ungrammatical and obviously a gloss. Against Starcky (*Pétra* 887–888) the Masoretic text as well as LXX B are to be accepted, since they give a good meaning.

42 Numbers 34:3–4.

43 Chronicles 26:7; see p. 137.

44 Diodorus 20.73.1. Barathra is west of the Sirbonian lake.

45 Diodorus 5.41–46; 6.1–11; Jacoby, *Fragmente* I 300–313 (no. 63); idem, *Euemeros*.

46 Jacoby, *Euemeros* 953.

47 Diodorus 5.41.1–3.

48 Diodorus 5.41.4; 42.3, 4.

49 Diodorus 5.42.2.

50 Diodorus 5.44.3.

51 Diodorus 5.46.7; 6.1.8–9.

52 Eusebius, *Commentary* 1.67 (p. 100).

53 Eusebius, *Praeparatio* 2.55.

54 One might also adduce the lines from Catullus' poem no. XI where he describes the extremest parts of the world: 'whether he reaches India//the shore where long resounding Eoa's//wave breaks//or the Hyrcanians or the *Arabes*//or the Scythians (Sacae) and the arrow-carrying Parthians . . .' The Arabs in this poem seem to dwell between Indian and the Iranian peoples, a geography reflecting that of Euhemerus.

55 On the other hand, the impression is that the islands were seen as quite close which makes the location of one of them to Rās Musandam less likely. There is, however, a tradition documented in later texts to call the southern half of the Arabian peninsula India. This is found in both Jewish and Christian tradition. Thus, for example, the targum (Yerushalmi, Chronicles) translate Ḥawilah in Genesis with HNDQY/HNDQʔY, i.e.' Indica' (cf. Krauss, *Völkertafel* 56). There might have been an original confusion between India and the south-eastern part of the Arabian peninsula, which is explicable considering the fact that at least the peoples in the Mediterranean had no clear idea about the extension or even the existence of this continent until the time of Alexander.

56 Cf. p. 242.

57 Diodorus 5.41.3; 6.1.4. Pliny's *Natural History* (6.97) mentions an *insula quae Solis appellatur*, 'an island which is called [that] of the sun'. The sentence is part of Pliny's digest of Nearchus' and Onesicritus' journey from India and is not located inside the Gulf. It is, however, likely that the name belongs to Euhemerus' island and was inserted wrongly by Pliny.

58 Cf. Jacoby, *Euemeros* 952.

59 The text is found in Diodorus 2.55–60. See in general Kroll, *Iamboulos*. Jacoby supposes a form of the root YBL. It could rather be from NBL, which is well known in the Arabic

onomasticon (cf. Altheim/Stiehl, *Araber* I 82). It could in that case be an imperfect *yābul* from YBL or *yanbul/yabbul* from NBL. The prefix vowel *-a-* indicates Arabic, like Iamblikhos (*yamlik*). The assimilation of *-n-* points to a dialect in the western or north-western part of Arabia. Altheim/Stiehl (loc. cit.) believe he came from Nabataea

60 Diodorus 2.55.4.
61 Diodorus 2.57.3.
62 Diodorus 2.58.7.
63 Diodorus 2.59.2.
64 Diodorus 2.55.1.
65 Diodorus 2.60.2.
66 It has often been supposed that the island Panchaea in Euhemerus and the Happy Island in Iambulus would be Soqotra. A suggested etymology of Soqotra is that it is the Sanskrit *dvīpa sukhatare*, 'the happy island', which, unfortunately, is most uncertain (Glaser, *Geographie* 11). It is perhaps an old popular etymology of the name of the island ultimately derived from the accounts of the two utopists.
67 Aristophanes, *Birds* 144–145.
68 Euripides, *Bacchae* 15–17; cf. p. 242. In a scholion to Aristophanes' *Birds* 44–45 it is said: 'The Red Sea is in the east. According to others he speaks about *Arabía eudaímōn*' (*Scholia in Aves* 145.3). This scholion is from a time when Happy Arabia was located in South Arabia but the original meaning of the verse was still remembered. The scholiast had to link differing views together.
69 Cf. Potts, *Gulf* I 85 ff. for references.
70 Potts, *Gulf* I 86.
71 Pritchard, *Texts* 44.
72 Translation according to Kramer/Maier, *Myths* 24. Cf. Pritchard, *Texts* 38.
73 Tarn/Griffith, *Civilisation* 121–125; Altheim/Stiehl, *Araber* I 80–92.
74 Qurʔān 27:24: *yasǧudūna li-š-šamsi min dūni l-lāhi. min dūn* is to be taken negatively as 'instead of': they did not worship God but the sun.
75 See p. 425, n. 66.
76 Ibn Hishām, *Tīǧān* 162.
77 Cf. Philby, *Queen*, colour illustration, Section I 2c.
78 Raschke, *Studies* 657.
79 Jones, *Cities* 239–240.
80 Jacoby, *Hekataios* 2758 ff.; Jacoby, *Fragmente* 3A 11–64 (no. 264).
81 Diodorus 1.19.6: Osiris marches through Arabia on his way to India; 45.2: The king Tnephakhthos (= Tef-Sukht twenty-third dynasty?) was near dying from thirst in Arabia during a campaign there; 53.5–6: Sesoōsis (= Sesostris?) marches to Arabia and subdues the people of the *árabes*; 57.4 (cf. Strabo 16.4.4): the same king builds a wall to defend the road from Syria and Arabia from Pelusium to Heliopolis; 63.6: king Khemmis the Memphite (= Cheops?) takes stones for his buildings in Arabia, i.e. the Mukattam mountain east of Cairo; 89.1–2: robbers from Libya and Arabia do not dare to cross the Nile because of the crocodiles.
82 Cf. Tarn, *Ptolemy* 11.
83 Cf. Diodorus 3.42.1; Strabo 16.4.4; cf. Tarn, *Ptolemy.*
84 Diodorus, 3.42–47; Strabo, 16.4.18–19; Photius, 7.134–189 (Codex 250); Jacoby, *Fragmente* 2A 211–222 (no. 86); Altheim/Stiehl, *Araber* I 65–69.
85 See Burstein, *Agatharchides* 37–38.
86 Burstein, *Agatharchides* 147.
87 Burstein, *Agatharchides* 147 note 3.
88 Burstein, *Agatharchides* 148 with references. The reading *nēssa*, 'duck', is said to be a mistake for *nēsos*, 'island' (Burstein, loc. cit.). Musil (*Ḥeǧâz* 302) says that the word *tīrān* means a kind of sea-bird, which would give a meaning to the Photius text. The word is, however, not documented in any Arabic dictionary.
89 For Rās al-Qaṣba, see Musil, *Ḥeǧâz* 302. For Rās Muhammed, see Noth, *Zur Geschichte* 139. There are no forests on either the Arabian or the Sinai side of the inlet. Around Rās Muhammed there are, however, large areas of mangrove along the sea shore.

90 The obscurity of the passage in all three witnesses may be due to the fact that Rās Muhammed is an elevation connected with the mainland by a narrow, sandy isthmus. Diodorus says the island is at (*pròs*) the *akrōtērion* of the mainland. Photius says it is close to (*engys*) the *akrōtērion*; Strabo says near (*plēsíon*). Only Strabo says that the *akrōtērion* stretches towards the north; the two others say it stretches from the island towards the north. Diodorus adds that the *akrōtērion* projects from (*prókeitai*) the island. The partly contradictory statements can be harmonized if we assume that the *akrōtērion* in fact is the isthmus itself that stretches from both the island and the mainland, whereas the island is the present-day Rās.

91 Cf. Noth, *Zur Geschichte* esp. p. 140. Noth takes 'the straight line' of Agatharchides as a description of maritime and overland routes (*geraden Weges*) from South Arabia via (Nabataean) Petra to Gaza, since Petra to him, as to everybody else, must be the Nabataean capital. But Agatharchides' text does not speak about trade routes or roads. The word *eutheía* means 'straight', not 'road'. Instead the word *grammē*, 'line', is to be understood. The word *theōrouménē*, 'observed', refers to some kind of visual observation. The impression is that Agatharchides has referred to some kind of map, perhaps that of Eratosthenes, which must have been known to him. It is clear that he, in this passage, has added information from other sources to that derived from Ariston. Stern, *Authors* 3–4, 6–7 note 3 (referring to Aristotle, *Meteorology* II 359a), 348–349, 515–520 (referring to Statius, *Silvae* 2.1.161, 3.2.105, 5.1.213) etc. points out that there are signs that the Greeks in Aristotle's time could already include Judaea in Palaistínē. Cf. also Philo, *De Virtutibus* 221; idem, *Vita Mosis* 1.163; Josephus, *Antiquities* 1.145, 20.259. This would be in line with the tendency observed already in Herodotus of calling even the lands behind Arabia by the same name. This does not, however, contradict the arguments here about the location of the Rock, since there are no indications that Palaistínē included Transjordan. The arguments by Jacobson (*Palestine*) that the very name Palaistínē is a cover term for Israel in Herodotus are not convincing.

92 See p. 369.

93 Burstein, *Agatharchides* 150 note 2. There is obviously an early confusion between the name Ayla/Elat and Liḥyān. The latter name is reflected in the form of the name in Diodorus and Photius. This confusion is evident in a passage in Pliny's *Natural History* (6.156):
There is an interior bay in which the Laeanitae [live] who have given it their name. Their capital is Agra and on the bay is Laeana or, as others [call it] Aelana; for the [name of] the bay our people write Laeaniticum, Artemidorus [writes] Alaeniticum and Iuba Leaniticum.
We notice that Artemidorus' form is in agreement with that of Strabo. Agra is probably Ḥiğr, the capital of the Liḥyanite kings near present-day al-ʕŪlā.

94 Cf. p. 137.

95 Burstein, *Agatharchides* 152 note 2.

96 This sanctuary may also be referred to by Pliny (6.155) when he mentions the island Sygaros near the bay of the Laeanitae 'which dogs do not enter'.

97 Photius seems to have repeated himself when copying Agatharchides and has not realized that the Bythemanéoi and the Batmizomaneîs refer to the same group.

98 2 Chronicles 14:15; 2 Chronicles 22:1, cf. pp. 137, 142, 144.

99 Cf. Musil, *Ḥeğâz* 292–293, 304; cf. p. 149.

100 Burstein, *Agatharchides* 154 note 2.

101 Burstein, *Agatharchides* 156 note 2.

102 Burstein, *Agatharchides* 167.

103 The texts from Dedan, Liḥyān and the Thamudic and Safaitic epigraphic texts all show the prefixed *h-* as the definite article.

104 The Pithom stele; see Tarn, *Ptolemy* 9.

105 References in Burstein, *Agatharchides* 150 note 2.

106 P. Revenue Laws col. 65 = Kiessling, *Sammelbuch* 26.

107 Manetho § 82 = Josephus, *Apion* 1.14.

108 LXX Genesis 45:10, 46:34.

109 P.I.S 558 (= Vitelli, *Papyri* V 123).

110 P. Edgar 59230 (Edgar, *Catalogue* II 85–86).
111 P. Edgar 59296 (= Edgar, *Catalogue* II 162).
112 P. Zenon 53 (= Kiessling, *Sammelbuch* III 6759); P. Edgar 59328 (= Edgar, *Catalogue* III 46); P.S.I 367 (= Vitelli, *Papiri* IV 97).
113 P. Michigan 67 (= Edgar, Papyri 144–146); P. Edgar 59433 (= Edgar, Catalogue III:161–162).
114 P.S.I. 388 (= Vitelli, Papiri IV 115).
115 P. Edgar 59425 (Edgar, *Catalogue* III 155–156); Kiessling, *Sammelbuch* III 6801; P. Edgar 59394, 59425 (= Edgar, *Catalogue* III 132, 155–156); P. Zenon 107 (Kiessling, *Sammelbuch* III 6990).
116 P. Magdola 15 (= Jouguet, *Papyrus* 115–116).
117 Cf. Knaack, *Eratosthenes* 371–372.
118 For the preserved explicit quotations from Eratosthenes, see Berger, *Fragmente*, especially pp. 233–302 for the Middle East and Arabia. For an analysis of the sources to Book XVI, see Aly, *Strabon* 157–164. Cf. also Honigmann, *Strabo* 100, and Dueck, *Strabo* 186.
119 Strabo 16.4.2; cf. Berger, *Fragmente* 288 ff. The explicit quotation from Eratosthenes containing the whole survey of Arabia runs from Chapters 2 to 4 in Book XVI. In Chapter 4, Strabo has supplemented the account with two short references to Anaxicrates and Hecataeus of Abdera, dealing with the western shore of the Red Sea/the Arabian Gulf. After them follows the extensive quotation from Agatharchides; see pp. 296–299.
120 Theophrastus, *Plants* 9.4.2; cf. p. 566.
121 See Tarn, *Ptolemy* 14.
122 Strabo 16.3.1.
123 Strabo 16.2.1.
124 Strabo 16.1.8.
125 Strabo 2.1.31.
126 It may be doubted whether Strabo's text is in order. The *autèn* in 16.4.2 occupied by 'the first ones after the Syrians and Judaeans' should probably refer to the northern, desert part of Arabia, and the whole passage from *ékhousi d'autèn* . . . to . . . *kamēloboskoí* should be moved back and inserted after *agraíōn*. This fits the structure in 16.3.1. The present contradictions might go back to Strabo himself, who perhaps was not familiar with all the details of the geography and ethnography of the Syrian desert.
127 Cf. von Wissmann, *Geschichte* I 39.
128 Strabo 16.3.3.; cf. pp. 273 f.
129 Agatharchides § 89b = Strabo 16.4.18; Diodorus 3.42.5; cf. Burstein, *Agatharchides* 149.
130 Wenning, *Nabatäer* 139.
131 Wenning, *Nabatäer* 159.
132 Pliny, 12.80.
133 Sprenger, *Geographie* 136 f.; von Wissmann, *Geschichte* I 43.
134 Ptolemy, 5.18; von Wissmann, *Geschichte* I 43, 35 note 2; Potts, *Routes* 131–133.
135 The route seems to run along the dividing line between Eratosthenes' *Arabia Deserta* and *Arabia Felix*. The division of Arabia into a northern and a southern part, separated by a line running from the north-west (the Gulf of ʕAqabah) towards the south-east in the direction of Ḥāyil, is strikingly similar to the border between the Semites and the Hamites in the P Table of Nations in Genesis 10 (see pp. 214–215). This division of the Arabian peninsula may thus not be the invention of the great Cyrenian scientist but go back to earlier Oriental traditions. The route may in that case be much older than the third century BC, although its role was drastically increased in that period.
136 Cf. von Wissmann, *Geschichte* I 39.
137 von Wissmann (*Geschichte* I 12) has suggested that HGR is mentioned in another passage from Eratosthenes, namely the one quoted about Gerrha (Strabo 16.3.3). After the mention of Gerrha, 'a city situated on a deep gulf' built from salt, Strabo says that *hē pólis*, 'the town', is 200 *stadia*, i.e. *c*. 40 kilometres, from the sea. 'The town' would thus be different from Gerrha on the seashore. This reading of Strabo is, however, doubtful. The natural meaning would be that it is Gerrha which is situated inland; see pp. 273 f.

138 Robin, *Monnaies* 87–88; von Wissmann, *Geschichte* I 31–43. The Agraei are also mentioned in Pliny 6.159 as well as in Ptolemy 6:18.
139 Pliny 6.157.
140 According to Knaack, *Dionysios*, the work is from the time of Hadrian and is built on Eratosthenes via a second hand which may have been Posidonius.
141 Dionysius 954–960.
142 The passage quoted has usually been translated as indicating that the term *árabes* is a comprehensive term for those following: 'the Arabian tribes, I mean the Nabataeans and the Chaulotaeans and the Agraeans' (Loeb). The wording of the Greek text, however, is more naturally rendered as has been done here: *tōn Arabíōn éthnōn Nabataíōn te kaì Khaulotaíōn kaì Agraíōn*. Cf. the same translator in Strabo 16.1.1: *kaì tà perì tēn Nínon pedía Dolomēnē te kaì Kalamēnē*, 'the plain in the neighbourhood of Ninos and also Dolomene and Kalamene'. The words *te kaì* may mean (1) 'and also' (2) 'namely', of which (1) is the more common (cf. Diodorus 40.4.1). The translator has been led astray by the presupposition that there existed an Arab 'people' occupying the whole peninsula, divided into smaller tribes, of which the Nabataeans were one.
143 Strabo, 16.4.21.
144 Pliny 5.65.
145 Strabo 16.4.2, middle section.
146 Josephus, *Antiquities* 15.8.5; idem, *War* 2.18.1; Ptolemy 5.16.4; cf. Jones, *Cities* 274 and note 64.
147 For the identity of the Agraeans, see pp. 585–587.
148 The part of the route from the Euphrates to Gerrha is described in Pliny 6.145.
149 Thus, Meineke's edition followed by the Loeb text. For the location of Mesene see Weissbach, *Mesene* 1082–1088.
150 The oldest extant MS to Book XVI of Strabo, the F MS, has *elesēnōn*; the others have *alesēnōn*. The difference between Mesene and al-Ḥasā is evident in Ptolemy's *Geography* 6.7.18, where he makes a clear distinction between *asanitōn pólis*, 'the town of the Ḥasaites', and *asanítēs kólpos*, 'the bay of the Ḥasaites', on the one hand, and *ho Maisanítēs kólpos*, 'the bay of the Mesenians', on the other. The latter should be identified with the present-day Bay of Kuwayt.
151 Appian, *History: Syrian wars* 9.9 (55).
152 Brodersen, *Abriss* 125.
153 Cf. Walbank, *Commentary* I 32.
154 Polybius 5.71.1.
155 Polybius 5.71.4.
156 *Rabbat ʕAmmān. According to Bowersock, *Roman Arabia* 17, these Arabs were Nabataeans, which is unlikely. For this problem, see the discussion about the Nabataeans pp. 378–385.
157 See Tcherikover, *Civilisation* 64–65; Schürer, *History* I 144; Jones, *Cities* 238–241.
158 Polybius 5.79.8; 82.12.
159 Polybius 5.85.4.
160 Polybius 13.9. Cf. Walbank, *Commentary* II 421–422; Schmitt, *Untersuchungen* 49 n. 1.
161 Walbank, *Commentary* II 252.
162 Schürer, *History* I 144.
163 Kraeling, *Gerasa* Inscr. no. 19, 20, 21, 22 (pp. 385–386).
164 Kraeling, *Gerasa* 22.
165 See p. 317.
166 The chronology of this story in Josephus is confused; see Tcherikover, *Civilisation* 140–142; Hengel, *Judentum* 490.
167 Josephus, *Antiquities* 12.229.
168 Josephus, *Antiquities* 12.233.
169 Tcherikover, *Civilisation* 130.
170 Livy 37.12.
171 Appian, *History: Syrian wars* 6.32.

172 The earliest occurrence of the word in Latin texts is in Plautus' plays: *Curculio* 443; *Miles gloriosus* 412; *Poenulus* 1179; cf. *Persa* 506, 522, 541; *Trinummus* 845, 933, 934; *Truculentus* 539; cf. fragm. Corn. 7; cf. Dangel, *Du Nil.* 324 ff. It can be assumed that its use as an exotic gloss reflects a similar usage in the New Attic Comedy, which was Plautus' main source of inspiration. This picture of Arabia as a distant exotic land goes well with the picture found in the Greek sources before Alexander. In Rome, Arabia and Arabs remained more or less unknown until the time of Augustus; see pp. 400 ff.

173 Josephus, *Antiquities* 12.236.

174 See Schürer, *History* I 148–154, especially notes 32 and 37 for the problems of chronology.

175 2 Maccabees 5:8.

176 Starcky, *Pétra* 904; Abel, *Livres* 351 (comm. ad loc.); idem, *Histoire* 1 250–255; Bowersock, *Arabia* 18; Negev, *Nabateans* 532; Kasher, *Jews* 24.

177 Schürer, *History* III.1 180–181 with further references. According to Wacholder, (*Eupolemus* 28–32), 1 Maccabees was written under John Hyrcanus (135–104 BC) and based upon a source describing the deeds of Judas Maccabaeus, which in its turn used a work by Eupolemus that ended around 159 BC, cf. 1 Maccabees 9:73. Eupolemus is probably identical with the leader of the delegation to Rome dispatched by Judas Maccabaeus in 161 BC (cf. 1 Maccabees 8:17). This source was also used by Jason of Cyrene, cf. Hengel, *Judentum* 180–181.

178 Schürer, *History* III.1 531–534; Hengel, *Judentum* 176–183. Also Jason used Eupolemus extensively; cf. Wacholder, *Eupolemus* 38–40.

179 1 Maccabees 5:6–8; Josephus, *Antiquities,* 12.329.

180 1 Maccabees 5:9–13; Josephus, *Antiquities* 12.330. Dathema is by Abel (*Histoire* 1 144, *Géographie* 2 303) with Shaykh Miskīn 50 kilometres north-west of Bosra.

181 1 Maccabees 5:24–36; Josephus, *Antiquities* 12.336–340. According to Wacholder, *Eupolemus* 34, the geographical notes betray the hand of Eupolemus. Abel (*Histoire* 1 145) identifies Khaspho/Kaspin with Tall Miqdād north of Bosra, Rapho/Romphon with ar-Rāfeh 5 kilometres north of Shaykh Miskīn and Karnion/Karnain with Shaykh Saʕad 15 kilometres east of ar-Rāfeh.

182 1 Maccabees 5:37–44; Josephus, *Antiquities* 12.341–344.

183 2 Maccabees 12:10–12.

184 2 Maccabees 12:13–26.

185 2 Maccabees 8:32.

186 Kasher, *Jews* 30, against Schürer, *History* I 140 note 5.

187 Bowersock, *Arabia* 19–20, assumes a different identity.

188 1 Maccabees 9:35.

189 According to Josephus (*Antiquities* 13.18) the sons of Amaraios were attacked when marrying one of their daughters to an Arab. 1 Maccabees has a Kanaanite instead. Both terms are likely to be literary and not political: that of 1 Maccabees from Biblical terminology (cf. Abel, *Livres* 168; Kasher, *Jews* 35) and that of Josephus from his general concept of ethnological conditions in Transjordan; cf. pp. 334 ff.

190 1 Maccabees 9:36; Josephus, *Antiquities* 13.10–11, 18–21. See Kasher, *Jews* 34–35.

191 The name occurs in different forms. One is found in an inscription: YʕMRW, which is a good Arabic word: *yaʕmuru*. There is, however, now ample documentation of a tribe ʕMRT in Transjordan (Milik, *Tribu*). Both names could refer to the same tribe. For the different form, cf. Iamblikhos (= Yamlik) – Malikhos (Malik) see p. 316. It has, of course, nothing to do with Amorites, as still maintained by Kasher (*Jews* 35). They were also distinct from the Nabataeans.

192 For a characterization of Jason as belonging to the Cleitarchus tradition in Greek historiography, see Wacholder, *Eupolemus* 28 note 4; Hengel, *Judentum* 181.

193 Cf. Wolski, *Empire* 79 ff.

194 Wolski, *Seleucids* 107.

195 1 Maccabees 11:15–19.

196 Josephus, *Antiquities* 13.116–118.

197 Diodorus 32.27.9d–10.1.

198 Cf. p. 310.
199 1 Maccabees 11:39–40.
200 Josephus, *Antiquities* 13.131–132 (v.1).
201 Diodorus 33.4a.
202 Cf. Merkel, *Festsetzungen* 277 ff.
203 For the expeditions of Jonathan, see Kasher, *Jews* 34–41.
204 1 Maccabees 12:31–32.
205 Against Abel, *Livres* 212, and Kasher, *Jews* 38 ff.
206 Josephus has obviously misunderstood his source here. According to him (*Antiquities* 13.179), the Arabs defeated by Jonathan were Nabataeans, which is impossible for many reasons; see p. 367.
207 According to Unger (*Umfang* 92) it is based on Book III of Posidonius' world history; cf. Theiler, *Poseidonios* I 84–85, II 65; see pp. 351 ff.
208 Grainger, *Cities* 40–42, cf. Strabo 16.2.2.
209 Unger, *Umfang* 92–93; Grainger, *Cities* 39; Dussaud, *Topographie* 199–200. There was also another Chalcis in Syria, namely in the Biqāʕ valley.
210 Strabo 16.2.10 has a note on the career of Tryphon which clearly shows that the geographical basis of his operations was the lower Orontes and adjacent territories:

> He was born at Casiana, a fortress of the Apamaean country, and, having been reared at Apamaea and closely associated with the king and the king's court, when he set out to effect a revolution, he got his resources from this city and also from its dependencies: Larisa, Casiana, Megara, Apollonia and other places like them, all of which were tributary to Apamaea. So Tryphon was proclaimed king of this country and held out for a long time.

For the location of Megara (= Maʕarra?) and Apollonia in the Apamene, see Dussaud, *Topographie* 199–200; Grainger, *Cities* 42–43. It is likely that the notice in Pliny (6.32) about the three Greek cities Arethusa, Larisa and Chalcis in Arabia destroyed in various wars are in fact the well-known Syrian cities which figure in the Tryphon story and other accounts of Syria with Arabs involved. Pliny mentions them together with places and peoples in South Arabia, where they definitely do not belong. For this location of Abai, see also Unger, *Umfang* 93, and Merkel, *Festsetzungen* 296.
211 For a suggested route, see Kasher, *Jews* 40.
212 The pre-Islamic poet Ṣakhr al-Ghayy from the tribe Hudhayl, pouring his scorn over an enemy, 'a chief of cocks, whose head is felt', says:

> His place of refuge is the Romans or Tanūkh or
> fortresses from Ṣawwarān or Zabad. (*Diwan,* poem 3:4 = Kosegarten 13)

The meaning is, of course, that this contemptible chief is a coward, who seeks refuge with others as soon as there is danger. The reference to Romans and Tanūkh gives the verse an archaic ring. The impression is that the Tanūkh tribe dwells in Syria. We then observe the juxtaposition of Zabad and Ṣawwarān. The latter is a village in the Ḥimṣ area according to the commentary to the verse by as-Sukkarī (Kosegarten Poems 13, 14. The notice is repeated by Yāqūt, *Muʕǧam* s.v. Ṣawwarān).
213 *Megillat Taʕanît* § 33; Schürer, *History* I 185 note 34; Kasher, *Jews* 41. For the text, see Schäfer, *Einführung* 44–45.
214 Abel, *Livres* 226. Merkel, *Festsetzungen* 356 note 9, mixes it up with Chalcis in northern Syria as do Abel, *Livres* 212, and Kasher, *Jews* 38–39. The matter is not made clearer by the confusion with the Ituraeans (Kasher, *Jews* 39). In other works, Abel seems not to exclude a location of Chalkis and Zabad in southern Syria cf. *Histoire* 1 184, 188; *Géographie* 2 137.
215 Honigmann (*Stephanos* 2387) suggested that Antigonus the Macedonian, who, according to the Uranius fragment (25) preserved by Stephanus of Byzantium (*Ethnika* 466), was killed by Rabilos the king of the *arábioi* at a place called Motho, is identical with Alexander Balas and that Rabilos is a corruption of Zab(d)ēlos; cf. Bellinger, *End* 78 note 85. If this is true, Uranius would thus reflect the anti-Zabadaean tradition represented by Josephus and 1 Maccabees.
216 See p. 306. A king ḤRTT of NBṬW is mentioned in an inscription from Elusa in the central Negev, which is usually dated to the second or third century BC. Apart from the

uncertainty of the dating (the inscription is now lost and known only through copies), it is no definite testimony of a Nabataean kingdom in the Negev, since we do not know much about the context of the inscription. That an Arabo-Nabataean co-operation existed along the route from Heroonpolis to the Gulf is probable, and individual Nabataeans could have been active along the road from Reqem to the Mediterranean. For the relationship betwen Arabs and Nabataeans, see pp. 366 ff.

217 Knauf, *Supplementa* 8 23–24; Bulliet, *Camel* 95; Högemann, *Alexander* 37–39.

218 Bulliet, *Camel* 91–92.

219 Bulliet loc. cit.

12

BETWEEN THE GREEKS AND THE ROMANS

The Middle East in the second half of the second century BC

When Demetrius II was taken prisoner by the Parthians under Mithradates II in 140/139 BC on a campaign in the east, in a futile attempt at restoring the empire of his predecessors, this was the death knell not only for Seleucid power but for the entire system created by Cyrus the Great and Darius I, 400 years earlier. It was a sign that the political set-up of the Middle East had entered a phase of change that would result in a new constellation of political powers. When Demetrius was captured, the Parthian armies had reached the Euphrates. From now on, this was to become the border between Graeco-Roman and Iranian spheres of interest. These decades witnessed events which were to be a turning point in the history of the region, determining its development for centuries to come: the political division of the Middle East into an Iranian and a Mediterranean sphere, a division which turned out to be extremely stable. The border between these two regions remained on the whole unchanged for more than seven centuries. As will become apparent, the division had far-reaching consequences for politics and culture, not only in Syria and Mesopotamia, the countries immediately affected, but for the whole area stretching from South Arabia to the Caspian Sea.

The political vacuum created by the collapse of the rule in Antioch around 130 BC created an unstable situation in Syria which lasted eighty years. In the end it had to be filled out by an exterior force. The political fragmentation of Syria and adjacent areas lasted for a while even after the heavy hand of Rome had been laid on everybody's shoulder. After their arrival in 63 BC, the Romans sought in many ways to preserve the local dynasties that had mushroomed during the preceding eighty years of total anarchy, hoping that they would maintain security without too much patronizing by Rome. The Oriental question, however, gave most Roman rulers grey hairs, and we can observe a continuous process of more or less reluctant incorporation by the Romans of one local realm after the other, culminating in the annexation of the Nabataean kingdom in AD 106. The border between the Iranian and Roman spheres of interest had then been stable for more than a century and remained so for several centuries to come.

The upheavals around 100 BC were paralleled by changes in trade routes hinting at fundamental processes in the various societies. As we have suggested earlier, there is evidence that during the Seleucid period there existed a trade route through northern Arabia from Gerrha to Egypt which the Seleucids in vain tried to control. The rise of this road was due to the rivalry between the two independent Oriental powers, the Seleucids and the Ptolemies, where the latter tried to circumvent the traditional route to the Persian Gulf now controlled by the former. The breakdown of Seleucid power in

Mesopotamia and the rise of Parthia seem to have changed the scenario. The Parthians were successful in diverting at least part of the trade from the Gerrha–Dumah–Petra route to a northern one from the Persian Gulf through Mesopotamia. Some of the trade was probably continued though Anatolia to the Black Sea. Other parts of it went through the desert to central Syria and the Mediterranean. The mystical town of Gerrha began to lose its importance. Instead, settlements at the estuary of the Twin Rivers started to blossom. The dominating tendency thus seems to have been the concentration of the main routes to Parthian territory. The appearance of delegations from China in the Parthian kingdom, as well as the testimonies of large amassment of gold and silver there, are testimonies to the new economic world-order emerging in the last pre-Christian century, which also resulted in a new political world-order.[1]

An important factor connected with these changes was the discovery by a certain Hippalus of the regular monsoon winds in the Indian Ocean, which enabled sailors from Egypt to sail directly to India without being dependent on land routes controlled by intermediaries in Arabia.[2] The Red Sea now became a main thoroughfare of far-reaching economic importance. This discovery was made *c.* 100 BC and was probably also the signal for changes in South Arabia, where the overland frankincense road began to lose its importance. Frankincense was from now on mainly exported from Dhofar directly to the port of Qana without being transported overland to Syria. The old kingdoms situated along the frankincense road faced new competitors in the highlands of Yemen, where we know that the state of the Himyarites was founded *c.* 115 BC. From the highlands of Yemen one was in a better position to control the dwindling frankincense route as well as the straits between the Red Sea and the Indian Ocean. This imposed new military demands on the empire-builders in Yemen, which was soon to have consequences also for the Arabs. South Arabia seems to have become more militarized than before, which is reflected in the growing number of votive inscriptions.

The importance of the overland routes through Arabia thus began to decline in favour of the sea transport in the Red Sea and the roads through Parthian Mesopotamia. With this goes the apparent lack of interest in controlling Arabia on the part of the empires. The pressure against Arabia, documented from the days of Nabonidus to the late Ptolemies, now ceases.[3]

The breakdown of Seleucid power and the arrival of the Romans in the Middle East made Arabs more visible in the sources, since they were drawn into the political convulsions in Syria that lasted from *c.* 130 BC until the end of the Roman civil wars in 31 BC. During this period, Arabs were involved in four great series of events: the wars waged by the Jewish king Alexander Jannaeus during the first quarter of the first century BC, the rise and fall of the Armenian king Tigranes the Great and his short-lived Oriental empire *c.* 83–67 BC, the Roman conquest of Syria by Pompey 65–61 BC, and, finally, the Parthian war launched by Licinius Crassus in 53 BC. After that we have a few sporadic appearances of Arabs in connection with events during the final phase of the Roman civil wars.

Sources for the events down to the battle of Actium

As during the previous periods, we see these Arabs through the eyes of others. There are no remaining original documents written by Arabs from which we can reconstruct their history. A possible exception is a series of inscriptions on monuments and coins in Nabataean Aramaic which, as we shall see, shed some light on the structure of the kingdom governed from Petra/Reqem. Even from the outsiders there are extremely few documents that can be called remains from this period. A couple of Cicero's letters written during the Parthian war, in which he was an eye-witness and also a participant, are the only examples of direct remains of events involving Arabs.

Our knowledge is thus almost wholly dependent on the narrative literary sources dealing with the period. We know that several accounts were written by people who were directly involved in some of the events mentioned above. Thus, the story of the war of the Romans against Tigranes and Mithradates of Pontus was written by the Roman historian Sallust, who knew the Roman general Lucullus personally and probably had access to documents from the campaign.[4] The story of Pompey's conquest of Syria was written by Theophanes of Mytilene, who took part in the campaign.[5] The Parthian campaign of Crassus was likewise documented by someone who had participated, perhaps Longinus Cassius, the later assassin of Julius Caesar.[6] Part of the account of the wars of the Jewish king Alexander Jannaeus probably goes back to a document from his reign.[7]

Unfortunately, none of these accounts is preserved. As we have pointed out earlier, this also holds for the great historian of this period, Posidonius of Apamaea, whose world history, which went down to the year 86 BC and dealt extensively with conditions in Syria and adjacent lands, is irretrievably lost, as is his biography of Pompey, written around 60 BC.[8]

All these works were, however, still extant when, at the end of the first century BC, four historians wrote comprehensive works which contained large sections on Middle Eastern affairs. The earliest one is Diodorus Siculus, who was followed by Strabo, Nicolaus of Damascus and Livy. The works of the two first were world histories, drawing heavily on Posidonius and in different ways continuing his work. The two others are national histories of Judaea and Rome respectively.[9] Unfortunately, these works too are either lost completely or preserved in mutilated, abbreviated or distorted shapes in later authors.[10] Of these, Josephus gives large sections from Strabo and Nicolaus and is our main witness for these two writers.[11] After him, Plutarch used all the sources mentioned, which makes the evaluation of his information very difficult. The same partly holds for his colleague Appian, who seems to have known his sources via some kind of digest.[12] Justinus' abbreviation of Pompeius Trogus' Roman history, made at the beginning of the second century, has some passages of interest for our theme. Both Appian and Trogus used sources dependent on Posidonius' works. Also the giant among Roman historians, Tacitus, has vouchsafed the Arabs a few notices. Both Trogus and Tacitus are probably based upon Livy, who in his turn was also dependent on Posidonius. In the third century, Cassius Dio, who also dealt extensively with our period in his Roman history, used the same variegated source material, although he seems to have had the tradition from Livy as his basis.[13] This also holds for the two compendia on Roman history by Festus and Eutropus from the fourth century AD, which are based on the summaries of Livy's work.[14]

None of these works was dedicated to the Arabs. They are seen flashing by in connection with the main events. They are also seen through a veil of transmission from an original source. One of the main tasks of source criticism is to try to determine from which lost work a notice relevant for our subject originates. This is then a prerequisite for a judgement of its historical value.

Apart from the historical sources there were two books written in the time of Augustus on geography where the Middle East loomed large: Strabo's *Geography* and

Iuba's *Arabica*. The *Geography*, which is preserved, also contains a lot of historical notices, taken from Posidonius and other sources from the first century BC.[15] Iuba's book was the first known monograph dedicated to Arabia and its inhabitants, and the fact that the original text is no longer extant is a great loss. Parts of it were used by Pliny the Elder in his *Natural History*, written in the middle of the first century AD. This work is a bewildering collection of information about geography, gleaned from a mass of earlier sources from Alexander's admirals to Pliny's own time. The material is rich but unfortunately uncritically mixed together into a not very appetizing hash. Even worse is the enumeration of series of names, often distorted beyond recognition. All this taken together makes the work unreliable and difficult to evaluate in spite of the valuable material originally used in it. Most of what Pliny tells about Arabia seems to come from Iuba.

A special problem is constituted by the Jewish sources. A very important source for the early Jewish traditions is the Christian author Eusebius, writing in the reign of Constantine the Great. In his work called *Praeparatio Evangelica*, he told the 'Christian prehistory', i.e. the story of the chosen people before the advent of Christ, in which he used several works by Hellenistic Jewish writers from the third century BC onwards which are otherwise lost. Also in his Bible commentaries Eusebius used these sources. Most of them he knew via a digest by Alexander Polyhistor, who lived *c*. 80–40 BC. Those relevant for this study are two works by Eupolemus and Artapanus respectively, both written in Greek in the second century BC. Also the Jewish philosopher Philo of Alexandria, writing in the first part of the first century AD, has some historical notes worth attention. Most of the concrete information in these sources concerning our theme seems to be derived from early Jewish commentors of the Bible, who tended to interpret geographical and ethnic passages in the Old Testament in terms of contemporary conditions. It seems then that many of these pieces of information were frozen and repeated through the centuries. A task is thus to try to find out in which period a certain comment was originally formulated.

The history of the Arabs in the Middle East in the century that saw the Roman conquest of Syria and Egypt has to be patched together from this quite difficult source material. We will start with an account of the testimonies about Arabs during the period from the fall of Demetrius II to the Roman occupation of Syria in 63 BC, starting from the east and describing conditions in the Parthian empire before proceeding to Syria and Palestine.

Mesene

We have earlier seen an ambition on the part of the Seleucid kings to control the inner shores of the Persian Gulf. Antiochus III had tried to take the town of Gerrha in 204 BC. The new town Alexandria, perhaps present-day Abadan, founded by Alexander the Great, was then refounded by Antiochus IV in 166/165 BC and was the capital of the eparchy *Erythrà thálassa*, 'The Red Sea Province'.[16]

The Parthian control of Mesopotamia seems to have been quite loose in the beginning, and always remained more lax than the grip of the Romans on their provinces. The Parthians thus in certain respects continued the praxis of the Achaemenids.[17] The instability of Parthian control of Mesopotamia during the decades after 140 BC enabled the Seleucid eparch in Alexandria, Hyspaosines, son of Sagdodonacus, to carve out a kingdom for himself in the area called Mesene.[18] This is documented mainly through the coins minted by him.

Hyspaosines managed to survive not only Mithradates II but also his successors Phraates II (138/137–129/128) and Artabanus I/II and was still on the throne during the reign of Mithradates III (*c.* 124–88 BC). In the 120s BC Hyspaosines controlled Mesopotamia from the Gulf to beyond Babylon and founded the town Charax on the seashore.[19] While he had to recognize Mithradates III as the formal overlord of the Mesenian kingdom, the Parthian kings did not regain control of the whole of Babylonia until *c.* 80 BC. Mesene remained semi-independent and had a monopoly on minting down to the end of the first century BC.[20]

The rise of the Mesenian kingdom goes together with the decline of the town of Gerrha, observable after *c.* 120 BC.[21] We have a list of kings in Characene from 127 BC to AD 116 reconstructed from numismatic evidence. None of the names in it are what we would call Arabic, although the name Attambelos, used by at least five of them, is Semitic. In Pliny's *Natural History* we read that *Arabia eudaemon* begins (*excurrit*) from the inner part of the Persian Gulf where the town Alexandria was situated. But then he goes on to say that the town was refounded by Hyspaosines as Charax and calls it 'a city of Arabia' (*oppidum Arabiae*).[22] In another notice Hyspaosines is described as king of the bordering *arabes* (*finitimorum arabum*).[23] These notices are taken by Pliny from Iuba's *Arabica*. Iuba in turn had his information from a work by a Mesenean native, Isidorus of Charax, which was also known to Pliny in its original form.[24] Unfortunately we can never be sure whether Pliny copied his source correctly, and the claim that Hyspaosines was king of Arabs cannot be verified from the Plinian passage alone. Still more unfortunate is that we cannot be certain about the meaning of this notice.[25] Even though the kings in Charax were not Arabs in any sense of the word, it cannot be ruled out that they employed, for example, Arab mercenaries. In that case, these must have come from Alesēnē/al-Ḥasā, where we know there were Arabs in the time of Eratosthenes. This cannot, however, be verified by evidence available at present, and the existence of Arabs in the Mesenian kingdom remains uncertain. It is more likely that these remarks in Pliny/Iuba/Isidorus ultimately go back to the idea that the people along the southern shore of the Persian Gulf were Arabs, a concept we have found originating in the last years of Alexander the Great. Charax was seen as situated on the border to *Arabia eudaemon*. Hyspaosines is then said to have been king of the bordering Arabs. They must be those living in the part of Arabia stretching along the Persian Gulf, deriving their Arabness from their habitat in Arabia, not from actually being Arabs. The Arabs ruled by Hyspaosines were thus Arabs to the Greeks. From the second century AD we have clear indications that the authority of the kings in Charax extended over most of the southern shore of the Gulf, i.e. Alexander's Arabia. This land was obviously, already in the first century and onwards, called Oman(a).[26] It is not impossible that the rule of the kings of Charax had been established long before Pliny/Iuba. The passage about the bordering Arabs seems to indicate Characene rule over at least parts of the southern shore of the Gulf before the time of Augustus. Whether the 'real' Arabs in Hağar were subject to the king of Charax we do not know.

Osrhoene

In 132 BC a new dynasty was established in the town of Edessa in northern Mesopotamia.[27] This town had been founded or at least refounded by Seleucus I and there are coins from the time of Antiochus IV minted there.[28] As we have seen, this king also showed a special interest in Mesene. Then the new dynasty was established at the same time as that in Mesene. It is tempting to see a connection. The Parthians treated the Edessan kings like those in Mesene: they were allowed to continue as vassals under the King of Kings.

The rise of Edessa goes together with the appearance of other kingdoms as well in northern Mesopotamia: Adiabene, Commagene and Gordyene. All of them were Parthian vassals but seem to have been given large elbow-room. Unfortunately we do not know much about these states during the period treated here; they are mentioned in much later sources. As we shall see, Arabs are later mentioned in connection with the kings in Edessa and Adiabene.

Syria-Palestine until the age of Alexander Jannaeus

To this period belongs the emergence of Palmyra, although it is poorly documented for the pre-Christian century.[29] The intimate connection between Characene and Palmyra is well documented from later periods and must go back to the apogee of Charax under Hyspaosines.[30] With the re-emergence of Mesopotamia as the main trade route also goes the rise of the new dynasties in northern Mesopotamia in Osrhoene and Adiabene. Not only the establishment of Palmyra as a caravan-station, but also the growing importance of Emesa in central Syria between Palmyra and the coast, is directly connected with developments further east.[31]

The situation prevailing in Syria at the end of the second century BC is characterized by the gradual emergence of at least three powers in the south trying to expand northwards: the Hasmonaeans in Palestine, the Ituraeans in the Antilebanon and the Biqāʕ, and the Arabo-Nabataeans south and south-east of Palestine. In central Syria as well as in the north, Arabs also continue to get involved in the chaotic political situation. The northern Arabs seem to have connections across the Euphrates with their namesakes in the Ǧazīra, whereas those in the south appear to have good ties with the Ptolemies in Egypt.

The successor to Demetrius II, his brother Antiochus VII Sidetes, managed to uphold Seleucid interests in Palestine, but when he fell in the last campaign against Parthia in 130/129 BC the ruler of Judaea, John Hyrcanus, could start expanding in all directions, conquering Transjordan and Samaria. In 103 BC his son Aristobulus could conquer parts of Ituraea north of Palestine and Judaize the inhabitants together with his incorporation of Galilee. But the Hasmonaean ambition to fill the vacuum after the Seleucids was not to remain unchallenged. The actions against Ituraea seem to have triggered the emergence of a strong ruler there, Ptolemy, son of Mennaeus, who played a central role in the struggle for power during the first half of the last pre-Christian century.

In Josephus' rendering of the ancient history of Israel in his *Antiquities of the Jews* we have several mentions of Arabs around Palestine. These notices probably reflect conditions in the Hellenistic period projected backwards into Biblical times. It is clear that these notices come from different sources, since there are some contradictions between them.

According to Josephus, Amram, Moses' father, recalled the story of Abraham:

> how he [Abraham] had begotten sons and left the land of the *árabes* to Ishmael and his descendants, Troglodytis to those of Katoura, and Khananaia to Isaac.[32]

In another passage it is told that the descendants of Qeṭurah were given Troglodytis and the part of *Arabía eudaímōn* which extends to the Red Sea, which is equivalent to Biblical Midian.[33] It can be assumed that these two pieces come from the same source, which thus separated the land of the Arabs (*tēn arábōn khōran*) from Midian, the north-western corner of *Arabía eudaímōn*.[34] The land of the Arabs must thus have been a rather limited area and probably outside *Arabía eudaímōn*. It is most likely that we meet these Arabs in Josephus' version of the story of Gideon:

> Barak and Debora having died simultaneously, thereafter the Madianites, calling the Amalekites and the *árabes* to their aid, marched against the Israelites, defeated in battle all who opposed them, plundered the crops and carried off the cattle.[35]

> In the preceding combat there had fallen of the Madianites and of their *árabes* comrades-in-arms about 120 000.[36]

The Hebrew version of the story has *bnê qedem*, 'sons of the east', for the allies of the Midianites.[37] This term in the Old Testament refers to people just south and south-east of Bashan. This makes it likely that the *árabes* mentioned in Josephus' updated version of the story are those found in Transjordan. In all the passages quoted, Midianites and *árabes* are kept apart. It is thus probable that they come from the same source. Since the *árabes* are identified with Israel's enemies, it is tempting to assume that the terminology reflects the conflicts between Jews and Arabs in Transjordan at the time of Judas Maccabaeus. The separation between Midianites and Arabs also points to a date before the middle of the second century BC.

Josephus does not indicate from which source he had his version of the war of Gideon or the distribution of land between Abraham's descendants.[38] But the Arabs in Transjordan also appear in another source from the second century BC which can be identified. In a Graeco-Jewish work ascribed to a certain Artapanus, which is lost except for quotations in Eusebius, originally written in that century, we have information about Arabs in the countries around Palestine in this period. When giving his version of the story of Joseph, Artapanus said:

> Having foreseen the conspiracy [of his brothers] he (Joseph) asked the neighbouring *árabes* to carry him to Egypt. These did what they were asked. For the kings of the *árabes* were the descendants of Ishmael, the son of Abraham and the brother of Isaac.[39]

Artapanus' work was also used by Josephus via Alexander Polyhistor's digest. It is very likely that the following passage, where Josephus tells the Joseph story, in fact goes back to this source or one they had in common:

> But Judas, another son of Jacob, having seen some *árabes*, merchants of the *génos* of the *ismaēlîtai* conveying spices and Syrian merchandise from Galadēnē for the Egyptian market, advised his brethren after Rubel's departure to draw up Joseph and to sell him to the *árabes*.[40]

The same identification is hinted at in Philo's version of the Joseph story:

> On that day by chance some merchants of those whose custom it was to bring goods from Arabia to Egypt came travelling.[41]

The form of the name of Gilead, Galadēnē, is interesting. This country is usually called Galaaditis in Greek sources, which reflects the terminology of the Ptolemies.[42] The form found in Josephus looks more like a Seleucid designation and seems to represent a terminology used after the Seleucid conquest of Palestine and adjacent lands in 202 BC.[43] Since the Seleucid designation obviously did not survive, it can be assumed that its occurrence in Josephus reflects official terminology shortly after the conquest, i.e. in the second century BC.

The passages from these two sources, the anonymous one and Artapanus, are in fact the first documented instances where Arabs are made descendants of Ishmael and it should be noticed that the identification clearly pertains to people in Transjordan, the original home of Ishmael. This identification, which is only made indirectly in the Old Testament, was to have great significance in the future. It is not certain that it was made by Artapanus or by the author of the anonymous source.[44] The identification could have been made in pro-Maccabaean circles inspired by the hostility between Jews and Arabs in Transjordan in the time of Judas Maccabaeus and the negative Ishmael oracle in Genesis 16:12. In any case, it is a testimony to the Arab presence in Transjordan already documented in the third century BC.[45]

Artapanus also reported about other Arabs than those in Transjordan. In his Egyptianizing novel about Jewish history, Moses is said to have fled to Arabia after having made a nuisance of himself in Egypt. His father-in-law, Ragouel, is then said to have recommended that he plunder Egypt 'commanding the *árabes*'.[46] The meaning must be that Midian is identified as Arabia. This identification reappears around two centuries later in the writings of the Jewish philosopher Philo of Alexandria. In three passages when referring to the history of Moses' escape to Midian he mentions Arabia and its inhabitants:

> When they had told this, he secretly escaped to neighbouring Arabia, where he could stay safely.[47]

Before telling the story of Moses' encounter with Jethro's daughters the following preparation is given:

> The *árabes* raise cattle, and not only men but also women, young men and young women shepherd animals among them, not only the neglected and the simple ones but also the very noble ones.[48]

The identity of these *árabes* is clear in Philo:

> The *árabes* are a most numerous people who in old times had the name *madiēnaîoi*.[49]

It seems reasonable to assume that the Alexandrine Jewish philosopher had this information from his compatriot and co-religionist Artapanus or from the same source as he. Artapanus has thus extended the concept of Arabs to encompass the Midianites. In Egypt the lands east of the delta were traditionally seen as Arabia. With this goes the idea that the Hyksos were Arabs, as reported by Manetho a century earlier.[50] Artapanus also confirms the existence of an Arabia in Wādī Tumaylāt when he says that the Israelites followed 'the river of Arabia' when they left Egypt.[51] It would thus seem that, according to these two Jewish writers, Moses' refuge could, in fact, have been in northern Sinai. In any case, this identification must have been made by Jews in Egypt in Ptolemaic times.

These Arabs would be those described by Herodotus, Hieronymus and Agatharchides. They are documented for this period in a Greek inscription in Priene in Asia Minor written shortly after 129 BC. It is in honour of a certain Moschion who, among several merits, was member of a delegation

> to Alexandria, to king Ptolemaíos, and to Petra of Arabia.[52]

The king is probably Ptolemy VIII Euergetes II (145–116 BC) or, less likely, his predecessor Ptolemy VII Philometor (180–145). It is natural that this text has been seen as a testimony to the existence of the Nabataean kingdom in Petra at this time.[53] Since, as we have seen, there are good reasons to suspect that the Arabia and the Arabs spoken about in the sources dealing with this period refer to Arabs, not Nabataeans, we should not be too certain about this passage either. We should remember that Moschion's visit was undertaken around the time when Agatharchides wrote his book on the Red Sea, where he no doubt mentioned Arabia in the Negev with a Petra as its capital which cannot be identical with the later Nabataean Petra. Instead this testimony fits rather well with the picture of a close connection between the Ptolemies and the Arabs in the Negev/northern Sinai.

From Egypt itself we have evidence in contemporary documents about continued Arab presence in Fayyūm in the second century BC. In a papyrus dated to the year 151 BC we hear about a garden (*parádeisos*) rented to two *árabes*, Asōpeús and Stotoētís, 'outside the village' near the city of Philadelphia.[54] In a papyrus from 143 BC we hear about the sending out of *árabes* belonging to the *árabes* of Ptolemais, present-day Madīnat al-Fayyūm.[55] These Arabs are well integrated in the Egyptian society, using Greek names in the papyrus documents as is documented already in the preceding century. The Arabs in Fayyūm could be the descendants of those mentioned there in the Zenon papyri. It cannot be verified but it is very likely that they originally belonged to the Arabs in the *nomós Arabía* in Wādī Tumaylāt. These documents are a testimony to the continued good relations between Arabs and the Egyptian government in the Ptolemaic age, which lasted during the Roman period.

The identification of Midianites as Arabs by Artapanus and Philo contradicts Josephus' source about the war in Gideon's day, where they are distinguished. In that source, Arabs were people east of Jordan only. There were obviously divided opinions among the Jews on how to adjust the ethnic notes of the Old Testament to contemporary conditions. In the middle of the second century BC, a Greek-speaking Jew, Eupolemus, wrote a history of the Jewish kings, which is known mainly through some quotations by Eusebius more than 400 years later.[56] He mentions the town of *Elanoí*, i.e. Elat, as being in Arabia.[57] This could reflect the same view as in Artapanus of Arabia as Midian, the Sinai peninsula or both. On the other hand, Eupolemus uses the ethnology of his own age when he describes David's conquests in Transjordan. The king 'campaigned against Idoumaîoi, Ammanîtai, Mōabîtai, Itouraîoi, Nabataîoi, and Nabdaîoi'.[58] The order in which these peoples are mentioned clearly indicates that the

Nabataeans are to be found close to the Ituraeans, and thus in northern Transjordan. Arabs are not mentioned. This confirms the picture of the Nabataeans given in the other documents from the third and second centuries BC.[59]

In these Jewish documents, which probably reflect conditions in the second century BC, we thus see contradicting views on how to update ethnic data in the Old Testament. On the other hand, it seems clear that they contain genuine documentation of Arabs in Transjordan and east of Egypt, which fits very well into the picture drawn from other sources in this period. We find the Arabs in Transjordan identified as descendants of Ishmael, but no similar indication concerning the Arabs east of Egypt. In the Book of Jubilees, an embellished retelling of Genesis written between 170 and 150 BC,[60] it seems that we have an attempt to make a more comprehensive classification of the closest neighbours of the Jews. The book was originally written in Hebrew but is preserved completely only in a Geez version. Parts of a Latin translation are also preserved. It is told that Abraham summoned his descendants through Qeṭurah and Hagar and gave them gifts:

> Ishmael, his sons, Keturah's sons, and their sons went together and settled from Farmon as far as the entrance to Babylon in all the land towards the east opposite the desert. They mixed with one another and were called *ʕarab* and Ishmaelites.[61]

As in Artapanus we find Arabs encircling Palestine from the south-west to the north-east but now they are all incorporated among the descendants of Hagar and her son. The Midianites have been arabicized. It looks like a development of the ethnic ideas in Artapanus. The identification between Arabs and Midianites is reflected in the Jewish Bible exegesis both in the paraphrases known as targums and in the midrashim. In the Fragment-Targum, the Targum Neophyti, and the targum of Jonathan as well as in early midrashic material preserved in *Bereshit Rabbah* and *Midrash Tanḥumah*, Qeṭurah is explicitly identified with Hagar.[62] The rabbinic documentation indicates that the identification is early and it can be traced back to at least the second century BC.[63]

An interesting geographical detail in the verse in Jubilees is the name Far(a)mon. Its Coptic equivalent is Peremoun, which is identical with Pelusium, the well-known city in the extreme north-eastern corner of the Nile Delta.[64] Originally, the north-eastern arm of the river reached the Mediterranean here, and the city was a border-post towards Syria-Palestine. The site is still called Tall al-Faramā. In the early Islamic tradition this town is associated with Arab origins. A saying attributed to Ibn Lahīʕa (*c.* AD 715–790) runs:

> The mother of Ismāʕīl, Hāǧar, mother of the *ʕarab*, was from a village which was in front of al-Faramā in Egypt.[65]

Ibn Lahīʕa belonged to the school of Yemeni story-tellers who spread ancient lore, Jewish and other, among the early Muslims, and undoubtedly the contents of this passage have the same origin as the saying in Jubilees. This means that the association between Hagar, Arabs and Pelusium may be very ancient. We remember that the Egyptians in the Achaemenid period called Arabia between the delta and Palestine by a name most probably derived from Hagar, and that one Egyptian ruler of the twenty-eighth dynasty, Achoris, carried a name probably derived from it.

In Josephus' story of Abraham and Ishmael there is a passage that stands very close to the one in Jubilees:

> When the child [i.e. Ishmael] reached manhood, his mother found him a wife of that Egyptian race whence she herself had originally sprung; and by her twelve sons in all were born to Ishmael: Nabaiothes, Kedaros, Abdeelos, Massamos, Masmasos, Idoumas, Masmesos, Khodamos, Thaimanos, Ietouros, Naphaisos, Kadmasos. These occupied the country from the Euphrates to the Red Sea and called it Nabatēnē; and it is these who conferred their names on the people (*éthnos*) of the *árabes* and the tribes from them (var.: on the various tribes of the *éthnos* of the *árabes*), in honour of their own prowess [*arētē*] and of the fame of Abraham.[66]

We find here the same relationship between Hagar, Ishmael and the Arab tribes in the Syrian desert as in Jubilees, although Midian is not mentioned, and it is likely that they both originate in early midrashic expositions of Genesis. It is interesting that the etymology of Arab (ar-ab) suggested in Josephus as a combination of 'virtue', *ar*-ētē and '*Ab*-raham' presupposes a Greek midrash.[67] This method of etymologizing Hebrew names appears in some passages in Eusebius' *Praeparatio* explicitly ascribed to a certain Apollonius Molon, a rhetor who wrote a polemic work against the Jews in the first half of the first century BC.[68] In one of the preserved fragments he tells the following:

> After three generations, Abraam was born [whose name] means 'beloved of a father'. He was a wise man and sought solitude. Having taken two wives, one indigenous relative and one Egyptian slave-girl, he begat twelve sons with the Egyptian one. They set out for Arabia and divided the region and reigned as kings as the first ones of the natives. Because of this, even until our time there are twelve kings of the *árabes* with the same names as these ones.[69]

The connection between this passage and that from Josephus is obvious, and it can be assumed that the one in Josephus also comes from Molon. The latter passage implies some knowledge of a Semitic language and it can be assumed that Molon had some of his information about the Jews from trustworthy sources. An important aspect of Molon's work is that it shows that from now on, the descent of the Arabs from Ishmael was also known outside Jewish circles.

The term 'Nabatēnē' in the Josephus passage, designating the whole area from the Red Sea to Babylonia, would indicate a terminus *post quem* about 200 BC, i.e. the Seleucid conquest of Palestine and Transjordan. The term 'as far as the entrance to Babylonia' or 'from the Euphrates to the Red Sea' expresses the same geographical idea. It is clearly an updating of the passage in Genesis 25 on the habitat of the Ishmaelites 'from Shur to Ḥawilah towards Asshur'. It seems that at least some learned Jews in the second century BC identified all tribes from Egypt to the Euphrates as descendants of Ishmael and Hagar and also as Arabs. This is a speculative identification in the spirit of the genealogical system of the priestly writer, not based on the actual ethnic conditions. The idea behind this extension of the concept of Ishmaelites could, in fact, be a combination of the area of the Ishmaelites and that of the sons of Qeṭurah in Genesis 25. Even though Nabatēnē is mentioned, this genealogy cannot be said to represent the later Arabo-Nabataean kingdom, since as far as we know the kings in

Petra/Reqem never ruled the Syrian desert 'from the Red Sea to the Euphrates'. Neither is the existence of twelve Arabian kings with the names of Ishmael's sons in the second century BC documented or even likely.

Alexander Jannaeus and the Arabs: the course of events according to Josephus

From the Moschion inscription one can conclude that the Arabs were closely connected with the Ptolemaic rulers in Alexandria, a pattern that is well documented at this time. This is the background for the events at the beginning of the reign of the Jewish king Alexander Jannaeus (103–76 BC). This king was involved in severe conflicts with his neighbours, among whom we also find Arabs.[70] Our only source for this period of Jewish history is Josephus. For the period 134–4 BC he mainly used two works now lost: Strabo's world history, completed during Augustus' reign, and the universal history of Nicolaus of Damascus, including the *Life of Herod the Great*, finished shortly after the king's death in 4 BC.[71] It seems that Josephus in his first work, *The Jewish War*, exclusively used Nicolaus for the period after 134 BC.[72] In the later *Antiquities*, he supplemented Nicolaus' history with extracts from Strabo.[73] Strabo's source for this period was Posidonius' *History*, practically contemporary with the events.[74] Nicolaus' sources for the pre-Herodian period are difficult to discern, but he probably had access to documents from the Hasmonaean kings.

In his account of the reign of Alexander Jannaeus in *War*, Josephus used Nicolaus exclusively. In the parallel account in *Antiquities* he still follows Nicolaus: the text of *War* is reproduced almost literally. There are, however, certain passages that seem expanded, and the impression is that in *Antiquities* we have a fuller quotation of Nicolaus' text than in *War*.[75] But there are also several passages which are definitely additions from other sources, i.e. Strabo's *History*.[76] This means, however, that in the main outline and disposition Josephus' account of this period in both works follows Nicolaus.

The events at the beginning of Alexander's reign are hinted at in *War* by two cryptic statements which become intelligible only when one reads the more complete and expanded version in *Antiquities*. Alexander attacked Ptolemais, present-day Acco, taking advantage of the ongoing civil war in Syria. Also in Egypt there was a civil war between the reigning queen Cleopatra III and her son Ptolemy Lathyrus, who was governor in Cyprus.[77] The people of Acco now called upon Ptolemy for help. Gaza, Joppa and Dor also supported Ptolemy against the Jewish king as well as against Cleopatra. Ptolemy made a campaign in Galilee, possibly crossing into Transjordan, and then devastated Judaea.[78] Meanwhile Cleopatra had marched northwards along the coast. Ptolemy subdued Gaza and then headed for Egypt. He was, however, driven out and ended up in Gaza. Needless to say, Cleopatra and Alexander Jannaeus had by now, at least politically, fallen into each other's arms.[79]

The further history of Alexander Jannaeus can, for our purpose, be divided into a series of episodes where Arabs are involved.

1. Allied with Cleopatra, Alexander went into Transjordan and conquered the cities Gadara and Amathus. At the latter, he was attacked by the ruler of Philadelphia, Theodorus, who defeated him.[80]

2. Then he marched against the coastal cities Raphia, Anthedon and Gaza and

conquered them. *War* only mentions Gaza as one of the conquered cities. *Antiquities* has a large addition about the events at Gaza.[81] We hear about the siege of the town:

> Their [i.e. the Gazaeans'] courage was heightened by the expectation that Aretas, the king of the *árabes*, would come to their assistance.[82]

Aretas did not arrive, however, and Gaza was taken.[83]

3. These successes were followed by an insurrection against Alexander by his own Jewish subjects. Alexander managed to subdue the insurgents by the use of mercenaries from Pisidia and Cilicia. He did not use Syrians 'because of their enmity against the Jewish people' (*War*), 'because he was at war with them' (*Antiquities*).[84]

4. Then followed new operations in Transjordan:

War:

> . . . he attacked Arabia; there he subdued the Galaadites and the Moabites and imposed tribute upon them and then turned against Amathus.[85]

Antiquities:

> And after subduing of the *árabes* of Moabitis and Galaaditis, whom he forced to pay tribute, he demolished Amathus.[86]

Theodorus is said to have kept away in fear of Alexander's military successes.

5. Immediately after this notice we are informed about further activities in the same area:

War:

> Afterwards he clashed with Obaidas, the king of the *árabes*, who had made an ambush near Gaulanē. Having lost his entire army, which was pressed together in a deep ravine and was torn asunder by a multitude of camels, he (Alexander) fled to Jerusalem.[87]

Antiquities:

> Having engaged in a battle with Obedas, the king of the *árabes,* and having fallen into an ambush in a rough and difficult region, he was pushed by a multitude of camels into a deep ravine near Garada/Gadara/Kharadra, a village of Galaaditis/Ioudanis, and barely escaped with his own life and fleeing from there came to Jerusalem.[88]

The site of this fight is located in the Golan, although the exact identification of the name is uncertain.[89]

6. Alexander's defeat by the *árabes* was one main factor behind the insurrection against

him that broke out shortly afterwards. The civil war in the Hasmonaean kingdom lasted around six years, and the king was in dire straits. The insurgents called upon the Seleucid Demetrius III Eukairos for assistance. *Antiquities* has an additional notice:

> [this] reduced him (Alexander) to the necessity of surrendering to the king of the *árabes* the territory which he had conquered in Moabitis and Galaaditis and the strongholds therein, in order that he might not aid the Jews in the war against him.[90]

Although Demetrius was victorious in a battle at Sichem, Alexander managed to survive and continue the fight. This resulted in Demetrius' withdrawal and Alexander's final victory over the Jewish insurgents.[91]

7. Demetrius returned to the chaos in Syria where his brother Philippus resided in Beroea/Aleppo. *Antiquities* here inserts an account of the growing political chaos in Syria. At the beginning of the 80s BC the conflict between Demetrius in Damascus and Philippus in Beroea came to a decisive point:

> When Demetrius returned from Judaea to Beroea he besieged his brother Philippus with ten thousand foot soldiers and a thousand horsemen. Thereupon Straton, the *tyrannos* of Beroea, allied with Philippus, called in Azizus, the *phylarkhos* of the *árabes*, and Mithridates, the *hyparkhos* of the Parthians. And so they came and besieged Demetrius in his barricaded camp, and under pressure of arrows and thirst they compelled the men inside with him to surrender.[92]

This information is found only in *Antiquities* and can thus safely be assumed to originate in Strabo's *History* and, ultimately, in Posidonius' *History*. This Azizus is probably the one who reappears some fifteen years later, also then as a king-maker.[93] From the geographical location of the events (Aleppo) it is likely that Azizus had his domicile not far from there, i.e. in Chalcis/Qinnasrīn.

8. The vacuum created by the disappearance of Demetrius was soon filled out in Damascus by a new pretender, Antiochus (XII). Damascus was, however, under growing threat not only from the *árabes* expanding northwards in Transjordan, but also from the Ituraeans in the north-west, who had now started to expand in all directions from their base in the Biqāʕ valley. *Antiquities* tells us that Antiochus set out on a campaign against the *árabes* immediately after his accession.[94] In his absence, Philippus took Damascus but was chased out:

> When Antiochus heard of Philippus' experience, he returned from Arabia and at once took the field, marching on Judaea.[95]

This then is the background for the next episode involving Arabs. Alexander Jannaeus, who had seemed to be down for the count, now interfered in the fight between Antiochus XII and the king of the *árabes*.

War:

> He (Alexander) feared that he (Antiochus) was going to march against the *árabes* and had a deep ditch dug between the hill-country at Antipatris and coast land at Joppe . . . he (Antiochus) deferred his vengeance upon the author of these obstructions and pushed on against the *árabes*. Their king started to retire to territory more favourable for battle and then, suddenly wheeling round, his cavalry ten thousand strong fell upon the troops of Antiochus while in disorder. A hard-fought battle ensued. So long as Antiochus lived, his forces held out, though mercilessly cut up by the *árabes*. When he fell, after constantly exposing himself in the front while rallying his worsted troops, the rout became general.[96]

Antiquities:

> Thereupon Alexander, who feared an invasion of him, dug a deep trench beginning at Khabarsaba, which is now called Antipatris, as far as the sea by Joppe . . . But Antiochus burnt all these constructions and so made his army pass through this way to Arabia. At first the Arab (*ho áraps*) retreated but afterward suddenly appeared with ten thousand horsemen, and though Antiochus on meeting them fought gallantly, he was killed just as he was gaining victory and was coming to the aid of part of his army which was in difficulties. And when Antiochus fell, his army fled to the village of Kana.[97]

We notice that Antiochus marched along the coast and it looks as if he was bound for Gaza and the Negev. The final battle was fought near a place called Kana of unknown location.[98] The plan could have been to circumvent the Arabs and attack them from the south, but the enterprise was obviously too large for the now anaemic Syrian army.

9. The scene lay open to new actors. The people of Damascus called upon a certain Aretas to reign over them out of fear of the ruler of the now expanding Ituraeans: Ptolemy son of Mennaeus. It is explicitly said that Aretas ascended the vacant throne in Damascus. Then comes a short notice that he marched against Alexander and defeated him at a place called Adida.[99] He made some kind of a treaty with the Hasmonaean and then retired from Judaea. Then we hear how Alexander started to expand again in Transjordan, although it is not said against whom he fought.[100] These events would have occurred in the latter half of the 80s BC. Alexander's conquests in Transjordan seem to have been considerable and perhaps put an end to Arab independence there.[101] These conquests are referred to later at the beginning of Salome Alexandra's reign.[102]

Evaluation of the evidence

The common opinion among scholars has always been that Alexander Jannaeus fought against the Arabo-Nabataean kingdom, stretching from the northern Sinai to southern Syria with its kings residing in Petra. Thus all kings mentioned in the account of Alexander – Aretas who failed to turn up at Gaza, Obaidas/Obedas against whom Alexander fought, and Aretas reigning in Damascus – are identified as Nabataean kings residing in Reqem/Petra, and they are equipped with numbers indicating successive reigns: Aretas II, Obodas I, Aretas III. Our previous investigation should by now, however, have made us somewhat more cautious than to assume an unproblematic series of Nabataean kings. One observation can be made immediately: no Nabataeans are mentioned as involved in these events. We only hear about *árabes*. Another is that Aretas the Damascene is not even called Arab, let alone identified with kings in Petra. The impression given by the text is that he is the local ruler of Damascus, nothing else. In episode 8 above, we are told that Antiochus first marched against Arabia, then returned to Damascus and then set out on a campaign against 'the *árabes*'. We notice that in episode 4 Arabia is definitely located in Transjordan which is also the case in episode 8. The *árabes* of that episode, on the other hand, seem to be in the Negev. Arabia of episode 8 is thus in Transjordan, which is where king Obaidas/Obedas in episode 5 is found. In the south we hear about one Aretas who was supposed to support Gaza, which fits very well with the interests of the Arabs in the Negev. To these is added Aretas the Damascene.

There are thus several cracks in the account, which should induce some scepticism against the concept of a streamlined series of Nabataean kings acting all around Palestine from their eagle's nest in Petra, even capturing Damascus. If we take a closer look at the whole narrative about Alexander Jannaeus, one cannot escape observing the similarities between episodes 1 and 3 on the one hand, and 4–6 on the other. They constitute two series of events which have many parallels. Both start with activities in Transjordan. In both, the town of Amathus and the ruler of Philadelphia, Theodorus, play important, although somewhat different roles. A town called Gadara is also mentioned in both of them. In both, Alexander suffers some kind of defeat, which somehow is not a real defeat. In both, these operations are followed by a Jewish insurrection in which the Syrians side with the insurgents. Amathus is taken by Alexander in the first series, but is also taken in the second one without any explanation of why it was necessary to attack it once more.[103] Episode 2 seems clearly out of context and belongs to the story about the conflict with Ptolemy Lathyrus.

All this leads to the conclusion that the story of Alexander Jannaeus as told by Nicolaus, who is the basic source for the sequence of events in Josephus' two works, has been heavily redacted and is definitely no journalistic report. For the first part of his reign, in fact, we have two variants of the same events: A = episodes 1 and 3, and B = episodes 4–6. B is very negative towards the king and paints his actions in the darkest possible colours, whereas A is more neutral. One may notice in A the absence of any reference to military clashes with Arabs. This version, instead of the report about the war with Obedas, inserts the remark about Aretas not turning up at Gaza. This episode probably belongs to the preceding paragraph which deals with the war with Ptolemy. *Antiquities* explicitly mentions the retirement of Ptolemy Lathyrus as the pretext for Alexander's attack.[104] In version A, Theodorus in Philadelphia is the main antagonist and the conflict with the Arabs is played down.

The firm ground for a retelling of the career of Alexander Jannaeus as a harmonizing paraphrase of Josephus' text thus crumbles away. Instead the following tentative series of events is suggested. Ptolemy Lathyrus had support from the coastal cities of the southern Levant in his struggle for power in Egypt. One might suspect that people in Syria also supported him. Against him stood Cleopatra III and the Jewish king. After having captured the cities, including Gaza, Alexander turned against Transjordan. The operations failed, however, and the defeats changed the scenario. He had to fight a severe insurrection, generated by ideological opposition and supported by foreign intervention. He obviously made some kind of treaty with the Arabs in Transjordan to secure their neutrality and even, perhaps, their help against his adversaries. The result of Alexander Jannaeus' defeat and domestic problems was the emergence of a southern Syrian alliance between Arabs in the Negev and Transjordan, and the Jewish state, probably with Arab dominance. One should not exclude the possibility that even the Ituraeans were in the same camp. This constellation of powers triggered off the campaigns of Antiochus Dionysius, the first against the Arabs in Transjordan, the second against those in the Negev. We catch a glimpse of Alexander Jannaeus as a loyal ally of the Arabs when he tries to stop this last Seleucid attempt to control southern Syria. Antiochus fell against the Negev Arabs. The desperate Damascenes, surrounded by Arabs, now installed Aretas to ward off the threats. This Aretas, an heir of the politics of Antiochus, managed to attack Alexander Jannaeus (the weakest link in the Arabo-Jewish league?) and get him over on his side. Alexander now turned against his former allies in Transjordan and started conquests there which seem to have been quite successful. Perhaps he made an end to Arab rule there.

The two versions of the account of Alexander Jannaeus' reign should be seen in the light of these events. One could see version A as reflecting the official policy during the period of the Arab alliance: military clashes with the allies are played down or ignored completely. Instead Theodorus of Philadelphia, perhaps an enemy also to Obaidas/Obedas in Transjordan, is made the main antagonist and responsible for the doubtful outcome of Alexander's activities in Transjordan. Alexander's disastrous defeat by Obaidas/Obedas is transformed/transferred to the benevolent neutrality of Aretas, helping Alexander to take Gaza. This neutrality looks very similar to the neutrality of the Transjordanian Arabs during the insurrection in Judaea.[105] Version B, which is very anti-Alexander, presents the Arabs as his main enemies, who first inflict humiliating defeats upon him and then make him their obedient servant.

In this context a passage from the the Roman history written by Trogus Pompeius in the time of Augustus should be commented. This work is, like so many others, lost and is known mainly through an abbreviation by a certain Justinus, whose time is most uncertain.[106] Trogus/Justinus, after having reported the story of the power struggle in Egypt under Cleopatra III at the end of the second century BC, proceeds by telling about the arrival of the Romans in the eastern Mediterranean: Cyrene (= Libya), Crete and Cilicia became provinces, which actually happened between the years 80 and 69 BC. According to Trogus/Justinus, the Roman presence caused the Syrians and Egyptians to start fighting with each other instead of with their neighbours. It also had another effect:

> They also became a prey to the people of the *Arabes*, until then peaceful, whose king, Herotimus, with support (*fiducia*) from seven hundred sons, whom he had begotten with concubines, having divided his troops, attacked now Egypt, now Syria and made the name of the *Arabes* great because of the weakened force of his neighbours.[107]

This Erotimus has usually been identified with (the Nabataean king) Aretas 'II', the one who did not turn up at Gaza.[108] Others have identified him with the later Aretas 'III'.[109] If we are to believe the chronological hints given by Trogus/Justinus, the activities of this king would be somewhat later and fit better into the later period of Alexander's reign. We notice that there is no talk about Nabataeans, only *Arabum gens*. We also know that just after Alexander's death in 76 BC there was a king Aretas 'the Arab' (*ho áraps*), who is usually seen as the one reigning when the Romans came to Syria in 64 BC, the so-called Aretas 'III'.

The strong position of the Arabs indicated in the Trogus/Justinus passage seems to fit well into the scenario we have reconstructed for the reign of Alexander Jannaeus. This also means that version B of his reign, in spite of its negative picture of him, would be closer to the historical events than version A, at least as far as his clashes with the Arabs are concerned. Alexander Jannaeus seems to have been more or less a vassal to his Arab neighbours during a period of his reign.[110]

Even though there is a massive opinion among scholars in favour of identifying Aretas the Damascene as the successor of Obaidas/Obedas the Transjordanian and as the Aretas known from the events during the Roman conquest twenty years later, and seeing both Obaidas/Obedas and Aretas reigning as Nabataean kings in Petra, it is worth pointing out that Aretas the Damascene is designated neither as Nabataean, Arab nor king in Petra in the relevant passages in Josephus' two works, which are the only narrative sources we have. The coins usually ascribed to this king and minted in Damascus have no special Nabataean characteristics and his epithet on them is *philél-lenos*, 'friend of the Greeks', not MLK NBṬW 'king of the *nabaṭ*', which is common later on.[111] It is also somewhat difficult to understand how Alexander Jannaeus, after a treaty with a king in Petra who controlled the whole area from Elat to Damascene, could embark on conquests in Transjordan without this king raising objections. Evidence points to Aretas as a local ruler in the Damascene, who had made a treaty with the Hasmonaean giving him a free hand in dealing with the imminent threat: the Ituraeans in Antilebanon and the Arabs in Transjordan. He might well have been a real Arab and his name well suits the onomasticon among the *árabes* at this time, but we have no explicit statement of his Arabness.[112]

Alexander Jannaeus became involved in a major conflict with his Arab neighbours which brought an end to the relatively peaceful relations that had existed until then. It has been assumed that these events can be explained by the need to control trade routes.[113] It is true that the dwindling of the old route through northern Arabia and its transference to the Land of the Two Rivers and northern and central Syria must have affected the Arabs, who had played an important role in the overland traffic from Gerrha to Heroonpolis. That this affected political developments remains a hypothesis not directly supported by the written sources.

One of Alexander's main ambitions was to wipe out the Arab dominance in Transjordan, which can be explained by purely strategic considerations. We have assumed that Arab rule in Transjordan was a result of the policy of Ptolemy II Philadelphus, who had settled Arabs there as a bulwark against the Seleucids in Coele Syria. The struggle for the hegemony in Transjordan now raged for almost half a century, until the Romans under Pompey settled the question by throwing out both Jews and Arabs and establishing the ten independent cities, the so-called Decapolis.

Tigranes the Great

The reason for the Roman intervention in Syrian affairs was the great spectacle taking place in Middle Eastern politics after the Parthian recovery of Mesopotamia from Mesene, namely the formation of the alliance between Mithridates VI Eupator of Pontus (121–63 BC) and Tigranes the Great of Armenia (94–63) and their joint venture of establishing a new Oriental empire. This brought the local power struggle in southern

Syria to a temporary standstill. The whole series of events that ultimately led to the Roman conquest of all Asia Minor and Syria, ending the struggle for this area, initiated by Cyrus the Great and Croesus half a millennium earlier, has epic dimensions, which unfortunately did not have a Thucydides or a Caesar to depict them. Our main sources for these dramatic events consist of the biographies of two Roman generals, Lucullus and Pompey, written by Plutarch at the beginning of the second century AD, and Cassius Dio's Roman history, written a hundred years after Plutarch. For his biography of Lucullus, Plutarch used Sallust's history of the Mithridates war that went down to the year 66 BC. He also had access to original letters from Lucullus to the Senate as well as an epic poem, the Luculliad, composed by a certain A. Licinius Archias, who took part in the Oriental campaign.[114] The passage dealing with Pompey's Oriental expedition was also founded upon the report of an eye-witness, Theophanes of Mytilene.[115] Plutarch's text thus appears to be based on quite good sources. Cassius Dio seems to belong to another tradition, and it has been assumed that for this period he, like Livy, leaned heavily on earlier Roman historians writing annals. It has even been suggested that Dio used Livy directly. The ultimate base for this tradition may have been Posidonius.[116]

To westerners, Mithridates is the better known of the two Oriental rulers because of his clash with the Roman generals Marius, Sulla, Lucullus and Pompey. For the Middle East, Tigranes was the more important. When the Parthian king Mithradates II/III died in 88 BC, Tigranes, who had actually been installed as king of Armenia by him, took his chance, occupied northern Mesopotamia and started to expand towards Syria, while Mithridates Eupator was engaged with Rome in the west.

In the year 83 BC Tigranes invaded Syria.[117] At the end of the 80s BC, the pitiful remains of the Seleucid empire were thus being wiped out, Tigranes advancing in northern Syria and the southern parts being divided between the Ituraeans and the Arab (?) rulers in Damascus. The Jews under Queen Salome Alexandra, Alexander Iannaeus' widow, kept a low profile during these dramatic events.

The two main sources each give a somewhat different picture of the role of the Arabs during these upheavals. According to the Plutarchian strain, Tigranes made a special use of Arabs:

> He removed from their wonted haunts the tent-dwelling *árabes* and brought them to an adjacent settlement, that he might employ them in trade and commerce.[118]

Just before, Plutarch has told how Tigranes moved Greeks away from Cilicia and Cappadocia. The word 'adjacent' (*plēsíon*) must refer to an area not far from there. In his biography of Pompey, Plutarch reports how Pompey's general Afranius in the mid-60s BC subdued 'the *árabes* at Amanus'.[119] Thus it seems certain that Tigranes settled Arabs in the Amanus region, a strategically important point, guarding one of the main roads between the Middle East and the Aegean world. Tigranes and the Arabs were obviously on good terms.

In his *Natural History* Pliny has preserved a notice which comes from Iuba's *Arabica*, reflecting conditions at the time of Augustus:

> Arabia . . . descends very long from Mount Amanus, Cilicia and Commagene, as we have said, many inhabitants of which were brought there by Tigranes the Great.[120]

These Arabs were thus still there at the beginning of our era. After that, we do not hear anything about them.

When Lucullus, after a dramatic campaign through Asia Minor, in 69 BC reached Tigranes in his new capital Tigranocerta, he was confronted with Tigranes' allies from other parts of the Middle East:[121]

> Lucullus, however, gave him (Tigranes) no time for preparation, but sent Murena to harass and cut off the forces gathering to join Tigranes, and Sextilius again to hold in check a large body of *árabes* which were drawing near the king. At one and the same time Sextilius fell upon the *árabes* as they were going into camp and slew most of them.[122]

We get a piece of information about the origin of these Arabs:

> But when the . . . kings of the Medes and the Adiabeni came up with all their hosts, and many *árabes* arrived from the sea of Babylonia.[123]

When he had conquered Tigranocerta, Lucullus was approached by former allies of the enemy:

> The kings of the *árabes* came to him (Lucullus), and handed their possessions over to him and the people of the Sopheni joined in. The Gordyeni were so affected by his kindness that they were ready to abandon their cities and follow him.[124]

The Arabs supporting Tigranes are mentioned together with Mesopotamian peoples: Sopheni, Gordyeni and Adiabeni. The context indicates that all were from the same area, which points to the northern Ǧazīra. This goes well with reports in some sources which indicate that Tigranocerta was situated south of Ṭūr ʕAbdīn at Tell Armen on the river Zergan, west of Nisibis.[125] The *árabes* from 'the Sea of Babylonia' could be people from Charax-Mesene and, perhaps, from al-Ḥasā. Tigranes obviously enjoyed the support of large parts of Mesopotamia, where Parthian supremacy was at least temporarily suspended.

Cassius Dio gives some supplementary information. When Lucullus had taken Tigranocerta it is said:

> He (Lucullus) received the king of Commagene, Antiochus . . . and a certain *arábios dynástēs* Alkhaudonios, who formerly, as I have said, was allied with the Parthians.[126]

This Alchaudonius, who will reappear later in this story, is further characterized in a note in Strabo in connection with the Bassus insurrection in Syria in the 40s BC.[127] He is there called Alkhaídamnos, king of the Rhambaîoi, who were nomads 'on this side of the river'. At that time, this ruler thus dwelt on the western side of the Euphrates but, as we shall see, he obviously had good connections with those on the other side and probably originally came from there.[128]

After his conquest of Tigranocerta in 69 BC, Lucullus laid siege to Nisibis.[129] His achievements in Mesopotamia are summarized in a late source, Festus' *Breviarium*, written at the end of the fourth century AD, where it is said that Lucullus was the first who led Roman arms across the Taurus mountains and defeated the '*phylarchi Saracenorum* in Osrhoena'.[130] The term 'Saracens' does not belong to this period but is an updating of earlier terminology made in late antiquity. More interesting is the term 'Osrhoena', the area around Edessa, west of Tigranocerta. Osrhoene is mentioned in connection with Pompey's activities a couple of years later, and it is not improbable that his conflict with Osrhoene has been secondarily transferred to Lucullus. Since Lucullus was dismissed from his command and replaced by Pompey, it is not unlikely that this notice reflects some anti-Pompeian propaganda.[131]

The Arabs supporting Tigranes were thus at least two groups: one from 'the Babylonian Sea', i.e. the Persian Gulf, probably al-Ḥasā, and one from the Ǧazīra. The latter may be connected with those mentioned by Xenophon 300 years earlier. There is good evidence for Tigranes' policy of transferring different ethnic groups in his kingdom. Perhaps even Arabs were settled around the new capital who were brought there from Xenophon's Arabia further south in the Ǧazīra and perhaps also from al-Ḥasā.[132] We would suggest that the Arabs settled by Tigranes in the Amanus, those commanded by Alchaudonius and parts of those taking part in the defence of Tigranocerta, all originated from Xenophon's Arabia. From the information found in Xenophon and later writers such as Pliny, we begin to discern an Arabia delimited by the Singār mountains in the north, the Khābūr river in the west, the Euphrates in the south and the Tigris in the east.[133]

The reports about Tigranes are the earliest instances where we hear about Arabs north of Sinǧār. During the following centuries we often find references to Arabs east of Edessa, i.e. in the area of Tigranes' capital. This country was called 'The land of the Arabs' (*ʔaṯrā ḏa-ʕraḇ*) in later Syriac sources and should be distinguished from Bêt ʕArbāyē between Nisibis and the Tigris further eastward.[134] At least the first goes back to the settlement programmes of Tigranes the Great, and it could be suggested that the Arabs in both these regions originally came from the Arabia transversed by Xenophon.

The arrival of the Romans

When the empire of Tigranes had been crushed by the Romans, Syria was again facing political chaos. Cassius Dio reports about Publius Clodius Pulcher, a notorious troublemaker who had been with Lucullus on his campaign across the Taurus but who left the army in 67 BC:

> Now Clodius, after being captured by the pirates and released by them in consequence of their fear of Pompey, came to Antioch in Syria, declaring that he would be their ally against the *arábioi*, with whom they then were at variance.[135]

The same source has the following general remark about conditions in Syria at this time:

> Coele-Syria and Phoenicia . . . had lately rid themselves of their kings and had been ravaged by the *arábioi* and Tigranes.[136]

Diodorus Siculus has more details about this chaotic period. A restoration of the

Seleucid dynasty was attempted. A Seleucid, Antiochus XIII Asiaticus, was propped up in Antioch. The choice of pretenders was, however, hampered by an *embarras de richesse*, and soon an anti-Seleucid appeared. Philippus, grandson of Antiochus Grypus, was launched as a candidate:

> Philippus proved receptive to the proposal and arranged a meeting with Azizus the *áraps*, who gave him a ready welcome, set a diadem on his head and restored him to the kingship. Pinning all his [i.e. Antiochus XIII's] hopes on the alliance with Sampsikeramos, he sent for him to come with an army. He [Sampsikeramos], however, having made a secret agreement with Azizus to do away with the kings, came with his army and summoned Antiokhos to his presence. When the king, knowing nothing of this, complied, Sampsikeramos acted the part of a friend but placed him under arrest, and though for the time being he merely held him closely guarded in chains, he later had him put to death. So, too, in accordance with the agreement to divide up the kingdom of Syria, Azizus intended to assassinate Philippus, but Philippus got wind of the plot and fled to Antioch.[137]

It is likely that Azizus is the same man who was already active in 87 BC and thus had survived the storms of the 80s and 70s to reappear once more as a king-maker. As we have pointed out already, he is likely to have dwelt not far from Aleppo, which probably makes him a successor of the Arabs in Chalcis known from the story of Alexander Balas.[138] Sampsiceramus is known from later events to have been the ruler of Arethusa, present-day ar-Ristan, and Emesa, present-day Ḥimṣ.[139] It is generally supposed that his rule in Emesa was established in the 60s in the aftermath of Tigranes. This makes it a likely hypothesis that he represented the Zabad Arabs, whom we have found documented in central Syria a century earlier.[140]

The shadow of Cnaeus Pompeius had already fallen over Syria. After his success against the pirates in the eastern Mediterranean he was appointed leader of the Roman military operations in the east in 66 BC. He took swift action in the Syrian chaos:

> After his legate Afranius had subdued for him the *árabes* about Amanus, he himself went to Syria.[141]

His arrival in Syria was in the spring of 64 BC. Cassius Dio gives the following report, which must refer to the earliest stage of Pompey's presence in Syria:

> He [Abgar of Osrhoene] had pledged himself to peace with the Romans in the time of Pompey . . . The same was done by Alkhaudonios, the *arábios* who always attached himself to the stronger party.[142]

Dio's report stands in connection with his account of the Parthian war in 53 BC when Abgar sided with the Parthians against the Romans. This is actually the first event where we hear about the kings in Edessa. The king is Abgar II, who according to the Edessan king-list reigned between 68 and 53 BC.[143] Alchaudonius had already submitted to the Romans at Tigranocerta.[144]

We have a notice explicitly stating that Pompey pacified the Ituraeans whose hostility, as we remember, had been the cause of putting Aretas on the throne in Damascus.[145]

One source indicates that Pompey, having reached Damascus, 'found the *árabes* ready to carry out any orders he might give'.[146] This might indicate that there were Arabs in Syria who now paid allegiance to the new ruler of the troubled land. If this notice has any historical value, it could refer to Alchaudonius, who by now had shown himself a loyal supporter of any strong man in sight. Twenty-five years later Caecilius Bassus was joined in his insurrection, in addition to Alchaudonius/Alchaedamnus, by Sampsiceramus, the phylarch of Emesa, and a phylarch from Lysias in the area of the Ituraeans.[147] It is very likely that Sampsiceramus also belonged to those *árabes* who submitted to Pompey.

The new Roman province, Syria, was an interim settlement which was to be revised many times during the 150 years to come. It was less a military occupation and administration of a territory than a general surveillance by a Roman governor residing in Antioch over a traditional Syrian patchwork of local principalities, city-states and allies with different degrees of independence. The Romans were unwilling to change the local structure of the Seleucid state. Their main ambition was not to let any local ruler get the upper hand.[148]

The Arabs in Syria were thus left on their own and continued their life as they had done before. Those in the north kept up their relations with Arabs on the Parthian side of the Euphrates, while those in Emesa had growing economic links with the now rising Palmyra and the trade route eastwards into the Parthian empire down to the Persian Gulf. The Ituraeans and the Arabs in the Biqāʕ were encircled by Romans on at least three sides and were probably checked by the rulers of Damascus in the east.[149]

Posidonius of Apamaea

The first half of the first century BC saw the floruit of one of the most important philosophers and scientists of antiquity, namely Posidonius of Apamaea in Syria. We have already referred to his *History* as a main source for our knowledge about Middle Eastern history from 146 BC down to the Roman conquest, since it was copied by Strabo and Diodorus as well as their successors.[150] Of his other known writings, the one entitled *Perì Okeanoû*, 'On the Ocean', would have been of special interest for us, since it dealt with world geography, the differences between peoples and the influence of environment on civilization. Large parts of it were based on autopsy: Posidonius had himself visited many of the countries he described. This book, like all others by Posidonius, is lost.[151] In Strabo's *Geography*, however, we find several explicit quotations from *Perì Okeanoû*, and there are several other passages in the same work which, in all likelihood, come from the same source. Also Diodorus Siculus used Posidonius' writings. The important thing for us is that Posidonius obviously had a lot to say about the Arabs in Syria in his day. Since he himself was a native of that country, he may be supposed to have had first-hand information. The passages in Strabo explicitly and implicitly from Posidonius give a surprisingly detailed picture of the ethnic conditions in Syria and Northern Mesopotamia. They are mostly taken from *Perì Okeanoû*, which is supposed to have been written in the 80s BC.[152] The information about the Arabs may serve as a suitable basis for conclusions and a summary of the history of the Arabs in the Middle East on the eve of the Roman conquest.

A starting point in Posidonius' sketch of the ethnic conditions in the Middle East, which was then used as an illustration of his thesis about the influence of climate upon the development of civilization, was the verse in Homer's *Odyssey* where Menelaus tells Telemachus and Thrasymedes about his journey back from Troy:

> 'I came to the *aithíopes* and the *sidónioi* and the *eremboí*'.[153]

Many speculated about the identity of the Erembians. We have seen that Hellanicus 200 years earlier had read *eremboí* as Arabs. According to Strabo, Zeno, the founder of the Stoa, changed *eremboí* in this passage in the Odyssey to *árabes* and this emendation was accepted by many. Then Strabo refers to Posidonius:

> It would seem that the view of Posidonius is best, for here he derives an etymology of the words from the kinship of the peoples and their common characteristics. For the nation of the Armenians and that of the Syrians and *arábioi* betray a close affinity, not only in their language, but in their mode of life and in their bodily build, and particularly wherever they live as close neighbours. Mesopotamia, which is inhabited by these three nations, gives proof of this, for in the case of these nations the similarity is particularly noticeable . . . Indeed, Posidonius conjectures that the names of these [three] nations are also akin; for, says he, the people whom we call Syrians are by the Syrians themselves called *arimaîoi* and *arammaîoi*; and there is a resemblance between this name and those of the *arménioi*, the *arábioi* and the *eremboí*, since perhaps the ancient Greeks gave the name of *eremboí* to the *arábioi*, and since the etymology of the word *erémbios* contributes to this result. Most scholars (*hoi polloí*) indeed derive the name *eremboí* from *éran embaínein* [= to go into the earth], a name which later peoples changed to Troglodytae [= cave-dwellers] for the sake of greater clearness. Now, these Troglodytae are that tribe of *arábioi* who live on the side of the Arabian Gulf [= the Red Sea] next to Egypt and Ethiopia.[154]

At the end of his *Geography*, Strabo gives another quotation evidently from the same passage in *Perì Okeanoû*:

> Posidonius more plausibly [than the emendation made by Zeno] writes with only a slight alteration of the text [i.e. *Odyssey* IV:84]:
>
> 'and *sidónioi* and *aramboí*'
>
> on the ground that the poet so called the present *árabes* just as they were named by all others. He says that they [the Ara(m)bians] are three peoples (*éthnē*), that they are situated in succession, one after the other, and that this indicates that they are homogeneous with one another, and that for this reason they were called by similar names – one tribe *arménioi*, another *aramaîoi*, and another *aramboí*. And just as one may suppose that they [the Arabians] were divided into three tribes, according to the differences in the latitudes, which ever vary more and more, so also one may suppose that they used several names instead of one.[155]

The passage is not altogether clear, which may be due either to Strabo or to Posidonius himself.[156] A plausible interpretation is that Posidonius considered *arambioí* a Homeric cover term for the three peoples known in his day, the Armenians, the Aramaeans and the Arabians, all these three names being ultimately derived from the Homeric term. It thus seems that he considered the three peoples as neighbours and living in three contiguous areas from north to south, representing differentiation in culture and language due to the influence of the environment. Their original unity is indicated by their similar names.

Posidonius' idea of the origin and distribution of the three peoples bears the stamp of typical Hellenistic desk-top speculation and systematization. It is more interesting to see what he actually had to say about the concrete details of ethnic conditions in the Middle East. Of the passages in Strabo the following one about Syria has strong claims to be a genuine quotation from Posidonius.[157] The passage is here rendered as literally as possible in order to show the problems in it:

> Bordering on the country of the Apamaeans, on the east, is Parapotamia, as it is called, of the *phylarkhoi* of the *árabes*, and Khalkidike, stretching down from Massyas and all [the country] towards the south of the Apamaeans, mostly [belonging to/consisting of] tent-dwelling [*skēnîtai*] men. These *skēnîtai* are similar to the nomads in Mesopotamia; and those more close to the Syrians are always more mild and less [so?] the *árabes* and the *skēnîtai* who have commonwealths (*hēgemoníai*) more complex (*syntetagménai*), such as Arethousa of Sampsikeramos and that of Gambaros and that of Themellas and others of this kind.[158]

The most likely interpretation is that Apamene is delimited in the east by the Arab phylarchs along the Euphrates and in the south by the tent-dwellers, the *skēnîtai*. The Chalcidice mentioned must be the one in the Biqāʕ valley (Massyas) mentioned by Strabo as Chalcis, the capital of the Ituraeans, although it has been claimed that it is the Chalcidice south-east of Beroea (Aleppo).[159] There is further no doubt that Posidonius makes a distinction between *skēnîtai* and *árabes*, a distinction which, as we shall see, he also upholds when describing Mesopotamia. The *árabes* have phylarchs, the *skēnîtai* live in tents. It seems evident from this passage that the *skēnîtai* live closer to the Syrians than the *árabes* do.

The problems are in the latter part of the text. What is meant by the statement that the *hēgemoníai* of the *árabes* are more *syntetagménai*?[160] And how can it be said that the *skēnîtai* on the one hand are 'milder' than those more distant from the Syrians, i.e. the *árabes*, and on the other hand that the *árabes* as well as the *skēnîtai* are less so?[161] This may not be a problem at all if one does not acknowledge that there is a difference between *árabes* and *skēnîtai* in Posidonius. But a plain reading of the text without preconceived definitions of these two terms must definitely lead to the conclusion that there is a difference according to Posidonius. This must be the starting point of the interpretation.

In another passage, Strabo gives a description of conditions in Mesopotamia which also seems to have been taken from Posidonius:

> The *skēnîtai* [living between the Two Rivers] are peaceful and moderate towards travellers in the exaction of their tribute, and on this account, merchants avoid the land along the river and risk a journey through the desert, leaving the river on the right for approximately three days' journey. For the *phylarkhoi* who

> live along the river on both sides occupy country which, though not rich in resources, is less resourceless than that of others, and are each invested with their own sovereignty (*dynasteía*) and exact tribute of no moderate amount. The Euphrates and the land beyond it constitute the boundary of the Parthian empire. But the parts on this side of the river [the west bank] are held by the Romans and the *phylarkhoi* of the *árabes* as far as Babylonia, some of these preferring to give ear to the Parthians and others to the Romans of whom they are neighbours; less so *skēnîtai*, the nomads who are close to the river, but more so those that are far away and near *Arabía eudaímōn*.[162]

The distinction made in the first part of the passage here between the phylarchs along the river (Parapotamia) and the peaceful *skēnîtai* is strongly reminiscent of that which we found in Syria. Strabo then adduces something that looks like a description of the conditions after 63 BC but fits well into the picture. Even though the latter part of the passage explicitly talks about the presence of the Romans in Syria, the rest is in full harmony with the picture, emerging from the two other fragments from Posidonius. If it was written in a later period. the conditions had obviously not changed since the days of Posidonius. The passage may, in fact, be from Posidonius but brought up to date by Strabo by inserting the note on the presence of the Romans.[163] It is thus a description of the situation at the beginning of the first century BC.[164]

A third fragment from Posidonius mentioning the Arabs may be the following:

> For the parts [of Mesopotamia] on the other side [the east bank] of the Euphrates, those near its outlets are occupied by the Babylonians and the tribe of the Chaldaeans of whom I [Strabo] have already spoken; and of those parts that follow after Mesopotamia as far as Coele-Syria, the part that lies near the river, as well as Mesopotamia, is occupied by tent-dwelling (*skēnîtai*) *árabes*, who are divided off into small sovereignties (*dynasteía*) and live in tracts that are barren for want of water. These people till the land either little or not at all, but they keep herds of all kinds, particularly of camels.[165]

This last passage is obviously very close to the one about the *skēnîtai* having phylarchs and dynasties. In that one the difference between *árabes* and *skēnîtai* is blurred. But from the two others quoted it is completely clear that *skēnîtai* and *árabes* are not identical. The *árabes* have phylarchs and dwell along the river Euphrates; the tent-dwellers, the *skēnîtai*, live south of Apamene, i.e. in central Syria and between the Two Rivers, in present-day al-Ǧazīra. When it is said that the phylarchs along the river are each invested with their own *dynasteía* this sounds reminiscent of the *hēgemoníai syntetagménai* mentioned in the first passage. But if we take the distinction between the phylarch-governed entities and the *skēnîtai* in the two latter passages into account, there may be something wrong in the first passage. Those with *hēgemoníai syntetagménai* cannot be the *árabes and* the *skēnîtai* but the *árabes* only. This means that the word *skēnîtai* should be deleted and the passage paraphrased thus: the tent-dwellers in Syria are peaceful like those in Mesopotamia, this being because of their proximity to the Syrians, i.e. the Aramaic-speaking sedentary population in Syria and northern Mesopotamia. The *árabes* are less so because they dwell farther away from the civilized Syrians. Their political system is more complex than that of the peaceful *skēnîtai* and the Syrians, since they are governed by several independent chieftains. Among these are counted, apart from those along the river, also Sampsiceramus of Arethousa/ Emesa.[166]

There is no doubt that Sampsiceramus and his two colleagues (whose habitat we unfortunately know nothing about, but who carry good Arabic names) are characterized by Posidonius as Arab phylarchs. We have also met with Azizus the phylarch, who, in light of his good connections with the Parthians, should be placed among the phylarchs in Parapotamia. Since both he and Sampsiceramus are designated Arabs in other sources, Posidonius appears as a trustworthy source. There are, in fact, two more passages in Strabo which betray the same distinctive insight into the ethnic conditions of Syria, and which thus probably also come from the great Stoic:

> After Macras one comes to the Massyas plain, which also contains some mountainous part, among which is Khalkis, the acropolis, as it were, of the Massyas. The beginning of this plain is the Laodicea near Libanus. Now all the mountainous parts are held by Ituraeans and *árabes* all of whom are robbers, but the people of the plain are farmers; and when the latter are harassed by the robbers, they require different kinds of help. These robbers use strongholds as basis of operations; those, for example, who hold Libanus possess high up on the mountain, Sinna and Borrama and other fortresses like them, and down below, Botrys and Gigartus and the caves by the sea and the castle that was erected on Theuprosopon.[167]

> Above Massyas lies the Royal Valley, as it is called, and also the Damascene country . . . and above it are situated two *Trákhōnes* (rugged, stony tracts) as they are called. And then, towards the parts of the mixed (*anamíx*) *árabes* and Ituraeans are mountains hard to pass, in which there are deep-mouthed caves.[168]

This passage shows a detailed knowledge about local geography in present-day Lebanon.[169] The clear distinction between Arabs and others, in this case the Ituraeans, must thus be considered to be a valuable piece of information. Both notices are followed with a commentary by Strabo himself, stating that in his day the robbers were pacified by the activities of Pompey during his conquest of Syria when the Ituraean kingdom became a Roman client. We may thus conclude that it is quite certain that Posidonius distinguished between *árabes* and other groups like the *skēnîtai* and Ituraeans. When the distinction is sometimes blurred in Strabo's text this is probably due to the fact that the distinction was unknown to him, since his great authority in geography, Eratosthenes, did not have it. As we have seen, Eratosthenes started with a definition of Arabia as an area and then called those living there Arabs. Posidonius' distinction did not fit into this picture and Strabo's pen slipped when paraphrasing the passages in *Perì Okeanoû*. Strabo may perhaps be excused: most modern geographers and scholars have not been able to make the distinction between Arabia and its inhabitants either.

It can safely be assumed that Posidonius also said something about other parts of Arabia. In Strabo's *Geography* we find a description which is probably derived from Posidonius:

> Egypt is difficult to enter from the eastern regions towards Phoenicia and Judaea, and from the Arabia of the *nabataîoi* which is next to Egypt. Through

> these regions is the route to Egypt. The country between the Nile and the Arabian Gulf is Arabia, and at its extremity is Pelusium, but the whole of it is desert and impassable for an army. The isthmus between Pelusium and the recess of the gulf at Heroonpolis is one thousand *stadia*, but, according to Posidonius, less than one thousand five hundred.[170]

The notice about Arabia between the Nile and the Red Sea with the mention of Pelusium, together with the information on the distance, is probably ultimately from Strabo's main source for the description of Egypt, namely Eratosthenes.[171] But Posidonius also is explicitly quoted, which shows that Strabo was familiar with his description of this part of the world. It is not impossible that the Eratosthenian material was quoted by Posidonius himself.[172] The passage just quoted is preceded by a lengthy description of the water conditions around Pelusium, which is most likely to come from Posidonius' *Perì Okeanoû*, and Strabo may have had the whole passage directly from Posidonius who, in his turn, quoted Eratosthenes.[173]

It could be argued that the quoted passage deals with two parts of Arabia: the Arabo-Nabataean one in the east, and the one between Pelusium, the Nile and the Arabian Gulf, i.e. the Gulf of Suez, in the west. The latter would have had its centre in Wādī Tumaylāt and correspond to the Arabia visited by Herodotus. The division between an Egyptian and a Nabataean Arabia is also found in Diodorus' Book II. In this part of his *Bibliotheca*, there is a long description of Arabia which is considered a digest from Posidonius' *Perì Okeanoû*.

> The description of Arabia in Diodorus' Book II goes from chapter 48 to chapter 54. Of these, 49–53 are ascribed to Posidonius by Jacoby.[174] There is no doubt that 48 is closely connected with the reports ascribed to Hieronymus of Cardia in Book XIX. We find a similar description of *árabes* in a waterless desert, building ingenious water reservoirs, unconquerable in wars, with an inaccessible rock as refuge, and a lake full of asphalt. On the other hand, it can be asked why Diodorus copied the same passage twice. It is more likely that chapter 48 is from Posidonius, showing that the great Stoic was well familiar with Hieronymus' writings. We happen to know that Posidonius wrote extensively about asphalt and other uncommon materials in *Perì Okeanoû*.[175] This means that he certainly used Hieronymus' description of the asphalt at the Dead Sea. In short: the differences between the two descriptions of Arabia in Diodorus' Book II:48 and Book XIX:94–95 is due to the fact that in Book XIX Diodorus copied Hieronymus of Cardia directly, while in Book II he followed Posidonius' *Perì Okeanoû*.[176]
>
> Chapters 49–53 in Book II are not unitary. First, 49–51.2 is a fanciful description of strange natural phenomena in an Arabia which remains geographically vague. Many of the data can be identified as borrowings from Theophrastus and Agatharchides.[177] Others are reminiscent of Euhemerus' and Iambulus' descriptions of the Happy Island. In contrast, 51.3–53 describe the results of the strong sun of Arabia on metals and animals in terms which seem to go well with what we know about Posidonius' teachings on the effects of different climates. It is likely that 49–51.2 is taken from some popular Hellenistic book about oddities in nature with facts gathered from several works, which Diodorus saw fit to be inserted in the digest of Posidonius' description of Arabia, which he might

have feared to be too dry and scientific to some of his readers.

The remaining chapter 54 is a brief but careful description of different parts of Arabia written by someone who has both interest in and knowledge about geography. The careful distinction between different regions and their characteristics is paralleled in chapter 48, and brings to mind the Posidonian passages in Strabo about Arabs in Syria quoted earlier. It is thus plausible that the entire passage 48–54 is from Posidonius except the fantasies in 49–51.2.

The most interesting part for our theme in Diodorus' Book II is the following:

> It [Arabia] lies between Syria and Egypt and is divided between many peoples of different characteristics. Now the eastern parts are inhabited by *árabes* whom they name *nabataîoi* and range over a country which is partly desert and partly waterless, though a small section of it is fruitful.[178]

This passage is very close to the one in Strabo quoted above, and it can be assumed that both authors have copied the same passage in Posidonius. Both attribute 'the eastern part of Arabia' to 'the Arabs called Nabataeans'. This means that the phrases 'the *árabes* whom they name *nabataîoi*' in Diodorus and 'the Arabia of the *nabataîoi*' in Strabo stand in a Posidonian context. Now it will be shown in the next chapter that this phrase seems to go back to the evidence transmitted by members of the Roman army in southern Syria in Pompey's campaign there in 64–63 BC. It has been assumed that Posidonius wrote *Perì Okeanoû* and the *History* before 65 BC.[179] On the other hand, we also know he wrote the history of Pompey's campaign around 60 BC.[180] The mention of *nabataîoi* by both Diodorus and Strabo in a passage dependent on Posidonius may thus reflect the great Stoic's last historical work where he took the new evidence from Syria into account. It cannot, however, be ruled out that the connection between *árabes* and *nabataîoi* had already been made in the book *On the Ocean*. In that case, Posidonius is our first witness about the close connection between the Arabs and the Nabataeans.[181]

The last chapter on Arabia in Diodorus' Book II contains a short but detailed description of the country. It is divided into six parts:

1. The Arabia towards the south called *eudaímōn*.
2. The interior part inhabited by *árabes* leading a nomadic life in tents.
3. The region between this part and *Arabía eudaímōn*. This is deserted and waterless.
4. The part lying towards the west which is full of sand dunes.
5. The part lying towards Syria, inhabited by farmers and merchants.
6. The Arabia lying along the ocean 'above the happy [one]' (*hyperánō tēs eudaímonos*).

It seems that no. 1 is identical with Eratosthenes' *Arabía eudaímōn*. This Arabia is also referred to in similar terms in chapter 49.1, which thus also probably comes from Posidonius and, ultimately, from Eratosthenes.[182] No. 2 may reflect Eratosthenes' *árabes skēnîtai*, thus the Syrian desert. No. 3 is terminologically (*érēmos* and *ánydros*) connected with the Arabs called Nabataeans in chapter 48 and must refer to the areas which Ptolemy much later named *Arabía petraía*, i.e. the main part of the Arabo-Nabatean kingdom. No. 4 is more difficult to identify but may perhaps be the 'Egyptian Arabia', i.e. the area between Arabo-Nabataea and the Nile Delta. No. 5 fits into the descriptions of the *árabes* around Antilebanon, who were characterized as farmers by some authors.[183] Finally, no. 6 is probably the 'real' Happy Arabia, i.e. the southern shore of the Persian Gulf opposite the *eudaímōn pólis* on Baḥrayn and close to Babylonia.

If this admittedly tentative interpretation is correct, we have a description of Arabia influenced by Eratosthenes but with a clear Syrian perspective. This, together with the Posidonian features in the passage about Arabia of the Nabataeans in Strabo and Diodorus with which this description is clearly connected, makes it likely that we have here an abbreviation of Posidonius' view on Arabia. It was obviously influenced by earlier authorities whom he quoted extensively, but his personal acquaintance with the Middle East enabled him to give a very variegated picture of the ethnic conditions. The disappearance of his books on geography and history is a great loss.

Notes

1 Cf. Wolski, *Empire* 94.
2 Pliny 6.104; *Periplus* § 3; Ptolemy 4.7.12; cf. Strabo 2.5.12; 17.1.13.
3 The Roman expedition to Yemen in 24 BC is an exception and was probably due to specific strategic factors; see pp. 402 f.
4 Peter, *Quellen* 106–108; Plutarch, *Lucullus* 50–52.
5 See p. 368.
6 Peter, *Quellen* 110–112.
7 See the discussion pp. 443 f.
8 For the scope of this work, see Unger, *Umfang* 79–86; Schürer, *History* I 20–21.
9 For Nicolaus, see Schürer, *History* I 28–32.
10 Diodorus is the best preserved one but mutilated for the period concerning us here. Livy is also lost for the first century BC, and we only have short summaries, so-called *periochae*, of the books dealing with the period. Strabo and Nicolaus are known only through lengthy quotations of varying quality in Josephus' works.
11 Schürer, *History* I 43–63.
12 Schwartz, *Appianus*, esp. 222; Schürer, *History* I 65.
13 Schwartz, *Cassius Dio* 1698–1705.
14 Cf. Schwartz, loc. cit.
15 We have already seen that Strabo also used valuable older texts from the third and second centuries, such as Eratosthenes and Agatharchides.
16 Pliny 6.138, 139; cf. Merkel, *Festsetzungen* 337; Potts, *Gulf* II 6–10, 15–20.
17 Cf. Wolski, *Seleucids* 109.
18 See Weissbach, *Mesene* 1082–83, for the extent of the area called Mesene.
19 Bellinger, *End* 60.
20 Nodelman, *Charakene*; Merkel, *Festsetzungen* 317–343.
21 Potts, *Gulf* II 97.
22 Pliny 6.136.
23 Pliny 6.139.
24 Pliny mentions two writers from Charax: Isidorus and Dionysius. The latter has always been considered identical with the former, and his name has been emended. The arguments are, however, doubtful. Dionysius wrote a book on Arabia, but Pliny says that he did not use it, preferring that of Iuba instead (6.141). There are preserved two short texts ascribed to Isidorus from Charax: the 'Parthian Stations', a description of the route from Antioch to Seleucia on the Tigris, and a treatise on the longevity of Oriental monarchs. They seem to be later than the Isidorus mentioned by Iuba and Pliny. There are no parallels between these

texts and Pliny's work. They are probably pseudepigraphs attributed to the famous Isidorus (cf. Weissbach, *Isidoros* 2055–2067).

25 Bosworth's characterization of the Characenian kingdom as 'an Arab principality' (*Iran* 594) and Wolski's appointment of Hyspaosines as *l'arabe* (*Empire* 87) are thus premature.

26 See Potts, *Gulf* II 324–328.

27 Cf. Duval, *Histoire* 20 ff.; Merkel, *Festsetzungen* 309–313; Drijvers, *Hatra* 867–868.

28 Drijvers, *Hatra* 863–867.

29 Février, *Essai* 1–7; Watzinger, *Palmyra* 264; Starcky, *Palmyre* 1078–1080.

30 Cf. Potts, *Arabia* 150 ff.; id., *Gulf* II 145–148.

31 Merkel, *Festsetzungen* 141, 371–372.

32 Josephus, *Antiquities* 2.213.

33 Josephus, *Antiquities* 1.239.

34 From the context of *Antiquities* 1.239–240 it is clear that this source was not found in Alexander Polyhistor. That source is explicitly quoted immediately after the remark about the descendants of Qeṭurah.

35 Josephus, *Antiquities* 5.210.

36 Josephus, *Antiquities* 5.229.

37 Judges 6:3.

38 Wacholder (*Nicolaos* 57–58) supposes that the expansions of the Biblical stories in Josephus come from Nicolaus of Damscus.

39 Eusebius, *Praeparatio* 9.23.1 (p. 516) = Freudenthal, *Alexander* 232.

40 Josephus, *Antiquities* 2.32.

41 Philo, *De Iosepho* 15.2/4.

42 Cf. Jones, *Cities* 242 and note 19; Abel, *Histoire* 1 61.

43 Cf. the *zabdēnoí* in Syria, in Josephus, *Antiquities* 13.179.

44 The identification is found in the targumic tradition as well; see both *Onqelos* and *Jonathan* ad loc. The targums are, however, almost impossible to date exactly, although it has been suggested that the original *Onqelos* is from the Hasmonaean period; cf. Beyer, *Texte* 37. Also the Peshitta makes this identification in Genesis 37:25, 28, where the Ishmaelites are translated as *ʕarḇayyê*.

45 A further possibility is that the identification of the hostile Arabs with Ishmael was already being made in the time of Nehemiah when the Arab Geshem, king of Qedar, son of Ishmael, opposed the building of the walls of Jerusalem. There is, however, no documentation of such an identification from the fifth century BC.

46 Eusebius, *Praeparatio* 9.27.17–19 (pp. 521–522); cf. Freudenthal, *Alexander* 234.

47 Philo, *Vita Mosis* 1.47.

48 Philo, *Vita Mosis* 1.51.

49 Philo, *De Virtutibus* 34 (7).

50 Manetho § 82 (= Josephus, *Contra Apionem* I.14).

51 Eusebius, *Praeparatio* 9.27.34 (= Freudenthal, *Alexander* 236).

52 Priene no. 108:168.

53 Bowersock, *Arabia* 22.

54 Kiessling, *Sammelbuch* III no. 7188.

55 P. Tebtunis no. 736 (= Hunt/Smiley, *Tebtunis* 145).

56 Schürer, *History* III.1 517–521; Hengel, *Judentum* 169–175; Wacholder, *Eupolemus*.

57 Eusebius, *Praeparatio* 9.30.7 (p. 539) = Freudenthal, *Alexander* 226.

58 Eusebius, *Praeparatio* 9.30.3. = Freudenthal, *Alexander* 225.

59 Cf. Wacholder, *Eupolemus* 133–134. According to Freudenthal, *Alexande*r 115 this passage represents an updating of Psalm 83:7-9 by Eupolemus (or his source).

60 *Jubilees*, Introduction V–VI.

61 *Jubilees* 20:12–13. The Latin version runs: *et filii eius et filii Cetturae et filii sui inhabitaverunt a Faramon usque ad introitum Babyloniae in omni terra orientali super faciem deserti et commixti sunt isti illis et adhesit nomen ipsorum arabiis et ismaelite usque in diem hanc*.

62 *Fragment-Targum* I:55; *Neophyti* 151; *Pseudo-Jonathan* 48; *Bereshit Rabbah* 661 (ascribed

to Rabbi Yehuda at the end of the second century AD); *Midrash Tanḥumah*: Ḥayyê Sarā 8 (ascribed to 'the rabbis' (*rabbôtênû*) and Rabbî [Yehuda]).

63 According to Beyer (*Texte* 35–37) the earliest layer in the Onkelos targum goes back to Hasmonaean times.

64 The name goes back to Ancient Egyptian Pʔ-ʔr-ʔmn. Vanderkam in his translation of Jubilees renders the name with Paran, the name of a desert south of the Negev. This translation has no support in any source: the Geez Bible has Fārān in the passages where it is mentioned. The LXX has Pharan and the name obviously has nothing to do with Pharamon/Pelusium.

65 Ibn Hishām, *Sīra* I:3; ʕAbd al-Ḥakam, *Futūḥ* 4 ll. 10–11.

66 Josephus, *Antiquities* 1.220–221.

67 Cf. Josephus, *Antiquities*, Loeb edition, p. 109 note m.

68 Cf. Schürer, *History* III.1 511, 598–600.

69 Eusebius, *Praeparatio* 9.19 = Jacoby, *Fragmente* III C Frgm. 728 = pp. 688–689.

70 Cf. Bellinger, *End* 71f.

71 Schürer, *History* I 30–32; 64–65; 43–63.

72 Hölscher, *Josephus* 1944–49; Schürer, *History* I 51; Wacholder, *Nicolaos* 54–60.

73 Schürer, *History* I 25.

74 Alexander Jannaeus was treated in book 47 of Posidonius' work; cf. Unger, *Umfang* 118 ff.

75 Thus the remarks in *War* about the war between Cleopatra III and Ptolemy Lathyrus are very short and incoherent. They are comprehensible only when compared to *Antiquities*. It is likely that in *Antiquities* we have a fuller quotation of Nicolaus' work, supplemented with extracts from Strabo. The same holds for the activities of Antiochus Dionysius, where the remarks in *War* become comprehensible in the light of *Antiquities*.

76 Such as *Antiquities* 13.324–55, 357–371 (the war of Ptolemy Lathyrus, the war between Seleucus and Antiochus Cyzicus), 384–89 (the war between Demetrius, Philippus and Antiochus Dionysius).

77 See in general Kasher, *Jews* 86.

78 *Antiquities* (13.338) mentions a battle between Alexander and Ptolemy at the town of Asophon, which has been identified with Tell as-Saʕīdiyye in the Jordan valley.

79 Of these events told in *Antiquities* 13.324–355, *War* only mentions that Ptolemy took the town of Asochis in Galilee and that he, feeling pursued by Cleopatra, went to Egypt (*War* 1.86). That the account in *War* is an abbreviation of Nicolaus is clear from Josephus' remark in *Antiquities* 13.347. From that remark we also learn that *Antiquities*, together with a fuller report of Nicolaus, also contains material from Strabo.

80 Josephus, *War* 1.86-87; idem, *Antiquities* 13.356.

81 Josephus, *War* 1.87 end; idem, *Antiquities* 13.358–364.

82 Josephus, *Antiquities* 13.360–64.

83 According to Kasher (*Jews* 89–90) Alexander installed Antipas as governor of Idumaea at this time. He also built the fortresses at Masada and Machaerus (ibid. 87–88). The latter is said to be 'on the border of Arabia' (Josephus, *Antiquities* 14.83). After this account, *Antiquities* inserts a passage about the developments in Syria after the death of Antiochus VIII Grypus, which resulted in the division of the crumbling Seleucid power by the two brothers Philippus in Beroea and Demetrius III in Damascus (*Antiquities* 13.365–371).

84 Josephus, *War* 1.88–89 beginning; idem, *Antiquities* 13. 372–374.

85 Josephus, *War* 1.89. The verb *anastréphō* is in the Loeb text translated 'returned once more', but in the German Michel/Bauernfeind edition rendered 'wandte sich gegen'.

86 Josephus, *Antiquities* 13.374.

87 Josephus, *War* 1.90.

88 Josephus, *Antiquities* 13.375. There are variations in the manuscripts in the names of the sites.

89 Schürer, *History* I 223 note 17; Kasher, *Jews* 92–95.

90 Josephus, *Antiquities* 13.382.

91 Josephus, *War* 1.91–98; idem, *Antiquities* 13.376–383.

92 Josephus, *Antiquities* 13.384–385.

93 The name of the *tyrannos* of the *árabes* in the MSS to Josephus' *Antiquities* is Deizos or

Zizos but is emended to Azizus according to Diodorus 40.1b. For the further career of Azizus see p. 350.

94 Josephus, *Antiquities* 13.387.

95 Josephus, *Antiquities* 13.389.

96 Josephus, *War* 1.99–102, which is very abbreviated here; the reasons for both Antiochus' and Alexander's actions are not clarified.

97 Josephus, *Antiquities* 13.390–391.

98 Abel, *Géographie* II 149, suggests a place, Qīna, south-east of the Dead Sea. Others have associated this battle with the story of how Rabelos defeated Antigonus at Mōthō, mentioned by Uranius. The site has been identified with Imtān in Ḥawrān (Roschinski, *Geschichte* 16; Negev, *Nabateans* 537; Wenning, *Nabatäer* 47). This is, however, unlikely; see p. 287.

99 Josephus, *War* 1.103; idem, *Antiquities* 13.392. Only *Antiquities* mentions the name of the site, which has been located near Lydda (Abel, *Géographie* II 340).

100 Josephus, *War* 1.103; idem, *Antiquities* 13.392. *Antiquities* (13.393–394) tells about new conquests of Alexander in Transjordan after this defeat.

101 Josephus, *Antiquities* 13.395; cf. 14.18. For the lists of the conquered cities, see Kasher, *Jews* 97–103.

102 Josephus, *Antiquities* 14.18.

103 Cf. the translations of the verb *anastréphō* (note 81) in the different editions. The Loeb translator gives an exegetic translation based on the common assumption of two different actions: 'he . . . returned once more [to Amathus]'. Even though this translation is defensible, it is not the only one possible from this verb. Josephus' phrasing does not necessarily indicate a second attack against the town.

104 Josephus, *Antiquities* 13.358.

105 According to Unger (*Umfang* 118 ff, cf. 79–86), Posidonius told the story about Alexander Jannaeus in Book 47 of his *History*. Version A is thus likely to originate from that work; cf. Theiler, *Poseidonios* II 81–82.

106 Suggestions range between the first and the fourth centuries AD. Trogus was ultimately based on Posidonius, cf. Theiler, *Poseidonios* II 35–40, possibly via Timagenes, who wrote the history of the Orient for Augustus; cf. Laqueur, *Timagenes*.

107 Iustinus, *Epitome* 39.5.5–6.

108 Starcky, *Nabatéens* 905; Bowersock, *Arabia* 23; Schürer, *History* I 577.

109 Merkel, *Festsetzungen* 290–293; Täubler, *Nabatäerkönig*.

110 According to Josephus/Nicolaus (*War* 1.91; *Antiquities* 13.376), the insurrection lasted six years, and Alexander's subjugation to the Arabs may have lasted at least that long and probably longer since Antiochus' campaign took place after that.

111 Meshorer, *Coins* 12–16; 86–87.

112 Also the name Obaidas/Obedas of the Transjordanian ruler could indicate that he was different from the later kings in Petra, who are called Obodas by Josephus.

113 So Kasher, *Jews* 89, 99, 101–103. Cf. Wenning, *Nabatäer* 139.

114 Plutarch, *Vies* VII 49–52; Peter, *Quellen* 106–109.

115 Plutarch, *Vies* VIII 152–158; Laqueur, *Theophanes* 2122. Cf. p. 368.

116 Schwartz, *Cassius* 1697–1705. See Theiler, *Poseidonios* II 59 f., 78–80.

117 Bellinger, *End* 80.

118 Plutarch, *Lucullus* 21:4–5.

119 Plutarch, *Pompey* 39:2.

120 Pliny, 6.142.

121 For Lucullus' campaign across the Taurus to Tigranocerta, see Dillemann, *Haute-Mésopotamie* 263–268.

122 Plutarch, *Lucullus* 25:5–6.

123 Plutarch, *Lucullus* 26:4.

124 Plutarch, *Lucullus* 29.5–6.

125 For a discussion of all the partly contradictory evidence, see Dillemann, *Haute-Mésopotamie* 247–271. Tigranocerta has also been located at Farqin on the southern slopes

of the Taurus mountains north-east of Diyarbakır and north of the Tigris. The earliest source is Strabo 11.14.15, which supports the southern location (Dillemann, *Haute-Mésopotamie* 247–248). Cf. also Tacitus, *Annals* 15.5, and Dillemann, *Haute-Mésopotamie* 252–262.

126 Cassius Dio 362.5.
127 Strabo 16.2.10.
128 See p. 397.
129 Plutarch, *Lucullus* 31.1; Cassius Dio 36.6.1.
130 Festus, *Breviarium* XIV.
131 Drijvers (*Hatra* 870) claims that people from Osrhoene took part in the defence of Tigranocerta. Although not impossible, the sources do not explicitly mention any participation of the Edessenians.
132 Dillemann, *Haute-Mésopotamie* 250–251.
133 See pp. 415 f.
134 Dillemann, *Haute-Mésopotamie* 75–78.
135 Cassius Dio 36.16.3.
136 Cassius Dio 37.7a (Xiphilinus).
137 Diodorus 40.1a–1b.
138 Cf. pp. 314 ff.
139 Cf. Merkel, *Festsetzungen* 144.
140 Cf. pp. 316 ff.
141 Plutarch, *Pompey*, 39:2; see p.347.
142 Cassius Dio 40.20.1.
143 Drijvers, *Hatra* 870.
144 Cassius Dio 36.2.5.
145 Strabo 16.2.18; Eutropius 6.14.1; Appian, *Mithradates* 16.106.
146 Florus 1.40.30.
147 Strabo 16.2.10; cf. Merkel, *Festsetzungen* 144.
148 For a survey of Pompey's settlement, see Jones, *Cities* 256–260, and Wenning, *Dekapolis* 6–8.
149 For the history of the lands between Damascus and northern Transjordan from this time onwards, see MacAdam, *Studies* 47–57.
150 Reinhardt, *Poseidonios* 638–39, 663; Schürer, *History* I 20–22.
151 Reinhardt, *Poseidonios* 662 ff.
152 Theiler, *Poseidonios* 6.
153 *Odyssey* IV:84.
154 Strabo 1.2.34.
155 Strabo 16.4.27.
156 Cf. the discussion by Merkel, *Festsetzungen* 159.
157 So Merkel, *Festsetzungen* 160. Strabo mentions Posidonius as an introduction to the passage (16.2.10): 'Posidonius, the Stoic, the most learned of all philosophers of my time, was a native of Apamaea.'
158 Strabo 16.2.11.
159 So Merkel, *Festsetzungen* 157–158, but cf. Dussaud, *Topographie* 399 ff. The expression in the Greek is not as clear as one would have wished but the juxtaposition of Chalcidice and Massyas leaves no reasonable doubt. Strabo must have confused the names.
160 According to Merkel, *Festsetzungen* 154, the expression *syntetagménai mállon* describes 'die einfache Verfassung nomadischer Stämme'. This is, however, not the only way of reading it and in light of the next passage becomes an unlikely interpretation.
161 The participle *ékhontes*, 'having', as it stands, must refer either to *árabes kaì skēnitai* or to *hoi plēsiaíteroi*, 'those more close to'. The translation in the Loeb edition is unnecessarily unclear ('the former having governments').
162 Strabo 16.1.26–28.
163 *Perì Okeanoû* is usually dated to the 80s or the 70s BC. But Posidonius died *c.* 50 BC and was acquainted with Pompey during his conquest of Syria. The last passage could thus in fact belong to the book and originate with Posidonius himself. There are other clear instances where Strabo quotes Posidonius and then adds a note on the conditions in his day.

164 Cf. Merkel, *Festsetzungen* 273.
165 Strabo 16.3.1.
166 The suggested deletion of the words *kai skēnîtai* in Strabo 16.2.11 is not so difficult to defend. It is doubtful whether Strabo himself understood that there was a difference between *árabes* and *skēnîtai* in Posidonius. We have already seen that Strabo made ample use of Eratosthenes and for that author *árabes* and *skēnîtai* were obviously the same, cf. 16.3.1. The MSS to Strabo's book 16 all have the phrase, which is probably a very early gloss. It is worth observing that it is not Eratosthenian: *árabes* and *skēnîtai* are kept apart.
167 Strabo 16.2.18.
168 Strabo 16.2.20.
169 Makras is the river Eleutherus, present-day Nahr al-kabīr (Dussaud, *Topographie* 91); the Massyas plain is the northern Biqāʕ (ibid. 399 f.); Khalkis may be present-day ʕAnǧar (ibid.); Laodicea is Tell Nabi Mend (ibid. 114); Botrys is present-day Baṭrūn just south of Tripolis (ibid. 71); Gigartus is the present-day castle of Musayliḥa (ibid. 81–82); and Theouprosopon is Rās aš-Šaqqa (ibid. 71) on the coast north of Baṭrūn.
170 Strabo 17.21.
171 Cf. Strabo 17.1.1.
172 For Posidonius' dependence on Eratosthenes, see Reinhardt, *Poseidonios* 663, and Theiler, *Poseidonios* II 66–67.
173 Strabo's description of Lake Sirbonis: 16.2.32–33a, 42; cf. 16.2.43 for the reference to Posidonius. For Strabo's use of Posidonius, see Reinhardt, *Posidonios* 663, and Theiler, *Poseidonios* II 66. The story of Moses told by Strabo in 16.2.35–37, which shows detailed acquaintance with conditions in Lake Sirbonis close to Pelusium, comes from *Perì Okeanoû* (Reinhardt, *Poseidonios* 638–639).
174 Jacoby, *Fragmente* 2A (no. 87) F 114.
175 Reinhardt, *Poseidonios* 640.
176 For Posidonius in Diodorus 2.49–53 see Reinhardt, *Poseidonios* 662 ff, and Theiler, *Poseidonios* II 77.
177 See the references to Theophrastus in the Loeb edition, Vol. II pp. 47–49. Agatharchides is identifiable in 51.1 and, above all, in 50.1 where there is a literal quotation from Agatharchides' description of the 'fireless gold' of Arabia, quoted by Diodorus in 3.47.7.
178 Diodorus 2.48.1.
179 So Unger, *Umfang* 83; Merkel, *Festsetzungen* 162; Theiler, *Poseidonios* 80. Reinhardt (*Poseidonios* 38–639) assumes that the story of Pompey was a continuation of the *History*.
180 Cf. Unger, *Umfang* 80. That Posidonius was active as late as 60 BC is documented by the fact that Cicero asked him to write the history of his consulate in 63 BC (ibid.).
181 The Posidonian origin of the identification is, of course, far from certain. It should be remarked that the phrase about the rock 'in the land of the *nabataîoi*' in the description in Diodorus 2.48.6 is suspect. The oldest MS (D) of Diodorus has *en tēi khōrai tōn anabatōn* where the last word is emended to *nabataíōn*. Since it is most likely that Hieronymus did not make the identification between Arabs and Nabataeans, not even mentioning the latter, the emendation can be doubted. Further, *anabátēs* means 'rider' or 'charioteer' but it remains uncertain what 'the land of the charioteers' would mean. A somewhat fanciful suggestion is to associate it with a Semitic word from the root RKB. It should be remembered that a group of people in ancient Israel with strong resemblance to the *árabes* on the Rock as described by Hieronymus were called 'sons of Rekab' and that their eponymous ancestor was associated with a chariot, *merkabā* (2 Kings 10:15–16). Both words are derived from the root RKB. Could the *anabatōn* refer to this or a similar group, i.e. Hieronymus' *árabes*? In the immediately following lines are found the words *anábasin*, 'ascendance', and *anabaínontes*, 'those ascending', which look like a pun on the emendated word. Perhaps Posidonius knew more than Hieronymus about these people and their traditions and added a note on his own.
182 For Posidonius' dependence upon Eratosthenes, see Reinhardt, *Poseidonios* 663.
183 For example, Curtius 4.2.24.

13

THE NABATAEAN PROBLEM

Arabs, Nabataeans and Jews during the Roman conquest: the events

The Roman presence in Syria also had a lasting influence on the Arabs further south. The spectacular rise of Petra begins after the arrival of the Romans. Since Arabs were closely involved in the history of the kingdom governed from the town, this phenomenon should be treated in some detail. Our main narrative source for the events is Josephus, writing 150 years later. His account has to be the starting point for our understanding of the ethnic and political situation in the region. His evidence is complemented by some notes in other writers: Diodorus, Strabo, Plutarch and Appian. We shall first give a summary of the events during the years 65–62 BC as they are told in the literary sources. Apart from Diodorus and Strabo, they were written more than a century and a half later.

The Romans had landed in the middle of a civil war in Palestine. According to Josephus' account, in the year 67 BC the conflict in Judaea between the two sons of Alexander Jannaeus, Hyrcanus and Aristobulus, had become acute. Hyrcanus had a counsellor, Antipatros, whose father had been *stratēgós* of Idumaea.

War:

> Antipatros persuaded Hyrcanus to flee to Aretas, the king of Arabia, to get back the kingship, and Aretas to receive Hyrcanus and help him to power . . . Then he defected in the night together with Hyrcanus and with a straining flight they escaped to the so-called 'Rock' (*pétra*). This is the royal residence (*basíleion*) of Arabia.[1]

Antiquities:

> By dint of constant pressure he [Antipatros] persuaded him [Hyrcanus] to take his advice and flee to Aretas, king of the *árabes*, promising that, if he followed his advice, he too would be his ally. When Hyrcanus heard that this would be to his advantage, he was ready to flee to Aretas, for Arabia borders on Judaea. However, he first sent Antipatros to the king of the *árabes* to receive sworn assurances that if he came as a suppliant, Aretas would not deliver him up to his enemies. When Antipatros had received these sworn assurances, he returned to Hyrcanus in Jerusalem; and not long afterward he slipped out of the city by

> night, taking Hyrcanus with him, and after travelling a great distance, brought him to the so-called 'Rock' (*pétra*), where the royal residence (*basíleia*) of Aretas was.[2]

Hyrcanus now promised to give Aretas the cities and territories that Alexander Jannaeus had taken from the *árabes*, possibly in both Transjordan and the Negev.[3] The alliance was formed; Aretas mustered an army of 50,000 men and started a siege of Jerusalem at the time of the Jewish *pesaḥ* in 65 BC.[4]

That same spring Marcus Aemilius Scaurus, one of Pompey's generals, arrived in Damascus. Both Hyrcanus and Aristobulus called on him, eager to seek support from the new military power in Syria. According to *War*, Hyrcanus' performance was the least convincing. One of Aristobulus' arguments was the offer of a bribe of 300 talents, which turned out to be an irrefusable offer. In *Antiquities*, on the other hand, Scaurus is said to have accepted 400 talents from both contenders but decided to support Aristobulus because of 'his great soul and his moderateness'. He set off towards Judaea to settle the matter. In his first version of this event, Josephus wrote the following:

> Scaurus made known by messengers to Hyrcanus and the *árabes* that the Romans and Pompey would interfere if the siege was not lifted. So Aretas withdrew from Judaea to Philadelphia and Scaurus back to Damascus.[5]

In *Antiquities*, Josephus gives us a more elaborate account:

> Hyrcanus was poor and niggardly and held out untrustworthy promises for greater concessions. For it was not the same to take a town among the most strongly fortified and powerful as to drive out refugees (*phygádes*) together with the host of *nabataîoi* not well fitted for warfare. And so he (Scaurus) took Aristobulus' side and, accepting the money, put an end to the siege by commanding Aretas to withdraw or else to be declared an enemy of the Romans. Then Scaurus withdrew to Damascus.[6]

Aretas withdrew to Philadelphia, i.e. Amman in Transjordan. Aristobulus inflicted a defeat on his enemies, although it is not clear whether they were the Arabs or the people of Hyrcanus and Antipatros.

When Pompey arrived in Damascus the next year, the two parties appealed to him for support as they had done with Scaurus. Aristobulus, according to *War*, trusted the corruptedness of Scaurus. This time the Roman general opted for Hyrcanus, being upset by Aristobulus' pursuit of his enemies and his general conduct. According to the account in *War*, which is somewhat confused here, a military conflict soon broke out between Pompey and Aristobulus.[7] After negotiations had failed, Aristobulus took refuge in Jerusalem, which was besieged and captured by the Romans in 63 BC.[8] Afterwards Scaurus was made governor in Syria. In the next year, 62 BC, we hear the following:

> Meanwhile Scaurus, having attacked Arabia, was held back by the difficult terrain of Petra. He then devastated the surroundings but was struck by difficulties because the army suffered famine. Because of that, Hyrcanus sent help through Antipatros sending the necessary alimentation. Since he was a friend of

> Aretas, Scaurus sent him there so that he should ward off the war with a sum of money. The *áraps* was persuaded to give three hundred talents and therefore Scaurus led the troops out of Arabia.[9]

Antiquities has some additions to the story about Pompey which are important. It is said that Aristobulus' messengers to Pompey accused Scaurus and Gabinius, another general, of having taken bribes, which was a bad move since it made the two enemies of Aristobulus. Then we hear that Pompey intended to go against the Nabataeans when he was distracted by Aristobulus' activities and had to make the army prepared for action against Judaea instead.[10] After that, we hear about Scaurus' campaign in Arabia:

> Scaurus now made an expedition against Petra in Arabia and because of the difficulty of access to it he ravaged its surroundings. And as his army was pinched by famine, Antipatros, at the command of Hyrcanus, furnished him with grain from Judaea and with whatever else he wanted. And when he [Antipatros] was sent to Aretas as an ambassador by Scaurus because he had lived with him formerly, he persuaded him [Aretas] to give Scaurus a sum of money to prevent the ravaging of the country and undertook to be his security for three hundred talents. So Scaurus upon these terms broke off the war no less eager to have this come about than was Aretas.[11]

The last appearance of the Nabataeans in Josephus is when he refers to the activities of the Roman governor Gabinius in Syria in 55 BC. It is said that this general conquered the *nabataîoi*.[12] The notice about this operation is found both in *Antiquities* and in *War* and it is one of the two occurrences of the term in the latter.[13] The term does not occur any more in *Antiquities*.

The problem: were the Nabataeans Arabs?

From what has been said, several questions arise when we read about these dramatic events: Who is Aretas? Which Petra is meant? Who are the Arabs and the Nabataeans? The most important question arises from the fact that, if we read *War* and *Antiquities* together, we get the impression that *árabes* and *nabataîoi* are somehow identified in the accounts about the Roman conquest of Palestine. From the passage in *War*, it is obvious that Aretas is king of the *árabes*.[14] In *Antiquities* Aretas is said to command 'refugees and a host of *nabataîoi* not well fitted for warfare'. If, for the moment, we assume that by the refugees are meant Hyrcanus and Antipatros and their followers, it appears that in *War*, Aretas' troops are *árabes* whereas in *Antiquities* they are *nabataîoi*.[15] The question is whether the Nabataeans whom Pompey planned to attack, and the Arabs who paid Scaurus off, are identical. For the reader of this book the problem becomes even more prominent if the identification of the Rock mentioned in accounts of the preceding period as situated in the Negev is accepted.

In fact, Antipatros' good relations with the Arab king, as well as the information that Judaea borders on Arabia fit very well if it is Arabia in the Negev which is meant.[16] Antipatros, son of the governor of the southernmost Judaean province, and the Arab Aretas would thus have been close neighbours.

The main question is, however, whether the apparent terminological variation between *árabes* and *nabataîoi* is only a rhetorical device or whether it reflects some reality. It could, of course, reflect the Erastothenic concept of everybody living in the Arabia of the geographers, including the Nabataeans, being an Arab. But the relationship between the Arabs in the Negev and the Arabo-Nabataeans remains to be clarified.

Nabataeans and Arabs before 65 BC: the literary sources

In order to front on the problem we shall start with a closer look at the use of the terms in the most important source, i.e. Josephus. With two exceptions he uses the term 'Nabataeans' in *Antiquities* only. In that work, Nabataeans are mentioned sporadically in the parts dealing with the history of the Jews down to the Roman conquest of Syria. After that, the name does not occur. When telling about the friendship between Jonathan Maccabaeus and the Nabataeans in Transjordan in *Antiquities*, Josephus calls them *nabataîoi árabes* or just *nabataîoi.*[17] In 1 Maccabees, however, the friends of Jonathan are called *nabataîoi* whereas his enemies are the *árabes*, a distinction which thus is blurred in Josephus.[18] When referring to the victory of Jonathan over Demetrius I he says that Jonathan, returning from Syria, made war against the *nabatēnoí* in Arabia.[19] In 1 Maccabees, however, Jonathan defeats the *árabes zabdēnoí*, whom we have earlier placed in Syria north of Damascus. There is no doubt that Josephus has his information about these events from 1 Maccabees. It is, however, also obvious that to him there was no real distinction between Arabs and Nabataeans and that he did not understand or pay attention to the distinction found in his sources. This is corroborated by one remarkable passage in *Antiquities*, namely in the quotation of Molon's story of the descendants of Ishmael. Their land from the Red Sea to the Euphrates is called Nabatēnē.[20] This is the first reference to Nabataeans in *Antiquities* and it probably well represents Josephus' own opinion on the question, based upon Jewish exegesis during the preceding centuries.[21] It is not unlikely that Josephus' change of *zabdēnoí* to *nabatēnoí* in the report about Jonathan is influenced by this passage from Molon: these *árabes* in southern Syria could well be seen as living in Nabatēnē, which by Molon and the tradition behind him was defined as encompassing the entire habitat of the sons of Qeṭurah, i.e. the Syrian desert from Midian to the Euphrates.

But there is no doubt that the appearance of Nabataeans in the part of *Antiquities* dealing with the pre-Roman history of Jewish Palestine reflects Josephus' source, namely the first book of Maccabees. This means that the other occurrences of that term are also likely to reflect the sources used, i.e. Strabo and Nicolaus. The unique occurrence of Nabataeans in *War*, paralleled in *Antiquities*, must reflect the main source of that work, i.e. Nicolaus of Damascus. Since it is generally agreed that Josephus for the period 134–4 BC used Nicolaus as his main source for the history of Judaea, the mention of Nabataeans in both *War* and *Antiquities* must reflect Nicolaus' own text which, in its turn, must be based upon a special source used in that passage. This source has been identified as a panegyric of Gabinius.[22] Apart from this instance, the *nabataîoi* in Josephus' work dealing with the period of the Roman conquest, i.e. *Antiquities*, must originate from Strabo's lost *History*. Since *War* does not say anything about Pompey's planned campaign against the Nabataeans/Arabs, this notice was probably not found in Nicolaus; consequently it comes from Strabo. Strabo also used the term *nabataîoi* in his *Geography* when quoting or paraphrasing earlier writers like Eratosthenes, Agatharchides and Athenodorus. It was thus familiar to him. On the other hand, we have also seen that, as far as the two first-mentioned writers are concerned, an analysis of Strabo's text does not lead to the conclusion that they presented *nabataîoi* and *árabes* as identical. But it seems that in the passages from Strabo's *History* preserved by Josephus dealing with the events in the 60s BC they are somehow identical.

From his *Geography* we can see that Strabo worked with earlier sources which he copied. We further know that Pompey's campaign in the East was recorded by a certain Theophanes of Mytilene who accompanied him. The only explicit quotations from Theophanes are found in Strabo's *Geography*. Theophanes was thus well known to Strabo and we can be quite certain that his account of Pompey's campaign was built on Theophanes.[23] Also Plutarch's report about this adventure in his biography on Pompey goes back to Theophanes.[24] It should be observed that the story about Scaurus' campaign in 62 BC mentions Arabia and Aretas the Arab in its two versions, in both *War* and *Antiquities*. The only source common to both is Nicolaus of Damascus; consequently, this information comes from him and his sources and not from Strabo and his source, namely Theophanes. The conclusion must be that the chronicler of Pompey's eastern campaign, Theophanes, called the enemy *nabataîoi*, not *árabes*.[25]

The relationship between *árabes* and *nabataîoi* at the time of the Roman conquest of Syria is highlighted by a passage in Diodorus where he reports the triumph celebrated by Pompey on his return from the Oriental campaigns in 61 BC. It is said that Pompey had written on a tablet the names of the conquered peoples and rulers:

> Pompey the Great, son of Cnaeus . . . who brought into subjection Darius, king of Medes (*sic!*), Artoles, king of the Iberians, Aristobulus, king of the Jews, king Aretas of *nabataîoi*, king of *árabes*, Syria bordering on Cilicia, Judaea, Arabia . . .[26]

We have here an official document which Diodorus could have seen with his own eyes, since such documents were preserved. He could, in fact, also have witnessed the triumph himself. This document seems to be quoted in another later literary work, namely Appian's account of the Mithradatic war in his Roman history, which is independent of the Theophanes tradition.[27] Appian tells that Pompey, when planning his campaign to Petra, waged war 'against the *árabes*, the *nabataîoi*', which sounds like an echo of the inscriptions quoted by Diodorus.[28] The passage in Appian can be seen as a confirmation that the double designation, after all, was used officially. The evidence from the official documents shows that, unlike the usual Greek manner of calling everybody in Arabia *árabes*, this juxtaposition of the two terms must have had some background in political realities. It thus seems fairly certain that the Nabataeans were mentioned together with Arabs in official documents as well as by eye-witness reports on the Roman conquest of Palestine by Pompey in the 60s BC. We must now try to find out why.

The Nabataeans before 65 BC: the non-literary testimony

The use of the two terms 'Nabataeans' and 'Arabs', seemingly for the same political entity in the reports originating from the Roman operations in Palestine around 60 BC, stands in contrast to documents from the preceding periods where they clearly refer to separate entities. In his treatment of that period, Josephus has obviously mixed them up. We have already referred to the papyrus from Zenon's archive dated to 259 BC as well as to the Books of Maccabees and other early Jewish documents such as Eupolemus, where there is no trace of identification of the Nabataeans as Arabs. Further, we have some inscriptions which, by palaeographic criteria, are dated to the time before the Roman conquest of Syria. Two of them mention the names of two kings of NBṬW: ḤRTT, i.e. Aretas, and ʕBDT, Obodas. The first one was found in Elusa in the Negev and the other one is still visible in Petra/Reqem.[29] The dating of them is uncertain although they might well be from the second half of the second century BC. A third early text mentions RBʔL MLK NBṬW, [BR . . .]T MLK NBṬW, 'Rabbʔil, king of the Nabaṭ, [son of . . .]t, king of the Nabaṭ'. The text has the date 'year 18 (or 16) of ḤRTT the king'. It has been tentatively dated to the beginning of the first century BC.[30]

These documents, which perhaps all belong to the pre-Roman period in Palestine, do not mention Arabs. Unfortunately, we know nothing about the provenance of the Elusa text, which nowadays is lost. If the dating of the Rabbʔil text is correct, it is tempting to identify ḤRTT with Aretas, the Arab king of Damascus in the 80s BC. We have a series of coins from Damascus, in the style of the Seleucid coins but with the inscription '[belonging to] king Aretas, the friend of Hellenes'.[31] There is no reason to doubt that this Aretas is identical to the one called in by the Damascenes to protect them against the Ituraeans. This Aretas is called neither 'king of the *árabes*' nor 'king of the *nabataîoi*' on the coins attributed to him. In short, there is no support for seeing this Aretas as a Nabataean king identical with the one who supported Hyrcanus.

Arabs and Nabataeans: a first evaluation

Apart from the accounts preserved by Josephus, there is thus no immediate documentation that straightforwardly identifies Nabataeans as Arabs before the Roman conquest of Syria. When Diodorus uses the term 'the *árabes* called *nabataîoi*', which he puts as a headline to his digest of Hieronymus of Cardia and which reappears in a couple of other passages, it can be suspected that he is dependent on the reports by Theophanes and, ultimately, the signs carried in Pompey's triumph.[32] The same holds for Strabo's use of the phrase in his digest of Agatharchides as well as for Plutarch in the *Life of Pompey*.[33] Both Diodorus and Strabo have used the phrase for updating the reports of Hieronymus and Agatharchides, the same tendency that we can discern in Josephus' *Antiquities*. In particular Strabo, like Josephus, has not understood or cared about the distinction between Arabs and Nabataeans obviously found in some of his sources, and Josephus' neglect may, in fact, be influenced by him.

We have already pointed out one of Strabo's quotations from Eratosthenes where it seems that his source (and probably Eratosthenes' source) distinguished between Arabs and Nabataeans.[34] From this source could also come the note in a Greek botanical text from the middle of the first century AD, Dioscurides' *De materia medica*, where we hear about different species of rush:

> One grows in Libya, one in Arabia and another in the so-called Nabataîa; that one is the most powerful.[35]

Libya and Arabia are likely to be the areas separated by the Nile, as in Herodotus. In that case one could expect Arabia to be more or less identical with that of Herodotus. The land of the Nabataeans is thus separated from it and situated further east. We have earlier referred to a passage in Pliny's *Natural History*, probably from Eratosthenes, in which the Nabataei dwell east of the Canchlei and Cedreni, which goes well with Dioscurides.[36]

It thus turns out that the identification of Nabataeans as Arabs can be seen as originating in texts dealing with the Roman conquest of Syria in 65–62 BC. A closer look at the text of Pompey quoted by Diodorus does not, however, support the intepretation that the Nabataeans were seen as a group subsumed under a larger category of Arabs. The text rather says that Aretas was king of Arabs *and* Nabataeans. If read as it stands in the manuscripts to Diodorus, it rather supports the distinction between the two. It is the literary writers, starting with Diodorus himself, who tend to blur the distinction. The impression from Pompey's text is of a kind of personal union between Arabs and Nabataeans incarnated by Aretas.

A central issue in the story is Pompey's Arab campaign. In the additional material used by Josephus when writing *Antiquities* it is said that Pompey himself intended to go against the Nabataeans. This notice comes from Theophanes, Pompey's own chronicler. The account of Scaurus' operations in *Antiquities*, on the other hand, comes from an anti-Scaurus source, emanating from the circles around Antipatros and Hyrcanus. From Pompey's inscription it is, however, clear that Scaurus implemented Pompey's Nabataean plans: Pompey in his triumph claimed to have subjected 'King Aretas of Nabataeans, king of the Arabs'. The reference must be to Scaurus' achievement. Theophanes must have told about Pompey's plans for a campaign against the Nabataeans. Josephus describes a campaign against Arabia and its Arab king.[37] The different terminology reflects different sources: the one emerging from Antipatros' circle, around the man who was married to a noblewoman from Arabia and who had been a 'friend' of their king, the other from the chronicler of the Roman conqueror. The terminology of the latter is also reflected in the characterization of Aretas' Arabs as Nabataeans at the siege of Jerusalem, a notice which comes from Theophanes.

Even though the depiction of the very campaign in 62 BC in Josephus' *Antiquities* is heavily biased by the Antipatros–Hyrcanus party, some observations can be made. The inaccessibility of 'the Rock' is spoken of. Compared to the description by Hieronymus of Cardia 250 years earlier, it seems strange that the Roman army, by now the conquerors of the entire East, could not perform what Athenaeus had done in 312 BC. From the use of the word *dyskhōría*, 'rough terrain', for the areas around 'the Rock', it looks as if this time we do not have to do with the Rock in the Negev, around which there is not much to burn down either, whereas the land around Petra has several permanent settlements.[38] The conclusion is thus that the campaign in 62 BC was undertaken against present-day Petra, also known as Reqem. Now according to the admittedly difficult fragments in Pliny and Eratosthenes as well as, perhaps, the hints in the Books of Maccabees, this is an area where we should expect to find the Nabataeans, i.e. east of the southern ʕArabah and the Dead Sea.

Theophanes has thus reported a campaign against the Nabataeans and their centre in present-day Petra south-east of the Dead Sea. At the same time there seems to be no doubt that these Nabataeans were governed by Aretas the Arab, king of the Arabs, probably with their centre on *their* rock in the Negev. This dichotomy is confirmed by Pompey's own inscription and it explains the varying terminology in the sources. The question that remains is why the Romans chose to attack Petra and not the rock in the Negev. This question can only be answered after an investigation of the sources dealing with the period after the Roman conquest.

In *War* Scaurus is described very negatively. He is presented as a corrupt, incompetent scoundrel. Both his main actions, the support for Aristobulus and the campaign in Arabia, are described as failures. The former is adjusted by Pompey and the latter is implemented by Gabinius. These two are described in neutral or even positive terms. There is no doubt that this reflects a pro-Hyrcanus–Antipatros source used by Nicolaus, very negative towards Aristobulus and, consequently, also against his Roman supporter, Scaurus. The negative picture of Scaurus' Arab campaign makes Hyrcanus and Antipatros appear in a rosy light as altruistic and generous helpers of the man who had treated them so badly. The same positive image is given of Gabinius, a tool for Hyrcanus.[39]

In the story of the siege of Jerusalem in *Antiquities*, Josephus has added material much more positive towards Scaurus and also Aristobulus. Scaurus reluctantly receives the sum paid by both contenders; Hyrcanus is portrayed as a simple bum, whereas Aristobulus is virtue incarnate. Also the final sentence in the account of the Arab campaign could be interpreted as a positive evaluation of the general: as during the siege of Jerusalem, he shows himself as a man practising the virtues of *clementia* and *moderatio*, seeking the least costly solution to a military conflict.

Arabs and Nabataeans after the Roman conquest: the sources

From the period following the Roman conquest of Syria, we have a series of coins and inscriptions from the area that became the Roman province of Arabia in AD 106, mentioning several 'kings of NBṬW'. Of these there are one or perhaps two ʕBDT, two MLKW, one ḤRTT and one RBʔL.[40] There are also two queens, ḤLDW and ŠQYLT, who are 'queens of the NBṬW'.[41] There is no inscription mentioning a 'king of the Arabs'. The word ʕRBY(ʔ) occurs in some inscriptions from Nabataean territory but they are all probably later than the period treated here.[42] It always designates an individual, not the Nabataean people as such.[43] It is thus the equivalent of the Arabic nisba-formation *ʕarabī*, or the Aramaic *ʕarbāy*, '[an, the] Arab'.

Hence, as far as the royal titulature is concerned, there seems to be some continuity from *c.* 100 BC to RBʔL, evidently the last king to carry the title 'king of the NBṬW' before the Romans converted the regions south-east and south of Palestine to a province in AD 106. The kings of the NBṬW are thus documented during two centuries. Neither Arabs nor their kings are mentioned in epigraphic and numismatic documents from the period. If these texts were the only ones we had, few would identify the NBṬW with the Arabs in antiquity.

In the literary sources dealing with events after Pompey, the term 'Arabs' dominates as a designation for the people in Reqem/Petra. Strabo has, however, preserved a description of the *nabataîoi* and their metropolis Petra, which is undoubtedly the site known by that name today. The description is based on an eye-witness report by Strabo's friend Athenodorus, who had visited the city. Into Athenodorus' account is inserted the report about Aelius Gallus' campaign to Yemen in 24 BC, an enterprise supported by the kings in Petra.[44] They are called *nabataîoi* although their country is situated in *Arabía eudaímōn*. This report also stems from eye-witnesses who took part in the expedition.[45]

Pliny's *Natural History,* compiled in the 70s AD, has a lot of material about the Arabo-Nabataean kingdom. Most of it is taken from Iuba writing in the time of Augustus, who, in turn, used older sources. In the passage about the aromatics, which Pliny mostly had from Iuba, the Nabataeans are said to be from Arabia bordering on Syria.[46] Iuba obviously also mentioned the Nabataeans in connection with the description of the caravan road from Syria to South Arabia, which has been dated to the first century BC.[47] Here they are said to dwell north of the earlier Timani (Taymāʔ). Unfortunately, we only know Iuba through Pliny's digest, which mostly gives a badly corrupted version of geographical and ethnic names.

Florus Annaeus at the beginning of the second century AD mentions *Arabes* siding with Mark Antony at Actium.[48]

Plutarch tells that the *árabes* around Petra burnt Cleopatra's fleet in the Red Sea after her fatal defeat by Octavian.[49] Cassius Dio, at the beginning of the third century AD, has some notes about the people of Nabataea: Aretas 'III' is *arábios;*[50] Malichus 'I', the *nabataîos*, supported the Parthians in 39 BC;[51] in the aftermath of Actium the *arábioi* are instigated to burn the Egyptian fleet, a piece of information shared with Plutarch and perhaps derived from him.[52]

To both Strabo and Pliny, the Nabataeans lived within the borders of larger Arabia. Here they both follow the tradition from Eratosthenes. On the other hand it seems clear that they used sources which did not see Nabataeans as Arabs. These sources, like Hieronymus of Cardia, Agatharchides of Cnidus and Athenodorus, were of good quality, written by eye-witnesses or based on first-hand sources. One such source is preserved in the *Periplus Maris Erythraei* written around AD 70. There we hear about a Malikhas, king of the *nabataîoi*, reigning in the latter part of the first century AD.[53] This Malikhas must be identical with MLKW, king of NBṬW, in the inscriptions from Madāʔin Ṣāliḥ and one of the MLKW MLK NBṬW on the coins.

Arabs and Nabataeans after the Roman conquest: Josephus' account

The main literary source for the political history of the Nabataeans is, however, Flavius Josephus. The picture of 'Arabo-Nabataean' political history given by all modern textbooks is chiefly founded upon the notices found in *The Jewish War* and *Antiquities,* which represent the most extensive source material extant for a reconstruction of the history of the area which later became *Provincia Arabia*.[54] In both works the designation 'Arabs' is used exclusively for the period after the Roman conquest.[55] The appearance of Arabs in that part of Josephus' works is confined to four main episodes in the reign of Herod the Great: Herod's flight during the Parthian invasion in 40–39 BC; his dealings with Antony and Cleopatra during the last years before the battle of Actium in 31 BC; Herod's settlement with the new ruler of Rome, Octavian, after Actium; and Herod's conflict with the prime minister in Petra, Syllaeus, around 10 BC.[56]

A survey of the terminology used in these parts of Josephus' works gives the impression that it is more exact than that of any other Greek or Latin source. He uses the designation *árabes* consistently for the inhabitants of the land he calls Arabia.[57] But we also find the term *ho áraps*, 'the Arab', quite often for the king or higher officials. When Herod fled to Arabia before the Parthians, he brought his nephew as ransom to *ho áraps* for his brother Phasael whom he believed to be his prisoner.[58] From the context it is clear that this 'Arab' was Malchus, 'king of the *árabes*'. Syllaeus is called *ho áraps* on several occasions.[59] One *áraps*, Corinthus, and two other *árabes* are condemned to death for a conspiracy against Herod.[60] The new king in Petra, Aretas 'IV', who supported the Roman governor Varus during the revolts after Herod's death in 4 BC, is called *ho áraps*.[61]

In one passage it is said that the king, Malchus, *ho áraps*, to whom Herod fled from the Parthians, had *hē arabarkhía*, 'the rule of the Arabs'.[62] A general at the same time, named Nakebos, is called *hēgouménos* or *stratēgòs tōn arábōn*, 'commander of the *árabes*'.[63] He is also said to command the *arabikē dynamis*, 'the Arab force'.[64]

Josephus mentions two persons, Malkhos *ho áraps* and Obadas, who are said to be 'kings of the *árabes*'.[65] To them is added Aretas, Varus' supporter, who is called *ho áraps* or *ho petraîos*, 'the one from Petra/the Rock'.[66] These three have long since been identified with MLKW, ʕBDT and ḤRTT, who are called 'kings of NBṬW' on the coins from the so-called Nabataean kingdom, supposed to have ruled from *c.* 60 BC to AD 40 as Malchus 'I' (*c.* 58–28 BC), Obodas 'III' (*c.* 28–9 BC) and Aretas 'IV' (9 BC–AD 40).[67] Other sources, namely Appian and Cassius Dio, call Malchus both 'king of the Nabataeans' and 'the Nabataean'.[68] Obodas 'III', who obviously followed Malchus 'I', appears as a ruler of the Nabataeans in Petra in Strabo's summary of the Gallus expedition.[69]

The epigraphic and numismatic evidence for the period, i.e. the primary documents, thus speaks unequivocally about Nabataeans, not Arabs. Also in the literary sources Nabataeans appear sporadically even though Arabs dominate. Taking the documentation of the titles of these kings on coins and in inscriptions into consideration, it is remarkable that, in both of Josephus' works, we not only find the Nabataean kingship over the *árabes* mentioned only rarely, but actually miss the Nabataeans altogether. Malchus, like Obodas, is by Josephus called *basileùs tōn arábōn*, 'king of the Arabs', only once and on two occasions 'their king' referring to the *árabes*. Instead the designation *ho áraps* is used.[70] This king is known as Malichus I in the commonly accepted series of Nabataean kings.

Since the documents left by the kings themselves (among which we must count the coinage) designate them 'kings of the Nabataeans' and since that title even appears in some literary sources, there is a discrepancy between these and Josephus, which presents itself as a larger problem than usually noticed, the more so since Josephus is the fullest documentation we have of the political history of this entity. On the whole, it is noteworthy that the very title 'king' seems to be avoided by Josephus as a designation of the supposed rulers in Petra. This is, in fact, a feature which closes the gap between Josephus and the numismatic and epigraphic evidence somewhat, but the problem remains: if the official title of the kings in Petra was 'king of the Nabataeans', why does not our main source for their political history, Josephus, also call them so?

It could be argued that Josephus' almost exclusive use of the term 'Arab' is due to the influence from Greek geographical literature where, as we have seen, there is a clear tendency to call everybody in Arabia 'Arab'. If the Nabataeans were a subdivision of a larger ethnic entity 'Arabs', Josephus' terminology would not pose a problem. But it could still be asked why he does not mention the Nabataeans since, after all, he seems to deal with them. It is also striking that the formula 'the *árabes* called *nabataîoi*' is absent in his works, although he must have been familiar with it since at least one of his main sources, namely Strabo, used it. Josephus is, in fact, our best source for the history of the rulers who seem to have called themselves 'kings of NBṬW'. In spite of this, Nabataeans are not mentioned.

The solution: Herod's legacy

In order to grasp something of the historical realities behind Josephus' account, we have once more to take a closer look at his work. As mentioned earlier, the book on the

Jewish War is the earliest of the two works. There is agreement that the part dealing with the reign of Herod, i.e. 1.30–2.116, is based almost entirely on Nicolaus of Damascus, Herod's own court historian.[71] This part is reproduced in *Antiquities* book 14–17, which, however, has much additional material on Herod's activities. Especially important for us are some of the sections on Herod's dealings with Cleopatra and the whole section about Syllaeus, episodes which are treated more summarily or only hinted at in *War*. There are also, mostly in *Antiquities*, passages which are strongly anti-Herodian. Most are, however, neutral or even positive towards the king. The latter is not surprising when we keep in mind that Nicolaus was Herod's own chronicler.

If we take a look at Josephus' handling of Nicolaus, we have already noted that the mention of Nabataeans, both in *Antiquities* and in *War* in the Gabinius story, is an indication that Nicolaus himself reflects a special source in that passage. Nicolaus thus seems to have been a truthful copyist of his sources. Now Josephus explicitly refers to Herod's own memoirs, and it is usually assumed that Nicolaus' entire biography of Herod was largely built upon them.[72] This means that the neutral passages about Herod in Josephus are likely to be based upon Herod's own documents, and the positive ones, to which the Arab passages belong, are more or less direct quotations or, at least, close paraphrases of Herod's own writings.[73] From this the following conclusions can be drawn: (1) Josephus is a quite faithful copyist of his sources, at least as far as terminology is concerned. (2) Nicolaus also quite faithfully reflected the ethnic terminology of his sources. (3) The fact that the Arabs are mentioned especially frequently in the pro-Herodian passages, especially the flight episode and the Syllaeus story, shows that they were mentioned as such in Herod's own memoirs. This means that it is none other than Herod the Great who has spoken about Arabs instead of Nabataeans, and that the terminology in Josephus' *War* and *Antiquities* represents that of the king himself. Why did he use this terminology?

Herod's mother was Cyprus, a woman 'from the distinguished (*episēmos*) ones from Arabia'.[74] Herod's father, Antipatros, was very close to Aretas, 'the Arab' (*ho áraps*), king of Arabia at the time of the coming of the Romans, and it is not unlikely that Cyprus was related to the royal house.[75] At the time of Caesar's final war with Pompey, Antipatros, who is said to have been the *xénos* of the *árabes*, came with support of *árabes* to Caesar.[76] We have already pointed out that the description of Scaurus' campaign against the Nabataeans in Petra as being directed against Arabia probably comes from circles around Antipatros.

Herod's Arab background explains his flight during the Parthian attack in 40–39 BC. He is said to have fled to 'the Arabian Petra/Rock' (*eis tēn arabikēn pétran*) or 'the Petra of Arabia' (*epì Pétras tēs Arabías*).[77] When he arrived, he received a message from Malchus, the king of the *árabes*, ordering him to leave the country. Without meeting the king, he set off for Egypt and reached Rhinocorura, present-day al-ʕArīsh, in two days.[78]

This story is of considerable interest not only for our subject.[79] The note about the two days' journey from Petra to al-ʕArīsh makes the identification of the former with present-day Petra very unlikely. From there to al-ʕArīsh is almost 180 kilometres of partly quite rough terrain. Judging from the testimony of modern travellers using riding animals, it is very doubtful, to say the least, if it is possible to make that journey in two days.[80] It is more likely that Malchus, known from the coins as the king of the Nabataeans, was in Nabataean Petra, i.e. Reqem. One should observe that Herod did not meet him, which is somewhat strange if he had reached Nabataean Petra, the residence of the Nabataean king.[81] In short: Herod did not go to Nabataean Petra but to the Rock of the Arabs in the Negev, the by now age-old residence of the kings of Arabia. This is also what the text actually says: Petra in Arabia.

All this explains why Herod talked about Arabs and not Nabataeans in his *Memoirs*: the Arabs were his close relatives and he turned to them, not to the Nabataeans, when he was in dire straits. This also explains the position of Syllaeus. This man, called *ho áraps*, was coveted as husband by none less than Salome, Herod's sister. We see a circle of people calling themselves Arabs to which Herod's family as well as Syllaeus belonged, linked to the ancient capital in the Negev but also to the Nabataean king, Malchus.

It seems that the Arabs, whom we have followed in the region between Palestine and Egypt during half a millennium, were still around even after the Roman conquest of Syria. Herod talks about Arabs because they were the group with which he dealt. He does not mention Nabataeans because he had no dealings with them. Arabs and Nabataeans were still two separate groups, although, as far as we can see, united under one king.

There are other details in Herod's testimony that become comprehensible in this perspective. When it is said that Malchus, officially called 'king of the Nabataeans', possesses the 'command of the Arabs' (*hē arabarkhía*) or when we later hear about a general, Nakebos, commanding 'the Arabic force' being 'the leader of the *árabes*', the picture emerges of the Arabs as a special sector of society with a predominantly military function. The word *nakebos* is probably not even a name but a title, appearing in the *ʕArabiyya*-language as *naqīb*, a highly venerable title.[82]

The Arabo-Nabataean kingdom

Starting from the fact that Arabs and Nabataeans are treated as separate entities before the 60s BC, then appear as juxtaposed terms in contemporary literary sources, we venture the following hypothesis: the kings of the *árabes*, until now having had their main stronghold in Petra in the Negev, having faced the ambitions of Alexander Jannaeus followed by the invasion of Tigranes and the arrival of the Romans in Syria, left their old residence and moved over to Reqem on the other side of the ʕArabah, until that date inhabited mostly by peaceful traders and farmers who were called Nabataeans. It is also very likely that a great many Arabs followed their kings to the new residence. On the other hand, it seems from the story of Herod's flight that Arabs remained in the old stronghold even after the transfer; and it can be asked if the Arabs around Petra who burnt Cleopatra's ships, when she tried to carry them from the Red Sea across the Suez isthmus after Actium, were not in fact those still settled in the ancient Petra in the Negev.[83]

It is not unlikely that some connection between the Arab kings and the Nabataeans had existed before this transfer, although its exact nature remains to be determined.[84] From now on we can speak of the Arabo-Nabataean kingdom. Its main manifestation was the moving of the royal residence from the 'Rock' in the Negev to Reqem in ancient Edom, a site which offered far better defensive advantages than the site in the Negev. It is likely that the name Petra for Reqem shows that the very name was also transferred to the new capital. We should thus distinguish between the Arabian Petra and the Nabataean Petra.

The name Reqem is already found in the Old Testament as the name of a king in

Midian, i.e. east of the ʕArabah.[85] According to Josephus the town was named after this king. In the Old Testament it is also the name of a son of Hebron and a brother of Qoraḥ.[86] The name RQM appears in the Targum, the Jewish Aramaic translations of the Old Testament, as well as in the Peshitta. In those texts, the Masoretic name Qadesh is rendered as RQM. Qadesh Barneaʕ is rendered RQM GYʔH.[87] In Eusebius' *Onomasticon* it is said that 'Gaîa [is] a city lying at Petra'.[88] There is still today a place named al-Ǧī close to modern Petra. It thus seems that in the Targum we have a testimony of an early identification of Qadesh Barneaʕ, the scene of many dramatic events during the Israelite desert wanderings, with Nabataean Petra/Reqem, an identification which must have been made before AD 300.

In a tannaitic description of the borders of the Promised Land we find two sites mentioned with the name RQM: RQM ṬRKWN, situated near Qanawāt in Trachonitis, and RQM DGYʔH, Reqem d-Gīʔā between Zered (= Wādī l-Ḥaṣā) and Ashqelon.[89] In another rabbinic passage, we hear about ha-Reqem and ha-Ḥeger as two different sites. Of these, Reqem is clearly east of the ʕArabah and likely to be Nabataean Petra.[90] The differentiation is also found in the Targum Onqelos to Genesis, where the well found by Hagar is said to have been situated between RQM and ḤGRʔ, and Abraham is said to have pitched his tent between these two sites.[91] In that latter passage, the Masoretic text has Shur and in the Targum Shur is regularly rendered ḤGRʔ. Shur is a term for the border against Egypt. A plain reading of the Biblical text leads to the conclusion that both Shur and Qadesh are thought to be situated somewhere in the northern Sinai/southern Negev, and that these were designated by the term ḤGRʔ by the Targumists.[92] But it is also clear that Qadesh Barneaʕ with all its events has been relocated to RQM DGYʔH, i.e. Nabataean Petra at a certain time. It is very plausible to assume that ḤGRʔ was originally the name of a site in the Negev, early identified with Shur and Qadesh Barneaʕ but different from RQM.[93]

It should be noticed that ḤGRʔ is connected with RQM only in a few instances. The decisive argument is the word ḤGR(ʔ). It is obviously the same as the Arabic root ḤǦR. This has two derivations: *ḥaǧar* meaning 'stone' and *ḥiǧr* meaning 'enclosure'.[94] It is likely that the latter meaning has led to its use as a replacement of Shur, which means 'wall'. It is difficult to avoid connecting the word 'stone' with the name of the stronghold of the Arabs in the Negev called 'the rock'. We would thus venture the following hypothesis: ḤGRʔ is the original Semitic name of the Rock of the Arabs in the Negev. Reqem is the original name of the valley just west of al-Ǧī and east of the ʕArabah. At a certain time, probably under Aretas 'III', the royal residence of the Arab kings was transferred from ḤGRʔ to Reqem. The transfer included the name 'the Rock', ḤGRʔ, in Greek *pétra*, which was applied to Reqem. It also affected the Israelite traditions around Qadesh Barneaʕ, since these traditions, probably long before, had been associated with ḤGRʔ in the Negev. Their transfer to Reqem has been remembered to this day: the modern visitor to Petra is confronted not only with the tomb of Aaron, but also with highlights such as the treasury of Pharaoh and his daughter's palace, and the whole region is named Wādī Mūsā, 'the Valley of Moses'.[95]

The evidence in Josephus supports this scenario. He says explicitly that Petra is a new name for the former Reqem.[96] He also identifies it with a site in the Negev formerly called Arkē, 'which the *árabes* have considered their metropolis'.[97] The perfect tense (*nenomíkasi*) is worth noticing: it is no longer considered so. Josephus has obviously mixed up the two sites: the Rock in the Negev, the stronghold of the Arabs, also known as Arkē; and Petra, the capital of the Nabataeans, formerly known as Reqem.

This shows that both the transfer and identification were made long before his time.

An Aretas figures in a remarkable notice originating from Uranius' book *Arabica*, written around AD 300.[98] It is told that Aretas, son of Obodas, received a prophecy from his father about the founding of a city in Arabia which Aretas named Auara, 'the white'. Aretas in a vision saw a man dressed in white on a white dromedary as a sign of the site of the new city, which was on a rock (*skópelos*) 'firmly rooted in the ground'.[99] In yet another notice, Uranius mentions the city of Oboda, 'a place of the Nabataeans in which the deified Obodas is buried'.[100] Instead of trying to identify these two kings with those mentioned in the sources, we should rather see them as mythical figures.[101] The city mentioned is most likely to be the royal residence of the Arab kings, i.e. the place called 'the rock' in our texts.[102] If the two passages belong together, we have a clear indication that 'the rock' is in fact identical with Avdat which, by the way, is situated on a rock of very bright limestone.[103] If Obodas and Aretas are mythical names, it explains the occurrence of these names among the kings of Arabs and Nabataeans.[104]

We have no explicit report in any source about the actual events sketched here. It should, however, be kept in mind that our knowledge of Arabo-Nabataean affairs in general is scanty in the extreme. Archaeology clearly shows that Reqem/Petra experienced a rapid development from the middle of the first century BC onwards.[105] One of our few glimpses of the inner structure of the Arabo-Nabataean state is the information from Athenodorus, who visited 'the metropolis of the *nabataîoi*, the so-called Rock (Petra)', at the end of the first century BC.[106] From the description it is clear that it is Reqem, present-day Petra, that is described, not the Petra described by Hieronymus.[107] The king is said to belong to a special royal family or clan (*génos*). He officiates at ritual drinking ceremonies. The participants are sometimes served by him and his conduct is an object of observation and scrutiny by the *dēmos*. The impression from this description is that the king was more a ceremonial figure than a ruler. Even Petra is described as a place for negotiations and peaceful meetings like some kind of sanctuary or asylum. The realm is ruled by an *epítropos*, an administrator, called 'the king's brother'.[108] It is unfortunate, but perhaps symptomatic, that Athenodorus does not mention the name of the king in Petra. It is, however, very likely that he was the Obodas mentioned by Josephus/Nicolaus/Herod. In that case, the *epítropos* was Syllaeus, *ho áraps*, who carries that title in Josephus.

The dichotomy in the terminology of the written sources themselves, and between them and the epigraphic and numismatic evidence, thus seems to have a background in political structures in the Arabo-Nabataean kingdom. It is possible to discern a combination of the peaceful Nabataeans and the Arab warriors making up this state.[109] Finally, the moving of the residence to Transjordanian Petra gives an excellent explanation of the campaign against the Nabataeans planned by Pompey and undertaken by Scaurus and Gabinius. The Romans tried to reach the new royal residence situated in the land of the Nabataeans and inhabited by them. It seems that the Arab kings had made the right calculation. The Romans could not take the Pink City, which turned out to provide a safe haven for the rulers of Arabs and Nabataeans.

The king of Arabs and Nabataeans

The Nabataeans called their kings 'king of the Nabataeans'. To outsiders they were known as 'king of the Arabs'. This sounds familiar. The same terminology was found with Qedar: they were called Arabs by Babylonians, Achaemenids and Greeks. Their king Geshem/Gashmu is, however, called king of Qedar in domestic texts. This goes back to the earliest known king of Qedar: Hazaʔil in the days of Sennacherib and Esarhaddon. He is called king of Qedar in some texts and king of the Arabs in others.

Relevant to this is another fact. We have seen that the Nabataean king is often called 'the Arab'. So is the Qedarite king Geshem in the book of Nehemiah: Geshem/Gashmu *haʕarbī*. And we now remember that far back in time Gindibu at Qarqar was also called 'the Arab', *arbāya*. This usage thus recurs in the text going back to Herod the Great, who probably knew very well what he was talking about. It increases the value of Herod's testimony of political terminology, which turns out to represent not only an age-old tradition in the region but probably also some kind of political continuity.

Without anticipating all the final conclusions of this study, a preliminary suggestion would be that in the Arabo-Nabataean kingdom, 'Arabs' was the designation of the army or, at least, parts of it. The king as the head of the army would then naturally be called 'king of the Arabs' and it is even understandable that he could be called 'the Arab', i.e. the foremost of the warriors. In the inscriptions, which are almost all funerary, he appears instead in civil apparel as king of the Nabataeans. Also on the coins his 'civilian' title is used. The term 'Nabataean' seems to be a more local usage, especially in Petra.[110]

A plausible interference is that this transfer of the royal residence, the name of the capital and large parts of the army was effected by Aretas 'III'. Aretas was obviously ruling both Arabs and Nabataeans, although he is not documented with the title 'King of Nabataeans'.[111] As we have pointed out, a plain reading without preconceived ideas of the writing carried in Pompey's triumph gives the impression that Aretas was king of Nabataeans *and* Arabs. The king, who could have been his direct successor, Malchus, is known with both titles in the literary sources. The obscure Obodas 'II', supposed to have reigned between Aretas 'III' and Malchus, is documented only as Nabataean king and he was perhaps not recognized as king of the Arabs.[112] If the Arab ruler in his role as Nabataean king had mainly ceremonial functions, one could imagine him residing at Reqem with the leader of the Arabs acting in war against neighbouring rulers. Malchus obviously united the two functions as did most of his successors. Under Malchus' successor, Obodas 'III', we catch a glimpse of how the Arabs were organized under special commands, a system which might have continued during the first century AD. To outsiders, the kingdom was known as Arabia, which was natural since this political entity had been known as Arabia at least since the days of Darius the Great and Arabs continued to play a main political and military role in it. This also explains why the Romans called it *Provincia Arabia*, not *Nabataea*, when they annexed it in AD 106.

Excursus: who were the Nabataeans?

Scholars have long since identified the Nabataeans not only with the Arabs appearing in the history of Herod, but also with the Arabs around Palestine appearing in the narrative sources from the time of Hieronymus of Cardia onwards. Historians have even constructed a list of kings of the Arabo-Nabataeans, starting with the Aretas to whom Iason fled in 168 BC, making him the first documented Arabo-Nabataean king, and continuing down to the year AD 106.[113] The fact that they seem to be called Arabs in Greek and Latin texts has been accepted as a true designation of their ethnicity: they were Arabs.[114] A support for this has been the obvious fact that the majority of personal names in the Nabataean inscriptions are found both in Islamic sources and in pre-Islamic inscriptions from other parts of the Arabian peninsula.[115] From the end of the sixth century BC there are traces of people in the Arabo-Nabataean area, especially in the Negev, carrying names of an 'Arabic' type. Such names documented in Nabataean inscriptions appear in other areas some centuries later.[116] Arabic names are, in fact, documented for Transjordan and areas south of Palestine already in the Pentateuch, and it is very likely that this represents ancient tradition.[117] A closer look shows that the 'Nabataean' onomasticon from the very beginning is strongly differentiated regionally, which gives the impression that Arabic names had been in use for a very long time in different parts of the area.[118] At the same time we can see survivals of Edomitic elements as well as influences from Syria in Nabataea. Archaeologists have stressed the cultural continuity in the area from Edomitic times down to the 'Nabataean' era, and a massive invasion of people from the Arabian peninsula seems not to be documented even though an influx of Arabisms is discernible from the sixth century BC.[119] It cannot be doubted that the Arabo-Nabataean kingdom inherited a multi-ethnic and multilingual territory from the very beginning.[120]

The problem has not been brought closer to its solution by the rather futile discussion of the original homeland of the Nabataeans, which indeed presupposes several unverified assumptions: that they were a 'people', that they were immigrants in Nabataea etc., assumptions which, in fact, continue national mythologies of exodi and conquests from antiquity.[121] The cultural continuity in Nabataea demonstrated by modern archaeology indicates that we should not automatically operate with concepts like migration, or ethnic units in the modern sense. We should look in another direction.

We have documentation of people called *nabaṭu* in Ssouthern Mesopotamia from the days of Tiglath Pileser III and Sennacherib in the eighth century BC.[122] The *nabaṭu* lived in the same area as the 'town of Arab(s)' (*uru/ālu ša arbāya*) in southern Mesopotamia near the town of Nippur.[123]

Josephus mentions a man from Adiabēnē on the upper Tigris, a participant in the great Jewish rebellion in AD 66–73, who was son of Nabataîos.[124] It is likely that this, in fact, does not refer to the name of his father but to the group he belonged to.[125] As we shall see later, Josephus also tells us about the presence of Arabs in that area shortly before. According to Quintus Curtius, Arabs may already have been in Adiabene in the time of Alexander the Great.[126] This information may, however, refer to Curtius' own time, i.e. the first century AD.

In southern Syria/northern Transjordan the Nabataeans appear in the third century BC.[127] As has been pointed out, there is also evidence for the existence of a region called Arabia south-east of Damascus in the days of Alexander Jannaeus, i.e. the area where the Nabataeans appear in the Zenon papyrus in 259 BC. The leader of these Arabs, Aretas, became king of Damascus, and it is worth noting the existence until this day of a quarter in that town called an-Naybaṭūn. From Aretas until Imruʔ al-Qays, 'the king of all Arabs' in AD 328, we have ample evidence of Arabs in this part of southern Syria.[128]

Claudius Ptolemy in his book on world geography, written in the second century AD, mentions *apataîoi* west of the mountain Zames.[129] The mountain has been identified with the present-day Shammar mountains, and the word, which probably refers to Nabataeans, designates dwellers west of the mountain probably close to, or even in, the Dedan oasis.[130] These Nabataeans must have lived close to or together with Thamūd, who in their turn seem to have been associated with Arabs.[131] Near Dedan we find today a Nabataean necropolis still more spectacular than Petra. The word NBṬ is even documented together with the Shalamians in an inscription from the necropolis.[132]

Ptolemy further mentions a people called *arabanîtai* near Nağrān in South Arabia. The presence of ʕRB there is confirmed by South Arabian inscriptions.[133] In three of them we also hear about NBṬ as enemies of the inhabitants of the town. One of the texts is dated to the year AD 547.[134]

Outside 'classical Nabataea' we thus find Nabataeans documented in southern Mesopotamia, Adiabene, Ḥawrān, Ḥiğāz and at Nağrān. It is striking that, in these six regions (including classical Nabataea), we can also document Arab presence. Arabs and Nabataeans seem to follow each other.

It is worthwhile to compare this evidence with the documentation of *nabaṭ* or *nabīṭ* in early Islamic times. As is well known, *nabaṭ* was the designation used in that period for the peasantry of present-day Iraq and Syria.[135] There are, however, remarks which give the picture of a somewhat more limited settlement. Thus it is stated that the *nabaṭ* belong to the marshes of southern Iraq.[136] We also hear about them in what is more or less Xenophon's Arabia, namely along the Khābūr river.[137] One notice mentions the *nabīṭ* in Ḥawwārīn, the area of the *árabes zabadaîoi* near Emesa in the Seleucid period.[138] According to an Arabic verse, the descendants of the founder of Quraysh in Mecca, Quṣayy b. Kilāb, were 'like Nabataeans', *mutanabbiṭūn*.[139] A verse preserved by al-Bakrī alludes to *nabīṭ* in Yathrib.[140] Another mentions the *nabīṭ* from the *ʔanṣār,* i.e. the Muslims in Medina.[141] The *ʔanbāṭ* of Yathrib took part in the events leading to the murder of ʕUthmān.[142] In Medina there was a *sūq an-nabaṭ*, a 'Nabataean bazar', at the beginning of the seventh century and *nabīṭ* sold food there at the same time.[143] At least some of these *nabīṭ*, however, are said to come from Syria.[144] The indisputable information from these early Islamic notes about *nabaṭ* is that they were active as tradesmen between Ḥiğāz and Syria. But they may also have been indigenous to the two holy cities. Finally, in eastern Arabia, we find *an-nabīṭ* mentioned in Arabo-Islamic sources. According to *Kitāb al-ʔAghānī*, *nabaṭ* lived in Hağar in the Hufūf oasis.[145] The *Lisān* refers to ʔAyyūb b. Qirriyya (dead AD 703): 'The people of Oman are *ʕarab* who have become *nabaṭ* (*istanbaṭū*); the people of Baḥrayn are *nabīṭ* who have become *ʕarab* (*istaʕrabū*).' In the same manner a ḥadīth ascribed to ʕUmar b. al Khaṭṭāb says: 'Make yourselves Maʕadd (*tamaʕdadū*) and do not make yourselves *nabaṭ* (*tastanbiṭū*) which means: be like the Maʕadd and do not be like the Nabaṭ.'[146]

As far as the language of the *nabaṭ* is concerned, in Arabo-Islamic sources it is usually identified as Aramaic (*suryānī*). This characterization might have been valid when more or less the entire population in the Fertile Crescent was seen as *nabaṭ*. But it becomes very unlikely that the *nabaṭ*, for example, in Medina, Nağrān, Hağar or Oman were Aramaic-speakers.[147]

Their main distinguishing characteristic was their way of living by farming and trading, which is confirmed by the two quotations from the *Lisān*.[148] In Yāqūt's dictionary we find a very clearcut definition of the *nabaṭī*: everyone who has not been a shepherd or a warrior with the *ʕarab* of the dwellers of the lands (*al-ʕarab min sākinī l-ʔaraḍīn*) is a *nabaṭī*.[149] al-Ǧāḥiẓ even mentions a *yahūdiyyun min ʔanbāṭi š-šām*, 'a Jew from the *nabaṭ* of Syria'.[150] The *ʔAghānī* has preserved a verse by Abū Yaʕqūb al-Khuraymī (– AD 829), a contemporary of ʕAlī b. Haytham from Taghlib, saying that he was an *ʕarabī* although his grandfather had been a *nabaṭī*.[151]

We also notice that the *nabaṭ/nabīṭ* in the Arabo-Islamic sources tend to appear in exactly the regions where we have found the Arabs in pre-Islamic times.[152] In these areas we also find that *nabataîoi* tend to appear as well.[153] This leads to the conclusion that Arabs and Nabataeans are somehow connected although not identical and, further, that there is a direct continuity between the Nabataeans in pre-Islamic times and the *nabaṭ/nabīṭ* in the Arabo-Islamic sources.

In the light of what has been said, it becomes very unlikely that these designations indicate ordinary tribes with their fictitious genealogical ancestry.[154] Since we have shown that the genealogical definition of Arabs is very late, it is quite certain that such a definition did not exist during the period dealt with here, which also explains their appearance in different, limited parts of Arabia. In that case, the Nabataeans are likely to have been something similar. Both groups look more like some kind of social states between which single individuals could switch.[155] This is explicitly said about the *nabaṭ* of the Arabo-Islamic authors, and is very likely to be true for the pre-Islamic Nabataeans as well. We are far away from the 'races' and 'stocks' so prominent in the minds of many modern scholars.

The distinction between Nabataeans and Arabs in both Islamic and pre-Islamic times was underlined by Quatremère, the first modern Western scholar who investigated the question. To him the Nabataeans in Petra were basically of the same kind as those documented in the Arabo-Islamic sources, i.e. Aramaic-speaking peasants and traders. The distribution of Nabataeans in several regions was explained by migration: since Quatremère defined both Arabs and Nabataeans as ethnic groups with distinct languages and cultures, this was the natural conclusion. The kingdom in Petra was characterized by being composed of two nationalities: Arabs and Nabataeans.[156]

This picture was revised by Nöldeke, who had access to the new epigraphical evidence from Nabataea. He interpreted the domination of Arabic in the onomasticon as an indication that the Nabataeans in Petra were Arabs.[157] This did away with the separation between the two advocated by Quatremère, blurred the distinction between Arabs and Nabataeans in the sources, made scholars neglect the evidence for Nabataeans in other regions, and led to the denial of connections between Nabataeans in antiquity and Nabataeans in Islamic times. This has hardened into something like a dogma with later scholars.[158] The Nabataeans in Petra are still seen as Arabic-speakers, and consequently as Arabs, whereas the *nabaṭ/nabīṭ* are explicitly said to have spoken Aramaic. This means that they belong to two different ethnic groups or 'nations'. The Petraean Nabataeans spoke Arabic and, consequently, belonged to the Arab 'race' or 'stock'; the *nabaṭ/nabīṭ* belonged to the Aramaic species. Consequently, there can be no direct links, let alone identity between them.

For the sake of justice, it should be pointed out that the great Nöldeke himself was aware of the problems with the identification of the Petraean Nabataeans as Arabs based on linguistic criteria. He realized that the concrete evidence of language in Nabataea, apart from the onomasticon of the inscriptions, does not support the view of her inhabitants as Arabic-speakers. The information we get, mostly through the rabbinic literature, shows that the language spoken in Nabataea must have been something between Arabic and Aramaic.[159] As a matter of fact, the linguistic arguments for defining the ethnicity of the Nabataeans in both antiquity and the Islamic period fall apart since the onomasticon is a very fragile ground upon which to build hypotheses of ethnicity. A comparison with the onomasticon in most modern European countries calls for caution. The Arabic onomasticon in Nabataea is a fact, but it shows only that the inhabitants had had long and intimate relations with a language we today would call Arabic. Such a language may very well have been spoken among them, but so were many others. This does not say much about how ethnicity and social institutions were conceived by them.

The picture of the relations between Arabs and Nabataeans, emerging from an unprejudiced reading of Josephus and other ancient sources, instead suggests very strong resemblances between the Nabataeans in those texts and the picture of them given by the Arabo-Islamic historians. In both, the peacefulness of the *nabaṭ* is emphasized and they are dependent on a political and military élite of people called Arabs. This holds for both the *nabaṭ* appearing in limited regions and those inhabiting the entire Fertile Crescent according to the Arabo-Islamic sources. We have hinted that the former are remnants of pre-Islamic conditions remembered by the Arabo-Islamic tradition, whereas the latter may represent conditions created by the rule of the Umayyads. In both groups of sources, the role of the Aramaic language is dominant, although it is evident that Nabataeans cannot be defined by linguistic criteria.

We would suggest that Quatremère was basically right when he assumed a dichotomy in the Arabo-Nabataean kingdom and that Arabs and Nabataeans were essentially two distinct groups. But the kingdom was not composed of two nationalities, one of which had immigrated from Mesopotamia and the other one from Arabia, as he thought.[160] Instead we see a political entity organized in two different states or castes between which individuals in certain cases could switch, very much as in the later Umayyad empire. If the *nabaṭ* in fact were those standing under some kind of protection by others, namely the *ʕarab*, which seems to be the most likely solution, this could explain why they both appear together at different sites: there were *ʕarab* at many places in the peninsula and adjacent regions and the *nabaṭ* followed them like a shadow.[161] When the designation *ʕarab* was expanded to encompass the entire ruling élite in the Umayyad empire, the status of *nabaṭ* was widened correspondingly. This would also explain why the Nabataeans disappeared from the *Provincia Arabia* after 106: like the *ʕarab* they disappeared because they too were a kind of institution which ceased to function when the Romans took over.[162]

The exact meaning of the word *nabaṭ* as designating a group of people is not altogether transparent. According to the Arab lexicographers, the root means 'water coming up from the earth' and from that: 'people who make water come up'.[163] A similar meaning is documented from South Arabia.[164] In some Aramaic dialects it is documented with the meaning 'to grow', 'to sprout', which is also found in Geez.[165] In Akkadian it means 'to shine', 'to beam'.[166] In Biblical Hebrew the root is used in the causative conjugation *hibbaṭ-* (< **hanbaṭ-*). The verb means 'to observe' and might be derived from 'be visible'. The Hebrew and Akkadian meanings belong together and stand against the meaning 'sprout' etc. even though both are related. The root belongs to the oldest layers of Semitic and is not alive in more modern languages. The root NBṬ occurs not infrequently in theophoric names in South Arabia.[167] A Sabaean name like NBṬ ʔL must mean 'the god ʔIl has [done something]'. A proper translation of the G-stem could be 'bring forth', which matches the meaning in Arabic 'bringing forth water'.[168] From this, the meaning 'to blossom' could be derived. In that case, the personal names would mean 'the god has brought forth', a type of Semitic name which has many parallels.[169]

The term *nabaṭ* for a group of people is likely to be the same formation as *ʕarab*. It is not very likely that it is an eponym or even a hypochoristicon.[170] This brings to mind a notice in the dictionary of Stephanus of Byzantium which probably goes back to the *Arabica* of Uranius written around AD 300 but which preserves older material not found anywhere else. It is said that *Nabatēs* is Arabic (*arabistí*) for 'born out of wedlock'.[171] We remember the 700 sons born to the king of the Arabs, Herotimus, by his concubines as told by Trogus/Iustinus.[172] The form of his name in Iustinus is probably a distortion based upon this piece of information. The original name could have been Ḥārithat, the name carried by the king of the Arabs who encountered the Romans at the walls of Jerusalem in 64 BC and to whom we have attributed the moving of the royal residence from Petra of the Arabs to Petra of the Nabataeans.[173] Does this somehow express the relationship between the Arabs and the Nabataeans, perhaps described by a pagan myth? What would then be the meaning of it? In the story of Abraham in Genesis, we hear about his engendering of a number of sons with a woman named Qeṭurah. These sons were seen as the patriarchs of the inhabitants of the Syrian desert from Dedan to the Euphrates by the Biblical writers. We have pointed out that there is an early, post-Biblical Jewish identification of Ishmaelites/Arabs/Nabataeans with the inhabitants of exactly this area, making them the sons of Hagar the concubine. The story could go back to ancient mythology, expressing the views of some about the low rank of the peoples living east of the Jordan and the Dead Sea. If the Nabataeans were somehow related to the Arabs by being their subjects or at least of lower status, these old myths could have been reused. An incitement may have been the fact that the basic idea of the myth was originally not the low rank of the offspring of the actors but a way of expressing their being autochthonous, born out of the land. We have the story about the origins of Ammon and Moab in the Old Testament, the forebears of whom are not only born out of wedlock but from incest. This could be the original meaning of the word *nabaṭ*: those who are born out of the earth by a promiscuous act of the Lord of Heaven, a motif well known from the eastern Mediterranean mythologies, later transformed by the monotheists into the story of a human patriarch. With this admittedly speculative but not unlikely suggestion we close the account of the Nabataeans.

Notes

1 Josephus, *War* 1.125–126.
2 Josephus, *Antiquities* 14.14.
3 Josephus, *Antiquities* 14.18. The translation in the Loeb edition is based on the idea that Alexander Jannaeus had taken the cities in Transjordan from Aretas and that he consequently now received them back. This view is followed by, for example, Kasher, *Jews* 96 ff. The verb translated as 'give back' is in Greek *apodōsein* (from *apodídōmi*), which can also mean 'give away', 'deliver, render'. There is no linguistic support for the idea that Aretas 'III' had once ceded these cities to Alexander and there are arguments against him being involved in Alexander's operations; cf. pp. 343–346.
4 Josephus says (*War* 1.126) that Aretas mustered 50,000 men including infantry and cavalry. In *Antiquities* (14.19) we hear that there were 50,000 cavalry plus an unspecified number of infantry.
5 Josephus, *War* 1.128–129.
6 Josephus, *Antiquities* 14.31–32.
7 See Kasher, *Jews* 111 ff., 116–118.
8 Strabo 16.2.40 gives a condensed version of Pompey's conquest, excluding many details. Cf. also the fragment in Diodorus 40.2.
9 Josephus, *War* 1.159.
10 Josephus, *Antiquities* 14.46, 48.
11 Josephus, *Antiquities* 14.80–81.
12 Josephus, *War* 1.178; idem, *Antiquities* 14:103.
13 *War* mentions later a certain Adiabenian, son of Nabataîos (5.474); see p. 379.

14 Cf. ibid. 1.131.
15 Cf. Kasher, *Jews* 112.
16 Cf. Strabo 16.2.34. This notice presupposes that Idumaea was counted as a Judaean province. In reality, Idumaea, the region between Hebron, Beer Sheba, Philistaea and the Dead Sea, separated Judaea proper from Arabia. Antipatros was married to a woman, Cyprus, from the nobles of Arabia who became the mother of his sons, among them Herod, and was thus related to the kings (Josephus, *War* 1.181).
17 Josephus, *Antiquities* 13:10–11.
18 1 Maccabees 5:25, 39.
19 Josephus, *Antiquities* 13:179.
20 Josephus, *Antiquities* 1.12.4; cf. p. 339.
21 Cf. p. 527 for identification in rabbinic sources of Nabataea with the whole Syrian desert unto the Euphrates.
22 See the remarks in the Loeb edition, ad loc.
23 Laqueur, *Theophanes* 2101. Cf. note to *Antiquities* 14:31 in Loeb. It is possible that Strabo knew Theophanes via Posidonius, who could have used it for his history of Pompey, a continuation or an appendix to his great *History*, which Strabo used extensively.
24 Laqueur, *Theophanes* 2122.
25 A report on the Roman conquest of Palestine of quite similar wording is also found in Diodorus 40.2 and Strabo 16.2.40 but neither mentions Arabs or Nabataeans. Both passages are probably derived from Posidonius' *Perì Okeanoû*; see p. 354.
26 Diodorus 40.4.1; cf. Plutarch, *Pompey* 45.2. The MSS have the title 'king' twice, one of which is usually deleted by modern editors. For Aretas' title, see p. 372.
27 Laqueur, *Theophanes* 2122.
28 Appian, *History: Mithradates* 16:106. The source may have been Posidonius' *History of Pompey* written around 60 BC (Unger, *Umfang* 80).
29 Cantineau, *Nabatéen* II 43–44 (Elusa; cf. Negev, *Nabateans* 545–546; Wenning, *Liste* 28–29. The original is lost and the reading of the name is not certain) 2–3 (Petra). For the dating of the Petra inscription, see Naveh, *History* 154; Fiema/Jones, *King-list* 244.
30 Cantineau, *Nabatéen* II 1–2; Naveh, *History* 154.
31 Meshorer, *Coins* 86–87; cf. 9–10, 12–14.
32 Diodorus 2.48.1; 3.43.4; 19.94.1. For the literary origin of the phrase, see p. 357.
33 Strabo 16.4.18; Plutarch, *Pompey* 45.2.
34 Cf. pp. 302, 307.
35 Dioscurides, *Materia* 1.17.2.
36 Pliny 5.12; cf. p. 306.
37 The only first-hand evidence for this campaign is the coinage minted by Scaurus in 58 BC, showing King Aretas kneeling beside a camel at a date-palm; cf. Kasher, *Jews* 118 n. 215.
38 Cf. the description of Petra in Pliny 6.32, which fits the present-day site very well. Cf. also Negev, *Beginnings* 127–128.
39 Josephus, *War* 1.169, 175, 177.
40 In the inscriptions published by Healey, most of which are from Madāʔin Ṣāliḥ, only three royal names are found: ḤRTT RḤM ʕMH, MLKW and RBʔL (Healey, *Inscriptions* 250). They all belong to the first century AD.
41 See Meshorer, *Coins*, *passim*, and Healey, *Inscriptions*, *passim*. For the full list, see Wenning, *Liste*.
42 Knauf, *Origins* 56–57.
43 Negev, *Names* 54 nr. 939.
44 Strabo 16.4.22–25. See pp. 401–403.
45 Strabo 16.4.21, 26. The description of Petra as a smooth place surrounded by mountains fits very well with Petra in Jordan but is very different from the description of 'the rock of the Arabs' in Hieronymus. The description of Petra in Pliny 6.32 is probably derived from that of Athenodorus.
46 Pliny 12.73.
47 Pliny 6.157; cf. von Wissmann, *Zamareni* I, II.

48 Florus 2.21.7.
49 Florus 2.21.7; Plutarch, *Antony* 69.3.
50 Cassius Dio 37:1.
51 Ibid. 48.41.5.
52 Ibid. 51.7.1.
53 *Periplus* §19.
54 The main modern presentations of the history are: Kammerer, *Pétra* (1929); Grohmann, *Nabataioi* (1935); Starcky, *Pétra* (1966); Hammond, *Nabataeans* (1973); Negev, *Nabateans* (1977); Roschinski, *Geschichte* (1980); Schürer, *History* (1973); Bowersock, *Arabia* (1983).
55 For the few cases of 'Nabataeans', see p. 367.
56 For Josephus' report about Abias, 'king of the Arabs' in Adiabene (*Antiquities* 20.77–79), see p. 413. In his report of the insurrection in AD 66–73 to which he was an eye-witness, he mentions both *árabes* and Malkhos *ho áraps*, who is probably identical with Malikhas, king of the *nabataîoi*, in the *Periplus*. See p. 421.
57 *War* 1.99, *Antiquities* 13.387; *War* 1.131, 276, *Antiquities* 14.18, 20; *War* 1.380, *Antiquities* 15.108 ff.; *War* 1.380; *Antiquities* 15.189, 351; *War* 1.566, 577, *Antiquities* 16.276, 295; *War* 2.68 ff., *Antiquities* 17.287. Arabia: *War* 1.117 (Hyrcanus escapes to Aretas 'III', king of Arabia 67 BC), 1.181 (Herod's mother was from Arabia), *Antiquities* 14.15 (Arabia borders on Judaea); *Antiquities* 14:80 (Scaurus' campaign to Petra 62 BC); *Antiquities* 14.128 (Antipatros gets troops from Arabia); *Antiquities* 15.361 (Cleopatra gets parts of Arabia from Antony); *Antiquities* 16.23 (Obodas 'II' is king of Arabia).
58 Josephus, *War* 1.274.
59 Josephus, *War* 1.534, 566, 574; idem, *Antiquities* 16.224, 227; 17.54.
60 Josephus, *War* 1.576–577.
61 Josephus, *War* 2.68. Malkhos, the supporter of the Romans in 66 BC, is called *ho áraps* (*War* 3.68; 5.290). Also Abias, the king in Adiabene, is called *ho áraps*; see p. 414.
62 Josephus, *Antiquities* 15:167, 172.
63 Josephus, *Antiquities* 16:284.
64 Josephus, *Antiquities* 16:289.
65 Josephus, *War* 1.276; idem, *Antiquities* 14.370 (Malchus); *War* 1.487 (Obaidas); *Antiquities* 14.220 (Obadas/Obodos/Obedos).
66 Josephus, *War* 2.68; idem, *Antiquities* 17.287.
67 Cf. Schürer, *History* I 580–583.
68 Appian, *Alexander* 1.1; Cassius Dio 48.41.5.
69 Strabo 16.4.24. Strabo seems to include him among the kings of the *árabes*, which, however, could be due to geographical systematization rather than ethnicity.
70 Josephus, *War* 1.274–278; idem, *Antiquities* 14.270, 272; cf. ibid. 14.128.
71 Hölscher, *Josephus* 1944–1947; Laqueur, *Nikolaos* 394; Wacholder, *Nicolaos* 62 ff.
72 Josephus, *Antiquities* 15.174, cf. Laqueur, *Nikolaos* 394; Hölscher, *Josephus* 1979–1980. There has been a discussion whether Josephus had access to the original memoirs or if he knew them through Nicolaus (Laqueur, *Nikolaos* 399–400).
73 Cf. Kasher, *Jews* 130–131.
74 Josephus, *War* 1.181; idem, *Antiquities* 14.121. Cf. Abel, *Histoire* 1 261–264. The word *epísēmos* means literally 'having a sign or a mark'.
75 Josephus, *War* 1.124; idem, *Antiquities* 14.122. Cf. Kasher, *Jews* 126–130.
76 Josephus, *War* 1.187–188; cf. *Antiquities* 14.128. The same word *xénos* is used by Herodotus for he who enters the *pístis* of the Arabs.
77 Josephus, *War* 1.267; idem, *Antiquities* 14.362.
78 Josephus, *War* 1.274–277; idem, *Antiquities* 14.370–374.
79 The flight of Herod the tyrant to Egypt away from the liberating Iranians could very well be the blueprint of the story of Jesus' birth under Herod, the adoration by the Iranian magi, and the flight of Joseph and Mary to Egypt in Matthew 2:1–15. The story, which must have been known among common people very early, perhaps through royal propaganda spreading a picture of Herod as a romantic hero, has been cleverly transformed by the evangelical tradition.
80 Cf. the time indications in Musil, *Arabia Petraea* I 401–408; II:1 340–343; II:2 249–252.

Shivta-Avdat: *c.* 4 hours = *c.* 25 kilometres (plain ground); Avdat-Qadesh Barnea (= ʕAyn Qudayrāt): between 11 and 13 hours = *c.* 70 kilometres; Wādī Mūsā-Wādī al-Ḥasā: 18 hours = *c.* 75 kilometres (rough terrain); ʕAqaba-Maʕān: 25 hours = 100 kilometres; Avdat-ʕAqaba: 43 hours = 140 kilometres. Davies (*Way* 23) indicates 32 kilometres as a normal figure for a day's journey in the ancient world. In *Targum Pseudo-Yonathan* to Numbers 10:33 three days' journey, probably on foot, in the desert is said to be equivalent to 36 Roman miles = *c.* 53 kilometres. Both *War* (1.122) and *Antiquities* (14.374) mention that Herod spent one night in a temple on the way. This could be Nessana in the upper course of Wādī al-ʕArīsh.

81 According to Kasher (*Jews* 124–125), Malchus supported the Parthians during the invasion and therefore did not want to have any dealings with Herod. This might be true and would, in fact, have given Herod very good reason to go to Petra where Malchus was.

82 The word is documented in Nabataean inscriptions (NQYBW) and interpreted as a personal name; cf. Cantineau, *Nabatéen* II:122. It is documented in Arabic for the first time about the twelve men from Medina coming to make the agreement with Muhammed in AD 622; cf. Watt, *Mecca* 147–148.

83 Plutarch, *Antony* 69; Kasher, *Jews* 150–151.

84 If the Elusa inscription is as old as is claimed, it could refer to such a relationship between Arabs and Nabataeans long before Aretas 'III'. For the possible nature of the ties between the two, see the following excursus.

85 Numbers 31:8; Joshua 13:21.

86 1 Chronicles 2:43-44.

87 Cf. Targum Jonathan and the Peshitta to Genesis 16:14 and Numbers 32:8 etc.

88 Cf. Davies, *Way* 16–18; 33–34.

89 This tannaitic *barayta* is found in several versions in the rabbinic texts, namely *Tosephta Shviʕit* 4.11 (Zuckermandel 66 l. 10–11), *Sifrê Devarîm ʕEqeb* 51 (Finkelstein 117–118), *Talmud Yerushalmi Sheviʕit* VI.1.36c and *Yalqûṭ Shimʕônī ʕEqeb* § 874. The last one is derived from *Sifrê*. For these testimonies, see Hildesheimer, *Beiträge* 51–55, 66–72. Since the mss. to Tosephta show two deviating versions of the list of names (Sussmann, *Barayta'* 223), the rabbinic literature presents four different versions of the list. During excavations in Rehov in lower Galilee carried out in 1974–76, a mosaic floor of a synagogue probably built in the fifth century AD was uncovered which contains the same list of names delineating the borders of the Holy Land according to early rabbinic tradition. The Rehov text must be considered the most trustworthy of all five versions. It turns out that of the literary texts the *Sifrê* version stands closest to the Rehov text.

90 *Mishnah Giṭṭin* 1.1–2.

91 *Targum Onqelos* to Genesis 16:14, 20:1.

92 The order of names in the literary transmitted versions can now be shown to be corrupt. The RQM in Trachonitis is given the epithet DḤGRʔ in *Sifrê* and *Tosephta* and a RPYḤ DḤGRʔ is located between Zered and RQM DGYʔ by *Tosephta* and *Yerushalmi.* The former is probably identical with the Reqem mentioned in 1 Chronicles 2:43 and 7:16 in northern Transjordan. The latter is obviously misplaced but since ḤGRʔ stands for Shur in the Old Testament and refers to the western Negev (cf. Hildesheimer, *Beiträge* 67) where we also find Raphia, this misplaced name probably represents a memory of the Negevite Ḥeger which we suppose is originally a place in the central Negev. The adornment of the Reqem in Trachonitis with the same epithet may be due to its being mixed up with Nabataean Reqem, a further indication of the transfer of the name Ḥagar/Petra from the Negev to the Nabataean capital. One might also suspect that the RQM DGYʔH in the border-list is in fact the site in the Negev and not Nabataean Petra. Otherwise the list would not mention any name between Petra and Ashqalon, which is strange. It might also be asked why Nabataean Petra would be considered a border town of the Promised Land by the rabbis. In the two Biblical border descriptions in Numbers 34 and Joshua 15, Qadesh Barneaʕ is a prominent southern border marker and it thus becomes very likely that RQM DGYʔH in the Rehov inscription in fact refers to the Negevite site. A Reqem is, in fact also mentioned in the family of Kaleb/Hebron, the patriarchs of the northern Negev (1 Chronicles 2:43). Once again we have a testimony

of the early confusion between the two 'Rocks'. The sites NYMRYN, MLḤ RZYZʕ and perhaps also ʔYGR SHDWTH between Zered and Reqem in the list should be looked for between the southern tip of the Dead Sea and Qadesh in the southern Negev. Eusebius (*Onomasticon* 138.21) mentions a Nimrin near Zoora/Zoʕar by the Dead Sea. 1 Chronicles 2:33 mentions a Zazah which should be located in the eastern Negev (belonging to the Yeraḥmeʔel-group). Cf. also Gazez in v. 46. Is G in Chronicles and R in the Rehov inscription a mispelling for D?

93 Cf. Davies, *Hagar*, especially 160–163. Mazar, *Reqem*, suggested that ḤGR was a term for 'fortified frontier' used for the entire borderline east and south of Palestine, which would explain why it occurs at different locations in the rabbinical text. Against this stands the fact that the texts themselves clearly indicate that there are two distinct places with this name. The reference to the term P-ḤQR in Sheshonq's description of his campaign in Palestine in the tenth century BC is not convincing.

94 Lane, *Lexicon* s.v. ḤǦR.

95 RQM DḤGRʔ is thus not Nabataean Petra (against Hartmann, *Namen* 144), nor is it Ḥiǧr in the Ḥiǧāz (correctly rejected by Davies, *Hagar* 158, 162). But the equation of ḤGRʔ with Petra is nevertheless correct, although not with Nabataean Petra but the Rock in the Negev. Hartmann (*Namen* 145) was more right than he realized when seeing that Diodorus (= Hieronymus) did not describe Nabataean Petra. Cf. Negev, *Beginnings* 127; idem, *Nabateans* 527.

96 Josephus, *Antiquities* 4.161.

97 Josephus, *Antiquities* 4.82.

98 For Uranius, see pp. 491 ff.

99 Stephanus 144.19–26.

100 Stephanus 482.15–16.

101 Negev identifies them with Obodas 'I', Alexander Jannaeus' adversary, and Aretas 'III' (*Nabateans* 537–538). The god ʕBDT is mentioned in the ʕEn Avdat inscription (Negev, *Obodas*). The name is also documented from Dedan/Liḥyān ʕBD/ʕBDH (Sima, *Inschriften* 59). For the documentation of the cult of Obodas, see Healey, *Religion* 147–151. For Obodas as a deity rather than a king, see Dijkstra, *Life* 319–321.

102 Negev's identification of it with 'Ḥauara' (= ʕAyn al-Hawāra?) north-east of ʕAqaba (Negev, *Nabateans* 538) is not very likely. It is difficult to see why the mythological apparatus was necessary to establish a military station.

103 The inscription mentioning the god ʕBDT is, in fact, found close by the ruins of the town Avdat; cf. Negev, *Obodas* and Healey, *Religion* 148.

104 Healey (*Religion* 148, 151) seems to be sceptical about the identification of Obodas the god with a historically documented/documentable king. Instead he assumes some kind of deity connected with the royal dynasty. Cf. also Dijkstra, *Life* 319–321. For the documentation of the names, see Weippert, *Jahresbericht* 296–299. The transfer of whole complexes of legends, including geographical names, to new political centres is not an isolated phenomenon. Suffice it to refer to the association of Biblical persons with Mecca or the recreation of Jerusalem in Ethiopia by king Lalibela.

105 Wenning, *Nabatäer* 200–204.

106 Strabo 16.4.21, 26.

107 Cf. p. 371. If the name followed the kings and Reqem was also renamed Petra, this could mean that the designation 'Rock' had some special, perhaps religious significance. The old residence in the Negev would have remained a centre for some time, probably with a cultic function. The present-day acropolis at Avdat with its agglomeration of churches rests upon an older structure going back to at least the first century AD, and it can be assumed that there are older layers under it. It gives the impression of having been a religious site for a long time, which is an argument for identifying it with the original 'rock'.

108 Strabo, 16.4.21. The existence of this title is confirmed by an inscription (RÉS 1100) by Syllaeus himself; cf. Bowersock, *Arabia* 51 n. 25; Hammond, *Nabataeans* 23; Kasher, *Jews* 163 note 86.

109 A dichotomy running through many aspects of 'Nabataean' culture is emphasized by Knauf,

Dushara 178. Cf. also Kasher, *Jews* 111. The analysis carried out here explains many of the inconsistencies in the picture of the 'Nabataeans' correctly pointed out by Dijkstra, *Life* 297–307.

110 This is probably also reflected in the passage in Apuleius' *Florida*, a collection of rhetorical successes by this author from the 160s AD. In one instance he refers to 'the Nabataean merchants, the Ituraeans poor in goods and the *arabes* rich in perfumes (*odorum divites arabas*)' (Apuleius, *Florida* 6.1). By *arabes* are here probably meant the South Arabians (Sabaeans etc.) whereas the people in Petra/Reqem are Nabataeans. It is not unlikely that Apuleius' source was Iuba or Athenodorus.

111 Unless he, in fact, is the king mentioned in the Elusa inscription.

112 There exist six coins with the inscription ʕBDT MLK NBṬW which differ from the others with this inscription (Meshorer, *Coins* 87–88). This has led scholars to postulate the existence of a king Obodas 'II', a son of Aretas 'III' and reigning 62–60 BC. (Meshorer, *Coins* 16–20). This king, however, is not documented in any other source and his existence remains somewhat uncertain. For a discussion, see Fiema/Jones, *King-list* 243–244, and Wenning, *Liste* 32–33.

113 For the latest versions of the list, see Fiema/Jones, *King-list* 245, and Wenning, *Liste* 38.

114 Cf. Starcky, *Pétra* 900, 924; Grohmann, *Nabataioi* 1454–1456; Roschinski, *Geschichte* 133; Bowersock, *Arabia* 11, 12; Shahid, *Prolegomena* 3–6; Healey, *Nabataeans*, more cautious in *Religion* 25 f.; cf. Knauf, *Origins* 57.

115 Nöldeke, *Inschriften,* especially 705 ff.; idem, *Namen* 122 ff. Cf. Healey, *Nabataeans*; Schürer, *History* I 575–576; Müller, *Altarabische* 30.

116 See in general Negev, *Names*; Müller, *Altarabische*.

117 See especially Knauf, *Midian* pp. 64–96; idem, *Edom* 66.

118 See Negev, *Names* pp. 4–5; Healey, *Religion* 10–11.

119 Cf. Knauf, *Edom* 76–77; idem, *Origins* 58–61; idem, *Ismael* 106 ff.; Bartlett, *Edom* 165–174; idem, *Edomites* I, *Edomites* II. The debate is somewhat distorted by the ideas of the Nabataeans being originally 'Arabs', i.e. bedouin and, consequently, immigrants, or the linking of Nabataeans with Nebayot, obviously a thought dear to many (cf. Knauf, *Edom* 76, and Graf, *Nabaṭ*). It is probably found for the first time in the targumic tradition (*Targum Jonathan* to Genesis 25:13 where Nebayot is Nabaṭ and Qedar is ʕArab) and taken up by Hieronymus (*Quaestiones in Genesim*, 31; cf. Quatremère, *Mémoire* 97). The identification is, however, linguistically impossible and was rejected as early as by Quatremère (*Mémoire* 97–98) but still supported, against all linguistic evidence, by for example Grohmann, *Nabataioi* 1454–1455, and Graf (*Nabaṭ*). For caveats against these concepts, see for example Parr, *Pottery* 204; MacDonald, *Kingdom* 106 ff.; Healey, *Religion* 25. It should be remarked that the Arabo-Islamic authors always make a clear distinction between *Nābit* = the eldest son of Ismāʕīl = Nebayot, the *Nabayāte* of the Assyrian inscriptions, and *nabaṭ/nabīṭ* = the farmers and tradesmen dealt with here.

120 Knauf, *Herkunft*; idem, *Dushara* 175; Graf, *Origin*; MacDonald, *Kingdom* 108. Healey, *Nabataeans*, on the other hand is a step backwards, working with antiquated concepts like 'race' and 'stock' and vague characterizations ('Nabataeans . . . might in fact have been Arabs of one sort or another' (2c), 'common basic culture' (1d) etc.). He is more cautious in *Religion* 9 ff.

121 Different ideas about their original homeland: Mesopotamia (Quatremère, *Mémoire* 100 ff.); South Arabia (Starcky, *Pétra* 903; Negev, *Beginnings*); the Persian Gulf (Milik, *Origines*; Healey, *Religion* 25); central Arabia (Roschinski, *Geschichte* 134); Arabia in general (Shahid, *Prolegomena* 11; Negev, *Nabateans* 527; Bartlett, *Edom* 174).

122 Tiglath Pileser: *Summary* 2:5 (Tadmor 130), 7:6 (Tadmor 158), 11:6 (Tadmor 194); Sennacherib: *Annals* H2 I:48 (Luckenbill 25), *Campaign* 1: A1:14 (Luckenbill 49) A1:56 (Luckenbill 54); *Bellino Cylinder* 15 (Luckenbill 57); cf. Dougherty, *Sealand* 58–60, 70–71; Brinkman, *History* 267–285, especially 270; Graf, *Origin* 59–60.

123 Zadok, *West Semites* 224–225. For the identity between these *nabaṭu* and the later Nabataeans, see Hommel, *Ethnographie* 193, 590 f.

124 Josephus, *War* 5.474.

125 The passage is in disorder and obviously contained some information that was not properly understood by the Greek translator. The MSS read: 'a certain Adiabenian (*Adiabēnós tis*) son of Nabataîos named according to/because of fate (*apò tēs tykhēs*) and *agiras/agēras/ageiras*, which means "lame" (*khōlós*)'. The last gloss is based upon the Aramaic word *ḥgīrā*, 'lame'. This interpretation is, however, somewhat absurd since it is told in the context of how this lame Adiabenian takes part in a rush with torches against the Romans. The word 'and' (*kai*) is difficult to account for and, for example, the Latin translation has read it together with the following as Ceagiras, i.e. another name. It is likely that neither *agiras* nor *nabataîos* is to be read as a personal name. The latter must mean 'Nabataean'. It is likely that the former is to be understood as the 'name': the Nabataean was called *agiras* for some special reason. The possible meaning of *agiras* will be discussed pp. 585 ff.

126 Cf.p. 266.

127 It is worth pointing out that the occurrences of the word 'Nabataean' in inscriptions all come from the northern borders of the Provincia Arabia, i.e. from the area where they first appear in texts from the third and second centuries BC; see Graf, *Nabaṭ*.

128 See pp. 462 ff.

129 There is an uncertain variant to the text: *napataioi*; see Sprenger, *Geographie* no. 331 (pp. 204–205). Cf. also Pliny 12.98.

130 Sprenger, *Geographie* § 274 p. 171. It is likely that the word in Ptolemy goes back to a plural of *nabaṭ*: *ʔanbāṭ* with an assimilation of the *n*, a sound-change characteristic of later dialects of western Arabia: *ʔabbāṭ*. Glaser (*Skizze* 213 ff.) opted for Ṭuwayq further east and located the *apataioi* south-east of Mecca (ibid. 256). This seems less likely. Ptolemy locates them close to the Athrîtai, Maisaimanoi and Oudenoi. It seems plausible to associate these names with Yathrib, Marsiman and Wādī respectively, which brings us to the central Ḥiǧāz.

131 See pp. 000–000.

132 CIS II:199; cf. Cantineau, *Nabatéen* II:28–29; Healey, *Inscriptions* 68–80. The tomb is made by a man originating from Taymāʔ and it is said to be ḤRM KḤLYQT ḤRM NBṬW WŠLMW LʕLM, 'holy according to the rule of holiness of the Nabataeans and the Shalamians for ever'. The king in Petra, Aretas 'IV', is mentioned in the dating of the inscription. For the closeness of Salamians and Nabataeans, see Stephanus 550.

133 Cf. pp. 149, 298.

134 CIH 541:32, 38-39; Philby 103, 135a (= Philby/Tritton, *Inscriptions* 123, 127); cf. Ryckmans, *Notes* 150, 152; Jamme, *Désastre*.

135 For example, al-Masʕūdī, *Murūǧ* II:78, 94; III:106–107; al-Bakrī, *Muʕǧam* 33; Ḥamza, *Tārīkh* 76. A useful survey is still Quatremère, *Mémoire* 100–113; cf. Nöldeke, *Namen* 123–124; Fahd, *Nabaṭ*.

136 According to Yāqūt (*Muʕǧam* 5:566) the *nabaṭ* are identical with the *Ṣābiʔa* in southern Iraq, i.e. the Mandaeans. According to *Lisān* (s.v. NBṬ) they inhabit the *baṭāʔiḥ* (= the stagnant waters) of the two ʕIrāq.

137 al-Masʕūdī, *Murūǧ* V:119 (a village near Mosul inhabited by *nabīṭ*); cf. Yāqūt, *Muʕǧam* 2:384 (s.v. Khābūr: *nabaṭ* navigating on the river) = verse from Ibn al-ʔAʕrābī.

138 Yāqūt, *Muʕǧam* 2:355 (s.v. Ḥawwārīn) = verse from Zufar b. al-Ḥārith.

139 *ʔAghānī* 18:52: 'From which region (*ṭaniyya*) rose Quraysh//they were a bunch, *nabaṭ*-like (*maʕšaran mutanabbiṭīnā*).' Cf. Fahd, *Divination* 123 n. 2. The *Lisān* (s.v. NBṬ) quotes Ibn ʕAbbās saying that Quraysh were *nabaṭ* from Kutha in Iraq.

140 al-Bakrī, *Muʕǧam* s.v. Zandaward.

141 Mubarrad, *Kāmil* 388:7.

142 al-Balādhurī, *ʔAnsāb* V:99; Iṣfahānī, *ʔAghānī* 15:72.

143 Ibn Hishām, *Sīra* 911 = Wāqidī, *Maghāzī* III:1051; ibid. I:395; III:989. This reminds us of the special Nabataean quarter in Damascus, *an-Naybaṭūn*.

144 For other references to *nabaṭ* in early Islamic tradition, see Bashear, *Arabs* 79–80; Hamarneh, *Nabateans*.

145 Iṣfahānī, *ʔAghānī* 13:80.

146 *Lisān* s.v. NBṬ.

147 The *Kitāb al-ʔAghānī* (5:288) has a note about the speech of the *nabaṭ* in Iraq. They say *ḍahabtū* instead of *ḍahabtŭ*, which shows (a) that they spoke Arabic, (b) that their speech had characteristics preserved in the modern *qəltu* dialects, the ancient vernacular of Iraq, cf. Corriente, *Marginalia* 55–56 note 2.
148 Cf. Morony, *Iraq* 170, 214.
149 Yāqūt, *Muʕǧam* III:634 ll. 16–17 (s.v. *ʕarabatun*).
150 Ǧāḥiẓ, *Ḥayawān* 4:377.
151 Iṣfahānī, *ʔAghānī* 11:344: 'You are for me from the ʔArāqim [a tribe in Taghlib]/ an *ʕarabī* while your grandfather (*ǧadduka*) was a *nabaṭī*.'
152 Cf. the notice in aṭ-Ṭabarī (*Tārīkh* I:830) where the city founded by Shāpur II in Mayshan (Mesene) was called Dīma/Rīma in *nabaṭiyya*, which could refer to the language of a Nabati population who need not necessarily have spoken Aramaic.
153 An interesting case is the eastern Naǧd, where we have previously located villages inhabited by *ʕarab* at the beginning of the seventh century AD (cf. p. 50). According to *Lisān* (s.v. NBṬ) there was in that area, the Dahnāʔ, a sandy desert called Waʕsāʔ an-Nabīṭ (*waʕs* means quicksand).
154 Cf. Fahd, *Nabaṭ* 836. In an inscription in Syria (*Inscriptiones Graecae ad res Romanas pertinentes* III:1257, cf. Knauf, *Origins* 57; Graf, *Nabaṭ* 834) a man identifies himself as being from the *genos nabas*. The same word is used by Josephus for two of the conspirators against Herod, who were *árabes to génos* 'Arabs according to *génos*' (*War* 1.576–577). It is also noteworthy that the Nabataean king reigning during Athenodorus' visit is said to belong to a special *génos*. The word *génos* may mean 'birth, genealogy' but can also mean 'rank, social class': the *génos* of philosophers, fishmongers, peasants etc. (Liddell/Scott, *Lexicon* s.v. génos V).
155 Nöldeke observed this very clearly; cf. *Namen* 124. Cf. also Macdonald, *Kingdom* 107 f.
156 Quatremère, *Mémoire* 130–131.
157 Nöldeke, *Inschriften;* idem, *Namen* 122–126.
158 Cf. the basic arguments in Cantineau, *Nabatéen et arabe*. Knauf seems to be the only one not quite comfortable with received opinion. Even though he tries to uphold the traditional view he has noted the problem; see *Origins* 61. We should also note the obvious difficulties in defining Nabateans in modern national terms demostrated by Healey, *Religion* 9–12.
159 Nöldeke, *Namen* 123–124; Krauss, *Nachrichten* 338. Cf. also O'Connor, *Loanwords*.
160 Also Nöldeke operated with an immigration hypothesis: the Nabataeans were what could be called 'versunkene Araber', having left traditional Arab ways of life, and were found as such by later invading tribes. This was the reason for the spread of the term *nabaṭ* as a designation for settled farmers in other parts of the Middle East (*Namen* 124). Healey seems to incline towards a similar view, cf. *Religion* 9f., 25.
161 This may explain a curious note in Strabo where it is said that 'the Idoumaîoi are *nabataîoi*' (16.2.34). The Elusa inscription mentions a ḤRTT MLK NBṬW. If this refers to one of the Arab rulers in the Negev half a century before the Roman conquest of Syria, the Idumaeans may well have been 'Nabataeans' to the Arab ruler, namely in the meaning established here: peaceful subjects under the protection of a ruling caste of warriors. The title of the Arab rulers 'king of the Nabataeans', may thus have been used long before the transfer of the residence to Reqem.
162 There are a few instances in later inscriptions where individuals appear as Nabateans (cf. Healey, *Religion* 9). The most interesting is the Palmyrene inscription CIS II 3973, where someone called himself NBṬY RWḤYʔ, i.e. belonging both to the Nabataeans and to the tribe or group called RWḤ. Healey (*Religion* 9, 145) translates 'A Nabataean of the Rawāḥ tribe'. This might be correct and could be easily explained if Nabataean is a term indicating a kind of juridical state, not an ethnic identity. In that case we do not have to assume some kind of double allegiance to two different tribes. We do not even have to assume that these Nabataeans came from the Arabo-Nabataean kingdom.
163 Cf. *Lisān* s.v. NBṬ.
164 Beeston *et al.*, *Dictionary* s.v. NBṬ; Ricks, *Lexicon* s.v. NBṬ.
165 Hoftijzer/Jongeling, *Dictionary* s.v. NBṬ (= Imperial Aramaic, cf. Jewish Babylonian

Aramaic in T.B. *Taʕanît* 4a which might be an ancient Aramaic proverb); Leslau, *Dictionary* s.v. NBṬ. In Geez it also has the meaning 'to boil (over)' .

166 von Soden, *Handwörterbuch* s.v. nabāṭum.

167 Cf. Tairan, *Personennamen* 212–214; Said, *Personennamen* 165–166.

168 Cf. Tairan, *Personennamen* 212.

169 Tairan (*Personnennamen* 212) translates NBṬʔL as 'ʔIl has appeared' or 'has brought forth'.

170 Assumed by Starcky, *Pétra* 900. Both ʕRB and NBṬ occur as a verbal element in personal names, but there is no evidence for the existence of an eponym to either of the two groups.

171 Stephanus 466: *ho ek moikheías genómenos*.

172 See p. 345.

173 A Nabataean name RTYMW is documented (Cantineau, *Nabatéen* II 148, Arabic *raṯīm* 'having a broken nose') and Merkel suggests that this might have been an epithet of the king (*Festsetzungen* 305). It remains uncertain and, in any case, the name in Iustinus is a popular etymology or a pun on *érōs*. For the identity of the king see Merkel, *Festsetzungen* 290–-293.

14

ARABS AND ROMANS UNTIL THE TIME OF TRAJAN

Arabs and Romans in the Middle East

The picture of the ethno-political conditions of Arabs in Syria and Mesopotamia in the first half of the first century BC is fairly coherent. We find the Arabs governed by phylarchs along the river Euphrates, but we also find them around Emesa. They were probably also present in Chalcis south-east of Beroea/Aleppo. These latter would have been in close contact with those along the river. There was further a wedge of Arabs and *skēnîtai* from the central Syrian steppe into the green land on the Emesa plain. The Arabs here were thus very close to the Arabs living in the Antilebanon together with the Ituraeans. The presence of all these Arabs in Syria was the result of the policy of the Seleucid rulers. A similar policy had been followed by Tigranes by settling Arabs in Amanus on the border to Cilicia. The Arabs in Transjordan, implanted there by the Ptolemies, are not mentioned after the time of Alexander Jannaeus. We do not have any certain evidence for the presence of Arabs in Osrhoene near Edessa from this period, although it is likely that they were there already. They will be documented more that half a century after the Roman conquest. Neither do we have any reliable information about the presence of groups designated as Arabs from the rest of Mesopotamia and southern Babylonia during this period.

The Roman conquest of Syria created stability, at least compared to what the situation had been like before. Pompey's settlement consisted of a Roman military presence in Syria proper, transformed to a Roman province, and a system of alliances with local rulers forming a *cordon sanitaire* around it. Of these, the weakest links were the restless southern rulers, the new dynasty of the Idumaeans in Jerusalem and the Arabo-Nabataeans in Petra. The Ituraeans remained in charge of large parts of the Lebanon, and the new dynasty of Sampsiceramus ruled Emesa and its surroundings. Thus, the 'Arab wedge', obviously established in the turmoil during the first half of the first century BC, was preserved and cemented by the Romans. The remains of the imperial institutions in Syria, ultimately going back to the days of the Achaemenids, had broken down for good and were successively replaced by Roman administration. The phylarchs and ethnarchs of the Arabs that had established themselves in the very heart of Greater Syria were allowed to continue, and became part of the system created by the Romans. On the other side of the Euphrates, the Abgarids in Edessa (together with other local rulers further north) in the same way were backed up as a Roman ally in order to function as a buffer against Parthia. The river itself, which was the formal boundary between the two empires, was guarded by the same Arab phylarchs.

The Roman conquest of Syria did not, however, automatically bring peace and stability to the troubled land. It took some time before the situation was settled. One of the main reasons for the troubles was the ongoing birthpangs bringing forth the new political system in the Roman empire, known as the principate, an order that would turn out to be more apt to govern the vast empire than the old republic. The new provinces in the East, including their Arab inhabitants and their neighbours, had to try to catch up with the different strongmen regularly appearing and disappearing during the entire first century BC: Crassus, Pompey, Caesar, Cassius, Mark Antony together with Cleopatra VII, until one of them remained, Octavian.

The Syrian province had a precarious position as the outpost against the only rival of the Roman empire that remained: Parthia. To this came the fixation of many Romans with the image of Alexander the Great. The idea of becoming a new Alexander was to haunt the minds of many Roman generals and lead them to launch more or less well-planned campaigns against the heirs of Darius III, as a rule with disastrous results.

Arabs and the battle of Carrhae

From the first ten years of Roman rule in Syria we have some notes about the Arabs in the Middle East in Appian's history of the Syrian wars:

> . . . Marcius Philippus . . . and Lentulus Marcellinus . . . spent the whole of [their] two years in warding off the attacks of the neighbouring *árabes*.

Marcius and Lentulus were the direct successors of Scaurus, Pompey's general who was the first governor of Syria. Lentulus' successor, Aulus Gabinius, appointed in 58 BC, may have belonged to those suffering from the Alexander-complex:

> As [their successor Aulus Gabinius] was setting out for the war with Parthia, Mithradates, king of the Parthians, who had been driven out of his kingdom by his brother Orodes, persuaded him to turn his forces from the *árabes*, against the Parthians.[1]

These passages have been interpreted as dealing with Arabs somewhere in Syria, for example, in al-Lağā.[2] From what is told in Josephus it is more likely that they are about the Arabo-Nabataeans.[3]

In 55 BC the new governor of Syria, Licinius Crassus, one of the members of the first triumvirate, arrived in the East, eager to take up the competition with Caesar and Pompey by conquering new provinces as they had done. Our main source for his activities is the passage dealing with the Parthian war in Plutarch's biography of Crassus. Plutarch obviously had before him a very good source, in which Caius Cassius Longinus, Julius Caesar's future murderer, plays a prominent role. He was an officer in Crassus' campaign, and it has been assumed that the account is ultimately based on a *Memoria* written by him.[4] Plutarch may have known it via Livy, who told of the war in 53 BC in book 106 of *Ab urbe condita*. Also Cassius Dio's account probably follows Livy, whereas Annaeus Florus and Appian, who both mention the war briefly, have had another source, very negative towards Crassus.

Having spent his first year as governor plundering Syrian temples in order to finance his expedition, Crassus crossed the Euphrates in the spring of 53 BC.[5] He thus found himself in the same geographic position as Cyrus the Younger in 401 BC. According to

Cassius Dio, Alkhaudonios the *arábios* now defected, whereas Abgar (II) of Edessa supported the enterprise with money.[6] It is said that Crassus' counsellors wanted him to follow the river Euphrates when marching against Seleucia, the residence of the Parthian king on the lower Tigris. But he followed the advice of another:

> While Crassus was still investigating and considering these matters, there came a *phylarkhos* of *árabes*, Ariamnes by name, a crafty and treacherous man, and one who proved to be, of all the mischiefs which fortune combined for the destruction of the Romans, the greatest and most consummate.[7]

According to Plutarch, this phylarch advised Crassus to march through the steppe of the Ǧazīra, leaving the Euphrates, heading for the upper Balīkh near Harran. Cassius Dio, however, blames Abgar of Edessa for having given this advice and accuses him of foul play with the Parthians.[8] In two less renowned historians, Florus and Festus, we find a certain Mazarus, a Syrian refugee, blamed as the origin of the bad advice.[9] We are thus confronted with a classic source problem, which can be solved only when we have surveyed the whole campaign.

The Roman army now faced the same hardships as Cyrus the Younger had done in 401 BC. In Plutarch's account, the 'treacherous Arab' is said to have given a piece of geographical information in order to encourage the thirsty legionaries:

> 'Is it through Campania that you think you are marching, yearning for its fountains and streams and shades and baths and taverns? Do you not remember that you are traversing the borderland between the land of the *árabes* and that of the Assyrians?'[10]

The *árabes* could very well be those mentioned by Posidonius and refer to the phylarchs in Parapotamia.

The confrontation with the Parthian *cataphracti* south of Carrhae, present-day Harran, ended with a disaster for the Romans. According to Cassius Dio, the Romans were attacked from behind by the Osrhoenians, whereas Plutarch only mentions an attack by the light cavalry.[11]

Crassus survived and took refuge on a hill nearby, starting negotiations with the Parthian general. Plutarch tells us that Cassius, who had now abandoned the army and was heading for Carrhae and Syria, had guides who were *árabes* and who gave him astrological advice.[12] While this was going on:

> after a short time there came *árabes* from the barbarians who knew Crassus and Cassius well from sight in the camp before the battle.[13]

These Arabs induced Crassus to negotiate with the Parthians, which turned out to be a trap. The negotiations ended with Crassus being killed by the treacherous Parthians and then followed a general massacre of the surviving Romans. In connection with this Plutarch says:

> Some of them [the Romans] went down and delivered themselves up, but the rest scattered during the night, and of these a very few made their escape; the rest of them were hunted down by the *árabes*, captured and cut to pieces.[14]

Instead of constructing a harmonizing account from the contradictory sources, we should try to find out what the contradictions mean. It is immediately clear that in Cassius Dio's account Abgar, the king of Osrhoene, is the traitor. In Plutarch, the role of the traitor is played by the Arabs. There is no reason to assume that Ariamnes, the phylarch of the Arabs, is identical with Abgar II of Edessa. The fact that Florus and Festus have an otherwise unknown Syrian as the giver of the bad advice makes the blaming of Abgar and the Arabs look like an attempt to put the blame on more important protagonists than the insignificant Mazarus, who may thus have been the real culprit.[15] Crassus may have made a mistake which had such disastrous consequences that it was necessary to find a more plausible explanation.[16] We observe that the Arabs blamed by Plutarch's source, which is pro-Cassian, in the aftermath of Carrhae sided with the Parthians and became Cassius' main enemy. The pro-Cassian source used by Plutarch may have had an interest in painting the Arabs in dark colours. Cassius Dio's *History* was written when the kings of Edessa had supported the wrong side in the struggle for the imperial Roman throne after Commodus, and Osrhoene, except Edessa, had been made a Roman province in the 190s AD. In 214 AD Edessa was made a Roman colony and the last king deposed.[17] Dio's account could thus represent a legitimation for the incorporation of the notoriously unreliable ally Edessa into the empire.

The important fact for this investigation is that Abgar and the Arabs appear as two different entities. It is clear that Arabs were employed by the Parthians: these used camels for transport, which were probably handled by Arabs.[18] It is tempting to look for our old friend Alkhaudonius in the Parthian ranks. The most trustworthy indication of Arabs on the Roman side is the passage about the Arab astrologers. Soothsayers of all kinds seem to have played a prominent role in this campaign, and their comments are continuously referred to by the sources. We know from Cicero that the Arabs were renowned as soothsayers, and it is likely that their knowledge of these things became known to the Romans at this time.[19] Since all the other mentions of Arabs in Plutarch's report about this campaign aim at pointing out a scapegoat, they should be read with some scepticism. The only thing we can say is that it is not unlikely that the Romans had Arab scouts, since they were passing through their territory and had Arabs as allies. Their role has, however, been strongly distorted by the tendentious reports of the campaign. The same holds for the role of Abgar of Edessa.

Arabs and the Parthian invasion after Carrhae

The Roman débâcle at Carrhae sent waves of unrest through the Middle East for several years afterwards. The Roman commander of the army after Crassus, Cassius, spent the whole year 52 BC skirmishing with Parthian troops. In 51, when the new governor of Syria, Bibulus, arrived, a large Parthian army crossed the Euphrates. We have first-hand documentation of this through the letters sent by the new governor of Cilicia, Marcus Tullius Cicero, where the spirit of the dramatic course of events can still be felt:

> [To the consuls, praetors and tribunes, autumn 51 BC]
>
> I received a dispatch from Tarcondimotus, who is regarded as our most loyal ally beyond Mount Taurus, and the best friend of the Roman people. He

> reported that Pacorus, son of Orodes, king of the Parthians, had crossed the Euphrates with a very strong force of Parthian cavalry and pitched his camp at Tyba, and that a serious uprising had been stirred up in the province of Syria. On the same day I received a dispatch dealing with the same incidents from Iamblichus, the leading *phylarchus* of the *Arabes*, a man who is generally considered to be loyally disposed and friendly to our Republic.[20]

Tyba is a location in northern Syria, perhaps not far from Aleppo.[21] A couple of months later the situation had changed; Cassius had already defeated the Parthians in October 51. In Cicero's letters, it seems rather as if he himself was the victor:

> [To Cato, January 50 BC]
>
> Meanwhile I was informed by written and oral messages from many quarters that strong forces of Parthians and *Arabes* had approached the town of Antioch, and that a large body of their cavalry which had crossed over into Cilicia had been cut to pieces by some squadrons of my cavalry and a praetorian cohort which was on garrison duty at Epiphanea.[22]

That Arabs played an important role in the campaign is evident from another passage in a letter by Cicero:

> [To Appius Pulchrus, October 51 BC]
>
> You ask about the Parthians; I do not think there were any Parthians; *Arabes* they were, partially equipped as Parthians, but it is said that they have all returned. There is not a single enemy, they tell me, in Syria.[23]

Cicero obviously tries to play down the importance of the Parthian presence, since his own contribution to the fighting was on a rather modest scale. We know instead that it was Cassius who rolled back the Parthians and the Arabs who had reached the walls of Antioch. Cassius' victory led Orodes to call off the operations in the summer of 50 BC, and the Euphrates remained the border between the two empires.

It is reasonable to assume that the Arab phylarchs around the Euphrates, as well as the kings of Osrhoene, from now on sided with the Parthians. From Cicero's letter it appears that only the dynast of Emesa, Iamblichus, remained loyal to Rome. The result of Crassus' attempt to become a new Alexander was thus the weakening of Roman positions in the east, probably including the loss of Osrhoene as an ally.

Arabs and the anti-Caesarians

After the death of Crassus, Caesar and Pompey were left as rivals for the power in Rome. The pattern in the power struggle leading to the final establishment of the principate was that one pretender had support in the West, mainly Italy and Spain, the other in the Orient, mainly Egypt and Syria. Pompey's position in the East was largely due to what he had performed there in the 60s. The decisive battle between Caesar and Pompey was fought at Pharsalus in Macedonia in 48 BC. Here Pompey seems to have had massive support from the East, among whom we note both Jews and Arabs. Two sources have preserved this information, both probably built on Livy, who described Pompey's final battle at Pharsalus in book 111 of his great work.[24] One is Appian, who in the second century AD described the allies:

> All the nations sent aid to Pompey . . . Syria, Phoenice, the people of the Hebrews, and *árabes*.[25]

The other is Lucan, who in the 60s AD wrote an epic poem, the *Pharsalia*, about the civil war between Pompey and Caesar, in which he mentions Arabs as Pompey's allies on several occasions:

> He [the East wind] drove all the clouds he found in his own clime
> to the west with Nabataean blasts,
> all the mists that *Arabes* feel and which the land
> of Ganges breathes forth.[26]
> . . .
> Next, the Ituraeans and Medes and the free *Arabes*,
> formidable archers, shot their arrows at no mark,
> aiming only at the sky overhead.[27]

The most remarkable point about these two passages is the distinction between Arabs on the one hand, and Ituraeans and Nabataeans on the other.

After Pharsalus, Pompey fled to Egypt. When Caesar came there to fight him, he received support from several local rulers who felt the new direction of the political winds. Their leader was Antipatros, head of the rising family of Idumaeans in Judaea. Among the allies were people from Nabataea, where Antipater had family connections, as well as Ptolemy, son of Soaemus, living in Mount Lebanon, and a certain Iamblichus.[28] The latter appears to be coming from Emesa but this is not certain. The general picture is, however, that the local dynasts in Syria now changed sides and sought recognition from the new strongman of the empire.

The loyalty of those mentioned was, however, not very reliable. In 46 BC a supporter of Pompey, Caecilius Bassus, started an insurrection in Apamaea in Syria, which lasted for three years. Among his allies we find many old acquaintances: Sampsiceramus and his son Iamblichus of Emesa and Arethusa; Ptolemy, son of Mennaeus in the Lebanon; and last but not least, Alchaedamnus, king of the Rhambaei. The latter is said to have been the friend of the Romans but to have retreated into Mesopotamia after a conflict with them.[29] We have suggested that this defection from Rome occurred in connection with the venture of Crassus in 53 BC. The participation of Alchaedamnus in the revolt indicates that there might have been Parthian interests involved in the Bassus revolt, since Alchaedamnus resided on the Parthian side of the river.

Bassus received unexpected support through the murder of Caesar in 44 BC. One of Caesar's murderers was Cassius, whose performance in the events of 53–50 BC we have heard about. He now arrived in Syria and took control of Bassus' men. This explains the note in Appian about the troops of the anti-Caesarians at Philippi in 42 BC:

> Cassius had . . . four thousand mounted bowmen, *árabes*, Medes and Parthians.[30]

From what has been said, the presence of Parthians together with Arabs at Philippi is not surprising. The anti-Caesarians were obviously ready to use even the Parthian enemy and his allies as a weapon in their struggle against Caesar's heirs, Octavian and Mark Antony. It would be interesting to know who the Arabs were. They could be the same ones who had supported Pompey at Pharsalus, then sided with Bassus, finally to end up with Cassius and Brutus at Philippi. At any rate, the same names tend to appear again and again.

When Antony and Cleopatra ruled the East

Cassius and Brutus lost at Philippi, and so did their allies. Antony was already in Syria in 41 BC, touring the country and taking Palmyra, which however had already been deserted.[31] He purged Syria of local politicians with doubtful loyalty, some of whom we have already met with. Many of them fled to Parthia. This was one of the reasons why the Parthians tried to stop the two conquerors from the West by launching a new invasion of the Roman Orient in 40 BC, led by Pacorus and the Roman defector Labienus. The Parthians this time took all of Syria as well as Palestine. The tide was, however, turned once again, this time by Antony's legate Publius Ventidius Bassus. After a decisive victory in 38 BC, Syria and Palestine were again under Roman control.

For the next few years the Orient was under the sway of Mark Antony and his ally, the queen of Egypt, Cleopatra VII. It was dominated by the ambitions of both to carve out an Oriental empire for themselves. Antony made two great campaigns in Armenia and came close to the Caspian Sea. He is said to have given Cleopatra large parts of Syria, in 34 BC, including parts of the Judaean and Arabo-Nabataean kingdoms, as a gift to his queen. It encompassed the whole coast of Palestine as far as the Eleutherus river, stretching across the Lebanon and down the Jordan valley including Transjordan:

> He had presented them [the children of Cleopatra] with extensive portions of Arabia in the districts both of Malchus and of the Ituraeans, for he executed Lysanias, whom he himself had made king over them.[32]

This was actually the end of the Ituraean principality, which from now on was divided in at least four different tetrarchies with different destinies during the hundred years that followed.[33] The notice in Dio Cassius is interesting in that it shows that Arabia was a term for an area larger than the two kingdoms mentioned. Herod managed to rent the Jericho oasis as well as the administration of the tribute from Malchus in Petra.[34]

The liquidation of the ruling house of Ituraea shows that Antony had misgivings about the loyalty of the local potentates in his realm. His last documented dealing with Arabs also shows that their relationship was somewhat strained. In 31 BC, when the decisive moment was approaching and Antony and Octavian stood against each other at the mouth of the Gulf of Corinth preparing for the battle at Actium, Antony is said to have become nervous when Agrippa had crushed his cavalry and the king of Cappadocia had defected:

> And because of this, he killed others, and also Iamblichus, the king of some *árabes*, after having tortured him.[35]

Also according to Plutarch, Antony had *árabes* in his army in the final battle.[36] It is not certain who this Iamblichus was, but he could very well belong to the rulers of Emesa, who had a tradition of being pro-Roman. It is not very likely that the torturing and killing of his allies was due to Antony's bad temper alone. He might have had suspicions that they were not all too trustworthy, especially after the defection of the Cappadocian king. We notice, however, that Arabs did take part in the battle that ended the Roman civil wars and that they supported the strongman in the East. According to a late source, the sea at Actium after the battle:

> continually yielded up the purple and spoils of the *Arabes* and the Sabaeae and a thousand other Asiatic peoples.[37]

This picture is somewhat hyperbolic, and the presence of Sabaeans at Actium is not verified and not very likely. But it seems certain that some Arabs, probably those from Emesa, took part and had to pay dearly for it.[38] The Arabs in Syria had once again backed the wrong horse. After Actium, everybody in the East, most of whom had made the same mistake as the Arabs, had to come to terms with the new strongman, this time the only one remaining in the whole empire: Caius Iulius Caesar Octavianus.

Rome and the Arabs in the reign of Augustus

When Rome finally took control of Egypt, she inherited the traditional Egyptian ambitions in the Red Sea, including Arabia. This also meant that the Romans from now on needed more systematic knowledge about the peninsula and adjacent lands. This is reflected in three literary works that were written in Latin in Augustus' time. Two of these, Marcus Vipsanius Agrippa's world survey and the geographical compendium later used by Pomponius Mela in the middle of the first century AD, were based on summaries of earlier Hellenistic world geographies which included descriptions of Arabia. The third one, Iuba's *Arabica*, was a monograph describing not only Arabia but also the Middle East. Through these works Romans could for the first time get an idea about Arabia (and other countries as well) in their own language.

All these three original sources are lost, and we know them only through later authors: Pomponius Mela and Pliny the Elder or, as far as Agrippa is concerned, through later maps partially based upon it, as well as some preserved parts of the text itself. Agrippa's Arabian geography is not altogether clear, since the text is not well transmitted. In it we find Eratosthenian terms like *Scenitae* and *Arabia Eudaemon*.[39] There seems to have been a difference between the *Scenitarum Arabia* immediately east of lower Egypt (i.e. the delta), and a larger Arabia (*Eudaemon*?) east of upper Egypt, limited by the Arabian and the Persian Gulf.[40] There is also mention of an Arabia 'close to Egypt', which is the land between the Nile and the Red Sea.[41] These two Arabias are part of an area stretching from the Nile to the Persian side of the Persian Gulf consisting of Arabia, Nubia and upper Egypt.[42] The northern border of this area is unclear in the preserved text. It is said to be limited in the north 'by Pharon and by Arabia (*ab Arabia*)'. The latter is emendated by modern editors to Nabataean Arabia (*Nabataea Arabia*). It is well in accordance with Eratosthenes to locate the Arabia of the *Scenitae* between the peninsula and Syria, although the emendation is more doubtful. The identity of Pharon is unknown and may be a distortion of some other name, perhaps Pelusium, in Coptic Peremon. It seems that Agrippa had some acquaintance with Erastothenian geography, but it is not evident how much of it he knew.

It has been assumed that a shadowy picture of Agrippa's survey has been preserved in a group of medieval maps from western Europe.[43] The most striking feature in these is the apparent absence of the Arabian peninsula or at least its minimal size. With this go the insignificant dimensions of the Persian Gulf, which is the more remarkable since the Red Sea seems to have the correct proportions. The surprising impression is thus that the picture of the world was largely based on a pre-Eratosthenian picture at least as far as the Orient was concerned, and leaned heavily on a tradition that goes back to Hecataeus.

From what has been said about Agrippa, the tracing of this chartographic tradition to him remains doubtful. It is more likely that it goes back to another geographical survey, compiled in Rome at the same time. The source used by Pomponius Mela for his *Chorographia*, written in the 40s AD, which was also used by Pliny, seems to have been a summary of Greek geographical knowledge compiled at the beginning of the first century BC.[44] As far as Arabia is concerned, it can be stated that the author did not use Eratosthenes. At least the expected terminology, *Scenitae*, *Deserta*, the four kingdoms in South Arabia and also *Eudaemon* in the Erastothenian meaning, is lacking. Arabia seems to be used for three main areas. One is described as stretching to the Mediterranean between Egypt and Syria/Palestine, containing the city of Pelusium as well as the mountain Casius. This is clearly taken from Herodotus or a source based on him.[45] The Red Sea is called *Sinus Arabicus* and is named after this Arabia, which is the Herodotean view.[46] It is further said to be surrounded by *Arabes*, which is relevant for the northern parts of the Red Sea, representing Arabia as visited by Herodotus.[47]

The description of the Euphrates belongs to the descriptions of the two gulfs. The Arabian Gulf is said to be narrow, stretching to the Casius mountain in Arabia. The Persian Gulf is said to be circular in shape with an outlet 'with straight shores' to the ocean.[48] Opposite the outlet (*in parte quae pelagi ostio adversa est*) is the land of Babylonians, Chaldaeans and the Two Rivers.[49] Of the Euphrates it is said that, having left the Anatolian mountains, it turns towards the south and having passed by the Syrians and then the *Arabes* dies out in the desert.[50] This remark must refer to the Arabia between the rivers described by Xenophon.[51]

Pomponius then continues:

> The other shore [of the Persian Gulf] is limited by a plain which stretches between both oceans (*pelagi*). It is called Arabia with the surname *eudaemon*. It is narrow but a great producer of cinnamon, frankincense (*tus*) and other perfumes. The Sabaei occupy the largest part, the Macae the part closest to the outlet and opposite the Carmanians. The sea-front between the outlets is full of forests and dangerous reefs. There are some islands in the middle: the most famous of them is Ogyris, since on it is the tomb of the King Erythras.[52]

The notice about the island and the royal tomb comes from Nearchus.[53] This, together with the geographical description, makes it clear that it deals with the southern shore of the Persian Gulf, not the Arabian peninsula as a whole. The two oceans are not the Red Sea and the Persian Gulf but rather the latter and the Indian Ocean. The outlets are those of the Gulf and of the Tigris. Pomponius and his source have thus preserved for the Romans a description of the original *Arabia Eudaemon*, not the Eratosthenian transformation.[54] The description of the Persian Gulf looks very much like the picture shown on the Peutinger map, which seems to reflect Hecataeus.

Pomponius says about the Bāb al-Mandab:

> From the part (*ab ea parte*) which is on the right to those entering, there are the towns Charra, Arabia and Adanus.[55]

The *Periplus Maris Erythraei*, written in the latter half of the first century AD, describes the same area, this time starting from the north: along the strait is Okelis, 'a village of *Arabes*'. Then comes *Eudaímōn Arabía*, a good harbour. Then after a long stretch of coastline is Kanē, the main port for export of frankincense.[56] It is likely that *Eudaímōn Arabía* is Aden. Ptolemy mentions an *Arabía* as an *empórion* whose location fits well with Aden.[57] There is, however, good evidence that the town's proper name was Aden.[58] The name in the *Periplus* is explicable as a translation of the Semitic name from the root ʕDN and launched by the international community of sailors, who used the harbour for a stop-over during the journey to and from India. It is a sign of the quality of Pomponius' source that it, unlike the otherwise very trustworthy *Periplus*, has mentioned the original name of the town.[59] In that case it can be wondered if Arabia in the *Chorographia* is not identical with Okelis in the *Periplus*, in that work characterized as 'a village of *árabes*'. Unfortunately, the town Charra remains unidentified.

Pomponius' source shows a surprisingly old-fashioned view of Arabia, largely untouched by Eratosthenes' work. Arabia still appears Hecataean. Agrippa seems somewhat more up to date although an exact picture of how Arabia was viewed is impossible to get. Agrippa's work was probably made known at the beginning of the 20s BC and also Pomponius' source must have been available to the reading public of Rome in the early reign of Augustus. Agrippa's geography must have been easily accessible to his closest friend, Augustus. Both sources are a testimony to the growing concern for world geography in Rome. As far as Arabia is concerned, the knowledge gathered by the two sources must have been studied closely in the Roman Ministry of Defence in connection with the great military expedition to South Arabia planned by Augustus and led by Aelius Gallus in 25–24 BC.

For the expedition of Gallus to Arabia we have four versions and some literary echoes. The official one is the passage in Augustus' own record of his reign, represented today by the *Monumentum Ancyranum*. The text was probably more or less finished in 2 BC but became public after the death of Augustus in AD 14:

> On my command and auspices, armies were conducted at the same time to Nubia and Arabia, which is called *Eudaemon* . . . the army proceeded into Arabia to the lands of the Sabaeans, to the town of Mariba.[60]

To this are added three literary sources. The earliest one is Strabo, who knew the general Gallus personally. According to him, the expedition was launched against the *árabes*, which may be a general reference to the inhabitants of the peninsula.[61] In Pliny's *Natural History* we find a reference to a report from Gallus himself, from which we get some more details than in Strabo. The expedition is made against Arabia.

The inhabitants are divided into two categories: nomads and *reliqui*, 'others'. The *reliqui* are divided into several groups: Homeritae, Minaei, Cerbani, Agraei, Chatramotitae, Carrei, and Sabaei. At the end it is said about the *Arabes*:

> The *Arabes* wear turbans (*mitrati degunt*) or go with unshorn hair, the beard is shaved except on the upper lip – others are unshaven.[62]

Pliny has further notes about conditions in South Arabia which are derived from reports from the Gallus expedition. They do not contain much about ethnic conditions.[63] The name Agraei in the list of South Arabian peoples should be observed. It should not necessarily be identified with Egra in the north (Dedan, al-Ḥiğr). Instead, we should rather see it as a reflection of Hagar and a testimony of the existence of a place and/or a people known by that designation also in South Arabia. Hağar is a well-known term for a kind of city in Islamo-Arabic sources, and is there limited to a few locations of which one is near Nağrān.[64]

In the youngest source, Cassius Dio, the expedition is undertaken against *Arabía eudaímōn* controlled by a certain Sabos.[65] Compared with Strabo, this notice is not very precise, since in Strabo this king reigned over Ararene, which seems to be identical with modern ʕAsīr.

Common to all these versions is that they employ the Eratosthenian terminology, which is thus by now officially established. Especially in Pliny's text we see, however, that the Romans were aware of the ethnic complexity of the lands traversed by the expedition. It is unfortunate that it is not clear what the term *Arabes* in Pliny refers to. Does it include all the peoples mentioned or are they to be seen as only one of them? The Gallus expedition increased the knowledge of the Graeco-Roman world about conditions in Arabia and the reports constituted one of the most important sources for the first comprehensive treaty of Arabia ever written, namely Iuba's *Perì tēs Arabías*.[66]

Excursus: the expedition of Aelius Gallus to Yemen

The four widely differing accounts of the Gallus expedition have generated a long debate among modern scholars on the actual series of events, about which no complete agreement has been reached. One central issue has been whether the Romans reached the Sabaean capital Marib or not. The latest scholars who have discussed the matter agree that Gallus and his soldiers did indeed see the walls of Marib.[67] This is in accordance with the *Res Gestae* and Pliny's account. Strabo's text mentions Marsyaba, which is usually seen as a corruption of Marib by later scribes. According to this view, Strabo is in harmony with the two others. Since the only site mentioned by Cassius Dio is Athloula, which is identifiable with present-day Barāqish, it can be argued that he does not speak against the testimony of the three others.

The current interpretation of the Gallus expedition is thus based on harmonizing the sources, which, however, is a very doubtful method in general and in this case in particular.[68] It must be emphasized that all the sources for the Gallus expedition are heavily biased. From both Strabo and Cassius Dio, though, one basic fact emerges clearly: the expedition was a catastrophe. Thousands of soldiers perished from thirst and pestilence, and no military or other results were achieved. Strabo puts the blame on the Nabataean guide, Syllaeus, who is accused of treason, whereas Gallus' role is seen in very positive terms. This is not surprising since we know that Gallus and Strabo were personal friends.[69] Strabo's account is clearly a defence for Gallus against criticism, which must have been launched against him after the failure of the expedition, a criticism that may be echoed in Cassius Dio's detailed account of the misery of the Roman army. Of this no traces are found in the *Res Gestae* and Pliny, which casts severe doubts on the reliability of these two sources, all the more since the former was the official account of the expedition, written by the emperor himself. Augustus had no interest in telling the whole *oikoumene* about the failure of his army in Arabia. One should compare his account about the Roman operations in Germany in the *Res Gestae*, where the catastrophe against Arminius in the Teutoburger forest is not mentioned. Instead he wants us to believe that the whole of Germania was subjected.[70]

It is very likely that Pliny's account reflects some official report which described the expedition in bright terms, being a cover-up of the disaster. Pliny's source was probably Iuba, who was close to Augustus and who is unlikely to have written anything going against the official view. Now the *Res Gestae* and Pliny are the only sources saying that the expedition was a complete success and that the Roman army reached Marib, the glorious capital of the mythical land of Saba. Since the town is mentioned neither by Strabo, who mentions it in other contexts, nor by Cassius Dio, who both acknowledge the catastrophe, it is most likely that the version emerging from Augustus and the circle around him is a propagandistic manipulation of uncomfortable facts.[71]

The arguments for emending Strabo's Marsyaba to Mari(a)b(a) are weak indeed. He explicitly says that Marsyaba was controlled by a certain Ilasarus, ruling the tribe of the Rhammanitae. It is very likely that this is ʔLŠRḤ, the KBR of the ʔRYMN mentioned in the Sabaean inscription RÉS 4085, i.e. a local governor in al-Ǧawf. The king residing in Marib is not mentioned at all in any of the accounts, which is quite remarkable if the Romans really had reached the city. There is thus no reason to read Strabo's Marsyaba as something else. It was probably a site in al-Ǧawf or not far from Barāqīsh. Most of the heroic military operations described by Pliny probably never occurred. That units of the army reached some of the towns mentioned in the sources is nonetheless likely. The town Athloula/Barāqīsh is mentioned by both Strabo and Cassius Dio, and some kind of Roman presence is verified by the finding of a Graeco-Latin inscription there with the name of a Roman soldier. What exactly happened there we do not know.[72]

Iuba's book on Arabia

The most lasting effect of the Gallus expedition was a wealth of new knowledge about Arabia, brought back by the survivors. Much of this information, together with a lot of earlier known facts, were compiled by Iuba in his book *On Arabia* (*Perì tē̂s Arabías*). Augustus' grandchild, Caius Caesar, was sent in AD 1 to the Orient basically in order to deal with the Armenian question. As a preparation for that expedition, the Mauritanian king Iuba, who also was a man of literature, composed a book about Arabia for the young prince. It is not immediately clear why Caius should be instructed particularly about Arabia, since his main goal was Armenia. We know, however, that he first went to Egypt and travelled through the land between the Red Sea and Palestine before reaching northern Syria. Iuba's book belongs to those lost, but we know a good deal about it since Pliny made ample use of it when he wrote about Arabia and Arabs in the *Natural History* in the 60s and 70s AD.[73] In fact, Iuba was his basic source in the passages about the Middle East and Arabia, and we can get a good picture from Pliny about the views on Arabia in the latter part of the reign of Augustus.[74]

Iuba used several sources for his description of Arabia, most of which seem to have been *períploi*, i.e. descriptions of sailing routes and also overland itineraries. The first one appears when he describes the shores of the Indian Ocean. Pliny starts with Iuba's description about Seleucid activities in Mesopotamia and the Gulf region, which we have quoted already.[75] Of the descriptions of navigation, we have already seen that he used Onesicritus' book for describing the Persian Gulf.[76] After the description based on him, there followed another *períplous*, describing the route from Rās Fartak in South Arabia with the monsoon to India.[77] This is followed by a third one describing the route from Egypt through the Red Sea via Aden and Qana to India.[78] These two must have been compiled during the preceding century, since the use of the monsoon started *c*. 100 BC.[79] Iuba also had a description of the Parthian empire, including notes on the conditions in southern Mesopotamia, i.e. the kingdom of Charax.[80] It is not quite clear where this information comes from but it is not impossible that it originates with Isidorus from Charax, whom Pliny mentions as one of the sources used by himself or by Iuba.[81]

Pliny also adduces a large part of Iuba's book when trying to give a comprehensive description of Arabia.[82] Unfortunately, the result is no success, and the passage mostly consists of a mess of more or less misunderstood names.[83] Anyway, he gives us a description of the *Scenitae* and the Nabataeans.[84] Then follows a description of the route between Charax and Petra via Duma and the lower Euphrates.[85] This route is more or less the same as described by Eratosthenes but the passage in Pliny may well originate from Isidorus.[86] There follows a *períplous* from Charax around the peninsula, which is partly based on the Seleucid source we have already mentioned.[87] This passage is completed by a presentation of the peoples in South Arabia, which does not seem to be based on descriptions of sea routes but instead gives the impression of being a caravan route from Sabota (Shabwa) to the Gulf of ʕAqaba, i.e. the classical frankincense road.[88] We are then given a description of another caravan route from the Yemeni highlands to Gerrha. This passage may also originate from Isidorus of Charax.[89] The following paragraph is the story of the Gallus expedition quoted earlier, which may well be taken by Iuba directly from the official report in a Roman archive.[90] In two other passages Pliny quotes from another work by Iuba, the *Libyca*, which included a description of the Arabs on the western shores of the Red Sea.[91]

In other parts of Pliny's *Natural History*, facts about Arabia pop up here and there. The most important are those where he writes about frankincense, myrrh and other perfumes.[92] Many of the facts found here come from Iuba, who in his turn had them from older authors like Theophrastus but also probably from merchants from the preceding century, as well as from Isidorus of Charax and the Gallus expedition.

It is clear that Iuba's work, in spite of its lack of originality and its compilatory character, contained a lot of highly valuable information on Arabia and represents the most important leap forward after Eratosthenes and Posidonius. It is most unfortunate that it is lost, since Pliny's digest often distorts the facts and names. What does it teach us, in its present shape, about Arabs in the time of Augustus?

Evidently Iuba had a very wide definition of Arabia, comprising the entire peninsula. Macae, i.e. Rās Musandam, is in Arabia as well as Cape Syagrus (Rās Fartak) and Ocelis (Aden).[93] Ḥaḍramawt as well as Nabataea are in Arabia.[94] So far Iuba follows the definition established from the time of Eratosthenes. More interesting is the northern border:

> Arabia, which as far as extent is concerned is not secondary to any nation (*gens*), slopes a long way down from Mount Amanus from the region of Cilicia and Commagene, as we have said, and many of its nations (*gentes*) have been brought there by Tigranes the Great or have by themselves reached the Mediterranean and the Egyptian shore, as we have explained; also the Nubei penetrate to Mount Lebanon, with whom the Ramisi, then the Teranei, then the Patami adjoin. The very peninsula of Arabia, however, projects between two oceans, the Red and the Persian, and by some device of nature being surrounded by sea to the likeness and extent of Italy. It looks in no different way towards the sky, and it is also prosperous in this position.[95]

It is also evident that Iuba included a description of lower Mesopotamia and Characene in his book on Arabia.[96] It thus seems that to him Arabia encompassed not only the peninsula and the Syrian desert but the whole of Syria and Mesopotamia as well. This implies that Arabia includes all kinds of peoples: Scenitae, Chaldaeans, Nabataeans, Omani and Characeni in the north, and then all the strange tribes known from the *períploi* around the coast, as well as the famous peoples in South Arabia.[97] It seems that the Ramisi and the Patami should be associated with the towns Raamses and Pithom in the eastern Nile Delta and that this area also belongs to his Arabia. It is then remarkable that the term 'Arabia' does not occur in the passage taken from the *Libyca*, where he mentioned a string of Arab tribes from the isthmus of Suez southwards along the western shore of the Red Sea.[98] He there gives the following names of tribes said to be Arabes: the Autaei (167), the Asarri (168), the Gebadaei close to the Autaei, the Ascitae (the 'rafters') living on the islands in the Bāb al-Mandab (176) and the tribes living along the Nile from Syene to Meroe (177).

In spite of these tribes being *Arabes*, they did not fit into Iuba's scheme, according to which Arabia was the land from the Anatolian and Iranian mountains to the Indian Ocean. It was quite abstract and not based on real ethnic conditions. This kind of geo-ethnic concept very much reminds one of Posidonius, and it can be supposed that Iuba was influenced by him. But it is evident, at the same time, that the northern borders of Iuba's Arabia are defined according to the actual existence of people called Arabs in that region. And this is the most valuable information contained in Iuba for our purpose.[99] The presence of Arabs in the Amanus region as well as in Osrhoene and perhaps also in Characene is documented, as we have already seen, in connection with political events there in the first century BC. These events are, however, recorded in sources written in the second century AD. Iuba is actually the earliest source we have mentioning Arabs in these regions.

The dates on the Arabs in Mesopotamia are taken from a source with good local knowledge, possibly the shadowy Isidorus of Charax:

> Besides the cities already mentioned it [Mesopotamia] has the towns of Seleucia, Laodicea, and Artemita; and also, in the territory of the tribe (*gens*) of *Arabes* called the Orroei and the Mandani, the town Antioch [called] Arabs, ['the Arab'] founded by the governor of Mesopotamia, Nicanor. Adjoining these, in the interior, are the *Arabes* called Eldamari above whom on the river Pallaconta is the town of Bura, and the *Arabes* called Salmani and Masei.[100]

This description is confused in the usual Plinian manner. The Antioch mentioned here is the present-day town of Viranshehir between Edessa/Urhāy and Mardin.[101] The *Arabes Orroei* are likely to be identical with those we encountered in connection with the events around Tigranocerta in 69 BC, which was probably situated just east of Viranshehir. The Mandani could be related to the name Mardin.[102] It is likely that this group of people were not Arabs originally.[103] Even though Pliny's text can be read to indicate that they were considered *Arabes*, other readings are possible. We would suggest that their Arabness is doubtful, since it has to be built on a reading of a not too clear Plinian text.[104]

The river Pallaconta could be identical with the Pollacopas canal, on which Alexander sailed from Babylon southwards, and where he built a sluice during his preparations for the Arabian campaign.[105] This canal stretched from *c.* 140 kilometres north of Babylon by ʔAnbār to the Persian Gulf.[106] The name is probably identical with that of the present-day town al-Fallūǧa on the Euphrates just west of Baghdad.[107] The town Bura could be identical with a town near Baghdad mentioned by Yāqūt.[108] From the context it follows that the Eldamari would be north of Bura and Pallaconta/Fallūǧa, and just south of the Arabs in Osrhoene. It is then close at hand to identify the *Eldamari Arabes* with those mentioned by Xenophon living in the Arabia between the two rivers.

The Salmani and Masei are difficult to locate, unless it is assumed that Masei has something to do with Mesene. It could thus refer to the kingdom of Charax and support the assumption of Arab presence in that area.[109]

Iuba had the following to say about conditions along the Euphrates:

> Where it [the Euphrates] ceases to afford protection by its channel, as it does when its course approaches the boundary of Charax, it immediately begins to be infested by the Attali robbers, a tribe (*gens*) of *Arabes*, beyond whom are the *Scenitae*. But the winding course of the Euphrates is occupied by the nomads of Arabia right to the desert of Syria, where, as we have stated, the river makes a bend to the south, quitting the uninhabited districts of Palmyra.[110]

The distinction between Arab robbers along the river and tent-dwellers further out in the desert is reminiscent of Posidonius, and Iuba may have taken the passage from him.

In a following passage we get details about conditions along the Shaṭṭ al-*ʕarab*:

> The town of Charax is situated in the innermost recess of the Persian Gulf, from which projects the country called *Arabia eudaemon* . . . The original town was founded by Alexander the Great with settlers brought from the royal city of Durine . . . The original town was destroyed by the rivers but was restored by Antiochus the fifth [i.e. Antiochus IV Epiphanes?] king of Syria, who gave the town his own name; and when it had been damaged again it was restored and named after himself by Spaosines son of Sagdonacus, king of the neighbouring *Arabes*.[111]

This passage has beeen quoted earlier as a possible indication of Arab involvement in the kingdom of Charax. The text we have is, unfortunately, quite confused, and no certain conclusions can be drawn from it about the role of Arabs in that kingdom. The inclusion of Characene in Iuba's Arabia might indicate that Arabs perhaps had an important political position there, which is not visible in our scanty sources but which was sufficient reason to label the area 'Arabia'. It would be an analogy to the case of Edessa.

Excursus: 'the Ituraeans, the Arabs'

We have previously pointed out the presence of Arabs in the Antilebanon area in the time of Alexander the Great and possibly earlier. After his time, that region became the borderland of the Ptolemies against the Seleucids. From the end of the third century BC we also hear about Arabs, and perhaps also about Nabataeans, in northern Transjordan, a land with a few scattered military colonies belonging to the king in Alexandria. From the Old Testament we also have testimonies, difficult to date exactly but probably reflecting conditions around Alexander's time, about the presence of a group called Yeṭur close to the *hagrîm* in the same area.[112] They are included among the sons of Ishmael by the P genealogist.[113] Eupolemus mentioned them in northern Transjordan in the middle of the second century BC.[114]

After the Seleucid conquest of Palestine, troubles in Transjordan continued surfacing in the events connected with the Maccabees. Alexander Jannaeus conquered parts of Ituraea and converted the inhabitants to Judaism.[115] In connection with this, there emerged an Ituraean principality with its base in the Biqāʕ.[116] The Ḥawrān was a theatre of war between Arabs, Ituraeans and Hasmonaeans until the first half of the first century BC. The Romans established a temporary peace by founding a system of cities, the Decapolis, as a buffer between the combatants and possibly as the prolonged arm of the governor in Syria.[117]

After the Parthian invasions we hear again about troubles in the northern Ḥawrān, and Mark Antony's giving parts of it to Cleopatra was perhaps a means of solving the problems. The Ituraean principality was dissolved, perhaps by Mark Antony.[118] Peaceful conditions seem to have been established when Herod took over the entire Trachonitis.

The impression from the history of the three centuries from Alexander to Herod is that the Ituraean principality in present-day Lebanon was united with the Ḥawrān and Bashan, and that this entire region constituted a belt of continuous unrest and unruliness, separating Palestine and Transjordan from Syria proper. In that area, different tribes and groups were moving to and fro, supplying the Ituraeans with fresh manpower. The Ituraeans meanwhile tried to keep the road towards the south-east free and under their control. This must have been the main reason for Pompey to pacify the Ituraeans and for Mark Antony to dissolve their principality, a measure which seems to have resulted in a state of complete lawlessness during more than two decades.

The Ḥawrān–Bashan area constitutes a large promontory of well-watered pasturages and fields extending eastwards into the desert, reaching the mouth of the Wādī Sirḥān. It was a natural landing spot for people coming from the east and south-east, as Qedar had probably done. We have a large number of inscriptions from exactly this area in a language closely related to the ones documented further south in pre-Islamic Arabia, in a variant of the South Semitic alphabet, from which we can discern a culture that has many chacteristics recognizable in later Arabic tradition. These inscriptions, the so-called Safaitic texts, are from a period later than the one treated here so far, but they show that the area was a centre for people coming in from the desert and also probably for people fleeing bad conditions in the sown.

The Ituraeans in the Biqāʕ valley are often considered Arabs.[119] The documentation of them as Arabs is, however, very scanty. Of the classical sources only Cassius Dio refers to them as Arabs in one passage where he reports that Caligula in the year AD 38 gave Sohaemus the land of the *Itouraîoi*, the *árabes*.[120] In another notice he says that Mark Antony gave large parts of 'the Arabia of the *Itouraîoi*' to Cleopatra's children in 36 BC. We have on the other hand several passages indicating the difference between Ituraeans and Arabs. The most important testimony is the one we have already adduced from Strabo, where the Ituraeans are said to live mixed with the Arabs in the Antilebanon, and another one telling that they and the *árabes* keep the mountains, all of them being robbers.[121] It is quite possible that this information comes from Posidonius and is to be judged trustworthy. It is supported by some passages in later writers. We have already quoted Lucanus' *Pharsalia*, where he clearly distinguishes between *Arabes* and *Ityraei*.[122] The same distinction is made by Apuleius in his *Florida*, which is probably based on the same source as Lucanus.[123] Finally, in some very late sources from the fourth century AD like the problematic *Historiae Scriptores Augustae*, in its biography of the emperor Aurelian, and in the *Breviarium* of Eutropius we find the same distinction between *Ityraei* and *Arabes*.[124] It is striking that we find this distinction continued in Latin authors over the centuries. Their most important source for the history of the Roman republic and the rise of Augustus was Livy's *Ab urbe condita*. We know that Livy used Posidonius for the events in the Orient. In that case, the distinction between Arabs and Ituraeans in both Strabo and the Latin authors goes back to the great Apamaean, which gives it increased value as historical evidence.

Among the names known from Ituraea we find several that are recognizable as Arab names, which would be a support for the claim that the Ituraeans were Arabs in the modern sense of the word.[125] It is not unlikely that in Ituraea there was spoken a Semitic language which we today would call Arabic on purely linguistic criteria. But even though such a language was spoken by both Ituraeans and Arabs in the principality, it would not make the former Arabs in the ancient sense. As we have seen, the sources make a clear distinction between the two. Since we, after all, know very little about the linguistic conditions in the area, we should beware of using modern linguistic criteria for identification of ethnic conditions in antiquity. There is no reason not to accept the testimony of the sources: Arabs constituted one group among the inhabitants of Ituraea, as they probably also did in the realm governed by the Nabataean kings.

According to the trustworthy sources, Arabs were people scattered among the inhabitants in Syria, such as the Ituraeans. The Arabs in Ituraea and those in Ḥawrān and northern Transjordan were probably related. This promontory of rainland into the Syrian desert is one of the most important 'Arabias' of antiquity. We have another such promontory pointing into the desert further north, east of Emesa. Also here we have found Arabs in the early Seleucid period exercising a sometimes decisive influence on the events in adjacent lands. Both areas were later to supply the Roman empire with emperors.

Excursus: Emesa

We have assumed that the Arabs who fought with Antiochus III at Raphia under their chief Zabdibelos, and the *árabes* called *zabadaîoi* who clashed with Jonathan Maccabaeus in the time of Alexander Balas, dwelt on the plains around present-day Ḥimṣ. It has been supposed that Arabs settled on the plain in the second century BC, but if they fought with Antiochus III in 217 BC. they could have arrived earlier.[126] These Arabs would then also be those mentioned in Strabo's quotation from Posidonius about the Arabs who had more complex forms of government.[127] Among these was Sampsiceramus of Arethusa, which is present-day ar-Ristan on the upper Orontes. There are also two other good Arabic names mentioned in the same context: Gambaros = Ğabbār and Themellas = Taym allāt.[128] Sampsiceramus is likely to be identical with the one who was an ally to the Arab phylarch Azizus in Qinnasrīn in the last struggle for the remains of Seleucid power after Tigranes' defeat in the early 60s BC.[129] From then on, the town of Emesa began to play an important role in Syrian politics which was to last well into the first century AD.[130] It was closely tied to the Roman power in Syria and used an era starting with the year 64/63, i.e. Pompey's conquest. The Emesenians seem to have had a very good relationship with him and Cicero even mockingly calls Pompey Sampsiceramus.[131]

The 'Arabness' of the rulers of Emesa remains to be proved. The name of the first one, Sampsiceramus, looks more Aramaic than Arabic, and he is never explicitly called Arab. As a matter of fact, Sampsiceramus' son and successor, Iamblichus (I), is the only Emesenian explicitly called so: Cicero calls him *phylarchus Arabum* during the dramatic events in 51 BC, and it is very likely that he was the Iamblikhos, 'king of some *arábioi*', killed by Mark Antony at Actium in 31 BC.[132]

Iamblichus' brother and successor Alexander was deposed by Augustus, who in 20 BC installed Iamblichus' brother Iamblichus (II) as ruler of Emesa. It is said that he was given back 'the land of the fathers (*hē patrōa*) of the *arábioi*'.[133]

It turns out that these are the only instances where Emesa is associated with Arabs. They are mentioned in connection with one ruler: Iamblichus I. Later rulers are called 'kings of the Emesenians', although they carry good Arabic names like Azizus (ʕAzīz) and Sohaemus (Suhaym).[134] There is no doubt that there was a strong admixture of Arabic-speaking people in Emesa and its surroundings, although the ancient name of the city itself looks more Aramaic: Ḥemṣā.[135] The city was not laid out as a Greek *pólis*, and its irregular plan differs from the one found in the other Hellenistic cities in Syria.[136] The fact that Emesa is not mentioned in any source before the first century AD indicates that it was a rather insignificant village.[137] It cannot be excluded that Emesa was a conglomeration of local Aramaic-speaking peasants and a group of Arabs who originally had their centre at Arethusa/ar-Ristan. We would venture the following hypothesis about the history of Emesa. Arabs were originally installed by the early Seleucids at Arethusa.[138] Then, probably under Sampsiceramus, a phylarchate was established in the little village of Emesa in the centre of the fertile plain with a garrison of Arabs from Arethusa and its surroundings. The breakdown of Seleucid power made possible the emergence of a city-state governed by Arabs. It was acknowledged by Pompey in 64/63 BC. This phylarchate supported Mark Antony and was dismantled after the defeat at Actium. Augustus then restored the independence of Emesa without the Arab garrison. This would be the meaning of the phrase in Cassius Dio about the '*patrōa* of the *arábioi*' being given back to the family of Sampsiceramus. That dynasty continued to rule but the Arab garrison was abolished. The rulers were kings of the Emesenians, not the Arabs. The two names thus stand for two different groups.[139]

We do not know exactly when Emesa was incorporated into the Syrian province, but it seems to have happened during the second century AD.[140] We know that the sun-god played a central role in the religion of Emesa. Members of his priesthood were to occupy the imperial throne in Rome during the third century AD.

Excursus: the *arabarchia*

Josephus says about the king Malchus, who is known from the coins as 'king of the

Nabataeans' and to whom Herod fled in 39 BC, that 'he had the *arabarkhía*'.[141] We have suggested that the meaning is that the king residing in Reqem/Petra, the centre of the Nabataeans, was also in commmand of the Arabs, who constituted a special sector of society in the Arabo-Nabataean kingdom. This suggestion is based on the evidence from this kingdom only. The term *arabarkhía* does, however, occur in other documents as well. It should be connected with the word *arabárkhēs*, which designated a person holding the office of *arabarkhía*. *Arabárkhēs* sounds very similar to *alabárkhēs*, which is also found in several documents, and there are weighty grounds for seeing them as identical.[142]

The *arabárkhēs* is mentioned for the first time in a letter by Cicero to his friend Atticus from May 59 BC, where he says the following about a person who is probably Pompey, now the strongman in Rome:

> If you do come as you say you will, I would like to fish out from Theophanes how the *arabarches* is disposed towards me.[143]

Theophanes is the man who wrote the history of Pompey's eastern conquests.[144] As has been shown, Pompey was heavily involved with Arabs who had supported him in his conquest of Syria. In this letter and some others, Cicero mentions Sampsiceramus, the *phylarches* of Emesa who had sided with Pompey. It is, however, likely that Cicero uses his name as a slightly scornful designation of Pompey himself. The term *arabárkhēs* means 'the commander of Arabs' and Pompey's connections with the Arabs in Syria could very well have given the pretext for its use by Cicero.

One century later we meet the term again, this time referring to a certain Alexander, who was *alabárkhēs* in Alexandria in the reign of Caligula.[145] This man was a Jew and brother of the famous philosopher Philo.[146] We hear of another *alabárkhēs*, Demetrius, appointed at the death of the emperor Claudius in 41 AD.[147] Both of these men were officials in Egypt. A third one is referred to by the Roman poet Juvenal, who in his first satire complains about upstarts showing themselves in Rome in different ways:

> and those triumphal statues, among which some Egyptian *arabarches* or other has dared to set up his titles, against whose statue more than one kind of nuisance may be committed.[148]

The man with the statue is probably Iulius Alexander, *praefectus Aegypti* in AD 67–70. Apart from these literary testimonies, the word occurs in some inscriptions of which two are dated. One is the so-called Coptos tariff, a text from upper Egypt dealing with the financial administration in the time of the emperor Domitian (AD 81–98).[149] The other one is a text in honour of an Ephesian magistrate, who is said also to have been *arabárkhēs* in Egypt in the reign of Marcus Aurelius.[150] There are several other undated texts mentioning the word which originate from or deal with Roman Egypt.[151]

It appears that most references to this office connect it with Egypt. It seems to be a designation of an official mainly dealing with fiscal matters all over the country. There is no doubt that the word *arabárkhēs* is derived from *áraps*. That does not mean that the arabarch was a governor of the region called Arabia in Egypt: the nome in the eastern delta or the desert between the Nile and the Red Sea. The documents show him as an official with jurisdiction over the entire country. He did not necessarily have any closer ties with the group of people we have been looking for in this study: the arabarch in Alexandria mentioned by Josephus was a Jew. In Roman times the arabarch was a post which could be filled by anyone seen by the authorities as fit for the task. But the very name of the office points to a period when the *arabárkhēs* was a leader of the *árabes* in Egypt. We have already seen that there is evidence from the early Ptolemaic period of Arabs acting as some kind of police force in Egypt, and the term *arabárkhēs* is most likely to have its origin in this arrangement.

The rulers of Egypt employed the *árabes* in Wādī Tumaylāt and further eastwards, not only as border guards but also as a police force in the country itself. This arrangement might very well go back to Achaemenid times, from which we have documentation about the presence of Arabs who had power in the Negev but also in the eastern Nile Delta. As late as the middle of the third century AD we hear about the *arabotoxótēs*, 'the Arab bowman', in a context which hints at some kind of police task.[152] The use of foreigners as border guards is well documented from Achaemenid times by the colony of Jewish mercenaries in Elephantine. The Persian rulers may have introduced the Arabs as a similar control instrument, useful since they had no immediate loyalties to the inhabitants of the country.

The term also occurs outside Egypt. Cicero's use of it could allude to a similar office in the Seleucid realm. His remarks could be seen as an indication that Sampiceramus of Emesa was an *arabárkhēs* and that the Seleucids had made the same arrangements as the Ptolemies in Egypt, an arrangement which might, in both cases, go back to the Achaemenids. A concrete testimony is a text from Dura Europus written in AD 121. The text, a contract of loan, mentions as one of the contrahents 'Phraates . . . collector of customs and military governor (*stratēgós*) of Mesopotamia and Parapotamia and *arabárkhēs*'.[153] Phraates was a Parthian official who fulfilled tasks quite similar to those mentioned from Egypt. His governorship was combined with the *arabarkhía*, which must have meant the leadership of the Arabs in Parapotamia mentioned by Strabo and, probably, also Arabs in the Ǧazīra itself. The whole terminology in the document points back to Seleucid times as testified by Strabo's digest of Posidonius and Eratosthenes. The organization of the areas around the middle Euphrates was inherited by the Parthians from the Seleucids.

The use of the term *arabarkhía* in connection with the king Malchus in Reqem/Petra should be read in the light of these documents. There is no reasonable doubt that the term refers to an authority over people called *árabes*. Both in Egypt and in Mesopotamia the *arabarkhía* meant the authority over Arabs integrated into the larger political entities of the Ptolemies and the Seleucids. In both countries the arrangements may go back to the Achaemenids. In that case it is very likely that the remark about the *arabarkhía* of Malchus, king of the Nabataeans, should be interpreted in the same way. In analogy with the conditions in Egypt and Mesopotamia, the *arabarkhía* in the Arabo-Nabataean kingdom was the office of commanding one sector of the society: the Arabs who probably constituted the army and the border guards, protecting the 'civilian' inhabitants known as Nabataeans. This arrangement is discernible from the time of Aretas 'III' onwards and represents an age-old system of military organization in the Middle East, documentable at least from the time of the Achaemenids. As we have seen, there is weighty evidence for the establishment of the Arabs in the Negev between Egypt and Palestine in the early Achaemenid period. The removal of their residence to Reqem in the middle of the first century BC was no major break in their history, although the civilian part of the state received increased prominence. We get a series of rulers called 'kings of the Nabataeans', who kept tight control of the Arab army. The Arabo-Nabataean kingdom emerges from the time of Aretas 'III' as a state in which the Arabs played a role resembling the one they had under the the Ptolemies and the Seleucids.

Arabs in the time of Claudius

We have seen that one of Iuba's sources located Arabs in the region of Edessa as well as in adjacent areas.[154] These Arabs were to become most important in the centuries to come. We have a document preserved by Pliny which was originally composed by Claudius, the man who was proclaimed Roman emperor in AD 41 after the murder of Caligula. In the 30s he had written a book which included a description of the Tigris area.[155] In Pliny, we find a note from it about Arabs:

> The Tigris, however, after receiving as tributaries from Armenia those notable rivers the Pathenias and Nicephorion, makes a frontier between the Orroei *Arabes* and the Adiabeni [*Arabes*] and forms the region of Mesopotamia.[156]

We learn from this passage that there were Arabs in Osrhoene, i.e. the area belonging to the Edessan kings, as well as on the eastern shores of the Tigris, in Adiabene. The exact location of these Arabs is not clear from Claudius' account, but we may note that Arabs on the eastern shores of the Tigris are mentioned in Quintus Curtius' story about the campaign of Alexander the Great, also written in the first century AD:

> As they [Alexander's army] went on [from Arbela], Arabia was on their left hand, a region famous for its abundance of perfumes; the route is through the plains in the land lying between the Tigris and the Euphrates.[157]

Since Arbela was the capital of Adiabene, the Arabia mentioned here must have been east of the Tigris. We cannot be sure if the Arabs really were in Adiabene in Alexander's days or if Curtius just projected conditions of his own day. The description of Arabia is obviously confused with that of Xenophon as well as with other descriptions of Arabia, but there may be a kernel of truth in the position of an Arabia south-east of Arbela, i.e. in Adiabene, in the first century AD. This is shown by events some years later.

In AD 49 the Romans attempted to put their own man, a certain Meherdates, on the Parthian throne instead of the successor of Artabanos II, Gotarzes.[158] Claudius sent Caius Cassius Longinus, a descendant of Caesar's murderer, with an army to support Meherdates' claims.[159] The story is told by Tacitus in his *Annales* written around AD 120. There are divided opinions about Tacitus' sources for this period of Claudius' reign: the historian Aufidius Bassus, who died *c.* AD 60 and had written a lost history of the Roman emperors, or Pliny, who wrote a continuation of Bassus.[160] Whoever was Tacitus' source, it can be assumed that the account is based on some kind of report by Cassius himself, who is later known as a writer on legal matters:

> Cassius . . . pitched his camp at Zeugma, the most convenient part to cross the river [Euphrates]. Then, when the Parthian noblemen and the king of the *Arabes*, Acbarus, had arrived, he cautioned Meherdates that the lively

> enthusiasm of barbarians grows chill with delay [of charge] and turns into treachery. So he urged to go on with the adventure. The advice was ignored through the dishonesty of Acbarus, who detained the inexperienced youth [Meherdates], who identified kingship with dissipation, for many days at the town of Edessa.[161]

The army made a *détour* through the mountains of the northern Ǧazīra and then reached Adiabene, whose king, Izates, reluctantly joined them. Cassius' warnings then seemed to be fulfilled:

> Gotarzes . . . had sent bribery agents to bid for the defection of his enemies. First, Izates with the Adiabenians, then Acbarus with the army of the *Arabes* took their departure, in accordance with the levity of their race and with the fact, proved by evidence, that barbarians are more inclined to seek their kings from Rome than to keep them.[162]

All commentators agree that this Acbarus is identical with Abgar V in Edessa.[163] As will become apparent, this would then be the only case where a king in Edessa is explicitly called an Arab. The details will be discussed in connection with the treatment of the epigraphic testimony from the surroundings of Edessa from the second century AD.[164] At this stage it should be noted that (a) the king is not said to be king of Edessa, and (b) his name is not Abgar.[165] If one has not made up one's mind in advance, and takes all evidence into account, it is more likely that Tacitus' text as we have it is right: there was a ruler of the Arabs named ʔAkbar, a good Arabic name, who sided with Meherdates and the Romans.[166] It is likely that he came from the Ǧazīra, although this is not explicitly stated. In the passage from Claudius already quoted it is said that there were two groups of Arabs in northern Mesopotamia: those in Osrhoene and those in Adiabene. It is likely that the former are the ones referred to by Tacitus. Commentators have been led astray by the remark that he delayed Meherdates at (not in) Edessa.[167] Since we know from the later inscriptions at Sumatar Harbesi near Edessa about rulers of Arabs who are not identical with the Edessan kings, it is likely that this ʔAkbar was such a ruler, perhaps associated with the Edessan kingdom in the same manner as Arabs in Syria were associated with Nabataeans and Ituraeans (and, as it seems, with Seleucids and Ptolemies as well). Acbarus' Arabs could be those settled there by Tigranes the Great.

Arabs in Adiabene

Arabs in the Tigris area, probably in the Ǧazīra, also appear in historical events some years later. At this time the king of Adiabene, Izates, and his mother, Helena, who had been involved in the failed venture of Meherdates, had converted to Judaism. Izates had been a vassal king to the Parthian King of Kings, Artabanus II, whom he had helped in regaining his throne. In return for this he had received the town of Nisibis. Around AD 51, under the new Parthian king, Vologases I, an insurrection broke out among the nobles of the kingdom of Adiabene. The story is told by Josephus. Helena spent her last years in Jerusalem and Josephus' account may well originate from her or the circles around her. According to Josephus the revolt was directed against the Judaizing policy of the royal house:

> They [the nobles] wrote to Abias, king of the *árabes*, promising him large sums if he would take the field against their king. They further offered to abandon the [latter] king at the first onset, for they wished to punish him because he had come to hate their way of life. Having bound themselves to mutual loyalty, they exhorted Abias to make haste. The Arab (*ho áraps*) consented and came marching with a great army against Izates.[168]

The insurrection turned out to be a failure. Izates pursued his enemies to the fortress of Arsamos, where 'the Arab' Abias killed himself before the others surrendered. The fortress Arsamus is probably Arsham, known in later Syriac sources between Mosul and Zakho.[169] Where the Arabs dwelt is not clear. Since the nobles wrote to Abias for help, it is reasonable to assume that he lived at some distance from their habitat and that he was more or less independent. It is then possible that he and his Arabs dwelt on the western side of the Tigris and thus were not identical with the Adiabenian Arabs. We have argued that Iuba's *Arabes Eldamari* must have lived in Xenophon's Arabia between the two rivers. Arsham is in fact quite close to this Arabia although on the other side of the river. Josephus seems to mention these Arabs in a notice in the introduction to *The Jewish War*, where he enumerates the peoples in Mesopotamia in the following order:

> Párthoi, Babylōnioi, the most distant *árabes*, our compatriots, Adiabēnoí.[170]

The *árabes* mentioned here seem to dwell in northern Mesopotamia, connected with the Jewish inhabitants of Abdiabene, whatever the term 'most distant' (*porrōtátō*) may mean. A strong argument for looking for Abias' Arabs on the western side of the Tigris is the very name of the Arab ruler, which appears in the inscriptions from Hatra from the second century AD where ʔBYʔ is a designation for some kind of chief or military leader.[171] We hear some sixty years after Abias that the king of Adiabene in the time of Trajan possessed not only Nisibis but also Singara and Ademystra.[172] The latter has been identified with a site a few kilometres north of Hatra.[173] This could be a result of Abias' failed intervention and thus represent his territory conquered in AD 51.[174] There are arguments in favour of seeing Hatra as the centre of Mesopotamian Arabia.

Arabs in the time of Nero: Corbulo's testimony

Another piece of information on the Arabs between the two rivers is preserved by Pliny and goes back to Nero's general Domitius Corbulo, who conducted three campaigns against the Parthian king Vologases I between AD 54 and 63.[175] The issue at stake was the control of Armenia, which after the fall of Tigranes the Great became a bone of contention between Rome and Iran for centuries. The important result of these activities for our purposes was the description of the Euphrates area composed by Corbulo in the 60s and incorporated in Pliny's *Natural History*.[176] The relevant parts are as follows:

> From this point [i.e. after the mountains of Taurus] it [the Euphrates] forms the frontier between the district (*regio*) Arabia called the country of the Orroeni on the left and Commagene on the right.

> . . .
>
> Arabia mentioned above contains the towns of Edessa, which was formerly called Antiochia, Callirrhoe, named from its spring, and Carrhae, famous for the defeat of Crassus there. Adjoining it is the prefecture of Mesopotamia, which derives its origin from the Assyrians and in which are the towns of Anthemousia and Nicephorium. Then comes the *Arabes* called *Praetavi*, whose capital is Singara.
>
> . . .
>
> The people contiguous to Mesopotamia are called the Rhoali. In Syria are the town of Europus and the town formerly called Thapsacus and now Amphipolis and the *Arabes scenitae*. So the river flows on to the place named Sura, where it takes a turn to the east and leaves the Syrian desert of Palmyra, which stretches right on to the city of Petra and the region called *Arabia Felix*.[177]
>
> . . .
>
> Both rivers [the Euphrates and the Tigris] rise in Armenia, and it forms the beginning of Mesopotamia, the tract of country lying between these two rivers; the intervening space is occupied by the *Arabes Orroei*.[178]

The last paragraph is obviously a condensed version of one of the preceding ones. We can see that from a Euphratean point of view it was the Arabs around Edessa who were the most prominent, but we note the mention of the ones in Singara as well. Unfortunately, the meaning of the epithet *Praetavi* is not known. There is little doubt that the *Arabes Praetavi* in Singara are related to the *Eldamari* Arabs mentioned by Iuba. This makes it likely that they are descendants of the Arabs between the rivers mentioned by Eratosthenes and, ultimately, Xenophon. They would be identical with those commanded by Abias, and they emerge in even brighter light during the next century in the texts from what was obviously their centre: Hatra. Like *Eldamari* the name *Praetavi* is not immediately informative. But unlike the former it contains an element which is recognizable: *-tav-* which could be related to *taiēnoí* and *ṭayyāyē*, which become a general designation for peoples living in the Syrian desert from the third century AD onwards.[179] The *taiēnoí* seem, in fact, to live close to Adiabene in a source from the third century.[180]

The presence of Arabs in Osrhoene is confirmed once again by Corbulo's report. These Arabs are thus well documented in the first century AD and show that the settlement in *ʔaṯrā ḏa-ʕrab*, which we have suggested goes back to the policy of Tigranes the Great, was well established.

The Arabs in Mesopotamia were important enough to receive attention from a professional general like Corbulo. They were also called in by the nobles of Adiabene, who must have trusted their military capacity. This can be seen in a wider perspective. During the first century AD the Arabs in Syria were pacified by the Romans. The unruly Ituraean and Ḥawrān areas were brought under control. The Arabs in central Syria are not heard of any more, except those in Emesa who seem to have become more interested in religion and trade than military ventures. And in 106 Nabataea is incorporated into the empire. Through the Roman annexation of Syria the Arabs there lose their importance and seem to disappear. Instead Arabs emerge in northern Mesopotamia: Edessa, Singara and later Hatra. Hatra and Singara were parts of an old Arab area, but not much had been heard from them since Xenophon's days. In the first century AD, Arabs appear all over the northern Ǧazīra, obviously playing a growing political role in the intricate power game between Rome, Parthia and the local rulers formally subject to the Parthians. Although we cannot say for sure, it is reasonable to assume that these Arabs had their origins in Xenophon's Arabia, i.e. east of the Khābūr river, which Eratosthenes also included in his Arabia. Without any documentation it is still reasonable to assume that the Arabs there received an increased political and military role after the break-down of the Seleucid power and the rise of local dynasts in the Ǧazīra at the end of the second century BC and the turmoil prevailing in central Syria during the first century BC. We have seen that in that period Arabs from the Euphrates and even from Mesopotamia took part in the struggle for power. In the second century AD they continued to play a prominent role in Mesopotamian politics, and now for the first time Arabs leave us their own contemporary documents in the form of inscriptions.

The reasons behind this shift of centre of gravity are not difficult to see. As the Roman grip on Syria tightened during the first century AD, the border against the Parthian provinces became sharper. Since the Euphrates constituted that border, the Ǧazīra became frontier land. The kingdom of Edessa constituted an advanced bastion of Roman influence on the eastern side of the river. The Parthian control was much more lax than the Roman one, allowing the existence of several vassal states. Since the northern Ǧazīra became a deployment zone for the regularly recurring Roman campaigns to Armenia, its military importance increased drastically. At the same time it remained a kind of Wild East, being a broad wedge of dry steppes and desert-like lands intruding into the Fertile Crescent from the south, difficult for both Romans and Parthians to handle. The militarization of the Arabs in this area is already under way on the evidence of Posidonius in the first century BC, whereas in Eratosthenes' time 100 years earlier the area seems to have been peaceful, as it was in Xenophon's days. The military capacity of the Arabs was to become manifest during Trajan's attempt to settle conditions in the East at the beginning of the second century.

Arabs in the New Testament

We have some testimonies about the more traditional Arabia from the first century, originating in Jewish circles. In the New Testament we find Arabia mentioned twice in the writings of Paul, both times in the letter to the Galatians written at the beginning of the 50s AD. When giving a short account of his career he tells about what happened after his conversion at Damascus:

> I did not go up to Jerusalem to those who were apostles before me; but I went into Arabia and returned again to Damascus.[181]

The common opinion is that this Arabia is Nabataea.[182] It is told in Acts that Paul came to the house of Ananias in Damascus after the revelation of Christ to him.[183] In one of his letters he himself tells the well-known story about his flight from the city; the *ethnárkhos* of King Aretas placed guards at 'the city of the Damascenes' in order to arrest him, and Paul escaped over the wall by means of a basket.[184]

There are many problems with these passages, but the presence of an ethnarch appointed by the king in Reqem/Petra in Damascus is not impossible.[185] The king must then be Aretas 'IV', king of the Nabataeans, who was on quite good terms with the Romans.[186] One must, however, ask if it is likely that a man wanted by the security service of the Nabataean king would go directly to his territory after having just escaped.

There was another Arabia at hand, namely that between Palestine and Egypt which encompassed the Sinai peninsula. A man like Paul may well, in the first enthusiasm after the Damascus incident, have tried to follow his master by going into the desert seeking further guidance. For a Jew like Paul it was natural to look for the source of divine guidance known to Israel, namely Mount Sinai or Horeb. The prophet Elijah had done so and travelled past Beer Sheba through the Negev to Mount Horeb.[187] Did Paul follow him?

In one of the most famous passages in Paul's writings, Mount Sinai and Arabia are mentioned together. In the allegorical description of the differences between the old and the new covenant, the two matriarchs, Hagar and Sarah, are used as representatives:

> For these are the two covenants: the one from the Mount Sinai, which gendereth to bondage, which is Hagar. This Hagar-Sinai mountain is in Arabia and answereth to the Jerusalem which now is and is in bondage with her children.[188]

There has been a debate around the geographical implications of these verses. Since Arabia is seen as a term for Nabataea, it has been taken as a proof that the Jews in the first century knew that Mount Sinai was in fact situated east of the Gulf of ʕAqaba, in the northern Ḥiǧāz, and not on the present-day Sinai peninsula.[189]

Josephus' opinion seems to have been that Sinai was east of the Gulf of ʕAqaba.[190] There were, however, others who thought Sinai to be somewhere between Egypt and 'Arabia'.[191] From a reading of the Biblical texts about the Exodus and the Sinai events as they now stand and had already stood for centuries by the first century AD, the normal conclusion for a contemporary reader would have been that Mount Sinai is situated somewhere between Egypt and Palestine, i.e. Herodotus' Arabia. This is also the Old Testament setting of the story about Hagar and Ishmael. There is no reason to doubt that Paul by the term 'Arabia' in Galatians 5:24 means Arabia between Egypt and Palestine.

If Paul followed Elijah, he would thus have gone to an area which had been known as Arabia at least since the days of Herodotus. The problem is that, in that case, he would probably have remained within the area at least formally controlled by the kings in Petra, although we do not know to what extent Aretas' policemen patrolled the deserted lands of the Sinai peninsula. On the other hand, there is not a word indicating that Paul had either Elijah or Moses in mind. The impression from the passage in Galatians is that Paul did not go so far from Damascus. Could he have gone to an Arabia closer to the city? As we have seen, the term *Arabía* could mean in Greek 'an area inhabited by *árabes*', an *arabía khōra*, an 'Arabian land'. In the following century we have documentation of Arab settlement in Trachonitis not far from Damascus.[192] Arabs had been in Transjordan since Seleucid and Ptolemaic times, and it is also likely that there was a connection between them and the Arabs of Ituraea. As we shall see later, there are reasons to assume that Trachonitis was a main centre for Arabs in southern Syria.[193] Paul could thus have gone out into the deserts east or south-east of Damascus.[194] From there it was easy to return to the city when everything had calmed down.

Another passage in the New Testament refers to a more traditional Arabia. In the story about the pouring out of the Holy Spirit at the Pentecost after Jesus' death, the amazed crowd says:

> How hear we every man in our own tongue, wherein we were born . . . Jews and proselytes, Cretans and *árabes*, we do hear them [the apostles] speak in our tongues the wonderful works of God?[195]

We may notice one more reference to an Arabic language. What actually happened on this occasion is, unfortunately, no longer possible to grasp. Acts was probably written after AD 70, and it is not quite clear what is meant by *árabes* and which language is referred to. The story of the Pentecost is highly legendary, being more a theological document than a historical one. The presence of representatives of peoples from all over the world is necessary for the theological point of the story, but most unlikely from a historical viewpoint. It can be observed that the list of names of the peoples present can be divided into several groups: the eastern peoples within the borders of the Parthian empire (Parthians, Medes, Elamites and Mesopotamians), the peoples of Asia Minor (Cappadocians, Pontines, Asians, Phrygians and Pamphylians) and those on the northern coast of Africa (Egyptians and Cyrenian Libyans together with Roman colonists). Judaea is mentioned together with the Asians, and then the Jews (Judaeans) occur together with the proselytes, the Cretans and the *árabes*, who constitute a fourth group. Why Cretans and Arabs are mentioned on the same line as Jews and proselytes needs clarification. Do the Cretans and the Arabs represent the sea peoples in the west and the land-dwellers in the east respectively? One could compare the antithetical position of Arabs and Sidonians in the sayings of Aḥiqar half a millennium earlier, as well as a close parallel in Jeremiah where Arabs are replaced by Qedar.[196] From this it is obvious that the two designations reflect a proverbial saying. In that case, the passage about the Holy Spirit in Acts has two lists of peoples: an original one mentioning Jews and proselytes together with all pagans on land and sea, and another with a more detailed enumeration of peoples with large Christian minorities. The latter list would then be younger, reflecting historical conditions at the end of the first century AD, whereas the former is older, expressing a more theological and wishful thinking prevalent in certain Judaeo-Christian circles before AD 50. The Arabs mentioned in the older list do not then represent a concrete Arabic group but stand for the land-dwellers around the Holy Land in general.[197]

Arabs and the Great Jewish Revolt

For his two books on Jewish history, Josephus used a lot of sources where Arabs were mentioned. But he also mentions them in connection with the dramatic events of AD 66–70, which he witnessed himself and also took part in. According to his account in *War*, Arabs played an important role in the war against the Jews. Thus, when the Great Revolt had started, Malkhos *ho áraps* sent 1,000 cavalry and 5,000 infantry, mainly bowmen, to Titus when the Roman general had reached Akko in the spring of AD 67. Among the Roman allies we also find Herod Agrippa, Antiochus of Commagene, and Soaemus of Emesa.[198] Later, in the summer of 67, the Romans beleaguered the town of Jotapata in Galilee, where the Jews were commanded by Josephus. On three occasions he mentions Arab bowmen (*árabes toxótai* or *tōn arábōn toxótai*) on the Roman side.[199] When Jotapata fell, Josephus was taken prisoner and then joined the Roman army under

Titus when he started the final siege of Jerusalem. During the final battles one *áraps* killed Johannes, the leader of the Idumaeans who had joined the insurrection.[200] The *árabes* and Syrians are then said to have committed atrocities during the final assault.[201]

This Malchus is usually identified with MLKW MLKʔ MLK NBṬW, 'Malik the king, king of the Nabataeans', documented in inscriptions and coins from the latter half of the first century and reigning until AD 70.[202] This identification is possible but not certain.

The destruction of the Jewish temple is, of course, often mentioned in the Jewish rabbinic literature. Historical references in this literature are mostly very difficult to date and are often quite general or vague. An exception are the stories told about the Great War, which refer to a dated event and sometimes preserve genuine historical memories. The Book of Lamentations was a text whose contents were applied also to the destruction of the Second Temple, and many stories about the events in AD 70 were attached to this text as commentaries. They were collected in the Midrash Rabbah to Lamentations, which was probably written down in the fourth century.[203] In a commentary to Lamentations 1:5, 'Her adversaries are the chief, her enemies prosper', these words are applied to the events in AD 70:

> And with him (Vespasian) were four *duces*: the *dux* of ʕRBYYH, the *dux* of ʔPNYQʔ, the *dux* of SYBYTYNY . . . The *dux* of ʕRBYYʔ, what was his name? Two had an opinion. One said: 'His name was ʔYLM'. One said: 'His name was ʔBGR'.[204]

This saying is anonymous, which is often an indication of age. One of the generals mentioned is obviously from Phoenicia. SYBYTYNY is uncertain but obviously reflects the name of a region ending in *-ēnē*. The second name of the *dux* of the ʕRBYYH, Abgar, is a well-known name among Arabic-speaking groups in antiquity, the Nabataeans included. It is, however, not a typical Nabataean name, but is more frequent in the Safaitic inscriptions as well as in Palmyra.[205] The other name is also found in inscriptions as ʔYLMY, and in Safaitic and Ḥawrān.[206]

Another reference to this event is found in a commentary to Lamentations 3.7, 'He hath hedged me about', which is explained thus:

> Rabbi Abahu said: This is the *qu/inṭrā* of the Persians. Rabbi Berekhyah said: This is the *sugar* of the ʕRBYYM. The rabbis said: This is the enclave of the Kutiyyim.[207]

Sugar means 'muzzle' or 'cage'. The context as well as the meaning indicate an oppression of the Jews or Jerusalem by Arabs which makes it very likely that it refers to the events in AD 70.[208] We thus have one more confirmation of the participation of Arabs in this event.

Another saying ascribed to an authority at the beginning of the third century AD alludes to the same events:

> Rabbi Yehoshua ben Lewi once visited GBLʔ when he saw vines laden with clusters of ripe grapes standing up like calves. 'Calves among vines!' he exclaimed. 'These', they told him, 'are clusters of grapes'. 'Land, o land!' he exclaimed, 'withdraw thy fruit; for whom art thou yielding this fruit? For those ʕRBYYM who rose up against us on account of our sins?'[209]

The word GBLʔ, Gablā, 'mountain', has been identified as Gebalēnē, the area around Petra, which still is called Ǧibāl, 'mountains'.[210] The Arabs in question would thus be the Nabataeans or the Nabataean Arabs in Petra/Reqem, and these notices may preserve a memory of the participation of Nabataeans in the operations during the Great War. This identification is, however, dependent upon the identity between Gablā in the Talmudic text and the area around Petra. As we have suggested already, this could be explained if we assume that 'Arab' was a term connected with the Nabataean army. There is, however, another possibility, namely that these Arabs were not connected with the Nabataeans but came from another area. The word Gablā could be the name of many places. As we shall see later on, the Arabs are often seen as low-standing people in the Jewish tradition, whereas there are no negative statements about Nabataeans. If the latter took part in the destruction of the Temple it is at least worth noticing that they are not mentioned in connection with it. Josephus himself does not mention Nabataeans as participants in the Great War. If we keep in mind that (a) there is no self-evident identity between Nabataeans and Arabs, and (b) there were Arabs outside Nabataea, it could be asked if *Málkhos ho áraps* did not come from somewhere else. After all, the name Malik is found all over the Arabic-speaking region in antiquity and is not limited to Nabataea.[211] As was pointed out above, there is good evidence for the existence of an Arabia in Trachonitis.[212] The vine-growing GBLʔ looks more like the present Ǧabal in southern Syria than the austere region around Petra.[213] As we have seen earlier, there are reasons to assume that the Arabs were warriors sometimes closely associated with the kings in Petra but also operating on their own. The Arab participants in the Great War of 66–73 AD are said to be archers, a characteristic of the Ituraean Arabs, not the Nabataean ones. They also appear in Akko, not too far from Ḥawrān, together with rulers of areas north and north-east of Palestine. Even though Malkhos in Josephus was indeed the Nabataean king Malchus II, his Arabs were perhaps not from Nabataea but from southern Syria. There are thus arguments in favour of identifying this Arabia of the vines with the Arabia where Paul sought refuge from the police in Damascus. In that case, the *árabes* encountered by the Jewish insurgents came from al-Laǧā.

In Josephus' account of the Jewish war of AD 66–73 there are several paragraphs with geographical remarks about Palestine and its surroundings. We are informed that Peraea, i.e. the east bank of the Jordan river and the adjacent mountain slopes, borders on Arabia, Hesbonitis, Philadelphia, and Gerasa.[214] On the southern border of Judaea there is a village Iardan 'on the border of the *árabes*'.[215] The name has been identified with Arad in the eastern Negev. In a description of the ʕArabah it is said that Petra belongs to Arabia.[216] This Petra is probably Reqem. The town Zoara just south of the Dead Sea likewise belongs to Arabia.[217] Machaerus south-west of Heshbon is said to be close to the region of the *árabes*.[218] From a tower in Jerusalem one can see Arabia.[219]

The geographical commentaries seem to come from a common source. We know that Josephus used something which may be called the area handbook of the Roman army for the campaign in Palestine during 66-73.[220] Some of the information in that work may come from Pliny. There are, however, some hints that the facts represent an earlier period. The remark about Machaerus and the one about the tower view are explicitly connected with the building acitivities of Herod the Great. This, together with the border description, might have belonged to a work describing the kingdom of Herod. A candidate for the authorship is consequently Nicolaus of Damascus. His work on the history of Herod's reign must have contained a geographical description of his kingdom, including an outline of the borders.

The *Periplus Maris Erythraei*

The last source from the first century AD giving information about Arabs and Arabia is the Greek *Períplous* of the Red Sea, composed by an anonymous author in the latter half of the century, a description of the sailing routes in the Red Sea and the seaway to India.[221] The author is well informed about conditions and has perhaps made the trip himself. He is also familiar with the geographical literature, reminiscences of which are found here and there in his text.

According to the author, Arabia commences just south of Leukē Kōmē, present-day ʕAynūna. The harbour was controlled by Malikhas, king of the Nabataeans.[222] This king is identified with the Nabataean king MLK who, according to most scholars, sent the Arab bowmen to the Romans in Judaea. To Leukē Kōmē came goods from Arabia:

> Immediately after this harbour begins the Arabian country (*arabikē khōra*), extending lengthwise far down the Erythraean Sea.[223]

At a first glance, the author of the *Periplus* seems to see Arabia as the entire peninsula, although, interestingly enough, the Nabataean kingdom seems not to be included: Arabia commences where that kingdom ends. Further on he says that the Arabian coast (*ēpeiros*) is close to Africa at the Bāb al-Mandab;[224] the harbour Ommana in Gedrosia exports pearls to Arabia.[225]

At the same time, he knows that ethnic conditions are complicated with many tribes and languages. This gives his account a somewhat contradictory character. He says that inland two different languages are spoken by villagers and pastoralists. These people are called *kanraïtai*, a word of unknown meaning, and they stand in opposition to the kings of Arabia, who constantly make them prisoners[226]; the town of Muza in present-day Yemen is said to teem with *árabes*, shipowners or charterers and sailors;[227] Ocelis is a village of *árabes*[228]; another town is called *Arabía eudaímōn* and is identical with present-day Aden[229]; the island of Dioscurides, i.e. Soqotra, is inhabited by a mixture of *árabes* and Indians and even Greeks, and is subject to king Eleazos of the frankincense land.[230]

From these passages it becomes clear that what is called Arabia in the *Periplus* is mainly South Arabia. As a matter of fact, the description skips over the entire coast from ʕAynūna/Leukē Kōmē to the 'Burnt Island', a rock in the middle of the Red Sea opposite al-Luḥayya, starting again with Muza, identified as present-day Mukhā. In accordance with this it is said that the region of Azania on the African side is subject to the kingdom of Arabia, which is represented by the ruler Cholaibos of Mapharitis.[231]

On the other hand, it is worth observing that the author seems to characterize the towns Muza, Ocelis and Aden as Arab. His terminology is a little unexpected. It is as if a skipper, having visited Liverpool, Newcastle and London, reported that the towns were full of Englishmen. Were not all the other inhabitants Arabs as well to our author? Possibly, but he does not say so. We are, in fact, reminded of the usage documented from Yemen until our time as well as evidence from Arabia in the earliest decades of

Islam, namely that a characteristic of the *ʕarab* was that they dwelt in towns or cities. We also recall the *uru ša arbāya*, 'the town of the Arabs' in Babylonia in the time of Sennacherib. From South Arabia we have a notice by the writer Ibn Ḥabīb, living in the ninth century AD, who says that there were two harbours belonging to the *ʕarab* in Oman at the coming of Islam.[232]

The most remarkable notice in the *Periplus* for our theme is perhaps what is said about the the island of Sarapis, present-day Maṣīra in Oman:

> It is populated by three villages and by holy men of the Fish-eaters (*ikhthyóphagoi*). They use an Arabic language (*arabikē glōssa*) and wear loin-cloths of palm-leaves.[233]

A sanctuary on this island is mentioned a century later by Ptolemy in his *Geography*.[234] The question is, of course, which language is meant: some ancient South Arabian language, or a North Arabian one related to that used in the Qurʔān? The impression is that these people used a language different from what would be expected, which is a South Arabian one. If our author called southern languages Arabic, it is remarkable that he saw it necessary to state that the inhabitants spoke one. Would our skipper, having visited the Isle of Wight, have found it interesting or necessary to report that the inhabitants spoke English?

The *Periplus* is a very thorough and exact description of the coasts of the Red Sea and South Arabia. Anyone who has visited some of the sites described can testify to its trustworthiness. Even though the author was familiar with the geographical theories of his time, he was a solid empirist with a keen interest in geographical facts. We have already seen several examples of conflict between theoretical geographical schemes and realities in the sources used for this investigation. Contradictions in terminology have turned out to be important for our theme. When geographical and ethnological facts tend not to fit into the larger schemes of the geographers, the former should be paid attention to. We believe that the *Periplus* has preserved some very valuable facts about the position of Arabs in South Arabia in the first century AD. Their importance will become evident when we try to make a synthesis of our findings.

Arabs in the Middle East from the end of the Seleucids to Trajan: a summary

The period between *c.* 130 BC and the end of the first century AD is the most complicated to handle as far as the Arabs are concerned. Several Arab groups played an important role in the history of Syria and the surrounding countries. The sources are, however, problematic. Almost all of them are literary, often known through second- or third-hand extracts and digests written centuries afterwards. It is not easy to get a structured picture from the fragmentary evidence.

It seems that the Greek monarchs of the east inherited Arabs in the northern Sinai and around Antilebanon from the Achaemenids. At least the latter were probably settled there by the Persian rulers. Arabs also lived in the central Ǧazīra, although we do not hear much about them until the first century AD. We then find Arab groups in Syria: in the north at Chalcis (Qinnasrīn), in the centre close to Emesa, and probably also not far from Damascus. It is likely that these groups were settled there by the Seleucids for different purposes, one of which might have been guarding the borders.

In the same way, the Ptolemies used Arabs as guards within the Nile valley. They also seem to have settled Arabs in Transjordan as a counterweight to those of the Seleucids. These Arabs were most likely to have come from the bastion of Arabism in the Middle East for centuries, the Arab kingdom between Egypt, Palestine and the Red Sea, with its centre somewhere in the southern Negev, which must have been in close alliance with the Ptolemaic rulers in Alexandria.

This policy of using Arabs as border guards and police forces was probably taken over by the Seleucids and Ptolemies from their Achaemenid predecessors. When Tigranes settled Arabs in the Amanus mountains and around Tigranocerta, he thus followed ancient Iranian practice. As a matter of fact, this period represents a heyday of Arab influence within the empires: they were settled in the middle of the most important parts of the two Greek Oriental empires and, as is clearly seen from the Seleucids, were able to interfere considerably in politics when the central power started to crumble.

When the Romans took over, they seem to have tried not to interfere too much in local politics, which meant that the Arabs continued to play a role in the power struggle in Syria. Gradually, however, the Romans abolished the independence of local groups, especially when, on several occasions, it turned out that the Arabs sided with their brothers on the other side of the new border that divided the Middle East. On the Roman side, the Arab influence was waning and we hear less and less about them in the first century AD. On the Parthian side, the development was the opposite: the new borderline demanded competent guards against the Roman threat, since Rome was full of generals suffering from an Alexander the Great complex. Consequently, the Arabs in the Ǧazīra, who had been there for a long time without playing any prominent role, were now drawn into politics. When Tigranes mobilized the Arabs in the east for his struggle with Rome, he showed the way for his Parthian successors. During the first century AD we can observe the rise of Arabs to prominence as auxiliaries of the Parthians and their vassals close to the Roman border. The Arabs in the Ǧazīra reached the climax of influence and power in the second century AD, when they were able to ward off the attacks by two Roman armies.

There is no doubt that there were Arabs in other regions of Arabia. We know about those in al-Ḥasā, and there is perhaps in Agatharchides a hint of people called Arabs in the Ḥiǧāz closely associated with Thamūd. But since most of the peninsula lay outside the control of the empires we do not hear much about its inhabitants, and it can be assumed that they were not affected in the same way as those in the north by the vicissitudes of superpower politics. From the first century AD we also begin to hear more about Arabs in Yemen when they, like their colleagues in the north, were drawn into the life of the empires.

Notes

1 Appian, *Syrian War* 7 (51).
2 Bowersock, *Arabia* 33.
3 Josephus, *War* 1.178; idem, *Antiquities* 14.103.
4 Peter, *Quellen* 110–111; Plutarch, *Vies* VII 191–195.
5 For the campaign, see in general Regling, *Partherkrieg*.
6 Cassius Dio 40.20.1.
7 Plutarch, *Crassus* 21.1.
8 Cassius Dio 40.20.3–4. Regeling deals with the differing information of the sources by

identifying Ariamnes with Abgar II (*Partherkrieg* 370) and is followed by Drijvers (*Hatra* 871; cf. p. 350).
9 Florus I.46.8; Festus 17.
10 Plutarch, *Crassus* 21.5.
11 Cassius Dio 40.23.1–21; Plutarch, *Crassus* 27.1–2.
12 Plutarch, *Crassus* 29.4.
13 Plutarch, *Crassus* 28.5.
14 Plutarchus, *Crassus* 31:7.
15 Cf. Drijvers, *Hatra* 871 note 301.
16 Crassus is usually seen as an incompetent general; cf. Duval, *Histoire* 43–44; Drijvers, *Hatra* 871, a view which, however, may be exaggerated; cf. Regeling, *Partherkrieg*.
17 Drijvers, *Hatra* 876–880.
18 Plutarch, *Crassus* 21.6; 25.1.
19 Cicero, *De Divinatione* 1.42 (92, 94). See further p. 594.
20 Cicero, *Ad Familiares* 15.1.1; cf. 15.3.1; 15.4.3.
21 Dussaud identified it with Dabiq north of Aleppo. Also ʕAynṭāb further north and aṭ-Ṭayyibe in the Palmyrean desert have been suggested (*Topographie* 472, 474).
22 Cicero, *Ad Familiares* 15.4.7.
23 Cicero, *Ad Familiares* 3.8.10.
24 Plutarch does not specify the allies of Pompey at Pharsalus.
25 Appian, *History: Civil Wars* 2.71.
26 Lucan, *Pharsalia* 4.64.
27 Lucan, *Pharsalia* 7.514; cf. also 2.590: 'Me the domesticated *Arabs* know' (Pompey before the battle); 3.247: 'To an unknown land you have come, o *Arabes*!' (to the participants in Pompey's army).
28 Josephus, *Antiquities* 14.128–129.
29 Strabo 16.2.10.
30 Appian, *History: Civil Wars* 4.88.
31 Appian, *History: Civil Wars* 5.7, 9. This is the first mention of Palmyra in any source after the passage in II Chron. 8:4.
32 Cassius Dio 49.32.5. Cf. Josephus, *War* I.361–362; idem, *Antiquities* 15.79, 93–96; Plutarch, *Antony* 36:2.
33 Cf. Schürer, *History* I 561–573.
34 Josephus, *War* 1.362, idem, *Antiquities* 15.107.
35 Cassius Dio 50:13:7.
36 Plutarch, *Antony* 61.
37 Florus 2.21.7.
38 It is noticeable that the king in Petra, Malikhos, seems to have kept himself out of the war. He had been maltreated by Antony and Cleopatra and had no reason to support them. This was also the reason why Herod did not turn up at Actium: he was entrusted with the task to punish the Nabataean king (Josephus, *War* 1.364 ff; idem, *Antiquities* 15.108 ff.). These operations mainly took place in Transjordan.
39 *Agrippa, Map: Demensuratio* 29; *Divisio* 20, 21.
40 Ibid., *Divisio* §29.
41 There has for a long time been a general consensus that Agrippa constructed a map together with a written commentary which were displayed in a portico in Rome. This has, however, been put into serious doubt by Brodersen (*Terra* 268–285). He shows that the testimonies do not support the assumption of the existence of a map, only of a written list of landmarks with short commentaries. On the whole it turns out that the Roman political and military leadership were largely ignorant of the scientific geography persued by Eratosthenes and his followers. They worked with intineraries and lists of landmarks (ibid. 139–194). Strabo's *Geography* was the first scientific description of the world which made Eratosthenes accessible to the Romans. Typically, the work was largely ignored until late antiquity: For example, Pliny did not use it.
42 Ibid., *Demensuratio* § 29.

43 Reproduced by Philippi, *Weltkarte*.
44 Pomponius, Introduction (Silbermann) XXXIII–XXXIV; XXXVII. The source has been completed with later material for certain areas but the data for the Orient are from the early first century BC.
45 Pomponius 1.14, 49, 60, 61, 63, cf. 3.74.
46 Pomponius 3.74; cf. pp. 243 f.
47 Pomponius 3.80.
48 Pomponius 3.73.
49 Pomponius 3.76.
50 Pomponius 3.78.
51 The idea about the disappearance of the Euphrates is found in Polybius (9.43). Strabo has the information that the river empties into the Gulf (11.12.3), which is likely to be the Eratosthenian view.
52 Pomponius 3.79.
53 Cf. Strabo 16.3.5.
54 Strabo (16.3.6) quotes Eratosthenes just after the passage on Ogyris when referring to the Red Sea and the Persian Gulf. But it is still likely that Pomponius' source did not use Eratosthenes. Instead both he and the Alexandrian geographer used the same source, namely Nearchus.
55 Pomponius 3.80.
56 *Periplus* §§ 25–27.
57 Ptolemy 6.7.9.
58 Cf. Casson's commentary in *Periplus* 158–159.
59 Ptolemy (6.7.44) mentions the two Adanus islands, which could be taken from the same source as Pomponius.
60 *Res gestae* §5.18–23.
61 Strabo 16.4.22.
62 Pliny 6:162.
63 With one possible exception; see pp. 565 f.
64 Cf. pp. 585 f.
65 Cassius Dio 53.29.3–8.
66 There is some evidence that the location of *Arabia eudaemon* to Yemen is connected with the Gallus expedition. Augustus explicitly identifies the land of the Sabaeans with *Arabia eudaemon*, which is the earliest clear example of this identification. This is probably reflected in Strabo 1.2.32 where it is said that the spice-producing part (of Arabia) is small and that the whole region has got its name after it. The notice may well be earlier than Strabo and originally refer to the 'real' *Arabía eudaímōn* at the Persian Gulf (against W. Müller, *Frankincense* 84). It is, however, clear from Strabo that to him the spice-producing land was Yemen, where his friend Aelius Gallus had almost reached the frankincense land. The confusion between *Arabía eudaímōn* and the frankincense-producing regions in Yemen seem to be very old, already documented in Euhemerus, although there is no doubt about the geographical separation between the two. The reason may have been the fact that frankincense from Dhufar first reached the Middle East via Gerrha and Baḥrayn long before the route through Ḥiğāz was established; cf. Nicander, *Alexipharmaca* 107, written perhaps around 200 BC, where it is stated that frankincense grows at Gerrha. The idea that *Arabía eudaímōn*, Gerrha and the frankincense land were more or less adjacent is observable in many passages in ancient literature; see, for example, Dionysius Periegetes p. 305.
67 Dihle, *Daten* 82; Pirenne, *Royaume* 93–124; von Wissmann, *Geschichte* III 10–11, 89–91; Robin, *Sheba* 1132; Müller, *Marib* 561; Sidebotham, *Aelius Gallus* 591.
68 Cf. Dihle, *Daten* 83.
69 Strabo 2.5.12.
70 *Res Gestae* § 26.6: . . . *Germaniam . . . ad ostium Albis flumen pacavi*. The only hint at the catastrophe in the year AD 9 is the absence of the word *provincia* in connection with the pacification of Germania. The *Res gestae* were finally redacted in the year before Augustus' death in AD 14 (Gagé's edition, 16; cf. 22 note 2 for the discussion of the passage).

71 Marek (*Expedition* 138 ff., 142–144) shows a healthy scepticism towards Strabo's account but instead places a too uncritical confidence in Pliny and the *Res Gestae*.

72 The most important echo in *belles-lettres* of the Gallus expedition is in Horace's odes. In one (I:XXIX), written just before the expedition, (26–25 BC; cf. Nisbel/Hubbard, *Commentary* 337–339) Horace asks his friend, the philosopher Iccius, why he wants to leave the comfortable life in Rome: 'O Iccius, do you long for the wonderful treasures/of the *Arabes*? and, preparing a harsh war,/for the not earlier defeated kings/of the Sabaeans? and for the terrible Mede / forging chains?'. In another (I:XXXV), written shortly before (cf. Nisbel/Hubbard, *Commentary* 387) he prays the goddess of Fortune to give success to the Roman weapons: 'O may you on a new/anvil reforge blunted swords against/the Massagetae and the *Arabes*.' Both poems show that the campaign was seen in Rome as an attack on the Arabs in general, i.e. the inhabitants of the Arabian peninsula. The linking of Arabs and 'Medes' (i.e. Parthians) in I:XXIX is noteworthy. Since the Massagetae, according to Herodotus, lived between the Caspian and the Aral Sea, they could here stand for the Parthians, who originated in that area. This is a support for Marek's hypothesis that the Arabian campaign was a preparation for a war in the East (Marek, *Expedition*). It was already suggested by Kiessling (*Horatius* 128). This speaks against the claim by Altheim/Stiehl (*Araber* II 56) that the expedition was a continuation of the Red Sea policy of the Ptolemies.

73 Cf. Jacoby, *Iuba* 2391–2392; idem, *Fragmente* 3A 127–155 (no. 275).

74 Cf. Pliny 6.141.

75 Pliny 6.124, 138–139, 147–152.

76 Pliny 6.96–100, 107 (from Nearchus).

77 Pliny 6.100–101.

78 Pliny 6.101–106.

79 For the Hippalus wind, see Otto, *Hippalos*; Diehle, *Voraussetzungen*.

80 Pliny 6.117–118, 138–140.

81 For Isidorus see p. 358, n. 24.

82 Pliny 6.142–162.

83 The introductory passage (141) is a resumé of what Pliny has said in other parts of his book together with undigested fragments from Posidonius, Varro and other writers.

84 Pliny 6.143 (end)–144.

85 Pliny 6.145–146.

86 See p. 302.

87 Pliny 6.147–156.

88 Pliny 6.153–156. von Wissmann (*Geschichte* II 15, 39–40) assumes that part of Iuba's information on South Arabia goes back to report from *c.* 400 BC.

89 For this text, see the studies by von Wissmann, *Zamareni* I, II.

90 Pliny 6.160–162.

91 Pliny 6.167–171, 176–177.

92 Pliny 12.50–65, 66–73, 77–78.

93 Pliny 5.98, 100, 104.

94 Pliny 12.50, 73.

95 Pliny 6.142–143. The passage is an explicit quotation from Iuba: ibid. 6.141.

96 Pliny 6.139.

97 Pliny 6.144, 149–151 (eastern Arabia), 154–159 (southern and western Arabia).

98 Pliny 6.165–179.

99 The importance and value of Iuba's information on conditions in the interior parts of Arabia is exemplified by von Wissmann's studies on the caravan routes described in Pliny 6.157–159.

100 Pliny 6.117–118.

101 Dillemann, *Haute-Mésopotamie* 78 and map 76. According to Dillemann, Pliny has mixed up this city with Nisibis.

102 Dillemann, *Haute-Mésopotamie* 98.

103 They are already mentioned by Xenophon, *Anabasis* 4.3.4.

104 Dillemann (*Haute-Mésopotamie* 98–99) translates 'chez les Arabes appelés Orroens et Mardanes'. It is also possible to see Mar/ndani as inserted: the town is situated in the territory inhabited by the *Arabes Orroei* together with the Mar/ndani, *Arabes* thus only referring to the Orroei. Such distinctions were not important to Pliny, who loved name dropping.
105 Arrian, *Anabasis* 7.21. In the MSS to Arrian there is a variant Pollakottas to Pollakopas, which is reflected in Pliny's text and is probably a better reading. The same form is found in Appian, *History* 2.153; cf. Meissner, *Pallacottas* 7; Sturm, *Pallakontas*. The -kopas could be a popular Greek etymology from *koptō* 'dig'.
106 Meissner, *Pallacottas* 8.
107 In Akkadian texts it is called Pallukkatu(m); cf. Meissner, *Pallacottas* 8 ff. For the identity with Fallūǧa, see ibid. 10–11.
108 Yāqūt, *Muʕǧam* I:755.
109 Cf. pp. 332–333.
110 Pliny 6.125.
111 Pliny 6.139; cf. 6.145.
112 1 Chronicles 5:18–22.
113 Genesis 25:15.
114 Eusebius, *Praeparatio* 9.30.3.
115 Josephus, *Antiquities* 13.11.3.
116 For the history, see Jones, *Urbanization*; Schottroff, *Ituräer*; Schürer, *History* I 561–563.
117 Cf. Bietenhard, *Dekapolis* 33–39.
118 Schürer, *History* I 565.
119 Beer, *Ituraea* 2378; Schürer, *History* I 563; Knauf, *Ituraea*.
120 Cassius Dio 59:12:2.
121 Strabo 16.2.18, 20; cf. p. 355.
122 Lucan 7.514; cf. p. 397.
123 Apuleius 6.1.
124 *Historia Augusta*: *Aurelianus* 11.3. One should observe the consistent spelling with a *y* instead of (*o*)*u*, which indicates a common source, probably Livy. Eutropius 6.14.1: *Arabes* and *Ituraei*. Festus' *Breviarium* (3.14.16) instead distinguishes between *Saraceni* and *Arabes* in the same area; cf. Bowersock, *Arabs* 75.
125 Schottroff, *Ituräer* 125–127, 149–152.
126 Merkel, *Festsetzungen* 150.
127 Strabo 16.2.11; cf. pp. 353 ff.
128 Merkel, *Festsetzungen* 153.
129 Diodorus 40.1a–1b; cf. p. 350.
130 For its history, see Sullivan, *Dynasty*, *passim*.
131 Cicero, *Ad Atticum* 2.162.
132 Cicero, *Ad Familiares* 15.1–2; Cassius Dio 50.13.7; cf. pp. 398 f.
133 Cassius Dio 54.9.20.
134 Sullivan, *Dynasty* 215–218.
135 Cf. Merkel, *Festsetzungen* 146–148.
136 Cf. Seyrig, *Antiquités* 76 186. It is difficult to agree with Eliséeff's claim (*Ḥimṣ* 397) that one can still see traces of Roman town planning.
137 Merkel, *Festsetzungen* 141.
138 Cf. Seyrig, *Antiquités* 76 186.
139 Against Merkel, *Festsetzungen* 150–151.
140 Cf. Chad, *Dynastes* 103–127.
141 Josephus, *Antiquities* 15.167.
142 Cf. Lesquier, *L'arabarchès*; Schürer, *History* III 136 n. 43.
143 Cicero, *Ad Atticum* 2.17.3.
144 Cf. Laqueur, *Theophanes* 2127.
145 Josephus, *Antiquities* 18.159, 259; 19.276.
146 Cf. Schürer, *History* I 456–457. His son Tiberius Alexander became procurator of Judaea *c.* AD 46–48.

147 Josephus, *Antiquities* 20.147.
148 Juvenal 1.130.
149 OGIS no. 674 (= Dittenberger, *Inscriptiones* 2 413–419).
150 *Supplementum* 100–101.
151 For example, OGIS 202 (Dittenberger, *Inscriptiones* 1 311) and OGIS 685 (Dittenberger, *Inscriptiones* 2 427–428); the latter is still to be read on one of the Memnon statues opposite Luxor in Egypt. The two texts are undated but are ascribed to the time of Augustus by Rostovtzeff/Welles (*Parchment* 49); P.I.S. no. 305 (= Vitelli, *Papiri* IV 38) from the second or third century AD. For further references, see Lesquier, *L'arabarchès*; Schürer, *History* III 136–137.
152 Bilabel, *Sammelbuch* no. 7244 (p. 254).
153 Dura parchment X:5 = Rostovtzeff/Welles, *Contract* 6–7.
154 Pliny 6.117–118; cf. p. 405.
155 Cf. Gehais, *Claudius* 2837; Detlefsen, *Anordnung* 155.
156 Pliny 6.129.
157 Curtius 5.1.11–12.
158 For the course of events, see Debevoise, *History* 172–173; Wolski, *Empire* 162 ff.
159 Cassius was governor of Syria; cf. Josephus, *Antiquities* 20.1 and 15.406 f.
160 Cf. Koestermann, *Erläuterungen* III 18. For Pliny's lost continuation of Aufidius, see Gundel, *Plinius*.
161 Tacitus, *Annales* 12.12.
162 Tacitus, *Annales* 12.14.
163 Duval, *Histoire* 48; Debevoise, *History* 172; Drijvers, *Hatra* 872; Koestermann, *Cornelius Tacitus* ad loc.
164 See pp. 440 ff.
165 Acbarus has been emended to Abgarus by modern editors of Tacitus; this has, however, no support in the MSS.
166 Cf. Harding, *Index* s.vv. ʔKBR (p. 61) and KBR (p. 493).
167 Tacitus has *apud oppidum Edessam.*
168 Josephus, *Antiquities* 20:77–78.
169 Fiey, *Assyrie* II 389–390.
170 Josephus, *War* 1.3.
171 See Segal, *Arabs at Hatra* 59–60, and p. 443.
172 Cassius Dio 68.22.2–3.
173 Dillemann, *Haute-Mésopotamie* 285 and 149 (map XVIII).
174 For the history of this area, see Teixidor, *Kingdom.*
175 For this campaign, see Dillemann, *Haute-Mésopotamie* 268–272.
176 Pliny 5.83–90; 6.24–25; cf. Detlefsen, *Anordnung* 86–87, 155–156.
177 Pliny 5.85, 86, 87. Anthemusia is Sarūğ and Nicephorium is Raqqa on the Euphrates. The meaning of the term 'Rhoali' is unknown. Dillemann's suggestion (*Haute-Mésopotamie* 77 n. 3) that it is a distortion of Orhoeni is only a guess.
178 Pliny 6.25.
179 In another, very confused passage (6.157) Pliny reports a people named *Taveni* living near the Nabataeans: *Nabataeis Timaneos iunxerunt veteres; nunc sunt Taveni, Suelleni, Araceni, Arreni oppida in quod negotiatio omnis convenit.* 'The ancient [authorities] joined the Timanei to the Nabataeans. Now there are the Taveni, Suelleni, Araceni, Arreni – in (?) a city into which all business is concentrated' (the syntax of the passage is not clear).The name Araceni is reminiscent of Aragdos and Rugdini mentioned in the sixth century BC (cf. p. 186) which should be looked for somewhere in the western Syrian Desert. In that case, the Taveni should also be found there. One should observe that the names are all derived from regional names ending in -ēnē̆, which points to the Seleucid sphere of the Syrian desert. One could imagine a migration from the Syrian desert into the Ğazīra in the Roman period which seems to be what Pliny says. If the Taveni/Praetavi are identical with the *ṭayyāyē̆,* it would explain why this latter term in later Syriac literature is the cover term for all the tribes in the Syrian desert: they had achieved quite a dominant position in the early Roman period.

180 Namely Hippolytos' *DiamerismOs*; see pp. 487–490.
181 Galatians 1:17.
182 Bruce, *Epistle* 95–96.
183 There are two versions of the story differing slightly from each other: Acts 9 and 22.
184 2 Corinthians 11:32.
185 Ananias' house is shown today in the quarter of Damascus still in the Middle Ages called *an-Naybaṭūn*, 'the Nabataeans'. The authenticity is, of course, not possible to prove, but it is quite certain that the house is an ancient Christian sanctuary probably going back to the first century. It has been shown that this quarter (between present-day Bāb Tūmā and Bāb aš-šarʔi) is an addition to the Greek city, whose plan is still very visible in the Old City of Damascus. It has been assumed that this quarter was established during the Nabataean occupation of the city between 85 and 72 BC (Sauvaget, *Plan* 343–345). As we have shown, there was no Nabataean occupation in this period (above, pp. 343 f). On the other hand, Nabataeans are documented in northern Transjordan as early as the third century BC (above, p. 294) and a Nabataean settlement in Damascus may have existed very early which remained a closed quarter reserved for Nabataeans under an ethnarch, just as is known from Alexandria. The expression 'city of the Damascenes' in 2 Cor. in fact becomes comprehensible if one assumes that the city of the Nabataeans was separated from the city of the (other) Damascenes (see Sack, *Damaskus* 11 and n. 66 for further references). The medieval name of the quarter is a testimony to a long Nabataean presence.
186 Schürer, *History* I 581–583; Negev, *Nabateans* 567; Bruce, *Epistle* 96.
187 1 Kings 19:3–4, 8–9.
188 Galatians 4:24–25. The translation of the beginning of verse 25 is difficult, and the meaning of the whole passage is far from clear. There are also several variant readings in MSS and versions. The reading with *tò* is *lectio difficilior* and should be retained; cf. Bruce, *Epistle* 219. If so, *tò* must refer to *óros*, 'mountain', and the two words *Agar* and *Sina* in between must be some kind of attribute to it. The interpretation here takes Hagar, Sinai and covenant to be more or less identical (cf. Burton, *Galatians* ad loc. p. 258 f. and Bruce, loc. cit.). Bruce renders: 'Now Hagar is Mt Sinai in Arabia.'
189 For the arguments, see Gese, *tò dè Agár*, especially 88–94.
190 Josephus, *Antiquities* 2.257, 264; cf. 6.140 and the discussion of these passages in Gese, op. cit. W. W. Müller (*Araber*) suggests that Hagar is a play on al-Ḥiğr in the Ḥiğāz, which is rightly rejected by Bruce (*Epistle* 219–220).
191 Josephus, *Contra Apionem* 2.25.
192 Ptolemy 5.15.20; Iustinus 283, 275; cf. p. 437. As late as around AD 500 we hear about 'an ancient fortress' near Bosra built by 'Arabian kings', *arabikoì basileîs*, before the reign of a Severus (Damascius, *Vita Isidori* § 191). This is also the area where we find the inscription of AD 328 from a 'king of all ʕRB' (see pp. 467 ff).
193 See pp. 612 f. It is worth pointing out that the present-day name of Trachonitis, al-Lağā, means 'refuge', 'asylum', showing that it has been a haven for people on the run for a long time.
194 For a similar interpretation, see Agrain, *Arabie* 1160.
195 Acts 2:8–11.
196 Ahiqar l. 208; see p. 190 and Jeremiah 2:10.
197 Cf. Eissfeldt, *Kreter*, for a similar analysis of this passage.
198 Josephus, *War* 3.68.
199 Josephus, *War* 3.168, 211, 262.
200 Josephus, *War* 4.290.
201 Josephus, *War* 4.551, 556.
202 Schürer, *History* I 583; Meshorer, *Coins* 63–70; Negev, *Nabateans* 569–570.
203 Strack/Stemberger, *Einleitung* 263–266.
204 *Ekhah Rabbati* 33a. A reference to this event is also found in the midrash to Psalms. In a commentary to Psalm 18:48, 'thou hast delivered me from the violent man', it is said that this expression stands for Edom = Rome and Ishmael, which is likely to be the Arabs mentioned in connection with the destruction of the Temple (*Midrash Tehillim* ad loc.).

205 See Negev, *Names* no. 5 and 6 (p. 9). It is of course best known as the most frequent name of the kings in Edessa.
206 Negev, *Names* no. 74 (p. 11).
207 *Ekhah Rabbati* 124–125.
208 The Kutiyym are the people settled by the Assyrians in Samaria after the fall of the northern kingdom of Israel (2 Kings 17:24–41). Later, the word was used for the Samaritans whose settlement in Sikem was a continuous cause of irritation for the Jews. *qu/inṭrā* is translated differently (Krauss: 'needle', Jastrow: 'knot') but the expression here could refer to the plight of the Jews told in the book of Esther. Krauss' opinion (*Nachrichten* 330) that the whole passage refers to the situation of the Jews in the diaspora in different countries is less likely.
209 *T.B. Ketubbot* 112a. For the dating of Rabbi Yehoshua, see Strack/Stemberger, *Einleitung* 89–90.
210 Cf. Eusebius, *Onomasticon* 96:18, 124:20; cf. Psalm 83:8.
211 There is even a rabbinic authority named MLWK ʕRBʔH, 'Mallukh the Arab' (*T.B. Ḥullin* 49a).
212 Cf. Ptolemy 5.15.20; cf. pp. 417, 467, 613 f.
213 Cf. also Krauss, *Nachrichten* 328.
214 Josephus, *War* 3.47.
215 Josephus, *War* 3.51.
216 Josephus, *War* 4.454.
217 Josephus, *War* 4.482.
218 Josephus, *War* 7.172.
219 Josephus, *War* 5.160.
220 Cf. Thackeray's Introduction in Josephus, *War* xx–xxii. Tacitus also used this source.
221 There has been considerable discussion about the dating of the *Periplus*; see Dihle, *Daten* 9–35, who argues for a dating in the first century AD. Decisive arguments based on epigraphical evidence from South Arabia have been proposed by Robin, *L'Arabie*, idem, *Date*, giving a date for the composition of the *Periplus* between 40 and 70 AD. Cf. also Kitchen, *Documents* 22–25, 28–29.
222 According to Strabo 16.4.23, this harbour was already under Nabataean control in the days of Aelius Gallus.
223 *Periplus* § 20. For the identification of Leukē Kōmē with ʕAynūna, see Casson's commentary to *Periplus* § 29 (pp. 143–144) and Kirwan, *Port*, but see the objections by Gatier/Salles, *L'emplacement*, who suggest al-Wağh further south.
224 *Periplus* § 25.
225 *Periplus* § 36. Potts' claim (*Gulf* II 306–310) that this Ommana is inside the Hormuz straits, perhaps identifiable with ad-Dūr in the emirate of Umm al-Qaywayn, is not tenable. His conclusion is based on an incorrect translation of the Greek text. The text mentions the mountains called Asabo, which are identified with those forming Rās Musandam. Then, after mentioning the Persian Gulf, it says: 'after having sailed by (*parapleúsanti*) the mouth of the Gulf, six runs further, you come to another port of trade of Persis called Ommana' (§ 36). For *parapléō* cannot mean anything else than 'sailing past, by' or perhaps 'close to' ('sailing through' would be *diapléō*). Since it is also said that Ommana exports goods to Arabia as well as to India, it must be outside Arabia. One should compare the wording in the letter from Faylaka (Piejko, *Inscriptions* 95–97): 'Do not permit anyone to collect tax for exportation [from Icarus/Failaka] to the mainland of Arabia (*eìs dè tēn en ēpeírōi Arabían*).' On the other hand, there seems also to have existed an Oman within the Gulf (Potts, *Arabia* 152 ff.; *Gulf* II 302–305) which, however, is not the Oman mentioned in the *Periplus*. We have to accept that the name Oman was used for several locations inside and outside the Straits of Hormuz.
226 *Periplus* § 20.
227 *Periplus* § 21.
228 *Periplus* § 25.
229 *Periplus* § 26.

230 *Periplus* §§ 30–31; cf. Casson ad loc. For the identity of this Hadrami king, see Robin, *L'Arabie* 13.
231 *Periplus* § 16. For the identification of this ruler, see Robin, *L'Arabie* 11–12.
232 Ibn Ḥabīb, *Muḥabbar* 265–266.
233 *Periplus* § 33; cf. Casson's commentary p. 175.
234 Ptolemy 6.7.47.

15

ARABS IN THE AGE OF THE GOOD EMPERORS

Sources for the second century AD

The most important sources for the history of Arabs in the second century AD are the contemporary inscriptions, where Arabs now begin to appear for the first time since the days of the Achaemenids. Arabs are mentioned in two groups of inscriptions: texts from the northern Ǧazīra (Hatra and Sumatar Harbesi) and the inscriptions in Yemen originating from kings and noblemen in the South Arabian kingdoms. We shall treat the history of the Arabs in the north and in the south separately, since they developed rather independently of each other during this period.

From the north we also have literary sources. The most important is Cassius Dio's Roman history, complemented by the two *Breviaria* of Festus and Eutropius from the fourth century AD. These sources give information about the historical events involving Arabs. Cassius' original text is unfortunately lost for the years AD 46–217.[1] For that period, his text has to be reconstructed from excerpts and abbreviations made from the books before they were lost.[2] A very special source, the *Scriptores Historiae Augustae*, becomes useful for the latter half of the second century. This work is a collection of biographies of Roman emperors from Hadrian to Carus, claiming to be written by different authors, but probably the work of one man at the end of the fourth century AD, composing a collection of stories by fictitious authors.[3] The value of the work is very uneven but, especially in the first part, the author seems to have used some good sources which can be discerned.[4]

Apart from these historians we have sources of other types. A very important one is the world geography of Claudius Ptolemy, written shortly after AD 150, which contains much data on Arabia not found in Pliny's sources. Some time in the same century another monograph on Arabia was compiled by a certain Glaucus, which is quoted by Stephanus of Byzantium in the sixth century.

A very special type of sources are the Jewish ones. After Josephus the Jews gradually ceased to use Greek. Instead we have a large corpus of texts in Hebrew ascribed to Palestinian Jewish rabbis mostly living after AD 70. This corpus, preserved in two large collections, the Mishna and the Tosephta, contains material from the period until *c.* AD 200 when, according to tradition, the Mishna was finally written down. The Tosephta was codified around a century later. There is also a great deal of further material ascribed to these authorities as well as to their successors, preserved in Jewish texts written down much later, like the Babylonian Talmud and the expositions of the Biblical texts known as midrash. This entire material contains not a few references to Arabs which, however, are most difficult to date exactly. The sayings of the rabbis were often transmitted for a very long time, and we can never be certain that the earliest identified transmitter also formulated the saying. The rabbinic references to Arabs will be dealt with in a separate chapter and not spread into the chronological frame of this study.

The reign of Trajan and its results

The accession of Marcus Ulpius Traianus in the year AD 98 as *princeps* of the Roman empire initiated a more aggressive Roman *Ostpolitik*. The latter half of the first century had already witnessed an ambition on the part of the Romans to simplify the map of the Roman sphere of interest in the Middle East. The buffer kingdoms of Commagene and Emesa as well as the remains of Ituraea and the entities of the Herodians disappeared. Palmyra had already become Roman in the time of Augustus.[5] After his campaigns in Dacia, Trajan took action against the last Middle Eastern Roman ally of any importance. Cassius Dio gave only a short notice about the event, which is also echoed in Eutropius' *Breviarium*:

> About this same time, Palma, the governor of Syria, subdued the part of Arabia around Petra and made it subject to the Romans.[6]

> After that he (Trajan) made Arabia into a province.[7]

On coins issued for the occasion we read *Arabia adquisita*, which has been interpreted as an indication of a peaceful annexation rather than a large military operation.[8] The end of the Arabo-Nabataean kingdom led to the establishment of a new Roman province which, interestingly enough, was called Provincia Arabia (not Nabataea). The acquisition of the province was the logical conclusion of a long development where the economic importance of the overland roads to the Arabian peninsula had been steadily decreasing, paralleled by a Roman build-up on the eastern Syrian border, mainly for strategic reasons: the incessant struggle between Rome and Parthia for the Armenian throne made it necessary for the Romans also to strengthen their southern flank.[9]

In AD 113 Trajan set out for the great eastern campaign. The trigger was once again Armenia, where a man of the Parthians had been installed. The campaign lasted till August 117, when Trajan died in Cilicia on his way back to Rome. Our main source of the events is Cassius Dio, who may have had access to reliable information from Arrian's *Parthica*, now lost apart from a few names quoted by Stephanus of Byzantium in his ethnic and geographical encyclopedia.[10] Arrian, whom we have already met as the biographer of Alexander the Great, was proconsul in Cappadocia AD 131–137 and obviously had access to reliable information.[11] Unfortunately, book 68 in Cassius Dio, which contained the account of the Parthian campaign, is known only through the digests of later writers, the most important being that of the Byzantine Xiphilinus in the eleventh century, who was a rather faithful copyist. Other material comes from panegyrical biographies of Trajan, a genre with little historical value except for political terminology and some notices on conquests. Especially the former tends to reflect actual political conditions, not manipulated in accordance with the theories of geographers. This material turns up in the historical compendia of Festus and Eutropius.[12]

The details of the campaigns will not be traced here.[13] The Romans clashed with Arabs twice during the operations. The first occasion was sometime in the winter of

114–115 when Armenia had been conquered and Trajan had advanced southwards and taken Nisibis. Cassius says, according to Xiphilinus:

> Trajan came to Edessa, and there he saw Abgarus for the first time. For although Abgarus had previously sent envoys and gifts to the emperor on numerous occasions, he himself, first on one excuse and then another, had failed to put in an appearance, as was also the case with Mannus, the [*phylarkhos*] of neighbouring Arabia, and Sporaces, the *phylarkhos* of Anthemousia.[14]

The Edessan king, who was Abgar VII (*c.* 109–116) and who had been installed as a puppet of the Parthians, now received the victorious Roman emperor and offered him everything he wanted in order to placate his ire. Other local potentates in upper Mesopotamia were also now eager to show their loyalty, with varying success:

> When Trajan had come into Mesopotamia, Mannus sent a herald to him . . . He was suspicious of Mannus, the more so as this king had sent an auxiliary force to Mebarsapes, king of Adiabene, on which occasion he had lost it all at the hands of the Romans. Therefore Trajan at this time also did not wait for them to draw near, but made his way to them at Adiabene. Thus it came about that Singara and some other places were occupied by Lusius without a battle.[15]

Trajan's activities during the winter of 114–115 are also reflected and summarized in the comentaries in the two *Breviaria*:

> He occupied the areas (*loca*) of the Osrhoeni and the *árabes*[16]

> He received the submission (*fides*) of *árabes* and Osdroeni[17]

Notable in the *Breviaria* is the distinction between Arabs and Osrhoeni. The phylarch of Arabia has a name well known from domestic sources, MʕNW = Maʕnū, which appears as the name of several kings of Edessa. But from Dio's account it is obvious that this Mannus did not reign in the city. It has been assumed that Mannus resided in the area south of Mardin, thus the land of the Osrhoenian Arabs mentioned in the sources from the preceding century. In Uranius' *Arabiká* written in the fourth century we hear about *árabes manneōtai* close to a town called Mannakarta, 'the city of Maʕn(u)', situated on the river Zergan just below Mardin, which would then be the same region.[18] This information probably comes from Arrian's *Parthica*. The account also shows that the Arabia of Mannus was connected with Adiabene in an alliance. We have seen earlier that this was probably the outcome of the episode between Izates and Abias in AD 49.[19] The campaign against Adiabene was not directed against Adiabene Transtigrim exclusively; that was attacked one year later when Trajan initiated the large operations that ended with the capture of Ctesiphon.[20] The aim of Lusius' expedition, which was probably undertaken at the beginning of AD 115, was Singara, which was called Arabia and was allied to the king of Adiabene. In the quotations from Arrian's *Parthica* preserved in Stephanus of Byzantium, we find Thebeta, Hatra and Libanai mentioned.[21] The latter is identical with present-day Qalʕat Sharqāṭ, which is the site of Asshur, the ancient capital of Assyria, on the western bank of the Tigris.[22]

The first is somewhere between Wādī Ǧarrāḥ and Ǧabal Singār on the present Syro-Iraqi border.[23] Lusius thus reached the Tigris after a march through the whole of Arabia west of the river. We have already observed that there is plenty of evidence for the Arabs in the Singara area from the time of Claudius, and for their close alliance with the kings in Adiabene. This evidence also shows that the Arabs in Osrhoene had tight links with Singara. The activities of Mannus appear as directed from Singara; at least this is how the Romans understood it. Singara emerges as a centre of Arab politics in the Ǧazīra: the Arabs there were on good terms with the rulers both in Adiabene and in Edessa. Our assumption that the Arabs in Osrhoene as well as those allied with Adiabene in fact came from Singara and its capital Hatra seems to be supported by the reports from the campaigns in AD 115.

When Trajan had conquered lower Mesopotamia and had reached the Persian Gulf in the first half of AD 116, insurrection broke out in the conquered territories. The Roman army turned back and crushed the insurrection. The operations lasted from the summer of AD 116 to the summer of AD 117. Trajan sent Lusius Quietus to Upper Mesopotamia to crush the revolt, which he did. Nisibis was captured and Edessa was burnt. Abgar VII was probably killed. In connection with this we read the following in Xiphilinus' version of Cassius Dio's text:

> Next he [Trajan] came into Arabia and began operations against the *atrēnoí/agarēnoí*, since they too had revolted. This city is neither large nor prosperous, and the surrounding country is mostly desert and has neither water (save a small amount and that poor in quality) nor timber nor fodder. These very disadvantages, however, afford it protection, making impossible a siege by a large multitude, as does also the Sun-god to whom it is consecrated; for it was taken neither at this time by Trajan nor later by Severus.[24]

In the modern editions of Cassius Dio the reading *atrēnoí* is usually given instead of *agarēnoí*.[25] The former is derived from the name of the city, Hatra. The two basic manuscripts to Xiphilinus' digest have the latter, which indeed looks like somehow being derived from Hagar. But *atrēnoí* is found in another source for this passage in Cassius Dio's lost text, namely in a collection of excerpts from different historians called *De virtutibus et vitiis*, 'On virtues and vices', in which there are 415 excerpts from Dio.[26] The questions are thus: which is the original reading and which is the town?

The answer to the latter question also gives the answer to the first one. The Roman historian Ammian Marcellinus, who wrote the history of Julian the Apostate in the fourth century, says when describing the campaign of that emperor in Mesopotamia in 362–363: 'We came near to Hatra, an old city placed in the middle of solitude and deserted since a long time ago . . . Trajan and Severus, warlike rulers, were almost annihilated here.'[27] As we shall see later on, it is explicitly told that the emperor Septimius Severus also laid siege to Hatra during his campaign in the east at the end of the second century. In the light of Ammian's remark it is clear that Cassius Dio's account refers to Trajan's siege of the town.[28] Important for the interpretation of the passage about the siege of Hatra is, however, the fact that there has been a confusion between the two emperors in the textual tradition of Cassius Dio's work. In one passage preserved in another collection of excerpts from different historians, the so-called *Excerpta Ursiniana*, it is said that Vologaesus, the son of Sanatruces, one of the Parthian governors, arrayed himself against Severus. This is obviously a mistake for Trajan, and the note belongs to the account of Trajan's campaign.[29] In the account of Severus' campaign, Hatra is mentioned by name several times in Cassius Dio's text. Since it was known that this passage about Trajan also dealt with a siege of Hatra, the confusion is explicable, as is the introduction of the name of the inhabitants of the town in the story of Trajan. The reading *atrēnoí* can be explained as an intrusion from the account about Severus' siege of the town eighty years later. This means that the reading *agarēnoí* in the account of Trajan's siege is probably the original one, since its presence cannot be explained otherwise. The consequence is that, according to Cassius Dio (or rather his source), in the days of Trajan the town of Hatra was situated in Arabia and was inhabited by people called *agarēnoí*, i.e. Hagarenes.[30] The implications of this mention of Hagarenes in Hatra will be returned to later in this study.

The failure to take Hatra must have greatly increased the reputation of the town among the tribes around it. We know of a ruler in Hatra at the beginning of the second century, named WRD = Worodes in the inscriptions from the town, who might have been the one who withstood the Roman assault. This WRD had the title MRY, 'lord', and both his son and his grandson are documented with the same title. They all seem to have constituted a dynasty ruling in Hatra during the first half of the second century AD.[31] Both the term *agarēnoí* and the name 'Arabia' for the area indicate the presence of Arabs in or around Hatra. It should, however, be noted that there is no indication that the rulers in the time of Trajan were Arabs, although this cannot be ruled out. Whatever identity they had, they were obviously some kind of Parthian vassals, serving as guards of the central Ǧazīra.

Trajan's successor, Hadrian, gave up the conquests in the east. He withdrew the Roman army to the Euphrates line. There are several possible reasons. Apart from the purely strategic ones, there had obviously been resistance in certain circles against Trajan's Oriental project. In the insurrection Jews played a prominent role, and we know that the Palmyrenes also sympathized with it. It is clear that the division of the Middle East cemented in 63 BC had created a growing class of go-betweens who handled the traffic across the border. Among these the Jews were important since they lived on both sides. Also Palmyra profited from its position as a border town. Palmyrenes, Jews and others profiting from the border traffic suffered a major setback when Trajan abolished the border and moved it to the Persian Gulf. In addition, of course, the Jews had other reasons to hate the Romans. During the insurrection, Charax remained calm, probably because in the new world order, which happened to last only two years, it had become a new Palmyra on the new Roman border to the east. We may notice the overwhelming reception given to Hadrian when he visited Palmyra and other cities in Syria in AD 129. Some of the monuments erected for the occasion by enthusiastic local politicians are still standing.[32] More important for us is the fact that the restitution of the border made permanent the role of the Arabs. The following century became the great age of the Arabs in the Ǧazīra.

Claudius Ptolemy

The historical events in the second century involving Arabs are known through sources written much later. In Ptolemy's book on geography, *Geographikē hyphēgēsis*, we have a contemporary source. This is the last great independent scholarly work on world geography and ethnology in antiquity and sums up the information gathered during the preceding centuries.[33] The book was written after the year AD 141, and we know that Ptolemy died under Marcus Aurelius (AD 161–180). It was thus completed shortly after the middle of the second century AD. It was based on the work of earlier geographers, among whom was a certain Marinus from Tyre.[34] This man wrote a collection of notes and commentaries on a world map in the time of Trajan.[35] Marinus' map and notes were an exhaustive summary of geographical knowledge at the beginning of the second century AD.[36] Ptolemy drew heavily on Marinus, and most of the geographical names in Ptolemy's *Geography* are likely to come from him.[37] Ptolemy's work consists of eight parts or 'books', of which book V describes the Middle East west of the Euphrates and book VI contains a survey of Arabia. To this was added a large map including Arabia, which can be restored and which contained several additional names of peoples in Arabia.[38] The map was also based on that by Marinus.[39] There are, however, many problems with Ptolemy's *Geography*. We lack a proper edition of the text, which is crucial for the identification of the geographical names. There is, further, very little study of the sources for the work of both Ptolemy and Marinus. This means that judgements and assertions based on the *Hyphēgēsis* are provisional.[40]

In Ptolemy we find the classical division of Arabia into three parts. Two of them are well known: *Arabía érēmos* and *Arabía eudaímōn*, a division going back to Eratosthenes. In Ptolemy we have a third Arabia: *Arabía petraía*. This latter should not, as is often done, be translated as 'Rocky Arabia' but rather 'The Arabia belonging to Petra'. It is, however, not identical with the Arabo-Nabataean kingdom, in Ptolemy's days the Arabian province.[41] From the description of the borders it seems that the southern border of *Arabía petraía* ran eastwards from the gulf of ʕAqaba.[42] In the north, Gerasa is part of it, whereas Philadelphia = ʕAmmān belongs to Syria, distinct from *Arabía érēmos* like most of Transjordan.[43] Interesting is that *Arabía petraía* is said to continue to the Egyptian border and that the entire Sinai peninsula is included. The mountains there seem to be those called 'The Black Mountains'. Between these mountains and Egypt is the land of Sarakēnē, which is now mentioned for the first time.[44] The term for the inhabitants, *sarakēnoí*, was later to be extended to all tribes in the Syrian desert.[45]

Arabía érēmos encompasses the Syrian desert from Judaea and former Nabataea to the Persian Gulf. Its northern border is the Euphrates up to Thapsacus.[46] Its southern border is a line from the Persian Gulf in present-day Kuwait westwards until it touches the eastern border of *Arabía petraía*.[47] Of peoples mentioned we may note the *masanoí* in the east, probably identical with the Mesenians, and the *agraîoi* close to the *batanaîoi*. These latter are probably the inhabitants of Bashan, present-day Ǧabal ad-Durūz. The *agraîoi* are then the Hagarenes, mentioned already in Old Testament sources.[48]

Outside Ptolemy's Arabia, in Syrian territory close to the border of *Arabía érēmos*, we find the following:

> . . . the region of Batanaía, eastwards from which there is Sakkaía and from which, under the (ou)alsadamos mountain the Trakhonîtai *árabes*.[49]

This is the only passage where Ptolemy explicitly speaks about Arabs. There is no doubt that we are in the same area as the *agraîoi*, mentioned in the passage about *Arabía érēmos*, i.e. around Ǧabal ad-Durūz, which is probably identical with the Alsadamos mountain.[50]

The largest part is *Arabía eudaímōn*, which encompasses the entire Arabian peninsula.[51] Ptolemy has gathered an astonishing number of names of places and peoples from Arabia and put them together into a rather confusing picture.[52] The enumeration of names is divided in three main parts: one containing the peoples and places along the coasts of Arabia, where he starts with the Gulf of ʕAqaba and ends with the Maesanite Gulf.[53] Then follow the peoples in the hinterland, starting with the *skēnîtai* in the north-west, ending with the Hadramites.[54] Next comes a list of towns from Midian to Ḥaḍramawt.[55] The passage ends with a list of islands around Arabia.[56]

The locations of the sites and peoples on Ptolemy's map can be restored with a high degree of certainty. The scheme is rather rigid and it has been observed that the same peoples often seem to occur in different lists, such as the *thamydîtai*/*thamydēnoí*, *atramîtai*/*khatramōnîtai* and *khitibanîtai*/*kottabánoi*.[57] Among these are probably the *elisároi* and the *asarîtai* in Yemen, who are probably identical with the (al-)ʔAshʕarī tribe known from both Sabaean and Arabic sources.[58] This indicates that Ptolemy (and Marinus) had several different sources for the compilation.[59] Of other peoples mentioned one could note the *kinaidokolpîtai* south of present-day Yanbuʕ, and Lathrippa which must be Yathrib, i.e. Medina.[60] A site called Makoraba in the Ḥiǧāz has been identified with Mecca; this is, however, not quite certain.[61] In eastern Arabia we find the *tanouîtai* on Ptolemy's map, seemingly north-west of Gerrha, who have been identified with Tanūkh of the Arabo-Islamic tradition.[62] We also read the name *asatēnoí* which could be the later ʔAsad, the name of a large tribe in central Arabia.[63] The Sabaean capital Marib is not mentioned; at least the name is not immediately recognizable in Ptolemy's rendering.[64]

The most interesting name from South Arabia on the map is the *arabanîtai* located between Laththa/Mara in the north-west and Mariama/Thumna in the south-east. The last is Timnaʕ, the capital of Qatabān. Laththa could be Yathull, the Ath(r)oula of the Graeco-Roman geographical literature, i.e. present-day Barāqīsh. We could thus locate the *arabanîtai* along or outside the border of the Sabaean kingdom towards the north-eastern desert.[65] This is, in fact, where we find the ʕRB(N) and the ʔʕRB in the Sabaean texts from this period onwards.[66] The form of the word in Ptolemy could be a Sabaean noun with the definite article -*(ā)n*. This is hypothetical but not at all unlikely if we accept the notion that 'Arabs' referred to small groups living on the peninsula and is not a term for all its inhabitants.[67]

Ptolemy's *Geography* is a most valuable source for the ethnic conditions in Arabia and the Syrian desert, but it does not give as much for the theme of this study as could be expected. The most valuable notice is the one about the Arabs in Trachonitis, interestingly enough outside Arabia proper, besides perhaps the testimony of Arabs on the Sabaean border. We also have names of some tribes and places which were to reach fame in the following centuries.

An anonymous source on Arabs from the second century AD

At the end of the sixth century AD a Byzantine scholar named Stephanus compiled a large dictionary of geographical names culled from older sources. Unfortunately, Stephanus' *Ethnica* is not preserved in its original shape. Our text is an abridged version made in later Byzantine times, of which there is no satisfactory modern edition. This is a great loss because the work contains a lot of valuable material.

Stephanus refers to many ancient writers as his sources.[68] There are, however, a large number of place-names in the *Ethnica* which have no reference.[69] An example is the notice about Antiokhía, 'the fifth [town with that name] between Coele Syria and

Arabia, of Semiramis'.[70] This sounds like a description of Antiochia Arabis, mentioned by Pliny east of Edessa 'among the people of *Arabes* called Orroei', but the wording in Stephanus' text as well as the reference to the Semiramis legend point to another source.[71] Among the anonymous data about Arabia one could further notice Sampsa, 'a village in Arabia', which is explained as derived from a word meaning 'sun'. In the account about Trajan's operations around Hatra the town is said to be protected by the sun-god Šamaš or, with a more Aramaic form: Šamšā. There is also a notice about the *Salamioi*. Their name is said to be derived from the word *salama* meaning 'peace', originating in their alliance with the Nabataeans.[72] This is a piece of information describing conditions before AD 106, which an author on Arabia after the annexation might well have included.

Both these latter data are based on a source written by someone with knowledge of Middle Eastern languages. It has been assumed that data from the same source were used by the grammarian Herodian, who at the end of the second century wrote a handbook on the morphology of Greek.[73] One of the main interests of Stephanus was the formation of derived adjectives from names of places and peoples. For example, the article *Arabía* is concluded with the comment: 'the ethnikon is *arábios*, *árabos* and *arabíssa*'.[74] This could be an argument in favour of the assumption that he used Herodianus' *Catholic Prosody* as a source, since this work dealt extensively with such forms.[75] The anonymous information in the *Ethnica*, on the other hand, seems to reflect conditions around AD 100. Suggested candidates as authors of the anonymous source are Uranius and Glaucus. Of these Uranius is better known and datable to the fourth century and Glaucus must have been written at least after AD 250 and probably much later.[76] From the Uranius fragments it seems that this author was not very well informed about Arabia.[77] It is likely that the anonymous material comes from Philo of Byblus who died around AD 160 and who wrote a large work on cities in the ancient world with notes on their history and mythology. Philo's book was a collection of information from many earlier writers from Herodotus to Philo's own time.[78] The Semitic etymologies point to him since we know that Stephanus made extensive use of Philo's work.[79] In that case, his explicit reference to Glaucus and Uranius would show that he also checked their works for the geographical comments when he found it necessary.

Arabs between Romans and Parthians before the Severian dynasty

When Hadrian decided to withdraw to the former Euphrates line, the Parthians seem to have tried to take a firmer grip on the borderlands. Edessa managed to keep a precarious independence between the two superpowers. Further south along the Euphrates the Parthians installed a special governor to handle the border. In a Greek document from Dura Europus dated AD 121 we read about a certain Manesos, who is *strategós* of Mesopotamia and Parapotamia as well as *arabárkhēs*, 'arab-ruler', under the King of Kings, who at this time was Vologases II, Osroes' successor.[80]

The presence of an arabarch at the Euphrates sounds familiar. We remember that Posidonius in the first century BC mentioned the Arab phylarchs along the Euphrates.[81] We have also seen the term *arabarkhía* used in connection with Nabataean troops.[82] At least after the Roman attack under Trajan, the Arabs in the Euphrates region were under the command of a Parthian military governor in Dura Europus, which had reverted to Parthian control after Trajan.[83] In two other documents from Dura, one from

AD 133/134 and another from AD 180, they are said to have been written 'in Europos at (*pròs*) *Arabía*'.[84] Dura Europus is situated on the southern shore of the Euphrates. On the other side were the Arabs in Singăr and Hatra, east of the Khābūr. This Arabia thus looks very much like that of Xenophon. It is also likely that the Arabs commanded by Manesos were related to those described by Posidonius almost 200 years earlier living along the river, ruled by phylarchs and creating problems for both Romans and Parthians in those days. Now obviously the Parthians tried to control them more tightly, since they constituted a spearhead directed against Roman Syria and, not least, the emerging glorious city of Palmyra. The notice in Corbulo's description of the Euphrates could indicate that the *Arabes Praetavi*, whose capital was Singara, were actually spread over a large area even down to the Euphrates, and that the Arabs at Hatra belonged to them.

The document from AD 180 is in fact Roman, not Parthian. An important change had occurred in upper Mesopotamia during the 160s AD. In 162 the Parthian king Vologases III attacked Edessa, deposed Mannus VIII and installed his own man there, Wael son of Sahru. Syria was then devastated. The Roman counterattack was formally led by the emperor colleague of Marcus Aurelius, Lucius Verus, who, however, found more amusement in erecting statues of himself than taking part in military operations. Those were led by Avidius Cassius, who in the summer of 164 occupied Dura Europus and later took Ctesiphon.

The story of the Parthian war in the 160s was originally told by Cassius Dio and Asinius Quadratus, both writing in the first half of the third century AD.[85] Dio quotes a speech by Marcus Aurelius where the emperor alludes to the operations in the east as 'that Arabian and Parthian war'.[86] An echo from Quadratus' *Parthica* is heard in the *Historia Augusta* when the following is said about Avidius:

> Having stiffened military discipline he performed well in Armenia, Arabia and Egypt.[87]

In Stephanus' *Ethnica* we have two references to Arabia explicitly taken from Quadratus' *Parthica*. It is said that Thelamouza is 'a castle in the Arabia on the Euphrates' and that Maskhanē is 'a town near the *skēnîtai árabes*'.[88]

These passages show clearly that the war of 163–165 involved Arabia, which must be Arabia between the two rivers. The disappearance of Quadratus' *Parthica* is one of the losses for our subject, since it probably contained an ethnographic excursus on the Arabs. At the end of the fourth century the great Roman historian Ammian Marcellinus used Quadratus' work as one of his sources for the history of the reign of Marcus Aurelius. In that part he gave a description of Arabia and its inhabitants which could have been based on Quadratus.[89] Unfortunately, that part of Ammian is also lost.[90] There is some supplementary information on Arabia in other parts of Ammian's work, but it cannot be proved that it is taken from Quadratus. If these passages are really based on that writer, it shows that he in his turn took most of his information about the people of the desert from still earlier writers.[91]

The Arabs at Edessa

The result of the operations in the 160s was that the Roman border was now moved eastwards and established along the Khābūr.[92] The Romans took firmer control of

Edessa, where Mannus was reinstalled.[93] The consequence of these events was that the strategic importance of the Arabs in Singǎr and Hatra increased, since they now formed the Parthian vanguard against Rome.

Edessa was in the middle of the turmoil during this war. We have from the period a number of inscriptions from a site today called Sumatar Harbesi, east of present-day Urfa, former Edessa. Sumatar was a kind of sanctuary, which was clearly in use for centuries.[94] The inscriptions cut in the rock are among the oldest testimonies of the Syriac Aramaic dialect. Among the texts from Sumatar there are five where the word 'Arab' occurs. Four of them are found in a cave and one on a low mountain nearby where a temple stood. Unfortunately, only the latter is dated:

> At the New Moon of Shebat in the year 476 I, Tiridates, son of Adona, ruler of the ʕRB, built this altar and set a pillar to Marilaha for the life of my Lord the king and his sons and for the life of Adona my father and for the life of MLYWR my brother and of our sons.[95]

The year is equivalent to AD 165. The title of Tiridates is in (Syriac) Aramaic *šallīṭāʔ da-ʕrab*, which corresponds to the Greek *arabárkhēs*. Marilaha (the Lord God) is one of the gods worshipped at Sumatar. We know from another inscription that the temple on the hill was dedicated in this year, which is the year when Avidius Cassius conquered Edessa and defeated the Parthians.[96] We have another inscription by Tiridates from the same year, and there is no doubt that the consecration of the temple and the inscriptions of Tiridates are connected with the dramatic events unfolding around the sanctuary.[97] It is most unfortunate that Tiridates did not find it worthwhile to mention the name of his king. It could have been the king of Edessa, although we do not know for sure. The question is then if it was the Parthian Wael or the Roman Mannus VIII. Most reasonable is to assume that it was the latter, and that the temple was consecrated as a celebration of the restoration of the old dynasty in Edessa by the Romans.[98] This would imply that the site was an old sanctuary which had been in use earlier and continued to be used afterwards. The remaining inscriptions, all in the cave, may thus have been put up before or after the Parthian interlude in the 160s:

> This is the statue which Wael, son of MWTRW, made . . . RD for Wael, ruler of the ʕRB, son of Wael, and for Wael, his son, *nuhadra* of SHWR . . .[99]

> [This is the statue] that Barnahar, son of RYNY, made, ruler of the ʕRB, to Aurelius Hafsay, son of Barkalba, the manumitted by Antoninus Caesar, his lord . . .[100]

> This is the statue that Maʕnū, son of Moqimi, made for Abgar, ruler of the ʕRB[101]

> This is the statue that MLH, son of ŠYLʔ, made to Barnahar, son of RYNY, ruler of the ʕRB[102]

The only indication of a date in the remaining texts is the mention of the Roman emperor Antoninus in Barnahar's text. Unfortunately, all emperors from Antoninus Pius to Alexander Severus, except Septimius Severus, carried that name, so it is not of much help. It is, however, probable that this text originates from after the Roman conquest in 165, which would exclude Antoninus Pius.[103] If the Tiridates inscription is connected with the restoration of the dynasty in Edessa, it seems likely that the inscriptions in Sumatar are from the period after 165 until the abolition of the kingdom by Caracalla or Heliogabalus at the beginning of the third century.

The inscriptions from Sumatar are of great importance for our subject. They confirm the existence of people called Arabs in the surroundings of Edessa, which we have heard about twice in Pliny's *Natural History* (*Arabes Orroei*) and also, perhaps, in Tacitus' account of the campaign in AD 49.[104] The very title of the individuals mentioned gives the impression of these Arabs being some kind of military units, perhaps attached to the Edessenian kings. It should, however, be pointed out that the evidence for such an attachment is rather weak: nowhere in the inscriptions do we find explicit reference to the Abgarids. Finally, it should be stressed that we have no indication that the Abgarids were Arabs. The fact that they have names classified as Arabic by modern linguists has nothing to do with their identity in antiquity.

The Arabs at Hatra

The epigraphic evidence from Sumatar is supplemented by the texts found at Hatra during this period. Among the almost 400 Aramaic inscriptions from the town, we have twenty-one in which Arabs are explicitly mentioned. From the texts we can also to a certain extent reconstruct some of the history of the town. We know that the dynasty of rulers, starting with WRD in the time of Trajan, lasted at least until the year AD 149. From that year there is an inscription in which perhaps Arabs appear for the first time in the texts from Hatra. The text is fragmentary and difficult to understand. A suggested reading of two lines is that someone has dedicated an altar 'to GNDʔ DY ʕRB', 'the Fortune of the Arabs'.[105] The expression occurs twice. 'The Fortune' (if correctly read) could be a divinity well known from pre-Islamic Arabia by the name GD(D) and related to the goddess of fortune, Manāt. Another suggestion is that the word GNDʔ is the same as *ǧund* in Arabic, meaning 'army', 'troops'.[106]

An easier text is one dated to AD 151. It exists in two copies, H 336 and H 343, of which the first is somewhat longer:

1. In the month of Kanun in the year 463 [AD 151] in the rule of

2. the gods there agreed ŠMŠBRK, the *rabbayt*[*ā*

3. and the Hatrans, old and young, and the ʕRBY[

4. all of them, and all who

[enter and go out of Hatra and all who]

dwell in Hatra decreed thus:

5. that all who steal inside this store

6. and inside the outer wall, if he is a

7. native he shall be killed by the death of

8. the gods, and if he is a foreigner

9. he shall be stoned.[107]

The expression 'old and young' is in Aramaic QŠYŠʔ W DRDQʔ. Of these the first term is a well-known Aramaic word with the meaning 'priest' in later Christian texts. Here it probably stands for some kind of official.[108] The most interesting aspect of this text is the picture it gives of the variegated demographic conditions in Hatra. It is clear that the Arabs constituted only a part of the inhabitants of the town. One should observe the expression 'the ʕRBYʔ, all of them', which also seems to appear in the famous Namāra inscription one and a half centuries later.[109]

In this text no king is mentioned, and the impression is that ŠMŠBRK is some kind of official. The word *rabbaytā* is, according to another inscription, a high official, the second in the realm. Both *qašīšā* and *rabbaytā* occur together in that text.[110]

We also have a series of inscriptions mentioning a certain SNṬRWQ, son of NṢRW. In eleven texts he appears as SNṬRQ MLKʔ D(Y) ʕRB, Sanaṭrūq, king of ʕRB.[111] In one text he has the epithet ZKYʔ, 'victorious'.[112] A more elaborate collection of epithets is found in the last text:

> . . . SNṬRWQ, king of the ʕRB, the great ʔBYʔ, the great ʔPKLʔ to ŠMŠ the god.[113]

The term ʔBYʔ is likely to be the one we have encountered in Josephus, in the form Abias, king of the Arabs in Adiabene.[114] It is clear from this text that it is not a name but rather a title designating a chief of some kind. The word ʔPKLʔ is the masculine form of *apkallatu*, the title of the queens in Dumah in Assyrian times.[115] Sanaṭrūq's father, Naṣr, is documented with the same title.[116] In a damaged inscription we read:

> . . . ʔ RBʔ D-ʕRB
>
> W-SNṬRWQ MLKʔ D-ʕRB
>
> BR NṢRW MRYʔ
>
> the great . . . ā of the ʕRB
>
> and Sanaṭrūq, king of the ʕRB
>
> son of NṢRW, the lord.[117]

In light of the evidence from Dumah, as well as other texts from Hatra, it can be argued that the missing word in the first line is ʔPKLʔ, thus 'the great *ʔaphkelā* of the ʕRB', designating some kind of high priest attached to the ʕRB.[118] We observe that the *ʔaphkelā* and the king of the ʕRB are two different persons.

In another text, Sanaṭrūq is said to have reigned in the year AD 177/178.[119] His father, Naṣr, is called MRY, 'lord', not king. This title does not occur together with the title 'king'.[120] Sometime between the years AD 151 and 177/178 kings of the Arabs were obviously installed in Hatra. The first of which was Sanaṭrūq, son of Naṣr, who also performed some kind of priestly function in the cult of the sun-god. There was also another priest with the same title connected with the Arabs. We should observe that Sanaṭrūq is not called king of Hatra but king of the Arabs.

There is an otherwise undated ruler possibly following Sanaṭrūq, son of Naṣr, likewise king of the Arabs: WLGŠ MLKʔ DY ʕRB, Vologases, king of ʕRB.[121]

From the period after the Partho-Roman war we have several inscriptions mentioning another ruler:

> [ʕBDSMY PŠ]GRYBʔ son of SNṬRWQ king of ʕRB son of NṢRW the lord.[122]

The word PŠGRYBʔ is an Iranian word of uncertain meaning. A suggested translation is 'heir to the throne'.[123] We have two texts dealing with an official from the reign of this king:

> Statue of ʔPRHṬ,
>
> *rabbaytā* of the ʕRB
>
> which ʕQBʔ put up for him,
>
> the *rabbaytā* of BRMRYN son of
>
> ŠMŠY the *rabbaytā*, for
>
> the life of ʕBDSMYʔ
>
> the king, his lord, and for the life
>
> of his sons.[124]

The following text, which does not mention the king, nevertheless must belong to the same period:

> Statue of ʔPRHṬ,
>
> *rabbaytā* of the ʕRB
>
> which ʔLYHBW erected for him,
>
> the *rabbaytā* of Our Lady,
>
> his ʔŠPZKN.[125]

The office of the *rabbaytā* of the *ʕarab* could be similar to the *šallīṭā* of the *ʕarab* mentioned in the texts from Sumatar Harbesi. It is clear from the texts that there were several different officials with the title *rabbaytā*.[126] ʕBDSMYʔ is mentioned in an inscription dated to the year AD 193/194, and he has been identified with Barsemias, who aided the Roman pretender Pescennius Niger.[127] This would fit well with the chronology in the inscriptions from Hatra.

The next king, SNṬRWQ son of ʕBDSMYʔ, is mentioned in dated inscriptions from AD 231 and 238.[128] From his time we have four texts where Arabs are mentioned:

> SNṬRWQ, the king, son of ʕBDSMYʔ, king of the ʕRB[129]

> Statue of ʕBDŠLMʔ son of BRʕY
> MRBYNʔ of SNṬRQ, king

> of ʕRB, the victorious, son of ʕBDSMYʔ . . .[130]

> [Statue of SNṬRWQ, the king],
>
> 1. the victorious whose fortune (GNDHʔ) is with
>
> 2. the god(s), son of ʕBDSMYʔ
>
> 3. the king . . .
>
> 9. By our lord the Eagle and by his kingship and by the Fortune (GNDʔ)
>
> 10. of the ʕRB and by the sign of MŠKNʔ and by the fortune
>
> 11. of SNṬRWQ and his descendants and all his sons
>
> 12. so that never MʕNʔ son of SNṬRWQ the king may lead them, or anyone of their sons (?)
>
> 13. BQTYRʔ
>
> 14. May they be remembered forever in Hatra and ʕRBYʔY.[131]

The ethnic mixture of Hatra is obvious from the different types of personal name found in the texts. We find both Iranian and Semitic names. The latter are mostly of a type which is found in inscriptions from all over Arabia and it was, undoubtedly, possible to hear in the streets of Hatra many forms of a language we today would call Arabic. This fits well into the religious conditions: there are temples to several gods known from Arabia but also from Mesopotamia and Syria. The religion of Hatra is, however, almost purely Semitic; no Iranian gods are documented. On the other hand, the kings Sanaṭrūq and Vologases have Iranian names whereas Sanaṭrūq's father has a genuine Arabic name: Naṣrū. Onomastics is, however, no certain indicator of ethnicity. Although it cannot be ruled out that the carriers of these names were what we would call Arabs but had adopted Iranian names, the question for us is: what is the meaning of ʕRB in these texts?

The texts from Sumatar and Hatra constitute a unique contemporary documentation of Arabs in antiquity. Not even in the Assyrian documents, which otherwise are comparable in documentary value, do we come this close to the protagonists of our investigation. Only in the texts from South Arabia, which start to flow at this time, do we find something similar. The interpretation of this material is thus crucial to our subject.

In Cassius Dio's account of Trajan's campaign we hear about an Arabia stretching from north of Edessa to somewhere north of Ctesiphon.[132] At Edessa Trajan met with an Arab ruler. This extension of the land of the Arabs in Mesopotamia fits well into what we have learnt from earlier periods. Xenophon's Arabia extends from Khābūr to al-Hīt. We remember Eratosthenes including the central Ǧazīra in his Arabia. It is also likely that these Arabs, originally from the other side of the Euphrates, were those installed at Chalcis/Qinnasrīn by the Seleucids and that they took part in the two large-scale Parthian invasions in Syria in the first century BC. Posidonius mentioned Arab phylarchs along the Euphrates. We also remember Pliny's *Arabes praetavi*, whose capital was Singara, as well as the *Arabes eldamari* in the same area. The Arabs at Edessa are documented from AD 49, and we are told that they had a close relationship with the kings in Adiabene. After the withdrawal of the Romans after Trajan's death, we hear about an Arabia on the shore of the Euphrates opposite Dura Europus. It is governed by an arabarch who must have been a Parthian official. These Arabs seem thus to be documented during a very long time, and there seems to be solid evidence for a continuous Arab presence in this area, which makes it well deserve the designation *Arabía*, 'Arab land'.

It is worth observing that until the time of Sanaṭrūq I, Arabs mostly appear on the fringes of this Arabia: north of Sinǧār and along the Euphrates. From the time of Trajan we hear about a town under the protection of the sun-god inhabited by Hagarenes. There is no doubt that this place is Hatra. We would thus venture the hypothesis that Hatra was the central sanctuary of the Arabs between the two rivers, and that the Arabs appearing at Edessa, on the Euphrates as well as in Adiabene, all had some kind of main cultic centre at Hatra. The expression 'the Arabs, all of them' in our texts could indicate this.

The Roman attack in the east in AD 164 caused changes. A king was set up in Hatra, probably with the support of the Parthian king Vologases III. The title 'victorious' of the first Sanaṭrūq could have something to do with the war against the Romans. It is less likely that he received it for incorporating the Arabs around Hatra in the new kingdom.[133] Sanaṭrūq I was entrusted with the area bounded by Sinǧār in the north, the Khabūr in the west, the Euphrates in the south and the Tigris in the north-east. As we have seen, inscriptions were put up at Sumatar at the same time, and one would very much have liked to know something about the connections between these Arabs and those at Hatra. Is the king mentioned in the Sumatar texts the 'king of the Arabs' in Hatra? The apparent splendour of Hatra from the middle of the second century AD onwards is a sign of a strong, local government and a political entity with considerable resources. The obscure last word in the inscription H 79 could be the name of the kingdom: Arabia written in Aramaic. The Arabs mentioned in the inscriptions would thus not be the inhabitants in and around Hatra only, but all Arabs in the Ǧazīra subject to the new kingdom.

The kings of Hatra were soon to show their strength in a confrontation with the world's foremost military machine. Their successful resistance against the Roman imperial armies in the end of the second century AD could be seen as a confirmation of the real strength indicated by the splendid architecture of the Holy City of the Sun. This Arabia was thus in a certain sense the heir to the Arabs in Petra. The outer magnificence of their capitals is similar, and one could speculate whether the embellishment of Hatra may have been influenced by what was known about the capital of the Arabian kingdom in the west. Unlike the Arabs close to Palestine, the kings of Hatra were remembered until Islamic times: as we shall see, the Arab kings in Syria in the third century, as well as those in al-Ḥīra, claimed descent from the kings at Hatra, who by then were shrouded in the mists of legends.

Excursus: *ʕarab* in the Hatra texts: region or people?

Several scholars have claimed that ʕRB = *ʕarab* in the Hatra texts stands for the territory of the town, not a group of people. The most important arguments have been presented by J. Teixidor.[134] He has two arguments: (1) The use of the particle D(Y) as a genitive exponent occurs only with names of regions in Nabataean and Palmyrene Aramaic inscriptions, not with ethnic terms. We thus have MLK NBṬW, 'king of the Nabataeans', but RYŠ DY ḤGRʔ, 'the chief of Hegra'. MLKʔ D(Y) ʕRB in Hatra would thus mean 'the king of (the region) ʕRB'. (2) Arabs in Mesopotamia were known by specific names like Scenitae, Orroei, Praetavi etc. It is thus unlikely that the Hatreans would call themselves just Arabs and nothing else.[135] One could continue his argumentation by claiming that the same would hold for the texts from Sumatar Harbesi: ŠLYṬʔ D-ʕRB would then mean 'the ruler of (the region) ʕArab'. Moreover, a support can be found in a late Aramaic source, the *Chronicle* ending with the year 1234. There we read:

> In that region (northern Mesopotamia) there were many kings: in Urhay [Edessa] kings of the family of Abgar, in *ʕrab* kings of the family of Sanaṭrūq who reigned in the town of Hatra.[136]

The expression *ba-ʕrab* could mean 'in ʕRB' and indicate a site, not a group of people. One could also adduce the evidence from the Assyrian scribes who wrote the name *arab-* preceded by the determinative for 'people' or for 'land' alternatively. The same expression seems to be found in the obscure oracle in Isaiah 21.

We should, however, keep in mind that the word itself can hardly be a place-name from the beginning. The later Arabic usage seems to exclude this. It is easier to imagine an unchanged gentilic being used as a name for a dwelling than vice versa.[137] It is possible that the Assyrian scribes were not too certain about or even interested in the status of the Arabs, whether they were a people or a country. That *ʕarab* could be used as a designation for a region by outsiders, i.e. non-Arabs, is possible and seems to be confirmed by the Assyrian texts as well as perhaps the Syriac 1234 Chronicle. But this is no decisive argument for the claim that the *ʕarab* themselves did so, or that the word really had this meaning for those who used it.[138] The argument that the Arabs would preferably use specific tribal names is dependent on the assumption that *ʕarab* in this period is a general ethnic designation or stands for a region. Since the first argument is far from certain, that explanation is weak. We have, in fact, no evidence whatsoever that the names Orroei, Praetavi etc. were used by the Arabs themselves. They are more likely to be labels given them by outsiders, not only geographers but also travelling merchants who needed to distinguish between the Arabs in different regions. But there is no support in the sources that the people called Arabs at this time were actually divided in different tribes, as they were in the late Umayyad period. On the contrary, everything speaks in favour of their being one group among innumerable others.

The grammatical argument is to be taken more seriously. One should, however, be very cautious in making any general statements based on the grammar of epigraphic Aramaic texts from this period, since the syntax of those dialects remains unexplored. Nabataean and Palmyrene Aramaic are dialects based upon Imperial Aramaic, whereas the language of the Hatra inscriptions has many affinities with eastern Aramaic.[139] Now it is well known that the classical *smîkhûtā* construction, i.e. the so-called synthetic genitive construction, is more frequent in older forms of Aramaic, including Imperial Aramaic, than in the eastern dialects like Syriac, Talmudic and Mandaic. In these dialects, the so-called analytic genitive, i.e. the periphrastic construction with *d* as a linking particle, is dominant. Thus, for example, in Daniel 7:1 we read in the original Biblical (= Imperial) Aramaic *mlek Babel*, 'the king of Babylon', but in the Syriac (= eastern Aramaic) Peshitta *malkā d-Babel*. The latter is also found already in Ezra 5:13. In Ezra 6:14 we read in the Masoretic version *mlek Pras*, 'king of the Persians', but in the Peshitta *malkā da-fras*.[140] The Syriac, an eastern Aramaic dialect spoken *west* of Hatra, thus uses the analytic construction with names of regions as well as of peoples. These examples are, of course, not decisive, but it is at least more likely that the expression MLKʔ DY ʕRB in the Hatra texts means exactly the same thing as *malkê ʕrab* in the Aramaic Targum to Jeremiah 25:24, by the Peshitta rendered as *malkē d-ʕarbāyē*, 'the kings of the Arabs'. In Hatra, the analytic construction seems to dominate, as in Syriac.[141] This shows that syntactic studies of these Aramaic dialects are a desideratum and may also throw light on ethnic and political conditions.

Notes

1 Also the first thirty-six books are lost, and Dio's text starts with the year 68 BC; see Millar, *Dio Cassius*.
2 See Lepper, *War* 2–6.
3 See the survey in Barnes, *Sources* 32–78.
4 Barnes, *Sources*, especially 98–113.
5 Février (*Essai* 19–24) assumed the year AD 114 and was followed by Watzinger, *Palmyra* 263. Starcky (*Palmyre* 1080), building on new evidence, claims a date before AD 19, as does Teixidor (*Port* 10; cf. Starcky/Gawlikowski, *Palmyre* 37–40). Also Will (*Les Palmyréniens* 39 ff.) puts the annexation in the first century AD.
6 Cassius Dio 68.15 according to Xiphilinus.
7 Eutropius 8.3.2.
8 Cf. Bowersock, *Annexation*, idem, *Report* 228. Wenning, *Ende*, claims that there was a military conquest of Nabataea triggered by an emerging nationalistic movement. The evidence in favour of this argument is, however, weak.
9 That the acquisition of Nabataea was directed eastwards and not southwards is clearly shown by the absence of Roman fortresses against the desert, especially in the south, which has always been a puzzle (Bowersock, *Limes*; Graf, *Saracens*; Parker, *History* 866). It shows, however, that the idea of a continuous pressure of wild bedouin against the borders of the empires is unfounded; cf. Graf, *Rome*; Briant, *État* 9–56.
10 Cf. Jacoby, *Fragmente* II B 853–878, for quotations from this work by Stephanus of Byzantium. The fragments of the *Parthica* were edited by Roos (*Arrianus* II 224–231).
11 Lepper, *War* 1–2.
12 The Chronicle of Malalas, written in the end of the sixth century AD, is important for the chronology of the campaign but has nothing about Arabs.

13 For a decisive treatment of the campaigns and the chronological problems, see Lepper, *War* 28–96. Cf. also Dillemann, *Haute-Mésopotamie* 273–289. Lepper's chronology seems to have been universally accepted; see Wolski, *État* 178–182; Drijvers, *Hatra* 872–875; Teixidor, *Kingdom* 6–7; idem, *Notes* 282, and the Loeb editor of Cassius Dio.
14 Cassius Dio 68:21.1. Anthemousia is Sarūğ; cf. Dillemann, *Haute-Mésopotamie* 102.
15 Cassius Dio 68:22.
16 Festus 20.
17 Eutropius 8.3.1. In Hieronymus' Latin version of Eusebius' chronicle we find the identical wording (Eusebius, *Chronicle* 194).
18 Stephanus, 285; cf. Dillemann, *Haute-Mésopotamie* 77.
19 See pp. 413 f.
20 Cassius Dio 68:26.2–4.
21 Hatra: Stephanus 143: 'Atrai, close to Libanai' (ibid. 274); cf. Jacoby, *Fragmente* II B 860–861 (F 48).
22 Stephanus 414: 'Libanai; a town of Syria neighbouring Atrai (= Hatra)'; Dillemann, *Haute-Mésopotamie* 284–285.
23 Dillemann, *Haute-Mésopotamie* 166 and map XVIII (p. 149).
24 Cassius Dio 68 [75:31].
25 See Boissevain ad loc.
26 It is usually called *Excerpta Valesiana* nowadays, since the manuscript was owned by a prince of Valois in the sixteenth century.
27 Ammian 25.8.5.
28 Cf. Streck, *Hatra* 2517; Herzfeldt, *Hatra* 656; Drijvers, *Hatra* 816–817.
29 See Boissevain, *Fragment*.
30 It could be argued that the reading *agarēnoí* is an interpretation by a later, Christian copyist familiar with the Judaeo-Christian tradition of Hagar as the mother of all Arabs. The change of the original *atrēnoí* would thus have been triggered by the mention of Arabia in the context. Against this goes the fact that Arabia and Arabs are also mentioned in the account about Septimius Severus and more often than in the one about Trajan. The *agarēnoí* do not occur in that context and a copyist influenced by the Judaeo-Christian scriptures could also be expected to make this change in the passages about Severus. A similar isolated occurrence of a term derived from Hagar is found in Ptolemy (see p. 4370). The influence of Judaeo-Christian terminology is as unlikely there as in Cassius Dio.
31 Cf. Drijvers, *Hatra* 821.
32 There is evidence from coins that he visited 'Arabia' during his trip in the East (Millar, *Near East* 106). This would have been the newly established province.
33 For a thorough analysis of the entire work, see Polaschek, *Ptolemaios*.
34 Cf. Honigmann, *Marinos*.
35 According to Honigmann (*Marinos* 1768), the work was compiled around AD 110, i.e. before Trajan's eastern campaign. This explains, for example, the absence of Hatra in Ptolemy.
36 Honigmann, *Marinos* 1790 ff.
37 Honigmann, *Marinos* 1772; cf. Ptolemy 1.6.1, 1.19.
38 The part containing Arabia is attached to Sprenger, *Geographie*.
39 Honigmann, *Marinos* 1779 and 1785–1786, for a reconstruction of Marinus' map.
40 Cf. MacAdam, *Strabo* 305–313, 316–320.
41 Sprenger (*Geographie* 8) asserts that the tripartition reflects the political division of the lands controlled by Arabs, which is untenable.
42 Ptolemy 5.16.1.
43 Ptolemy 5.14.4.
44 Sprenger, *Geographie* 200. The word *Arraceni* in Pliny 5.16.4 and 6.7.19 has sometimes been seen as a corruption of the name, but this cannot be proved. For another suggestion, see p. 209, n. 458.
45 The meaning of this term is debated. For a detailed survey of the debate see Shahid, *Rome* 123–141. It is usually seen as a reflection of an Arabic word: 'thieves' (from *saraqa* 'steal'),

'confederation' (from *šarika*, 'be a partner'), 'east' or 'the easterners' (from *šarq*, 'east' or 'sunrise'), or an Aramaic *srāq*, 'desert'. No agreement has been reached. Shahid (op. cit. 126–127) suggests that it is the name of a tribe in the area called Sarakēnē by Ptolemy (cf. Sprenger, *Geographie* 200). The form of the name points to a derivation from the name of a region ending in -ēnē. We would then expect that name in its turn to be derived from a name of some locality in analogy to most other names of this kind, such as Damaskēnē and Palmyrēne. As has been remarked already, these names seem to belong to the areas outside the sway of the Ptolemies but not necessarily under the control of the Seleucids.

46 Ptolemy 5.16.4–5; 5.18; 6.7.19.

47 Ptolemy 5.18. For the borders and sites of Arabia Deserta in Ptolemy, see Musil, *Arabia Deserta* 502–508; MacAdam, *Strabo* 319 (map).

48 Cf. Sprenger, *Geographie* 288–2898 (no. 421).

49 Ptolemy 5.15.20.

50 MacAdam, *Studies* 6–9, argues that Alsadamos is Ǧabal Says north-east of Ǧabal ad-Durūz. Sakkaía is present-day Shaqqa. For further references to Arabs in this region from the same time, see Robert, *Épitaphe*.

51 Ptolemy 6.6. For a thorough study of this chapter, Sprenger's *Geographie* is still fundamental.

52 For the disposition, cf. MacAdam, *Strabo* 310–313.

53 Ptolemy 6.7.1–20.

54 Ptolemy 6.7.20–26.

55 Ptolemy 6.7.27–42.

56 Ptolemy 6.7.43–47.

57 Sprenger, *Geographie* 27–28 (no. 27) and 202–203 (no. 329); ibid. 81 (no. 95) and 305–308 (nos. 438, 439); ibid. 304 (no. 436) and 263–264 (no. 398).

58 Sprenger, *Geographie* 63–64 (no. 61). Glaser (*Skizze* 237–238) suggested a derivation from a personal name ʔIlšaraḥ.

59 Cf. Honigmann, *Marinos* 1791–1793.

60 Sprenger, *Geographie* 155 (no. 231). Sprenger's identification of the *kinaidokolpîtai* with Kināna and Kalb (ibid. 31–33 no. 30) is too far-fetched. Glaser (*Skizze* 232 f.) suggested Kinda which is also somewhat unlikely.

61 Sprenger, *Geographie* 155–156 (no. 233). The word is not the same but an old South Semitic word for 'sanctuary' preserved in Geez: *mak*^{w}*rāb* 'temple', 'synagogue'. A support for the identification could be a passage in al-ʔAzraqī's history of Mecca written in the ninth century AD. It is told that after the Flood of Noah, people used to seek asylum on the hill where the Temple had been built 'and they invoked by it *al-makrūb* and there were few who invoked and did not get any answer' (ʔAzraqī, *ʔAkhbār* I 20). The word *makrūb* was obviously no longer understood by the Muslims, who seem to have considered it the name of a divinity or a demon.

62 Sprenger, *Geographie* 208 (no. 340); Glaser, *Skizze* 283.

63 So Sprenger, *Geographie* 206 (no. 337); Glaser, *Skizze* 282.

64 Possible candidates on the map are Mara and Mariama.

65 Cf. Ryckmans, *Royaumes* 94–95 who, however, thinks they lived along the coast at Ǧīzān.

66 See Chapter 19.

67 Sprenger, *Geographie* 304 (no. 437) also locates them in this region but identifies them with ʔArḥab. Glaser (*Skizze* 289) reads *rabanîtai* and identifies them with RʔBN in the Sabaean texts.

68 Cf. Honigmann, *Stephanos* 2379–2389.

69 Cf. Honigmann, *Stephanos* 2369; Schultz, *Herodian* 959 f.

70 Stephanus 99.

71 Pliny 5.21.1; 6.30. Pliny is never referred to by Stephanus.

72 Stephanus 550.

73 Cf. Schultz, *Herodian* 963–965. Herodian is extensively quoted by Stephanus, and some of the place-names in the Orient are taken from him: Synages in Phoenicia (591), Atharrabis in Egypt (33), Phres in Libya (672) and Solima in India (596).

74 Stephanus 108.
75 Lentz' reconstruction of Herodian from Stephanus was rejected by both Honigmann (*Stephanos* 2338) and Schultz (*Herodian* 961–962).
76 See pp. 491–493.
77 Cf. Honigmann, *Stephanos* 2387.
78 Honigmann, *Stephanos* 2382–2384. According to him, Philo's main source was Alexander Polyhistor.
79 Von der Mühll, *Herennius* 654–655. Philo is mentioned thirty-three times in the *Ethnika*.
80 Welles, *Parchments*: Civil Texts no. 20:4–5 (pp. 109–116); cf. Rostovtzeff/Welles, *Contract* 6, 46–51.
81 See pp. 354–354.
82 Josephus, *Antiquities* 15.17; see pp. 409 ff.
83 Millar, *Near East* 102.
84 Welles, *Parchments*: Civil Texts 119–120; 126 ff.
85 Barnes, *Sources* 108.
86 Cassius Dio 72.25.2: *Arabikòn tón te parthikòn ekeînon pólemon*; cf. Bowersock, *Arabia* 115 n. 25.
87 *Historia Augusta: Avidius* 6.5–6.
88 Stephanus 308; 437.
89 Ammian 14.4.2.
90 Barnes (*Sources* 108) assumes that the author of the *Historia Augusta* knew Quadratus through Ammian's digest.
91 For the passages on Arabia in Ammian, see pp. 514 ff.
92 For suggestions of the exact running of the border, see the maps in Dillemann, *Haute-Mésopotamie* 202 (fig. XXVII) and 205 (fig. XXVIII).
93 For the events at Edessa, see Drijvers, *Hatra* 875–876. For the whole war, see Millar, *Near East* 111–114.
94 See Segal, *Monuments*, especially 104–116.
95 Drijvers, *Inscriptions* no. 23 = Segal, *Inscriptions* no. 11; Drijvers/Healey, *Inscriptions* As36 (104–107).
96 Drijvers, *Inscriptions* no. 16 = Segal, *Inscriptions* no. 4; Drijvers/Healey, *Inscriptions* As29 (93–94).
97 Drijvers, *Inscriptions* no. 24 = Segal, *Inscriptions* no. 12; Drijvers/Healey, *Inscriptions* As37 (108–114).
98 Segal (*Monuments* 105–106) argues for the Parthian period 162–64, claiming the temple to have been established after the Roman conquest of Edessa and before they reached Sumatar. This sounds very unlikely. Everybody, especially in the crumbling kingdom of Wael, must have been occupied with other business than temple building in that year when the Roman armies were rapidly approaching.
99 Pognon, *Inscriptions* no. 5 = Drivers, *Inscriptions* no. 5; Drijvers/Healey, *Inscriptions* As47 (128–130); *nuhadra* is an Iranian designation for some kind of military commander; cf. Drijvers/Healey, *Inscriptions* 47.
100 Pognon, *Inscriptions* no. 7 = Drijvers, *Inscriptions* no. 7; Drijvers/Healey, *Inscriptions* 132–133 (As49).
101 Pognon, *Inscriptions* no. 9 = Drijvers, *Inscriptions* no. 9; Drijvers/Healey, *Inscriptions* As50 (135–136). Segal (*Monuments* 105) claims that Abgar is the king of Edessa, which would then mean the successor of Mannus VIII, Abgar VIII(?). In that case one has to explain why his title is not mentioned. Since clearly none of the other 'Arab rulers' mentioned in these inscriptions is king, there is no reason to believe that Abgar was king either. After all, Abgar was a very common name.
102 Pognon, *Inscriptions* no. 10 = Drijvers, *Inscriptions* no. 10; Drijvers/Healey, *Inscriptions* As52 (137).
103 The identification of this Aurelius with the first Roman governor in Osrhoene mentioned by Michael Syrus in his chronicle (6.5 pp. 77–78), suggested by Pognon (*Inscriptions* 37–38) and accepted by Segal (*Monuments* 107), raises problems. Michael's account does not

seem to be in order, having confused the events in 165, 212 and 241. If Aurelius was the governor, one would like to have his title mentioned. He is only characterized as the manumitted one.

104 Cf. pp. 405, 412.

105 H 288:A8–B1, C3; Safar, *Kitābāt* V 8–10; Degen, *Weitere Inschriften* 79–84.

106 Altheim/Stiehl, *Araber* IV 243–244, in a discussion of H 79 where the word is also found; see below.

107 H 336 and H 343 = Ibr. I; Safar, *Kitābāt* VI 69–71; Segal, *Texts* 109–111; idem, *Arabs* 75; cf. ibid. 60.

108 Segal, *Arabs* 65–66.

109 See p. 468.

110 H 342; cf. Segal, *Arabs* 65. The word also seems to occur in the ʔUmm Gimāl inscription; see p. 481.

111 H 196, 197, 199 (Safar, *Kitābāt* I 58–59; Caquot, *Inscriptions* VI 269), 231 (Safar, *Kitābāt* 7); cf. Segal, *Arabs* 64, 347 (Aggoula, *Remarques* 355), 353 (Aggoula, *Remarques* 357), 373, 375, 376, 378, 379 (Aggoula, *Remarques* 365–366).

112 H 194 (Safar, *Kitābāt* 26–27; Caquot, *Inscriptions* 268).

113 H 345 = Ibr. IV (Aggoula, *Remarques* 353; Segal, *Arabs* 74–75).

114 Josephus, *Antiquities* 20.77–78; cf. p. 414.

115 Aggoula translates them 'patrice' and 'juge' respectively, which is questionable; cf. Segal, *Arabs* 59–60.

116 H 67; cf. Segal, *Arabs* 61.

117 H 231 (Safar, *Kitābāt* IV 5); Degen, *Inscriptions* 403.

118 The word RBʔ is found with ʔPKLʔ in the text Ibr. IV and IX (ʔPKLʔ RBʔ D-ŠMŠ, 'the great *ʔaphkelā* of (the god) ŠMŠ; Segal, *Arabs* 74) and with ʔLHʔ 'god(s)' in H 25. Segal (*Arabs* 64) has to reject this evidence, seemimgly because of his opinion that ʕRB in the Hatra texts stands for a territory, not a group of people.

119 H 82 (Safar, *Kitābāt* I 21–25; Caquot, *Inscriptions* V 7–8). For the dating, see Drijvers, *Hatra* 820.

120 Segal, *Arabs* 61.

121 H 193 (Safar, *Kitābāt* II 55–56; Caquot, *Inscriptions* VI 268); cf. Drijvers, *Hatra* 824.

122 H 375 (Aggoula, *Remarques* 366). The reading of the first name is not certain.

123 Maricq, *Hatra* 275–280; Segal, *Arabs* 61.

124 H 223 (Safar, *Kitābāt* III 38–39); Degen, *Inschriften* 228–229.

125 H 364 (Aggoula, *Remarques* 362).

126 Segal, *Arabs* 65.

127 H 290; cf. Drijvers, *Hatra* 823–824.

128 Drijvers, *Hatra* 823–825; Dijkstra, *State* 87–88.

129 H 195 (Safar, *Kitābāt* II 57; Aggoula, *Inscriptions* 269). H 287 (Safar, *Kitābāt* V 7–8), which probably also belongs to the reign of this king (Segal, *Arabs* 64), has the same formula except for the form ʕRBYʔ, which looks like a plural.

130 H 203 (Aggoula, *Inscriptions* 271).

131 H 79 (Safar, *Kitābāt* I 11–17; Caquot, *Inscriptions* V 2–6; Teixidor, *Notes* 2).

132 Cassius Dio 68.21, 31.

133 Aggoula, *Remarques* III 202; Segal, *Arabs* 63.

134 Cf. also the argumentation by Zwettler, *Imra'alqays* 8–12.

135 Texidor, *Bulletin* 484–485. Cf. Dillemann, *Haute Mésopotamie* 75–78; Degen, *Inscriptions* 403; Segal, Arabs 65 (probably); Dijkstra, *State* 95; Zwettler, *Imra'alqays* 10. For arguments against, see Chaumont, *Chute* 226–227.

136 *Chronicle 1234* I 114:1–3.

137 An example of the first is the old name for Russia, *Rus'*, which was originally a gentilic. This probably also holds for the name China. An example of the opposite is perhaps the name of the Israelite tribe Judah, originally the name of the area south of Jerusalem.

138 According to Dijkstra (*State* 95–96) it must mean 'desert', since 'Arabs' means 'nomads', an argument which is accepted by Zwettler (*Imra'alqays* 8–12 and Hoyland, *Arabia* 78).

From what has been shown in the present investigation, this appears very unlikely.

139 Cf. Caquot, *Inscriptions* I 110–111.

140 In Ezra 4:24 M has *melek Pārās*, i.e. *smîkhûthā*, but the Peshitta has an attributive construction: *malkā parsāyā*.

141 Caquot, *L'araméen* 39; cf. Starcky, *Palmyre* 1082.

16

FROM THE SEVERIANS TO CONSTANTINE THE GREAT

Sources for the period from Septimius Severus to Theodosius

The end of the second century AD saw the ascendancy of the military men as rulers of the Roman empire. This was accompanied by inner and outer convulsions that a century later had transformed it into something new. The foundation was laid for what we could call the Byzantine version of the Roman empire, which was to last until the Moslem conquests. Also other parts of the Orient saw convulsions: a new dynasty took power in Iran, and an empire was formed in South Arabia. These three were now to dominate political events in Arabia and adjacent lands until the whole scenario was drastically changed by the Moslem conquerors.

The period from Septimius Severus to Muhammed can, from our viewpoint, be divided into two parts. The first 200 years saw major changes in Arabia and the role of the Arabs. As will become evident, the end of that period saw the emergence of new sociopolitical structures affecting the lives of the inhabitants of the peninsula. The following two centuries, from the division of Rome until the time of Heraclius, witnessed the consolidation of structures established in the previous period and the build-up in the peninsula for what was to break forth with astounding power at the beginning of the seventh century. It will become clear that it is the first period which concerns us here and we shall present the sources relevant for our subject for the entire period and then deal with the two centuries separately.

Of contemporary testimonies reflecting political events involving Arabs, we have only a few, sometimes badly preserved, texts originating in Iranian territory: two royal inscriptions, one by Shāpur I from *c.* AD 260 and one by Narses at the very end of the century. The inscription from Sanaṭrūq son of ʔBYʔ in Hatra belongs to the 230s AD. To these is added a Manichaean text from the end of the century. From Palmyra we have an extensive corpus of inscriptions in Palmyrene Aramaic which, however, do not mention Arabs explicitly, although they contain a lot of Arabic personal names. Two inscriptions from Syria, the Umm Ǧimāl text and the Namāra inscription, are crucial but short, ambiguous and difficult to interpret. For the fourth century, a few references to Arabia are found in official Roman documents, namely panegyric speeches delivered to emperors. An interesting source is the *Notitia dignitatum*, a description of the Roman army reflecting conditions in the fourth century.[1]

Apart from Cassius Dio's Roman history, which ends in AD 220, the main narrative sources available to us were all, except one, written during the latter half of the fourth century, although often building on older texts.

The account of the perhaps most spectacular events in the third century, namely the history of Palmyra, was told by Dexippus of Athens in two books, the *Historiae* going up to AD 270, dealing with the lives of the emperors, and the *Scythica*, covering the years AD 238–275 and treating the history of the eastern frontiers.[2] Another source for Palmyra was a *Historia Caesarum*, a collection of imperial biographies written just after AD 337.[3] These three sources are lost. They were, however, used by historians in the latter half of the fourth century AD, like the compilers of the *Breviaria* of Festus and Eutropius (*c.* AD 370) or the author of the pseudepigraphic work *Scriptores Historiae Augustae* (*c.* AD 390), which give us some idea of what they contained. A fourth-century source which probably preserves data from the *Historia Caesarum* is Aurelius Victor's collection of imperial biographies from Augustus to Constantine written around AD 360. The valuable material in the account about the Orient in the *Scriptores Historiae Augustae* comes from Dexippus. The main source for our knowledge of the history of Palmyra, Zosimus' *Historía néa* from around AD 500, is also based on Dexippus' writings together with the *Historia Caesarum*. Dexippus was also used as late as the end of the sixth century AD by the Byzantine chronicler Malalas.

Our knowledge of the events around Palmyra thus comes from Dexippus' lost works. Around AD 400. Eunapius wrote a continuation of Dexippus' *History*, which is likewise lost. Zosimus at the beginning of the sixth century follows Eunapius for the history after AD 275. The greatest historian of the fourth century, Ammian Marcellinus, is a first-hand source for the reign of Julian the Apostate, who had a lot to do with the Saracens. Both Eunapius and Ammian were pagans and admirers of Julian. Also Zosimus was a non-Christian.[4]

The extant sources telling about the political events are thus all from the end of our period, i.e. the latter half of the fourth century. From the Greek- and Latin-speaking world, a few relevant contemporary texts are preserved. Most of them were written by the early Christian thinkers, like Clement of Alexandria, Origen and Hippolytus from the third century and Eusebius and Basil the Great from the fourth. These texts contain some remarks about Arabs of an ethnographic or theological nature, usually in connection with Bible exegesis. This means, however, that their contents are difficult to date, since this kind of commentary tends to contain and repeat material from widely differing periods.[5] To this category also belongs a text originating from the school of the Syrian philosopher and gnostic Bardesanes of Edessa from the beginning of the third century: *The Book of the Laws of Countries*. The geographical tradition was continued by Uranius, whose book on Arabia is unfortunately lost and known only through a few quotations. Its dating is also uncertain but there are good arguments for locating it around AD 300.

Finally, a source that stretches over the entire period, and perhaps reaches far back, is the literature of rabbinic Judaism consisting of Bible commentaries as well as codifications of tradition and lore of the Jews in Palestine and Mesopotamia. Like the information given by the Christian authors mentioned, this material is very difficult to date accurately, since it has often been transmitted from authority to authority for a long time, without indication of its actual origin. All these non-historical literary sources are best treated on their own, independently of the historical account.

The course of events from Septimius Severus to Diocletian: general outline

The takeover by the new emperor, Septimius Severus, in AD 193 was in many ways the beginning of a new era. He was the first emperor (except Vespasian a hundred years earlier) to take power by arms. This procedure opened the way for the Parthians to interfere for the first (and only) time in a Roman succession. The result for the Orient was then the confirmation of a political vacuum: Severus' campaigns demonstrated the weakness of the Parthian power, which had not been able to defend Mesopotamia and its own capital. As a matter of fact, this had now occurred three times in eighty years, and the growing weakness of the Arsacids became more and more evident. This must have reduced the authority of the dynasty in Iran, where the power-base for all Iranian rulers lay. On the other hand, it was also evident that the Romans were not ready, willing or able to fill the vacuum in the Orient. A couple of decades later, a new Iranian dynasty had overthrown the old one, and an ideologically and militarily restored Iran became a deadly threat to the Roman empire.[6] Severus' campaigns had opened the gates for the Sassanids.

The accession of Severus implied the takeover by the non-European provincials in the empire. Severus himself was from Cyrenaica, i.e. Africa, and during his governorship in Syria he had, in the year AD 185, married into the leading family of priests in Emesa. Through the empress Iulia Domna and her sister Iulia Maesa, the Syrians received a key position in the empire. For the East one can surely speak of the Syrian century *c.* AD 190–270 when Syria enjoyed not only economic strength but also considerable political influence in the Roman empire. For more than forty years the family of the rulers of Emesa was in power in Rome, delivering three emperors. From developments in the third century it is obvious that the role of the Emesans was not the result of hazardous factors. The economic prosperity of Syria had been increasing for centuries, and the eastern provinces constituted the financial and economic centre of the empire for a long time. The construction of the enormous temples in Syria, such as at Damascus and Palmyra, as early as the first century AD, and Baalbek in the second, is a lasting testimony not only to religious fervour but also to continuous economic progress.

From the middle of the first century, Palmyra had become the main transit centre for the traffic between the Persian Gulf and the Mediterranean.[7] The second century witnessed a prosperity in the town the traces of which are still visible today. Emesa had always had close relations with Palmyra, and the rise of the ruling family there to the highest position in the empire was not only noticed in Palmyra but probably also exploited. When the Emesan dynasty was overthrown, Palmyra began to emerge as an independent political power. Between the rule of the Emesan dynasty and the heyday of Palmyra we find the reign of another Syrian, Philippus. It seems as if in the first half of the third century there was a kind of attempt from Syria to seize power in the Roman empire. This attempt was thwarted by the emergence of a series of generals from the Danube region in Europe. The latter half of the century can in some ways be seen as the time of struggle between the ambitions of the Syrians on the one hand, the ambitions of the Illyrian and Pannonian generals on the other. The outcome was the military victory of the Balkans over Syria in AD 272. The Syrians successively lost their political position and, finally, all political independence. Landmarks of this story are the murder of Alexander Severus, the last Emesan imperial ruler, in 235, the death in battle of Philippus, the last Syrian on the imperial throne, in 249, and the fall of Palmyra in 272. From other viewpoints, Syria was victorious: the sun-cult from Emesa also became the ideology for the Europeans and its gradual transformation into orthodox Christianity in the fourth century was a confirmation of the Syrian ideological connection – the founders of Christianity were after all a kind of Syrians.

The third century saw several changes of the border between Rome and Iran which affected the Arabs. Septimius Severus conquered upper Mesopotamia and made the Tigris the eastern border of a new province, Mesopotamia, with its capital at Nisibis. The kingdom of Edessa was reduced to the town itself, and it was finally abolished by Severus' successor Caracalla. Then, in the 250s, the new Iranian king Shāpur I conquered Mesopotamia and Syria. The Roman power broke down, but the tide was stemmed by the rulers in Palmyra who seem to have recaptured parts of the Transeuphratean province. The Romans recaptured Mesopotamia west of the Balīkh river, including Osrhoene, in a peace treaty with the Sassanid ruler Vahram II in AD 283. Finally, Diocletian defeated the Sassanid king Narses in 297 and incorporated not only Mesopotamia but also areas east of the Tigris into the empire. At the end of the century the Roman empire reached its furthest extension eastwards.[8] This political situation in the east was to remain stable until 361 when the emperor Julian tried to implement Trajan's old project of also incorporating lower Mesopotamia. The attempt was a failure; the Romans lost Diocletian's conquests, and the border was rolled back to a line following the Khābūr, leaving Nisibis in Iranian hands.

Septimius Severus and the Arabs

After the activities formally headed by Lucius Verus in the 160s, Edessa remained within the Roman sphere of interest. It is not quite clear whether there was any Roman military presence east of the Euphrates. The Osrhoenian kingdom seems to have included Nisibis. The Ǧazīra was to become a theatre of war once again, and Hatra was to be attacked a second time by a Roman army. The year AD 193 was filled with the struggle between three pretenders for the empire after the epoch of Marcus Aurelius and his circle. One of them, Pescennius Niger, had his base in the eastern provinces and was backed by Abgar IX of Edessa, Barsamius of Hatra, Narses of Adiabene and also a brand new King of Kings, Vologases IV.[9] The *Historia Augusta* refers to an attack on Pescennius Niger's army in Egypt by *Saraceni*.[10] Unfortunately we have no means of checking this information and determining who these Saracens were. From the context they could be located on the Sinai peninsula. We do, in fact, have a text that could be connected with these events. In a Nabataean inscription in Wādī Mukattab in the eastern Sinai peninsula which is a memorial to a certain WʔLW [Wāʔil] we read:

> This was written in the year 85 by the HPRKYH in which the ʕRBYʔ devastated the land.[11]

It is most likely that the text is dated according to the so-called Bosra era starting in AD 106 and we are thus in the year AD 189/190. The title mentioned is the *eparkhía*, which is the Greek term for the office of the governor of a province, in this case probably the *Provincia Arabia*. The identification of the Arabs and the land devastated remains obscure, but it is tempting to see a connection with the events around the rise and fall of Pescennius Niger. The *Historia Augusta* in that case has transformed the Arabs in its source to the more contemporary Saracens. But the identity of the Arabs/Saracens is still problematic. The inscription must be considered a better source for the terminology than the *Historia Augusta* written 200 years later. It seems unlikely that there were still independent Arabs between Palestine and Egypt but it cannot be excluded that they had survived further south on the Sinai peninsula.

Pescennius Niger and the second pretender were swept away by the third one, Septimius Severus, who emerged as the new strongman of the empire. Instigated by Vologases, the Osrhoenians and the Adiabenians had laid siege to Nisibis. Now they refused to give up what they had taken and Severus had to take action. In AD 195 he crossed the Euphrates and attacked the Osrhoenians, the Adiabenians and the Arabs.[12] Severus lifted the siege of Nisibis and obviously pacified the Osrhoenians and Adiabenians. Our source is Cassius Dio, who now speaks as an eye-witness:

> The *arábioi*, inasmuch as none of their neighbours was willing to aid them, sent envoys again to Severus with more reasonable offers; nevertheless, they did not obtain what they wanted, as they had not come along themselves.[13]

Cassius Dio has no clear information about operations against Arabs.[14] It is, however, found in the *Historia Augusta*:

> Next [i.e. after having defeated Niger] he engaged in further operations around (*circa*) Arabia and brought the Parthians back to allegiance and also the Adiabeni all of whom had sided with Pescennius.[15]

It so happens that the *Historia Augusta* in the passages about the Parthian wars in the second century is directly or indirectly based on a good source, namely Quadratus' *Parthica*, which makes this report trustworthy.[16] That Severus must have directed some military operations against Arabs is confirmed by contemporary documentation. On the coins issued in 195 he is called *Parthicus Arabicus*, *Parthicus Adiabenicus* or *Arabicus Adiabenicus*, which must indicate the main theatres of operations in this campaign.[17] In the *Breviaria* we have similar indications which seem to refer to the campaigns in 195 rather than to the ones in 197–200:

> He defeated the Parthians, the inner *Arabes* and the Azabeni; the *Arabes* he subdued (*superavit*) so that he made a province there. Then (*idcirco*) he was called *Parthicus Arabicus Azabenicus*.[18]

> He defeated the Parthians harshly, annihilated the Aziabeni, received the inner *Arabes* and made a province in Arabia. Therefore the epithets were claimed from the victories; for he was called *Aziabenicus*, *Parthicus*, *Arabicus*.[19]

Both *Breviaria* thus say that Severus made a province in Arabia, a piece of information derived from their common source, probably the *Historia Caesarum*. A similar note is found in Aurelius Victor.[20] Also the *Historia Augusta* mentions the sway over the Arabs, which may be derived from the same source:

> He defeated Abgarus, the king of the Persians. He extended his sway over the *Arabes*.[21]

Festus' version gives a hint that the Arabs surrendered without struggle, which might also be reflected in Eutropius. The question is who the 'inner Arabs' were. It is not likely that the term refers to Hatra, since this town was never conquered by Severus. In the passage in Dio about the army units sent against *arkhén*, it is said that he bestowed some dignity upon Nisibis and that Severus boasted that he had added a vast area to the empire. It is thus likely that Severus dealt with Arabs near Nisibis. The 'inner Arabs' would then be those in the Ǧazīra, living within the Roman border established in the 160s. This would mean the Arabs documented at Sumatar.

The victory is mentioned in a more or less contemporary document. In the excavations at Dura Europus a calendar of the festivals in the town was found, which is dated to the reign of Alexander Severus (AD 222–235). According to it, on 28 January were celebrated 'the Arabian, Adiabenian and great Parthian victories of the divine Severus'.[22]

A new province was created between the Euphrates and Edessa.[23] Severus had to cut short his eastern campaign because of unrest in Gaul. In his absence an insurrection broke out in the west, led by a certain Albinus and supported *inter alia* by the legion III Cyrenaica in Arabia, i.e. former Nabataea.[24] The revolt failed but it led the new Parthian king Vologases IV to make another attempt at abolishing the Roman presence and influence east of the Euphrates. Adiabene was plundered and Nisibis was beleaguered once more. In 198 Severus was back in the east and lifted the siege to the lock of the Orient once again. Then he proceeded along the Euphrates, reached Ctesiphon and plundered it. He did not attempt to occupy the whole of Mesopotamia but returned along the Tigris.[25] At the beginning of AD 199 he reached Hatra, which was attacked but could not be taken.[26]

The importance of controlling Hatra was obvious and becomes comprehensible if, with the incorporation of the region between Osrhoene and the Tigris, many of the Arabs with traditional loyalty to the kings in Hatra had come to live within the Roman border. In the year AD 200 Severus set out once again to take Hatra. This time a siege was undertaken, lasting for twenty days but without success:

> A good many [soldiers] were lost on foraging expeditions, as the barbarian cavalry, I mean that of the *arábioi*, kept assailing them everywhere in swift and violent attacks. The archery, too, of the *atrenoí* was effective at very long range.[27]

After having waited in vain for the surrender of the Hatrans, Severus had to call off the operation and return to Syria. Hatra remained independent and the Khābūr–Singǧār line remained the south-eastern border of the new province of Mesopotamia, which reached the Tigris.[28] In the year AD 203 Severus erected his triumphal arch on the Forum Romanum. On it we can still read his own summary of the Oriental campaign and the military achievements he found worth mentioning:

> To the Imperator Caesar Lucius Septimius, son of Marcus, Severus Pius Pertinax Augustus, Father of his country (*pater patriae*), *Parthicus Arabicus* and *Parthicus Adiabenicus*.[29]

Severus received the title *Parthicus Maximus* after the conquest of Ctesiphon.[30] It is worth noticing, though, that this title is not mentioned in his own official inscription. This is not a coincidence but represents a conscious policy. The ambitions of Trajan, inherited from earlier Roman rulers, are emphatically rejected. Severus had demonstrated Roman power by advancing to the Parthian capital but he did not try to keep Mesopotamia. The Roman military apparatus was not capable of solving the problem of holding that province. Strategically, an occupation of all Mesopotamia would create a very difficult defence situation, since the land of the Two Rivers could not be held unless the Iranian plateau was also pacified. Severus wisely refrained from that venture.

The *Historia Augusta* has a notice on the reign of the emperor Opellius Macrinus (AD 217–218), Caracalla's successor:

> He fought against the Parthians, the Armenians and the *Arabes* whom they call *eudaemones*, with no less bravery than success.[31]

We know that Macrinus fought a war with the Parthians during which Nisibis was besieged.[32] Our main sources for Macrinus, namely Cassius Dio (book 79) and Herodian (book 5), do not, however, mention any Arabs in connection with Macrinus. The *Historia Augusta* is a muddy source, and the mention of *Arabes eudaemones* does not increase confidence, since a Roman campaign to that country, whether in Yemen or in the Persian Gulf at this time, is very unlikely. On the other hand, it is not at all impossible that the operations in 217–218 involved the Arabs under Parthian rule, mainly those around Hatra. When he describes Septimius Severus' operations in the Ǧazīra, Herodian calls the Arabia around Hatra *eudaímōn*, and the *Historia Augusta* may well have the phrase from that source.[33] Even though Macrinus fought with Arabs in Mesopotamia, it was not a prominent part of the operations: the only honorary name he is known to have been given is *Parthicus Maximus*.[34] From the inscriptions of Macrinus' predecessor, Caracalla, we know that this ruler applied the honorary titles of Septimius Severus on himself, among them *Arabicus*, without activities against any Arabs being otherwise documented.[35] The inflation in honorary titles in the Severian age may well lie behind the notice about Macrinus' dealings with Arabs and Armenians.

Philippus *Arabs*

There were not only generals from the Balkans who were interested in governing the rich Syrian provinces. The new vigorous dynasty in Iran showed a keen interest in the same region. The third century was also dominated by the Iranians' attempts at extending their sway to the Mediterranean and thus revising the order of Pompey, now 300 years old.

Edessa had already become a Roman colony in 214, and the last vestiges of its independence were abolished. In AD 230, the founder of the Sassanid dynasty, Ardashir, initiated the now traditional siege of Nisibis. This time the threat was turned away by the Roman army under Alexander Severus. Ardashir tried to take Hatra once again in 238 but failed.[36] In 240 Hatra was finally taken by the Sassanids.[37] This occurred as Ardashir's successor Shāpur I had been enthroned and when a new grand-scale attack was launched by him against Syria.[38] The counterattacks were led by Gordianus III and his prefects of the Praetorian guard, which in this century was one of the most important political institutions of the empire. For a short while, the kingdom of the Abgarids was revived during the campaign against the Sassanids in 240–43.[39] Syria was liberated and Edessa was finally incorporated into the Mesopotamian province and the dynasty abolished. The prefect Timesitheus died suddenly, and was succeeded by Marcus Iulius Philippus from Trachonitis in Syria.

The disappearance of Edessa and Hatra as independent political entities is an event of crucial importance for the history of the Arabs. These two had obviously been a centre for Arabs for centuries. Their disappearance was a symptom that changes were going on, not only in the political structures of the surrounding empires but also among the inhabitants of the Syrian desert.

The Syrian emperor who ascended the throne in 244, Philippus, is known by his nickname, *Arabs*. The only ancient source where that name is mentioned is the *Historia Augusta*.[40] As has been pointed out, this text was written 150 years after Philippus and is notoriously unreliable. In Zosimus' *Historía néa*, written *c*. AD 500, it is said that the emperor came from 'the very bad people of Arabia'.[41] The information about Philippus' humble origins has been cast into doubt by modern historians.[42] The information in these two works probably comes from the lost history of Eunapius and the lost parts of Ammian Marcellinus. Both were pagans, admirers of Julian the Apostate and negative against the Christians. There was a rumour, at least from the time of Constantine, that Philippus had been a Christian.[43] For a pagan author in the fourth century AD, Philippus' successor, Decius, must have been a hero since he initiated the first large-scale persecution of the Christians. In Aurelius Victor's collection of imperial biographies written *c*. AD 360, it is alleged that Philippus was born in a very insignificant place and that his father, although a nobleman, had been leader of robbers.[44] According to the same source, Philippus founded a town, 'Philippopolis by Arabia', present-day Shahbāʔ, and it is likely that this was his home town.[45] Aurelius Victor's information may be closer to the truth than that of the later authors. All this, together with the fact that Philippus' home town, according to Aurelius Victor, was in the *Provincia Arabia*, and that, according to Ptolemy, there were Arabs in nearby Trachonitis, makes it likely that the nickname is the result of a *damnatio memoriae* of the Syrian emperor by the pagan party at the end of the fourth century. As a matter of fact, we have no means of verifying whether Philippus was an Arab and, in that case, what kind of Arab he was.[46]

The Orient in turmoil: Shāpur I and Palmyra

In 253, when Philippus and his successor Decius had passed away, Ardashir's son and successor Shāpur I launched a new violent attack against Syria. This time the result was disastrous to the Romans, and the Iranians overran the whole country and also invaded the Arabian province in the south, as well as Asia Minor. The struggle lasted an entire decade and ended with the capture by the Iranians of the Roman emperor Valerian in AD 260. In an inscription put up by Shāpur in Naqsh-e-Rustam, close to that of his great predecessor Darius I, he summarized the achievements of his reign. Like Darius' inscription, this one is in three languages, Parthian, Middle Persian and Greek, of which the Middle Persian is the basis.[47] This important text encompasses seventy lines, of which the first thirty-six deal with the political history of Shāpur's reign. He enumerates the lands subject to him, among which Arabia is found:

> I possess the lands of Persis, Parthia, Susania, Mesanéne, Assyría, Adiabéne, Arabía/ʔRBYSTNY, Adourbadéne, Armenía, Ibería . . .[48]

After the enumeration of the lands possessed is an account of the campaigns undertaken by the King of Kings.[49] There are three campaigns altogether. In the third one, that against Valerian, Shāpur had to confront an army composed of many peoples in the Roman empire:

> [from the people of] Phrygía, Syría, Phoineikē, Joudaía, Arabía, Mauritanía . . .[50]

The order of names in the first passage clearly follows geography. The countries mentioned must be those considered integral parts of the Iranian empire, the inheritance of the King of Kings, the lands he possessed lawfully and independently of the three great campaigns. Shāpur describes the traditional borders of the empire governed from Ctesiphon. Assyria is the central part of Mesopotamia where the capital was, bordering Mesene in the south. Hence Arabía/ʔRBSTNY is an area within the traditional borders of Shāpur's realm. Since it stands beside Adiabene, it is reasonable to assume that it is the Parthian province that was named Arabia, i.e. the land of the Arabs between Khābūr, Singăr, the Euphrates and the Tigris, whose capital had been Hatra, conquered by Shāpur in the first year of his reign. This further means that this Arabia has nothing to do with the 'Arabias' within the Roman border in Osrhoene.[51]

Since the Arabia mentioned in the next part of the text, dealing with the military operations against Rome, comes immediately after Judaea, it probably refers to the former Arabo-Nabataean kingdom, since AD 106 called *Provincia Arabia*. It should be observed that Shāpur uses an old-fashioned terminology: there was no official Judaea at this time. This inscription is also a confirmation of the existence of at least two Arabias of rather small extent in this period: one Roman and one Iranian.

The rise and fall of Palmyra

The breakdown of Roman power in Syria in the 250s led to the definitive emergence of Palmyra. The dramatic story of the Palmyrene decade, ending in AD 272 with the Roman conquest of the city, is known only from much later sources.[52] Only three inscriptions mentioning the rulers in Palmyra are relevant to our investigation. The basic narrative is found in Zosimus' *Historía néa*. It is paralleled by two chapters in the *Scriptores Historiae Augustae*: *The Thirty Tyrants* and *Aurelian*. Both of these are from the end of the fourth century, i.e. more than a century after the events. Zosimus based his report on Dexippus' *Historia* and *Scythica* together with the *Historia Caesarum*.[53] The latter was used by the author of the *Historia Augusta*.[54] For the story of the emperor Aurelian, the author of this work also had another source before him, which has been identified with Dexippus via Eunapius.[55] Lately another suggestion has been made, namely Nicomachus Flavianus.[56] Also Malalas' *Chronography* and Syncellus' *Ecloga*, written three centuries after the events, are witnesses of Dexippus and the *Historia Caesarum*.[57]

The unfavourable source situation has the effect of veiling many details in the history of Palmyra which we would have liked to know more about.[58] From the narratives we have, we can see how the Palmyrene king, Odenathus, emerged as the saviour of Rome and the conqueror of Shāpur. The Palmyrenians threw out the Iranians and established themselves as the rulers of the East. Odenathus invaded Mesopotamia and reached Ctesiphon in 262. During the following decade the Palmyrenians dominated the East. Odenathus was murdered in 267 and succeeded by his son Vaballatus, although the real power was in the hands of his widow, Zenobia. She initiated the conquest of Egypt in 270 but seems to have given up Odenathus' conquests in Mesopotamia. Instead she expanded Palmyrene power into Asia Minor. Finally, the new Roman emperor,

Aurelian, defeated the Palmyrenians. Zenobia fled but was caught on the Euphrates and taken to Rome.

In the Aramaic inscriptions from Palmyra we find many Arabic names. This does not mean that the inhabitants were Arabs. It does not even mean that those carrying these names were necessarily Arabs in any sense of the word.[59] Our task is not to retell the story of Palmyra but to clarify the role of Arabs in its history. We first have to turn to the contemporary documents. The formal successor of Odenathus, Vaballatus, is presented as the conqueror of Arabia in an inscription as well as on milestones in Transjordan:

> Imperator Caesar L. Iulius Aurelius Septimius Vaballatus Athenodorus, *Persicus Maximus*, *Arabicus Maximus*, *Adiabenicus Maximus* . . .[60]

The reason for Vaballatus' title is not quite clear. We know from a late source that Palmyra took control of Roman Arabia.[61] That conquest is also confirmed by an inscription in a temple in Bosra.[62] On the other hand, we have seen that the title *Arabicus* was used by Septimius Severus as an indication of the conquest of areas in upper Mesopotamia. This makes it likely that Vaballatus' title also indicates military triumphs in Mesopotamia, not the conquest of the Roman province of Arabia.[63] His father, Odenathus, had made conquests in Mesopotamia. It has been supposed that the Palmyrenians kept at least some of their conquests on the other side of the Euphrates until the time of Zenobia.[64] When Palmyra was defeated by Aurelian in AD 272 Zenobia fled eastwards and tried to cross the Euphrates.[65] This could indicate that she counted on support there and not necessarily Sassanid support. What remains certain is that there is no indication that Vaballatus, his father or his mother or the Palmyrenians in general were seen as Arabs.

Zenobia's conqueror, Aurelian, was also decorated with titles after his achievements in the East, and among them we find *Arabicus Maximus* mentioned twice in the inscriptions.[66] It is very unlikely that this title refers to Aurelian's conquest of Palmyra. It must rather refer to some achievement in Mesopotamia, where it is said in the *Historia Augusta* that he had defeated the Persians.[67] If the title refers to Palmyra, it would be a completely unique designation for that area. As a matter of fact, Aurelian also carried the title *Palmyrenicus*, which definitely shows that Palmyra was something different from Arabia.[68] It cannot be ruled out that the titles of Septimius Severus lie behind those of Aurelian. Anyone who marched through upper Mesopotamia with an army became an *Arabicus*.

There are thus no certain indications in contemporary documents about Arabs in Palmyra and even less about the Palmyrenians being Arabs themselves. In the literary sources available, all written at least a century after the events, we find Arabs mentioned in two: the *Historia Augusta* written around AD 400 and Johannes Malalas' world chronicle from the sixth century. In both works, the term 'Saracens' is also found. In the *Historia Augusta*, *Arabes* occur three times in connection with Zenobia and Aurelian. The first is in a letter said to have been sent by Aurelian to the Senate, where he describes the qualities of the Palmyrene queen:

> I might even say that such was the fear that this woman inspired in the peoples of the east and also the Egyptians that neither *Arabes*, nor *Saraceni*, nor Armenians ever moved against her.[69]

Another letter is quoted in the biography of Aurelian, said to be sent to him by the emperor Valerian, i.e. before AD 260:

> The command of the troops will be vested in you. You will have three hundred Ituraean bowmen, six hundred Armenians, one hundred and fifty *Arabes*, two hundred *Saraceni*, and four hundred *auxilia* from Mesopotamia.[70]

Lastly, after the victory in the east we have an exuberant description of Aurelian's triumph in Rome:

> [the captives from the barbarian peoples] Blemmyes, Axomitae, *Arabes eudaemones*, Indi, Bactriani, Hiberi, Saraceni, Persi . . .[71]

The evidence in Malalas is more bewildering:

> Then rose Enathos [Odenathus] the ally of the Romans, king of the barbarian *sarakēnoí*, ruler (*kratōn*) of the land of the *árabes* who had Zenobia, the Saracen, as wife and queen.[72]

> . . . as imperator he (Aurelian) went to Arabia. There he initiated war with Enathos, the king of the *sarakēnoí* barbarians, killed him and took Arabia.[73]

> At that time, Zenobia, the widow of Enathos, the *sarakēnós*, in order to take revenge for her husband . . . occupied Arabia, which belonged to the Romans.[74]

The main difference between the *Historia Augusta* and Malalas is that the latter identifies the Palmyrenians and probably all inhabitants in the Syrian desert as Saracens, whereas the former distinguishes between Arabs and Saracens and does not see any of them as identical with Palmyrenes or the subjects of Zenobia. We know that the term 'Saracen' as a general designation for 'desert-dwellers' in the Syrian desert does not belong to the third century. It was introduced in the fourth century, and its use in Malalas reflects the terminology of later periods.[75] Our main source for the introduction of the term 'Saracen', Ammian Marcellinus, the historian of Julian the Apostate, writing at the end of the fourth century, says that the term 'Saraceni' has replaced *Arabes scenitae*.[76] Zosimus, our main narrative source for the history of Palmyra, does not mention either Saracens or Arabs.

Malalas is a very confused source and is not very reliable. Aurelian did not kill Odenathus and the chronological framework is opaque. The claim that Aurelian took Arabia could be the result of a misunderstanding of his title *Arabicus*. It is most likely that there is a confusion between Odenathus and his wife in Malalas' account. The Arabia occupied by Zenobia is clearly the Roman province. More problematic is the claim that Odenathus was 'ruler of the Arabs'. It could refer to the Mesopotamian Arabia. One late source, Georgius Syncellus, says that Odenathus conquered Mesopotamia and besieged Ctesiphon. It is not impossible that Odenathus had conquered the areas around Singār when defeating Shāpur in the 260s. It is thus probable that the Palmyrenians kept control over the northern Ğazīra and that Vaballatus' title *Arabicus Maximus* is somehow connected with that. Important is, however, that even

Malalas does not explicitly say that the rulers of Palmyra were Arabs. They are Saracens, which thus reflects the views described by Ammianus Marcellinus.

In the *Historia Augusta* the author in the three quoted instances makes a clear distinction between *Arabes* and *Saraceni*. The passage about the composition of Aurelian's army has an authentic ring, although it has been clearly shown that the letter in which it occurs is a concoction of the author and does not originate in Aurelian's time.[77] As we shall see, the distinction between Arabs, Ituraeans and Saracens is found in the *Notitia dignitatum*, a document describing the composition of the Roman army, going back to the time of Diocletian around AD 300.[78] Since this piece of information is found in a spurious letter, it is likely that the author has drawn on facts known by him and transposed conditions in the Roman army as reflected in the *Notitia dignitatum* back into the times of Aurelian.[79] This would, however, mean that the word *Saraceni* in the passage in the *Historia Augusta* is not the general designation for the inhabitants in the Syrian desert as used by Ammian but represents special units in the Roman army at the beginning of the fourth century AD.[80] This then also holds for the *Arabes* in Aurelian's army. The distinction between *Arabes* and *Saraceni* in the *Historia Augusta* clearly reflects an earlier terminology than the one used by Ammian Marcellinus. Since the closest parallel is the *Notitia dignitatum*, this terminology reflects conditions during the first decades of the fourth century AD. The composition of Aurelian's army in the 270s AD remains undocumented.

The presence of Axumites, Bactrians and Indians in Aurelian's triumph sounds quite unlikely, and it is clear that the author has gathered names found in earlier descriptions of triumphs combined with reports of visiting embassies. The *Arabes eudaemones* thus belong to the same category as the other peoples mentioned and represent the exotic inhabitants in the outskirts of the *oecumene*.[81] Like the Blemmyes and the Axumites, they here give a special performance coming directly out of Heliodorus' novel *Aethiopica*, written around AD 350![82]

In the letter from Valerian, the Arabs (as well as the Saracens) are on the Roman side, and in the letter to the Senate they seem to be seen as Zenobia's enemies, which is in accordance with the conditions in the *Notitia dignitatum*. On the other hand, the *Historia Augusta* also mentions *Saraceni* on Zenobia's side together with the Armenians and Persians.[83] This is a relapse of the author into the terminology of his own time and is in accordance with Ammian and Malalas.[84]

One might wonder which terminology was used by the original sources for the events around the rise and fall of Palmyra, i.e. Dexippus and Nicomachus Flavianus. In Malalas we find the Saracens characterized as *bárbaroi*, a term also used by Zosimus. According to the latter, Zenobia had an army of Palmyrenians, Syrians and barbarians, or Palmyrenians and 'others'.[85] Other writers from the fourth century, such as Aurelius Victor and Eutropius, mention Arabs in other contexts but not in connection with Palmyra.[86] We can thus assume that both sources in their account of the Roman–Palmyrene war used terms like *bárbaroi* or, less likely, *skēnîtai* as a designation for the allies of the Palmyrenians. They thus probably did not mention either Arabs or Saracens.

It can be concluded that there is no indication in any source that the Palmyrenians had Arabs on their side.[87] Arabs seem to have played no significant role in the story of the rise and fall of Palmyra. It is likely that Odenathus conquered Mesopotamian Arabia and that it was held for a while by the Palmyrenian troops. Zenobia's army captured the Roman province of Arabia. We hear nothing about Arabs in the ranks of her or her husband's army, let alone that the rulers themselves were considered Arabs. The fact that they all carry good Arabic names does not change this conclusion. The obscure references to Arabs, both in contemporary inscriptions and in the written sources, all refer to the Arabs on the other side of the Euphrates, the Mesopotamian Arabia.

The author of the *Historia Augusta* depicts Zenobia as a heroine similar to Cleopatra, another notorious female enemy of Rome. There are, however, several elements which are reminiscent of the later legend of Bilqīs, the legendary Queen of Sheba, rather than of the Egyptian queen: sexual restraint, fondness of hunting, endowment with wisdom, possession of physical beauty, calling descriptions of women in later Arabic poetry to mind.[88] It looks as if we, in the description of this woman in the *Historia Augusta*, have a substantial piece of Middle Eastern folklore preserved.[89] There is a tradition told by the *Historia Augusta* and Eutropius' *Breviarium* that Zenobia lived many years in Rome and that her descendants lived in her house there long after her death.[90] This story has been cast into doubt, since Zosimus says she died during her voyage to Rome.[91] Be that as it may, it seems that the author of the *Historia Augusta* has known legends about the queen, perhaps told by Palmyrenians in Rome, and incorporated their panegyric remembrances of the queen in his account.[92]

The three empires: interaction around AD 300

The fall of Palmyra had secured the Roman grip on the Oriental provinces for more than 300 years to come. After the death of Aurelian, there again followed some years of interior convulsions. Under the emperor Carus, a new violent attack was undertaken against Persia in the year AD 283, and the Roman army once again reached Ctesiphon. The emperor's sudden death caused the cancellation of the enterprise. The border between Rome and Iran was established along the Balīkh river and running to Amida.[93] Edessa remained under Roman rule but was an outer bulwark, difficult to defend.

In 284 after the Mesopotamian campaign and Carus' death, Diocletian became emperor. From the year AD 290 there are indications of an active Roman policy against the peoples of the Syrian desert.[94] Diocletian's activity against the desert is mentioned only in a *praeteritio* in a swaggering panegyric referring to the deeds of a campaign in Syria. The defeated enemy is called Saracens.[95] The relationship between Rome and Iran remained on the whole peaceful during these years.[96]

In 293 a new Iranian king, Narses, took power, probably by a *coup d'état*. In the inscription put up by him at Paikuli in Kurdistan we find, among the rulers said to have acknowledged his kingship, two kings with the Arabic name ʕAmr, one called the Lakhmid, ʔMRW LHMʔČ/ŠYN, and another called the Abgarid, ʔMRW ʔPGRNʔN.[97] Judging by the order of names in the inscription, they dwelt west of the Sassanid empire proper. It is not necessary to assume that they were obedient servants of the King of Kings.[98] They seem rather to have been allies. One of the ʕAmrs, probably the Lakhmid, also appears as Amarō, 'king [of the sons of the L]ahim', in a fragment of a Manichaean chronicle.[99] This king is mentioned together with 'Queen Thadamor', i.e. probably Zenobia of Palmyra, which indicates a Syrian rather than a Mesopotamian location.[100]

In 296 Narses initiated a war against Rome by attacking Armenia. The Roman response was powerful. Diocletian dispatched a new ruler to Armenia, Tiridates, who took part in the operations in Mesopotamia. He is known as the king who Christianized Armenia. The Romans were victorious and took Nisibis in 297/298. In the peace treaty, the Ǧazīra between the Euphrates and the Tigris and north of Sinǧār became Roman. Also parts of Adiabene on the eastern side of the Tigris came under Roman sway.[101] Diocletian thus succeeded in vindicating Roman power in the east, and Roman positions were advanced considerably. Diocletian's border was to last until the 360s, and the mighty hand of the reinvigorated Roman empire lay over the Middle East for more than half a century.

The tetrarchy of Diocletian was, after years of convulsions, followed by the reign of Constantine the Great. Constantine was the last Roman emperor to carry the title *Arabicus Maximus*.[102] The reason for this is unknown. We have no indication of any military operations against Arabs of any kind. It has been suggested that some of his other titles were inherited from his father, Constantius. He did not, however, take part in Diocletian's operations in the east. The title is documented only in one inscription in North Africa.[103] It should be pointed out that if the title represents the military achievement of somebody, it must refer to operations in the Ǧazīra. As has been shown in this study, all the preceding emperors who carried this title received it after victories in the area between Edessa, Sinǧār and Hatra. It could thus refer to the war between 296 and 299. But as far as we know, neither Constantine nor his father were there then.[104] There are, however, a couple of passages referring to Constantine's activities against the Persians.[105] The title *Arabicus* could refer to these events, which would confirm that the title has to do with Arabia in the Ǧazīra.

The king of all Arabs: the text from an-Namāra

From the time of Constantine the Great dates the most famous text from the pre-Islamic period dealing with Arabs. The text was originally found at an-Namāra north-east of present-day Ǧabal ad-Durūz a few kilometres east of the Roman borderline.[106] The dating is clear: the year AD 328. The writing is Nabataean but the language is a form of Arabic related to the ʕArabiyya known from the earliest Arabic poetry and the Qurʔān.[107] Since the Nabataean script has only twenty-two signs, several of them in the inscription have two values in order to render the twenty-eight or twenty-nine consonants of this Arabic dialect. In fact, many of the twenty-two signs are very similar and often impossible to distinguish from each other. The result is that the text contains several passages that can be read in different ways and there is no consensus about the readings of many of them. We shall not undertake another analysis with suggestions of even more readings here. We will instead try to establish a picture of the interpretations given and which historical conclusions can be drawn from them. The following passages seem to be those about which most scholars agree[108]:

> Ia. This is the tomb of MRʔLQYŠ, son of ʕMRW, b: king of the ʕRB . . . c: . . . the TG
>
> IIa: and he ruled the two ʔŠD and NZRW and their kings b: and he . . . MḤGW c: . . .
>
> IIIa: . . . b: in . . . of NGRN the town of ŠMR c: and he ruled MʕDW d: and . . . his sons
>
> IVa: over the tribes b: and . . . c: and no king achieved his achievement

Va: . . . b: he died in the year 223 on day 7 of KSLWL c: . . .[109]

Ib. Most commentators read KLH as 'all of them', i.e. 'all Arabs'. One has read FLH 'and to him';[110] another, WLQBH 'and his title of honour'.[111] The traditional reading is, however, to be followed.[112] The expression 'Arabs, all of them' is found in inscriptions 336 and 343 at Hatra and it is likely that there is a connection.[113]

Ic. Most commentators see this phrase as a reference to an endowment of royal insignia. TG is usually seen as the word *tāǧ*, a word of Iranian origin borrowed into Aramaic and Arabic, designating the headgear of an Iranian king. It is a tiara, i.e. a kind of helmet, rather than a diadem, which was originally a band around the head.[114] The meaning of the preceding letters is, however, debated. They have been read ʔŠR, 'bind', or ʔŠD.[115] The syntax of the phrase is usually seen as that of a relative clause reading DW *ḏū* as relative particle. It is, however, also possible to read it with the well-attested meaning 'possessor of'.[116] In that case the following ʔŠR(ʔŠD) must be a nominal form: 'the one with the ʔŠR/D of the *tāǧ*'.

IIa. All commentators except one agree on the reading of this passage.[117] The crux is the meaning of the ʔLʔŠDYN. Suggestions range between 'the two ʔAs(a)ds', 'the two tribes ʔAsad and Tanūkh', 'the tribesmen of ʔAsad', 'the ʔAzd in ʕAsīr' and 'the ʔAzd in ʕUmān'.[118] The latest suggestion is to read ʔLʔŠRYN as 'the two (As)Syrias'.[119]

IIb. The interpretation of the verb in this phrase is usually 'disperse', 'put to flight'. Two commentators have read HḎB as *haḏḏaba* 'chastise', instead of HRB, *harraba*, 'make flee'.[120] The word MḤGW was early emended to MḎḤGW, i.e. Madhḥiǧ, the name of a well-known South Arabian tribe, by one of the earliest commentators, who has been followed by almost everyone ever since.[121]

IIc–IIId. This is one of the two most discussed passages in the inscription and interpretations differ widely:

> who brought success/was lucky in the siege/conquest of Naǧrān, the city of Shammar, king of Maʕadd.[122]

> He came scattering the densely living inhabitants of Naǧrān, the city of Shammar, king of Maʕadd.[123]

> He pushed forward with success to the siege of Naǧrān, the capital of [the region of] Shammar and installed his son Maʕadd [and Banān] as kings.[124]

> He came back boasting about the attack on Naǧrān the city of Shammar, and the kingdom of Maʕadd.[125]

> and he entered without any difficulty into Ẓarbān of Naǧrān, the city of Shammar who subdued Maʕadd.[126]

> He collected/imposed tribute in the ḤBG of Naǧrān.

> He came with ease to Nağrān.[127]

> . . . so that he successfully smote, in the irrigated land of Nağrān, the realm of Shammar, and ruled Maʕadd.[128]

> and he came driving them into the gates of Nağrān, the city of Shammar, and he subdued Maʕadd.[129]

> . . . until he knocked them down with his iron spearhead at the gates of Nağrān, the city of Shammar, king of Maʕadd.[130]

> . . . until he hit with his lance the gates of Nağrān, city of Shammar [and] became king of Maʕadd.[131]

It is easily seen that the letters preceding the name Nağrān are problematic. Only the fourth and sixth words are agreed upon: *fī . . . madīnat*(*i*), 'in the town'. The first word must be a conjunction or a sentence-initial particle, since it occurs as such also in the last line, although its meaning remains obscure.[132] In the last line it is followed directly by a finite verb. This makes it likely that the following letters in line IIc should be read *wağaʔ*(*a*) *bi*, 'smite with' and not 'bring' (*wa-ğāʔ*(*a*) *bi*).[133] The next group has been read as *bi-zağāʔ/y*, 'with success', 'victoriously' etc. but the interpretation is very uncertain.[134]

The other main problem is the relationship between the two personal names MRʔ ʔLQYŠ and ŠMR and the following phrase in IIIc, WMLK MʕDW. Depending on the function of W, it can be read 'and he ruled Maʕadd' or '[Shammar], the king of Maʕadd'. In the first reading, the problem arises whether it is the king of the Arabs who rules Maʕadd or it is Shammar. This question cannot be answered with grammatical arguments. An opinion must be built upon the general historical interpretation of the text.

IId–IVc. Opinions remain divided on the following part:

> who distributed the tribes among his sons and installed these as cavalry in the service of the Romans.[135]

> who installed his sons over the tribes and entrusted them to Persians and Romans.[136]

> who entrusted his sons to the tribes and made them (the tribes) cavalry for the Romans.[137]

> [who entrusted to his sons Maʕadd] and Bayān the government of the great tribes whose delegates formed a cavalry corps in the service of the Romans.[138]

> and [who] when the tribes separated from him [Shammar] for Persia had handed them over to Rome.[139]

> [Shammar, the king of Maʕadd and] the . . . tribes when the Persians had handed them over to Rome.[140]

> [who installed his sons Maʕadd] and Banān [as kings] and ordered them as horse-riders for Rome.[141]

> The tribes acknowledged his sons and he trusted them so they sided with Rome.[142]

> the tribes being divided between his sons and all of them served as horsemen for the Romans.[143]

> He handed over the sedentary communities to his sons when he had been given authority over the latter on behalf of Persia and Rome.[144]

> and he dealt gently with the nobles of the tribes and appointed them viceroys and they became phylarchs for the Romans.[145]

> He handed over the sedentary communities to his sons and made them governors. Thus his reign was consolidated and that forever.[146]

> and he divided between his sons the tribes and the auxiliary troops of the Persians and the Romans.[147]

As can be seen, the first part of this passage contains a series of letters which are very ambiguous. The main problem, however, is the interpretation of the letters PRŠW, which have been read 'Persians' or 'riders'. Later commentators have suggested a verb meaning 'become steadfast' (RSW) or 'rule' (RʔS).[148]

Historical interpretation of the text

The historical interpretation of the Namāra inscription should start with the parts about which there is a fairly high degree of consensus. One should then try to relate the contents to what is known from contemporary documents about conditions in Arabia and the Syrian desert. As will be shown below, there is also a tradition in Arabo-Islamic historical writing about events in this period. Since those texts were written down at the beginning of the ninth century AD, i.e. half a millennium later, they should not automatically be adduced as sources on the same level as the comtemporary documents. These latter have to be evaluated first. Then the later Arabo-Islamic tradition should be studied and compared with the contemporary evidence.

The interpretation should start with three basic facts: the location of the inscription, its structure, and those parts of its contents which can be determined with a fair degree of consensus.

1. The text was found in southern Syria north-east of the Ǧabal ad-Durūz, only a few kilometres from the Roman forts marking the *limes* area towards the Syrian desert. It was put up not in Roman territory but very close to it.[149] It should be noted, however, that the exact origin of the text is somewhat obscure. If the word NPŠ (Ia) means 'tomb', the exact location of the tomb remains to be determined. The location of the inscription makes it very likely that the king was also politically on good terms with the Romans. Since the text refers to the king as having a wide-ranging influence in Arabia, it is very unlikely that he was not a Roman ally of some kind. Diocletian and

Constantine would not have tolerated a large, completely independent Arab kingdom in the Syrian desert. The text was evidently put up when the Romans controlled the northern Ǧazīra as far as Adiabene. In spite of his royal title, MRʔ LQYŠ is likely to have been a Roman ally.[150] This speaks in favour of the reading of the letters in IVb as RWM, i.e. Rūm.[151]

2. The text is clearly divided in three parts: an introduction, presenting the names and the titles of the king (Ia–c), followed by a section dealing with his *res gestae* (IIa–IVc) and concluding with the announcement of his death (Va–c). This is strikingly reminiscent of the disposition in Shāpur's inscription at Naqsh-e-Rustam. In that text, we have an enumeration of the king's titles and the provinces of the realm ruled by him, followed by an account of his wars and other activities.[152] This analogy leads us to the conclusion that MRʔ LQYŠ' title 'king of all ʕRB' is not derived from his activities described in the second part. His rule of the Arabs therefore does not have anything to do with his campaigns against the tribes mentioned in the second part.[153] He was king of all Arabs, like the kings in Hatra, and in addition he achieved successes in the peninsula.[154]

3. In spite of the many ambiguities of the second part, all commentators agree that it deals with military activities against tribes most of which can be identified from the later Arabo-Islamic historical tradition. Among the names, Nizār and Maʕadd, the reading of which is agreed upon, point to western Arabia, which is supported by the interpretation of ʔLʔŠDYN as referring to al-ʔAzd in the ʕAsīr.[155] The mention of Naǧrān, which is not seriously contested either, supports the picture of a large military operation mainly going through western Arabia down to the Gateway of Yemen.[156] This also makes it very likely that the ʔLʔŠDYN are groups later known as al-ʔAzd, i.e. people in the ʕAsīr, rather than ʔAsad in central Arabia.[157] It is, further, unlikely that such an enterprise would have been undertaken without the consent and support, and even initiative, of Rome. The whole picture of a campaign from Syria through western Arabia down to Yemen in the footsteps of Aelius Gallus more than three centuries earlier is another strong support for the assumption that Imruʔ al-Qays was in fact an agent of Roman power.[158] It is then very likely that the passage IIId–IVc deals with his role as military agent for Rome, although unfortunately the exact nature of this relationship escapes us.

MRʔ LQYŠ's father was, according to the text, ʕMRW, i.e. ʕAmr. This is a common Arabic name in the pre-Islamic period but it is most tempting to associate it with one of the two ʕAmrs mentioned in the Paikuli inscription. The question is which one of them was the predecessor of MRʔ LQYŠ: the Lakhmid or the Abgarid? It seems unlikely that an Arab king allied with Rome in the 320s could be located at al-Ḥīra and in that case, the presence of his tomb on the Roman *limes* becomes difficult to explain.[159] In the document on the establishment of Manichaeism in Palmyra, Amarō, son of Lahim, appears who must be identical with the Lakhmid in Paikuli.[160] The Paikuli inscription was put up just after the accession of Narses. Most of the traditional Arab lands in the Ǧazīra would by then still be outside Roman territory proper. After the capture of Nisibis and the peace treaty in 298, the entire Arab area north of Sinǧār was incorporated with Rome. We should imagine ʕMR and his son as leaders of the Arab warriors along the border from Nisibis in the north to the Ǧabal in the south: an-Namāra is situated in an area where, according to Ptolemy, there were Arabs in the second century AD and which is probably the Arabia to which Paul fled from Damascus.[161] It is not unlikely that the Romans also took some control of the Arabia south of Singăr.[162] This order would have been established from the year 299 at the latest. This means that the title 'king of all Arabs' in the Namāra inscription does not refer at all to a supremacy over the whole of North Arabia but only over the Arabs in Syria and the northern Ğazīra.[163] MRʔ LQYŠ' title is a phrase found in the texts from Hatra where it cannot refer to a supremacy over the whole of North Arabia. This is also the most natural reading of the text in spite of all its uncertainties.

According to the inscription, MRʔ LQYŠ ruled during the first half of the reign of Constantine the Great. It is tempting to connect the king of all Arabs with Constantine's activities in the east against the Iranians and with his title *Arabicus*, although our knowledge about his eastern dealings is scanty.[164]

The reasons and background for such an undertaking escape us as well, since sources are lacking. One could point to some contemporary pieces of information that may have to do with this campaign. The most important is a Sabaean inscription which says that the king ŠMR YHRʕŠ, king of Sabaʔ, Dhū Raydān, Ḥaḍramawt and Yamnat sent a delegation 'to the two royal cities of of PRS and the land of TNH̱ as well as to the king of [ʔ]LʔSD' and MLK from K . . .'[165] It is most tempting to read the latter as KDT, i.e. Kinda, well known from Sabaean inscriptions in the third century. It is worth remarking that in this text we find a tribal name which looks very like one of those in the Namāra inscription: LʔSD – ʔLʔŠD.

We know that Shammar reigned in Yemen *c.* AD 275–310.[166] He was the unifier of all Yemen, conquering ancient Saba and Ḥaḍramawt and creating the Himyarite empire, which was to play a crucial role in world politics until the beginning of the sixth century. The meaning of the inscription must be that around AD 300 there were diplomatic ties between the Himyarite empire and not only large tribes like Kinda and ʔLʔŠD in Arabia, but also the Sassanian kings in Ctesiphon. Even though it is speculative, it is reasonable to assume that Shammar sought political support against enemies from other areas. The arch-enemy against all efforts to establish a strong political power in South Arabia was the kingdom in Axum, which in its turn was usually supported by Rome. The unification of South Arabia under Shammar created a new situation that was uncomfortable for Rome and its allies. The Axumites had been thrown out of Yemen at the end of the third century, and it can be assumed that the Romans thought it necessary to take action. It was natural for the Yemeni rulers to seek support from Rome's arch-enemy, a policy which was to be repeated in the future. The campaigns described in the Namāra inscription should be seen in the light of this development.

Of much more uncertain importance is another inscription, this time from Eritrea, put up by a king named Sembrouthēs who calls himself 'king of kings of Axum . . . the great king.'[167] This king is not known from Ethiopian evidence either of coins or of mention in inscriptions or the king-lists. The name could well be a Greek rendering of ŠMR, which would imply that the great Shammar for a while even conquered Axum on the African side of the Red Sea. The title 'king of kings' does indeed sound like an echo of the epithet of the Iranian kings, and is encountered in Ethiopia with Ezana in the middle of the fourth century.[168] If the Himyarites had been lords of Axum, this could explain the titles documented for the later Axumite king Ezana, who adopted the titulature of the Himyarite rulers. A crux here is, however, that the title 'king of kings' is not documented for any ruler in Yemen proper.

The existence of a large anti-Roman power on the shores of the Red Sea would definitely trigger off a Roman counterattack. Shammar's reign ceased around AD 310. He was succeeded by two kings, ḎMR ʕLY YHBR and his son and successor ṮʔRN YHNʕM, whose monumental statues are preserved and kept in the National Museum in Ṣanʕāʔ. They are completely Hellenistic in style, belonging to the end of the third century AD and they are even cast by a Greek. They were put up before the year AD 319.[169] These statues represent a dynasty that was to take over after Shammar Yuharʕish.[170] Unfortunately, the transition between these two dynasties is totally obscure, but the Hellenistic flavour of the monuments of the founders is provocative and points to good connections with the Roman cultural sphere. Did the Romans topple Shammar's dynasty and replace it with rulers more friendly to Rome? Ḥaḍramawt seems to have been lost and the unification had to be renewed by later kings. The king of all Arabs could indeed have been a protagonist in a great political drama in the years around AD 300 that was the first Roman attempt to curb the ambitions of creating a larger empire in Arabia. This was also to be repeated two centuries later.

The picture emerging is one of great military mobility. The Arabian campaign of MRʔ LQYŠ was a considerable enterprise. We catch a glimpse of how the Arabian peninsula is divided into spheres of interest: the western parts belonging to the Romans and the eastern and central parts to the Iranians. The empire in the southern peninsula could balance between the two, but the politics of Shammar was to become the main trend: the Romans were closer to Yemen through the Red Sea and constituted a more direct threat than the Iranians, separated from Yemen by vast deserts which the Yemenites could handle better than the Sassanids. The Roman presence in the Red Sea made it more profitable for the king in Yemen to seek support from Iran, which could irritate the Romans' flank in the north if they became too intrusive in the southern Red Sea or western Arabia.

Shammar's policy showed that the Romans needed a foothold in the Red Sea region in order to preserve their influence there and counterbalance the Yemeni ally in the north. Perhaps the embassy sent by Shammar to the Iranian vassals in north-eastern Arabia triggered off not only MRʔ LQYŠ' campaign but also other activities aiming at a more permanent Roman presence in the Red Sea: the following period witnessed a quite intense Christian missionary effort in the area, leading to the introduction of Christianity in Axum.

In AD 326 the new Iranian king, Shāpur II, undertook a major operation against Arabia. The sources for this event are late, but there is no reason to doubt that the account is based on real events. According to aṭ-Ṭabarī, Shāpur, because the Arabs used Fars as pasture ground, crossed the sea to Baḥrayn, took Hağar in al-Ḥasā, crossed the Yamāma and reached the land close to Yathrib/Medina.[171] We have no means of verifying this account. Such a campaign against peaceful shepherds seems to be an overreaction from the king of kings. If such a campaign was undertaken and if the king tried to reach western Arabia, the goals must have been different.[172] In the light of the preceding analysis it is tempting to see Shāpur's action as a response to the Roman policy in western and southern Arabia. Unfortunately, the results of these events are not documented.

The Namāra inscription and the kings of al-Ḥīra: the Arabic tradition

The Islamic historians starting with Ibn al-Kalbī (– AD 819) have preserved a list of the kings of al-Ḥīra, the centre of a Sassanid vassal kingdom near the middle Euphrates, which seems to start in the third century. The third king on this list is an Imruʔ al-Qays, whose father is ʕAmr ibn ʕAdī, who, according to the Islamic historians, was the founder of the dynasty reigning until the rise of Islam. This king fits quite well chronologically with the king of the Namāra inscription. In 1903, Peiser identified MRʔ LQYŠ in that text with Imruʔ al-Qays al-badʔ, son of ʕAmr, king of al-Ḥīra.[173] The identification was connected with his reading of PRŠW as 'Persians', a reading which has been followed by several scholars after him. Even those who have not followed the reading of PRŠW as Persians have accepted the identification of the king of all Arabs with Imruʔ al-Qays al-badʔ who, according to a note in the king-list, was a vassal (*ʕāmil*) of the Iranian king. Since the inscription was found at an-Namāra, which is fairly distant from Mesopotamia but close to Roman territory, this identification creates a problem which has been tackled in different ways. Imruʔ al-Qays is thought either to have been completely independent and played a game with both Romans and Persians, or to have been a Persian vassal who defected and fled to the Romans.[174] The former scenario is somewhat unlikely since there does not seem to be much room for an independent ruler between Iran and Rome around AD 300. The latter solution, apart from the fact that such a flight is undocumented even in the Arabo-Islamic tradition, raises the question of how Imruʔ al-Qays' dynasty could stay on in al-Ḥīra in spite of his defection. All answers to this question have remained completely speculative and unverified.[175]

The oldest complete list of the kings of al-Ḥīra originating from Hishām ibn al-Kalbī is preserved in slightly varying shapes by two historians from the tenth century AD, aṭ-Ṭabarī and Ḥamza al-ʔIṣfahānī, in their world histories.[176] The former introduces the list of the kings in al-Ḥīra with a long story about the foundation of the dynasty which is also attributed to Ibn al-Kalbī. It is likely that the whole complex as told by aṭ-Ṭabarī is patched together from several of Ibn al-Kalbī's books. We know that Ibn al-Kalbī told the early history of the Arabs in several lost books and it is obvious that aṭ-Ṭabarī used several of them.[177]

The whole Ḥīra complex as told by Ibn al-Kalbī and reproduced in at-Ṭabarī's world history can be divided into five main parts: (1) the settling of the *ʕarab* in Iraq by Bukhtunuṣṣur, i.e. Nebuchadnezzar of Babylon; (2) the migrations of the sons of Maʕadd from Mecca, leading to the formation of Tanūkh and their settlement along the Euphrates; (3) the story of the first Arab kings in Iraq, including Ǧadhīma al-ʔabraṣ/ʔabraš, king of Tanūkh; (4) the rise of ʕAmr b. ʕAdī and the establishment of the kingdom of al-Ḥīra; (5) the story of the kings of al-Ḥīra until the rise of Islam.[178] Part 2 of the story is found in a parallel version attributed to az-Zuhrī (–741), the first who wrote a chronological biography of the Prophet, which also included stories about the pre-Islamic period. His version of the events is preserved in the *Kitāb al-ʔaghānī* and al-Bakrī's geography, both compiled in the tenth century AD. In a non-Ḥīra-context aṭ-Ṭabarī also adduces a couple of passages about the history of Hatra atrributed to Ibn al-Kalbī, which turn out to have some importance for this theme.

1a) The first part is already known to us: it was shown earlier in this study that it contains elements going back to a novel about Nebuchadnezzar preserving memories from the late Assyrian and Babylonian kings.[179] According to Ibn al-Kalbī's account, Bukhtunuṣṣur settled some of the tradesmen of the *ʕarab* in a *ḥayr*, a kind of fenced-in camp near Naǧaf in Iraq. Other *ʕarab* from the tribes of the *ʕarab* in the countryside of Iraq then submitted to him and these were settled in a place close to the Euphrates called al-ʔAnbār. After Nebuchadnezzar's death the *ʕarab* in the *ḥayr* moved to al-ʔAnbār and united with the *ʕarab* living there. The *ḥayr* remained abandoned for a long time.[180]

1b) Immediately after this passage aṭ-Ṭabarī gives another version of how the first *ʕarab* ended up in Iraq, namely the story about Nebuchadnezzar's war against Israel and the *ʔarab*. This story does not come from Ibn al-Kalbī but preserves memories of the actual campaign against Qedar in 599 BC.[181] The operations are said to be God's revenge on people, killing their prophets. Only Maʕadd, who was a prophet, was spared. He was miraculously saved from Nebuchadnezzar's destruction by the Burāq, the animal that later brought Muhammed to Jerusalem. Many *ʕarab* from the land between ʕAraba and Ḥadūr gathered. Some left before the battle: those led by ʕAkk, those who went to Wabār and those who went to *ḥaḍr* (var. *ḥiṣn*) *al-ʕarab*. Nebuchadnezzar then, after the battle, brought some of his prisoners from ʕAraba and settled them in ʔAnbār which was called *ʔanbār al-ʕarab*. Here they later mixed with the *nabaṭ*. Maʕadd with the remaining prophets came to Mecca and then settled in Raysūb, the location of which is unknown. Maʕadd married Maʕāna, the daughter of the last survivor of Ǧurhum, the ancient inhabitants of Mecca. She became the mother of Nizār.[182] This story is thus the explanation of how Maʕadd ended up in western Arabia.

The second part of the story about the foundation of al-Ḥīra begins in Tihāma, close to Mecca, where Maʕadd and his descendants live. Ibn al-Kalbī seems not to have told about how they got there in the book which aṭ-Ṭabarī used, and this is probably one of the reasons why he adduced the other variant about the *ʕarab* and Nebuchadnezzar, which gives the necessary background.

2a) Ibn al-Kalbī's version reports that a conflict arose between the sons of Maʕadd. The result was the emigration of Quḍāʕa and others from the Tihāma. Clans from two sub-tribes of Quḍāʕa, the sons of Wabara belonging to the Ḥulwān group, set out for Baḥrayn. They were led by the two descendants of Fahm from the Wabara tribe, Mālik and ʕAmr. Mālik ibn Zuhayr was ʕAmr's descendant. The Quḍāʕa people were followed by two other sons of Maʕadd, Qanaṣ and ʔIyād, together with groups from the Yemeni ʔAzd. Tanūkh was formed by *ʕarab* in Baḥrayn where they were joined by clans (*buṭūn*) from Lakhm b. Numāra. Then followed the migration from Baḥrayn to Iraq which took place in the time of the *ṭawāʔif* kings. A war is said to have raged between them and the ʔArmāniyyūn at this time. The first group to arrive was Qanaṣ, who were absorbed by the *ʕarab* in al-ʔAnbār and al-Ḥīra. Then came Tanūkh, led by the Fahmids and Mālik b. Zuhayr, which settled in the deserted *ḥayr*.

2b) az-Zuhrī gives a version which basically follows the outlines of that of Ibn al-Kalbī. There are, however, many important differences. He gives a detailed background for the conflict between Nizār and Quḍāʕa which need not concern us here. He does not mention the Fahmids at all, only Mālik b. Zuhayr. The emigrants from Tihāma are only the Wabara tribe and the Yemeni ʔAšʕariyyūn. To this version belongs the important notice that when they reached Hağar it was inhabited by *nabaṭ*.[183] Both the name Tanūkh and the idea of an immigration to Iraq come from a soothsayer named az-Zarqāʔ, the sister of Mālik. They are now joined by a group from the Yemeni ʔAzd and they set out for Iraq.[184]

3a) Ibn al-Kalbī now tells the story of the first kings of Tanūkh. This tribe united the lands between ʔAnbār and al-Ḥīra and were called *ʕarab aḍ-ḍāḥiya*, 'the Arabs of the outskirts'. They did not live in houses of clay and did not mix with the locals. The Fahmids Mālik and ʕAmr ruled as kings over them.[185] Mālik b. Zuhayr called on Ǧadhīma/Ǧudhayma al-ʔabraš, the son of Mālik, son of Fahm, son of Ghānim, son of

Daws, the ʔAzdī, to settle with him. Ǧadhīma got married to Mālik's daughter Lamīs. ʔAzd and the Fahmids become allies 'in front of the rest of Tanūkh'.[186] Mālik b. Fahm is said to have been the first king, living near al-ʔAnbār. He was followed by his brother ʕAmr b. Fahm. Ibn al-Kalbī then probably told how the Quḍaʕa parts of Tanūkh, led by the Fahmids, emigrated to the Quḍaʕa, who were in Syria because of attacks from Aradashir, the first Sassanian king.[187] Ǧadhīma, son of Mālik b. Fahm, from ʔAzd succeeded him. He was the first king in Iraq.[188] His realm encompassed the area between al-ʔAnbār and al-Ḥīra, the areas of Baqiyya, Hīt, ʕAyn Tamr and the steppes at Ghuwayr, Quṭquṭāna, and Khafiyya south-west of the Euphrates.[189] An anonymous verse says his dwelling was in Yabrīn, the great oasis between Yamāma and Haǧar.[190] Ǧadhīma acted as a *kāhin* and a *nabī*. He had two idols called 'the two Ḍayzan'. He made war against ʔIyād in ʕAyn ʔUbāgh. The ʔIyād in ʕAyn ʔUbāgh captured his idols but Ǧadhīma brought them back and received ʕAdī b. Naṣr from the clan of Numāra b. Lakhm, who was related to ʔIyād on his mother's side, as a hostage. In another note it is said that ʕAdī b. Naṣr from Numāra b. Lakhm descended from Qanaṣ, the first Arab immigrants to Iraq. During a drinking bout, Ǧadhīma's sister Riqāsh, who had fallen in love with ʕAdī, made her brother promise her to marry him. ʕAdī was then killed during a hunt before Riqāsh gave birth to a son named ʕAmr b. ʕAdī. This boy became the favourite with Ǧadhīma. He was caught by ǧinns but was brought back by two men from the Wabara tribe from Quḍāʕa.[191]

3b) az-Zuhrī's version is quite different. Tanūkh arrive at al-Ḥīra, which is founded by them. They are then attacked by Sābūr the Great and, led by Ḍayzan, they leave for Hatra which has been built by as-Sāṭirūn.[192] az-Zuhrī has a complementary note about the rest of the Quḍāʕa. One branch of the Ḥulwān, Tazīd, goes to the Ǧazīra. When they are attacked there by the Turks, they are aided by the Bahrāʔ tribe who also kill ʔUbāgh b. Salīḥ, after whom the famous oasis ʕAyn ʔUbāgh is named. The tribe of Salīḥ then goes to Palestine and joins the clan of ʔUdhayna b. Samaydaʕ from the ʕĀmila tribe. Other groups from Quḍāʕa go to Ḥiǧāz.

4) Ibn al-Kalbī now proceeds to tell the story of the rise of ʕAmr b. ʕAdī. Initially, ʕAmr b. Ẓarab b. Ḥassān b. ʔUdhayna b. Samaydaʕ was the king of the *ʕarab* of Syria and the Ǧazīra. Ẓarab was killed by Ǧadhīma and was followed by his daughter Zabbāʔ. She enticed Ǧadhīma to her town and tricked him into a trap and killed him. Her army consisted of *ʕamālīq*, *ʕarab al-ʔūlā* and Tazīd and Salīḥ, who both descend from Quḍāʕa. ʕAmr took revenge for his uncle by killing Zabbāʔ. He then became king of Tanūkh and settled in the hitherto abandoned al-Ḥīra. All the later kings descend from him. They were the vassals (*ʕummāl*) of the Sassanids.

5) ʕAmr was followed by ʔImruʔ al-Qays al-badʔ, 'the beginning', who was the first king of al-Ḥīra to become a Christian. He is said to have reigned over most Arab tribes, being the vassal (*ʕāmil*) of the Sassanid kings Sābūr (I), Hurmuzd (I), Bahrām (I) and Bahrām (II). He was followed by his son, ʕAmr, who was the *ʕāmil* of Sābūr *ḏū l-ʔaktāf*, 'he with the shoulders', who undoubtedly is Shāpur II in the fourth century.[193] Ibn al-Kalbī then goes on enumerating the kings in al-Ḥīra, often with some notes on historical events.

Analysis of the story

In order to grasp the historical value of the account by Ibn al-Kalbī and the more fragmentary pieces found in other writers, it must be critically scrutinized before being compared with contemporary sources for the events told. In aṭ-Ṭabarī the story of Ǧadhīma and ʔAmr b. ʕAdī as well as the king-list itself, i.e. parts 4 and 5, and the introduction (part 1(a)) are probably taken from Ibn al-Kalbī's *Kitāb al-Ḥīra*. Parts 2 and 3 seem to be patched together from other books: *Kitāb iftirāq Maʕadd*, *Kitāb Tanūkh*, *Kitāb Quḍāʕa*.[194] There is no doubt that the purpose of the main cycle of stories, i.e. parts 1(a), 3 and 4 which in Ibn al-Kalbī form one literary composition and are reproducing the *Kitāb al-Ḥīra*, is to tell about the origins of al-Ḥīra. The tendency is evident in the parallel between Nebuchadnezzar's *ḥayr*, the earliest Arab settlement in Iraq, and the name al-Ḥīra, and there is no doubt that the story-teller wants us to accept the identity between the two names. The dynasty in al-Ḥīra is said to go back to ʕAmr b. ʕAdī, who appears as the main hero. At the same time it is clear that the account as we have it in Ibn al-Kalbī's version is composed of several elements with different origins. We are already acquainted with the use of the Nebuchadnezzar novel for part 1. The list of the kings of al-Ḥīra, part 5, is treated as a separate unit by other Muslim historians and could even be an addition to the main tale by Ibn al-Kalbī. The story of the immigration of Tanūkh from Baḥrayn to Iraq and the first Arab kings there (part 3) is likely to be a separate element as well, since we find it in a different context in az-Zuhrī's version, which is also quite different in many details. The romance about ʕAmr and his revenge on Zabbāʔ (part 4) is obviously a story not necessarily connected with the other elements. It is documented as a separate tale in several other sources.[195] Good arguments have been presented in favour of its being based on an epic story which was obviously known in al-Ḥīra at the end of the sixth century, when it is referred to in some detail by the Christian poet ʕAdī b. Zayd.[196]

The main difference between az-Zuhrī and Ibn al-Kalbī is that in the latter the story leads to the establishment of the royal house of al-Ḥīra. The list of the kings of this dynasty is connected with the tale of the wanderings of Tanūkh by the novel about Ǧadhīma al-ʔabraṣ/ʔabraš, making up the third part of the story. This may indicate that parts 1(a), 3 and 4 of the story as told by Ibn al-Kalbī are a fairly late composition, probably made by a Christian in al-Ḥīra, who used the Nebuchanezzar novel and the epic Ǧadhīma-ʕAmr romance as well as other devices to compose a story glorifying the origins of the great kings of the sixth century AD.[197] The pro-Ḥīra tendency of the story is obvious and it should be read from that perspective. The work was probably a written account which was used by Ibn al-Kalbī.

We do not know how old this tradition is. It is evident that it comes to us from al-Ḥīra. Ibn al-Kalbī states explicitly that he has the story from ecclesiastical books in al-Ḥīra.[198] His account has a definite pro-Ḥīra tendency, and the whole story, as we have it, could very well represent an official version of the foundation of the kingdom of al-Ḥīra, giving the dynasty of Naṣr a glorious past and projecting it to earliest pre-Islamic times. The Kalbī tradition emphasizes the Christianity of several kings: Imruʔ al-Qays al-badʔ is said to have been the first Christian king in the dynasty. There was also, in the dynastic history, a legend about the Christianity of Nuʕmān of al-Ḥīra, reigning at the beginning of the fifth century AD.[199] On the other hand, Mundhir III around AD 550 is described as an ardent pagan. It seems clear, however, that there was a tradition in Ḥīra, perhaps created by Christians close to the royal house, about the glorious past of the kings. The fact that the history of Nebuchadnezzar's campaign against Qedar in 599 BC stood as an introduction to the history of Ḥīra indicates that it was transmitted by Christians in Mesopotamia.

We have already analysed part 1 of the story and since it has no relevance for the history of the third century AD it can be left out here.[200] In part 2 the common features of both az-Zuhrī and Ibn al-Kalbī are the emigration from the Tihāma to Baḥrayn, the formation there of the Tanūkh, and the migration from Baḥrayn to Iraq and settlement along the Euphrates. The first part about the emigration belongs to the so-called *iftirāq* theme, which deals with the dispersion of the tribes from their original habitat around Mecca.[201] That idea follows from the concept of the descent of the tribes of Arabia from a common forefather living in Mecca: Ismāʕīl or his offspring Maʕadd. It explains the participation of Qanaṣ and ʔIyād in the Ibn al-Kalbī-version: since they too according to the genealogical scheme were sons of Maʕadd, they must have emigrated from Tihāma as well. Since the *iftirāq* theme is dependent on the sanctity of Mecca and its position as the centre of the world, its historicity is highly suspect. It can be assumed that the story of the migration from Baḥrayn should be separated from that about the emigration from Tihāma, which is a theoretical construction by early Muslim genealogists.

The Yemenis appearing here and there in the story are also suspect. The tribe ʔAzd joins the migration at different moments in the two versions, and Ğadhīma as well as ʕAmr b. ʕAdī are said to be of ʔAzdī descent. It should be remembered that ʔAzd was a dominant tribe in Basra in the early Islamic period and its presence in the story may very well be an intrusion in line with the Yemeni propaganda documented elsewhere. Possibly it did not belong to the original written docment but was supplied by Ibn al-Kalbī.

More complicated is the presence of Quḍāʕa. This name is a label for tribes in Syria, Palestine and north-western Arabia in the early Islamic period.[202] Since the emigration of Quḍāʕa groups from Tihāma to Baḥrayn clearly belongs to the *iftirāq* theme, there are good arguments to eliminate them from that event. The activities of Quḍāʕa in Baḥrayn and in the foundation of al-Ḥīra, both locations far away from Syria, may well belong to the tendency to give everybody a share in the story of the legendary founders of al-Ḥīra, which is also shown by the fact that Ibn al-Kalbī makes the Fahmids end up among the Quḍaʕa in Syria. This puts a question-mark over the role of the Fahmids in Ibn al-Kalbī's version. This scepticism is supported by az-Zuhrī's version, where the Fahmids are completely absent.[203] Instead we read about the presence of Quḍāʕa groups like Bahrāʔ and the Ḥulwān at ʕAyn ʔUbāgh, as well as the dispersion of Quḍāʕa from the Ğazīra to Ḥiğāz.[204] According to the Arabo-Islamic geographic tradition, ʕAyn ʔUbāgh was somewhere west of al-ʔAnbār.[205] According to al-Bakrī, Ḥulwān is 'the beginning of Iraq and the end of the mountain', which may indicate the border between Anatolia and the Ğazīra.[206] The impression we get from this tradition is rather that the groups to which the Fahmids belonged are originally located in northern Syria and the northern Ğazīra, and from there had contacts with western Ḥiğāz. The role of the Fahmids in the whole migration story of Tanūkh may well be secondary.

Striking is the disagreement about Ğadhīma's genealogy, which is traceable in other historical works as well. He is often made an ʔAzdī, i.e. of Yemeni descent.[207] Another tradition says he was from Qanaṣ.[208] Some say he belongs to *al-ʕāriba al-ʔūlā*, i.e. *al-bāʔida*, descending from ʔUmaym, son of Lawdh. With this goes the claim that he came from Yabrīn which is on the road to Wabār, the mythical town of ʔUmaym. It is also explicitly said that he was the first king in Iraq, in blatant contradiction to the statement that the Fahmids were the first rulers who represent Quḍāʕa. Ğadhīma is made a Fahmid in a rather clumsy way.[209] Instead he appears closer to Mālik b. Zuhayr whose attachment to the Fahmids likewise appears brittle. It is also noteworthy that Ǧadhīma's enemies in the armies of Zabbāʔ belong to Quḍāʕa. It is obvious that he, like Mālik b. Zuhayr and az-Zarqāʔ, did not belong to this family in an older version of the story.[210] Ǧadhīma was obviously a legendary hero whose origin was unknown and to whom several later groups wanted to be related: Yemenis, Syrians and Iraqis.

About ʕAdī and his son ʕAmr there are many conflicting traditions. ʕAdī is son of Naṣr, son of ar-Rabīʕa, and the genealogy ends with Numāra, son of Lakhm.[211] His immediate ancestors belong to a very special tradition, namely the legend about the emigration of ar-Rabīʕa b. Naṣr (sic) from Yemen before the bursting of the the great dam. This story is told by many Arabic writers.[212] From these it is clear that this event is thought to have occurred around AD 400. There is no doubt that the presence of these two names as the immediate ancestors of ʕAmr b. ʕAdī is secondary and belongs to another tradition.[213]

In most versions their ultimate forebear is Numāra b. Lakhm. They are said to have joined Tanūkh at an early stage.[214] Not surprisingly, the name Numāra also appears as a Yemeni tribe, i.e. descendants of Qaḥṭān, in the *ḥayr* that Buxt Nuṣṣur had built.[215] In this we recognize the Yemeni propaganda which strove to turn every prominent person in the history of Arabia into a Yemeni.[216] Instead Numāra looks very similar to the name of the site in Syria where Imruʔ al-Qays' inscription was found.

According to the later Muslim genealogists, Lakhm is a tribe living in Palestine and adjacent areas, i.e. in southern Syria. We are not so far from Na/umāra. It is the brother of Ǧudhām and ʕĀmila.[217] It is noteworthy that Lakhm are never explicitly said to belong to Tanūkh.[218] The Lakhmids are also closely related to ʔIyād: according to Ibn al-Kalbī, Ǧadhīma made a raid against ʔIyād in ʕAyn ʔUbāgh and ʕAdī was taken hostage by him while sojourning with his uncles among ʔIyād. This tribe is linked to the areas west and north-west of the middle Euphrates.[219] They are also connected with the oasis ʕAyn ʔUbāgh, the location of which is not known exactly.

From a scrutiny of the texts we thus see a series of tribes along the western shore of the Euphrates, Tanūkh, Qanaṣ, and ʔIyād, settled in an area from al-Ḥīra to the westernmost point of the Euphrates in Syria. At that point there is contact with a group of Syrian tribes, among them Ḥulwān, with its subgroups Wabara, the tribe of the Fahmids and Salīḥ, Bahrāʔ and Lakhm. The central point is ʕAyn ʔUbāgh where groups of the later Quḍāʕa formation like Ḥulwān and Bahrāʔ dwelt and ʔIyād is also found.

There is another line of names and events which belongs to this complex, involving people in the Ǧazīra. az-Zuhrī tells how Tazīd, a branch of Ḥulwān, i.e. close relatives to the Fahmids, settle at a place in the Ǧazīra called ʕAbqar, of unknown location. They are attacked by Turks and Bahrāʔ comes to their assistance. At the same time they defeat ʔUbāgh b. Salīḥ who belong to the Ḥulwān branch as well and after whom the oasis is named. His relatives take refuge in Syria with ʔUdhayna b. Samaydaʕ. In this story a connection, albeit hostile, is established between the Ǧazīra, perhaps somewhere around Ǧabal Singǎr, and the oasis ʕAyn ʔUbāgh on the Syrian side of the river.

It is further told by az-Zuhrī how Tanūkh in Iraq were attacked by Sābūr and moved, led by Ḍayzan, to Hatra, built by as-Sāṭirūn.[220] Ibn al-Kalbī has more to tell about this. According to him Ḍayzan, whose father was from Salīḥ and whose mother was from Tazīd, was a great king over Ǧazīra and the Quḍāʕa in Syria. A war broke out with Sābūr, who conquered Hatra and destroyed it.[221] In the fragment in ad-Dīnawarī it is told that Zabbāʔ was the daughter of Ḍayzan, the last ruler in Hatra, who was killed by Sābūr.[223]

One tradition says that ʕAmr b. ʕAdī and his family, i.e. the Lakhmids, were also descendants of as-Sāṭirūn, 'king of Syria' and 'lord of the fortress', i.e. Hatra.[223]

Disregarding the pro-Ḥīra tendency, there is in the texts an obvious connection between Ǧadhīma-Tanūkh geographically belonging to the middle Euphrates, Numāra b. Lakhm with its origins around Palestine, and [Quḍāʕa-]Ḥulwān to which the Fahmids belonged, with its domicile somewhere in northern Syria. The meeting point between the Mesopotamian Arabs and those in Syria was ʕAyn ʔUbāgh, a place which emerges as one of the great sites in Arab pre-Islamic history. These connections have no immediate function as glorification of the dynasty in al-Ḥīra, and it can be argued that they belong to the given tradition which was used by the author of the epic story of the foundation of al-Ḥīra.

The picture emerging from the texts analysed here is that of an immigration of Tanūkh from Baḥrayn to the middle Euphrates in the time of the *tawāʔif* kings. When Ardashir became king, many Tanūkh fled to Hatra, which is described as a power ruling on both sides of the Euphrates. The ruler, Ḍayzan, belonged to Salīḥ, a group associated with the Syrian tribes. This rule of Salīḥ is abolished by the attack of Sābūr, who may be the one hidden behind the 'Turks' mentioned by az-Zuhrī. The Salīḥ are also driven away from ʕAyn ʔUbāgh by Bahrāʔ, a name standing for a tribe from northern Ḥiǧāz. From that region also comes the tribe of Lakhm who appear to have relations with ʔIyād, who live in the desert west of the Euphrates and whose presence at ʕAyn ʔUbāgh may be the result of the fall of the rule of Salīḥ. It cannot be ruled out that the name Bahrāʔ in fact represents Islamic times when we know that this tribe was in northern Syria, and that other groups from southern Syria and northern Ḥiǧāz, among them the tribe of Lakhm, were the ones originally figuring in the traditions.

Into this picture then comes Ǧadhīma al-ʔabrash. He appears as an enemy of ʔIyād and possibly a preserver of the memories of the rulers in Hatra. It is striking that he is not a real military man. He is not an empire-builder. Instead he is associated with cult. He is connected with the people in northern Syria in two ways: as an ally of the Fahmids and as the protector of the Lakhmid ʕAdī and his son ʕAmr.

The tradition describes the rise of Zabbāʔ as the restorer of the power of Quḍāʕa in Syria and the Ǧazīra: among her ardent supporters are the Salīḥ. It is thus quite logical that the Lakhmid ʕAmr b. ʕAdī is the one who brings her and her empire down. Ǧadhīma appears as a very ambiguous figure: he is described both as a supporter of the traditions from Hatra and a close ally of the Ḥulwān to which Salīḥ belonged, and as a protector of the anti-Quḍāʕa dynasty of ʕAdī.

The evidence from contemporary documents

This is the picture found in the Arabic texts from the first Islamic centuries put together by a philologist working in Basra until AD 819. The question now is how much of this narrative can be related to what is known about historical events in the third century AD, about which period the narrative obviously claims to be reporting. It turns out to contain several names that we find in sources from the third century AD.

Tanūkh, as we have seen, is probably already mentioned in eastern Arabia in the second century AD by Ptolemy.[224] According to Ibn al-Kalbī, Tanūkh arrived in Iraq during the time of the *tawāʔif* kings, who, in Arabo-Islamic historical writing, stand for the Parthians. Tanūkh would then have been in southern Iraq before AD 220. Their presence there at the end of the third century is confirmed by the mention of the ʔRḌ TNḪ, 'the land of Tanūkh', in the inscription about Shammar Yuharʕish's ambassadors to the Persians. Further, from the site identified as Thāǧ in eastern Arabia we now have a handful of texts in South Semitic script with names among which we find the expression D̲ʔT ʔL YNH̲ʔL, 'she who belongs to the tribe of Yanūh̲-ʔil'.[225] The archaeological remains on the site originate from the period 300 BC – 300 AD with a main expansion of settlements in the Seleucid period.[226] The last word looks very much like a variant of the name of the tribe figuring in the accounts of az-Zuhrī and Ibn al-Kalbī. It is worth observing that this name is only one of several tribal names documented at Thāǧ. In early Islamic times we find a small tribe named Tanūkh in northern Syria, in the area of Qinnasrīn, as well as a small group in al-Ḥīra on the middle Euphrates.[227]

The name Sābūr figuring in the account of the conquest of Hatra must be identical with Shāpur I, the conqueror of Hatra in AD 240. It can be assumed that the name aṣ-Ṣāṭirūn is somehow connected with SNṬRQ, the name of several rulers of Hatra.[228]

As far as the enigmatic Ǧadhīma is concerned, he appears as a figure whom it would have been easy to dismiss as pure legend. He is the protagonist of a romance filled with folkloristic and even mythical elements. It shows him as an almost Homeric hero, founder of the pagan cults in al-Ḥīra and the originator of proverbs. The name Ǧadhīma appears, however, in a bilingual Nabataean–Greek inscription from ʔUmm Ǧimāl in Jordan dated to the third century AD. It is by a certain FHRW, son of ŠLY, who has been the RBW of GDMT TNWH̲. The Greek version says that he was *tropheús* of Gadimato[s] *basileùs thanouēnōn*, 'king of Tanūkh'.[229] The exact meaning of the word RBW/*tropheús* is not clear but it has something to do with 'nourisher', 'educator' or the like, and this concept recurs in Ibn al-Kalbī's Ǧadhīma story.[230] We remember that Ǧadhīma is said to have nourished and educated ʕAmr. Even though the roles in the inscription are different, it is remarkable that the concept is found in a document contemporary with Ǧadhīma and related to him.

A Lakhmid named ʕAmr is mentioned in the Paikuli inscription and it seems very likely that the same ruler is mentioned in the Manichaean Coptic chronicle.[231] In the latter, he appears together with the queen of Palmyra and it is indeed tempting to identify him with ʕAmr b. ʕAdī in Ibn al-Kalbī's story, as well as with the father of the king of all Arabs in the Namāra inscription. The chronology fits nicely.

Finally, Zabbāʔ belongs to the family of ʔUdhayna, which is connected with Palmyra in the time of Odenathus and Zenobia, and the identification of her with the famous Palmyrene queen lies close at hand.[232] We have already pointed out that there are traces of a Zenobia legend as early as in the *Historia Augusta.*

The general historical background should be kept in mind when we try to judge the historical value of this account. The main events in the history of the Middle East in the third century AD were the fall of the Parthian dynasty and the rise of the house of Sasan under Ardashir, followed by the capture of Hatra in 241 by Shāpur I. This was followed by growing Iranian supremacy, culminating in the Roman defeat in 253. This triggered off the rise of Palmyra, whose ruler Odenathus with the consent of the Romans conquered the Ǧazīra around 262. The fall of Palmyra was effected by the Romans with, it seems, the silent permission of the Iranians. There seems to have been an uncertain equilibrium between the two superpowers after the fall of Palmyra, giving rulers in Syria and the Ǧazīra quite free hands for some decades. A new era was inaugurated by the war at the end of the 290s, ending with the peace in 298 which extended Roman power across the northern Ǧazīra to the Tigris, incorporating most of Mesopotamian

Arabia in the new province, Assyria. The Roman control of the western shore of the upper Tigris lasted until AD 363.

The main outline of the story of the Arabs in Mesopotamia given in the Arabic sources fits surprisingly well into this picture, especially when the accretions obviously reflecting later ages have been peeled off.

The presence of Tanūkh on the middle Euphrates at the beginning of the third century AD should not be doubted. They did, according to the az-Zuhrī version, have connections with the last rulers of Hatra. It is said that they were attacked by Shāpur I, which seems to reflect the conquest of Hatra in AD 240.

The very terminology used in both versions of the story points to their being real *ʕarab*, not belonging to any of the large tribes. So does their origin in Hağar, one of the earliest settlements of Arabs known. The story of az-Zarqāʔ also has an archaic ring. Mālik b. Zuhayr, who is mentioned in both variants and is the brother of az-Zarqāʔ, may well belong to the original Tanūkh tradition and his relationship to the Fahmids is secondary. Qanaṣ are said to have immigrated into Iraq like Tanūkh and to survive among the inhabitants of al-Ḥīra.[233] It can be assumed that their story was not originally connected with that about Tanūkh. But both migrations may well be historical events, having occurred in the later part of the Parthian period.

Ǧadhīma could have been installed as king of Tanūkh after these events. We should believe the notice about Ǧadhīma's operations against ʔIyād, which was outside the Iranian sphere of interest. The notice in az-Zuhrī about the attack from 'the Turks' could be connected with this operation. According to him, these events effected the siding of several Quḍāʕa groups with ʔUdhayna, i.e. Palmyra.

Thus, in the middle of the third century a certain Ǧadhīma was king of a group called Tanūkh, settled in Mesopotamia along the Euphrates, which had emigrated from eastern Arabia, perhaps as early as Parthian times. His influence must have been considerable, encompassing at least the area around the middle Euphrates and possibly far into the Syrian desert. The nature of his kingdom is impossible to discern from the legends preserved about him. The story of Ǧadhīma's death is pure legend, and his dealings with Palmyra may be the result of the activities of later story-tellers. It is more likely that he was somehow attached to Shāpur I.[234]

The tradition about the emigration of Tanūkh from al-Ḥasā/Baḥrayn to the Euphrates valley and to Syria seems thus to be confirmed. It is also confirmed that Ǧadhīma was a king of Tanūkh who could have reigned in the middle of the third centuryAD. On the other hand, he remains an obscure figure.

Ǧadhīma seems firmly rooted in Mesopotamia but is mentioned in a contemporary document from southern Syria. The ʔUmm Ǧimāl inscription is by someone who had been closely attached to the king of Tanūkh in Mesopotamia. We do not have to assume that Fihr, son of Shullay was an inhabitant of the area where the inscription was found. We do not know anything about this Fihr apart from the facts that (a) his grave was in southern Syria, (b) the author of his inscription knew little Nabataean and less Greek, and (c) his tombstone was reused in building a house which, unfortunately, is difficult to date.[235] Now the legend of Ǧadhīma speaks about wars with powers in Syria: Zabbāʔ as well as Numāra b. Lakhm. A speculative but plausible occasion for such operations by a king of immigrants in Mesopotamia in the third century AD would have been during the invasions of Syria by Shāpur the Great in the 250s AD. Did Ǧadhīma take part in the great invasion which, as we know, reached Bosra, i.e. even beyond the region where an-Namāra is found? Did his *tropheús* find his death there during these operations? Speculative but not implausible.

According to the Arabic account, ʕAmr b. Ẓarib b. ʔUdhayna controlled Syria and the Ğazīra at the time of Ğadhīma. Translated into historical facts, this corresponds to the conquests of the Ğazīra by Odenathus, *corrector totius orientis* and the prolonged arm of Rome after Shāpur's devastations in the Orient. Behind ʕAmr may lurk the figure of Vaballatus, the son of Odenathus and Zenobia. According to one Arabic source, ʕAmr was made king by the Romans.[236] Ğadhīma's death through Zabbāʔ may thus reflect the conquest of the old realm of the kings of Hatra by the Palmyrenians in AD 262. The Arabic story may well preserve a political scenario where the destruction of Hatra by the Iranians and their Mesopotamian allies demanded revenge.

The Paikuli inscription mentions two ʕAmr, one of whom is called the Lakhmid. This ruler is also probably mentioned in the Manichaean Coptic chronicle. The existence of this dynasty in the third century AD is thus also confirmed, as well as the existence of a ruler named ʕAmr of this family in the beginning of the 290s AD. It is therefore very likely that ʕAmr ibn ʕAdī of the Ğadhīma story is in fact identical with ʕAmr the Lakhmid in the Paikuli inscription and in the Coptic chronicle. If we look at the Arabic sources, we find that there are four main names among the forefathers of ʕAmr b. ʕAdī which figure as a designation for the royal house in al-Ḥīra: Rabīʕa, Naṣr, Numāra and Lakhm. Of these, Naṣr and Rabīʕa always go together as father and son, as do Numāra and Lakhm. According to Ḥamza al-ʔIṣfahānī, ʕAmr b. ʕAdī is the first king mentioned in the books in Ḥīra, and the kings of Iraq are said to be his descendants and their name is Naṣr.[237] Dīnawarī says that ʕAmr b. ʕAdī is the *ǧudd* of Nuʕmān b. al-Mundhir. The first king in the list with this name reigned at the beginning of the fifth century.[238] Now in the so-called South Arabian version of the king-list, Nuʕmān is said to descend directly from ʕAdī via his son ʕAmr.[239] No other kings are mentioned in between, and we especially miss Imruʔ al-Qays al-badʔ, the third king in Ibn al-Kalbī's list.

A closer look at the successon of kings in Ḥīra after ʕAmr ibn ʕAdī shows a great confusion, with several Imruʔ al-Qays interspersed with *ʕamāliqa* kings.[240] In the more sober list given by Ibn al-Kalbī there are only three kings between ʕAmr and Nuʕmān, and two of these are called Imruʔ al-Qays al-badʔ.[241] Finally, there is even a tradition saying that ʕAmr ibn ʕAdī was succeeded not by Imruʔ al-Qays but by his brother al-Ḥārith.[242] It is obvious that there is a large break in the list here, and there is no doubt that at least the first part of the list of kings in Ḥīra from Ğadhīma to Nuʕmān b. Mundhir is a construction of doubtful historicity. Story-tellers and historians have tried in different ways to mend the break.[243]

This explains the complications of ʕAmr's descent. The names Rabīʕa and Naṣr belong to a legend about the emigration of the house of Rabīʕa from Yemen before the breaking of the dam in Marib. The whole context of this legend shows that it was thought to belong to the era of king ʔAbū Karib ʔAsʕad. This king, identical with ʔSʕD KRB in the South Arabian inscriptions, reigned in the first half of the fifth century AD, which fits well with the more or less explicit chronology of the Arabic sources.[244] An invasion of al-Ḥīra by this king is, in fact, mentioned by Ibn al-Kalbī. This puts the origin of the dynasty in al-Ḥīra in a new light. From the kings reigning there at the beginning of the fifth century there are two main lines backwards: one connecting them with South Arabia, another connecting them with ʕAmr b. ʕAdī. It can be doubted whether any of them are historical. At a fairly early stage they have been fused into one line of descent. But this shows (a) that the historical dynasty of al-Ḥīra probably began around AD 400 and (b) that it did not have any connections with ʕAmr b. ʕAdī and the Lakhmids in the third century. The house of Lakhm and the house of Naṣr should be kept apart. Their connection as well as their ultimate origin from Ǧadhīma is the result of manipulation much later by story-tellers, royal propagandists and historians and does not reflect any direct historical connection, except that all these rulers lived in more or less the same geographical area.[245]

A tentative reconstruction is that a kingdom was established in al-Ḥīra around AD 400 in the reign of the Sassanid hero-king Vahram V. The appearance of *ʕamāliqa* kings in the list immediately before the reigns of Mundhir and Nuʕmān is a sign that, in fact, we have to do with a new beginning, a new line of kings. The name of this family was probably Naṣr and it reigned until the suspension of the kingdom around AD 600. It is not unlikely that this dynasty was already artificially connected with the earlier rulers in Mesopotamia by chroniclers already before the rise of Islam.

There are two hard facts in ʕAmr's history: he was a Lakhmid, thus clearly belonging to Syria, and he did homage to the Iranian king in AD 293 together with another ʕAmr, probably belonging to the ancient royal house of Edessa. Both of them seem to have had a relatively independent position in the Syrian desert before the Roman expansion in the 290s. Afterwards the Roman grip tightened and we do not hear more about the Abgarids. ʕAmr the Lahkmid was obviously more successful and established a closer alliance with the Romans. With his position is also connected his relationship to Ǧadhīma in the legend. The Syro-Mesopotamian dichotomy is also visible in the picture of Ǧadhīma: he was king of Tanūkh. Everything told about him, albeit legendary, locates him in the middle Euphrates region.[246] At the same time he is mentioned in a text found in Syria. The question is then: what is the connection between the Mesopotamian Ǧadhīma and the Lakhmids?

As far as the ʔUmm Ǧimāl text is concerned it does not mean that Ǧadhīma had been in Syria. Fihr may have had a wide-ranging career. On the other hand, it is reasonable to assume that Fihr was from Ḥawrān or the Ǧabal area if his tomb is found there. The legend says that Ǧadhīma was married into a family from Quḍāʕa, i.e. Syrian tribes. He had relations with the rulers in Palmyra and he nourished an heir from a Syrian tribe. The reality behind this Syrian connection of the enigmatic Ǧadhīma from Mesopotamia escapes us, yet he appears not as a military conqueror but as a religious figure.

The association between the Lakhmid rulers and Ǧadhīma may be quite ancient and perhaps go back to the Lakhmids themselves. It seems that ʕAmr the Lakhmid came to prominence in connection with the fall of Palmyra. He may have established himself as a ruler of several tribes in the Syrian desert on both sides of the Euphrates. Undoubtedly he was on good terms with the Iranians, although the claim that he resettled or even founded the town of al-Ḥīra cannot be verified. It seems, however, that the Lakhmids claimed some kind of succession to the rulers of Hatra: the title of Imruʔ al-Qays, probably the son of ʕAmr the Lakhmid, in the Namāra inscription 'king of all Arabs', as well as the term *tāǧ* used in it, definitely point eastwards.

ʕAmr, the Lakhmid, or his son Imruʔ al-Qays became a close ally of Rome at least after the peace treaty in AD 298. We do not have to assume any defection and even less a dramatic flight through the desert from Iranian to Roman territory. The Lakhmids were Syrians who conformed to the new geopolitical situation after 298. They also had ancient relations with groups in the south-western Syrian desert, where they originally came from. As a Roman ally, Imruʔ al-Qays became the ruler of all Arabs along the

Roman eastern border. He and his troops were employed in a large campaign initiated by Constantine to increase Roman pressure in the Red Sea area and to curb the newly emerged Himyarite empire, which sought support from the Iranians and their Tanūkh vassals in Mesopotamia. The spread of Roman power on the western side of the peninsula was countered by a strengthened Iranian grip on its eastern side: Shāpur II made a military expedition across the Persian Gulf and might even have penetrated deeper into Arabia in an attempt to check Roman interests.

In the Arabic tradition the king of an-Namāra does not play any prominent role. Since MRʔ LQYŠ was obviously (a) the man of the Romans, (b) a great warrior who had had a prominent position in the Syrian desert and the northern Ǧazīra at the beginning of the fourth century, it must have been an irresistible temptation for the later kings in al-Ḥīra, or their propagandists, to adopt him into their genealogy as they did with Ǧadhīma al-ʔabraṣ and ʕAmr b. ʕAdī the Lakhmid.[247]

Since he had been a Roman vassal, this could explain why his position was toned down, perhaps in contrast with ʕAmr. It explains why Numāra stands under Lakhm in the final genealogy. Since ʕAmr the Lakhmid had probably had some influence in Mesopotamia reflected in his legendary descendance from Ǧadhīma, he could be seen as a more direct predecessor to the Naṣrids than the king at Namāra.[248]

The result of this critical scrutiny of the sources is that the scenarios where MRʔLQYŠ is ruling the entire Syrian desert from al-Ḥīra to Ḥawrān, working as a go-between for the two empires, or where he has been installed as king by the Sassanids but pulled out and defected to the enemy, turn out to be unlikely, built as they are on harmonizing readings of sources of very uneven historical value.

There has been a fundamental methodological weakness in all treatments of this question, namely the assumption that aṭ-Ṭabarī and his colleagues somehow tell the correct story and that the Namāra inscription should be inserted into it. The result has been all kinds of more or less forced harmonizing between the different sources. But it must be a fundamental principle in reconstruction of historical events that contemporary testimonies, such as documents of a more or less official although propagandistic character, must be assigned greater weight than narrative sources 500 years younger which are full of legends and all kinds of distortion. This does not exclude the possibility that even the narrative sources have preserved historical memories, but the contemporary documents must have the final word. The solution to the problem treated here is that MRʔ LQYŠ, king of all Arabs, and Imruʔ al-Qays al-badʔ in the king-list of al-Ḥīra are probably identical but did not have anything to do with the dynasties in Mesopotamia. The insertion of this name in the king-list of al-Ḥīra is the work of much later times, when the ancient rulers around the Syrian desert were still remembered, although vaguely. They could easily be arranged into a genealogical tree ending with the rulers in al-Ḥīra in the sixth century. This was neither the first nor the last time in Middle Eastern history that such an operation was performed.

Arabs in literary texts from the third century

The events told in the Namāra inscription and the Arabo-Islamic traditions about the foundation of the dynasty in al-Ḥīra reflect a new age with great changes in Arabia. Unfortunately, the sources dealing with political events in Arabia in the third and at the beginning of the fourth centuries are scanty. More light is thrown on the processes by the literary texts from the period, from which we get valuable details about ethnic and social movements not visible in the other texts. The material found in these sources is, however, often difficult to date. Much of it is probably taken from sources which are lost and difficult to identify. Noteworthy is how we encounter in Greek and Latin texts from this period information about Arabia and its inhabitants which is not mentioned earlier. Some of it, especially that found in Christian literature, may have been taken from Jewish sources. It also seems that the Helleno-Roman world received new information about Arabia from the time of Marcus Aurelius onwards. The Parthian wars in the third century must have stimulated interest and demand for such knowledge. The repeated operations around Hatra, the incorporation of Edessa and the establishment of the Mesopotamian province probably gave the Romans access to new information about their future heirs.

Arabs in the outgoing second century: the testimony of Clement of Alexandria

Christianity's first great writer, Clement of Alexandria (*c.* AD 150–214), mentions Arabs on a few occasions in his works. His notices are, as a rule, echoes from Herodotus and Strabo and have no independent value for Clement's own time. There is, however, one passage in his *Paedagogus* well worth looking at:

> The youths of the *arábioi* fit for bearing arms are camel riders. They mount the camels while these are pregnant. They pasture and run at the same time as they carry their masters and the house together with them. And if these barbarians lack drink, they give their milk even when they are empty of food; they do not even spare their blood, as it is said of raging wolves. They are indeed more mild-tempered than the barbarians, not getting ill-minded when maltreated, but run through the desert courageously, carrying and nourishing their masters.[249]

The passage contains some identifiable literary reminiscenses which make it likely that it is based on an earlier text.[250] This realistic description of the life of the camel riders in the North Arabian desert is a unique documentation of the relationship between the Arabs and the camel. It must go back to a source giving information about Arabia which has not been preserved. Since this picture appears for the first time in Clement, it is likely that it was not written considerably earlier.

Origen

The famous Alexandrine theologian is said to have visited the Arabian province three times: around AD 215, in 247 and in 249.[251] The first time he was invited by the governor; the other two visits were made because of heretical tendencies among the Christians in the province which was to become well known for its heresies. He thus must have had a good idea of conditions in Roman Arabia. In a commentary to Genesis 25, the list of the sons of Qeṭurah, he says:

> From the sons of Khettoura many peoples arose who inhabit the desert of the Troglodytae, *Arabía eudaímon* and that which stretches past Madianitis, the town Madiam being situated beyond (*hypèr*) *Arabía eudaímōn*, opposite Pharan to the east of the Red Sea.[252]

In an excerpt from the famous apologetic work *Contra Celsum* where the circumcision is discussed, the difference between the Jews' custom, by which boys are circumcised at eight days old, and their cousins is emphasized:

> Among the Ismaelites opposite (or in the direction towards: *katà* + acc.) Arabia, they are circumcised in the same manner at the age of thirteen.[253]

The impression from these passages is that Ismaelites are not identified as Arabs, although they live close to each other. For Origen, Arabs were obviously people in the province. He does not, then, follow Jewish *haggadah* on this point.

In a commentary (the attribution of which to Origen is somewhat uncertain) to Ps. 137:7, 'Remember, o Lord, the children of Edom in the day of Jerusalem', it is said:

> [These are] the *árabes*, he says, who were allied to the Babylonians, whom the prophet continuously mentions as being relatives and being worse than the enemies; he says: 'demand revenge on them!'[254]

The Edomites are thus identified as Arabs, which must mean the inhabitants of the Roman province of Arabia encompassing ancient Edom.[255] The Edomites had been identified with Nabataeans at an early stage, which contributed to their becoming Arabs.[256] It is likely that Origen here is dependent on Jewish *haggadah*, with which he was familiar. The identification of the Edomites with Arabs could also reflect the participation of Arabs in the events in AD 70.

More interesting are the remarks indicating the limits of Origen's Arabia. In a commentary to Ps. 120:5, 'Woe is me, that I sojourn in Mesech/That I dwell in the tents of Qedar', it is said:

> This is a people of barbarians with an animal-like disposition, in the same manner as the *árabes* who use tents and huts.[257]

This also looks as if it is taken from some Jewish midrash to Psalms. In the Jewish targum to the psalm, Qedar are identified with Arabs.[258] The impression from Origen is that they are not identical: Qedar live in tents *like* the Arabs.

Hippolytus' *Diamerismós*

More fruitful for our study is the information given by the Christian writer Hippolytus, who lived during the first half of the third century. In the introduction to his Chronicle, the so-called *Diamerismós*, 'the distribution', we find a grand exposition of the peoples of the earth according to the Table of Nations in Genesis 10.[259] Hippolytus has, however, added a lot of material to the Biblical scheme, which contains data from many different sources.[260] The background for Hippolytus' text is complicated and hardly yet investigated. We have to be content with referring to what is said about Arabs and Arabia.

Part I of Hippolytus' text (§§ 44–197) contains lists of (a) the descendants of each of Noah's sons, (b) peoples descending from them but without specific forefathers, and (c) countries inhabited by other peoples, sometimes descending from the sons, sometimes not. The descendants of Shem are found in §§ 158–188 (a), §§ 189–195 (b), §§

193–197 (c). In part II (§§ 198–237) we find five other lists: (a) the seventy-two peoples spread over the earth after the tower of Babel (§§ 198–201), (b) a list of colonies of peoples otherwise unmentioned (§§ 202–223), (c) the zones of unknown peoples (§§ 224–234), (d) the twelve most famous mountains (§§ 235–235), (e) a list of rivers (§§ 236–237).

In part I Arabs are mentioned in all three passages dealing with the Semites:

> 178 [Iektan gave birth to] Aram; from him are the *árabes*.
>
> 184 [Iektan gave birth to] Sabat; from him are the Alamousinoí (the first *árabes*).
>
> 190 [From Sem are descended]: . . . [the] first *árabes* called Kedroúsioi (*árabes*, Kedroúsioi), [the] second *árabes* called 'the naked philosophers' (*gymnosophístai*).
>
> 194 [The countries of the Semites] Persis with the peoples neighbouring it, Bactria, Babylonia, Cordylia, Assyria, Mesopotamia, Ancient *Arabía*, Elymais, India, *Arabía eudaímōn*, Coele Syria Commagene and Phoenicia.

In the same way, they occur in §§ (a)–(d) in part II:

> 200 [the 72 peoples] Hebrews, who also are Jews, Assyrians, Chaldaeans, Medes, Persians, first and second *árabes*, first and second Madiēnaîoi, Adiabēnoi, Taiēnoi, Salamoúsioi, Sarakēnoí.
>
> 205 [unknown peoples] *árabes hoi eudaímones* have become the colonies of the *árabes*; *Arabía eudaímōn* is called by this name.
>
> 226 [zones of the unknown peoples] Adiabēnoí beyond (*péran*) the *árabes*, the Tainoí below (*katantikrys*) them (Adiabēnoí and Tainoí are beyond the *árabes*).
>
> 227 Alamosinoí beyond (*péran*) the *árabes*.
>
> 228 Sakkēnoí (Sarakēnoí) beyond the Tainoí.
>
> 235 [famous mountains] Nausaion (Nyssus) and Sina in Arabía.

The most concrete information from the text as it stands is that the Adiabenians and the Taienians are adjacent to but not identical with the *árabes* (226). The Adiabenians are, of course, on the upper Tigris. The term 'Taienians' must be identical with the designation *ṭayyāyē* used in Syrian sources for tribes operating in the central Ǧazīra and later used as a general term for all tribes in the Syrian desert. This would mean that the *árabes* mentioned are in the upper Ǧazīra, i.e. in the ancient Parthian province of Arabia with its capital Hatra. This would then explain the note 178 that the Arabs were sons of Aram, since the upper Ǧazīra was considered the home of Biblical Aram. This interpretation is further supported by the list of the seventy-two peoples in § 200. Here, the *árabes* are clearly integrated in an Iranian group of peoples: they stand between Medes, Persians, Adiabenians and Taienians.[261] The 'Ancient Arabia' mentioned in 194 fits well into the picture of the Arabs within the Iranian sphere: it stands between the provinces of Mesopotamia and Elymais (Elam).

We may thus draw the conclusion that Hippolytus had access to a source with information about ethnic conditions in the Parthian or Sassanid empire. We should observe the parallels between his ethnography and that found in Shāpur's inscription at Naqsh-e-Rustam. An important point is the differentiation between *árabes* and *taiēnoí*, as well as the fact that they both seem to belong to the Iranian sphere.

A most interesting detail is that the (Iranian) Arabs are made descendants of Aram. This reappears in the genealogies of the early Islamic historians, where one of the two branches of the *ʕarab ʕāriba* are descendants of ʔRM, which is identified with both the Aramaeans and ʔIram mentioned in the Qurʔān. This identification is probably not the work of the Islamic genealogists but was made long before their time. One could suspect some Jewish midrash as the ultimate source via a Syrian Christian writer.

Hippolytus has also integrated elements containing information about conditions in the west. This is most apparent in the location of the two mountains in Arabia in § 235, of which that of Sinai of course goes back to Paul. As will be apparent later, there are good reasons to locate Mount Nausaíon/Nyssus in Trachonitis, i.e. the Arabia south-east of Damascus. In this area we also find the Sakkēnoí in Ptolemy's *Geography*.[262] Hippolytus or his copyists seem to have mixed up this name with another western designation, the Sarakēnoí. In § 200 the Taiēnoí are followed by the Salamoúsioi and the Saracens, which probably refer to peoples of more or less similar status and way of living between the northern Ǧazīra and the northern Ḥiǧāz. The Salamusi should then be looked for in the Syrian desert.

Hippolytus notes the existence of two groups of Arabs: first (*prōtoi*) and second (*deúteroi*). This division is also found with some other peoples. The first *árabes* are associated with Kedroúsioi and Alamousinoí (§§ 184, 190 cf. 227). In one version they are identical with the Kedrousians; in the other they are adjacent. The same with the Alamousinoí: in § 184 they are identical with the first Arabs, in § 227 they are separated. Hippolytus could have used contradictory sources here.

An attempt to identify the *árabes* should start with the Kedroúsioi, a name which looks like a distortion of Qedar. The next step is to note that Iektan gave birth to Sabat, from whom the Alamousinoí descended. These latter are said to be beyond the *árabes*. If Sabat is Sheba in Genesis 10, we are in western or southern Arabia. The latter is unlikely, although it cannot be ruled out that Hippolytus (or his source) had mixed up the two Shebas. As a support for the westerm Arabian interpretation we would suggest that behind the Alamousinoí hide the Alimazoneîs mentioned by the LXX Chronicler in the Old Testament. This name turns up in many different forms in Greek sources.[263] They lived in the north-western Ḥiǧāz. If this identification is tenable, we have in Hippolytus a testimony about Arabs in the northern Ḥiǧāz. These Arabs we have identified earlier as mentioned by Agatharchides of Cnidus in the third century BC (who also mentions the Alamousinoí) and probably as early as by Sargon II (the Marsimani).

Hippolytus thus turns out to be an excellent source in spite of the problematic state of his text. Since he obviously based his work on sources different from the Greek geographical literature, his picture of Arabs and their neighbours is astonishingly independent and informative. This does not mean that it reflects conditions in the third century AD in all details. The impression is that Hippolytus has had access to much older sources, especially for western Arabia. The picture emerging from the

Diamerismós is that the area from the northern Ḥiǧāz across the Syrian desert into the northern Ǧazīra was inhabited by several different groups of people: Taienians, Salamusians, Saracens and others. *árabes* are found in the Ǧazīra in the ancient Parthian province of Arabia and in the northern Ḥiǧāz. These Arabs appear to be quite small groups limited to these geographic areas. There is no trace of an Arabia encompassing the entire peninsula inhabited by Arabs.

The Book of the Laws of Countries

One of the oldest extant texts in Syriac is a description of the customs and laws of different peoples originating from the school of the Syrian philosopher and gnostic Bardesanes (Bar Dayṣān). The text was probably written by one of his disciples and composed before the fall of Hatra in AD 241. Apart from a Syriac version, we have several quotations from a Greek version, mostly by the church historian Eusebius, a version which, obviously, was very widespread. It became popular among Christians because its main point is that the customs and institutions of different peoples are determined not only by the stars but also by climate and other natural factors. Since the work is a kind of ethnographic description, it is not surprising that we find notes about Arabs of different kinds in it.

When presenting the laws and customs of different peoples and how they differ independently from the influence of the stars, the author enumerates some well-known names:

> The laws of the RQMYʔ, the ʔWRHYʔ and the ʕRBYʔ. Among the RQMYʔ not only the adulterous wife is killed, but even she who is suspected of adultery is punished.

> The stars do not have any influence upon customs such as circumcision:

> Recently, the Romans have conquered ʕRB and done away with all the laws there used to be, particularly circumcision, which was a custom they used.[264]

> The Romans could thus abolish this custom without any interference from the stars. On the other hand, the Jews practise circumcision regardless of which stars they live under:

> But whether they [the Jews] live in Edom or in ʕRB, in Greece or in Persia, in the North or the South, they keep to the law laid upon them by their fathers.[265]

The ʔWRHYʔ are the inhabitants of Edessa, ʔUrhay, which is also correctly translated by Eusebius (or his *Vorlage*) as Osrhoene. RQMYʔ are probably the inhabitants of Petra and its surroundings.[266] In accordance with both contemporary and later Syriac usage, the ʕRBYʔ should be the inhabitants of the areas east and south-east of Edessa. This is confirmed by the note that the Romans have recently conquered Arabia, which must refer to the Mesopotamian campaigns by Septimius Severus, which brought parts of this Arabia under Roman sway. The expression B-ʕRB is also found in the inscriptions from Hatra, where it refers to the Parthian province in the upper Ǧazīra.[267] There is thus no reason to assume that this text operates with an Arabia encompassing much or all of the peninsula and its inhabitants.

The author of the *Book of the Laws* enumerates a series of countries where there is no visible trace of the alleged influence of constellations and planets. Among them are 'the land (*ʔaṯrā*) of ṬYYʔ and SRQYʔ'.[268] It is completely clear that these two entities are not identical with the ʕRBYʔ. Instead they represent inhabitants of the Syrian desert and the Ǧazīra. The author of this text follows the same terminology as Hippolytus, and it is not unlikely that they are mutually dependent on each other. The SRQYʔ are likely to be identical with the *sarakēnoí* in Hippolytus and Ptolemy, who are separate from Arabs.

Uranius' *Arabica*

We have already encountered one example of an ethnological monograph in ancient literature dealing with Arabia, namely the one by Iuba.[269] We know about a few more which are lost and the scanty references to them in other preserved books do not contain much information.[270] From one of these lost books, however, we can still profit through quotations by later authors. A certain Uranius from Apamea in Syria is said to have written an *Arabica*, which seems to be datable to *c.* AD 300 or slightly later. From this work we have some quotations preserved in the *Ethnica* by Stephanus of Byzantium, written in the sixth century AD. Stephanus has thirty-two short passages from Uranius, from which some idea of Uranius' views on Arabs and Arabia can be gleaned.[271]

There has been a protracted debate about the dating of the Uranius fragments. Received opinion was for a long time that it was written in the days of Diocletian.[272] This was challenged in 1908 by Domaszewski who argued for a date during the reign of the Nabataean king Aretas 'III'.[273] Another attempt at an early dating was made by W. Aly, who claimed that there were quotations from Uranius in Strabo's descriptions of the Red Sea which would go back to information from the Gallus expedition.[274] He dated Uranius to the reign of Augustus.[275] These early datings were adjusted somewhat by H. von Wissmann, who in a lengthy article presented arguments, mainly from the South Arabian material in the fragments, arguing for a dating later than Strabo and Pliny but before the conquest of Nabataea in AD 106.[276] Recently, West has revived the later dating, suggesting a time after AD 337, based on the note about a town named after Constantius II.[277]

It seems clear that the early datings suggested by Domaszewski and Aly are untenable. This also holds for that of von Wissmann, although some of his arguments, for example his observation that neither Strabo nor Pliny had read Uranius, are solid. These three scholars all find passages in the fragments describing conditions much earlier than the assumed fourth century AD. For both Domaszewski and von Wissmann the prominence of the Nabataeans is decisive. For Aly the undeniable parallel between the passages in Strabo and Uranius about the Red Sea was the main point. But it is obvious that there is always the possibility that a fourth-century writer copies and quotes older material without much change. The impression gained from the fragments is of an author with a strong linguistic and archaeological/historical interest. He may thus have incorporated ancient material without necessarily having tried to adjust it to the conditions of his own day. West's dating seems to be the best solution.

From the fragments the general outline of Uranius' book can be reconstructed. It consisted of five books, I: Arabs along the Euphrates, peoples in South Arabia; II: Peoples in North Arabia: Nabataea, Palmyra, Moab; III: Aromatics; IV–V: History: Nabataeans, the Gallus expedition.[278]

The term 'Arabia' is, in the fragments, used as a designation for an area along the Euphrates (2), around Singara (3), South Arabia with the epithet *eudaímōn* (13–18), and the land where Motho (25) and Moba (9, 32) are situated. The last two belong to the former Nabataea, and Uranius gives several names of towns said to be 'in the land of Nabataeans' (6–8, 24), among them Madaba and Oboda (Avdat). In connection with the Thamouda it is said that they are the neighbours of the Arabian Nabataeans (12). From this it is clear that, for Uranius, Arabian matters encompassed the whole peninsula. He thus operates with the Eratosthenic concept of Arabia, which, after all, is not surprising.

In the preserved fragments, Arabs are mentioned in five:

> 12: Thamouda: neighbour of the Nabataean *arábioi*. Ouranios Arabika III. The inhabitant [is called] *thamoudēnós*.
>
> 22: Akkhēnoí, an Arabian (*arábion*) people as Uranius says in Book IV [living] on the neck (*aukhēn*) of the Red Sea.
>
> 23: Edoumaîoi, an Arabian (*arábion*) people as Uranius says in Book IV.
>
> 25: Mōthō, a village of Arabia in which Antigonus the Macedonian was killed by Rabilos, the king of the *arábioi*, which, as Uranius [says] in Book IV, in the language of the *árabes* is 'place of death'.
>
> 28: Mánneōs, a region in the middle of the rivers in which the *manneōtai árabes* dwell, as Uranius says.

Those mentioned in 28 can be identified with Arabs already known by us. A city named Mannakarta is known on the Zergan river on the plain south of present-day Mardin, and it is very likely that these *árabes* belong to that area.[279] We are thus east of Edessa and west of Nisibis and it is likely that we have to do with the Arabs documented in the inscriptions from Sumatar.[280] The name of the area as well as that of the city appears to be derived from a personal name Maʕn(ū), well known from the onomasticon of the kings in Edessa. It is likely that the town is a royal foundation by an Edessan king or another king with an Arabic name.[281]

That the Edomites are identified as Arabs is an interpretation of a passage in Strabo.[282] This interpretation is also found in Origen and may go back to Jewish sources. The notice about Motho is difficult to interpret. Contrary to what is usually assumed, there are no certain indications that Motho and its Arabs are identical with the Nabataeans and that Rabilos is the first known Nabataean king. Neither do we know who was Antigonus the Macedonian. That he is identical with Antigonus Monophthalmus, the successor of Alexander the Great, and that we have to do with a legend about his death as is usually assumed, is unproved.[283] The name Rabbilos = Rabb-ʔil is documented from Transjordan in the third century BC and later appears as the name of the last king in Petra.[284] There is, however, no mention of Nabataeans in the passage. Motho may well be in Arabia south-east of Damascus, and the death of

Antigonus the Macedonian an event not recorded anywhere else.[285]

The Akkhēnoí are said to live 'on the neck of the Red Sea'. The word *aukhēn* as a geographical term in Greek can stand for an isthmus, a strait or a mountain pass. A tribe named ʕAkk is known from pre-Islamic South Arabian inscriptions, living in the Yemeni Tihāma. In the genealogical system of the Islamic historians, ʕAkk is the brother of Maʕadd, and they are said to have taken part in the pagan cult in Mecca.[286] We obviously have to do with inhabitants somewhere on the Red Sea coast.

Also Uranius mentioned the Saracens and Taieni. In fragment 10 he says that the *taínoi* are a people beyond the *sarakēnoí* towards the south. According to what we know, it is likely that it is the Saracens who are towards the south, although this is not clear from the text. What should be noticed is that neither of them is explicitly said to be an *arábion éthnos*, 'an Arabian people'. The testimony of Uranius can thus be considered to be in accordance with that of Hippolytus and the *Book of the Laws* distinguishing *árabes* from everybody else.

Glaucus

In the geographical encyclopaedia written by Stephanus of Byzantium in the sixth century AD there are thirteen references to a work called *Arabikē arkhaiología* by a certain Glaucus, who is otherwise unknown. This was obviously a treatise on the history and geography of Arabia, divided into at least four books. Unfortunately, the dating of Glaucus is most uncertain.

The place-names in Stephanus taken from Glaucus are locations in the Arabo-Nabataean kingdom or its immediate vicinity.[287] From the commentaries in Stephanus, it is evident that Glaucus' third and fourth books were dedicated to that area. We hear about Gea, 'a city near "Rocks" in Arabia',[288] Karakmōba,[289] Ailanon,[290] Doumatha[291] and Arindēla,[292] which can all be located in or close to the Arabian Province. Also Ertha and Omana are quoted from Glaucus, which shows that he treated Mesopotamia and the Gulf as well in his work.[293] The other names are more uncertain.[294]

The predominance of names from the Arabo-Nabataean kingdom could be an indication that the work was written after the establishment of the Provincia Arabia in AD 106. Omana is explicitly located in *Arabía eudaímōn* and perhaps identical with the Omana on the southern shore of the Persian Gulf mentioned by Pliny. Remarkable is the town of Ertha, mentioned as a town in Parthia on the Euphrates.[295] It is difficult to avoid the conclusion that this must be the town known in later Aramaic sources as Ḥer̲tā and in Arabic as al-Ḥīra, the capital of the Lakhmids in the fifth and sixth centuries AD. In that case we should compare a notice in the Shahrīhā ī Erān, a middle Persian list of cities in the Sassanian realm, which says:

> The capital of Hērt was built by Shāpur the son of Ardashir and he appointed Mihrzād marzban of Hērt on the lake of the *tāzīgān*.[296]

tāzīgān is the Middle Persian term corresponding to Saracens and *ṭayyāyē*.[297] If the identification of Hērt with al-Ḥīra is correct, this means that Glaucus wrote in the time of Shāpur I or later.[298] It has even been suggested that the Iranian king is in fact Shāpur II, which would bring us to the fourth century.[299] As has been pointed out, the picture from the Arabic sources does not make it likely that this town had any importance before AD 400.[300] This is an argument for dating Glaucus to the fifth century AD.

Notes

1 For the South Arabian texts from this period, see pp. 543 ff.
2 Barnes, *Sources* 108–113.
3 Barnes, *Sources* 91–94.
4 For this whole complex of sources, see Barnes, *Sources* 90–123.
5 For this problem, which is also relevant for the Jewish sources from this period, see pp. 485 f., 526 f.
6 Cf. Wolski, *Empire* 190 note 31, 194.
7 The trade routes in the Middle East underwent changes at certain crucial points. The overland trade from the east around 300 BC took a southern route in order to avoid the control of the Greeks (Alexander, the Seleucids). The route from Gerrha via Duma to Petra prospered for 200 years, and the Seleucids tried in vain to control it. Around 100 BC the Seleucids were gone, and the Parthians took loose control of Mesopotamia. It became profitable again to go along the rivers. For 150 years there were two routes: one from Charax to Petra and one from Charax to Palmyra. Around AD 50 the southern route had played out its role and the northern route became the main one. Together with the establishment of the northern route *c.* 100 BC goes the discovery of the sea-route to India. From 100 BC there were thus three ways of trading with India, of which the one via Dumah and Petra dwindled away.
8 Cf. Frézouls, *Fluctuations* 195–214.
9 For the course of events, see Debevoise, *History* 255 ff.
10 *Historia Augusta: Pescennius Niger* 7.8.
11 Euting, *Inschriften* no. 463 (p. 61) and Tafel 26. There is a crack in the rock which damaged the two letters RB and the reading is not 100 per cent certain.
12 Cassius Dio 75.1.1 (= Xiphilinus). For the course of events, see Kneissl, *Siegestitulatur* 126–128; Millar, *Near East* 120–122.
13 Cassius Dio 75.3.2 (= Excerpta Ursiniana).
14 It is said in 75.3.2 that Severus sent three divisions of the army against a place whose name is unfortunately corrupt; the MSS have *arkhén*, which gives no meaning. It has been suggested as reading Atrene, which would indicate operations against Hatra. This is, however, not likely from the context. The impression is that this notice refers to activities in the region of Nisibis.
15 *Historia Augusta: Severus* 9.9.
16 Barnes, *Sources* 108.
17 Kneissl, *Siegestitulatur* 129, 136. The *Historia Augusta* (*Severus* 9.11.) says that he received the titles *Arabicus Adiabenicus Parthicus*, which is somewhat confused.
18 Eutropius 18.4.
19 Festus 21.10.
20 Aurelius Victor 20.15.
21 *Historia Augusta: Severus* 18.1. This is confused since Abgarus was not king of the Persians. Herodian mentions the episode with a correct location of Abgar (Herodian 3.9.2.).
22 *Feriale Duranum* I.14 (= Welles *et al.*, *Excavations* 198); cf. Rubin, *Dio* 431–437.
23 According to Drijvers (*Hatra* 878) the province was established after the second campaign. According to Millar (*Near East* 125) it was set up already in AD 195.
24 *Historia Augusta: Severus* 12.6.
25 Cassius Dio 76.9 (= Xiphilinus and Excerpta).
26 Cassius Dio 76.10. Herodian (3.9.3) says that Severus overran *Arabía eudaímōn*. This is probably derived ultimately from Xenophon's description of Mesopotamian Arabia as full of odoriferous herbs, which led to the confusion with the assumed *Schlaraffenland* on the peninsula.
27 Cassius Dio 76.11.2.
28 Bowersock, *Arabia* 114–115; Millar, *Near East* 125–126.
29 CIL VI.1033; cf. Brilliant, *Arch* 91–95, and Kneissel, *Siegestitulatur* 126–137, 211 ff. It has been argued that one of the panels on the triumphal arch (the southern one on the Capitol side) shows the siege of Hatra; see Rubin, *Dio* 425–431. According to Brilliant (*Arch* 207–217) it shows the capture of Ctesiphon; cf. *ibidem* 171–182.

30 Cf. Kneissel, *Siegestitulatur* 126 ff.
31 *Historia Augusta: Opellius Macrinus* 12.5.
32 For Macrinus' reign, see Millar, *Near East* 144–146.
33 Herodian 3.9.3; cf. Barnes, *Sources* 54 ff., 80 ff.
34 Kneissl, *Siegestitulatur* 166–167.
35 Kneissl, *Siegestitulatur* 149.
36 Cassius Dio 80.3.2.
37 *Codex Manichaeus Colonensis* 18.1–16. Cf. Heinrichs/Koenen, *Mani-Kodex* 125–132. For the discussion of the date, see Chaumont, *Chute*; Wiesenhöfer, *Anfänge*; and Tardieu, *L'Arrivée* 23 n. 34.
38 The king in Hatra was probably SNṬRWQ, son of ʕBDSMʔ, mentioned in the inscriptions H 195 and 203; cf. pp. 445 f.
39 For the problems concerning the end of Edessa, see Drijvers, *Hatra* 879–885.
40 *Historia Augusta: Gordiani tres* 29.1.
41 Zosimus, I:18.3: *ex Arabías éthnous kheirístou.*
42 Cf. Millar, *Near East* 530–531.
43 Eusebius, *History* 6.34, 38, 39, 41.9; 7.10.3. For a discussion of the evidence for Philippus' Christianity, see Shahid, *Rome* 65–93.
44 Aurelius Victor 28.4: *humillimo locus orto . . . pater nobilissimus latronum ductor.*
45 Aurelius Victor 28; cf. the *Oracula Sibyllina* 13.64–70 where Bosra and Philippopolis are 'cities of the *Arabes*'. According to Aigrain (*Arabie* 1163), Severus moved the frontier of the Arabian province northwards, incorporating Ḥawrān/Trachonitis; cf. Bowersock, *Arabia* 113–116.
46 Cf. the remarks by Millar, *Near East* 531. For Arabs in this region, see Robert, *Épitaphe.*
47 Maricque, *Classica* 5 296–299.
48 Shahpur, *Res gestae* 2–3. Cf. Maricque, *Classica* 5 336, for the Middle Persian and Parthian forms of the names of the regions. The enumeration goes from line 2 to line 6.
49 Lines 6–36.
50 Shāpur, *Res gestae* 23, the Greek text. The Persian version does not have these names.
51 This also means that it is not immediately connected with the ecclesiastical province *bēṯ ʕarbāyē* documented in the fifth century in Nestorian ecclesiastical documents, as is often assumed: at the synod in AD 497 the bishop of Nisibis is metropolitan of *ʔaṯrwāṯā ḏa-ʕrab*, 'the lands of [the] Arab' (Chabot: *Synodicon* 62 l. 17, cf. 311), or *ʔaṯrā ḏ-bēṯ ʕarbāyē*, 'the land of the house of the Arabs' (ibid. 66 ll. 1–2 cf. 315, cf. Honigmann/Maricq, *Recherches* 98; Maricq, *Classica* 5 305 n. 5). It is reasonable to assume that the name reproduces an Iranian designation where *bēṯ* stands for the Persian *istān*, a common element in the Parthian and Sassanid province names. The borders of the ecclesiastical province do not, however, coincide with anything known from the time of Shāpur I (see p. 518).
52 For a survey, see Equini Schneider, *Septimia Zenobia* 34–52.
53 According to Paschoud, *L'histoire* (224–229), Zosimus knew Dexippus only through an intermediary, which explains the differences between the *Historía néa* and the *Historia Augusta*: the latter used Dexippus directly (ibid. 229–233).
54 For all these sources, see Barnes, *Sources* 110–113.
55 Barnes, *Sources* 112–113; Schwartz, *L'Histoire.*
56 Cf. Paschoud, *Histoire Auguste: Introduction* XXXIX–XLI; Préface 12.
57 Cf. Février, *Essai* V–VI.
58 The most thorough account of the history of Palmyra is still Février's *Essai.*
59 Cf. Starcky's cautious remark in *Palmyre* 1081. According to Altheim/Stiehl, *Araber* III 254, 270, there is no doubt that Odainatus was 'beduinischen Ursprungs'.
60 *Inscriptiones* 8924 (Dessau III p. XXI), RÉS 562; cf. Février, *Essai* 114.
61 Malalas 12 p. 229.3–10.
62 IGLS 9107: 'the temple of Iuppiter Hammon, destroyed by the Palmyrene enemies'; cf. Dodgeon/Lieu, *Frontier* p. 86 (4.6.4).
63 Against Equini Schneider who claims that the title is connected with the conquest of the Provincia Arabia in AD 270 (*Septimia Zenobia* 70).

64 Février, *Essai* 106.
65 *Historia Augusta: Aurelianus* 28.1–3. This is a passage derived from Nicomachus Flavianus; cf. Paschoud, *Histoire Auguste* 12.
66 Kneissl, *Siegestitulatur* 177, 237.
67 *Historia Augusta: Aurelianus* 28.4; 35.4–5. The passage is derived from the *Historia caesarum*; see Paschoud, *Histoire Auguste* 12.
68 *Inscriptiones* no. 579 p. 134; cf. Kneissl, *Siegestitulatur* 177, 237.
69 *Historia Augusta: Triginta tyranni* 30.7.
70 *Historia Augusta: Aurelianus* 11.3.
71 *Historia Augusta: Aurelianus* 33.4.
72 Malalas 12.297.
73 Malalas 12.298, cf. 300.
74 Malalas 12.299.
75 Cf. Bowersock, *Arabs* 71 ff. See pp. 505 ff.
76 Cf. p. 516.
77 den Hengst, *Verba* 170–173; Paschoud, *Histoire Auguste* 88 ff.
78 See pp. 511 f.
79 Cf. Paschoud, loc. cit.
80 Also Paschoud (*Histoire Auguste* 89–90) associates the units with the *Notitia dignitatum.*
81 For an analysis of the account, see Paschoud, *Histoire Auguste* 160–169, who emphasizes its composite character with elements from different Roman ceremonies (reception of ambassadors, parade of gladiators etc.). Equini Schneider (*Septimia Zenobia* 62 ff.; cf. 81) is more positive and points to the Palmyrene connections with the Red Sea area.
82 Paschoud, *Histoire Auguste* 165–166.The whole description of the siege and capture of Palmyra in the sources seems to be very exaggerated; cf. Equini Schneider, *Septimia Zenobia* 82.
83 *Historia Augusta: Aurelianus* 27.5; 28.2, 5.
84 Cf. Paschoud, *Histoire Auguste* 148.
85 Zosimus 1.44.1, 52.3.
86 Cf. Bowersock, *Arabs* 74.
87 For the memories of these events in Arabic sources, see pp. 476, 482 f.
88 *Historia Augusta: Triginta tyranni* 30.12–22.
89 The chastity motif also appears in the story about Ǧadhīma al-ʔabraṣ and az-Zabbāʔ, as told by al-Yaʕqūbī (*Tārīkh* I:237). The figure of az-Zabbāʔ contains memories about Zenobia; see p. 481.
90 *Historia Augusta: Triginta tyranni* 309.24–27; Eutropius 9.13.2.
91 Zosimus 1.59; cf. Paschoud, *Histoire Auguste* 147–148.
92 Cf. Bowersock, *Arabs* 77-80.
93 Frézouls, *Frontière* 195 (map), 214 n. 148.
94 Ensslin, *Ostpolitik* 15; Millar, *Near East* 177.
95 *Panegyrici* III:V (Galletier 53): . . . *omitto Sarmatiae vastationem oppressumque captivitatis vinculis Sarracenum.*
96 Ensslin's claim (*Ostpolitik* 16) that Diocletian's title *Persicus* derives from his dealings with the Saracens in 290 is not convincing. There is no hint that the Saracens were agents of the Sassanids.
97 *Paikuli* § 92 (Humbach/Skjaervö, *Inscription* 3.1 71).
98 Cf. Skjaervö, *Inscription* 126. Cf. Chaumont, *États* 94–97.
99 This chronicle, preserved in a Coptic version, disappeared in World War II; see Schmidt/Polotsky, *Mani-Fund* 28–29. A fragment reappeared later in Dublin, see Tardieu, *L'arrivée* 16–17.
100 For the text, see Tardieu, *L'arrivée* 16–17. The text is discussed by de Blois (*King Amarō*), who is sceptical about the location of this king in Mesopotamia. His doubts about the emendation of the king's title '[L]ahim' may be partially due to this. As we shall see, there are good arguments in favour of a Syrian location for this king, which increases the likeliness of Tardieu's emendation.

101 Frézouls, *Frontière* 195 (map), 214.
102 *Inscriptiones* no. 696 p. 157; Kneissl, *Siegestitulatur* 178.
103 See Shahid, *Byzantium* I 56–59.
104 Shahid (*Byzantium* I 73) suggests that the *cognomen* could refer to the expedition of Imruʔ al-Qays mentioned in the Namāra inscription (see the following). This is based on the idea that Imruʔ al-Qays fought against Arabs, i.e. tribes in the Ḥiǧāz and South Arabia. There is, however, no evidence that the term 'Arabs' was used as a political term with this meaning. If it refers to the inhabitants of the peninsula conquered by Imruʔ al-Qays in the name of the Roman emperor, it would be a completely new employment of the term for which there is no other evidence.
105 Cedrenus I 496–497; Malalas 317–318. Cf. Dodgeon/Lieu, *Frontier* 146–147.
106 Cf. MacAdam, *Nemara* 9–13, and the map in idem, *Studies* 63.
107 It deserves to be emphasized that the language of the Namāra inscription is not the *ʕArabiyya* (against, for example, Bellamy, *Reading* 33; cf. Macdonald, *Reflections* 50: 'more or less "pure" Old Arabic'). Apart from several deviating lexemes and morphemes (the conjunction ʕKDY, poss. pronominal suffix -HN for masc. plur.), two of the most characteristic grammatical features of this language are absent, namely the case system and the *tanwīn*. The nominal declension in an-Namāra is reminiscent of that found in the Nabataean inscriptions, which is different from that of the *ʕArabiyya*. The distinction between these dialects is blurred by the fact that the *ʕArabiyya* in the Qurʔān and most later forms of that language is written with an orthography which reflects a language much closer to that of an-Namāra than to the *ʕArabiyya* itself. When this orthography was to be used for writing the *ʕArabiyya*, it soon had to be adjusted by a system of diacritical signs marking vowels and other features. Why this orthography was used for writing the 'Arabic Qurʔān' remains a mystery. There is, however, no reason to assume that the inscription was read with an *ʕArabiyya* pronunciation.
108 Cf. Kropp, *Vassal* 68.
109 The text has been published many times. The basic text has been that by Dussaud, who was the first publisher and who revised his interpretations of it several times. His final word on the text was given in *Arabes* in 1907. Dussaud's text was used by everyone until Bellamy's new study in 1985, which was based on a study of the physical text. Since then, Kropp, Zwettler and Calvet/Robin have also submitted the stone in the Louvre to renewed scrutiny. It should be observed that we should render the twenty-first letter of the Aramaic alphabet by *š* and not *s* as is usually done with this text. The *š* in the forms of Arabic known to us is pronounced as [s] but we do not know for sure how it was pronounced by the writer of this inscription and his readers. There are, in fact, reasons to assume that the change *š* to *s* is late in Arabic. It is wise to make a transliteration, not a transcription of a supposed pronunciation.
110 Peiser, *Inschrift*.
111 Bellamy, *Reading*.
112 Cf. the thorough discussion by Zwettler, *Imra'alqays* 15–18.
113 Cf. pp. 442, 468. The Hatran connection has been observed by Zwettler, *Imra'alqays* 10–13. Kropp, *Vassal* 67, rejects the two readings.
114 Cf. Fraenkel, *Fremdwörter* 62; Monneret de Villard, *Tāǧ*; Lidzbarski, *Ephemeris* 35, 375–376; Caskel, *Inschrift* 376–377. According to *Lisān* (s.v. TWǦ), the *ʕarab* call the *ʕamāʔim at-tāǧ*. The *ʕimāma* is a band that is tied around the head of chiefs as a sign of their rank. It seems, however, that this terminology is later than our inscription and that the *tāǧ* was originally different from the *ʕimāma* and the *ʔiklīl*. The former is said to be made of gold and jewels and is identified with an *ʔiklīl*. Dussaud (*Inscription* 414) claims that the Nabataean kings wore a *tāǧ*. On the coins they wear a diadem which is an *ʕimāma* rather than a tiara; see the plates in Meshorer, *Coins*. In later Arabic texts the *tāǧ* and the *ʕimāma* are identified as a sign for both the Iranian kings and their vassals in Arabia, cf. Athamina, *Kings*, and Chaumont, *Chute* 219.
115 The latter is suggested by Calvet/Robin, *Catalogue* no. 205 p. 267, seeing it as a causative of ŠDD. The G-stem can mean 'tighten', 'tie', 'bind', which would suit well. The causative

does not, however, have this meaning, or the meaning 'raffermir' given by Calvet/Robin. Kropp (*Re*, *Vassal*) reads it as a *maṣdar*: 'quello col cerchio del diadema', the one with the circle of the diadem. Beeston's suggestion (*Nemara*) to read it *ʔasrā*, 'to make travel by night', which gives the meaning 'who sent his troops to Thaǧ', seems not to have caught on. Bellamy (*Reading* 36) reads D̲W ʔŠD W-MD̲ḤG 'his title of honour was master of Asad and Madhḥiǧ', rejected by Kropp and Calvet/Robin.

116 So Kropp, *Vassal* 72–73.

117 The exception is Bellamy (*Reading*) who reads BHRW instead of NZRW, 'arriving at': 'and he subdued the Asadīs and they were overwhelmed (*buhirū*) together with their kings'. His reading is not accepted by the later commentators Kropp and Calvet/Robin. The argumentation is, in fact, weakly based on the claim that Nizār and Maʕadd, mentioned further down, are identical. They are never identified in the genealogies, Maʕadd being the father of Nizār, which is not identification but rather political ranking. Historically they were definitely two separate groups.

118 Lidzbarski, *Ephemeris* 35; Caskel, *Inschrift* 371; Bellamy, *Reading* 36–37; Shahid, *Observations* 35–37, Müller, *Gesandtschaft* 160–161.

119 Calvet/Robin, *Catalogue* 267.

120 Hartmann, *Inschrift* 578–579, rejected by Lidzbarski, *Ephemeris* 376, but repeated by Beeston, *Nemara* 4.

121 Peiser, *Inschrift* 279. Exceptions are Hartmann (*Inschrift* 578), who did not accept Peiser's emendation, and Altheim/Stiehl, *Araber* II 313, who associate it with ḤGG (*ḥaǧǧ* etc.).

122 Transformed to *ʕArabiyya*: *wa-ǧāʔa bi-zaǧāʕin fī ḥabǧi Naǧrāna, madīnati Šammarin, maliki Maʕaddin*. This is basically Dussaud's reading (*Inscription, Arabes* 35), which was followed by Peiser and Rodinson.

123 Hartmann, *Inschrift* 579–581, reading *wa-ǧāʔa yuzǧī ḥibǧa Naǧrāna*.

124 Lidzbarski, *Ephemeris* 35–36.

125 Altheim/Stiehl, *Araber* II 313–314. They read: *wa-ǧāʔa bāziǧan fī* . . . and: *mulki Maʕadd*.

126 Caskel, *Inschrift* 374, reading *wa-ǧāʕa bi-zuǧāʔin fī Ẓarbān*.

127 Shahid, *Observations*, gives two suggestions of *bi-zaǧāʔin*: 'with ease' or 'with tax-collecting' (?). No reference is given for the last meaning.

128 Beeston, *Nemara*, taking WGʔ as one verb *waǧaʔa* and reading ḤBG as ḪLG [ḫuluǧ], 'irrigated land'.

129 Bellamy, *Reading*, reading BZGY as YZGY = *yazuǧǧuhu* and ḤBG as RTG [rutūǧ] 'gates'.

130 Kropp, *Re*; idem, *Vassall*, reading BZGY as *bi-zuǧǧihi*, 'with spearheads'.

131 Calvet/Robin, *Catalogue* 267–268, thus following Bellamy and Kropp.

132 From the reading ʕKDY Dussaud suggested 'ever' (*Inscription*) or 'until' (*Arabes*). Hartmann read *ʕal ka-ḏā* 'in this way'. Halévy compared it with Aramaic ʕD KDWN, 'until'. Beeston followed by Kropp and Calvet/Robin read ʕDKDY as 'until', which is found in the inscription from Qaryat al-Fāw. Caskel and Rodinson understood it as a postponed emphatic particle, developing an idea from Lidzbarski and Dussaud (*Inscription, Ephemeris* 35). Bellamy suggested *ʕan kā-ḏā*, 'hereafter'.

133 Suggested by Beeston (*Nemara*) and supported by Kropp (*Vassal* 71) against Bellamy (*Reading* 39), who has no good arguments against Beeston's reading.

134 The reading *bi-zuǧǧihi*, 'with his spears', is attractive from the context but does not fit the spelling of the text. The first signs in line II have been read BZGY, YZGY, BZGH, BZGʔ and YZGH, the main crux being the last sign. It is definitely not a Y, although the arguments for an H are not totally convincing either: the text contains several final Hs which do not have much resemblance to this sign.

135 Dussaud, *Inscription*.

136 Dussaud, *Arabes* 35; Caskel, *Inschrift*.

137 Rodinson, *Kitābāt* 143.

138 Halévy, *Inscription*, reads WKL not as a verb, 'hand over' etc., but as a noun, *wukalāʔ*, 'entrusted ones, delegates'. He also reads PRŠW not as a noun meaning 'cavalry' but as a verb *farrasa*, 'form cavalry'.

139 Peiser, *Inschrift* 280. Peiser read BYN BYNH [bayna baynihi] 'between his separation'

instead of BYN BNYH [bayyana banīhi]. The reading is grammatically awkward.

140 Hartmann, *Inschrift*.

141 Lidzbarski, *Ephemeris* 35–36.

142 Altheim/Stiehl, *Araber* II 314–316, reading for BYN BYʕ [bāyaʕa] and F-RSW as a finite verb [fa-rasaw].

143 Shahid, *Observations* 39–40. He reads BYN as a preposition here in an adverbial complement: 'the tribes being [divided] between his sons'.

144 Beeston, *Nemara*, reading NYL [nāyala] instead of BYN. This form seems not to be documented. ŠʕWB is interpreted according to an assumed Sabaean meaning which, however, is based upon the interpretation of ʕRB as nomads, i.e. non-sedentary, which is obviously erroneous.

145 Bellamy, *Reading*, taking Dussaud's BYN as NBL [nabala] and BNYH as BNH [bi-nabah(in)]. The verb WKL is taken as denominative (from *wakīl*) and PRŠW is read as a verb: *fa-rasaw*, 'and they became steadfast, anchored'.

146 Kropp, *Re*; idem, *Vassall*. He returns to the reading of BNYH as 'his sons'. The main innovation in this reading is the interpretation of LRWM, by everybody else read [li-Rūm], 'to Rome', as LDWM [li-dawām], 'forever'. Otherwise Bellamy's readings are more or less followed.

147 Robin/Calvet, *Catalogue* 268–269. BYN is here read NḤL, 'give'. WKL is taken as *wukalāʔ* and the last L is read twice as a definite article to PRŠW.

148 Cf. Bellamy, *Reading* 42–43; Kropp, *Vassal* 76–77.

149 Cf. MacAdam, *Nemara* 10 (Poidebard's map); Rodinson, *Kitābāt*; Kropp, *Vassal* 65.

150 MacAdam, *Nemara* 13.

151 For weighty arguments against the reading 'Persians', see Lidzbarski, *Ephemeris* 377–378. The idea of kingship as 'eternal' is known from the Old Testament and Mesopotamia but seems alien to the world of ancient Arabia.

152 Bellamy, *Reading* 46, sees everything after ʕMRW as belonging to the account of the king's activities. Against is Kropp, *Vassal* 72. This latter understanding is also supported by the disposition of the text (see below): line I: introduction; lines II–IV: *res gestae*; line V: conclusion. The parallel to Iranian royal inscriptions has also been pointed out by Zwettler, *Imra'alqays* 5.

153 Against Altheim/Stiehl, *Araber* II 314; Shahid, *Byzantium* I 35; and Kropp, *Vassal* 73. These scholars see the title as a result of the *res gestae*, since they believe that NZR, ʔŠD etc. are names of Arab tribes, i.e. tribes considered Arabs at this time. Zwettler has clearly seen the problem (*Imra'alqays* 7–8) but gives an explanation different from the one suggested here.

154 The parallel between the title of the kings in Hatra and that of Imruʔ al-Qays was observed by Altheim/Stiehl (*Araber* II 269; cf. also Zwettler, *Imra'alqays* 10–11) but their interpretation of it cannot be upheld.

155 Caskel (*Inschrift* 372; cf. idem, *Gamhara* II 379) locates Maʕadd in central Arabia. In the Arabic tradition, Maʕadd is associated with western Arabia/Tihāma and tribes around Mekka. He is the brother of ʕAkk, which is a tribe in the Tihāma; cf. Bräu, *Maʕadd*; Watt, *Maʕadd*; Shahid, *Byzantium* 1 43; idem, *Byzantium* 3 151, 160–166, whose location of the Maadenoi mentioned by Procopius (*History* 1.19.14) must be correct. The original location of Nizār is problematic; cf. Levi della Vida, *Nizār*. Caskel (*Gamhara* II 448) locates a Nizār in north-eastern Arabia, but it is doubtful if this is the one mentioned at Namāra. Even though Nizār is mentioned rather late in Islamic sources, it tends to be associated with tribes from western Arabia (Thaqīf, Ǧurhum, Bağīla, Khathʕam), which could indicate that it was remembered that there had been an ancient tribe with that name in western Arabia.

156 Ryckmans (*Royaumes* 92) doubted that ŠMR in the Namāra inscription is identical with the great Shammar Yuharʕish. Instead he supposed a local ruler in Nağrān. Kropp (*Vassal* 74) assumes that ŠMR was somewhere in northern Arabia. Beeston rejected the identification of Nağrān in South Arabia because it is called MDYNT [madīna] which, according to him, must mean a capital, which Nağrān was not. According to Beeston, a *madīna* must be either founded or the headquarters of a specific individual. This is, however, doubtful.

Neither David nor Muhammed founded their respective *madīnas*. They changed the place's status when moving there. The meaning of *madīna* is probably 'a place where a certain person has special jurisdiction'. This holds for the best-known *madīnas* in the Middle East, Jerusalem and Yathrib, which stood under the jurisdiction of David and Muhammed respectively. Nağrān could very well have been something of that kind. von Wissmann (*Zur Geschichte* 191, 405–408) pointed out that according to the inscription Ja 658 ŠMR YHRʕŠ fought against troops belonging to NŠDʔL 'in the wādī ʕTWD in the north'. The name of the enemy is said only to occur in Safaitic inscriptions, which may indicate that the events referred to in the text could have something to do with the events in the Namāra inscription.

157 For ʔLʔSD in the inscription Ja 635 dated to *c*. AD 220, see von Wissmann, *Zur Geschichte* 185, 397. He locates them north of the Bisha oasis, identifying them with the ʔAsad tribe known from the Arabo-Islamic historical tradition. The name ʔSD is also mentioned in the inscription 'Sharafaddin p. 44', which deals with expeditions by ŠMR YHRʕŠ III against MLK son of K . . . king of ʔLʔSD. W. Müller points out that ʔL read as the definite article never occurs in Arabic texts together with ʔAsad, but reads well with al-ʔAzd, the tribe in ʕAsīr and Oman whose name is derived from the root ʔSD (W. Müller, *Gesandtschaft* 159–160). According to Müller, ʔLʔSD in this text must be ʔAzd ʕUmān, which is difficult to see. From Ja 635 it is clear that ʔLʔSD is to be located at the Thumāl oasis in Wādī Bīsha and it is most likely that the expedition in Sharfaddin p. 44 also went there. This oasis was in Islamic times inhabited by descendants of Naṣr b. al-ʔAzd (al-Hamdānī, *Ṣifa* 211). It is probable that ʔLʔSD in the two Sabaean texts is identical with or a forefather to ʔAzd ʕAsīr and also is the one mentioned in the Namāra inscription.

158 Shahid (*Byzantium* 1 72–73) suggests that the Latin inscription found in Baraqish in Yemen originates from the expedition of Imru al-Qays. There seems to be some foundation for this assumption in the palaeography of the text. It should, however, be pointed out that there is no indication that (a) Roman soldiers took part in the expedition or (b) Imru al-Qays reached Baraqish/Yathull. In this light, the suggestion appears less likely; cf. Marek, *Inschrift*, and Bowersock, *Arabia* 148–153.

159 He is usually identified with the Lakhmid; cf. Chaumont, *États* 94–95. From this originates the idea of his defection from the Iranians (for which there is no documentation) or scepticism of his Lakhmid identity (de Blois, *King Amarō*). For the solution of this problem, see pp. 483 ff. Cf. also Skjaervö, *Inscription* 126.

160 See the text published by Tardieu, *L'Arrivée* 16.

161 Cf. pp. 416 f.

162 There are some indications in the Arabo-Islamic tradition that Hatra was considered Roman at the time of ʕAmr b. ʕAdī; see pp. 479 f.

163 Halévy (*Inscription* 59) already considered the Arabs of MRʔ LQYŠ a small tribe not including the others mentioned in the inscription. Shahid (*Byzantium* 1 34–35) claims that the Arabs of MRʔ LQYŠ were not bedouin but both settlers and nomads.

164 Cf. p. 467.

165 Ryckmans, *Texte*, ll. 5–11; for the translation, see Müller, *Gesandtschaft* 162–163. Caskel's dating to the second century AD (*Inschrift* 367) cannot be maintained.

166 See e.g. Kitchen, *Documentation* 14–16.

167 Cf. Munro-Hay, *Aksum* 73–74; Kitchen, *Documentation* 40.

168 In the inscriptions in Axum the title is found both in the (pseudo-) Sabaean texts DAE IV:I.2 (Aksoum 195), Axoum 185bis I.3: MLK MLKN and in the Geez texts DAE VIII.4 (Aksoum 186), DAE IX.3 (Aksoum 187), DAE XI.4 (Aksoum 189): *negusa nagast* (*Recueil* 239–267). The title occurs only in Ezana's texts.

169 Cf. Weidemann, *Könige* 8–18; Kitchen, *Documentation* 14–15.

170 Cf. the inscriptions Ja 668, 669, 670, 671.

171 aṭ-Ṭabarī, *Tārīkh* I:836-840; cf. also *Commentaria* II:14. Nöldeke's doubts about the historicity of the events (*Geschichte* 57 n. 1) were rejected by Altheim and Stiehl (*Araber* II 346), rightly as it seems; cf. Shahid, *Byzantium* 1 62–63. The inscription Ry 535 does not, however, have anything to do with these events. It is about events around AD 250.

172 Cf. Potts, *Gulf* II 139–140.

173 Peiser, *Inschrift*.
174 Most commentators have seen MRʔ LQYŠ as balancing between the two world powers; cf. Dussaud, *Arabes* 37–38; Bowersock, *Bilingual*. The defection theory was launched by Altheim/Stiehl (*Araber* II 318 ff.) and is followed by Caskel and Shahid.
175 Both Caskel (*Inschrift* 377–379) and Shahid (*Byzantium* 31–47) have tried to sketch a possible scenario based on the defection theory. The result is, however, more fiction than history.
176 See Rothstein, *Dynastie* 52 ff. Most of the other variants of the list are built upon the versions given by these two writers or on Ibn al-Kalbī directly (Rothstein, *Dynastie* 55 f.). There is, however, one variant, the 'South Arabian' (Rothstein, *Dynastie* 59–60), which is quite different and which has some importance for the history of al-Ḥīra; see pp. 478 f.
177 Rothstein, *Dynastie* 50 f.
178 An indication that parts 1(a) and 3 in aṭ-Ṭabarī are copied from one continuous text is the overlapping between the quotations in, for example, I:672 and 745.
179 See pp. 184–189.
180 aṭ-Ṭabarī, *Tārīkh* I:671.5–672.8; 744.19–745.3.
181 See pp. 176–180.
182 aṭ-Ṭabarī, *Tārīkh* I:672.
183 Cf. p. 380.
184 The account of the actual journey and settlement in Iraq is found only in al-Bakrī (*Muʕǧam* 35).
185 aṭ-Ṭabarī, *Tārīkh* I:745–746.
186 aṭ-Ṭabarī, *Tārīkh* I:746:8–747:2.
187 aṭ-Ṭabarī, *Tārīkh* I:822. This episode is inserted in a wrong context in aṭ-Ṭabarī, but is clearly connected with the Ḥīra complex.
188 The word *ʔabraš*, 'spotted', is said to be a euphemism for *ʔabraṣ*, 'leprous'. The wording in aṭ-Ṭabarī introducing his kingship shows a clear break, and the emigration story of the Fahmids should probably be inserted just before it.
189 Yāqūt, *Muʕǧam* 2.457, 3.867, 4.137.
190 Yāqūt, *Muʕǧam* 1005–06; aṭ-Ṭabarī, *Tārīkh* I:749:14–752:1.
191 aṭ-Ṭabarī, *Tārīkh* I:752:2–756:7.
192 Iṣfahānī, *ʔAghānī* 13:80–81; al-Bakrī, *Muʕǧam* 14–17.
193 aṭ-Ṭabarī, *Tārīkh* I:745 sqq., 834, 845–846.
194 For the Ǧadhīma-ʕAmr story, cf. Piotrovskij, *Versija* 174–175. For the lost books of Ibn al-Kalbī, see Ibn an-Nadīm, *Fihrist* I 95–98. Nöldeke (*Geschichte* xxvii f.) assumed that only the Ḥīra book was used, but it is most likely that the background to aṭ-Ṭabarī's text is more complicated.
195 There are three main variants preserved by Mufaḍḍal aḍ-Ḍabbī, Ibn al-Kalbī and Ibn Ḥabīb respectively. The differences between them are insignificant and they go back to a common source. In Dīnawarī, *ʔAkhbār* 56, there is a fragment of a quite different version; see Piotrovskij, loc. cit.
196 Piotrovskij, *Versija* 173–174.
197 Cf. Piotrovskij, *Versija* 181. Unlike part 1(a), part 1(b) has a clear Islamic flavour (the prophethood of Maʕadd, the appearance of the Burāq etc.). On the other hand, it contains the references to Nebuchadnezzar's campaign against Qedar. It is possible that both parts ultimately come from the same source, namely the Nebuchadnezzar novel.
198 aṭ-Ṭabarī, *Tārīkh* I:770.
199 Nöldeke, *Geschichte* 85.
200 See, pp. 184–189.
201 For the dispersion theme in early Islamic historiography, see Caskel, *Gamhara* I 41–44.
202 See Caskel, *Gamhara* I 32, II 73–76, 470; Kister, *Ḳuḍāʕa* 315. The name itself probably belongs to Ḥiǧāz and may have been an old designation of a tribal cultic association around a sanctuary there, encompassing tribes like ʕUdhra, Balī, Ǧuhayna and Bal-Qayn.
203 In al-Bakrī, Mālik b. Zuhayr is made a Fahmid, but this genealogy is absent in the *Kitāb al-ʔaghānī*.

204 al-Bakrī, *Muʕǧam* s.v. ʔUbāgh.
205 Yāqūt, *Muʕǧam* III:756. There is a possibility that it should be sought further upstream of the Euphrates. One of the most famous battles of pre-Islamic Arabia was the *yawm* Ḥalīma, in which the king of al-Ḥīra, Mundhir 'III', was killed by the king of Ghassān, al-Ḥārith b. Ǧabala. This battle is well documented in contemporary non-Arabic sources and took place in the year AD 554 not far from Khalkis, i.e. Qinnasrīn, south of Aleppo; see Shahid, *Byzantium* 3:1 240 ff.
206 al-Bakrī, *Muʕǧam* s.v. Ḥulwān.
207 Cf. Ibn Qutayba, *Maʕārif* 107–108; Dīnawarī, *ʔAkhbār* 55. Ḥamza tried to find his way out of the genealogical mess by dividing both Mālik and Ǧadhīma into two (*Tārīkh* 74–75). Kawar's (i.e. Shahid) claim that tradition makes him an ʔAzdī (*Djadhīma*) is a simplification.
208 Ibn Qutayba, *Maʕārif* 646.
209 The genealogy tries to sit on two chairs at the same time by making Ǧadhīma both an ʔAzdī and a Fahmid. The result is that the latter become ʔAzdīs as well.
210 Ǧadhīma is married to Lamīs, Mālik's sister. The *kāhina* az-Zarqāʔ is also a sister of Mālik and it is likely that the two female names stand for the same person.We also notice that Ǧadhīma is a *kāhin* and a *nabī*.
211 Yaʕqūbī, *Tārīkh* 237; aṭ-Ṭabarī, *Tārīkh* I:746.
212 The earliest version may be the one in Ibn Hishām's *Kitāb at-tīǧān* 273–303.
213 See pp. 483 f.
214 aṭ-Ṭabarī, *Tārīkh* I:746:5–8.
215 aṭ-Ṭabarī, *Tārīkh* I:748:10–749:14.
216 Cf. Dīnawarī, *ʔAkhbār* 55.
217 The Lakhmids, according to al-Hamdānī (*Ṣifa* 129–131), are settled in and around Palestine, where they are especially allied with the tribe of Ǧudhām (cf. Lammens/Shahid, *Lakhm*, for other references).
218 Rothstein, *Dynastie* 41.
219 According to al-Bakrī, ʔIyād was connected with a place called as-Samāwa between Mosul and Syria in the land of the tribe of Kalb (*Muʕǧam* s.vv. Samāwa and ʔIyād).
220 Also Ibn al-Kalbī also knew about an emigration of the Quḍāʕa element of Tanūkh to the Quḍāʕa in Syria. According to Ibn al-Kalbī this took place during the reign of Ardashir, Shahpur's predecessor. His variant shows that the Fahmids were actually known as residing in Syria like the other parts of Quḍāʕa.
221 aṭ-Ṭabarī, *Tārīkh* I:827. This tale contains the famous episode about the love between Ḍayzan's daughter Naḍīra and Shāpur.
222 Dīnawarī, *ʔAkhbār* 56.
223 Ibn Qutayba, *Maʕārif* 645.
224 Cf. p. 438.
225 Gazdar *et al.*, *Excavations* text A:16 (p. 88), D:16 (p. 90). In Dedan/Liḥyān a name TNḪ is documented (Sima, *Inschriften* 87). Its meaning for the history of the tribe is still uncertain.
226 Gazdar *et al.*, *Excavations* 83; Potts, *Gulf* II 30–48.
227 Cf. Kindermann, *Tanūkh* 245.
228 Ḍayzan is a name that probably belongs to a later age. A Taizanes is mentioned in Malalas as a local ruler on the middle Euphrates at the beginning of the sixth century AD and it is not unlikely that he has been mixed up with the names and events of the third century; cf. Nöldeke, *Geschichte* 35 n. 1.
229 Littmann, *Bilinguen* 386–390. Cf. Sartre, *Tropheus*; Caskel, *Inschrift* 369–370.
230 Cf. Sartre, *Tropheus*. Both the Greek and the Nabataean are poor in this text and the author was obviously not good at either of them.
231 Thus Tardieu, *L'Arrivée* 16.
232 Cf. Rothstein, *Dynastie* 44.
233 aṭ-Ṭabarī, *Tārīkh* I:745:4–746:4.
234 Cf. aṭ-Ṭabarī, *Tārīkh* I:827–830, Nöldeke, *Geschichte* 33–40.
235 Most buildings in ʔUmm Ǧimāl are dated to late antiquity; cf. Wenning, *Nabatäer* 48–51.

236 al-Masʕūdī, *Murūǧ* III:274–275.
237 Ḥamza, *Tārīkh* 76; cf. Rothstein, *Dynastie* 45.
238 Rothstein (*Dynastie* 63) dates the transition between them to AD 413–420.
239 Dīnawarī, *ʔAkhbār* 56; cf. Rothstein, *Dynastie* 59–60.
240 Cf. Ḥamza, *Tārīkh* 77–79. For a survey see Rothstein, *Dynastie* 54–60.
241 aṭ-Ṭabarī, *Tārīkh* I:850.
242 Ibn Qutayba, *Maʕārif* 646.
243 Rothstein (*Dynastie* 64–65) suggested an interregnum in al-Ḥīra. His confidence in the number of regnal years given by the Arabo-Islamic historians as well as in the whole tradition was probably far too great.
244 Kitchen, *Documentation* 9.
245 This solves the problem of how the Lakhmid ʕAmr could operate on the Roman side of the Syrian desert: Lakhm has nothing to do with al-Ḥīra. The association between them and the royal house of Naṣr there is made much later. This makes it very likely that Tardieu's emendation of Amarō's patronymic in the Coptic chronicle to Lahim = Lakhm (*L'Arrivée* 16) is correct. de Blois' scepticism (*King Amarō*) is thus unfounded.
246 The geographical note that Tanūkh lived between al-Ḥīra and al-ʔAnbār 'and that which is above' is quite precise and is found in all versions of the story, and it may preserve a concrete memory.
247 The names of the kings of al-Ḥīra in the fourth century found in Ibn al-Kalbī (aṭ-Ṭabarī, *Tārīkh* I:845, 850) are suspicious: ʕAmr and Imruʔ al-Qays could be recycled names. It is, however, not impossible that there was indeed an Imruʔ al-Qays in al-Ḥīra some time before Nuʕmān. This could have facilitated the incorporation of the Arab king Imruʔ al-Qays in the dynastic line by the later propagandists.
248 That Imruʔ al Qays was indeed a Syrian king is perhaps also indicated by the tradition that his mother was from Ghassān (Rothstein, *Dynastie* 64) which probably means Syria.
249 Clement, *Paedagogus* 3.25.1.
250 The use of the Xenophontic term *arábioi* reflects Clement's classicistic ambitions. The mention of the wolves probably alludes to Aelian's *De natura animalium*; cf. the note to the passage in the edition of Marrou *et al.*
251 For Origen in Arabia, see Kretschmar, *Origenes*.
252 Origenes, *Selecta* 120:31.
253 Origenes, *Philocalia* 23.16.28–29.
254 Origenes, *Frgm. in Psalmos* ad loc.
255 According to Origen, Gerasa and Yabboq belong to Arabia (Origenes, *Selecta* 128.25; idem, *Commentarium in Euangelio Iohannis* 6:41:209:1).
256 Strabo 16.2.34.
257 Origenes, *Frgm. in Psalmos* ad loc.
258 'The tents of Qedar' = *mašknêhōn d-ʕarbāyē*.
259 Wolski-Conus, *Geographie* 214–216.
260 Cf. Scholten, *Hippolytos* 508–509 who supposes an older diamerismus as well as Ptolemy's map as two of the main sources.
261 The Madiēnoí could be derived from Matiēnē, adjacent to the south-western border of Atropatēnē (Dillemann, *Mésopotamie* 279–280).
262 Ptolemy 5.15.20: Sakkaía east of Batanaía; see p. 437.
263 Cf. 2 Chronicles 22.1 and pp. 150, 298.
264 *Book* 56:17 (603). Eusebius, *Praeparatio* 6.10.41: 'Recently, the Romans, having conquered Arabía . . .'
265 *Book* 58:2 (606).
266 For the Semitic name of Petra, RQM, see Josephus, *Antiquities* 4.4.7; 7:1. Cf. Numbers 31:8 LXX; Eusebius, *Onomasticon* 144:7; Starcky, *Pétra*.
267 Cf. pp. 447 f.
268 *Book* 50.11; cf. Eusebius, *Praeparatio* 6.10.31, who has *taiēnoí* and *sarakēnoí*.
269 See pp. 403 ff.
270 For these, see Jacoby, *Fragmente* 3C:1 338–344 (nos. 674–676).

271 Jacoby, *Fragmente* 3C:1 339–344 (no. 675).
272 Stemplinger, *Studien* 630.
273 Domaszewski, *Bedeutung* 239–242.
274 Aly, *Strabon* 179–180; cf. Strabo 16.4.20.
275 Aly's dating was followed by Pirenne, *Royaume* 128–129.
276 von Wissmann, *Uranios*.
277 West, *Uranius*. West's article is a digest of an unpublished thesis on Uranius.
278 Aly, *Strabon* 190.
279 Cf. Dillemann, *Haute-Mésopotamie* 77, for this identification.
280 Dillemann, loc. cit.
281 Dillemann compares it with the *Málioi skēnîtai* mentioned by Strabo (16.1.27) which, however, is more uncertain.
282 In Strabo 16.2.34 the Idumaeans are said to be Nabataeans. This must be the reason for their transformation into Arabs.
283 This holds, for example, for the identification of Motho with 'Mawtah' (Starcky, *Pétra* 904; Negev, *Nabateans* 529). No place with such a name is known today; 85 kilometres from Petra is al-Muʔta (suggested by Abel, *Géographie* II 187–188) but it means something else and there is no reason think that it is Uranius' Motho. The same holds for the name Imtān.
284 Edgar, *Catalogue* I:59004: *toîs parà Rabbēlou*. Cf. Negev, *Nabateans* 530. This king is usually called Rabbel II, based on the assumption that the king mentioned by Uranius was a 'Nabatean' king reigning in Petra.
285 For a possible interpretation of this event, see p. 327.
286 Caskel, *ʕAkk*; idem, *Ǧamhara* II 150.
287 The Glaucus fragments are collected in Müller, *Fragmente* IV 409.
288 Stephanus 200.
289 Ibid. 688.
290 Ibid. 48.
291 Ibid. 237.
292 Ibid. 118.
293 Ibid. 276, 491.
294 Negla (471), Gadda (193), Bassinoí (160), Eualēnoí (283), Athraphēnoí (142).
295 Herodianus 253.6; Stephanus 276.
296 Gignoux, *L'organisation* 14; cf. Potts, *Gulf* II 232. This text was compiled in the abbasid period. The 'lake of the *tāzīgān*' is interpreted as the Persian Gulf.
297 The text is written in the early abbasid period but contains older material. For the relation between these terms, especially the possible derivation of the Persian word from *ṭayyāyē*, see Sundermann, *Attestation*.
298 A place called ḤYRTʔ is also mentioned in a Palmyrene inscription dated to the year AD 132; see Littmann, *Inscriptions* 70; cf. Caskel, *Nemara* [6]. Since it occurs in the inscription together with ʕNʔ, it has been identified with al-Ḥīra downstream from al-ʕĀna on the Euphrates. That would mean that al-Ḥīra already existed at the beginning of the second century AD and would make possible an earlier dating of Glaucus. The identification of both sites with al-Ḥīra and al-ʔĀna respectively is, however, uncertain (see Littmann's commentary, ad loc.). *ḥerṯā* means '(movable) camp' and its use as a name for a town is secondary. According to the Arabo-Islamic historical tradition al-Ḥīra was founded by Tanūkh at the very end of the Parthian period, which could be a distortion of the historical truth that it was established by Shāpur, the enemy of Tanūkh (see pp. 475 f). According to the same tradition there was another older site in Mesopotamia named *ḥīr*, which could be the one mentioned in the inscription.
299 Nyberg, *Westgrenze* 318.
300 See p. 484.

17

THE DISAPPEARING ARABS

The emergence of the Taieni and the Saraceni

The most important information in Hippolytus, the *Book of the Laws of Countries* and the Uranius fragments is the appearance of the Saracens and the *taēnoí* together with the Arabs. All three authors make a clear distinction between the three groups. This is a trustworthy piece of information since it comes from literature which is more or less independent of the theoretical approach of the Hellenistic geographers.

The appearance of these two groups in the three texts shows that they were well known in the first half of the third century AD. There is no certain mention of the *taēnoī*/Taieni earlier than that. The earliest documentation of a *taiēnós* which can be combined with a certain date is the mention of a certain Pamphilus who participated in the consilium in Nicaea in AD 325. and was a *taēnós*.[1] It has long since been agreed that this term is identical with the name of the tribe known from later Arabic literature as Ṭayyiʔ, who had their habitat on the south-western and western shores of the northern Nafūd with Khaybar as the most important oasis.[2] Their traditional habitat, however, is said to have been larger, and it had probably been reduced in the east by their neighbours, ʔAsad. They also had close ties with the rulers in al-Ḥīra as late as the end of the sixth century.[3] If they once dominated both the south and the north of the Nafūd, this could be reflected in the quoted passages: they would be south of the Saracens in northern Ḥiǧāz and south of Adiabene, which is actually what Hippolytus says. It is clear that they must have had quite a dominating position in the eastern parts of the Syrian desert, reaching the Euphrates valley, since their name became the normal term for the tribes in the desert among the Syriac-speaking communities.[4] It should be noticed that unlike the Saracens, the *taiēnoí* are designated by a real tribal name which has survived into the Arabo-Islamic tradition and which is still in use today. There is no evidence that the Saracens themselves ever called themselves by this name or that there were ever people imagining themselves as members of a Saracen 'nation'. On the other hand, the *ṭayyāyē* of the Syrians was also probably a comprehensive term including those who considered themselves belonging to the Ṭayyiʔ but also others. The term reflects the importance of the tribe with that name in a certain period, which left the name as a legacy used also for their successors as well as less important contemporaries.

As far as Saracens are concerned, their first appearance in a datable context is more difficult to judge since their occurrence in the quoted texts may well be derived from other sources now lost. In Ptolemy, Sarakēnē is a region in the northern Sinai peninsula, probably named after the town Saraka there, but there is also a people called *sarakēnoí* in north-western Arabia.[5] Ptolemy's *Geography* is the earliest text where we find the

Saracens mentioned as a group of people.[6] Stephanus of Byzantium says that Saraka is a region beyond the *nabataîoi* whose inhabitants are the *sarakēnoí*, a note that may go back to Ptolemy via Uranius.[7] It is, however, somewhat unclear if it is Saracens in the Sinai or in the northern Ḥiǧāz who are intended. More precise is the remark by Ptolemy that the *sarakēnoí* live as neighbours of the *thamoudēnoí*. It occurs in his list of peoples of the hinterland of the Red Sea coast, starting with the *skēnîtai*.[8] According to Uranius, the *thamoudēnoí* were neighbours of the Nabataeans in Petra. We can locate the *Thamudeni* at the end of the second century with a high degree of certainty. The federation of Thamūd (*éthnos thamoudēnōn*, ŠRKT TMWDW) is mentioned in an inscription on a temple dedicated to the emperor Marcus Aurelius in AD 168 at Rawwāfa in the northern Ḥiǧāz.[9] The *Thamudeni* were most likely in some way allied to the Romans, probably as border guards.[10]

Saracens may figure in the report in the *Historia Augusta* about the revolt of supporters of Septimius Severus against the pretender Pescennius Niger in AD 193.[11] These are called *Saraceni*. The revolt is mentioned in connection with a similar revolt in Egypt and is followed by a report about complaints from people in Palestine. It could thus refer to Saracens on the Sinai peninsula. The Saracens there appear in Eusebius' *Ecclesiastical History* which quotes a letter from Dionysius, bishop of Alexandria AD 248–265, where he tells about the persecution under the emperor Decius (249–251). One of his colleagues, Chaeramon, takes refuge on the eastern shore of the Nile:

> Many were, in the Arabian mountain, enslaved by the barbarian *sarakēnoí*.[12]

The Saracens mentioned here could very well be those connected with Ptolemy's Saraka in the northern parts of the Sinai peninsula. This is the earliest reference to Saracens which can be dated more precisely. Both this reference and the one in the *Historia Augusta* (if it is genuine) deal with Saracens between Egypt and Palestine. In Hippolytus, the *Book of Laws* and Uranius it seems, however, that it is the Saracens in the northern Ḥiǧāz who are intended.

In AD 291, the rhetor Mamertinus delivered a speech before the Caesar Maximinianus, lauding his deeds:

> I omit your devastation of Sarmatia and the subjugation of the *Saraceni* with the bonds of captivity.[13]

The geographical location of these Saracens is uncertain. There is, however, definite proof that at the end of the third century AD there were people in north-western Arabia called Saracens, who had a certain military ability. Remarkable is that they appear as militant enemies of the Roman empire.

Eusebius of Caesarea

In the sources from the fourth century, we can observe how Saracens and Arabs are mentioned side by side by the authors. The earliest comprehensive source for the status of both Arabs and Saracens in that century is the church historian Eusebius from Caesarea (–339/340). In his extensive writings, he touches upon matters related to them on several occasions. We have earlier seen how he used older Jewish sources in his introductions to the Gospels, the *Praeparatio* and the *Demonstratio*. He also wrote a book on history, the *Chronicon*, and compiled a dictionary on Biblical geography, the *Onomasticon*, as well as commentaries to Psalms and Isaiah, in which he continued the tradition from Origen. It can be assumed that he has also gathered material from earlier periods in the *Onomasticon* and the Bible commentaries, although there are no references to sources. Eusebius thus represents the views of the Christian church in the third and at the beginning of the fourth centuries on the geography and ethnology of the Middle East. We will adduce a choice of the most important passages before evaluating the testimony in the light of what we have learnt from earlier sources.

According to the *Chronicon*:

> Abraham from the maid Agar gave birth to Ismahel from whom the lineage (*genus*) of the Ismaelites [came] who later were called *Agareni* and lately *Saraceni.*[14]

The *Chronicon* is an early work of Eusebius written before AD 303.[15] It is preserved only in a Latin translation. Arabs are mentioned twice in connection with the activities of Trajan and Septimius Severus in the Ǧazīra. Both references are to the Arabs there.[16] The impression is thus so far that in this work Eusebius (or his sources) saw the Arabs as dwelling in the Ǧazīra, the Saracens possibly between Egypt and Palestine.

The *Onomasticon* was compiled later, perhaps in the 320s AD after the *Praeparatio* and the *Demonstratio*.[17] Eusebius had obviously learnt a lot of facts from the old sources he had perused for these two works, and he is probably drawing on them for the *Onomasticon* as well as for the Bible commentaries:

> Kedar [in Hez. 27:21] is the region of the *sarakēnoí*; and Kedar was the son of Ismael son of Abraham.[18]

> Gerara: it lies close to two deserts: that lying along Egypt which the people who go to the Red Sea have in front of them, and that of Kades extending to the desert of the *sarakēnoí*.[19]

> Madiam: it lies beyond Arabia to the south in the desert of the *sarakēnoí* eastwards from the Red Sea.[20]

> Pharan: It is a town opposite (*hypèr*) Arabia, lying close to the *sarakēnoí* in the desert, in which the sons of Israel dwelt when they left Sinai. It lies even beyond Arabia towards the south and Aila is at a distance of three days . . . dwelt Ismael from whom the Ismaelites are.[21]

> Choreb: a mountain of God in the region of Madiam. It lies close to Mount Sinai opposite Arabia in the desert.[22]

According to the most plausible interpretation of this geography, the Saracens dwell east of the Gulf of ʕAqaba. Arabia is obviously the Roman province. The Saracens do not dwell there but they are considered descendants of Ismael through Kedar. These Saracens seem to be more or less identical with those mentioned by Ptolemy. In these passages there is no explicit identification of Arabs and Saracens. There is thus a transference of the Ishmaelitic descent from Arabs to Saracens.

The commentary to Isaiah belongs to the last works of Eusebius, written in the 330s.[23] It is a direct continuation of the genre initiated in Christian literature by Origen and many facts are taken from him:

> [to 11:11: the Lord shall save . . . those of the people left by the Assyrians, by Egypt, Babylonia, Ethiopia, the Elamites, the rising sun, and from Arabia (LXX)]. At that time (the time of the Assyrians) there were toparchs and ethnarchs and various kings like the ones of Egypt, of Arabia, of Tyre, of Sidon and other peoples.[24]

> [to 11:14: and they shall stretch out their hands to Edom, Moab, and the sons of Ammon]. The Moabites, the Idoumaeans and the Ammonites were Arabic peoples (*arabikà éthnē*) around Judaea in the time of the prophet . . . these peoples belonged to those who in old times inhabited Arabia; then they were demon-fearing, now they are subject/submissive to the teaching of Christ.[25]

The first of these passages looks like an enumeration of peoples along the Mediterranean shore from the south to the north. In that case it reflects quite early conditions, such as those described by Herodotus. It is likely that Eusebius here follows an old source dependent on Herodotus.

The second passage is more in tune with the period when the Arabo-Nabataeans held sway over the southern parts of Transjordan and, perhaps, the Negev. The Arabic peoples have their identity by living in Arabia, i.e. Nabataea or the Province.

> [to 13:20: [Babylon] shall not be inhabited to everlasting time; *árabes* shall not pass through it]. By this is meant, as far as I know, those by us called *sarakēnoí*, who, having business in old times, used to pitch their tents in Babylon. Thus deserted by neighbours visiting it as from a remote people, the shepherds from the *árabes* do not pasture any of their creatures therein because of its complete desertedness. It should be known that the peoples of the *sarakēnoí* and those Assyrians who extend to it (Babylon) and those shepherding the innermost desert are called *árabes* because they have the region of the *árabes* as neighbour. Because of this Symmachus says: no *áraps* shall pitch his tent. There is also another [region] called *Arabía eudaímōn* close to the region of the Persians so that also from this it is possible to explain the wording concerning them (the *árabes*).[26]

This passage is difficult, but Eusebius seems here to identify the Arabs who used to visit Babylon with the Saracens (or vice versa). The reason for the identification is given in the latter part. Saracens and Assyrians are called Arabs because their region borders on that of the Arabs. We know that there was an Arabia bordering on Assyria and that the land of the Saracens in the northern Sinai also bordered on Arabia. If 'they' refers to the Assyrians and the Saracens, it is clear that the two have received the designation without originally being Arabs.[27] The impression is that Eusebius has a problem with the Biblical text: it talks about Arabs in Babylon where, according to his knowledge, there were no Arabs. Now as far as we have seen from the other passages, and, in fact, according to the whole evidence from the preceding two centuries, there should be no Saracens either. The explanation is that Saracens might be called Arabs because of their closeness to Arabia. The transfer of the Saracens to Babylonia sounds like a strange emergency solution and is somewhat out of place. Even though we have here for the first time an identification of Saracens with Arabs, the passage, as a matter of fact, presupposes that they were originally two different groups.

> [to 15:7, 9 (LXX): I shall conduct *árabes* to the canyon and they shall take it . . . the water of Remmon shall be filled with blood; for I shall conduct *árabes* to Remmon]. This was fulfilled according to history (?) by the attack by Assyrians and Babylonians and by the *árabes* taking power over that region in later times, in which God threatens that He will conduct *árabes* over them; perhaps meaning the neighbouring *árabes* or the *sarakēnoí*, the more interior of them to which the Word says that He will deliver Moab.[28]

The passage in Isaiah deals with the destruction of Moab. The allusion to an Arab attack on Moab may well reflect the Arab presence in Transjordan from Ptolemy II until Alexander Jannaeus. We have no information on any other attack by people called Arabs in that area. Problematic is the relation between *árabes* and *sarakēnoí*. The most reasonable move is to take Arabs here as a more general term: Arabs consist of the neighbours of Moab and the Saracens, who are more distant.

> [to 42:11 (LXX): Rejoice, o desert and its villages, encampments and those who inhabit Kedar; may the inhabitants of Petra rejoice; they shout from the mountain tops]. Kedar possesses [the land] beyond Arabia at the farthest desert which the lineage of the *sarakēnoí* is said to have . . . the truth of these words is known through the fulfilment through deed (?) when churches to Christ are built both in the very town of Petra and in their region as well as in the deserts of the *sarakēnoí*.[29]

Here, the land of the Saracens is probably the one found in the *Onomasticon*, i.e. south of Nabataea/Provincia Arabia. Arabs are, consequently, not mentioned.

There is, in the evidence from Eusebius, as it seems, a clear difference between the *Onomasticon* and the Isaiah commentary. In the latter we find plain traces of an identification of Saracens as Arabs. The commentary was written in the 330s whereas the *Onomasticon* belongs to the first years of the century. The commentary is to a large extent founded upon the commentary to Isaiah by Origen. Until the text of Origen one day turns up we do not know exactly what it said. The only certain thing we can infer is that in Eusebius' day Saracens could be seen as a kind of Arabs, although it was still known that they were two different groups. The argument was that they lived close to regions called Arabia. According to Eusebius, Assyrians could also be called Arabs for the same reason. Eusebius gives a hint that this could be due to the fact that they lived in a larger Arabia, namely *Arabia Felix*. The fact remains that the mention of Arabs in connection with Babylonia in the Biblical text was a problem which had to be solved by commentators.

Basil the Great

It is of some interest to see how another Bible commentator in the same century handled Isaiah 15. In the commentary to Isaiah by Basil the Great (–379) it is said:

> [no Arab shall pass through]. It shall become a desert so that no shepherd will find an enclosure in it or *árabes*, those who dwell in the desert. These who take everything as booty, searching through cities and villages, they do not enter because of the despair of any inhabitants in it or finding anything for life.[30]

> [I will conduct upon them Arabs]. The former ones [i.e. the Moabites who will repent] will be saved through their weeping. The other ones who have an unrepenting heart [will be saved] through the conducted stroke of the *árabes*. The *árabes* are the westerners, or perhaps the forces similar to the darkness are said to be *árabes*.[31]

It is a very traditional picture of Arabs that is offered here. They are depicted as violent robbers. There is no talk about Saracens. Instead, in the second passage, the Arabs are abolished by an etymology: Arab is analysed as derived from *ġrb/ʕrb*, 'go down', 'set' (of the sun). The interpreter obviously knew some Hebrew or Aramaic, which may indicate that it ultimately comes from Origen.[32] Compared to these passages, those in Eusebius make a more 'modern' impression, trying to take in the new development where the Saracens are coming on stage.

Epiphanius

Epiphanius in the fourth century wrote a survey called *Panarion*, 'the Breadbasket', of the heresies flourishing in the fourth century. Already in Origen's time the Arabian province had been a home for Christian movements condemned by the emerging orthodoxy. When describing the career of the Manichaean Scythianus it is said:

> He originated from the *Sarakēnía* and was raised in the borderland of Palestine, that is, in Arabia.[33]

It is likely that the Arabia which is the border of Palestine is in fact those parts of the Arabian province which were severed from the old province and established as Palaestina II and III. It is clear that to Epiphanius, Arabia is the province as it was before the changes in Diocletian's time.[34] The land of the Saracens would according to this passage be somewhere outside Arabia, although bordering on it. We thus find the same view of Arabia and Saracens as in Eusebius.

Epiphanius has a most interesting notice about Arabia. He describes a heretic cult of a goddess giving birth to a divinity called *Aiōn*:

> This [divinity] is also born in the same way in the town of Petra (it is the main city in Arabia, which is the Edom written in the Scripture) in the idolatry practised there. They praise the virgin in Arabic speech (*arabikēi dialéktōi*) and call her in Arabic (*arabistí*) Khaamou, which means 'young woman', i.e. virgin, and also the one born by her called Dousares, meaning 'the lord's first-born'. This is also done in the town of Elousa and in the same night as in Petra and in Alexandria.[35]

We may notice the identification between Arabia and Biblical Edom which, as we have seen, is also found in earlier Christian commentaries to the Psalms. The most interesting element in this passage is of course the description of a pagan cult practised within the borders of the former Arabo-Nabataean kingdom in the fourth century AD. The implications of this description and its relevance for the identification of the Arabs will be discussed in the final part of this book.[36]

Other testimonies from the early fourth century

The expansion of the term 'Saracens' to warriors in the east, of which we have seen traces in Eusebius' writings, becomes apparent in the middle of the century. In a book on geography, the *Expositio totius mundi* written shortly after AD 347, it is said after the Persians have been treated:

> But close to them [the Persians] lives the people of the *Saraceni*, setting their hope to earn their living by bow and plundering. They are similar to the Persians as to illoyalty and treason, not keeping treaties of war nor of other business. And women are said to rule among them.[37]

The closeness of the Saracens to the Persians is similar to what we saw in Eusebius' Isaiah commentary. It is obvious that by the middle of the fourth century, the term 'Saracen' was no longer used only for people dwelling in the areas south of traditional Arabia, i.e. the Sinai and the northern Ḥiğāz. It could now also be applied to similar groups in Mesopotamia.

A different relationship between Rome and these groups in the Syrian desert and northern Arabia is found in the list of civil and military employees of the Roman state, called *Notitia dignitatum*. This text was compiled perhaps in the fifth century, but it is agreed that it reflects the structure of the army in a much earlier period, probably the reign of Diocletian.[38] In the list of the units of the eastern border troops, the *limitanei*, we find six which are of immediate interest. First there are three units of Arabs:

> Ala tertium Arabum in limes Aegypti
> Cohors quinquagenaria Arabum in Mesopotamia
> Cohors tertia felix Arabum in Arabia.[39]

We then have three units of Saracens:

> Equites Saraceni in Phoenicia
> Equites Saraceni indigenae in Phoenicia
> Equites Saraceni Thamudeni in limes Aegypti.[40]

There is no doubt about the differentiation between Arabs and Saracens in this list, which represents official terminology at the beginning of the fourth century. The Arabs are stationed where we expect to find them: Egypt, Mesopotamia and the Province. They are employed as infantry (*cohortes*) or light cavalry (*alae*). The Saracens, on the other hand, serve as heavy cavalry (*equites*). One of the Saracen units has the epithet *Thamudeni*. The same epithet is used for another unit, the *Equites Thamudeni Illyriciani*, stationed in Palestine.[41] The closeness between Saracens and *Thamudeni* is confirmed. The impression is that the name *Saraceni* in this text is beginning to be used as a more comprehensive term for a special kind of *equites* drafted among the inhabitants of the Syrian desert. Among the Saracens are distinguished *indigenae* and

Thamudeni. The former could be people recruited from Phoenicia itself. We are reminded of the Ituraeans who served in the Roman army earlier. The latter are people from Thamūd who are now included under the term 'Saracens'.[42] The *Saraceni* without an epithet may be the original ones mentioned by Ptolemy.

The picture of the Saracens emerging from these sources is that of unruly, violent desert people. They appear as enemies of Rome during the third century. Their defeat through Maximinianus could imply a change in their relations to Rome. We find them in the *Notitia dignitatum* as allies incorporated in the Roman army. At least parts of them were, from now on, tools of the emperors in keeping order along the eastern borders.

The fourth century: Arabs in the waning

After the rise of the political system created by Diocletian, the whole Arabian peninsula was drawn into world politics in a more definite way than before. Reborn Rome and renovated Iran stood against each other, ready to continue the struggle that had been going on since the days of Crassus.[43] That struggle was to continue until the eve of the Islamic conquest. Several devastating attacks were made from both sides but no substantial results were achieved. The border remained more or less stable except for the Roman loss of eastern Assyria including Nisibis in 363. The stalemate was in some ways due to weaponry: the Roman army was still dominated by infantry, which was vulnerable to the Iranian cavalry on the open plains of Syria and Mesopotamia. The latter, however, encountered insurmountable difficulties when it reached the mountainous regions of Syria and Anatolia, where the infantry had the upper hand. A definite breakthrough was made by the Iranians in AD 610 when they overran Syria and took Egypt. Iranian hegemony was impending in the eastern Mediterranean. The Romans managed to roll back the offensive, but by then the tipping of the balance by the Iranians had set new forces on the move from Arabia which, in an amazingly short time, were to tear down the wall that had divided the Middle East since the days of the last Seleucids.

The continuous attempts by the two superpowers to achieve a breakthrough on their common front-line had important consequences for the inhabitants on both sides. We see the emergence of allied troops recruited from the inhabitants of the deserts as professional soldiers on both sides, called Saracens by the Romans. These troops were to play an important role in the wars as allies, but also as warriors on their own. They turned out to be unreliable allies, and both Romans and Iranians on several occasions suffered from military enterprises undertaken by the Saracens without consulting their employers.

From the end of the third century there was clearly an increased Roman pressure on the Red Sea region. The possible campaign into South Arabia by Imruʔ al-Qays, which can be assumed from the testimony of the Namāra inscription, is a sign of this interest on the part of the Romans at the time of the tetrarchies. Rome's ambitions in the Red Sea may to some extent have been due to economic interests, but the decisive factor was strategy. Rome as well as Iran was governed by autocratic generals, and military thinking dominated foreign policy. The main point for Rome was how to circumvent the now dangerous Iranian enemy. Control, or at least influence, in Arabia was a major means for achieving what we today perhaps would call first-strike capability.

There is a long tradition in scholarship of seeing the policy of ancient empires as steered by the demand for trade routes.[44] This picture probably needs to be revised. In late antiquity Rome and Iran were both military powers and, unlike,

> for example, the merchant class in seventeenth- and eighteenth-century England, the merchant class had no political institutions through which it could exert influence on foreign policy. The ruling generals were landowners, interested in the money they could wring from peasants and merchants; they had no desire to let the interests of these groups govern their policy. This does not exclude the fact that the interests of merchants and generals could sometimes coincide. But we should beware of assuming that, for example, the increased Roman pressure against the Red Sea area after AD 300 was something similar to, let us say, the expansion of the British in India in the eighteenth and nineteenth centuries. Thus, the frankincense trade, which is often adduced as a major factor in Roman *Ostpolitik*, was declining in the fourth century because the conquering church abolished the pagan cults and was hostile to the use of frankincense in its own. In fact, we do not hear anything about the use of frankincense in a Christian cult before the funeral ceremonies of Justinian in AD 563. The market must thus have been strongly reduced during these centuries. It is most unlikely that the quest for this aromatic would have decided Roman politics in the Red Sea and Arabia before the end of the sixth century.[45]

With the new scenario is also connected the emergence of a new power at the Red Sea, namely the kingdom in Axum. The Axumite kings had taken part in the warfare between the South Arabian kingdoms in the third century and had clearly shown their imperial ambitions. Unfortunately, there is a blank spot in the sources for the crucial decades around the year AD 300, both in the north and in the south. This is the reign of Shammar Yuharʕish in Ḥimyar. Then, in the 340s, we have inscriptions from king Ezana in Axum where he uses the titulature of the Himyarite kings, showing that the king in Axum claimed the Himyarite throne as well. It is remarkable that the Himyarite title stands first in Ezana's inscriptions. The nature of this connection escapes us but the following pattern is discernible: Shammar – anti-Roman, seeking relations with Iran; Imruʔ al-Qays – agent for Rome waging war against Shammar; Shammar's successors – appearing as Roman emperors; the Iranian king Shāpur II – campaigning in Arabia against Himyarite and Roman influence. The explanation could be that there was an empire around AD 300 encompassing both sides of the Red Sea which was seen as a threat to Roman influence. It was divided in two, perhaps through Roman intervention in which Imruʔ al-Qays played an important role.

The Roman ambitions in the Red Sea and South Arabia, as well as in Ethiopia, are visible in the reign of Constantine's son, Constantius (337–359). We hear of two missionary expeditions, one initiated by the Arian emperor himself, who sent Theophilus as a missionary to the king of Ḥimyar and afterwards to his colleague in Axum.[46] The latter also received another expedition, led by Frumentius, sponsored by the patriarch of Alexandria, Athanasius, a staunch Nicene opponent of the emperor. King Ezana in Axum appears as a Christian ruler in some of his inscriptions, which presumably shows his predilection for Alexandrine Christianity. As far as we know, both these expeditions were failures, but they show very clearly the Roman ambitions.[47]

The time of Julian the Apostate: the testimony of Ammian Marcellinus

The new role of the Saracens emerges in full daylight in the testimonies about the campaign undertaken by the emperor Julian in the year 363. The main source for this dramatic event is the *Res Gestae* written by Ammian Marcellinus at the end of the century.[48] To this are added a letter from Julian himself and an oration by Libanius delivered some ten years after the emperor's death.

The letter from Julian to his friend Libanius was written in Hierapolis in Syria during the initial phase of the campaign. He says:

> I sent an embassy to the *sarakēnoí* and suggested that they should come if they wished.[49]

According to Ammian, 'the kinglets of the tribes of the Saraceni' came to Julian at Callinicus (present-day Raqqa) on the Euphrates, offering their service and a golden crown.[50] With the Saracens as auxiliary troops he marched on to Circesium (at present-day Deir ez-Zōr).[51] Further down the river, Anatha (present day al-ʕĀna) was conquered, and the Saracens took some skirmishers as prisoners.[52] After the Roman conquest of Ozogardana (near present-day Ḥabbāniyya) they were attacked by the Iranians together with the *Saraceni Assanitae* under a phylarch, 'Malechus with the name Posodaces'.[53] Ctesiphon was captured but the Romans had to retreat along the Tigris. They were harassed by the Saracens, and in a battle the emperor was killed.[54] At a town called Dura the Roman Saracens revolted, but the army was saved by the light cavalry.[55] When crossing the Tigris the Roman army was attacked by Iranians on one side and Saracens on the other side of the river and suffered serious losses.[56]

In Ammian's description, the Saracens play a considerable role as both Roman and Iranian allies. We hear about walls being built at a place called Charcha by the Tigris to hinder the Saracens from making raids into Assyria.[57] The Roman army was here still on Iranian territory, which shows that the locals had problems with the Saracens. But Shāpur II had managed to use them in the war with Rome, just as the Roman emperor did.

A tradition says that Julian was killed by a Saracen, although Ammian has nothing of this. The other contemporary, Libanius, says in a speech delivered to the emperor Theodosius that he was killed by a *taiēnós*.[58] Later, however, he talks about 'one from the Persian line of the so-called *sarakēnoí*' who shouted *malkhán* to him. The Saracen reappears in later sources.[59]

We find that in the reports about the military operations in 363 no Arabs appear. On both sides, Saracens constitute an important military asset for the imperial armies. Ammian himself took part in the campaign, and even if the book was written many years later it probably reflects actual conditions. From now on, 'Saracens' becomes the regular term for the desert-dwellers in the Middle East.

Excursus: Ammian's description of Arabia and Arabs and its background

Ammian makes some remarks on Arabia and Arabs in the preserved parts of his work in which he uses the older terminology and does not mention Saracens. These accounts are derived from earlier sources not representative of conditions in his time.[60] The information in Ammian about the inhabitants of Arabia is not very precise but contains some interesting details. There are two excurses on Arabia preserved. One follows the description of Persis:

> To these [the Persians], on the south-eastern part, border the *Arabes beati*, so called because they are rich in the fruits of the field as well as cattle, dates and many varieties of perfumes. A great part of their lands borders to the right on the Red Sea and to the left on the Persian Sea, and the people know how to avail themselves of all the advantages of both elements. On that coast there are both many anchorages and numerous safe harbours, trading cities in an uninterrupted line, uncommonly splendid and richly adorned residences of their kings, natural hot springs of remarkable curative powers, a conspicuous abundance of brooks and rivers, and a very salubrious climate, so that to men of good judgement they evidently lack nothing for supreme happiness. And while they have an abundance of towns inland and on the coast as well as fruitful plains and valleys, yet the choicest cities are Geapolis, Nascos, Baraba and also Nagar, Maephe, Taphra and Dioscuris. Moreover, in both seas and near to the shore there are many islands which it is not worth while to enumerate. The most prominent among them is Turgana on which there is said to be a great temple to Serapis.[61]

Behind this somewhat fanciful description we recognize the original concept of *Arabía eudaímōn*. Apart from the enumerated cities, many of which can be identified with known sites in Yemen, the description clearly contains echoes from Euhemerus and Iambulus.[62] The geographical location clearly points to the Gulf area. Turgana is probably the island called Organa in Arrian's *Indica*, identical with the island of Qeshm in the Hormuz straits.[63] The passage is followed by a description of Carmania in southern Iran, which is said to be situated 'beyond the frontier of this people'. It is very likely that the Red Sea should be taken in its original meaning as the Indian Ocean. The list of cities is undoubtedly taken from Ptolemy's *Geography*.[64] They are included because of the close commercial relationship between the Persian Gulf and the frankincense lands. The rest of the description gives the impression of reflecting conditions earlier than the second century AD, and parallels with Arrian's account of Arabia along the southern shore of the Gulf are discernible.

The other remark on Arabia is the following:

> Adjacent to this area [i.e. Palestine] is Arabia, which on the other side is contiguous with the *Nabataei*, [a land] of rich variety of wares and filled with strong castles and fortresses, which the watchful care of the old ones erected in suitable and defendable defiles for repelling the outbursts of neighbouring peoples. Among some villages, this area also has great cities: Bostra, Gerasa and Philadelphia, very well defended by the solidness of walls. This region, being given the name of province and attributed a governor, the emperor Traianus compelled to obey our laws after having frequently crushed the arrogance of its inhabitants, when he waged glorious war with Media and the Parthians.[65]

This description of the old Arabo-Nabataean kingdom looks more contemporary than the one of *Arabia Felix*.[66] Remarkable is the absence of Petra. The singling out of three cities as well built and defended seems to reflect the building activities there in the second century.[67] The Nabataeans seem to be separated from the province. If this is not a misunderstanding by Ammian and/or his source, the existence of Nabataeans south of

Provincia Arabia is quite possible.[68] We have already pointed out that there are traces of Nabataeans far south in the Ḥiǧāz.

Ammian thus describes two distinct Arabias, one on the Persian Gulf and one east and south of Palestine. The descriptions are compilations from different sources, of which Ptolemy is identifiable for the Gulf area. But even for that area he is not the only one. There are clear reminiscences of earlier, Hellenistic works. The descriptions of the two Arabias are part of a larger complex of geographical notes in Ammian's work. Its framework was a catalogue of Roman provinces compiled *c.* AD 340–350.[69] Apart from this work there are traces of other sources. The description of the eastern provinces is dependent on Ptolemy.[70] It has been supposed that Ammian's coastal descriptions owe much to Timagenes' *Circumnavigation of the Entire Sea*, written in the time of Augustus. Timagenes seems to have been strongly dependent upon the early Hellenistic geographical tradition, like Eratosthenes and his predecessors.[71]

The division of Arabia in two, one western and one eastern, is also found in Stephanus' *Ethnica*:

> *Arabía* . . . There are two: one perfume-producing between the Persian and the Arabic seas, another more western, bordering in the west to Egypt and in the north to Syria.[72]

The picture is quite similar to the one found in earlier Latin geographers such as Pomponius Mela and the work of Agrippa. There thus seems to be an interference in Ammian from the non-Eratosthenian view of Arabia as two areas, one on the shore of the Persian Gulf and one on the Sinai peninsula, a testimony of the erudition of this last great historian of antiquity.

Ammian explicitly identifies the Arabs treated in his geographical commentaries with the Saracens, whom he had met during the campaigns in the east:

> [Egypt looks] to the *Scenitae Arabes,* whom we now call the *Saraceni.*[73]

> On the west [Persia] touches . . . the Red Sea and the *Scenitae Arabes,* whom men of later ages called *Saraceni.*[74]

Here we encounter terminology going back to Eratosthenes. Ammianus further says that he has given a description of the *Saraceni* when telling the story of the reign of Marcus Aurelius.[75] Unfortunately, this part of his work is lost. But there is a remarkable excursus on the Saracens in the preserved part of his book:

> Among those tribes (*gentes*) whose original dwelling extends from the Assyrians to the cataracts of the Nile and the frontiers of the Blemmyae, all are warriors of equal rank, half nude, clad in dyed cloaks as far as the loins, ranging widely with the help of swift horses and slender camels in time of peace or of disorder. No man ever grasps a plough-handle or cultivates a tree, none seeks a living by tilling the soil, but they rove continually over wide and extensive tracts without a home, without fixed abodes or laws; they cannot endure the same sky nor does the sun of a single district ever content them.
>
> Their life is always on the move, and they have mercenary wives, hired

> under a temporary contract. But in order that there may be some resemblance of matrimony, the future wife, by way of dowry, offers her husband a spear and a tent, with the right to leave him after a stipulated time, if she so chooses: and it is unbelievable with what ardour both sexes give themselves up to passion.
>
> Moreover, they wander so widely as long as they live, that a woman marries in one place, gives birth in another, and rears her children far away, without being allowed any opportunity for rest.
>
> They all feed upon game and an abundance of milk, which is their main sustenance, on a variety of plants, as well as on such birds as they are able to take by fowling, and I have seen many of them who were wholly unacquainted with grain and wine.[76]

Ammian's account contains a few elements which might reflect a more developed stage of life in Arabia than heard of before: the use of horses together with camels is similar to the classic warfare of the tribes known in the *ʔayyām al-ʕarab* literature, as well as among the Islamic conquerors. The extensive and aimless wanderings of the Saracens partly reflect the later warrior-caste and partly the view of the Hellenistic urban bourgeois. On the other hand, there are several other features which give a more archaic impression: the rejection of wine and agriculture, and the sparse clothing. The temporary marriage resembles the *mutʕa* marriage well known from later Arabo-Islamic tradition and could be a 'progressive' feature.[77] The statement that all were warriors may be an exaggeration. Ammian has probably inserted elements from his own time when composing an ethnographic excursus with some elements taken from earlier works.[78]

The description of the Saracens thus contains some 'modern' features revealing that changes had taken place in Arabia before the time of Ammian. From the preserved fragments we can get an idea of the character of the lost passage on the Saracens. The *Historia Augusta* mentions how Avidius Cassius 'made it well' in Arabia in AD 164–165.[79] This conflict was described by Quadratus, whose *Parthica* may have been edited before AD 210. We would venture the guess that this work contained an ethnographic account about Avidius' adversaries in the operations in the Ǧazīra in the 160s and that this description is reflected by Ammian.

It seems therefore that Ammian's account of the Saracens to some extent represents conditions in the fourth century AD, when the ancient Arabs were on the wane in the Syrian desert and the new Saracen culture was rising, which was to culminate in the classical culture of the bedouin, documented in the poems and stories of the earliest Arabic literature.[80] The teetotallers would then be a survival of the ancient Arab custom described by Hieronymus. These ancient Arabs also appear in Ammian's two descriptions of Arabia.

Arabs and Saracens from the end of the fourth century

The campaign of Julian is the earliest occasion when we hear about an alliance between the Saracens and the empires which can be dated.[81] It is very clear that they were difficult and unreliable allies for both sides. The Saracens burst into Roman history anew around AD 371, when the border regions of Palestine and Arabia were devastated by Saracens led by a queen, Mavia.[82] These Saracens are said to have been *hypóspondoi* to the Romans, which shows that they were allied, probably as *foederati*.[83] Their warrior-like qualities are evident and the parallel to those employed by Julian is obvious. During the siege of Constantinople by the Goths in 378, the emperor Valens called in reinforcements of Saracens, who made a spectacular performance in the combats.[84]

The Saracens had, around the turn of the century 300–400, emerged as an important ally to the Romans along the eastern border. We hear about another group led by a chief Zōkomos who, like Mavia's Saracens, turned Christian in the reign of Arcadius (394–408).[85] In the *Vita* of Pelagia, written in Syria or Palestine in the fifth century, it is told about thirty Saracens who were baptized by the bishop of Antioch at the same time.[86] Not all Saracens turned Christian, though. We hear about them killing monks in the Judaean desert at the same time.[87] According to Hieronymus, there were *Arabes* and *Agareni* in the vicinity of Jerusalem who in his days were called *Saraceni*.[88] He thus follows the terminology known from Ammian.

Arabs seem to disappear completely from the sources written around 400 and later. When Egeria made her pilgrimage to the Holy Land around that year, she went from Egypt through the eastern delta into the Sinai desert. The eastern delta and the lands to the plains of Moab she calls Arabia but the inhabitants are the Saracens, who are said to make incursions into Egypt.[89] As we have seen, the *Notitia dignitatum*, which was probably written down in this period, distinguishes between Arabs and Saracens, and it is likely that there were still units in the Roman army which carried the Arab name at the turn of the century. When Synesius of Cyrene sailed to his homeland from Egypt in the year AD 404, he says that with them on the ship were many *arábioi* from the cavalry regiment.[90] These may in fact have been troopers from the *Ala tertia Arabum*, which was stationed in the delta.

Synesius may be the last instance when we hear about Arabs as a distinct group from the Graeco-Roman viewpoint. Arabs, as far as the term occurs, is a general designation for the inhabitants of the province of Arabia or sometimes the original Arabia, i.e. the former Nabataean realm. It is said that the bodies of the monks killed by the Saracens in the Judaean desert were venerated *a universa plebe Arabum*.[91] These Arabs must then be the by now largely Christian inhabitants of the province and adjacent areas and not the Saracens.[92] The formula '*Arabes* [*scenitae*] whom we now call Saracens' is found in later literature as a reminiscence.[93] Also the other occurrences of the term must be considered literary survivals, not reflecting contemporary realities.[94]

In Syriac literature, too, the Arabs gradually disappear, being replaced by the term *ṭayyāyē*.[95] The area between Nisibis and the Tigris continued, however, to carry the name *Bēt ʕarbāyē*, 'the house of the Arabs', or simply *ʕārāb*, through the centuries.[96] For a long time, however, the two terms *ʕarbāyē* and *ṭayyāyē* were used together, like Arabs and Saracens in Roman sources.

From the middle of the fifth century we have a testimony from Isaac of Antioch, who in poems lamented the destruction of the town Bêth Ḥûr on the border east of Nisibis, which is said to have been pagan. This event probably took place in the war between Rome and Iran during AD 440–442.[97] The pagan inhabitants of Bêth Ḥûr are said to have been attacked by their co-religionists, the pagan Arabs:

> And as the Persians have taken her [Bêth Ḥûr] prisoner//who worship the sun like her,
> Lo, even the ʕRBYʔ took her prisoner//who honour Balti together with her;
> the Persians did not let her escape//who prostrate to the sun together with her;
> and the ʕRBYʔ did not pardon her//who sacrificed with her to ʕUzzay.[98]

> Lo, captivity and exile//with theft of all possessions;
> the ʕRBYʔ upset the land//the part of which they had taken;
> the whole oecumene is perturbed//for they have transcended the hedge of peace,
> the murderous wild-asses, the sons of Hagar//and they have destroyed the good ones with the bad ones.[99]
>
> We give praise to Assyria//when an angel has taken revenge on its blasphemers.
> We give woe to the land//whose sins ʕRBYʔ punish,
> and to our unhappy land//which legions of the sons of Hagar [destroy].[100]

The Biblical reminiscence is clear when the Arabs are called 'wild-asses, sons of Hagar'.[101] Did the poet use the actual terminology of his day, or does Isaac's terminology constitute a poetic, ancient-sounding term for the *ṭayyāyē* of his day, a memory of those days when the inhabitants of the plains between Hatra and Nisibis were called Hagarene Arabs? From another passage in his poems it seems that the Arabs attacking Bêth Ḥûr may also be called *ṭayyāyē*. Isaac's Arabs thus belong to poetry, not to reality.[102]

In sources dealing with the war between Rome and Iran in AD 502–506, our term appears once more. In the chronicle written by Joshua the Stylite shortly after the events, there is a report about a swarm of locusts occurring in the year 502:

> They ate and destroyed the whole ʕRB and the whole of Bêth Reshayna [= present-day Raʔs al-ʕAyn], Bêth Talyā [between Mardin and Edessa] and Bêth Urhāyē [the area of the Edessenians].[103]

The impression is that Joshua uses *ʕārāb* as a geographical term. A slightly more complex picture is given in the ecclesiastical history of Zacharias Rhetor from Mytilene, dealing with the same event. The relevant passages were written in the end of the sixth century:[104]

> And the locusts came to the ʕRB of Bêth Nahrîn [= the Ǧazīra] and a famine arose in the ninth year about which Jacob the Teacher wrote a book, in the eleventh year of the reign of Anastasius. And many ʕRBYʔ died.[105]

Later it is told about the foundation of the fortress Dara around AD 507–508:

> And they asked him [namely the Roman emperor Anastasius] that a town be built in protection at the mountain-side as a refuge for the army and for its rest and for preparing the weapons and for the guarding of the land of the ʕRBYʔ against the robbers of the Persians and the *ṭayyāyē*.[106]

To these passages should be contrasted another one where it it is said that during the Samaritan uprising in AD 528. the Romans sent troops against them, consisting of Roman forces and '*ṭayyāyē* who are in Arabia' (ʔRBYʔ). Arabia is here definitely the province.[107] There is no doubt that Zacharias here translates *sarakēnoí* with *ṭayyāyē*.[108] It is thus evident that Zacharias called the inhabitants of the area east of Nisibis *ʕarbāyē* and those along the Roman border and within the empire *ṭayyāyē*.

Isaac, Joshua and Zacharias preserve an ancient term for the inhabitants of a certain area in the Ğazīra. In the fifth century it is evident that *ṭayyāyē* had become the standard Syriac term for different kinds of desert-dweller, the equivalent to the Saracens of the Romans. In a source contemporary with Isaac, namely the *Vita* of Simeon the Stylite, *ṭayyāyē* are mentioned on several occasions as seeking the saint and becoming Christians.[109] According to the chronicle of Joshua the Stylite both sides employed *ṭayyāyē* as allies.[110] *ʕarbāyē* are not heard of. This usage corresponds to the term *sarakēnoí* in the Roman sources for the same period. The famous letter G by Simeon of Bêth Arsham describing the martyrs in Nağrān tells how the author met *ṭayyāyē* in the camp of al-Mundhir III by al-Ḥīra.[111] Arabs have also disappeared as contemporaries from the Syriac texts. But in the fifth century the Nestorian metropolite in Nisibis was still called 'Metropolite of the land of ʕRB' [ʕārāb].[112]

The *ṭayyāʕē*

In the Amoraitic parts of the Talmudic literature we find one more designation which is usually translated as Arabs, namely masculine sg. *ṭayyāʕā*, feminine sg. *ṭayyāʕṯā*, masculine pl. *ṭayyāʕē*.[113] A handful of these instances are found in sayings attributed to Palestinian *amoraim* of the second to the fifth generation, i.e. roughly AD 230–340. Most of them, however, belong to the Babylonian Amoraitic tradition. These *ṭayyāʕē* have swords or spears;[114] they ride on camels;[115] they have goats;[116] they often travel together with Jews;[117] they can make gifts to a synagogue;[118] they make *tefillîn* and *mezûzôt* and sell them to Jews;[119] their rams are slaughtered by a Jew;[120] they dress in black;[121] they are consulted about medical treatment;[122] they know the meaning of some Biblical words which the Rabbis do not know.[123] There is a story attributed to Rabba bar Ḥana, a third-generation Babylonian *amora* (i.e. in the end of the third century AD), where a *ṭayyāʕā* shows him the place in the desert where Qoraḥ and his followers were devoured by the earth or where the bones of the Israelites who died during the forty years are found.[124]

The picture is thus contradictory. The *ṭayyāʕē* are engaged in several different activities, peaceful and warlike, and they are found in Babylonia as well as in the Sinai desert. It is unlikely that the translation 'Arab' is correct. The word *ṭayyāʕā* is probably derived from a root *ṭwʕ*, 'to roam', 'to wander about'. It is thus a designation for all kinds of movable people including peaceful merchants, trigger-happy Saracens/*ṭayyāyē* and shepherding nomads. In Syriac literature we have an incident from the time of the emperor Leo I (474–91) when it is said that 'Persian *ṭūʕāyē*' from the south make raids across the border into Roman territory and that the Romans and their allies, the *ṭayyāyē*, demand compensation from the Iranian king. The negotiations take place in Nisibis between the Iranian *marzuban* of Bêth Aramāyē and the king of the Roman *ṭayyāyē*. The *ṭūʕāyē* attack them while negotiating.[125] It is thus clear that there is no immediate identity between the *ṭayyāyē* and the *ṭūʕāyē*.

Arabs versus *Saraceni* and *ṭayyāyē*

Ammian uses the term *Saraceni* when describing actualities. The ethnographic expositions, where he speaks about Arabs, are, at a closer look, based on his reading of earlier writers. Ammian's terminology shows that the term 'Arabs' was disappearing and only lived on as a traditional ornament which could give a modern text a more antique flavour. From his time onwards, every instance of the word 'Arab' in Greek,

Latin and, as it seems, also in Syriac texts can be explained as an antiquated, stylistic variant which, when it occurs, is always a reminiscence of ancient terminology. After Ammian, the normal term for the warriors in the desert was Saracens. In the middle of the fifth century, similarly, *ṭayyāyē* was the normal Syriac term.[126]

The question to be posed is, of course, why the terminology was changed. Is there an unproblematic identity between the ancient Arabs, whom we have followed from the days of Shalmaneser III, and the Saracens from the third century onwards, as Ammian Marcellinus wants us to believe, and which has been accepted by almost everyone ever since, including all modern scholars? Or does the changed terminology reflect a real ethnic or some other change among the populations along the imperial borders dividing the Middle East, from Pompey to Muhammed? If so, what was the change? And why was the term *sarakēnós* or *ṭayyāyā* chosen?

We have thus, at last, reached the central issue of this investigation.

Notes

1 Honigmann, *Liste* nr. 91. Another reading is, however, *taknós*.
2 Cf. Honigmann, *Taiēnoí*; Nöldeke, *Taiēnós*.
3 Cf. Bräu, *Ṭaiy*; Caskel, *Ǧamhara* II 555.
4 A somewhat speculative scenario arises if it is assumed that the name Praetavi in the Singăr mentioned by Pliny originating from Corbulo is connected with the Taieni (cf. p. 415). The presence of people with that name in Mesopotamian Arabia would explain why the word in Syriac became the general term for inhabitants in the Syrian desert. There is an isolated saying going back to al-Qatāda describing the situation of 'this tribe of *al-ʕarab*' before Islam when they were 'confined on a top of a rock between Fāris (= Iran) and Rūm' (quoted by Kister, *al-Ḥīra* 143; cf. aṭ-Ṭabarī, *Tafsīr* to sura VIII:26). According to Pliny, Mount Singăr was a centre for the *Praetavi Arabes*, i.e. Mesopotamian Arabia, which was a border country between Iran and Rome for seven centuries. The saying would thus have preserved a memory of the situation of the Taieni/Ṭayyiʔ during a long period of their history. The Ṭayyiʔ later had a traditional centre around the two mountains Salmā and ʕAǧā, hich in the early Islamic period were inhabited by ʔAsad. The Ṭayyiʔ would thus originally have had a more eastern habitat than they had later, which would explain why they are not mentioned in the Namāra inscription. The ʔAsad seem to have old connections with the ʔAzd in ʕAsīr, and these would be the ʔŠDYN mentioned in the Namara inscription. ʔAsad's occupation of the area around the two mountains would have occurred between the time of the Namāra inscription and the beginnings of tribal history recorded in Arabic.
5 Ptolemy 5.16.3; 6.7.19. See p. 437.
6 The adjective *sarakēnós* occurs for the first time in Dioscurides' *Materia medica* (see p. 369), written *c.* AD 50, as an attribute of a herb growing on the Sinai peninsula.
7 Stephanus, 566:3–4.
8 Ptolemy 6.7.20.
9 Beaucamp, *Rawwafa*; Bowersock, *Inscription*.
10 Cf. Graf, *Saracens*; Bowersock, *Limes*; Graf/O'Connor, *Origins*.
11 *Historia Augusta: Pescennius Niger* 7.8.
12 Eusebius, *History* 6.42.4.
13 *Panegyrici* 11 (3) 5.4.
14 Eusebius, *Chronicle* 23b.
15 Schwartz, *Eusebios* 1376.
16 Eusebius, *Chronicle* 162, 211. See pp. 433 ff., 457 ff.
17 Schwartz, *Eusebios* 1434; Morau, *Eusebius* 1063.
18 Eusebius, *Onomasticon* 118:22.
19 Eusebius, *Onomasticon* 60:7.
20 Eusebius, *Onomasticon* 124:10.

21 Eusebius, *Onomasticon* 166:13.
22 Eusebius, *Onomasticon* 172:9.
23 Morau is cautious and only dates it after AD 315 (*Eusebius* 1064).
24 Eusebius, *Commentary* I:62 (p. 80). The Masoretic text has 'the islands of the ocean' instead of Arabia.
25 Eusebius, *Commentary* I:63 (p. 86).
26 Eusebius, *Commentary* 67 (p. 100).
27 There is no better solution: Babylon is referred to as 'she' (*autē*). The text says: . . . *árabas onomázei geítona gar ékhousi tēn arábōn khōran*. The *gar* must be explicative in this position, and the subject of *ékhousi* cannot be anyone else than the Saracens, the Assyrians and the shepherds mentioned in the preceding clause.
28 Eusebius, *Commentary* I:70 (p. 108). The Masoretic text has 'the brook of the willows' (hāʕᵃrābīm).
29 Eusebius, *Commentary* II:23 (p. 273).
30 Basil, *Commentary* 599 C.
31 Basil, *Commentary* 641 C.
32 The same interpretation is found in the *Enarratio in Isaiam* ascribed to Basil; see *San Basilio: Enarratio in prophetam Isaiam*, ed. P. Trevisan, Torino 1939 ad loc. A similar understanding is found in a fragment of a commentary to Psalms by Didymus Caecus (to Ps. 72:10: 'kings of *árabes* and Saba . . .'); *árabes* . . . means Westerners.
33 Epiphanius 66:1:7 (p. 16).
34 Epiphanius 51:30 (p. 301); Gerasa is in Arabia; ibid. 55:1 (p. 325). In the synod at Seleucia in 359 one Berochius, bishop of Arabia, and one Adraon, bishop of the *árabes*, took part (Epiphanius 73:20). Berochius would then have come from the capital of the province, Bostra. The church historian Socrates mentions another bishop of the *árabes*, Theotimus, who participated in the synod in Antioch in 363. He would have come from the same area as Adraon (Socrates, *History* III:25). Eusebius already mentions a bishop Beryllus of the *árabes* at Bostra/of the Bostrans of Arabia in the reign of Alexander Severus (222–235): Eusebius, *History* 6.20.1–2. A certain Zeuxius from Arabia took part in the consilium in Nicaea (Honigmann, *Liste* nr. 93).
35 Epiphanius 286–287.
36 See pp. 602 ff.
37 *Expositio* XX (p. 154).
38 Polaschek, *Notitia* 1081–1097.
39 *Notitia dignitatum: Oriens* XXVII:24; XXXVI:35; XXXVIII:17.
40 *Notitia dignitatum* XXXII:27, 28; XXVII:17.
41 *Notitia dignitatum* XXXIV:22.
42 In Festus' *Breviarium* (3.14.16) we hear about *Saraceni et Arabes*. In the parallel passage in Eutropius (6.14.1) we read *Ituraei et Arabes*. Both texts are built on Livy, but Festus has updated the terminology in accordance with usage in the latter half of the fourth century AD.; cf. Festus 14 (anachronistic *Saraceni* defeated by Lucullus). On the other hand, both *Breviaria* have Arabs and Osrhoenians in the notice about Trajan's eastern campaign (Festus 57; Eutropius 8.3.1).
43 See the survey in Retsö, *Road*.
44 A recent study of Roman policy in Arabia following this tradition is Simon, *Trade*.
45 Cf. Marek, *Expedition* 125 ff., for a similar view.
46 Cf. Fiaccadori, *Teofilo* 5 ff.
47 It seems clear that re-Christianization attempts were resumed in the fifth century AD. Around 450 the community in Nağrān was established and Ethiopia received a new wave of missionaries, documented in the legend of the Nine Saints. This new wave was Monophysite, which perhaps explains the absence of Ezana and his Christianity from the later Ethiopian king-lists and ecclesiastical tradition.
48 The *Res Gestae* were completed between AD 395 and 400; see Seyfarth's introduction to Ammianus' *Res gestae* (I 24–27).
49 Julian, *Letters* 98 p. 183.

50 Ammian 23.3.8: *reguli Saracenorum gentium.*
51 Ammian 23.5.1.
52 Ammian 24.1.10.
53 Ammian 24.2.4.
54 Ammian 25.1.3; 3.6 sqq.
55 Ammian 25.6.8–10.
56 Ammian 25.8.1.
57 Ammian 25.6.8.
58 Libanius, *Oration* 24:6.
59 First by Philostorgius, *History* 7.15 (*c.* AD 430). Theodoretus (end of the fifth century) says that he was killed by a nomad called *Ismaelitēs* (*History* 3.20). The Saracen returns in Sozomenus (*History* 6.1) and Johannes Lydus (*De Mensibus* 4.95). The word *malkhán* looks like Aramaic for 'our king'. Julian's death is discussed by Shahid, *Byzantium* 1 124–132. His conclusion is that it is likely that Julian was killed by an 'Arab'. Since Shahid uses this term in its modern sense, his conclusion does not shed light on the problem discussed here.
60 Cf. Isaac, *Limits* 171.
61 Ammian 23.6.45–47.
62 Of the cities Nascos is NŠQ in al-Ǧawf, Nagar is Naǧrān, Maephe is Mayfaʕa inland from Qane, Taphra is Ẓafār, the residence of the Himyarites, and Dioscuris is Soqoṭra. Baraba could be a distortion of Marib(a).
63 Arrian, *Indica* 37. There is a confusion between this island and Maṣīra on the coast of Oman; cf. Sprenger, *Geographie* 98–102.
64 Cf. Ptolemy 6.7. 29, 35, 37, 41, 45 and Fontaine, *Commentaire* 94–95.
65 Ammian 14.8.13.
66 Mommsen (*Geographica* 609) assumed that this passage was a quotation from the relevant account on Trajan in Ammian's own book, without suggesting any other source.
67 Cf. Bowersock, *Arabia* 111–112.
68 The first sentence is, in fact, reminiscent of the passage in Pliny 5.65, which we have assumed goes back to Eratosthenes. Mommsen assumed that Ammian knew Pliny via Solinus' *Collectanea rerum memorabilium.* This work, written shortly after AD 200, was especially used for the geographical descriptions of, for example, the Orient (Mommsen, *Geographica* 627 ff.). The rest of the passage definitely describes conditions after AD 106.
69 Gardthausen, *Quellen* 512–538, modified by Mommsen, *Geographica* 610 ff.
70 Mommsen, *Geographica* 612–618.
71 Mommsen, *Geographica* 618 ff., especially 626–627.
72 Stephanus 107.
73 Ammian 22.15.1.
74 Ammian 23.6.13.
75 Ammian 14.4.2.
76 Ammian 14.4.3–6. The borders are also mentioned in 14.8.5, where the Saracens are said to live along the eastern border from the Euphrates to the borders of the Nile.
77 Robertson-Smith (*Kinship* 88 ff.) identified it with the *mutʕa* marriage known from Islamic legislation. Heffening (*Mutʕa*) has pointed out that there seem to be some differences.
78 Millar, *Near East* 484–485.
79 *Historia Augusta: Avidius* 6.5–6. Cf. p. 440.
80 Cf. Shahid, *Byzantium* 1 239–250. So Gardthausen (*Quellen* 510) who pointed out the parallels between Ammian's description of the Saracens and the Huns.
81 The dating of the contents in the *Notitia dignitatum* is more uncertain, although there are good reasons to assume that the employment of Saracens there goes back to the time before Julian; cf. p. 511 and Shahid, *Rome* (Ch. 5); idem, *Byzantium* 1 485–486.
82 The sources: Rufinus, *History* 11.6 (pp. 1010–1012); Socrates, *History* 36 (pp. 556–557); Sozomenos, *History* 6.38.1–4; Theodoros Anagnostes, *History* 185–186; Theophanes, *Chronographia* 64. The three oldest sources were written in the first half of the fifth century. By and large, they go back to an almost contemporary text by Gelasius of Caesarea which is lost (cf. Bowersock, *Mavia*). For analyses see Sartre, *Études* 140–144 and Shahid,

Byzantium I 139–169. The latter identifies Mavia's Saracens with Tanūkh. This identification has no support in the sources and is problematic also from other viewpoints. Palestine and Arabia mentioned in the sources may well be the historic areas and not the provincial borders at the time. The revolt is also mentioned in connection with events in Alexandria, and the Christian monk sent to the Saracens comes from an area close to Egypt. It is thus likely that Mavia's Saracens are the 'real' ones, i.e. those in the northern Sinai. One of Shahid's arguments is the inscriptions in Ansartha in Syria from AD 425 mentioning a Maouia and a Silvanus who is *kratéōn aeì en Eremboîs*, which he translates *semper victor in Arabibus*. Silvanus would thus be identical with the Victor marrying Mavia's daughter, according to Socrates. All this is very hypothetical and unverified. Mavia is a common name in North Arabia and could stand for Māwiyya or Muʕāwiya; *kratéō* is not quite the expected Greek counterpart to Latin *vinco*; the Homeric term *Ermboí* is strange and it is not clear why it was chosen to designate the Saracens. The conclusions are not entirely impossible but built, as it seems, on a somewhat strained argumentation.

83 Cf. Shahid, *Rome* 30–32, 54–55; idem, *Byzantium* 1 16–25, 113–115, 140 ff., 498–510.

84 Ammian 31.16:5–6; Eunapius, *History* 64–65; Sozomenos, *History* 7.1.1; Zosimus, *History* 4.22; Theodoros Anagnostes, *History* 219 (p. 75); Theophanes, *Chronographia* 65. Perhaps the panegyric to Theodosius I (*Panegyrici* III:12 p. 189) refers to this event. Cf. Shahid, *Byzantium* 1 138–202.

85 Sozomenus, *History* 299–300; cf. Shahid, *Byzantium* 1 274–277.

86 *Vita Pelagiae* § 32 (= 87–88, Greek pi; 116 Greek alpha). The Georgian version (146) translates Saracen with *taičʔ* = camel (in the modern Latin translation (157) rendered 'camel driver'). The ancient Latin versions 175, 209, 267 have *Saraceni*. The Armenian translates *Tačka* (283); the Arabic version (330) has *al-ʕarāb* (sic). The Syriac text is not given in the modern edition. Its modern Latin translation (306) has *arabes*. The work was originally written in Greek (Introduction 15–16).

87 Iohannes Cassianus, *Collocatio* col. 643–644.

88 Hieronymus, *Epistula ad Dardanum* 4 (pp. 161–162).

89 *Peregrinatio Egeriae* 7.1, 6; 8.1, 4; 9.6–10.1, 4; 11.3.

90 Synesius, *Epistula* 5.16.

91 Iohannes Cassianus loc. cit.

92 Thus in Justinian's time the province is said to be 'the region of the Arabes' (*Novella* 102, prooemium). A similar term is found in the so-called Pella inscription from AD 521/522 where the relevant phrase can be restored as *apò khōrōn tōn arábōn éthnous*. For this text as well as a similar interpretation, see Shahid, *Byzantium* 3 56–59.

93 Malchus, *Byzantiaca* 404–406; Iohannes Lydus, *De Mensibus* 4.53; Euagrius, *History* 5.20, 6.2; Theophanes, *Chronographia* 218.

94 Thus, the classicist Theodoretus of Cyrrhus: *Therapeutica* 1.19, 10.53; *Isaiah* to 13:20–23, ibid. 15:6–16:2; 21:13–17; *Paralipomena* 272, 280, 286; *Jeremiah* 637; *Daniel* 1440 l. 45; Sozomenos, *History* 1.3.3 (on Herod's descent).

95 For a general survey of 'Arabs' in Syriac sources, see Segal, *Syriac Sources*, and Pigulevskaja, *Araby*. Neither of these authors pays any attention to the different terms for 'Arabs'.

96 Cf. *Thesaurus Syriacus* s.v. ʕRB. For *ʕārāb* as a geographical designation we have documents from around 500: Joshua the Stylite, *Chronicle* 38, 50.

97 Cf. Nöldeke, *Geschichte*, 116 n. 2; Shahid, *Byzantium* 2 37–39.

98 Isaac XI:89 (Bickell I:210).

99 Isaac XI:36 (Bickell I: 207–208 (227).

100 Isaac XI:331 (Bickell I: 220).

101 Genesis 16:12. Isaac has also preserved a memory of the distinction between Arabs and others; see p. 604.

102 *ṭayyāyē* is found once in another of Isaac's poems (XII:100 = Bickell I:230). Here it is said that Bêth Ḥûr was captivated by 'mimers' (*raqqādē*) and *ṭayyāyē*.

103 Joshua, *Chronicle* § 38.

104 For the complex history of this work see Baumstark, *Geschichte* 183–184.

105 Zacharias, *History* 7.2 (= Brooks II p. 20).
106 Zacharias, *History* 7.6 (= Brooks II p. 35 ll. 16–17); 12.7 (Brooks II p. 208).
107 Zacharias, *History* 9.8 (Brooks II p. 100); cf. 10.12 (Brooks II p.193) where it is said that bishops were sent from Arabia to Persia.
108 Cf. the other sources for this uprising where the assisting troops are called *sarakēnoí* (Malalas 657). When adducing an abbreviation of Ptolemy's description of the Middle East, Zacharias likewise renders Sarakēnē by *ṭayyāyē* (Zacharias, *History* 12.7 = Brooks II p. 207).
109 Simeon, *Vita* 546 (Hilgenfeldt 108:13, 20), 555 (Hilgenfeldt 114:21), 596 (Hilgenfeldt 146 f.). Arabia is mentioned only once as a geographical term, probably the area between Egypt and Palestine (Simeon, *Vita* 604 l. 3 = Hilgenfeldt 151 l. 18.).
110 Joshua, *Chronicle* §§ 22, 24, 51, 52, 54, 57.
111 Simeon, *Letter* 502 ll. 3, 6–7; 507 l. 16. It should be observed that Simeon distinguishes between ṬYYʔ and MʕDYʔ = Maʕadd.
112 *Synodicon orientale* 62. l.17.
113 A feminine plural **ṭayyāʕāṯā* seems not to be documented.
114 Sword: *T.B. Sanhedrin* 67b (Pal.); *T.B. Yebamot* 120b (Bab.); spear: *T.B. Taʕanit* 22b (Bab.).
115 *T.B. Baba Meṣiʕa* 86a; *T.B. Moʕed Qaṭan* 25b; *T.B. Shabbat* 155b (Pal); *T.B. Taʕanit* 22b; *T.B. Baba Qamma* 55a; *T.B. Yebamot* 120b (Bab.).
116 *T.B. Baba Bathra* 36a; *T.B. Bekorot* 44a (Bab.).
117 *T.B. Ḥullin* 7a (Pal., Bab.); *T.B. Rosh ha-Shanah* 26b.
118 *T.B. ʕArakin* 6b (Bab.). This is also possible for other non-Jews.
119 *T.B. Giṭṭin* 45b (Bab.).
120 *T.B. Ḥullin* 39b (Bab.).
121 *T.B. Niddah* 20a (Bab.). In this case it is only one *ṭayyāʕā*, and it is not certain how representative he is.
122 *T.B. ʕAvodah Zarah* 28a, 29a; *T.B. Yoma* 84a, cf. *T.B. Shabbat* 110b (Bab.).
123 *T.B. Bekorot* 44a: *ṣimmeaḥ*; *T.B. Rosh ha-Shanah* 26b: *yehab* in Ps. 55:23.
124 *T.B. Sanhedrin* 110a; *T.B. Baba Bathra* 73b–74a.
125 *Synodicon orientale* 526–527/532–534. See Segal, *Syriac Sources* 109; Shahid, *Byzantium* 2 38.
126 According to Sundermann and others (Sundermann, *Attestation*) the modern Persian word *tāzī*, 'arab', going back to Middle Persian *tāzīg*, is ultimately the tribal name Ṭayy- with an Iranian suffix. The word Tağik, nowadays a designation of Iranian groups in central Asia, could possibly have the same origin via another dialect (Sogdian). The word would ultimately go back to Parthian times.

18

ARABS IN TALMUDIC SOURCES

After the destruction of the Jewish temple in AD 70, the rabbinic movement became dominant in Judaism, and its world-views and attitudes became the foundation of all later developments. The bearers of the rabbinic tradition were at first a group of teachers in Palestine, the so-called *tannaim*. They were active from the destruction of the temple until *c*. AD 200. The tannaim were followed by another group of teachers, the *amoraim*, who lived both in Palestine and Mesopotamia. The teachings of the *tannaim* are mostly in Hebrew, whereas the *amoraim* used both Hebrew and Aramaic. The main rabbinic (tannaitic and amoraitic) documents are codified from *c*. AD 200 and onwards. Rabbinic teaching is at this stage found as commentaries to Biblical texts, *midrash*, or in discussions about the practical performance of the commandments. Even though the earliest rabbinic document, the *Mishnah*, is codified around AD 200, and most of the material is found in much younger texts, the contents are often old, going back even to pre-tannaitic times.

In the rabbinic texts we find sayings mentioning Arabs, some of which are anonymous, some of which are ascribed to known rabbis.[1] The earliest named authority is Yoḥanan ben Zakkai, who lived through the destruction of the temple, and the latest belong to the third generation of Palestinian *amoraim* and the fourth of Babylonian *amoraim*.[2] This means a time span from *c*. AD 70 to 350. Most of the references with the word 'Arabs' or 'Arabia' (ʕRB, ʕRBY, ʕRBYʔ) come from Palestinian authorities. Designations derived from this root are not unknown to the Babylonian *amoraim*, but the instances are rather few. Instead, the Babylonians sometimes refer to a group called ṬYʕʔ, which has usually been seen as identical with the ʕRB. The term is also rendered 'Arabs' in modern translations of rabbinical texts.

The anonymous sayings where Arabs are mentioned are found in tannaitic sources and in amoraitic ones mostly of Palestinian origin. Most of the latter occur in the compilations of biblical commentaries to Genesis and Lamentations gathered in the two collections *Bereshit Rabbah* and *Ekhah Rabbati*. These two are the oldest of the amoraitic collections of midrash, which received their final redaction *c*. AD 400.[3]

The word 'Arab' belongs to the oldest layer of rabbinical literature. It seems to disappear in the fourth century AD, which agrees with the testimony of other sources.[4] As far as the exact dating of the sayings is concerned, this raises some special problems. The attribution of a saying to a named authority does not necessarily mean that it was formulated originally by him. Apart from the fact that the attribution may be of doubtful historicity, rabbinic material was handed down through generations, and we can never be sure if a saying ascribed to a rabbi was formulated by him or was given to him by his predecessors or attributed to him by later generations. In short, the chronology of rabbinic material is difficult, if not impossible to pinpoint. This means that the material has to be studied thematically.[5] Within a theme a tentative chronology may in some cases be attempted, but it should be kept in mind that rabbinic material is basically tradition literature, which can often be supposed to have had a very long history before the earliest written evidence available to us. This means that even though most of the mentions of Arabs are found in texts much later than the year AD 200, it cannot be excluded that they often reflect conditions before that time.

Apart from the term ṬYʕʔ used by the Babylonian *amoraim*, we also find in rabbinical literature the term Yishmaʕʔel or Yishmeʕʔelim used for groups identical with or close to the Arabs. The relationship between Ismaelites and Arabs has been treated earlier, where it was shown that early Hellenistic Jewish circles had seen Arabs and Ishmaelites as identical. This must be analysed in the rabbinic sources, and the first theme of our investigation will be the question of the identity of the Arabs in rabbinic literature and the relationship between the different terms.

In Genesis 15:18 ff., the inhabitants of the land promised to Abraham are enumerated. Among these are 'the Kenites, the Kenizzites, and the Kadmonites'. The comment is:

> The rabbis said: [these are] ʕRWYYH, ŠLMYYH, NWṬYYH.[6]

In another context, the same saying is ascribed to a tannaitic authority.[7] The last name should be read as Nabataeans or Nabataea.[8] The middle name indicates the Shalamians, the people living south of the Nabataeans around al-Ḥiğr, known from the Late Assyrian period down to Nabataean inscriptions.[9] We notice that Nabataeans and Arabs are two different groups with the Shalamians in between. A similar picture is given in the targumic tradition where *Targum Jonathan* in the genealogy of Ishmael distinguishes between Nabaṭ = Nebayot and ʕArab = Qedar. If we assume that the order of names in the midrash corresponds to the order of names in the Old Testament text, there is no doubt about the whereabouts of these Arabs. They stand for the Kenites, the descendants of Kain who, according to the information available to us, as well as to the rabbis, from the Old Testament, lived in the Negev. That the Arabs are to be found in this region is also indicated by the Biblical context. In the preceding verse the Promised Land is said to stretch 'from the river of Egypt unto the great river, the river Euphrates'. The three peoples mentioned in the midrash seem to stand for those inhabiting the border regions of the Promised Land from the south-west to the north-east. The Nabataeans are thus seen as inhabiting the Syrian desert east of Palestine. It is likely that the Biblical word Kadmonites, *ha-qadmônî*, has been associated with 'the sons of the east', *bnê qedem*, the Israelite term for those who dwelt in that area in Biblical times. According to this exposition, the Nabataeans lived east of Palestine and perhaps inhabited the whole Syrian desert to the Euphrates. This perspective reminds us of Josephus' description of the dwelling places of the Arab sons of Ishmael, paralleled by a passage in the Book of Jubilees.[10] A remarkable difference is that in both Jubilees and Josephus the easterners are Arabs, whereas in the rabbinic passage Arabs and Nabataeans are kept apart: Arabs live south of Palestine, the Nabataeans east of it. Both Jubilees and Josephus make the Arabs descendants of Ishmael, which they are not in the rabbinic passage. The rabbinic saying thus gives a very archaic impression and may reflect conditions earlier than the second century BC.

Another early definition of Arabia is found in an anonymous commentary to Genesis 41:56: 'And the famine [in the days of Joseph] was over all the face of the earth'.

> [this means] in PNWQYH, in ʕRBYH, in PLSṬYNY.[11]

To this commentator, the world consists of Phoenicia, Arabia and Palestine. The anonymous saying quoted cannot, of course, be that old in its present shape, which is seen from the Greek forms of all three country names mentioned. The last seems even to reflect a pronunciation [palestini]. Both the names Arabia and Palestine reflect conditions after Hadrian when the Holy Land for the first time was officially named *Palaestina* and a province officially named Arabia had been established shortly before.

The names are thus modern, i.e. from the second century AD, but the perspective is older. Phoenicia stands for the coastal regions of the eastern Mediterranean and Arabia for the region inland. This reminds us very strongly about the geographical perspective in the pentecostal story in Acts and reaches back to the Aḥiqar proverbs.[12] It is by the rabbis combined with a traditional view of the borders of the Holy Land: Phoenicia and Arabia are regions beyond Dan and Beer Sheba respectively, the ancient frontier points of the land of Israel in the Old Testament. Arabia is thus, according to this saying, the region south of Beer Sheba.

That Arabs in early rabbinic literature are to be sought south and south-west of Palestine is also evident from the targum Pseudo-Jonathan to Genesis 25:13. This Aramaic paraphrasing of the Pentateuch is of Palestinian origin. In it, the two eldest sons of Ishmael, Nebayot and Qedar, are rendered as NBṬ and ʕRB.[13] The identification of Nebayot with Nabataeans is here met with for the first time and has followed scholarship ever since, in spite of the impossible etymology.[14] Apart from the differentiation between Nabataeans and Arabs we notice that the identification of Arabs with Qedar makes it reasonable to look for these Arabs between Egypt and Palestine. For the targumist, it was natural to identify Qedar and Arabs which may indicate that the targumic interpretation is ancient, preserving the memories of the power of Qedar.[15]

In this targum we have a link between Ishmael and the Arabs. It should be noticed that, according to the targum, Arabs are Ishmaelites but not all Ishmaelites are Arabs. There are other ancient rabbinic sayings where the Arabs are seen as descendants of Ishmael. One is a commentary to the story about the three men visiting Abraham in Genesis 18, attributed to Rabbi Yishmael, a tanna of the first generation, i.e. the beginning of the second century AD.[16] The commentary is to Abraham's words in v. 4: 'let a little water, I pray, be fetched, and wash your feet':

> They [the three men] said to Abraham: 'Do you suspect us of being ʕRBYYM who worship the dust of their feet?'. Ishmael had [just] issued from him.[17]

The meaning of the saying is: we are not human beings, especially not like those low-standing Arabs, who walk without shoes or sandals so that they have to wash their feet when visiting more civilized people. The main point for us is that Ishmael here is seen as the father of the Arabs, although it is not explicitly said that he was the father only of the Arabs.[18]

We have several instances where the Ishmaelites in Genesis 37:25, who come from Gilead and buy Joseph from his brethren at the well of Dothan, are transformed into Arabs. The targum Pseudo-Jonathan has ʕRBʔN and Onqelos has ʕRBʔY where the Biblical text has *yišmʕʔelîm*.[19] There is then a more haggadic rabbinic version:

> Rabbi Tarfon said [concerning the effects of the merits of the righteous]: even

> though this dear and beloved one [Joseph] descended [to Egypt] together with ʕRBYYM, he was not killed by the stench of their camels and the smell of tar; no, the Holy One, blessed be His Name, prepared sacks full of perfumes and all kinds of lovely incense so that he [Joseph] did not die from the stench of the camels and the smell of the tar.[20]

Rabbi Tarfon was a contemporary of Rabbi Aqiba in the first half of the second century AD.[21] The haggadah, which is thus explicitly tannaitic, obviously takes the identification for granted and as a starting point, which indicates that the targumic tradition is pre-tannaitic. We have already pointed out that this tradition is documented in passages in Josephus and Eusebius, originating from Artapanus in the middle of the second century BC.[22] It is, however, worth observing that the interpretations of Genesis 37:25 do not necessarily assume full identity between all the descendants of Ishmael and the Arabs. Nothing excludes the possibility that the interpreters saw the Arabs in Genesis 37:25 as only one group among the presumed descendants of Ishmael, as stated in the targum to Genesis 25:13.

To a named authority is attributed another exposition of Genesis 18:2 where Abraham, sitting in his tent door, 'lifted up his eyes and looked and lo, three men stood by him':

> R. Lewi said: one was like a SRQY, one like a NWWṬY, and one like a ʕRBY.[23]

Rabbi Lewi was a Palestinian amora of the third generation, which means that he lived at the end of the third century AD.[24] The saying reflects conditions later than those in the preceding quotations. We here have the Saracens mentioned together with the Nabataeans and the Arabs. We notice that Arabs and Nabataeans are still two different groups. The Saracens we have already encountered in the *Geography* of Ptolemy, where they are said to live in the western part of the Sinai peninsula and in the northern Ḥiǧāz.[25] Ptolemy's information represents the situation in the first part of the second century AD. The distinction between Arabs and Nabataeans in Rabbi Lewi's statement is, however, remarkable and must reflect conditions much earlier. There is no indication here that the Nabataeans are Arabs. This saying may well be the earliest mentioning of the Saracenes.

We have already adduced some traditions about the role of Arabs during the Great Revolt in AD 66–73.[26] These are important because they refer to a dated event. Rabbi Aqiba, one of the most famous *tannaim* in the first half of the second century AD, is said to have visited Arabia, and there are several reports attributed to him about conditions there.[27] These reports can thus also be dated. An important question is which Arabia is meant.[28] Of the sayings attributed to him only one gives a geographical hint. In this statement he is commenting on the words in Numbers 5:19 dealing with how to find out if a wife has committed adultery:

> Can there be a woman who commits adultery while 'under her husband?' The story is about the king of the ʕRBYYM who asked Rabbi Aqiba: 'I am black (kûšī) and my wife is black (kûšīt) but she has given birth to a white son. Shall I kill her for having played the harlot while lying with me?' Said the other [R. Aqiba]: 'Are the figures painted in your house black or white?' He said: 'White'. The other answered him: 'When you had intercourse with her, she

> fixed her eyes on the white figures and bore a child like these'.[29]

This *histoire piquante* plays with ancient magic beliefs already known in the Old Testament.[30] It is probably completely legendary but it gives some hints about Arabia. The information that the king of the Arabs is black is curious. The key is the use of the adjective *kûšī*, a derivation of Kûš, the Biblical name for Nubia as a designation also for Arabia. In the targumic tradition, Cush in the Table of Nations (Genesis 10:6 = 1 Chronicles 1:8) is translated as Arabia (ʕRB, ʕRBYʔ).[31] In the targum to the Song of Songs it is said that when the Israelites had made the golden calf their faces became black 'like the sons of Kush who dwell in the tents of Qedar'.[32] This is an exposition of the verse 'I am black but handsome . . . like the tents of Qedar'. This blackness of Qedar in the Biblical text is the origin of the identification of Cush with Arabia and the idea that the king of Arabia is black.[33] The blackness of the Arabian king is due to his dwelling in the land of Qedar whose inhabitants are black, according to the Song of Songs. The existence in northern Arabia of a Kushan, remembered in the Old Testament, may also have played a role for the rabbinic exegesis. Rabbi Aqiba's Arabia is thus identical with that of Qedar, which was the area between Egypt and Palestine, i.e. the same Arabia where Aqiba's colleague, Paul of Tarsus, had located Mount Sinai.

Another Arabia far from Palestine may be documented in a strange dictum ascribed to a Palestinian *amora* of the second generation:[34]

> [About the Garden of Eden] Resh Laqish said: If it is in the Land of Israel its gate is Beth Shean; if it is in ʕRBYʔ its gate is Beth Gerem.[35]

The same Arabia is hinted at in the following dictum:

> Rabbi Ḥanan ben Rabah (or: ben Ḥisdah) said in the name of Rab: There are five appointed temples of idol-worship. They are: [That of] Bel of Babylon, the temple of Nebo in Kursi, [that of] Tarʕata which is in Mapug, [that of] Ṣerifa which is in Ashqelon [and that of] NŠRʔ which is in ʕRBYʔ.[36]

Rab is the great *amora* of the first generation in Babylonia, i.e. at the beginning of the third century AD, and it can be assumed that we here have a Mesopotamian viewpoint.[37] If we look for a temple with a god called 'the eagle' (Nešrāʔ), it is not difficult to find. A god was worshipped under this name in one of the large temples at Hatra, i.e. in an area which is explicitly named Arabia.[38] We would then suggest that Resh Laqish' saying also refers to the same area. Bêt Garmāi is the southern province of Adiabene in upper Mesopotamia, thus close to the area called ʕRB in the inscriptions from Sumatar and Hatra. There seems to have been a discussion in rabbinic Judaism about the exact location of the Garden of Eden, where one school maintained that it was somewhere in Mesopotamia and the other claimed the Promised Land.[39] We should notice the expression 'in Arabia', B-ʕRB, which is exactly the same as found in the texts from Sumatar. As a matter of fact, we do find in rabbinic literature the term ʕRBYʔ [ʕaraviyyā] as a designation for a place or a region (*ʔaṯrā*).[40]

A picture of the Arabs in Babylonia is found in an anecdote from the first half of the fourth century AD:

> To Pumbeditha came ʕRBʔY who confiscated land of [ordinary] people.[41]

It is said that the inhabitants of this town, one of the main Jewish centres in Mesopotamia in Sasanian times, came to Abaye, an *amora* of the fourth generation, to complain.[42] We are thus in the reign of Shāpur II. To this passage there is a commentary by the medieval commentator Gershom ben Yehuda (dead 1028 in Mainz) worth quoting:[43]

> ʕRBʔY: Ishmaelites who used to assist the king when he went to war and used to remain in his kingdom for a long time before they returned to their dwelling. They came with him to Pumbeditha, and he gave them permission to confiscate land surrounding the city from people in order to live from it as long as they were there.[44]

The commentary sounds very authentic, although we do not know from where Gershom had his information. The Arabs as allies of the Sassanid king are well known from the fifth and sixth centuries and may be an institution that is earlier. It is probably a good snapshot of the relationship between the warring tribes of northern Arabia and the sedentary inhabitants, at least from the third century AD onwards.

In the Talmudic literature there are quite a few references to the language of Arabia which, at a first glance, looks like a mixture of Arabic and Aramaic. This would fit very well into known linguistic conditions in Nabataea/Provincia Arabia in the second century AD.[45]

It is possible to collect several more references to Arabs from the rabbinic literature. They were circumcised;[46] they had tents;[47] they had special shields;[48] they had camels, horses and cattle and, according to one tradition, the Jews used to buy the red heifer from them;[49] they used waterskins with a special knot;[50] they had a special oven dug in the ground;[51] they wore a special headgear;[52] their women went out veiled;[53] there was a coinage named after them, the Arabian denar;[54] they had special sorcerers;[55] they practised hepatoscopy.[56]

There are frequent expressions of a low opinion of them. A famous one is a story where Yoḥanan ben Zakkai is the protagonist:

> The rabbis told a story about Yoḥanan ben Zakkai, who one day was riding his donkey and left Jerusalem with his students following after him. He saw a girl (*ribba*) who was collecting grains from the dungheaps of the animals of the ʕRBYYM . . . and Yoḥanan ben Zakkai wept and said: ‘Happy are you, o Israel, when you do the will of the Place and no people or tongue has power over you, but when you do not do the will of the Place, He delivers you into the hand of a low people’.[57]

A quite frequent item is their reputation for sexual indulgence:

> Ten *qabs* of adultery descended to the world; nine were taken by ʕRBYʔ, one by the rest of the world.[58]

This accusation is found in several passages in rabbinic literature.[59] The rabbis also go to great lengths to exclude Arabs from taking part in eating the pascal lamb, in spite of their being circumcised.[60] This negative attitude is, however, countered by other passages where there are traces of a more neutral or even positive attitude. The buying of the red heifer from Arabs has already been mentioned. The tents of the Arabs do not defile;[61] bridegift of Arabian camels is valid, and as we have seen, the gates of Paradise could be in the land of the Arabs.[62] The ranging of Arabs among the descendants of Ishmael is probably connected with the more positive attitude. We have suggested above that this identification took place early in the Maccabaean period and lived long after. The Jewish attitude hovers between enmity towards the Arabs, as already reflected in the book of Nehemiah, and the feeling towards close relatives. The impression is that the neutral and positive statements in rabbinic literature are, on the whole, old and the negative ones younger. It is very likely that the Arab participation in the events of AD 70 contributed to the strengthening of the negative attitude. This was to change once again: the Moslem empire of the Ishmaelites was in the beginning greeted by the Jews as a liberation from the yoke of the evil Esau.

The Talmudic literature in general is characterized by a lack of precision when it comes to historical and geographical matters. That was not the concern of the rabbis. This material is, however, of considerable interest for our subject. It is not influenced by the systematic and theoretical thinking of Greek geographers. As is evident from the quotations, it also contains quite unique insight into what could be called Arab civilization, which we do not find in most of the other sources, which tend to pay attention only to the military and political role of the Arabs. An important detail is that in the rabbinic sources we find a derivation of the word ʕRB as a designation for their habitat: *ʕAr(a)biyyā*. Another is, of course, that Arabs were not as a rule identified with Nabataeans or Saracens. The description of them does not fit very well into what we know about the Nabataeans. The picture is of people with a rather low standard of living: tents, ovens in the ground, shepherds, trading in despised goods like camel hides and tar. There is no trace of the spendour of the Nabataeans as described by Athenodorus. The Arabs are seen as descendants of Ishmael but are not necessarily identified with all Ishmaelites. Even the Nabataeans are on a couple of occasions given Ishmaelite descent but distinguished from the Arabs. Arabia is to the rabbis primarily the area between Palestine and Egypt but there were also Arabs in Mesopotamia. A striking fact is that the picture of Arabs and other groups around them, gained from rabbinic literature, sometimes gives an archaic impression. Noteworthy also is that there are no sayings with explicit reference to Arabs datable to authorities after *c.* AD 340.

The picture of Arabs in rabbinic sources fits neatly into the 'reductionist' view that is emerging in this study. The rabbis knew about Arabs between Egypt and Palestine, in Transjordan and in upper Mesopotamia. In the lands surrounding the Holy Land there were also other groups like Nabataeans and Shalamians, who were not Arabs, even though they could be seen as descendants of Ishmael. The Ishmaelite ancestry of the Arabs results from the parallel between Qedar and Arabs, which is ancient, going back to Assyrian times. Compared to the Hellenistic authors quoted by Josephus, the extension of 'Arabness' by the rabbis is more restricted and, as it seems, never extended to encompass the Nabataeans.

Notes

1 For a survey of the passages about different kinds of 'Arabs', Krauss, *Nachrichten*, is still essential. He has not, however, made any distinction between different terms for 'Arabs' and

does not attempt any chronological order. A smaller collection of passages from rabbinic literature is found in Funk's *Monumenta* 63–66, which does not make any distinction between different terms either.

2 For the system of generations of rabbinic authorities, see Streck/Stemberger, *Einleitung* 71–103.

3 For the dating, see Schürer, *History* I 93, 95; Streck/Stemberger, *Einleitung* 259–261, 264–265.

4 See pp. 505 ff.

5 This explains why Krauss discarded chronology altogether in his study.

6 *Bereshit Rabbah* 446.

7 In a tannaitic saying, a so-called *baraita*, in *T.B. Baba Bathra* 56a a similar exposition is attributed to a Rabbi Meir who could be Meir the miracle-maker (*baʕal ha-nes*), living in Palestine in the middle of the second century AD (Streck/Stemberger, *Einleitung* 82): R. Meir says: [they are] NPTWḤʔ, ʕRBʔH, and ŠLMʔH.

8 So Krauss, *Nachrichten* 323.

9 Cf. p. 439. For the Shalamians, see Langdon, *Shalamians*; Pope, *Song* 320.

10 Josephus, *Antiquities* 1:220–221; Jubilees 20:12–13, cf. p. 438.

11 *Bereshit Rabbah* 1106.

12 Acts 2:11; see pp. 190, 418.

13 Pseudo-Jonathan in fact translates all the names of the Ishmaelites into Aramaic. Only the two first ones are identified with peoples. Qedar is also rendered as Arabs in the targum to Psalms 120:5 (cf. Krauss, *Nachrichten* 322).

14 al-ʔAzraqī in his *ʔAkhbār Makka* (81) has preserved a notice that is perhaps related to this one. It is said about the sons of Ismāʕīl: 'The eldest of them were Qaydhār and Nābit, and from these two God made the *ʕarab* spread forth.'

15 Even though the targumic texts have been revised over centuries, there seems to be a fair consensus that the basic haggadic contents are pre-tannaitic. See Schürer, *History* 104–105. Krauss says that the replacement of Qedar by Arabs is a modernization. It is, however, unclear what that means. We know that Qedar between Egypt and Palestine were known as Arabs by foreigners. So were the Nabataeans. The latter did not, however, occupy the same area as Qedar. Arabs-Qedar and Nabataeans are clearly distingushed in this saying. It is difficult to see the targumic terminology as a modernization. It rather reflects a period where there probably were both Nabataeans and Qedar-Arabs south of Palestine, and is thus to be connected with Pliny 5.65. We have suggested above (p. 306) that this scenario corresponds to the situation at the time of Eratosthenes, i.e. the beginning of the third century BC.

16 Streck/Stemberger, *Einleitung* 78.

17 *T.B. Baba Meṣīʕa* 86b. The translation follows Goldschmidt, which gives a better meaning than the Soncino translation. The word *mimmennû* is ambiguous, meaning either 'from us' or 'from him'.

18 According to targum Pseudo-Jonathan ad loc., Ishmael was standing behind the door listening to the conversation between Abraham and his visitors.

19 The Peshitta has *ʕarbāyē*; the LXX has *ismaēlîtai* and Neophyti has SRQYN, i.e. Saracens.

20 *Mekhilta Be-Shallaḥ* VI (Lauterbach 235). Versions of the same commentary are found in *Tosefta Berakhot* IV:16 (Lieberman 10) and *Bereshit Rabbah* 84:17 (Theodor/Albeck 1021). The stench of the Arabs is in these passages said to come from the hides they carry as merchandise.

21 Streck/Stemberger, *Einleitung* 79.

22 Cf. pp. 335 f.

23 *Bereshit Rabbah* 485–486.

24 Strack/Stemberger, *Einleitung* 94.

25 Ptolemy 5.14.4. See p. 437.

26 Above, pp. 418–421.

27 See Strack/Stemberger, *Einleitung* 79, for the dating of Rabbi Aqiba.

28 This is usually not seen as a problem since Arabia is interpreted as a designation for the entire peninsula. Thus Aqiba could have travelled anywhere from Nabataea to Yemen.

29 *Tanḥumah Nasōʔ* 7 (Buber 13); cf. *Ba-Midbar Rabbah* 9:34.
30 Cf. Genesis 30.
31 *Targum Jonathan* ad loc.; *Targum to Chronicles* ad loc.; cf. Krauss, *Völkertafel* 55.
32 *Targum Shir ha-Shirim* 1.5.
33 It is thus a vain task to try to locate Aqiba's Arabia somewhere in Yemen or to search for 'black Arabs' like Japhet, *Chronicles* 710, or to identify Kush with Ethiopia like Ryckmans, *Royaumes* 95, and Altheim/Stiehl, *Araber* III 21–22. The latter point to an interesting parallel to the story in Heliodorus' novel *Aithiopiká* but this only shows that we have to do with a widely spread motif.
34 Streck/Stemberger, *Einleitung* 91.
35 *T.B. ʕErubin* 19a.
36 *T.B. ʕAvodah Zarah* 11b.
37 Streck/Stemberger, *Einleitung* 90.
38 For the relationship between this god and the others in Hatra, see Drijvers, *Hatra* 828 sqq. Attempts at locating this temple in Nabataea must be rejected (Krauss, *Nachrichten* 350, who even wants to change the reading NŠRʔ to DŠRʔ, the name of the Nabataean god Dusares. The temples at Hatra were not known in Krauss' days). Even though the eagle is known as a divine designation elsewhere, the most spectacular sanctuary is the one in Hatra, partly still standing. For a Mesopotamian it must have been the first one worth mentioning, since in Rab's time it was brand new. The temple of Nebo is likely to be that in Borsippa, his main sanctuary since time immemorial (KWRSY is a misspelling of BWRSY[P]); the temple in Ashqelon is mentioned because it was closely associated with the cult of Athargatis (Tarʕata) in the temple at Hierapolis = Mabbug (MPG). The location of the temple of the Arabs in Mesopotamia is definitely verified by a passage in the *Doctrina Addai*, a Syriac text from the beginning of the fifth century AD (Baumstark, *Geschichte* 28) based upon older material. In his exposition of Christian doctrine before the king of Edessa, the apostle Addai says:

> For I saw in this city [Edessa] that it abounded greatly in paganism, which is against God. Who is Nebo, an idol made which ye worship, and Bel, which ye honour? Behold, there are those among you who adore Bath Nikal, as the inhabitants of Harran, your neighbours, and Tarʕata, as the people of Mabbug and the eagle as the ʕRBYʔ. (*Doctrina Addai* 24 Vrs. 24 transl.)

There is no doubt that in both passages, we have to do with a traditional summary of the main cults in upper Mesopotamia.
39 The common assumption that Beth Gerem would be somewhere in our Arabia – Gurhum in Mecca (Krauss, *Nachrichten* 352) or Yarīm in Yemen – should be rejected.
40 *T. B. Shabbat* 144b, cf. *T. Y. Taʕanit* II:1/ 65a (left. col. middle); *T. B. Ketubbot* 67a.
41 *T. B. Baba Bathra* 168b.
42 Streck/Stemberger, *Einleitung* 99.
43 Streck/Stemberger, *Einleitung* 209.
44 Cf. Funk, *Monumenta* no. 364 p. 63.
45 Cohen, *Arabisms*; Krauss, *Nachrichten* 338–349. It is not necessary to see this as a reflex of a 'Mischsprache' between Arabic and Aramaic in Nabataea. Also the place-names from the area found in sources from the second century AD like Ptolemy, Glaucus and also Uranius, show the same mixture of Arabic and Aramaic elements. Especially eye-catching among the latter is the frequency of the suffix *-a* in toponymics: Karakmoba, Sampsa, Galada etc., which, however, is not employed according to the rules of Aramaic. There are weighty reasons to assume that the language in Nabataea was made up by a bundle of isoglosses different from those making up Arabic and Aramaic. But there is no reason to believe that there was a sharp geographical boundary between Arabic, Aramaic and Mishnaic Hebrew in Syria at this time (or any time). The linguistic map looked more or less as it does today with a continuum of isoglosses where it is not possible to say where one language ends and another begins. Cf. Retsö, *Kaškaša* and Contini, *Hawran*.
46 *T. B. Yebamot* 71a; ibid. *ʕAvodah Zarah* 27a.
47 *Mishnah Oholot* 28:10; *Targum Tehillim to* Ps. 120:5 (Krauss, *Nachrichten* 322).
48 *Mishnah Kelaʔim* 24:1.
49 *T. B. Ketubbot* 67a; ibid. *Baba Bathra* 156b; ibid. *Shabbat* 144b (camels), *Mekhilta* II:193

(horses); *Yalquṭ Shimʕoni* Ḥuqqat waydabber end p. 512 (the red heifer). According to *Tosefta Parah* II:1 (Liebermann p. 631) and *T. B. ʕAvodah Zarah* 24a it was bought from the gentiles in Sidon.

50 *Mishnah Kelim* 26:4; *T. B. Menaḥot* 5a.

51 *Mishnah Kelaʔim* 5:10. The utensil is called 'the oven of Ben Dînā', the meaning of which is uncertain. Funk's suggestion (*Monumenta* 65) that it is a misspelling of BYDWNʔ, 'bedouin', is impossible.

52 *Mishnah Kelaʔim* 29:1. The GMDYM/N of the ʕRBYYM is known in Arabic as *ǧimād*. Also Pliny (6.32) mentions a *mithra arabum*.

53 *Mishnah Shabbat* 6:6.

54 *T. B. Bekorot* 49b.

55 *T. B. Sanhedrin* 65b.

56 *Ekhah Rabbati* 23 (Buber p. 20), *Qohelet Rabbah* to 12:7.

57 *Sifre Devarim* 305 (Finkelstein p. 325); *T. B. Ketubbot* 66b; cf. *Tosefta Ketubbot* 5 (Zuckermandel 267 ll. 9–10), where this episode is explained as a fulfilment of Song of Songs 1:8: 'If thou know not, O thou fairest among women, go thy way forth by the footsteps of the flock and feed thy kids beside the shepherds' tents.' Cf. also *Mekhilta* (Lauterbach) II:193 ff.

58 *T. B. Qiddushin* 49b; cf. *ʔAbot d-Rabbi Natan* A:25 (Schechter p. 85). This saying belongs to a genre characterizing peoples and places in a very distinct manner. Related to this one is one about Ishmael (*T. B. Sukkah* 52b):

> There are four things the Holy One, blessed be His Name, regrets that he created: the Exile, the Chaldaeans, the Ishmaelites, and the Evil inclination . . . the Ishmaelites since it is written: 'the tabernacles of robbers prosper, and they who provoke God are secure' (Job 12:6).

59 *T. B. Ketubbot* 36b = ibid. *Giṭṭin* 81a; ibid. *ʕAvodah Zarah* 22b; ibid. *Niddah* 47a.

60 *T. B. Yebamot* 71a

61 *Mishnah Oholot* 18:10.

62 *T. B. Ketubbot* 67a.

19

ARABS IN SOUTH ARABIA

Introduction

The Greeks had extended the designation Arabia to encompass the whole peninsula when they realized the existence of this large land mass beyond the area between Egypt and Palestine. This occurred at the latest in the time of Alexander. There is no doubt that the Greeks even before that time had vague notions of a larger Arabia. The frankincense route from South Arabia, which was established in the seventh century BC, had made it known to them, even though it took some time before they realized the dimensions of this new continent. As has become evident from the preceding survey, the Greeks tended to call all inhabitants of the area Arabs, even though there are sporadic hints in the sources that the Greeks, too, had information that Arabs were in fact a group among others in the frankincense land.

The differentiation between Arabs and other inhabitants in Arabia emerges with indisputable clarity in the large amount of epigraphical material which has come to light during 150 years of research in the history of South Arabia. We now possess a corpus of more than 10,000 inscriptions from the southern parts of the peninsula in different local Semitic languages, mostly Sabaean, from which it is possible to reconstruct the history of this area. The history is still rather sketchy for many periods, and definite datings are not possible for the pre-Christian era. For the six centuries before the rise of Islam we can now pinpoint at least some important historical events chronologically, and a general picture of political and religious developments is now available, although there are still many *lacunae*.[1]

Arabs are mentioned in about forty inscriptions among the many thousand. All of them, except one, can be dated to the Christian era, i.e. the first century AD and onwards. Even though definite years can be ascribed to only a handful of them, almost all testimonies of Arabs can now be set into a historical context and dated at least to specific centuries and in many cases also within decades. It is now possible to sketch a picture of the history of the Arabs in Yemen in pre-Islamic times.[2] All inscriptions are official documents, i.e. they are dedications to gods, set up by officials or kings in South Arabia. They can thus be considered as giving a rather true picture of the role and position of Arabs in South Arabian society and politics, not influenced by the theories and schemes of armchair philosophers and geographers. This evidence is thus crucial for the determination of what the word 'Arab' stands for in the pre-Islamic period.

The earliest phases of South Arabian political history are still shrouded, if not in darkness, at least in mist. The earliest secure date is the evidence from the expeditions of Alexander, documented in the writings of Theophrastus where we find South Arabia divided into four kingdoms: Mamáli, Sabá, Kitíbaina and Hadramyta.[3] If we assume that

Mamáli is the kingdom of the *minaîoi* mentioned somewhat later by Eratosthenes, this evidence is in agreement with what we find in the South Arabian inscriptions from the three pre-Christian centuries.[4] There we find the names of the four kingdoms MʕN in present-day al-Ǧawf, SBʔ with the capital Marib, a town still existing, QTBN in present-day Wādī Bayḥān, and HḌRMT, which still today carries the ancient name Ḥaḍramawt.[5]

The earliest traces of writing in South Arabia have now been dated to the twelfth century BC.[6] We have to wait several centuries, however, until texts with historical information appear. The earliest ones contain names of rulers of Saba, from which a tentative series of successive rulers can be established, starting perhaps at the beginning of the eighth century BC.[7]

Arabs in South Arabia until the end of the third century

Among the earliest inscriptions from South Arabia is a group of texts originating from a king named KRBʔL WTR, conventionally pronounced Karibʔil Watar, from which it is evident that he had conquered areas known to be controlled by the Minaeans and the Qatabanians.[8] This ruler appears as the first empire-builder in Arabia, and he is important for our study since Arabs in South Arabia are probably mentioned for the first time by him. In his largest inscription, set up at the old sanctuary of Ṣirwāḥ west of Marib, he describes his campaigns against neighbouring rulers. After an introduction about the building of irrigation devices (ll. 1–3), the traditional duty of a South Arabian ruler, there follows a description of his dealings with kings of Qatabān and ʔAwsān to the south-east of his capital (ll. 3–14). Then he tells about operations in the north against the cities NŠN, NŠQ and KMNHW, all in the area of al-Ǧawf, the latter two known from the campaign of Gallus in 24 BC. Then it is said:

> and when he slew YDHN and GZBT and ʕRB-M and imposed tribute upon them to ʔLMQH and SBʔ.[9]

Then follows the conquest of HRM and NGRN.[10]

Since there is no trace of such a conquest in the inscriptions from the time after Alexander, the empire of this king must have existed at an earlier date, i.e. before 300 BC. This is also supported by the comparative study of the development of the South Arabian script, where the style of Karibʔil's inscriptions points to a rather early date.[11]

The dating of Karibʔil Watar has been a bone of contention among historians for a long time. Suggestions have oscillated between the early seventh century and the late fifth century BC.[12] There is no doubt that his reign falls within this time span. Most scholars seem now to favour the beginning of the seventh century BC.[13] For this dating two main arguments are given: (1) The archaeological evidence in general supports the dating of the beginning of monumental architecture and script in South Arabia to the eighth century BC, and the palaeography of the inscriptions from Karibʔil Watar's time belong to the two earliest centuries of monumental architecture and script. (2) Karibʔil Watar was early identified with the Sabaean king Ka-ri-bi-ilu mentioned in an Assyrian inscription from 685 BC, bringing gifts to Sennacherib.[14]

> To start with the latter argument, the synchronism is highly uncertain. There is no indication in the Assyrian text that this was a South Arabian ruler, and there is no hint in Karibʔil Watar's own texts that he had anything to do with Assyria

or that there were any political connections that far north. The Assyrian Ka-ri-ib-ilu could as well have been a ruler of the Sabaeans further north.[15] Sennacherib's predecessor Sargon II in 715 BC mentions a Sabaean named It-'a-am-a-ra.[16] That name looks very similar to ʔItāmār, son of Aaron the priest.[17] The latter name is definitely North Arabian and its connection with Sabaean YṮʕʔMR is uncertain. The name YṮʕʔMR is in fact also documented in Dedan.[18] In South Arabia the name Karibʔil was very common among rulers.

The arguments for the dating of Karibʔil Watar to around 685 BC, based on the archaeological material published, still appear somewhat brittle. There are basically two arguments. The first is based on the Italian excavations at Wādī Yalā, south of Wādī Dhana. According to calibrated radio carbon dating, this settlement was abandoned *c*. 535 BC at the latest (the destruction of house A). An inscription found in a creek nearby belongs to Pirenne's style B4, dated by her to *c*. 380 BC, but must, according to the excavators, have been written before 535. This would make the inscriptions of Karibʔil Watar (Styles A2–B1) belong to a time several generations earlier, i.e. the seventh century.[19] It is obvious that there are too many 'ifs' here to make the argument solid. As the scholars themselves admit, it is based on two assumptions: (a) that the destruction of house A coincides with the abandonment of the site, and (b) that the inscription has some connection with the site and house A. None of them is proved. To this can be added the problems with radio carbon dating in general together with the development of South Arabian epigraphy, where we should beware of claiming to know much about the duration of different styles.[20]

The second argument is based on the French excavations in as-Sawdāʔ in al-Ǧawf, ancient NŠN. In this temple, inscriptions in the style of Karibʔil Watar were found on monoliths in the interior, mentioning a ruler SMHYFʕ YSRN, son of LBʔN, king of NŠN, and members of his family. At the entrance there are inscriptions in a very archaic style from the builder of the temple and obviously older than those in the interior. The walls are dated with calibrated radio carbon dating to 830–450 BC. According to the excavators, this means that the temple was built in the eighth century BC and that SMYFʕ ruled a couple of generations later, i.e. in the seventh. Now Karibʔil Watar reports in his inscription that he warred against SMYFʕ in NŠN.[21] This would place Karibʔil Watar in the seventh century BC.[22] The excavator admits that the argument is fragile, built upon radio carbon dating only. To this it may be commented that the temple could as well have been built in the ninth century as well as in the fifth, according to this dating. It is difficult to see why the seventh century has to be chosen, unless one has already made up one's mind, which indeed seems to be the case, since the synchronism with Sennacherib's inscription is accepted. Even though there are now weighty arguments in favour of rejecting the 'short' chronology, dating Karibʔil Watar to the end of the fifth century, one should be most cautious in using the new evidence as a decisive argument for the dating of Karibʔil Watar to the seventh century, even though one accepts the identity of the king of Nashan in the inscriptions. The hypothesis that the time span between the two epigraphic styles in the temple is 'two or three generations, not more' definitely remains to be proved. The impression is that the building inscription is far older than that of SMYFʕ.

The dating of Karibʔil Watar should be made without paying attention to the

Assyrian texts. The latest attempt by K. Kitchen, built on South Arabian epigraphic evidence only, dates him to the end of the sixth century.[23]

The information about the ʕRB-M and the two others in Karibʔil's inscription is tantalizingly short, and we are not informed what these three names stand for. Both before and after this passage ʔHGR-M, plural of HGR-M, are mentioned. This word is usually translated 'town' but may have had a more specific meaning, indicating not only an urban agglomeration but also a special kind of juridical or religious status.[24] Since the word is not mentioned in connection with the three names in line 17, it is likely that they are tribes or the like. From the context it seems that the three are found between the main river of al-Ğawf and Nağrān, i.e. between the urbanized areas of these two oases. The importance of the passage is its mention of Arabs in the area just north-east of al-Ğawf. Arabs appear in that region in later texts and it is likely that the word ʕRB-M here also refers to them.[25] Prior to the establishment of the Minaean kingdom the al-Ğawf area seems to have been divided into several petty states along the river Madhāb.

From al-Ğawf we have a text, MAFRAY ash-Shaqab 3, which has been dated by Ch. Robin to the sixth century BC or a couple of generations after Karibʔil Watar, and which, according to him, is the earliest mention of Arabs in South Arabia.[26] According to Robin the relevant passage runs:

> And all MʕN, free and clients and settlers and ʕRB contributed (?) five ceremonies [in honour] of WD from them, and he gave them a temple and a sacrifice.

It is, however, more likely that ʕRB here is a verb meaning 'to offer', 'to give'. The text thus means: 'and all MʕN, free and dependants, have FQḌ (a verb of unknown meaning) and gave five incense-offerings for WD'. It is thus irrelevant for our theme.[27]

We hear nothing more about Arabs in South Arabia until perhaps the first century AD. Around 100 BC a small region in the western part of the Qatabanian kingdom seems to have acquired independence. The kings of Ḥimyar in the fortress of Raydān started a career which in due time led to the unification of Yemen under their sway. As has been suggested earlier, this was probably the time when the Ptolemies started to sail through the Bāb al-Mandab to India.[28] The power base in South Arabia consequently started to move from the irrigation-based areas on the brim of the desert along the frankincense road towards the highlands in the west, from which both the desert and the coast could be controlled. On the other side of the Red Sea, the kingdom in Axum arose at the same time.

Sometime around the beginning of our era, Yemen seems to have been united by a king named ḎMRʕLY WTR YHNʕM, tentatively vocalized Dhamarʕaliyy Watar Yuhanʕim. He was the first king to be called king of Saba and Dhū Raydān, which indicates that Saba and Ḥimyar were united under him.[29] It would be interesting to know if there is any connection between this unification and the campaign of Aelius Gallus, which probably took place just before Dhamarʕaliyy's reign. Perhaps from this period we have a Sabaean inscription, CIH 79, where Arabs seem to appear again:

> 1) RBB-M YʔZM from of ʔH̲RF dedicated
>
> 2) this inscription to ʔLMQH of HRN . . .
>
> 8) . . . because he saved his servant

9) RBB-M in an attack which he made against the

10) ʕRB in the region of MNHT-M.[30]

The region of MNHT-M is in the upper al-Ǧawf, west of the main towns.[31] RBB-M was from Wādī ʔAkhrūf north-west of ʕAmrān.[32] The god is the main god of Saba. HRN is the temple to this god in the town of ʕAmrān.[33] RBB-M mentions his lord YFRʕ. This name occurs also in the inscription Ry 591, which most probably is from the time of Dhamarʕaliyy.[34] The Arabs mentioned here could thus very well be related to those subjugated by Karibʔil Watar many centuries earlier, who now confronted Karibʔil's late successor, the new empire-builder in Yemen. We know that Dhamarʕaliyy had special interests in the Ǧawf area, shown by his revival of the old cult-site at Ǧabal al-Lawdh.[35]

The first century AD is dominated by the united kingdom of Saba and Dhū Raydān. Among the kings we find one KRBʔL WTR YHNʕM = Karibʔil Yuhanʕim, who is probably identical with Kharibael, mentioned in the *Periplus Maris Erythraei*, reigning *c.* AD 40–70.[36] At the end of the first century AD a king named NŠʔKRB YHʔMN = Nashaʔkarib Yuhaʔmin reigned, who was a grandson of Kharibael.[37] In an inscription from his time, Ja 560, Arabs are mentioned:

1) GWṮM . . . and ʔSLM and their son ʔBKRB . . . ʔKBR . . .

3) of the tribe MYDʕM have dedicated to

4) ʔLMQH . . . these two statues . . .

8) because he has given success in the campaign and the mission on which his

9) lord NŠʔKRB YHNʕM king of Saba, son of ḎMRʕLY ḎRḤ, sent him

10) against the land of the ʕRB to seek out and capture

11) some ʔṢḤB who ṢḤBW (were attached to? belonged to?) the people (ḪLF) [in?] the town (HGR) Marib,

12) and they sought out and captured and seized these soldiers, their

13) ʔṢḤB, and confiscated their riding animals for the soldiers had captured

14) the land and their riding animals; and they brought them home to the town Marib.[38]

The text is difficult and it is not easy to grasp exactly the series of events referred to. The text seems to talk about an operation against ʔṢḤB, 'followers', people who stood in some kind of dependency upon those dwelling in towns.[39] One is reminded of the 'followers' of Muhammed, who early were called *ʔaṣḥāb*.[40] The relationship between these ʔṢḤB, the 'soldiers' (ʔSD) and the ʕRB is, however, not clear. It is not immediately comprehensible what these ʔṢḤB were doing in the land of the ʕRB if they belonged to the region of Marib. We hear for the first time about 'the land of the ʕRB'. It can be assumed that this land was north of Marib, although this is not explicitly said.[41] This is supported by the general picture in the inscriptions treated further below. A possible but uncertain explanation is that these ʔṢḤB had fled to the land of the ʕRB because of some offence (perhaps referred to in lines 13–14) and now were brought back.

Some time after Nashaʔkarib Yuhanʕim, the first Himyarite empire burst into two. This may have occurred after king ʔLŠRḤ YḤḌB = ʔIlsharaḥ Yaḥḍub and his son and co-regent WTR YHʔMN = Watar Yuhaʔmin, whose reigns seem to have ended in turmoil around AD 130. According to later Arabo-Islamic sources, Watar was deposed. Nashaʔkarib had belonged to the tribe of GRT (Gurat) south of Ṣanʕāʔ.[42] ʔIlsharaḥ and Watar seem to have belonged to another group, namely the sons of Marthad, the leading family in the town of ʕAmrān, belonging to the large tribe of Bakīl.[43] Their successor, SʕDŠMS = Saʕdšams, is the first Sabaean king for whom we have a definite date. We know that he reigned in the year AD 141/142.[44] Saʕdshams was probably not a member of the royal dynasty, although this is claimed in some inscriptions. This might be the reason for the wars reported between him and another king of Saba and Dhū Raydān, ḎMRʕLY YHBR = Dhamarʕaliyy Yuhabirr, who is the second documented ruler of Ḥimyar.[45] From several inscriptions we hear about a massive attack on Saʕdshams by a coalition of powers consisting, apart from Ḥimyar, of Ḥaḍramawt, Qatabān and Radmān.

One inscription dealing with this war, Ja 629, mentions Arabs. The author, Marthad, together with his son ḎRḤN from the tribe of YHBʕL, praise the god in the ʔAwwām temple in Marib because he has helped ḎRḤN while the latter was serving the kings of Saba and Dhū Raydān, Saʕdshams and Marthad:

> 6) . . . in/against the land of the ŠʕB of RDMN during the war that WHBʔL from MʕHR had caused/initiated
>
> 7) [together with] ḎḪWLN, ḤḌRMWT, QTBN, RDMN, MḌḤY, and all officers (ʔNS) and ʔʕRB
>
> 8) who supported them against their lords, the kings of Saba.[46]

The inscription then proceeds to enumerate the activities of ḎRḤN in more detail. The operations took place in the south-east against the king of Ḥaḍramawt, YDʕʔL = Yadaʕʔil, and the chief of Maʕāfir, present-day Ḥuğariyya, WHBʔL.[47] One episode is the following:

> 32) because he [the god] has protected and saved his worshipper ḎRḤN ʔŠWʕ from GRF and [also] RBŠMS YʕRR
>
> 33) son of/from ʕLFQM from an attack (ʕNT) which they made, pursuing Ḥaḍramis and ʕRB, who had advanced to
>
> 34) the region of Timnaʕ.[48]

We notice here for the first time the occurrence of the plural ʔʕRB (line 8). These appear as supporters of the kings that were the enemies of Saba, and they stood in the same category as the ʔNS, a term for warrior, probably an officer of some kind. The ʔʕRB are thus allies of the South Arabian kings and on this occasion rallying against the kings in the northern highlands. In the second passage (line 33) the ʕRB are not attached to any special local rulers and give the impression of operating on their own. The scene is the region around the Qatabanian capital of Timnaʕ in Wādī Bayḥān.[49]

We thus find 'Arabs' as both enemies and allies of the rulers of South Arabia in the first half of the first century AD. Arabs around Timnaʕ are mentioned in a text called Doe 2, originating from that very area, written in the local language, Qatabanian. It could then be assumed to come from the period when the Qatabanian kingdom still existed. This kingdom was conquered by Ḥaḍramawt sometime in the second century AD.[50] The palaeography of the text would also favour a dating to the second century AD.[51] It should thus be connected with the preceding text. It goes as follows:

> 1) HWŠʕ ʔŠWʕ son of/from ʔH̱RN, ʕRB of DWNM from ṮMD and protected by ʕM
>
> 2) of ibexes in the town H̱ḎRY has dedicated to his god and lord ʕM of ibexes
>
> 3) in his sanctuary, ŠʕBN in the town H̱ḎRY, a statue of gold/bronze because he had promised him for his
>
> 4) protection and the protection of his safety (?) and his ability and for the protection of the masters of their house and all that he owns
>
> 5) and possesses; and [on the day] when ʕM delivered and helped his servant HWŠʕ, his domestics and slaves and
>
> 6) the subjects (RʕM) he had brought with him when he campaigned; and he celebrated a feast to the Master of BŠRM in the sanctuary of
>
> 7) ṢNʕ when he had given them victory in a razzia against the ʕRB in the valley of KLS^{3}FM, and there was
>
> 8) a killing behind them and before them in this battle; and ʕM instructed and delivered his servant . . .[52]

This refers to religious acts in two different sanctuaries. The first one is in the town of H̱ḎRY, which is situated in Wādī Bayḥān, south of Timnaʕ.[53] The other one is in an unidentified area but probably also within the confines of Qatabān.[54] The latter part speaks about a razzia against Arabs in an unidentified valley. If this is in Wādī Bayḥān, we are reminded of the ʕRB in Jamme 629 who are said to operate near Timnaʕ. If they are identical with those mentioned here, which is not impossible although not provable at the moment, the events would have happened *c.* AD 140.

The crux in the text is the identification of the protagonist. The name ṮMD is probably an area north-west of Ḥaḍramaut. DWN-M is found in the expression ʕM ḎDWNM, '[the god] ʕAmm from DWN', and would thus be the name of a sanctuary or a place. According to two Qatabanian inscriptions, the god had a sanctuary in Timnaʕ, the capital of Qatabān.[55] The temple of DWN was, however, somewhere else in Qatabān.

Most difficult are the two words ʔH̱RN and ʕRB. The latter is undoubtedly part of a genitive construction with the following word thus giving the meaning 'the ʕRB of DWN-M'. ʔH̱RN could mean 'lineage' or be a proper name of a tribe or the like. It has been suggested that ʕRB here does not mean 'bedouin' but 'hostage'.[56] It is then obscure what 'the hostage of DWN-M from ṮMD' would mean. The full meaning of this passage cannot be established until a thorough discussion of the meaning of the root ʕRB is made, as also the relationship between the meaning 'hostage', 'pledge' on the one hand, and 'Arab' on the other. It should, however, be noted that the form ʕRB is documented from the area of Timnaʕ in both MAFRAY Miʕsāl 3 and Ja 629.[57]

The result of the conflict in the middle of the second century AD, which evolved around the dissolution of the first empire of united Saba and Dhū Raydān, was a short Himyaritic rule in Marib by Dhamarʕliyy Yuhabirr, which was then ended by a new ruler from the northern highlands: WHBʔL YḤZ.[58] The division was made permanent for more than a century. The political centre had definitely moved into the highlands of Yemen, which from now on were divided between two political centres: one south of the Yislaḥ pass, whose kings resided in the castle of Raydān carrying the name of Ḥimyar, the other one north of the pass, where we find a series of dynasties from different tribes, mostly from the plains just north of Ṣanʕāʔ. The old centre in Marib continued to be some kind of ceremonial capital for the northern kingdom. A factor which has caused much confusion among modern scholars is that both the northern and southern kings often called themselves by the same title 'king of Saba and Dhū Raydān', and that control of Marib was a main target for the Himyarite kings in Raydān as well as those residing in the northern highlands.

WHBʔL YḤZ, who called himself king of Saba, was from the Bataʕ family of the Ḥumlān tribe. The Ḥumlān tribe belonged to the Sumʕay federation, north of Ṣanʕāʔ.[59] These events might have occurred around the middle of the second century AD. We have an inscription, Ja 561 bis, originating from a chief in the Hamdān clan, leaders of the Ḥāšid tribe, which was another part of the Sumʕay federation. This chief, YRM ʔYMN, had earlier acted as an arbiter in the war between Saʕdshams and Ḥimyar, and now appears together with his brother BRG as the *condottiero* of the pretender from Bataʕ.[60] When thanking the god of Marib for his protection in warfare, he reports two military operations in which he has taken part: one against the king of Dhū Raydān and the other one as follows:

> 6) because ʔLMQH has granted favours and protected his subjects (ʔDM) from
>
> 7) HMDN and their ŠʕB ḤŠD with triumph
>
> 8) and killing . . .
>
> 10) in all the combats for which
>
> 11) they joined for war against some ʔʕRB on
>
> 12) the borders of the ŠʕB of ḤŠD, and some from the lands of the ʕRB,
>
> 13) ʔʕRB who had committed offences against their lords, the kings

> 14) of SBʔ and Ḏ RYDN, and some of the lands of the ʔŠʕB of the king of SBʔ.[61]

In this not too easy text there is talk about two groups: one group of ʔʕRB on the border of the land of the Ḥāshid, and another living in the land of the ʕRB.[62] If we assume that these are not identical and that the border regions of Ḥāshid are different from the land of the ʕRB, it is likely that those who have 'sinned' against the kings of Saba are those on the borders of Ḥāshid. If we are to judge from the texts treated so far, it can be assumed that 'the lands of the ʕRB' (ʔRḌT ʕRB-N) lie farther north. If it is identical with 'the land of the ʕRB' (ʔRḌ ʕRB-N) in Ja 560, it would be located in the region of al-Ǧawf or not far from there. We find once again that the Arabs who are allied with or dependent upon the kings are called ʔʕRB, i.e. a plural form, whereas those dwelling further out are designated with a singular or collective form: ʕRB.

In a text from roughly the same period, CIH 353, we hear once more about YRM and BRG.[63] The text, which is slightly damaged, is a thanksgiving by a certain SʕDTʔLB YHŠʕ and someone else and their sons to their god Taʔlab Riyyām, who was the main god of the Sumʕay federation. Saʕdtaʔlab has taken part in a war with Ḥimyar. There is talk about a siege of a fortress in the town ḌHR by the two kings of the Raydanites (= Himyarites): MLKKRB and ŠMR YHRʕŠ:

> 8) . . . and they beleaguered them in it [the fortress] until they were close to death . . .
>
> 9) . . . they made a pact with their two lords YRM and BRĠ, sons of BTʕ and HMDN . . .
>
> 10) . . . the Raydanites and a tenth of SFLN and the ʔʕRB of Marib and Ḏʔ BN, the land . . .
>
> 11) . . . their two lords ŠFʕṮT ʔŠWʕ and YRM ʔYMN helped after them/afterwards
>
> 12) . . . and he pursued them on the two hills and liberated them, their prisoners . . .[64]

Due to the lacunae in the text, the course of events is not altogether clear. From another text, obviously dealing with the same events, we know that the lords ŠFʕṮT ʔŠWʕ and YRM ʔYMN are chiefs in the Ḥāshid tribe, namely the clans of Dhū Raydat.[65] ḌHR is the present-day well-known Wādī Ẓahr, north-west of Sanʕāʔ.[66] A plausible reconstruction of the events is that the Ḥimyar kings attacked, and the author and his men were besieged in the town of ḌHR. The Himyarites had support from SFLN. This group is somewhat difficult to locate. According to some, they originally belonged to the Sumʕay, but according to al-Hamdānī, they also settled around Ẓafār, the Himyarite capital.[67] Others locate them on the edge of the desert.[68] To the allies of Ḥimyar also belonged the ʔʕRB around Marib. When the siege had been lifted with the aid of the chiefs YRM and BRG, who had established the alliance between Bataʕ and Hamdān, the leading clans of the tribes Ḥumlān and Ḥāshid respectively, there followed a campaign against the allies of the Himyarites, now together with other chiefs from Ḥāshid.

To the same period probably belongs the inscription Ryckmans 502 = Jamme 2131 = Glaser 1177. Unfortunately it is damaged like CIH 353 but according to G. Ryckmans it should be supplemented by the inscription RÉS 4658, together with which it forms the fragments of a larger text.[69] The reconstruction runs as follows:

> . . . have dedicated to TʔLB [RYMM, the lord of KBDM]
>
> 2) . . . SM when they set out and attacked in their east, when the ŠʕB had revolted . . .
>
> 3) . . . in ḤRB east of YRSM, and they annihilated and defeated this army of . . .
>
> 4) . . . SẖYMM, the chiefs (ʔQYL) of the tribe . . . and LḤYʕṮT from SẖYMM and with them five horses and two hundred soldiers . . .
>
> 5) . . . LḤYʕṮT and their tribe . . . they killed of the army of these ʔʕRB two hundred soldiers, apart from those who returned wounded . . .
>
> 6) . . . hundred men to . . . and the baggage-train, which had set out with this army; and LḤʕṮT praised the power and force of his patron-god T[ʔLB RYMM . . .
>
> 7) . . . after this troop (GYŠ) . . . and captured the army of these SFLN and the one who supported them from the ʔʕRB . . .[70]

The last three lines speak about further operations on the borders of SẖYM. This group was a clan of chiefs in ḎHGR, north-east of Ṣanʕāʔ, which constituted the third part of the Sumʕay federation (the other two were Ḥāshid governed by Hamdān and Ḥumlān governed by Bataʕ).[71] We recognize the SFLN, together with the ʔʕRB in CIH 353, as the enemy of the Bataʕ/Hamdān chiefs. It seems that the events reflected in Ry 502/Ja 2131/RÉS 4658 are the same as in CIH 353.[72] Thus, in a war between the Sumʕay tribes and the Himyarites, we find the SFLN and the ʔʕRB as allies of the latter. The Arabs in Ry 502/Ja 2131(/RÉS 4658) would in that case be the 'Arabs of Marib' mentioned in CIH 353.[73]

We see in these texts the emergence of the supremacy of the Sumʕay tribes in the highlands against the dominance of Ḥimyar as well as against the Bakīl group. The Arabs around Marib sided with the tribes further north (SFLN, ḎʔBN) against the new power in the northern highlands, just as the ʔʕRB in the borderlands of Ḥāshid had done in the days of Saʕdshams.

With WHBʔL the Bataʕ clan, belonging to the Sumʕay tribe, had taken power in the north. There seems to have been a smooth transfer of power from his descendants to the YRM ʔYMN mentioned in Ja 561 bis, who apparently played an important role during the rise of the Sumʕay kings.[74] With YRM, whose access can be dated to around AD 180, the Hamdān clan from the Ḥāshid tribe became dominant. The pressure from Ḥimyar continued under YRM's grandson ʕAlhān Nahfān. During his reign (*c.* AD 190–205) we find Saba seeking alliances against the Himyarites, re-establishing ties with Ḥaḍramawt and, more fatefully, calling in the new vigorous rulers on the other side of the Bāb al-Mandab in Axum.[75] Thus the rising kingdom of Ḥimyar now met with a massive alliance of opponents.

From the reign of ʕAlhān we have a royal text, Nami 72+73+71, which unfortunately is fragmentary. The reconstructed reading of the extant pieces runs:

1) . . . over them ʕLHN, king of Saba and the troops (ḪMYS) and the ʔʕRB of the king of Saba

2) . . . MḎḤY and QTBN and chiefs and leaders and ʔŠʕB of the king of ḤBŠT

3) . . . land and pasture (NWYN) of ḎRYDN, subjected people and troops and the ʔʕRB of the king

4) . . . RYDN for the safety of their property/kingdom (MLKHMW) at the time when . . .

5) and the ʔʕRB of the king of ḤḌRMWT and the tribes

6) . . . and the troops of the Raydanites and then . . .[76]

In spite of the disconnected fragments we can discern some facts of interest. The text probably deals with the rule of ʕAlhān after his victory over most of his enemies. Important for us is the presence of Arabs as allies to the kings of Saba, of Ḥaḍramawt and, perhaps, also of Ḥimyar (ḎRYDN). The latter could be mentioned in line 3. The main powers of South Arabia did have Arabs as allies at the end of the second century BC, and they are mentioned together with troops of different kings. In Ja 629 we already found ʔʕRB together with Qatabān and Ḥaḍramawt around AD 140. This shows that the Arabs were mainly used as soldiers of some kind.

Another text ascribed to the reign of ʕAlhān is CIH 350.[77] The author, ʔBKRB YHSKR, is from the tribe of Ḥāshid and has taken part in military operations against Himyarites and Habashites around the town of NʕṬ, south-east of Ṣanʕāʔ, which was a major centre in the Gurat area, and further south in MRD in the land of ʔLHN, on the south-eastern border of Sumʕay:[78]

7) . . . and because they advanced against the ḤBŠT in the region . . .

8) and one man/officer was killed there; and because a column of support advanced [against]

9) the ʕRB, ten and [one] hundred soldiers, and they advanced a[gainst]

10) BRQ-N, and one man/officer was killed there . . .[79]

It seems that this passage refers to three attacks, one of them against Arabs.[80] The context is, as often in these texts, not clear.

We possess a unique text which may give a hint about an Arabia outside the kingdoms of Yemen. The Christian author Cosmas Indicopleustes visited the port of the

Axumite kingdom Adoulis around AD 530. There he saw two Greek inscriptions, which he copied and included in his book on Christian geography. One of these inscriptions was by an Axumite king who, judging from the text, was a great conqueror. Unfortunately, his name is missing in Cosmas' text, probably because the inscription was already damaged when Cosmas saw it. Most scholars nowadays think that the author of the text could very well have been GDRT, the king of the ḤBŠT mentioned in Sabaean inscriptions as the ally of ʕAlhān.[81] He says that he was the first king in his kingdom to extend his sway to the Arabian peninsula. This goes nicely with the evidence from Yemen, where GDRT is the first Axumite king who is mentioned and who had troops on the Yemeni side of the Bāb al-Mandab.[82]

The author tells about his military exploits on the African side of the Red Sea, which obviously extended as far as the Nile. Then he says:

> And to the *arabîtai* and the *kinaidokolpîtai* living on the other side of the Red Sea I dispatched an army of ships and infantry and subjected their kings and ordered them to pay tribute from their land and travel and sail in peace. I waged war from Leukē Kōmē unto the land of the *sabaîoi*.[83]

Here three peoples are mentioned, one of which are the *arabîtai*. It is clear that these live outside the Sabaean territory and north of it.[84] We know that the Axumites penetrated unto Nağrān, i.e. the area where the land of the Arabs seems to have been situated according to the inscriptions treated so far.[85] We have also found evidence in Ptolemy's *Geography* of Arab presence in this area.[86] In that case, the author of the Adulis inscription has penetrated inland to Nağrān and even further eastwards. There is, however, another possibility, namely that this is a reference to Arabs living in the Tihāma. The title of the later Himyaritic kings in the fifth century AD seems to indicate some kind of Arab presence there.[87] Much later al-Hamdānī commented on the names Qanawnā, Dawqa, al-Līth, ʕAšm as-Sirrayn and as-Sarāʔ, all names in the Tihāma south of Ğidda, mentioned in a poem by the Yemeni poet Abū l-Ḥayyāsh:

> These are names of the land (*bilād*) of the *ʕarab*: waterholes, wādīs of the Tihāma and the *sarwiyya*, known, famed, mentioned, which the *ʕarab* from the people (*ʔahl*) of Tihāma, both their *bādī* and their *ḥāḍir* occupy.[88]

The impression from this text is, once again, that the *ʕarab* are one section or group of the inhabitants in the Tihāma. Otherwise it is difficult to understand why it is necessary to single out these places as inhabited by them in particular. No one can allege that these *ʕarab* are identical with nomads or bedouin. Presence of a special group of people called *ʕarab* in the Tihāma was obviously well documented for al-Hamdānī. Such a presence is probably supported by the title of the Himyaritic rulers. The earliest documentation may thus be the Adulis inscription, which confirms the picture given by the Sabaean texts in seeing Arabs as one group among many others in south-western Arabia.

ʕAlhān's successor ŠʕR ʔWTR = Shaʕr ʔAwtār was the great conqueror among the kings of the Bataʕ/Hamdān dynasty. We know that he reigned in the year AD 217/218.[89] He continued the alliance with Ḥaḍramawt and Axum but in the later years of his reign the alliance seems to have broken up, and we hear about conflicts with Ḥaḍramawt and the tribes in the north-east as well as with the Axumites.[90] The Ethiopians had a strong influence in the Nağrān area, and Shaʕr's ambition was to break this encirclement. We know that Shaʕr captured the Ḥaḍramī capital of Shabwa and undertook two large campaigns against Kinda and one against Nağrān, where the Ethiopians were.

We have two texts made by officers who took part in these campaigns, which are of interest for this study. The first one, Iryani 12, is from an officer, WFYM ʔḎRḤ, who was entrusted by Shaʕr ʔAwtār to guard the boundaries of the Ḥāshid tribe during the war with the ʔḤBŠ, the Habashites:

> 2) and he [WFYM ʔḎRḤ] protected all the boundary stones of the HGR and of the countryside-dwellers (ʔHL) of the ŠʕB of ḤŠD and those who supported them from 'the sons of the ʔʕRB' during all the years when he performed his commission to provide protection guarding the boundary stones of ḤŠD until the ʔḤBŠ made peace . . . the ʔḤBŠ invaded (crossed the boundaries) and attacked with five hundred and two thousand soldiers; and they attacked some of the ʔʕRB in the wādī of Ḏ WʕRM in western ḤŠD
>
> 3) and WFYM ʔḎRḤ came to help against them, and with him were seventy and one hundred soldiers of the [ʔ]ʕRB; and he pursued/reached them in the second night in MʕQR Ḏ ŠRḤT; and they attacked in the middle of their camp in the night, and they killed and routed them out of their camp and they captured from them five hundred and seventy captives.[91]

The other one, Ja 635, is from a certain ʔBKRB ʔḤRS who took part in the campaigns against Nağrān, where the Habashites were, and further the operations against the king of Kinda in Qaryat al-Fāw:[92]

> 29) . . . because ʔLMQH protected his servant ʔBKRB
>
> 30) so as to return with booty, captives, loot,
>
> 31) booty, and horses which they killed and which they captured
>
> 32) alive, when (BKN) his lord had sent him to fight
>
> 33) and to take command of some from ḪWLN ḪḌLM and some
>
> 34) from NGRN and some from the ʔʕRB in order to wage war against the
>
> 35) tribe (ʕŠRT) of YḤBR, soldiers who gave support to the sons of YW[N]M
>
> 36) and QRYTM.[93]

In both these texts, the ʔʕRB are the allies of the Sabaean king.[94] They are explicitly associated with the border of one of the great tribes on the plateau in Ir 12. In Ja 635 they are said to live in ḪWLN ḪḌLM. This is the present-day Ḫawlān Ṭiyāl, the area and the tribes in the mountains between Ṣanʕāʔ and Marib.[95] There is no doubt that these Arabs were well integrated in the military system of the Sabaean monarchy and took part in operations as some kind of auxiliary troops. We have already observed that the allied Arabs are usually designated with the plural form ʔʕRB. In Ir 12 we have the form ʕRB once. Due to the strange history of the documentation of the Iryani texts there are several misspellings in Iryani 12, and it cannot be taken as a strong argument against the claim that the plural form is the proper designation for the allied Arabs.[96]

From the time of these Sabaean kings we have Arabs appearing in another part of South Arabia. At al-ʕUqla, not far from Shabwa, the capital of Ḥaḍramawt, there is a large rock with inscriptions. From the kings mentioned in them we can see that this was a kind of sanctuary in use at least from the time of the Sabaean king YRM ʔYMN until the end of the third century AD.[97] Among the inscriptions we find the two following:

ʔTYBT son of ʕMRM, the ʕRBY, the MQTWY[98]

GDWT and ŠNDM, the two ʕRBYT, the two MBNYT[99]

MQTWY is a term for some kind of subordinate officer or official.[100] MBN is a name of some kind, perhaps that of a tribe. An exact dating of these two texts is not possible, but they certainly belong to the decades around AD 200.[101] Here we meet with adjectives, masculine singular and feminine singular, the latter with the dual affix (*-yhn*) added, formed from the root ʕRB. The first person is actually the son of someone with a genuine (North) Arabic name, ʕAmr. There are, in fact, plenty of such names in the ʕUqla texts. In the north, we have already found several cases of individuals designated by an adjective derived from the noun 'Arab', from Gindibu the Arab to the Nabataean kings. The ʕUqla texts seem to indicate that, whatever the word actually means, it appears in connection with people with names of a North Arabian type. It should also be observed that we now once more have women explicitly called Arabs.[102]

The inscription CIH 343 is not possible to date exactly but seems to belong to the period of the Bataʕ/Hamdān dynasty, although it cannot be ascribed to the reign of a definite king. Its authors, HʕN YʔZM and his sons, are subjects of the BTʕ clan, the leaders of the ḤMLN tribe. It is a series of thanksgivings to the god of SMʕY, TʔLB in the temple in Riyam, among which is the following:

13) . . . and because he protected them

14) in the land of ḤMYR-M and (of?) the ʕRB and in all the campaigns

15) they undertook . . .[103]

The Arabs mentioned here are definitely the enemies of the authors. The Ḥimyar and the ʕRB are obviously two different regions, although they seem to be allied. There is an inscription which might fit into the same scenario of growing pressure against Saba from Ḥimyar and their allies, among them the ʕRB. It was found at Khadaqān in the area of Sumʕay, the large tribal federation north of Ṣanʕāʔ not far from where the author of CIH 343 lived:

. . . son of ʔLŠRḤ son [of]

. . . dedicated to their [goddess] ŠMS the statue

. . . of warriors whom he killed from the ŠʕB of ḤMYRM and ḤḌRMWT and the ʕRB in a war which the kings of Saba waged against these

ʔŠʕB . . .[104]

The dating is uncertain, although the paleography allows a dating to the end of the third century AD. The text speaks about a war against Saba by the Himyarites and their allies in Ḥaḍramawt. On their side are also the ʕRB. We notice that the latter word has the same form as in CIH 343 and seems to play the same role. The two texts should probably be read together with those from al-ʕUqla as a testimony to the growing integration of ʕRB into the kingdoms east of Saba.

After the reign of Shaʕr ʔAwtār the Sabaean kingdom seems to have started its way downhill. Perhaps around AD 230 we have a new dynasty, that of FRʕ YNHB, residing in Marib, controlling the northern and central highlands.[105] Under his sons, ʔIlsharaḥ Yaḥḍub and Yaʔzil Bayyin, the last great confrontation with the rivals in Ẓafār took place. The king of Ḥimyar called in the Ethiopian king ʕḎBH against the Sabaeans. The kings in Marib tried under these circumstances to keep peace on the northern flank. This is the background of the inscription Jamme 2110, a dedication from a certain MQTWY, WFYM to the god in Marib as fulfilment of a promise he had made to the god:

6) when they thirsted in the north for three days and nights

7) when he was sent to the kings of the north

8) ʔL-ḤRṮ son of KʕB, king of ʔSD and MLK

9) son of BD, king of KDT, MḎḤG and some of

10) the ʔʕRB . . .[106]

WFYM was sent by ʔIlsharaḥ Yaḥḍub and Yaʔzil Bayyin, the two kings of Saba and Dhū Raydān. The names of the kings and tribes in the north are partly familiar. Mālik was king of Kinda, and he was obviously acknowledged by the Madhḥiğ tribe as well. The ʔSD is most likely to be the ʔAzd, well known from Islamic sources, who inhabited the Sarāt area, i.e. the mountainous lands between Ṭāʔif and Nağrān, known today as ʕAsīr.[107] The king has a pure Arabic name with the definite article *ʔl*. A tribe named Balḥārith is known from the Nağrān area in Islamic sources.[108] They were called 'sons of al-Ḥārith son of Kaʕb' which is exactly the name found in the inscription, and it is likely that they were related to the king in the middle of the third century AD.[109]

To these come the Arabs who are clearly different from the two tribes. From the context it seems that the Arabs were subjects or allies to Mālik, the king of Kinda, but it is evident that, at least according to our inscription, there is no identity between the two named tribes and the Arabs here.[110]

Two more inscriptions from the time of ʔIlsharaḥ Yaḥḍub are relevant for our theme. They are by an officer (MQTWY) of the local rulers of Ḫalīl and Suḫaym in the northern highlands named SʕD ŠMS giving thanks to the god in Marib:

Now he has protected his servant SʕDŠMS in all the expeditions he has

> undertaken and fought against the ʔʕRB in the land of MḌḤY, RDMN and QTBN.[111]

The expedition was undertaken against the areas south and south-east of Marib in the area originally governed by the kings of Qataban and was possibly connected with the larger operations against the Himyarite kings in Ẓafār. The second inscription gives a more precise geographical location:

> . . . when they made an expedition and fought and raided in the land of RDMN, MḌḤY and the valleys of ʔH̲R of QTBN against the ʔʕRB.[112]

The ʔʕRB apparently belonged to the areas of the large tribes enumerated in the texts. The 'valleys of ʔH̲R' are identical with present-day Wādī Khirr, which is the upper course of Wādī Bayḥān.[113] Like the ʔʕRB in the north, these also seem to be integrated in the military system of the three enumerated tribes and do not appear as roaming nomads in the desert.

There exists an inscription roughly contemporary with the preceding ones, but written by a Himyarite local ruler over Radmān. The inscription MAFRAY Miʕsāl 3 is still unpublished, but there is mention of a certain T̲WBSY, who has the title SWD ʕRBN.[114] The exact meaning is difficult to determine with the text still inaccessible, but it could mean 'the leaders of the Arabs' or the like.[115] At least it shows that people thus designated were found far south-east of the Himyarite capital.

Around AD 275 the kingdom of Saba disappeared and evidently was finally conquered by the Himyarite king ŠMR YHRʕŠ = Shammar Yuharʕish (III). This king also took Ḥaḍramawt and thus created a South Arabian empire that was to play a crucial role in the history of Arabia during the two following centuries. We know from one inscription that he continued the policy in the north which was initiated by the Sabaean kings Shaʕr ʔAwtār and ʔIlsharaḥ Yaḥḍub (II). He sent an embassy to the Iranian court in Mesopotamia and to the land of Tanūkh.[116] The new empire in Arabia showed its ambition to take a part in the world politics of late antiquity.

From Shammar's operations in Ḥaḍramawt, we have one text where 'Arabs' appear. The text, originally published by A. H. Sharafaddin (No. 32), goes as follows:

> 8–9) and their lord ŠMR YHRʕŠ, king of Saba and D̲RYDN, son of YSR YHNʕM king of Saba and D̲RYDN, ordered them
>
> 10) to make an expedition and a war and to put themselves as leaders of the ŠʕB of Saba
>
> 11) and some from the H̲MS and the ʔʕRB and to go to war with eight
>
> 12) hundred warriors, mounted, from the ŠʕB of Saba and six
>
> 13) hundred warriors, mounted, from ḤMLN, H̲WLN and
>
> 14) ʔWSQN and the ʔʕRB of KDT and with six [hundred] horsemen and to march

15) and to get water supply from the wādī of ʕBRN. From there they were to march

16) and supply themselves with corn and to make a raid on the town (HGRN) of ʕBRN with its [surrounding] valleys, and

17) the town of ŠBM and the town of RṬGTM and SʔYN and all the towns

18) and . . . and towns . . . in the region of the town ŠBM . . .

19) . . . from the owners of ŠBM and to make a raid in its valleys . . .

20) and from it . . . , and they returned with their spoils . . .[117]

From the names of the towns mentioned, it is clear that the operations took place in Ḥaḍramawt.[118] We notice that the army of the Himyarite king is divided into several kinds of troops: mounted warriors (ʔSD RKB) from Saba itself; and mounted warriors from the regions of the highlands, Ḥumlān and Ḫawlān, which perhaps constituted the ḪMS.[119] Then come the ʔʕRB, which are two different groups: one from Saba and one from Kinda. It is likely that the mounted warriors, in fact, were camel riders and thus distinguished from the horsemen.[120] It seems, however, that the camel riders were not necessarily ʔʕRB. Shammar thus continued the policy of his predecessors by employing ʔʕRB from different regions for military purposes. It was also to be the policy of his successors.

Arabs in South Arabia from the fourth to the sixth century

The unification of Saba, Ḥimyar and Ḥaḍramawt around AD 275 under Shammar Yuharʕish was followed by an obscure period in South Arabian history. It seems that Ḥaḍramawt was lost and had to be reconquered by Shammar's successors.[121] The main documents for the reconquest are three inscriptions by two officers who took part in the operations. There seem to have been two campaigns. The first was undertaken under a king named YSR YHNʕM, who was the successor of Shammar Yuharʕish.[122] It would have occurred during the first decade of the fourth century AD:

Ja 665:

1) SʕDTʔLB YTLF from GDN, KBR

2) of the ʔʕRB of the king of Saba and [of] KDT, MḎḤG, ḤRM,

3) BHL, and ZYDʔL and all ʔʕRB of Saba and ḤMYR,

4) ḤḌRMWT and YMNT, has dedicated to

5) ʔLMQH, the Lord of Awwam, this statue of gold in praise, because

6) their lord ʔLMQH, the Lord of Awam, has protected him

7–8) when their lord YSR YHNʕM and his son ḎRʔʔMR, the two kings of Saba ḎRYDN and

9) ḤḌRMWT and YMNT, ordered them to fight and precede their two lords YSR

10) YHNʕM and his son ḎRʔʔMR, the two kings of Saba, ḎRYDN,

11) ḤḌRMWT and YMNT, against the land of ḤḌRMWT;

12) and their lord YSR YHNʕM ordered them to make war and and to precede them and his

13) corps of mercenaries, the ʔʕRB of the king of Saba and KDT and the lords of NŠQ

14) and NŠN.[123]

Saʕdtaʔlab belonged to Gadan, one of the leading clans in the land of Ḥāshid.[124] He appears in another operation against Ḥaḍramawt, perhaps a decade later:

Iryani 32:

1) SʕDTʔLB from GDN, KBR of the ʔʕRB

2) of the king of Saba and KDT, MḎḤG, ḤRM,

3) BHL, ZYDʔL and all ʔʕRB of Saba,

4) ḤMYR, ḤḌRMWT and YMNT, has dedicated

5) to his Lord, ʔLMQH lord of Awam, this statue of gold in

6) praise, because his servant SʕDTʔLB from GDN was sent

7) and his corps of mercenaries, the ʕRB, as protection of NŠQ against

8) ḤḌRMWT. And to them came a message and a call

9) from their lord ḎMRʕLY YHBR, king of Saba,

10) ḎRYDN, ḤḌRMWT and YMNT that SʕDTʔLB from GDN should make an expedition

11) and wage a war, and that he should make himself leader of the ŠʕB

12) of Saba, the lords of Marib, and the ʔʕRB of the king of Saba and [of] KDT,

13) NGRN, and SFLN. And they departed to the sanctuary of

14) GRW, and all their troops waited seven days.

15) And from Saba went only three hundred

16) warriors and from the ʕRB only three hundred and

17) twenty warriors as horsemen . . .[125]

From that campaign we also have one further text from another participant:

CIH 397:

1) ʔLRM YḤMD . . .

2) and ŠRḤʕLY . . .

3) subject to the king dedicated . . .

4) to ʔLMQH, lord of the ibexes of Ṣirwāḥ [this statue]

5) of gold in praise because ʔLMQH showed him favour

6) through his oracle to Saba. And

7) this ʔLRM marched together with the people of Saba and

8) the ʕRB and SʕDTʔLB from GDN was made their leader.

9) The day they marched and fought in

10) SRRN indeed ʔLMQH then was merciful towards his servant;

12) ʔLRM wounded men deadly in the region of

13) the town MRYMTM and took prisoners and

14) booty which he [ʔLMQH] vouchsafed him . . .[126]

The dating of these texts is made possible by the mention of the king ḎMRʕLY YHBR in the first of them. The son of this king, ṮʔRN YHNʕM, is mentioned in a text dated to the year AD 319/324.[127] Both texts deal with operations in the central Ḥaḍramawt: the town MRYMTM is mentioned in both and is identified with a ruin between Sayʔūn and Tarīm.[128] SRRN, 'the valley', is probably Ḥaḍramawt itself.[129]

We are here confronted with a KBR, some kind of high military official who is the commander of ʔʕRB, who seem to be special troops to the kings.[130] Unfortunately, the syntax of the first lines of Ja 665 and Ir 32 is not so clear to us that we can define the exact position of these Arabs. The ʔʕRB belonging to the king of Saba we have met before. The problem is whether Saʕdtaʔlab, KBR of the Arabs, belongs to the king of

Saba and, further, KBR of KDT, MḎḤG etc., or whether he is KBR of the ʔʕRB of the king as well as KBR of the ʔʕRB of KDT etc. In the latter case, the passage 'all ʔʕRB of Saba, Ḥimyar, Ḥaḍramawt and YMNT' would be a summary of the preceding tribes. It is clear that the interpretation depends on preconceived ideas about the identity of the ʔʕRB. The ʔʕRB could be a group separated from the enumerated tribes (Kinda etc.).[131] But the meaning could also be that some ʔʕRB belonged to the king of Saba, others belonged to the tribe of KDT etc. ʔʕRB would then be a part of KDT but not identical with them. A similar hint is given in the text Sharafaddin 32. In that case, Ir 32 would refer to Arabs at Nağrān as well as among the SFLN. According to al-Hamdānī, a group called Sufl dwelt in the westernmost part of al-Ğawf and were probably related to those around Ẓafār.[132] As we have seen, CIH 79 refers to ʕRB in that area. The view of Arabs as a section of the tribes enumerated is thus possible from the texts and fits well into the general picture emerging from the sources.

Later in the fourth century we hear about further activities involving Arabs. A certain MLŠN, from the clan of YZʔN in the region of Mayfaʕ between Ḥaḍramawt and Dathīna at a place called ʕAbadān, put up a text which originally encompassed forty-four lines, but which now is damaged, dealing with the deeds of MLŠN and his sons. We hear about military operations, among them against central and eastern Arabia. The most interesting parts for this study are the following:

> 6) And after this MLŠN and his sons ḪWLY
>
> 7) and ŠRḤBʔL made a campaign against the land . . . and the ʔʕRB of ḤḌRMWT . . . and from the land of MHRT against ʔWʕRN (?) and they reached YBRN and from YBRN
>
> 8) . . . of the ʕRB . . . and they . . . the towns, and they gathered and came back
>
> 9) . . . they took all the camels of the lords of ṢDYN (?) . . . as booty
>
> 10) . . . they came back to the fortress of ʕBDN in the seventh month . . .[133]
>
> 12) ḪWLY ŠRḤBʔL and MʕDKRB made a campaign, and MRṮD their brother took part with them for the first time
>
> 13 . . . and MRD, MŠRQN, ḌYFTN and the ʔʕRB of ḤḌRMWT; and the YZʔN-ites preceded them as vanguard.[134]

The text is dated to the year AD 360, but the events told in it probably happened earlier.[135] Three kings are mentioned in this text. The first one is ṮʔRN YNʕM, who was a co-regent with YSR YHNʕM in Ja 665, who reigned in the year AD 319/324.[136] Later, we encounter two more kings: ṮʔRN ʔYFʕ and ḎMRʕLY ʔYFʕ.[137] The first is mentioned in a few other inscriptions together with a YSR YHNʕM. The relation between these kings remains somewhat uncertain.[138] The clan of YZʔN was closely related to GDN, to which Saʕdtaʔlab YTLF in Ja 665 and Ir 32 belonged.

It seems likely that we here have the account of two campaigns towards central Arabia in which the ʔʕRB from Ḥaḍramawt and possibly Mahrat took part. At least the first campaign reached eastern Nağd. YBRN is probably identical with Yabrīn, two days' journey south-west of al-Hufūf.[139] There is little doubt that we have here documentation of the presence of ʔʕRB as auxiliaries not only in Saba but also in Ḥaḍramawt, and possibly other places as in Ja 665. The ʔʕRB at this time were auxiliaries of the kings of South Arabia, standing under the command of a special officer, the *kabīr*. This indicates that they have become an important factor for the South Arabian kings after the unification.

The mention of ʕRB in a context together with YBRN is worth noticing. An interpretation remains somewhat speculative, due to the damage of the text, but it should be remembered that Yabrīn is in an area where *ʕarab* are also mentioned in connection with the 'villages of the *ʕarab*' in al-Yamāma in the earliest Islamic period.[140] Now al-Hamdānī says explicitly that Yabrīn was inhabited by clans (*buṭūn*) of *ʕarab* who have been expelled by Qushayr, a tribe belonging to the Kaʕb group in the ʕĀmir b. Ṣaʕṣaʕa federation.[141] This remark becomes somewhat enigmatic if one assumes that *ʕarab* was the term for everybody on the peninsula or for bedouin or all the tribesmen. But if we assume that *ʕarab* was originally the designation of certain small groups living in certain settlements among the tribes in Arabia, al-Hamdānī's note becomes very comprehensible and fits well with the other data about this part of Arabia. It also gives an interesting clue to the understanding of the ʕAbadān inscription, which fits into the larger picture of the roles of the ʔʕRB and ʕRB in the South Arabian texts. The ʕRB and the ʔʕRB in the ʕAbadān inscription would thus not be identical. The former belong to the troops of the Himyarites; the latter are the *ʕarab* living in an oasis in al-Yamāma.

A king named ṮʔRN YHNʕM is further known from a series of inscriptions in Marib, together with his son and successor MLKKRB. This king is usually seen as identical with the one mentioned in Ja 665 and the ʕAbadān inscription. In one of these texts, Ja 671, an official from SẖYM, whose name is lost, describes a task he has performed for the two kings:

> 7) . . . when their lord
>
> 8) ṮʔRN YHNʕM and his son MLKKRB
>
> 9) YNʕM, the two kings of SBʔ, ḎRYDN,
>
> 10) ḤḌRMWT and YMNT, ordered him to take command of a troop of (?) the ʕRB
>
> 11) when the dam in ḤBBḌ and RḤBM hade been crushed
>
> 12) and the whole MḌRF had been crushed separating ḤBBḌ and
>
> 13) RḤBM and when seventy ŠWḤṬ of the dam was crushed . . .[142]

The dam in question is no less than the most famous antiquity of Arabia, the one in Marib. This is the first bursting we hear of and it would have occurred sometime in the middle of the fourth century AD. Unfortunately, the grammar of the crucial passage is problematic. Is the troop composed of ʕRB or is it to be deployed against them? The preposition B in line 10 is ambiguous. This could, however, be the first instance when we hear about the use of ʕRB for peaceful purposes. It should be noticed, however, that they are called ẖMS, which is a term for some kind of military unit, directly under the command of the Himyaritic king.[143] We should perhaps imagine these Arabs as a garrison permanently stationed at Marib.

MLKKRB YʔMN was followed by his son ʔBKRB ʔSʕD, the ʔAsʕad Kāmil in later Arabo-Islamic tradition, a conqueror shrouded in legends.[144] He is mentioned together with his father in an inscription dated to AD 378/384.[145] and later in another one, this time together with his sons and successors ḤSN YHʔMN and ŠRḤBʔL YʕFR, dated AD 428.[146] In Islamic legend, ʔAsʕad Kāmil is said to have conquered Ḥiǧāz including Mecca. There is, undoubtedly, some historical foundation for this: inscriptions from the king are found in Wādī Māsil, 1,000 kilometres north of Marib, a testimony to the extended Himyaritic influence on the peninsula.[147]

We do have one inscription from ʔAbukarib/Asʕad Kāmil, Ry 509, where he tells directly about Arab involvement in his campaigns. It is found in present-day Wādī Māsil, on the road between Riyādh and Mecca, and describes a campaign in that region:

1) ʔBKRB ʔSʕD and his son ḤSN YHʔMN, the two kings of Saba,

2) ḎRYDN, ḤḌRMWT, YMNT and the ʔʕRB of the highland and in the low-land,

3) the two sons of ḤSN MLKKRB YHʔMN, king of Saba, ḎRYDN

4) ḤḌRMWT and YMNT wrote this text in the wādī

5) of MʔSL GMḤN when they were campaigning and pitched camp in the land

6) of MWDM/MʕDM ḌMW, descending together with (?) their tribes and with the tribes

7) of ḤḌRMWT, Saba, the sons of Marib and the lesser of

8) their governors, their workers, their functionaries, their rear-

9) guard, their hunters, their militia, and with their ʔʕRB:

10) KDT, SʕD, W[ʕ?]LH, . . .[148]

As in many of the texts from the fifth century onwards, this one contains an increasing number of difficult words and expressions. In particular, line 6 is obscure. It seems, though, that we have a testimony about the employment of ʔʕRB as mercenaries of the king, or rather, the employment of some tribes as ʔʕRB, which is the literal meaning of lines 9–10. The only tribe that can be identified with certainty is KDT, the tribe of Kinda known from the Arabo-Islamic tradition. The SWD reminds one of the SWD ʕRBN in the inscription Miʕsāl 3.[149]

In this text we find the ʔʕRB mentioned in the title of the king: ʔʕRB ṬWDM WTHMT 'the Arabs of ṬWDM and Tihāma'. This phrase was obviously introduced in the royal title by ʔAbukarib. In the other inscriptions from him he carries a slightly different title:

MLK SBʔ W-ḎRYDN W-ḤḌRMWT W-YMNT W-ʔʕRBHMW ṬWDM WTHMT.

king of Saba, Dhū Raydān, Ḥaḍramawt, Yam(a)nat and their *ʔaʕrāb*, Ṭawd and Tihāma.[150]

The first four names in the title were also used by ʔAbu Karib's predecessors from Shammar Yuharʕish onwards and reflect the development of the Himyarite kingdom by the annexation of Ḥaḍramawt and adjacent areas. Yam(a)nat is usually identified with the area between Wādī Ḥaḍramawt and the ocean, with a centre in Mayfaʕa.[151] The last three elements are added by ʔAbu Karib. The last two literally mean 'highland' and 'lowland', but their exact meaning in the royal title has been debated.[152] According to al-Hamdānī, *ṭawd* means the mountains 'that cut through Yemen, belonging to the mountains of as-Sarāt, which is between its inner plateau and its [coastal] lowlands (its Tihāma)'.[153] In a poem by a Muslim Yemeni poet, quoted by al-Hamdānī, it is said that the tribe of ʔAzd 'ruled *aṭ-ṭawd* from Sarūm to aṭ-Ṭāʔif', i.e. the entire ʕAsīr.[154] It seems, then, that it is the areas north of the Yemeni highlands, the mountains of ʕAsīr and the Tihāma, which are meant by the royal title.

The most interesting question for us is the meaning of ʔʕRBHMW, 'their ʔʕRB'. Who are 'they'? One would have liked to have the possessive suffix in dual -HMY and not plural -HMW if it refers to the two areas. It should also be noticed that the last two terms are not introduced with the particle W-, 'and', like the other ones.

The most likely interpretation is that the suffix refers to the four preceding names of former independent kingdoms.[155] ʔʕRB are thus those who were in some way dependent upon or subject to those kingdoms. In Ja 665 and Ir 32 we find a similar summary of all ʔʕRB associated with the same kingdoms as in the royal title. There we also find the Arabs of Kinda and Madhḥiǧ, two large tribal groups north of Yemen. The last two terms, ṬWDM and THMT, look like an explanation of the preceding and should perhaps be read as adverbs: the ʔʕRB of the mentioned kingdoms, [those] in the highland as well as [those] in the lowland. This would also neatly explain the variant without the suffix: the ʔʕRB of the highland and the lowland.[156]

In spite of this evidence, the identity of these ʔʕRB is not certain. From the context and the terminology it is less likely that they are identical with those around Naǧrān. If the ʕRB, as we have hinted during this investigation, was an institution rather than an ethnic or social group, it could be imagined that the Himyaritic kings introduced ʕRB, used by them as auxiliaries and border-guards, in the newly conquered territories north of Saʕda. Another possibility is that the 'Arabs of the lowland' are the *arabîtai* mentioned in the Adulis inscription, who could have dwelt along the coast.[157]

There is no doubt that the introduction of the ʔʕRB in the royal title reflects their increased importance in the new Himyaritic empire. The ʔʕRB continue to occur in the royal title during the fifth century, but we have no other concrete information on their role until the beginning of the sixth century.[158] They appear in an inscription, Ry 510, by the king Maʕdīkarib Yaʕfur, dated to the year AD 516. This text is found in the same area as the preceding one, which is actually mentioned in line 3:

1) MʕDKRB YʕFR king of SBʔ, ḎRYDN,

2) ḤḌRMWT, YMNT and their ʔʕRB in the highland and the lowland

3) made public (?) and wrote this inscription in MʔSLM GMḤN

4) concerning/during (?) the campaigns on the ʕRQ of KTʔ because (?)

5) the ʕRB, rebelling, drove them out (?); and MḎR

6) fought them, and they campaigned against them with their ŠʕB: Saba, Ḥimyar, RḤBTM,

7) ḤḌRMWT and YḤN and together with their ʔʕRB: KDT and MḎḤG

8) and together with the sons of ṮʕLBT and MḎR and-SBʕ

9) in the month of ḎQYḎN in six hundred and thirty one.[159]

There are many words in this inscription of uncertain reading and meaning. It seems certain that the ʔʕRB in line 7 are the allies of the South Arabian king. MḎR has been identified with Alamoundaros, the Saracen of the Iranians in the first half of the sixth century and the great Munḏir III of al-Ḥīra in the Arabo-Islamic tradition, reigning during the first half of the sixth century.[160] If that reading is correct, we would have a documentation of conflicts between the Himyaritic empire and the kings in al-Ḥīra, who were the prolonged arm of Iran.[161] The ʕRB are mentioned in line 5, which is the one most difficult to interpret.[162] The ʕRB would then be the allies of MḎR against the Himyarites. Later Arabic tradition has a lot to tell about the breakdown of the rule of the kings from Kinda, the vassals of the Himyarites in central Arabia at the beginning of the sixth century AD. Even though it is likely that this inscription refers to the events connected with those reflected in later Arabic legends, the interpretation of the text remains uncertain.[163] The ʔʕRB in this text seem to play the same role as in Ry 509:9–10. Kinda and Maḏḥiğ are classified as the ʔʕRB of the traditional provinces of South Arabia. As in ʔAbū karib's time, these tribes serve the king as ʔʕRB.

MʕDKRB YʕFR carries the title mentioning the ʔʕRB.[164] It is absent with his successor, YWSF ʔSʔR YṮʔR, Dhū Nuwās of the Arabo-Islamic tradition, the most famous king of pre-Islamic South Arabia through his anti-Christian policy.[165] His first name YWSF shows his adherence to Judaism. His policy was strongly anti-Roman. YWSF was ousted from power by an invasion from Axum in the first year of his reign but returned to power after a while. In the autumn of 523, he annihilated the Christian community in Nağrān, probably because they were seen as a Roman fifth column. This event sent shock-waves through all Christendom and triggered off a new expedition from the Roman allies in Axum, now led by the king himself, Kaleb. The invasion was probably undertaken in the spring of AD 525 and resulted in the fall of YWSF and the instalment of a king from the YZʔN clan, SMYFʕ ʔSWʕ, son of ŠRḤBʔL YKML, one of YWSF's officers, who was to be a puppet of the Ethiopians.[166]

There are several contemporary texts preserved dealing with these dramatic events. Those from the Christian side are to some extent based on reports by eye-witnesses about what happened in Nağrān.[167] From YWSF himself we do not have texts dealing with the massacre in Nağrān, except a letter preserved by a Christian writer, which is probably a distorted version.[168] We do, however, have three inscriptions from the king dealing with his campaigns in which Arabs are mentioned. All three mention the defeat of the Ethiopians and actions against Naǧrān. They are dated to the year AD 518.[169]

Ry 507 (= Ry 444)

This text is damaged and contains several obscure words. It is dated to 633 Himyaritic era which is equivalent to AD 518, and was written by a certain ŠRḤʔL ḎYZʔN who took part in operations against Naǧrān. Arabs are mentioned together with other military men:

1) [May the God, to whom the heaven and the earth belong, bless king YWSF ʔSʔR YṮʔR king of all] tribes [and may he bless] their governors (ʔQL), and their chiefs (MRʔS), and their ʕRBN . . .

8) and then the king mustered what he had taken as booty and who had died (?) and all governors (ʔQWLN), and ʔʕRB and fighters, fourteen thousand killed and eleven thousand prisoners and two hundred and ninety

9) thousand camels, cattle and goats. And ŠRḤʔL ḎYZʔN, the governor (QL), had this inscription written when he had made an attack with the tribes of ḎHMDN and the ʔʕRB against Naǧrān, until the king gave order that he was satisfied (?).[170]

Ry 508

This inscription is better preserved than the preceding one. It is dated to the year 633, Himyaritic era, thus AD 518, and was written by ŠRḤʔL YQBL, son of ŠRḤBʔL, from the family GDN in the tribe of YZʔN. He is likely to be identical with the author of Ry 507. The text describes a campaign by the king Y(W)SF against ʔḤBŠN, i.e. the Abyssinians in Ẓafār and in the lowlands around Mukhā. After that

6) the king sent him (ŠRḤʔL) to fight against NGRN among/together with

7) the chief of ʔZʔN (= the Yazʔanites) and with the tribes (ʔŠʕB) of HMDN, their townspeople (HGR-HMW) and their ʔʕRB and the ʔʕRB of KDT and MRD and MḎḤG . . .[171]

Ja 1028

The third text was found in the same area as Ry 507. It is dated to the same year as Ry 508, and its content is very close to the latter. In certain passages there is verbal identity. The author is also the same. Like Ry 508 it starts with the operations against the Ethiopians in Ẓafār and Mukhā. Then the author presents himself:

6) . . . ŠRḤʔL from YZʔN, the governor (QYLN) wrote this inscription when he fought against NGRN with

7) the tribes (ʔŠʕB) of HMDN, the townspeople (HGRN) and the ʕRB, and the forces from ʔZʔN and the ʔʕRB of KDT (Kinda), and MRD, and MḎḤG and

the governors (ʔQWLN), his brothers.[172]

The (ʔ)ʕRB constitute a military unit, fighting together with other units of the army of the Himyaritic king. The ʔʕRB taking part in the operations against Nağrān are closely associated with the Hamdān rulers in the northern highland. To them are added those from Kinda and possibly other tribes north of Yemen proper. As in the royal title, we can see that these Arabs are 'owned' by Hamdān: the word has the plural possessive suffix referring to the tribes governed by the Hamdān clan. From Ry 508 it is clear that there is no identity between the ʔʕRB and the ʔŠʕB of Hamdān. From this text and Ja 1028 the impression is that Hamdān consists of the ʔŠʕB and the HGR with the ʔʕRB associated.[173]

YWSF is not documented with the long royal title. We do not know if this is a coincidence due to the lack of inscriptions or if it has some other meaning. Around AD 530, the Ethiopian general ʔAbrahā took power in Ṣanʕāʔ, reassuming the imperial policy of the Himyaritic kings. From him we have three inscriptions where he uses the long title of ʔAbu Karib ʔAsʕad and his dynasty.[174] In CIH 541, one of the longest Sabaean inscriptions preserved and dated to the year AD 543/548, ʔAbrahā first describes an insurrection by a certain YZD, a chief of the Kinda tribe, together with several others, among them MʕDKRB, son of SMYFʕ from YZʔN. The latter was the son of the king installed by the Ethiopians in 525 and we have here an attempt from nationalistic circles to throw off the regime of the usurper. After several operations YZD made a pact with the king:

41–42) And then a cry came to them from Saba that

43) the dam, the overland wall,

44) and ḪBŠM and the sidewall of

45) the [water] distributor had been crushed in the month ḎMḎRʔN

46) in the year seven. After

47) this order having reached him

48) he sent messengers to sub-

49) jugate the ʕRB who

50) had not returned with YZD

51) and then all of them assured their

52) loyalty and gave hostages through the messengers.

The king then requests material and support for the repair of the destruction in Marib:

63) And after he had

64) dispatched a monition and the ʕRB had submitted,

65) he went to the town of Marib.

Peace being restored, a church is consecrated in Marib, the town is restored, and ʔAbrahā receives delegations from the kings of Rome and Iran as well as the rulers of Ghassān and al-Ḥīra, Ḥārith b. Ğabala and Mundhir III.[175]

The most natural interpretation is that by ʕRB is meant a group closely associated with the tribe of Kinda but not identical with them. These ʕRB would not have been identical with the ʔʕRB who had been in the service of the Sabaean and Himyaritic kings for centuries. Instead, the arrangement between them and Abrahā was an agreement new in its kind, in that it involved ʕRB not previously serving the kings. Since the centre of Kinda was north of Nağrān, these ʕRB could very well be those dwelling somewhere not far from the city. It is in this area that the ʕRB of Karibʔil Watar should be looked for. Thus, with the last mention of ʕRB in a South Arabian inscription, we are brought back to where we started: the ʕRB living in what was known to the Islamic traditionists as *ʔarḍ al-ʕarab* close to Nağrān.

Arabs in South Arabia: survey and summary

When we take a comprehensive look at the Arabs in the South Arabian inscriptions it is evident that we have a unique series of documents about Arabs, going into the sixth century BC. Unlike in the north, where, as we have seen, the Arabs disappear from the sources from the fourth century onwards, being replaced by Saracens and *ṭayyāyē*, they live on in South Arabia until the eve of the rise of Islam. Since the term *ʕarab* and its derivations were well known in Arabia in the time of Muhammed, the South Arabian evidence seems to constitute a major link of documentation between the Arabs of antiquity and the Arabs of the Islamic period.

Nothing in the South Arabian texts themselves indicates that either of the two terms ʕRB and ʔʕRB means nomads or bedouin. Allegations that this is the case are based on sources which are not from South Arabia and not from the period when the texts were written.[176] As has become evident from the preceding investigation, nor is there any support in other ancient sources for ascribing such a meaning to these terms. Only in the Greek texts do we here and there find passages where such a claim is made. These passages are, however, often contradicted by others in the same texts. All explanations based on the assumption of South Arabian Arabs being identical with nomads or bedouin should be discarded.

Basic for the further analysis is that in the South Arabian texts we have two terms derived from the same root: ʕRB and ʔʕRB.[177] From a grammatical viewpoint the two terms ʕRB and ʔʕRB are derivable from the same root according to the morphology of the South Arabian languages. There is no doubt that ʔʕRB is the plural of ʕRBY, i.e. a plural of a nisba adjective.[178] This kind of plural to nisba adjectives is paradigmatic in Sabaean.[179] The (singular feminine) nisba ʕRBY-T is documented in the two texts from al-ʕUqla and the so-called List of Hierodules. ʕRB is thus a collective and probably the basis for all the derivations. This is strikingly reminiscent of the Arabic words *ʕarab* and *ʔaʕrāb*. The latter is given a nisba form *ʔaʕrābī* by the Arab lexicographers.[180] This seems, however, to be a secondary adaptation to the Arabic morphology. It is likely that *ʔaʕrāb* as plural of *ʕarabī*, in fact, is a South Arabian borrowing into Arabic.

The documentation of the two words in South Arabian texts can be divided in two groups, one containing the texts dated before the reign of Shammar Yuharʕish III (*c.* AD 275–300), the other consisting of the texts from after that time.

In the first group a basic pattern emerges: ʕRB are the enemies of the South Arabian kings, ʔʕRB are their allies. The latter word tends to stand in a genitive construction to a following noun: 'the ʔʕRB of . . .'

The ʕRB are mentioned in connection with the ʔṢḤB in Marib (Ja 561 bis) and they appear at Timnaʕ (Ja 629, Doe 2). Twice we hear about a 'land of the ʕRB'. The oldest text we have, RÉS 3945, seems to speak about ʕRB between al-Ǧawf and Naǧrān.

The ʔʕRB on one occasion give support to Saba's enemies Ḥaḍramawt and Qatabān (Ja 629, Ja 739, Ja 758). They are found on the northern border of Ḥāshid in the central highlands (Ja 561 bis, Ir 12). They belong to Marib (CIH 353) and SFLN (CIH 353, Ry 502) or they are, together with Naǧrān and Ḫawlān aṭ-Ṭiyāl (east of Ṣanʕāʔ), allied to Saba (Ja 635). They are found in the upper Wādī Bayḥān and they belong to the kings of Saba, Ḥaḍramawt and Dhū Raydān (Nami 72+73+71).

At the beginning of the second period the ʔʕRB still belong to Saba and/or the king of Saba (Ja 665, Ir 32, Sharafaddin 32). These ʔʕRB now stand under a special official, the KBR, who commands them in battle. At the same time we hear about ʔʕRB belonging to Ḥaḍramawt (ʕAbadān, Ir 32). But we also hear about ʔʕRB belonging to new entities: Kinda and Maḏḥiǧ (Ja 665, Ry 510) or the king of Kinda (loc. cit., Ir 32) as well as Hamdān (Ja 1028, Ry 508). The latter may be those earlier said to dwell on the borders of Ḥāshid. Their relationship to Kinda and Maḏḥiǧ is, however, not completely clear: in some instances these tribes are ʔʕRB, in others the ʔʕRB are part of them.[181] This contradiction reminds us of the Ituraeans in Syria who on occasion are called Arabs but on others are said to have Arabs living among them.

The ʕRB are still independent and wage war against Ḥimyar (Ry 510). But a new feature is that they are not principal enemies of the imperial rulers: they can function as mercenaries (Ir 32, CIH 397, 541, Ry 510).

There is no reason to claim that the ʔʕRB and the ʕRB are identical or replaceable in the texts. A plain reading of them makes it evident that we have to do with two groups with different relations to the kings of Saba and Dhū Raydān.[182] The first ones are called ʔʕRB, a plural of ʕRBY; the other ones ʕRB, which seems to be a collective noun. We thus have two types of 'Arab': one is principally closely allied with kings and tribes, living on or inside the borders and found in many parts of South Arabia. The other is principally independent, living outside the territory of the kingdoms and, as it seems, in a special area called 'the land(s) of the ʕRB'. That area can tentatively be located somewhere between Naǧrān and Ǧawf.

We should, in this context, once again look at the passage in Ibn Saʕd's *Ṭabaqāt* referring to the delegation of Hamdān coming to the Prophet to embrace Islam. This passage is obviously based on a document well informed about conditions in Yemen. We learn from it that Hamdān, which by the time of the Prophet was the name for the former Sumʕay federation, which by now ruled large parts of the northern Yemeni plateau, consisted of four groups: the *ʔaḥmūr*, which was the aristocracy; the *ʕarab*; the *xalāʔiṭ*, meaning 'the mixed ones'; and the *mawālī*, those under protection.[183] That the *ʔaḥmūr* are the aristocrats is evident from the following passage in Ibn Saʕd where it is said that they were composed of the *ʔaḏwāʔ* of Hamdān. *ʔaḏwāʔ* is the designation for the leading families of the Himyarite empire in the Arabo-Islamic tradition, which makes it likely that the name *ʔaḥmūr* is connected with Ḥimyar. The *ʕarab*, according to Ibn SaʕTd, consisted of groups known by names, most of which can be located from evidence in Sabaean texts or by modern place-names: ʔArḥab, which was the original kernel of the Ḥāshid tribe in the northern SMʕY;[184] Nihm, which was the name of two distinct groups, one north-east of Ṣanʕāʔ and another one on the northern slopes of the land of ʔAmīr, centred in the oasis of Khabb;[185] Shākir, which was the name of the entire land of ʔAmīr in al-Hamdānī's time;[186] Wadāʕa, which was an area in ʔAmīr;[187] Yām, which is the name of a tribe around Nağrān and east of it, in later times considered a part of Shākir;[188] Murhiba, which was a small area *c.* 40 kilometres north-east of Khamir, an area where we also find a Wādī Kharfān, which could be identical with Khārif, also belonging to the *ʕarab* according to Ibn Saʕd;[189] ʕUdhar, which belonged to Nihm and consequently was found both in the southern and northern Nihm;[190] Dālān, which can be located in the upper al-Ğawf not far from MNHYTM;[191] and finally Ḥağūr, which was a tribe living in the mountains north-west of Ḥāshid, thus not too far from Dālān.[192]

The names enumerated can all be located in a few specific geographical areas: the borderland west, south and north of al-Ğawf and in the Nağrān oasis. The centre seems to be the land of ʔAmīr, the mountainous area north-east of al-Ğawf. This is the area where we assumed that we should look for the centre of the ʕRB in the South Arabian inscriptions. Even though the location of 'Arabs' and delimitation of tribal areas are still somewhat uncertain, there are reasons to assume that the *ʕarab* mentioned in Ibn Saʕd's document are in fact more or less identical with the ʕRB mentioned in the inscriptions. 'The land of the ʕRB' is thus perhaps ʔAmīr, an area with special features in religion and way of living.[193] There we should perhaps look for the *arabanîtai* in Ptolemy and, perhaps less likely, also the *arabîtai* in the Adulis inscription, both from the second century AD.

In very early Islamic tradition, we hear about the land of the *ʕarab* at Nağrān. Wahb b. Munabbih told about the Christianization of the town through Faymiyyūn and Ṣāliḥ, a story which was preserved by Ibn Isḥāq. It is said that the people of Nağrān followed the religion of the *ʕarab*, worshipping a palm tree. The town itself was situated 'in the middle of the land of the *ʕarab*'.[194] In another context, Wahb reported that in olden times there was a mythical ruler known by the strange name 'the snake of Nağrān', who was the foremost judge of the *ʕarab*, to whom they used to appeal in legal cases.[195] There is no need to assume that these passages refer to the Arabs of the entire peninsula. Instead, it seems that there was a special region at Nağrān belonging to the *ʕarab*, thus a confirmation of the picture emerging from the epigraphic South Arabian evidence.

Ibn Saʕd also mentions the ʔArḥab in the northern part of Sumʕay not far from Murhiba. To Sumʕay also belonged the southern Nihm, occupying its north-eastern corner. The ʔArḥab corresponds neatly to the ʔʕRB along the border of Ḥāshid in the inscriptions. According to the texts, however, these ʔʕRB had a close relationship to the ʕRB further north. Thus, Ir 12 mentions the ʔʕRB living in the countryside along the border of Ḥāshid. Ja 561bis talks about 'the ʔʕRB on the borders of Ḥāshid and some from the land of the ʕRB'. CIH 79 mentions the ʕRB in the region of MNHYT-M in the upper al-Ğawf. Ja 635 indicates that the ʔʕRB live near Khawlān, which could be southern Nihm.

There is not only a linguistic correspondence between South Arabian ʕRB – ʔʕRB and Arabic *ʕarab* – *ʔaʕrāb*. The *ʔaʕrāb* mentioned in the Qurʔān have a position strongly reminiscent of that of the South Arabian ʔʕRB.[196] They live outside the city (of Medina) but are associated with it in different ways and have an obligation of military service to its ruler.[197] This similarity is so striking that we have to assume that the *ʔaʕrāb* in Medina at the time of the Prophet must represent the survival of a South Arabian institution going back to the ancient kingdoms of South Arabia, which engaged people called ʔʕRB as auxiliaries and border-guards.[198] This makes it likely that the very term *ʔaʕrāb* in the Qurʔān is, in fact, a South Arabian word like the institution itself.

Hence there is indeed a tight continuity between the Arabs as documented in ancient South Arabia and those appearing in the sources dealing with or stemming from the very beginning of the Islamic period. This connection becomes even more interesting and important when we remember that the employment of the term 'Arab' underwent dramatic changes during the Umayyad period and that the use of it in Arabia until modern times is probably the outcome of this process.

The exact relationship between the ʕRB and the ʔʕRB in South Arabia is not yet clear. But judging from the very morphology of the terms, ʕRB must be the original one, from which the other is derived. This would then also represent a real procedure. A hypothesis is that the ʔʕRB were individuals originally belonging to the ʕRB, who for different reasons became the servants of the big chiefs of the Yemeni ʔŠʕB and the kings in Marib and elsewhere. The texts clearly indicate that the ʕRB belonged to an area north-east of Yemen, whereas the ʔʕRB are spread out in the entire region, preferably along borders. This is explicable by the fact that they were employed by the kings and chiefs in different parts of the country and that they were garrisoned or settled where there was need for them.

The role of Arabs as employees of the South Arabian kings is, in fact hinted at in a very early source originating outside Arabia. In Theophrastus' *Book of Plants*, written around 300 BC, which derives much of its information on the flora of Arabia from the expeditions dispatched by Alexander the Great, we read the following about the frankincense land:

> The whole range of frankincense-bearing mountains, they said, belongs to the Sabaeans; for it is under their sway.
>
> The myrrh and the frankincense are collected from all parts into the temple of the sun; and this temple is the most sacred thing which the Sabaeans of that region possess, and it is guarded by certain *árabes* in arms.[199]

The Sabaeans in Marib never, as far as we know, ruled the frankincense-producing areas in Mahra and Dhufār. The story of the sun-temple also sounds legendary and may be a confusion with the description of the Island of the Sun in the Persian Gulf. It should be observed that the reference is to a *lógos* from the sailors who only knew the coastal areas. There is, however, in a later source, namely Pliny's *Natural History*, a passage that is clearly connected with the one in Theophrastus, which contains further details:

> Eight days' journey [from Sabota] is a frankincense-producing region belonging to them [the Sabaeans] called Sariba/Arabia/Saba. The Greeks say it means *mysterium*.[200]

It is not impossible that the word 'Sabaeans' in Theophrastus is, in fact, a distortion of Sabota, the capital of the kingdom of Ḥaḍramawt, which would then give a good meaning to the passage.[201] The textual tradition is uncertain as far as the name of this region is concerned. In Solinus' book on curious geographical matters, written perhaps in the third century AD, of which more than three-quarters is a reproduction of Pliny, it is said that the frankincense region 'is called *Arabia*, i.e. sacred' (*sacra*).[202] Also Isidorus of Seville, who in his *Etymologica* written at the beginning of the seventh century AD copied Pliny, has the same reading: *Arabia* meaning sacred (*sacra*).[203] It could thus be argued that Arabia is the original reading of the name of the district.[204] Pliny has further details about the frankincense region:

> It is said that there are not more than three thousand families who retain the right of trading in it [the frankincense] and that consequently the members of these families are called sacred (*sacros*) and are not allowed to be polluted by ever meeting women or funeral processions when they are engaged in making incisions in the trees in order to obtain the frankincense.[205]

Pliny has this information from unnamed Greek sources which are not Theophrastus. Herodotus had already heard stories about Arabs gathering frankincense and the trees being guarded by mythical beings.[206] We have no documentation from South Arabian inscriptions yet about such an arrangement for frankincense production. On the other hand, the archaeological investigation of Mahra and Dhufār is still in its beginnings. If, as we have suggested, the Arabs in South Arabia were some kind of guards, and if we combine this with what we know about the taboos impendent upon Arabs in the north, as told by Hieronymus of Cardia, the description of their role in Theophrastus and Pliny may not be wholly taken out of the air. It is not impossible that Arabs were used as guardians of the holy trees just as they were used as border-guards later on by the kings in South Arabia. We shall return to this information in our final discussion of what the Arabs originally were.

Theophrastus has a further note about the political conditions in South Arabia:

> Now frankincense, myrrh, cassia, and also cinnamon are found in the Arabian peninsula about Saba, Hadramyta, Kitibaina, and Mamali.[207]

Unlike the preceding one, this note comes from a good informant and describes well the known political conditions in South Arabia in Alexander's time. Sabaean dominance is gone, Karibʔil's empire is broken up and Qatabān is independent. Mamali refers to the areas north of Saba, possibly including Maʕīn and southern ʕAsīr.[208] The statement about the Sabaeans and their Arab guards may, however, represent conditions before the division of the first Sabaean empire which were still remembered at the time of the Greek expeditions. Even though the trustworthiness of the information is somewhat uncertain, it fits well with the documented role of the ʔʕRB in South Arabia in later times.[209] Theophrastus' notice could be the earliest attestation of the integration of Arabs into the political system of the South Arabian empire-builders.

Was the relationship between the ʕRB, the ʔʕRB and the rulers of Yemen the same as that between the people in the *qurā al-ʕarab*, the *ʔaʕrāb* and the ruler of Medina? Such a conclusion seems near at hand, even though the evidence is, admittedly, still somewhat scanty. We are now approaching a synthesis of the results of our investigation, which will create a picture with most of the pieces falling into place. This will be the task of the last part of this book.

Notes

1 The basic handbook on chronology is now Kitchen, *Documentation* 1–41 for AD 0–600 and 81–119 for the preceding period.
2 The first observations were made in 1899 by Halévy, *Arabes*. The latest surveys are by Alsekaf, *Géographie* 36–40, Bāfaqīh, *Unification* 271–288, and Robin, *Pénétration*. None of these is complete in that they take all texts into consideration.
3 Theophrastus, *Plants* I9.4.2.6. See pp. 271, 566.
4 For the identification of Mamáli, see von Wissmann, *Ophir.*
5 Eratosthenes (= Strabo 16.4.2) mentions the following: Minaîoi with the capital Kárna; Sabaîoi with Maríaba, Kattabaneîs with Támna and, in the Far East, Khatramōtîtai with Sábata as capital.
6 Isolated letters occur on ostraca from Raybūn in Ḥaḍramawt and Yalā west of Marib dated to this period; cf. Garbini, *Iscrizioni*; idem, *Yalā*, esp. 87–91.
7 von Wissmann, *Geschichte* II 8240 (chart), dates the earliest ruler in Saba around 775 BC. Kitchen, *Documentation* 110 ff., in an alternative dating, tries to extend the list further backwards until 900 BC, which, however, seems less likely.
8 For the inscriptions, see Kitchen, *Documentation* 196–197.
9 RÉS 3945 ll.17.
10 Lines 18–29.
11 von Wissmann, *Geschichte* II 145–151, 175–176.
12 For the debate and the arguments, see Avanzini, *Chronologie*.
13 Cf. von Wissmann, *Geschichte* II 145–150; Avanzini, *Chronologie*; Lemaire, *Histoire* [38]; Robin, *Cités* 50 ff.; idem, *Épisodes* 55; idem, *Sheba* 1120 (more hesitant).
14 Sennacherib, Foundation Stela I 2:48–49 (= Luckenbill, *Annals* 138; cf. Frahm, *Einleitung* 173–174). The name Ka-ri-bi-ilu also appears in some other Assyrian texts, the so-called 'pearl-inscriptions'; see Frahm, *Einleitung* 145–146.
15 For the 'northern' Sabaeans, see pp. 134 f., 217 f.
16 Cf. p. 149.
17 Exodus 6:23.
18 For the identification of It-'a-am-a-ra with Sabaean YṮʕʔMR and its documentation in North Arabia (JS 130, 379, 526), see Müller, *Abyaṯaʕ* 26. For a different view, see Propp, *Ithamar* 579, who sees it as a Gt-form of the verb *ʔamara*, 'he appeared' or 'he obeyed'. Similar names are found in Amoritic and Egyptian execration texts, but it is very doubtful whether the Old Testament name goes back to such an early period. The North Arabian origin seems more likely.
19 de Maigret/Robin, *Fouilles* esp. 283 ff.
20 Cf. Robin, *Cités* 50–51.
21 RÉS 3945:14, 17.
22 Robin/Breton, *Sanctuaire* esp. 445–450.
23 Kitchen, *Documentation* 80–145, especially 114.
24 Cf. Beeston, *Significance*, and Puin, *Hijrah*, who suggests a connection between the ancient South Arabian HGR and the Yemeni *hiǧra* institution.
25 For other testimonies see p. 564. According to W. Müller, *Araber* 143, the word ʕRB-M in the inscription refers to bedouin from northern or central Arabia who immigrated into South Arabia.
26 Robin, *Pénétration* 72.
27 Observed by W. Müller, *rev. L'Arabie Antique* (472). For an analysis and a new translation of this text, see Al-Said, *Verben* 263–264.
28 Above, p. 330.
29 Robin/Breton, *Sanctuaire*; Robin, *Sheba* 1133–1134; Kitchen, *Documents* 29–31.
30 CIH 79:1–2, 8–10. In connection with the verb QDM, 'confront, do battle', the preposition BʕM should mean 'against' in l. 9; cf. Jamme, *Désastre* 168. Beeston *et al.*, *Dictionary* s.v. ʕm. Jamme (*Désastre*, 167–168) translates ll. 8–9 'because he withdrew his servant from an attack', which, however, does not give a good meaning in the context. Robin dates the text to the first century BC (*Pénétration* 77; *Royaumes* 185); cf. a general dating in von

Wissmann, *Zur Geschichte* 354. In idem, *Geschichte* [93] the text is dated to the second half of the second century AD on palaeographic grounds.

31 Cf. Robin/Brunner, *Map* E4. von Wissmann, *Zur Geschichte* 355–356, assumed that MNHTM is much further north, in the area of Mekka. This is unlikely and was corrected in *Geschichte* [93] note 189.

32 von Wissmann, *Zur Geschichte* loc. cit.

33 Höfner, *Religion* 258.

34 Ryckmans, *Inscriptions* 17 172–174: ʕLHN BN YHFRʕ ŠʕBN MHFRʔM. It should be observed that Ry 591 has the Sabaeic form YHFRʕ, whereas RBB-M uses YFRʕ, which could indicate a northern influence. For the identification of the king in Ry 591 with ḎMRʕLY WTR YHNʕM, see Robin/Breton, *Sanctuaire* 592, 606–610. Cf. also Bāfaqīh, *Unification* 120–125.

35 See in general Robin/Breton, *Sanctuaire*.

36 *Periplus* § 19; pp. 144–145.

37 Kitchen, *Documentation* 19–20, 25; cf. Bāfaqīh, *Unification* 128–129.

38 Ja 560:1–4, 8–15 = Jamme, *Inscriptions* 31. The text is translated in Beeston, *Warfare* 57–58.

39 Beeston (*Warfare* 57–58) translates ʔṢḤB as 'bedouin auxiliaries', suggested also in the Sabaean dictionary (s.v. ṣḥb). He is followed by Bāfaqīh, *Unification* 279. The word occurs also in Ry 533:21: BN ʔGYŠ WʔṢḤB ʔḤBŠN. Cf. also CIH 26:4. The word is here contrasted to GYŠ, which is a special task force of some kind (Beeston, *Warfare* 10; idem, *Ḥimā* 43); see p. 545). Both are here parts of the army of the Habashites, which makes the translation 'bedouin' appear somewhat too hasty.

40 The Qurʔān mentions *ʔaṣḥāb al-qarya* (XXXVI:13), which is a parallel to the phrase in Ja 560:11. It also mentions *ʔaṣḥāb Mūsā* (26:61), and Muhammed is called the *ṣāḥib* of his compatriots (81:22). The term *ʔaṣḥāb* for the early Muslims is, however, later than the Qurʔān.

41 Jamme's translation is not comprehensible in all details. Especially in lines 12 and 13 the relationship between 'soldiers' (ʔSD) and ʔṢḤB is obscure. In line 12 they seem to be identical, which might then also hold for the soldiers in line 13. Beeston (*Warfare*) ignores 'soldiers' in line 12, translating 'bedouin auxiliaries'. The role of these soldiers/ʔṢḤB is, however, not clear. Another alternative is to read 'soldiers' as the acting subject: these soldiers saved and captured their ʔṢḤB, confiscated their riding animals, took the land and their animals and brought them to Marib. Beeston instead renders 'the men had made off into the desert', which seems a very free guess. None of the readings solves all difficulties of the text.

42 GRT was a tribe on the plain south of Ṣanʕāʔ; see von Wissmann, *Zur Landeskunde* 366–368; Bāfaqīh, *Unification* 128–129.

43 Cf. Robin, *Hautes-terres* 45–46; Bāfaqīh, *Unification* 161–163.

44 The basic study of the absolute chronology and the identification of the different eras used in the South Arabian inscriptions is Robin, *Miʕsâl*, especially 331–338. For the year 141/142, see Kitchen, *Documentation* 1–9, 17.

45 Bāfaqīh, *Unification* 351–357; Kitchen, *Documentation* 27–28.

46 Ja 629:6–8 (= Jamme, *Inscriptions* 128). Jamme translates KWN KWNHMW in line 8 'who were with them'. We now know that this expression has a more concrete meaning; cf. Beeston *et al.*, *Dictionary* s.v. KWN and Beeston's translation in *Warfare* 44. For some reason, Beeston translates ʔʕRB with 'communes'.

47 Robin/Brunner, *Map* D10.

48 Ja 629:32–34 = Jamme, *Inscriptions* 128. Jamme translates ʔḤḌR with 'dwellings', which is obviously wrong; cf. Robin, *Pénétration* 78. For a translation of the whole text, see Beeston, *Warfare* 43–45.

49 Bāfaqīh, *Unification* 352–353.

50 Kitchen, *Documentation* 36–37, dates the fall of Qatabān to *c.* AD 160.

51 Cf. the photograph in Beeston, *Notes*, with those of the Qatabanian inscriptions in Jamme, *Miscellanées* IX Pl. a (Ja 2826) and Pl. e (TTI 100) dated to the reign of ŠHR HLL YHQBḌ *c.* AD 120–135 (Jamme, op. cit. 42–43, 60; Kitchen, *Documentation* 187–188).

52 Beeston, *Notes* 10–13.
53 Robin/Brunner, *Map* H7.
54 A ṢNʕ is situated in the extreme south of the Radmān plateau on the southern confines of Qatabān; see Robin/Brunner, *Map* G9.
55 RÉS 3566:4; 3689:1.
56 Beeston, *Notes* ad loc.
57 W.W. Müller (private communication) points out that both these two texts are in Sabaean, not Qatabanian. All three texts, however, seem to refer to the same geographical area.
58 Bāfaqīh, *Unification* 353–357; Kitchen, *Documentation* 27–28.
59 For a description of the geography of this tribal area, see von Wissmann, *Zur Geschichte* 271–387. Cf. also Robin, *Hautes-terres* 42–45, and Bāfaqīh, *Unification* 163–169.
60 Kitchen, *Documentation* 18.
61 Ja 561 bis 5–8, 10–14 (= Jamme, *Inscriptions* 37) and Beeston, *Warfare* 22–23. Robin, *Pénétration* 78, translates ʔʕRB as 'Arabes' and ʕRB as 'nomades'.
62 Bāfaqīh (*Unification* 280) does not make any distinction between the two terms here, and sees the operations as directed against bedouin who have made an incursion and who are now chased out. This reading does not take all distinctions in the text into consideration.
63 For the dating of CIH 353, see von Wissmann, *Himyar* 457, 462; idem, *Zur Geschichte* 53–54; Bāfaqīh, *Unification* 361–362.
64 CIH 353: 6–12. For the interpretation and dating, see von Wissmann, *Zur Geschichte* 339–340, especially note 212.
65 Originally published by M. al-Iryani, *Fī tārīkh al-Yaman*, commented upon by J. Ryckmans in *Himyaritica* 4 pp. 500–502.
66 von Wissmann, *Zur Geschichte* 338–340.
67 al-Hamdānī, *Ṣifa* 103, 110; cf. W.W. Müller, *Ende* 235–236.
68 According to Bāfaqīh (*Unification* 280–281 following Beeston, *Warfare* 6) the SFLN lived in the lowlands between al-Ǧawf and Naǧrān.
69 Ryckmans, *Inscriptions historiques* 321–322; cf. the publication by Schaffer, *Inschriften* 14–20.
70 Ry 502:1–4 (Ryckmans, *Inscriptions* 10 270–273, Pl. 312); Ja 2131 = Jamme, *Pre-islamic Inscriptions* 117; Glaser 1177 = Schaffer, *Inschriften* 14–20. The translation of the first word in line 3, *ḥsq*, is uncertain. G. Ryckmans compares it to different roots in other Semitic languages (*ḥšq*, *ḥzq*) meaning 'adhere to', 'attach to' and translates it 'faire cause commune'. Jamme translates it as 'prisoner-keepers' without giving any reasons. Also Beeston *et al.* take it as a noun meaning 'baggage-train' (*Dictionary* s.v.). Schaffer (*Inschriften* 17–18) suggests 'baggage' (of an army). She also reads SBʔ as a verb whereas the earlier commentators took it as the name Saba. Ryckmans' rendering of line 4 cannot be maintained. The SFLN are not said to be ʕRB, and the phrase Ḏ-KYN KWNHMW does not mean 'ce qui était compté comme des leurs (parmi les Arabes)' but 'those who supported them (from among the ʔʕRB)'.
71 See note 59.
72 G. Ryckmans (*Inscriptions historiques* 325) dated it to the first century AD, mainly on palaeographic grounds. This can now be corrected from the more exact dating of YRM and BRG in CIH 353.
73 An inscription dealing with the same events is Ir 17. Iryani's identification of the tribe SFLN with the *ʔaʕrāb* (Iryani, *Nuqūš* 136; cf. Ryckmans, *Himyaritica* 4, 501) led Bāfaqīh (*Unification* 280) to claim that the word ʔʕRB SFLN occurs in Ir 17, which is wrong; cf. Beeston, *Warfare* 32.
74 Bāfaqīh, *Unification* 359–360; Kitchen, *Documentation* 18.
75 See Robin, *Abyssins* 149 ff.
76 For this text, see the reconstruction by von Wissmann, *Himyar* 470.
77 For the dating, see von Wissmann, *Zur Geschichte* 67, dating it between AD 180 and 215; cf. Robin, *Abyssins* 2–3; Bāfaqīh, *Unification* 266–267.
78 von Wissmann, *Zur Geschichte* 364 f.
79 CIH 350:7–10. For a translation, see Beeston, *Warfare* 45.

80 The translation in the CIH takes the word 'column of support' (ŠRḤT) as a part of ʕRB supposing the preposition BN 'from, out of' in between: *progressa est extenta turba ex Arabibus*. This reading is also followed by Beeston (*Warfare* 45). At least in the transcription only the letter B is visible, and the text is obviously damaged. The analogy with the preceding and following passages makes the suggested reading more plausible, supposing the preposition BʕM instead: BḎT TQDMW BʕM ḤBŠT, 'because they went against the Abyssinians'; BḎT TQDM ŠRḤT B[ʕM] ʕRBN, 'because the column went against the ʕRB'; WTQDMW BʕM BRQN 'and they went against BRQN'.

81 Drewes (*Inscriptions* 103–107) claims that the author was Shammar Yuharʕish III but he has not received any backing on this hypothesis.

82 von Wissmann, *Zur Geschichte* 67–69; Robin, *Intervention* 154–155; Munro-Hay, *Aksum* 42.

83 Cosmas, *Topographie* II:62 (Vol. I p. 376); Drewes *et al.*, *Recueil* I 378–382.

84 Cf. Frézouls, *Cosmas* 456. Cosmas makes his own comment on the inscription: 'By *arabîtai, kinaidokolpîtai* and the land of the *sabaíoi* he means the *homērîtai*', which might indicate the extension of the empire of the rulers in Yemen of his day.

85 Cf. von Wissmann, *Himyar* 470–474.

86 Ptolemy 6.7.24; see p. 438; von Wissmann, *Himyar* 474. The identification of the Kinaidokolpîtai, also mentioned by Ptolemy, with the tribe of Kinda suggested by Olinder (*Kings* 36 note 1) is less likely. They lived south of Yanbuʕ; von Wissmann, *Zur Geschichte* 64, 66.

87 See p. 438.

88 al-Hamdānī, *Ṣifa* 217.

89 Robin, *Miʕsâl* 4.

90 Bāfaqīh, *Unification* 369 ff.

91 Ir 12:2–3 (Iryani, *Nuqūš* 100); cf. Ryckmans, *Himyaritica* 3 245–247. The text is translated by Beeston, *Warfare* 23–24.

92 Bāfaqīh, *Unification* 285–286, 304, 308–309. He assumes (312) that this is the earliest mention of Kinda in any text.

93 Ja 635: 28–36 (Jamme, *Inscriptions* 137). The text is translated by Beeston, *Warfare* 24–25. Bāfaqīh (*Unification* 308–309) suggests the reading ṮWRM, the name of the dynasty in Qarya, instead of YWNM without, however, being able to check the original text.

94 Robin (*Abyssins* 150) assumed that the Arabs supported the Abyssinians. The passage Iryani 12:2: ḎKWN BʕMHMW BN Ḏʔ BNW ʔʕRBN must, however, mean 'those who supported them (i.e. the dedicant and his people) from (among) ḎʔBNW, [viz.] the ʔʕRBN'. This is also Iryani's interpretation, supported by Beeston, *Warfare* 24: 'their supporters among the . . . Arab'. Robin follows the two in *Pénétration* 79. Beeston (*Warfare* 24; cf. ibid. 3) defines the supporters as 'second-generation Arab immigrants'. Iryani, Beeston (*Warfare*) and Bobin (*Pénétration* 79) make the ʔʕRB in Ir 12:2 (end) attack together with the Abyssinians. Only Ryckmans (*Himyaritica* 3 246) sees the ʔʕRB as being attacked. We have followed his translation here, fitting better into the general picture of the ʔʕRB given in the ancient South Arabian texts.

95 Robin, *Hautes-Terres* 27. Cf. von Wissmann, *Zur Geschichte* 171 ff.

96 Cf. Ryckman's commentary (*Himyaritica* 3 245). The misspellings: ʔLMN l. 1 and ʔLQH l. 5 for ʔLMQH. In the first occurrence of the word ʔʕRBN in line 2, the copyist forgot the ʔ and had to add it afterwards.

97 See Ryckmans, *Rois*.

98 Ja 950 (= Jamme, *al-ʕUqla* 50).

99 Ja 961 (Jamme, *al-Uqla* 53).

100 According to Beeston, *Warfare* 11, the MQTWY was second-in-command to a king or a *qayl*.

101 Cf. Ryckmans, *Rois* 277.

102 Women are mentioned several times as queens of the Arabs in Dumah (p. 154) and once as an ʕRBYT from Qedar in the so-called Hierodul lists (Mlaker, *Hierodulenlisten* 34.

103 CIH 343:12–15.

104 Gr 124 = Bauer/Lundin, *Pam'atniki* 29 and photos 120a and b.

105 Bāfaqīh, *Unification* 380 f.
106 Ja 2110: 6–10 (= Doe/Jamme, *Inscriptions* 15–16; *Corpus*, 39.11/02 (II:33, Beeston)).
107 Cf. Strenziok, *Azd*; W.W. Müller, *Gesandschaft* 160. In Sabaean ʔSD is a term for 'warrior' and it is not unlikely that both tribal names ʔAsad and ʔAzd originally had this meaning. The Arabic meaning 'lion' would thus be a metonym (Beeston, *Warfare* 11 and note 20).
108 A ḤRṮ-N BN KʕBM is mentioned in Ja 660:11, 15 as the enemy of Shammar Yuharʕish (III) a decade later and it is likely that he is identical with the one mentioned here.
109 Cf. Schleifer, *Ḥārith*.W. Müller (*Gesandschaft* 160) identifies ʔSD in this text with the tribe ʔAsad in central Arabia, since this tribe's name in later Arabic is said never to contain the definite article L-, whereas ʔAzd (from ʔAsd) usually has it. To this it could be objected that, in order to make the argument valid, it should be shown that ʔAzd never occurs without the article. The *Lisān* (s.v ʔZD) knows both. But even though it could be shown that the distinction between ʔSD and (ʔ)LʔSD is always made in Arabic, thus distinguishing the two tribes, one should not take for granted that the Sabaeic-speakers always made it as well. The crucial elements are the name and pedigree of the king, which, by the Arabo-Islamic tradition, are explicitly connected with ʔAzd as-Sarāt and not with ʔAsad. The linguistic argument is here weaker than the historical one.
110 It is well worth noticing that Beeston, when retranslating Ja 2110, has added the word 'other' before ʔʕRBN (*Corpus*, loc. cit.), which is not found in the text and is contrary to the whole meaning. He is followed by W. Müller (*Gesandschaft* 160). The translators, like everybody else, are governed by the idea that all these tribes must be 'Arabs', in spite of what the sources say.
111 Ja 739:8–10. ʔIlsharaḥ Yaḥḍub is not mentioned in the inscription but SʕDŠMS is mentioned in Ja 594:4–5, which also mentions the king.
112 Ja 758:7–9.
113 Robin/Brunner, *Map* H7.
114 Robin, *Inscriptions* 326; Bāfaqīh, *Unification* 287–288.
115 Cf. W. Müller, *Frühnordarabisch* 27.
116 Documented in the inscription 'Sharafaddin p. 44'; cf. W. Müller, *Gesandtschaft*, and pp. 551 ff.
117 Translation according to the Sabaean text in Beeston, *Warfare* 59, which is improved by comparison with a photo.
118 ʕBRN is located north of Shabwa (von Wissmann, *Zur Geschichte* 201; Beeston, *Warfare* 6–7; Robin/Brunner, *Map* L4). Shibam, Raṭgha and Sayʔūn are all in the central Ḥaḍramawt (Robin/Brunner, *Map* O5).
119 Cf. Beeston, *Warfare* 7–8.
120 Cf. Beeston, *Warfare* 12.
121 Cf. W. Müller, *Ende* 248–251.
122 von Wissmann, *Himyar* 491; Kitchen, *Documentation* 14–15.
123 Ja 665:1–14 (= Jamme, *Inscriptions* 169–172); translated anew by Beeston, *Warfare* 52–53; cf. Robin, *Pénétration* 80. For the translation of TMHRT (l. 13) as 'mercenaries' (Beeston: 'trained band'), see W. Müller, *Ende* 233–234.
124 Cf. W. Müller, *Ende* 232.
125 ʔIryānī, *Nuqūš* 199–205. Commented by Ryckmans, *Himyaritica* 5 209–215. Translated anew by Beeston, *Warfare* 53–55. The definitive publication is W. Müller, *Ende*. Iryani's publication as ʔʕRBN in line 16 was corrected (?) by Müller to ʕRBN.
126 The CIH writes the name in line 2 as ŠHRʕLY, corrected by Beeston (*Warfare*). The translation of TQDM-HMW in line 8 in the CIH as 'et aggressus est ipsos (scil. Saba et Arabes) Saʕdtaʔlab' interprets the text as a testimony of a war between Hamdān and Himyar/Saba. It is, however, clear from Schreyer/Geukens = Iryani 32:11 that the verb TQDM with direct object must mean 'to put oneself as leader for someone' whereas with a prepositional object (BʕM) it means 'to attack someone' (cf. Beeston *et al.*, *Dictionary* s.v. QDM). In this text it must thus mean 'he put himself as leader for them', or perhaps 'he was made leader for them' (namely the Sabaeans and their Arabs). Beeston (*Warfare* 55) translates 'under the command of S'.

127 For the dating of Ja 665, cf. von Wissmann, *Zur Geschichte* 63. Cf. Müller, *Felsinschrift* and Kitchen, *Documentation* 14–15.
128 Ir 32:30. Cf. Müller, *Ende* 241.
129 Beeston, *Warfare* 7; von Wissmann, *Zur Geschichte* 198.
130 Cf. Beeston, *Warfare* 10, and von Wissmann, *Zur Geschichte* 188–189, 194 f., 201.
131 Cf. Ryckmans, *Himyaritica* 4 501; Müller, *Ende* 231–232.
132 al-Hamdānī, *Ṣifa* 110.
133 ʕAbadān l. 6–10. For a facsimile of the text, see Pirenne, *Prospections* 235; for a transcription to Arabic and a commentary, see Bāfaqīh, *Hawāmiš*. Our reading follows the new edition by Robin and Gajda (*Inscription*).
134 ʕAbadān 12–13.
135 Robin/Gajda, *Inscription* 132–133.
136 ʕAbadān 5, 16; cf. Kitchen, *Documentation* 16 (Table D); Robin/Gajda, *Inscription* 133.
137 ʕAbadān 24, 26.
138 Cf. the discussion in Robin/Gajda, *Inscription* 133.
139 al-Hamdānī, *Ṣifa* 137:25–26; 149:22–24; 165:4–15; Yāqūt, *Muʕǧam* IV:1006; cf. Robin/Gajda, *Inscription* 122. A̧ YBRN is also mentioned in Ja 555:3 and CIH 368:2, which seems to be located in al-Ǧawf.
140 Cf. pp. 48, 50, 78, 84.
141 al-Hamdānī, *Ṣifa* 165:9–11; Caskel, *Gamhara* II 473, 365. According to al-Hamdānī, the word for these clans was *luḥūm* or *ṭuxūn*.
142 Ja 671 (= Jamme, *Inscriptions* 176 sqq.). MḌRF is a part of the dam, translated by W. Müller as 'Seitenmauer' (*Stele*). ŠWḤṬ is a measure of length equivalent to *c.* 5 cubits.
143 Beeston, *Warfare* 7. The expression is LQTDMN ḪMSN BʕRBN. Jamme compared the expression in CIH 350:8–9: TQDM ŠRḤTM BN ʕRBN. The reading of CIH 350 is, however, not certain (see p. 546).
144 For the traditions about him, see Piotrovskij, *Predanije* 45 ff.
145 Bayt Ashwal 2 (= Garbini, *Bilingue* 162 ff.).
146 Ry 534; cf. Kitchen, *Documentation* 9.
147 See Robin, *Royaume* 680–682.
148 Ry 509 (= Ryckmans, *Inscriptions* 10 270–273 = Ry 445 (Ryckmans, *Inscriptions* 9 99–102); cf. Ryckmans, *Inscriptions historiques* 327–328 and Robin, *Royaume* 675–680. The meaning of the verb RQD, describing what the army did in Wādī Māsil, is debated. G. Ryckmans took it as a synonym for SṬR, 'write'. Caskel (*Entdeckungen* 9) suggested 'ascend'. The Sabaean Dictionary has 'traverse'. Robin (*Royaume* 677–678 cf. n. 50) supports Ryckmans' interpretation. In line 6 Robin reads MʕD instead of Ryckmans' MWD. This makes Maʕadd a tribe in eastern central Arabia which, however, raises some problems. The phrase ḌMW NZLM BN in line 6 is also unclear. Robin (*Royaume*) reads BMW 'à l'occasion même de', thus 'at the same time as the settling of some of their tribes'.
149 See p. 551. According to W. Müller, the reading could be SʕD (personal communication); cf. Robin, *Royaume* 679 f.
150 Ry 446:2; Ry 534:2; [RÉS 4105]; Fakhry 60:2. Cf. Ryckmans, *Institution* 215–216.
151 See Robin/Brunner, *Map*.
152 Ryckmans, *Institution* 216, suggests that ṬWDM is 'tout le plateau central de l'Arabie'. Robin (*Pénétration* 81) suggests 'les arabes de la montagne et de la plaine côtière', i.e. Tihāma and ʕAsīr. His latest suggestion is that 'the highland' is the whole of central Arabia or Naǧd and identical with the kingdom of Kinda, established there by Abū karib (*Royaume* 681, 693). This idea is partly built on the assumption that the 'Arabs' in the title refer to all the tribes in central Arabia. As is evident from the present study, this is very unlikely. Also the reading of the inscriptions Ry 509 and Ry 510 is uncertain, and neither the kingdom of Kinda nor Arabs in central Arabia are mentioned.
153 al-Hamdānī, *Ṣifa* 208:8–10.
154 al-Hamdānī, *Ṣifa* 210. Sarūm is a town near Saʕda: ibid. 114; cf. Yāqūt, *Muʕǧam* 3:556.
155 So Halévy, *Arabes* 152.
156 Cf. al-Hamdānī (*Ṣifa* 217): 'the *ʕarab* from the inhabitants (*ʔahl*) of Tihāma and its

Sarwiyya (= as-Sarāt belonging to Tihāma), their *bādī* and their *ḥāḍir*'.

157 For these, see p. 547. al-Hamdānī (*Ṣifa* 68, 72, 103) also mentions *ʕarab* in the land of ʕAkk on the Tihāma, just west of present-day Ḥarāz.

158 CIH 540; Garbini, *Iscrizione*; Dostal 1 (= Müller, *Inschrift* l. 6) from ŠRḤBʔL YʕFR, son of ʔBKRB ʔSʕD. Ry 264 = RÉS 4969 [RÉS 4298, CIH 537, 644] from ŠRḤBʔL YKF, the successor of ŠRḤBʔL YʕFR. Ry 203 = RÉS 4919 from LḤYʕT YNWF, son of ŠRḤBʔL YKF AD 467/472. Fakhry 74 from MRṮDʔLN YNF AD 499/504. From the king MʕDKRB YNʕM, reigning after ŠRḤBʔL YNF around AD 490, we have no inscription with the long title, although it may have been found in CIH 620.

159 Ry 510 (= Ryckmans, *Inscriptions* 10 307–310) = Ry 446 (= Ryckmans, *Inscriptions* 9 103–106). The text is also known as Philby 228; cf. Ryckmans, *Inscriptions historiques* 328–330, and Garbini, *Osservazioni*. For the latest translation, see Robin, *Royaume* 686. In line 7 YḤN should not be read YḤNN (W.W. Müller, personal communication).

160 Ryckmans, *Inscriptions historiques* 329; Robin, *Royaume* 689, reads it MḌR, i.e. Muḍar. The reading is, however, uncertain.

161 This is an argument in favour of Robin's reading of the latter part of line 4 as 'on the ʕIrāq of Kūṯā'.

162 The most difficult phrase is ḎNDYNHMW, which has been read in different ways: Ḏ NDYN-HMW, 'when [the Arabs] demanded their help' (Ryckmans); 'when [the Arabs] pursued them' (Beeston *et al.*, *Dictionary* s.v. NDY); 'when [the Arabs] gathered' (Garbini, *Osservazioni*); ḎN DYN-HMW, '(because of) this submission to him (*sic*!) of the revolting Arabs', (Robin, *Royaume* 668). None of them is a satisfactory solution.

163 Cf. in general Robin, *Royaume* 691 ff., an interpretation with many question marks remaining.

164 Cf. also Ry 446:2; Ja 2483 (= Jamme, *Miscellanées* III 85–87).

165 This king is known under several names: Finḥas in the Ethiopian tradition, Masrūq in the Syriac, and Zurʕa Dhū Nuwās, 'the one with the bang', in the Arabic. In Greek he is called Dounaas, clearly dependent on the Arabic. See Shahid, *Martyrs* 260–266.

166 For the sequence of events and their dating, see de Blois, *Date*, and Kitchen, *Documentation* 1–9.

167 For the documents, see Shahid, *Documents*.

168 Cf. Simeon, *Letter*; Shahid, *Martyrs*.

169 de Blois, *Date*; Kitchen, *Documentation* 5–6.

170 Ryckmans, *Inscriptions* 10 284–295. For some phrases see Beeston, *Biʔr Ḥimā*, commentary to lines 4–5.

171 Ryckmans, *Inscriptions* 10 295–303. For further commentaries on Ry 507 and 508, see Ryckmans, *Inscriptions historiques* 330–339.

172 Jamme, *Sabaean Inscriptions* 39–55. The text is commented upon by Rodinson (*Inscription*) and Beeston (*Biʔr Ḥimā*).

173 Jamme's commentary (Ja 1028 ad loc.) that ʔʕRB are the nomads and the HGR is the settled population, thus including the ʔŠʕB, seems too hasty. His reference to Lundin, *Aravija* 107 sq. and note 56 is not quite to the point. The problem is connected with the use of the connective particle W-; does its absence signal a following specification or is it dropped haphazardly? A comparison between Ry 508 and Ja 1028 gives support for the latter interpretation.

174 CIH 541:6–9; Ry 506:1–2; Ja 546:2–3.

175 For the dating to AD 543 see Kitchen, *Documentation* 8–9. This text, which disappeared a long time ago, was published anew by Piotrovskij in *Yémen* 218–219 (photo and translation) and by W. Müller, *Stele*, with a translation which is followed here.

176 This is the commonly accepted meaning: cf. Halévy, *Arabes* 155 (ʔʕRB = nomades); Müller, *Araber* 143. Bāfaqīh, *Unification*, 271–288, bases his claim on much later Arabic sources. Apart from the methodological doubtfulness of this procedure, the testimony of those sources, as we have seen, is far from unequivocal. Robin, *Pénétration* 73–74 is very confused; see p. 110.

177 Cf. Robin, *Pénétration* 73–74.

178 In South Arabian the nisba adjectives ending in -Y were obviously formed only in the singular. For the plural, 'broken plurals' were used. In Arabic the plural of nisbas in *-iyyūn/-iyyīn* was disliked by many grammarians who prescribed the use of broken plural or circumscriptions like *ʔahl al-Yaman*, 'people of Yemen', instead of *yamaniyyūn* 'Yemenites'. The avoidance of plurals of nisba adjectives could very well be a South Arabian influence in the ʕArabiyya.
179 Beeston, *Grammar* 26.
180 *Lisān* s.v. ʕRB
181 Cf. Caskel, *Ǧamhara* II 371–372. As has been shown, it is not correct to say that 'Kinda werden in den südarabischen Inschriften *ʔaʕrāb* genannt'.
182 Halévy (*Arabes* 152–153) underlined that the 'Arabs' in South Arabian inscriptions were defined according to their relation to the kings and the noblemen and not according to language or ethnicity.
183 Ibn Saʕd, *Ṭabaqāt* I:73. See p. 32.
184 von Wissmann, *Zur Geschichte* 98, 242, 297–318, 374–383. The name was especially attached to a sanctuary in the northern part of SMʕY.
185 von Wissmann, *Zur Geschichte* 87 f., 96 f. (the northern Nihm), 322 f. (the southern Nihm).
186 von Wissmann, *Zur Geschichte* 81 f., 87 f., 98, 148, 155.
187 von Wissmann, *Zur Geschichte* 93 f., 113, 157, 190.
188 von Wissmann, *Zur Geschichte* 122f., 148.
189 von Wissmann, *Zur Geschichte* 33, 315, 352 Anm. 249.
190 von Wissmann, *Zur Geschichte* 158 Anm. 281.
191 al-Hamdānī, *Ṣifa* 83.
192 al-Hamdānī, *Ṣifa* 113; von Wissmann, *Zur Geschichte* 352.
193 Cf. von Wissmann, *Zur Geschichte* 81–206.
194 Ibn Hishām, *Sīra* 20–22.
195 Ibn Hishām, *Tīǧān* 163; cf. Ibn al-Kalbī, *Nasab* I.134.
196 Cf. pp. 87–93.
197 See p. 92.
198 Cf. also the passage in aṭ-Ṭabarī (*Tārīkh* I:955) where the Persians in AD 572 encountered an army of Yemenis consisting of Ḥabaša, Ḥimyar and *ʔaʕrāb*.
199 Theophrastus, *Plants* 9.4.5–6.
200 Pliny 12.52.
201 Suggested by W. Müller, *Frankincense* 80.
202 Solinus 33.5.
203 Isidorus, 14.15.
204 The reading Arabia is found in the R 2 MS (Codex Florentinus Riccardianus 488, written *c.* AD 100). The MSS D1, E, F and a have different variants of Sarib-. The MSS T1 and several old fragments have Saba; cf. Pliny, ed. Ernout, ad loc.
205 Pliny 12.54.
206 Herodotus 3.107.
207 Theophrastus, *Plants* 9.4.2.
208 Cf. von Wissmann, *Ophir*.
209 There is a passage in Strabo (16.4.19) originating from Artemidorus (cf. Potts, *Gulf* II 90) saying that 'from their trafficking, the Gerrhaeans and the Sabaeans have become richest of all'. This is part of the description of South Arabia originally found in Agatharchides. This description does not fit very well with known conditions in South Arabia in 280 BC (the other three kingdoms are not mentioned) and may, in fact, go back to the source quoted by Theophrastus. It also indicates that the ties between Gerrha and South Arabia may be much older than the time of Alexander.

Part III

THE SOLUTION OF AN ENIGMA?

20

THE PICTURE OF ARABS IN PRE-ISLAMIC SOURCES

A final evaluation of the sources

Arabs are mentioned in sources from the 850s BC until the rise of Islam. The preceding penetration of them has shown that they are of quite varying value for the historian. The first reflection is that there are extremely few primary remains from the Arabs themselves or events which involved them. Perhaps the only identifiable ones are the papyrus documents from Ptolemaic Egypt and, possibly, some of the inscriptions from Hatra. There are, of course, artefacts around that may have been used or produced by Arabs; but since Arabs so far are not identifiable archaeologically and no texts are found connecting any artefact with those called Arabs in the texts, the protagonists of our story remain anonymous in the archaeological evidence.

Almost the entire source material we possess is thus to be classified as textual or narrative, i.e. textual accounts referring to people called Arabs in different ways. Of these the Greek sources are those which cover the longest time span: from *c.* 500 BC until the Prophet. The Latin texts are to a large degree founded upon Greek ones and should be judged together with them. The Graeco-Latin texts are also the most problematic ones. The acquaintance of the writers with the Arabs varies from the first-hand knowledge of writers like Herodotus, Xenophon, Hieronymus of Cardia, Posidonius and perhaps Josephus, to only literary acquaintance. The latter is the most common. The classical sources are informative as far as political relations between the Arabs and the empires are concerned, but are as a rule silent about cultural conditions. This is connected with the fact that Arab affairs are usually referred to *en passant* along with the description of political events in which they happened to be involved. There are some remarkable exceptions: Herodotus, Hieronymus of Cardia and Josephus have preserved unique material which allows us to catch some glimpses of the nature of these Arabs. But since much of the evidence given by the classical writers is known to us through digests and selections from original texts which have disappeared, we are dependent upon the attitudes and evaluations of those writers whose books are extant. No information from a Greek or Latin text can be used without minute source criticism. It also turns out that quite unsophisticated authors like Diodorus and Cosmas Indicopleustes are more valuable than relatively reflective authors like Strabo who tend to filter the information through minds full of preconceived ideas about geography and ethnology. Worst of all is Pliny. Most information that passed through his boiling brain was destroyed or confused beyond recognition, which is a great loss since he obviously had access to sources of great value. His general picture of the geography of the Middle East seems to have been sketchy, and practically every 'barbarian' place-name is distorted. But a more sober writer like Strabo is also full of mistakes and unclear contexts. The much criticized and ridiculed Diodorus, on the other hand, stands out as a faithful and careful copyist in the cases where we can check him, and his accounts in general give a trustworthy impression even though he has often abbreviated and summed up his sources. This also holds to a large extent for Josephus.

Of the Oriental sources, the ones in Akkadian, South Arabian languages and the texts from Hatra have a high degree of authenticity. Unlike the Graeco-Latin material, they are almost all official documents reflecting the current political terminology of their time. They are rarely if ever influenced by literary or academic ideas about ethnic and political conditions, and they can thus be assumed to give a faithful picture of the status of the Arabs. Unfortunately the value of most of those documents is limited to the political sphere. Only the Assyrian texts contain several pieces of information about religious, social and economic conditions among the 'Arabs'. Such information is also found in the Jewish sources from the Old Testament to the Talmud and in the texts dependent upon them, like the Christian Bible commentaries. References to actual political conditions are mostly absent in this material.

The conclusion from this evaluation of the sources is that the picture of the Arabs emerging from the Oriental sources must have precedence over that in the Graeco-Latin sources. More exactly, if there is a discrepancy between them, the Oriental sources are to be preferred.

The lands of the Arabs

The difference between the sources becomes evident in the general picture of the land called Arabia. Arabia appears as two different kinds of entity: one which encompasses the entire peninsula and adjacent lands which are inhabited by Arabs, and another where the lands of the Arabs are several different regions on the peninsula in which the Arabs are spread as numerous smaller groups. The former picture is found in the Greek sources at least from Eratosthenes onwards. The latter occurs in the Oriental sources and, since it can also be traced in various Graeco-Latin texts where it stands in contradiction to the more comprehensive one, there are reasons to infer that it is the correct one, especially as it can be traced in the Arabo-Islamic texts. A general conclusion is thus that the term 'Arabs' in the ancient world from Shalmaneser III and well into early Islamic times was the designation of groups of people living in certain limited areas on the Arabian peninsula and in adjacent regions in the Middle East.

It may well be that the Greek term *Arabía* was originally a term for such a region: *hē arabía khōra*, 'the Arabian region'. There seem to be several instances in the Greek texts where Arabia is used with this meaning. In Semitic we hear in Sabaean texts about 'the land(s) of the *ʕarab*', ʔRḌ(T) ʕRBN, referring to a specific area by Nağrān. It can even be suspected that the Arabic term *ğazīrat al-ʕarab*, 'the part' or 'the lot of the *ʕarab*', originally referred to the same kind of region and not to the entire peninsula.

There would thus originally have existed several 'Arabias', settlements of the *ʕarab*. The earliest one appearing in our documents is Dumah, which obviously for several centuries was a settlement of *ʕarab*. From the Neo-Babylonian period we also hear about an *ālu ša arbāya*, 'town of the Arabs', near Nippur in lower Mesopotamia. A third major Arab area is between Palestine and Egypt where there is already a trace of Arab settlement in the time of Tiglath Pileser III. Arabs are referred to there in the time of Esarhaddon. But they appear in full light in the days of the Achaemenids when it was visited by Herodotus, and are found there down to Roman times.

A fourth Arabia is described by Xenophon in 401 BC but may already be referred to in texts from the time of Cyrus the Great. It stretched between the Khābūr and the Euphrates rivers and was probably limited to the north by the Singăr mountains. We do not hear anything more about it until the time of Augustus when it was described by Iuba. It is well documented in the second century AD through the campaigns of the Roman emperors in Mesopotamia, and the texts from Hatra constitute a unique first-hand documentation. As a matter of fact, this Mesopotamian Arabia is the only one from which we possess original documents written by the inhabitants themselves.

A fifth Arabia is documented in Transjordan near the Ğabal ad-Durūz or Bashan. There seem to be several different regions of Arab settlement in this part of southern Syria documented at least from the time of Alexander the Great. One group lived in some kind of symbiosis with the Ituraeans in the Antilebanon. They are certain to have emerged from the Ğabal. The rugged area called Trachonitis connects their habitat with the area south-east of Damascus called Arabia in early Christian writings. This is the region where we find the tomb of Imruʔ al-Qays, 'king of all *ʕarab*'.

The Arabia south-east of Damascus is situated on the tip of a piece of fertile, rain-watered land stretching into the Syria desert. A similar green promontory is found east of Ḥimṣ/Emesa in central Syria, where we also find Arabs settled at least from the beginning of the second century BC. There was also an Arab settlement in northern Syria south-east of Aleppo. These Arabs played an important role in the politics of the Seleucid kingdom during its last phase and the beginning of Roman rule in Syria. Those in the north may have fulfilled some task of guarding the heartland of the Seleucid rulers in northern Syria.

An Arab settlement is found in Gilead or ʕAğlūn during the third century BC and a couple of centuries onwards. An Arab settlement in al-Ḥasā in eastern Arabia is well documented from the early Hellenistic period into Islamic times. There also seems to have been a group of Arabs in the western Ḥiğāz close to Thamūd already in the time of Sargon II. Finally, we hear about a 'land of the *ʕarab*' somewhere near Nağrān, perhaps as early as the sixth century BC until the time of the kings of Ḥimyar. At the same time, people called ʔʕRB were widely employed by the South Arabian kingdoms as border-guards and auxiliaries of different kinds. The most important of these Arabias was the third one. It seems that this Arabia was in some way established by the Achaemenid rulers. It is evident that the Arabs there were closely united with the empire and played a crucial strategic role, situated as they were between Egypt, Asia and western Arabia. A scrutiny of the sources has shown that this Arabia survived the downfall of the Achaemenid empire, withstood the attacks of the successors of Alexander the Great and was even able to preserve its independence until AD 106. Contrary to what has been hitherto assumed, there is no break between Achaemenid Arabia and the so-called Nabataeans of the Hellenistic age. It is unfortunate that we do not know more about the inner life of this entity, which shows such remarkable stability over more than six centuries. Apart from its strategic importance, it played a significant economic role from the days of the Achaemenids down to the Hellenistic era. From both Herodotus and Agatharchides it appears that this Arabia was a gateway to the trade-routes through Arabia to the Persian Gulf as well as South Arabia. Its final downfall may have been caused by the dwindling importance of this trade. Obviously the tribe of Qedar played a crucial role at least during the early history of this Arabia, leading us to suspect that these Arabs also had something to do with Dumah, with which Qedar was intimately connected.

There might be a linkage of the Arabs between Palestine and Egypt with those around the Ǧabal ad-Durūz. From the Assyrian records it appears that Qedar originally had its domicile somewhere in that area, perhaps in the Wādī Sirḥān. The Old Testament writers also connect Qedar with tribes in northern Transjordan in the Ishmaelite genealogy. The Ituraeans and the Arabs in Antilebanon lived along the border between the Ptolemies and the Seleucids. The Arab groups in Syria may thus have been installed there by these rulers as guards of their borders. The employment of Arabs as border-guards is well documented from South Arabia. Since Arabs were obviously already in Antilebanon in Alexander's time, they may have been stationed there by the Achaemenids, perhaps during the great satrap revolt in the fourth century BC. It can also be assumed that the Arabs in Mesopotamia were established there by those rulers. In that case it may be suggested that the Arabs in central and northern Syria were installed there by the Seleucids as a counterweight to the Ptolemies in Lebanon and Palestine. If so, these Syrian Arabs were presumably brought from the other side of the Euphrates. We have indications of good relations between the Syrian Arabs and those east of the great river. This system of employing Arabs as guards in strategic places may go back to the Assyrians, who implanted Arabs south of Gaza as well as in lower Mesopotamia. This policy was clearly continued on a large scale by the Achaemenids, who were followed by their heirs, the Ptolemies in Egypt and the Seleucids in Syria. The employment of Arabs as a police force in Egypt, a system which lasted into late antiquity, might have been initiated by the Achaemenids. There are also traces of a similar system in the Seleucid realm.

This involvement of Arabs with the politics of the great empires in the Middle East is the main reason for the quite ample documentation we have of them in the ancient sources. Outside the main areas we find only hints of Arabias on the peninsula.

How the Arabs lived

Many details about the Arab's way of living can be found in the texts. The most informative are the most ancient ones, i.e. the Akkadian texts. Arabs with small cattle are documented in the reliefs of the capture of Shamsi by Tiglath Pileser III in 733 BC, showing sheep and goats being led towards the king.[1] In the other tribute lists, small cattle are absent. They are, however, mentioned in some of Assurbanipal's texts.[2] In the Old Testament the *ʕarbîm* are said to have given king Jehoshaphaṭ of Judah 7,700 rams and the same number of bucks.[3] In the same manner both Qedar and the *ʕarab* are said to trade in sheep and goats with Tyre in the days of Ezechiel.[4]

The use of the one-humped dromedary as a riding animal is first documented in two reliefs from Carchemish and Tell Ḥalaf in northern Syria around 900 BC. It also appears on the Balawāt gates from the time of Shalmaneser III.[5] Camels appear for the first time with Arabs at Qarqar in 853 BC. In the reign of Tiglath Pileser III they are pictured together with Shamsi in 733. It is said in the texts that she gave *gamalī* and *anāqāti*, i.e. male and female camels, as tribute.[6] Sargon II says that he received *gamalī* from 'the kings of the shore of the sea and the desert'. The latter are Shamsi and Itamra of Saba.[7] Sennacherib takes a number of camels from Telhunu.[8] Esarhaddon imposes a tribute of sixty-five camels on Hazaʔil and fifty on his son Yaʕlu added to an earlier tribute.[9] He also requires camels from the Arabs for his campaign to Egypt.[10] During Assurbanipal's war with the Arabs, camels are a constant booty.[11] In Assyrian texts, camels are very rarely mentioned together with peoples other than Arabs.[12]

In the Old Testament the association between camels and the *ʕarab* is less evident. In fact, camels are mentioned in texts reflecting conditions in the seventh and sixth centuries BC with Qedar, Ishmael, Midian, Ephah and Sheba, not with *ʕarab* proper.[13] The Israelites themselves seem not to have used domesticated camels until the time of the exile.[14]

The slight difference between the pictures in Akkadian and Old Testament texts should not conceal certain basic facts. One is that the Arabs used the camel extensively. Another is that widespread use of the camel for civil transport is not documented before 700.[15] This goes with the fact, well documented from Assyrian sources, both written and pictorial, that the camel was in use from 900 BC down to 650 mainly for military purposes.[16] The Assyrian interest in the animal is thus easily explained, as is the role of the tribes who knew how to handle the animal.

It must, however, be emphasized that the picture of Arabs as primarily busy with camel-breeding or even shepherding is not unequivocal in the Akkadian texts. In the documents from southern Mesopotamia, Arabs are active as both tradesmen and landowners. The latter is remarkable since later sources say that they do not farm. But they might have been owners of land without working there themselves. In the same letters they appear as sellers of small cattle, which makes the picture similar to the one in the Old Testament. Camels are not mentioned with the Arabs from southern Mesopotamia. It seems that the Arabs in the Syrian desert during the earliest documented period were participants in a larger economic system supplying the kingdoms in the surrounding Fertile Crescent with animals, small cattle for food, wool production and perhaps also currency. These activities brought them into close contact with the settled communities, as we can see clearly in southern Mesopotamia. A speciality was the camel, which had to be handled in a special way and which turned out to have military importance, for the Assyrians as transport, for the Arabs themselves and other camel-breeding tribes also as a weapon.

Camels appear regularly together with the Arabs in later ages. Herodotus mentions them together in the Persian army.[17] They appear in the Seleucid army at Raphia, and the Nabataean king Aretas 'III' is shown on Scaurus' coins kneeling beside a camel. Later, camels and Arabs are mentioned together by Clement of Alexandria and Ammian. They also accompany each other in the Jewish literature, both the Greek and the rabbinic. Judging from the picture given by the sources, the handling of the camel was the main and most exotic characteristic of the Arabs as seen by the surrounding communiites.

Hieronymus of Cardia mentions Arabs as farmers in Syria, a testimony supported by Quintus Curtius. Both references are to the time of Alexander the Great and we thus have a parallel to the picture of the Arabs in southern Mesopotamia. Also from that time is the report about the Arabs in the Gulf area and their fertile land. The fact that some of the Arabs are explicitly said to live in oases like Dumah and al-Ḥasā is an argument in favour of their being farmers. We remember Euhemerus' depiction of the fertility of *Arabía eudaímōn* as well as the villages of the *ʕarab* in the early Islamic sources probably to be situated in oases. We may also remember the Arabs in Ptolemaic Egypt who operated as policemen and were involved in business of the same kind as in southern Mesopotamia. On the other hand, Hieronymus also says that the Arabs in the Negev did not plant or sow. The Talmudic sources do not mention any agricultural products from the Arabs. The picture is thus contradictory and a solution may be suggested only after this survey. But there is one thing that appears with undeniable clarity: the Arabs in the ancient sources do not appear as nomads, let alone bedouin. Shepherding is only one of their ways of living. Further, they do not live in 'deserts'. Both in Egypt and in Mesopotamia we find them in the middle of settled lands.

Tiglath Pileser III received gold but no perfumes (*riqqē*) from Shamsi.[18] *Riqqē,* gold and silver are mentioned as tribute from the nine tribes in 733 BC.[19] These goods are also recorded by Sargon in 716 BC from the Arabs, the Sabaeans and Muṣur.[20] Gold and *riqqē* are included in the tribute from Hazaʔil to Esarhaddon and the latter imposed a tribute of 10 talents of gold on Yaʕlu.[21] Gold and perfumes are not mentioned in Assurbanipal's records of the war with the Arabs.

Neither in the Old Testament nor in the Akkadian texts do we find any association between Arabs and frankincense before the fifth century BC. The frankincense trade was a completely South Arabian business that emerged suddenly in western Arabia in the middle of the seventh century BC. From Herodotus onwards we have ample evidence of the Arabs being involved in the frankincense business. It is mentioned together with Arabs in the Sinai and in al-Ḥasā, naturally enough since they both lived where the two main caravan routes from South Arabia reached the north.

This brings us to the military aspects of the culture of the Arabs. We have already pointed out that the camel was used by the Assyrians mainly for military purposes down to the fifth century BC. The way it was used is mainly shown in the Assyrian illustrations of the Arab campaigns. From these it can be seen that the animal was ridden with a cushion-saddle placed on the hump on which one or two riders were placed. The cushion-saddle seems to have been an invention made in the north; its earliest representations are the camels on reliefs from Carchemish and Tell Ḥalaf, both from *c.* 900 BC.[22] The Assyrians used it only for transport.[23] The Arabs are shown riding and shooting with arrows. On Assurbanipal's reliefs they are also equipped with short swords, or rather daggers with a broad blade, when dismounted. The bow seems to be a traditional hunting bow made from one piece of wood. There is an obvious difference on the reliefs between the bows of the Assyrians and those of the Arabs. Those of the former are larger and are considerably deformed when stretched. This indicates that the Assyrians had composite bows which could shoot larger arrows further than that of the Arabs.[24] The armoury of the Arabs appears rather primitive compared to that of the Assyrians. In spite of this we have seen that the Arabs dared to challenge the Assyrian army on several occasions. That the bow was seen as a characteristic weapon of certain groups in the wilderness is indicated by the fact that Ishmael is called an archer, *qaššāt*.[25] The main asset, however, was the camel. Its advantages must then have been considerable and outweighed the light armoury. The advantages were the elevated position of the rider/shooter and the mobility of the animal. In particular, the possibility of swift escape from the battle into desert lands made the camel riders an elusive enemy. How this worked can be seen from the story of David's war with the Amalekites, a story which reflects conditions in the seventh century BC.[26] Four hundred men are said to have escaped a defeat by riding on camels. It is evident from the context of this story that the Israelites had neither camels nor horses.

One should keep in mind that the Assyrians were slowly developing the art of riding horses by this time, with support from horse riders in the north. The horse, however, was not very useful in the dry and hot desert and steppe areas south of the Fertile Crescent. The ability of quick withdrawal into areas where no pursuit was possible made the Arabs almost impossible to control. There are thus certain characteristics already visible now which later became dominant in the picture of the Arabs. But it should be underlined that this is no bedouin culture. We are still far from the razzia-loving warrior caste that was to take power in Arabia many hundred years later and which built its power on the introduction of the horse as well as new weapons. The Arabs and their neighbours in this period were basically peaceful cattle-breeders. They were involved in the life of the empires by their handling of the camel, which was a useful asset to the armies for transport, and as providers of cattle to the kings.[27] The fact that Ishmael is depicted as a wild and warrior-like individual in the famous oracle to Hagar about her son is due more to the view of the settled, urban society of the desert-dwellers than reality.[28] Civilized life outside the cultivated, urbanized land was considered impossible and those dwelling there consequently must needs live in anarchy.[29] But the important fact was that the Arabs by their breeding of the new animal had in their hand a tool that could be well used for military purposes, which drew them into war with the empires several times.

The differences between the Arabs in our period and the classical bedouin are also evident in their dress. On the reliefs we see the males dressed in short loincloths only.[30] In the *Periplus* it is said of the Arabic-speaking holy men living on the island of Sarapis that they are dressed in loin cloths of palm-leaves.[31] There is no trace of the wide mantle and the head-cloth characteristic of modern bedouin, but neither of the heavy armour with helmets and breast-plates known from the Arabic texts about the events in the sixth and seventh centuries AD. The female figure on Tiglath Pileser's reliefs from 733, which may well be a picture of Queen Shamsi herself, is dressed in a long gown which also covers her head and her arms. There is a striking resemblance between this dress and the *ʔiḥrām* clothing demanded for the performance of the *ʕumra* and the *ḥaǧǧ* at Mekkah today. The *ʔiḥrām* thus gives the impression of being an archaic dress preserved in the rituals around the ancient Mekkan sanctuary even after the emergence of classical bedouin culture with its quite different dress. The sparse dressing is a trait found with several of the so-called pariah tribes in Arabia in modern times, which have preserved many archaic features in their culture.[32]

We may also note the absence of head-covering for the men on Tiglath Pileser's and Assurbanipal's reliefs.[33] With this go the traces of shaving along the forehead which is clearly visible on the Assyrian pictures.[34] We know that, in the oracle against Qedar in Jeremiah 49 as well as the passage in Jeremiah 25, the Qedarites and the *ʕarab* and the desert inhabitants are said to be *qṣūṣē peʔā*. The meaning of this must be 'shaved on one's forehead'. This must thus have been an eye-catching characteristic of the Arabs and their neighbours which separated them from the settled peoples. It is also mentioned by Herodotus.[35] This custom is explicitly forbidden for the Israelites.[36] With the later bedouin the hair of the forehead was cut off on slaves and prisoners of war, whereas the preservation of the forelock was a sign of the free aristocrat.[37]

The Arabs lived in tents. This is another characteristic which is emphasized in Assyrian texts, the Old Testament and Greek sources. Telhunu and Hazaʔil leave their tents when they flee from Sennacherib's attack.[38] Assurbanipal burnt the tents of Aṭiya, queen of the Arabs.[39] Burning of tents is shown on the reliefs from Assurbanipal's palace.[40] In Assurbanipal's reliefs we have pictures of tents used by the Arabs which are small, polygonal structures with a central pole, quite different from the long, rectangular tents known from later epochs.[41] Hieronymus of Cardia emphasizes the fact that Arabs do not live in built houses. In the old Testament, Qedar are said to live in tents.[42]

The Arab tent-dwellers were identified by Eratosthenes with the *skēnîtai*, the tent-dwellers in the Syrian desert. It is, however, worth noticing that Posidonius seems to have distinguished the Arabs from the *scenitae* in general. He did not necessarily mean that they did not live in tents, only that this was not their main characteristic. And the living in tents does not imply that they must have been nomads or lived in the 'desert'.

In a famous Biblical passage, the tents of Qedar are said to be black.[43] This might indicate that tents made of goat's hair were already in use in northern Arabia around 600 BC. Such material was used for covering the cloth on the priestly Tabernacle.[44] The pieces of goat's hair are called in Hebrew *yerīʕōt*.[45] The same word is used for the tents of Qedar in Jeremiah 49.[46] In the description of the construction of the Tabernacle curtains of linen and coverings of rams' skins dyed red are also mentioned.[47] It is likely that parts of the equipment of this edifice reflect the tents in the Syrian desert from the seventh century BC and later.

Two other words connected with the settlements in the Syrian desert appear in the Old Testament. In the list of the Ishmaelites in Genesis 25 it is said that they live in *ṭîrōt*. The same word designates the dwellings of the *bnê Qedem* in Hezechiel.[48] In a poetic OT text it stands in parallelism with tents: 'let their *ṭîrā* be desolate/let none dwell in their tents'.[49] Since the word in other Old Testament passages means fence or wall, it must be a designation for a camp closed in by a low wall.[50] Such camp-sites are in fact known from Arabia in later periods.[51]

In the list of the Ishmaelites it is further said that they live in *ḥaṣerōt*.[52] As we have seen, the same word lies behind *ḥaṣor* in the oracle about Qedar in 599 BC. The meaning of this term is indicated by the description of the priestly Tabernacle, where it is the designation of the courtyard surrounding the *miškan* proper, which was fenced off by poles and curtains of linen.[53] In Arabic we have the word *ḥaẓīra* or *ḥiẓār*, 'enclosure for sheep' etc.'[54] Of these two, the latter is the linguistic equivalent to the *ḥaṣor* in Jeremiah 49. The whole arrangement with fences and walled-in courtyards points to the importance of cattle-raising with the tribes in question, thus confirming the other information given by the sources.

Political structure

We know less about the social and political structure within the Arab communities.[55] In the Assyrian texts we find 'kings' (*šarrū, šarrāni*) as rulers among the Arabs.[56] Also in the Old Testament the *ʕarab* are said to have 'kings' (*melakîm*).[57] The title 'king of the ʕRB' is also prominent in the texts from Hatra. There is, however, another title, namely *dynástēs* in Greek, which is equivalent to the Aramaic *šallîṭā*. This title is found among Arabs around the Euphrates, in northern Syria and in Sumatar. According to Posidonius, the rule of the *dynástai* was a characteristic of the Arabs in Syria distinguishing them from other tent-dwellers. We have no information about the ruler of the Arabs in al-Ḥasā but in South Arabia we hear about a KBR as a special commander of the Arabs in the service of the kings. This reminds us of the *arabárkhēs* found in both Ptolemaic and Roman Egypt as well as in the Arabo-Nabataean kingdom, who seems to have occupied a position similar to the South Arabian KBR: an officer in command of the Arabs as a kind of special troops serving as police or border guards. The *dynástai/šallîṭē* in the north fulfilled a similar role. This office is probably already mentioned in southern Mesopotamia in the sixth century BC where a *ḥaṭru* fulfilled the tasks of the above-mentioned officials. We should thus distinguish between the Arab kingdoms in

Dumah, Hatra and probably also in the Negev, which were more or less independent of the empires, and the Arabs governed by *haṭrū/arabárkhai/dynástai/šalliṭē/*ʔKBR, who were more definitely under the formal rule of an empire and integrated into the imperial armies.

A title difficult to interpret is the one found in Hatra: *rabbaytā* of the Arabs.[58] It might be suggested that it is a religious title of some kind. Also the term 'Abias' mentioned by Josephus and occurring in the Hatrene inscriptions may be a religious title. In the earliest period there is another kind of ruler found among the Arabs. As we have seen, the *apkallatu* were probably some kind of priestesses with sacral functions in the oasis of Dumah. The exact function of these remains obscure.[59] The same title is found with the king of the Arabs in Hatra.[60] Since their title definitely has to do with religion and cult, it should be seen in the light of what we know about the religious conditions of the Arabs.

Arabs, Hagar, Nabaṭ

One feature that deserves to be pointed out is the apparent connection between the Arabs and the terms/names Hagar and *nabaṭ*/Nabataeans. The link between the first and the last has already been observed. A close reading of the texts shows that the derivation from the root HGR should be included in the complex. Between Egypt and Palestine there is a figure called Hagar documented in the Old Testament who has clear mythical features. The name seems to appear also in the Egyptian name for the area: HKR. We should also remember the term NBṬ in the Elousa inscription as well as the notice by Strabo that the Idumaeans, in his time living in the northern Negev, were Nabataeans.[61] In Transjordan *árabes*, *hagrîm* and *nabataîoi* are well documented in the Hellenistic period. The HGR in southern Syria may even be reflected in the name Hukkarina mentioned by Assurbanipal as a stronghold of the Arabs. The link between the Arabs in Antilebanon and the farmers in the Biqāʕ valley, where there is still a city called Nabaṭiyye, is more uncertain but not without interest.[62] The constellation of the three may also be documented from the region around Hatra, i.e. Mesopotamian Arabia, and certainly in al-Ḥasā and Nağrān.[63] Also Dumah might be connected with the *agraîoi* mentioned by several sources. In southern Mesopotamia *hagaranu* are mentioned together with *nabaṭ* and Arabs between the seventh and the fifth centuries BC. And the connection between the three is confirmed beyond doubt in the Islamic sources.

A last observation before a synthesis is suggested is the curious fact that the term *ʕarab* seems to disappear in the north after AD 300. We have observed that *ʕarab*, *sarakēnoí* and *ṭayyāyē* originally referred to three distinct groups. Of these, the latter two become current in northern sources in the fourth century AD and onwards. In South Arabia, the Arabs remain in the texts. It is easy to associate this change with the suggestion by W. Caskel and W. Dostal of a major socio-political change in northern and central Arabia in the third century AD. The introduction of the horse, heavy armament and new weaponry from Iran created a new class of warriors in the north, who very soon became the allies of the empires and organized in buffer-states in Iraq and Syria and later also in central Arabia. This revolution also changed the internal political organization of the inhabitants of the area, and it can be no coincidence that the earliest documentation of the tribal names known from the Arabo-Islamic tradition is from around AD 300.[64] The historical memory of the tribes making up the Islamic state did not go further back than the third century AD. This supports the assumption that a major change took place in that period and that the structures created then lived on into the Islamic age.[65] Classical Arabia as we know it from the tradition preserved in the early Arabo-Islamic sources arose in the third and fourth centuries AD, culminating in the creation of the Islamic empire in the seventh century. There are thus good reasons to call this period in the history of northern and central Arabia the 'age of the Saracens', distinguishing it from the preceding 'age of the Arabs', lasting from 850 BC to AD 300.

The change of the terminology in the sources thus seems to reflect a major transformation of society in Arabia. It is extremely unlikely, to say the least, that the replacement of *ʕarab* with Saracen represents some major migration of 'peoples'. Instead we have a change of social structure and political institutions. It is not easy to say why the terms 'Saracens' and *ṭayyāyē* became the new ones. Perhaps both were originally used locally and then extended as terms for the new groupings. Saracens may have been a term for people on the border line of the *Provincia Arabia*, perhaps along the border to Egypt, having some kind of alliance with the Romans which would explain why it was later expanded to cover all the allied tribes as well as their neighbours. In the same manner, the *ṭayyāyē* could originally have been a tribe employed by the Parthians as border-guards around Mount Sinğār. But the important thing is that this means that the term *ʕarab* must have designated something else than an ethnic group. Since the word definitely does not mean 'nomad', let alone 'bedouin', and the sources, both pre-Islamic amd Islamic, do not present a picture of Arabs as nomads, we should look in the direction of some kind of institution which disappeared in the north but was obviously preserved in South Arabia and even in central Arabia until the rise of Islam, when both the institution and the designation were revived and transformed.

There are many indications in favour of such a solution. The institutional nature of the *ʕarab* in the early layers of Arabo-Islamic sources is clearly visible, as we have pointed out. The synonymity between *muhāğirūn*, *ʕarab* and Muslim is a clear indication that all terms refer to membership in institutionally rather than ethnically or genealogically defined groups: unlike the tribes in Arabia, the *muhāğirūn* and the Muslims are not even in fiction descendants of patriarchs named Muhāğir or Muslim. The existence of communities based on common cult is well documented through the existence of the *ḥums* in Mecca and the *ṭuls* in south-western Arabia in pre-Islamic times.[66] According to Caskel, both Muḍar and Madhḥiğ were originally cultic associations around the sanctuaries at Mecca and Ğurash respectively.[67] A similar picture of the Arabs emerges from the documentation in the pre-Islamic sources: the absence of a genealogy going back to a patriarch with the same name, the traces of wine prohibition and exclusive cult, the role of female priestesses as rulers, the taboos against building houses and tilling the soil, the special hair-dress indicating status as possessions of a god or a ruler, the clothing hinting at some kind of religious sanctity, the living in borderlands between the desert and the sown and the negative evaluation of them by the settled ones, and their role as guardians of borders. To this might be added the unique relationship between the Arabs and the camel and their very special function in warfare. The documentation of the Arabs is predominantly in military contexts. From Achaemenid times onwards they appear as auxiliaries of all empires of the Middle East. On the other hand, their military performance is not always impressive and it can be doubted if it was their capacity as soldiers that was the only impetus for the empires to hire them. Sometimes they seem to function as scarecrows in the imperial armies, and their function almost as apotropaeic auxiliaries goes well together with their guarding function, which could point to some kind of religious significance. The contrast to the Muslim warriors in the seventh century is indeed striking.

There emerges the picture of a socio-religious association of warriors, subject to a divinity or a ruler as his slaves, who are separate from ordinary settled farmers and city-dwellers, living in their own lots often outside the border between the desert and the sown. Their way of life is described in surprising detail by Hieronymus of Cardia. Even though they do not till the soil they do not appear as pure nomads. If the Arabs were some kind of religious institution, it must have been possible to become one through initiation. It is very likely that the initiation is described by Herodotus in his account of the *pístis* of the *arábioi*: the cutting of the hair, the obligation of exclusive cultic practice and the acceptance into a fellowship of 'friends', *phíloi*. It is suggested that the name of the sanctuary where the initiation took place was HGR. It becomes very likely that the *hagrîm* mentioned by the Chronicler as living on the border between the desert and the sown in northern Transjordan are in fact the *ʕarab* known to have dwelt there. There might thus be a direct link between the personification of this place as a woman named Hagar, the mother of the bowmen in the Paran desert, and the female *apkallatu* of the *ʕarab* archers in Dumah.

Even though the Arabs as an institution may have declined in northern Arabia in late antiquity, customs connected with them lived on. There is a remarkable story told in the *Kitāb al-ʔagānī* about how Labīd b. Rabīʕa became a poet, in fact one of the most famous in Arabia. It is said that, as a very young man, he accompanied some of his relatives on a visit to the king of al-Ḥīra, an-Nuʕmān b. al-Mundhir. In the company of the king was a man named ar-Rabīʕ who was an enemy of Labīd's paternal family and who spoke against them in front of the king. Labīd offered to his kinsmen to compose invective verses against their enemy which would annihilate him morally in front of the king. In order to prove his ability as a future poet, he spent one whole night awake, riding his camel until dawn. Then his relatives shaved his head, except a lock of his hair (*ḏuʔāba*), dressed him in a ceremonial dress (*ḥulla*) and presented him to the king. Labīd then recited verses of such vituperative force that the king lost all his appetite, not only for his breakfast but also for ar-Rabīʕ. By this Labīd had proved that he was a real poet and acceptable into the company of warriors.[68]

It is difficult, when reading this story, not to think of what Herodotus wrote about the *pístis* of the Arabs. The hair-shaving leaves a lock which is not necessarily the forelock (*nāṣiya*).[69] But even though the meaning is that the forelock was left, this would be an important mark of the free man who, unlike the ancient *ʕarab*, always guarded the hair on his forehead as a token of his independence even when undergoing rituals inherited or copied from earlier cults and customs. In this case, a young man is initiated into the guild of those who were entitled to use the ancient language of the *ʕarab*, the most important survival of their culture in northern Arabia. It is interesting to observe that when Labīd's relatives before the ritual test him by ordering him to compose a lampoon, he gives an example in rhymed prose, *sağʕ*. When appearing in front of the king, now as a poet, he recites a piece of *šiʕr*, poetry according to the rules.[70] The shaving of the head is also mentioned in his poem as a sign of military prowess. The anecdote thus preserves several features which originally belonged to the initiation ceremony described by Herodotus. Remarkable is the nightly vigil with the camel riding, which connects the ancient Arabic *qaṣīda*, the main poetical form in ancient Arabic poetry, with the initiation rite.[71] It also gives us the only real glimpse of a possible ceremonial link between the camel and the Arab initiate.

Notes

1 Barnett/Falkner, *Sculptures* plates XXVI–XXX (pp. 74–75).
2 Prism B VIII:12 (= Piepkorn, *Inscriptions* 82, 83); Assur-letter I:54–55; III:54–55 (Weippert, *Kämpfe*); Rassam VIII:114; IX:5; IX:42 (= Streck, *Assurbanipal* 72, 74, 75; Weippert, *Kämpfe* 45).
3 2 Chronicles 17:11.
4 Hezechiel 27:21. For the background to this text see p. 177.
5 See Retsö, *Domestication* 200.
6 Tiglath Pileser, *Summary inscription* (= Tadmor, *Inscriptions* 228, 229 §§ 5, 8).
7 Sargon, *Annals* 125 (= Lie, *Annals* 22, 23); 'Prunkinschrift' § 27 =Winckler, *Keilschrifttexte* 100, 101).
8 Sennacherib, *Annals* H5 rev. 22–26 (= Luckenbill, *Annals* 92).
9 Heidelprism III:6–8 (= Heidel, *Prism* 20–21); Nin. A IV:17–18 (= Borger, *Inschriften* 53); Fragm. B rs. 6–7 (= Borger, *Inschriften* 110).
10 Fragm. F rs. 2 (= Borger, *Inschriften* 112).
11 Cf. references in note 2 above.
12 The nine tribes mentioned by Tiglath Pileser in 733 BC in the Summary inscriptions (Tadmor, *Inscriptions* 228, 229 § 7; Eph'al, *Arabs* 94). Cf. the tribute from Suhu (Nimrud letter XVII).
13 Jeremiah 49:38 (Qedar), Genesis 37:25 (Ishmael), Isaiah 60:6 (Midian, Ephah, Sheba), 1 Kings 10:10/2 Chronicles 9:9 (the queen of Sheba), 2 Chronicles 14:15 (Cush).
14 For the camel and the Israelites, see see Retsö, *Domestication* 201–205.
15 The Ishmaelites in Genesis 37 reflect conditions in the seventh century BC or later. Camels as pack animals are pictured on the Balawāt gates from *c.* 850 BC but this is surely in a military context.
16 For the documentation, see Retsö, op. cit.
17 Herodotus 7.86, 87.
18 Tadmor, *Inscriptions* Stele III A:20–23.
19 Eph'al, *Arabs* 94; Tadmor, *Inscriptions* 228–229 (§§ 7–8).
20 Sargon, Annals § 124 (= Lie, *Inscriptions* 22, 23).
21 Heidelprism III:5–7 (Heidel, *Prism* 20, 21); cf. Annals Nin. A IV:20–21 (= Borger, *Inschriften* 53).
22 For the development of the cushion-saddle, see Dostal, *Evolution* 15; idem, *Frage*; Bulliet, *Camel* 78 ff.; Knauf, *Midian* 9–15. For its military function, see ibid. 84.
23 Balawāt gates *c.* 850 BC (King, *Reliefs* plates XXIII, XXIV); cf. the Lachish reliefs of non-Assyrian refugees, Bulliet, *Camel* 81.
24 For the bow in the Middle East and Arabian peninsula, see Rausing, *Bow* 81–90; Knauf, *Ismael* 22–23; cf. Opitz, *Darstellungen* 9.
25 Genesis 21:20.
26 I Samuel 30:17. The Amalekites in this passage clearly reflect later conditions than the time of David: their roaming area as indicated in 1 Samuel 15 coincides with that of the Ishmaelites in Genesis 25.
27 Cf. Dostal, *Development* 128.
28 Genesis 16:11–12. A similar characterization is made in Sargon's Annals (94–97), where the *arbāya* are said 'to dwell in the distant desert not knowing the art of writing'.
29 For the artificiality of the urban view of nomadic societies in antiquity, see especially Briant, *État* 12–42.
30 For the classical clothing of the bedouin, see Jacob, *Beduinenleben* 43–45.
31 *Periplus* § 33: *perizōmasi phyllōn kounikōn.*
32 See Henninger, *Pariastämme* 520 (237) Sherārāt; Oppenheim, *Beduinen* IV 1 119 (Hutēm); Dostal, *Ṣulubba* esp. III and the Arabs in the *Periplus* (§ 33).
33 Cf. Henninger, loc. cit.
34 See the illustrations in Knauf, *Supplementa* 5.
35 Herodotus 3.8.
36 Leviticus 19:27; see Knauf, *Supplementa* 5.

37 Wellhausen, *Reste* 198; Henninger, *Frage* 293 note 35; Knauf, *Supplementa* 5 n. 15. For the role of the forelock in later culture, see, for example, Qurʔān, sūra XCVII.
38 Sennacherib, Annals H5 rev. 22–26 (= Luckenbill, *Annals* 92).
39 Rassam cylinder V:28; cf. ibid. VII:121.
40 Opitz, *Darstellungen* 12 and Tafel I:1, III:1.
41 Cf. Knauf, *Ismael*, 60; Alt, *Zelte* 235 f.; Opitz, loc. cit. This tent may be preserved in the wedding tents of the modern bedouin; see Dalman, *Arbeit* VI 26.
42 Psalm 120:5; Jeremiah 49:38.
43 Song of Songs 1:5.
44 Exodus 26:7 ff.; 36:14 ff.
45 Exodus 26:7.
46 Jeremiah 49:29.
47 Exodus 26:1 ff., 14 ff.; 36:8 ff., 19 ff. In Psalm 104:2 God is said to stretch out heaven like a *yerīʕā*.
48 Hezechiel 25:4.
49 Psalm 69:26.
50 Cf. Hezechiel 46:23; Song of Songs 8:9.
51 Knauf, *Ismael* n. 287. Knauf's rejection of this meaning of *ṭīrā* seems ill founded (*Ismael* 59–60). The reference to modern bedouin is of course not to the point, since in this period we have another half millennium to go before the bedouin appears. It is very likely that our word is of the same root as South Arabian MṬWR, 'enclosure'. In Arabic we have *ṭawr*, 'the yard of a house; limit', the verb *ṭāra*, 'go around something'. In Syriac, *ṭawrō*, 'territory, limit', *ṭyorō*, 'crates'. The existence of such camps is fully comprehensible when we consider that the cattle-breeders in this period were more stationary than the later bedouin.
52 Genesis 25:16.
53 Exodus 27:9 ff.
54 Lane, Lexicon s.v. ḤẒR.
55 P says in the list of Ishmael's sons that they are divided into *ʔummōt*. Also the Midianites are said to consist of *ʔummōt*, which is a term peculiar to P and equivalent to the Hebrew *bêt ʔab* (Numbers 25:15); for the meanings of *bêt ʔab*, 'family', see Lemche, *Israel* 245–259. Since the Ishmaelites and probably also the Midianites are here used as umbrella terms by the Priestly writers, the only secure information we get from this is that *ʔummā* may have been a term associated with the tribes in question. It recalls the Arabic term *ʔumma*, well known from the Qurʔān (cf. Knauf, *Ismael* 59 note 280). Since *ʕarab* is never explicitly identified with either the sons of Ishmael or the Midianites, the term *ʔummōt* is no clue to their organization.
56 Esarhaddon, *Annals*, Frgm. F (= Borger 112); Jeremiah 25:20; 1 Kings 10:15 = 2 Chronicles 9:14.
57 According to P, the Ishmaelites had *nesîʔîm*, plural of *nasîʔ*, as leaders. This is a term peculiar to P and, like *ʕummôt*, it does not tell us anything about the *ʕarab.* Cf., for example, Numbers 7 where it stands for the leaders of the twelve Israelite tribes.
58 Hatra 364; cf. pp. 442 ff.
59 It might be remembered that women among the classical bedouin in general have had a more independent position than their sisters in the towns. This also holds for the so-called pariah tribes who have preserved some very archaic features of pre-bedouin society; cf. Henninger, *Pariastämme;* Dostal, *Sulubba*.
60 Hatra 345; cf. p. 443. For Dedan/Liḥyān see Sima, *Inschriften* 89.
61 Strabo 16.2.34.
62 Strabo 16.2.20.
63 Cf. von Wissmann, *Zur Geschichte* 156 note 263.
64 I.e. Nizār, Maʕadd, ʔAsad, Tanūkh.
65 Caskel, *Bedeutung*; idem, *Beduinisierung*; Dostal, *Development* 130; Knauf, *Midian* 19–15. The two latter scholars see three phases in the development of bedouin life: 1) a proto-bedouin phase from *c.* 1100 to 400 BC; 2) an early bedouin phase *c.* 400 BC to *c.* AD 200; 3) the full bedouin phase from the third century onwards. The main characteristic of the latter

is the introduction of the horse. It can, however, be assumed that the development was somewhat more complicated. The shadād-saddle did not have the impact on warfare often assumed and the horse was obviously in use, especially among the Arabo-Nabataeans, several centuries earlier; see Macdonald, *Hunting*, and p. 255 (Pseudo-Scylax, *c*. 350 BC) The changes that undoubtedly took place in northern Arabia in the third century AD had several causes, not the least political ones. Dostal is probably right in emphasizing the importance of the Iranian influence for the rise of a professional warrior-class in Arabia (*Development* 132–135). Hoyland (*Arabia* 231 ff.) still believes in a massive migration.

66 See Watt, *Ḥums*.

67 Caskel, *Bedeutung* 15, 16.

68 Iṣfahānī, *ʔAghānī* 15:363–365.

69 According to Lane (*Lexicon* s.v. Ḏʔ B) the word may signify any hanging lock of hair, from the forehead or the top of the head.

70 The metre of the poem is *rağaz*.

71 See Stetkevych, *Immortals* especially 3–86, for a somewhat fanciful but stimulating study of the link between ancient Arabic poetry and pagan ritual. The story of Labīd's initiation is treated on pp. 46–51.

21

THE LINGUISTIC ISSUE

The language of the Arabs

A language of the Arabs is hinted at already in an Assyrian letter from the time of Assurbanipal.[1] But the earliest clear reference is in Agatharchides, who mentioned a plant named *larimna* in *arabistí*, 'Arabic'.[2] This stands in the context of a description of the Sabaeans and it can be doubted whether 'Arabic' is really a language especially connected with Arabs. The next occurrence is in the New Testament. In Acts it is told how everyone at the Pentecost, due to the miraculous effect of the Holy Spirit, heard the gospel preached in their own language, including that of the people from Arabia.[3] In the *Periplus* written at the same time as Acts, we hear about the Fish-eaters on the island of Sarapis, probably present-day Maṣīra in Oman, who are said to be holy men wearing loincloths and using the 'Arabic language', *hē arabikē glōssa*.[4] In a quotation from Uranius in Stephanus of Byzantium we hear that the name Mōthō means 'place of death' in the language of the *árabes*, *hē arábōn phōnē*.[5] The place was probably somewhere in southern Syria. From a region nearby also come the many 'Arabic' words adduced in the Talmud.[6] In Christian authors we have several references to an Arabic language used in the Arabian province. In the fourth century Epiphanius tells how the pagans celebrate a ritual in Elusa in the Negev, praising a virgin goddess in 'Arabic dialect', *arabikē diálektos*, and calling her *khaamou* in Arabic, *arabistí*, meaning 'young woman'.[7] Finally, Hieronymus, familiar with the languages of Palestine and its surroundings, refers to the *Arabicus sermo* or *Arabica lingua*, the latter in connection with a remark on the linguistic peculiarities of the book of Job.[8]

There are three observations that can be made from this survey. The first is that there is no certain indication that the Arabic language referred to is one and the same. The only linguistic evidence is found in the Talmud, from which the impression is that of a dialect standing somewhere between what we would call Arabic and Aramaic. Since the term 'Arabic language' in the Qurʔān clearly refers to another language than the one discernible in the Talmud, the epithet 'Arabic' may not have been above all a linguistic characterization but a sociolinguistic one: the language(s) associated with the Arabs. Since Arab communities were found in several regions far away from each other, the language must also have differed. The second point is that almost all references to an Arabic language are to the Arabo-Nabataean area or close to it. Agatharchides and the *Periplus* may be the only exception. This could be a coincidence, since the most detailed documentation we have about the Arabs in general comes from that region. The third observation is that the mention of an Arabic language tends to connect it with religion. The passage in Epiphanius is the most explicit, describing the Arabic language as a language used in liturgy or cult. In the *Periplus*, it is used by 'holy men' dressed in a peculiar way. Even the indirect reference in Acts actually makes it the result of divine inspiration. It is more uncertain whether the Arabic referred to in the Talmud and by Hieronymus is the same as that mentioned by Epiphanius, although it is not at all unlikely.

Since Arabs were evidently a non-ethnic community which existed in many parts of Arabia, the characterization of a language as Arabic must mean that it has a special relationship to Arabs, not necessarily that it has a distinct linguistic structure which was more or less the same everywhere. At the same time, the description in Epiphanius gives a clear hint that it was still something specific, deviating from something else: if the language used in the pagan cult in Elusa was the everyday speech in the cities in the Negev, why does Epiphanius have to make the remark about it? From his description one may draw two further conclusions: there was a special language used in the cult in Elusa which differed from the common speech of the region, and that language was named after the Arabs, who had been a distinct community in the Negev for many centuries.

In the Qurʔān, the *ʕarabī*-language is used as a proof that the message is divine. This would be an absurd argument if this language was the normal everyday speech in Mecca and its surroundings. Instead it refers to a language connected with the *ʕarab* which was known as a vehicle for messages from the non-human world. Like the language used in Elusa the one used in the Qurʔān was named after the Arabs. But since the Arabs in Ḥiǧāz and the Yamāma lived in the *qurā ʕarabiyya*, the Arab villages, which were obviously spread around among the settlers, it is highly unlikely that these Arabs spoke differently from the surrounding settlers. This becomes even more unlikely if, as we have suggested, Arab was something one could become by initiation. It is rather improbable that the initiate would change his speech (even though the possibility cannot be completely excluded). The question thus remains: why was there a language in Arabia named after the Arabs, a language which obviously had some status as a sacred tongue used in pagan cults and for divine messages?

According to the lore preserved in the traditions about the *ʕarab bāʔida* and the *ʕarab ʕāriba* as claimed by the Yemeni party in the later Umayyad age, the Arabic language was given by God to the earliest Arabs. The Yemenis claimed their forefather Yaʕrub to have been its first speaker.[9] Considering the more historical evidence presented above, this tradition comes into some new light. The Arabic language was, at least in certain early Muslim circles, seen as a miraculous revelation from above. Behind this could lie the existence of a specific language form used since ancient times by people who transmitted messages from the world of spirits and gods. Such people are, in fact, well known in the Arabo-Islamic traditions about the pre-Islamic age. There are plenty of instances where the activities of the oracle-giving *kāhin* are described.[10] Another figure was the *šāʕir*, who gave similar performances. The later tradition made a separation between the utterances of the *kāhin* formed as *saǧʕ*, 'rhymed prose', and those of the *šāʕir* formed according to the rules of *raǧaz*, rhymed verses or *qarīḍ* poetry with its variegated metres.[11] There is no doubt that these designations both stand for oracle-givers and soothsayers who transmitted messages from the spiritual world in a language with specific characteristics and in a stylized poetic form. There seems to have been a certain antagonism between these two 'schools' and it is noteworthy that the Qurʔān, which clearly uses the poetic form of the *kāhin*, the *saǧʕ*, delivers a scorching critique of the *šāʕir*.[12] It thus seems to side with one of the schools. At the same time, the *šuʕarāʔ* were also the carriers of the Holy Tongue and this term, as is well known, later became the proper designation for a poet using the *ʕArabiyya* of the *kuhhān* and the *šuʕarāʔ*. The ancient language of gods and spirits was, at a certain time, secularized together with the spread of the forms of classical Arabic poetry which used the Holy Tongue for quite everyday themes. This may be connected with the rise of 'Saracen' culture, which clearly took over many cultural features of the ancient Arabs, among them the language of the *kuhhān* and the *šuʕarāʔ*.

It is very tempting to associate the most prestigious poetic form in ancient Arabic poetry, the *qaṣīda*, directly with the ancient Arabs, and more specifically, with the initiation we have identified. One variant of the *qaṣīda* begins by describing a nightly vigil which may represent a ritual seclusion from association with others, especially with women, followed by the description of a camel ride and finishing with a panegyric of a tribe or a chief, thus very similar to the description of how Labīd became a *šāʕir*.[13] On the other hand, the *qaṣīda*s we have show no concrete awareness of a ritual background. It seems that this background was forgotten and a poetic form lived on (in fact until the present day) which preserved the ancient structure but was used for new purposes.

It has been assumed that the earliest trace of the existence of the *šāʕir* poetry is the mention in Sozomenus about how the Saracens in the fifth century AD celebrated the memory of their queen Mawia, who had led them against the Romans in the 370s, with *ōdai*, 'songs'.[14] Against this assumption it may be argued that the classical Arabic *qaṣīda* is not an epic account of the achievements of kings and chiefs from the past. It is rather a panegyrical ode directed towards a contemporary chief, tribe or even the poet himself with enumerations of his virtues in war and peace and lacking narrative elements. The historical contents are, in fact, quite meagre, most often made *en passant*. The songs of the Saracens in Sozomenus' time might well have sounded more like the poems with long narrative sections dealing, above all, with the legends about the Yemeni kings and attributed to poets from the seventh century AD onwards, which are documented in the works of Wahb b. Munabbih and his followers. This poetry, which is likely to have had a long history before its appearance in the Arabic texts we possess, later developed into the large epic compositions of the oral literature in Arabic. Like the latter, the early narrative poems were looked down upon by the literary arbiters of later ages and have also been neglected by Western scholarship. Considering the Yemeni origins of, for example, the rhyme technique of Arabic poetry in general, the strong element of loan-words from South Arabian languages in the *ʕArabiyya*, the heroic contents and the Yemeni themes of this poetry, the age of this tradition is without doubt, which makes it likely that queen Mawia was celebrated with poems like these, not by *qaṣīdas* as we know them from the classical tradition. It could also be pointed out that Mawia's Saracens lived in the north-west, probably in the Negev, whereas the earliest centre for *ʕArabiyya* poetry is in eastern Arabia.

It is, on the whole, striking that the *kuhhān*, when they appear in the texts dealing with the pre-Islamic period, are often explicitly called Arabs or are closely associated with the term.[15] And the *šuʕarāʔ* are well known as the main arbiters of linguistic questions about the *ʕArabiyya* far into the Abbasid age. In most cases they are poets, but one could sometimes suspect that the formula 'said the *šāʕir*' refers not to a composer of poems in the classical forms but rather to *šāʕir* of the original type.

The Arabo-Islamic tradition thus has ample documentation about diviners and soothsayers, as well as the language of gods used by them, among the pre-Islamic Arabs. But such documentation might be much earlier. Cicero already mentions the divinatory skills of the Arabs:

> Phrygians, Pisidians, Cilicians and the people of the *Arabes* chiefly rely on the meaning of birds.
>
> . . .
>
> For the *Arabes*, Phrygians and Cilicians because they mainly use pasture for cattle, wandering through fields and mountains winter and summer, more easily have observed the singing of birds and flying creatures.[16]

The divination among the Arabs was also observed by other writers in Graeco-Roman antiquity. Thus, Clement of Alexandria makes the following remark when claiming that all philosophy and art are invented by barbarians:

> Isaurians and *árabes* have developed the observation of birds.[17]

Similarly, Philostratus, at the beginning of the third century AD, wrote a biography about a remarkable wandering philosopher Apollonius of Tyana in Cappadocia. This forerunner of later Christian ascetics lived during the first century AD and was famed for his knowledge about magic as well as foreign languages:

> For he learnt this on his way through the region of the *arábioi* who best know and practise it. For it is quite common for the *arábioi* to listen to the birds prophesying like any oracles but they acquire this faculty of understanding them by feeding themselves, so they say, either on the head or the liver of serpents.[18]

The art of ornithomancy, *ʕiyāfa*, among the Arabs is also known from later Arabic sources.[19] The connection between *ʕiyāfa* and *kahāna* is, however, not immediately visible. On the other hand, in the legend about the wise Luqmān who is said to have been 'a son of ʕĀd' there is a story about how he managed to lead a very long life by associating with birds, perhaps eagles (*nusūr*) hatched on a high mountain, a story behind which may lie mantic practices in pre-Islamic Arabia.[20] Luqmān is also seen in the Qurʔān as a true prophet and one of the predecessors of Muhammed, and his wisdom is said to have been given by ʔAllāh.[21]

If the Arabs were a community of the kind we have suggested here, it might be imagined that soothsayers of different kinds were found among them, since the Arabs, to a certain extent, were set apart from normal society.[22] The use of a special language by soothsayers and mantics is a well-known phenomenon in many parts of the world.[23] This does not mean that the language was invented. The *ʕArabiyya* was undoubtedly a language originally spoken somewhere in Arabia but which probably died out quite early. It was preserved by the mantics and soothsayers who were closely associated with the original Arab community. It is tempting to look to Dumah as the original home of this language, but it should be emphasized that no direct evidence exists for it there, or anywhere else in pre-Islamic times. The language in the Namāra inscription is close to, but not identical with, the language of the Qurʔān or of the poetic texts codified by the later grammarians in Iraq. Also the latter two are not quite identical. The onomasticon from Arabo-Nabataea shows traces of a language different from the *ʕArabiyya* but with certain phonetic, morphological and lexical features in common. It is worth noticing that strikingly many of the features characteristic of the language of the *rağaz* poetry, sometimes assumed to be the most original poetic form of the *šuʕarāʔ*, are found in the language called Himyaritic by the Arab lexicographers, which represents a speech close to the languages in South Arabia. One must imagine that there existed several 'languages of the Arabs' in pre-Islamic Arabia which had two characteristics in common: they were distinct from everyday speech, and they were connected with the Arab communities through being used by the *kuhhān* and the *šuʕarāʔ* who lived among them.

The name and its linguistic background

If the Arabs were originally an association of sanctified warriors, it might be asked if this is reflected in the very term used for them. In all languages the word appears both as a collective noun and as a designation of an individual. In Akkadian *arab-* is written with the determinative LÚ for humans or KUR for land, but it is difficult to see whether any difference in meaning is intended. In both cases the reading of *arab-* as a collective noun is the most likely. There is then another term, *arbāya*, derived from the collective noun by adding the nisbah-suffix *-āya*. It is the designation for one member of the collective but can also be used in the plural meaning: several individuals. *arbāya* seems to be used when referring to people in the service of, or subject to, the rulers. Thus the individuals in the letters from Mesopotamia, who often appear as officials or servants of the kings, are called *arbāya*. Also Gindibu, the provider of camels to the allies at Qarqar, is called by this epithet. On the other hand, those fighting directly against the Assyrians from Tiglath Pileser III to Nabonidus are always *arab*. This differentiation is similar to the one we found in the South Arabian inscriptions, where ʕRB is a general term used mostly for those outside the borders of the South Arabian kingdoms, whereas ʔʕRB are those in service of the kingdoms.

The derivation of *arb-āya* from *arab* is in full accordance with the rules of Akkadian morphology. The monosyllabic form of the word [*ʕ*]*arb-* is explicable from the rules of Akkadian, which deletes the second short vowel in an open syllable thus: *ʕărăbāy* > *ʕărbāy*.[24] The Tiberian Hebrew vocalization of ʕRBY(M) [ʕarḇī(m)] is somewhat more difficult to explain. If we assume a proto-Arabic form *ʕarab* with a nisbah-form *ʕarabī/iyy*, the expected proto-Tiberian form would be **ʕărāb ʕărābī*(*m*). The consonantal text, however, has the variants ʕRBʔYM, ʕRBYYM. It seems that it is the latter form that was the basis for other variants in the Tiberian reading. Thus **ʕarabiyyīm* would regularly give the documented Tiberian *ʕarḇiyyîm* with the variant *ʕarḇiʔîm*. The variant *ʕarḇîm* could be a back-formation in analogy with other cases where the nisbah-plural *-iyyîm* alternates with the plural *-îm*. It could, however, also reflect a pronunciation close to Aramaic where the regular nisbah-formation with *-iyy* from *ʕarab* would give *ʕarḇî*. It is somewhat difficult to explain, though, why an Aramaizing reading of this word would have been introduced. Such a reading is undoubtedly present in the form of the collective *ʕ*^{a}*rāḇ* where the expected Tiberian form would be **ʕārāb*. The collective could have been seen as a loan-word. It is noteworthy that the correct, or at least explicable, form *ʕarbiyyîm* etc. occurs throughout the work of the Chronicler and Nehemiah except in the passage about the tribute to Solomon.

The identity between the Akkadian *arab*/*arbāya* and the Arabs mentioned in the Greek texts is confirmed through the undeniable identity between the *arabāya* in the

Achaemenid inscriptions and the *arábioi* in Herodotus. Further, there is no reasonable doubt about the identity between the word occurring in the pre-Islamic sources and the *ʕarab* we have investigated in Part I of this book. The only rub is the absence of a reflex of the laryngal [ʕ] in the Assyrian texts. We would have expected **ẖarab* in Akkadian. Thus, the Israelite king whose name was pronounced [ʕUmrī] appears as Ḫumri in Assyrian texts. It seems, though, that the laryngal often remained unwritten before an [a].

The form *arábios* (plur. *arábioi*) is the earliest one used by the Greeks and appears in Herodotus and Xenophon. The earliest dated occurrence of the form *áraps* (plur. *árabes*) is in the First Delphic Hymn from the fourth century BC but it may have been in use earlier.[25] This form then becomes the normal one in Greek texts and was also taken over into Latin. Greek and Latin do not have a collective noun similar to *ʕarab.* Instead they use a normal plural of a consonantal stem. It seems that the Greeks from the beginning borrowed the collective noun *ʕarab* as a designation of an individual: *áraps* must be the Greek form of the Semitic collective.[26] *arábios* may be a Greek formation from *ʕarab* as well, but could also reflect a Semitic nisbah-adjective *ʕarabī/iyy*. *arábios* occurs sporadically in later Greek writers from the third century AD onwards, probably as an echo from Xenophon, whose style and vocabulary were imitated by the Atticists. Thus Dio Cassius uses it consistently and it also occurs in Clement of Alexandria and, as it seems, in Uranius' *Arabica* and occasionally in other Atticizing writers. According to the quotations in Strabo and Diodorus, Posidonius talked about *arábioi* when discussing the meaning of the Homeric term *eremboí*, probably because of the similar suffix; otherwise he used *árabes*. Coincidentally, the last Greek writer to mention 'genuine Arabs', Synesius, employs the same form as Herodotus.

In Aramaic the collective form *ʕarab* is almost completely absent. It is also clear that the Greek form *áraps* etc. is not borrowed from Aramaic. Otherwise, the Greeks would have talked about **arabaîoi* as they talked about *aramaîoi*, *nabataîoi* etc. In the earliest Aramaic documentation of the word in the ʔAḥiqar text, an individual ʕRBY [ʕarbāy] is mentioned. In the Jewish targums the plural form *ʕarbāyē* is regularly used as a rendering of the Hebrew collective *ʕarab*. This is also the regular form in Syriac literature. Only in the inscriptions from Mesopotamia from the second century AD do we find the form ʕRB, which is always connected with a title of a ruler: king or governor of the ʕRB. As we have argued above, there is no reason to assume that this form means anything but 'the people of ʕRB'. Since this term is linked to one of the 'Arabias' outlined above, it is very likely that it reflects the official title of the rulers in Hatra and Sumatar being an Arabic word, not an Aramaic one. An Arabic pronunciation may also be the explanation of the irregular appearance in Biblical Hebrew described above.

We must now turn to the etymology, a task which receives increased importance since the word evidently does not refer to ethnic identity or lifestyle. If, as suggested here, the word refers to a group of initiates of a fellowship of warriors or guards around a divinity, one might expect that this would be reflected much more directly in the etymology of the word than is usually the case with ethnic names.

Nominal and verbal derivations from the root ʕRB occur in all ancient Semitic languages with several divergent meanings. Most of them might be derived from a basic meaning 'enter', 'go in'.[27] In Akkadian, *erēbu*(*m*) is the normal verb for 'to enter', which is also known from Ugaritic and Qatabanian.[28] The other languages have employed other verbs for the concept, but the original meaning of ʕRB has survived in a very ancient specialization of the root as a term for 'to set' (of the sun) and then the noun 'evening' or 'west' found in Ugaritic, Hebrew, Aramaic (Syriac), Sabaean and Qatabanian.[29]

With the meaning 'to enter' may be connected the meaning 'to mix', which is documented from Hebrew, Palestinian Aramaic and Syriac. From this some other specialized usages may be derived, such as 'woof', documented from Mishnaic Hebrew and Palestinian Aramaic.[30] Also the *ʕArabiyya* usage 'clear', 'unmixed' is explicable from this meaning. For some languages (Phoenician and Sabaean) the dictionaries note a further variant 'to offer' with the G-stem of the root.[31] But in most languages the root has a much better-defined meaning, namely: 'to guarantee' or 'give a pledge or security', 'to pay in advance earnest-money'. With this is connected the noun meaning 'pledge, security'. It appears in two main forms, one like the Hebrew *ʕerabôn*, the other like the Syriac *ʕrābā*. The *ʕArabiyya* knows *ʕarabūn* and *ʕurbān*, of which the first is an obvious borrowing from the languages in Syria, whereas the second looks like a genuine Arabic form.[32] This noun (with the *n*-suffix) was borrowed into Greek, probably in the fourth century BC, in the form *ar(r)abōn* with the same meaning as in Semitic.[33] The Geez verb *ʕarba*, 'trade', 'be a merchant', must be derived from this meaning.

The question is now whether any of these meanings would be connected with the concept of Arabs as a community of the kind we have outlined above.[34] In Akkadian we find the words *erbum*, 'gift to a temple', and *ērib bītim*, 'temple official'.[35] The same category is referred to in Ugarit: ʕRBM is 'a group of temple servants that entered the sanctuary'.[36] In Akkadian there are many terms indicating close relationship to or submission under gods or human beings formed with the verb *erēbum*: *ana ṣēr NN erēbum*, 'to get married to someone' (about a woman); *ana mārūtīšu erēbum*, 'to enter his sonship', i.e. 'to be adopted by someone'; *ana mamman ana wardūtim erēbum*, 'to become the slave of someone'; *ana ilkim erēbum*, 'to become the vassal of someone'; *ana libbi adê erēbum*, 'to swear an oath' and several others.[37]

In the Ancient South Arabian languages there are many instances of the root ʕRB meaning 'to give to a god'. This is especially frequent in Minaean. A typical case is a sentence like: YWM ʕRB MṮʕY ʕṮTR, 'when he offered incense to ʕAthtar'.[38] The verb in Minaean is often used in the causative: ḎBḤHY YSʕRB MʕN, 'the slaughtering sacrifice which Maʕīn offers'.[39] In Qatabanian the verb means 'to pay tax'.[40] This meaning is close to what seems to be the normal one in Sabaean: 'to give hostage, pledge' etc.[41] But there are also cases in Sabaean where it must mean 'to dedicate, offer'.[42] In Biblical Hebrew, the verb from the root ʕRB is found as a term for 'pay', as in Qatabanian in Ezechiel's Song of Tyre.[43] Apart from the most frequent meaning 'give as a pledge, guarantee' one may notice some cases where it is used as a term for mixing, namely with foreign peoples.[44]

It seems that the usage in Akkadian and South Arabian gives a meaning from which the word *ʕarab* could well be derived. The nominal pattern *qătăl* in Semitic is found as an abstract noun often as an infinitive to intransitives with the a-imperfect. Thus Hebrew *ʔašam*, 'guilt'; *raʕab*, 'hunger'; Arabic *ʕamal*, 'work'; *ḥarağ*, 'fear'; Geez *nagar*, 'speech'; *šaraq*, 'lightning' etc.[45] What is especially interesting is the use of this pattern in Arabic, not only as abstract nouns but also as collectives in accordance with the general plural-formation in that language. Thus we have words like *ṭalab*, 'search' and then 'those who search'; *ḥaras*, 'guarding' and then 'guards'; *ġalab*, 'noise' and then 'the noisy ones'.[46] Words from this pattern are not very frequent, but on the other hand they belong to the basic vocabulary. It must thus be an ancient morphological pattern in Semitic into which the word *ʕarab* fits very well. There are no linguistic arguments against an interpretation of the word as meaning 'those who have entered into the service of a divinity and remain his slaves or his property'. We are reminded of Herodotus' account of the *pístis* ceremony of the Arabs, a word which in Greek may mean 'pledge, guarantee' etc.[47]

Notes

1 Harper letter 259, see p. 591.
2 Photius, *Bibliotheca* 459a; cf. Burstein, *Agatharchides* 167.
3 Acts 2:11–12.
4 *Periplus* § 33.
5 Uranius Frg. 25 = Stephanus 466.
6 See p. 531.
7 Epiphanius 51.22.11. The passage is quoted by several later writers, such as Johannes Damascenus, Cosmas of Jerusalem and Bartholomaeus of Edessa; see the notes to the passage quoted. Hieronymus also mentions the cult in Elusa but quotes a word in Syriac, *voce Syra* (*Vita Hilarionis* 42).
8 Hieronymus, *Divina Bibliotheca* 1139; idem, *Daniel*: *Praefatio* 1358.
9 Ibn Hishām, *at-Tīǧān* 40; al-ʕAṣmaʕī, *Tārīkh* 7–8; Diʕbil, *Waṣāyā* 27; al-Hamdānī, *ʔIklīl* I 37.
10 See Wellhausen, *Reste* 134–140, and Fahd, *Divination* 92 ff.
11 Fahd, *Divination* 150 ff.
12 It must be emphasized that the meaning of the word *šuʕarāʔ* in XXVI:224 is definitely not 'poets' but rather 'soothsayers', which is the original meaning of the word.
13 For similar ideas, although even more fanciful, see Stetkevytch, *Immortals*, especially 3–54.
14 Cf. Shahid, *Byzantium* 1 443–455.
15 Cf., for example, Ibn Hishām, *Sīra* 129–130.
16 Cicero, *De Divinatione* 1.42 (92, 94).
17 Clement, *Stromata* 1.16 (74).
18 Philostratus, *Vita Apollonii* 1.20 (33). It should be observed that this notice stands in a context talking about Apollonius' wanderings through Mesopotamia. The region must thus be the Arabia between the Khābūr and the Tigris. Philostratus' work is said to have used a source written by a certain Damis from Nineveh who would have been well informed about the geography of his homeland. For further references, see Robert, *Épitaphe*.
19 Fahd, *Divination* 432–450. For parallels between the method described by Philostratus and documented shamanistic practices, see Eliade, *Chamanisme* 93 (note 1).
20 For the frequent links between shamans and birds, see Eliade, *Chamanisme* 136–137.
21 For the complex about Luqmān, see Horowitz, *Untersuchungen* 132–136.
22 One could compare the figure of Apollonius of Tyana who, according to Philostratus, behaved like a drop-out from society, abstained from wine and learned occult wisdom and speech from the Arabs in Mesopotamia. A Greek Cynic or Pythagorean could obviously feel at home with Arabs and learn from them.
23 Eliade, *Chamanisme* 91–93.
24 von Soden, *Grammatik* 14. The statements in Retsö, *Arabs* should be corrected. The Akkadian form does not represent the Aramaic reduction of short vowels in open syllables. This process started much later in Aramaic (sometime after the second century BC, perhaps as late as the second century AD; cf. Beyer, *Texte* 128–136), although it is not impossible that the process in both languages is part of a common drift or adstratum influence.
25 The Hellanicus fragment quoted on p. 243 has *árabes*.
26 It should be noticed that there is no trace of a case-vowel which could have appeared in Greek as **árabos*, **árabis* or **árabas*. This shows that it was probably borrowed not from Akkadian but from a West Semitic language.
27 Many of the meanings given for the root and its derivations in the *ʕArabiyya* are difficult to

explain. Of the verb we find: G-stem: 'to become swollen'; 'to be abundant'; the D-stem: 'to upbraid someone'; 'lopping of a palm-tree'; the causative stem: 'make one's horse run'. Cf. also the noun *ʕirb*, 'dried grass'. There is a long series of derivations from the meaning 'pure', 'unmixed'. For an interesting explanation for some of these see Rotter, *Veneris Dies* 122 ff.

28 For a similar view of the original meaning and the South Arabian evidence, see Lundin, *Notes* 50–51. Arabic has a word *ʕarāba*, 'coition' (Lane, *Lexicon* s.v.), which must be a survival of the ancient meaning.

29 In Arabic there is a phonetic differentiation between ʕRB and ǦRB, the latter having the meaning 'to set' (of the sun) etc. In Ugaritic, however, ʕRB is used with this meaning (Aistleitner, *Wörterbuch* s.v. ʕRB) even though that language had the phoneme /Ǧ/ and the differentiation in Arabic might be secondary. In Sabaean there is only one very uncertain instance of ǦRB with an assumed meaning 'west' (CIH 149:2–3; cf. Biella, *Dictionary* s.v. ǦRB). Otherwise, Sabaean has MʕRB for 'west' (not *MǦRB).

30 Jasrow, *Dictionary;* Sokoloff, *Dictionary*. Perhaps the word *ʕarabah* with the meaning 'willow' is connected with the concept of weaving.

31 Hoftijzer/Jongeling, *Dictionary* ʕRB 4; Beeston *et al.*, *Dictionary* s.v. ʕRB.

32 From this word a denominal verb is formed: *ʕarbana*.

33 See Liddell/Scott, *Lexicon* s.v. *arrabōn*. The word also occurs in Latin as *arrapho* in the same meaning.

34 Lundin stated that since the word ʕRB(ʔʕRB) in the South Arabian languages means 'Arabs', 'bedouin' and this cannot be related to the other documented meanings of the words derived from the root, the word must be a loan-word in Sabaean and should not be included in the Sabaean dictionary (Lundin, *Dictionary* 50). This reasoning is correct so long as its starting point is accepted. Since it is quite evident that the word ʕRB does not mean 'Arab', 'bedouin' in the sense assumed by Lundin (and everybody else), it immediately becomes clear that this word might well also belong to the semantic sphere of the root. At least it must be investigated.

35 von Soden, *Handwörterbuch* s.v. *erēbum*.

36 Aistleitner, *Wörterbuch* s.v. ʕRB (item 2093).

37 *Assyrian Dictionary* 4 262 ff., 290f., 292; von Soden, *Handwörterbuch* s.v. *erēbum* G 4, 5.

38 Robin, *Inabba'* 179–180: Kaminahu 9. Cf. RÉS 2789:3; 2924:5; 2975:13; 3890 no. 5; Shaqaf 3:8 (= Robin, *L'Arabie* 72); CIH 428:2.

39 RÉS 3306A:2; cf. 3427:1; 3695:2. Cf. Al-Said, *Verben* 262–264.

40 RÉS 4337A:8. The text deals with the rules for transactions on the market in Timnaʕ (Beeston, *Code* 5).

41 See, for example, Ja 735:9; 574:11; 578:22; cf. also RÉS 4773:1; 4767:5; CIH 308:24; 308bis.

42 Thus Mashamayn 4 (= Robin/Ryckmans, *L'attribution* 45). It is also worth reminding of the notice in Pliny and his successors about the meaning 'mysterium' or 'sacred' of the word *Arabia* when applied to those entrusted with the guardianship of the frankincense tree in Ḍufār, see p. 565. Both words may well go back to the meaning 'dedicated', 'initiated'.

43 Ezechiel 27:9, 27.

44 Psalm 106:35; Proverbs 20:19, 24:2; Ezra 9:2.

45 Barth, *Nominalbildung* 14, 105–106.

46 Barth, *Nominalbildung* 14; Fleisch, *Traité* 305, 475–476.

47 Liddell/Scott, *Lexicon* s.v. especially II.1. Cf. Herodotus 9.91, 92.

22

THE ARABS AND THEIR RELIGION

The six gods of Dumah

From what has emerged in the preceding paragraphs, the religious conditions among the Arabs in antiquity acquire new interest. The Arabs appear as a segment of society in Arabia, sharing many features of life-style and economy with other inhabitants of that area. Their distinctive features are not found in their way of living as nomads or shepherds, but in certain more subtle characteristics differentiating them from ordinary nomads and shepherds. In the same way, it cannot be assumed that a general description of what we know about religion in pre-Islamic Arabia will give us a true picture of the religious customs of the Arabs. We have now seen that there are strong indications that the Arabs in antiquity were indeed a group with a special status, expressed in features very possibly linked to religious concepts: initiation and taboos manifest in outer signs. The question must be: is there any hint that the Arabs, as they appear in this investigation, did have a cult of their own distinguished from that of the other inhabitants of Arabia? Did they have their own gods or did they have a special relationship to some of the gods worshipped in Arabia?

The answer must be found by studying what is said in the sources about the religion of the Arabs proper, not of all the inhabitants of the peninsula.[1] From a methodological point of view, testimonies about religious ideas must be weighed even more critically than those on political and other conditions. Testimonies from Arabs themselves, as far as they are extant, should be the yardstick according to which all others must be measured. It is to be expected that information of the kind we possess about religious concepts from outsiders are haphazard and distorted. Great scepticism must be shown towards Greek data, where we often have to deal with rationalistic or pseudo-rationalistic explanations and/or interpretations according to Greek mythology. That does not exclude the preservation of hard-core facts in Greek texts, but they must always be evaluated against the testimony coming from the protagonists themselves.

Unfortunately, evidence of the latter kind is extremely sparse. From Gerash we have dedicatory inscriptions in Greek to 'the Arab god', perhaps from pre-Christian times.[2] At Hatra one of the Aramaic texts has been supposed to mention 'the Fortune (GND?) of the Arabs' in a context that clearly refers to divinities or heroes.[3] The interpretation of this text is, however, uncertain.

These two texts, or one of them, seem to be the only first-hand testimonies about the religion of the Arabs. They both come from official inscriptions at cultic sites where the Arab presence is well documented. We learn from them that, in Transjordan in the centuries at the turn of the era, there was a male divinity explicitly characterized as an Arab god, and that in Hatra there was perhaps a similar figure, although the exact meaning of the name is not immediately clear.[4]

Everything else consists of remarks produced by outsiders.[5] Since the picture they give is quite contradictory, it should be evaluated very critically. The evidence is also spread out in time. There are two important notes in Assyrian texts and Herodotus. Then we have to wait until the fourth century AD before further information starts to appear.

The earliest pieces of information about religion explicitly involving Arabs are the passages about the gods in Dumah in the inscriptions of Esarhaddon and Assurbanipal. Esarhaddon tells how his father, Sennacherib, captured six gods from Dumah, 'the gods of the Arabs', and brought them to Assyria: Attarshamāyīn, (A-tar-sa-ma-a-a-in), Dāya (?Da-a-a), Nuhā (Nu-ha-a), Ruḍāw (Ru-ul-da-a-u), Abbīr-ʔilu (?A-bi-ri-il-lu) and Attar qurūmā (A-tar-qu-ru-ma-a).[6] They were then returned by Esarhaddon to Ḥazaʔil together with the priestess Tabua. Later, when Ḥazaʔil's son Yawthaʕ revolted against Esarhaddon and was defeated, the gods were recaptured by the Assyrians. When Yawthaʕ sought peace with Assurbanipal, Attarshamāyīn was given back.[7]

A divinity ʕTRSM appears in one of the oldest inscriptions in northern Arabia, an invocation from Ǧawf, i.e. Dumah, dated to the sixth century BC together with two others: RḌW and NHY.[8] The identity between Attarshamāyīn and ʕTRSM as well as between the two others and Ruḍāw and Nuhā is thus fairly certain, as is the location of all three in Dumah, but we hear no details about their cult.[9]

These three divinities then appear in the earliest epigraphic texts documented from the area around Dumah and Taymāʔ (Thamud A) and somewhat later (Thamud B–D) from Naǧd and around al-ʕUlā. The dating of the Thamudic texts is from around 500 BC to the turn of the era.[10] The names occur in the Safaitic texts in the Syrian desert at least until the third century AD.[11] They also spread to the south-western and central parts of the peninsula. The Assyrian evidence from Dumah is thus the earliest textual testimony of religion in northern and central Arabia.

The three names, especially RḌW and NHY, are very often invoked in the Thamudic inscriptions but tend to become more infrequent in the later texts, being replaced by other divine names.[12] The only name that lived on until late antiquity was RḌW, who is very prominent in the so-called Ṣafaitic texts from Syria and northern Arabia in the centuries up to AD 300.[13] This divinity was the most vital of the six gods from Dumah.

It has been suggested that the appearance of these gods of Dumah in the Thamudic texts is due to the fact that Dumah was drawn into 'Thamudic' influence after 400 BC.[14] According to a notice in Pliny reflecting conditions in Seleucid times, the Thamudaei controlled Hegra (Dedan) and Domatha (Dumah) in that period.[15] The worship of the gods of Dumah would thus have been restricted to the area of al-Ǧawf for a long period and then started to spread along the caravan roads a couple of centuries after Sennacherib's time. Support for this hypothesis is that both Dedan and Taymāʔ show a different set of gods from the beginning.[16]

All six gods of Dumah are said to be 'the gods of [the land of] the Arabs' (*ilāni* KUR *aribi*). Attarshamāyīn, whose name must mean 'ʕAthtar of heaven', is especially associated with Qedar and their king. The goddess 'Ishtar of Heaven' is documented from Assyria, in the time of Sennacherib when she appears distinguished from other Ishtars like Ishtar of Nineveh and Ishtar of Arbela.[17] It is very likely that this goddess is the one that was taken from Dumah by Sennacherib and that Attar (= ʕAthtar) and Ishtar is the same name. We also have documentation in the Old Testament of a cult to 'the queen of heaven' in the late seventh century BC who must be the goddess ʕAshtoret/Ishtar.[18]

It thus seems clear that Attarshamāyīn of the Arabs was a goddess.[19] Both the *arab* and Qedar had had centuries of close contacts with the settled lands of Syria and Mesopotamia, and it is not unlikely that the epithet 'heaven' reflects Syrian or Mesopotamian theological/mythological terminology. There were others than Arabs in the oasis, such as Qedar, who were led by someone with what looks like a Syrian name, Hazaʔil, and it has been assumed that the goddess Attarshamāyīn especially belonged to them.[20] On the other hand, the 'host of Attarshamāyīn' mentioned in Assurbanipal's texts is not identical with Qedar. Since there are clear signs that Arabs and Qedar are not identical although they are closely connected, the question still arises of which relations existed between Arabs and others in and around Dumah.

There were obviously two Attars in Dumah: Attarshamāyīn and Attarqurūmā. The epithet *qurūmā* can mean 'cut off', 'peel off'. It is known from Arabic in the meaning 'chief' but also 'stud, stallion'.[21] The connection between these is not immediately visible but we shall suggest one further below.

The name Nuhā/NHY seems to mean 'the wise'.[22] One early inscription mentions NHY with the epithet 'the elevated sun'.[23] This god could thus be associated with the sun. The word could, however, also refer to a divinity connected with a special kind of wisdom. In the Old Testament there are traditions of wisdom in Temān, which may be a region south of Edom, such as Taymāʔ, and the god could have some connection with these traditions.[24]

The two gods of Arabo-Nabataea

The next information about the religion among Arabs is two centuries later. Herodotus says that the Arabs worship only two deities: *hē ouranía*, 'the heavenly', and Dionysus. These deities are called by the Arabs *Alilat* and *Orotalt* respectively.[25] Dionysus is said to have cropped hair like the Arabs themselves.[26] In another passage he says that the Arabs call Aphrodite by the name Alilat and the Assyrians call the same goddess Mylitta.[27] The statement of Herodotus is repeated by Origen in his *Contra Celsum* with the addition that 'the *arábioi* worship *Ouranía* as a female and *Diónysos* as a male'.[28]

The information Herodotus had about Arabia, including its deities, is most likely to come from his visit in the eastern Nile Delta and is relevant for the Arabia situated between Egypt and Palestine, later known as the Arabo-Nabataean kingdom. Documentation of religion in this area begins to appear with the Nabataean inscriptions in the first century BC. In them we find two divinities dominant: the female ʕWZY, ʕUzzay, and the male DŠRY, Dhū Sharay. The joint cult of these two seems to belong to Arabo-Nabataea.[29] There are no traces of it in other parts of Arabia.[30] ʕUzzay alone appears sporadically in Mesopotamia. Her cult in al-Ḥīra is well known from both Muslim writers and earlier Christian ones.[31] She is mentioned by Isaac of Antioch, who says that the Arabs worship two goddesses: Baltî and ʕUzzay.[32]

The existence of a special cult in Arabo-Nabataea of a female and a male deity is well-documented from the fourth century AD. From that century we have a testimony from the Christian writer Epiphanius describing a cult in Arabia. After having described the celebrations in Alexandria of Korē, 'the young girl', giving birth to *Aíōn*, 'Time', he says:

> This also takes place in the same idolatrous manner in Petra, which is the capital of Arabia, which is Edom in the Scriptures; they praise the virgin in Arabic

> language, calling her in Arabic *khaamou* which means *korē* (young girl) and virgin, and also Dousarēs born by her which means the single-born of the Lord. This also takes place in the town of Elousa on the same night as in Petra and Alexandria.[33]

This cult was obviously well known in late antiquity and is often referred to.[34] Hieronymus of Bethlehem, in his *Vita Hilarionis*, tells how his hero, Hilarion, came to Elusa on the very day of the celebration of the goddess Venus, when everybody had congregated in the temple, 'for they worship her [i.e. Venus] because of Lucifer, to whose cult the people of the *Saraceni* are much dedicated'.[35] In a commentary to the hymns of Gregory of Nazianz, Cosmas from Jerusalem, living in the middle of the eighth century AD, describes how the pagans celebrate Aphrodite. They are said to come out from temples at midnight shouting: 'The virgin has given birth, the light has increased!'. According to him, this is the feast described by Epiphanius as celebrated by the *sarakēnoí* in honour of Aphrodite worshipped by them 'whom they in their own language call *khamara*'.[36] This worship is also reflected in a passage in a work about heresies by the Christian writer Johannes Damascenus at the beginning of the eighth century AD:

> They [i.e. the Ishmaelites who are called *sarakēnoí*] worship and prostrate to the star of dawn [*ho eōsphoros astēr*] and to Aphrodite whom they call *khabar*, which in their language means 'great'.[37]

The same expression occurs in a Christian ritual for abjuration of Islam where one of the prescribed formulas runs:

> I anathemize those who prostrate to the morning star, that is Eōsphoros, and Aphrodite whom they in the language of the *árabes* call *khabar*, that is 'great'.[38]

The divine child is by Epiphanius identified as Dusares, who is the main divinity DŠRY in the Arabo-Nabataean kingdom and who also appears with Dionysiac features.[39] This divinity is said by Hesychius, the author of a dictionary in early Byzantine times, to be the Dionysus of the Nabataeans. His information comes from Isidorus of Alexandria living at the end of the fifth century AD.[40] Dusares' female counterpart is identified by several authors as Aphrodite. There is thus no doubt that the domestic divinities in the Arabo-Nabataean kingdom, ʕWZY, ʕUzzay and DŠRY, Dhū Sharay, were seen as counterparts to the Greek Aphrodite and Dionysus.[41]

When Herodotus mentions Urania/Aphrodite and Dionysus as the two divinities of Arabia, it thus lies near at hand to see them as cover terms for ʕUzzay and Dhū Sharay who were worshipped in the Arabo-Nabataean kingdom, which already existed in his day. A continuity of their cult in Elusa and Petra from the time of Herodotus until late antiquity is not at all unlikely. It should, however, then be observed that the roots of this cult are hardly to be found in Arabia.[42] The goddess giving birth to a young god is documented from other parts of Syria such as Emesa and Byblos and probably also Bethlehem. Close parallels are found in Egypt, which has been suggested as the origin of this myth of the divine birth, which received such a pervasive force in Hellenistic and Roman antiquity and is still celebrated in large parts of the world.[43]

But Herodotus' claim that these two deities, Aphrodite and Dionysus, who can be identified with ʕUzzay and Dhū Sharay, were worshipped by the Arabs in the Arabo-Nabataean area as Alilat and Orotalt raises problems. Ruḍā is never mentioned in the later Nabataean inscriptions.[44] Also ʔAllāt seems to be absent in the core areas.[45] This goddess, in fact, appears in Greek disguise as Athena, not as Aphrodite.[46] The divine name ʔLT is well documented in the Thamudic inscriptions from the fifth century BC onwards. She becomes one of the two main divinities mentioned in the Safaitic texts. Orotalt has convincingly been analysed as a distortion of Ruldaw/RḌW/Y and thus identical with one of the deities from Dumah.[47] This deity appears together with ʔAllāt in the Thamudic and Safaitic inscriptions. In the latter, ʔAllāt and Ruḍā appear together as the main divinities. But they are not documented where Herodotus claims they are worshipped. The only remarkable exception is that Alilat, 'the goddess', is probably the one who appears in the name HN-ʔLT, 'the goddess', from the sacrificial bowl offered at a temple in the Nile Delta in the fifth century BC by a chief of Qedar.[48] This is probably the deity referred to by Herodotus which, however, does not appear in this area in later documents.

Further, Herodotus' allegation that the Arabs worship Dionysus is somewhat surprising since this god is connected with viniculture and the Arabs in the Negev are said by Hieronymus of Cardia to abstain from wine. Also the cropping of his hair is unknown in Greek mythology.

The solution to this problem is that ʕUzzay and ʔAllāt are two separate deities, as are Dhū Sharā and Ruḍā.[49] We would thus have to do with two pairs: ʕUzzay/Aphrodite and Dhū Sharay/Dionysus on the one hand, associated with Herodotus' Arabia, and ʔAllāt and Ruḍā on the other, whose cult originated in Dumah and then spread in Arabia and in the Syrian desert.

In the Syriac Bible commentary by Theodorus bar Kônî from the eighth century AD, it is explicitly said that the *ṭayyāyē* worship ʕUzzay, whereas the *ʕarbāyē* worship Nanî.[50] It is likely that Isaac of Antioch also describes the two different cults when he mentions two female deities worshipped by the Arabs and the sons of Hagar: ʕUzzay and Baltî. The second would then be the one called Nanî by Theodorus. This name most likely designates the divinity known among Semitic-speaking Mesopotamians as Ishtar, in this case Ishtar of Heaven, i.e. the divinity of the Arabs in Dumah: Attarshamāyīn.[51]

The epithet *ouranía* given to the Arabian goddess by Herodotus belongs to Aphrodite, who according to the myth was the daughter of Uranus, the god of heaven. But it can also be applied to other divinities, and it is perhaps significant that Herodotus adduces only the epithet 'heavenly', not the name Aphrodite, when he identifies her with Alilat.[52] The name Attarshamāyīn, which must mean 'Attar of Heaven', appears in Assyria as Ishtar of Heaven, i.e. the name of a female deity. It has therefore been concluded that Attarshamāyīn in Dumah was a goddess identical with ʔAllāt/Alilat.[53] This is also the most likely solution, although it cannot be ruled that the two names ʔAllāt and ʕAthtar(t) in a distant past may have stood for different divinities.[54]

It is then worth pointing out that the cult of ʔAllāt is especially well documented in places where Arabs also lived. There was a temple to ʔAllāt in Hatra.[55] Her cult was sparse in South Arabia except in the Naǧrān area.[56] She is very prominent in the cults in Ḥawrān.[57] There was a sanctuary to ʔAllāt outside Emesa.[58] And, finally, a person named Theimallatos, 'the slave of ʔAllāt', is explicitly characterized as being a Gerrhaean.[59]

If Attarshamāyīn/ʕTRSM in northern Arabia is identical with ʔAllāt, it fits well with Herodotus and it also follows that the Arabs had a special relationship to this goddess during their earliest documented history.

In the late Graeco-Latin sources it is the Saracens that appear as the ardent worshippers of the other two deities, Aphrodite/Venus/ʕUzzay and Dionysus/Lucifer/Dhū Sharay. If this is to be understood literally and in the light of the results of this investigation, it confirms the hypothesis that we have to do with two different pairs of deities.[60] But the problem remains. If the two divine couples represent different cults, why does Herodotus identify the deities of the Arabs with those of the later Saracens? Was there any connection between them and, if so, what kind of connection? In order to solve this problem we have to take a closer look at the Saracen cult.

The cult of the Saracens

The cult of the young goddess giving birth to a divine child manifest as the morning star is part of a complex of religious ideas current in the eastern Mediterranean in antiquity. Isaac of Antioch describes how women belonging to 'the sons of Hagar' worship 'the star', *kawkabtā*.[61] We also hear how the Saracens in Elusa worship Lucifer, Venus' son. According to Hieronymus, 'in Hebrew' he is called *Chocab* which means 'star'.[62] His name is a Latin translation of the Greek *phōsphoros*, 'light-carrier', a term for the planet Venus as morning star. A god manifest in the morning star is well documented in ancient epigraphic monuments, in Latin by the name *bonus puer phosphorus*, 'the good lad, the light-carrier'.[63] This makes it likely that Isaac of Antioch also refers to a cult of the new-born child manifest in the morning star. The star, *kawkabtā*, would thus be the male god, Dusares/Dionysus/Phosphoros/Eōsphoros/Lucifer, not the female ʕUzzay/Aphrodite. The feminine form of the word belongs to Syriac grammar, not to Arabian mythology. Contrary to what was assumed by earlier scholarship, it has become clear that there is no definite evidence for an identification between the morning star and the main female gods of Arabia.[64]

The emperor Julian tells us that in Palmyra and Edessa there were two divinities, Azizos and Monimos, 'the strong' and 'the giver of mercy or pleasure', who accompanied the main god *hēlios aníkētos*, *Sol invictus*, 'the unconquered sun'. Azizos is identified by Julian with Ares, and Monimos with Hermes, and it is generally assumed that the two are manifest in the morning star and the evening star respectively.[65] Azizos as the morning star is thus a close relative to Phosphorus/Lucifer as worshipped in Elusa, and ʕAzīz is probably another epithet of the young god born under the rising morning star.[66] Both Azizos and his colleague are documented in inscriptions from Palmyra as ʕZZ and ʔRṢW respectively.[67] The latter name stands for the god appearing as the evening star and is identical with Monimos. The name, which is the same as RḌW/Y found in the Thamudic and Safaitic inscriptions, must mean 'pleasure', 'delight'.[68] It can be interpreted as a variant of Monimos, which goes back to Arabic *munʕim*, 'he who gives *niʕma*', i.e. 'mercy' but also 'pleasure', 'well-being' etc.[69] The name, together with the association with the evening star, hints at a divinity connected with evening festivities.[70] Julian's identification of Monimos as Hermes should be observed as this divinity in his original homeland is intimately connected with border-crossing and passage rites.[71] This is a hint that the divinity RḌW/ʔRṢW/Ruḍāw can be assumed to be connected with transition from one state to another and the festivities connected with such ceremonies. Since his colleague is explicitly manifest in the morning star, this divinity may be supposed to be connected with evening ceremonies. Such ceremonies are well documented in the Middle East to this day, like weddings and circumcision, both typical examples of transition rituals.[72]

This mythology and cult can be traced far back in Semitic religion. In Ugarit the two deities are called ŠḤR and ŠLM, 'dawn' and 'peace', or perhaps better 'happiness', and they seem to have manifested themselves in the appearance of Venus as morning and evening star.[73] Also the name Attarshamāyīn points back to ancient cults. ʕAthtar and ʔIl/ʔEl belong to the oldest divine names in Semitic and represent a very archaic layer of gods which has been replaced by others during the millennia.[74] For our purposes it is important that the name ʕAthtar appears in Attarshamāyīn, the main deity of Dumah, who has no documented astral characteristics. We can assume that ʕAthtar was originally a celestial divinity of neutral or androgynous sex giving rain and fertility and, as it seems, subordinate to the god of creation and wisdom, ʔIl.[75] ʕAthtar may not have been associated with the morning star from the beginning.[76] In the Ugaritic myths he appears together with a female counterpart ʕṮTRT, ʕAthtart, and he is curiously presented as a child-like figure who is not fit to reign as king: his feet do not reach the floor when he sits on the throne. On the other hand, he early receives the morning star as his sign, which may be connected with his childishness: he is born to become the assistant and forerunner of the creator of the world.[77] The ancient figure of the young god as the divine forerunner appears in many places in the ancient Semitic world and reaches into the constitutive documents of monotheism: in the Book of Revelation, the conquering Christ is called the morning star.[78] The association between ʕAthtar as a new-born child, and later a conquering hero, and the morning star must be very ancient, although it seems that the planet Venus was not originally a manifestation of ʕAthtar.

The gods of the Arabs and the Saracen cult of the twin gods

The explicit connection made by Herodotus between the divinities involved in birth and transition rituals and the Arabs shows that the Arabs were not isolated from the cults of 'normal' society. The cult of Ruḍā among the Arabs makes them part of the mythological complex around the divine pair ʕZZ/Azizos and ʔRṢW/MNʕM/Monimos. The main meeting point between their cult and that of the surrounding society was the figure of Ruḍā. His identification with Dionysus is the clue to the nature of the cult among the Arabs.[79] According to Herodotus, the Arabian Dionysus had his hair cropped. This is a ceremony performed on bridegrooms in many parts of the Middle East to this day, and it is also well documented among modern bedouin as an initiation into the society of adults.[80] It is likely that the cropping of hair, like circumcision, originally belonged to the rites of puberty, wedding and entrance into adult society.[81] The nocturnal initiation of an *ʕarabī* poet is described in the story about Labīd, and it would seem that not only weddings and circumcisions but also this kind of initiation were performed at night, preferably under the evening star. Herodotus says that the hair-shorn Dionysus/Orotalt was connected with the *pístis* ritual. This may give a clue to the identification of the hair-cropped Arab with the Greek god. Dionysus was not only the god of wine. There was also a myth about his birth. The story of Dionysus' second birth from the thigh of Zeus hints at an initiation ritual, and it has perhaps a connection with a very special corps of warriors in Thebes.[82] This makes the connection between Arabs and Dionysus more palatable and it should be borne in mind that the role of Dionysus as the lord of wine does not give an exhaustive picture of his true nature in the fifth century BC.

If an initation ceremony was essential for the establishment of the Arab community, this deity would be the guardian of it. The parallel between the deities of the Arabs and the cults in Arabo-Nabataea, hinted at by Herodotus and supported by evidence from late antiquity, shows that the Arab initiation rite may even have been described in mythical terms as a birth from a goddess. The characteristics of the two divinities of the evening and morning star, Ruḍāw and ʕAzīz, i.e. initiation and birth, could be summarized through the figure of the Greek Dionysus. This means that the Arab initiate could be seen as new-born even though there is no explicit documentation of such a view.[83] It is, however, tempting to point to an obvious parallel to this cultic-mythical scenario in the same region, namely the story of Hagar and her son. That story deals with the birth of a kind of warrior, a bowman, which may well be the mythical expression of an initiation of the kind we have assumed for the Arabs. Ishmael is linked in a prominent way to an initiation rite, namely circumcision. According to the Biblical account, he is the first to be circumcised and thus stands as the predecessor of the Israelites, although not belonging to them. He is also circumcised at the age of thirteen, which clearly shows that the rite has to do with initiation into a society of adults. It is curious that the idea that the Ishmaelites are circumcised at this age lived on through the ages, and it gives the impression that the custom was still practised among those considered his descendants, who, by then, were identified as Arabs.

It thus seems that the Arabs were linked to the cults in Syria through the god Ruḍā, the guardian of ceremonies of initiation and passing from one state to another. But Herodotus indicates an even closer relationship of the Arabs to the cults of the Syrians. We should recall that there was a difference in the naming of the goddess: Alilat by the Arabs and HN-ʔLT by Qedar. The latter form is well documented and is the regular one in Thamudic and Safaitic texts, characterized by the definite article HN-. The former name has the definite article (ʔ)L and is, in fact, the earliest documentation we have of the *l*-dialects in Arabia, to which the later *ʕArabiyya* language belongs. This indicates a linguistic difference among the worshippers of this goddess. Now we have pointed out earlier that there was an intimate relationship between Qedar and the Arabs but that they were not identical. Herodotus is thus right when he links Alilat with the Arabs. That name belongs to Arabic, i.e. a language already at this period connected with the Arabs, whereas HN-ʔLT comes from the language used by Qedar, which belonged to another branch of languages spoken in northern and central Arabia.[84]

This leads us to the linguistic remarks in Epiphanius. Hieronymus says that the cult in Elusa was performed by Saracens. According to what we have found during this investigation, there is no doubt that the Saracens were different from the Arabs. When Epiphanius says that the cult was performed at least partly in Arabic language, there must have been some reason for him to point this out. The Arabs in the Negev by this time were probably long gone, but there lived on a language named after them which was an exotic feature of the cult worth mentioning. When Herodotus explicitly states that the Arabs call Aphrodite and Dionysus by names in a language which seems to be closely linked to the later *ʕArabiyya*, this might mean the same as in Epiphanius: the local cult of the birth-giving goddess contained a linguistic element associated with the Arabs. This implies that Arabs were originally somehow involved in the cult but that it was not exclusively theirs.[85] The gods of local cults could thus be labelled with Arabic names. The notice by Herodotus contains not only an *interpretatio graeca* but also an *interpretatio arabica* of local cults in the Arabo-Nabataean kingdom. The latter may have had its foundation in the use of an Arabic language in parts of the cult. It is worth observing that the divinities ʔAllāt and Ruḍāw predominantly belong to the Ḥawrān and southern Syria. This is where we have found ample documentation of Arabs from the time of Alexander the Great down to Imruʔ al-Qays. Considering what we have learned concerning the role of the Arabs in Nabataea, it is hardly surprising to find the local divinities there dressed in Arabic names. Also the Nabataean Aphrodite, whose original name we do not know for sure, later appears as an Arab: ʕWZY/al-ʕUzzā.[86]

Another interesting, and to the same degree speculative, association arises from the curious allegation by the Christian apologist Justine the Martyr, writing in the middle of the second century AD, that the *magi* adoring the new-born Christ came from Arabia.[87] Why from Arabia? To Justine, Arabia was obviously situated south-east of Damascus.[88] Now it should be obvious to everyone that the story about the birth of Christ in Bethlehem belongs to the complex of the birth of the divine child celebrated in pagan cults around the eastern Mediterranean.[89] We also have good reasons to assume that Arabs in some way were participants in this cult, at least in Elusa and Petra. Arabs could thus be expected to turn up when a divine child was born. The remarks by Justine may give a hint of the real function of the Arabs in this cult: they are the first to pay their respects by presenting gifts to the new-born god. It can be suggested that a ritual attendance on the divine neophyte was an integrated part of the ceremonies in the cults around Palestine. In Matthew, these attendants have been transformed into Iranian *magi* in accordance with certain apocalyptic ideas current in that age. Justine has remembered the Arabs taking part in the cult and since there was no concrete geographical identification of the country of the *magi* in the gospel text, they could be arabicized without any difficulty, the more so since there was a tradition of the Arabs being good at astrology and divination. In the gospel tradition there stand, beside the *magi* of Matthew, the simple shepherds of Luke. These two variants represent the differentiation of the same motif: the paying of respects to the new-born saviour by people not immediately belonging to the community. It cannot be denied that Justine's Arabs, who did not cultivate the earth or dwell in houses, stand closer to Luke's shepherds than do Matthew's *magi*. Luke's shepherds were perhaps Arabs after all.

We would thus suggest that behind Herodotus' notice about the hair-cropped Arabian Dionysus stands the initiate to the Arab community of *phíloi*, who could be seen mythically as a new-born child, just like his colleagues in Thebes. At this stage one may begin to suspect that Attar qurūmā from Dumah, whose epithet may well mean 'cut', namely the hair, is the same figure. It would thus seem that the cult of the Arabs in Dumah, as well as that described by Herodotus, was quite archaic in its worship of ʕAthtar as the divinity of heaven and Ruḍāw/Munʕim/ŠLM as the god of nightly initiation ceremonies. But since this latter divinity was early paired with ʕAthtar/ʕAzīz because of the ancient relationship between ŠLM of the evening and ŠḤR of the morning, the birth mythology could be integrated into the ideas around the initiation of the Arabs. It seems that this is the origin of Herodotus' identification of the two main divinities of the Arabs with those belonging to the cults in Elusa and Petra.

Both Strabo and Arrian have a notice about the two gods of the Arabs: according to Arrian, they are Uranius and Dionysus; according to Strabo, Zeus and Dionysus. Both give the information in connection with Alexander the Great and his ambitions in Arabia, and it is likely that both authors reflect a source from that period.[90] It is also interesting that they may be referring to another group of Arabs than Herodotus, namely in the Persian Gulf area where the cult of the birth-giving goddess did not exist. This may indicate that the involvement in the birth mythology documented in the west, which may have affected the original Arab initiation rite, was local and did not belong to it from the beginning. The attending Arabs may appear in their basic function although it can be suspected that the deity attended was not always or even originally a divine child. We may also notice that both divinities appear as males, which may be a very archaic feature: behind Zeus/Uranius stands an originally male ʕAthtar of Heaven worshipped by the Arabs as well as the peoples of South Arabia. This god is then most likely to be 'the Arabian god' mentioned in the inscriptions from Gerash.

The god ʕT̲TR in Ugarit and South Arabia appears as masculine. There is, however, a clear tendency for him to become female. In ancient Mesopotamia the goddess Ishtar/Inanna appeared as the planet Venus. Also in Syria it was ʕAthtart, not ʕAthtar, who survived and became a main divinity (Astarte, ʕAshtoret). A similar process has obviously occurred in Dumah. It can be assumed that it was this change, or rather, determination of the sex of the deity, which contributed to the abandonment in Arabia of the ancient name, replacing it with ʔAllāt, 'the goddess'.

It is, however, unlikely that this was an exclusively Arabic cult. ʔAllāt had a very prominent temple in Palmyra, but as we have seen there is no textual evidence for Arab presence there. The same might be said about the pre-Islamic sanctuary in Thaqīf, documented in Arabo-Islamic literature. The widespread occurrence of the name ʔLT on graffiti and in personal names all over western Arabia, culminating in the centuries around the turn of the era, also speaks against an exclusively Arab cult. But it appears without doubt that Arabs had a special involvement in the cult of ʔAllāt/Attar shamāyīn.

Another problem is the female name ʕUzzay/al-ʕUzzā, which seems to be derived from the male ʕAzīz. This would make the Nabataean goddess a feminine variant of ʕAthtar. The problem is that, according to what we can discern of the mythology, it would rather be Dhū Sharay who represents ʕAthtar/ʕAzīz/the morning star. The solution may be that the connection between ʕUzzay and Dhū Sharay and the birth mythology in Elusa and Petra is secondary after all. At least the latter seems to belong to the area equivalent to ancient Edom, not the Negev. As we have seen, there is some evidence that the Nabataean ʕUzzay was also known by another name and that there may have been two different divinities. ʕUzzay may then not originally be linked to the function of the birth-giving goddess but instead have been a local variant of ʕAzīz, made feminine due to the same development that affected Athtar in Dumah. It should be observed that the birth mythology documented in the literary sources is not mentioned in the inscriptions and is unknown in Arabia, including the sanctuary of al-ʕUzzā at an-Nakhla. Epiphanius' identification of the new-born god in Elusa and Petra with Dusares may be secondary, perhaps due to a syncretistic cult in Petra itself, from where the name Dusares was also absorbed in Elusa. This must then have occurred when Petra/Reqem became the stronghold of Arabo-Nabataea. It is thus quite possible that Herodotus did not hear the names ʕUzzay and Dhū Sharay as the alternative names of his Arab deities. These had not yet been renamed according to the local cult east of the ʕArabah.

Tracing the Arab god

The connection between Arabs, Nabataeans and the cults in the Negev was obviously not clear to everybody. When Maximus of Tyre in the middle of the second century AD says that the Arabs worship a god in the form of a square stone, he definitely refers to the cult of Dusares in Arabo-Nabataea.[91] The linking of Arabs with Dusares is also found in a remark by Eusebius, who has supplementary information. He says that 'the sons of *árabes* worship Dusares and Obodos'.[92] This certainly refers to Arabo-Nabataea. The worshipped Obodos we have met before. Uranius told that the deified Obodas was buried in the city in the Negev named after him, present-day ʕAvdat.[93] The kings of Nabataea/Arabia must have seen themselves somehow as successors or, perhaps, even as manifestations of this dead hero and his successor Aretas, as is visible from the names of the kings who were actually known as 'the kings of the Arabs'.[94] In the figure of Obodas we have a mythical character quite close to the Arabs, in fact identified with them.

The threefold role as carrier of a royal name, as prophet and as dead object of worship points to a hero-cult of a semi-human, semi-divine figure. Marinus of Neapolis in the fifth century says that the *arábioi* venerate a divinity called Thyandrítēs.[95] This stands in a context mentioning the gods of Ashqelon and Gaza, which might indicate that the Arabs mentioned by Marinus are those around Palestine. Since Marinus himself was of Samaritan origin, he is likely to have been well informed. In another text from the same period by Damascius, telling the story of Isidorus of Alexandria, we hear that in Bosra there was a male god called Theandrítēs 'inspiring souls with feminine life'.[96] The latter enigmatic statement reminds us of Origen's specification of the male and female gods of the Arabs. A god Theándrios is well documented from the Ḥawrān in inscriptions from late antiquity, and must be the one described by Marinus and Damascius.[97] The name of this divinity, 'God-man', indicates a semi-divine hero, thus a figure reminiscent of Obodas in the Negev.

In connection with the god in Bosra, Damascius has more to say about the cults practised there:

> He [i.e. Isidorus] went to Bostra in Arabia, a city not very old since the emperor Severus had founded it, but it is an ancient fortress provided with walls against the neighbouring 'Dionysians' (*dionysieís*) by the Arabic kings (*hypò tōn arabikōn basiléōn*).[98]

It is not immediately clear what is meant by the *dionysieís*, a plural of *dionysieús*. In an inscription from Suwayda, there is mentioned a *mágnos oikodómos dionysieús*.[99] The word seems to be a special designation for Dionysus-worshippers.[100] If we may dare to knit these facts together, we can see a semi-divine hero, the 'God-man' in Bosra venerated by Arabs defending themselves against the attacks of the worshippers of Dionysus. It cannot be denied that this picture fits better with what Hieronymus said about the non-wine-drinking Arabs than with Herodotus' presentation of them as followers of Dionysus the wine-god. As has been shown, Herodotus' statements may have another meaning and refer to something else than worship of a wine-god. But there emerges a picture of the Arabs, both in the Negev and in Ḥawrān, led or inspired by a semi-divine hero. In the Negev we discern a myth about birth which may refer to initiation. In Ḥawrān we see a struggle against the followers of Dionysus.

The Arabs and their god

In the last great epic work of Hellenistic antiquity, the *Dionysiaca* of Nonnus from Panopolis in Egypt, written in the middle of the fifth century AD, the travels of the god Dionysus around the world are described as a fantastic pageant, the last great appearance of the dying gods of antiquity. In this work, the Arabs in Ḥawrān enter the stage in a monumental way.

In song XX, Dionysus has reached the shores of the Levant. Having passed Tyre and Byblus, the god continues towards the source of Adonis in the mountain of Lebanon. Then he reaches Arabia and the region called Nysa with large forests and a city built on a mountain, known as the home of undaunted warriors. There lives Lycurgus, the son of Ares, a violent warrior who is called 'the ruler of Arabia' (*Arabíēs medéōn*). He is now urged by Hera to take up arms against Dionysus and his followers, and she makes bows of horn for the bowmen of the *árabes*. Dionysus descends from Mount Carmel and the battle commences. Dionysus is chased by Lycurgus and throws himself into the Red Sea and is received by Thetis and Nereus, 'the Arab'. One of Dionysus' companions, the nymph Ambrosia, attacks Lycurgus by transforming herself into a vine which entangles him. Then he is attacked by other Dionysiac nymphs. Now Rhea, the ruler of the mountains, sends Poseidon against Arabia. The earth trembles and the cloud-swept palace of Arabia falls. The ground of 'Nysios the Arab' is shaken, everybody is seized by bacchantic frenzy, and the 'Arab shepherd' runs amok. Lycurgus tells everybody to show the courage of the *árabes*. Hera comes to Arabia and saves Lycurgus by cutting the vines that have entangled him. The *árabes* then worship him with bloody sacrifices. He is made into a blind wanderer, while Dionysus celebrates his victory with the nereids in the Red Sea. The rumour about the events in 'inhospitable Arabia' is spread.[101]

In a later passage it is told how Dionysus returns to Arabia from India and Caucasia and teaches the people of the *árabes* the Dionysiac mysteries, and plants his herb (i.e. the vine) 'on the Nysian mountains'. Then he leaves the deep forests of Arabia on the road to Assyria and comes to Tyre.[102]

These events are referred to in several other passages in the poem.[103] The combat between Dionysus and Lycurgus was originally told in the *Iliad*, where Diomedes tells the following to Glaucus as a warning for a mortal not to attack a god, even though the god is a child:

> For the son of Dryas, the mighty Lykourgos, did not
> live long, he who fought the heavenly gods,
> who once drove the nurses of mad Dionysos
> down holy Nyseion; those all, at the same time,
> letting their *thysthla* fall to the ground, by man-slaughtering Lykourgos
> smitten with a *bouplēx*. Dionysos, frightened,
> dived into the salty billow, and Thetis received him in her bosom,
> frightened. For a mighty terror had hit him from the threat of a human.
> At him the easy-living gods were furious
> and the son of Kronos made him blind; not for long
> did he live hereafter; he was hated by all immortal gods.[104]

In the *Iliad*, there is not a word about Arabs, and most ancient commentators agreed that the scene is set in Thrace.[105] There is, however, already in the Homeric Hymn to Dionysus a polemic against a location of the Nyseion or Nysa in Greece. Instead, the hymn favours a place 'on a high mountain, far from Phoenicia, near the streams of Aigyptos'.[106] The reference looks as if Herodotus' Arabia is intended, and we should also observe what seems to be a rejection of a location in Phoenicia which, consequently, must have been current. When telling the story of Dionysus, Diodorus Siculus refers to a poet writing in the late fifth century BC named Antimachus. According to him, Lycurgus was king, not of Thrace but of Arabia, and the attack upon Dionysus and the *bacchae* took place in Nysa in Arabia.[107] Diodorus also reports that Dionysus as a child was brought by Zeus to Nysa in Arabia where he was brought up by nymphs, a piece of information likely also to originate from Antimachus.[108]

The version in the *Dionysiaca* contains several features which are not from the Homeric story, such as Lycurgus being the son of Ares, his custom of cutting off heads and suspending them on the city gate, his being led by Hera and the Ambrosia episode.[109] Specific also is the explicit enmity between Lycurgus and the wine as well as the cult established around him.[110] Also worth noticing are Lycurgus' words that he cannot control the sea.[111] And the most important addition is, of course, the Arab supporters around him. It is not impossible that all these elements go back to Antimachus. There is no doubt that the location of the events in Arabia goes back to him and was well established around 400 BC.

According to the geographical indications in Nonnus' story, Dionysus comes from a place named Carmel to the town of Lycurgus and his Arabs. From the information given, it does not seem that this Carmel should be identified with Mount Carmel at Haifa. The god travels northwards along the Levantine coast past Tyre, then turns inland to the sanctuary of Adonis, which is situated inland from Byblus. Then from Carmel he reaches Arabia. Now it is documented that Jupiter Heliopolitanus, the main god at Baalbek, was called *Zeus Heliopoleitēs Karmēlos*.[112] Since Carmel was probably originally a cultic name of a sanctuary of the gods of wine, it may well have been applied to different areas, among them Baalbek. The important role of wine is well documented in the artistic decoration of that great sanctuary, and it is even almost certain that the struggle between Dionysus and Lycurgus is depicted on one of the reliefs on the so-called Bacchus temple.[113] There are very good arguments in favour of locating Carmel, i.e. the residence of Dionysus in the Levant according to Nonnus' story, at Baalbek.[114]

This means that Nonnus'/Antimachus' Arabia should be looked for not too far away. The presence of Arabs in Antilebanon is documented from the time of Alexander the Great onwards. But there is also, as has been shown in this study, an Arabia south of Damascus to which Paul fled and from which the *magi* came according to Justine, and where we find the tomb of Imruʔ al-Qays, 'the king of all *ʕarab*'. We should also remember the saying of Rabbi Yehoshua ben Lewi about the abundant vines growing in an area called 'the Mountain', which can be identified with the present-day Ǧabal ad-Durūz and where there were obviously Arabs.[115] In this part of Syria there are other literary references to our story. The notice in Damascius sounds like a description of the scene in the *Dionysiaca* when Lycurgus, the king of the Arabs, is attacked by Dionysus and his followers. It should be kept in mind that the neighbouring city of Bosra, present-day Suwayda, was called Dionysias in antiquity.[116] It may also be noticed that the divine name Ares is documented in an inscription from Qanawāt, which seems to be the only documentation in southern Syria of this name outside Rabbathmoba, present-day Karak.[117] The myth about the struggle between Dionysus and Lycurgus with his Arabs was also told as having taken place in Damascus.[118] There is thus a series of locations from Baalbek to Bosra where the Lycurgus–Dionysus story was told, and it can be assumed with great certainty that this is the area described in Nonnus' epic as the region where the Arabs appear as supporters of the enemy of the god of wine.

The testimonies about Lycurgus are not only literary. There are six inscriptions from Ḥawrān dedicated to Lycurgus showing him to be a hero or a divinity of some importance in that region.[119] It is very likely that the Greek name, in fact, is a disguise for a local Semitic divinity. It was suggested a long time ago that Lycurgus is identical not only to the god ŠYʕ ʔL/HQWM mentioned in some inscriptions from Syria, but also to the god Theandrítēs.[120] Of the inscriptions, one in Palmyrene Aramaic is especially interesting, since the god in it has the epithet 'who does not drink wine'.[121] This divinity has a warrior-like appearance and the name, which is purely Arabic, means 'the leader of the people', which might be a military term.[122] It is difficult to avoid the conclusion that this is the original Semitic Lycurgus who was associated with the Arabs, who, according to Hieronymus of Cardia, did not drink wine or cultivate grapes.[123] In that case, it becomes likely that Dionysus is, if not identical with, then of the same kind as the god known from Nabataea and southern Syria by the name Dusares.[124] This divinity was especially worshipped by the Nabataeans, ruled by the kings from Petra/Reqem who, according to Strabo's friend Athenodorus, were great wine-drinkers.[125] From what we know, there seems to have been a dividing line in the Arabo-Nabataean kingdom between the wine-drinkers and the teetotallers. The latter were the Arabs originally living around the Rock in the Negev. But a similar dichotomy can clearly be discerned in the other Syrian Arabia, namely in Ḥawrān.[126]

From what has been said in this investigation, it becomes very unlikely that the conflict between the wine-god and the Arabs would reflect some kind of eternal conflict between settlers and nomads.[127] Instead we have here traces of a ritual which was spread in many places in Ḥawrān and, perhaps, also further south, in the Arabo-Nabataean kingdom. The exact contents and meaning of this ritual cannot be investigated here. But from all that has been said, it can be concluded that there is no doubt that the Arabs in Nonnus' *Dionysiaca* are not a purely literary ornament. Nonnus' story is based on earlier sources, datable as far back as 400 BC, which used a local ritual in southern Syria and its mythology as a complement to the Greek story of Dionysus' journeys around the world. We can dimly perceive a festival connected with viniculture where a section of the population refuses to take part in wine drinking. In Nonnus the teetotallers lose the fight, but this might well be attributed to the Greek Dionysiac mythology, according to which none could resist the power of the god. The story actually tells us that Lycurgus and his followers continued to exist: a cult is established in which Lycurgus is venerated by his followers. These followers are called Arabs, and there is no reason to doubt the correctness of that.[128] Worth noticing is the line about Lycurgus not being able to control the sea, which sounds like an echo of the saying in the proverbs of Aḥiqar where the alienness of the Arab to the sea is emphasized.[129]

We would then suggest that Nonnus in his epic has preserved a unique piece of information about the Arabs in southern Syria going back to the fifth century BC. It shows the Arabs as connected with a ritual involving a struggle between a wine-drinking community and a group of warriors belonging to a divinity or a mythical hero who is subject to certain taboos, among which the abstention from wine drinking plays a central role. This taboo may be connected with the picture of the Dionysiac frenzy affecting the inhabitants of Nonnus' Arabia. If this frenzy takes place in a festival or a ritual, the sober Arabs and their leader represent a segment of society which, for some reason, did not take part in the orgiastic Dionysiac rites. They appear as guardians of society and its order when the Dionysiac frenzy is let loose. The picture is once again strongly reminiscent of the Rechabites in the Old Testament. Did the Arabs play the role of protectors of a society temporarily running out of control during the festival? Such a role may well have led to their employment as protectors in other contexts too, as police forces and border-guards. [130]

Rendezvous in Mecca: the legend of Quṣayy b. Kilāb

In the legends about pre-Islamic Mecca there are some events which may be seen in a new light if compared to what has been said. The story, as told by Ibn Isḥāq, goes that Mecca was in the hands of three successive tribes: Ǧurhum, Khuzāʕa and Quraysh. According to the story, Ǧurhum mismanaged their custody of the Holy Place and made lawful things that were taboo.[131] With this goes the notice about ʔIsāf and Nāʔila, a man and a woman from that tribe said to have had sex in the sanctuary.[132] Two other clans expelled them from Mecca: the Bakr from Kināna and the Ghubshān from Khuzāʕa. Khuzāʕa are especially associated with the corruption of the religion of Abraham in Mecca and the introduction of idolatry through their hero ʕAmr b. Luḥayy.

The signal to leave from the plain of ʕArafa during the Great Pilgrimage belonged to a group called the Ṣūfa who were descendants of Ǧurhum and who, according to the story, remained in office even after the expulsion of Ǧurhum. Another group, the ʕAdwān, were in charge of the departure from Muzdalifa until the coming of Islam.

But the real hero of Mecca is Quṣayy b. Kilāb, who is said to have gathered Quraysh, who were spread out among the Kināna. He is called *al-muǧammiʕ*, 'the gatherer'.[133] Quṣayy was raised by his mother from Kināna and his step-father from the tribe of ʕUdhra, belonging to the Quḍāʕa, in his stepfather's tribe. When he had grown up, he raised the claim to rule in Mecca based on his ancestry. It is said that the *ʕarab* had been dissatified with the activities of the Ṣūfa.[134] His mother advised him to take action in connection with the pilgrimage in the holy month. Quṣayy now mobilized warriors with his half-brother Rizāḥ:

> Rizāḥ son of Rabīʕa went out and his brothers Ḥunn son of Rabīʕa, Maḥmūd son of Rabīʕa and Ǧulhuma son of Rabīʕa – these were not the sons of Fāṭima [the mother of Quṣayy and Rizāḥ] – went out with him among those who followed him [Quṣayy] from Quḍāʕa among the pilgrims of the *ʕarab* (*ḥāǧǧ al-ʕarab*).[135]

There follows a fight of Quṣayy and his followers from Quḍāʕa against the two clans in Mecca. Arbitration is entrusted to 'a man from the *ʕarab*', who gives Quṣayy the right to rule in Mecca. He is given the right to feed and water the pilgrims and rules as king.[136]

Certain doubts can be entertained about the historicity of this story. The succession of three possessors of Mecca may be a rationalization of a more complex or even completely different scenario. Both Ǧurhum and Khuzāʕa were, in fact, inhabitants of Mecca even into the Islamic period, the latter playing quite a prominent role in the history of Muhammed.[137] There are also totally different versions about the early history of Mecca: that its earliest inhabitants were the ʔIyād or that it was completely deserted before the arrival of Quraysh.[138] None of these versions should be taken as history at first glance. As far as the three successive inhabitants are concerned, they belong to the *bāʔida*, the *ʕāriba* and the *mustaʕriba* respectively. This sounds much like a construction of later times when this division had been established. It should also be observed that both Bakr and Quraysh belong to the Kināna. Among the sons of Quṣayy there is a ʕAbd Quṣayy. The conclusion must be that Quṣayy is a name of someone who is more a divinity than a human, and that the story of the three successive rulers of Mecca is a historification of mythology.[139] Important is that the events are intimately connected with the rituals in Mecca and its surroundings. The Ǧurhum belong to the *ʕarab al-bāʔida* and are thus in the same category as ʕĀd. Like them, Ǧurhum start to decline morally. Their successors represent dissolution, corruption and idolatry. The name Khuzāʕa is associated with the verb *taxazzaʕa*, which means 'to separate oneself from something', 'to cut oneself off'.[140] Quraysh is said to come from the verb *taqarrasha*, 'to gather', 'to come together'. In the history of Mecca, Ǧurhum represents the old order much like ʕĀd in other parts of Arabia. Khuzāʕa stands for a period of dissolution, and Quṣayy and his followers represent a new restored order. For once, the etymologies of the names might contain some truth.

Quṣayy comes from outside Mecca, even though he is said originally to have been born there. He is supported by the *ʕarab*.[141] In verses attributed to the poet Qays b. Ḥidādiyya quoted earlier, we hear him boast about how his tribe, the Khuzāʕa, has defended the Temple against *ʕarab*.[142] In the story of Quṣayy, the Quḍāʕa are connected with *ʕarab*: they take part in their *ḥaǧǧ*. One of the most prominent members of the Quḍāʕa group was the tribe of ʕUdhra. This is the tribe in which Quṣayy was brought up. Further, ʕUdhra lived in Wādī al-qurā, i.e. the valley where the 'villages of the *ʕarab*' were to be found.[143] We have heard about the *ʕarab* of Quḍāʕa before, and the term obviously means the *ʕarab* who lived among the tribes counted as Quḍāʕa.[144] There was thus no difficulty for a Ḥiǧāzī Lycurgus to find Arabs to support him. Or to put it differently: if there was a ritual of a similar kind in Ḥiǧāz like the one we have found in Ḥawrān, we should expect the *ʕarab* to turn up and play a similar role. This is also the case in the story of Quṣayy's conquest of Mecca. At this stage no one can be surprised to find even Lycurgus himself in Ḥiǧāz: of the two Nabataean inscriptions mentioning ŠYʕ ʔLQWM, one is found in Ḥawrān and the other in Madāʔin Ṣāliḥ, i.e. on the entrance to Wādī al-qurā.[145] And it is difficult not to point out that the leader of the *ʕarab* in Ḥiǧāz has a name which is probably derived from a verb meaning 'to cut off', especially the forelock.[146]

Notes

1 Of the general studies on religion in pre-Islamic Arabia, Wellhausen's classic, *Reste arabischen Heidentums*, originally from 1887, is founded on the testimonies of the Arabo-Islamic texts, although other sources are referred to. Of the modern studies, Ryckmans' *Réligions* (1951) treats the entire peninsula, including South Arabia. The same holds for Caskel's short sketch *Gottheiten* (1958) in which he gave a short survey of the main divinities in Arabia, including South Arabia. Henninger in his short but well-balanced sketch from 1959 shows an awareness of the regional complexities and limits himself to a description of 'la réligion bédouine'. Fahd's *Panthéon* (1967) is a fairly complete survey of names of divinities and sanctuaries according to inscriptions and Arabic sources. Höfner (1970) takes the epigraphic material into account, makes a distinction between South Arabia and the rest, and also describes the religions of Arabia, not 'les réligions arabes' as does Ryckmans. This distinction was already made in her section on Arabia in Haussig's *Wörterbuch der Mythologie* (1965 pp. 407–481 on North and Central Arabia (together with E. Merkel), pp. 483–567 on South Arabia) A major step forward since Wellhausen is Krone's monograph on the goddess ʔAllāt (1992), which, in fact, is a thorough survey and analysis of the main cults in pre-Islamic Arabia, based on both epigraphic and literary sources and well structured according

to both chronology and geography. The same holds for Healey's thorough and well-balanced study on religion in the Arabo-Nabataean area (2001). In spite of their great erudition none of these writers has had any clear idea about what the Arabs were. They all describe the religion of the people(s) living in Arabia, not that of the Arabs.

2 See pp. 309 f.

3 Hatra 79; see p. 442.

4 Höfner points out that Gad may stand for several different deities, Höfner/Merkel *Stammesgruppen* 438–439).

5 In Sumatar one text mentions MRʔLHʔ, 'the Lord God' (mār ʔallāhā), worshipped by the *šalliṭā* of the Arabs (Drijvers, *Inscriptions* no. 23 = Segal, *Inscriptions* no. 11; cf. p. 441). But it is uncertain whether this god really was worshipped by the Arabs themselves. The text says that the monument was put up for the account of the king, probably of Edessa.

6 Nin. A IV:10–12 (= Borger, *Inschriften* 53); Mon. B:10–11 (= Borger, *Inschriften* 100); see p. 158.

7 For the identification of the god returned with Attarshamāyīn, see Knauf, *Ismael* 82–84, and Krone, *Gottheit* 76–79.

8 The name RḌW also sometimes appears as RḌY, RḌʔ or RḌ (Höfner, *Religionen* 374). For the documentation, see Winnnett/Reed, *Records* p. 80; cf. Knauf, *Ismael* 86, for the dating.

9 ʕṮRSM is identified with Attar Shamāyīn, cf. Knauf, *Ismael* 82.

10 For the different types of Thamudic script and their dating, see Roschinski, *Sprachen* 165; Macdonald/King, *Thamudic*; and Macdonald, *Reflections* 33–35.

11 van den Branden, *Histoire* 109–110, 112–113; Knauf, *Ismael* 82–84.

12 Krone, *Gottheit* 80–83.

13 Krone, *Gottheit* 445.

14 van den Branden, *Histoire* 25.

15 Pliny 6.157. The information probably comes from Isidorus of Charax.

16 For the development in Taymāʔ, cf. Roschinski, *Sprachen* 176–183. The nature and identity of the two remaining gods of Dumah, Abirillu and Dāya, are difficult to grasp. The latter has been identified with both al-ʕUzzā and ʔAllāt (Krone, *Gottheit* 496–497; Ryckmans, *Religions* 22; cf. Knauf, *Ismael* 84, 86).

17 Tallqvist, *Götterepiteta* 333. One might also compare the cult of Baʕal Šamāyīn/Šamēm etc. in this period; see Gese, *Religionen* 182–185. For the background of Athtar/Athtart, see ibid. 137–139, 161–164.

18 Jeremiah 7:18; 44:17–19, 25; cf. Hezechiel 8:14 about the women bewailing Tammuz, which indicates a cult of Ishtar.

19 Caskel, *Gottheiten* 101; Knauf, *Ismael* 82–84; Krone, *Gottheit* 78 ff.

20 Krone, *Gottheit* 79.

21 *Lisān*, s.v. QRM; cf. South Arabian in Ry 508:7 where it could be translated 'chieftain'. The root has several meanings in Arabic, among them some derived from the meaning 'cut off': *qurma* means 'a spot above the nose where the skin is peeled off and folded, skin that is peeled off'; the verb *qarama* is 'scrape off from bread' and 'gnaw'; cf. Geez *qärämä*, 'to glean, to harvest'.

22 van den Branden, *Histoire* 104; Höfner, *Religionen* 374; Krone, *Gottheit* 348.

23 Hu. 327: B-NHY ŠMS ʕLY; cf. Knauf, *Ismael* 84 n. 461.

24 Jeremiah 49:7. For the wisdom tradition of northern Arabia in the book of Proverbs 30 and 31, see Albright, *Tribe* 6–11. Of the names ʔAgûr and Yaqē, the first one belongs to the onomasticon found in the Thamudic inscriptions; the second is clearly related to Sabaean WQH (Albright, op. cit. 7 n. 3). One might also adduce Job's satirical words about the wisdom of his friends (12:2), among whom we find one Têmanî. The idea of wisdom in Job is, on the whole, related to the concept in Proverbs 30–31. Also the linguistic peculiarities of these texts point to an Arabo-Aramaic milieu which fits well with north-western Arabia in the sixth century BC. Cf. Knauf, *Teman*; idem, *Husham*.

25 Herodotus 3.8; Fahd, *Panthéon* 144–45, Knauf, *Ismael* 85.

26 Jeremiah 7:18; 44:17 ff.; Herodotus 1.131; 3.8.

27 Herodotus 1:131. The MSS actually have Alitta but this has been emended to Alilat in accor-

dance with 3.8, and the fact that the same goddess is said to be called Mylitta in the same context can explain the distortion of the original name.

28 Origenes, *Contra Celsum* V:38.

29 Sourdel, *Cultes* 59–68; Krone, *Gottheit* 496 ff. There is some variation in the spelling of the names in the texts, cf. Healey, *Religion* 86–88; 114.

30 Outside northern Arabia, al-ʕUzzā was worshipped at the sanctuary in an-Nakhla north-east of Mekka, which represents a very special cult which seems to be quite isolated in Arabia; see Krone, *Gottheit* 500–508.

31 Evagrius, *History* 6.22; Procopius, *Wars* 2.28.13.

32 Isaac XI:89.

33 Epiphanius 51:22.

34 Cf. Mordtmann, *Dusares*; Healey, *Religion* 103–104.

35 Hieronymus, *Vita Hilarionis* 41.

36 Cosmas, *Synagoge* 38:342.

37 Johannes Damascenus, *De haeresibus* 764. Cf. Rotter, *Dies Veneris* 126.

38 *Taxis* 54:19–23. *Eōsphoros* literally means 'star of dawn'.

39 Sourdel, *Cultes* 59–68; Bowersock, *Cult*; Healey, *Religion* 100–101.

40 Hesychius, *Lexicon* s.v. Dousares (I 475). Also in Stephanus of Byzantium, Dusares is linked with the Nabataeans; cf. *Ethnika* 237 and 223 (s.v. Dakharēnoí) .This notice comes from Uranius.

41 For the documentation of the identification of ʕWZY with Aphrodite see Krone, *Gottheit* 512–517; Healey, *Religion* 117.

42 The cult of al-ʕUzzā at an-Nakhla north-east of Mecca, well known in Arabic literature, is not very typical for Arabia and is most likely to have been introduced from the north; cf. Krone, *Gottheit* 500–507. His scepticism about the identification is unfounded.

43 The classic study is Norden, *Geburt*.

44 Krone, *Gottheit* 73; Healey, *Religion* 94.

45 Krone, *Gottheit* 73, 542. ʔAllāt appears in the periphery of the Arabo-Nabatean area like Ḥawrān, Dedan, Wādī Ramm; cf. Healey, *Religion* 108.

46 Krone, *Gottheit* 303–313; Starcky, *Allath*. The identification with Athena is documented from the first century AD onwards; cf. Février, *Réligion* 11. ʕUzzāy is explicitly identified with Aphrodite in the bilingual inscription from Cos; cf. Healey, *Religion* 117.

47 Höfner/Merkel, *Stammesgruppen* 456–457; Knauf, *Ismael* 85.

48 Dumbrell, *Tell El-Maskhuṭa* 36. See p. 2500.

49 So Höfner/Merkel, *Stammesgruppen* 434. Krone, *Gottheit* 520. Starcky (*Pétra* 1003) and Healey (*Religion* 108, 133–134, 119, cf. 109–110) claim that the two female deities are identical and only differentiated at a late stage of 'Nabataean' religion. But the arguments (the identification between Ouraníē and Alilat by Herodotus, the frequent invocations of ʔUzzāy in Wādī Ramm close to the sanctuary of ʔAllāt) are weak. Knauf (*Ismael* 110) assumes that Ruḍā and Dhū Sharā were two names for the same god. But there is good evidence against this, as underlined by Healey, *Religion* 94–95, although it is very likely that the cults of the two gods influenced each other, just as did the cults of Aphrodite/ʕUzzāy and ʔAllāt.

50 Theodorus, *Scholia* 205.

51 The Akkadian Ishtar was very early identified with the Sumerian Inanna. That name originally meant 'the lady of heaven' (nin-an-ak; cf. Wilcke, *Inanna* 75). Another possibility is that Nanî is connected with Nanaia, a goddess belonging to the cult of Nabu. She is identified with Inanna/Ishtar in texts from the time of Sargon II (Stol, *Nanaja* 148). In both cases, the testimony of Theodorus shows that the Arabs worshipped Ishtar, not al-ʕUzzā. The goddess NNY is documented in the Aramaic inscriptions from Assur perhaps from the second century AD; see Beyer, *Inschriften* 13–14 and 7.

52 Liddell/Scott, *Lexicon* s.v. ouranía.

53 Thus emphatically Knauf, *Ismael* 82–84.

54 Krone (*Gottheit* 82–86) launches three arguments against the identification of Allāt and Attarshamāyīn: the absence of the latter name on the Tell al-Maskhūta bowls, the absence of the name ʔAllāt in the earliest Thamudic inscriptions, where ʕṮRSM occurs instead, and the

occurrence of both names together in some texts. But the hypothesis of the two being two different gods creates considerable difficulties, the most prominent of which is the fact that Qedar in Dumah are followers of Attarshamāyīn and in Tell al-Maskhūṭa of han-ʔilāt/ʔAllāt. If we assume that the two names in fact stand for the same divinity, Krone's arguments are still explicable.

55 Krone, *Gottheit* 146.

56 von Wissmann, *Geographie* 155 Anm. 261

57 Sourdel, *Cultes* 69–74; Krone, *Gottheit* 102 ff.

58 Krone, *Gottheit* 152–153.

59 Krone, *Gottheit* 102. In the story about the emigration of Quḍāʕa from Tihāma to Baḥrayn, where Tanūkh was to be formed, one of the emigrants belonging to the Wabara clan was Taym ʔAllāt (*ʔAghānī* 11.161 = 13:4592). To this clan belonged the Fahmids according to aṭ-Ṭabarī, *Tārīkh* I:745 (who, like al-Bakrī, has Taym ʔAllāh).

60 This is another argument in favour of the hypothesis that the last-mentioned pair originally belonged to the Arabo-Nabataean kingdom, where their cult continued until the rise of Islam. This might also explain the spread of the cult of ʕUzzay to Mesopotamia, which may be connected with the rise of the Saracen culture in the third and fourth centuries AD. As we have shown, the earliest documentation of people called Saracens points to north-western Arabia as the origin for this term.

61 Isaac XI:408–457 (= Bickell 244–247).

62 Hieronymus, *Amos* 1055 (a commentary to Amos 5:26).

63 Cf. Noiville, *Culte* 373 n. 7.

64 There is no certain evidence for al-ʕUzza/ʕUzzāy being connected with Venus; cf. Henninger, *Problem* 136–139, modifying his own earlier statements in *Sternkunde* 79 ff.; Hawting, *Idea* 142; Seidensticker, *Frage* 509; cf. the discussion in Drijvers, *Cults* 151 ff. (contradicting himself on p. 153); Healey (*Religion* 117) seems to stick to the old opinion. It is worth observing that the abjuration formula (*Taxis* 154) quoted by Healey as proof of the identification (*Religion* 118) distinguishes between Aphrodite (= ʕUzzāy) and the Morning star, Eōsphoros.

65 Julian, *Oration* 4.34 (p. 128), 40 (p. 133); Drijvers, *Cults* 159–163. Edessa is usually emended to Emesa but there are arguments against this emendation. It is, however, evident that the cult of the twin gods was well established even in Emesa. For this question, see Drijvers, *Cults* 149–159.

66 There is a Latin inscription in Dacia from the middle of the third century AD (CIL III 875) dedicated *Deo Azizo bono puero* (see Février, *Réligion* 21 note 5), which thus confirms the identiy of the god with the divine child; cf. also Höfner/Merkel, *Stammesgruppen* 428.

67 Février, *Réligion* 16–33.

68 In the *ʕArabiyya riḍā* is a verbal noun meaning 'state of well-being, being pleased, content'; see Lane, *Lexicon* s.v.

69 Cf. Lane, *Lexicon*, s.v. NʕM. The meaning is more 'active' than indicated by the usual translation 'the favourable one'; cf. Drijvers, *Cults* 161.

70 One should observe the prominence of the invocations to the evening star in wedding songs from the old Mediterranean cultures, such as the epithalamion by Catullus (no. LXII).

71 Burkert, *Religion* 243–247. For the rejection of the identification of Monimos with KTBY/ʔ/Nabu/the planet Mercury as suggested by Starcky, *Pétra* 988 ff., see the discussion by Drijvers, *Cults* 163–165.

72 Drijvers, *Cults* 166–169, pointing to the iconography, emphazises the warrior-like quality of Monimos/ʔArṣu which stands in some contradiction to the characteristics of the Greek Hermes. The interpretation of the role of this divinity in Arabia as presented here will provide an explanation of this fact.

73 Gese, *Religionen* 80–82, 139, 168–169. The linking of birth, youth, heroism and dawn is apparent in the most enigmatic verses in the book of Psalms, 110:2–3, where the god ŠḤR is probably mentioned.

74 Gese, *Religionen* 138.

75 Gese, *Religionen* 137–141, 94–106, 117–119.

76 Gese, *Religionen* 138.
77 Gese, *Religionen* 138–139.
78 Revelation 22:16: 'I, Jesus, have sent mine angel to testify to you these things in the churches. I am the root and the offspring of David and the bright and morning star.' Also 2:27 plays with the same symbol, although the reference is not completely clear: 'And he that overcometh and keepeth my works unto the end, unto him I will give power over the nations; and he shall rule them with a rod of iron; as the vessels of a potter shall they be broken to shivers even as I received of my father, and I will give him the morning star.' The figure of the divine child also lies behind the picture of primordial Wisdom in Proverbs 8:23–31, and the coming glorious conquering king of Israel is depicted as a rising star in Bileam's oracle in Numbers 24:17. Interestingly, Christ is called the forerunner in Hebrews 6:20. This is the only occurrence of the Greek word *pródromos* in the New Testament. This word in later Greek Christian tradition is used for John the Baptist and it might be speculated that John attracted this epithet, originally belonging to ʕAthtar the rain-giver, because of his activities as a water-man and forerunner of the real hero.
79 Starcky, *Palmyre* 103, 212, 225–226; Sourdel, *Cultes* 74–75; Winnett/Reed, *Records* 75–76; Henninger, *Sternkunde* 79–96; Höfner, *Religionen* 363; Knauf, *Ismael* 85. These two divinities are the companions of the sun-god Helios, who has another cult practised in Emesa.
80 Cf. Wellhausen, *Reste* 198; Henninger, *Frage* 296 and n. 52.
81 Henninger, *Frage* 303. Cf. the story of Labīd quoted p. 587.
82 Burkert, *Religion* 257, assumes a clear homoerotic meaning of the story of Dionysus' birth. The myth of Dionysus' birth belongs to Thebes. In that town there was a special corps of warriors consisting of homosexual couples, called 'the holy league' (*ho hieròs lókhos*). Although not stated explicitly, it can be expected that the story of Dionysus' second birth is connected with this institution. This is a Dionysus appearing not as a god of drinking but as a representative of ritual birth and initiation, which fits well into the picture of the Arab Dionysus. For the Holy League, see Ogden, *Homosexuality*, especially 111–115. There is, however, no evidence that the Arabs followed similar sexual regulations.
83 If Ruḍāw/Monimos was the deity of the initiation of the Arabs as a kind of sanctified warrior, this would also explain his war-like quality manifest in the iconography, as pointed out by Drijvers, *Cult* 166–169. Monimos/Ruḍāw thus combines the guiding function of the Greek Hermes and the warrior quality of Ares. Drijvers, in fact, identifies Dusareas and ʔRṢW/Ruḍāw (*Dusares*). Interestingly, Dhusharāy also seems to appear as a warrior. Drijvers claims that this divinity is the *theòs arabikós* documented from Gerasa. Nothing of this is implausible, although it must be assumed that Dusares and Ruḍāw are originally two separate divinities.
84 Languages in northern Arabia can be divided in at least two main groups, characterized among other things by the different form of the definite article H(N)- or (ʔ)L. Almost all modern forms of Arabic, including the *ʕArabiyya*, belong to the latter group, whereas the languages in the Thamudic, Liḥyanitic, Ḥasaitic and Ṣafaitic inscriptions belong to the former. For the languages in northern and central Arabia, see W.W. Müller, *Frühnordarabische* and Macdonald, *Reflections*, especially 41–45.
85 It is worth observing that the abjuration formula (*Taxis*) is directed against the religion of the Saracens but the name of the female goddess is said to be 'in the language of the *árabes*'.
86 The original name is badly transmitted by the Greek authors: Khaamou, Khaabou, Khamara, Khabar. Rotter (*Veneris Dies* 126–128) has some good arguments in favour of a connection with KBR. The original name of Dusares/Dhū Sharā was perhaps ʔAʕarā; see Sourdel, *Cultes* 59–60; Höfner/Merkel, *Stammesgruppen* 419, 433–435; Healey, *Religion* 97–100.
87 Justine, *Dialogue* 276–282.
88 Ibid., 282.
89 See Norden, *Geburt*, *passim*.
90 It is very unlikely that the source is Aristobulus; Arrian explicitly refers to another source: *lógos dè katékhei* . . . (cf. Arrian, *Anabasis* 7.20.1 with 7.19.3).
91 Maximus, *Oration* 2:8; cf. Healey, *Religion* 157.
92 Eusebius, *Tricennatsrede* § 13 (p. 237); cf. Healey, *Religion* 149.

93 Stephanus 144.19–26; 482:15–16; cf. Healey, *Religion* 147–151; see p. 377.
94 See p. 377 for the mythical nature of these two figures. It might be suggested that the royal names in the Arabo-Nabataean kingdom ʕBDT, ḤRTT and MLKW are all divine epithets referring to gods linked to the kingship. This would mean that proper names like ʕBDḤRTT and ʕBDMLKW do not show a special allegiance to the kings, as supposed by Dijkstra (*Life* 321 note 7), but are instead real theophoric names. It is tempting to draw the enigmatic book of Obadiah in the Old Testament into this complex. Obodas acts as a prophet in Uranius' notice and is definitely located in ʕAvdat. The book of Obadiah not only seems to share its name with the Negevite hero; it also deals with that area (Edom, Seʕir) and is formed as uttered by a prophet.
95 Marinus, *Vita Procli* 76 (ll. 481–482).
96 Photius, *Bibliotheca* 242: Damascius 196–197.
97 Sourdel, *Cultes* 78–81; Höfner/Merkel, *Stammesgruppen* 471.
98 Photius, *Bibliotheca* 242 Damascius 196.
99 Waddington 2299.
100 Sourdel (*Cultes* 63) assumes it to be the designation for the inhabitants of Dionysias, i.e. Suwayda.
101 Nonnus, *Dionysiaca* 20:142–21:325.
102 Nonnus, *Dionysiaca* 40:294–299.
203 Nonnos, *Dionysiaca* 26:23; 30:280; 32:196; 36:96; 43:180; 47:629.
104 *Iliad* VI:130–140. The exact meanings of the words *thysthla* and *bouplēx* are not certain. The former seems to be a term for some of the cultic equipment of the followers of Dionysus. The latter could be an ox-goad or an axe of some kind.
105 Chuvin, *Mythologie* 258.
106 *Homeric Hymn* I:8–9. These verses are preserved by Diodorus in the *Bibliotheca* 3.66.3.
107 Diodorus 3.65.7.
108 Diodorus 3.64.5–6. The Arabian Nysa is mentioned by Stephanus of Byzantium, who enumerates several places by that name (*Ethnica* 479). A Mount Nausaion in Arabia is also mentioned by Hippolytus (*Diamerismos* § 235).
109 The Ambrosia episode is documented in Hellenistic art and literature at least from the third century BC (Chuvin, *Mythologie* 256–257).
110 Nonnos, *Dionysiaca* 20:235 ff.: The fire of Arabia shall devour the vine.
111 Nonnos, *Dionysiaca* 21:1 ff.
112 Hajjar, *Triade* I 266–270; II pls. LXXI:187–192; LXXXVI:227.
113 Picard, *Frises* 331–335; cf. 337. The Ambrosia story is also found there; see Picard, *Frises* 339 ff.
114 Chuvin's arguments in favour of Scythopolis are not convincing (*Mythologie* 260–264). The town Beth Shean/Scythopolis was named Nysa after a member of the royal house of the Seleucids. This has obviously given the pretext for associating Dionysus with the town, as is documented from coins. But there is no trace of the Lycurgus story from Scythopolis and the town is not in Arabia. That the town was not Jewish either is irrelevant, and Klein's arguments against it (*Altertumskunde* 196) are still valid. Besides, Carmel in Nonnus is definitely not the mountain on the Palestinian coast, although an identification between the god of Baalbek and the one of Mount Carmel is not impossible; cf. Hajjar, *Triade* 267 ff.
115 *T.B. Ketubot* 112a; cf. pp. 419–420.
116 Cf. Sartre, *Bostra* 59.
117 Sourdel, *Cultes* 77; cf. Bowersock, *Ares* 43–44; Robert, *Épitaphe*.
118 Photius, *Bibliotheca* 242: Damascius 200; Stephanus 217.
119 Sourdel, *Cultes* 81–83.
120 Clermont-Ganneau, *Dieu* 392 ff.; cf. Cantineau, *Nabatéen* II 21; JS nab. 72 = Jaussen/Savignac, *Mission I* 221. Cf. Knauf, *Dushara* 176; Healey, *Religion* 143–147.
121 CIH 3973 (= Corpus II 156–157, cf. Littmann, *Inscriptions* 70–75): ʔLHʔ ṬBʔ WŠKRYʔ DY Lʔ ŠTʔ ḤMR. It is interesting that the name of the god in this text contains the Arabic definite article ʔL: ŠYʕ ʔLQWM.
122 Février, *Réligion* 33–38; Höfner/Merkel, *Stammesgruppen*. 465–466.

123 This identification has been doubted by Sourdel (*Cultes* 83–84), Dussaud (*Pénétration* 145–147) and Merkel (Höfner/Merkel, *Stammesgruppen* 451) but is supported by Healey, *Religion* 146. The claim is that the anti-Dionysiac myth in Nonnos has nothing to do with the Lycurgus cult in Syria and that Nonnos' (or his source) has transferred it there just because of the identity of names. There is thus no reason to identify Nonnos' Lycurgus with ŠYʕ LQWM. But the onomastic identity remains to be explained. The name is definitely Greek and has been applied to a local Syrian deity sometime before 400 BC. Since Lycurgus' main mythical role in Homer is that of the antagonist of Dionysus, it becomes very likely that it was this feature that gave the impetus for the identification. And the presence of the Arabs in Nonnos' story is difficult to explain unless it is acknowledged that they represent an essential part of the myth. The local Syrian god must thus have had a function similar to the Homerian Lycurgus, which makes the identity between Nonnos' Lycurgus and the Syrian god who does not drink wine very likely.

124 Cf. Sourdel, *Cultes* 63, and Knauf, *Dushares* 177–178. Starcky (*Pétra* 990) is more cautious.

125 Strabo 16.4.26. Remarkable is, however, that the author of the Palmyrene inscription to ŠYʕ ʔLQWM calls himself NBṬYʔ, 'Nabataean'. Even more interesting is that he says he has served at ḤYRTʔ = al-Ḥīra and ʕĀna, both on the middle Euphrates. His grandfather carried the Arabic name ŠʕDLT = Saʕd allāt. Obviously a *nabaṭī* could venerate the god of the Arabs just as the Arabs took part in the cult of the Nabataean gods in Elusa.

126 Cf. Clermont-Ganneau, *Dieu* 397; Knauf, *Dushara* 178. This god may have a different origin from Dionysus. He was represented by a standing stone, often with hints of a face engraved which does not immediately point to a wine-god. The cult of Dusares is also limited to an area commencing in the southern Ḥawrān and Ǧabal and southwards. It might well be that the role of Dionysus south of this line was played by Dusares and that the two were kept apart.

127 As assumed by Chuvin, *Mythologie* 267, Knauf, *Dushara* 178, and Healey, *Religion* 147. The widespread idea among scholars that 'nomads' do not drink wine or alcohol is curious. One does not have to read many lines of Arabic *Ǧāhiliyya* poetry, composed by alleged 'nomads', before one encounters lines describing wine drinking in the most glowing terms, let alone, for example, the kumys-imbibing nomads of central Asia. The whole idea of the eternal contrast and conflict between the peaceful, wine-cultivating farmers and the wild but sober 'nomads' or 'bedouin' belongs to the myths of scholarship which should definitely be discarded. It should also be observed that the wine prohibition in the Qurʔān has nothing to do with nomadism, since all scholars agree that the message in the Holy Book is not 'nomadic'. Instead the Qurʔān prescribes abstention from wine drinking for a religious community which, in fact, is an interesting and important parallel to the interpretation of the Lycurgus cult presented here.

128 To this can be added the worship of the dead Obodas in the Negev. Epiphanius (55.1.9) has a curious notice which should be connected with this complex. It is said that 'those who live in Arabia of the Petraeans called Rokom and Edom consider Moses a god because of the divine signs. They prostrate themselves to his picture which they have made as a copy. They err, not because of the right cause, but because the error has put together for them a fantasy of reality in their ignorance through that which is right'. This somewhat obscure description reflects the transfer of the Moses traditions to Petra, where he was the object of some kind of cult; cf. Mordtmann, *Dusares*.

129 See p. 190.

130 One should also observe the parallel between Lycurgus and Joseph in the ancient saying in Genesis 49:22–24 where the patriarch is likened with a vine which is assaulted by bowmen, a mythological scene which looks like a counterpart to Nonnos' account.

131 Ibn Hishām, *Sīra* 73.

132 Ibn Hishām, *Sīra* 54.

133 For the sources and the variants of the story of Quṣayy, see Levi della Vida, *Ḳuṣayy*.

134 Ibn Hishām, *Sīra* 79.

135 The text restored from the versions of Ibn Hishām (*Sīra* 75–76) and Ibn Saʕd (*Ṭabaqāt* I/1

38); cf. aṯ-Ṭabarī, *Tārīkh* I:1095.

136 Ibn Hishām, *Sīra* 79–80.

137 Kister, *Khuzāʕa* 78–79.

138 Kister, *Khuzāʕa* 77.

139 Symptomatic is that Ibn Isḥāq (or his editor Ibn Hishām) has suppressed the divine name, calling the son ʕAbd only. The original name is preserved, e.g. by Ibn Saʕd (*Ṭabaqāt* I:1 39) with a not too convincing attempt to explain it. Shahid (*Byzantium* 2 350–360) treats the story of Quṣayy as a quite trustworthy historical report. The notice in Ibn Qutayba's *Maʕārif* (640–641) about Byzantine involvement in Ḥiǧāzī politics may well be a memory of a fact. The dating of it remains uncertain.

140 Ibn Hishām, *Sīra* 59.

141 The word *ʕarab* appears more frequently in this story than in the surrounding texts in Ibn Hishām/Ibn Isḥāq. The same holds for the version in al-Yaʕqūbī, *Tārīkh* I:275–276 where it is obvious that *ʕarab* is a cultic term for those, or rather some of those, taking part in the pilgrimage, separate from Quraysh and Kināna. In the early part of the history of Ibn Isḥāq, the word *ʕarab* appears almost exclusively in cultic contexts; see e.g. the chapter on the *ḥums* (Ibn Hishām, *Sīra* 126, 128–129).

142 See p. 71.

143 The ʕUdhra tribe was not identical with the *ʕarab*. According to al-Bakrī (*Muʕǧam* 30), the ʕUdhra made a covenant with the Jews in the Wādī to protect them from the *ʕarab*.

144 See p. 55. It may be remarked that in Islamic tradition there was a Quḍāʕa also in Yemen, namely in the north around Saʕda. It is perhaps no coincidence that this is the region where we can discern an important Arab settlement, well-documented even in the pre-Islamic inscriptions; see p. 564 and Robin, *Hautes-terres* 27–39. Perhaps the term Quḍāʕa has something to do with this Arab presence. Unfortunately, its etymology is obscure.

145 Sourdel, *Cultes* 81; Cantineau, *Nabatéen* II 21 (= Jaussen/Savignac Nab 72).

146 Lane, *Lexicon* s.vv. QṢW and QṢṢ. The later legend says he got his name beacuse he was raised far away (QṢY) from Mecca, cf. Levi della Vida, *Ḳuṣayy*), which sounds very much like a popular etymology.

SUMMING UP: THE ARABS FROM THE ASSYRIANS TO THE UMAYYADS

The conclusion arrived at in this investigation, namely that the term 'Arab' designates a community of people with war-like properties, standing under the command of a divine hero, being intimately connected with the use of the domesticated camel, should not be misunderstood. It is obvious that in many instances, the originator of the ancient source did not have this meaning in mind. To many the meaning itself was probably unknown. But this does not necessarily mean that the word had a vague and general meaning to everybody. In the time of the Soviet Union the inhabitants were often designated Russians by outsiders. This did not mean that the word was a legitimate general designation for the inhabitants of the USSR and nothing else. In that empire of nationalities most people had very clear ideas about what a Russian was and almost half of them did not consider themselves to be Russians in any sense of the word. The word 'Arab' in antiquity would have had a similar status. We have pointed out at least one general usage which is clearly not the proper one, namely the general designation of the inhabitants of Arabia as defined by Greek geographers. The usage of the word in the ancient sources is thus variegated. This does not mean, however, that the word itself had a vague and general meaning for those who originally had coined it and who continued to use it in its original meaning. We think we have been able to point out a sufficient number of occurrences of the word 'Arab' where it has a very specialized and distinct usage and we think that there is little doubt that we here have its original and proper meaning. Finding out this was the main aim of this investigation.

A development of the meaning of the term in the period before the rise of Islam cannot be ruled out. Such a development is not, however, detectable in the sources and remains hypothetical. There is further no doubt that there is a continuity in the use of the term from the earliest times until the early Islamic period. This is evident from the documentation in Ancient South Arabian and explains the use of it in the early Islamic sources. For the Islamic period the documentation of the change of the meaning of the designation Arab is well documented and the variegated meaning of the term in these sources is an important indication that the large compilations of the Islamic historians contain materials originating in different stages of the earliest Islamic history.

This does not necessarily mean that every Arab mentioned in the pre-Islamic texts was an active member of the community we have suggested as the origin of the term. Some of the Arabs appearing, for example, in the Ptolemaic papyri are not immediately connected with either war or camels. We have no reason to assume that the ʕRBYT mentioned in some ancient South Arabian texts were Arab counterparts to the amazons. It could well be that the Arab identity once acquired became a characteristic that could not be deleted. It could perhaps be inherited. We have no indication of this in the sources but the application of the term 'Arab' on the tribal members in the later Umayyad period could have been facilitated if this had originally been the case. And the *ʕarabiyyāt* in the South Arabian texts could be women married to or descending from Arabs proper. In spite of the apparent variegated use of the term 'Arab' in ancient and early Islamic sources, there is no doubt about what it did *not* designate: nomad, inhabitant of the peninsula or even a nationality. In the cases where the ancient evidence becomes detailed and explicit enough it points in another direction.

We shall finally give a summary of what has been found during this investigation. At last we discard the use of modal auxiliaries and formulate a series of propositions which constitute the core of our conclusions, making up a plausible historical narrative of the rise and fall of the Arabs, and thus a history in the Herodotean sense of the word. That many of these propositions, in fact, must remain hypothetical in different degrees will be evident to whoever has read the preceding account.

The term 'Arab' originally designated a community which was the special property of a semi-divine hero, leading them as a kind of police force during certain renewal festivals. It existed in several places in Arabia as well as in the border regions. Membership was constituted by an initiation ceremony, which included a nightly vigil and cropping of one's hair as an outer sign of dependence on the semi-divine leader-hero. This figure was represented by an official or a chief, functioning as a commander. The initiation took place at a specific asylum or sanctuary named HGR. The Arabs remained a closed community, settled in special villages spread among the other settlers or situated on the border between the desert and the sown. They stood under special taboos which prohibited them from living in built houses, tilling the soil or using wine. Because of these taboos they tended to live in symbiosis with farmers and tradesmen, whom they served as protectors. These were called *nabaṭ*, Nabataeans. The Arabs were not the only community of their kind in Arabia or the ancient Middle East, but they had a characteristic feature not shared by others: their handling of the camel, an animal which already played a role in the initiation. Its preference for large pasture grounds and dry climate determined the whereabouts of the Arabs in regions outside the main settlements, wandering between the desert and the sown.

The Arab communities, as we know them, arose together with the final domestication of the camel and its use as a riding animal around 900 BC. Due to their status as partial outsiders in relation to the normal settlers, together with their control of 'the police car of the desert', the camel, they could function not only as guards and police forces in the original cultic contexts but also as regular employees of the rulers of the oases of Arabia or chiefs of peripheral agricultural regions of the Fertile Crescent and South Arabia. They were often individually recruited from the original Arab communities and were then designated by a term derived from the proper term *ʕarab*.

There was also a language associated with the Arabs and named after them. This, together with the frequent reference to Arab soothsayers and poets in early Islamic sources, indicates that some of them had special contact with the divine world and brought messages in a distinctive tongue. The language was not necessarily the same in all Arab communities but had the common features of being partly archaic and not spoken in everyday life either by the Arabs or by others. The separateness of the Arabs fostered the appearance of soothsayers and people mastering shamanistic techniques among them.

These communities were drawn into world history by the Assyrians, although the first states known to have employed Arabs as auxiliaries are the states in Syria in the ninth century BC. The Assyrians from Tiglath Pileser III onwards tried to control Arab communities in the Syrian desert and also employed them as guards against the Egyptian border, as a police force in Mesopotamia, and even as officials in the administration of the empire. These efforts culminated in the armed conflicts between the Assyrians under Sennacherib, Esarhaddon and Assurbanipal, and the Arabs in Dumah, their earliest known independent settlement.

The integration of Arabs into the military system of the great empires was continued and increased by the Achaemenids, who stationed Arabs around their empire. Apart from the border region between Syria and Egypt, they were established in Egypt proper, in the Antilebanon and in the northern Ğazīra. These Arab settlements played an important role in the history of the Middle East down to the breakdown of the Seleucids and the arrival of the Romans, and the period between 500 and 100 BC was the heyday of the Arabs in antiquity. Especially in Syria, the Arabs came to play a key role in the struggle between the direct heirs of the Achaemenid rulers: the Seleucids and the Ptolemies. The main centre of Arabs was the Arabo-Nabataean kingdom located between Palestine and Egypt, originally founded in the later Assyrian period and lasting until the first century AD. The core of this entity, apart from the farming and trading *nabaṭ*, was the tribe of Qedar, which in its turn was led by an Arab king. To this bastion of Arab presence was added the Arabia between the Two Rivers, the Khābūr and the Sinğar mountains, already existing in the late Assyrian period and living on until the third century AD. The increased importance of the Arabs effected by the Achaemenids is reflected in their appearances in Greek literature from Herodotus to Hieronymus of Cardia, which, in spite of being second-hand reports by outsiders, constitute the basic testimonies we have about the nature of the Arab communities.

The position of the Arabs in Syria and adjacent lands started to decline with the arrival of the Romans in the first century BC, culminating in the abolition of the Arabo-Nabataean kingdom in AD 106. The Arabs in the Ğazīra continued to play a key role for a century, due to the struggle between Rome and the Parthians. But during the third century AD the Arab kingdom in Hatra was dismantled like its Arabo-Nabataean colleague and disappeared from history. The last Arabs in the north comprised the kingdom of ʕAmr b. ʕAdī and Imruʔ al-Qays, established with Roman support in the aftermath of the fall of Palmyra. In the Middle East, the Arabs were replaced by a new military system, recruiting the inhabitants of the deserts called Saracens. Among them were, of course, many descendants of the Arabs, but the Arabs as an institution had lost importance due to the political changes and the development of new military technology: the introduction of the horse and armoured cavalry.

The South Arabian kingdoms also employed Arabs as border-guards and auxiliaries, at least from the first century AD. The Arab institution never became outdated in South Arabia but continued to operate until the rise of Islam. In other parts of Arabia too, such as Ḥiğāz, al-Ḥasā and the Yamāma, the ancient Arab communities continued to exist more or less unaffected by the rise and fall of the empires. Based in or around some of the main oases, they still functioned, for example, as guards during the festivals, as is visible from what is told about the early history of Mecca. Even though they had lost the military weight they originally possessed due to the process of 'Saracenization', i.e. the introduction of the new military technology into Arabia, they continued to enjoy some kind of status. But their most enduring influence was the spread of the language named after them, originally used by their soothsayers and oracle priests, now re-employed as the vehicle of an emerging tradition of oral poetry spreading rapidly among the tribes in Arabia after AD 450. The poetic tradition had many of its most important roots among the Arabs living in South Arabia in symbiosis with the empires and was diffused via the rule of the Himyarites and their agents in central and eastern Arabia.

The concept of *ʕarab* was on the verge of disappearing altogether when the major events started in the Ḥiǧāz in the first decades of the seventh century AD. The message of the prophet of the new religion was delivered in the language of the Arabs, a sign of its being of divine origin. When the Islamic community was established in Medina, it incorporated a segment of traditional Arabs, recruited as guardians of that oasis, who initially belonged to the lower ranks of the new movement. When the sanctuary of Mecca finally became the rallying point of Islam around AD 630, the Arabs who had functioned in the rituals as guardians and protectors, residing in the 'villages of the Arabs' in Ḥiǧāz, became attached to the new movement and played a certain role during its first decade. Besides, the term 'Arab' was revived as a designation for some of the tribes who emerged as supporters of the divinely inspired Prophet. The traditional Arabs from the villages in Ḥiǧāz belonged to those groups in early Islamic history who were steadily losing their influence upon the emergence of the aristocracy of Quraysh and the traditional aristocracy of the large tribes in central and eastern Arabia. From the 650s, these Arabs and the Muslims from Medina begin to appear together in an alliance of people with decreasing influence. Their alliance was natural since both had played the role of helpers and assistants to the core groups of the Islamic movement.

From now on, 'Arab' became a designation for a party within the Islamic community and could be used by groups dissatisfied with their position. This meant that it started to spread and was used by other groups as well, and it was gradually transformed into a status term. During the second Islamic civil war in the 680s it was adopted even by the tribal aristocracy itself, to a large extent triggered by the now fast-growing opposition of groups from Iraq and Iran, who had never had any connections with Arabia. A testimony of this is the promulgation of the language of the *ʕarab* as the official language of the Islamic empire under ʕAbd al-Malik. This development culminated in the reign of ʕUmar ibn ʕAbd al-ʕAzīz when 'Arab' was launched as a designation for the entire Muslim community. This was a propagandistic device which did not work in the long run, but henceforth 'Arab' became the proper and accepted designation for the full tribal members of the Islamic state, and it has lived on ever since as the term for a genuine tribesman, regardless of where or how he lives. The declining Yemeni party managed to convince at least the historians and genealogists of later times that they were those who were closest to the original Arabs, an institution which by then had disappeared completely even from Arabia, and whose characteristics were forgotten. They were remembered only as the vague figures of 'the lost Arabs', *al-ʕarab al-bāʔida*.

BIBLIOGRAPHY

Abbreviations

AA L'Arabie antique de Karib'îl à Mahomet. Nouvelles données sur l'histoire des Arabes grâce aux inscriptions (Revue du monde musulman et de la Méditerranée 61, Paris 1991).
AAW Die Araber in der Alten Welt 1–5 ed. F. Altheim and R. Stiehl Berlin 1965–1968.
ABD The Anchor Bible Dictionary vols 1–6 ed. by D. N. Friedman, New York 1992.
ADAJ Annual of the Department of Antiquities, Jordan.
AION Istituto Orientale di Napoli. Annali.
AfO Archiv für Orientkunde.
AMB L'Arabie et ses mers bordières I: Itinéraires et voyages ed. J.-F. Salles, Lyon/Paris 1988.
ANRW Aufstieg und Niedergang der Römischen Welt Berlin/New York 1972–.
APEHC L'Arabie préislamique et son environnement historique et culturel. Actes du Colloque de Strasbourg 24–27 juin 1987 ed. T. Fahd, Leiden 1989.
Arabia Felix = Arabia Felix. Beiträge zur Sprache und Kultur des vorislamischen Arabien. Festschrift Walter W. Müller zum 60 Geburtstag, Wiesbaden 1994.
ArAnt 1 Arabia Antiqua. Hellenistic Centres Around Arabia ed. A. Invernizzi/ J.-F. Salles, Roma 1993 (Serie Orientale Roma LXX, 2).
ArAnt 2 Arabia Antiqua. Early Origins of South Arabian States. Proceedings of the First International Conference on the Conservation and Exploitation of the Archaeological Heritage of the Arabian Peninsula Held in the Palazzo Brancaccio, Rome, by IsMEO on 28th–30th of March 1991 ed. Ch. Robin and I. Gajda, Roma 1996 (Serie Orientale Roma LXX, 1).
AS Joseph Henninger, *Arabica Sacra. Aufsätze zur Religionsgeschichte Arabiens und seiner Randgebiete*, Freiburg/Göttingen 1981 (Orbis Biblicus et Orientalis 40).
ASB L'Antica Società Beduina ed. F. Gabrieli, Roma 1959 (Studi Semitici 2).
AV Joseph Henninger: *Arabica Varia. Aufsätze zur Kulturgeschichte Arabiens und seine Randgebiete*, Freiburg/Göttingen 1989 (Orbis Biblicus et Orientalis 90).
BiOr Bibliotheca Orientalis.
BKAT Biblischer Kommentar zum Alten Testament.
BN Biblische Notizen.
BSOAS Bulletin of the School of Oriental and African Studies.
CIH = Corpus inscriptionum semiticarum pars quarta inscriptiones ḥimyariticas et sabaeas continens t. I–III, Paris 1889–1929.
CIH II = Corpus inscriptionum semiticarum pars secunda inscriptiones aramaicas continens, t. 3, Paris 1924.
CQ The Classical Quarterly.
CRAIBL Académie des Inscriptions et Belles-lettres. Comptes rendus.
CSCO Corpus Scriptorum Christianorum Orientalium.
EI [1] Enzyklopädie des Islam 1 ed. Leiden/Leipzig 1913–1938.
EI [2] Encyclopedia of Islam 2nd ed. Leiden 1960–.
EJ Encyclopaedia Judaica, corrected edition, Jerusalem 1996.
FHG Fragmenta Historicorum Graecorum I–IV ed. C. and Th. Mueller, Paris 1841–1868.
GAPh Grundriss der arabischen Philologie Bd. 1: Sprachwissenschaft hrsg. W. Fischer, Wiesbaden 1982.

GCS Die Griechischen Christlichen Schriftsteller.
JA Journal Asiatique.
JAOS Journal of the American Oriental Society.
JBL Journal of Biblical Literature.
JESHO Journal of the Economic and Social History of the Orient.
JJS Journal of Jewish Studies.
JRAS Journal of the Royal Asiatic Society.
JSAI Jerusalem Studies in Arabic and Islam.
JSOT Journal for the Study of the Old Testament.
JSS Journal of Semitic Studies.
KS Alt, A: *Kleine Schriften I–III*, München 1953–1959.
LÄ Lexikon der Ägyptologie I–, Wiesbaden 1975–.
LCL. Loeb Classical Library.
MGH Monumenta Germaniae Historica Auctorum Antiquissimorum t. XI: Chronica minora saec. IV, V, VI, VII Vol. II ed. Th. Mommsen, nova ed. Berlin 1961.
MGWJ Monatsschrift für Geschichte und Wissenschaft des Judentums.
MPMP Mythologie gréco-romaine, mythologies périphériques. Études d'iconographie Paris 17 mai 1979 ed. L. Kahil/Ch. Augé, Paris 1981 (Colloques internationaux du Centre national de la Recherche Scientifique 593).
MUSJ Mélanges de l'Université Saint-Joseph.
OrAnt Oriens Antiquus.
PA Présence arabe dans le Croissant fertile avant l'Hégire. Actes de la Table ronde internationale (Paris 13 novembre 1993), Paris 1995.
PG Patrologiae cursus completus. Series Graeca ed. J.-P. Migne.
PL Patrologiae cursus completus Series Latina ed. J.-P. Migne.
PSAS Proceedings of the Seminar for Arabian Studies.
RA Reallexikon der Assyriologie und vorderasiatische Archäologie I–, Berlin/Leipzig 1928–.
RACh Reallexikon für Antike und Christentum 1–, 1950–.
RE Paulys Real-Encyclopädie der klassischen Altertumswissenschaften hrsg. von G. Wissowa 1894–.
RÉS = *Répertoire d'épigraphie sémitique* t. V–VII, Paris 1928–1950.
SDB Supplément de la Dictionnaire de la Bible.
SHA I Studies in the History of Arabia Vol. 1: Sources for the History of Arabia Part 1, Riyadh 1979.
TUAT Texte aus der Umwelt des Alten Testament.
WMANT Wissenschaftliche Monographien zur Alten und Neuen Testament.
WO Die Welt des Orients.
WZKM Wiener Zeitschrift für die Kunde des Morgenlandes.
ZA Zeitschrift für Assyriologie.
ZAW Zeitschrift für alttestamentliche Wissenschaft.
ZDMG Zeitschrift der Deutschen Morgenländischen Gesellschaft.
ZDPV Zeitschrift des Deutschen Palästinavereins.

Sources

General

Dodgeon, M. and Lieu, S. N. C.: *The Roman Eastern Frontier and the Persian Wars (AD 226–363): A Documentary History*, London/New York 1991.
Fontes Historiae Nubiorum. Textual Sources for the History of the Middle Nile Region Between the Eighth Century BC and the Sixth Century AD Vol. I: From the Eighth to the Mid-Fifth Century AD ed. T. Eide. T. Hägg, R. H. Pierce and L. Török, Bergen 1994.
Kramer, S. N. and Maier, J.: *Myths of Enki, the Crafty God*, Oxford 1989.
Pritchard, J. B.: *Ancient Near Eastern Texts Relating to the Old Testament* 2nd edn., Princeton 1955.

Akkadian

Borger, R.: 'Assyrische Staatsverträge', *TUAT 1* 1987–85 155–177.
Borger, R.: 'Historische Texte in akkadischer Sprache aus Babylonien und Assyrien', *TUAT 1* 1987–85 354–407.
Cavigneaux, A. and Ismail, B. Kh.: 'Die Statthalter von Suhu und Mari im 8 JH. v. Chr. anhand neuer Texte aus den irakischen Grabungen im Staugebiet des Qadissiya-Damms', *Baghdader Mitteilungen* 21 (1990) 321–411.
Barnett, R. D. and Falkner, M.: *The Sculptures of Aššur-Naṣir-Apli (883–859 BC), Tiglath Pileser III (745–727 BC), Esarhaddon (681–669 BC) from the Central and South-West Palaces at Nimrud*, London 1962.
Fales, M./Postgate, J. N.: *State Archives of Assyria XI: Imperial Administrative Records Part I: Palace and Temple Administration,* Helsinki 1992; *Part II: Provincial and Military Administration*, Helsinki 1995.
Grayson, A. K.: 'Akkadian Treaties of the Seventh Century BC', *Journal of Cuneiform Studies* 39 (1987) 127–160.
Grayson, A. K.: *Assyrian and Babylonian Chronicles*, Locust Valley 1975 (Texts from Cuneiform Studies Vol. V).
Luckenbill, *Records = Ancient Records of Assyria and Babylonia* by D. D. Luckenbill, Vol. I: *Historical Records of Assyria from the Earliest Times to Sargon*, Chicago 1926 repr. London 1989; Vol. II: *Historical Records of Assyria from Sargon to the End*, Chicago 1927, repr. London 1989.
Parpola, S.: 'Neo-Assyrian Treaties from the Royal Archives', *Journal of Cuneiform Studies* 39 (1987) 161–189.
Parpola, S. and Watanabe, K.: *State Archives of Assyria II: Neo-Assyrian Treaties and Loyalty Oaths*, Helsinki 1988.
Saggs, H. W. F.: 'The Nimrud Letters, 1952 – Part II', *Iraq* 17 (1955) 126–160.
Waterman, L.: *Royal Correspondence of the Assyrian Empire* translated into English, with a transliteration of the text and a commentary I–IV, Ann Arbor 1930–1936.
Wiseman, D. J.: *Chronicles of the Babylonian Kings* (626–556 BC) in the British Museum, London 1956.

Assurbanipal

Bauer, Th.: *Das Inschriftenwerk Assurbanipals vervollständigt und neu bearbeitet* II Teil: Bearbeitung, Leipzig 1933 (Assyriologische Bibliothek N. F. Bd II).
Borger, R.: *Beiträge zum Inschriftenwerk Assurbanipals* mit einem Beitrag von A. Fuchs, Wiesbaden 1996.
Buis, P.: 'Un traité d'Assurbanipal', *Vetus Testamentum* 28 (1978) 469–472.
Deller, K. and Parpola, S.: 'Ein Vertrag Assurbanipals mit dem arabischen Stamm Qedar', *Orientalia* 37 (1968) 464–466.
Grayson, A. K.: 'Akkadian Treaties of the Seventh Century BC', *Journal of Cuneiform Studies* 39 (1987) 127–160.
Piepkorn, A. C.: *Historical Prism Inscriptions of Ashurbanipal*, Chicago 1933.
Streck, M.: *Assurbanipal und die assyrischen Könige bis zum Untergang Nineveh's II Teil: Texte,* Leipzig 1916.
Thompson, R. C. and Mallowan, M. E. L.: 'The British Museum Excavations at Nineveh', *Annals of Archaeology and Anthropology* 20 (1933) 71–186.
Weidner, E. F.: 'Assyrische Beschreibungen der Kriegs-Reliefs Aššurbânaplis', *AfO* 8 (1932/1933) 175–203.
Weippert, M.: 'Die Kämpfe des assyrischen Königs Assurbanipal gegen die Araber. Redaktionskritische Untersuchung des Berichts in Prisma A', *WO* 7 (1973–74) 39–85.

Esarhaddon

Borger, R.: *Die Inschriften Asarhaddons Königs von Assyrien*, Osnabrück 1967 (Neudruck der Ausgabe 1956).
Heidel, A.: 'A New Hexagonal Prism of Esarhaddon (676 BC)', *Sumer* 12 (1956) 9–37.

Nabonidus

The Nabonidus Chronicle = S. Smith, *Babylonian Historical Texts Relating to the Capture and Downfall of Babylon*, London 1924, repr. Hildesheim 1975 98–123.

The Royal Chronicle = Lambert, W. G.: 'A New Source for the Reign of Nabonidus', *AfO* 22 (1968/1969) 1–8.

Harran Stele nr 2 (H2) = Gadd, C. J.: 'The Harran Inscriptions of Nabonidus', *Anatolian Studies* 8 (1958) 35–92.

Salmaneser III

Grayson, A. K.: *Assyrian Rulers of the Early First Millenium BC II (858–745 BC)*, Toronto 1996 (The Royal Inscriptions of Mesopotamia: Assyrian Periods 3).

Michel, E.: 'Die Assur-Texte Salmanassars III. (858–824)', *WO* 2 (1947) 57–71.

King, *Reliefs* = King, L. W.: *Bronze Reliefs from the Gates of Shalmaneser, King of Assyria BC 860–825*, London 1915.

Sargon II

The Assur Charter = Winckler, H.: 'Zur babylonisch-assyrischen Geschichte', *Altorientalische Forschungen* I, Leipzig 1897 371–420.

The Inscriptions of Sargon II, King of Assyria Part I: The Annals. Transliterated and translated by A. G. Lie, Paris 1929.

Gadd, C. J.: 'Inscribed Prisms of Sargon II from Nimrud', *Iraq* 16 (1954) 171–201.

Parpola, S.: *State Archives of Assyria I: The Correspondence of Sargon II Part I: Letters from Assyria and the West*, Helsinki 1987.

Weidner, E. F.: 'Šilkan(he)ni, König von Muṣri, ein Zeitgenosse Sargons II', *AfO* 14 (1941/1944) 40–53.

Sennacherib

Luckenbill, D. D.: *The Annals of Sennacherib*, Chicago 1924.

Paterson, A.: *Assyrian Sculpture. Palace of Sinacherib. Plates and Ground Plan of the Palace*, The Hague 1912–1914.

Tiglath Pileser III

Annals = Tadmor, H.: *The Inscriptions of Tiglath-Pileser III, King of Assyria*, Jerusalem 1994 27–89.

Iran-Stela = ibid. 90–110.

Summary inscriptions = ibid. 117–204.

Tukulti Ninurta III

Tukulti Ninurta, *Annales = Annales de Tukulti Ninip II, Roi d'Assyrie 889–884* par V. Scheil et J.-Et. Gauthier, Paris 1909.

Weidner, Tiglatpileser = Weidner, E. 'Die Feldzüge und Bauten Tiglatpilesers I', *AfO* 18 (1957–58) 342–360.

Persian

Cyrus Cylinder = Weissbach, F. H.: *Die Keilinschriften der Achämeniden*, Leipzig 1911 2–9.

Gignoux, Ph.: 'L'organisation administrative sasanide: le cas de *marzbān*', *JSAI* 14 (1984) 1–29.

Hallock, R. T.: 'Selected Fortification Texts', *Cahier de la Délégation archéologique francaise en Iran* 8 (1978) 109–136.

Kent, R. G.: *Old Persian. Grammar, Texts, Lexicon*, 2nd edn., New Haven 1953.

Malbran-Labat, F.: *La version akkadienne de l'inscription trilingue de Darius À Behistun*, Roma 1994.

Paikuli = Humbach, H. and Skjaervö, P. O.: *The Sassanian Inscription of Paikuli 3:1: Restored Text and Translation*, Wiesbaden 1983.

Shahpur, *Res Gestae* = Maricq, A: 'Classica et orientalia 5: Res gestae Divi Saporis', *Syria* 35 (1958) 295–360.

Vallat, F.: 'Table accadienne de Darius Ier (DSaa)', *Fragmenta Historiae Aelamicae. Mélanges offerts à M.-J. Steve* ed. L. De Meyer, H. Gasche, H. and F. Vallat, Paris 1986 277–283.
Walser, G.: *Die Völkerschaften auf den Reliefs von Persepolis. Historische Studien über den sogenannten Tributzug an der Apadanatreppe*, Berlin 1966 (Teheraner Forschungen hrsg. vom Deutschen Archäologischen Institut, Abteilung Teheran Bd 2).
Yoyotte, J.: 'Une statue de Darius découverte à Suse: Les inscriptions hiéroglyphiques: Darius et l'Égypte', *JA* 260 (1977) 253–266.

Egyptian/Coptic

Spiegelberg, *Mythus = Der ägyptische Mythus vom Sonnenauge (der Papyrus der Tierfabeln – 'Kufi') nach dem Leidner demotischen Papyrus I 384* bearbeiter von W. Spiegelberg, Strassburg 1917, repr. Hildesheim 1994.
Tardieu, M.: 'L'arrivée des manichéens à al-Ḥīra', *La Syrie de Byzance à l'Islam VIIe–VIIIe siècles. Actes du Colloque international Lyon – Maison d'Orient Méditerranéen Paris – Institut du Monde Arabe 11–15 Septembre 1990* ed. P. Canivet and J.-P. Rey-Coquais, Damas 1992 15–24.

Hebrew and Judaeo-Aramaic

Epigraphic

Avigad, N.: *Hebrew Bullae from the Time of Jeremiah. Remnants of a Burnt Archive*, Jerusalem 1986.
Mosaic Inscription from the Synagogue of Rehov ed. Y. Israeli, The Israel Museum 1978 (Cat. No. 176).

Literary

Biblia Hebraica Stuttgartensia ed. K. Elliger/W. Rudolph, Stuttgart 1967/1977.
The Fragment-Targums of the Pentateuch According to the Extant Sources I–II ed. M. L. Klein (Analecta Biblica 76) Roma 1986.
Maseket Abôt d-Rabî Natan bi-štê nôsaḥôt ed. S. Schechter, Vienna 1887.
Mekilta de-Rabbi Ishmael I-III, ed. and transl. J. Z. Lauterbach, Philadelphia 1933–1935.
Midrash Bereshit Rabba. Critical edition with notes and commentary by J. Theodor and Ch. Albeck, 2nd edn. by Ch. Albeck, Jerusalem 1965.
Midrash Echa Rabbati. Sammlung agadischer Auslegungen der Klagelieder, hrsg. S. Buber, Vilna 1899.
Midrash rabbah 1–11 ed. M. A. Mirkin, Tel Aviv 1956.
Midrash Tanḥumā ed. Ḥ. Zundel B"R Josef, Yerûshalayim TWBB"?.
Midrash Tehillim ed. S. Buber, Vilna 1892 repr. Jerusalem 1966.
Monumenta Talmudica Bd 1: Bibel und Babel ed. S. Funk Wien/Leipzig 1913.
Pseudo-Jonathan (Targum Jonathan ben Usiël zum Pentateuch) hrsg. M. Ginsburger, Berlin 1903.
Sifrê ʕal sefer Devarîm ed. E. A. Finkelstein (Corpus Tannaiticum: Sectio Textus P. III: Siphre d'be Rab fasc. II: Siphre ad Deuteronomium) Berlin 1939, repr. New York 1969.
Šišā sidrê Mišnā mefûrašîm bîdê Ḥ. Albeq ûmenûqad bîdê Ḥ. Yalôn, Jerusalem 1959 repr. ibid. 1973.
Sperber, A.: *The Bible in Aramaic I–IV*, Leiden 1959–1973 repr. 1992.

Talmud Babli:
Talmûd Bavlî ʕim kol ha-mefarešîm kaʔašer nidpas mi-qedem, Yerûšalayyim TWBB"?.
Der Babylonische Talmud neu übertragen von L. Goldschmidt I–XII, Berlin 1930–1936.
Talmûd Yerûšalmî, Krotoshin 1866.
Targum Neophyti = Diez Macho, A.: *MS Neophyti I. Targum Palestinense MS de la Biblioteca Vaticana I: Genesis*, Barcelona 1968.
Targum Onkelos, hrsg. A. Berliner, Berlin 1884.
Tosephta ed. M. S. Zuckermandel. With Supplement to the Tosephta by S. Liebermann, new ed. Jerusalem 1970.

Yalquṭ Šimʕoni ʕim mavo we-hašlamot 1–2, Jerusalem 5720 [1960].

Ethiopic

Pereira, *Historia* = *Historia dos martyres de Nagran. Versâo ethiopica* ed. and trans. F. M. Esteves Pereira, Lisboa 1899.

Johannes, *Chronique* = *Chronique de Jean, éveque de Nikiou.* Texte éthiopien publié et traduit par M. H. Zotenberg, Paris 1883 (Notices des manuscrits T. 24:1).

Jubilees = *The Book of Jubilees.* A Critical Text ed. and trans. by J. C. Vanderkam, Louvain 1989 (CSCO Vol. 510–511: Scriptores Aethiopici t. 87–88).

Recueil des inscriptions de l'Éthiopie des périodes pré-axoumite et axoumite t. I: Les documents, t. II: Commentaire ed. E. Bernand, A. J. Drewes and R. Schneider, Paris 1991.

Greek

Papyri, parchments

Bell, *Aphrodito* = *Greek Papyri in the British Museum. Catalogue with Texts, Vol. IV: The Aphrodito Papyri* ed. by H. I. Bell. With an Appendix of Coptic Papyri, ed. by W. E. Crum, London 1910.

Bilabel, F.: *Sammelbuch Griechischer Urkunden aus Ägypten* Bd III:1, Berlin/Leipzig 1926.

Edgar, *Catalogue* = Edgar, C. C.: *Catalogue général des antiquités égyptiennes du Musée du Caire. Zenon papyri II–III*, Le Caire 1926–1928.

Edgar, *Papyri* = Edgar, C. C.: *Zenon Papyri in the University of Michigan Collection*, Ann Arbor 1931.

Codex Manichaeus Colonensis = Heinrichs, A. and Koenen, L.: 'Der Kölner Mani-Kodex (P. Colon. inv. nr. 4780 Perì tēs gennēs toû sōmátou autoû. Edition der Seiten 1–72', *Zeitschrift für Papyrologie und Epigrafik* 19 (1975) 1–85.

Hunt, A. S. and Smiley, J. G.: *The Tebtunis Papyri* Vol. III part I, London 1933 (University of California Publications, Graeco-Roman Archaelogy III).

Jouguet, P. *et al.*: *Institut Papyrologique de l'Université de Lille, t. II: Papyrus de Magdola 2* éd. par J. Lesquier, Paris 1912.

Kiessling, E.: *Sammelbuch Griechischer Urkunden aus Ägypten, Beiheft 1*, Göttingen 1952.

Kraemer, *Excavations* = *Excavations at Nessana Vol. 3: Non-literary Papyri* by C. J. Kraemer, Princeton 1958.

Rostovtzeff, M. and Welles, C. B.: 'A Parchment Contract of Loan from Dura-Europus on the Euphrates', *Yale Classical Studies* 2 (1931) 3–78.

Welles, C. B, Fink, R. O. and Gilliam, J. F.: 'The Parchments and Papyri', *The Excavations at Dura-Europos Conducted by Yale University and the French Academy of Inscriptions and Letters: Final Report V:1*, ed. A. Perkins, New Haven 1959.

Vitelli, *Papiri* = *Papiri greci e latini vol. IV–V* ed. G. Vitelli, Firenze 1917.

Epigraphy

Ḥammat Gader = Green, J. and Tsafrir, Y.: 'Greek Inscriptions from Ḥammat Gader', *IEJ* 32 (1982) 77–96.

Kraeling, *Gerasa* = *Gerasa: City of the Decapolis* ed. C. H. Kraeling, New Haven 1938.

OGIS = *Orientis Graeci Inscriptiones Selectae* ed. W. Dittenberger I–II Leipzig 1903, 1905.

Piejko, F.: 'The Inscriptions of Icarus-Failaka', *Classica et Medievalia* 39 (1988) 89–116.

Priene = *Königliche Museen zu Berlin: Inschiften von Priene* hrsg. von F. Frhr. Hiller von Gaertringen, Berlin 1906.

Robert, L.: 'L'épitaphe d'un arabe à Thasos', *Hellenica* 2 (1946) 43–50.

Supplementum Epigraphicum Graecum IV (1930).

Literary works: General

Jacoby, F.: *Die Fragmente der griechischen Historiker.*

I: *Genealogie und Mythographie*, Berlin 1923.

II *Zeitgeschichte*:

A: *Universalgeschichte und Hellenika*, Berlin 1926.

B: *Spezialgeschichte, Autobiographien und Memoiren. Zeittafeln*, Berlin 1929.
III: *Geschichte von Städten und Völkern (Horographie und Ethnographie)*:
A: *Autoren über verschiedene Städte (Länder)*, Leiden 1940.
a: *Kommentare zu 209–296*, Leiden 1943.
C: Autoren *über einzelne Länder Nr. 608–856 Bd. 1: Ägypten-Geten Nr. 608a–708*, Leiden 1958.

Thesaurus Liguae Graecae CD-ROM #D, University of California, Irvine.

Literary works: individual authors

Aeschylus: *Prometheus Bound*, ed. M. Griffith, Cambridge 1983.

Anastasius Sinaites:
Dialogus contra Iudaeos PG 89 1204–1281.
Sermo III, *PG* 89 1151–1180.
Viae dux, PG 89 36–309.

Appian:
Brodersen, K.: *Appianus Abriss der Seleukidengeschichte (Syriaca 45.237–70.369) Text und Kommentar*, München 1989.
Appian's Roman History vol. III–IV: The Civil Wars ed. and trans. H. White, London/Cambridge 1955 (LCL).

Aristophanes, *Birds* = *Aristophanis Comoediae* I ed. F. W. Hall/W. M. Geldart, Oxford 1906.

Aristotle:
Historia Animalium = Aristote: *Histoire des animaux* I-–III, ed. et trad. P. Louis, Paris 1964.
Meteorology = Aristote: *Météorologiques* I, ed. et trad. P. Louis, Paris 1982.

Arrian:
Arrien: *L'Inde*. Texte et traduction P. Chantraine, 2 éd. Paris 1952.
Arrian: *Anabasis Alexandri. Indica* with an English translation by E. I. Robson I–II, Cambridge Mass./London 1958, 1960 (LCL).
Arrian with an English translation II: *Anabasis Alexandri Books V–VII; Indica* trans. P. A. Brunt, Cambridge, Mass./London 1983 (LCL).
Flavii Arriani quae exstant omnia I–II ed. A. G. Roos, Lipsiae 1907, 1928 (Teubner).

Basilius, *Commentarium in Isaiam prophetam*, *PG* 30 117–668.
Berossos, *Babyloniaca* = Schnabel, P.: *Berossos und die babylonisch-hellenistische Literatur*, Leipzig 1923 repr. Hildesheim 1968.

Cassius Dio:
Cassii Dionis Cocceiani Historiarum Romanarum quae supersunt I–V ed. V. Ph. Boissevain, Berlin 1895-1955.
Dio's Roman History with an English translation by E. Cary, vol. 1–9 London/Cambridge, Mass. 1954–1961 (LCL).

Clement:
Paedagogus = Clément d'Alexandrie, *Le Pédagogue* I–III ed. et trad. H.-I. Marrou, M. Harl, C. Mondésat and Ch. Matray, Paris 1960–1970.
Stromata = Clément d'Alexandrie: *Les stromates* I–II ed. et trad. M. Caster, Paris 1951, 1954 (Sources Chrétiennes).

Corpus Iuris Civilis Vol. III: Novellae ed. R. Schöll and W. Kroll, Berlin 1912.
Cosmas, *Synagoge* = *Cosmae Hierosolymitani commentaria in S. Gregorii Nazianzeni carmina collecti et interpretati PG* 38:341–680.
Cosmas Indicopleustès: *Topographie Chrétienne* I–III ed. W. Wolska-Conus, Paris 1968–1973 (Sources Chrétiennes 141, 159, 197).
Ctesias, *Persica* = König, F.W.: *Die Persika des Ktesias von Knidos*, Graz 1972 (Archiv für Orientforschung Beiheft 18).

Damascius, *Vita Isidori* = *Damascii Vitae Isidori Reliquiae* ed. C. Zintzen, Hildesheim 1967 (Bibliotheca Graeca et Latina Suppletoria).
Delphi Hymn, I = *Collectanea Alexandrina* ed. J. U. Powell, Oxford 1925 141.
Dio Chrysostom, *Discourse 4* = *Dionis Prusaensis qui vocatur Chrysostomus quae exstat*, Vol. I ed. J. de Arnim, Berlin 1962.

Diodorus Siculus:
Diodori Bibliotheca Historica I–V, ed. F. Vogel, Lipsiae 1888–1906.
Diodore de Sicile: *Bibliothèque historique. Introduction générale. Livre I* par F. Chamoux, P. Bertracet et Y. Vernière, Paris 1993.
Diodore de Sicile: *Bibliothèque historique, Livre XIX* ed. F. Bizière, Paris 1975.
Diodorus of Sicily with an English translation by C. H. Oldfather I–XII, London/New York/Cambridge, Mass. 1933–67 (LCL).

Dionysius Periegetes Graece et Latine ed. and comm. G. Bernhardy, Leipzig 1828.
Dioscurides: *Materia* = Pedanii Dioscuridis Anazarbei: *De Materia Medica Libri Quinque* vol. 1–3 ed. M. Wellmann, Berlin 1906–1919.
Epiphanius, *Panarion* = Epiphanius II: *Panarion haeresium 34–64, III 65–80 De Fide* hrsg. K. Holt 2 Ausg. J. Dummer, Berlin 1980, 1985.
Eunapius, History = Blockley, R. C.: *The Fragmentary Classicising Historians of the Later Roman Empire: Eunapius, Olympiodorus, Priscus, and Malchus* 2, Liverpool 1983 pp. 2–150.
Euripides' Bacchae ed. with introduction and commentary by E. R. Dodds 2 ed., Oxford 1960.

Eusebius:
Chronicle = *Eusebius Werke 7 Band: Die Chronik des Hieronymus 1–2* hrsg. R. Helm, Leipzig 1913, 1926.
Commentary = *Eusebius Werke Bd. 9: Der Jesajakommentar* hrsg. J. Ziegler, Berlin 1975.
History = Eusèbe de Césarée: *Histoire ecclésiastique I–IV* ed. et trad. G. Bardy, Paris 1952–1971.
Tricennatsrede = *Eusebius Werke 1* ed. I. A. Heikel, Leipzig 1902 193–259.
Onomasticon = *Eusebius Werke 3.1*: *Das Onomastikon* hrsg. E. Klostermann, Leipzig 1904 (GCS 11.1).
Praeparatio = *Eusebius Werke: Die Praeparatio Evangelica I–II* hrsg. K. Mras, 2 Ausg. hrsg. E. des Places, Berlin 1982–1983 (Die Griechischen Schriftsteller. Die ersten Jahrhunderte: Eusebius 8:1–2).

Evagrius, *History* = *The Ecclesiastical History of Evagrius including the scholia* ed. J. Bidez and L. Parmentier, London 1898.
The Greek New Testament ed. K. Aland, M. Black, C. M. Martini, B. M. Metzger and A. Wikgren, 3rd edn. United Bible Societies 1983.
Herodian in two volumes I–II with an English translation by C. R. Whittaker, London/Cambridge, Mass. 1969 (LCL).
Herodianus, *Prosody* = *Herodiani Technici reliquiae* T. I, ed. A. Lentz, Leipzig 1867.

Herodotus:
Herodoti Historiae I–II ed. C. Hude, 3 ed., Oxonii 1927.
Herodotus with an English translation by A. D. Godley in four volumes, Cambridge Mass./London 1920-81 (LCL).

Hesychius, *Lexicon* = *Hesychii Alexandrini Lexicon* I–II ed. K. Latte, Copenhagen 1953, 1966.
Hippolytos, *Chronik* = *Hippolytus Werke vierter Band: Die Chronik* hergestellt von A. Bauer, Leipzig 1929 (GCS 36).
Johannes Damascenus, *De haeresibus compendium PG* 94:677–780.
Johannes, *Narratio* = *Joannis Hierosolymitani reverentissimi monachi narratio*, *PG* 109:517–520.
Johannes Lydus, *De mensibus* = *Iohannis Laurentii Lydi Liber de Mensibus* ed. R. Wuensch, Leipzig 1898.

Josephus:
Flavii Iosephi opera omnia 1–6 ed. S. A. Naber, Leipzig 1888–1896.

Josephus, *Apion* = Flavius Josèphe: *Contre Apion* ed. Th. Reinach, trad. L. Blum, Paris 1930.
Flavius Josephus De Bello Judaico Der jüdische Krieg, Griechisch und Deutsch Bd I–III, hrsg. O. Michel and O. Bauernfeind, Darmstadt 1959–1969.
Josephus with an English translation by H. St. Thackeray Vol. I–II: *The Jewish War*, London/Cambridge, Mass. 1961–1962 (LCL).
Josephus with an English translation by H. St. Thackeray, R. Marcus, A. Wikgren and L. H. Feldman Vol. V–IX: *Jewish Antiquities*, London/Cambridge, Mass. 1961–1981 (LCL).

Julian:
Letters = L'Empereur Julien: *Oevres complètes t. I:2: Lettres et fragments* ed. et trad. J. Bidez, Paris 1924 (Budé).
Oratio = L'Empereur Julien: *Oevres complètes t. II: Discours de Julien l'empereur* ed. et trad. Ch. Lacombrade, Paris 1964 (Budé).

Justine, *Dialogue = Iustini philosophi et martyris dialogus cum Tryphone. Iustinus philosophi et martyris opera quae ferenda omnia* ed. I. C. Th. eques de Otto 3 Aufl. 1876 repr. Wiesbaden 1969.
Libanius, *Orations = Libanii opera vol. II: Orationes XII–XXV* ed. R. Foerster, Leipzig 1904.

Malalas:
Chronographia, PG 97: 65–718.
The Chronicle of John Malalas. A translation by E. Jeffreys, M. Jeffreys and R. Scott, Melbourne 1986.

Malchus of Philadelphia, *Byzantiaca* = Blockley, R. C.: *The Fragmentary Classicising Historians of the Later Roman Empire: Eunapius, Olympiodorus, Priscus and Malchus II: Text, Translation and Historiographical Notes*, Liverpool 1983 402–462.
Manetho with an English translation by W. G. Waddell, Cambridge, Mass./London 1940 (LCL).
Marinus, *Vita* = Marino di Neapoli: *Vita di Proclo. Testo critico, introduzione, traduzione e commentario* a cura di R. Masullo, Napoli 1985.
Maximus Tyrius, *Philosophumena* ed. H. Hobein, Leipzig 1910 (Teubner).
Nicander. The Poems and Poetical Fragments ed., comm. and trans. A. S. F. Gow and A. F. Scholfield, Cambridge 1953.
Nonnus, *Dionysiaca* = Nonnos de Panopolis: *Les Dionysiaques t. VIII Chants XX–XXIV* ed. N. Hopkinson, trad. F. Vian, Paris 1994 (Budé).
Die Oracula Sibyllina ed. J. Geffcken. Leipzig 1902 (GCS 8).

Origenes:
Commentarium in Euangelium Iohannis ed. E. Preuschen, Leipzig 1903 (GCS 10 Origenes Werke 4).
Contra Celsum = Origène, *Contre Celse* I–V, ed. M. Borret, Paris 1967–1976 (Sources chrétiennes 132).
Fragmenta in Psalmos 1–150 ed. J. B. Pitra, Venezia 1883 (Analecta sacra spicilegio Solesmensi parata Vols. 2–3).
Selecta in Genesim, PG 12:91–146.
The Philocalia of Origen ed. J. Armitage Robinson, Cambridge 1893.

Pelagia, Vita = *Pélagie la pénitente. Métamorphoses d'une légende T. I: Les textes et leur histoire*, ed. P. Petitmengin, M. Cazacu, F. Dolbeau, B. Flusin, A. Guillamont, F. Guillamont, L. Leloir, C. Lévy, J.-P. Rotschild, J.-Y. Tilliette et M. van Esbroeck, Paris 1981.
Periplus = The Periplus Maris Erythraei. Text with Introduction, Translation, and Commentary by L. Casson, Princeton 1989.

Philo:
De Iosepho = Philonis Alexandrini opera quae supersunt IV, ed. L. Cohn, Berlin 1902 61–118.
De virtutibus = Philonis Alexandrini opera quae supersunt V, Berlin 1906 266–335.
De vita Mosis = Philonis Alexandrini opera quae supersunt IV ed. L. Cohn, Berlin 1902 119–268.

Philostorgius, *History* = *Philostorgius Kirchengeschichte* hrsg. J. Bidez 2 Aufl. F. Winkelman, Berlin 1972.
Philostratus, *Vita Antonii* = Philostratos: *The Life of Apollonios of Tyana* 1–2 with an English translation by F. C. Conybeare Cambridge, Mass./London 1960 (LCL).
Photius: *Bibliothèque* I–VII ed. et trad. R. Henry, Paris 1959–1974.

Plutarch:
Plutarque, *Vies* ed. et trad. R. Flacelière et E. Chambry:
Alexander = *Vies IX: Aléxandre-César*, Paris 1975.
Crassus, Lucullus = *Vies VII: Cimon-Lucullus - Nicias-Crassus*, Paris 1972.
Pompey = *Vies VIII: Sertorius-Eumène - Agésilas-Pompée*, Paris 1973.
Demetrius = *Vies XIII: Démétrios-Antoine*, Paris 1977.

Polybius:
Histoire Livre V ed. et trad. P. Pédech, Paris 1977.
Polybii Historiae ed. L. Dindorf, rev. Th. Büttner-Wobst vol. III Leipzig 1893.

Procopius, *Wars* = *Procopius* with an English translation by H. B. Dearing, Cambridge Mass./London 1954 vols. I–VI: *History of the Wars* (LCL).
Pseudo-Scylax = *Geographi Graeci Minores I* ed. C. Müllerus, Paris 1955 15–96.

Ptolemy:
Claudii Ptolemaei Geographica ed. C. F. A. Nobbe, Leipzig 1843–45 repr. Hildesheim 1966.
Claudius Ptolemy: *The Geography* transl. and ed. E. L. Stevenson, New York 1932 repr. Toronto 1991.

Scholia Graeca in Aristophanem ed. F. Dübner, Paris 1877 repr. Hildesheim 1969
Sebeos, *Histoire* = *Histoire d'Héraclius par l'éveque Sebéos* traduite de l' arménien et annotée par F. Macler, Paris 1904.
Septuaginta id est Vetus Testamentum Graece iuxta LXX interpretes ed. A. Rahlfs, Stuttgart 1935 Vol. I–II.
Socrates, *History* = *Socratis Historia Ecclesiastica PG* 67:33–842.
Sophronius, *Ad Sergium* = *Sancti Sophronii Hierosolymitani Epistola Synodica ad Sergium Patriarcham Constantinopolitanum PG* 87.III:3147–3200.
Sophronius, *Oratio* = *Sancti Sophronii Hierosolymitani Oratio I: In Christi Natalitia, PG* 87 III:3201–3212.
Sozomenus Kirchegeschichte hrsg. J. Bidez und G. Chr. Hansen, Berlin 1960 (GCS).
Stephanus = Stephan von Byzanz: *Ethnika. Stephani Byzantii Ethnicorum quae supersunt* ed. A. Meineke, Berlin 1849, repr. Graz 1958.

Strabo:
The Geography of Strabo with an English translation by H. L. Jones, London/Cambridge Mass. 1960–1969 (LCL).
Strabon: Géographie t. I 1re partie. Introduction par. G. Aujac et F. Lasserre, ed. G. Aujac, Paris 1969 (Budé).

Syncellus, *Ecloga* = *Gregorius Syncellus Ecloga Chronographica* ed. A. A. Mosshammer, Leipzig 1984.
Synesius, *Epistula* = *Synesii Cyrenensis Epistolae* ed. A. Garzya, Roma 1979.
Taxis = E. Montet: 'Un rituel d'abjuration des musulmans dans l'église grecque', *Revue de l'histoire der religions* 53 (1906) 145–163.

Theodoretus:
Daniel = *Theodoreti Episcopi Cyrensis Commentarius in Visionis Danielis Prophetae PG* 81:1255–1546.
Isaiah = Théodoret de Cyr, *Commentaire sur Isaïe* I–II ed. et trad. J.-N. Guinot, Paris 1980, 1982.
History = Theodoret, *Kirchengeschichte* hrsg. L. Parmentier 2 Aufl., Berlin 1954 (GCS 44).
Jeremiah = *Theodoreti Episcopi Cyrensis in Divinum Ieremiam Prophetam Interpretatio PG* 81:495–780.

Paralipomena = *Theodoreti Episcopi Cyrensis Quaestiones in Reges et Paralipomena* ed. N. Fernández Maria and J. R. Busto Saiz, Madrid 1984.
Therapeutica = Théodoret de Cyr: *Thérapeutique des maladies helléniques* I–II ed. P. Canivet, Paris 1958.

Theodorus Anagnostes, *History* = *Theodoros Anagnostes Kirchengeschichte* hrsg. G. Chr. Hansen, Berlin 1971.
Theophanis Chronographia I–II ed. C. de Boor, Leipzig 1883, 1885.
Theophrastus, *Plants* = Theophrastus: *De Causis Plantarum* I–III ed. with an English translation B. Einarson and G. K. Link, London/Cambridge, Mass. 1976–1990 (LCL).
Vita Gregorii Chozebitae = *'Sancti Gregorii Chozebitae confessoris et monachi vita auctore Antonio eius discipulo'*, Analecta Bollandiana VII, ed. C. de Smedt, J. de Becker, C. Houze et F. van Ortroy, Paris/Bruxelles 1888.

Xenophon:
Xenophontis Opera Omnia III: Expeditio Cyri ed. E. C. Marchant, Oxford 1904.
Xenophon: *Hellanica VI–VII. Anabasis I–III; Anabasis IV–VII. Symposion and Apology*. With an English translation by C. L Brownson, Cambridge, Mass./London 1961, 1957.
Xenophontis Opera Omnia IV: Institutio Cyri ed. E. C. Marchant, Oxford 1910.
Xenophon: *Cyropaedia* with an English translation by W. Miller I–II, Cambridge, Mass./London 1947, 1949 (LCL).

Zosimus:
Zosime: *Histoire nouvelle* I–III ed. et trad. F. Paschoud, Paris 1971–1986.
Zosimus' New History. A translation with commentary by R. T. Ridley, Sydney 1982.

Latin

Inscriptions

Inscriptiones Latinae Selectae Vol. I–III ed. H. Dessau, Berlin 1892–1916.
Res Gestae Divi Augusti. Texte établi et commenté par J. Gagé, 2me éd., Paris 1950.

Literary works: general

PHI CD-ROM # 5.3, The Packard Humanities Institute 1991

Literary works: individual authors

Agrippa, *Map* = Schnabel, P.: 'Die Weltkarte des Agrippa als wissenschaftliches Mittelglied zwischen Hipparch und Ptolemaeus', *Philologus* 90 (1935) 405–440.
Ammianus, *Res gestae* = Ammianus Marcellinus, *Römische Geschichte Lateinisch und Deutsch* 1–4 ed. W. Seyfarth, Berlin 1968–1971.
Apuleius, *Florida* = *Apulei Platonica Madaurensis: Opera quae supersunt* Vol. II:2 Florida, ed. R. Helm, Lipsias 1959.
Aurelius Victor: *Livre des césars* ed. et trad. P. Dufraigne, Paris 1975.
Avienus, *Descriptio* = Rufus Festus Avienus: 'Descriptio Orbis Terrae', *Dionysius periegetes Graece et Latine cum vetustis commentariis et interpretationibus* ed. and comm. G. Bernhardy, Leipzig 1828.
Biblia Sacra iuxta Vulgatam Clementina nova editio A. Colunga and L. Turrado, Madrid 1982.
Catullus = *C. Valerii Catulli Carmina* ed. R. A. B. Mynors, Oxford 1958.

Cicero:
Cicero's Letters to Atticus Vol. I 68–59 BC 1–45 (Book I and II) ed. by D. R. Shackleton Bailey, Cambridge 1965.
Cicero, *Epistulae ad familiares* I–II ed. D. R. Shackleton Bailey, Cambridge 1977.
Cicero, *De Divinatione* = *M. Tulli Ciceronis scripta quae manserunt fasc. 46: De divinatione. De fato. Timaeus* ed. R. Giomini, Leipzig 1975 (Bibliotheca Teubneriana).

Continuatio Byzantina Arabica, MGH IX 323–369.
Continuatio Hispanica, MGH IX 323–369.

Curtius = *Quintus Curtius* with an English translation by J. C. Rolfe I–II, London/Cambridge, Mass. 1956 (LCL).

Egeria = *Éthérie, Journal de voyage* ed. et trad. H. Pétré, Paris 1948.

Expositio totius mundi ed. et trad. J. Rougé, Paris 1966.

Festus = *The Breviarum of Festus.* A critical edition with historical commentary by J. W. Eadie, London 1967.

Florus: *Oevres I–II* ed. et trad. P. Jal, Paris 1967.

Hieronymus:

Amos = S.Eusebii Hieronymi Commentariorum in Amos Prophetam libri tres, PL 25:989–1096.

Epistula ad Dardanum = Saint Jérôme, *Lettres* t. VII ed. J. Labourt, Paris 1961 154–166.

Hebraicae quaestiones in libro Geneseos Corpus Christianorum Series latina LXXII pars I:1 1–56 ed. P. de Lagarde, Brepols 1959.

Praefatio in Danielem prophetam, PL 28:1291–1294.

Vita Sancti Hilarionis, PL 23:29–54.

Historia Augusta:

Histoire Auguste t. V:1: Vies d'Aurélien, Tacite ed., trad. et comm. F. Paschoud, Paris 1996.

Scriptores Historiae Augustae I–II ed. E. Hohl, add. et corr. Ch. Samberger/W. Seyfarth, Leipzig 1965.

The Scriptores Historiae Augustae with an English translation by D. Magie, London/Cambridge, Mass. 1921–1932 (LCB).

Horatius, *Opera* ed. D. R. Shackleton Bailey (2 ed.), Stuttgart 1991 (Teubner).

Isidorus Hispalensis episcopi Etymologicarum sive Originum libri XX ed. W. W. Lindsay, Oxford 1911.

Johannes Cassianus, *Collatio = Johannis Cassiani Collatio sexta: De nece sanctorum, PL* 49:643–668.

Iustinus, *Epitome = M. Iuniani Iustini Epitome Historiarum Philippicarum Pompei Trogi accedunt prologi in Pompei Trogi* ed. O. Seel, Leipzig 1935.

Juvenal and Persius with an English translation by G. G. Ramsay, London/Cambridge, Mass. 1950 (LCL).

Livy:

Titi Livi Ab urbe condita libri XXXI–XL t. II:XXXVI–XL ed. J Briscoe, Stuttgart 1991.

Periochae = Abrégés des livres de l'histoire de Tite-Live 34:2: 'Periochae' transmises par les manuscrits (70–142) et par le papyrus d'Oxyrynchos ed. et trad. P. Jal, Paris 1984.

Lucanus, *Pharsalia* = Lucain: *La guerre civile (la Pharsale)* ed. A. Bourgery et M. Ponchont, I Paris 1958, II, Paris 1948.

Peutinger Map = Miller, K.: *Die Peutingersche Karte oder Welkarte des Castorius*, Stuttgart 1916.

Notitia dignitatum ed. O. Seeck, Frankfurt/M. 1886.

Panegyrici = Panégyriques latines I (I–V) ed. et trad. E. Galletier, Paris 1949.

Plautus = Plaute, *Comédies* I–VII ed. et trad. A. Ernout, Paris 1961–1972 (Budé).

Pliny:

Pline l'ancien, *Histoire naturelle livre XII*, ed. A. Ernout, Paris 1949 (Budé).

C. Plinii Secundi Naturalis Historia Libri XXXVII Vol. I: Libri I–VI ed. C. Mayhoff, Leipzig 1906.

Pliny: *Natural History* in ten volumes with an English translation by H. Rackham, W. H. S. Jones and D. E. Eichholz, Cambridge, Mass./London 1949–1958 (LCL).

Pomponius Mela: *Chorographie* ed. A. Silbermann, Paris 1988 (Budé).

Priscianus, *Periegesis = Dionysius Periegetes Graece et Latine cum vetustis commentariis et interpretationibus* ed. and comm. G. Bernhardy, Leipzig 1828.

Rufinus, *Historia ecclesiastica, PL* 21:467–540.

Solinus = *C. Iulii Solini Collectanea rerum memorabilium* ed. Th. Mommsen, Berlin 1895 repr. Berlin 1953.

Tacitus, *Annals* = *Cornelii Taciti Annalium ab excessu Divi Augusti Libri* ed. C. D. Fischer, Oxford 1906.

Aramaic/Nabataean/Syriac

Epigraphy

Aggoula, B.: 'Remarques sur les inscriptions hatréennes', *MUSJ* 47 (1972) 3–81.

Aggoula, B.: 'Remarques sur les inscriptions hatréennes III', *Syria* 52 (1975) 181–206.

Aggoula, B.: 'Remarques sur les inscriptions hatréennes XII', *Syria* 63 (1986) 353–374.

Beyer, K.: *Die aramäischen Inschriften aus Assur, Hatra und dem übrigen Mesopotamien*, Göttingen 1998.

Cantineau, J.: *Le Nabatéen II: Choix de textes – lexique*, Paris 1932.

Caquot, A.: 'Nouvelles inscriptions araméennes de Hatra (V)', Syria 40 (1963) 1–16.

Caquot, A.: 'Nouvelles inscriptions araméennes de Hatra (VI)', *Syria* 41 (1964) 251–272.

Degen, R.: 'Neue aramäische Inschriften aus Hatra', (214-230) *WO* 5 (1969/1970) 222–236.

Degen, R.: 'New Inscriptions from Hatra (nos. 231–280)', *Jaarbericht van het Vooraziatisch-Egyptisch Genootschap Ex Oriente Lux* 23 (1973/1974) 402–422.

Degen, R.: 'Weitere Inschriften aus Hatra (Nr 281–335)', *Neue Ephemeris für semitische Epigraphik* 3 (1978) 67–111.

Drijvers, H. J. W.: *Old-Syriac (Edessean) Inscriptions*, Leiden 1972 (Semitic Study Series 3).

Drijvers, H. J. W. and Healey, J.: *The Old Syriac Inscriptions of Edessa and Osrhoene. Texts, Translations and Commentary*, Leiden 1999 (Handbuch der Orientalistik 1:42).

Dupont-Sommer, A.: 'L'ostrakon araméen d'Assour', *Syria* 24 (1944/1945) 24–61.

Euting, J.: *Sinaïtische Inschriften*, Berlin 1891.

Healey, J.: *The Nabataean Tomb Inscriptions of Mada'in Salih*, Manchester 1993 (JSS Supplement 1).

Littmann, E.: 'Nabatäisch-Griechische Bilinguen', *Florilegium ou recueil de travaux d'érudition dédiés à Melchior de Vogüé*, Paris 1909 375–390.

Pognon, H.: *Inscriptions sémitiques de la Syrie, de la Mésopotamie et de la région de Mossoul*, Paris 1907.

Rabinowitz, I.: 'Aramaic Inscriptions of the Fifth Century BCE from a North-Arab Shrine in Egypt', *JNES* 15 (1956) 1–9.

Safar, *Kitābāt* I = Safar, F.: 'Kitābāt al-Ḥaḍar', *Sumer* 17 (1961) 9–35.

Safar, *Kitābāt* II = Safar, F.: 'Kitābāt al-Ḥaḍar', *Sumer* 18 (1962) 21–64.

Safar, *Kitābāt* III = Safar, F.: 'Kitābāt al-Ḥaḍar', *Sumer* 21 (1965 31–43.

Safar, *Kitābāt* IV = Safar, F.: 'Kitābāt al-Ḥaḍar', *Sumer* 24 (1968) 3–32.

Safar, *Kitābāt* V = Safar, F.: 'Kitābāt al-Ḥaḍar', *Sumer* 27 (1971) 3–14.

Safar, *Kitābāt* VI = Safar, F.: 'Kitābāt al-Ḥaḍar', *Sumer* 34 (1978) 69–74.

Segal, J. B.: 'Aramaic Legal Texts form Hatra', *JJS* 33 (1982) 109–115.

Segal, J. B.: 'Some Syriac Inscriptions of the 2nd–3rd Century AD', *BSOAS* 16 (1954).

Teixidor, J.: 'Notes hatréennes 2 – l'inscription de Hatra no 79', *Syria* 41 (1964) 280–284.

Papyri

Cowley, A.: *Aramaic Papyri from the Fifth Century BC* Edited, with translation and notes, Oxford 1923.

Lindenberger, J. M.: *The Aramaic Proverbs of Ahiqar*, Baltimore/London 1983.

Porten, *Textbook* = *Textbook of Aramaic Documents from Ancient Egypt*. Newly copied, edited and translated into Hebrew and English by B. Porten and A. Yardeni vol. 3: Literature, Accounts, Lists, Jerusalem 1993.

Literary

Bardaisan, *Laws* = *The Book of the Laws of the Countries. Dialogue on Fate of Bardaiṣan of Edessa* by J. W. Drijvers, Assen 1965 (Semitic Texts with Translations vol. III, ed. by J. H. Hospers and Th. C. Vriezen).

Chronicle 1234 = *Anonymi auctoris Chronicon ad annum Christi 1234 pertinens* I–II, ed. et interpr. I.-B. Chabot, Louvain 1917–37 (CSCO: Scriptores Syri: Textus, ser. III t. XIV–XV).

The Doctrine of Addai, the Apostle ed. and trans. G. Phillips, London 1876.
Isaac of Antioch = *S. Isaaci Antiocheni Doctoris Syrorum Opera Omnia pars I* ed. G. Bickell, Giessen 1873.
Jaʕqub, *Chronicon* = 'Chronicon Iacobi Edesseni [Makhtbhūth zabhnē dh-Yaʕqubh ʔUrhāyā]' *Cronica Minora I*, ed. Ignatius Guidi Parisiis 1893 (CSCO: Scriptores Syri, Textus Ser. III t. IV) 261–330).
Johannes, *Colloque* = Nau, F.M.: 'Un colloque du patriarche Jean avec l'émir des agaréens et faits divers des années 712 à 716', *JA* 11:5 (1915) 225–279.
Joshua, *Chronicle* = *The Chronicle of Joshua the Stylite composed in Syriac* AD *507*, trans. and ed. by W. Wright, Cambridge 1882 repr. Amsterdam 1968.
'Liber Calipharum', *Chronica Minora II*, ed. E. W. Brooks (CSCO: Scriptores Syri, Textus Ser. III t. IV).
Michael Syrus, *Chronicle* = Michel le Syrien: *Chronique* ed. et trad. J. B. Chabot, Paris 1899–1910.
Nöldeke, *Kämpfe* = Nöldeke, Th., 'Zur Geschichte der Araber im 1. Jahrh. d. H. aus syrischen Quellen 1: Die letzten Kämpfe um den Besitz Syriens', *ZDMG* 29 (1876) 76–82.
Nöldeke, *Bruchstücke* = Nöldeke, Th., 'Zur Geschichte der Araber im 1. Jahrh. d. H. aus syrischen Quellen II: Bruchstücke einer syrischen Chronik über die Zeit des Moʕâwija', *ZDMG* 29 (1876) 82–98.
The Old Testament in Syriac according to the Peshîtta Version, Leiden 1966–.
Pseudo-Methodius, *Apokalypse* = *Die syrische Apokalypse des Pseudo-Methodius*, hrsg. und übersetzt von G. J. Reinink, Louvanii 1993 (CSCO Vol. 540–541 Scriptores Syri t. 220–221).
Simeon, *Letter* = Guidi, I.: 'La lettera di Simeon, vescovo di Bêth Aršâm, sopra i martiri omeriti', *Reale Accademia dei Lincei: Memorie. Classe di scienze morali, storiche e filologiche* Serie 3, 8 (1881) 471–515.

Simeon, *Vita*:
'Neṣḥāneh d-mār Šemʕōn rāšā d-ʔabīle' ed. P. Bedjan, *Acta Martyrum et Sanctorum IV*, Leipzig 1894 507–644.
Hilgenfeldt, H.: 'Lobrede auf den Herrn Simeon, das Haupt der Eremiten', *Das Leben des heiligen Symeon Stylites*, Leipzig 1908 (Texte und Untersuchungen zur Geschichte der altchristlichen Literatur 3 Reihe 2 Band Heft 4).

'Synodicon orientale ou Recueil de synodes nestoriens' ed. J. B. Chabot, *Notices et extraits des manuscrits de la Bibliothèque Nationale et autres bibliothèques* 37 (1902).

Theodorus, *Scholia* = *Theodorus bar Kōnī Liber scholiorum pars prior* ed. A. Scher, Paris 1910 (CSCO: Scriptores Syri Textus 2:65).
Zacharias Rhetor, *History* = *Historia ecclesiastica Zachariae Rhetori vulgo adscripta* ed. E. W. Brooks, Paris 1921 (CSCO: Scriptores Syri Textus Series tertia – tomus VI).

South Arabian: epigraphic

Arabie heureuse, Arabie déserte: Catalogue des antiquités arabiques du Musée du Louvre ed. Y. Calvet/Ch. Robin, Paris 1997 92–269 (Notes et documents des musées de France 31).
Bāfaqīh, M. ʕA. 'Hawāmiš ʕalā naqš ʕAbadān al-kabīr', *Raydān* 4 (1984) 29–48 (Arabic section).
Bauer, G. M. and Lundin, A. G.: *Epigrafičeskije pam'atniki drevnego Jemena (Južnaja Aravija: Pam'atniki drevnej istorii i kul'tury)* Sankt-Peterburg 1998.
Beeston, A. F. L.: 'Miscellaneous Epigraphic Notes', *Raydān* 4 (1984) 9–2.
Corpus des inscriptions et antiquités sud-arabes II: Le Musée d'Aden t. II:1: Inscriptions, Louvain 1986.
Doe, B. and Jamme, A.: 'New Sabaean Inscriptions from South Arabia', *JRAS* 1968 2–28.
Fakhry, A.: *An Archaeological Journey to Yemen II: Epigraphical Texts* by G. Ryckmans, Cairo 1952.
Garbini, G.: 'Una bilingue sabeo-ebraica da Ẓafar', *AION* 30 (1970) 153–167.
Garbini, G.: 'Una nuova iscrizione di Šaraḥbiʔil Yaʕfur', *AION* 29 (1969) 559–570.
Iryānī, M. A.: *Nuqūš musnadiyya wa-taʕlīqāt*, 2nd rev. edn Ṣanʕāʔ 1990.

Jamme, A.: 'Un désastre nabatéen devant Nagran', *Cahiers de Byrsa* 6 (1956) 165–171.
Jamme, A.: *Miscellanées d'ancient arabe* III, Washington 1972.
Jamme, A.: *Miscellanées d'ancient arabe* IX, Washington 1979.
Jamme, A.: 'The Pre-Islamic Inscriptions of the Riyâdh Museum', *Oriens Antiquus* 9 (1970) 115–139.
Jamme, A.: *Sabaean and Ḥasaean Inscriptions from Saudi Arabia*, Rome 1966 (Studi Semitici 23).
Ja 550–851 = Jamme, A.: *Sabaean Inscriptions from Maḥram Bilqîs (Mârib)* Baltimore 1962 (Publications of the American Foundation for the Study of Man vol. III).
Jamme, A.: *The Al-ʕUqla Texts,* Washington 1963 (Documentation Sud-Arabe, III).
Mlaker, K.: *Die Hierodulenlisten von Maʕīn nebst Untersuchungen zur altsüdarabischen Chronologie*, Leipzig 1943.
Müller, W. W.: 'Das Ende des antiken Königreichs Ḥaḏramaut. Die sabäische Inschrift Schreyer-Geukens = Iryani 32', *Al-Hudhud. Festschrift Maria Höfner zum 80. Geburtstag* hrsg. R. G. Stiegner, Graz 1981 225–256.
Müller, W. W.: 'Die sabäische Felsinschrift von Maṣnaʕat Māriya', *NESE* 3 (1978) 137–148.
Müller, W. W.: 'Eine sabäische Gesandschaft in Ktesiphon und Seleukeia', *NESE* 2 (1974) 155–165.
Müller, W. W.: 'Eine sabäische Inschrift aus dem Jahre 566 der ḥimjarischen Ära', *NESE* 2 (1974) 139–144.
Philby, H. St. J. B. and Tritton A. S.: 'Najran Inscriptions', *JRAS* 1944 119–129.
Pirenne, J.: 'Deux prospections historiques au Sud-Yémen', *Raydān* 4 (1981) 205–240.
Robin, Ch. and Gajda, I.: 'L'inscription du Wadi ʕAbadan', *Raydān* 6 (1994) 113–137.
Robin, Ch. and Ryckmans, J.: 'L'attribution d'un bassin à une divinité en Arabie du Sud antique', *Raydan* 1 (1978) 39–64.
Ryckmans, *Inscriptions* 9 = Ryckmans, G.: 'Inscriptions sud-arabes: Neuvième série', *Le Muséon* 64 (1951) 93–126.
Ryckmans, *Inscriptions* 10 = Ryckmans, G.: 'Inscriptions sud-arabes: Dixième série', *Le Muséon* 66 (1953) 267–317.
Ryckmans, *Inscriptions* 17 = Ryckmans, G.: 'Inscriptions sud-arabes: Dix-septième série', Le Muséon 72 (1959) 159–176.
Ryckmans, G.: 'Notes épigraphiques. Quatrième série VIII: Graffites rupestres de Nejran', *Le Muséon* 60 (1947) 149–170.
Ryckmans, J.: 'Le texte Sharafaddin, Yemen, p. 44, bas, droite', *Le Muséon* 80 (1967) 508–512.
Schaffer, B.: *Sabäische Inschriften aus verschiedenen Fundorten*, Wien 1972 (Sammlung Eduard Glaser VII. Österreichische Akademie der Wissenschaften, phil.-hist. Klasse, Sitzungsberichte Bd. 282.1).

Arabic: epigraphic

Harding, G. Lankester: *An Index and Concordance of Pre-Islamic Arabian Names and Inscriptions*, Toronto 1971.
Jaussen, A. J. and Savignac, R.: *Mission archéologique en Arabie (mars-mai 1907)I: De Jérusalem au Hedjaz Médain-Saleh*, Paris 1909; *II: El-'Ela, d'Hégra à Teima, Harrah de Tebouk*, Paris 1914 (Publications de la Société Française des Fouilles Archéologiques II).
Gazdar, M. S., Potts, D. T. and Livingstone, A.: 'Excavations at Thaj', *Atlal* 8 (1404/1984) 55–108.
Sima, A.: *Die lihyanischen Inschriften von al-ʕUḏayb (Saudi-Arabien)*, Jena/Berlin 1999 (Epigraphische Forschungen auf der arabischen Halbinsel Bd 1).
Winnett, F. V. and Reed, W. L.: *Ancient Records from North Arabia*, Toronto 1970.

Arabic: classical

ʕAbd al-Ḥakam, *Futūḥ = The History of the Conquest of Egypt, North Africa and Spain known as the Futūḥ Miṣr of Ibn ʕAbd al-Ḥakam* ed. by Ch. Torrey, New Haven 1922 (Yale Oriental Series Researches Vol. III).
ʕAbd al-Ḥakam, *Sīrat ʕUmar = Sīrat ʕUmar b. ʕAbd al-ʕAzīz ʕalā mā rawāhu l-ʔimām Mālik*

b. ʔAnas wa-ʔaṣḥābuhu, ed. ʔAḥmad ʕAbīd, Miṣr 1927/1346.
ʔAbū Dāwūd, *Sunan* 1–4, ed. M. M. ʕAbd al-Ḥamīd [s.a.].
ʔAbū ʕUbayd, *ʔAmwāl = Kitāb al-ʔamwāl taʔlīf ʔimām al-ḥadīṯ wa-l-fiqh wa-l-lugha wa-l-ʔadab li-ʔAbī ʕUbayd al-Qāsim b. Sallam*, ed. Muḥammad ʕImāra, Bayrūt/al-Qāhira 1409/1989.
Ahlwardt, *Divans* = W. Ahlwardt: *The Divans of Six Ancient Arabic Poets*, 1870 repr. Osnabrück 1972.
al-ʔAʕsha, *Dīwān = The Díwán of al-Aʕshà. Gedichte von ʔAbû Basîr Maimûn ibn Qais al-ʔAʕšâ* hrsg. von R. Geyer London 1928 (E. J. W. Gibb Memorial Series N.S. VI).
al-ʕAṣmaʕī, *Tārīkh* = ʕAbdallāh b. Qurayb al-ʔAṣmaʕī: *Tārīx al-ʕarab qabla al-ʔIslām*, ed. M. H. ʔĀl Yāsīn, Baghdad 1379/1959.
al-ʔAzraqī, *ʔAkhbār = Die Chroniken der Stadt Mekka I: Die Geschichte und Beschreibung der Stadt Mekka von al-Azraqī* ed. F. Wüstenfeld, Leipzig 1856.
al-Bakrī, *Muʕǧam = Das geographische Wörterbuch des Abu 'Obeid 'Abdallah ben 'Abd el-'Aziz el-Bekrî*, hrsg. von F. Wüstenfeldt, Göttingen 1876/77 repr. Osnabrück 1976.
al-Balādhurī, *ʔAnsāb* V = *The Ansāb al-Ashrāf of al-Balādhurī* Vol. V, ed. S. D. F. Goitein, Jerusalem 1936.
al-Balādhurī, *Futūḥ = Liber expugnationis regionum auctore Imāmo Ahmed ibn Jahja ibn Djábir al-Beládsori*, ed. M. J. de Goeje Leiden 1866 repr. Lugduni batavorum 1966.
Bayḍāwī, *Tafsīr = ʔAnwār at-tanzīl wa-ʔasrār at-taʔwīl al-maʕrūf bi-tafsīr al-Bayḍāwī*, Bayrūt s.a.

al-Bukhārī, *Ṣaḥīḥ*:
Le recueil des traditions mahométanes par Abou Abdallah Mohammed ibn Ismaîl el-Bokhâri ed. M. L. Krehl and Th. W. Juynboll, Vol. IV, Leiden 1908.
Ṣaḥīḥ al-Bukhārī Vol. 1–6 + fihrist ed. M. Dīb al-Bughā, Damascus/Beirut 1990/1410.
Commentaria = Maris Amri et Slibae de Patriarchis Nestorianorum Commentaria ed. H. Gismondi, Roma 1899.

Diʕbil, *Waṣāyā = Waṣāyā al-mulūk wa-ʔabnāʔ al-mulūk min walad Qaḥṭān b. Hūd al-mansūb ʔilā Diʕbil b. ʕAliyy al-Xuzāʕī* ed. N. ʔAbāẓa, Damascus 1997/1417.
ad-Dīnawarī, *ʔAkhbār* = Abū Ḥanīfa ad-Dīnawarī: *Kitāb al-ʔaxbār aṭ-ṭiwāl* ed. I. Kratchkovsky, Leiden 1912.
Dīwān al-Huḏayliyyīn = Kosegarten, J. G. L.: *The Hudsailian Poems Contained in the Manuscript of Leyden* Vol. I, London 1854.
Ǧāḥiẓ, *Bayān* = al-Ǧāḥiẓ: *al-Bayān at-tabyīn*, ed. ʕA. M. Hārūn, al-Qāhira 1985/1405.
Ǧāḥiẓ, *Ḥayawān* = al-Ǧāḥiẓ: *Kitāb al-Ḥayawān* 1-7, ed. ʕA. M. Hārūn, Bayrūt 1949–1950.
Ǧāḥiẓ, *Rasāʔil = Rasāʔil al-Ǧāḥiẓ* I, ed. ʕA. M. Hārūn, al-Qāhira 1964.
Ǧarīr, *Dīwān = Šarḥ dīwān Ǧarīr muḍāfan ʔilayhi tafsīr ʔAbī Ǧaʕfar Muḥammad b. Ḥabīb*, Vol. 1 ed. M. ʔI. ʕA. aṣ-Ṣāwī, Bayrūt s.a.
al-Hamdānī, *ʔIklīl* I = al-Hamdānī: *al-Iklīl. Erstes Buch in der Rezension von Muḥammad bin Našwān bin Saʕīd al-Ḥimyarī* ed. O. Löfgren, Uppsala 1954 (Bibliotheca Ekmania 58:1–2).
al-Hamdānī, *Ṣifa = Al-Hamdânî's Geographie der arabischen Halbinsel* hrsg. D. H. Müller, Wien 1884–1891, repr. Leiden 1968.
Ḥamīdullah, *Waṯāʔiq* = M. Ḥamidullah: *al-Waṯāʔiq as-siyāsiyya li-l-ʕahd an-nabawī wa-l-xilāfa ar-rāšidiyya*, Beyrut 1387.
Ḥamza, *History = Hamzae Ispahansesis Annalium Libri X* T 1: *Textus arabicus,* T. II: *Translatio latina*, ed. I. M. E, Gottwaldt, Leipzig 1848, 1849.
Ibn ʕAbd Rabbihi, *ʕIqd* = ʔAbū ʔAḥmad b. Muḥammad b. ʕAbd Rabbihi al-ʔAndalusī: *Kitāb al-ʕiqd al-farīd*, ed A. ʔAmīn/A. Zayn/I. al-ʔAnbārī, al-Qāhira 1940?.
Ibn Durayd, *Ištiqāq = al-Ištqāq li-ʔAbī Bakr Muḥammad b. al Ḥasan b. Durayd* ed. ʕA. M. Hārūn al-Qāhira 1979.
Ibn Ǧinnī, *Sirr ṣināʕat al-ʔiʕrāb* 1–2 ed. Ḥ. Hindāwī, Damascus 1993/1413.
Ibn Ḥabib, *Muḥabbar = Kitāb al-muḥabbar li-ʔAbī Ǧaʕfar Muḥammad b. Ḥabīb riwāyata as-Sukkarī* ed. I. Lichtenstädter, Hydarabad 1942, repr. Bayrūt s.a.
Ibn Ḥazm, *Ǧamhara = Ǧamharat ʔansāb al-ʕarab li-ʔAbī Muḥammad b. ʔAḥmad b. Saʕīd b.*

Ḥazm al-ʔAndalusī ed. A. S. M. Hārūn, al-Qāhira 1982.
Ibn Hishām, *Sīra* = *Das Leben Muhammed's nach Muhammed Ibn Ishâk bearbeitet von Abd el-Malik Ibn Hischam*, hrsg. F. Wüstenfeld, I:1 Göttingen 1858 I:2 ibid. 1859, II ibid. 1860 repr. Frankfurt/M 1961.
Ibn Hishām, *Tīǧān* = *Kitāb at-tīǧān fī mulūk Ḥimyar riwāyata Muḥammad ʕAbd al-Malik b. Hišām* 1 ed. 1347 H. repr. Ṣanʕāʔ 1979.

Ibn Khaldūn, *ʕIbar*:

ʕAbd ar-Raḥmān b. Khaldūn, *Kitāb al-ʕibar wa-dīwān al-mubtadaʔ wa-l-xabar fī ʔayyām al-ʕarab wa-l-ʕaǧăm wa-l-barbar wa-man ʕāšarahum min ḏawī s-sulṭān al-ʔakbar*, 1–7 Būlāq 1284.
Ibn Khaldun: *The Muqaddimah. An Introduction to History* vol. 1–3 translated by F. Rosenthal, New York 1958.

Ibn al-Kalbī, *ʔAṣnām* = *Das Götzenbuch Kitāb al-ʔaṣnām des Ibn al-Kalbī* ed., trans. and comm. by Rosa Klinke-Rosenberger, Leipzig 1941.
Ibn al-Kalbī, *Nasab* = *Nasab Maʕadd wa-l-Yaman al-kabīr li-ʔAbī l-Munḏir Hishām b. Muḥammad as-Sāʔib al-Kalbī* 1–2 ed. N Ḥasan, Bayrūt 1988/1408.
Ibn Manẓūr, *Lisān* = *Lisān al-ʕarab li-ʔAbī Faḍl Ğamīl ad-Dīn b. Makram b. Manẓūr al-ʔIfrīqī al-Miṣrī*, Bayrūt s.a.
Ibn Muǧāwir, *Tārīkh* = Ibn al Muǧāwir: *Descriptio Arabiae Meridionalis* ed. O. Löfgren, Leiden 1951–1954.

Ibn an-Nadīm, *Fihrist*:
Kitâb al-Fihrist mit Anmerkungen hrsg. G. Flügel Bd I Text, Leipzig 1871; Bd II Anmerkungen und Idices, Leipzig 1872.

Ibn Qutayba, *Maʕārif* = *al-Maʕārif li-bn Qutayba, ʔAbī Muḥammad ʕAbd allāh b. Muslim*, ed. Tharwat ʕUkāša, Miṣr 1960.
Ibn Qutayba, *ʕUyūn al-ʔaxbār*, ed. ʕAbd al-Qādir Ḥāṭim al-Qāhira 1963/1383.
Ibn Saʕd, *Ṭabaqāt* = Ibn Saad: *Biographien Muhammeds, seiner Gefährten und der späteren Träger des Islams bis zum Jahre 230 der Flucht* I–IX hrsg. E. Sachau e.a., Leiden 1905–.
Ibn Saʕīd, *Nashwa* = Kropp, M.: *Die Geschichte der 'reinen Araber' vom Stamme Qaḥṭān aus dem Kitāb našwat aṭ-ṭarab fī taʔrīx ǧāhiliyyat al-ʕarab des Ibn Saʕīd al-Maghribī* 2 Aufl., Frankfurt/M 1982 (Heidelberger orientalistische Studien Bd 4).
Iṣfahānī, *ʔAghānī* = *Kitāb al-ʔaġānī taʔlīf ʔAbī l-Faraǧ al-ʔIṣfahānī* 1–24, al-Qāhira 1927/1345–1974/1394.
al-Khalīl, *Kitāb al-ʕayn* = *Kitāb al-ʕayn li-ʔAbī ʕAbd ar-Raḥmān al-Xalīl* 1–9 ed. M. al-Makhzūmī/I. as-Sāmarrāʔī, Qum 1409 [1989].
Masʕūdī, *Murūǧ* = Maçoudi: *Les prairies d'or*. Texte et traduction par C. Barbier de Maynard et Pavet de Courteille 1–9 Paris 1861–1872.
Masʕūdī, *Tanbīh* = *Kitâb at-tanbîh wa'l-ischrâf auctore al-Masûdî* ed. M. J. de Goeje, Leiden 1894 (Bibliotheca Geographorum Arabicorum VIII).
al-Minqarī, *Ṣiffīn* = Naṣr ad-Dīn b. Muḥāzim al-Minqarī: *Waqʕat Ṣiffīn* ed. A. Hārūn, al-ʔIskandariyya 1365.
Mubarrad, *Kāmil* = *The Kāmil of el-Mubarrad* ed. W. W. Wright 1–2, Leipzig 1874–1892.
Naqāʔiḍ = *The Naqāʔiḍ of Jarīr and al-Farazdaq* 1–3, ed. A. A. Bevan, Leiden 1905–1912.
Nöldeke, *Delectus* = *Delectus veterum carminum arabicorum*, sel. et ed. Th. Nöldeke, Berlin 1890 repr. 1961.

Nuʕaym, *Kitāb al-fitan*:
MS British Museum Or. 9449.
Kitāb al-fitan li-ʔAbī ʕAbdallāh Nuʕaym b. Ḥammād al-Marūzī ed. S. Zakkār, Makka al-Mukarrama s. a.

Samuel, *Apocalypse* = 'L'Apocalypse de Samuel, supérieur de Deir-el-Qalamoun', ed. and trans. by J. Ziadeh, *L'Orient chrétien* 10 (1915/17) 374–407.
aṭ-Ṭabarī, *Tafsīr* = *Tafsīr aṭ-Ṭabarī al-musammā Ğāmiʕ al-bayān fī taʔwīl al-Qurʔān* vol.

1–12, Bayrūt 1992/1412.
aṭ-Ṭabarī, *Tārīkh* = *Annales auctore Abu Djafar Mohammed Ibn Djarir at-Tabari* ed. M. J. de Goeje *et al.*, Leiden 1879–1901.
Ṭirimmāḥ, *Poems* = *The Poems of Ṭufail ibn Auf al-Ghanawī and aṭ-Ṭirimmāḥ ibn Ḥākim aṭ-Ṭāʔyī* ed. and trans. by F. Krenkow, London 1927.
The History of al-Ṭabarī Vol. X: The Conquest of Arabia trans. and annot. by F. M. Donner, New York 1993.
Wāqidī, *Maghāzī* = *The Kitāb al-maghāzī of al-Wāqidī* 1–3, ed. M. Jones, London 1966.
ʕUbayd, *ʔAkhbār* = ʕUbayd b. Šarya al-Ǧurhumī: *ʔAxbār al-Yaman wa-ʔašʕāruhā wa-ʔansābuhā*, ed. Ṣanʕāʔ 1979.
Wahb, Papyrus I = N. Abbott: 'An Arabic papyrus in the Oriental Institute. Stories of the Prophets', *JNES* 5 (1946) 169–180.
Wahb, Papyrus II = R. G. Khoury: *Wahb b. Munabbih Teil 1: Der Heidelberger Papyrus PSR Heid. Arab. 23*, Wiesbaden 1972.
Yaʕqūbī, *Tārīkh* = *Ibn-Wādhih qui dicitur Al-Jaʕqubī: Historiae* 1–2 ed. M. Th. Houtsma, Lugduni Batavorum 1883.
Yāqūt, *Muʕǧam* = *Jacut's geographisches Wörterbuch Kitāb muʕǧam al-buldān* 1–6 hrsg. von F. Wüstenfeld, Leipzig 1866–1873, repr. Leipzig 1924.
az-Zamakhsharī, *Kashshāf* = *al-Kaššāf ʕan ḥaqāʔiq ġawāmiḍ at-tanzīl wa-ʕuyūn al-ʔaqāwīl fī wuǧūh at-taʔwīl li-Maḥmūd b. ʕAmr az-Zamaxšarī* 1–4 ed. M. Ḥusayn ʔAḥmad, Bayrūt 1987/1407.

Arabic: modern colloquial

Bailey, C.: *Bedouin Poetry from Sinai and the Negev*, Oxford 1991.
Behnstedt, P.: *Die nordjemenitischen Dialekte Teil 2: Glossar: ḏāl-ġayn,* Wiesbaden 1996 (Jemen-Studien Bd 3).
Ingham, B.: *Bedouin of Northern Arabia. Traditions of the Āl-Ḍhafīr*, London 1986.
Kurpershoek, P. M.: *Oral Poetry and Narratives from Central Arabia 1: The Poetry of ad-Dindān, a Bedouin Bard of Southern Najd*, Leiden 1994.
Kurpershoek, P. M.: *Oral Poetry and Narratives from Central Arabia 3: Bedouin Poets from the Dawāsir Tribe. Between Nomadism and Settlement in Southern Najd*, Leiden 1999 (Studies in Arabic Literature XVII/III).
de Landberg, C.: *Langue des Bédouins ʕAnazeh. Texte arabe avec traduction, commentaire et glossaire. 1: Texte arabe et traduction,* Leide 1919.
de Landberg, C.: *Études sur les dialectes de l'Arabie méridionale I: Ḥadramoût*, Leide 1901.
Marçais, W. and Guîga, A.: *Textes arabes de Takroûna II: Glossaire* 1–8, Paris 1958–1961.
Montagne, R.: 'Le ghazou de Šāyèʕ Alemṣāḥ. Conte en dialecte des Šemmar du Neǧd des Rimāl', *Mélanges Maspéro III*, Le Caire 1935–1940, 411–416.
Palva, H.: *Artistic Colloquial Arabic. Traditional Narratives and Poems from al-Balqāʔ (Jordan): Transcription, Translation and Metrical Analysis*, Helsinki 1992 (Studia Orientalia 69).
Palva, H.: *Narratives and Poems from Ḥesbān. Arabic Texts Recorded Among the Semi-Nomadic əl-ʕAǧārma Tribe (al-Balqāʔ District, Jordan)*, Göteborg 1978 (Orientalia Gothoburgensia 3).
Palva, H.: *Studies in the Arabic Dialect of the Semi-Nomadic əl-ʕAǧārma Tribe (al-Balqāʔ District, Jordan)*, Göteborg 1976 (Orientalia Gothoburgensia 2).
Rosenhouse, J.: *The Bedouin Arabic Dialects. Central Problems and a Close Analysis of North Israel Bedouin Dialects*, Wiesbaden 1984.
Schmidt, H. and Kahle, P.: *Volkserzählungen aus Palästina gesammelt bei den Bauern von Bir-Zet und in Verbindung mit Dschirius Jusif herausgegeben* II, Göttingen 1930.
Sinaceur, Z. I. (ed.): *Le dictionnaire Colin d'arabe dialectal marocain* 1–8 Rabat/Paris 1993.
Sowayan, S.A.: *The Arabian Oral Historical Narrative. An Ethnographic and Linguistic Analysis*, Wiesbaden 1992 (Semitica Viva Bd. 6).
Stewart, F. H.: 'A Bedouin Narrative from Central Sinai', *Zeitschrift für arabische Linguistik* 16 (1987) 44–92.
Stewart, F. H.: *Texts in Sinai Bedouin Law* Part 1: *The Texts in English Translation,* Wiesbaden

1988, Part 2: *The Texts in Arabic. Glossary*, Wiesbaden 1990 (Mediterranean Language and Culture Monographs Vols 3, 5).
Taine-Cheikh, C.: *Dictionnaire ḥassāniyya-francais. Dialecte arabe de Mauritanie* 1–, Paris 1988–.
Wetzstein, J. G.: 'Sprachliches aus den Zeltlagern der syrischen Wüste', *ZDMG* 22 (1868) 69–194.

Secondary literature

Abel, F.-M.: 'L'expédition des grecs à Pétra en 312 avant J.-C. (1)', *Revue Biblique* 46 (1937) 373–391.
Abel, F.-M.: *Géographie de la Palestine* I–II Paris 1933, 1938.
Abel, F.-M.: *Histoire de la Palestine depuis la conquête d'Alexandre jusqu'à l'invasion arabe* I–II, Paris 1952.
Abel, F.-M.: *Les livres des Maccabées*, Paris 1949.
Abū Lughod, L.: *Veiled Sentiments. Honor and Poetry in a Bedouin Society*, Berkeley/Los Angeles/London 1986.
Aharoni, Y.: *The Land of the Bible. A Historical Geography*, London 1967.
Aharoni, Y.: 'The Land of Gerar', *IEJ* 6 (1956) 26–32.
Aigrain, R.: 'Arabie', *Dictionnaire d'histoire et de géographie ecclesiastiques* t. III 1924 col. 1158–1339.
Aistleitner, J.: *Wörterbuch der ugaritischen Sprache* hrsg. von O. Eissfeldt, Berlin 1963 (Berichte über die Verhandlungen der Sächsischen Akademie der Wissenschaften zu Leipzig Phil.-hist. Klasse Bd 106:3).
Albright, W. F.: 'The Biblical Tribe of Massa' and some Congeners', *Studi Orientalistici in Onore di G. Levi della Vida* I, Roma 1956 1–14.
Albright, W. F.: 'Dedan', *Geschichte und Altes Testament*, Tübingen 1953 (Beiträge zur historischen Theologie 16) 1–12.
Alsekaf, A. A.: *La géographie tribale du Yémen antique*, diss. Paris III 1985.
Alt, A.: 'Irrige Meinungen über Gerar', *Journal of the Palestine Oriental Society* 18 (1937) 218–235 (= *KS* III:435–449).
Alt, A.: 'Judas Nachbarn zur Zeit Nehemias', *Palästinajahrbuch* 27 (1931) 66–74 (= *KS* II:338–345).
Alt, A.: 'Neue assyrische Nachrichten über Palästina und Syrien', *ZDPV* 67 (1944/1945) 128–159 (= *KS* II:226–241).
Alt, A.: 'Zelte und Hütten', *Alttestamentliche Studien Friedrich Nötscher zum sechzigsten Geburtstag gewidmet*, Bonn 1950 16–25 (= *KS* III:233–242).
Altheim, F. and Stiehl, R.: *Die Araber in der alten Welt* I–V, Berlin/New York 1964–1969.
Altheim, F. and Stiehl, R.: *Christentum am Roten Meer* 1–2, Berlin/New York 1971, 1973.
Aly, W.: *Strabon von Amaseia. Untersuchungen über Text, Aufbau und Quellen der Geografika* (Strabonis Geographica. Strabons Geografika in 17 Büchern. Text, Übersetzung und erläuternde Anmerkungen von W. Aly Bd. 4), Bonn 1957 (Antiquitas, Reihe 1: Abhandlungen zur alten Geschichte Bd 5).
Arberry, A.: *The Koran Interpreted*, London 1964.
von Arnim, H.: 'Skylax', *RE* 3 (1929) 619–646.
Aro, S.: *Tabal. Zur Geschichte und materiellen Kultur des zentralanatolischen Hochplateaus von 1200 bis 600 v.Ch.*, Diss., Helsinki 1998.
al-ʔAsad, N.: *Maṣādir aš-šiʕr al-ǧāhilī wa-qīmatuhā at-tārīxiyya*, al-Qāhira 1956.
The Assyrian Dictionary of the Oriental Institute of the University of Chicago 1–, Chicago 1964–.
Astour, M. C.: 'Sabtah and Sabteca', *JBL* 84 (1965) 422–425.
Athamina, Kh.: 'Aʕrāb and Muhājirūn in the Environment of Amṣār', *Studia Islamica* 66 (1987) 5–25.
Athamina, Kh.: 'The Tribal Kings of Arabia', *Al-Qantara* 19 (1998) 19–37.
Avanzini, A.: 'La chronologie 'courte': un réexamen', *ArAnt* 2 [7–22].
Bacijeva, S. M.: 'Bor'ba meždu Assiriej i Urartu za Siriju', *Vestnik Drevnej Istorii* 2 [44] (1953) 17–36.

Bāfaqīh, M. A.: *L'unification du Yémen antique. La lutte entre Saba', Ḥimyar et le Ḥaḍramawt du Ier au IIlme siècle de l'ère chrétienne*, Paris 1990.

Barnes, T. D.: *The Sources of the Historia Augusta*, Bruxelles 1978 (Collection Latomus 155).

Barth, J.: *Die Nominalbildung in den semitischen Sprachen* 2 Aufl., Leipzig 1894.

Bartlett, J. R.: *Edom and the Edomites*, Sheffield 1989 (JSOT Supplement 77).

Bartlett, *Edomites* I = Bartlett, J. R.: 'From Edomites to Nabataeans. A Study in Cultural Continuity', *Palestine Exploration Quarterly* 111 (1979) 53–66.

Bartlett, *Edomites* II = Bartlett, J. R.: 'From Edomites to Nabataeans: the Problem of Continuity', *Aram* 2 (1990) 25–34.

Bartlett, J. R.: 'The Land of Seir and the Brotherhood of Edom', *Journal of Theological Studies N.S.* 20 (1969) 1–20.

Bashear, S.: *Arabs and Others in Early Islam*, Princeton 1997 (Studies in Late Antiquity and Early Islam 8).

Baumstark, A.: *Geschichte der syrischen Literatur mit Ausschluss der christlich-palästinensischen Texte*, Bonn 1922.

Beaucamp, J.: 'Rawwafa', *SDB* 9 (1979) 1467–1475.

Beaulieu, P.-A.: *The Reign of Nabonidus, King of Babylon 556–539 BC*, New Haven/London 1989.

Beer, G.: 'Ituraea', *RE* 17 (1914) 2377–2380.

Beeston, A. F. L.: 'Functional Significance of the Old South Arabian "Town"', *PSAS* 2 (1971) 26–28.

Beeston, A. F. L.: *The Mercantile Code of Qataban*, London 1959 (Qahtan. Studies in Old South Arabian Epigraphy fasc. 1).

Beeston, A. F. L.: 'Nemara and Faw', *BSOAS* 42 (1979) 1–6.

Beeston, A. F. L.: *Sabaic Grammar*, Manchester 1984.

Beeston, A. F. L.: 'Some Observations on Greek and Latin Data Relating to South Arabia', *BSOAS* 62 (1979) 7–12.

Beeston, A. F. L.: 'Two Biʔr Ḥimā Inscriptions Reexamined', *BSOAS* 48 (1985) 42–52.

Beeston, A. F. L.: *Warfare in Ancient South Arabia (2nd–3rd centuries AD)*, London 1976 (Qahtan. Studies in Old South Arabian Epigraphy fasc. 3).

Beeston, A. F. L., Ghul, M. A., Müller, W. W. and Ryckmans, J.: *Sabaic Dictionary (English–French–Arabic)*, Louvain/Beyrout 1982.

Bell, *Commentary* = *A Commentary on the Qurʔān* Vol. I: surahs I–XXIV, Vol. II: surahs XXV–CXIV prepared by Richard Bell, ed. C. Bosworth and M. E. J. Richardson, Manchester 1991 (Journal of Semitic Studies Monographs 14).

Bellamy, J. A.: 'A New Reading of the Namārah Inscription', *JAOS* 105 (1985) 31–51.

Bellinger, A. R.: 'The End of the Seleucids', *Transactions of the Connecticut Academy of Arts and Sciences* 38 (1949) 51–120.

Bellinger, A. R.: 'Hyspaosines of Charax', *Yale Classical Studies* 8 (1942) 53–67.

Berger, H.: *Die geographischen Fragmente des Eratosthenes neu gesammelt, geordnet und besprochen*, Leipzig 1880.

Beyer, K.: *Die aramäischen Texte vom Toten Meer samt den Inschriften aus Palästina, dem Testament Levis aus der Kairoer Genisa, der Fastenrolle und den alten talmudischen Zitaten*, Göttingen 1984.

Biella, J. C.: *Dictionary of Old South Arabic, Sabaean Dialect*, Chico 1982 (Harvard Semitic Studies 25).

Bietenhard, H.: 'Die Dekapolis von Pompeius bis Trajan. Ein Kapitel aus der neutestamentlichen Zeitgeschichte', *ZDPV* 79 (1963) 24–58.

von Bissing, Fr.-W.: 'Die Bedeutung der geographischen Termini Muṣr und Miṣraim. Eine Nachlese', *Recueil de travaux relatifs à la philologie et à l'archéologie égyptiennes et assyriennes* 33 (1911) 125–152.

Blachère, R.: 'L'allocution de Mahomet lors de pélérinage d'Adieu', *Mélanges Louis Massignon*, Damas 1956 223–240, repr. idem, *Analecta*, Damas 1975 121–143.

Blachère, R.: *Le Coran* vol. 1, Paris 1949, vol. 2, Paris 1950.

de Blois, F.: 'The Date of the "Martyrs of Nagrān"', *Arabian Archaeology and Epigraphy* 1

(1990) 110–128.
de Blois, F.: 'Who is King Amarō?', *Arabian Archaeology and Epigraphy* 6 (1995) 196–198.
Boese, J. and Rüss, U.: 'Gold', *RA* 3 504–531.
Boissevain, U. Ph.: 'Ein verschobenes Fragment des Cassius Dio (75, 9, 6)', *Hermes* 25 (1890) 329–339.
Borger, R.: 'Assyriologische und altarabische Miszellen', *Orientalia* 26 (1957) 1–11.
Borger, R. and Tadmor, H.: 'Zwei Beiträge zur alttestamentlichen Wissenschaft aufgrund der Inschriften Tiglatpilesers III: II: Die Meuniter', *ZAW* 94 (1982) 250–251.
Bosworth, A. B.: *Conquest and Empire: The Reign of Alexander the Great*, Cambridge 1988.
Bosworth, A. B.: 'The Government of Syria under Alexander the Great', *The Classical Quarterly N.S.* 24 (1974) 46–64.
Bosworth, C. E.: 'A Note on taʕarrub in Early Islam', *JSS* 34 (1989) 355–362.
Bosworth, C. E.: 'Iran and the Arabs before Islam', *The Cambridge History of Iran 3 (1) The Seleucid, Parthian and Sasanian Periods* ed. E. Yarshater, Cambridge 1983 593–612.
Bowersock, G. W.: 'The Annexation and Initial Garrison of Arabia', *Zeitschrift für Papyrologie und Epigraphik* 5 (1970) 37-47.
Bowersock, G. W.: 'The Arabian Ares', *Tri corda. Scritti in onore di Arnaldo Momigliano, Bibliotheca di Athaeum* 1 (1983) 43–47.
Bowersock, G. W.: 'Arabs and Saracens in the Historia Augusta', *Bonner Historia-Augusta-Colloquium 1984/1985*, Bonn 1987 (Antiquitas Reihe 4: Beiträge zur Historia-Augusta-Forschung Bd 19 ed. J. Straub) 71–80.
Bowersock, G. W.: 'The Cult and Representation of Dusares in Roman Arabia', *Petra and the Caravan Cities* ed. F. Zayadine 1993 31–36.
Bowersock, G. W.: 'The Greek–Nabataean Inscription at Ruwwāfa, Saudi Arabia', *Le monde grec. Pensée, littérature, histoire, documents. Hommage à Claire Préaux* ed. J. Bingen, G. Gambier et G. Nachtergael, Bruxelles 1975 513–522.
Bowersock, G. W.: 'Limes arabicus', *Harvard Studies in Classical Philology* 80 (1976) 219–229.
Bowersock, G. W.: 'A Report on Arabia Provincia', *Journal of Roman Studies* 61 (1971) 219–242.
Bowersock, G. W.: Review of Högemann: Alexander der Grosse und Arabien, *Gnomon* 59 (1987) 508–511.
Bowersock, G. W.: *Roman Arabia*, Cambridge, Mass./London 1983.
van den Branden, A.: *Histoire de Thamoud* 2ème éd., Beyrouth 1966 (Publications de l'Université Libanaise, Études historiques VI).
Brandis, C. G.: 'Arabarches', *RE* II (1896) 342–343.
Bräu, H. H.: 'Maʕadd', EI^1 III 62–63.
Bräu, H. H.: 'Ṭaiy', EI^1 VI 675.
Braun, R.: *1 Chronicles*, Waco 1986 (World Biblical Commentary 14).
Bräunlich, E.: 'Beiträge zur Gesellschaftsordnung der arabischen Beduinenstämme', *Islamica* 6 (1934) 68–111, 182–229.
Breton, J.-F.: 'Le sanctuaire de ʕAthtar Dhū Riṣāf d'as-Sawdāʔ (République du Yémen)', *CRAIBL* 1992 429–453.
Briant, P.: *État et pasteurs au Moyen Orient ancien*, Paris/Cambridge 1982.
Briant, P.: *Histoire de l'empire perse de Cyrus à Alexandre* I–II Leiden 1996 (Achaemenid History X).
Bright, J.: *Jeremiah. Introduction, translation and notes*, 2nd edn, Garden City, NY 1965 (The Anchor Bible 21).
Brilliant, R.: *The Arch of Septimius Severus in the Roman Forum*, Rome 1967 (American Academy in Rome, Memoirs XXIX).
Brinkman, J.: 'A Further Note on the Date of the Battle of Qarqar', *JCS* 30 (1975) 173–175.
Brinkman, J.: *A Political History of Post-Kassite Babylonia 1158–727 BC*, Roma 1968 (Analecta orientalia 43).
Brinkman, J.: *Prelude to Empire. Babylonian Society and Politics 747–626 BC*, Philadelphia 1984.
Brodersen, K.: *Terra incognita. Studien zur Römischen Raumerfassung*, Hildesheim 1995 (Spudesmata 59).

van den Broek, R.: *The Myth of the Phoenix According to Classical and Early Christian Traditions*, Leiden 1972 (Études préliminaires aux réligions orientales dans l'empire romain 24).

Bron, F.: 'Vestiges de l'écriture sud-sémitique dans le Croissant fertile', *PA* 82–91.

Bruce, F. F.: *The Epistle of the Galatians. A Commentary on the Greek Text*, Exeter/Grand Rapids 1982 (New International Greek Testament Commentary).

Brunner, G.: *Der Nabuchodonosor des Buches Judith* 2 Aufl., Berlin 1959.

Buhl, F.: *Geschichte der Edomiter*, Leipzig 1893.

Buhl, F.: *Muhammeds religiöse Forkyndelse efter Qurânen*, Köbenhavn 1924.

Bulliet, R.: *The Camel and the Wheel*, Cambridge, Mass. 1981.

Burkert, W.: *Griechische Religion der archaischen und klassischen Epoche*, Berlin 1977 (Die Religionen der Menschheit 15).

Burstein, *Agatharchides* = *Agatharchides of Cnidus: On the Erythraean Sea*. Translated from the Greek and edited by S. M. Burstein, London 1989 (The Hakluyt Society 2 ser. 172).

Cameron, G. G.: 'The Persian Satrapies and Related Matters', *JNES* 32 (1973) 47–56.

Campbell, A. F.: 'An Historical Prologue in a Seventh-Century Treaty', *Biblica* 50 (1969) 534–535.

Cantineau, J.: 'Nabatéen et arabe', *Annales de l'Institut d'Etudes Orientales, Alger* 1 (1934/1935) 77–97.

Caquot, A.: 'L'araméen de Hatra', *Groupe linguistique d'études chamito-sémitiques* 9 (1960–1963) 87–89.

Caquot, A.: 'Nouvelles inscriptions araméennes de Hatra I', *Syria* 29 (1952).

Caskel, W.: 'Aijām al-ʕArab. Studien zur altarabischen Epik', *Islamica* 4 (1931) 1–99.

Caskel, W.: 'ʕAkk' *EI* 2 I 340–341.

Caskel, W.: 'Der arabische Stamm vor dem Islam: Gesellschaftliche und juristische Organisation', *Atti del convegno internazionale sul tema: Dalla tribù allo stato, Roma 13–16 aprile 1961*, Rome 1962 139–151.

Caskel, W.: 'Die alten semitischen Gottheiten in Arabien', *Le antiche divinità semitiche* ed. S. Moscati, Roma 1958 (Studi semitici 1) 95–117.

Caskel, W.: *Die Bedeutung der Beduinen für die Geschichte der Araber*, Opladen/Köln 1953 (Arbeitsgemeischaft für Forschung des Landes Nordrhein-Westfalen: Geisteswissenschaft Heft 8).

Caskel, W.: *Entdeckungen in Arabien*, Köln/Opladen 1954 (Arbeitsgemeinschaft für Forschung des Landes Nordrhein-Westfalen. Geisteswissenschaften, Heft 30).

Caskel, W.: 'Zur Beduinisierung Arabiens', *ZDMG* 28 (1953) *28*–*36*.

Caskel, W.: *Ǧamharat an-nasab. Das genealogische Werk des Hišām Ibn Muḥammad al-Kalbī* I-II, Leiden 1966.

Caskel, W.: 'Die Inschrift von en-Nemāra - neu gesehen', *Mélanges de l'Université Saint-Joseph* 45 (1969) 367–379.

Caton, S. C.: *Peaks of Yemen I Summon. Poetry as Cultural Practice in a North Yemeni Tribe*, Berkley 1990.

Chad, C.: *Les dynastes d'Emèse*, Beyrouth 1972.

Chaumont, M. L.: 'A propos de la chute de Hatra et du couronnement de Shapur Ier', *Acta Antiqua Academiae Scientiarum Hungaricae* 27 (1979) 207–237.

Chaumont, M. L.: 'États vassaux dans l'empire des premiers sassanides', *Monumentum H. S. Nyberg* = *Acta Iranica* 4 (1975) 89–156.

Choueiri, Y. M.: *Arab Nationalism. A History,* Oxford 2000.

Christensen, A.: *Les gestes des rois dans les traditions de l'Iran antique*, Paris 1936.

Chuvin, P.: *Mythologie et géographie dionysiaques. Recherches sur l'oevre de Nonnos de Panopolis*, Clermont-Ferrand 1991 (Vates 2).

Clermont-Ganneau, C.: 'Le dieu nabatéen Chaîʕ al-Qaum', *Recueil d'archéologie orientale* 4 (1901) 382–402.

Cleveland, W. L.: *The Making of an Arab Nationalist. Ottomanism and Arabism in the Life and Thought of Sati' Al-Husri*, Princeton 1971.

Cogan, M.: *Imperialism and Religion: Assyria, Judah, and Israel in the Eighth and Seventh*

Centuries BCE, Missoula 1974 (Society of Biblical Literature Monograph Series Vol. 19).
Cohen, A.: 'Arabisms in Rabbinic Literature', *Jewish Quarterly Review* 1912/1913 221–233.
Cole, S.: *Nippur in Late Assyrian Times c. 755–612 BC*, Helsinki 1996.
Conrad, L. I.: 'The Arabs', *Cambridge Ancient History* XVI, Cambridge 2000 678–700.
Conti Rossini, M. Ch.: 'Les listes des rois d'Aksoum', *JA* 10 (1909) 263–320.
Contini, R.: 'Linguistic Conditions in Hawran', *Felix Ravenna* 233–234 (1989) 25–79.
Conzelmann, H.: *Die Apostelgeschichte*, Tübingen 1963 (Handbuch des Neuen Testaments).
Corriente, F.: 'Marginalia on Arabic Diglossia and the Evidence Thereof in the Kitab al-Aghani', *JSS* 20 (1975) 38–61.
Crone, P.: 'The First Century Concept of Hiǧra', *Arabica* 41 (1994) 352–387.
Crone, P.: 'Mawlā', *EI* [2] VI 874–882.
Crone, P.: *Meccan Trade and the Rise of Islam*, Oxford 1987.
Crone, P.: *Slaves on Horses. The Evolution of the Islamic Polity*, Cambridge 1980.
Crone, P.: 'Were the Qays and Yemen of the Umayyad Period Political Parties?', *Der Islam* 71 (1994) 1–57.
Crone, P. and Cook, M.: *Hagarism. The making of the Islamic World*, Cambridge 1977.
Cook, J. M.: 'The Rise of the Achaemenids and Establishment of their Empire', *The Cambridge History of Iran* Vol. 2: *The Median and Achaemenian Periods*, Cambridge 1985 200–291.
Crosby, E. W.: *Akhbar al-Yaman wa-ash'aruha wa-ansabuha: The History, Poetry, and Genealogy of Yemen of 'Abid b. Sharya al-Jurhumi*, Diss. Yale 1985.
Cross, F. M.: 'Geshem the Arabian, Enemy of Nehemiah', *BA* 18 (1955) 46–47.
Curtis, E. L. and Madsen, A. A.: *A Critical and Exegetical Commentary on the Books of Chronicles*, Edinburgh 1910 (The International Critical Commentary).
Dagorn, R.: *La geste d'Ismaël d'après l'onomastique et la tradition arabes*, Genève/Paris 1981.
Dalman, G.: *Arbeit und Sitte in Palästina* I–VII, Gütersloh 1927–1942, repr. Hildesheim/New York 1987.
Dandamaev, M. A.: 'Aravit'ane v Mesopotamii novovavilonskogo i axemenidskogo vremeni', *Vestnik Drevnej Istorii* (in press).
Dandamaev, M. A.: *A Political History of the Achaemenid Empire*, Leiden/New York/Köbenhavn/Köln 1989.
Dangel, J.: 'Du Nil à l'Euphrate dans l'imaginaire des poètes latins de l'époque républicaine', *APEHC* 321–339.
Davies, G. I.: 'Hagar, el-Heǧra and the Location of Mount Sinai', *Vetus Testamentum* 22 (1972) 152–163.
Davies, G. I.: *The Way of the Wilderness. A Geographical Study of the Wilderness Itineraries in the Old Testament*, Cambridge 1979 (Society for Old Testament Study Monograph Series 5).
Debevoise, N. C.: *A Political History of Parthia*, Chicago 1938.
Detlefsen, D.: *Die Anordnung der geographischen Bücher des Plinius und ihre Quellen*, Berlin 1909 (Quellen und Forschungen zur alten Geschichte und Geographie Heft 18).
Dhorme, E.: 'Les peuples issus de Japhet', *Syria* 13 (1932) 28–49.
Dietrich, A.: 'Geschichte Arabiens vor dem Islam', *Orientalische Geschichte von Kyros bis Mohammed 2*, Leiden 1966 (Handbuch der Orientalistik 1 Abt. Bd 2: Keilschriftforschung und alte Geschichte Vorderasiens 4) 291–336.
Dihle, A.: 'Arabien und Indien', *Hérodote et les peuples non grecs.* Neuf exposés suivis de discussions . . . entretiens preparés de G. Nenci et présidés par O. Reverdin, Vandoevres-Genève 22–26 août 1988, Genève 1990 42–61.
Dihle, A.: 'Die entdeckungsgeschichtlichen Voraussetzungen des Indienhandels der römischen Kaiserzeit', *ANRW* II 9:2 (1976) 546–580.
Dihle, A.: *Umstrittene Daten. Untersuchungen zum Auftreten der Griechen am Roten Meer*, Opladen 1965 (Wissenschaftliche Abhandlungen der Arbeitsgemeinschaft für Forschung des Landes Nordrhein-Westfalen Bd 32).
Dijkstra, K.: *Life and Loyalty. A Study in the Socio-religious Culture of Syria and Mesopotamia in the Graeco-Roman Period Based on Epigraphic Evidence*, Leiden 1995 (Religions in the Graeco-Roman World 128).

Dijkstra, K.: 'State and Steppe. The Socio-political Implications of Hatra Inscription 79', *JSS* 35 (1990) 81–98.
Dillard, R. B. L.: *2 Chronicles*, Waco 1987 (World Biblical Commentary 15).
Dillemann, L.: *Haute Mésopotamie orientale et pays adjacents. Contribution à la géographie historique de la région du Ve siècle avant l'ère chrétienne au VIe de cette ère*, Paris 1962 (Institut Français d'Archéologie de Beyrouth: Bibliothèque archéologique et historique 72).
Dillmann, A.: 'Zur Geschichte des abyssinischen Reichs', *ZDMG* 7 (1853) 338–364.
Dillmann, A.: *Lexicon linguae aethiopicae* 1865, repr. Osnabrück 1970.
von Domaszewski, A.: 'Die politische Bedeutung der Religion von Emesa', *Archiv für Religionswissenschaft* 11 (1908) 223–242.
Donner, F. M.: *The Early Islamic Conquests*, Princeton 1981.
Donner, F, M.: *Narratives of Islamic Origins. The Beginnings of Islamic Historical Writing*, Princeton 1998 (Studies in Late Antiquity and Early Islam 14).
Dostal, W.: 'The Development of Bedouin Life in Arabia Seen from Archaeological Material', *SHA* I 125–144.
Dostal, W.: 'Die Araber in vorislamischer Zeit', *Der Islam* 74 (1997) 1–63.
Dostal, W.: 'The Evolution of Bedouin Life', *ASB* 11–34.
Dostal, W.: 'Die Ṣulubba und ihre Bedeutung für die Kulturgeschichte Arabiens', *Archiv für Völkerkunde* 11 (1956) 15–42.
Dostal, W.: 'Zur Frage der Entwicklung des Beduinentums', *Archiv für Völkerkunde* 13 (1958) 1–14.
Dougherty, R. Ph.: *The Sealand of Ancient Arabia*, New Haven 1932 (Yale Oriental Series 19).
Dozy, R.: *Supplément aux dictionnaires arabes* t. 1–2, Leyden 1881.
Dresch, P.: *Tribes, Government, and History in Yemen*, Oxford 1989.
Drijvers, H. J. W.: *Cults and beliefs at Edessa*, Leiden 1980 (Ètudes préliminaires aux religions orientales dans l'empire romain 82).
Drijvers, H. J. W.: 'Dusares', *Lexicon iconographicum mythologiae classicae* III:1 670–672.
Drijvers, H. J. W.: 'Hatra, Palmyra und Edessa. Die Städte der syrisch-mesopotamischen Wüste in politischer, kulturgeschichtlicher und religionsgeschichtlicher Beleuchtung', *ANRW* II 8 799–906.
Drinkard, J. F.: 'ʕal pĕnē as "east of"', *JBL* 98 (1979) 285–286.
Dumbrell, W. J.: 'Jeremiah 49:28–33; An Oracle Against a Proud Desert Power', *Australian Journal of Biblical Archaeology* 2 (1972) 99–109.
Dumbrell, W. J.: 'Midian – a Land or a League?', *Vetus Testamentum* 25 (1975) 323–337.
Dumbrell, W. J.: 'The Tell el-Maskhuṭa Bowls and the "Kingdom" of Qedar in the Persian Period', *BASOR* 203 (1971) 33–44.
Duri, A. A.: *The Rise of Historical Writing among the Arabs*, ed. and trans. L. I. Conrad, Princeton 1983.
Dussaud, R.: *Les arabes en Syrie avant l'Islam*, Paris 1907.
Dussaud, R.: 'Inscription nabatéo-arabe', *Revue archéologique* 41 (1902) 409–421.
Dussaud, R.: *La pénétration des Arabes en Syrie avant l'Islam*, Paris 1955.
Dussaud, R.: *Topographie historique de la Syrie antique et médiévale*, Paris 1927.
Duval, R.: *Histoire d'Édesse, politique, religieuse et littéraire*, Paris 1892, repr. Amsterdam 1975.
Edelman, D. V.: 'Edom. A Historical Geopgraphy', *You Shall Not Abhor an Edomite for He is Your Brother: Edom and Seir in History and Tradition* ed. D. V. Edelman, Atlanta 1995 1–11 (Archaeology and Biblical Studies 3).
Edens, Ch. and Bawden, G.: 'History of Taymāʔ and Hejazi Trade During the First Millennium BC', *JESHO* 32 (1989) 48–103.
Eissfeldt, O.: 'Kreter und Araber', *Theologische Literaturzeitung* 4 (1947) 207–212.
Eissfeldt, O.: 'Protektorat der Midianiter über ihre Nachbarn im letzten Viertel des 2 Jahrtausends v. Chr.', *JBL* 87 (1968) 383–393.
Elat, M.: 'The Campaigns of Shalmaneser III against Aram and Israel', *IES* 25 (1973) 25–35.
Eliade, M.: *Le chamanisme et les techniques archaïques de l'extase*, 2 éd. Paris 1968.
Eliséeff, N.: 'Ḥimṣ', *EI*² III 397–402.

Ensslin, W.: *Zur Ostpolitik des Kaisers Diokletian*, München 1942 (Sitzungsberichte der Bayerischen Akademie der Wissenschaften Phil.-hist. Abt. 1942:1).
Eph'al, I.: *The Ancient Arabs. Nomads on the Borders of the Fertile Crescent 9th–5th Centuries* BC, Jerusalem/Leiden 1982.
Eph'al, I.: '"Arabs" in Babylonia in the 8th Century BC', *JAOS* 94 (1974) 108–115.
Eph'al, I.: "Ishmael" and "Arab(s)": A Transformation of Ethnological Terms', *JNES* 35 (1976) 225–235.
Eph'al, I.: 'Ishmaelites', *EJ* IX 87–90.
Equini Schneider, E.: *Septimia Zenobia Sebaste*, Rome 1993.
Fahd, T.: *La divination arabe. Études religieuses, sociologiques et folkloristiques sur le milieu natif de l'Islam*, Leiden 1966.
Fahd, T.: 'The Nabaṭ al-ʕIrāq', *EI*[2] VII:835–838.
Fahd, T.: *Le panthéon de l'Arabie centrale à la veille de l'Hégire*, Paris 1968.
Février, J. G.: *Essai sur l'histoire politique et économique de Palmyre*, Paris 1931.
Février, J. G.: *La réligion des palmyréniens*, Paris 1931.
Fiaccadori, G.: *Teofilo Indiano*, Ravenna 1992 (Bilioteca di 'Felix Ravenna' 7).
Fiema, Z. T. and Jones, R.: 'The Nabataean King-list Revised: Further Observation on the Second Nabataean Inscription from Tell esh-Shuqafiya, Egypt', *ADAJ* 34 (1990) 239–248.
Fiey, J. M.: *Assyrie chrétienne. Contribution à l'étude de l'histoire et de la géographie ecclésiastiques et monastiques du nord de l'Iraq* I–II, Beyrouth 1965.
Fleisch, H.: *Traité de philologie arabe I: Préliminaires, phonétique, morphologie nominale*, Beyrouth 1961 (Recherches publiées sous la direction de l'Institut de Letters Orientales de Beyrouth t. XVI).
Fontaine, *Commentaire = Ammien Marcellin: Histoire t.IV:1–2 (Livres XVIII–XXV)* Commentaire par J. Fontaine, Paris 1977.
Forrer, G.: *Die Provinzeinteilung des assyrischen Reiches*, Leipzig 1920.
Frame, G.: Review of Eph'al, I: The Ancient Arabs, *JAOS* 107 (1987) 130–131.
Fraenkel, S.: *Die aramäischen Fremdwörter im Arabischen*, Leiden 1886.
Freudenthal, J.: *Alexander Polyhistor und die von ihm erhaltenen Reste judäischer und samaritanischer Geschichtswerke*, Breslau 1875.
Frézouls, E.: 'Cosmas Indicopleustès et l'Arabie', *APEHC* 441–460.
Frézouls, E.: 'Les fluctuations de la frontière orientale de l'empire romain', *La géographie administrative et politique d'Alexandre à Mahomet. Actes du colloque de Strasbourg 14–16 juin 1979*, Leiden 1981 177–225.
Frick, F. S.: 'Rechab', *ABD* V:630–632.
Galil, G.: *The Chronology of the Kings of Israel and Judah*, Leiden/New York/Cologne 1996 (Studies in the History and Culture of the Ancient Near East IX).
Galling, K.: 'Jesaia 21 im Lichte der neuen Nabonidtexte', *A. Weiser Festchrift*, Göttingen 1963 49–62.
Galter, H. D.: '". . . an der Grenze der Länder im Westen". Saba' in den assyrischen Königsinschriften', *Studies in Oriental Culture and History. Festschrift for Walter Dostal* ed. A. Gingrich, S. Haas, G. Paleczek and Th. Fillitz, Frankfurt/M 1993 29–40.
Garbini, G.: 'Le iscrizioni su ceramica da ad-Durayb - Yalā', *Yemen* 1 (1992) 79-91.
Garbini, G.: 'Le iscrizioni proto-arabe', *AION* 36 (1976) 165–174.
Garbini, G.: 'Osservazioni linguistiche e storiche sull'iscrizione di Maʕdkarib Yaʕfur (Ry 510)', *AION* 39 (1979) 469–475.
Garbini, G.: 'I Sabei del Nord come problema storico', *Studi in onore di Francesco Gabrieli nel suo ottantesimo compleanno* Vol. I, ed. R. Traini Roma 1984 373–380.
Gardiner, A.: *Egypt of the Pharaohs*, Oxford 1961 repr. ibid. 1978.
Gardthausen, V.: 'Die geographischen Quellen Ammians', *Jahrbücher für klassische Philologie: Supplement 6* (Leipzig 1872–73) 509–556.
Garrelli, P.: 'Muṣur', *SDB* 5 (1957) 1468–1474.
Gatier, P.-L. and Salles, J.-F.: 'L'emplacement de Leuké Komé', *L'Arabie et ses mers bordiers I Itinéraires et voisinages* ed. J.-F. Salles, Paris 1988 186–187.
Gauthier-Pilters, H. and Dagg, A. I.: *The Camel: Its Evolution, Ecology, Behavior and*

Relationship to Man, Chicago/London 1981.
Gaheis, A.: 'Claudius: Schriftstellerische Tätigkeit', *RE* 3 (1899) 2836–2839.
Gerholm, T.: *Market, Mosque and Mafrag. Social Inequality in a Yemeni Town*, Stockholm 1977.
Gese, H.: 'Die Religionen Altsyriens', in H. Gese, M. Höfner, and K. Rudolph, *Die Religionen Altsyriens, Altarabiens und der Mandäer*, Stuttgart etc. 1970 1–232.
Gese, H.: 'tò dè Agár Sinà óros estìn en tēi Arabíai', *Das Ferne und Nahe Wort. Festschrift Leonhard Rost zur Vollendung seines 70 Lebensjahres 1966 gewidmet* ed. F. Maass, Berlin 1967 (BZAW) 105) 81–94.
Gibb, H. A. R.: 'Tarikh', *EI*[1] *Supplement*, Leiden 1938 233–245.
Giesinger, F.: 'Skylax' *RE Zweite Reihe* III (1929) 619–646.
Gihon, M.: 'Idumea and the Herodian Limes', *IEJ* 17 (1967) 26–42.
Glaser, E.: *Skizze der Geschichte und Geographie Arabiens von den ältesten Zeiten bis zum Propheten Muḥammad* 2 Bd, Berlin 1890.
Goldziher, I.: *Muhammedanische Studien* I–II, Halle 1888 repr. Hildesheim 1971.
Graf, D. F.: 'Arabia During Achaemenid Times', *Achaemenid History IV: Centre and Periphery. Proceedings of the Groningen 1986 Achaemenid History Workshop* ed. H. Sancisi-Weerdenburg and A. Kuhrt, Leiden 1990 131–148.
Graf, D. F.: 'The Nabaṭ al-Shām', *EI*[2] VII 834–835.
Graf, D. F.: 'The Origin of the Nabataeans', *Aram* 2 (1990) 45–75.
Graf, D. F.: 'Rome and the Saracens: Reassessing the Nomadic Menace', *APEHC* 341–400.
Graf, D. F.: 'The Saracens and the Defense of the Arabian Frontier', *BASOR* 229 (1978) 1–26.
Graf, D. F. and O'Connor, M.: 'The Origin of the Term Saracen and the Rawwāfa Inscription', *Byzantine Studies* 4 (1977) 52–66.
Grainger, J. D.: *The Cities of Seleucid Syria*, Oxford 1990.
Gray, J.: *I and II Kings. A Commentary*, 3rd edn, London 1977 (Old Testament Library).
Grayson, A. K.: 'Studies in Neo-Assyrian History: The Ninth Century BC', *Bibliotheca Orientalis* 33 (1976) 134–145.
Grohmann, A.: *Kulturgeschichte des Alten Orients: Arabien*, München 1963 (Handbuch der Altertumswissenschaft 3 Abteilung 1 Teil 3 Band 3 Abschnitt 4 Unterabschnitt).
Grohmann, A.: 'Nabataioi', *RE* 16 (1935) 1453–1468.
Groom, N.: *Frankincense and Myrrh. A Study of the Arabian Incense Trade*, London/New York 1981.
Grünfeld, H. Y.: 'Masaʕ Nevûxadneʔṣar be-sefer Yehûdît', *Yediʕôt. Bulletin of the Israel Exploration Society* 28 (1964) [204]–[208].
Guidi, I.: *L'Arabie antéislamique. Quatre conférences données à l'Univerité Égyptienne au Caire en 1909*, Paris 1921.
Guillaume, A: *The Life of Muhammad. A Translation of Ibn Isḥāq's Sirat rasul allah*, Oxford 1955 repr. Karachi 1967.
Gundel, H.: 'Plinius d. ä.: A fine Aufidii Bassi XXXI', *RE* 21 (1952) 289–294.
Guthrie, D.: *Galatians* (revised edition), London 1974 (The Century Bible N.S.).
Hajjar, Y.: *La triade d'Héliopolis-Baalbek. Son culte et sa diffusion à travers les textes littéraires et les documents iconographiques et épigraphiques* I–II, Leiden 1977.
Háklár, N.: 'Die Stellung Suhis in der Geschichte: Ein Zwischenbilanz', *OrAnt* 22 (1983) 25–36.
Halévy, J.: 'Les arabes dans les inscriptions sabéennes', *Revue sémitique d'épigraphie et d'histoire ancienne* 7 (1899) 146–157.
Halévy, J.: 'L'Inscription nabatéo-arabe d'En-Némara', *Revue sémitique d'épigraphie et d'histoire ancienne* 11 (1903) 58–62.
Hallock, R. T.: 'The Evidence of the Fortification Tablets', *The Cambridge History of Iran* Vol. 2: *The Median and Achaemenian Periods* ed. I. Gershevitch, Cambridge 1985 588–609.
Halpern, B.: 'Kenites', *ABD* IV:17–22.
Hamarneh, S. K.: 'The Nabataeans after the Decline of their Political Power: From the Arabic Islamic Sources', *Aram* 2 (1990) 425–436.
Hamarneh, S. K.: 'The Role of the Nabateans in the Islamic Conquests', SHAJ 1 (1982) 347–349.
Hamilton, J. M.: 'Hormah', *ABD* III:288–289.

Hammond, N. G. L.: *Sources for Alexander the Great: An Analysis of Plutarch's Life and Arrian's Anabasis Alexandrou*, Cambridge 1993.
Hammond, N. G. L.: *Three Historians of Alexander the Great: The so-called Vulgate Authors, Diodorus, Justin and Curtius*, Cambridge 1983.
Hammond, Ph.: *The Nabataeans – Their History, Culture, and Archaeology*, Göteborg 1973 (Studies in Mediterranean Archaeology 37).
Hampl, F.: 'Alexanders des Grossen Hypomnemata und letzte Pläne', *Studies presented to D. M. Robinson* Vol. II 816–829, Washington, DC 1953.
Hartmann, M.: 'Zur Inschrift von Namāra', *OLZ* 9 (1906) 573–584.
Hartmann, R.: 'Die Namen von Petra', *ZAW* 30 (1910) 143–151.
Hawting, G. R.: *The Idea of Idolatry and the Emergence of Islam*, Cambridge 1999.
Healey, J.: *The Religion of the Nabataeans. A Conspectus*, Leiden 2001.
Healey, J. F.: 'Were the Nabataeans Arabs?' *Aram* 1:1 (1989) 38–44.
Heinrichs, A. and Koenen, L.: 'Ein griechischer Mani-Kodex', *Zeitschift für Papyrologie und Epigraphik* 5 (1970) 97–214.
Hengel, M.: *Judentum und Hellenismus*, 3 Aufl., Tübingen 1988 (Wissenschaftliche Untersuchungen zum Neuen Testament 10).
den Hengst, D.: 'Verba, non res. Über die Inventio in den Reden und Schriftstücken in der Historia Augusta', *Bonner Historia-Augusta-Colloquium 1984/1985*, Bonn 1987 (Antiquitas, Reihe 5: Beiträge zur Historia-Augusta-Forschung Bd 19).
Henninger, J.: 'Altarabische Genealogie. (Zu einem neuerschienen Werk)', *AV* 49–82.
Henninger, J.: 'Pariastämme in Arabien', *AV* 180–304.
Henninger, J.: 'Über religiöse Strukturen nomadischer Gruppen', *AS* 34–47.
Henninger, J.: 'Über Sternkunde und Sternkult in Nord- und Zentralarabien', *AS* 48–117.
Henninger, J.: 'Zum Problem der Venussterngottheit bei den Semiten', *Anthropos* 71 (1976) 129–168.
Henninger, J.: 'Zur Frage des Haaropfers bei den Semiten', *AS* 286–306.
Herzfeldt, E.: 'Hatra', *ZDMG* 68 (1914) 655–676.
Herzfeldt, E.: *The Persian Empire. Studies in Geography and Ethnography of the Ancient Near East* ed. by G. Walser, Wiesbaden 1968.
Hidal, S.: 'The Land of Cush in the Old Testament', *Svensk Exegetisk Årsbok* 41–42 (1976–1977) 97–106.
Hildesheimer, H.: *Beiträge zur Geographie Palästinas*, Berlin 1886.
Hinds, M.: 'Kūfan Political Alignments and their Background in the Mid-Seventh Century AD.', *IJMES* 2 (1971) 346–367.
Hitti, Ph.: *History of the Arabs from the Earliest Times to the Present*, 10th edn, London 1970.
Höfner, M.: 'Die vorislamischen Religionen Arabiens', *Die Religionen Altsyriens, Altarabiens und der Mandäer*, ed. H. Gese, M. Höfner and K. Rudolph, Stuttgart/Berlin/Köln/Mainz 1970 (Die Religionen der Menschheit Bd 10:2) 233–402.
Höfner, M. and Merkel, E.: 'Die Stammesgruppen Nord- und Zentralarabiens in vorislamischer Zeit', *Wörterbuch der Mythologie I Bd 1: Götter und Mythen im Vorderen Orient* ed. H. W. Haussig, Stuttgart 1965 407–481.
Hoftijzer, J. and Jongeling, K.: *Dictionary of the North-West Semitic Inscriptions* 1–2, Leiden 1995 (Handbuch der Orientalistik 1 Abt. Bd 21:1–2).
Högemann, P.: *Alexander der Grosse und Arabien*, Munich 1985 (Zetemata Heft 82).
Holladay, W. L.: *Jeremiah. A Commentary on the Book of the Prophet Jeremiah* 1: Chapters 1–25, Philadelphia 1986, 2: Chapters 26–52, ibid. 1989.
Hölscher, G.: 'Josephus', *RE* 9 (1914) 1934–2000.
Hommel, F.: *Ethnologie und Geographie des alten Orients*, München 1926 (Handbuch der Altertumswissenschaft 3 Abt., Teil 1, Bd 1).
Honigmann, E.: 'La liste originale des pères de Nicée', *Byzantion* 14 (1935) 17–76.
Honigmann, E.: 'Marinos von Tyros', *RE* 14 (1930) 1767–1796.
Honigmann, E.: 'Strabo', *RE* (2 Reihe) 4 (1932) 76–115.
Honigmann, E.: 'Stephanos Byzantios', *RE* (2 Reihe) 3 (1929) 2369–2399.
Honigmann, E.: 'Taiēnoí', *RE* (2 Reihe) 4 (1932) 2025–2026.

Honigmann, E. and Maricq, A.: *Recherches sur les Res Gestae Divi Saporis*, Bruxelles 1953 (Académie Royale de Belge, Classe des lettres et de sciences morales et politiques, Mémoires t. 47:4).
Hornblower, J.: *Hieronymus of Cardia*, Oxford 1981.
Horowitz, J: *Koranische Untersuchungen*, Berlin/Leipzig 1926 (Studien zur Geschichte und Kultur des islamischen Orients IV).
Hoyland, R. G.: *Seeing Islam as Others saw It. A Survey and Evaluation of Christian, Jewish and Zoroastrian Writings on Early Islam,* Princeton 1997 (Studies in Late Antiquity and Islam 13).
Hoyland, R. G.: *Arabia and the Arabs from the Bronze Age to the Coming of Islam,* London 2001.
Humphreys, R. S.: 'Taʔrīkh: Historical writing', *EI*[2] X 271–276.
Irvine, A. K.: 'The Arabs and the Ethiopians', *Peoples of Old Testament Times* ed. D. J. Wiseman, Oxford 1973 287–312.
Jacob, G.: *Altarabisches Beduinenleben nach den Quellen geschildert* 2 Aufl., Berlin 1897 repr. Hildesheim 1967.
Jacobson, D.: 'When Palestine Meant Israel', *Biblical Archaeological Review* 27:3 (2001) 43–47.
Jacoby, F.: 'Euemeros', *RE* 6 (1909) 952–972.
Jacoby, F.: 'Hekataios aus Abdera', *RE* 7 (1910) 2750–2769.
Jacoby, F.: 'Hekataios aus Milet', *RE* 7 (1910) 2667–2750.
Jacoby, F. 'Hellanikos', *RE* 8 (1912) 104–153.
Jacoby, F.: 'Herodotos', *RE Supplement* 2 (1903) 205–520.
Jacoby, F.: 'Hieronymos von Kardia', *RE* 15 (1912) 1540–1560.
Jacoby, F.: 'Iuba', *RE* 9 (1914) 2384–2395.
Jamieson-Drake, D. W.: *Scribes and Scholars in Monarchic Judah. A Socio-Archaeological Approach*, Sheffield 1991 (JSOTS 109).
James, W. E.: 'On the Location of Gerra', *AAW* V/2 36–57.
Japhet, S.: *I&II Chronicles. A Commentary*, London 1993 (Old Testament Library).
Jastrow, M.: *A Dictionary of the Targumim, the Talmud Babli and Yerushalmi, and the Midrashic Literature* 1–2, New York 1886–1903, repr. New York 1975.
Johnson, M. D.: *The Purpose of the Biblical Genealogies with Special Reference to the Setting of the Genealogies of Jesus*, Cambridge 1969.
Jones, A. H. M.: *The Cities of the Eastern Roman Provinces* 2nd rev edn. by M. Avi-Yonah *et al.*, Oxford 1971.
Jones, A. H. M.: 'The Urbanization of the Ituraean Principality', *Journal of Roman Studies* 21 (1931) 265–275.
Junge, P. J.: 'Satrapie und Natio. Reichsverwaltung und Reichspolitik im Staate Dareios' I', *Klio* 34 (1941/1942) 1–55.
Juynboll, G. H. A.: 'The Qurrāʔ in Early Islamic History', *JESHO* 16 (1973) 113–129.
Juynboll, G. H. A., 'The Qurʔān Reciter on the Battlefield and Concomitant Issues', *ZDMG* 125 (1975) 1–27.
Kammerer, A.: *Pétra et la Nabatène* I–II, Paris 1929, 1930.
Kasher, A.: *Jews, Idumaeans, and Ancient Arabs*, Tübingen 1988 (Texte und Studien zum antiken Judentum 18).
Katzenstein, H. J.: *The History of Tyre from the Beginning of the Second Millennium* BCE *until the Fall of the Neo-Babylonian Empire in 538* BCE, Jerusalem 1973.
Kawar (= Shahid), I.: 'Djadhīma al-Abrash or al-Waḍḍāḥ', *EI*[2] 2 365.
Kennedy, H.: *The Prophet and the Age of the Caliphates. The Islamic Near East from the Sixth to the Eleventh Century*, London/New York 1986.
Kiessling, A.: *Q. Horatius Flaccus: Oden und Epoden* 7 Aufl. ed. R. Heintze, Berlin 1930.
Kindermann, H.: 'Tanūkh', *EI*[1] *Supplement* 243–246.
Kirwan, L.: 'Where to Search for the Ancient Port of Leuke Kome', *SHA* II 55–61.
Kister, M. J.: 'Land Property and Jihād', *JESHO* 34 (1991) 270–311.
Kister, M. J.: 'Khuzāʕa', *EI*[2] 5 76–80.
Kister, M. J.: 'Ḳuḍāʕa' *EI*[2] 5 314–318.
Kitchen, K.: *Documentation for Ancient Arabia Part I: Chronological Framework and Historical Sources*, Liverpool 1994.

Klein, S.: 'Zur jüdischen Altertumskunde 2–4', *MGWJ* 41 N.F. (1933) 180–198.
Klengel, H.: *Syria 3000 to 300 BC. A Handbook of Political History*, Berlin 1992.
Knaack, G.: 'Dionysios [Periegetes]', *RE* 5 (1905) 915–924.
Knaack, G.: 'Eratosthenes', *RE* 6 (1909) 358–387.
Knauf, E. A.: 'Bedouin and Bedouin States', *ABDI* 634–638.
Knauf, E. A.: 'Dushara and Shaiʕ al-Qaum', *Aram* 2 (1990) 175–183.
Knauf, E. A.: 'Herkunft der Nabatäer', *Petra. Neue Ausgrabungen und Entdeckungen* hrsg. von M. Lindner, München/Bad Windsheim 1986 74–86.
Knauf, E. A.: 'Husham', *ABD* III 339.
Knauf, E. A.: 'Ishmaelites', *ABD* III 513–520.
Knauf, E. A.: *Ismael. Untersuchungen zur Geschichte Palästinas und Nordarabiens im 1 Jahrtausend v. Chr.*, Wiesbaden 1985 (Abhandlungen des Deutschen Palästinavereins).
Knauf, E. A.: 'Ituraea', *ABD* III 583–584.
Knauf, E. A.: 'Madiáma', *ZDMG* 135 (1985) 16–21.
Knauf, E. A.: *Midian. Untersuchungen zur Geschichte Palästinas und Nordarabiens am Ende des 2 Jahrtausends v.Cr.*, Wiesbaden 1988 (Abhandlungen des Deutschen Palästinavereins).
Knauf, E. A.: 'Midianites and Ishmaelites', *Midian, Moab and Edom. The History and Archaeology of Late Bronze and Iron Age Jordan and North West Arabia* ed. J. A. Sawyer and D. J. A. Clines, Sheffield 1983 (JSOTS 24) 147–162.
Knauf, E. A.: 'Mu'näer und Meuniter', *WO* 16 (1985) 114–122.
Knauf, E. A.: 'Nabataean Origins', *Arabian Studies in Honour of Mahmoud Ghul: Symposium at Yarmouk University December 8–11, 1984* ed. M. M. Ibrahim, Wiesbaden 1989 56–61.
Knauf, E. A.: 'Nodab', *ABD* IV 1134.
Knauf, E. A.: 'The Persian Administration in Arabia', *Transeuphratène* 2 (1990) 202–217.
Knauf, E. A.: 'Supplementa Ismaelitica 1: Ein keilschriftlicher Beleg für den Stamm Naphis', *BN* 20 (1983) 34–36.
Knauf, E. A.: 'Supplementa Ismaelitica 4: Ijobs Heimat', *BN* 22 (1983) 25–29.
Knauf, E. A.: 'Supplementa Ismaelitica 5: Die Haartracht der alten Araber', *BN* 22 (1983) 30–33.
Knauf, E. A.: 'Supplementa Ismaelitica 8: Philisto-arabische Münzen', *BN* 30 (1985) 19–28.
Knauf, E. A.: 'Supplementa Ismaelitica 12: Camels in Late Bronze and Iron Age Jordan: The Archaeological Evidence', *BN* 40 (1987) 20–23.
Knauf, E. A.: 'Supplementa Ismaelitica 13: Edom und Arabien', *BN* 45 (1988) 62–79.
Knauf, E. A.: 'Teman', *ABD* VI 347–348.
Kneissl, P.: *Die Siegestitulatur der römischen Kaiser. Untersuchungen zu den Siegerbeinamen des ersten und zweiten Jahrhunderts*, Göttingen 1969 (Hypomnemata 23).
Koestermann, E.: *Cornelius Tacitus: Annales. Erläuterungen mit einer Einleitung versehen*, I–IV, Heidelberg 1963–1968.
Köhler, L. and Baumgartner, W.: *Hebräisches und aramäisches Lexikon zum Alten Testament* 3 Aufl., Leiden 1967–1990.
Krauss, S.: 'Die biblischen Völkertafel im Talmud, Midrasch und Targum', *MGWJ* 19 (1895) 1–11, 49–63.
Krauss, S.: 'Talmudische Nachrichten über Arabien', *ZDMG* 70 (1916) 321–353.
Kretschmar, G.: 'Origenes und die Araber', *Zeitschrift für Theologie und Kirche* 50 (1953) 258–279.
Kroll, W.: 'Iamboulos', *RE* 9 (1914) 681–683.
Krone, S.: *Die altarabische Gottheit al-Lāt*, Frankfurt/M 1992 (Heidelberger orientalistische Studien 23).
Kropp, M.: 'Grande re degli arabi e vassallo di nessuno: Mar´ al-Qays ibn 'Amr e l'iscrizione ad en-Nemara', *Quaderni di Studi Arabi* 9 (1991) 3–27.
Kropp, M.: 'Vassal – neither of Rome nor Persia. Marʔ-al-Qays the great king of the Arabs', *PSAS* 23 (1993) 64–93.
Kuan, J. K.: *Neo-Assyrian Historical Inscriptions and Syria-Palestine*, Hong Kong 1995 (Jian Dao Dissertation Series 1: Bible and Literature 1).
Lambert, W. G.: 'Nabonidus in Arabia', *PSAS* 2 (1972) 53–64.

Lammens, H. and Shahid, I.: 'Lakhm', *EI*² 5 632.
de Landberg, Le Comte: *Étude sur les dialectes de l'Arabie Méridionale Vol. I: Ḥaḍramoût*, Leide 1901.
Lane, E. W.: *Arabic–English Lexicon*, London/Edinburgh 1863–1893, repr. Cambridge 1984.
Langdon, S.: 'The "Shalamians" of Arabia', *JRAS* 1927 529–533.
Laqueur, R.: 'Nikolaos von Damaskos', *RE Zweite Reihe* 17 (1937) 362–424.
Laqueur, R.: 'Theophanes von Mytilene', *RE Zweite Reihe* 5 (1934) 2090–2127.
Laqueur, R.: 'Timagenes', *RE Zweite Reihe* 6 (1937) 1063–1071.
Lecker, M.: *The Banū Sulaym. A Contribution to the Study of Early Islam*, Jerusalem 1989 (The Max Schloessinger Memorial Series Monograph IV).
Lecker, M.: 'Wādī 'l-ḳurā', *EI*² XI 18–19.
Lemaire, A.: 'Histoire du Proche-Orient et chronologie sudarabique avant Alexandre', *ArAnt* 2 [35–48].
Lemche, N.-P.: *Early Israel. Anthropological and Historical Studies on the Israelite Society Before the Monarchy*, Leiden 1985 (Supplements to Vetus Testamentum vol. 37).
Lemche, N.-P.: *The Israelites in History and Tradition*, Louisville/London 1998.
Lendle, O.: *Kommentar zu Xenophons Anabasis (Bücher 1–7)*, Darmstadt 1995.
Lepper, F. A.: *Trajan's Parthian War*, Oxford 1948.
Leslau, W.: *Comparative Dictionary of Geʕez (Classical Ethiopic)*, Wiesbaden 1987.
Lesquier, J.: 'L'arabarchès d'Égypte', *Révue archéologique* Sér. 5:5 (1917) 95–103.
Leuze, O.: *Die Satrapieeinteilung in Syrien und im Zweistromlande von 520 bis 320*, Halle/Saale 1935 (Schriften der Königsberger Gelehrten Gesellschaft 11, Geisteswiss. Klasse Heft 4).
Levi della Vida, G.: 'Nizār b. Maʕadd', *EI*¹ 3 1015–1016/*EI* ² 8 82–83.
Levin, A.: 'Sibawayhi's Attitude to the Spoken Language', *JSAI* 17 (1994) 204–243.
Lewis, I. M.: *Peoples of the Horn of Africa. Somali, Afar and Saho*, 4th edn., London 1998.
Lewy, J.: 'Enthält Judith I–IV Trümmer einer Chronik zur Geschichte Nebukadnezars und seine Feldzüge von 597 und 591?', *ZDMG* 81 (N.F. 6) 1927 LII–LIV.
Lewy, J.: 'Nāḫ et Rušpān', *Mélanges syriens offerts à Mr Dussaud* I (1939) 273–275.
Liddell, H. G. and Scott, R.: *Greek–English Lexicon*. New edn. by H. S. Jones, Oxford 1940.
Lidzbarski, M.: *Ephemeris für semitische Epigraphik* II, Giessen 1908.
Lindner, M.: 'Die Geschichte der Nabatäer', *Petra und das Königreich der Nabatäer*, 3 Aufl. hsrg. von M. Lindner, Nürnberg 1970 38–103.
Lipinski, E.: 'Arabie, Arabes', *Dictionnaire Encyclopédique de la Bible*, Brepols 1987 123–125.
Liverani, M.: 'Early Caravan Trade between South-Arabia and Mesopotamia', *Yemen. Studi archeologici, storici e filologici sull'Arabia Meridionale* 1 (1992) 111–115.
Livingstone, A.: 'Arabians in Babylonia: Some Reflections à propos New and Old Evidence', *APEHC* 97–105.
Lloyd, A. B.: *Herodotus Book II: Introduction, Leiden 1975; Commentary 1–98*, Leiden 1976 (Études préliminaires aux religions orientales dans l'empire romain t. 43).
Lundin, A. G.: 'Južnaja Aravija v VI veke', *Palestinskij Sbornik* 8 (71) 1961.
Lundin, A. G.: 'Sabaean Dictionary. Some Lexical Notes', *Ṣayhadica. Recherches sur les inscriptions de l'Arabie préislamique offertes par ses collègues au professeur A. F. L. Beeston* ed. Ch. Robin et M. Bâfaqîh, Paris 1987 49–56.
MacAdam, H. I.: 'The Nemara Inscription: Some Historical Considerations', *Al-Abhath* 28 (1980) 3–16.
MacAdam, H. I.: 'Strabo, Pliny the Elder and Ptolemy of Alexandria: Three Views of Ancient Arabia and its Peoples', *APEHC* 289–320.
MacAdam, H. I.: *Studies in the History of the Roman Province of Arabia: The Northern Sector*, Oxford 1986 (BAR International Series 295).
Macdonald, M. C. A.: 'Hunting, Fighting, and Raiding: The Horse in Pre-Islamic Arabia', *Furusiyya. The Horse in the Art of the Near East* Vol. 1 ed. D. Alescander, Riyadh 1996 73–83.
Macdonald, M. C. A.: 'Reflections on the Linguistic Map of Pre-Islamic Arabia', *Arabian Archaeology and Epigraphy* 11 (2000) 28–79.
Macdonald, M. C. A.: 'Trade Routes and Trade Goods at the Northern End of the "Incense Road"

in the First Millennium BC', *Profumi d'Arabia.* Atti del convegno a cura di A. Avanzini, Rome 1997 333–349.
Macdonald, M. C. A.: 'Was the Nabataean Kingdom a "Bedouin State"?', *ZDPV* 107 (1991) 102–119.
Macdonald, M. C. A. and King, G. M. H.: 'Thamudic', *EI*² X 436–438.
Madelung, W.: 'Apocalyptic Prophecies in Ḥimṣ in the Umayyad Age', *JSS* 31 (1986) 141–185.
Madelung, W.: 'Has the *Hijra* Come to an End?', *Revue des études islamiques* 54 (1986) 225–237.
Madelung, W.: 'The Sufyānī Between Tradition and History', *Studia Islamica* 63 (1986) 5–48.
de Maigret, A./Robin, Ch.: 'Les fouilles italiennes de Yâlâ (Yémen du nord): Nouvelles données sur la chronologie de l'Arabie du sud pré-islamique', *CRAIBL* 1989 255–291.
Malamat, A.: *Das davidische und salomonische Königreich und seine Beziehungen zu Ägypten und Syrien. Zur Entstehung eines Grossreichs*, Wien 1983 (Österreichische Akademie der Wissenschaften. Phil.-hist. Klasse, Sitzungsberichte, Bd 407).
Mārbākh, ʕA.: 'Maʕnā l-muṣṭalaḥ "ʕarab" ḥasba l-maʕāǧim wa-l-Qurʔān wa-l-Kitāb li-Sībawayhi wa-Muqaddimat Ibn Xaldūn', *Al-Karmil. Studies in Arabic Language and Literature* 13 (1992) 145–178.
Marek, Ch.: 'Die Expedition des Aelius Gallus nach Arabien im Jahre 25 v.Chr.', *Chiron* 23 (1993) 121–156.
Marek, Ch.: 'Der römische Inschriftenstein von Barāqīš', *Arabia Felix* 178–189.
Maricq, A.: 'Hatra de Sanatrouq', *Syria* 32 (1955) 273–288.
Marx, E.: *Bedouin of the Negev*, Manchester 1967.
Marx, E.: 'The Organization of Nomadic Groups in the Middle East', *Society and Political Structure in the Arab World* ed. M. Milson, New York 1973 305–336.
Marx, E.: 'The Tribe as a Unit of Subsistence: Nomadic Pastoralism in the Middle East', *American Anthropologist* 79 (1977) 343–363.
Mattingly, G. L.: 'Amalek', *ADB* 1 169–171.
Mayzler, B (= Mazar, B.): 'Ha-Reqem we-ha-Ḥeger', *Tarbiz* 20 (1949) 316–319.
Meier, F.: 'Über die umstrittene Pflicht des Muslims bein nichtmuslimischer Besetzung seines Landes auszuwandern', *Der Islam* 68 (1991) 65–86.
Meissner, B.: 'Pallacottas', *Mitteilungen der Vorderasiatischen Gesellschaft* 4 (1896) 1–13.
Merkel, E.: 'Erste Festsetzungen im fruchtbaren Halbmond', *AAW* I 139–180, 268–372.
Meshorer, Y.: *Nabataean Coins*, Jerusalem 1975 (Qedem. Monographs of the Institute of Archaeology, The Hebrew University of Jerusalem 3).
Meyer, E.: *Der historische Gehalt der Aiyām al-ʕArab*, Wiesbaden 1970.
Meyer, E.: *Die Israeliten und ihre Nachbarstämme. Alttestamentlichen Untersuchungen.* Mit Beiträgen von B. Luther, Halle 1906.
Milik, J. T.: 'Origines des Nabatéens', *SHAJ* I 1982 261–265.
Milik, J. T.: 'La tribu des Bani ʕAmrat en Jordanie de l'époque grecque et romaine', *ADAJ* 24 (1980) 41–54.
Millar, F.: *A Study of Cassius Dio*, Oxford 1964.
Millar, F.: *The Roman Near East 31 BC – AD 337*, Cambridge, Mass./London 1993.
Miller, J. M. and Hayes, J. H.: *A History of Ancient Israel and Judah*, Philadelphia 1986.
Mittmann, S.: 'Die Küste Palästinas bei Herodot', *ZDPV* 99 (1983) 130–140.
Mittmann, S.: 'Ri. 1,16f und das Siedlungsgebiet der kenitischen Sippe Hobab', *ZDPV* 93 (1977) 213–235.
Mommsen, Th.: 'Ammians Geographica', *Hermes* 16 (1881) 602–636.
Monneret de Villard, U.: 'Il Tāǧ di Imru' l-Qays', *Atti della Academia Nazionale dei Lincei, Rendiconti. Classe di scienze morali, storiche e filologiche* 8 (1953) 224–229.
Montgomery, J. A.: *Arabia and the Bible*, Philadelphia 1934.
Montgomery, J. A.: *A Critical and Exegetical Commentary on the Books of Kings* ed. by H. S. Gehman, Edinburgh 1951 (The International Critical Commentary).
Moore, C. A.: *Judith. A New Translation with Introduction and Commentary*, Garden City, New York 1985 (The Anchor Bible 40).
Mordtmann, J. H.: 'Dusares bei Epiphanius', *ZDMG* 29 (1876) 99–106.

Moreau, J.: 'Eusebios von Caesarea', *RACh* 6 (1966) 1052–1088.
Morkot, R.: 'Nubia and Achaemenid Persia: Sources and Problems', *Achaemenid History VI: Asia Minor and Egypt: Old Cultures in a New Empire* ed. H. Sancisi-Weerdenburg and A. Kuhrt, Leiden 1991 321–336.
Morony, M. G.: *Iraq After the Muslim Conquest*, Princeton 1984.
Müller, D. H.: 'Arabia', *RE* 2 (1896) 344–359.
Müller, H.-P.: 'Arabien und Israel', *Theologische Realenzyklopädie* hrsg. von G. Krause und G. Müller Bd. III, Berlin/New York 1978 571–577.
Müller, W. W.: 'Abyaṯaʕ und andere mit yṯʕ gebildete Namen im Frühnordarabischen und Altsüdarabischen', *WO* 10 (1979) 23–29.
Müller, W. W.: 'Das Altarabische der Inschriften aus vorislamischer Zeit', *GAPh* 30–36.
Müller, W. W.: 'Altsüdarabien als Weihrauchland', *Theologische Quartalschrift* 149 (1969) 350–368.
Müller, W. W.: 'Araber', *Neues Bibel-Lexikon* hrsg. von M. Görg und H. Lang Benziger, Zürich 1988 143–145.
Müller, W. W.: 'L'écriture zabur du Yémen pré-islamique dans la tradition arabe', Ryckmans, *Textes* 35–39.
Müller, W. W.: 'Arabian Frankincense in Antiquity According to Classical Sources', *SHA* 1 79–87.
Müller, W. W.: 'Das Frühnordarabische', *GAPh* 17–29.
Müller, W. W.: 'Marib', *EI*² VI 559–567.
Müller, W. W.: 'Obal', *ABD* V:4–5.
Müller, W. W.: 'Die Stele des 'Abraha, des äthiopischen Königs von Jemen', *Im Land der Königin von Saba. Kunstschätze aus dem antiken Jemen* hrsg. vom Staatlichen Museum für Völkerkunde München, München 1999 268–272.
Müller, W. W.: review of L'Arabie Antique ed. Ch. Robin, *BiOr* 51 (1994) 468–475.
Munro-Hay, S.: *Aksum. An African Civilisation of Late Antiquity*, Edinburgh 1991.
Musil, A.: *Arabia Deserta. A Topographical Itinerary*, New York 1927 (American Geographical Society: Oriental Explorations and Studies No. 2).
Musil, A.: *Arabia Petraea I: Moab. Topographischer Reisebericht*, Wien 1907.
Musil, A.: *Arabia Petraea II; Edom. Topographischer Reisebericht* 1-2, Wien 1907.
Musil, A.: *The Manners and Customs of the Rwala Bedouins*, New York 1928.
Musil, A.: *The Northern Ḥeğâz. A Topographical Itinerary*, New York 1926 (The American Geographical Society: Oriental Explorations and Studies No. 1).
Myers, J. M.: *I Chronicles. Introduction, Translation and Notes*, Garden City, New York 1965 (The Anchor Bible 12).
Myers, J. M.: *II Chronicles. Translation and Notes*, Garden City, New York 1965 (The Anchor Bible).
Myers, J. M.: *Ezra, Nehemiah. Introduction, Translation and Notes*, Garden City, New York 1965 (The Anchor Bible).
Na'aman, N.: 'Nawwadîm-rôʕîm bi-sfar ha-drômî šel memlexet Yehûdā bi-tqûfat ha-memlexet ha-mefûleget', *Zion* 52 (1987) 261–278.
Na'aman, N.: 'Two Notes on the Monolith Inscription of Shalmaneser III from Kurkh', *Tel Aviv* 3 (1976) 89–106.
Nagel, T.: 'Qurrāʔ', *EI*² V 499–500.
Nallino, C. A.: 'Arabi', *Raccolta di scritti editi e inediti III,* Roma 1941 179–193.
Nallino, C. A.: 'L'Arabia preislamica', *Raccolta di scritti editi e inediti III*, Roma 1941 1–47.
Naveh, J.: *Early History of the Alphabet. An Introduction to West Semitic Epigraphy and Paleography*, Jerusalem/Leiden 1982.
Negev, A.: 'The Early Beginnings of the Nabataean Realm', *PEQ* 108 (1976) 125–133.
Negev, A.: 'The Nabateans and the Provincia Arabia', *ANRW* II:8 520–686.
Negev, A.: 'Obodas the God', *IEJ* 36 (1986) 56–60.
Negev, A.: Personal Names in the Nabataean Realm, Jerusalem 1991 (Qedem 32).
Neiman, D.: '"Urbi" = "irregulars" or "Arabs"', *JQS* 60 (N.S.) 1969/1970 237–258.
Newby, G. D.: *A History of the Jews of Arabia*, University of South Carolina 1988.

Newby, G. D.: *The Making of the Last Prophet. A Reconstruction of the Earliest Biography of Muhammad*, University of South Carolina 1989.
Nisbel, R. G. M. and Hubbard, M.: *A Commentary on Horace's Odes Book I*, Oxford 1970.
Nodelman, S. A.: 'A Preliminary History of Characene', *Berytus* 13 (1959–1960) 83–121.
Noiville, J.: 'Le culte de l'étoile du matin chez les arabes préislamiques et la fête de l'épiphanie', *Hespéris* 8 (1928) 363–384.
Nöldeke, Th.: 'Der Araberkönig von Namāra', *Florilegium ou recueil de travaux d'érudition dédiés à Melchior de Vogüé*, Paris 1909 463–466.
Nöldeke, Th,: 'Arabia, Arabians', *Encyclopaedia Biblica* Vol. I ed. T. K. Cheyne and J. S. Black London 1899 cols. 272–275.
Nöldeke, Th.: *Beiträge und Neue Beiträge zur semitischen Sprachwissenschaft*, Strassburg 1904, 1910; repr. Amsterdam 1982.
Nöldeke, Th.: *Geschichte des Korans* I, Leipzig 1909 repr. Hildesheim 1961.
Nöldeke, Th.: *Geschichte der Perser und Araber zur Zeit der Sasaniden aus der arabischen Chronik des Tabari übersetzt und mit ausführlichen Erläuterungen und Ergänzungen versehen*, Leyden 1879, repr. Graz 1973.
Nöldeke, Th.: 'Die Namen der aramäischen Nation und Sprache', *ZDMG* 25 (1871) 113–131.
Nöldeke, Th.: 'Taïēnós tis', *Philologus* 52 (1894) 736.
Nöldeke, Th.: 'Ueber die Amalekiter und einige andere Nachbarvölker der Israeliten', *Orient und Okzident* 2 (1864) 614–655.
Nöldeke, Th.: 'Zu den nabatäischen Inschriften', *ZDMG* 17 (1863) 703–708.
Norden, E.: *Die Geburt des Kindes. Geschichte einer religiösen Idee*, Leipzig/Berlin 1924.
Norris, H. T.: 'Mūrītāniyā', *EI*[2] VII 611–628.
Noth, M.: 'Beiträge zur Geschichte des Ostjordanlandes III: Die Nachbarn der israelitischen Stämme im Ostjordanlande', *ZDPV* 68 (1951) 1–50.
Noth, M.: 'Das Deutsche Evangelische Institut für Altertumswissenschaft des Heiligen Landes. Lehrkursus 1954', *ZDPV* 71 (1955) 1–59.
Noth, M.: 'Ismael', *Die Religion in der Geschichte und Gegenwart* III, 3 Aufl., 935–936.
Noth, M.: *Die israelitischen Personennamen im Rahmen gemeinsemitischer Namengebung*, Stuttgart 1928, repr. Hildesheim/New York 1980.
Noth, M.: 'Das Reich von Hamath als Grenznachbar des Reiches Israel', *Palästinajahrbuch* 33 (1937) 36–51.
Noth, M.: 'Zur Geschichte des Namens Palästina', ZDPV 62 (1939) 125–144.
Nyberg, H. S.: 'Die sassanidische Westgrenze und ihre Verteidigung', *Septentrionalia et orientalia. Studia Bernardo Karlgren a. d. III Non. oct. anno MCMLIX dedicata*, Stockholm 1959 (Kungl. Vitterhets Historie och Antikvitets Akademiens handlingar 91) 316–326.
O'Connor, M.: 'The Arabic Loanwords in Nabataean Aramaic', JNES 45 (1986) 213–229.
Ogden, D.: 'Homosexuality and Warfare in Ancient Greece', *Battle in Antiquity* ed. A. B. Lloyd, London 1996 107–168.
Olinder, G.: *The Kings of Kinda of the Familiy of Ākil al-Murār*, Lund/Leipzig 1927 (Lunds universitets Årsskrift N.F. Avd. 1, Bd 23, Nr 26).
Opitz, D.: 'Die Darstellungen der Araberkämpfe Aššurbânaplis aus dem Palaste zu Ninive', *AfO* 7 (1931/1932) 7–13.
Oppenheim, M.: *Die Beduinen Bd I: Die Beduinenstämme in Mesopotamien und Syrien*, Leipzig 1939.
Otto, W.: 'Hippalos', *RE* 15 (1912) 1660–1661.
Parr, P.: 'Aspects of the Archaeology of North-West Arabia in the First Millennium BC', *APEHC* 39–66.
Paret, R.: *Der Koran. Kommentar und Konkordanz*, Stuttgart 1971.
Paret, R.: *Der Koran. Übersetzung*, Stuttgart 1962.
Parker, Th.: 'Towards a History of the Limes Arabicus', *Roman Frontier Studies 1979 XII: Papers presented to the 12th International Congress of Roman Frontier Studies part 3*, 1980 865–878.
Parr, P.: 'Pottery, Peoples and Politics', *Archaeology in the Levant. Essays for Kathleen Kenyon* ed. P. R. G. Moorley and P. Parr, Warminster 1978 203–209.

Parr, P.: 'Pottery of the Late Second Millennium BC from North West Arabia and its Historical Implications', *Araby the Blest: Studies in Arabian Archaeology* ed. D. T. Potts, Copenhagen 1988 72–89.
Paschoud, F.: 'À propos des sources du récit des campagnes orientales d'Aurélien dans l'*Historiae Augustae*', *Historiae Augustae Colloquium Maceratense* a cura di G. Bonamenti e G. Paci, Bari 1996 281–295.
Paschoud, F.: 'L'histoire Auguste et Dexippe', *Historiae Augustae Colloquium Parisinum*, Macerata 1991 (Historiae Augustae Colloquia N.S. 1: Colloquium Parisinum MCMXC) 217–269.
Paschoud, F.: 'Nicomaque Flavien et la connexion byzantine (Pierre le Patrice et Zonaras): à propos un livre récent de Bruno Bleckmann', *Antiquité Tardive* 2 (1994) 71–82.
Payne, E.: 'The Midianite Arc in Joshua and Judges', *Midian, Moab and Edom. The History and Archaeology of Late Bronze and Iron Age Jordan and North West Arabia*, Sheffield 1983 (JSOTS 24) 163–172.
Pearson, L.: *Early Ionian Historians*, Oxford 1939.
Pearson, L.: *The Lost Histories of Alexander the Great*, New York/Oxford 1960.
Pedersen, J.: *Israel* vol. 1 and 2, Köbenhavn 1934.
Pedersen, J: Review of E. Meyer: Ursprung und Geschichte der Mormonen, *Der Islam* 5 (1914) 110–115.
Peiser, F. E.: 'Die arabische Inschrift von En-Nemâra', *OLZ* 6 (1903) 277–281.
Peter, H.: *Die Quellen Plutarchs in den Biographien der Römer*, Halle 1865.
Petráček, K.: 'Gindibu' Arbaija – ein Ṣafā-Araber?', *Archiv Orientální* 27 (1959) 44–53.
Philby, H. S.: *The Queen of Sheba*, London 1981.
Philippi, F.: *Zur Reconstruktion der Weltkarte des Agrippa*, Marburg 1880.
Piamenta, M.: *Dictionary of Post-Classical Yemeni Arabic* 1–2, Leiden 1990.
Picard, Ch.: 'Les frises historiées autour de la cella et devant l'adyton dans le temple de Bacchus à Baalbek', *Mélanges syriens offerts à M. René Dussaud* I, Paris 1939 319–343.
Pigulevskaja, N. V.: 'Araby VI v. po sirijskim istočnikam', *Trudy 2 sessii Associacii Arabistov 19–23 okt'abr'a 1936 g.*, Leningrad 1941 49–70.
Piotrovskij, M. B.: 'Arabskaja versija istorii caricy Zenobii (az-Zabby)', *Palestinskij Sbornik* 21/84 (1970) 170–184.
Piotrovskij, M. B.: *Predanije o ximjaritskom care As'ade Kamile*, Moskva 1977.
Pirenne, J.: *Le royaume sud-arabe de Qatabân et sa datation*, Louvain 1976.
Pitard, W. T.: *Ancient Damascus. A Historical Study of the Syrian City-State from the Earliest Times until its Fall to the Assyrians in 732 BCE*, Wiona Lake 1987.
Polaschek, E.: 'Notitia Dignitatum', *RE* 17 (1937) 1077–1111.
Polaschek, E.: 'Ptolemaios: Das geographische Werk', *RE Supplement* X (1965) 680–833.
Posener, G.: 'Achoris', *Revue d'égyptologie* 21 (1969) 148–150.
Potts, D. T.: 'Arabia and the Kingdom of Characene', *Araby the Blest: Studies in Arabian Archaeology* ed. D. T. Potts, Copenhagen 1988 137–167.
Potts, D. T.: *The Arabian Gulf in Antiquity I: From Prehistory to the Fall of the Achaemenid Empire; II: From Alexander the Great to the Coming of Islam*, Oxford 1990.
Potts, D. T.: 'Thaj and the Location of Gerrha', *PSAS* 14 (1984) 87–91.
Potts, D. T.: 'Trans-Arabian Routes of the Pre-Islamic Period', *AMB* 127–162.
Priebatsch, H. Y.: 'Das Buch Judith und seine hellenistische Quellen', *ZDPV* 90 (1974) 50–60.
Propp, W. H.: 'Ithamar', *ABD* III:579–581.
Puin, G.-R.: *Der Dīwān von ʕUmar ibn al-Ḫaṭṭāb. Ein Beitrag zur frühislamischen Verwaltungsgeschichte*, Diss. Bonn 1970.
Puin, G.-R.: 'The Yemeni Hijrah Concept of Tribal Protection', *Land Tenure and Social Transformation in the Middle East* ed. T. Khalidi, Beirut 1984 483–494.
de Pury, A.: 'Yahwist ("J") Source', *ABD* VI 1012–1020.
Quatremère, M.: 'Mémoire sur les nabatéens', *JA* 15 (1835) 4–55, 97–137.
von Radinger, K.: 'Hekataios', *RE* 7 (1912) 2667–2750.
Radner, K. (ed.): *The Prosopography of the Neo-Assyrian Empire* I:1–2, Helsinki 1998, 1999.
Raschke, M. G.: 'New Studies in the Roman Commerce with the East', *ANRW* 9:2 604–13–78.

Rashīd, S.: *Al-Rabadha. A Portrait of Early Islamic Civilisation in Saudi Arabia*, Riyadh 1984.
Rausing, G.: *The Bow. Some Notes on its Origin and Development*, Bonn/Lund 1967 (Acta Archaeologica Lundensia 8:6).
Redmount, C. A.: *On an Egyptian Asiatic Frontier. An Archaeological History of Wādi Tumīlāt*, Diss. Chicago 1989.
Regeling, K.: 'Crassus Partherkrieg', *Klio* 7 (1907) 357–394.
Reinhardt, K.: 'Poseidonios', *RE* 22 (1954) 558–826.
Retsö, J.: 'The Arab Connection. Political Implications of Frankincense in Early Greece', *Profumi d'Arabia*. Atti del convegno a cura di A. Avanzini, Roma 1997 473–480.
Retsö, J.: 'The Domestication of the Camel and the Establishment of the Frankincense Road from South Arabia', *Orientalia Suecana* 40 (1991) 187–219.
Retsö, J.: 'The Earliest Arabs', *Orientalia Suecana* 39 (1989–1990) 131–139.
Retsö, J.: 'kaškaša, t-passives and the Dialect Continuum in Ancient Arabia', *Oriente Moderno* 19 N.S. (2000) 111–118.
Retsö, J.: 'The Road to Yarmūk. The Arabs and the fall of the Roman Power in the Middle East', *Aspects of Late Antiquity and Early Byzantium. Papers read at a Colloquium held at the Swedish Research Institute in Istanbul 31 May–5 June 1992* ed. by L. Rydén and J. O. Rosenqvist, Stockholm 1993 (Swedish Research Institute in Istanbul Transactions vol. 4) 31–41.
Retsö, J.: 'Xenophon in Arabia', *Greek and Latin Studies in Memory of Cajus Fabricius* ed. by S.-T. Teodorsson, Göteborg 1990 122–133 (Studia graeca et latina gothoburgensia LIV).
Ricks, S. D.: *Lexicon of Inscriptional Qatabanian*, Roma 1989 (Studia Pohl 14).
Ringgren, H.: *Islam, ʔaslama and muslim*, Uppsala 1949 (Horae Soederblomianae II).
Roaf, M.: 'The Subject Peoples on the Base of the Statue of Darius', *Cahiers de la délégation archéologique francaise en Iran* 4 (1974) 73–160.
Robertson Smith, W.: *Kinship and Marriage in Early Arabia*, London (?) 1903.
Robertson Smith, W.: *The Religion of the Semites. The Fundamental Institutions*, 2nd edn. Edinburgh 1894.
Robin, Ch.: 'La première intervention abyssine en Arabie méridonale (de 200 à 270 de l'ère chrétienne environ)', *Proceedings of the Eighth International Conference of Ethiopian Studies University of Addis Ababa 1984* vol. 2, Addis Ababa 1989 147–162.
Robin, Ch.: 'L'Arabie du sud et la date du Périple de la Mer Érythrée (Nouvelles données)', *JA* 279 (1991) 1–30.
Robin, Ch.: 'Cités, royaumes et empires de l'Arabie avant l'Islam', AA 45–54.
Robin, Ch.: 'The Date of the *Periplus of the Erythraean Sea* in the Light of South Arabian Evidence', *Crossings. Early Mediterranean Contacts with India* ed. F. de Romanis and A. Tchernia, New Delhi 1997.
Robin, Ch.: *Les hautes-terres du Nord-Yémen avant l'Islam* I–II, Istanbul 1982.
Robin, Ch.: 'Les inscriptions d'al-Miʕsâl et la chronologie de l'Arabie Méridionale au IIIe siècle de l'ère chrétienne', *CRAIBL* 1981 315–339.
Robin, Ch.: 'Les langues de la péninsule Arabique', *AA* 89–111.
Robin, Ch.: 'Monnaies provenant de l'Arabie du Nord-est', *Semitica* 24 (1974) 82–125.
Robin, Ch.: 'Quelques épisodes marquants de l'histoire sudarabique', *AA* 55–70.
Robin, Ch.: 'Le royaume hujride, dit 'royaume de Kinda', entre Himyar et Byzance', *CRAIBL* 1996 665–714.
Robin, Ch.: 'Les royaumes combattants', *Yémen* 180–187.
Robin, Ch.: 'Sheba', *SDB* 17 (1996) 1047–1254.
Robin, Ch.: 'La pénétration des arabes nomades au Yémen', *AA* 71–88.
Robin, Ch./Breton, J.-F.: 'Le sanctuaire préislamique du Ǧabal al-Lawḏ (Nord-Yémen)', *CRAIBL* 1982 590–629.
Robin, Ch. and Brunner, U.: *Map of Ancient Yemen/Carte du Yémen Antique*, Staatliches Museum für Völkerkunde, München 1997.
Rodinson, M.: 'Sur une nouvelle inscription du règne de Dhou Nowâs', *Bibliotheca Orientalis* 26 (1969) 26–34.
Röllig, W.: 'Erwägungen zu neuen Stelen König Nabonids', *ZA* N.F. 22 (1964) 218–260.

Romane, P.: 'Alexander's Siege of Gaza', *The Ancient World* 18 (1988) 21–30.
Roschinski, H. P.: 'Geschichte der Nabatäer', *Bonner Jahrbücher* 180 (1980) 129–154.
Roschinski., H. P.: 'Sprachen, Schriften und Inschriften in Nordwestarabien', *Bonner Jahrbücher* 180 (1980) 155–188.
Rosenthal, F.: *A History of Muslim Historiography* 2 rev. edn., Leiden 1968.
Rothenberg, B. and Glass, J.: 'The Midianite Pottery', *Midian, Moab and Edom. The History and Archaeology of late Bronze and Iron Age Jordan and North-West Arabia* ed. by J. F. A. Sawyer and D. J. A. Clines, Sheffield 1983 65–124.
Rothstein, G.: *Die Dynastie der Lahmiden in al-Ḥîra. Ein Versuch arabisch-persischer Geschichte zur Zeit der Sasaniden*, Berlin 1899 repr. Hildesheim 1968.
Rotter, G.: 'Der *veneris dies* im vorislamischen Mekka, eine neue Deutung des Namens "Europa" und eine Erklärung für *kobar* = Venus', *Der Islam* 70 (1993) 112–132.
Rowton, M.: 'Autonomy and Nomadism in Western Asia', *Orientalia N.S.* 42 (1973) 247–258.
Rowton, M.: 'Dimorphic Structure and Topology', *OrAnt* 15 (1976) 2–31.
Rowton, M.: 'Enclosed Nomadism', *JESHO* 17 (1974) 1–30.
Rowton, M.: 'The Physical Environment and the Problem of the Nomads', *La civilisation de Mari. XVe Rencontre Assyriologique Internationale* ed. J.-R. Kupper Paris 1967 109–121.
Rowton, M.: 'Urban Autonomy in a Nomadic Environment', *JNES* 32 (1973) 201–215.
Rubin, Z.: 'Dio, Herodian, and Severus' Second Parthian War', *Chiron* 5 (1975) 419–441.
Rudolph, W.: 'Der Aufbau der Asa-Geschichte (2 Chr. XIV–XVI)', *VT* 2 (1952) 367–371.
Rudolph, W.: *Chronikbücher*, Tübingen 1955 (Handbuch zum Alten Testament Erste Reihe 21).
Rudolph, W.: *Jeremia*, Tübingen 1947 (Handbuch zum Alten Testament Erste Reihe 12).
Rüger, H.-P.: 'Araber, Arabien', *Bibelhistorisches Handwörterbuch* Bd I hrsg. von B. Reicke und L. Rost, Göttingen 1962, 118.
Ryckmans, G.: 'Inscriptions historiques sabéennes', *Le Muséon* 66 (1953) 319–342.
Ryckmans, G.: *Les religions arabes préislamiques*, Louvain 1951 (Bibiothèque du Muséon 26).
Ryckmans, J.: *L'Institution monarchique en Arabie Méridionale avant l'Islam (Maʕîn et Saba)*, Louvain 1951.
Ryckmans, J.: 'Petits royaumes sud-arabes', *Le Muséon* 70 (1957) 75–96.
Ryckmans, J.: 'Himyaritica 3', *Le Muséon* 87 (1974) 237–263.
Ryckmans, J.: 'Himyaritica 4', *Le Muséon* 87 (1974) 493–521.
Ryckmans, J.: 'Himyaritica 5', *Le Muséon* 88 (1975) 199–219.
Ryckmans, J.: 'Les rois de Hadramawt mentionnès à ʕUqla', *Bibliotheca Orientalis* 221 (1964) 277–282.
Ryckmans, J., Müller, W. W. and ʕAbdallāh, Y. M.: *Textes du Yémen Antique inscrits sur bois*, Louvain-la-neuve 1994.
Sack, D.: *Damaskus. Entwicklung und Struktur einer orientalisch-islamischen Stadt*, Mainz 1989 (Damaszener Forschungen 1).
Sahas, D.: *John of Damascus on Islam. 'The Heresy of the Ishmaelites'*, Leiden 1972.
Al-Said, S. F.: *Die Personennamen in den minäischen Inschriften*, Wiesbaden 1995 (Akademie der Wissenschaften und der Literatur, Mainz: Veröffentlichungen der Orientalischen Kommission Bd 41).
Al-Said, S. F.: 'Die Verben rtkl und s^1ʕrb und ihre Bedeutung in den minäischen Inschriften', *Arabia Felix* 260–267.
Sartre, M.: *Bostra des origines à l'Islam*, Paris 1985 (Institut Français d'archéologie du Proche-Orient. Bibliothèque archéologiqie et historique 117).
Sartre, M.: *Trois études sur l'Arabie romaine et byzantine*, Bruxelles 1982 (Collection Latomus 178).
Sartre, M.: 'Le tropheus de Gadhimat, roi de Tanukh: une survivance en Arabie d'une institution hellenistique', *Liber Annuus* 29 (1979) 253–258.
Sass, B.: *Studia alphabetica. On the Origin and Early History of the Northwest Semitic, South Semitic and Greek Alphabets*, Freiburg/Göttingen 1991.
Sauvaget, J.: 'Le plan antique de Damas', *Syria* 26 (1949) 314–358.
Säve-Söderberg, T.: 'Kusch', *RÉ* 888–893.
Savignac, R.: 'Notes de voyage – le sanctuaire d'Allat à Iram', *RB* 41 (1932) 581–597.

Savignac, R.: 'Le sanctuaire d'Allat à Iram (1)', *RB* 42 (1933) 405–422.
Scagliarini, F.: 'La chronologie dédanite et liḥyanite: mise au point', *Présence arabe dans le Croissant fertile avant l'Hégire. Actes de la Table ronde internationale (Paris, 13 novembre 1993)* ed. H. Lozachmeur, Paris 1995 (Editions Recherche sur les Civilisations) 119–132.
Schachermeyr, F.: *Alexander der Grosse. Das Problem seiner Persönlichkeit und seines Wirkens*, Wien 1973 (Österreichische Akademie der Wissenschaften, Phil.-hist. Klasse, Sitzungsberichte 285).
Schachermeyr, F.: 'Die letzten Pläne Alexanders des Grossen', *Jahreshefte des Österreichischen Archäologischen Instituts* 41 (1954) 118–140.
Schedl, C.: 'Nabochodonosor, Arpakšad und Darius', *ZDMG* 115 (1965) 242–254.
Schleifer, J.: 'Ḥārith b. Kaʕb', *EI*[2] III:223.
Schmidt, C. and Polotsky, H. J.: 'Ein Manifund in Ägypten', *Sitzungsberichte der Preussischen Akademie der Wissenschaften Jahrgang 1933 Phil.-hist. Klasse*, Berlin 1933. PPP.
Schmitt, H. H.: *Untersuchungen zur Geschichte Antiochos des Grossen und seiner Zeit*, Wiesbaden 1964.
Schmitt, R.: 'Medisches und persisches Sprachgut bei Herodot', *ZDMG* 117 (1967) 119–145.
Scholten, C.: 'Hippolytos II (von Rom)', *RACh* 15 (1991) 492–551.
Schottroff, W.: 'Die Ituräer', *ZDPV* 98 (1982) 125–152.
Schramm, W.: *Einleitung in die assyrischen Königsinschriften. Zweiter Teil: 934–722 v. Chr.*, Leiden/Köln 1973 (Handbuch der Orientalistik 1 Abt. Ergänzungsband 5:1).
Schultz, H.: 'Herodian', *RE* 8 (1912) 959–973.
Schürer, E.: *The History of the Jewish People in the Age of Jesus Christ* I–III. A new English version revised and edited by G. Vermes, F. Millar, M. Black and M. Goodman, Edinburgh 1973–1987.
Schwartz, E.: 'Appianus', *RE* 2 (1896) 216–237.
Schwartz, E.: 'Cassius Dio', *RE* 3 (1899) 1684–1722.
Schwartz, E.: 'Diodorus', *RE* 5 (1905) 663–704.
Schwartz, E.: 'Ephoros', *RE* 6 (1909) 1–16.
Schwartz, E.: 'Eusebios', *RE* 6 (1909) 1370–1439.
Schwartz, J.: 'L'Histoire Auguste et Palmyre', *Bonner Historia-Augusta-Colloquium 1964/1965*, Bonn 1966 (Antiquitas Reihe 4) 185–195.
Scott, R. B. Y.: 'Solomon and the Beginnings of Wisdom in Israel', *Wisdom in Israel and in the Ancient Near East Presented to H.H. Rowley*, Leiden 1955 (Supplement to Vetus Testamentum 3) 262–279.
Segal, J. B.: 'Arabs at Hatra and the Vicinity: Mariginalia on New Aramaic Texts', *JSS* 31 (1986) 57–80.
Segal, J. B.: 'Arabs in Syriac Sources before the Rise of Islam', *JSAI* 4 (1984) 89–123.
Segal, J. B.: 'Pagan Syriac Monuments in the Vilayet of Urfa', *Anatolian Studies* 3 (1953) 97–119.
Seidensticker, T.: 'Zur Frage eines Astralkultes im vorislamischen Arabien', *ZDMG* 136 (1986) 493–511.
Seyrig, H.: 'Antiquités syriennes 76: Charactères de l'histoire d'Emèse', *Syria* 36 (1959) 185–192.
Shaban, M. A.: *Islamic History. A New Interpretation* AD *600–750* 1–2, Cambridge 1971.
Shahid, *Byzantium 1* = Shahid, I.: *Byzantium and the Arabs in the Fourth Century*, Washington, DC 1984.
Shahid, *Byzantium 2* = Shahid, I.: *Byzantium and the Arabs in the Fifth Century*, Washington, DC 1989.
Shahid, *Byzantium 3* = Shahid, I.: *Byzantium and the Arabs in the Sixth Century* I:1, Washington, DC 1995.
Shahid, I.: *The Martyrs of Najrân. New Documents*, Bruxelles 1971 (Subsidia Hagiographica 49).
Shahid, I.: 'Philological Observations on the Namāra Inscription', *JSS* 24 (1979) 33–42.
Shahid, I.: 'Pre-islamic Arabia', *The Cambridge History of Islam* Vol IA ed. P. M. Holt, A. K. S. Lambton and B. Lewis, Cambridge 1970 3–29.
Shahid, I.: *Rome and the Arabs. A Prolegomenon to the Study of Byzantium and the Arabs*,

Washington, DC 1984.
Sidebotham, S.: 'Aelius Gallus and Arabia', *Latomus* 45 (1986) 590–602.
Skjaervö, P. O.: *The Sassanian Inscription of Paikuli part 3.2 Commentary*, Wiesbaden 1983.
von Soden, W.: *Grundriss der Akkadischen Grammatik*, Roma 1952 (Analecta orientalia 33).
von Soden, W.: *Akkadisches Handwörterbuch* 1–3, Wiesbaden 1965–81.
Sokoloff, M.: *A Dictionary of Jewish Palestinian Aramaic*, Ramat-Gan 1990.
Sourdel, D.: *Les cultes du Hauran à l' époque romaine*, Paris 1952 (Institut Français d'Archéologie de Beyrouth. Bibliothèque archéologique et historique t. LIII).
Spencer, J. R. 'Aaron', *ABD* I 1–6.
Sprenger, A.: *Die alte Geographie Arabiens als Grundlage der Entwicklungsgeschichte des Semitismus*, Bern 1875.
Springberg-Hinsen, M.: *Die Zeit vor dem Islam in arabischen Universalgeschichten des 9. bis 12. Jahrhunderts*, Würzburg 1989 (Würzburger Forschungen zur Missions- und Religionswissenschaft 1:2 Religionswissenschaftliche Studien 13).
Starcky, J.: 'Allath, Athèna et la déesse syrienne', *MGMP* 119–133.
Starcky, J.: 'Palmyre', *SDB* 6 (1957–60) 1066–1103.
Starcky, J.: 'Pétra et la Nabatène', *SDB* 7 (1966) 886–1017.
Starcky, J. and Gawlikowski, M.: *Palmyre*, Paris 1985.
Stemplinger, E.: 'Studien zu Stephanos von Byzanz', *Philologus* 63 (1904) 615–630.
Stern, M.: *Greek and Latin Authors on Jews and Judaism I: From Herodotus to Plutarch*, Jerusalem 1976.
Stetkevych, S. P.: *The Mute Immortals Speak. Pre-Islamic Poetry and the Poetics of Ritual*, Ithaca 1993.
Stol, M.: 'Nanaja', *RA* 9 146–151.
Strack, H. L. and Stemberger, G.: *Einleitung in Talmud und Midrasch*, 7 Aufl. München 1982.
Streck, M.: 'Das Gebiet der heutigen Landschaften Armenien, Kurdistân und Westpersien nach den babylonisch-assyrischen Keilschriften', *ZA* 15 (1900) 257–382.
Streck, M.: 'Hatra', *RE* 7 (1910) 2516–2523.
Strenziok, G.: 'Azd', *EI²* I 811–812.
Stummer, F.: *Geographie des Buches Judith*, Stuttgart 1947 (Bibelwissenschaftliche Reihe Heft 3).
Sturm, J.: 'Pallakontas', *RE* 18:2 (1949) 229.
Sullivan, R. D.: 'The Dynasty of Emesa', *ANRW* II:8 198–219.
Sundermann, W.: 'An Early Attestation of the Name of the Tajiks', *Medioiranica. Proceedings of the International Colloquium Organized by the Katolieke Universiteit Leuven from the 21st to the 23rd of May 1990* ed. W. Skalmowski and A. van Tongerloo, Leuven 1993 (Orientalia Lovansensia Analecta 48) 163–171.
Sussmann, Y.: 'Baraytaʔ d-tḥûmê ʔereṣ Yisraʔel', *Tarbiz* 45 (1976) 213–257.
Sweet, L. E.: 'Camel Pastoralism in North Arabia and the Minimal Camping Unit', *Man, Culture, and Animals. The Role of Animals in Human Ecological Adjustments* ed. A. Leeds and A. P. Vayda, Washington, DC 1965 129–152.
Sweet, L. E.: 'Camel Raiding of North Arabian Bedouin: A mechanism of Ecological Adaptation', *American Anthropologist* 67 (1966) 1132–1150.
Tadmor, H.: 'Assyria and the West. The Ninth Century and its Aftermath', *Unity and Diversity. Essays in the History, Literature, and Religion of the Ancient Near East* ed. H. Goedicke and J. J. M. Roberts, Baltimore/London 1975 36–48.
Tadmor, H.: 'The Campaigns of Sargon II of Assur. A Chronological Study', *Journal of Cuneiform Studies* 12 (1958) 22–40, 77–100.
Tadmor, H.: 'Hameʕûnîm be-D[ivrê] H[a]-Y[amîm] le-ʔôr teʕûdā ʔašûrît', *Bible and Jewish History Dedicated to the Memory of J. Liver* ed. B. Uffenheimer, Tel-Aviv 1971 222–230.
Tadmor, H.: 'The Inscriptions of Nabunaid: Historical Arrangement', *Studies in Honor of Benno Landsberger on his 75 Birthday, April 21, 1965* ed. H. Gütenbock and Th. Jacobsen, Chicago 1965 (Assyrian Studies 16).
Tadmor, H.: 'Que and Muṣri', *IES* 11 (1961) 143–150.
Tadmor, H.: 'Introductory Remarks to a New Edition of the Annals of Tiglath-Pileser III',

Proceedings of the Israel Academy of Sciences and Humanities 2 (1968) 168–187.
Tadmor, H.: 'Philistia under Assyrian Rule', *The Biblical Archaeologist* 29 (1966) 86–102.
Tairan, S. A.: *Die Personennamen in den altsabäischen Inschriften*, Hildesheim/Zürich/New York 1992 (Texte und Studien zur Orientalistik Bd 8).
Tallqvist, K.: *Akkadische Götterepiteta mit einem Götterverzeichnis und einer Liste der prädikativen Elemente der sumerischen Götternamen*, Helsinki 1938 (Studia orientalia 7).
Tarn, W. W.: *Alexander the Great I–II*, Cambridge 1948.
Tarn, W. W.: 'Ptolemy II and Arabia', *Journal of Egyptian Archaeology* 15 (124) 9–25.
Tarn, W. W. and Griffith G. T.: *Hellenistic Civilisation* 3rd edn, London 1952.
Täubler, E.: 'Der Nabatäerkönig Erotimus', *Klio* 10 (1910) 251–253.
Tcherikover, V.: *Hellenistic Civilisation and the Jews*, JPSA 1959, repr. New York 1975.
Teixidor, J.: 'Bulletin d'épigraphie sémitique', *Syria* 48 (1971) 453–493.
Teixidor, J.: 'The Kingdom of Adiabene and Hatra', *Berytus* 17 (1967) 1–11.
Teixidor, J.: 'Notes Hatrénnes 3–4', Syria 43 (1966) 91–97.
Teixidor, J.: *Un port romain du désert: Palmyre*, Paris 1984 (Semitica 34).
Theiler, W.: *Poseidonios: Die Fragmente II: Erläuterungen*, Berlin/New York 1982 (Texte und Kommentare Band 10, 2).
Thesaurus Syriacus I–II ed. R. Payne Smith, Oxford 1879, 1901.
Thompson, Th. L.: *Early History of the Israelite People from the Written and Archaeological Sources,* Leiden/New York/Köln 1994 (Studies in the History of the Ancient Near East IV).
Thompson, Th. L.: *The Historicity of the Patriarchal Narratives*, Berlin/New York 1974.
Tkač, J.: 'Eremboi', *RE* 6 (1909) 413–417.
Tkač, J.: 'Gerrha', *RE* 7 (1912) 1270–1272.
Toynbee, A.: *A Study of History* Vol. VII, London 1954.
Trimingham, J. S.: *Christianity Among the Arabs in Pre-Islamic Times*, London/Beirut 1979.
Unger, G. F.: 'Umfang und Anordnung der Geschichte des Poseidonios', *Philologus* 55 (1896) 73–122.
Untersteiner, M. and Calderini, A.: 'Ricerche etnografiche sui papiri greco-egizî: Introduzione; Africa, Arabia', AAW I (1964) 373–391.
Von der Mühll, F.: 'Herennios Philon von Byblos', *RE* 8 (1912) 650–661.
Von Grunebaum, G.: 'The Nature of Arab Unity Before Islam', *Arabica* 10 (1963) 5–23.
Wacholder, B.: *Eupolemus. A Study of Judaeo-Greek Literature*, Cincinnati 1974 (Monographs of the Hebrew Union College III).
Wacholder, B.: *Nicolaus of Damascus*, Berkeley and Los Angeles 1962 (University of California Publications in History LXXV).
Wagner, E.: *Grundzüge der klassischen arabischen Dichtung Bd I: Die altarabische Dichtung*, Darmstadt 1987.
Walbank, F. W.: *A Historical Commentary on Polybius I, II* Oxford 1957, 1967.
Wallis, G.: 'Die Tradition von den drei Ahnvätern', *ZAW* 81 (1969) 18–40.
Wapnish, P.: 'Camel Caravans and Camel Pastoralists at Tell Jemmeh', *JANES* 13 (1981) 101–121.
Watt, W. M.: *Bell's Introduction to the Qurʔān*, Edinburgh 1970.
Watt, W. M.: 'Ḥums', *EI*² III 577–578.
Watt, W. M.: 'Maʕadd', *EI*² V 894–895.
Watt, W. M.: *Muhammed at Mecca*, Oxford 1953.
Watt, W. M.: *Muhammed at Medina*, Oxford 1956.
Watt, W. M.: 'Ḳays ʕAylān' *EI*² IV 833–834.
Watzinger, C.: 'Palmyra', *RE* 18 (1949) 262–277.
Weidemann, K.: *Könige aus dem Yemen. Zwei antike Bronzestatuen*, Mainz 1983.
Weidner, E. F.: 'Šilkan(he)ni, König von Muṣri, ein Zeitgenosse Sargons II nach einem neuen Bruchstück der Prisma-Inschrift des assyrischen Königs', *Archiv für Orientforschung* 14 (1941/1944) 40–53.
Weippert, M.: 'Archäologischer Jahresbericht', *ZDPV* 82 (1966) 274–330.
Weippert, M.: 'Die Kämpfe des assyrischen Königs Assurbanipal gegen die Araber. Redaktionsgeschichtliche Untersuchung des Berichts in Prisma A', *WO* 7 (1973–1974) 39–85.

Weippert, M.: 'Menahem von Israel und seine Zeitgenossen in einer Steleninschrift des assyrischen Königs Tiglath-Pileser III aus dem Iran', *ZDPV* 89 (1973) 26–53.
Weiss-Rosmarin, T.: 'Aribi und Arabien in den babylonisch-assyrischen Quellen', *JSOR* 16 (1932) 1–37.
Weissbach, F. H.: 'Isidoros', *RE* 9 (1914) 2064–2068.
Weissbach, F. H.: 'Mesene', *RE* 15 (1931/1932) 1082–1095.
Welch, A. T.: 'al-Ḳurʔān', *EI*[2] V 400–429.
Wellhausen, J.:'Medina vor dem Islam', *Skizzen und Vorarbeiten* 4, Berlin 1889, repr. Berlin/New York 1985.
Wellhausen, J.: *Die religiös-politischen Oppositionsparteien im alten Islam*, Berlin 1901.
Wellhausen, J.: *Reste arabischen Heidentums gesammelt und erläutert*, 2 Aufl., Berlin 1897, repr. Berlin 1961.
Welten, P.: *Geschichte und Geschichtsdarstellung in den Chronikbüchern*, Neukirchen-Vluyn 1973 (WMANT 42).
Wenning, R.: 'Die Dekapolis und die Nabatäer', *ZDPV* 110 (1994) 1–35.
Wenning, R.: 'Das Ende des nabatäischen Königreichs', *ArAnt* 1 [81] – [103].
Wenning, R.: 'Eine neuerstellte Liste der nabatäischen Dynastie', *Boreas* 16 (1993) 25–38.
Wenning, R.: *Die Nabatäer – Denkmäler und Geschichte*, Freiburg/Göttingen 1987.
West, J. M. I.: 'Uranius', *Harvard Studies in Classical Philology* 78 (1974) 282–284.
Westermann, C.: *Genesis 1 Teilbd.: Genesis 1–11* 3 Aufl. Neukirchen-Vluyn 1983 (BKAT I/1).
Westermann, C.: *Genesis 2 Teilbd.: Genesis 12–26* 2 Aufl. Neukirchen-Vluyn 1989 (BKAT I/2).
Westermann, C.: *Genesis 3 Teilbd.: Genesis 37–50* 2 Aufl. Neukirchen Vluyn 1992 (BKAT I/3).
Wiesehöfer, J.: 'Die Anfänge sassanidischer Wetspolitik und der Untergang Hatras', *Klio* 64 (1982) 437–447.
Wilcke, C.: 'Inanna/Ištar', *RA* 5 74–87.
Wilcken, U.: 'Die letzten Pläne Alexanders des Grossen', *Sitzungsberichte der Preussischen Akademie der Wissenschaften. Philosophisch-historische Klasse*, Berlin 1937 192–207.
Will, E.: *Les palmyréniens. La Venise des sables (Ier siècle avant-IIIème siècle après J.-C.)*, Paris 1992.
Williamson, H. G. M.: *1 and 2 Chronicles* (The New Century Bible Commentary), London 1982.
Wilson, R. R.: *Genealogy and History in the Biblical World*, New Haven/London 1977 (Yale Near Eastern Researches 7).
Winckler, H.: 'Das nordarabische Land Muṣri in den Inschriften und der Bibel', Winckler, H.: *Altorientalische Forschungen* I (1893–97), Leipzig 1897 24–41, 337–338.
Winnett, F. V.: 'The Arabian Genealogies in the Book of Genesis', *Translating and Understanding. Essays in Honor of Herbert Gordon May*, ed. by H. T. Frank and W. I. Reed, Nashville, New York, 1970 171–196.
Winnett, F. V.: 'A Reconsideration of Some of the Inscriptions from the Taymā' Area', *SHA* I 69–78.
von Wissmann, *Geschichte* = von Wissmann, H.: 'Die Geschichte des Sabäerreichs und der Feldzug des Aelius Gallus', *ANRW* III: Principat Bd 9:1, Berlin/New York 1976 308–544.
von Wissmann, *Geschichte I* = von Wissmann, H.: *Über die frühe Geschichte Arabiens und der Entstehung des Sabäerreiches. Die Geschichte von Saba I*, Wien 1975 (Österreichische Akademie der Wissenschaften, Phil.-hist. Klasse, Sitzungsberichte 301 Bd 5 Abh. Sammlung Eduard Glaser XIII).
von Wissmann, *Geschichte II* = von Wissmann, H.: *Die Geschichte von Saba' II: Das Grossreich der Sabäer bis zu seinem Ende im frühen 4. Jh. v. Chr.*, hrsg. von W. Müller, Wien 1982 (Österreichische Akademie der Wissenschaften. Phil.-lhist. Klasse, Sitzungsberichte 402 Band).
von Wissmann, H.: 'Geographische Grundlagen und Frühzeit der Geschichte Südarabiens', *Saeculum* 4 (1963) 61–114.
von Wissmann, H.: 'Ḥimyar, Ancient History', *Le Muséon* 77 (1964) 429–497.
von Wissmann, H.: 'Madiáma und Modiána', *RE Supplement* 12 (1970) 525–551.
von Wissmann, H.: 'Ōphīr und Ḥawīla', *RE Supplement* 12 (1970) 925–967.
von Wissmann, H.: 'Uranios', *RE Supplement* 11 (1968) 1278–1292.

von Wissmann, *Zamareni I* = von Wissmann, H.: 'Zamareni', *RE Supplement* 11 (1968) 1322–1337.
von Wissmann, *Zamareni II* = von Wissmann, H.: 'Zamareni', *RE Supplement* 12 (1970) 1709–1712.
von Wissmann, H.: *Zur Geschichte und Landeskunde von Alt-Südarabien*, Wien 1964 (Österreichische Akademie der Wissenschaften, Phil.-hist. Klasse, Sitzungsberichte 246).
von Wissmann, H.: 'Zur Kenntis von Ostarabien, besonders al-Qaṭīf, im Altertum', *Le Muséon* 80 (1967) 489–508.
de Witt Burton, E.: *A Critical and Exegetical Commentary on the Epistle to the Galatians*, Edinburgh 1921 (The International Critical Commentary).
Wolski, J.: *L'Empire des Arsacides*, Leuven 1993 (Acta Iranica 3me série: Textes et mémoires vol. XVIII).
Wolski, J.: *The Seleucids. The Decline and Fall of their Empire*, Kraków 1999.
Wolski-Conus, W.: 'Geographie', *RACh* 10 (1978) 155–222.
Wörterbuch der klassischen arabischen Sprache I–, Wiesbaden 1970–.
Yamada, Sh.: *The Construction of the Assyrian Empire: A Historical Study of the Inscriptions of Shalmaneser III (859–824 BC) Relating to his Campaigns in the West*, Leiden 2000.
Yeivin, Sh.: 'Yehôšafaṭ ha-melex', *Eretz-Israel* 7 (1964) 6–17, 165*.
Yémen. Au pays de la reine de Saba'. Exposition présentée à l'Institut du monde arabe du 25 octobre 1997 au 28 février 1998, Paris 1997.
Young, T. C.: 'The Persian Empire: The Consolidation of the Empire and Its Limits of Growth under Darius and Xerxes', *The Cambridge Ancient History* Vol. IV*: Persia, Greece and the Western Mediterranean c. 525 to 479 BC* 2nd ed. Cambridge 1988 53–111.
Zadok, R.: 'Arabians in Mesopotamia during the Late-Assyrian, Chaldaean, Achaemenian and Hellenistic Periods Chiefly According to Cuneiform Sources', *ZDMG* 131 (1981) 42–84.
Zadok, R.: *On West Semites in Babylonia During the Chaldean and Achaemenian Periods. An Onomastic Study*, Jerusalem 1977.
Zayadine, F.: 'L'iconographie d'al-Uzza-Aphrodite', *MGMP* 113–120.
Zetterstéen, K. V. and Lewis, B.: 'al-ʔAbnāʔ', *EI*² I 102.
Zimmerli, W.: *Hezekiel, 2 Teilband: Hezechiel 25–48*, 2 Aufl. Neukirchen/Vluyn 1979 (Biblischer Kommentar zum Alten Testament XIII/2).
Zwettler, M.: 'Imra'alqays, son of 'Amr: King of . . .???', *Literary Heritage of Classical Islam. Arabic and Islamic Studies in Honor of James A. Bellamy* ed. M. Mir, Princeton 1993 3–37.

GENERAL INDEX

The general index contains important names and terms not immediately accessible through the Table of Contents. The ordering is according to the Latin alphabet without regard to the Arabic or Greek definite article. The words beginning with ʔ and ʕ are listed separately after A. Semitic words beginning with consonants marked with diacritic signs follow those with unmarked ones.

INDEX LOCORUM

The index lists all passages from the sources quoted directly or otherwise commented upon in the text.

HEBREW/ARAMAIC (JEWISH POSTBIBLICAL)

LATIN

Inscriptions

Literary texts

OLD TESTAMENT (MT, LXX)

PERSIAN

SOUTH ARABIAN

SYRIAC